THE 1991
INFORMATION PLEASE®
SPORTS
ALMANAC

P9-CSB-316

Mike Meserole
EDITOR

PRODUCTION SUPERVISOR
Michael Michaud

Research assistance by
Howie Schwab and **Edward R. Pete**

Typesetting by
CopyRight of Bedford, Mass.

HOUGHTON MIFFLIN COMPANY   BOSTON

The Information Please Sports Almanac

ISSN: 1045-4980

Comments and Suggestions

Comments and suggestions from readers are invited. Because of the many letters received, however, it is not possible to respond personally to every correspondent. Nevertheless, all letters are welcome and each will be carefully considered. **The Information Please Sports Almanac** does not rule on bets or wagers. Address all correspondence to Houghton Mifflin Company, 2 Park Street, Boston, Massachusetts 02108.

Additional copies of **The 1991 Information Please Sports Almanac** may be ordered directly by mail from:
Customer Service Department
Houghton Mifflin Company
Burlington, MA 01803
Phone toll-free (800) 225-3362 for price and shipping information. In Massachusetts, phone (617) 272-1500.

C O N T E N T S   3

Major League Cities & Teams

There are 110 major league sports teams playing baseball, basketball, football and hockey in 61 cities and towns in the United States and Canada. Listed below are the cities and the teams that play there. If a team actually plays in a nearby suburb, that town is in parentheses. San Jose begins NHL play in 1991.

Anaheim
AL   California Angels
NFL L.A. Rams

Arlington
AL   Texas Rangers

Atlanta
NL   Braves
NBA Hawks
NFL Falcons

Baltimore
AL   Orioles

Boston
AL   Red Sox
NBA Celtics
NFL N.E.Patriots (Foxboro)
NHL Bruins

Buffalo
NFL Bills (Orchard Park)
NHL Sabres

Calgary
CFL Stampeders
NHL Flames

Charlotte
NBA Hornets

Chicago
AL   White Sox
NL   Cubs
NBA Bulls
NFL Bears
NHL Blackhawks

Cincinnati
NL   Reds
NFL Bengals

Cleveland
AL   Indians
NBA Cavaliers (Richfield)
NFL Browns

Dallas
NBA Mavericks
NFL Cowboys (Irving)

Denver
NBA Nuggets
NFL Broncos

Detroit
AL   Tigers
NBA Pistons (Auburn Hills)
NFL Lions (Pontiac)
NHL Red Wings

East Rutherford
NBA New Jersey Nets
NFL New York Giants
NFL New York Jets
NHL New Jersey Devils

Edmonton
CFL Eskimos
NHL Oilers

Green Bay
NFL Packers

Hamilton
CFL Tiger-Cats

Hartford
NHL Whalers

Houston
NL   Astros
NBA Rockets
NFL Oilers

Indianapolis
NBA Pacers
NFL Colts

Kansas City
AL   Royals
NFL Chiefs

Los Angeles
NL   Dodgers
NBA Clippers
NBA Lakers (Inglewood)
NFL Raiders
NHL Kings (Inglewood)

Miami
NBA Heat
NFL Dolphins

Milwaukee
AL   Brewers
NBA Bucks

Minneapolis
AL   Minn. Twins
NBA Minn. Timberwolves
NFL Minn. Vikings
NHL Minn. North Stars
     (Bloomington)

Montreal
NL   Expos
NHL Canadiens

New Orleans
NFL Saints

New York
AL   Yankees
NL   Mets
NBA Knicks
NHL Rangers

Oakland
AL   Athletics
NBA Golden St. Warriors

Orlando
NBA Magic

Ottawa
CFL Rough Riders

Philadelphia
NL   Phillies
NBA 76ers
NFL Eagles
NHL Flyers

Phoenix
NBA Suns
NFL Cardinals (Tempe)

Pittsburgh
NL   Pirates
NFL Steelers
NHL Penguins

Portland
NBA Trail Blazers

Quebec City
NHL Nordiques

Regina
CFL Saskatchewan Roughriders

Sacramento
NBA Kings

St.Louis
NL   Cardinals
NHL Blues

Salt Lake City
NBA Utah Jazz

San Antonio
NBA Spurs

San Diego
NL   Padres
NFL Chargers

San Francisco
NL   Giants
NFL 49ers

San Jose
NHL Sharks (1991-92)

Seattle
AL   Mariners
NBA SuperSonics
NFL Seahawks

Tampa
NFL Buccaneers

Toronto
AL   Blue Jays
CFL Argos
NHL Maple Leafs

Uniondale
NHL N.Y.Islanders

Vancouver
CFL B.C. Lions
NHL Canucks

Washington
NBA Bullets (Landover, Md.)
NFL Redskins
NHL Capitals (Landover, Md.)

Winnipeg
NHL Jets
CFL Blue Bombers

Back in the mid-1950s, Roger O'Gara, the late sports editor of the *Berkshire Eagle* in Pittsfield, Mass., would adjourn to a local watering hole for a quick beer on Friday nights with the admonition, "I'll be at the Rosa. Call me if the Yanks trade Mantle."

At the time, Mickey Mantle was the best player in the American League and the chances of the Yankees trading him were about the same as the Russians pulling out of Eastern Europe. Needless to say, nobody ever called.

Those were simpler times. These days, even Wayne Gretzky gets traded. And Pete Rose gets five months for tax evasion. And a woman reporter is the most talked about person in pro football. Blame it on whatever and whoever you like—free agency, Astroturf, ESPN, autograph shows, steroids, luxury suites, square-grooved golf clubs, the DH, the DL, the DeBartolos, the hole in the ozone layer—but sports has definitely gotten confusing.

The Information Please Sports Almanac is an attempt to bring some clarity to this confusion by combining a chronicle of the year at hand with a comprehensive review of what has gone on before. This unique coverage is enhanced by over 150 photos and 17 year-in-review essays from many of the country's top sportswriters.

This year there are also contributions from two Pulitzer Prize winners—editorial cartoonist Jeff MacNelly of the *Chicago Tribune*, whose hilarious view of 1990 appears on page 13, and architecture critic Paul Goldberger of *The New York Times*, whose piece on arenas and ballparks begins on page 419.

Readers of last year's almanac will notice that this year's edition is thicker (by 96 pages) and that chapter tabs have been added to the front and back covers to take the guesswork out of thumbing through the book. Also, last year's special chapter on Divison I college football, which reviewed every season from 1936-88, has been replaced by a chapter recounting every Division I college basketball season from 1938-89.

If you're picking up the **Sports Almanac** for the first time, I hope you like it. If you enjoyed last year's book and have come back for more, your continued interest is appreciated.

That said, I'll be at the Rosa. Call me if the Red Sox or the Cubs win the World Series.

—Mike Meserole

Wolcott, Conn.
October, 1990

Almanacs are like golf tournaments—you shouldn't call one an annual or the other a classic until at least the second year. The **Information Please Sports Almanac** becomes an annual with this edition, a milepost attained not without a lot of help.

My thanks to all the cooperative souls in public relations offices, sports information departments, libraries, halls of fame, chambers of commerce and newsrooms around the country—and, in some cases, around the world—who took my calls, put up with my requests and came through with the needed material.

If there was a game ball involved in putting this book together, it would go to my production supervisor Michael Michaud for the second year in a row. He held the project together. As I write this on Halloween night in Marblehead, Mass., I am again the guest of Mike, his wife Lynn and their daughters Annie and Molly. Whenever I'm up here, they make me feel like one of the family and with Lynn pregnant, soon we'll be six.

It's impossible to thank everybody who has contributed to the success of this book over the last two years, but there are a few folks who deserve to be mentioned: Charley Monagan; Dawn Longo; everybody at CopyRight typesetting in Bedford, Mass.; Steve Lewers and his troops at Houghton Mifflin, especially Margaret Ann Miles, Chris Leonesio and Marya Labarthe; Jim Murphy of Western Publishing; Nat Andriani of Wide World Photos; Maggie Hearn of the Bettmann Archives; Cynthia Gable and Jim Van Valkenburg of the NCAA; my agent Tom Hart; my mailman George Dostaler; and Mary Vaughn at the Wolcott, CT, post office.

Many thanks to the best batting order in sports bookdom: Bill Connors, Eric Duhatschek, Bernard Fernandez, Paul Gardner, Paul Goldberger (now the cultural editor of *The New York Times*), Mike Harris, Phil Hersh, Tim Kurkjian, Jeff MacNelly, Jim Martz, John McManus, Gary Myers, Scott Ostler, Marino Parascenzo, Dave Petruska, Billy Reed, Bob Ryan, Sharon Smith and Caulton Tudor.

Finally, a belated thanks to my brothers Cork and Brooke and my sisters Bam and Hilary for their encouragement and support. This second annual almanac is dedicated to them.

—M.M.

UPDATES

Matt Mendelsohn/UPI/Bettmann News Photos

Holyfield dethrones Douglas

Evander (The Real Deal) Holyfield knocked out **James (Buster) Douglas** at 1:10 of the third round on Oct.25 to win the undisputed heavyweight championship of the world. The fight, billed "The Moment of Truth," was held before a stunned crowd of 16,000 at the Mirage in Las Vegas and came eight months and two weeks after Douglas upset Mike Tyson in 10 rounds to win the title in Tokyo.

The 30-year-old Douglas was the underdog, entering the ring for his first defense at a roly-poly 246 pounds—14½ pounds heavier than when he fought Tyson. Holyfield, 28, came in at 208 pounds and easily controlled the first two rounds. In the third, Douglas tried to land the same right uppercut that floored Tyson, but Holyfield was ready for it. The challenger stepped back and countered with a straight right that connected with the middle of the champion's face and sent him to the canvas until he was counted out by referee Mills Lane.

Holyfield, now 25-0 with 21 knockouts, will make his first title defense against another bulky heavyweight when he meets 42-year-old former champion **George Foreman** on Friday, April 19, 1991, at Caesars Palace in Las Vegas. Foreman, who ruled the division from 1973-74, won five times in 1990 to run his record to 24-0 since launching his comeback in 1987.

Baseball

Jim Leyland of the Pittsburgh Pirates and **Jeff Torborg** of the Chicago White Sox were named managers of the year the last week in October by the Baseball Writers Association of America.

Leyland, who was 64-98 in his first year as Pirates' skipper in 1986, guided the Bucs to a 95-67 record and their first NL East title in 11 years. He outpolled Cincinnati's Lou Piniella, 99-49. Torborg turned Chicago around in only his second year at the helm, going from 69-92 in 1989 to 94-69 this year. Unfortunately, the White Sox were in the same division with the AL champion Oakland A's (103-59) and finished nine games back. A's manager Tony LaRussa placed second to Torborg in the voting, 128-72.

The remainder of the BWAA's annual baseball awards were given out in November.

Shortly after the World Series, the Associated Press released its 1990 Major League All-Star Team, based on a nationwide vote by national sportswriters and broadcasters who regularly cover the sport.

C—Carlton Fisk, Chicago-AL
1B—Cecil Fielder, Detroit
2B—Ryne Sandberg, Chicago-NL
SS—Barry Larkin, Cincinnati
3B—Matt Williams, San Francisco
DH—Dave Parker, Milwaukee

OF—Ricky Henderson, Oakland
OF—Barry Bonds, Pittsburgh
OF Bobby Bonilla, Pittsburgh
RHP—Bob Welch, Oakland
LHP—Frank Viola, New York-NL
RP—Bobby Thigpen, Chicago-AL

College Football

Virginia held the high ground in the AP Top 25 poll with a 7-0 record through October. The Cavaliers, who began the season ranked No.15, were followed in order by **Notre Dame, Nebraska, Auburn** and **Illinois.**

Notre Dame was upset by Stanford, 36-31, in South Bend on Oct.6, but rebounded by beating Miami of Florida, 29-20, at home two weeks later in the last regular season meeting between the two schools. It was the second loss of the season for Miami, the 1989 national champ and consensus preseason No.1. The Hurricanes were jolted, 28-21, by **Ty Detmer** and **BYU** in their opening game Sept.8 in Provo. With five weeks left in the season, the Heisman Trophy competition centered on quarterbacks Detmer, Shawn Moore of Virginia, and David Klingler of Houston, who replaced 1989 Heisman winner Andre Ware. All-purpose back Raghib (Rocket) Ismail of Notre Dame was also a strong contender.

AP Top 25
(as of Monday, Oct.29, 1990)

Writers' poll, including games through Oct.27, 1990. First place votes in parentheses, followed by record, total votes and ranking in preseason poll.

	Record	Pts	Pre-Season			Record	Pts	Pre-Season
1 Virginia (44)	7-0-0	1462	15	14 Texas	5-1-0	742	35
2 Notre Dame (6)	6-1-0	1380	2	15 Florida	6-1-0	638	31
3 Nebraska (5)	8-0-0	1350	7	16 Georgia Tech	6-0-1	612	34
4 Auburn (2)	6-0-1	1284	3	17 Mississippi	7-1-0	519	36
5 Illinois	6-1-0	1230	11	18 Clemson	7-2-0	424	10
6 Houston (2)	7-0-0	1196	24	19 Wyoming	9-0-0	407	—
7 Washington (1)	7-1-0	1189	20	20 Michigan	4-3-0	403	6
8 Miami,FL	5-2-0	1074	1	21 Southern Cal	6-2-0	333	9
9 Colorado	7-1-1	1009	5	22 Oregon	6-2-0	230	37
10 BYU	6-1-0	943	16	23 Arizona	6-2-0	225	26
11 Tennessee	4-1-2	870	8	24 Penn State	5-2-0	123	21
12 Florida St	5-2-0	807	4	25 Louisville	7-1-1	108	33
13 Iowa	6-1-0	759	—				

Colleges

The reshuffling of major college conferences begun earlier in the year by **Penn State** (to the Big Ten) and **Arkansas** (from the Southwest to the Southeastern), continued into the Fall, with independents Miami of Florida, Florida State and South Carolina all moving to established leagues.

Florida State became the ninth member of the Atlantic Coast Conference on Sept.14, **South Carolina** made the SEC a 12-team league on Sept.25, and **Miami** threw in with the Big East on Oct.10, making that previously basketball-only conference a 10-team group. Boston College, Pittsburgh and Syracuse are the Big East's other major football schools and conference plans call for an aggressive marketing strategy, possibly with TV and bowl alliances with the ACC, SWC and others.

On the probation front, the NCAA Infractions Committee handed down two-year probations on Sept.20 to both the football and basketball programs at

Wide World Photos

Miami joins Big East
Latest major conference call.

Florida. The football team, 6-1 under new coach Steve Spurrier and ranked 15th in the country going into November, was prohibited from participating in a bowl game this season.

Pro Football

San Francisco and the **New York Giants** were 7-0 at the end of October and the only unbeaten teams left in the NFL. Each held comfortable leads in their divisions—the 49ers by 4 games in the West, the Giants by three in the East—and were scheduled to meet Monday night, Dec.3, at Candlestick Park. Three teams had 6-1 records—**Buffalo** and **Miami** in the AFC East, the **LA Raiders** in the AFC West, and **Chicago** in the NFC Central.

Near or at the bottom of the heap were Cleveland (2-5), Minnesota (1-6) and New England (1-6). AFC finalists in 1989, the Browns headed into November with head coach Bud Carson seemingly one defeat away from losing his job. One year after the Herschel Walker-for-the-future trade with Dallas, the Vikings were so bad that GM Mike Lynn jumped ship on Oct.10 to take over as president of the new World League of American Football.

And the Pats? Their contribution to the season was the Zeke Mowatt-Lisa Olson controversy, involving Patriot receiver Mowatt's alleged sexual harassment of *Boston Herald* reporter Olson in the team's locker room, Sept.17. Two weeks later, Cincinnati coach Sam Wyche banned another woman reporter from the Bengals' locker room and was fined $30,000 by league commissioner Paul Tagliabue.

Otherwise, after announcing that he planned to move the Raiders back to Oakland, managing partner Al Davis says that his club will remain in Los Angeles for the next 20 years, provided the LA Coliseum undergoes a promised $145 million renovation. Stay tuned.

Pro Basketball

When the 1990-91 season opened up on Nov.2, both **Pat Riley** and **Doug Moe** were out of coaching. Riley, who led the LA Lakers to four NBA titles in 10 years, quit on June 11 to take a studio host job with the NBA's new TV network NBC. Moe was fired by the Denver Nuggets on Sept.6, after 14 consecutive seasons coaching San Antonio and then Denver.

On July 31, the NBA salary cap rose to $12 million per team, setting off a flurry of trades that sent **Danny Ainge** to Portland, **Paul Pressey** to San Antonio and **Manute Bol** to Philadelphia. Other major off-season deals included a 3-way exchange between Utah, Washington and Sacramento that ended up with **Jeff Malone** going to the Jazz, **Pervis Ellison** to the Bullets, and **Eric Leckner** and **Bob Hansen** to the Kings. The Lakers signed free agent **Sam Perkins** of Dallas for $19 million over six years. Dallas signed free agent **Alex English** of Denver for one year. Cleveland won a $26.5 million bidding war with Miami (Sept.6) for the services of Cavs' forward **John (Hot Rod) Williams**. And Portland signed Clyde Drexler to a contract extension (Oct.12) that will pay him $8 million a year in 1995-96.

Hockey

Wayne Gretzky scored his 2000th career regular season point with an assist against Winnipeg (Oct.26). Going into November, the NHL's all-time leading scorer was tied with Pittsburgh's John Gullen for the league lead in points with 26.

Off the ice, on Sept.27 the NHL suspended Edmonton goalie **Grant Fuhr** one year for admitted cocaine drug use during the 1980s; and the Pittsburgh Penguins announced that, despite successful surgery, recurring back problems would keep **Mario Lemieux** out of the lineup until at least January.

Gretzky (8-17—25) trailed only Pittsburgh's **John Cullen** (5-21—26) in scoring after one month. **Brett Hull**, last season's goal-scoring leader with 76, started off the new year with 15 in the first 12 games.

Off-season deals included: Winnipeg trading captain **Dale Hawerchuk** to Buffalo for **Scott Arniel**, **Phil Houseley** and **Jeff Parker**; Chicago and Montreal exchanging stars **Denis Savard** and **Chris Chelios**; St.Louis signing free agent defenseman **Scott Stevens** of Washington, to a 4-year, $5 million deal; the Detroit Red Wings firing coach **Jacques Demers** and replacing him with coach and GM **Bryan Murray**.

Soccer

Olimpia of Paraguay defeated Barcelona of Ecuador by a 3-1 aggregate to win South America's **Copa Libertadores**. Olimpia shut out Barcelona, 2-0, at home (Oct.3) then played to a 1-1 draw on the road (Oct.10) to win the two-leg championship.

Next stop for Olimpia is the **Toyota Cup** in Tokyo (Dec.9), where it will meet European Cup champion **AC Milan** for the world club championship. Milan won the Toyota Cup last year.

Bowling

Chris Warren overtook Amleto Monacelli as the PBA's leading money winner by winning the Japan Cup in Tokyo (Oct.14). Warren defeated Dave Husted, 226-163, in the final to collect $18,500 and boost his overall winnings to $190,825. Monacelli did not compete in the tournament. Meanwhile, the PBA fall tour got underway with the Budweiser Challenge in Rochester, N.Y. (Oct.29-Nov.3).

Jimmy Certain won the final PBA Seniors event of the year (Oct.25), taking the Treasure Coast Open and $7500 with a 218-202 victory over Bob Hart.

On the women's tour, **Tish Johnson** joined **Lisa Wagner** and **Patty Costello** as the only women to win three consecutive pro titles when she began the LPBT fall tour with victories in the Cobra Classic, Delaware Open and Eastern Open. Johnson's three winner's checks improved her 1990 earnings to $71,420. Her bid for a fourth straight title the following week at the Brunswick Open in Hammond, IN, failed when she finished out of the money. **Leanne Barrette**, **Lorrie Nichols** and **Nikki Gianulias** also registered wins in October.

Horse Racing

Death rode in the seventh Breeders' Cup at Belmont Park on Oct.27, as thoroughbreds **Go For Wand** and **Mr. Nickerson** died in separate races.

Mr. Nickerson died in the first race of the day, suffering a heart attack at the start of the Breeders' Cup Sprint and dying on the track.

Go For Wand, the champion 3-year-old filly who was a solid Horse of the Year candidate, shattered her right front ankle in the Breeders' Cup Distaff. Go For Wand was locked in a stretch duel with eventual winner **Bayakoa** when the injury occurred and she fell, throwing jockey Randy Romero. Romero was only shaken up but Go For Wand, her leg "torn to shreds" as one vet put it, had to be humanely destroyed.

Go For Wand's demise was the latest and most dramatic in a racing season cursed by bad luck and injuries that forced horses the caliber of Sunday Silence, Easy Goer, Criminal Type and Summer Squall to pass up the Breeders' Cup.

In harness racing, **Jake And Elwood** won the Messenger Stakes (Sept.8) and **Beach Towel** won the Little Brown Jug (Sept.20) to wrap up the pacing Triple Crown races, while Star Mystic won the final leg of the trotting Triple Crown, the Kentucky Futurity (Oct.5).

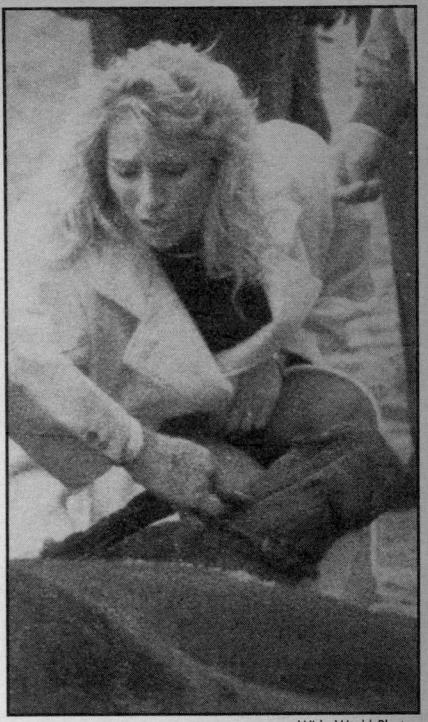

Wide World Photos

Exercise rider Rose Badgett
Grieves for Go For Wand.

7th Breeders' Cup

Results from the seven Breeders' Cup races held Saturday, Oct.27,1990, at Belmont Park in Elmont, NY.

Race	Time	Top 3 Finishers	Jockeys	Trainers	Money won
Sprint (6 furlongs)	1:09⅗	1 Safely Kept 2 Dayjur 3 Black Tie Affair	Craig Perret Willie Carson Laffit Pincay,Jr	Alan Goldberg W.R.Hern Ernie Poulos	$450,000 225,000 108,000
Juvenile Fillies (1¹⁄₁₆ miles)	1:44	1 Meadow Star 2 Private Treasure 3 Dance Smartly	Jose Santos Jerry Bailey Sandy Hawley	LeRoy Jolley Joseph Pierce James Day	$450,000 225,000 108,000
Distaff (1⅛ miles)	1:49⅕	1 Bayakoa 2 Colonial Waters 3 Valay Maid	Laffit Pincay,Jr Jose Santos Marco Castaneda	Ron McAnally LeRoy Jolley Carlos Garcia	$450,000 225,000 108,000
Mile	1:35⅕	1 Royal Academy 2 Itsallgreektome 3 Priolo	Lester Piggott Corey Nakatani Cash Asmussen	M.V.O'Brien Wallace Dollase Francois Boutin	$450,000 225,000 108,000
Juvenile (1¹⁄₁₆ miles)	1:43⅖	1 Fly So Free 2 Take Me Out 3 Lost Mountain	Jose Santos Bill Smith Chris McCarron	Scotty Schulhofer William Mott Tom Bohannan	$450,000 225,000 108,000
Turf (1½ miles)	2:29⅗	1 In the Wings 2 With Approval 3 El Senor	Gary Stevens Craig Perret Angel Cordero,Jr	Andre Fabre Roger Attfield William Wright	$900,000 450,000 216,000
Classic (1¼ miles)	2:02⅕	1 Unbridled 2 Ibn Bey 3 Thirty-Six Red	Pat Day Randy Quinn Jimmy Smith	Carl Nafzger Paul Cole Nick Zito	$1,350,000 675,000 324,000

Tennis

Playing one of his best indoor matches of the year, **Boris Becker** beat **Stefan Edberg** 6-4,6-0,6-3 to win the Stockholm Open (Oct.28). Going into November, Becker and Edberg were two of four men's players who had secured berths in the first ATP Tour World Championship scheduled for Nov.13-18 in Frankfurt. **Ivan Lendl** and **Andre Agassi** were the others. The remaining four positions figured to go to **Pete Sampras**, **Andres Gomez**, **Thomas Muster** and **Emilio Sanchez**, but **Brad Gilbert** and **Goran Ivanisevic** were still in contention.

On the women's tour, 14-year-old **Jennifer Capriati** won her first pro title at the Puerto Rico Open (Oct.28), beating **Zina Garrison** 5-7,6-4,6-2. The victory clinched Capriati a berth in the 16- player Virginia Slims Championship, set for Nov.12-18 at Madison Square Garden in New York.

Golf

Jodie Mudd shot a final round 68 and birdied the last three holes to win the $2.5 million Nabisco Golf Championships (Oct.28) at Champions Golf Club in Houston. Mudd caught Billy Mayfair on the 18th, then beat him on the first hole of sudden death. The $450,000 winner's check gave Mudd a total of $911,746 for the year and moved him from 21st to 5th on the PGA money list. **Greg Norman**, who tied for 7th in the tournament, won the overall earnings title with $1,165,477. Other PGA winners since the Canadian Open: **Nolan Henke** at the B.C.Open (Sept.23), **Kenny Knox** in a playoff at the Southern Open (Sept.30), **Mark O'Meara** at the Texas Open (Oct.7), **Bob Tway** in a playoff at the Las Vegas International (Oct.14), and **Tim Simpson** at the Disney World/Oldsmobile Classic (Oct.20).

Lee Trevino turned in a nine-birdie 65 on the final day of the Transamerica Championship (Oct.21) to win his 7th PGA Seniors title of the year. Trevino, in his rookie year with the Seniors, increased his earnings for the season to $922,352. Other PGA Seniors winners since the Greater Grand Rapids Open: **Jim Dent** at the Crestar Classic (Sept.23), **Mike Hill** in a playoff at the Space Coast Classic (Sept.30), **Charles Coody** at the Vantage Championship (Oct.7), and **Bruce Crampton** at the Gatlin Brothers Classic (Oct.14).

Beth Daniel kept pace with Trevino as pro golf's top winner in 1990, taking her 7th title at the Centel Classic (Oct.7). The victory also pushed Daniel's record one-year prize money total over the $800,000 mark. Other late season winners on the LPGA tour were **Nancy Lopez** at the MBS Classic (Sept.23), and Cathy Gerring at the Trophee Urban World Championship in Paris (Oct.14).

Auto Racing

Al Unser Jr. became the first second generation driver to win the CART points championship when he clinched his first Indy car title at the Bosch Spark Plug 200 in Nazareth, PA. Unser's father is a three-time CART champion. Little Al crashed on lap 109 of the 200- lap race and placed 16th, but points challenger Michael Andretti couldn't take advantage and finished 5th. **Emerson Fittipaldi**, the 1989 CART champion, won the race. Two weeks later, Unser finished second to Danny Sullivan in the Champion 300k to close the season.

Only 45 points separated Winston Cup points leader **Mark Martin** and **Dale Earnhardt** as they headed into November and the last two races of the 1990 NASCAR season. Martin and Earnhardt finished 1-2 in the Holly Farms 400 (Sept.30), but Martin was able to increase his lead from 16 to 49 points the following week by placing 14th in the Mello Yello 500 while Earnhardt came in 25th. Earnhardt was 10th in the AC Delco 500 (Oct.21), but Martin was 11th and lost only four points. Those two October races, by the way, were won by **Davey Allison** and **Alan Kulwicki**.

In Formula One, archrivals **Ayrton Senna** and **Alain Prost** crashed into each other at the Japan Grand Prix for the second year in a row (Oct.21), only with much different results. Last year, the collision knocked Senna out of the race for the World Driving Championship and allowed Prost to clinch the title. This time, it was Prost who was eliminated and Senna who won. Only two months before, both drivers had agreed to end their feud and become friends. No such luck.

THE YEAR IN REVIEW

*Park yourself curbside, folks,
it's time for another year
to pass in review.*

The Big Sports Parade of 1990

by Scott Ostler

Hello, ladies and gentlemen, and welcome to the Big Sports Parade, celebrating the heroes and villains of 1990 in a spectacular floral pageant that, quite frankly, makes all other parades look cheap and insignificant.

Remember, folks, please! No flash photography, no alcoholic beverages except those of our kind sponsors, and no pestering the athletes for autographs until after the parade, when you can buy all you want down at the big Autograph-o-Rama.

Now, let's all stand, and cover our ears for the National Anthem, performed by the lovely and cumbersome Roseanne Barr. She was chosen for the honor because our theme this year is "Sweat and Inspiration," and Ms. Barr's screeching, scratching and spitting rendition of the Star Spangled Banner before a San Diego Padres game in July inspired a lot of sweaty debate. Congress briefly considered replacing the anthem with a tune less musically challenging, like "A Hundred Bottles of Beer on the Wall."

As Ms. Barr is being led away in a large paper bag, I see that George Steinbrenner, our Grand Marshall, is about to fire the starting gun, setting in motion this colossal beast of an event.

You'll observe that George is standing under a banner that bears our motto for 1990—words spoken by Bucky Dent just before he became Steinbrenner's 19th managerial change in 17 years: "I don't know what's happening, but it's been happening all year."

Steinbrenner was the runaway choice for Grand Marshall because he brought so much happiness to the hearts of baseball fans this year. Who can forget the night of July 30 at Yankee Stadium when denizens of the Bronx Zoo rose as one, cheering and weeping with joy at the announcement that The Boss had been banished from baseball for life?

Steinbrenner's crime was giving $40,000 to lowlife gambler Howie Spira, allegedly in payment for information that could be used to discredit Yankee outfielder Dave Winfield. Summoned to

Scott Ostler is a columnist for The National, the nation's first sports daily newspaper. Before that his column appeared in the Los Angeles Times and was syndicated nationally for six years.

Jeff MacNelly, whose cartoon appears on page 13, is an editorial cartoonist for the Chicago Tribune. He has won three Pulitzer Prizes and is the creator of the comic strip "Shoe."

Yankee fans of all ages had their prayers answered on July 30 when **George Steinbrenner** was forced out after 17 years as boss of the Bronx Zoo.

commissioner Fay Vincent's office to explain himself, George claimed he gave the money to Spira "out of the goodness of my heart," whereupon the commissioner spit out a mouthful of coffee. Public opinion was divided on the harshness of Steinbrenner's lifetime sentence. Many felt it was too short.

Meanwhile, New York finished with the worst record in the American League, despite the inspirational visit in June of South African anti-apartheid leader Nelson Mandela, who pulled on a team jacket and cap and proclaimed, "I am a Yankee." The next day Mandela was gone, like Winfield, Rickey Henderson, Doug Drabek and countless other all-stars before him.

Ah, the parade is moving toward us and I see there's been a lineup change. The first float was supposed to be the world champion Oakland Athletics' salute to great baseball dynasties, but we've received a report that the A's float was blindsided by a Big Red Machine with Ohio plates and swept off the parade route.

The new lead-off float is a large, bloated floral rendering of a yacht dubbed "Collusion III" with the tanned and smiling former baseball commissioner Peter Ueberroth at the helm. For the third straight year, an independent arbitrator found baseball owners guilty of conspiring to keep the cost of free agents down during the reign of Peter the Suave. This year's judgement cost the owners $103 million. Note how the ship is sinking in a bed of roses labeled "The Sea of Chutzpah."

Towed along behind our lead float is a little, boarded-up outhouse entitled "Locked Out." That's in honor of the owners' 32-day shutdown of spring training this year. Does anybody remember what that was all about? Ever get the impression the owners are just in this for laughs?

15

Nolan Ryan
Six no-hitters and two Advil.

Bill McCartney
Fifth down and goal to go.

Ah, but you can't keep a good sport down. Here comes the baseball float, called—what else?—''The Hunt for Red October.'' There's World Series MVP Jose Rijo and his father-in-law Juan Marichal, the Nasty Boys, Billy Hatcher, Barry Larkin and manager Lou Piniella, who escaped George Steinbrenner's doghouse to share a victory Milkbone with Marge Schott's slobbering St. Bernard, Schottzie. Elsewhere on the float we see Cecil Fielder, the Hanshin and Detroit Tiger who came back from exile in Japan to sock 51 homers; 27-game winner Bob Welch and 57-game savior Bobby Thigpen; the wondrous Rickey Henderson; Barry Bonds and ageless White Sox catcher Carlton Fisk surrounded by eight of the nine pitchers who threw no-hitters this year.

Just coming into view is our first musical ensemble—the Witnesses Against Pete Rose Glee Club, out on parole and giving forth with a stirring rendition of ''Ain't It Good to Know You've Got a Friend?'' A funny thing happened to Rose on his way to the Baseball Hall of Fame—some of his close friends testified against him in court and helped send him on a five-month vacation to the federal slammer in Marion, Ill.

Yes, the man who remembers each of his 4256 base hits forgot each of the 354,968 dollars he collected in paper bags at various autograph shows and was convicted of income tax evasion. If you're scoring at home, charge Rose with an error, a double felony and a caught stealing. Baseball's all-time driller of base hits was given a job in the prison machine shop, drilling holes for 11 cents an hour. Tax free.

Speaking of bad judgement, let's have a big hand for our next float, titled: ''Brothers Under the Skin''—a truly mammoth representation of Hall Thompson and Zeke Mowatt, slam-dunking the U.S. Constitution into a paper shredder.

Thompson, you may remember, is the founder of the Shoal Creek Country Club, site of the 1990 PGA Championship in August. Two months before the tournament, Thompson explained to *Birmingham Post-Herald* reporter Joan Mazzolini that not only did his club not have any black members, but would not be pressured into admitting blacks, even as luncheon guests. ''That's just not done in Birmingham, Alabama,'' he said.

It's doubtful that a lot of black people in Birmingham were clamoring to have lunch with Thompson, either, but his quotes stirred the slumbering conscience of the golf world. Journalists got to nosing around and found out that Shoal Creek was the norm rather than the exception here in the land of the free. Should race-restricted clubs be chosen to host major golf tournaments? The answer was provided by big money TV sponsors. When IBM and Toyota started to pull out over the bad publicity, golf quickly saw the error of its ways.

The PGA promised to choose future tournament sites with an eye to fairness in membership practices, and clubs like Shoal Creek and Augusta National scurried to find a black member or two. Some critics felt that these actions were a matter of too little, too late.

''You need a tub of water,'' said black touring pro Charlie Owens, ''and you get a teardrop.''

Most of the PGA touring pros, including Jack Nicklaus, either defended Thompson or refused to get involved in the whole dicussion. But the final scorecard showed clearly that golf's claim to being an equal-opportunity sport was an unplayable lie.

Selectivity was also a big issue in pro football, where Mowatt, the New England Patriots' tight end, led the fight to keep NFL locker rooms safe from women. Zeke and four teammates, all naked, allegedly surrounded *Boston Herald* sportswriter Lisa Olson one day after practice and presented themselves as a sort of sexual smorgasbord. When Patriots' owner Victor Kiam was told that Olson wanted to throw a penalty flag at his players for illegal use of glands, he referred to the writer as ''a classic bitch,'' and said of his naked warriors, ''They can wiggle their waggles in front of her face as far as I'm concerned.''

Faced with the threat of a female boycott of his Remington electric shavers, Kiam had a change of heart. He got down on bended knee and faxed an apology to Olson.

That didn't solve the big problem, however. That being how to grant women reporters equal access to news-rich locker

Wide World Photos

Nelson Mandela
''I am a Yankee.''

Wide World Photos

Lee Trevino
Million dollar Señor.

17

Wide World Photos

The Ken Griffeys
Side by side in Seattle.

rooms without sacrificing the virginal modesty of the Zeke Mowatts of the sports world. Sam Wyche hit on one solution.

The Bengals' coach was determined to shield his showering stallions from the eyes of female reporters, but how? Bar women from the locker room? No, Wyche tried that and it cost him a $30,000 fine from the league. Order his players to shower in raincoats? Nah, too silly, even for football.

Then, Eureka! Wyche was struck by an inspiration. He put up a shower curtain.

And coming down the street right now is a man who is seldom sent to the showers. Let's have a big hand for the ever-popular Nolan Ryan One-Man Band. Ryan has been working without a team behind him for much of his 24-year major league career, but he won his 300th game this season. He also threw his sixth career no-hitter and led the league in strikeouts for the 11th time. More importantly, he finally divulged the secret of his incredible longevity as a power pitcher.

"For me," Ryan said on one of his many TV commercials, "it's two Advil, and all those aches and pains are long gone."

If you believed that, you probably also believed Jennifer Capriati, the 14-year-old tennis queen, when she revealed her secret for staying so doggone youthful—Oil of Olay.

Do you suppose Ryan was secretly massaging his right arm with Oil of Olay? Other pitchers begged to know. For all those victims of shredded rotator cuffs, ruptured tendons and killer bone spurs, it's major surgery. For Ryan, it's two lousy pills. Look, nobody ever said life was fair.

Ryan refused to ride on our next entry, the "Golden Geezers of 1990," because his right arm is still going through puberty. But just look at these inspirational senior citizens, coming over the hill and into view. There's Hale Irwin, the U.S.Open golf champ at 45, and 50-year-old Lee Trevino, who joined the Seniors Tour and won nearly a million bucks. Jack Nicklaus also turned 50, but, unlike the Merry Mex, had to be pulled kicking and screaming on to the Senior circuit. He won twice as a golden oldie, but enjoyed his 6th place finish at the Masters more. There are two other old timers you might remember: 40-year-old Olympic great Mark Spitz, who is back in the water and swimming for Barcelona, and NASCAR driver Harry Gant, who won a race at age 50.

18

Martina Navratilova
Centre Court dynasty.

Some of these guys have hung around so long, they're competing with their own kids. Ken Griffey, 40, came out of a brief retirement in September to join Ken, Jr., 20, in the Seattle outfield. How did Griffey, Sr., do as an Ancient Mariner? Not bad. He hit .377 in 21 games.

Dinosaur drivers Al Unser and Mario Andretti were still leadfooting it in 1990, but they couldn't catch their sons. Little Al and Michael finished 1-2 in the CART standings.

The largest float in the parade is up next, a gigantic steamroller titled, "Tribute to Dynasties: from Ming to Motown."

You know how the experts have been telling us that sports dynasties are dead? That revenue sharing, drafting, free agency, computer scouting and computer dating have brought about an insidious and bland parity? Well, what do the experts know?

Behold, the San Francisco 49ers. Led by Joe Montana, the mild-mannered Quarterback From Hell, the Niners rolled into their second decade of NFL domination with a 55-10 busting of the Broncos in January's Super Bowl. And then there are the ruthlessly efficient Detroit Pistons. With Isiah Thomas running the show, the Pistons were one bad boy short of a load

after they dumped Ricky Mahorn, but they were still able to crunch the Portland Trail Blazers in five games to win their second straight NBA title.

Elsewhere, the Edmonton Oilers bubbled up again in the NHL and skated off with their fifth Stanley Cup in seven years—and their first title of the post-Gretzky era. And the Miami Hurricanes were college football's No.1 team for the third time since 1983.

You want more? How about individual dynasties like Martina Navratilova and Greg LeMond? Martina won the women's singles championship at Wimbledon for the ninth time since 1978, while LeMond cycled to his third title in five years in the grueling Tour de France.

Jogging alongside the dynasty float is the Little League baseball team from Taipei, Taiwan, representing maybe the most awesome sports dynasty of all. In 1990, Taiwan won the Little League World Series for the 14th time in 17 appearances, outscoring its last three opponents, 43-1. The Taiwanese own Williamsport, Pa. Maybe not to the extent that the Japanese came to own the golf links at Pebble Beach this year, but close.

The Little League World Series, incidentally, featured the return to network

Don King
Right there in the thick of it.

Jane Fonda and Ted Turner
A fun couple.

broadcasting of Brent Musburger. Brent was sportscasting's version of a one-man dynasty—the main man with the mike for football, college basketball and baseball on CBS—until he asked for too much money and was shown the door on April Fool's Day. ABC picked him up, dusted him off and sent him to central Pennsylvania in August. Hey, Brent, a World Series is a World Series.

Next up in our floral flotilla of the year's flotsam and jetsam is an exact replica of the *Love Boat* with many of 1990's fun couples huddled together on the poop deck. Let's see, there's Bill Laimbeer and Charles Barkley, Jose Canseco and Will Clark, and NFL coaching pals Buddy Ryan and Jimmy Johnson.

We are informed by the cruise director that earlier in the parade Kareem Abdul-Jabbar was heard reading selections of his autobiography to Wilt Chamberlain while Gary Kasparov and Anatoly Karpov were engaged in a friendly game of Chutes and Ladders. Finally, at the helm of this love feast is none other than yachtsman and cable TV mogul Ted Turner with main squeeze Jane Fonda. Turner had a tough year. He lost $40 million on the Goodwill Games, his Hawks missed the NBA playoffs and his Braves finished last in the NL West with the worst record in baseball. Poor Ted.

You may be interested to know that this year's parade is the most expensive ever. Just ask the driver of our next float, CBS Sports president Neil Pilson. This entry, which depicts the famous Brink's Heist of 1950, cost a zillion dollars, a little more than Pilson paid for Major League Baseball, NFL football and the NCAA basketball tournament. Riding on this one, you'll recognize baseball pitchers Mark Langston and Mark Davis, co-captains of this year's All-Overpaid team. Back in December, 1989, Langston of the Angels and Davis of the Royals signed contracts worth a combined $29 million over nine years. Their combined stats in 1990, however, came to 12 wins, 24 losses, six saves and an ERA of 4.63. The Brink's robbers only stole about $3 million.

This is a mighty crowded float. Look at all those $600,000-a-year utility infielders. And what about those $1 million-a-year NBA bench warmers? Well, what do you expect from a league that pays its commissioner $3.5 million a year and where Clyde Drexler can get a contract extension that will pay him $8 million in 1996? Then there's Al Davis, the Raider boss. Al has been searching for the fabled Seven Cities of Gold, and found most of them—Irwindale, Oakland, Sacramento—but he agreed to stay in Los Angeles when the city agreed to rebuild the Coliseum and make it look like a giant Raider helmet.

The huge trash dumpster coming our way is actually a float, covered with wilted flowers and titled ''Send in the Clowns.'' It's a bin for the dishonored, discarded and discredited personalities of 1990.

But don't let boxing promoter Don King hear you say that. There's no other place he'd rather be. Right there in the thick of it with his good buddy, World Boxing Council president Jose Sulaiman.

Take Andre Agassi. Please. The dashing racqueteer called French Open officials ''a bunch of Bozos,'' spit in the face of an official at the U.S. Open, choked in the Davis Cup and boycotted Wimbledon again because a man's got to stand up for his right to wear hot lava-colored underpants.

Quite a collection in that dumpster. Next to Agassi is Boston Red Sox pitcher Roger Clemens, whose opinion of American League umpire Terry Cooney was lower than his league-leading ERA. In Game 4 of the AL playoffs, Clemens verbally attacked Cooney in a tirade so vile and vulgar that had he been a pro tennis player, he might have received a warning from the chair.

Also crammed into the dumpster are a whole bunch of college coaches, like N.C.State's Jim Valvano and Clemson's Danny Ford who were driven from their jobs by picky NCAA investigators and school administrators. There's Jerry Tarkanian—wave your towel to the fans, Tark!—whose Runnin' Rebels ran off with the NCAA basketball championship then were banned from defending their title in 1991 for a 13-year-old rule infraction that finally came home to roost.

But this float's sorriest occupant is Colorado football coach Bill McCartney. On Oct.6, McCartney's team beat Missouri, 33-31, on a referee's mistake—scoring the winning TD in the closing seconds on a

Wide World Photos

Andre Agassi
Hot lava underpants.

Wide World Photos

Roger Clemens
Hot under the collar.

George Foreman
No glass love handles

Wide World Photos

fifth down. McCartney could have been a hero. He could have struck a long overdue blow for integrity and fair play in college football. He could have forfeited the game. Of course, if he had done that, Colorado fans would have ridden him out of Boulder on a rail.

One thing we know about this garbage —the broken rules, twisted ethics, spoiled brats and rotting moral standards—is that it is sure to be recycled.

No less depressing is the box score from the streets of Detroit the night the Pistons won the NBA title: eight dead, 127 injured (23 from gunshot wounds), and 100 stores looted. Surprisingly, the carnage wasn't nearly as bad at the World Cup in Italy. Oh, there were a few skirmishes between the anti-terrorist police and barnstorming hooligans and neo-Nazis, but offensive fan behavior in the stands seemed to be as far removed from the World Cup as offensive play on the fields. What other event this year made the world championship chess match between Kasparov and Karpov seem so darn, well, spine-tingling?

But we never end The Big Sports Parade on a down note. Inspiration is our theme, remember? Speeding past the reviewing stand at about 70 mph is the 1989-90 Loyola Marymount basketball team, which swept into the NCAA Regionals before losing to UNLV. The incredibly overachieving Lions did it all in tribute to teammate Hank Gathers. Late in the season, Gathers threw down a thunderous dunk in a conference tournament game and then collapsed. He died moments later of a rare heart defect. The Lions decided to accept a bid to the NCAA playoffs in Hank's honor, and seldom has a young athlete's sad passing been mourned so magnificently.

Our final entry may look like a runaway balloon from the Macy's Thanksgiving Day parade, but it's really George Foreman.

Foreman was Boxer of the Year by default. The invincible Mike Tyson was vinced by Buster Douglas in Tokyo, but Buster's eight-month reign ended in Las Vegas when he went belly up in the third round against Evander Holyfield.

By all accounts, Douglas is a decent sort, but he took us all for a ride. He didn't get knocked out, he got beached. A lot of people were offended when he struggled to lose weight in training camp and still had to be practically forklifted into the ring with Holyfield. Foreman, a heavyweight's heavyweight, disagreed. "He was too light," said George. "He should have been at 270 and comfortable."

At 42, Foreman is comfortable in his second coming as boxing's Cholesterol Kid. He has been waging his comeback at around 255 and remains undefeated and undieted. One sportswriter sized up the acreage of George's once-chiseled physique and wrote, "His chest sagged and his love handles jiggled."

So what? George doesn't have glass love handles. He won five fights in 1990 and no athlete ate better, laughed more or flaunted convention, logic and Father Time more recklessly and successfully.

Closing in on a shot at regaining the heavyweight crown, Foreman seemed to echo the sentiments of Andre Agassi, who, after winning a minor tennis tournament, said, "I've just begun to scratch the iceberg."

Or was it the captain of the Titanic who said that? Or Roseanne Barr? □

Wisconsin's **Suzy Favor**, seen here winning the women's 800-meters at the NCAA Track & Field Championships in June, also won her fourth straight 1500 to end her college career with a record nine individual titles.

1989-90 CALENDAR

Sun	Mon	Tue	Wed	Thu	Fri	Sat
			1	2	3	4
5	6	7	8	9	10	11
12	13	14	15	16	17	18
19	20	21	22	23	24	25
26	27	28	29	30		

Wide World Photos

Kent Desormeaux
Boots home record 547th

1 Eighth US Circuit Court in St. Louis overturns lower court ruling of Aug.31, 1987 and grants NFL free agency restraints and immunity from antitrust statutes.

2 Center Jimmy Carson, who went from LA to Edmonton in Wayne Gretzky trade of Aug.9, 1988), is sent to Detroit in six-player deal.

4 Sunday Silence, with jockey Chris McCarron replacing suspended Pat Valenzuela, edges archrival Easy Goer by a neck in Breeders' Cup Classic at Gulfstream Park. Sunday Silence beat Easy Goer in both the Kentucky Derby and Preakness but lost Belmont to Easy Goer by 8 lengths.

5 Tanzania's Juma Ikangaa wins New York City Marathon in 2:08:01, a new course record, while Ingrid Kristiansen of Norway misses setting new women's mark by one second (2:25:30).

7 NFL Players Assn. announces it is abandoning all bargaining rights with NFL Management Council and will move to decertify itself in an attempt to force league to deal with players individually—as free agents.

San Francisco voters reject $115 million bond issue to build a new downtown baseball stadium. Giants owner Bob Lurie says team will play in Candlestick Park for at least one more season and then move.

9 East Germany declares end of restrictions on emigration and travel to West. Within hours thousands of East Germans swarm across and through Berlin Wall (built in 1961) to celebrate new freedom.

NBC Sports acquires broadcast TV rights of NBA basketball for $600 million over four years. Winning bid is a 350 percent increase over current CBS pact.

18 Dexter Manley banned for life by NFL after the Washington defensive end's third violation of league's substance abuse policy.

19 US soccer team qualifies for first World Cup since 1950, beating Trinidad & Tobago, 1-0, in Port of Spain. Paul Caligiuri scores winning goal.

Rusty Wallace captures his first NASCAR Winston Cup title, placing 15th in the year's final race, the Atlanta Journal 500. Dale Earnhardt wins race marred by death of Grant Adcox in crash on 198th lap.

Steffi Graf wins Virginia Slims Championship in New York, beating Martina Navratilova in best-of-5 final 6-4,7-5,2-6,6-2. Graf finishes year with 14 singles titles and an 85-2 record.

21 Kevin Mitchell & Will Clark of SF Giants finish 1-2 in NL Most Valuable Player voting. Earlier, baseball's other major awards went to Milwaukee's Robin Yount (AL MVP), San Diego's Mark Davis (NL Cy Young) and KC's Bret Saberhagen (AL Cy Young).

CBS Sports holds on to NCAA basketball tournament, gaining exclusive TV rights from 1991-97 for $1 billion. New contract is a 260 percent increase over current deal.

22 Kirby Puckett cracks $3 million-a-year barrier in baseball, re-signing with Minnesota for $9 million over next three seasons.

24 Tulane returns to Division I basketball after a four-year absence following a point-shaving scandal. Green Wave loses season opener to TCU, 83-63.

25 No.7 Miami routs No.1 Notre Dame, 27-10, before 81,634 at the Orange Bowl. Hurricanes halt Irish winning streak at 23.

Pat Porter wins record 8th straight US Cross-Country title in San Francisco, covering 6.2-mile course in 32:08. Lynn Jennings is the women's champion for third year in a row.

26 Willie (Flipper) Anderson of LA Rams sets a new NFL record for receivers with 336 yards (15 catches) as Rams rally to defeat New Orleans in OT, 20-17.

30 Kent Desormeaux rides filly Gilten to victory at Laurel (Md.) Race Course, setting new one-year world record for jockeys with 547th win. Chris McCarron won 546 in 1974.

Sun	Mon	Tue	Wed	Thu	Fri	Sat
					1	2
3	4	5	6	7	8	9
10	11	12	13	14	15	16
17	18	19	20	21	22	23
24	25	26	27	28	29	30
31						

Wide World Photos

George Allen
Takes 49er job at 71

1 **Free agent pitcher** Mark Langston signs a 5-year, $16 million contract with California Angels, making him baseball's highest paid player at $3.25 million-a-year.

2 **Junior Andre Ware** of Houston becomes first black QB to win Heisman Trophy as nation's outstanding college football player.

   Auburn stuns No.2 Alabama, 30-20, ties Bama and Tennessee for SEC title. Contest played at Auburn for first time in 54-game rivalry.

3 **Stefan Edberg** upsets Boris Becker 4-6,7-6, 6-3,6-1 to win Nabisco Masters in New York. Edberg is first Swede to win event since Bjorn Borg in 1981.

5 **Pittsburgh Penguins** fire GM Tony Esposito and coach Gene Ubriaco, replacing them both with former NY Rangers GM Craig Patrick. Fifth place Pens are 10-14-2 in Patrick Division (named after Craig's grandfather Lester).

6 **Joe Carter signs** 3-year, $9.2 million deal with San Diego to finalize Dec.5 three-for-one trade with Cleveland. Indians got catcher Sandy Alomar Jr. and two others.

7 **Sugar Ray Leonard** wins unanimous decision in his third bout with Roberto Duran—this one for Leonard's WBC super middleweight title in Las Vegas.

8 **FIFA bans Chile** from 1994 World Cup soccer tournament after goalkeeper Roberto Antonio Rojas is judged to have faked a head injury in Sept.3 Cup qualifying match against Brazil.

9 **NHL board of governors** votes to expand league from 21 to 28 teams by year 2000. Entry fee set at $50 million per franchise, with first teams to join by 1992-93 season.

10 **Seattle receiver** Steve Largent catches 100th career touchdown pass, overtaking Green Bay legend Don Hutson for 1st place on NFL's all-time list.

11 **Free agent reliever** Mark Davis signs 4-year deal with KC Royals for $13 million. Davis had 44 saves for San Diego in 1989.

12 **North Carolina State's** basketball program placed on two years' probation by NCAA for allowing players to sell shoes and tickets. Wolfpack is also barred from 1990 NCAA tournament.

13 **Bo Schembechler**, head football coach at Michigan since 1969, announces he'll retire after Wolverines' Rose Bowl date with Southern Cal.

14 **Pitt football coach** Mike Gottfried fired despite 7-3-1 record and 26-17-2 mark over four years.

17 **West Germany** wins Davis Cup for second year in a row as Boris Becker defeats Sweden's Mats Wilander in straight sets to clinch final in Stuttgart.

18 **Harness racing** driver Herve Filion becomes first in sport to win 800 races in one year, driving two winners at Freehold (N.J.) Raceway. Filion, 49, now has 11,993 career victories.

19 **Penn State joins** Big Ten. Nittany Lions expected to compete for conference title in basketball by 1991-92 season, but full integration into football schedule won't come until mid-1990s.

   Former NFL coach George Allen, 71, named head football coach at Long Beach State.

25 **Billy Martin killed** in one-vehicle accident near his home in upstate New York. Martin, 61, the 5-time NY Yankees manager, was passenger in pickup truck driven by friend William Reedy of Detroit.

26 **Olympic champion** John Smith beats 6-time world champ Sergei Beloglazov, 6-2, in 136.5-lb match at World Grand Wrestling Championships in Pittsburgh.

31 **Steve Spurrier**, 1966 Heisman Trophy-winning QB at Florida, signs a 5-year contract to coach the Gators. Spurrier coached at Duke for the last three seasons.

Sun	Mon	Tue	Wed	Thu	Fri	Sat
	1	2	3	4	5	6
7	8	9	10	11	12	13
14	15	16	17	18	19	20
21	22	23	24	25	26	27
28	29	30	31			

© The National

The National
Debut is front page news

1 Top-ranked Colorado falls to Notre Dame and No.2 Miami beats Alabama in Orange and Sugar Bowl games; No.3 Michigan loses to USC as Bo Schembechler retires with 2-8 Rose Bowl record.

2 Miami named No.1 in final AP and UPI college football polls, national championship is Hurricanes' third in 1980s.

4 Sacramento Kings pick Dick Motta as new head coach. Motta is NBA's third all-time winningest coach behind Red Auerbach and Jack Ramsay.

8 Bill Curry, who quit as Alabama football coach on Jan.7, is named head coach at Kentucky, succeeding Jerry Claiborne.

9 Baseball writers elect 3-time AL Cy Young Award winner Jim Palmer and 2-time NL MVP Joe Morgan to Baseball Hall of Fame.

Houston Oilers hire Houston Cougars' Jack Pardee as head coach two days after firing Jerry Glanville.

Distance runner Vicki Huber of Villanova, holder of record eight individual NCAA titles, wins Honda-Broderick Award as nation's top collegiate woman athlete of 1989.

11 Bear Bryant protege Gene Stallings named head coach at Alabama, replacing Bill Curry.

14 NFL Conference titles decided as Denver beats Cleveland, 37-21, in AFC and San Francisco routs LA Rams, 30-3, in NFC.

15 Former heavyweight champion George Foreman, 41, scores 2nd round TKO over Gerry Cooney, 33, in Atlantic City.

Washington Capitals, last in NHL's Patrick Division, replace 9-year coach Bryan Murray with his younger brother Terry.

18 Clemson football coach Danny Ford, whose program is faced with allegations of 14 NCAA rules violations from 1984-88, resigns. Ford led Tigers to national title in 1981.

Indiana swimming coach James (Doc) Counsilman, 69, announces his retirement after 33 years, six national titles and two stints as US Olympic men's coach.

21 John McEnroe disqualified from Australian Open for cursing supervisor of referees Ken Farrar during 4th round match with Mikael Pernfors.

Mario Lemieux scores four goals to lead the Wales Conference to a 12-7 win at the NHL All-Star game in Pittsburgh.

NY Rangers deal wingers Tomas Sandstrom and Tony Granato to LA for center Bernie Nicholls.

Jack Nicklaus turns 50, becomes eligible for PGA Seniors tour.

27 Steffi Graf wins third straight Australian Open with 6-3, 6-4 victory over Mary Joe Fernandez in final.

Pro Football Hall of Fame announces election of six players—Buck Buchanan, Bob Griese, Franco Harris, Ted Hendricks, Jack Lambert, Bob St. Clair—and coach Tom Landry.

28 Joe Montana throws record five TD passes as San Francisco routs Denver, 55-10, to win record-tying 4th Super Bowl title.

Ivan Lendl captures second consecutive Australian Open title when challenger Stefan Edberg is forced to retire in third set with Lendl leading 4-6, 7-6, 5-2.

31 The National, America's first daily sports newspaper, debuts in New York, Chicago, and Los Angeles.

Sun	Mon	Tue	Wed	Thu	Fri	Sat
				1	2	3
4	5	6	7	8	9	10
11	12	13	14	15	16	17
18	19	20	21	22	23	24
25	26	27	28			

Wide World Photos

Players locked out
Fans fed up

1 Wayne Gretzky signs two-year contract extension with LA Kings that will make him NHL's first $4 million-a-year player in 1996-97.

Illness forces Sebastian Coe, 33, of Britain to withdraw from 1500 meters at Commonwealth Games in Auckland, NZ. Race would have been last for retiring 2-time Olympic champion.

3 All-time leading jockey Bill Shoemaker, winner of 8833 stakes races, ends 41-year career finishing 4th aboard Patchy Groundfog in "Legend's Last Ride" Stakes at Santa Anita.

4 Danny Everett sets world indoor record of 45.04 seconds in 400 meters in Stuttgart.

NFC wins Pro Bowl with 27-21 win over AFC. LA Rams cornerback Jerry Gray is MVP.

5 Notre Dame breaks away from CFA-ABC TV package to sign 5-year, $30 million deal with NBC to show 30 home games from 1991-95.

6 St.Louis Blues right wing Brett Hull scores 50th goal of season at home against Toronto to join father Bobby in NHL's 50-Goal Club.

8 Steffi Graf chips bone in right thumb trying to avoid photographers while skiing in St.Moritz. Injury will sideline tennis star for two months.

Basketball Hall of Fame announces election of Elvin Hayes, Earl Monroe, Dave Bing, and late Neil Johnston.

9 Romanian miler Doina Melinte earns $100,000 bonus for setting world indoor records in both 1500 (4:00.27) and mile (4:17.13) in same race at Vitalis/Meadowlands (NJ) Invitational.

10 Underdog Buster Douglas knocks out previously undefeated Mike Tyson at 1:23 in 10th round to win heavyweight title in Tokyo.

11 Eastern Conference defeats West, 130-113, in NBA All-Star Game at Miami. West's Magic Johnson scores 22, gets MVP nod.

13 NY Islanders center Bryan Trottier scores 500th goal of NHL career at home against Calgary, but Flames win, 4-2.

14 Mario Lemieux's point-scoring streak ends at 46 games—five shy of Wayne Gretzky's record—when back injury forces him to leave game with NY Rangers in second period.

15 Owners' lockout of baseball spring training camps officially begins as contract impasse with players' union continues.

16 NFL gives in, says it will no longer oppose juniors who wish to enter draft.

18 Derrike Cope drives to victory in Daytona 500 when leader Dale Earnhardt blows tire on last lap.

21 NY Knicks send disgruntled 23-year-old Rod Strickland to San Antonio for Maurice Cheeks, 33, in an exchange of guards.

Minnesota North Stars' owners George and Gordon Gund threaten to move club to San Jose after their demands for $15 million in Met Center improvements are rejected.

22 LaSalle All-America Lionel Simmons becomes only fifth basketball college player to score 3000 career points, getting 27 at home against Manhattan.

25 Mark Martin wins Pontiac 400 at Richmond, but is fined $40,000 when NASCAR inspectors discover an illegal carburetor spacer in his engine.

27 Baseball owners cancel more than 100 exhibition games as lockout continues.

NFL announces plans to play 16-game regular season schedule over 17 weeks, giving each team a week off and eliminating the off-week between conference championship games and Super Bowl.

New England Patriots name former defensive coordinator Rod Rust, 61, head coach one day after firing Raymond Berry over what are termed "philosophical differences."

Britain's Peter Elliot sets world indoor record of 3:34.21 for 1500 meters during meet in Seville, Spain.

Sun	Mon	Tue	Wed	Thu	Fri	Sat
				1	2	3
4	5	6	7	8	9	10
11	12	13	14	15	16	17
18	19	20	21	22	23	24
25	26	27	28	29	30	31

AAU

Janet Evans
Receives Sullivan Award

1 **Two wildcard games** added to NFL playoff schedule as postseason field grows to 12 teams. Expanded playoffs part of new 4-year, $950 million deal with ABC Sports.

4 **All-America forward** Hank Gathers of Loyola Marymount dies of heart failure after collapsing during West Coast Conference tournament game with Portland in LA.

6 **Thirteen-year-old** Jennifer Capriati defeats Mary Lou Daniels, 28, in straight sets (7-6,6-1) in pro debut at Va.Slims of Florida in Boca Raton.

8 **CBS Sports** agrees to pay NFL more than $1 billion for four more years of NFC games and 1992 Super Bowl. A day later, NBC gets four more years of AFC coverage and 1993 Super Bowl for $752 million.

9 **NHL reinstates** Detroit forward Bob Probert after he served a 90-day sentence in Rochester, Minn., state prison for cocaine possesion.

10 **Jill Trenary** of US wins Women's World Figure Championship in Halifax, Nova Scotia, outpointing defending champion Midori Ito of Japan.

12 **Swimmer Janet Evans** receives 60th annual Sullivan Award as 1989's outstanding American amateur athlete.

LA Raiders owner Al Davis informs NFL of his desire to return to Oakland as local politicians agree to welcome team back with 15-year, $602 million deal.

NFL owners, meeting in Orlando, approve replay rule for fifth season. Commissioner Paul Tagliabue asks expansion committee to consider divisional realignment.

14 **Susan Butcher** sets new record of 11 days, one hour, 53 minutes and 23 seconds in winning her fourth Anchorage-to-Nome Iditarod Trail Sled Dog Race.

16 **Formal baseball talks** resume after 9-day layoff. Players reject new owners' proposal, which offers to increase pension benefits and minimum salary but makes no concessions on key sticking point—arbitration eligibility.

17 **Julio Cesar Chavez** defeats Meldrick Taylor when referee Richard Steele stops their junior welterweight title fight with two seconds left in the 12th round and Taylor ahead on points.

18 **Baseball lockout ends** after 32 days. Owners and players settle on new 4-year basic agreement which hikes minimum salary (to $100,000) and pension contributions and makes top 17 percent of second-year players eligible for arbitration. Opening Day pushed back a week, missed games to be made up.

22 **Twenty-two juniors** officially cleared by NFL to enter 1990 college draft on April 22. Among them are QBs Andre Ware of Houston and Jeff George of Illinois, RB Emmitt Smith of Florida, and LBs Keith McCants of Alabama and Junior Seau of USC.

24 **Mike Barrowman** of Michigan breaks Steve Lundquist's 9-year-old American record in the 200-meter breaststroke with a 1:53.77 at the NCAA men's swimming championships in Bloomington, Ind. Texas wins its third straight team title one week after the Texas women upset Stanford.

Oklahoma State wins 29th NCAA Division I wrestling championship, and second in a row, outpointing Arizona State and Iowa at College Park, Md.

27 **NY Rangers win** first title in NHL since 1942, clinching Patrick Division regular season pennant with 7-4 victory over Quebec.

28 **Bulls' Michael Jordan** scores career-high 69 points in Chicago's 117-113 overtime win at Cleveland.

31 **Devils and Rebels** win NCAA Semifinals in Denver, move on to championship game. Duke beats Arkansas, 97-83, UNLV downs Georgia Tech, 90-81.

Sun	Mon	Tue	Wed	Thu	Fri	Sat
1	2	3	4	5	6	7
8	9	10	11	12	13	14
15	16	17	18	19	20	21
22	23	24	25	26	27	28
29	30					

Wide World Photos

Jack Nicklaus
An immediate success

1 **CBS Sports fires** Brent Musburger after 15 years as principal anchorman, but will allow him to call NCAA final on Apr.2.

Jack Nicklaus wins PGA Seniors debut, taking the Tradition in Scottsdale, Ariz., by four strokes.

Stanford beats Auburn, 88-81, to win NCAA Women's Division I Basketball Championship in Knoxville, Tenn.

Wisconsin routs Colgate, 7-4, in Detroit for fifth NCAA Division I hockey title.

2 **Nevada-Las Vegas** records most lopsided win ever in NCAA Final, crushing Duke, 103-73 in Denver. Sophomore guard Anderson Hunt scores 29 and is named Most Outstanding Player.

TV sitcom producer Tom Werner ("Roseanne," "The Cosby Show") signs agreement to purchase San Diego Padres for $75 million.

7 **Jim Valvano agrees** to $213,000 buyout of his contract by N.C.State. Popular Wolfpack basketball coach forced out after 10 years for presiding over academically irresponsible program that was also tainted by unproven charges of point-shaving and booster payments.

8 **Nick Faldo** defeats Raymond Floyd on 2nd hole of sudden death playoff to win second straight Masters.

9 **Baseball opens** 1990 season one week late with 10 games and a rainout at Wrigley Field.

11 **California pitchers** Mark Langston and Mike Witt combine to no-hit Seattle, 1-0, in Anaheim.

14 **Stanley Cup** champion Calgary eliminated in first round of playoffs by Los Angeles. Kings' goal in double-overtime of Game 6 sends Flames packing.

15 **Steffi Graf** returns two months after breaking thumb to win Bausch & Lomb Championships, routing Aranxta Sanchez in final, 6-1, 6-0.

16 **Boston Marathon** won by 1988 Olympic champions Gelindo Bordin (2:08:19) and Rosa Mota (2:25:24).

17 **Bowing to pressure** from an enraged electorate, Oakland city council votes to rescind approval of $602 million deal to bring back the LA Raiders and offers $428 million instead.

19 **Indianapolis Colts** trade Pro Bowl tackle Chris Hinton and WR Andre Rison to Atlanta for overall No.1 pick (QB Jeff George of Illinois) in NFL Draft. Colts sign George following day for $15 million over 6 years.

20 **Pete Rose pleads** guilty to two charges of filing false income tax returns, faces strong possibility of jail term and fines of up to $500,000.

Pistons and 76ers fined a total of $50,000 by NBA for Apr.19 fight in Philadelphia. Bill Laimbeer and Charles Barkley fined $20,000 each.

Hank Gathers' family files $32.5 million suit against Loyola Marymount coaches, doctors and trainers.

22 **Five juniors** among first seven players chosen in NFL Draft. Group includes No.1 pick QB Jeff George, linebackers Keith McCants and Junior Seau, safety Mark Carrier and QB Andre Ware.

San Antonio Spurs beat Phoenix on last day of regular season to clinch Midwest Division and complete biggest turnaround in NBA history—35 games (from 21-61 to 56-26).

24 **LA Lakers** fined $25,000 by NBA for not playing starters in final regular season game against Portland. Blazers won, 130-88.

26 **New York Appeals Court**, in 5-2 vote, awards America's Cup to San Diego Yacht Club, ending 2½-year legal battle with New Zealand.

27 **Pitcher Orel Hershiser** of LA Dodgers will miss rest of baseball season after rotator cuff surgery on right shoulder.

Sun	Mon	Tue	Wed	Thu	Fri	Sat
		1	2	3	4	5
6	7	8	9	10	11	12
13	14	15	16	17	18	19
20	21	22	23	24	25	26
27	28	29	30	31		

Stephen Parker/Syracuse U.

Gary and Paul Gait
Had Loyola seeing double

2 Brent Musburger signs 6-year, $11 million contract with ABC Sports, 30 days after being let go by CBS. He remains TV's highest-paid sportscaster.

Gund Brothers agree to sell North Stars to Morris Belzberg and former Hartford Whalers owner Howard Baldwin for $31.5 million. In return, NHL grants Gunds expansion team in San Jose for 1991-92.

5 Kentucky Derby won by Unbridled, a 10-1 shot ridden by Craig Perret and owned by 92-year-old Frances Genter. Summer Squall is second and Pleasant Tap third.

7 Calgary Flames fire 3rd-year coach Terry Crisp three weeks after having their Stanley Cup title defense cut short in opening round.

8 Cleveland voters endorse downtown stadium-arena complex for baseball Indians and NBA Cavs, by voting in favor of cigarette and alcohol tax that will pay for half of estimated $200 million construction costs.

13 Sixteen-year-old Monica Seles upsets Martina Navratilova, 6-1, 6-1, to win Italian Open.

14 LA Lakers' Pat Riley named NBA Coach of Year after leading club to 63-19 record and 9th straight Pacific Division title.

15 Lakers eliminated from NBA playoffs in second round. Phoenix eliminates defending Western champs in five games.

Edmonton beats Bruins, 3-2, in triple overtime to open Stanley Cup finals in Boston Garden. Game-winner netted by Petr Klima with 4:47 left in third OT.

19 Preakness Stakes finish a reversal of Kentucky Derby as Summer Squall edges Unbridled. Summer Squall, however, will pass up Belmont because New York is a non-Lasix state.

20 Monica Seles strikes again, upsetting Steffi Graf, 6-4, 6-3 to win German Open and end Graf's 66-match winning streak.

World shotput record broken by American Randy Barnes with toss of 75-feet, 10¼-inches at meet in Los Angeles.

22 Magic Johnson of LA Lakers wins NBA Most Valuable Player vote by 22 votes over Philadelphia's Charles Barkley, who received 11 more first place votes. Bulls' Michael Jordan places third.

23 Atlanta named host of 1994 Super Bowl by NFL owners. Super XXVIII will be played in new Georgia Dome.

24 Edmonton reclaims Stanley Cup, beating Boston in five games. NHL title is fifth in seven years for Oilers and first without Wayne Gretzky.

27 Arie Luyendyk wins fastest and richest Indianapolis 500 ever, averaging 185.981 mph and taking home over $1 million.

28 Gary and Paul Gait lead Syracuse to third straight NCAA Division I lacrosse title, trouncing Loyola (Md.), 21-9. The Gait Bros. scored eight times and finished their 4-year careers with a combined 319 goals and 146 assists.

29 Top seeds Stefan Edberg and Boris Becker beaten in first round of French Open. Sergi Bruguera downs Edberg in straight sets while Goran Ivanisevic bests Becker in four.

Rickey Henderson becomes AL's all-time stolen base leader, overtaking Ty Cobb with steal No.893 against Toronto in Oakland. He still trails Lou Brock's record major league total by 45.

NY Mets fire Davey Johnson, name Bud Harrelson manager. Johnson was the winningest Met manager ever and led club to 1986 World Series title.

30 Big East commissioner Dave Gavitt named head of basketball operations by Boston Celtics.

31 NCAA places Clemson football program on one-year probation, but issues no major sanctions.

Sun	Mon	Tue	Wed	Thu	Fri	Sat
					1	2
3	4	5	6	7	8	9
10	11	12	13	14	15	16
17	18	19	20	21	22	23
24	25	26	27	28	29	30

Wide World Photos

Mike Dunleavy and Pat Riley
Changing of the ex-guards

2 **Seattle's Randy Johnson** throws second no-hitter of season, blanking Detroit, 2-0, at the Kingdome.

Suzy Favor of Wisconsin completes 800-1500 meter double, winning her fourth straight 1500 title in NCAA Track & Field Championships at Duke. Nine overall individual titles make her the winningest athlete in NCAA history. Meanwhile, LSU takes men's and women's team titles.

4 **ABC Sports** and ESPN sign former N.C.State coach Jim Valvano to contract worth $900,000 over three years.

6 **NY Yankees** fire Bucky Dent in Boston, name Stump Merrill to replace him. Managerial change is 19th in 17 years for owner George Steinbrenner.

NHL Hart Trophy goes to Edmonton center Mark Messier, who beats out Boston's Ray Bourque by two votes in league's closest MVP vote ever.

Al Michaels becomes highest-paid sportscaster on TV, signing new 5-year deal with ABC for $2.5 million a year.

8 **World Cup soccer** tournament opens in Italy, with Cameroon stunning defending champion Argentina, 1-0, at Milan.

Duke coach Mike Krzyzewski turns down 4-year, $2 million offer to become coach of Boston Celtics. Celts fired Jimmy Rodgers on May 8.

9 **French Open** women's title won by Monica Seles, who defeats Steffi Graf 7-6, 6-4. Seles, at 16, is youngest player ever to win the French.

Irish thoroughbred Go And Go wins Belmont Stakes as favorite Unbridled finishes fourth, 13 lengths back.

Georgia captures College World Series, beating Oklahoma State, 2-1, to become first SEC team to win baseball championship.

St.Louis Blues sign 73-goal scorer Brett Hull to 3-year contract. Hull's salary goes from $125,000 to $1.5 million a year.

10 **Thirty-year-old** Andres Gomez defeats Andre Agassi in four sets to win French Open men's title.

US soccer team routed, 5-1, by Czechoslovakia in America's first World Cup soccer match in 40 years.

11 **Nolan Ryan tosses** record 6th no-hitter, striking out 14 and walking two, as Texas beats A's, 5-0, in Oakland.

Pat Riley resigns as coach of LA Lakers after winning four NBA titles in nine seasons. Milwaukee assistant Mike Dunleavy named as replacement.

12 **Baltimore shortstop** Cal Ripken moves into second place behind Lou Gehrig on baseball's all-time consecutive game list with 1308th straight appearance.

Boston Celtics end search for new coach, name assistant Chris Ford.

14 **Detroit Pistons** get last-second basket from Vinnie Johnson to beat Portland, 92-90, and win their second straight NBA title in Game 5. Isiah Thomas is playoff MVP.

18 **Hale Irwin wins** third US Open golf title, beating Mike Donald on first hole of sudden death after extra round. At 45, Irwin is oldest Open champion.

27 **New Jersey Nets** select Syracuse forward Derrick Coleman with 1st pick of NBA draft. Three underclassmen picked in first round: Chris Jackson, Dennis Scott and Jerrod Mustaf.

Oakland outfielder Jose Canseco becomes baseball's first $5 million-a-year player, signing 5-year, $23.5 million contract.

29 **Two no-hitters** thrown on the same night as Oakland's Dave Stewart blanks the Blue Jays, 5-0, in Toronto and LA's Fernando Valenzuela stifles St.Louis, 6-0, at Dodger Stadium.

Chicago Blackhawks trade star center Denis Savard to Montreal for star defenseman Chris Chelios.

Sun	Mon	Tue	Wed	Thu	Fri	Sat
1	2	3	4	5	6	7
8	9	10	11	12	13	14
15	16	17	18	19	20	21
22	23	24	25	26	27	28
29	30	31				

Wide World Photos

Pete Rose
Caught stealing

1 New York hurler Andy Hawkins pitches no-hitter and loses, 4-0, as Yankees make three errors in 8th inning at Comiskey Park.

Lee Trevino holds off Jack Nicklaus to take US Senior Open, becoming 5th golfer to win both US and US Senior opens.

5 Baseball commissioner Fay Vincent fines NY Yankees $25,000 and orders them to pay California $200,000 for tampering in May 11 Dave Winfield trade.

Washington Capitals' defenseman Scott Stevens signed to 4-year, $5 million offer sheet by St. Louis Blues.

6 Whitey Herzog quits as manager of St. Louis Cardinals, saying he's "embarrassed" by team's play. Cards are 33-47 and 15 games out in NL East. Herzog led club to three pennants and one world title in 1980s.

7 Martina Navratilova wins Wimbledon singles title for record 9th time, beating Zina Garrison 6-4, 6-1.

8 West Germany captures third World Cup championship, beating Argentina, 1-0, on a penalty kick by Andreas Brehme. Crowd of 73,603 on hand at Rome's Olympic Stadium.

Stefan Edberg outlasts Boris Becker 6-2, 6-2, 3-6, 3-6, 6-4 to win second Wimbledon singles title in three years.

10 Julio Franco's 2-run double off Rob Dibble in top of the 7th paces AL to 2-0 victory over NL in rain-delayed All-Star game at Wrigley Field.

11 San Diego changes managers, Jack McKeon stepping down in favor of coach Greg Riddoch.

12 Melido Perez of White Sox throws season's 7th no-hitter, a rain-shortened six-inning job at Yankee Stadium.

13 Detroit Red Wings fire two-time Coach of Year Jacques Demers, make general manager Jim Devellano a Senior VP, and bring in Bryan Murray as combined head coach and GM.

14 PGA of America amends site selection criteria for championship after complaints are raised about racial policies at Shoal Creek C.C. in Birmingham, Ala.

15 Defending champion Betsy King comes from 11 shots back in last 36 holes to win rain-interrupted US Women's Open. Second round leader Patty Sheehan blows 9-shot lead in two-round final day.

18 Easy Goer forced to retire due to foot injury. Four-year-old colt won 1989 Belmont and 14 of 20 career starts.

19 Pete Rose sentenced to five months in federal prison and fined $50,000 for tax evasion.

20 NCAA bans Nevada-Las Vegas from defending Division I basketball title in 1991 tournament. Penalty comes 13 years after NCAA ordered UNLV to suspend coach Jerry Tarkanian for recruiting violations and Tarkanian was able to get a court injunction prohibiting his suspension.

22 Nick Faldo wins British Open at St. Andrews, becomes first men's golfer in eight years to win two majors in same season.

American cyclist Greg LeMond wins second straight Tour de France and third in five years. Italian Claudio Chiappucci is second, 2:16 back.

23 Leroy Burrell outruns Carl Lewis to win 100-meters in 10.05 at Goodwill Games in Seattle.

30 George Steinbrenner agrees to resign as general managing partner of NY Yankees by Aug. 20, after commissioner Fay Vincent finds him in violation of "best interests of baseball" rule for dealings with admitted gambler Howard Spira.

31 Nolan Ryan registers 300th win in Milwaukee, going 7⅔ innings in 11-4 Texas victory over Brewers.

Shoal Creek extends honorary membership to black businessman Louis J. Willie. Protesters agree to call off boycott of PGA Championship.

Sun	Mon	Tue	Wed	Thu	Fri	Sat
			1	2	3	4
5	6	7	8	9	10	11
12	13	14	15	16	17	18
19	20	21	22	23	24	25
26	27	28	29	30	31	

Wide World Photos

George Steinbrenner
No longer the boss

1 Arkansas leaves SWC after 75 years to become 11th member of Southeastern Conference.

NBA salary cap raised over $2 million to nearly $12 million per team.

Joe Torre, who won NL batting title and MVP award as St.Louis 3rd baseman in 1971, is named manager of Cardinals.

2 Sunday Silence, 1989 Horse of Year, joins archrival Easy Goer in retirement after tearing ligament in left foreleg. Four-year-old won Kentucky Derby, Preakness and Breeder's Cup Classic in '89.

4 Hambletonian harness race won by Harmonious in 1:54.2. Victory is third in four years for driver John Campbell.

5 LA attorney Alan Rothenberg elected president of US Soccer Federation, outpolling incumbent Werner Fricker at USSF meeting in Orlando.

US women beat Soviet Union, 82-70, to win basketball gold medal at Goodwill Games.

8 Pete Rose begins serving 5-month prison sentence for income tax evasion at Marion (Ill.) Federal Prison Camp. Release date set for Jan.7, 1991.

9 All-Pro quarterback Joe Montana of SF 49ers agrees to 4-year, $13 million contract, making him NFL's highest-paid player.

Canadian track officials say banned sprinter Ben Johnson should be welcomed back into international competition when his 2-year IAAF suspension for steroid use ends on Sept.24.

11 Lightweight champion Pernell Whitaker knocks out Juan Nazario in 1st round at Lake Tahoe to unify the WBC, WBA and IBF titles.

12 Wayne Grady wins PGA Championship by three strokes over Fred Couples, who bogeys four straight holes on back nine at Shoal Creek.

13 Stefan Edberg replaces Ivan Lendl as No.1 player on ATP computer. Lendl had been ranked first for 80 consecutive weeks.

15 Terry Mulholland no-hits former San Francisco teammates, 6-0, in Philadelphia for record 8th no-hitter of season.

George Steinbrenner chooses theatrical producer Robert Nederlander to succeed him as managing general partner of NY Yankees.

17 Carlton Fisk's 349th career home run against Texas is also his record-setting 328th as a catcher.

19 Yugoslavia routs USSR, 92-75, to win World Men's Basketball Championship in Buenos Aires.

22 Miami Heat signs Cleveland forward John Williams to offer sheet worth $26.5 million over seven years.

US Olympic Committee executive committee, places vice president George Steinbrenner on inactive list in wake of his baseball difficulties.

26 Jose Maria Olazabal of Spain wins World Series of Golf in Akron with record 18-under 262.

Taiwan shuts out Shippensburg, Pa., 9-0, to win Little League World Series. Title is Taiwan's 14th in 17 trips to Williamsport.

28 Stefan Edberg upset by Alexander Volkov 6-3, 7-6, 6-2 in opening round of US Open.

29 Oakland A's deal for NL batting leader (.335) Willie McGee of St.Louis and Texas DH Harold Baines before trading deadline.

Indianapolis Colts suspend running back Eric Dickerson for six weeks, putting him on non-football injury list after his refusal to take physical exam.

31 Seattle Mariners start first father-son combination in history of major leagues with Ken Griffey Sr. and Jr. in Kingdome outfield. Both single and score in first inning against Kansas City.

Boston Bruins sign all-star defenseman Ray Bourque to 4-year, $5 million contract.

Sun	Mon	Tue	Wed	Thu	Fri	Sat
						1
2	3	4	5	6	7	8
9	10	11	12	13	14	15
16	17	18	19	20	21	22
23	24	25	26	27	28	29
30						

Wide World Photos

Doug Moe
Nuggets say "Aloha"

2 Dave Stieb throws season's 9th and final no-hitter, as Toronto shuts out Indians, 3-0, in Cleveland.

3 Bobby Thigpen notches 47th save out of White Sox bullpen to set new major league record. Chicago beats KC, 4-2.

4 NFL fines SF 49ers $500,000 for transferring ownership of team to DeBartolo Corp. in 1986 without league permission. DeBartolo Corp. also owns NHL Pittsburgh Penguins. NFL does not permit either corporate or cross-ownership.

5 NY Giants sign holdout linebacker Lawrence Taylor to 3-year contract worth $4.95 million making him NFL's highest-paid defensive player.

6 Doug Moe fired by Denver Nuggets after 10 years and nine trips to playoffs. Moe ranks 11th in all-time NBA coaching wins with 642 (including playoffs).

Cleveland matches Miami's offer sheet ($26.5 million for 7 years) to Cavs' forward John Williams.

7 Wasting little time, Denver names Loyola Marymount coach Paul Westhead to replace Doug Moe as coach. Westhead led LA Lakers to 1980 NBA title.

8 Gabriela Sabatini wins US Open, defeating defending champion Steffi Graf 6-2, 7-6 (7-4) for first Grand Slam title.

BYU quarterback Ty Detmer throws for 406 yards and three TDs as Cougars upset No.1 Miami, 28-21, in Provo, Utah.

9 Nineteen-year-old Pete Sampras becomes youngest men's US Open champion ever, recording 13 aces in 6-4, 6-3, 6-2 rout of Andre Agassi.

11 LA Raiders agree to 20-year deal that will keep them in Los Angeles, provided 67-year-old Memorial Coliseum undergoes a promised $145 million renovation.

14 Florida State accepts invitation to become 9th member of Atlantic Coast Conference.

17 Arbitrator George Nicolau awards baseball players $102.5 million in damages, after finding owners violated collective bargaining agreement in 1987 and '88 by suppressing free agent market.

18 IOC chooses Atlanta over Athens and four other cities to host 1992 Summer Olympic Games. Decision announced at IOC meeting in Tokyo.

20 NCAA Infractions Committee hands down two-year probations to both football and basketball programs at Florida. Football team is barred from bowl game this season.

22 Illinois running back Howard Griffith scores eight touchdowns for 48 points, breaking NCAA records for TDs and points in a single game. Illini beat Southern Ill., 56-21.

24 Michael Chang concludes two-day, 3-6, 6-7, 6-4, 6-4, 6-3 victory over Austria's Horst Skoff in Vienna. USA advances to Davis Cup final against Australia.

25 South Carolina accepts invitation to become 12th member of Southeastern Conference.

27 NHL suspends Edmonton goalie Grant Fuhr for one year for admitted drug use. Fuhr can apply for reinstatement as soon as Jan.15, 1991.

NFL to appoint special counsel to investigate sexual harassment charges leveled by *Boston Herald* reporter Lisa Olson against receiver Zeke Mowatt and other New England Patriots players.

28 Canadian Olympic Association votes, 9-3, to rescind its ban on sprinter Ben Johnson, for testing positive for steroids during 1988 Seoul Olympics.

30 Comiskey Park closes its doors after 80 seasons with 2-1 White Sox victory over Kansas City. Crowd of 42,849 pushes 1990 attendance over 2 million mark.

Sun	Mon	Tue	Wed	Thu	Fri	Sat
	1	2	3	4	5	6
7	8	9	10	11	12	13
14	15	16	17	18	19	20
21	22	23	24	25	26	27
28	29	30	31			

Wide World Photos

Jose Rijo
World Series Hero

1 **Head coach** Sam Wyche refuses to allows *USA Today* reporter Denise Tom into Cincinnati locker room after Bengals' 31-16 loss to Seattle in Kingdome.

3 **Boston Red Sox** win AL East with 3-1 victory over Chicago on final day of regular season. Tom Brunansky's sliding catch in Fenway Park right field corner with two on and two out in 9th saves game.

Cecil Fielder of Detroit belts home runs No.50 and 51 at Yankee Stadium, becoming 11th hitter to reach 50 homers and first since George Foster in 1977.

Nevada-Las Vegas coach Jerry Tarkanian offers to sit out upcoming postseason if NCAA will lift ban and allow defending national champion UNLV to play in 1991 basketball tournament.

5 **NFL commissioner** Paul Tagliabue fines Cincinnati coach Sam Wyche $30,000 for excluding woman reporter from locker room on Oct. 1.

6 **Oakland blanks** Boston, 7-0, in first game of AL Championship series at Fenway Park.

Top two teams beaten in college football as Stanford edges No.1 Notre Dame, 36-31, in South Bend and Miami downs No.2 Florida State, 31-22, at Orange Bowl.

Fifth down TD allows Colorado to defeat Missouri, 33-31, on last play of their Big 8 game in Columbia, Mo.

7 **Al Unser Jr.** clinches CART driving championship despite crashing on lap 109 of 200-lap Bosch Spark Plug 200 in Nazareth, Pa.

8 **Gravelly voiced** Johnny Most, 67, retires after 37 years as radio play-by-play man for Boston Celtics.

World Chess Championship between defender Gary Kasparov and former champion Anatoly Karpov begins best-of-24 game match in New York. Contest will switch to Lyons, France, after 12 games.

10 **Oakland sweeps** Boston in four games to win third straight AL pennant. Red Sox starter Roger Clemens thrown out of finale in 2nd inning for cursing plate umpire Terry Cooney.

Miami accepts Big East invitation to become 10th member. Known as basketball conference, Big East includes football schools Boston College, Pitt and Syracuse.

NFL's fledgling WLAF spring league fires Tex Schramm as president and names Minnesota general manager Mike Lynn to replace him.

12 **Cincinnati beats** Pittsburgh, 2-1, to wrap up first NL pennant since 1976 in six games.

Portland guard Clyde Drexler signs contract extension that will pay a reported $8 million in 1995-96, making him highest paid team sport athlete ever.

13 **No. 1 Michigan** a 28-27 loser to Michigan State after 2-point conversion try fails in final seconds. Refs miss interference call on play.

16 **World Series** opens in Cincinnati with Reds routing heavily-favored Oakland, 7-0.

18 **Michael Nunn** stops Donald Curry in 10th round to retain IBF middleweight title in Paris.

20 **Cincinnati completes** four-game sweep of favored Oakland to win World Series. Reds' starter Jose Rijo named MVP.

No. 2 Notre Dame gets 5 field goals from Craig Hentrich, beats No. 2 Miami, 29-20, in South Bend.

25 **Evander Holyfield** knocks out champion Buster Douglas at 1:10 in 3rd round to win undisputed heavyweight title in Las Vegas.

26 **Wayne Gretzky** reaches 2000 regular season points with first period assist, but visiting LA Kings lose to Winnipeg, 6-2.

27 **Two horses die** in Breeders' Cup races at Belmont Park: Horse of the Year hopeful Go For Wand breaks ankle in Distaff and is humanely destroyed, while Mr. Nickerson has heart attack and dies in Sprint. Unbridled wins $3 million Classic.

JANUARY

1 Bowl games (8): Cotton (Dallas); Citrus (Orlando); Fiesta (Tempe,AZ); Gator (Jacksonville,FL); Hall of Fame (Tampa); Orange (Miami); Rose (Pasadena); Sugar (New Orleans).
3 World Swimming Championships begin (Perth, Australia).
5 NFL playoffs (2): AFC/NFC wildcard games.
6 NFL playoffs (2): AFC/NFC wildcard games.
8 NCAA Convention begins (Nashville).
12 NFL playoffs (2): AFC/NFC semifinals.
13 NFL playoffs (2): AFC/NFC semifinals.
13 Australian Open tennis begins (Melbourne).
19 NHL Hockey All-Star Game (Chicago).
20 NFL playoffs (2): AFC/NFC championship games.
27 Super Bowl XXV (Tampa).

FEBRUARY

2 24 Hours at Daytona begins (Daytona Beach).
3 NFL Pro Bowl (Honolulu).
10 NBA All-Star Game (Charlotte).
10 US Figure Skating Championships begin (Minneapolis).
11 Westminster Dog Show begins (New York).
17 Daytona 500 (Daytona Beach).

MARCH

2 Iditarod Trail Sled Dog race begins (Anchorage to Nome).
10 US Grand Prix Formula One auto race (Phoenix).
11 World Figure Skating Championships begin (Munich).
13 NCAA Women's Division I Basketball tournament begins.
14 NCAA Men's Division I Basketball tournament begins.
14 NCAA Division I Wrestling Finals begin (Iowa City).
17 NFL Annual Meeting begins (Kona, HI).
24 PBA National bowling begins (Toledo).
28 LPGA Dinah Shore golf begins (Rancho Mirage,CA).
28 NCAA Division I Hockey Final Four begins (St.Paul, MN).
29 NCAA Women's Basketball Final Four begins (New Orleans).
30 NCAA Men's Basketball Final Four begins (Indianapolis).
31 NHL regular season ends.

APRIL

3 NHL Stanley cup playoffs begin.
3 US Spring Nationals swimming begins (Seattle).
7 US Men's Open bowling begins (Indianapolis).
8 Baseball Opening Day.
11 Masters golf begins (Augusta, GA).
15 Boston Marathon.
17 US Indoor Diving Championships begin (Minneapolis).
21 NFL Draft begins (New York).
21 NBA regular season ends.
23 PBA Firestone Tournament of Champions begins (Akron).
25 NBA playoffs begin.
30 ABC Masters bowling begins (Toledo).

MAY

4 Kentucky Derby (Louisville).
18 Preakness Stakes (Baltimore).
25 NCAA Lacrosse Final Four begins (Syracuse).
25 US Women's Open bowling begins (Los Angeles).
26 Indianapolis 500.
27 French Open tennis begins (Paris).
29 NCAA Track & Field Championships begin (Eugene, OR).
31 NCAA College Baseball World Series begins (Omaha).

JUNE

6 US Gymnastics Championships begin (Cincinnati).
8 Belmont Stakes (Elmont, NY).
8 Cincinnati Collegiate Rowing Regatta Rowing Finals.
13 US Open golf begins (Chaska, MN).
22 24 Hours of Le Mans auto race begins (France).
24 Wimbledon tennis begins.
27 LPGA Championships golf begins (Bethesda, MD).

JULY

3 US Pro Cycling Road Championships begin (Salt Lake City).
6 Tour de France cycling race begins (through July 28).
9 Baseball All-Star Game (Toronto).
11 US Women's Open golf begins (Ft. Worth).
12 US Olympic Festival begins (Los Angeles).
18 British Open golf begins (Royal Birkdale).
25 US Senior Open golf begins (Detroit).

AUGUST

3 Pan American Games begin (Havana).
3 Hambletonian harness race (E. Rutherford, NJ).
5 US Women's Amateur golf begins (Hutchinson, KS).
8 PGA Championship golf begins (Carmel, IN).
10 All-American Soap Box Derby (Akron).
12 US Summer Nationals swimming begins (Boca Raton, FL).
14 US Outdoor Diving Championships begin (Bartlesville, OK).
16 Women's Major Fast Pitch softball tournament begins (Decatur, IL).
20 US Amateur golf (Coltewah, TN).
20 Little League Baseball World Series begins (Williamsport, PA).
22 Pan Pacific Swimming Championships begin (Edmonton).
24 World Track & Field Championships begin (Tokyo).
26 US Open tennis begins (Flushing, NY).

SEPTEMBER

1 NFL regular season opens
6 Men's Major Fast Pitch softball tournament begins (Midland, MI).
6 World Gymnastics Championships begin (Indianapolis).
12 LPGA du Meurier Classic golf begins (Vancouver).

OCTOBER

6 Baseball regular season ends.
8 Baseball AL/NL Championship Series begin.
12 College football: Oklahoma vs Texas (Dallas).
19 World Series begins (in city of AL champion).
19 Ironman Triathlon (Kailua-Kona, HI).
26 College football: USC at Notre Dame.

NOVEMBER

2 Breeders' Cup horse racing (Louisville).
3 New York City Marathon.
11 ATP Men's Tennis Championships begin (Frankfurt).
16 College football: Miami, FL at Florida St.
18 Virginia Slims Tennis Championships begin (New York).
23 College football: Harvard at Yale; Ohio St. at Michigan; Oklahoma at Nebraska; UCLA at USC.
24 CFL Grey Cup Championship (Winnipeg).
29 US Open swimming begins (Minneapolis).
30 College football: Alabama vs Auburn (Birmingham).

DECEMBER

6 National Finals Rodeo (Las Vegas).
7 Army-Navy Game (Philadelphia).
23 NFL regular season ends.
28 NFL playoffs begin.

With manager **Lou Piniella** throwing numerous fits and an occasional base, the Cincinnati Reds played with a season-long intensity that enabled them to sweep heavily-favored Oakland in the World Series.

BASEBALL

*Cincinnati ends Hunt for Red October
by sweeping A's in World Series;
Ryan records 6th no-hitter and 300th win;
Fielder hits 51, Steinbrenner hits road.*

BASEBALL

1990 YEAR IN REVIEW

by Tim Kurkjian

The major league baseball season ended much as it began, with observers shaking their heads in amazement.

How could the Cincinnati Reds stumble so badly down the stretch of the regular season, then sweep the mighty Oakland Athletics in the World Series? In March, the same heads shook when the owners locked the players out of spring training. How could this be allowed to happen while the game was reaching an all-time high in popularity?

It was an amazing year. Off the field, the lockout, the jailing of Cincinnati legend Pete Rose for tax evasion, and the permanent suspension of New York Yankees' owner George Steinbrenner attracted a great deal of attention. Fortunately, there was more than enough going on down on the field to compensate.

The 1990 season was filled with achievements and thrills—both great and goofy. Detroit Tigers first baseman Cecil Fielder, who spent 1989 playing in Japan, became the first major leaguer since George Foster in 1977—and first AL player since Roger Maris and Mickey Mantle in 1961—to hit 50 homers in a season. He did it in style, pounding Nos. 50 & 51 at Yankee Stadium on the final night of the season. Fielder also led the AL with 132 RBIs. That's one more than the top two RBI men (Lou Whitaker and Fred Lynn) had combined in the Tigers' awful 1989 season.

Oakland Athletics pitcher Bob Welch won 27 games—the most in the AL since Denny McLain won 31 in 1968. And that still didn't guarantee him the Cy Young, which gives you an idea of the individual pitching performances this season. Chicago White Sox reliever Bobby Thigpen shattered the record for saves in a season with 57—11 more than Dave Righetti posted in his record-setting season in 1986.

Tim Kurkjian writes the "Inside Baseball" column for *Sports Illustrated*. He joined *SI* last year after covering the major leagues for *The Baltimore Sun* from 1986-89.

Detroit's favorite Japanese import, first baseman **Cecil Fielder** of the Tigers, hit home runs No.50 and 51 on the last night of the regular season.

Kansas City's George Brett, believed by many to be washed up after hitting .220 for the first two months, batted .390 the second half of the season to win the AL batting title at .329. He became the only man in history to win a batting title in three decades. The National League batting crown went to St. Louis' Willie McGee, who finished the year with Oakland in the AL.

A record nine no-hitters were thrown (see box), including No.6 by Nolan Ryan of the Texas Rangers. Ryan also won his 300th game and struck out 16 batters in one outing—giving him fifteen 16-strikeout games. All other AL pitchers have combined for 15 in the last 25 years. The ultimate compliment for Ryan came from Toronto Blue Jays infielder Rance Mulliniks, who was asked what it would be like if every player were like Nolan Ryan. He said, "Everyone would like each other, and no one would get a hit."

Carlton Fisk, 11 months younger than the 43-year-old Ryan, enjoyed what was arguably his finest season in 21 years behind the plate, guiding the young White Sox pitching staff to over 90 wins, hitting .285 and breaking the major league record for career home runs by a catcher. He also stole seven bases.

Fisk wasn't in the line-up on July 1, when Andy Hawkins of the Yankees threw a no-hitter at the White Sox—and lost, 4-0. On July 6, he pitched 11 shutout innings (the longest outing by an AL pitcher in four years), but lost to the Twins in the 12th, 2-0. On July 12, he was the losing pitcher in the rain-shortened no-hitter thrown by the White Sox's Melido Perez. On July 17, he gave up three home runs in six innings to Kansas City's Bo Jackson. On July 22, his team scored 10 unearned runs against Minnesota, but he didn't get the win. Surprisingly, he didn't oppose Nolan Ryan in Ryan's first bid to win his 300th game on July 25. Hawkins said with a smile, "I can't believe I'm not pitching this game."

The Cubs' Ryne Sandberg led the NL with 40 homers, the first second baseman since Rogers Hornsby to do so. Sandberg had five times as many home runs as errors. Barry Bonds of the Pirates and Ron Gant of the Braves joined the prestigious 30-30 (homers and steals) Club. The Cubs' Andre Dawson joined Willie Mays in the 300-300-2000 Club (homers, steals, hits), although it should be pointed out that Mays finished his career at 660-338-3283. Rickey Henderson of Oakland stole 65 bases to pull within two of tying Lou Brock's all-time record of 938. He'll probably break the record in the first inning of his first game in 1991.

The season also had its share of surprises, including Whitey Herzog quitting as manager of the last place St.Louis Cardinals in July; Wade Boggs of the Red Sox failing to get 200 hits for the first time in eight years; Boston hitting into two triple plays in one game against Minnesota; Oakland reliever Dennis Eckersley having more saves (48) than hits and walks combined (45); Vince Coleman outhomering Don Mattingly, 6-to-5; and 64 pitchers winning more games than the Angels' $3 million a year lefthander Mark Langston, who was 10-17.

The retirement of Dan Quisenberry and the release of Mike Flanagan gave us a new Funniest Player in the Game—outfielder Andy Van Slyke of the Pirates. The best of his one-liners came early in the season when he went 0-for-5 in a spring training game and said, "I couldn't drive Miss Daisy home."

Then there was Richard Griffin, the hilarious public relations director of the Montreal Expos. He ordered pizza for the entire team from 30,000 feet over Cleveland. When L.A.'s Ramon Martinez started a mid-week afternoon game against Dennis Martinez, Griffin called it the "Two Martinez Businessman Special." When Zane Smith was dealt from the Expos to the Pirates on Aug. 8, Griffin determined that the distance traveled by Smith the two times he was traded in his career was 453 feet (in each deal, Smith was sent to the team on the opposite side of the field, so Griffin walked off the clubhouse-to-clubhouse distance in Montreal, and had Braves public relations director Jim Schultz do the same in Atlanta). Griffin also researched that Montreal's Otis Nixon had more 30-0 seasons (30 steals, no HRs) than anyone in history. And, finally, after Expos farmhand Antonio Alfonseco—who has six toes on each foot and six fingers on each hand—made his professional debut this year, Griffin put in his daily notes than Alfonseco's favorite player was Sixto Lezcano and his favorite movie is The Dirty Dozen.

Baseball even gave us four pretty good pennant races in 1990.

In the AL East, it was Boston and Toronto. The resistible force meets the movable object. Not a lot of nobility, but the best pennant race in town for passion and emotion. Think about it. No other team but the Red Sox had to contend with a maniacal Boston-hater at Yankee Stadium flashing a sign that read "1918" into their dugout during a key game down the stretch. No team but the Blue Jays had to put up with everybody calling them underachievers, chokers or, simply, the Blow Jays.

The AL East race went down to the final pitch of the final game. The Red Sox led by one game with one to play, but needed to beat the hungry Chicago White Sox, the year's most improved team. In the top of the ninth, Boston had a 3-1 lead with two out and one on. Then Jeff Reardon gave up a single to Sammy Sosa on an 0-2 pitch. The assembled at Fenway groaned. One strike away. It couldn't happen again, could it? Reardon then hit Scott Fletcher. It was happening again! Ozzie Guillen followed with a line drive into the right field corner. Had it fallen, it would have been a sure two-run triple, "probably a home run," said Boston Red Sox manager Joe Morgan. But right fielder Tom Brunansky, who played like Roberto Clemente the final 10 days of the season after stumbling through the first four months, made a terrific sliding catch to save the game and escape what would have been perhaps the second-worst collapse in the often gruesome history of the team.

Has a better catch ever been made at a more crucial time in major league history?

Maybe not.

The Catch provided more proof that this was the Red Sox' year in the AL East. When the season started, they weren't even expected to contend for the division crown, what with a patchwork starting rotation, two closers (Reardon and Lee Smith), no DH and an unproven first baseman (Carlos Quintana). But Boston got miraculous efforts from unlikely people. Greg Harris, a journeyman reliever, became the No. 3 man in the rotation and wound up winning more games (13) than people like Langston, Bruce Hurst, Joe Magrane and Gregg Swindell. Tom Bolton, a career minor leaguer who said in 1988 that the reason he hadn't retired was "I'm too lazy to work and too scared to steal," won 10 games. Quintana manned first base admirably, Lee Smith was traded for Brunansky and the great Roger Clemens was unhittable en route to a 21-6 record with a 1.93 ERA and four shutouts.

But when Clemens was sidelined with a right shoulder injury on Sept. 4, the Red Sox watched their 6½-game lead disappear. By Sept. 23, they trailed Toronto by one game. But the Blue Jays, too, have a history of folding. They lost six of their last eight games and eight of their last 12 to hand the title to the Red Sox.

No one handed anything to Oakland in the AL West. The mighty Athletics were just too good. They were, however, ruffled along the way by the pesky White Sox, whose 94 wins was the third most in baseball. The A's started September 5½ ahead, but with the crushing acquisitions of McGee and Harold Baines at the end of August, the A's pulled away. Chicago shortstop Ozzie Guillen put it best when he said of Oakland's maneuvering, "They get McGee and Baines, we get Jerry Hairston and Minnie Minoso."

Even though the White Sox didn't win the division, they won the hearts of millions in the final year at venerable Comiskey Park. Jeff Torborg's team improved its record from 64-92 to 94-68, showing that hustle, desire, speed and pitching can go a long way.

But the A's were a machine. They got off to their usual great start (winning 22 of 28), held off the White Sox until September, then put it in a gear that only they know. In doing so, Rickey Henderson made a strong bid to become only the third leadoff man in AL history to win the MVP (Zolio Versailles and Phil Rizzuto were the others). Welch won 27, but the ace of the staff, Dave Stewart, won 20 games for the fourth straight year—the first pitcher since Jim Palmer to accomplish that.

Everyone picked the Mets to win the NL East. They had the power and the pitching, plus they had a mental hold on the Pirates. But Pittsburgh won two out of three in New York in the first series of the season, which Pirate Manager Jim Leyland would later say was the biggest series of the season. Others disagreed,

Oakland pitcher **Bob Welch's** 27 wins were the most by an AL pitcher since 1968.

the biggest series came Sept. 5-6 at Three Rivers Stadium. The Pirates entered that three-game set with a half-game lead and won three straight: 1-0, 3-1, 7-1. Whatever psychological headlock the Mets had on them had been broken for good.

The Mets came back to pull within a half-game on Sept. 18, but the Pirates—as they did all season—won when they had to. From Sept. 23-30, they took 10 out of 11 to clinch the division. Doug Drabek, the Cy Young-in-waiting, pitched a brilliant three-hitter to beat the Cardinals, 2-0, in the clincher. It was the Bucs' first division title since the "We Are Family" days of 1979. It was greeted with tears by many Pirates, who had endured a lot of losing before winning.

"We've come a long way since those funny-looking hats," said coach Rich Donnelly.

The pill-box shaped caps with the hideous yellow pinstripes were last worn in 1986, a 98-loss debacle in Leyland's first

Pittsburgh prided itself on teamwork, but the Pirates' two best players were outfielders **Bobby Bonilla** (left) and **Barry Bonds**, who combined for 65 homers and 234 RBIs.

year. "I told my brother (who is a priest)," said Leyland, "that if we lost 100 games, I would resign."

That season began the rebuilding of the Bucs, but the job was not completed until Aug. 8 when general manager Larry Doughty sent pitcher Scott Ruskin and two minor leaguers to Montreal for left-hander Zane Smith. Even though the Mets Darryl Strawberry said "Zane Smith, he ain't s——" on the day of the trade, Smith went 6-1 with Pittsburgh to help sew up the title.

The Pirates were led by left fielder Barry Bonds, the MVP-to-be. After a few years of unfulfilled potential, the enigmatic Bonds hit .301 with 33 homers, 114 RBIs and 52 steals. He was clearly the best player in the league, although teammate Bobby Bonilla (.280-32-120) might have been the second best. But the Pirates won because everyone contributed. "We are a *team*," said catcher Don Slaught. "I've never been on a team that was such a team." Nineteen different Pirate pitchers won a game and nine different Pirate relievers saved a game. A shuttle operated between the Bucs' Triple-A club in Buffalo and Three Rivers, but everyone who was called up helped. The

Mets didn't exhibit the teamwork that the Pirates did. The Montreal Expos, picked for last, were close, but ran out of horses at the end.

In the NL West, "The Hunt for Red October" began with nine straight victories at the start of the season. By June 3, Cincinnati was 33-12 and nine games in front. The Reds' lead never dipped below three games as they became the first NL team ever to lead wire-to-wire. Early, it was pitcher Jack Armstrong and "The Nasty Boys"—relievers Randy Myers, Rob Dibble and Norm Charlton—who grabbed most of the attention. But through it all, it was shortstop Barry Larkin who was easily the Reds' best player. He batted .301, provided great defense, leadership, class, speed and savvy.

Manager Lou Piniella added the needed intensity to push the Reds over a hump that had seen them finish second for four straight years (1985-88). Piniella drew criticism with his base-throwing, cooler-kicking and umpire-berating tantrums, but as first baseman Todd Benzinger said, "they might not have been good for Lou's life expectancy, but they helped the team." And the team needed help.

Slumps by Armstrong, Eric Davis and a bunch of others allowed the San Francisco Giants—the defending West champs—and the Los Angeles Dodgers to enter the race during the summer. The Giants made a few gallant runs at the Reds, but too many injuries to the pitching staff left them short. How the Dodgers ever pulled within three games in late September is a tribute to their heart and manager Tommy Lasorda. Lasorda was without ace right-hander Orel Hershiser for most of the season, then lost pitcher Tim Belcher for the final 1½ months. He didn't have Kirk Gibson for the first half and bullpen closer Jay Howell was injury-plagued for much of the season. The Dodgers even rebounded from a 12-11 loss to Philadelphia on Aug. 21—a game they led, 11-3, entering the ninth inning. Phillies pitcher Roger McDowell said he had never seen such a comeback since "Strat-O-Matic, against my brother."

Back in March, it didn't look like there would be a regular season. Representatives for baseball's owners and players negotiated into the night in countless sessions, but could not reach an accord on baseball's next Basic Agreement. The key sticking point was salary arbitration, the issue that everyone knew it would come down to in the end, but wasn't properly addressed until it almost jeopardized the season. As the sessions dragged on, the lockout of the players—instituted by the owners—remained in effect. They would not lift the lockout until an agreement was reached.

Finally, after an all-night bargaining session, the two sides reached agreement on March 19. Half of spring training had been lost, and the first week of the regular season was canceled. There was serious concern whether the players—especially the pitchers—could get in shape in time. There were only minor problems, however. The season started April 9, and all the canceled games were made up.

The owners' inability to deal with the players resurfaced on Sept.17, when they were found guilty of collusion—conspiring to hold down player salaries—the third straight year. Arbitrator George Nicolau awarded the players $102 million in damages and could possibly grant a number of players free agency in the off season.

The season was further soiled by the controversy involving George Steinbrenner, who was forced to remove himself from the day-to-day operation of the New York Yankees for acting contrary to the best interests of the game—specifically, his "undisclosed working relationship" with admitted gambler Howard Spira. Steinbrenner paid Spira $40,000 in January for damaging information about the Boss's longtime nemesis, former Yankee outfielder Dave Winfield, and about the charitable David M. Winfield Foundation.

Baseball commissioner Fay Vincent ordered an investigation of the Steinbrenner-Spira-Winfield case and questioned the Yankees' owner at length. Finally, on July 30, it was announced that Steinbrenner had agreed to step down permanently—ending his sometimes successful, always turbulent, 18-year reign as principal owner of what was once the game's proudest franchise. The news was cheered heartily that night at Yankee Stadium, where fans had been cheering "George Must Go" for most of the season—the Yankees' worst (67-95) in over 70 years.

Steinbrenner wanted his son, Hank, to replace him at the helm of the team, but Hank said he wasn't interested. Steinbrenner finally decided on theatrical producer Robert Nederlander, a close friend and member of the Yankees' board of directors. Nederlander is certainly no baseball man, and it was clear from the start that he wouldn't have anything to do with the baseball operations. Some believed Nederlander would be Steinbrenner's puppet, but Vincent was doing his best to make sure Steinbrenner had nothing to do with the Yankees.

On his way out the door Aug.20, Steinbrenner changed general managers for the 14th time (Pete Peterson out, Gene Michael in) and extended the contract of Stump Merrill, who became the 13th man to manage the Yanks under Steinbrenner when he replaced Bucky Dent in June.

In October, the AL Championship turned out to be every bit the mismatch many had predicted.

The mighty A's swept Boston in four games, and ran their postseason winning streak to 10 games. The unfortunate Red Sox have not won a postseason game since their infamous Game 6 loss to the Mets in the 1986 World Series.

The final scores were 9-1, 4-1, 4-1, 3-1, but they don't tell the true story. The A's, who bludgeoned the Toronto Blue Jays in the 1989 ALCS, swept Boston without hitting a homer. No team since the 1919 Cincinnati Reds has won a postseason series without a home run. "You'll never see that again," said Blue Jays scout Gordon Lakey. Oakland won even though Jose Canseco and Mark McGwire had a combined three RBIs, and Rickey Henderson only stole two bases. The A's won because they played great defense and did all the little things, which are often overshadowed by their bashing.

And the A's got great pitching, as usual. The Red Sox managed only one hit with a runner in scoring position in the series and had only three hits with men on base.

The A's were so good (or the Red Sox so bad), this series was somewhat of a dud. In Game 1, Dave Stewart, the ALCS MVP, and Roger Clemens, the ALCS villain, staged a terrific pitching duel for the first six innings. Wade Boggs' fourth-inning homer gave Boston a 1-0 lead. Clemens was at his mitt-popping best for five innings, but he was taken out in the seventh with a 1-0 lead because manager Joe Morgan said "he was cooked."

So were the Red Sox for the rest of the series. When Clemens came out, the Fenway faithful deflated. The overworked Boston bullpen gave up nine runs in the final three innings, turning what had been a dream game into a nightmare. Stewart pitched eight innings, running his career record against Clemens to 8-0.

Game 1 essentially ended the ALCS. Oh, the Red Sox scored first in Game 2, and rookie Dana Kiecker pitched 5⅔ gutsy innings, but it was clear that the A's were going to win no matter what. In Game 2, they got into the Boston bullpen again, scoring three times in the last three innings for a 4-1 win behind Bob Welch. When the scene shifted to Oakland for Game 3, nothing changed. The Red Sox jumped to a 1-0 lead against winning pitcher Mike Moore, but the A's scratched and clawed for three tainted runs to beat hard-luck Mike Boddicker, 4-1.

"It's over," said Canseco.

Variety marks record-setting no-hit binge

No doubt about it, 1990 was The Year of the No-Hitter. Not just because of the volume—a major league record nine were thrown—but because of the variety: a combined no-hitter, the tallest pitcher to pitch one, the oldest to pitch one, two no-hitters in one night, a pitcher who threw a no-hitter and lost, a rain-shortened no-hitter and one by a pitcher who two times in 1988 had come within one out of a no-no, then lost it.

The Honor Roll:

April 11—In his first start at Anaheim Stadium as a member of the California Angels, Mark Langston combined with Mike Witt for a no-hitter over the Seattle Mariners. Langston pitched the first seven innings, Witt the last two in the 1-0 win. It was the first time that the Mariners have been involved in a no-hitter. It was Langston's finest hour. He would not win another home game until Aug. 15. Witt, meanwhile was traded to the Yankees for Dave Winfield on May 11.

June 2—Randy Johnson of Seattle became the tallest man—6-foot-10—ever to throw a no-hitter, beating Detroit, 2-0. Johnson, who is learning to play the drums, said he kept calm between innings by tapping his thigh to a drum beat. "After the game," he said laughing, "I called my parents. My mom was crying. My dad, who's my biggest critic, wanted to know why I walked six batters."

June 11—Nolan Ryan of Texas threw his sixth career no-hitter, extending his major league record. He beat Oakland, 5-0, striking out 14 along the way. At age 43, he became the oldest pitcher ever to throw a no-hitter. His catcher this night was John Russell, who had been released by the Braves earlier in the season and was completely out of baseball. In May, he was painting houses and hoping a team would call. The Rangers did. A month later, he caught Ryan's no-no. Russell called it the "greatest thrill of my career."

Ryan started accumulating no-hitters

Of the year's nine no-hit pitchers, the Yankees' **Andy Hawkins** was the only one who lost.

17 years ago, throwing four with California and one with Houston before ringing up No.6 with Texas. His five victims before the A's were the Royals and Tigers in 1973, the Twins in '74, the Orioles in '75 and the Dodgers in '81.

June 29—For the first time in modern major league history, two nine-inning no-hitters were thrown in the same day. Oakland's Dave Stewart threw the first one of his career, fanning 12 as he beat Toronto, 5-0, before 49,817 at the SkyDome. A few hours later, Fernando Valenzuela threw the first no-hitter of his career, beating the Cardinals, 6-0, in L.A. Valenzuela and Stewart were rookies together with the Dodgers in 1981.

July 1—One of the strangest no-hitters in history. The Yankees' Andy Hawkins held the White Sox hitless, but lost, 4-0. Chicago scored four runs in the bottom of the eighth inning on errors by third baseman Mike Blowers and left fielder Jim Leyritz. Hawkins' pitching line: 81 P, 0 H, 4 R, 0 ER, 3 SO. "Usually when someone pitches a no-hitter, he walks off the mound happy," said Hawkins.

July 12—Melido Perez of the White Sox pitched a rain-shortened, six inning no-hitter against the Yankees in New York, winning, 8-0. Perez joined his brother, Pascual, on the all-time no-hit list. Pascual's no-hitter (in 1988) was also rain-shortened. "I called my brother Vladamir," said Melido, speaking of his younger brother on the New York Mets Class AA Jackson (Miss.) team. "I told him it was his turn next."

Aug.15—Terry Mulholland of Philadelphia no-hit his former teammates, the Giants, 6-0. "If we have to get no-hit," said San Francisco manager Roger Craig, "I'm glad it was by Terry." Mulholland, who had fewer than 20 major league wins at the time, said, "This is supposed to happen to Nolan Ryan, not Terry Mulholland." Mulholland said the last time he got this much notoriety was in 1987 when, as a pitcher with the Giants, he fielded a grounder, got the ball stuck in the webbing of his glove, and tossed the glove to first for the out. After that game, Giants pitcher Mike Krukow told first baseman Bob Brenly, "You blew it, you should have whipped the glove around the infield."

Sept.2—It was fitting that Dave Stieb finally threw one. In 1988, he twice came within one pitch of a no-hitter only to lose it with two outs in the ninth. Cleveland's Julio Franco ruined the first bid on a bad-hop grounder. In the second one, Jim Traber of Baltimore hit a 120-foot flare over first base that dropped in. There would be no ruining this one. Stieb no-hit the Indians, in Cleveland, 3-0. "I had better stuff in the other two," said Stieb. Seconds after getting the elusive final out, Stieb pointed to the press box where a writer named Kevin Boland was sitting. Boland co-authored Stieb's autobiography, *Tomorrow, I'll Be Perfect.*

That day, he almost was.

Actually, this series was just starting. Clemens, who was managing the team by this time, said before Game 3 that he would only start Game 4 if his team was in danger of being swept. Down 3-0, he started against his nemesis, Stewart. What took place after that might never be explained, but it was clearly one of the most bizarre happenings in postseason history. Behind, 1-0, in the second inning, Clemens walked Willie Randolph on a close pitch, putting runners at first and second with one out.

Suddenly, from behind home plate, umpire Terry Cooney ejected Clemens. Morgan rushed out of the dugout to argue. Boston reserve infielder Marty Barrett tossed a tub of Gatorade out of the dugout at first base umpire Vic Voltaggio. Cooney would later say that Clemens—from the stretch position—had assaulted him verbally with a battery of swear words. Cooney provoked Clemens, saying "you better not be shaking your head at me." Clemens did more than shake his head. TV replays show curse words spewing from his mouth.

"It's unbelievable," said Clemens, who claims he never swore at Cooney. "If I didn't eject him," said Cooney, "I would have lost the respect of the players."

Clemens lost some respect around the nation as well. Was he so spooked by Stewart that he snapped? Did he intentionally get ejected? Does he really need counseling, as one high ranking member of the Red Sox front office suggested? We might never know. All we know for sure is that the Red Sox—riding high after dramatically edging Toronto for the AL East title—finished the season on an ugly note.

A's third baseman Carney Lansford called the Red Sox "an embarrassment to the game I play.'"

For this series, he was right.

Over in the National League, Pittsburgh was supposed to win the pennant. They had momentum, superior starting pitching and better health. But they didn't have the Cincinnati bullpen, and lost in six games.

Pittsburgh won the opener, 4-3, in Cincinnati, behind starting pitcher Bob Walk, a two-run homer by Sid Bream and a hideous misplay of a fly ball by Reds' left fielder Eric Davis, allowing the eventual winning run to score in the seventh. But the Reds won Game 2, beating 22-game winner Doug Drabek, 2-1. Pirates left fielder Barry Bonds lost Paul O'Neill's double in the sun in the fifth inning, allowing the eventual winning run to score. O'Neill also drove in the Reds' other run, and threw out Andy Van Slyke at third in the sixth, killing a rally.

The key game of this series was the third one—the first postseason contest played in Pittsburgh since 1979. The Pirates were starting Zane Smith, who might have been the best pitcher in the league the second half of the season. But he gave up a two-run homer to ex-Pirate Billy Hatcher in the second and a three-run homer to Mariano Duncan in the fifth to fall behind 5-2. The Cincinnati bullpen of Rob Dibble, Norm Charlton and Randy Myers—the famed Nasty Boys—teamed up to save Danny Jackson's victory. Myers and Dibble also played a key role in Game 4, a 5-3 Reds' victory. Drabek won Game 5 by a 3-2 margin, but it took reliever Bob Patterson to get Jeff Reed to ground into a bases-loaded double play in the ninth inning to end it.

The NLCS ended after shifting back to Cincinnati for Game 6. Pirates manager Jim Leyland chose reliever Ted Power to start instead of Smith, feeling the Reds were more vulnerable to right-handed pitching. The strategy worked, but Cincinnati's pitching was again too much. Jackson, Charlton and Myers combined on a one-hitter, and pinch-hitter Luis Quinones delivered the game-winning RBI with a single in the seventh for a 2-1 win. It wasn't over, however, until Reds right fielder Glenn Braggs made a leaping catch at the right field wall in the ninth inning, taking a possible two-run homer away from Carmelo Martinez. It was fitting that such a tight, hard-fought series would be decided on such a play. It was also fitting that the co-MVP's were two members of the bullpen that led the Reds all season—the nastiest of the Nasty Boys, righty Dibble and lefty Myers.

"I'm not worried about them (the A's)," said Dibble, heading into the World Series, "I'll let them worry about us."

Meanwhile, shortstop and clubhouse leader Barry Larkin mentioned the man who wasn't there—Pete Rose, the former

Cincinnati's celebrated "Nasty Boys," relievers **Norm Charlton** (left), **Randy Myers** (center) and **Rob Dibble**, share a hug after wrapping up the NL pennant on Oct.12.

Reds' manager who was banned from baseball for life in 1989 for betting on games and began serving a five-month jail term in August for income tax evasion. "I really wish Pete was here today in uniform to enjoy what we have," said Larkin. "He molded the nucleus of this team."

Cincinnati had a date with destiny in the World Series, but all the talk beforehand was about Oakland's date with dynasty.

Sure, the Reds were a gritty bunch with a terrific bullpen, good speed and more than a little punch, but, after all, they were up against the mighty A's. The World Champions. An all-star team back in the Series for the third straight year and determined to repeat so that all the talk about greatness and all the comparisons to the A's of 1972-74 would be warranted.

They never had a chance.

They couldn't stop Reds center fielder Billy Hatcher, who reached base in his first nine World Series plate appearances and wound up going 9-for-12 (.750)—the highest batting average ever in a four-game series, breaking Babe Ruth's record (.625). They couldn't stop third baseman Chris Sabo, who hit .563 with two home runs and five RBIs. They couldn't hit Series MVP Jose Rijo, who was 2-0, allowed one run in 15⅓ innings and had 14 strikeouts —five more than the A's staff combined.

The A's didn't just lose, they got swept. The Series was over, some believe, in the first inning of Game 1. Reds center fielder Eric Davis, whose damaged left shoulder hurt when he spoke, let alone played, drew a few boos as he walked to the plate to face Dave Stewart, the guts of the Oakland staff and the best pitcher in baseball over the last four years. Davis had been so unproductive, manager Lou Piniella asked him if he would rather hit leadoff than fourth. Davis chose fourth. So he hit a two-run homer over the center field fence, keying an easy 7-0 victory behind Rijo and Hatcher (3-for-3). Davis said "when I hit, it gives the rest of the guys confidence." And when Stewart loses a big game—does it ever happen?—it makes the A's wonder.

The A's really had to be wondering after Game 2. Stewart had been hit this season, but A's relief ace Dennis Eckersley had barely been touched. Yet there he was giving up three straight hits in the 10th inning to lose, 5-4.

It was a game for the ages, certainly the best Series game since the sixth game of the 1986 Series. The A's scored in the top of the first, but that man Hatcher doubled home a run in the bottom half, then scored for a 2-1 lead. The A's hit their first postseason homer—a bases-empty blast by Jose Canseco in the third inning, then took a 4-2 lead off Danny Jackson. But Bob Welch, the A's 27-game winner, gave up a run in the fourth. Then Hatcher opened the eighth with a triple that tipped off Canseco's glove in right field. After the game, A's manager Tony LaRussa said Canseco got a bad jump on the ball.

"If you're going to win," said LaRussa, "you have to make that play." Well, that started an A's controversy. LaRussa rarely scolds his players publicly, but frustration had already set in. Hatcher scored on Glenn Braggs' fielder's choice grounder, tying the score. Where was Eckersley? Why hadn't he pitched in the eighth? Why hadn't LaRussa pitch-run for Ron Hassey in the top of the eighth? Why did he have Carney Lansford bunt with none out and Rickey Henderson on in the first inning? The game's best manager was being second-guessed liberally.

The game ended abruptly in the 10th. Reserve infielder Billy Bates, whom teammates thought was a clubhouse kid when he was acquired during the summer from the Milwaukee Brewers, beat out an Astroturf chopper with one out in the inning off Eckersley. It was Bates' first hit as a Red and only his third in 31 major league at bats this season. Sabo followed with a single and then catcher Joe Oliver singled over third to end it.

"I guess this is my first walk-off since Gibson," said a shocked Eckersley, referring to walking off the mound as a losing pitcher for the first time since allowing the two-run homer to the Dodgers' Kirk Gibson in Game 1 of the 1988 Series. "But I don't want to bring that s——— up. . . nothing was worse than Gibson."

It was starting to look as if the Reds were destined to win.

That was clear after Game 3 in Oakland. Reds' starter Tom Browning, whose wife, Debbi, had given birth to a son two nights earlier, was given a 1-0 lead on Sabo's homer in the second off Mike Moore. After Harold Baines' two-run homer in the bottom of the second made it 2-1, the Reds exploded for seven runs on seven hits in the third, including another Sabo homer. The A's barely threatened the rest of the way. They were now down, three games to none.

For Game 4, LaRussa benched Canseco, whose back and finger injuries had turned him from the game's most feared hitter into an easy out. But all would be well, thought A's fans, Stew was pitching. But so, too, was Rijo.

The A's scored in the first, then never came close again. Davis suffered a rib and kidney injury diving for a ball in the first, and Hatcher suffered an injured left hand when hit by a Stewart pitch in the first. Each was removed in the second.

It didn't matter.

Stewart had a 1-0 lead, but he lost it in the eighth. Barry Larkin drilled a leadoff single. Hatcher's replacement, Herm Winningham, dumped a bunt single on an 0-2 pitch. Paul O'Neill bunted, but reached base when Stewart's throw pulled second baseman Willie Randolph off the bag for an error. Braggs followed with a bases-loaded ground out that scored a run. And Hal Morris hit a sacrifice fly to put the Reds in front, 2-1. Rijo got the first out in the ninth—the 20th straight hitter he had retired. Myers then came on to get the last two hitters for the save, and the Reds were World Champs.

"A team of destiny bunts 0-2," said Reds first baseman Todd Benzinger, "and beats it out."

Maybe the Reds were a team of destiny. Perhaps that's the only way to explain how they completely dominated the A's.

As for the entire season, there is no explanation. And that's what makes the game so great. □

BASEBALL STATISTICS

THE SEASON IN REVIEW
1990
LEAGUE LEADERS • POSTSEASON

THE 1991 INFORMATION PLEASE SPORTS ALMANAC

SEC A

PAGE 49

Final Major League Standings

Division champions (*) are noted. Number of seasons listed after each manager refers to current tenure with club.

American League

East Division	W	L	Pct	GB	Home	Away
*Boston	88	74	.543	—	51-30	37-44
Toronto	86	76	.531	2	44-37	42-39
Detroit	79	83	.488	9	39-42	40-41
Cleveland	77	85	.475	11	41-40	36-45
Baltimore	76	85	.472	11½	40-40	36-45
Milwaukee	74	88	.457	14	39-42	35-46
New York	67	95	.414	21	37-44	30-51

West Division	W	L	Pct	GB	Home	Away
*Oakland	103	59	.636	—	51-30	52-29
Chicago	94	68	.580	9	49-31	45-37
Texas	83	79	.512	20	47-35	36-44
California	80	82	.494	23	42-39	38-43
Seattle	77	85	.475	26	38-43	39-42
Kansas City	75	86	.466	27½	45-36	30-50
Minnesota	74	88	.457	29	41-40	33-48

1990 Managers: Bos—Joe Morgan (3rd season); **Tor**—Cito Gaston (2nd); **Det**—Sparky Anderson (12th); **Cle**—John McNamara (1st); **Bal**—Frank Robinson (3rd); **Mil**—Tom Trebelhorn (5th); **NY**—replaced Bucky Dent (2nd, 18-31) with Stump Merrill (49-64) on June 6.

1989 Standings: 1.Toronto (89-73); 2.Baltimore (87-75); 3.Boston (83-79); 4.Milwaukee (81-81); 5. New York (74-87); 6.Cleveland (73-89); 7.Detroit (59-103).

1990 Managers: Oak—Tony LaRussa (5th season); **Chi**—Jeff Torborg (2nd); **Tex**—Bobby Valentine (6th); **Cal**—Doug Rader (2nd); **Sea**—Jim Lefebvre (2nd); **KC**—John Wathan (4th); **Min**—Tom Kelly (5th).

1989 Standings: 1.Oakland (99-63); 2.Kansas City (92-70); 3.California (91-71); 4.Texas (83-79); 5.Minnesota (80-82); 6.Seattle (73-89); Chicago (69-92).

National League

East Division	W	L	Pct	GB	Home	Away
*Pittsburgh	95	67	.586	—	49-32	46-35
New York	91	71	.562	4	52-29	39-42
Montreal	85	77	.525	10	47-34	38-43
Philadelphia	77	85	.475	18	41-40	36-45
Chicago	77	85	.475	18	39-42	38-43
St.Louis	70	92	.432	25	34-47	36-45

West Division	W	L	Pct	GB	Home	Away
*Cincinnati	91	71	.562	—	46-35	45-36
Los Angeles	86	76	.531	5	47-34	39-42
San Francisco	85	77	.525	6	49-32	36-45
Houston	75	87	.463	16	49-32	26-55
San Diego	75	87	.463	16	37-44	38-43
Atlanta	65	97	.401	26	37-44	28-53

1990 Managers: Pit—Jim Leyland (5th season); **NY**—replaced Davey Johnson (7th, 20-22) with Bud Harrelson (71-49) on May 29; **Mon**—Buck Rodgers (6th); **Phi**—Nick Leyva (2nd); **Chi**—Don Zimmer (3rd); **StL**—Whitey Herzog (11th, 33-47) resigned on July 6, replaced by interim Red Schoendienst (13-11) who was replaced by Joe Torre (24-34) on Aug.1.

1989 Standings: 1.Chicago (93-69); 2.New York (87-75); 3.St.Louis (86-76); 4.Montreal (81-81); 5.Pittsburgh (74-88); 6.Philadelphia (67-95).

1990 Managers: Cin—Lou Piniella (1st season); **LA**—Tom Lasorda (15th); **SF**—Roger Craig (6th); **Hou**—Art Howe (2nd); **SD**—Jack McKeon (3rd, 37-43) resigned on July 11, replaced by Greg Riddoch (38-44); **Atl**—replaced Russ Nixon (3rd, 25-40) with Bobby Cox (40-57) on June 22.

1989 Standings: 1.San Francisco (92-70); 2.San Diego (89-73); 3.Houston (86-76); 4.Los Angeles (77-83); 5.Cincinnati (75-87); 6.Atlanta (63-97).

Home Attendance

Overall 1990 attendance in Major League Baseball was 54,871,718 in 2060 games for an average per game crowd of 26,637. Teams in each league are ranked by attendance over the regular season.

American League
Based on tickets sold.

	Attendance	Gm	Average
1 Toronto	3,885,284	81	47,966
2 Oakland	2,900,217	80	36,253
3 Boston	2,528,986	80	31,612
4 California	2,555,688	81	31,552
5 Baltimore	2,415,189	79	30,572
6 Kansas City	2,244,956	78	28,781
7 Texas	2,057,887	81	25,406
8 Chicago	2,002,359	79	25,346
9 New York	2,006,436	80	25,080
10 Milwaukee	1,752,900	79	22,189
11 Minnesota	1,750,964	80	21,887
12 Detroit	1,495,785	80	18,697
13 Seattle	1,509,705	81	18,638
14 Cleveland	1,225,241	75	16,337
TOTAL	30,331,597	1114	27,228

National League
Based on turnstile count.

	Attendance	Gm	Average
1 Los Angeles	3,002,396	81	37,067
2 New York	2,732,745	77	35,490
3 St.Louis	2,573,495	81	31,772
4 Cincinnati	2,400,892	78	30,781
5 Chicago	2,243,291	77	29,140
6 Pittsburgh	2,049,908	78	26,281
7 Philadelphia	1,992,484	77	25,876
8 San Francisco	1,975,571	80	24,695
9 San Diego	1,856,395	79	23,499
10 Montreal	1,421,388	81	17,548
11 Houston	1,310,927	81	16,184
12 Atlanta	980,129	76	12,896
TOTAL	24,540,121	946	25,941

American League Individual Leaders

Batting
(Minimum of 502 plate appearances.)

	Avg	AB	R	H	HR	RBI
George Brett, KC	.329	544	82	179	14	87
Rickey Henderson, Oak	.325	489	119	159	28	61
Rafael Palmeiro, Tex	.319	598	72	191	14	89
Alan Trammell, Det ..	.304	559	71	170	14	89
Wade Boggs, Bos ...	.302	619	89	187	6	63
Edgar Martinez, Sea	.302	487	71	147	11	56
Ken Griffey,Jr, Sea...	.300	597	91	179	5	63
Fred McGriff, Tor	.300	557	91	167	35	88
Chris James, Cle	.299	528	62	158	12	70
Kirby Puckett, Min ...	.298	551	82	164	12	80
Mike Greenwell, Bos .	.297	610	71	181	14	73
Ellis Burks, Bos ...	.296	588	89	174	21	89
Julio Franco, Tex ...	.296	582	96	172	11	69
Brian Harper, Min ...	.294	479	61	141	6	54
Gary Sheffield, Mil ...	.294	487	67	143	10	67

Pitching
(Minimum of 162 innings pitched)

	ERA	W-L	IP	H	SO
Roger Clemens, Bos....	1.93	21-6	228.1	193	209
Chuck Finley, Cal.....	2.40	18-9	236.0	210	177
Dave Stewart, Oak....	2.56	22-11	267.0	226	166
Kevin Appier, KC......	2.76	12-8	185.2	179	127
Dave Stieb, Tor	2.93	18-6	208.2	179	125
Bob Welch, Oak	2.95	27-6	238.0	214	127
David Wells, Tor	3.14	11-6	189.0	165	115
Greg Hibbard, Chi	3.16	14-9	211.0	202	92
Erik Hanson, Sea......	3.24	18-9	236.0	205	211
Kirk McCaskill, Cal.....	3.25	12-11	174.1	161	78
Mike Boddicker, Bos ..	3.36	17-8	228.0	225	143
Bobby Witt, Tex	3.36	17-10	222.0	197	221
Nolan Ryan, Tex	3.44	13-9	204.0	137	232
Matt Young, Sea	3.51	8-18	225.1	198	176
Bud Black, Cle-Tor.....	3.57	13-11	206.2	181	106

Home Runs
Fielder, Det 51
McGwire, Oak.....39
J.Canseco, Oak....37
McGriff, Tor.......35
Gruber, Tor 31
R.Henderson, Oak..28
Jackson, KC.......28
Deer, Mil 27
Barfield, NY 25
Incaviglia, Tex 24
Parrish, Cal 24

Runs Batted In
Fielder, Det 132
Gruber, Tor 118
McGwire, Oak.....108
J.Canseco, Oak....101
Sierra, Tex 96
Maldonado, Cle ...95
Parker, Mil........92
Burks, Bos 89
Palmeiro, Tex......89
Trammell, Det 89
McGriff, Tor.......88

Wins
Welch, Oak 27-6
Stewart, Oak 22-11
Clemens, Bos ...21-6
Stieb, Tor 18-6
Finley, Cal 18-9
Hanson, Sea 18-9
Boddicker, Bos ...17-8
Witt, Tex........17-10
Sanderson, Oak ..17-11
Candiotti, Cle 15-11
Morris, Det 15-18

Saves
Thigpen, Chi 57
Eckersley, Oak....48
Jones, Cle 43
Olson, Bal 37
Righetti, NY 36
Aguilera, Min 32
Henke, Tor.......32
Schooler, Sea.....30
Harvey, Cal......25
Montgomery, KC....24
Plesac, Mil 24

Stolen Bases
	SB	CS
R.Henderson, Oak	65	10
Sax, NY	43	9
Kelly, NY	42	17
Cole, Cle	40	9
Pettis, Tex	38	15
Johnson, Chi	36	22
Calderon, Chi	32	16
Sosa, Chi	32	16
Franco, Tex	31	10
Reynolds, Sea	31	16

Hits
Palmeiro, Tex....191
Boggs, Bos.......187
Kelly, NY 183
Greenwell, Bos ..181
Brett, KC 179
Griffey Jr, Sea....179
Parker, Mil.......176
Fernandez, Tor ...175
Burks, Bos 174
Jo.Reed, Bos 173
Franco, Tex 172

Games
Thigpen, Chi 77
Montgomery, KC...73
Ward, Tor 73
Henneman, Det ...69
Rogers, Tex 69
Murphy, Bos 68
Crim, Mil 67

Innings
Stewart, Oak 267.0
Morris, Det 249.2
Welch, Oak 238.0
Finley, Cal 236.0
Hanson, Sea 236.0
Clemens, Bos ...228.1
Boddicker, Bos ..228.0

Games Started
Morris, Det 36
Stewart, Oak 36
Perez, Chi 35
Welch, Oak 35
Boddicker, Bos 34
Sanderson, Oak...34
Swindell, Cle 34

Games Finished
Thigpen, Chi 73
Jones, Cle 64
Eckersley, Oak.....61
Montgomery, KC....59
Henke, Tor.......58
Olson, Bal 58
Henneman, Det 53

Triples
Fernandez, Tor 17
Sosa, Chi 10
Johnson, Chi 9
Liriano, Tor-Min......9
Polonia, NY-Cal 9

Doubles
Brett, KC 45
Jo.Reed, Bos 45
Boggs, Bos 44
Calderon, Chi 44
Harper, Min 42

Complete Games
Morris, Det 11
Stewart, Oak 11
Clemens, Bos 7
Finley, Cal 7
Robinson, Mil.......7
Witt, Tex 7
Young, Sea 7

Shutouts
Clemens, Bos 4
Stewart, Oak 4
Appier, KC.........3
Morris, Det 3
Perez, Chi 3
Ten tied with 2.

Runs
R.Henderson, Oak..119
Fielder, Det 104
Reynolds, Sea 100
Yount, Mil 98
Phillips, Det 97

On Base Pct.
R.Henderson, Oak .439
McGriff, Tor 400
E.Martinez, Sea... .397
Brett, KC 387
Davis, Sea 387

Strikeouts
Ryan, Tex........232
Witt, Tex 221
Hanson, Sea 211
Clemens, Bos 209
Langston, Cal 195

Walks
Johnson, Sea 120
Hough, Tex 119
Witt, Tex 110
Young, Sea 107
Langston, Cal 104

Total Bases
Fielder, Det 339
Gruber, Tor 303
McGriff, Tor......295
Griffey,Jr, Sea 287
Burks, Bos 286

Slugging Pct.
Fielder, Det ...... .592
R.Henderson, Oak .577
J.Canseco, Oak... .543
McGriff, Tor ...... .530
Brett, KC 515

Losses
Leary, NY........9-19
Anderson, Min ...7-18
Young, Sea.......8-18
Morris, Det......15-18
Langston, Cal 10-17
Stottlemyre, Tor ..13-17

HRs Given Up
Johnson, Bal 30
Sanderson, Oak....27
Swindell, Cle 27
Johnson, Sea 26
Morris, Det 26
Welch, Oak........26

Times Walked
McGwire, Oak.....110
Tettleton, Bal 106
Phillips, Det 99
R.Henderson, Oak..97
McGriff, Tor......94
Fielder, Det 90

Times Struck Out
Fielder, Det 182
Tettleton, Bal 160
J.Canseco, Oak....158
Barfield, NY 150
Sosa, Chi 150
Kelly, NY 148

National League Individual Leaders

Batting
(Minimum of 502 plate appearances.)

	Avg	AB	R	H	HR	RBI
Willie McGee, St.L	.335	501	76	168	3	62
Eddie Murray, LA	.330	558	96	184	26	95
Dave Magadan, NY	.328	451	74	148	6	72
Lenny Dykstra, Phi	.325	590	106	192	9	60
Andre Dawson, Chi	.310	529	72	164	27	100
Bip Roberts, SD	.309	556	104	172	9	44
Mark Grace, Chi	.309	589	72	182	9	82
Tony Gwynn, SD	.309	573	79	177	4	72
Brett Butler, SF	.309	622	108	192	3	44
Ryne Sandberg, Chi	.306	615	116	188	40	100
Lonnie Smith, Atl	.305	466	72	142	9	42
Ron Gant, Atl	.303	575	107	174	32	84
Barry Larkin, Cin	.301	614	85	185	7	67
Barry Bonds, Pit	.301	519	104	156	33	114
Kal Daniels, LA	.296	450	81	133	27	94
Tim Wallach, Mon	.296	626	69	185	21	98

Pitching
(Minimum of 162 innings pitched)

	ERA	W-L	IP	H	SO
Danny Darwin, Hou	2.21	11-4	162.2	136	109
Zane Smith, Mon-Pit	2.55	12-9	215.1	196	130
Ed Whitson, SD	2.60	14-9	228.2	215	127
Frank Viola, NY	2.67	20-12	249.2	227	182
Jose Rijo, Cin	2.70	14-8	197.0	151	152
Doug Drabek, Pit	2.76	22-6	231.1	190	131
Ramon Martinez, LA	2.92	20-6	234.1	191	223
Oil Can Boyd, Mon	2.93	10-6	190.2	164	113
Dennis Martinez, Mon	2.95	10-11	226.0	191	156
Bruce Hurst, SD	3.14	11-9	223.2	188	162
David Cone, NY	3.23	14-10	211.2	177	233
Mike Harkey, Chi	3.26	12-6	173.2	153	94
Terry Mulholland, Phi	3.34	9-10	180.2	172	75
Jack Armstrong, Cin	3.42	12-9	166.0	151	110
Sid Fernandez, NY	3.46	9-14	179.1	130	181
Greg Maddux, Chi	3.46	15-15	237.0	242	144

Home Runs
Sandberg, Chi	40
Strawberry, NY	37
Mitchell, SF	35
Bonds, Pit	33
Williams, SF	33
Bonilla, Pit	32
Gant, Atl	32
Justice, Atl	28
Daniels, LA	27
Dawson, Chi	27

Runs Batted In
Williams, SF	122
Bonilla, Pit	120
Carter, SD	115
Bonds, Pit	114
Strawberry, NY	108
Dawson, Chi	100
Sandberg, Chi	100
Wallach, Mon	98
Clark, SF	95
Murray, LA	95

Wins
Drabek, Pit	22-6
Martinez, LA	20-6
Viola, NY	20-12
Gooden, NY	19-7
Browning, Cin	15-9
Maddux, Chi	15-15
Burkett, SF	14-7
Rijo, Cin	14-8
Whitson, SD	14-9
Cone, NY	14-10
Smoltz, Atl	14-11

Saves
Franco, NY	33
Myers, Cin	31
L.Smith, St.L	27
Lefferts, SD	23
Smith, Hou	23
McDowell, Phi	22
Burke, Mon	20
Brantley, SF	19
Bedrosian, SF	17
Howell, LA	16
Williams, SF	16

Stolen Bases
	SB	CS
Coleman, St.L	77	17
Yelding, Hou	64	25
Bonds, Pit	52	13
Butler, SF	51	19
Nixon, Mon	50	13
Raines, Mon	49	16
Roberts, SD	46	12
DeShields, Mon	42	22
Samuel, LA	38	20
Johnson, NY	34	8

Hits
Butler, SF	192
Dykstra, Phi	192
Sandberg, Chi	188
Larkin, Cin	185
Wallach, Mon	185
Murray, LA	184
Grace, Chi	182
Clark, SF	177
Gwynn, SD	177
Bonilla, Pit	175
Gant, Atl	174

Games
Agosto, Hou	82
Assenmacher, Chi	74
Harris, SD	73
McDowell, Phi	72
Akerfelds, Phi	71
Bedrosian, SF	68
Dibble, Cin	68

Innings
Viola, NY	249.2
Maddux, Chi	237.0
Martinez, LA	234.1
Gooden, NY	232.2
Drabek, Pit	231.1
Smoltz, Atl	231.1
Whitson, SD	228.2

Triples
Duncan, Cin	11
Gwynn, SD	10
Butler, SF	9
Coleman, St.L	9
L.Smith, Atl	9

Doubles
Jefferies, NY	40
Bonilla, Pit	39
Sabo, Cin	38
Johnson, NY	37
Wallach, Mon	37

Games Started
Browning, Cin	35
Maddux, Chi	35
Viola, NY	35
Deshaies, Hou	34
Gooden, NY	34
Smoltz, Atl	34

Games Finished
McDowell, Phi	60
Myers, Cin	59
Bedrosian, SF	53
Franco, NY	48
L.Smith, St.L	45
Lefferts, SD	44

Runs
Sandberg, Chi	116
Bonilla, Pit	112
Butler, SF	108
Gant, Atl	107
Dykstra, Phi	106

On Base Pct.
Dykstra, Phi	.418
Magadan, NY	.417
Murray, LA	.414
Bonds, Pit	.406
Butler, SF	.397

Complete Games
Martinez, LA	12
Drabek, Pit	9
Hurst, SD	9
Maddux, Chi	8
De.Martinez, Mon	7
Rijo, Cin	7
Viola, NY	7
Five tied with 6.	

Shutouts
Hurst, SD	4
Morgan, LA	4
Boyd, Mon	3
Drabek, Pit	3
Gardner, Mon	3
Martinez, LA	3
Viola, NY	3
Whitson, SD	3

Total Bases
Sandberg, Chi	344
Bonilla, Pit	324
Gant, Atl	310
Williams, SF	301
Wallach, Mon	295
Bonds, Pit	293

Slugging Pct.
Bonds, Pit	.565
Sandberg, Chi	.559
Mitchell, SF	.544
Gant, Atl	.539
Justice, Atl	.535
Dawson, Chi	.535

Strikeouts
Cone, NY	233
Gooden, NY	223
Martinez, LA	223
Viola, NY	182
Fernandez, NY	181
Smoltz, Atl	170

Walks
Smoltz, Atl	90
Combs, Phi	86
DeLeon, St.L	86
Deshaies, Hou	84
Glavine, Atl	78
Rijo, Cin	78

Times Walked
Ja.Clark, SD	104
Bonds, Pit	93
Butler, SF	90
Dykstra, Phi	89
V.Hayes, Phi	87
Murray, LA	82

Times Struck Out
Galarraga, Mon	169
Williams, SF	138
Murphy, Atl-Phi	130
Presley, Atl	130
Samuel, LA	126
Stubbs, Hou	114

Losses
DeLeon, St.L	7-19
Magrane, St.L	10-17
Morgan, LA	11-15
Rasmussen, SD	11-15
Maddux, Chi	15-15

HRs Given Up
Rasmussen, SD	30
Scott, Hou	27
Browning, Cin	27
Martinez, LA	26
Five tied with 21	

AL Team by Team Statistics

At least 150 at bats or 50 innings pitched during the regular season. Players who played with more than one AL team during the season are listed with their final clubs. Players traded from the NL are listed with AL team only if they have 150 AB or 50 IP. Note that (*) indicates rookie.

Baltimore Orioles

Batting (150 AB)	Avg	AB	R	H	HR	RBI	SB
Billy Ripken	.291	406	48	118	3	38	5
Joe Orsulak	.269	413	49	111	11	57	6
Randy Milligan	.265	362	64	96	20	60	6
Steve Finley	.256	464	46	119	3	37	22
Tim Hulett	.255	153	16	39	3	16	1
Cal Ripken	.250	600	78	150	21	84	3
Sam Horn	.248	246	30	61	14	45	0
Bob Melvin	.243	301	30	73	5	37	0
Mike Devereaux	.240	367	48	88	12	49	13
Brady Anderson	.231	234	24	54	3	24	15
Ron Kittle	.231	338	33	78	18	46	0
Craig Worthington	.226	425	46	96	8	44	1
Mickey Tettleton	.223	444	68	99	15	51	2

Acquired: 1B-DH Kittle from Chisox (Jul.30) for OF Phil Bradley.
Traded: P Tibbs to Pit.(Jun.25) for minor leaguer.

Pitching (50 IP)	ERA	W-L	Gm	IP	BB	SO
Mark Williamson	2.21	8-2	49	85.1	28	60
Gregg Olson	2.42	6-5	64	74.1	31	74
Ben McDonald*	2.43	8-5	21	118.2	35	65
Joe Price	3.58	3-4	50	65.1	24	54
Dave Johnson	4.10	13-9	30	180.0	43	68
Pete Harnisch	4.34	11-11	31	188.2	86	122
Bob Milacki	4.46	5-8	27	135.1	61	60
Brian Holton	4.50	2-3	33	58.0	21	27
John Mitchell	4.64	6-6	24	114.1	48	43
Jeff Ballard	4.93	2-11	44	133.1	42	50
Jay Tibbs	5.68	2-7	10	50.2	14	23

Saves: Olson (37); Curt Schilling (3); Jay Aldrich, Kevin Hickey and Williamson (1). **Complete Games:** Johnson, Harnisch and McDonald (3); Milacki (1). **Shutouts:** McDonald (2); Milacki (1).

California Angels

Batting (150 AB)	Avg	AB	R	H	HR	RBI	SB
Luis Polonia	.335	403	52	135	2	35	21
Johnny Ray	.277	404	47	112	5	43	2
Brian Downing	.273	330	47	90	14	51	0
Lance Parrish	.268	470	54	126	24	70	2
Wally Joyner	.268	310	35	83	8	41	2
Rick Schu	.268	157	19	42	6	14	0
Dave Winfield	.267	475	70	127	21	78	0
Chili Davis	.265	412	58	109	12	58	1
Donnie Hill	.264	352	36	93	3	32	1
Max Venable	.259	189	26	49	4	21	5
Dante Bichette	.255	349	40	89	15	53	5
Dick Schofield	.255	310	41	79	1	18	3
Jack Howell	.228	316	35	72	8	33	3
Devon White	.217	443	57	96	11	44	21
Lee Stevens*	.214	248	28	53	7	32	1

Acquired: OF Polonia from NY Yanks (Apr.29) for OF Claudell Washington and a minor leaguer; OF Winfield from NY Yanks (May 11) for P Mike Witt.

Pitching (50 IP)	ERA	W-L	Gm	IP	BB	SO
Chuck Finley	2.40	18-9	32	236.0	81	177
Willie Fraser	3.08	5-4	45	76.0	24	32
Mark Eichhorn	3.08	2-5	60	84.2	23	69
Bryan Harvey	3.22	4-4	54	64.1	35	82
Kirk McCaskill	3.25	12-11	29	174.1	72	78
Mike Fetters*	4.12	1-1	26	67.2	20	35
Mark Langston	4.40	10-17	33	233.0	104	195
Jim Abbott	4.51	10-14	33	211.2	72	105
Bert Blyleven	5.24	8-7	23	134.0	25	69

Saves: Harvey (25); Eichhorn (13); Fraser (2); Fetters (1). **Complete Games:** Finley (7); Langston (5); Abbott (4); Blyleven and McCaskill (2); Scott Lewis (1). **Shutouts:** Finley (2); Abbott, McCaskill and Langston (1).

Boston Red Sox

Batting (150 AB)	Avg	AB	R	H	HR	RBI	SB
Wade Boggs	.302	619	89	187	6	63	0
Mike Greenwell	.297	610	71	181	14	73	8
Ellis Burks	.296	588	89	174	21	89	9
Jody Reed	.289	598	70	173	5	51	4
Carlos Quintana	.287	512	56	147	7	67	1
Tom Brunansky	.267	461	61	123	15	71	5
Tony Pena	.263	491	62	129	7	56	8
Dwight Evans	.249	445	66	111	13	63	3
Marty Barrett	.226	159	15	36	0	13	4
Luis Rivera	.225	346	38	78	7	45	4

Acquired: OF Brunansky from St.L. (May 4) for P Lee Smith; P Andersen from Hou. (Aug.31) for 2 minor leaguers.

Pitching (50 IP)	ERA	W-L	Gm	IP	BB	SO
Roger Clemens	1.93	21-6	31	228.1	54	209
Jeff Reardon	3.16	5-3	47	51.1	19	33
Mike Boddicker	3.36	17-8	34	228.0	69	143
Tom Bolton	3.38	10-5	21	119.2	47	65
Dana Kiecker*	3.97	8-9	32	152.0	54	93
Greg Harris	4.00	13-9	34	184.1	77	117
Jeff Gray	4.44	2-4	41	50.2	15	50
Dennis Lamp	4.68	3-5	47	105.2	30	49
Jerry Reed	4.82	2-2	33	52.1	19	19
Wes Gardner	4.89	3-7	34	77.1	35	58
Rob Murphy	6.32	0-6	68	57.0	32	54

Saves: Reardon (21); Gray (9); Murphy (7); Lee Smith (4); Reed (2); Larry Andersen (1). **Complete Games:** Clemens (7); Boddicker (4), Bolton (3); Harris (1). **Shutouts:** Clemens (4).

Chicago White Sox

Batting (150 AB)	Avg	AB	R	H	HR	RBI	SB
Frank Thomas*	.330	191	39	63	7	31	0
Carlton Fisk	.285	452	65	129	18	65	7
Lance Johnson	.285	541	76	154	1	51	36
Ozzie Guillen	.279	516	61	144	1	58	13
Dan Pasqua	.274	325	43	89	13	58	1
Ivan Calderon	.273	607	85	166	14	74	32
Phil Bradley	.256	422	59	108	4	31	17
Robin Ventura*	.249	493	48	123	5	54	1
Ron Karkovice	.246	183	30	45	6	20	2
Scott Fletcher	.242	509	54	123	4	56	1
Sammy Sosa	.233	532	72	124	15	70	32
Carlos Martinez	.224	272	18	61	4	24	0

Acquired: OF Bradley from Bal. (Jul.30) for 1B-DH Ron Kittle.

Pitching (50 IP)	ERA	W-L	Gm	IP	BB	SO
Bobby Thigpen	1.83	4-6	77	88.2	32	70
Barry Jones	2.31	11-4	65	74.0	33	45
Greg Hibbard	3.16	14-9	33	211.0	55	92
Wayne Edwards*	3.22	5-3	42	95.0	41	63
Eric King	3.28	12-4	25	151.0	40	70
Donn Pall	3.32	3-5	56	76.0	24	39
Ken Patterson	3.39	2-1	43	66.1	34	40
Alex Fernandez*	3.80	5-5	13	87.2	34	61
Jack McDowell	3.82	14-9	33	205.0	77	165
Adam Peterson*	4.55	2-5	20	85.0	26	29
Melido Perez	4.61	13-14	35	197.0	86	161
Scott Radinsky*	4.82	6-1	62	52.1	36	46

Saves: Thigpen (57); Radinsky (4); Edwards, Pall and Patterson (2); Jones (1). **Complete Games:** McDowell (4); Fernandez, Hibbard and Perez (3); King and Peterson (2). **Shutouts:** Perez (3); King (2), Hibbard (1).

Cleveland Indians

Batting (150 AB)	Avg	AB	R	H	HR	RBI	SB
Alex Cole*	.300	227	43	68	0	13	40
Chris James	.299	528	62	158	12	70	4
Brook Jacoby	.293	553	77	162	14	75	1
Sandy Alomar, Jr*	.290	445	60	129	9	66	4
Dion James	.274	248	28	68	1	22	5
Candy Maldonado	.273	590	76	161	22	95	3
Jerry Browne	.267	513	92	137	6	50	12
Tom Brookens	.266	154	18	41	1	20	0
Carlos Baerga*	.260	312	46	81	7	47	0
Felix Fermin	.256	414	47	106	1	40	3
Mitch Webster	.252	437	58	110	12	55	22
Cory Snyder	.233	438	46	102	14	55	1

Claimed: P Valdez on waivers from Atl. (Apr.30).

Pitching (50 IP)	ERA	W-L	Gm	IP	BB	SO
Doug Jones	2.56	5-5	66	84.1	22	55
Steve Olin*	3.41	4-4	50	92.1	26	64
Tom Candiotti	3.65	15-11	31	202.0	55	128
Jesse Orosco	3.90	5-4	55	64.2	38	55
John Farrell	4.28	4-5	17	96.2	33	44
Greg Swindell	4.40	12-9	34	214.2	47	135
Sergio Valdez	4.75	6-6	24	102.1	35	63
Mike Walker	4.88	2-6	18	75.2	42	34

Saves: Jones (43); Orosco (2); Olin and Colby Ward (1). **Complete Games:** Candiotti and Swindell (3); Farrell (1). **Shutouts:** Candiotti (1).

Detroit Tigers

Batting (150 AB)	Avg	AB	R	H	HR	RBI	SB
Alan Trammell	.304	559	71	170	14	89	12
Travis Fryman*	.297	232	32	69	9	27	3
Dave Bergman	.278	205	21	57	2	26	3
Cecil Fielder	.277	573	104	159	51	132	0
Mike Heath	.270	370	46	100	7	38	7
Larry Sheets	.261	360	40	94	10	52	1
Chet Lemon	.258	322	39	83	5	32	3
Gary Ward	.256	309	32	79	9	46	2
Tony Phillips	.251	573	97	144	8	55	19
Lloyd Moseby	.248	431	64	107	14	51	17
John Shelby	.248	222	22	55	4	20	3
Lou Whitaker	.237	472	75	112	18	60	8
Mark Salas	.232	164	18	38	9	24	0
Darnell Coles	.209	215	22	45	3	20	0

Acquired: P Parker and P Lance McCullers from NY Yanks (Jun.4) for C Matt Nokes; 3B Coles from Sea. (Jun.18) for OF Tracy Jones. **Signed:** P Terrell (Jul.28) after being released by Pit.

Pitching (50 IP)	ERA	W-L	Gm	IP	BB	SO
Edwin Nunez	2.24	3-1	42	80.1	37	66
Jerry Don Gleaton	2.94	1-3	57	82.2	25	56
Paul Gibson	3.05	5-4	61	97.1	44	56
Mike Henneman	3.05	8-6	69	94.1	33	50
Clay Parker	3.58	3-3	29	73.0	32	40
Dan Petry	4.45	10-9	32	149.2	77	73
Jack Morris	4.51	15-18	36	249.2	97	162
Walt Terrell	4.54	6-4	13	75.1	24	30
Steve Searcy*	4.66	2-7	16	75.1	51	66
Brian DuBois*	5.09	3-5	12	58.1	22	34
Frank Tanana	5.31	9-8	34	176.1	66	114
Jeff Robinson	5.96	10-9	27	145.0	88	76

Saves: Henneman (22); Gleaton (13); Nunez (6); Gibson (3); Tanana (1). **Complete Games:** Morris (11); Petry, Robinson, Searcy and Tanana (1). **Shutouts:** Morris (3); Robinson (1).

Kansas City Royals

Batting (150 AB)	Avg	AB	R	H	HR	RBI	SB
George Brett	.329	544	82	179	14	87	9
Willie Wilson	.290	307	49	89	2	42	24
Brian McRae*	.286	168	21	48	2	23	4
Jim Eisenreich	.280	496	61	139	5	51	12
Kevin Seitzer	.275	622	91	171	6	38	7
Pat Tabler	.272	195	12	53	1	19	0
Bo Jackson	.272	405	74	110	28	78	15
Danny Tartabull	.268	313	41	84	15	60	1
Mike Macfarlane	.255	400	37	102	6	58	1
Gerald Perry	.254	465	57	118	8	57	17
Kurt Stillwell	.249	506	60	126	3	51	0
Bill Pecota	.242	240	43	58	5	20	8
Frank White	.216	241	20	52	2	21	1

Traded: 1B Tabler to NY Mets (Aug.30) for minor leaguer.

Pitching (50 IP)	ERA	W-L	Gm	IP	BB	SO
Steve Farr	1.98	13-7	57	127.0	48	94
Jeff Montgomery	2.39	6-5	73	94.1	34	94
Kevin Appier*	2.76	12-8	32	185.2	54	127
Andy McGaffigan	3.09	4-3	24	78.2	28	49
Luis Aquino	3.16	4-1	20	68.1	27	28
Bret Saberhagen	3.27	5-9	20	135.0	28	87
Tom Gordon	3.73	12-11	32	195.1	99	175
Steve Crawford	4.16	5-4	46	80.0	23	54
Mark Gubicza	4.50	4-7	16	94.0	38	71
Storm Davis	4.74	7-10	21	112.0	35	62
Mark Davis	5.11	2-7	53	68.2	52	73

Saves: Montgomery (24); M.Davis (6); Crawford, Farr and McGaffigan (1). **Complete Games:** Gordon (6); Saberhagen (5); Appier (3); Gubicza (2); Aquino and Farr (1). **Shutouts:** Appier (3); Farr and Gordon (1).

Milwaukee Brewers

Batting (150 AB)	Avg	AB	R	H	HR	RBI	SB
Darryl Hamilton	.295	156	27	46	1	18	10
Gary Sheffield	.294	487	67	143	10	67	25
Dave Parker	.289	610	71	176	21	92	4
Paul Molitor	.285	418	64	119	12	45	18
B.J. Surhoff	.276	474	55	131	6	59	18
Mike Felder	.274	237	38	65	3	27	20
Edgar Diaz	.271	218	27	59	0	14	3
Jim Gantner	.263	323	36	85	0	25	18
Greg Brock	.248	367	42	91	7	50	4
Robin Yount	.247	587	98	145	17	77	15
Bill Spiers	.242	363	44	88	2	36	11
Greg Vaughn*	.220	382	51	84	17	61	7
Rob Deer	.209	440	57	92	27	69	2

Acquired: P Robinson and a minor leaguer from Cin. (Jun.10) for OF Glenn Braggs and INF Billy Bates.

Pitching (50 IP)	ERA	W-L	Gm	IP	BB	SO
Ron Robinson	2.91	12-5	22	148.1	37	57
Chuck Crim	3.47	3-5	67	85.2	23	39
Ted Higuera	3.76	11-10	27	170.0	50	129
Paul Mirabella	3.97	4-2	44	59.0	27	28
Bill Krueger	3.98	6-8	30	129.0	54	64
Chris Bosio	4.00	4-9	20	132.2	38	76
Mark Knudson	4.12	10-9	30	168.1	40	56
Dan Plesac	4.43	3-7	66	69.0	31	65
Tom Edens*	4.45	4-5	35	89.0	33	40
Jamie Navarro	4.46	8-7	32	149.1	41	75

Saves: Plesac (24); Crim (11); Julio Machado (3); Edens (2); Navarro and Randy Veres (1). **Complete Games:** Robinson (7); Bosio, Knudson and Higuera (4); Navarro (3); Bill Wegman (1). **Shutouts:** Knudson and Robinson (2); Bosio, Higuera and Wegman (1).

AL Team by Team Statistics (Cont.)

Minnesota Twins

Batting (150 AB)	Avg	AB	R	H	HR	RBI	SB
Junior Ortiz	.335	170	18	57	0	18	0
Shane Mack	.326	313	50	102	8	44	13
Kirby Puckett	.298	551	82	164	12	80	5
Brian Harper	.294	479	61	141	6	54	3
Kent Hrbek	.287	492	61	141	22	79	5
Dan Gladden	.285	534	64	147	5	40	25
Gene Larkin	.269	401	46	108	5	42	5
Randy Bush	.243	181	17	44	6	18	0
Al Newman	.242	388	43	94	0	30	13
Fred Manrique	.237	228	22	54	5	29	2
Greg Gagne	.235	388	38	91	7	38	8
Nelson Liriano	.234	355	46	83	1	28	8
Gary Gaetti	.229	577	61	132	16	85	6
John Moses	.221	172	26	38	1	14	2

Acquired: 2B Liriano from Tor. (Jul.27) for P John Candelaria and a minor leaguer.

Pitching (50 IP)	ERA	W-L	Gm	IP	BB	SO
Rick Aguilera	2.76	5-3	56	65.1	19	61
Scott Erickson*	2.87	8-4	19	113.0	51	53
Terry Leach	3.20	2-5	55	81.2	21	46
Juan Berenguer	3.41	8-5	51	100.1	58	77
Mark Guthrie	3.79	7-9	24	144.2	39	101
Kevin Tapani*	4.07	12-8	28	159.1	29	101
Tim Drummond*	4.35	3-5	35	91.0	36	49
Allan Anderson	4.53	7-18	31	188.2	39	82
Roy Smith	4.81	5-10	32	153.1	47	87
David West	5.10	7-9	29	146.1	78	92

Saves: Aguilera (32); Rich Garces* and Leach (2); Drummond, Jack Savage and Gary Wayne (1). **Complete Games:** Anderson (5); Guthrie (3); West (2); Erickson, Smith and Tapani (1). **Shutouts:** Anderson, Guthrie, Smith and Tapani (1).

New York Yankees

Batting (150 AB)	Avg	AB	R	H	HR	RBI	SB
Roberto Kelly	.285	641	85	183	15	61	42
Steve Sax	.260	615	70	160	4	42	43
Mel Hall	.258	360	41	93	12	46	0
Jim Leyritz*	.257	303	28	78	5	25	2
Don Mattingly	.256	394	40	101	5	42	1
Kevin Maas*	.252	254	42	64	21	41	1
Matt Nokes	.248	351	33	87	11	40	2
Oscar Azocar*	.248	214	18	53	5	19	7
Jesse Barfield	.246	476	69	117	25	78	4
Alvaro Espinoza	.224	438	31	98	2	20	1
Bob Geren	.213	277	21	59	8	31	0
Randy Velarde	.210	229	21	48	5	19	0
Steve Balboni	.192	266	24	51	17	34	0

Acquired: P Witt from Cal. (May 11) for OF Dave Winfield; C Nokes from Det. (Jun.4) for P Clay Parker and P Lance McCullers.

Pitching (50 IP)	ERA	W-L	Gm	IP	BB	SO
Eric Plunk	2.72	6-3	47	72.2	43	67
Lee Guetterman	3.39	11-7	64	93.0	26	48
Jeff Robinson	3.45	3-6	54	88.2	34	43
Dave Righetti	3.57	1-1	53	53.0	26	43
Mike Witt	4.00	5-9	26	117.0	47	74
Dave LaPoint	4.11	7-10	28	157.2	57	67
Tim Leary	4.11	9-19	31	208.0	78	138
Greg Cadaret	4.15	5-4	54	121.1	64	80
Chuck Cary	4.19	6-12	28	156.2	55	134
Andy Hawkins	5.37	5-12	28	157.2	82	74
Jimmy Jones	6.30	1-2	17	50.0	23	25

Saves: Righetti (36); Cadaret (3); Guetterman (2); Witt (1). **Complete Games:** Leary (5); Cary, Hawkins, LaPoint and Witt (2); Robinson (1). **Shutouts:** Hawkins, Leary and Witt (1).

Oakland Athletics

Batting (150 AB)	Avg	AB	R	H	HR	RBI	SB
Rickey Henderson	.325	489	119	159	28	61	65
Harold Baines	.284	415	52	118	16	65	0
Jose Canseco	.274	481	83	132	37	101	19
Dave Henderson	.271	450	65	122	20	63	3
Carney Lansford	.268	507	58	136	3	50	16
Walt Weiss	.265	445	50	118	2	35	9
Felix Jose	.264	341	42	90	8	39	8
Willie Randolph	.257	292	37	75	1	21	6
Terry Steinbach	.251	379	32	95	9	57	0
Mark McGwire	.235	523	87	123	39	108	2
Ron Hassey	.213	254	18	54	5	22	0
Mike Gallego	.206	389	36	80	3	34	5
Doug Jennings	.192	156	19	30	2	14	0

Acquired: 2B Randolph from LA (May 13) for OF Stan Javier; DH Baines from Tex. (Aug.29) for 2 minor leaguers. **Traded:** OF Jose and 2 minor leaguers to St.L. (Aug.29) for OF Willie McGee.

Pitching (50 IP)	ERA	W-L	Gm	IP	BB	SO
Dennis Eckersley	0.61	4-2	63	73.1	4	73
Gene Nelson	1.57	3-3	51	74.2	17	38
Dave Stewart	2.56	22-11	36	267.0	83	166
Rick Honeycutt	2.70	2-2	63	63.1	22	38
Bob Welch	2.95	27-6	35	238.0	77	127
Todd Burns	2.97	3-3	43	78.2	32	43
Scott Sanderson	3.88	17-11	34	206.1	66	128
Mike Moore	4.65	13-15	33	199.1	84	73
Curt Young	4.85	9-6	26	124.1	53	56

Saves: Eckersley (48); Honeycutt (7); Nelson (5); Burns (3); Joe Klink (1). **Complete Games:** Stewart (11); Moore (3); Sanderson and Welch (2). **Shutouts:** Stewart (4); Welch (2); Sanderson (1).

Seattle Mariners

Batting (150 AB)	Avg	AB	R	H	HR	RBI	SB
Edgar Martinez	.302	487	71	147	11	49	1
Ken Griffey,Jr	.300	597	91	179	22	80	16
Alvin Davis	.283	494	63	140	17	68	0
Jay Buhner	.276	163	16	45	7	33	2
Tracy Jones	.260	204	23	53	6	24	1
Henry Cotto	.259	355	40	92	4	33	21
Harold Reynolds	.252	642	100	162	5	55	31
Jeffrey Leonard	.251	478	39	120	10	75	4
Omar Vizquel	.247	255	19	63	2	18	4
Greg Briley	.246	337	40	83	5	29	16
Pete O'Brien	.224	366	32	82	5	27	0
Scott Bradley	.223	233	11	52	1	28	0
Dave Valle	.214	308	37	66	7	33	1

Acquired: OF Jones from Det. (Jun.18) for 3B Darnell Coles. **Signed:** OF Ken Griffey, Sr. (Aug.29) after being released by Cin. (Griffey Sr. batted .377 with 3 HR and 19 RBI in 21 games with Mariners).

Pitching (50 IP)	ERA	W-L	Gm	IP	BB	SO
Mike Schooler	2.25	1-4	49	56.0	16	45
Bill Swift	2.39	6-4	55	128.0	21	42
Keith Comstock	2.89	7-4	60	56.0	26	50
Erik Hanson	3.24	18-9	33	236.0	68	211
Matt Young	3.51	8-18	34	225.1	107	176
Randy Johnson	3.65	14-11	33	219.2	120	194
Brian Holman	4.03	11-11	28	189.2	66	121
Mike Jackson	4.54	5-7	63	77.1	44	69

Saves: Schooler (30); Swift (6); Jackson (3); Comstock (2). **Complete Games:** Young (7); Hanson and Johnson (5); Holman (3); Rich DeLucia*(1). **Shutouts:** Johnson (2); Hanson and Young (1).

Texas Rangers

Batting (150 AB)	Avg	AB	R	H	HR	RBI	SB
Rafael Palmeiro	.319	596	72	191	14	89	3
Jack Daugherty	.300	310	36	93	6	47	0
Julio Franco	.296	582	96	172	11	69	31
Ruben Sierra	.280	608	70	170	16	96	9
Geno Petralli	.255	325	28	83	0	21	0
Mike Stanley	.249	189	21	47	2	19	1
Jeff Huson*	.240	396	57	95	0	28	12
Gary Pettis	.239	423	66	101	3	31	38
Pete Incaviglia	.233	529	59	123	24	85	3
Steve Buechele	.215	251	30	54	7	30	1
Scott Coolbaugh*	.200	180	21	36	2	13	1
Jeff Kunkel	.170	200	17	34	3	17	2

Acquired: None.

Pitching (50 IP)	ERA	W-L	Gm	IP	BB	SO
Brad Arnsberg	2.15	6-1	53	62.2	33	44
Kenny Rogers	3.13	10-6	69	97.2	42	74
Bobby Witt	3.36	17-10	33	222.0	110	221
Nolan Ryan	3.44	13-9	30	204.0	74	232
Kevin Brown	3.60	12-10	26	180.0	60	88
Charlie Hough	4.07	12-12	32	218.2	119	114
Mike Jeffcoat	4.47	5-6	44	110.2	28	58
Jamie Moyer	4.66	2-6	33	102.1	39	58

Saves: Rogers (15); Jeff Russell (10); Arnsberg and Jeffcoat (2); John Barfield (1). **Complete Games:** Witt (7); Brown (6); Hough and Ryan (5); Jeffcoat and Moyer (1). **Shutouts:** Brown and Ryan (2); Witt (1).

Toronto Blue Jays

Batting (150 AB)	Avg	AB	R	H	HR	RBI	SB
Fred McGriff	.300	557	91	167	35	88	5
Pat Borders	.286	346	36	99	15	49	0
Tony Fernandez	.276	635	84	175	4	66	26
Kelly Gruber	.274	592	92	162	31	118	14
John Olerud*	.265	358	43	95	14	48	0
Mookie Wilson	.265	588	81	156	3	51	23
George Bell	.265	562	67	149	21	86	3
Junior Felix	.263	463	73	122	15	65	13
Manny Lee	.243	391	45	95	6	41	3
Greg Myers*	.236	250	33	59	5	22	0
Glenallen Hill*	.231	260	47	60	12	32	8
Kenny Williams	.161	155	23	25	0	13	9

Claimed: OF Williams on waivers from Det. (Jun.18). **Acquired:** P Candelaria from Min. (Jul.27) for 2B Nelson Liriano and a minor leaguer; P Black from Cle. (Sept.17) for 3 minor leaguers.

Pitching (50 IP)	ERA	W-L	Gm	IP	BB	SO
Tom Henke	2.17	2-4	61	74.2	19	75
Dave Stieb	2.93	18-6	33	208.2	64	125
David Wells	3.14	11-6	43	189.0	45	115
Duane Ward	3.45	2-8	73	127.2	42	112
Bud Black	3.57	13-11	32	206.2	61	106
Jim Acker	3.83	4-4	59	91.2	30	54
John Candelaria	3.95	7-6	47	79.2	20	63
Willie Blair*	4.06	3-5	27	68.2	28	43
Jimmy Key	4.25	13-7	27	154.2	22	88
Todd Stottlemyre	4.34	13-17	33	203.0	69	115
Frank Wills	4.73	6-4	44	99.0	38	72
John Cerutti	4.76	9-9	30	140.0	49	49

Saves: Henke (32); Ward (11); Candelaria (5); Wells (3); Acker (1). **Complete Games:** Black (5); Stottlemyre (4); Stieb (2). **Shutouts:** Black and Stieb (2).

NL Team by Team Statistics

At least 150 at bats or 50 innings pitched during the regular season. Players who played with more than one NL team during the season are listed with their final clubs. Players traded from the AL are listed with NL team only if they have 150 AB or 50 IP. Note that (*) indicates rookie.

Atlanta Braves

Batting (150 AB)	Avg	AB	R	H	HR	RBI	SB
Lonnie Smith	.305	466	72	142	9	42	10
Ron Gant	.303	575	107	174	32	84	33
Jeff Treadway	.283	474	56	134	11	59	3
Dave Justice*	.282	439	76	124	28	78	11
Jeff Blauser	.269	386	46	104	8	39	3
Tommy Gregg	.264	239	18	63	5	32	4
Greg Olson*	.262	298	36	78	7	36	1
Oddibe McDowell	.243	305	47	74	7	25	13
Jim Presley	.242	541	59	131	19	72	1
Mark Lemke*	.226	239	22	54	0	21	0
Andres Thomas	.219	278	26	61	5	30	2
Ernie Whitt	.172	180	14	31	2	10	0

Acquired: P Kerfeld from Hou. (Apr.29) for 2 minor leaguers; P Grant from SD (Jul.12) for P Derek Lilliquist; P Parrett and 2 minor leaguers from Phi. (Aug.3) for OF Dale Murphy and a minor leaguer.

Pitching (50 IP)	ERA	W-L	Gm	IP	BB	SO
Charlie Leibrandt	3.16	9-11	24	162.1	35	76
John Smoltz	3.85	14-11	34	231.1	90	170
Tony Castillo	4.23	5-1	52	76.2	20	64
Tom Glavine	4.28	10-12	33	214.1	78	129
Jeff Parrett	4.64	5-10	67	108.2	55	86
Mark Grant	4.73	2-3	59	91.1	37	69
Pete Smith	4.79	5-6	13	77.0	24	56
Steve Avery*	5.64	3-11	21	99.0	45	75
Marty Clary	5.67	1-10	33	101.2	39	44
Rick Luecken*	5.77	1-4	36	53.0	30	35

Saves: Kent Mercker* (7); Joe Hesketh (5); Grant (3); Charley Kerfeld, Parrett and Mike Stanton (2); Castillo, Marvin Freeman and Luecken (1). **Complete Games:** Smoltz (6); Leibrandt (5); Smith (3); Avery, Glavine and Paul Marak* (1). **Shutouts:** Leibrandt and Smoltz (2); Avery and Marak* (1).

Chicago Cubs

Batting (150 AB)	Avg	AB	R	H	HR	RBI	SB
Andre Dawson	.310	529	72	164	27	100	16
Mark Grace	.309	589	72	182	9	82	15
Ryne Sandberg	.306	615	116	188	40	100	25
Dave Clark	.275	171	22	47	5	20	7
Joe Girardi	.270	419	36	113	1	38	8
Domingo Ramos	.265	226	22	60	2	17	0
Jerome Walton	.263	392	63	103	2	21	14
Shawon Dunston	.262	545	73	143	17	66	25
Dwight Smith	.262	290	34	76	6	27	11
Luis Salazar	.254	410	44	104	12	47	3
Doug Dascenzo	.253	241	27	61	1	26	15
Curtis Wilkerson	.220	186	21	41	0	16	2
Marvell Wynne	.204	186	21	38	4	19	3

Acquired: P Long from Chisox (Apr.30) for a minor leaguer.

Pitching (50 IP)	ERA	W-L	Gm	IP	BB	SO
Paul Assenmacher	2.80	7-2	74	103.0	36	95
Mike Harkey*	3.26	12-6	27	173.2	59	94
Greg Maddux	3.46	15-15	35	327.0	71	144
Shawn Boskie*	3.69	5-6	15	97.2	31	49
Mitch Williams	3.93	1-8	59	66.1	50	55
Bill Long	4.37	6-1	42	55.2	21	32
Les Lancaster	4.62	9-5	55	109.0	40	65
Steve Wilson	4.79	4-9	45	139.0	43	95
Jeff Pico	4.79	4-4	31	92.0	37	37
Mike Bielecki	4.93	8-11	36	168.0	70	103
Jose Nunez	6.53	4-7	21	60.2	34	40

Saves: Williams (16); Assenmacher (10); Lancaster (6), Long (5); Pico (2), Bielecki, Dean Wilkins and Wilson (1). **Complete Games:** Maddux (8); Harkey (2); Boskie, Lancaster and Wilson (1). **Shutouts:** Maddux (2); Harkey and Lancaster (1).

NL Team by Team Statistics (Cont.)

Cincinnati Reds

Batting (150 AB)	Avg	AB	R	H	HR	RBI	SB
Hal Morris*	.340	309	50	105	7	36	9
Mariano Duncan	.306	435	67	133	10	55	13
Barry Larkin	.301	614	85	185	7	67	30
Bill Doran	.300	403	59	121	7	37	23
Ron Oester	.299	154	10	46	0	13	1
Glenn Braggs	.299	201	22	60	6	28	3
Billy Hatcher	.276	504	68	139	5	25	30
Paul O'Neill	.270	503	59	136	16	78	13
Chris Sabo	.270	567	95	153	25	71	25
Eric Davis	.260	453	84	118	24	86	21
Herm Winningham	.256	160	20	41	3	17	6
Todd Benzinger	.253	376	35	95	5	46	3
Jeff Reed	.251	175	12	44	3	16	0
Joe Oliver	.231	364	34	84	8	52	1

Acquired: OF Braggs and INF Billy Bates from Mil. (Jun.10) for P Ron Robinson and a minor leaguer; 2B Doran from Hou. (Aug.31) for 3 minor leaguers.

Pitching (50 IP)	ERA	W-L	Gm	IP	BB	SO
Rob Dibble	1.74	8-3	68	96.0	34	136
Randy Myers	2.08	4-6	66	86.2	38	98
Jose Rijo	2.70	14-8	29	197.0	78	152
Norm Charlton	2.74	12-9	56	154.1	70	117
Jack Armstrong	3.42	12-9	29	166.0	59	110
Tim Layana*	3.49	5-3	55	80.0	44	53
Danny Jackson	3.61	6-6	22	117.1	40	76
Tom Browning	3.80	15-9	35	227.2	52	99
Tim Birtsas	3.86	1-3	29	51.1	24	41
Rick Mahler	4.28	7-6	35	134.2	39	68
Scott Scudder	4.90	5-5	21	71.2	30	42

Saves: Myers (31); Dibble (11); Mahler (4); Charlton and Layana (2). **Complete Games:** Rijo (7); Armstrong, Browning and Mahler (2); Charlton (1). **Shutouts:** Armstrong, Browning, Mahler, Rijo and Charlton (1).

Los Angeles Dodgers

Batting (150 AB)	Avg	AB	R	H	HR	RBI	SB
Eddie Murray	.330	558	96	184	26	95	8
Stan Javier	.304	276	56	84	3	24	15
Lenny Harris	.304	431	61	131	2	29	15
Mike Sharperson	.297	357	42	106	3	36	15
Kal Daniels	.296	450	81	133	27	94	4
Hubie Brooks	.266	568	74	151	20	91	2
Mike Scioscia	.264	435	48	115	12	66	4
Kirk Gibson	.260	315	59	82	8	38	26
Juan Samuel	.242	492	62	119	13	52	38
Alfredo Griffin	.210	461	38	97	1	35	6

Acquired: OF Javier from Oak. (May 13) for 2B Willie Randolph; P Cook from Phi. (Sept.13) for C Darrin Fletcher.

Pitching (50 IP)	ERA	W-L	Gm	IP	BB	SO
Jay Howell	2.18	5-5	45	66.0	20	59
Tim Crews	2.77	4-5	66	107.1	24	76
Jim Gott	2.90	3-5	50	62.0	34	44
Ramon Martinez	2.92	20-6	33	234.1	67	223
Mike Hartley*	2.95	6-3	32	79.1	30	72
Jim Neidlinger*	3.28	5-3	12	74.0	15	46
Mike Morgan	3.75	11-15	33	211.0	60	106
Dennis Cook	3.92	9-4	47	156.0	56	64
Tim Belcher	4.00	9-9	24	153.0	48	102
F. Valenzuela	4.59	13-13	33	204.0	77	115

Saves: Howell (16); Crews (5); Don Aase and Gott (3); Cook, Hartley and Dave Walsh* (1). **Complete Games:** Martinez (12); Morgan (6); Belcher and Valenzuela (5); Cook (2); Hartley (1). **Shutouts:** Morgan (4); Martinez (3); Belcher and Valenzuela (2); Cook and Hartley (1).

Houston Astros

Batting (150 AB)	Avg	AB	R	H	HR	RBI	SB
Casey Candaele	.286	262	30	75	3	22	7
Craig Biggio	.276	555	53	153	4	42	25
Franklin Stubbs	.261	448	59	117	23	71	19
Rafael Ramirez	.261	445	44	116	2	37	10
Eric Yelding	.254	511	69	130	1	28	64
Glenn Davis	.251	327	44	82	22	64	8
Glenn Wilson	.245	368	42	90	10	55	0
Ken Caminiti	.242	541	52	131	4	51	9
Ken Oberkfell	.207	150	10	31	1	12	1
Eric Anthony*	.192	239	26	46	10	29	5
Gerald Young	.175	154	15	27	1	4	6

Traded: P Andersen to Bos. (Aug.31) for 2 minor leaguers.

Pitching (50 IP)	ERA	W-L	Gm	IP	BB	SO
Larry Andersen	1.95	5-2	50	73.2	24	68
Danny Darwin	2.21	11-4	48	162.2	31	109
Dave Smith	2.39	6-6	49	60.1	20	50
Mark Portugal	3.62	11-10	32	196.2	67	136
Jim Deshaies	3.78	7-12	34	209.1	84	119
Mike Scott	3.81	9-13	32	205.2	66	121
Bill Gullickson	3.82	10-14	32	193.1	61	73
Juan Agosto	4.29	9-8	82	92.1	39	50
Xavier Hernandez	4.62	2-1	34	62.1	24	24
Jim Clancy	6.51	2-8	33	76.0	33	44

Saves: Smith (23); Andersen (6); Agosto (4); Darwin (2); Clancy and Brian Meyer (1). **Complete Games:** Scott (4); Darwin (3); Deshaies and Gullickson (2); Portugal (1). **Shutouts:** Scott (2); Gullickson (1).

Montreal Expos

Batting (150 AB)	Avg	AB	R	H	HR	RBI	SB
Tim Wallach	.296	626	69	185	21	98	6
Delino DeShields*	.289	499	69	144	4	45	42
Tim Raines	.287	457	65	131	9	62	49
Dave Martinez	.279	391	60	109	11	39	13
Junior Noboa	.266	158	15	42	0	14	4
Marquis Grissom*	.257	288	42	74	3	29	22
Andres Galarraga	.256	579	65	148	20	87	10
Otis Nixon	.251	231	46	58	1	20	50
Mike Fitzgerald	.243	313	36	76	9	41	8
Mike Aldrete	.242	161	22	39	1	18	1
Larry Walker*	.241	419	59	101	19	51	21
Spike Owen	.234	453	55	106	5	35	8
Tom Foley	.213	164	11	35	0	12	0
Nelson Santovenia	.190	163	13	31	6	28	0

Acquired: P Ruskin and 2 minor leaguers from Pit. (Aug.8) for P Zane Smith.

Pitching (50 IP)	ERA	W-L	Gm	IP	BB	SO
Steve Frey	2.10	8-2	51	55.2	29	29
Tim Burke	2.52	3-3	58	75.0	21	47
Scott Ruskin*	2.75	3-2	67	75.1	38	57
Chris Nabholz*	2.83	6-2	11	70.0	32	53
Oil Can Boyd	2.93	10-6	31	190.2	52	113
Dennis Martinez	2.95	10-11	32	226.0	49	156
Bill Sampen	2.99	12-7	59	90.1	33	69
Dale Mohorcic	3.23	1-2	34	53.0	18	29
Mark Gardner*	3.42	7-9	27	152.2	61	135
Kevin Gross	4.57	9-12	31	163.1	65	111
Drew Hall	5.09	4-7	42	58.1	29	40

Saves: Burke (20); Dave Schmidt (13); Frey (9); Hall (3); Mohorcic, Ruskin and Sampen (1); Mel Rojas (1). **Complete Games:** Martinez (7); Boyd and Gardner (3); Gross (2); Brian Barnes and Nabholz (1). **Shutouts:** Boyd and Gardner (3); Martinez (2); Gross and Nabholz (1).

New York Mets

Batting (150 AB)	Avg	AB	R	H	HR	RBI	SB
Dave Magadan	.328	451	74	148	6	72	2
Mackey Sasser	.307	270	31	83	6	41	0
Gregg Jefferies	.283	604	96	171	15	68	11
Darryl Strawberry	.277	542	92	150	37	108	15
Daryl Boston	.273	366	65	100	12	45	18
Kevin McReynolds	.269	521	75	140	24	82	9
Tom Herr	.261	547	48	143	5	60	7
Keith Miller	.258	233	42	60	1	12	16
Mark Carreon	.250	188	30	47	10	26	1
Tim Teufel	.246	175	28	43	10	24	0
Howard Johnson	.244	590	89	144	23	90	34
Mike Marshall	.239	163	24	39	6	27	0
Kevin Elster	.207	314	36	65	9	45	2

Claimed: OF Boston on waivers from Chisox (Apr.31). **Acquired:** 2B Herr from Phi. (Aug.31) for 2 minor leaguers; P Dan Schatzeder from Hou. (Sept.10) for 2 minor leaguers.

Pitching (50 IP)	ERA	W-L	Gm	IP	BB	SO
Dan Schatzeder	2.20	1-3	51	69.2	23	39
John Franco	2.53	5-3	55	67.2	21	56
Frank Viola	2.67	20-12	35	249.2	60	182
Alejandro Pena	3.20	3-3	52	76.0	22	76
David Cone	3.23	14-10	31	211.2	65	233
Wally Whitehurst*	3.29	1-0	38	65.2	9	46
Sid Fernandez	3.46	9-14	30	179.1	67	181
Bob Ojeda	3.66	7-6	38	118.0	40	62
Dwight Gooden	3.83	19-7	34	232.2	70	223
Ron Darling	4.50	7-9	33	126.0	44	99

Saves: Franco (33); Pena (5); Whitehurst (2); Jeff Innis (1). **Complete Games:** Viola (7); Cone (6); Fernandez and Gooden (2); Darling (1). **Shutouts:** Viola (3); Cone (2); Fernandez and Gooden (1).

Philadelphia Phillies

Batting (150 AB)	Avg	AB	R	H	HR	RBI	SB
Lenny Dykstra	.325	590	106	192	9	60	33
John Kruk	.291	443	52	129	7	67	10
Darren Daulton	.268	459	62	123	12	57	7
Von Hayes	.261	467	70	122	17	73	16
Charlie Hayes	.258	561	56	145	10	57	4
Dickie Thon	.255	552	54	141	8	48	12
Dale Murphy	.245	563	60	138	24	83	9
Randy Ready	.244	217	26	53	1	26	3
Ricky Jordan	.241	324	32	78	5	44	2

Claimed: P Greene on waivers from Atl. (Aug.9). **Acquired:** P Boever from Atl. (Jul.23) for P Marvin Freeman; OF Murphy and a minor leaguer from Atl. (Aug.3) for P Jeff Parrett and 2 minor leaguers.

Pitching (50 IP)	ERA	W-L	Gm	IP	BB	SO
Jason Grimsley*	3.30	3-2	11	57.1	43	41
Terry Mulholland	3.34	9-10	33	180.2	42	75
Joe Boever	3.36	3-6	67	88.1	51	75
Jose DeJesus*	3.74	7-8	22	130.0	73	87
Darrel Akerfelds	3.77	5-2	71	93.0	54	42
Roger McDowell	3.86	6-8	72	86.1	35	39
Pat Combs*	4.07	10-10	32	183.1	86	108
Don Carman	4.15	6-2	59	86.2	38	58
Ken Howell	4.64	8-7	18	106.2	49	70
Tommy Greene*	5.06	3-3	15	51.1	26	21
Bruce Ruffin	5.38	6-13	32	149.0	62	79

Saves: McDowell (22); Boever (14); Akerfelds (3); Carman (1). **Complete Games:** Mulholland (6); Combs, and DeJesus (3); Howell and Ruffin (2). **Shutouts:** Combs (2); DeJesus, Mulholland and Ruffin (1).

Pittsburgh Pirates

Batting (150 AB)	Avg	AB	R	H	HR	RBI	SB
Barry Bonds	.301	519	104	156	33	114	52
Don Slaught	.300	230	27	69	4	29	0
Wally Backman	.292	315	62	92	2	28	6
R.J.Reynolds	.288	215	25	62	0	19	12
Andy Van Slyke	.284	493	67	140	17	77	14
Bobby Bonilla	.280	625	112	175	32	120	4
Sid Bream	.270	389	39	105	15	67	8
Jose Lind	.261	514	46	134	1	48	8
Mike LaValliere	.258	279	27	72	3	31	0
Jay Bell	.254	583	93	148	7	52	10
Gary Redus	.247	227	32	56	6	23	11
Jeff King	.245	371	46	91	14	53	3
Carmelo Martinez	.240	217	26	52	10	35	2

Acquired: P Smith from Mon. (Aug.8) for P Scott Ruskin and 2 minor leaguers; 1B Martinez from Phi. (Aug.30) for 2 minor leaguers.

Pitching (50 IP)	ERA	W-L	Gm	IP	BB	SO
Bill Landrum	2.13	7-3	54	71.2	21	39
Randy Tomlin*	2.55	4-4	12	77.2	12	42
Zane Smith	2.55	12-9	33	215.1	50	130
Doug Drabek	2.76	22-6	33	231.1	56	131
Bob Patterson	2.95	8-5	55	94.2	21	70
Bob Kipper	3.02	5-2	41	62.2	26	35
Neal Heaton	3.45	12-9	30	146	38	68
Stan Belinda*	3.55	3-4	55	58.1	29	55
Ted Power	3.66	1-3	40	51.2	17	42
Bob Walk	3.75	7-5	26	129.2	36	73
Rick Reed	4.36	2-3	13	53.2	12	27
John Smiley	4.64	9-10	26	149.1	36	86
Walt Terrell	5.88	2-7	16	82.2	33	34

Saves: Landrum (13); Belinda (8); Power (7); Patterson (5); Kipper and Vicente Palacios (3); Reed and Walk (1). **Complete Games:** Drabek (9); Smith (4); Smiley and Tomlin (2); Reed and Walk (1). **Shutouts:** Drabek (3); Smith (2); Reed and Walk (1).

St. Louis Cardinals

Batting (150 AB)	Avg	AB	R	H	HR	RBI	SB
Willie McGee	.335	501	76	168	3	62	28
Vince Coleman	.292	497	73	145	6	39	77
Rex Hudler	.282	220	31	62	7	22	18
Pedro Guerrero	.281	498	42	140	13	80	1
Tom Pagnozzi	.277	220	20	61	2	23	1
Ozzie Smith	.254	512	61	130	1	50	32
Jose Oquendo	.252	469	38	118	1	37	1
Todd Zeile*	.244	495	62	121	15	57	2
Terry Pendleton	.230	447	46	103	6	58	7
Milt Thompson	.218	418	42	91	6	30	25

Acquired: INF Hudler from Mon. (Apr.23) for P John Costello; P L.Smith from Bos. (May 4) for OF Tom Brunansky. **Traded:** OF McGee to Oak. (Aug.29) for OF Felix Jose and 2 minor leaguers.

Pitching (50 IP)	ERA	W-L	Gm	IP	BB	SO
Lee Smith	2.10	3-4	53	68.2	20	70
John Tudor	2.40	12-4	25	146.1	30	63
Tom Niedenfuer	3.46	0-6	52	65.0	25	32
Bob Tewksbury	3.47	10-9	28	145.1	15	50
Ken Dayley	3.56	4-4	58	73.1	30	51
Joe Magrane	3.59	10-17	31	203.1	59	100
Bryn Smith	4.27	9-8	26	141.1	30	78
Jose DeLeon	4.43	7-19	32	182.2	86	164
Frank DiPino	4.56	5-2	62	81.0	31	49
Scott Terry	4.75	2-6	50	72.0	27	35
Greg Mathews	5.33	0-5	11	50.2	30	18
Ken Hill	5.49	5-6	17	78.2	33	58

Saves: L.Smith (27); DiPino (3); Dayley, Niedenfuer and Terry (2); Ricky Horton, Mike Perez and Tewksbury (1). **Complete Games:** Magrane and Tewksbury (3); Hill and Tudor (1). **Shutouts:** Magrane and Tewksbury (2); Tudor (1).

NL Team by Team Statistics (Cont.)

San Diego Padres

Batting (150 AB)	Avg	AB	R	H	HR	RBI	SB
Bip Roberts	.309	556	104	172	9	44	46
Tony Gwynn	.309	573	79	177	4	72	17
Roberto Alomar	.287	586	80	168	6	60	24
Benito Santiago	.270	344	42	93	11	53	5
Jack Clark	.266	334	59	89	25	62	4
Mike Pagliarulo	.254	398	29	101	7	38	1
Garry Templeton	.248	505	45	125	9	59	1
Shawn Abner	.245	184	17	45	1	15	2
Fred Lynn	.240	196	18	47	6	23	2
Joe Carter	.232	634	79	147	24	115	22
Mark Parent	.222	189	13	42	3	16	1
Phil Stephenson	.209	182	26	38	4	19	2

Acquired: P Lilliquist from Atl. (Jul.12) for P Mark Grant. **Signed:** P Hammaker (Aug. 21) after being released by SF.

Pitching (50 IP)	ERA	W-L	Gm	IP	BB	SO
Greg Harris	2.30	8-8	73	117.1	49	97
Craig Lefferts	2.52	7-5	56	78.2	22	60
Ed Whitson	2.60	14-9	32	228.2	47	127
Bruce Hurst	3.14	11-9	33	223.2	63	162
Andy Benes	3.60	10-11	32	192.1	69	140
Atlee Hammaker	4.36	4-9	34	86.2	27	44
Calvin Schiraldi	4.41	3-8	42	104.0	60	74
Dennis Rasmussen	4.51	11-15	32	187.2	62	86
Derek Lilliquist	5.31	5-11	28	122.0	42	63
Eric Show	5.76	6-8	39	106.1	41	55

Saves: Lefferts (23); Harris (9); Rich Rodriguez*, Schiraldi and Show (1). **Complete Games:** Hurst (9); Whitson (6); Rasmussen (3); Benes (2); Lilliquist (1). **Shutouts:** Hurst (4); Whitson (3); Lilliquist and Rasmussen (1).

San Francisco Giants

Batting (150 AB)	Avg	AB	R	H	HR	RBI	SB
Brett Butler	.309	622	108	192	3	44	51
Will Clark	.295	600	91	177	19	95	8
Mike Kingery	.295	207	24	61	0	24	6
Rick Leach	.293	174	24	51	2	16	0
Kevin Mitchell	.290	524	90	152	35	93	4
Terry Kennedy	.277	303	25	84	2	26	1
Matt Williams	.277	617	87	171	33	122	7
Gary Carter	.254	244	24	62	9	27	1
Kevin Bass	.252	214	25	54	7	32	2
Jose Uribe	.248	415	35	103	1	24	5
Greg Litton	.245	204	17	50	1	24	1
Robby Thompson	.245	498	67	122	15	56	14
Ernest Riles	.200	155	22	31	8	21	0

Acquired: P Thurmond from SD (May 1) for minor leaguer; P Oliveras from Min. (May 30) for minor leaguer.

Pitching (50 IP)	ERA	W-L	Gm	IP	BB	SO
Jeff Brantley	1.56	5-3	55	86.2	33	61
Francisco Oliveras	2.77	2-2	33	55.1	21	41
Mark Thurmond	3.34	2-3	43	56.2	18	24
Kelly Downs	3.43	3-2	13	63.0	20	31
John Burkett	3.79	14-7	33	204.0	61	118
Rick Reuschel	3.93	3-6	15	87.0	31	49
Mike LaCoss	3.94	6-4	13	77.2	39	39
Trevor Wilson	4.00	8-7	27	110.1	49	66
Scott Garrelts	4.15	12-11	31	182.0	70	66
Steve Bedrosian	4.20	9-9	68	79.1	44	43
Don Robinson	4.57	10-7	26	157.2	41	78

Saves: Brantley (19); Bedrosian (17); Thurmond (4); Oliveras (2); Burkett, Rafael Novoa and Reuschel (1). **Complete Games:** Garrelts and Robinson (4); Wilson (3); Burkett (2); LaCoss (1). **Shutouts:** Garrelts and Wilson (2).

Team Batting

American League

	Avg	AB	R	H	HR	RBI	SB
Boston	.272	5516	699	1502	106	660	53
Cleveland	.267	5485	732	1465	100	675	107
Kansas City	.267	5488	707	1465	100	660	107
Minnesota	.265	5499	666	1458	100	625	96
Toronto	.265	5589	767	1479	167	729	111
California	.260	5570	690	1448	147	646	69
Seattle	.259	5474	640	1419	107	610	105
Texas	.259	5469	676	1416	110	641	115
Detroit	.259	5479	750	1418	172	714	82
Chicago	.258	5402	682	1393	106	637	140
Milwaukee	.256	5503	732	1408	128	680	164
Oakland	.254	5433	733	1379	164	693	141
Baltimore	.245	5410	669	1328	132	623	94
New York	.241	5483	603	1322	147	561	119

National League

	Avg	AB	R	H	HR	RBI	SB
Cincinnati	.265	5525	693	1466	125	644	166
Chicago	.263	5600	690	1474	136	649	151
San Francisco	.262	5573	719	1459	152	681	109
Los Angeles	.262	5491	728	1436	129	669	141
Pittsburgh	.259	5388	733	1395	138	693	137
San Diego	.257	5554	673	1429	123	628	138
New York	.256	5504	775	1410	172	734	110
St.Louis	.256	5462	599	1398	73	554	221
Philadelphia	.255	5535	646	1410	103	619	108
Atlanta	.250	5540	682	1376	162	636	92
Montreal	.250	5453	662	1363	114	607	235
Houston	.242	5379	573	1301	94	536	179

Team Pitching

American League

	ERA	W	Sv	CG	ShO	HR	BB	SO
Oakland	3.18	103	64	18	16	123	494	831
Chicago	3.61	94	68	17	10	106	548	914
Seattle	3.69	77	41	21	7	120	606	1064
Boston	3.72	88	44	15	13	92	519	997
California	3.79	80	42	21	13	106	544	944
Texas	3.83	83	36	25	9	113	623	997
Toronto	3.84	86	48	6	9	143	445	892
Kansas City	3.93	75	33	18	8	116	560	1006
Baltimore	4.04	76	43	10	5	161	537	776
Milwaukee	4.08	74	42	23	13	121	469	771
Minnesota	4.12	74	43	13	13	134	489	872
New York	4.21	67	41	15	6	144	618	909
Cleveland	4.26	77	47	12	10	163	518	860
Detroit	4.39	79	45	15	12	154	661	856

National League

	ERA	W	Sv	CG	ShO	HR	BB	SO
Montreal	3.37	85	50	18	11	127	510	991
Cincinnati	3.39	91	50	14	12	124	543	1029
Pittsburgh	3.40	95	43	18	8	135	413	848
New York	3.43	91	41	18	14	119	444	1217
Houston	3.61	75	37	12	6	130	496	854
San Diego	3.68	75	35	21	12	147	507	928
Los Angeles	3.72	86	29	29	12	137	478	1021
St.Louis	3.87	70	39	8	13	98	475	833
Philadelphia	4.07	77	35	18	7	124	651	840
San Francisco	4.08	85	45	14	6	131	553	788
Chicago	4.34	77	42	13	7	121	572	877
Atlanta	4.58	65	30	17	8	128	579	938

American League Championship Series

Composite Box Score

Oakland Athletics

Batting (1 AB)

	Avg	AB	R	H	HR	RBI
Jamie Quirk, ph	1.000	1	0	1	0	0
Terry Steinbach, c	.455	11	2	5	0	1
Carney Lansford, 3b	.438	16	2	7	0	2
Mike Gallego, ss	.400	10	1	4	0	2
Willie Randolph, 2b	.375	8	1	3	0	3
Harold Baines, dh	.357	14	2	5	0	3
Ron Hassey, c	.333	3	0	1	0	0
Rickey Henderson, lf	.294	17	1	5	0	3
Willie McGee, cf	.222	9	3	2	0	0
Jose Canseco, rf	.182	11	3	2	0	1
Dave Henderson, cf	.167	6	0	1	0	1
Mark McGwire, 1b	.154	13	2	2	0	2
Walt Weiss, ss	.000	7	2	0	0	0
Doug Jennings, rf	.000	1	0	0	0	0
Lance Blankenship, pr	—	0	1	0	0	0
TOTALS	.299	127	20	38	0	18

Pitching

	ERA	W-L	Gm	IP	H	BB	SO
Dennis Eckersley	0.00	0-0	3	3.1	2	0	3
Rick Honeycutt	0.00	0-0	3	1.2	0	0	0
Gene Nelson	0.00	0-0	1	1.2	3	0	0
Dave Stewart	1.13	2-0	2	16.0	8	2	4
Bob Welch	1.23	1-0	1	7.1	6	3	4
Mike Moore	1.50	1-0	1	6.0	4	1	5
TOTALS	1.00	4-0	4	36.0	23	6	16

Saves: Eckersley 2, Honeycutt.

Boston Red Sox

Batting (1 AB)

	Avg	AB	R	H	HR	RBI
Wade Boggs, 3b	.438	16	1	7	1	1
Mike Marshall, ph	.333	3	0	1	0	0
Ellis Burks, cf	.267	15	1	4	0	0
Dwight Evans, dh	.231	13	0	3	0	0
Luis Rivera, ss	.222	9	1	2	0	0
Tony Pena, c	.214	14	0	3	0	0
Jody Reed, 2b	.133	15	0	2	0	1
Tom Brunansky, rf	.083	12	0	1	0	1
Mike Greenwell, lf	.000	14	1	0	0	1
Carlos Quintana, 1b	.000	13	0	0	0	1
Danny Heep, ph	.000	2	0	0	0	0
Marty Barrett, 2b	—	0	0	0	0	0
Randy Kutcher, pr	—	0	0	0	0	0
TOTALS	.183	126	4	23	1	4

Pitching

	ERA	W-L	Gm	IP	H	BB	SO
Tom Bolton	0.00	0-0	2	3.0	2	3	3
Dana Kiecker	1.59	0-0	1	5.2	6	1	2
Mike Boddicker	2.25	0-1	1	8.0	6	3	7
Jeff Gray	2.70	0-0	2	3.1	4	1	2
Roger Clemens	3.52	0-1	2	7.2	7	5	4
Larry Andersen	6.00	0-1	3	3.0	3	3	3
Jeff Reardon	9.00	0-0	1	2.0	3	1	0
Rob Murphy	13.49	0-0	1	0.2	2	1	0
Greg Harris	27.27	0-1	1	0.1	3	0	0
Dennis Lamp	109.1	0-0	1	0.1	2	2	0
TOTALS	4.50	0-4	4	34.0	38	19	21

CG—Boddicker; **WP**—Clemens; **PB**—Pena; **HB**—Boddicker 2 (McGwire, D.Henderson), Kiecker (Gallego), Reardon (Hassey).

	1	2	3	4	5	6	7	8	9	Runs
Oakland	0	3	0	3	0	2	2	1	9 —	20
Boston	0	1	1	1	0	0	0	0	1 —	4

DP: Oakland 3, Boston 6. **LOB:** Oakland 29, Toronto 30. **2B:** Oakland—Baines, Gallego, Lansford, McGee; Boston—Burks 2, Boggs, Evans, Rivera; **SB:** Oakland—Canseco 2, R.Henderson 2, McGee 2, Baines, Blankenship, D.Henderson; Boston—Burks. **CS:** Oakland—Gallego, R.Henderson, Randolph; **S:** Oakland—Lansford 2, Baines, McGee; Boston—Reed. **SF:** Oakland—Canseco, D.Henderson, R.Henderson; Boston—Brunansky, Quintana.

Umpires: Terry Cooney, Jim Evans, Rich Garcia, John Hirschbeck, Larry McCoy, Vic Voltaggio.

Game 1
Saturday, Oct.6 at Boston

	1	2	3	4	5	6	7	8	9	R	H	E
Oakland	0	0	0	0	0	0	1	1	7 —	9	13	0
Boston	0	0	0	1	0	0	0	0	0 —	1	5	1

Win—Stewart, Oak.(1-0); **Loss**—Andersen, Bos.(0-1).
HR: Boston—Boggs (1).
RBI: Oakland—R.Henderson 3, Lansford 2, Canseco, Randolph, Steinbach; Boston—Boggs.
SB: Oakland—Canseco (1), R.Henderson (1), McGee (1).
Attendance—35,192. **Time**—3:26.

Game 2
Sunday, Oct.7 at Boston

	1	2	3	4	5	6	7	8	9	R	H	E
Oakland	0	0	0	1	0	0	1	0	2 —	4	13	1
Boston	0	0	1	0	0	0	0	0	0 —	1	6	0

Win—Welch, Oak.(1-0); **Save**—Eckersley, Oak.(1); **Loss**—Harris, Bos.(0-1).
HR: None.
RBI: Oakland—Baines 3, McGwire; Boston—Quintana.
SB: Oakland—McGee (2); Boston—Burks (1).
Attendance—35,070. **Time**—3:42.

Game 3
Tuesday, Oct.9 at Oakland

	1	2	3	4	5	6	7	8	9	R	H	E
Boston	0	1	0	0	0	0	0	0	0 —	1	8	3
Oakland	0	0	0	2	0	2	0	0	x —	4	6	0

Win—Moore, Oak.(1-0); **Save**—Eckersley, Oak.(2); **Loss**—Boddicker, Bos.(0-1).
HR: None.
RBI: Boston—Randolph 2, D.Henderson; Boston—Brunansky.
SB: Oakland—Canseco (2), Baines (1), D.Henderson (1).
Attendance—49,026. **Time**—2:47.

Game 4
Wednesday, Oct.10 at Oakland

	1	2	3	4	5	6	7	8	9	R	H	E
Boston	0	0	0	0	0	0	0	1	—	1	4	1
Oakland	0	3	0	0	0	0	0	x	—	3	6	0

Win—Stewart, Oak.(2-0); **Save**—Honeycutt (1); **Loss**—Clemens, Bos.(0-1).
HR: None.
RBI: Boston—Reed; Oakland—Gallego 2, McGwire.
SB: Oakland—R.Henderson (2), Blankenship (1).
Attendance—49,052. **Time**—3:02.

National League Championship Series

Composite Box Score

Cincinnati Reds

Batting (1 AB)	Avg	AB	R	H	HR	RBI
Luis Quinones, ph	.500	2	1	1	0	2
Paul O'Neill, rf	.471	17	1	8	1	4
Hal Morris, 1b	.417	12	3	5	0	1
Billy Hatcher, cf	.333	15	2	5	1	2
Todd Benzinger, 1b	.333	9	0	3	0	0
Ron Oester, 2b	.333	3	1	1	0	0
Mariano Duncan, 2b	.300	20	1	6	1	4
Herm Winningham, cf	.286	7	1	2	0	1
Barry Larkin, ss	.261	23	5	6	0	1
Chris Sabo, 3b	.227	22	1	5	1	3
Glenn Braggs, rf	.200	5	0	1	0	0
Eric Davis, lf	.174	23	2	4	0	2
Joe Oliver, c	.143	14	1	2	0	0
Jeff Reed, c	.000	7	0	0	0	0
Jose Rijo, p	.000	5	0	0	0	0
Tom Browning, p	.000	3	0	0	0	0
Danny Jackson, p	.000	3	0	0	0	0
Rob Dibble, p	.000	2	0	0	0	0
Billy Bates, pr	.—	0	1	0	0	0
TOTALS	.255	192	20	49	4	20

Pitching	ERA	W-L	Gm	IP	H	BB	SO
Rob Dibble	0.00	0-0	4	5.0	0	1	10
Randy Myers	0.00	0-0	4	5.2	2	3	7
Rick Mahler	0.00	0-0	1	1.2	2	0	0
Scott Scudder	0.00	0-0	1	1.0	1	0	1
Norm Charlton	1.80	1-1	4	5.0	4	3	3
Danny Jackson	2.38	1-0	2	11.1	8	7	8
Tom Browning	3.27	1-1	2	11.0	9	6	5
Jose Rijo	4.38	1-0	2	12.1	10	7	15
TOTALS	2.38	4-2	6	53.0	36	27	49

Saves: Myers (3), Dibble; **HB**—Browning (Bell).

Pittsburgh Pirates

Batting (1 AB)	Avg	AB	R	H	HR	RBI
Sid Bream, 1b	.500	8	1	4	1	3
Jay Bell, ss	.250	20	3	5	1	1
Carmelo Martinez, 1b	.250	8	0	2	0	2
Gary Redus, 1b	.250	8	1	2	0	0
Jose Lind, 2b	.238	21	1	5	1	2
Andy Van Slyke, cf	.208	24	3	5	0	3
R.J.Reynolds, rf	.200	10	0	2	0	0
Bobby Bonilla, rf-3b	.190	21	0	4	0	1
Barry Bonds, lf	.167	18	4	3	0	1
Doug Drabek, p	.167	6	0	1	0	0
Wally Backman, 3b	.143	7	1	1	0	0
Jeff King, 3b	.100	10	0	1	0	0
Don Slaught, c	.091	11	0	1	0	1
Mike LaValliere, c	.000	6	1	0	0	0
Bob Walk, p	.000	4	0	0	0	0
Zane Smith, p	.000	3	0	0	0	0
Ted Power, p	.000	1	0	0	0	0
TOTALS	.194	186	15	36	3	14

Pitching	ERA	W-L	Gm	IP	H	BB	SO
Bill Landrum	0.00	0-0	2	2.0	0	0	1
John Smiley	0.00	0-0	1	2.0	2	0	0
Bob Patterson	0.00	0-0	2	1.0	1	2	0
Doug Drabek	1.65	1-1	2	16.2	12	3	13
Stan Belinda	2.45	0-0	3	3.2	3	0	4
Ted Power	3.60	0-0	3	5.0	6	2	3
Bob Walk	4.85	1-1	2	13.0	11	2	8
Zane Smith	6.00	0-2	2	9.0	14	1	8
TOTALS	3.29	2-4	6	52.0	49	10	37

Saves: Patterson, Power; **WP**—Drabek; **HB**—Drabek (Morris).

	1	2	3	4	5	6	7	8	9	Runs
Cincinnati	6	2	0	2	4	0	3	1	2	20
Pittsburgh	3	0	1	6	2	0	1	2	0	15

DP: Cincinnati 3, Pittsburgh 4. **LOB:** Cincinnati 33, Pittsburgh 41. **2B:** Cincinnati—O'Neill 3, Larkin 2, Davis, Hatcher, Morris, Winningham; Pittsburgh—Martinez 2, Backman, Bell, Bonilla, Bream, Lind, Slaught, Van Slyke. **3B:** Pittsburgh—Lind, Van Slyke. **SB:** Cincinnati—Larkin 3, O'Neill, Quinones, Winningham; Pittsburgh—Bonds 2, Backman, Redus, Reynolds, Van Slyke. **CS:** Cincinnati—Bates, Davis, Winningham; Pittsburgh—Bonilla, Redus, Slaught. **S:** Cincinnati—Hatcher, Jackson, Morris. **SF:** Cincinnati—Quinones, Sabo, Winningham; Pittsburgh—Slaught.

Umpires: Jerry Crawford, Gerry Davis, John McSherry, Dutch Rennert, Paul Runge, Harry Wendelstedt.

Game 1
Thursday night, Oct.4 at Cincinnati

	1	2	3	4	5	6	7	8	9	R	H	E
Pittsburgh	0	0	1	2	0	0	1	0	0	4	7	1
Cincinnati	3	0	0	0	0	0	0	0	0	3	5	1

Win—Walk, Pit.(1-0); **Save**—Power, Pit.(1); **Loss**—Charlton, Cin.(0-1).
HR: Pittsburgh—Bream (1).
RBI: Pittsburgh—Bream 2, Lind, Van Slyke; Cincinnati—Davis, Morris, O'Neill.
SB: Pittsburgh—Redus (1); Cincinnati—Larkin (1).
Attendance—52,911. **Time**—2:51.

Game 2
Friday, Oct.5 at Cincinnati

	1	2	3	4	5	6	7	8	9	R	H	E
Pittsburgh	0	0	0	0	1	0	0	0	0	1	5	2
Cincinnati	1	0	0	0	1	0	0	0	x	2	5	0

Win—Browning, Cin.(1-0); **Save**—Myers, Cin.(1); **Loss**—Drabek, Pit.(0-1).
HR: Pittsburgh—Lind (1).
RBI: Pittsburgh—Lind; Cincinnati—O'Neill 2.
SB: Cincinnati—Larkin (2), O'Neill (1), Winningham (1).
Attendance—54,456. **Time**—2:38.

Game 3
Monday, Oct.8, at Pittsburgh

	1	2	3	4	5	6	7	8	9	R	H	E
Cincinnati	0	0	2	0	0	3	0	0	1	6	13	1
Pittsburgh	0	0	0	2	0	0	1	0	0	3	8	0

Win—Jackson, Cin.(1-0); **Save**—Myers, Cin.(2); **Loss**—Smith, Pit.(0-1).
HR: Cincinnati—Duncan (1), Hatcher (1).
RBI: Cincinnati—Duncan 4, Hatcher 2; Pittsburgh—Bonilla, Martinez.
SB: None.
Attendance—45,611. **Time**—2:51.

Game 4
Tuesday night, Oct.9, at Pittsburgh

	1	2	3	4	5	6	7	8	9	R	H	E
Cincinnati	0	0	0	2	0	0	2	0	1	5	10	1
Pittsburgh	0	1	0	0	1	0	0	1	0	3	8	0

Win—Rijo, Cin.(1-0); **Save**—Dibble, Cin.(1); **Loss**—Walk, Pit.(1-1).
HR: Cincinnati—O'Neill (1), Sabo (1); Pittsburgh—Bell (1).
RBI: Cincinnati—Sabo 3, O'Neill, Quinones; Pittsburgh—Bell, Bream, Van Slyke.
SB: Pittsburgh—Backman (1), Bonds (1), Van Slyke (1).
Attendance—50,461. **Time**—3:00.

Game 5
Wednesday night, Oct.10, at Pittsburgh

	1 2 3	4 5 6	7 8 9	R	H	E
Cincinnati	...1 0 0	0 0 0	0 1 0	—2	7	0
Pittsburgh	..2 0 0	1 0 0	0 0 x	—3	6	1

Win—Drabek, Pit.(1-1); **Save**—Patterson, Pit.(1); **Loss**—Browning, Cin.(1-1).
HR: None.
RBI: Cincinnati—Larkin, Winningham; Pittsburgh—Bonds, Slaught, Van Slyke.
SB: Pittsburgh—Bonds (2), Reynolds (1).
Attendance—48,221. **Time**—2:48.

Game 6
Friday night, Oct.12 at Cincinnati

	1 2 3	4 5 6	7 8 9	R	H	E
Pittsburgh	..0 0 0	0 1 0	0 0 0	—1	1	3
Cincinnati	...1 0 0	0 0 0	1 0 x	—2	9	0

Win—Charlton, Cin.(1-1); **Save**—Myers, Cin.(3); **Loss**—Smith, Pit.(0-2).
HR: None.
RBI: Pittsburgh—Martinez; Cincinnati—Davis, Quinones.
SB: Cincinnati—Larkin (3), Quinones (1).
Attendance—56,079. **Time**—2:57.

World Series

Composite Box Score

Cincinnati Reds

Batting (1 AB)	Avg	AB	R	H	HR	RBI
Billy Bates, ph	1.000	1	1	1	0	0
Ron Oester, ph	1.000	1	0	1	0	0
Billy Hatcher, cf	.750	12	6	9	0	2
Chris Sabo, 3b	.563	16	2	9	2	5
Herm Winningham, ph,cf	.444	4	1	2	0	0
Barry Larkin, ss	.353	17	3	6	0	1
Joe Oliver, c	.333	18	2	6	0	2
Jose Rijo, p	.333	3	0	1	0	0
Eric Davis, lf	.286	14	3	4	1	5
Todd Benzinger, ph,1b	.182	11	1	2	0	0
Mariano Duncan, 2b	.143	14	1	2	0	1
Paul O'Neill, rf	.083	12	2	1	0	1
Hal Morris, 1b,dh	.071	14	0	1	0	2
Glenn Braggs, ph,lf	.000	4	0	0	0	2
Danny Jackson, p	.000	1	0	0	0	0
TOTALS	.317	142	22	45	3	22

Pitching	ERA	W-L	Gm	IP	H	BB	SO
Rob Dibble	0.00	1-0	3	4.2	3	1	4
Jack Armstrong	0.00	0-0	1	3.0	1	0	3
Randy Myers	0.00	0-0	3	3.0	2	0	3
Scott Scudder	0.00	0-0	1	1.1	0	2	2
Norm Charlton	0.00	0-0	1	1.0	1	0	0
Jose Rijo	0.59	2-0	2	15.1	9	5	14
Tom Browning	4.50	1-0	1	6.0	6	2	2
Danny Jackson	.10.13	0-0	1	2.2	6	2	0
TOTALS	1.70	4-0	4	37.0	28	12	28

Saves: Myers (1); **WP:** Dibble (1).

Oakland Athletics

Batting (1 AB)	Avg	AB	R	H	HR	RBI
Doug Jennings, ph	1.000	1	0	1	0	0
Rickey Henderson, lf	.333	15	2	5	1	1
Ron Hassey, c,ph	.333	6	0	2	0	1
Carney Lansford, 3b	.267	15	0	4	0	1
Willie Randolph, 2b	.267	15	0	4	0	0
Dave Henderson, ph,cf	.231	13	2	3	0	0
Mark McGwire, 1b	.214	14	1	3	0	0
Willie McGee, cf	.200	10	1	2	0	0
Harold Baines, ph,dh	.143	7	1	1	1	2
Terry Steinbach, c	.125	8	0	1	0	0
Mike Gallego, ss	.091	11	0	1	0	1
Jose Canseco, rf,ph	.083	12	1	1	1	2
Jamie Quirk, c	.000	3	0	0	0	0
Bob Welch, p	.000	3	0	0	0	0
Lance Blankenship, ph	.000	1	0	0	0	0
Dave Stewart, p	.000	1	0	0	0	0
Mike Bordick, pr,ss	—	0	0	0	0	0
TOTALS	.207	135	8	28	3	8

Pitching	ERA	W-L	Gm	IP	H	BB	SO
Gene Nelson	0.00	0-0	2	5.0	3	2	0
Rick Honeycutt	0.00	0-0	1	1.2	2	1	0
Curt Young	0.00	0-0	1	1.0	1	0	0
Joe Klink	0.00	0-0	1	0.0	0	1	0
Dave Stewart	3.46	0-2	2	13.0	10	6	5
Bob Welch	4.91	0-1	1	7.1	9	2	2
Mike Moore	6.75	0-1	2	2.2	8	0	1
Dennis Eckersley	6.75	0-1	2	1.1	3	0	1
Scott Sanderson	10.80	0-0	2	1.2	4	1	0
Todd Burns	16.20	0-0	2	1.2	5	2	0
TOTALS	4.33	0-4	4	35.1	23	6	16

CG: Stewart (1); **HB:** Stewart (Hatcher); **WP:** Burns and Sanderson (1).

	1	2	3	4	5	6	7	8	9	10	Runs
Cincinnati	4	1	9	1	3	0	0	3	0	1	22
Oakland	2	2	4	0	0	0	0	0	0	0	8

E: Cincinnati—Oliver 3, Jackson; Oakland—McGwire 2, Gallego, Hassey, Stewart. **DP:** Cincinnati 2, Oakland 5. **LOB:** Cincinnati 32, Oakland 31. **2B:** Cincinnati—Hatcher 4, Oliver 3, Larkin, Sabo; Oakland—R.Henderson 2, D.Henderson, McGee. **3B:** Cincinnati—Hatcher, Larkin. **SB:** Cincinnati—Duncan, O'Neill; Oakland—R.Henderson 3, Gallego, Lansford, McGee, Randolph. **CS:** Cincinnati—Hatcher, Sabo. **S:** Cincinnati—O'Neill; Oakland—Lansford, Welch. **SF:** Cincinnati—Morris; Oakland—Hassey.
Umpires: AL—Larry Barnett, Ted Hendry, Rocky Roe; NL—Bruce Froemming, Randy Marsh, Frank Pulli, Jim Quick.

Game 1
Tuesday night, Oct.16 at Cincinnati

	1 2 3	4 5 6	7 8 9	R	H	E
Oakland	....0 0 0	0 0 0	0 0 0	—0	9	1
Cincinnati	...2 0 2	0 3 0	0 0 x	—7	10	0

Win—Rijo, Cin.(1-0); **Loss**—Stewart, Oak.(0-1).
2B: Oakland—R.Henderson 2; Cincinnati—Hatcher (2).
3B: None.
HR: Cincinnati—Davis (1).
RBI: Cincinnati—Davis 3, Sabo 2, Hatcher, O'Neill.
SB: Oakland—Lansford (1), McGee (1).
Attendance—55,830. **Time**—2:38.

Game 2
Wednesday night, Oct.17 at Cincinnati

	1 2 3	4 5 6	7 8 9	10	R	H	E
Oakland	...1 0 3	0 0 0	0 0 0	0	—4	10	2
Cincinnati	.2 0 0	1 0 0	0 1 0	1	—5	14	2

Win—Dibble, Cin.(1-0); **Loss**—Eckersley, Oak.(0-1).
2B: Cincinnati—Hatcher 2, Larkin, Oliver.
3B: Cincinnati—Hatcher.
HR: Oakland—Canseco (1).
RBI: Oakland—Canseco 2, Gallego, Hassey; Cincinnati—Braggs, Davis, Hatcher, Oester, Oliver.
SB: Oakland—R.Henderson (2).
Attendance—55,832. **Time**—3:31.

World Series (Cont.)

Game 3
Friday night, Oct.19, at Oakland

	1	2	3	4	5	6	7	8	9	R	H	E
Cincinnati	...0	1	7	0	0	0	0	0	0	—8	14	0
Oakland	0	2	1	0	0	0	0	0	0	—3	7	0

Win—Browning, Cin.(1-0). **Loss**—Moore,Oak.(0-1).
2B: Cincinnati—Oliver; Oakland—D.Henderson.
3B: Cincinnati—Larkin.
HR: Cincinnati—Sabo 2 (2); Oakland—Baines (1), R.Henderson (1).
RBI: Cincinnati—Sabo 3, Davis, Duncan, Larkin, Morris, Oliver; Oakland—Baines 2, R.Henderson.
SB: Cincinnati—Duncan (1), O'Neill (1); Oakland—R.Henderson (2), Randolph (1).
Attendance—48,269. **Time**—3:01.

Game 4
Saturday night, Oct.20, at Oakland

	1	2	3	4	5	6	7	8	9	R	H	E
Cincinnati	...0	0	0	0	0	0	2	0	0	—2	7	1
Oakland	1	0	0	0	0	0	0	0	0	—1	2	1

Win—Rijo, Cin.(2-0); **Save**—Myers,Cin.(1); **Loss**—Stewart, Oak.(0-2).
2B: Cincinnati—Oliver, Sabo; Oakland—McGee.
3B: None.
HR: None.
RBI: Cincinnati—Braggs, Morris; Oakland—Lansford.
SB: Oakland—Gallego (1), R.Henderson (3).
Attendance—48,613. **Time**—2:48.

All-Star Game

61st Baseball All-Star game. **Date:** July 10 at Wrigley Field in Chicago; **Managers:** Tony LaRussa, Oakland (AL) and Roger Craig, San Francisco (NL); **Most Valuable Player:** 2nd baseman Julio Franco, Texas (AL), 7th inning double knocked in game's only runs.

American League

	ab	r	h	bi	po	a
Rickey Henderson, Oak, lf	3	0	0	0	2	0
Ozzie Guillen, Chi, ss	2	0	0	0	0	2
Wade Boggs, Bos, 3b	2	0	2	0	0	4
e-Kelly Gruber, Tor, 3b	1	0	0	0	0	1
Jose Canseco, Oak, rf	4	0	0	0	1	0
Cal Ripken, Bal, ss	2	0	0	0	1	1
f-George Bell, Tor, lf	2	0	0	0	2	0
Ken Griffey Jr, Sea, cf	2	0	0	0	2	0
i-Kirby Puckett, Min, cf	1	0	1	0	1	0
Mark McGwire, Oak, 1b	2	0	0	0	7	0
g-Cecil Fielder, Det, 1b	1	0	0	0	3	1
Sandy Alomar, Cle, c	3	1	2	0	3	0
Bobby Thigpen, Chi, p	0	0	0	0	1	0
j-Alan Trammell, Det, ph	1	0	0	0	0	0
Chuck Finley, Cal, p	0	0	0	0	0	0
Dennis Eckersley, Oak, p	0	0	0	0	0	0
Steve Sax, NY, 2b	1	0	0	0	0	1
Bret Saberhagen, KC, p	0	0	0	0	0	0
h-Lance Parrish, Cal, c	1	1	1	0	3	0
Bob Welch, Oak, p	0	0	0	0	0	1
a-Brook Jacoby, Cle, ph	1	0	0	0	0	0
Dave Stieb, Tor, p	0	0	0	0	0	0
d-Julio Franco, Tex, 2b	3	0	1	2	1	0
Totals	32	2	7	2	27	11

National League

	ab	r	h	bi	po	a
Lenny Dykstra, Phi, cf	4	0	1	0	3	0
Ryne Sandberg, Chi, 2b	3	0	0	0	1	2
Roberto Alomar, SD, 2b	1	0	0	0	1	2
Will Clark, SF, 1b	3	0	1	0	6	0
Randy Myers, Cin, p	0	0	0	0	0	0
John Franco, NY, p	0	0	0	0	0	0
l-Matt Williams, SF, ph	1	0	0	0	0	0
Kevin Mitchell, SF, lf	2	0	0	0	1	0
Frank Viola, NY, p	0	0	0	0	0	0
Tim Wallach, Mon, 3b	2	0	0	0	0	0
Andre Dawson, Chi, rf	2	0	0	0	1	0
Darryl Strawberry, NY, rf	1	0	0	0	3	1
Chris Sabo, Cin, 3b	2	0	0	0	0	2
Dave Smith, Hou, p	0	0	0	0	0	0
Jeff Brantley, SF, p	0	0	0	0	0	0
Rob Dibble, Cin, p	0	0	0	0	0	0
Bobby Bonilla, Pit, 1b	1	0	0	0	1	0
Mike Scioscia, LA, c	2	0	0	0	6	0
k-Greg Olson, Atl, c	1	0	0	0	0	0
Ozzie Smith, St.L, ss	1	0	0	0	1	1
Dennis Martinez, Mon, p	0	0	0	0	0	0
Barry Bonds, Pit, lf	1	0	0	0	2	0
Jack Armstrong, Cin, p	0	0	0	0	1	0
Ramon Martinez, LA, p	0	0	0	0	0	0
b-Tony Gwynn, SD, ph	0	0	0	0	0	0
c-Barry Larkin, Cin, ss	0	0	0	0	1	2
Shawon Dunston, Chi, ss	2	0	0	0	0	0
Totals	29	0	2	0	27	10

a-Grounded out for Welch in 3rd; **b**-Walked for R.Martinez in 3rd; **c**-Ran for Gwynn in 3rd; **d**-Grounded out for Stieb in 5th; **e**-Ran for Boggs in 6th; **f**-Struck out for Ripken in 6th; **g**-Flied out for McGwire in 6th; **h**-Singled for Saberhagen in 7th; **i**-Singled and went to third on two-base error for Griffey in 8th; **j**-Popped out for Thigpen in 8th; **k**-Struck out for Scioscia in 8th; **l**-Called out on strikes for John Franco in 9th. **Players not used: AL**—batter Dave Parker, Mil., and pitchers Roger Clemens, Bos., Randy Johnson, Sea., Doug Jones, Cle., and Gregg Olson, Bal.; **NL**—pitcher Neal Heaton, Pit.

	1	2	3	4	5	6	7	8	9	R	H	E
American League	0	0	0	0	0	0	2	0	0	— 2	7	0
National League	0	0	0	0	0	0	0	0	0	— 0	2	1

E—Strawberry; **DP**—National (2). **LOB**—American (10), National (4); **2B**—Julio Franco. **SB**—Gruber (2), Sax, Larkin, Canseco.

AL Pitching

	IP	H	R	ER	BB	SO	HR
Welch, Oak	2.0	1	0	0	0	1	0
Stieb, Tor	2.0	0	0	0	1	1	0
Saberhagen, KC (W)	2.0	0	0	0	0	1	0
Thigpen, Chi	1.0	0	0	0	0	1	0
Finley, Cal	1.0	0	0	0	1	1	0
Eckersley, Oak (S)	1.0	1	0	0	0	1	0
TOTALS	9.0	2	0	0	2	6	0

NL Pitching

	IP	H	R	ER	BB	SO	HR
Armstrong, Cin	2.0	1	0	0	0	2	0
R.Martinez, LA	1.0	0	0	0	2	1	0
D.Martinez, Mon	1.0	0	0	0	1	0	0
Viola, NY	1.0	1	0	0	0	1	0
D.Smith, Hou	0.2	1	0	0	2	0	0
Brantley, SF (L)	0.1*	2	2	2	0	0	0
Dibble, Cin	1.0	0	0	0	1	0	0
Myers, NY	1.0	1	0	0	0	0	0
Franco, NY	1.0	0	0	0	0	1	0
TOTALS	9.0	7	2	2	7	5	0

*Pitched to two batters in 7th.

Umpires—Ed Montague (NL) plate; Dave Phillips (AL) 1b; Steve Rippley (NL) 2b; Mark Johnson (AL) 3b; Dana DeMuth (NL) lf; Tim Welke (AL) rf. **Attendance**—39,071. **Time**—2:53.

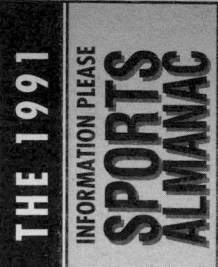

BASEBALL STATISTICS

THE 1991 INFORMATION PLEASE SPORTS ALMANAC

THROUGH THE YEARS 1900-1990

WORLD SERIES • ALL-TIMERS

SEC B

PAGE 63

The World Series

The World Series was started in 1903 when Pittsburgh of the older National League (founded in 1876) invited Boston of the American League (founded in 1901) to play a best-of-9 game series to determine which of the two league champions was the best. Boston was the surprise winner of the competition, 5 games to 3.

The 1904 NL champion New York Giants refused to play Boston the following year, so there was no series. Giants' owner John T. Brush hated AL president Ban Johnson and considered the junior circuit to be a minor league. By the following year, however, Brush and Johnson had smoothed over their differences and the Giants agreed to play Philadelphia in a best-of-7 game series.

Since then the World Series has been best-of-7 format, except from 1919-21 when it returned to best-of-9.

In the chart below, the National League teams are listed in capital LETTERS. Also, each World Series champion's wins and loses are noted in parentheses after the series score.

Year	Winner	Manager	Series	Loser	Manager
1903	Boston Red Sox	Jimmy Collins	5-3 (LWLLWWWW)	PITTSBURGH	Fred Clarke
1904	No Series				
1905	NY GIANTS	John McGraw	4-1 (WLWWW)	Philadelphia A's	Connie Mack
1906	Chi. White Sox	Fielder Jones	4-2 (WLWLWW)	CHICAGO CUBS	Frank Chance
1907	CHICAGO CUBS	Frank Chance	4-0-1 (TWWWW)	Detroit	Hugh Jennings
1908	CHICAGO CUBS	Frank Chance	4-1 (WWLWW)	Detroit	Hugh Jennings
1909	PITTSBURGH	Fred Clarke	4-3 (WLWLWLW)	Detroit	Hugh Jennings
1910	Philadelphia A's	Connie Mack	4-1 (WWWLW)	CHICAGO CUBS	Frank Chance
1911	Philadelphia A's	Connie Mack	4-2 (LWWWLW)	NY GIANTS	John McGraw
1912	Boston Red Sox	Jake Stahl	4-3-1 (WTLWWLLW)	NY GIANTS	John McGraw
1913	Philadelphia A's	Connie Mack	4-1 (WLWWW)	NY GIANTS	John McGraw
1914	BOSTON BRAVES	George Stallings	4-0	Philadelphia A's	Connie Mack
1915	Boston Red Sox	Bill Carrigan	4-1 (LWWWW)	PHILA. PHILLIES	Pat Moran
1916	Boston Red Sox	Bill Carrigan	4-1 (WWLWW)	BKLN. DODGERS	Wilbert Robinson
1917	Chi. White Sox	Pants Rowland	4-2 (WWLLWW)	NY GIANTS	John McGraw
1918	Boston Red Sox	Ed Barrow	4-2 (WLWWLW)	CHICAGO CUBS	Fred Mitchell
1919	CINCINNATI	Pat Moran	5-3 (WWLWWLLW)	Chi. White Sox	Kid Gleason
1920	Cleveland	Tris Speaker	5-2 (WLLWWWW)	BKLN. DODGERS	Wilbert Robinson
1921	NY GIANTS	John McGraw	5-3 (LLWWLWWW)	NY Yankees	Miller Huggins
1922	NY GIANTS	John McGraw	4-0-1 (WTWWW)	NY Yankees	Miller Huggins
1923	NY Yankees	Miller Huggins	4-2 (LWLWWW)	NY GIANTS	John McGraw
1924	Washington	Bucky Harris	4-3 (LWLWLWW)	NY GIANTS	John McGraw
1925	PITTSBURGH	Bill McKechnie	4-3 (LWLLWWW)	Washington	Bucky Harris
1926	ST. L. CARDINALS	Rogers Hornsby	4-3 (LWWLLWW)	NY Yankees	Miller Huggins
1927	NY Yankees	Miller Huggins	4-0	PITTSBURGH	Donie Bush
1928	NY Yankees	Miller Huggins	4-0	ST. L. CARDINALS	Bill McKechnie
1929	Philadelphia A's	Connie Mack	4-1 (WWLWW)	CHICAGO CUBS	Joe McCarthy
1930	Philadelphia A's	Connie Mack	4-2 (WWLLWW)	ST. L. CARDINALS	Gabby Street
1931	ST. L. CARDINALS	Gabby Street	4-3 (LWWLWLW)	Philadelphia A's	Connie Mack
1932	NY Yankees	Joe McCarthy	4-0	CHICAGO CUBS	Charlie Grimm
1933	NY GIANTS	Bill Terry	4-1 (WWLWW)	Washington	Joe Cronin
1934	ST. L. CARDINALS	Frankie Frisch	4-3 (WLWLLWW)	Detroit	Mickey Cochrane
1935	Detroit	Mickey Cochrane	4-2 (LWWWLW)	CHICAGO CUBS	Charlie Grimm
1936	NY Yankees	Joe McCarthy	4-2 (LWWWLW)	NY GIANTS	Bill Terry
1937	NY Yankees	Joe McCarthy	4-1 (WWWLW)	NY GIANTS	Bill Terry
1938	NY Yankees	Joe McCarthy	4-0	CHICAGO CUBS	Gabby Hartnett
1939	NY Yankees	Joe McCarthy	4-0	CINCINNATI	Bill McKechnie
1940	CINCINNATI	Bill McKechnie	4-3 (LWLWLWW)	Detroit	Del Baker
1941	NY Yankees	Joe McCarthy	4-1 (WLWWW)	BKLN. DODGERS	Leo Durocher
1942	ST. L. CARDINALS	Billy Southworth	4-1 (LWWWW)	NY Yankees	Joe McCarthy
1943	NY Yankees	Joe McCarthy	4-1 (WLWWW)	ST. L. CARDINALS	Billy Southworth
1944	ST. L. CARDINALS	Billy Southworth	4-2 (LWLWWW)	St. Louis Browns	Luke Sewell
1945	Detroit	Steve O'Neill	4-3 (LWLWWLW)	CHICAGO CUBS	Charlie Grimm

World Series (Cont.)

Year	Winner	Manager	Series	Loser	Manager
1946	ST.L.CARDINALS	Eddie Dyer	4-3 (LWLWLWW)	Boston Red Sox	Joe Cronin
1947	NY Yankees	Bucky Harris	4-3 (WWLLWLW)	BKLN.DODGERS	Burt Shotton
1948	Cleveland	Lou Boudreau	4-2 (LWWWLW)	BOS.BRAVES	Billy Southworth
1949	NY Yankees	Casey Stengel	4-1 (WLWWW)	BKLN.DODGERS	Burt Shotton
1950	NY Yankees	Casey Stengel	4-0	PHILA.PHILLIES	Eddie Sawyer
1951	NY Yankees	Casey Stengel	4-2 (LWLWWW)	NY GIANTS	Leo Durocher
1952	NY Yankees	Casey Stengel	4-3 (LWLWLWW)	BKLN.DODGERS	Charlie Dressen
1953	NY Yankees	Casey Stengel	4-2 (WWLLWW)	BKLN.DODGERS	Charlie Dressen
1954	NY GIANTS	Leo Durocher	4-0	Cleveland	Al Lopez
1955	BKLN.DODGERS	Walter Alston	4-3 (LLWWWLW)	NY Yankees	Casey Stengel
1956	NY Yankees	Casey Stengel	4-3 (LLWWWLW	BKLN.DODGERS	Walter Alston
1957	MILW.BRAVES	Fred Haney	4-3 (LWLWLWW)	NY Yankees	Casey Stengel
1958	NY Yankees	Casey Stengel	4-3 (LLWLWWW)	MILW.BRAVES	Fred Haney
1959	LA DODGERS	Walter Alston	4-2 (LWWWLW)	Chi.White Sox	Al Lopez
1960	PITTSBURGH	Danny Murtaugh	4-3 (WLLWLWW)	NY Yankees	Casey Stengel
1961	NY Yankees	Ralph Houk	4-1 (WLWWW)	CINCINNATI	Fred Hutchinson
1962	NY Yankees	Ralph Houk	4-3 (WLWLWLW)	SF GIANTS	Al Dark
1963	LA DODGERS	Walter Alston	4-0	NY Yankees	Ralph Houk
1964	ST.L.CARDINALS	Johnny Keane	4-3 (WLLWWLW)	NY Yankees	Yogi Berra
1965	LA DODGERS	Walter Alston	4-3 (LLWWWLW)	Minnesota	Sam Mele
1966	Baltimore	Hank Bauer	4-0	LA DODGERS	Walter Alston
1967	ST.L.CARDINALS	Red Schoendienst	4-3 (WLWWLLW)	Boston Red Sox	Dick Williams
1968	Detroit	Mayo Smith	4-3 (LWLLWWW)	ST.L.CARDINALS	Red Schoendienst
1969	NY METS	Gil Hodges	4-1 (LWWWW)	Baltimore	Earl Weaver
1970	Baltimore	Earl Weaver	4-1 (WWWLW)	CINCINNATI	Sparky Anderson
1971	PITTSBURGH	Danny Murtaugh	4-3 (LLWWWLW)	Baltimore	Earl Weaver
1972	Oakland A's	Dick Williams	4-3 (WWLWLLW)	CINCINNATI	Sparky Anderson
1973	Oakland A's	Dick Williams	4-3 (WLWLLWW)	NY METS	Yogi Berra
1974	Oakland A's	Al Dark	4-1 (WLWWW)	LA DODGERS	Walter Alston
1975	CINCINNATI	Sparky Anderson	4-3 (LWWLWLW)	Boston Red Sox	Darrell Johnson
1976	CINCINNATI	Sparky Anderson	4-0	NY Yankees	Billy Martin
1977	NY Yankees	Billy Martin	4-2 (WLWWW)	LA DODGERS	Tom Lasorda
1978	NY Yankees	Bob Lemon	4-2 (LLWWWW)	LA DODGERS	Tom Lasorda
1979	PITTSBURGH	Chuck Tanner	4-3 (LWLLWWW)	Baltimore	Earl Weaver
1980	PHILA.PHILLIES	Dallas Green	4-2 (WWLLWW)	Kansas City	Jim Frey
1981	LA DODGERS	Tom Lasorda	4-2 (LLWWWW)	NY Yankees	Bob Lemon
1982	ST.L.CARDINALS	Whitey Herzog	4-3 (LWWLLWW)	Milw.Brewers	Harvey Kuenn
1983	Baltimore	Joe Altobelli	4-1 (LWWWW)	PHILA.PHILLIES	Paul Owens
1984	Detroit	Sparky Anderson	4-1 (WLWWW)	SAN DIEGO	Dick Williams
1985	Kansas City	Dick Howser	4-3 (LLWLWWW)	ST.L.CARDINALS	Whitey Herzog
1986	NY METS	Davey Johnson	4-3 (LLWLWWW)	Boston Red Sox	John McNamara
1987	Minnesota	Tom Kelly	4-3 (WWLLLWW)	ST.L.CARDINALS	Whitey Herzog
1988	LA DODGERS	Tom Lasorda	4-1 (WWLWW)	Oakland A's	Tony LaRussa
1989	Oakland A's	Tony LaRussa	4-0	SF GIANTS	Roger Craig
1990	CINCINNATI	Lou Piniella	4-0	Oakland A's	Tony LaRussa

World Series Most Valuable Players

Currently selected by media panel made up of representatives of CBS Sports, CBS Radio, AP, UPI, and World Series official scorers. Presented by *Sport* magazine from 1955-88 and by Major League Baseball since 1989. Winners who did not play for World Series champions are in **bold type**.
Multiple winners: Bob Gibson, Reggie Jackson and Sandy Koufax (2).

Year		Year		Year	
1955	Johnny Podres, Bklyn, P	1968	Mickey Lolich, Det., P	1980	Mike Schmidt, Phi., 3B
1956	Don Larsen, NY, P	1969	Donn Clendenon, NY, 1B	1981	Pedro Guerrero, LA, OF;
1957	Lew Burdette, Mil., P	1970	Brooks Robinson, Bal., 3B		Ron Cey, LA, 3B;
1958	Bob Turley, NY, P	1971	Roberto Clemente, Pit., OF		& Steve Yeager, LA, C
1959	Larry Sherry, LA, P	1972	Gene Tenace, Oak., C	1982	Darrell Porter, St.L., C
1960	**Bobby Richardson**, NY, 2B	1973	Reggie Jackson, Oak., OF	1983	Rick Dempsey, Bal., C
1961	Whitey Ford, NY, P	1974	Rollie Fingers, Oak., P	1984	Alan Trammell, Det., SS
1962	Ralph Terry, NY, P	1975	Pete Rose, Cin., 3B	1985	Bret Saberhagen, KC, P
1963	Sandy Koufax, LA, P	1976	Johnny Bench, Cin., C	1986	Ray Knight, NY, 3B
1964	Bob Gibson, St.L., P	1977	Reggie Jackson, NY, OF	1987	Frank Viola, Min., P
1965	Sandy Koufax, LA, P	1978	Bucky Dent, NY, SS	1988	Orel Hershiser, LA, P
1966	Frank Robinson, Bal., OF	1979	Willie Stargell, Pit., 1B	1989	Dave Stewart, Oak., P
1967	Bob Gibson, St.L., P			1990	Jose Rijo, Cin., P

All-Time Individual World Series Leaders
CAREER
World Series leaders through 1990. Years listed indicate number of World Series appearances.

Hitting

Games

	Yrs	Gm
Yogi Berra, NY Yankees	14	75
Mickey Mantle, NY Yankees	12	65
Elston Howard, NY Yankees-Boston	10	54
Hank Bauer, NY Yankees	9	53
Gil McDougald, NY Yankees	8	53

At Bats

	Yrs	AB
Yogi Berra, NY Yankees	14	259
Mickey Mantle, NY Yankees	12	230
Joe DiMaggio, NY Yankees	10	199
Frankie Frisch, NY Giants-StL Cards	8	197
Gil McDougald, NY Yankees	8	190

Hits

	AB	H	Avg
Yogi Berra, NY Yankees	259	71	.274
Mickey Mantle, NY Yankees	230	59	.257
Frankie Frisch, NYG-StL Cards	197	58	.294
Joe DiMaggio, NY Yankees	199	54	.271
Hank Bauer, NY Yankees	188	46	.245
Pee Wee Reese, Brooklyn	169	46	.272

Runs

	Gm	R
Mickey Mantle, NY Yankees	65	42
Yogi Berra, NY Yankees	75	41
Babe Ruth, NY Yankees	41	37
Lou Gehrig, NY Yankees	34	30
Joe DiMaggio, NY Yankees	51	27

Batting Avg. (minimum 50 AB)

	AB	H	Avg
Pepper Martin, StL Cards	55	23	.418
Lou Brock, St.Louis	87	34	.391
Thurman Munson, NY Yankees	67	25	.373
George Brett, Kansas City	51	19	.373
Hank Aaron, Milwaukee	55	20	.364

Home Runs

	AB	HR
Mickey Mantle, NY Yankees	230	18
Babe Ruth, NY Yankees	129	15
Yogi Berra, NY Yankees	259	12
Duke Snider, Brooklyn-LA	133	11
Lou Gehrig, NY Yankees	119	10
Reggie Jackson, Oakland-NY Yankees	98	10

Runs Batted In

	Gm	RBI
Mickey Mantle, NY Yankees	65	40
Yogi Berra, NY Yankees	75	39
Lou Gehrig, NY Yankees	34	35
Babe Ruth, NY Yankees	41	33
Joe DiMaggio, NY Yankees	51	30

Stolen Bases

	Gm	SB
Lou Brock, St.Louis	21	14
Eddie Collins, Phi.A's-Chisox	34	14
Frank Chance, Chi.Cubs	20	10
Davey Lopes, Los Angeles	23	10
Phil Rizzuto, NY Yankees	52	10

Total Bases

	Gm	TB
Mickey Mantle, NY Yankees	65	123
Yogi Berra, NY Yankees	75	117
Babe Ruth, NY Yankees	41	96
Lou Gehrig, NY Yankees	34	87
Joe DiMaggio, NY Yankees	51	84

Slugging Avg. (50 AB)

	AB	Avg
Reggie Jackson, Oakland-NY Yankees	98	.755
Babe Ruth, NY Yankees	129	.744
Lou Gehrig, NY Yankees	119	.731
Al Simmons, Phi.A's-Cin	73	.658
Lou Brock, St.Louis	87	.655

World Series Appearances

In the 87 years that the World Series has been contested, American League teams have won 50 championships while National League teams have won 37.

The New York Yankees have appeared in the Series on 33 occasions and won a record 22 titles. The Brooklyn-Los Angeles Dodgers are second in appearances with 18, but the St.Louis Cardinals and Philadelphia-Kansas City-Oakland Athletics are second in championships with nine each.

The following teams are ranked by number of appearances through the 1990 World Series. Note that (*) indicates American League teams.

	App	W	L	Pct.	Last Series	Last Title
NY Yankees*	33	22	11	.667	1981	1978
Bklyn/LA Dodgers	18	6	12	.333	1988	1988
NY/SF Giants	16	5	11	.313	1989	1954
St.L.Cardinals	15	9	6	.600	1987	1982
Phi/KC/Oak.A's*	14	9	5	.643	1990	1989
Chicago Cubs	10	2	8	.200	1945	1908
Boston Red Sox*	9	5	4	.556	1986	1918
Cincinnati Reds	9	5	4	.556	1990	1990
Detroit Tigers*	9	4	5	.444	1984	1984
Pittsburgh Pirates	7	5	2	.714	1979	1979
St.L/Bal.Orioles*	7	3	4	.429	1983	1983
Wash/Min.Twins*	5	2	3	.400	1987	1987
Chi.White Sox*	4	2	2	.500	1959	1917
Bos/Mil/Atl.Braves	4	2	2	.500	1958	1957
Phi.Phillies	4	1	3	.250	1983	1980
Cle.Indians*	3	2	1	.667	1954	1948
NY Mets	3	2	1	.667	1986	1986
KC Royals*	2	1	1	.500	1985	1985
Sea/Mil.Brewers*	1	0	1	.000	1982	—
SD Padres	1	0	1	.000	1984	—

Pitching

Games

	Yrs	Gm
Whitey Ford, NY Yankees	11	22
Rollie Fingers, Oakland	3	16
Allie Reynolds, NY Yankees	6	15
Bob Turley, NY Yankees	5	15
Clay Carroll, Cincinnati	3	14

Wins

	Gm	W-L
Whitey Ford, NY Yankees	22	10-8
Bob Gibson, St.Louis	9	7-2
Allie Reynolds, NY Yankees	15	7-2
Red Ruffing, NY Yankees	10	7-2
Lefty Gomez, NY Yankees	7	6-0
Chief Bender, Philadelphia A's	10	6-4
Waite Hoyt, NY Yankees-Phi.A's	12	6-4

All-Time Individual World Series Leaders (Cont.)

Losses

	Gm	W-L
Whitey Ford, NY Yankees	22	10-8
Christy Mathewson, NY Giants	11	5-5
Joe Bush, Phi.A's-Bosox-NY Yanks	9	2-5
Rube Marquard, NY Giants-Brooklyn	11	2-5
Eddie Plank, Philadelphia A's	7	2-5
Schoolboy Rowe, Detroit	8	2-5

ERA (minimum 25 IP)

	Gm	IP	ERA
Jack Billingham, Cincinnati	7	25	0.36
Harry Brecheen, St.Louis	7	33	0.83
Babe Ruth, Boston Red Sox	3	31	0.87
Sherry Smith, Brooklyn	3	30	0.89
Sandy Koufax, Los Angeles	8	57	0.95

Innings Pitched

	Gm	IP
Whitey Ford, NY Yankees	22	146
Christy Mathewson, NY Giants	11	102
Red Ruffing, NY Yankees	10	86
Chief Bender, Philadelphia A's	10	85
Waite Hoyt, NY Yanks-Phi.A's	12	84

Saves

	Gm	IP	Sv
Rollie Fingers, Oakland	16	33	6
Allie Reynolds, NY Yankees	15	77	4
Johnny Murphy, NY Yankees	8	16	4
Seven pitchers tied with 3 saves.			

Strikeouts

	Gm	IP	SO
Whitey Ford, NY Yankees	22	146	94
Bob Gibson, St.Louis	9	81	92
Allie Reynolds, NY Yankees	15	77	62
Sandy Koufax, Los Angeles	8	57	61
Red Ruffing, NY Yankees	10	86	61

Bases on Balls

	Gm	IP	BB
Whitey Ford, NY Yankees	22	146	34
Allie Reynolds, NY Yankees	15	77	32
Art Nehf, NY Giants-Chi.Cubs	12	79	32
Jim Palmer, Baltimore	9	65	31
Bob Turley, NY Yankees	15	54	29

Complete Games

	GS	CG	W-L
Christy Mathewson, NY Giants	11	10	5-5
Chief Bender, Philadelphia A's	10	9	6-4
Bob Gibson, St.Louis	9	8	7-2
Whitey Ford, NY Yankees	22	7	10-8
Red Ruffing, NY Yankees	10	7	7-2

Shutouts

	GS	CG	ShO
Christy Mathewson, NY Giants	11	10	4
Three Finger Brown, Phi.A's	7	5	3
Whitey Ford, NY Yankees	22	7	3
Seven pitchers tied with 2.			

League Championship Series

Division play came to the major leagues in 1969 when both the American and National Leagues expanded to 12 teams. With an East and West Division in each league, League Championship Series (LCS) became necessary to determine the NL and AL pennant winners.

In the charts below, the East Division champions are noted by the letter E and the West Division champions by the letter W. Also, each playoff winner's wins and losses are noted in parentheses after the series score. Note that the LCS changed from best-of-5 to best-of-seven in 1985.

American League

Year Winner	Manager	Series	Loser	Manager
1969 E- Baltimore	Earl Weaver	3-0	W- Minnesota	Billy Martin
1970 E- Baltimore	Earl Weaver	3-0	W- Minnesota	Bill Rigney
1971 E- Baltimore	Earl Weaver	3-0	W- Oakland	Dick Williams
1972 W- Oakland	Dick Williams	3-2 (WWLLW)	E- Detroit	Billy Martin
1973 W- Oakland	Dick Williams	3-2 (LWWLW)	E- Baltimore	Earl Weaver
1974 W- Oakland	Al Dark	3-1 (LWWW)	E- Baltimore	Earl Weaver
1975 E- Boston	Darrell Johnson	3-0	W- Oakland	Al Dark
1976 E- New York	Billy Martin	3-2 (WLWLW)	W- Kansas City	Whitey Herzog
1977 E- New York	Billy Martin	3-2 (LWLWW)	W- Kansas City	Whitey Herzog
1978 E- New York	Bob Lemon	3-1 (WWLW)	W- Kansas City	Whitey Herzog
1979 E- Baltimore	Earl Weaver	3-1 (WWLW)	W- California	Jim Fregosi
1980 W- Kansas City	Jim Frey	3-0	E- New York	Dick Howser
1981 E- New York	Bob Lemon	3-0	W- Oakland	Billy Martin
1982 E- Milwaukee	Harvey Kuenn	3-2 (LLWWW)	W- California	Gene Mauch
1983 E- Baltimore	Joe Altobelli	3-1 (LWWW)	W- Chicago	Tony LaRussa
1984 E- Detroit	Sparky Anderson	3-0	W- Kansas City	Dick Howser
1985 W- Kansas City	Dick Howser	4-3 (LLWLWWW)	E- Toronto	Bobby Cox
1986 E- Boston	John McNamara	4-3 (LWLLWWW)	W- California	Gene Mauch
1987 W- Minnesota	Tom Kelly	4-1 (WWLWW)	E- Detroit	Sparky Anderson
1988 W- Oakland	Tony LaRussa	4-0	E- Boston	Joe Morgan
1989 W- Oakland	Tony LaRussa	4-1 (WWLWW)	E- Toronto	Cito Gaston
1990 W- Oakland	Tony LaRussa	4-0	E- Boston	Joe Morgan

ALCS Most Valuable Players

Year	Year	Year
1980 Frank White, KC, 2B	1984 Kirk Gibson, Det., OF	1988 Dennis Eckersley, Oak., P
1981 Graig Nettles, NY, 3B	1985 George Brett, KC, 3B	1989 Rickey Henderson, Oak., OF
1982 Fred Lynn, Cal., OF	1986 Marty Barrett, Bos., 2B	1990 Dave Stewart, Oak., P
1983 Mike Boddicker, Bal., P	1987 Gary Gaetti, Min., 3B	

National League Series

Year	Winner	Manager	Series	Loser	Manager
1969	E- New York	Gil Hodges	3-0	W- Atlanta	Lum Harris
1970	W- Cincinnati	Sparky Anderson	3-0	E- Pittsburgh	Danny Murtaugh
1971	E- Pittsburgh	Danny Murtaugh	3-1 (LWWW)	W- San Francisco	Charlie Fox
1972	W- Cincinnati	Sparky Anderson	3-2 (LWLWW)	E- Pittsburgh	Bill Virdon
1973	E- New York	Yogi Berra	3-2 (LWWLW)	W- Cincinnati	Sparky Anderson
1974	W- Los Angeles	Walter Alston	3-1 (WWLW)	E- Pittsburgh	Danny Murtaugh
1975	W- Cincinnati	Sparky Anderson	3-0	E- Pittsburgh	Danny Murtaugh
1976	W- Cincinnati	Sparky Anderson	3-0	E- Philadelphia	Danny Ozark
1977	W- Los Angeles	Tom Lasorda	3-1 (LWWW)	E- Philadelphia	Danny Ozark
1978	W- Los Angeles	Tom Lasorda	3-1 (WWLW)	E- Philadelphia	Danny Ozark
1979	E- Pittsburgh	Chuck Tanner	3-0	W- Cincinnati	John McNamara
1980	E- Philadelphia	Dallas Green	3-2 (WLLWW)	W- Houston	Bill Virdon
1981	W- Los Angeles	Tom Lasorda	3-2 (WLLWW)	E- Montreal	Jim Fanning
1982	E- St. Louis	Whitey Herzog	3-0	W- Atlanta	Joe Torre
1983	E- Philadelphia	Paul Owens	3-1 (WLWW)	W- Los Angeles	Tom Lasorda
1984	W- San Diego	Dick Williams	3-2 (LLWWW)	E- Chicago	Jim Frey
1985	E- St. Louis	Whitey Herzog	4-2 (LLWWWW)	W- Los Angeles	Tom Lasorda
1986	E- New York	Davey Johnson	4-2 (LWWLWW)	W- Houston	Hal Lanier
1987	E- St. Louis	Whitey Herzog	4-3 (WLWLLWW)	W- San Francisco	Roger Craig
1988	W- Los Angeles	Tom Lasorda	4-3 (LWLWWLW)	E- New York	Davey Johnson
1989	W- San Francisco	Roger Craig	4-1 (WLWWW)	E- Chicago	Don Zimmer
1990	W- Cincinnati	Lou Piniella	4-2 (LWWWLW)	E- Pittsburgh	Jim Leyland

NLCS Most Valuable Players

Year		Year		Year	
1977	Dusty Baker, LA, OF	1982	Darrell Porter, St.L., C	1988	Orel Hershiser, Los Ang., P
1978	Steve Garvey, LA, 1B	1983	Gary Matthews, Phi., OF	1989	Will Clark, San Fran., 1B
1979	Willie Stargell, Pit., 1B	1984	Steve Garvey, SD, 1B	1990	Rob Dibble, Cin., P
1980	Manny Trillo, Phi., 2B	1985	Ozzie Smith, St.L., SS		& Randy Myers, Cin., P
1981	Burt Hooton, LA, P	1986	Mike Scott, Houston, P		
		1987	Jeff Leonard, San Fran., OF		

Other Playoffs

American League

Year	AL	W	L	Manager
1948	Boston	96	58	Joe McCarthy
	Cleveland	96	58	Lou Boudreau
	Playoff: (1 game) Cleveland, 8-3 (at Boston)			
	AL East	**W**	**L**	**Manager**
1978	Boston	99	63	Don Zimmer
	New York	99	63	Bob Lemon
	Playoff: (1 game) New York, 5-4 (at Boston)			

Year	AL East	W	L	Manager
1981	(1st Half) N.Y.	34	22	Bob Lemon
	(2nd Half) Milw.	31	22	Buck Rodgers
	Playoff: (Best-of-5) New York, 3-2 (WWLLW)			
	AL West	**W**	**L**	**Manager**
	(1st Half) Oakland	37	23	Billy Martin
	(2nd Half) Kan.City	30	23	Jim Frey
	Playoff: (Best-of-5), Oakland, 3-0			

National League

Year	NL	W	L	Manager
1946	Brooklyn	96	58	Leo Durocher
	St.Louis	96	58	Eddie Dyer
	Playoff: (Best-of-3) St.Louis, 2-0			
	NL	**W**	**L**	**Manager**
1951	Brooklyn	96	58	Charlie Dressen
	New York	96	58	Leo Durocher
	Playoff: (Best-of-3) New York, 2-1 (WLW)			
	NL	**W**	**L**	**Manager**
1959	Milwaukee	86	68	Fred Haney
	Los Angeles	86	68	Walter Alston
	Playoff: (Best-of-3) Los Angeles, 2-0			

Year	NL	W	L	Manager
1962	Los Angeles	101	61	Walter Alston
	San Francisco	101	61	Al Dark
	Playoff: (Best-of-3) San Francisco, 2-1 (WLW)			
	NL West	**W**	**L**	**Manager**
1980	Houston	101	61	Bill Virdon
	Los Angeles	101	61	Tom Lasorda
	Playoff: (1 game) Houston, 7-1 (at LA)			
	NL East	**W**	**L**	**Manager**
1981	(1st Half) Phila	34	21	Dallas Green
	(2nd Half) Montreal	30	23	Jim Fanning
	Playoff: (Best-of-5) Montreal, 3-2 (WWLLW)			
	NL West	**W**	**L**	**Manager**
	(1st Half) Los Ang.	36	21	Tom Lasorda
	(2nd Half) Houston	33	20	Bill Virdon
	Playoff: (Best-of-5) Los Angeles, 3-2 (LLWWW)			

Major League Franchise Origins

Here is what the current 26 teams in Major League Baseball have to show for the years they have put in as members of the National League (NL) and American League (AL).

National League

	1st Year	Pennants & World Series	Franchise Stops
Atlanta Braves	1876	4 NL (1914,48,57-58) 2 WS (1914,57)	Boston (1876-1952) Milwaukee (1953-65) Atlanta (1966-)
Chicago Cubs	1876	10 NL (1906-08,10,18,29,32,35,38,45) 2 WS (1907-08)	Chicago (1876-)
Cincinnati Reds	1876	9 NL (1919,39-40,61,70,72,75-76,90) 5 WS (1919,40,75-76,90)	Cincinnati (1876-80) Cincinnati (1890-)
Houston Astros	1962	None	Houston (1962-)
Los Angeles Dodgers	1890	18 NL (1916,20,41,47,49,52-53,55-56,59,63, 65-66,74,77-78, 81,88) 6 WS (1955,59,63,65,81,88)	Brooklyn (1890-1957) Los Angeles (1958-)
Montreal Expos	1969	None	Montreal (1969-)
New York Mets	1962	3 NL (1969,73,86) 2 WS (1969,86)	New York (1962-)
Philadelphia Phillies	1880	4 NL (1915,50,80,83) 1 WS (1980)	Philadelphia (1883-)
Pittsburgh Pirates	1887	7 NL (1903,09,25,27,60,71,79) 5 WS (1909,25,60,71,79)	Pittsburgh (1887-)
St.Louis Cardinals	1892	15 NL (1926,28,30-31,34,42-44,46,64, 67-68,82,85,87) 9 WS (1926,31,34,42,44,46,64,67,82)	St.Louis (1892-)
San Diego Padres	1969	1 NL (1984)	San Diego (1969-)
San Francisco Giants	1883	16 NL (1905,11-13,17,21-24,33,36-37,51, 54,62,89) 5 WS (1905,21-22,33,54)	New York (1883-1957) San Francisco (1958-)

American League

	1st Year	Pennants & World Series	Franchise Stops
Baltimore Orioles	1902	7 AL (1944,66,69-71,79,83) 3 WS (1966,70,83)	Milwaukee (1901) St.Louis (1902-53) Baltimore (1954-)
Boston Red Sox	1901	9 AL (1903,12,15-16,18,46,67,75,86) 5 WS (1903,12,15-16,18)	Boston (1901-)
California Angels	1961	None	Los Angeles (1961-65) Anaheim, CA (1966-)
Chicago White Sox	1901	4 AL (1906,17,19,59) 2 WS (1906,17)	Chicago (1901-)
Cleveland Indians	1901	3 AL (1920,48,54) 2 WS (1920,48)	Cleveland (1901-)
Detroit Tigers	1901	9 AL (1907-09,34-35,40,45,68,84) 4 WS (1935,45,68,84)	Detroit (1901-)
Kansas City Royals	1969	2 AL (1980,85) 1 WS (1985)	Kansas City (1969-)
Milwaukee Brewers	1969	1 AL (1982)	Seattle (1969) Milwaukee (1970-)
Minnesota Twins	1901	5 AL (1924-25,33,65,87) 2 WS (1924,87)	Washington, DC (1901-60) Bloomington,MN(1961-81) Minneapolis (1982-)
New York Yankees	1901	33 AL (1921-23,26-28,32,36-39,41-43,47, 49-53,55-58,60-64,76-78,81) 22 WS (1923,27-28,32,36-39,41,43,47,49-53, 56,58,61-62,77-78)	Baltimore (1901-02) New York (1903-)
Oakland Athletics	1901	14 AL (1905,10-11,13-14,29-31,72-74,88-90) 9 WS (1910-11,13,29-30,72-74,89)	Philadelphia (1901-54) Kansas City (1955-67) Oakland (1968-)
Seattle Mariners	1977	None	Seattle (1977-)
Texas Rangers	1961	None	Washington, DC (1961-71) Arlington, TX (1972-)
Toronto Blue Jays	1977	None	Toronto (1977-)

Yearly Individual Batting Leaders (since 1900)

Batting Average

National League

Multiple winners: Honus Wagner (8); Rogers Hornsby and Stan Musial (7); Roberto Clemente, Tony Gwynn and Bill Madlock (4); Pete Rose and Paul Waner (3); Hank Aaron, Richie Ashburn, Jake Daubert, Tommy Davis, Ernie Lombardi, Willie McGee, Lefty O'Doul, Dave Parker and Edd Roush (2).

Year		Avg	Year		Avg	Year		Avg
1900	Honus Wagner, Pit	.381	1930	Bill Terry, NY	.401	1960	Dick Groat, Pit	.325
1901	Jesse Burkett, St.L	.382	1931	Chick Hafey, St.L	.349	1961	Roberto Clemente, Pit	.351
1902	Ginger Beaumont, Pit	.357	1932	Lefty O'Doul, Bklyn	.368	1962	Tommy Davis, LA	.346
1903	Honus Wagner, Pit	.355	1933	Chuck Klein, Phi	.368	1963	Tommy Davis, LA	.326
1904	Honus Wagner, Pit	.349	1934	Paul Waner, Pit	.362	1964	Roberto Clemente, Pit	.339
1905	Cy Seymour, Cin	.377	1935	Arkie Vaughan, Pit	.385	1965	Roberto Clemente, Pit	.329
1906	Honus Wagner, Pit	.339	1936	Paul Waner, Pit	.373	1966	Matty Alou, Pit	.342
1907	Honus Wagner, Pit	.350	1937	Joe Medwick, St.L	.374	1967	Roberto Clemente, Pit	.357
1908	Honus Wagner, Pit	.354	1938	Ernie Lombardi, Cin	.342	1968	Pete Rose, Cin	.335
1909	Honus Wagner, Pit	.339	1939	Johnny Mize, St.L	.349	1969	Pete Rose, Cin	.348
1910	Sherry Magee, Phi	.331	1940	Debs Garms, Pit	.355	1970	Rico Carty, Atl	.366
1911	Honus Wagner, Pit	.334	1941	Pete Reiser, Bklyn	.343	1971	Joe Torre, St.L	.363
1912	Heinie Zimmerman, Chi	.372	1942	Ernie Lombardi, Bos	.330	1972	Billy Williams, Chi	.333
1913	Jake Daubert, Bklyn	.350	1943	Stan Musial, St.L	.357	1973	Pete Rose, Cin	.338
1914	Jake Daubert, Bklyn	.329	1944	Dixie Walker, Chi	.357	1974	Ralph Garr, Atl	.353
1915	Larry Doyle, NY	.320	1945	Phil Cavarretta, Chi	.355	1975	Bill Madlock, Chi	.354
1916	Hal Chase, Cin	.339	1946	Stan Musial, St.L	.365	1976	Bill Madlock, Chi	.339
1917	Edd Roush, Cin	.341	1947	Harry Walker, St.L-Phi	.363	1977	Dave Parker, Pit	.338
1918	Zack Wheat, Bklyn	.335	1948	Stan Musial, St.L	.376	1978	Dave Parker, Pit	.334
1919	Edd Roush, Cin	.321	1949	Jackie Robinson, Bklyn	.342	1979	Keith Hernandez, St.L	.344
1920	Rogers Hornsby, St.L	.370	1950	Stan Musial, St.L	.346	1980	Bill Buckner, Chi	.324
1921	Rogers Hornsby, St.L	.397	1951	Stan Musial, St.L	.355	1981	Bill Madlock, Pit	.341
1922	Rogers Hornsby, St.L	.401	1952	Stan Musial, St.L	.336	1982	Al Oliver, Mon	.331
1923	Rogers Hornsby, St.L	.384	1953	Carl Furillo, Bklyn	.344	1983	Bill Madlock, Pit	.323
1924	Rogers Hornsby, St.L	.424	1954	Willie Mays, NY	.345	1984	Tony Gwynn, SD	.351
1925	Rogers Hornsby, St.L	.403	1955	Richie Ashburn, Phi	.338	1985	Willie McGee, St.L	.353
1926	Bubbles Hargrave, Cin	.353	1956	Hank Aaron, Mil	.328	1986	Tim Raines, Mon	.334
1927	Paul Waner, Pit	.380	1957	Stan Musial, St.L	.351	1987	Tony Gwynn, SD	.370
1928	Rogers Hornsby, Bos	.387	1958	Richie Ashburn, Phi	.350	1988	Tony Gwynn, SD	.313
1929	Lefty O'Doul, Phi	.398	1959	Hank Aaron, Mil	.355	1989	Tony Gwynn, SD	.336
						1990	Willie McGee, St.L	.335

American League

Multiple winners: Ty Cobb (12); Rod Carew (7); Ted Williams (6); Wade Boggs (6); Harry Heilmann (4); George Brett, Tony Oliva and Carl Yastrzemski (3); Luke Appling, Joe DiMaggio, Ferris Fain, Jimmie Foxx, Nap Lajoie, Pete Runnels, Al Simmons, George Sisler and Mickey Vernon (2).

Year		Avg	Year		Avg	Year		Avg
1901	Nap Lajoie, Phi	.422	1923	Harry Heilmann, Det	.403	1945	Snuffy Stirnweiss, NY	.309
1902	Ed Delahanty, Wash	.376	1924	Babe Ruth, NY	.378	1946	Mickey Vernon, Wash	.353
1903	Nap Lajoie, Cle	.355	1925	Harry Heilmann, Det	.393	1947	Ted Williams, Bos	.343
1904	Nap Lajoie, Cle	.381	1926	Heine Manush, Det	.378	1948	Ted Williams, Bos	.369
1905	Elmer Flick, Cle	.306	1927	Harry Heilmann, Det	.398	1949	George Kell, Det	.343
1906	George Stone, St.L	.358	1928	Goose Goslin, Wash	.379	1950	Billy Goodman, Bos	.354
1907	Ty Cobb, Det	.350	1929	Lew Fonseca, Cle	.369	1951	Ferris Fain, Phi	.344
1908	Ty Cobb, Det	.324	1930	Al Simmons, Phi	381	1952	Ferris Fain, Phi	.327
1909	Ty Cobb, Det	.377	1931	Al Simmons, Phi	.390	1953	Mickey Vernon, Wash	.337
1910	Ty Cobb, Det	.385	1932	Dale Alexander, Det-Bos	.367	1954	Bobby Avila, Clev	.341
1911	Ty Cobb, Det	.420	1933	Jimmie Foxx, Phi	.356	1955	Al Kaline, Det	.340
1912	Ty Cobb, Det	.410	1934	Lou Gehrig, NY	.363	1956	Mickey Mantle, NY	.353
1913	Ty Cobb, Det	.390	1935	Buddy Myer, Wash	.349	1957	Ted Williams, Bos	.388
1914	Ty Cobb, Det	.368	1936	Luke Appling, Chi	.388	1958	Ted Williams, Bos	.328
1915	Ty Cobb, Det	.369	1937	Charlie Gehringer, Det	.371	1959	Harvey Kuenn, Det	.353
1916	Tris Speaker, Cle	.386	1938	Jimmie Foxx, Bos	.349	1960	Pete Runnels, Box	.320
1917	Ty Cobb, Det	.383	1939	Joe DiMaggio, NY	.381	1961	Norm Cash, Det	.361
1918	Ty Cobb, Det	.382	1940	Joe DiMaggio, NY	.352	1962	Pete Runnels, Bos	.326
1919	Ty Cobb, Det	.384	1941	Ted Williams, Bos	.406	1963	Carl Yastrzemski, Bos	.321
1920	George Sisler, St.L	.407	1942	Ted Williams, Bos	.356	1964	Tony Oliva, Min	.323
1921	Harry Heilmann, Det	.394	1943	Luke Appling, Chi	.328	1965	Tony Oliva, Min	.321
1922	George Sisler, St.L	.420	1944	Lou Boudreau, Clev	.327	1966	Frank Robinson, Bal	.316

Batting Average (Cont.)

Year		Avg	Year		Avg	Year		Avg
1967	Carl Yastrzemski, Bos	.326	1975	Rod Carew, Min	.359	1983	Wade Boggs, Bos	.361
1968	Carl Yastrzemski, Bos	.301	1976	George Brett, KC	.333	1984	Don Mattingly, NY	.343
1969	Rod Carew, Min	.332	1977	Rod Carew, Min	.388	1985	Wade Boggs, Bos	.368
1970	Alex Johnson, Cal	.329	1978	Rod Carew, Min	.333	1986	Wade Boggs, Bos	.357
1971	Tony Oliva, Min	.337	1979	Fred Lynn, Bos	.333	1987	Wade Boggs, Bos	.363
1972	Rod Carew, Min	.318	1980	George Brett, KC	.390	1988	Wade Boggs, Bos	.366
1973	Rod Carew, Min	.350	1981	Carney Lansford, Bos	.336	1989	Kirby Puckett, Min	.339
1974	Rod Carew, Min	.364	1982	Willie Wilson, KC	.332	1990	George Brett, KC	.329

Home Runs

National League

Multiple winners: Mike Schmidt (8); Ralph Kiner (7); Gavvy Cravath and Mel Ott (6); Hank Aaron, Chuck Klein, Willie Mays, Johnny Mize, Cy Williams and Hack Wilson (4); Willie McCovey (3); Ernie Banks, Johnny Bench, George Foster, Rogers Hornsby, Tim Jordan, Dave Kingman, Eddie Mathews, Dale Murphy, Bill Nicholson, Dave Robertson, Wildfire Schulte and Willie Stargell (2).

Year		HR	Year		HR	Year		HR
1900	Herman Long, Bos	12	1930	Hack Wilson, Chi	56	1959	Eddie Mathews, Mil	46
1901	Sam Crawford, Cin	16	1931	Chuck Klein, Phi	31	1960	Ernie Banks, Chi	41
1902	Tommy Leach, Pit	6	1932	Chuck Klein, Phi	38	1961	Orlando Cepeda, SF	46
1903	Jimmy Sheckard, Bklyn	9		& Mel Ott, NY	38	1962	Willie Mays, SF	49
1904	Harry Lumley, Bklyn	9	1933	Chuck Klein, Phi	28	1963	Hank Aaron, Mil	44
1905	Fred Odwell, Cin	9	1934	Rip Collins, St.L	35		& Willie McCovey, SF	44
1906	Tim Jordan, Bklyn	12		& Mel Ott, NY	35	1964	Willie Mays, SF	47
1907	Dave Brain, Bos	10	1935	Wally Berger, Bos	34	1965	Willie Mays, SF	52
1908	Tim Jordan, Bklyn	12	1936	Mel Ott, NY	33	1966	Hank Aaron, Atl	44
1909	Red Murray, NY	7	1937	Joe Medwick, St.L	31	1967	Hank Aaron, Atl	39
1910	Fred Beck, Bos	10		Mel Ott, NY	31	1968	Willie McCovey, SF	36
	& Wildfire Schulte, Chi	10	1938	Mel Ott, NY	36	1969	Willie McCovey, SF	45
1911	Wildfire Schulte, Chi	21	1939	Johnny Mize, St.L	28	1970	Johnny Bench, Cin	45
1912	Heinie Zimmerman, Chi	14	1940	Johnny Mize, St.L	43	1971	Willie Stargell, Pit	48
1913	Gavvy Cravath, Phi	19	1941	Dolf Camilli, Bklyn	34	1972	Johnny Bench, Cin	40
1914	Gavvy Cravath, Phi	19	1942	Mel Ott, NY	30	1973	Willie Stargell, Pit	44
1915	Gavvy Cravath, Phi	24	1943	Bill Nicholson, Chi	29	1974	Mike Schmidt, Phi	36
1916	Dave Robertson, NY	12	1944	Bill Nicholson, Chi	33	1975	Mike Schmidt, Phi	38
	& Cy Williams, Chi	12	1945	Tommy Holmes, Bos	28	1976	Mike Schmidt, Phi	38
1917	Dave Robertson, NY	12	1946	Ralph Kiner, Pit	23	1977	George Foster, Cin	52
	& Gavvy Cravath, Phi	12	1947	Ralph Kiner, Pit	51	1978	George Foster, Cin	40
1918	Gavvy Cravath, Phi	8		& Johnny Mize, NY	51	1979	Dave Kingman, Chi	48
1919	Gavvy Cravath, Phi	12	1948	Ralph Kiner, Pit	40	1980	Mike Schmidt, Phi	48
1920	Cy Williams, Phi	15		& Johnny Mize, NY	40	1981	Mike Schmidt, Phi	31
1921	George Kelly, NY	23	1949	Ralph Kiner, Pit	54	1982	Dave Kingman, NY	37
1922	Rogers Hornsby, St.L	42	1950	Ralph Kiner, Pit	47	1983	Mike Schmidt, Phi	40
1923	Cy Williams, Phi	41	1951	Ralph Kiner, Pit	42	1984	Dale Murphy, Atl	36
1924	Jack Fournier, Bklyn	27	1952	Ralph Kiner, Pit	37		& Mike Schmidt, Phi	36
1925	Rogers Hornsby, St.L	39		& Hank Sauer, Chi	37	1985	Dale Murphy, Atl	37
1926	Hack Wilson, Chi	21	1953	Eddie Mathews, Mil	47	1986	Mike Schmidt, Phi	37
1927	Cy Williams, Phi	30	1954	Ted Kluszewski, Cin	49	1987	Andre Dawson, Chi	49
	& Hack Wilson, Chi	30	1955	Willie Mays, NY	51	1988	Darryl Strawberry, NY	39
1928	Jim Bottomley, St.L	31	1956	Duke Snider, Bklyn	43	1989	Kevin Mitchell, SF	47
	& Hack Wilson, Chi	31	1957	Hank Aaron, Mil	44	1990	Ryne Sandberg, Chi	40
1929	Chuck Klein, Phi	43	1958	Ernie Banks, Chi	47			

American League

Multiple winners: Babe Ruth (12); Harmon Killebrew (6); Home Run Baker, Harry Davis, Jimmie Foxx, Hank Greenberg, Reggie Jackson, Mickey Mantle and Ted Williams (4); Lou Gehrig and Jim Rice (3); Dick Allen, Tony Armas, Joe DiMaggio, Larry Doby, Frank Howard, Wally Pipp, Al Rosen and Gorman Thomas (2).

Year		HR	Year		HR	Year		HR
1901	Nap Lajoie, Phi	13	1911	Home Run Baker, Phi	11	1920	Babe Ruth, NY	54
1902	Socks Seybold, Phi	16	1912	Home Run Baker, Phi	10	1921	Babe Ruth, NY	59
1903	Buck Freeman, Bos	13		& Tris Speaker, Bos	10	1922	Ken Williams, St.L	39
1904	Harry Davis, Phi	10	1913	Home Run Baker, Phi	12	1923	Babe Ruth, NY	41
1905	Harry Davis, Phi	8	1914	Home Run Baker, Phi	9	1924	Babe Ruth, NY	46
1906	Harry Davis, Phi	12	1915	Braggo Roth, Chi-Cle	7	1925	Bob Meusel, NY	33
1907	Harry Davis, Phi	8	1916	Wally Pipp, NY	12	1926	Babe Ruth, NY	47
1908	Sam Crawford, Det	7	1917	Wally Pipp, NY	9	1927	Babe Ruth, NY	60
1909	Ty Cobb, Det	9	1918	Babe Ruth, Bos	11	1928	Babe Ruth, NY	54
1910	Jake Stahl, Bos	10		Tilly Walker, Phi	11	1929	Babe Ruth, NY	46
			1919	Babe Ruth, Bos	29			

Year	HR	Year	HR	Year	HR
1930 Babe Ruth, NY	49	1952 Larry Doby, Cle	32	1974 Dick Allen, Chi	32
1931 Lou Gehrig, NY	46	1953 Al Rosen, Cle	43	1975 Reggie Jackson, Oak	36
& Babe Ruth, NY	46	1954 Larry Doby, Cle	32	& George Scott, Mil	36
1932 Jimmie Foxx, Phi	58	1955 Mickey Mantle, NY	37	1976 Graig Nettles, NY	32
1933 Jimmie Foxx, Phi	48	1956 Mickey Mantle, NY	52	1977 Jim Rice, Bos	39
1934 Lou Gehrig, NY	49	1957 Roy Sievers, Wash	42	1978 Jim Rice, Bos	46
1935 Jimmie Foxx, Phi	36	1958 Mickey Mantle, NY	42	1979 Gorman Thomas, Mil	45
& Hank Greenberg, Det	36	1959 Harmon Killebrew, Wash	42	1980 Reggie Jackson, NY	41
1936 Lou Gehrig, NY	49	& Rocky Colavito, Cle	42	& Ben Ogilvie, Mil	41
1937 Joe DiMaggio, NY	46	1960 Mickey Mantle, NY	40	1981 Tony Armas, Bos	22
1938 Hank Greenberg, Det	58	1961 Roger Maris, NY	61	Dwight Evans, Bos	22
1939 Jimmie Foxx, Bos	35	1962 Harmon Killebrew, Min	48	Bobby Grich, Cal	22
1940 Hank Greenberg, Det	41	1963 Harmon Killebrew, Min	45	& Eddie Murray, Bal	22
1941 Ted Williams, Bos	37	1964 Harmon Killebrew, Min	49	1982 Reggie Jackson, Cal	39
1942 Ted Williams, Bos	36	1965 Tony Conigliaro, Bos	32	& Gorman Thomas, Mil	39
1943 Rudy York, Det	34	1966 Frank Robinson, Bal	49	1983 Jim Rice, Bos	39
1944 Nick Etten, NY	22	1967 Harmon Killebrew, Min	44	1984 Tony Armas, Bos	43
1945 Vern Stephens, St.L	24	& Carl Yastrzemski, Bos	44	1985 Darrell Evans, Det	40
1946 Hank Greenberg, Det	44	1968 Frank Howard, Wash	44	1986 Jesse Barfield, Tor	40
1947 Ted Williams, Bos	32	1969 Harmon Killebrew, Min	49	1987 Mark McGwire, Oak	49
1948 Joe DiMaggio, NY	39	1970 Frank Howard, Wash	44	1988 Jose Canseco, Oak	42
1949 Ted Williams, Bos	43	1971 Bill Melton, Chi	33	1989 Fred McGriff, Tor	36
1950 Al Rosen, Cle	37	1972 Dick Allen, Chi	37	1990 Cecil Fielder, Det	51
1951 Gus Zernial, Chi-Phi	33	1973 Reggie Jackson, Oak	32		

Runs Batted In

National League

Multiple winners: Hank Aaron, Rogers Hornsby, Sherry Magee, Mike Schmidt and Honus Wagner (4); Johnny Bench, George Foster, Joe Medwick, Johnny Mize and Heinie Zimmerman (3); Ernie Banks, Jim Bottomley, Orlando Cepeda, Gavvy Cravath, George Kelly, Chuck Klein, Willie McCovey, Dale Murphy, Stan Musial, Bill Nicholson and Hack Wilson (2).

Year	RBI	Year	RBI	Year	RBI
1900 Elmer Flick, Phi	110	1930 Hack Wilson, Chi	190	1962 Tommy Davis, LA	153
1901 Honus Wagner, Pit	126	1931 Chuck Klein, Phi	121	1963 Hank Aaron, Mil	130
1902 Honus Wagner, Pit	91	1932 Don Hurst, Phi	143	1964 Ken Boyer, St.L	119
1903 Sam Mertes, NY	104	1933 Chuck Klein, Phi	120	1965 Deron Johnson, Cin	130
1904 Bill Dahlen, NY	80	1934 Mel Ott, NY	135	1966 Hank Aaron, Atl	127
1905 Cy Seymour, Cin	121	1935 Wally Berger, Bos	130	1967 Orlando Cepeda, St.L	111
1906 Jim Nealon, Pit	83	1936 Joe Medwick, St.L	138	1968 Willie McCovey, SF	105
1907 Sherry Magee, Phi	85	1937 Joe Medwick, St.L	154	1969 Willie McCovey, SF	126
1908 Honus Wagner, Pit	109	1938 Joe Medwick, St.L	122	1970 Johnny Bench, Cin	148
1909 Honus Wagner, Pit	100	1939 Frank McCormick, Cin	128	1971 Joe Torre, St.L	137
1910 Sherry Magee, Phi	123	1940 Johnny Mize, St.L	137	1972 Johnny Bench, Cin	125
1911 Wildfire Schulte, Chi	121	1941 Dolph Camilli, Bklyn	120	1973 Willie Stargell, Pit	119
1912 Heinie Zimmerman, Chi	103	1942 Johnny Mize, NY	110	1974 Johnny Bench, Cin	129
1913 Gavvy Cravath, Phi	128	1943 Bill Nicholson, Chi	128	1975 Greg Luzinski, Phi	120
1914 Sherry Magee, Phi	103	1944 Bill Nicholson, Chi	122	1976 George Foster, Cin	121
1915 Gavvy Cravath, Phi	115	1945 Dixie Walker, Bklyn	124	1977 George Foster, Cin	149
1916 Heinie Zimmerman, Chi-NY	83	1946 Enos Slaughter, St.L	130	1978 George Foster, Cin	120
1917 Heinie Zimmerman, NY	102	1947 Johnny Mize, NY	138	1979 Dave Winfield, SD	118
1918 Sherry Magee, Cin	76	1948 Stan Musial, St.L	131	1980 Mike Schmidt, Phi	121
1919 Hy Myers, Bklyn	73	1949 Ralph Kiner, Pit	127	1981 Mike Schmidt, Phi	91
1920 George Kelly, NY	94	1950 Del Ennis, Phi	126	1982 Dale Murphy, Atl	109
& Rogers Hornsby, St.L	94	1951 Monty Irvin, NY	121	& Al Oliver, Mon	109
1921 Rogers Hornsby, St.L	126	1952 Hank Sauer, Chi	121	1983 Dale Murphy, Atl	121
1922 Rogers Hornsby, St.L	152	1953 Roy Campanella, Bklyn	142	1984 Gary Carter, Mon	106
1923 Irish Meusel, NY	125	1954 Ted Kluszewski, Cin	141	& Mike Schmidt, Phi	106
1924 George Kelly, NY	136	1955 Duke Snider, Bklyn	136	1985 Dave Parker, Cin	125
1925 Rogers Hornsby, St.L	143	1956 Stan Musial, St.L	109	1986 Mike Schmidt, Phi	119
1926 Jim Bottomley, St.L	120	1957 Hank Aaron, Mil	132	1987 Andre Dawson, Chi	137
1927 Paul Waner, Pit	131	1958 Ernie Banks, Chi	129	1988 Will Clark, SF	109
1928 Jim Bottomley, St.L	136	1959 Ernie Banks, Chi	143	1989 Kevin Mitchell, SF	125
1929 Hack Wilson, Chi	159	1960 Hank Aaron, Mil	126	1990 Matt Williams, SF	122
		1961 Orlando Cepeda, SF	142		

American League

Multiple winners: Babe Ruth (6); Lou Gehrig (5); Ty Cobb and Hank Greenberg (4); Sam Crawford, Jimmie Foxx, Jackie Jensen, Harmon Killebrew, Vern Stephens and Ted Williams (3); Home Run Baker, Cecil Cooper, Harry Davis, Joe DiMaggio, Buck Freeman, Nap Lajoie, Roger Maris, Jim Rice, Al Rosen, and Bobby Veach (2).

Year		RBI	Year		RBI	Year		RBI
1901	Nap Lajoie, Phi	125	1933	Jimmie Foxx, Phi	163	1963	Dick Stuart, Bos	118
1902	Buck Freeman, Bos	121	1934	Lou Gehrig, NY	165	1964	Brooks Robinson, Bal	118
1903	Buck Freeman, Bos	104	1935	Hank Greenberg, Det	170	1965	Rocky Colavito, Cle	108
1904	Nap Lajoie, Cle	102	1936	Hal Trosky, Cle	162	1966	Frank Robinson, Bal	122
1905	Harry Davis, Phi	83	1937	Hank Greenberg, Det	183	1967	Carl Yastrzemski, Bos	121
1906	Harry Davis, Phi	96	1938	Jimmie Foxx, Bos	175	1968	Ken Harrelson, Bos	109
1907	Ty Cobb, Det	116	1939	Ted Williams, Bos	145	1969	Harmon Killebrew, Min	140
1908	Ty Cobb, Det	108	1940	Hank Greenberg, Det	150	1970	Frank Howard, Wash	126
1909	Ty Cobb, Det	107	1941	Joe DiMaggio, NY	125	1971	Harmon Killebrew, Min	119
1910	Sam Crawford, Det	120	1942	Ted Williams, Bos	137	1972	Dick Allen, Chi	113
1911	Ty Cobb, Det	144	1943	Rudy York, Det	118	1973	Reggie Jackson, Oak	117
1912	Home Run Baker, Phi	133	1944	Vern Stephens, St.L	109	1974	Jeff Burroughs, Tex	118
1913	Home Run Baker, Phi	126	1945	Nick Etten, NY	111	1975	George Scott, Mil	109
1914	Sam Crawford, Det	104	1946	Hank Greenberg, Det	127	1976	Lee May, Bal	109
1915	Sam Crawford, Det	112	1947	Ted Williams, Bos	114	1977	Larry Hisle, Min	119
1916	Del Pratt, St.L	103	1948	Joe DiMaggio, NY	155	1978	Jim Rice, Bos	139
1917	Bobby Veach, Det	103	1949	Ted Williams, Bos	159	1979	Don Baylor, Cal	139
1918	Bobby Veach, Det	78		& Vern Stephens, Bos	159	1980	Cecil Cooper, Mil	122
1919	Babe Ruth, Bos	114	1950	Walt Dropo, Bos	144	1981	Eddie Murray, Bal	78
1920	Babe Ruth, NY	137		Vern Stephens, Bos	144	1982	Hal McRae, KC	133
1921	Babe Ruth, NY	171	1951	Gus Zernial, Chi-Phi	129	1983	Cecil Cooper, Mil	126
1922	Ken Williams, St.L	155	1952	Al Rosen, Cle	105		& Jim Rice, Bos	126
1923	Babe Ruth, NY	131	1953	Al Rosen, Cle	145	1984	Tony Armas, Bos	123
1924	Goose Goslin, Wash	129	1954	Larry Doby, Cle	126	1985	Don Mattingly, NY	145
1925	Bob Meusel, NY	138	1955	Ray Boone, Det	116	1986	Joe Carter, Cle	121
1926	Babe Ruth, NY	145		& Jackie Jensen, Bos	116	1987	George Bell, Tor	134
1927	Lou Gehrig, NY	175	1956	Mickey Mantle, NY	130	1988	Jose Canseco, Oak	124
1928	Lou Gehrig, NY	142	1957	Roy Sievers, Wash	114	1989	Ruben Sierra, Tex	119
	& Babe Ruth, NY	142	1958	Jackie Jensen, Bos	122	1990	Cecil Fielder, Det	132
1929	Al Simmons, Phi	157	1959	Jackie Jensen, Bos	112			
1930	Lou Gehrig, NY	174	1960	Roger Maris, NY	112			
1931	Lou Gehrig, NY	184	1961	Roger Maris, NY	142			
1932	Jimmie Foxx, Phi	169	1962	Harmon Killebrew, Min	126			

Stolen Bases
National League

Multiple winners: Max Carey (10); Lou Brock (8); Vince Coleman and Maury Wills (6); Honus Wagner (5); Bob Brescher, Kiki Cuyler, Willie Mays and Tim Raines (4); Bill Bruton, Frankie Frisch and Pepper Martin (3); George Burns, Frank Chance, Augie Galan, Stan Hack, Sam Jethroe, Davey Lopes, Omar Moreno, Pete Reiser and Jackie Robinson (2).

Year		SB	Year		SB	Year		SB
1900	George Van Haltren, NY	45	1920	Max Carey, Pit	52	1940	Lonny Frey, Cin	22
	& Patsy Donovan, St.L	45	1921	Frankie Frisch, NY	49	1941	Danny Murtaugh, Phi	18
1901	Honus Wagner, Pit	49	1922	Max Carey, Pit	51	1942	Pete Reiser, Bklyn	20
1902	Honus Wagner, Pit	42	1923	Max Carey, Pit	51	1943	Arky Vaughan, Bklyn	20
1903	Jimmy Sheckard, Bklyn	67	1924	Max Carey, Pit	49	1944	Johnny Barrett, Pit	28
	& Frank Chance, Chi	67	1925	Max Carey, Pit	46	1945	Red Schoendienst, St.L	26
1904	Honus Wagner, Pit	53	1926	Kiki Cuyler, Pit	35	1946	Pete Reiser, Bklyn	34
1905	Art Devlin, NY	59	1927	Frankie Frisch, St.L	48	1947	Jackie Robinson, Bklyn	29
	& Billy Maloney, Chi	59	1928	Kiki Cuyler, Chi	37	1948	Richie Ashburn, Phi	32
1906	Frank Chance, Chi	57	1929	Kiki Cuyler, Chi	43	1949	Jackie Robinson, Bklyn	37
1907	Honus Wagner, Pit	61	1930	Kiki Cuyler, Chi	37	1950	Sam Jethroe, Bos	35
1908	Honus Wagner, Pit	53	1931	Frankie Frisch, St.L	28	1951	Sam Jethroe, Bos	35
1909	Bob Bescher, Cin	54	1932	Chuck Klein, Phi	20	1952	Pee Wee Reese, Bklyn	30
1910	Bob Bescher, Cin	70	1933	Pepper Martin, St.L	26	1953	Bill Bruton, Mil	26
1911	Bob Bescher, Cin	81	1934	Pepper Martin, St.L	23	1954	Bill Bruton, Mil	34
1912	Bob Bescher, Cin	67	1935	Augie Galan, Chi	22	1955	Bill Bruton, Mil	35
1913	Max Carey, Pit	61	1936	Pepper Martin, St.L	23	1956	Willie Mays, NY	40
1914	George Burns, NY	62	1937	Augie Galan, Chi	23	1957	Willie Mays, NY	38
1915	Max Carey, Pit	36	1938	Stan Hack, Chi	16	1958	Willie Mays, SF	31
1916	Max Carey, Pit	63	1939	Stan Hack, Chi	17	1959	Willie Mays, SF	27
1917	Max Carey, Pit	46		& Lee Handley, Pit	17			
1918	Max Carey, Pit	58						
1919	George Burns, NY	40						

Year	SB	Year	SB	Year	SB
1960 Maury Wills, LA	50	1970 Bobby Tolan, Cin	57	1980 Ron LeFlore, Mon	97
1961 Maury Wills, LA	35	1971 Lou Brock, St.L	64	1981 Tim Raines, Mon	71
1962 Maury Wills, LA	104	1972 Lou Brock, St.L	63	1982 Tim Raines, Mon	78
1963 Maury Wills, LA	40	1973 Lou Brock, St.L	70	1983 Tim Raines, Mon	90
1964 Maury Wills, LA	53	1974 Lou Brock, St.L	118	1984 Tim Raines, Mon	75
1965 Maury Wills, LA	94	1975 Davey Lopes, LA	77	1985 Vince Coleman, St.L	110
1966 Lou Brock, St.L	74	1976 Davey Lopes, LA	63	1986 Vince Coleman, St.L	107
1967 Lou Brock, St.L	52	1977 Frank Tavares, Pit	70	1987 Vince Coleman, St.L	109
1968 Lou Brock, St.L	62	1978 Omar Moreno, Pit	71	1988 Vince Coleman, St.L	81
1969 Lou Brock, St.L	53	1979 Omar Moreno, Pit	77	1989 Vince Coleman, St.L	66
				1990 Vince Coleman, St.L	77

American League

Multiple winners: Rickey Henderson (10); Luis Aparicio (9); Bert Campaneris, George Case and Ty Cobb (6); Ben Chapman, Eddie Collins and George Sisler (4); Bob Dillinger, Minnie Minoso and Bill Werber (3); Elmer Flick, Tommy Harper, Clyde Milan, Johnny Mostil, Bill North and Snuffy Stirnweiss (2).

Year	SB	Year	SB	Year	SB
1901 Frank Isbell, Chi	52	1930 Marty McManus, Det	23	1960 Luis Aparicio, Chi	51
1902 Topsy Hartsel, Phi	47	1931 Ben Chapman, NY	61	1961 Luis Aparicio, Chi	53
1903 Harry Bay, Cle	45	1932 Ben Chapman, NY	38	1962 Luis Aparicio, Chi	31
1904 Elmer Flick, Cle	42	1933 Ben Chapman, NY	27	1963 Luis Aparicio, Bal	40
1905 Danny Hoffman, Phi	46	1934 Bill Werber, Bos	40	1964 Luis Aparicio, Bal	57
1906 Elmer Flick, Cle	39	1935 Bill Werber, Bos	29	1965 Bert Campaneris, KC	51
& John Anderson, Wash	39	1936 Lyn Lary, St.L	37	1966 Bert Campaneris, KC	52
1907 Ty Cobb, Det	49	1937 Ben Chapman, Wash-Bos	35	1967 Bert Campaneris, KC	55
1908 Patsy Dougherty, Chi	47	& Bill Werber, Phi	35	1968 Bert Campaneris, Oak	62
1909 Ty Cobb, Det	76	1938 Frank Crosetti, NY	27	1969 Tommy Harper, Sea	73
1910 Eddie Collins, Phi	81	1939 George Case, Wash	51	1970 Bert Campaneris, Oak	42
1911 Ty Cobb, Det	83	1940 George Case, Wash	35	1971 Amos Otis, KC	52
1912 Clyde Milan, Wash	88	1941 George Case, Wash	33	1972 Bert Campaneris, Oak	52
1913 Clyde Milan, Wash	75	1942 George Case, Wash	44	1973 Tommy Harper, Bos	54
1914 Fritz Maisel, NY	74	1943 George Case, Wash	61	1974 Bill North, Oak	54
1915 Ty Cobb, Det	96	1944 Snuffy Stirnweiss, NY	55	1975 Mickey Rivers, CA	70
1916 Ty Cobb, Det	68	1945 Snuffy Stirnweiss, NY	33	1976 Bill North, Oak	75
1917 Ty Cobb, Det	55	1946 George Case, Cle	28	1977 Freddie Patek, KC	53
1918 George Sisler, St.L	45	1947 Bob Dillinger, St.L	34	1978 Ron LeFlore, Det	68
1919 Eddie Collins, Chi	33	1948 Bob Dillinger, St.L	28	1979 Willie Wilson, KC	83
1920 Sam Rice, Wash	63	1949 Bob Dillinger, St.L	20	1980 Rickey Henderson, Oak	100
1921 George Sisler, St.L	35	1950 Dom DiMaggio, Bos	15	1981 Rickey Henderson, Oak	56
1922 George Sisler, St.L	51	1951 Minnie Minoso, Cle-Chi	31	1982 Rickey Henderson, Oak	130
1923 Eddie Collins, Chi	47	1952 Minnie Minoso, Chi	22	1983 Rickey Henderson, Oak	108
1924 Eddie Collins, Chi	42	1953 Minnie Minoso, Chi	25	1984 Rickey Henderson, Oak	66
1925 Johnny Mostil, Chi	43	1954 Jackie Jensen, Bos	22	1985 Rickey Henderson, NY	80
1926 Johnny Mostil, Chi	35	1955 Jim Rivera, Chi	25	1986 Rickey Henderson, NY	87
1927 George Sisler, St.L	27	1956 Luis Aparicio, Chi	21	1987 Harold Reynolds, Sea	60
1928 Buddy Myer, Bos	30	1957 Luis Aparicio, Chi	28	1988 Rickey Henderson, NY	93
1929 Charlie Gehringer, Det	28	1958 Luis Aparicio, Chi	29	1989 R.Henderson, NY-Oak	77
		1959 Luis Aparicio, Chi	56	1990 Rickey Henderson, Oak	65

Yearly Individual Pitching Leaders (since 1900)

Winning Percentage

At least 15 wins, except in strike year of 1981 when the minimum was 10 wins.

National League

Multiple winners: Ed Reulbach and Tom Seaver (3); Larry Benton, Harry Brecheen, Jack Chesbro, Paul Derringer, Freddie Fitzsimmons, Carl Hubbell, Sandy Koufax, Bill Lee, Christy Mathewson, Don Newcombe and Preacher Roe (2).

Year	W-L	Pct	Year	W-L	Pct
1900 Jesse Tannehill, Pittsburgh	20-6	.769	1910 King Cole, Chicago	20-4	.833
1901 Jack Chesbro, Pittsburgh	21-10	.677	1911 Rube Marquard, New York	24-7	.774
1902 Jack Chesbro, Pittsburgh	28-6	.824	1912 Claude Hendrix, Pittsburgh	24-9	.727
1903 Sam Leever, Pittsburgh	25-7	.781	1913 Bert Humphries, Chicago	16-4	.800
1904 Joe McGinnity, New York	35-8	.814	1914 Bill James, Boston	26-7	.788
1905 Christy Mathewson, NY	31-8	.795	1915 Grover Alexander, Phila.	31-10	.756
1906 Ed Reulbach, Chicago	19-4	.826	1916 Tom Hughes, Boston	16-3	.842
1907 Ed Reulbach, Chicago	17-4	.810	1917 Ferdie Schupp, New York	21-7	.750
1908 Ed Reulbach, Chicago	24-7	.774	1918 Claude Hendrix, Chicago	19-7	.731
1909 Christy Mathewson, New York	25-6	.806	1919 Dutch Ruether, Cincinnati	19-6	.760
& Howie Camnitz, Pittsburgh	25-6	.806			

Winning Percentage (Cont.)

Year		W-L	Pct	Year		W-L	Pct
1920	Burleigh Grimes, Brooklyn	23-11	.676	1957	Bob Buhl, Milwaukee	18-7	.720
1921	Bill Doak, St.Louis	15-6	.714	1958	Warren Spahn, Milwaukee	22-11	.667
1922	Pete Donohue, Cincinnati	18-9	.667		& Lew Burdette, Milwaukee	20-10	.667
1923	Dolf Luque, Cincinnati	27-8	.771	1959	Roy Face, Pittsburgh	18-1	.947
1924	Emil Yde, Pittsburgh	16-3	.842	1960	Ernie Broglio, St Louis	21-9	.700
1925	Bill Sherdel, St.Louis	15-6	.714	1961	Johnny Podres, Los Angeles	18-5	.783
1926	Ray Kremer, Pittsburgh	20-6	.769	1962	Bob Purkey, Cincinnati	23-5	.821
1927	Larry Benton, Boston-NY	17-7	.708	1963	Ron Perranoski, Los Angeles	16-3	.842
1928	Larry Benton, New York	25-9	.735	1964	Sandy Koufax, Los Angeles	19-5	.792
1929	Charlie Root, Chicago	19-6	.760	1965	Sandy Koufax, Los Angeles	26-8	.765
1930	Freddie Fitzsimmons, NY	19-7	.731	1966	Juan Marichal, San Francisco	25-6	.806
1931	Paul Derringer, St.Louis	18-8	.692	1967	Dick Hughes, St. Louis	16-6	.727
1932	Lon Warneke, Chicago	22-6	.786	1968	Steve Blass, Pittsburgh	18-6	.750
1933	Ben Cantwell, Boston	20-10	.667	1969	Tom Seaver, New York	25-7	.781
1934	Dizzy Dean, St.Louis	30-7	.811	1970	Bob Gibson, St. Louis	23-7	.767
1935	Bill Lee, Chicago	20-6	.769	1971	Don Gullett, Cincinnati	16-6	.727
1936	Carl Hubbell, New York	26-6	.813	1972	Gary Nolan, Cincinnati	15-5	.750
1937	Carl Hubbell, New York	22-8	.733	1973	Tommy John, Los Angeles	16-7	.696
1938	Bill Lee, Chicago	22-9	.710	1974	Andy Messersmith, Los Ang.	20-6	.769
1939	Paul Derringer, Cincinnati	25-7	.781	1975	Don Gullett, Cincinnati	15-4	.789
1940	Freddie Fitzsimmons, Bklyn	16-2	.889	1976	Steve Carlton, Philadelphia	20-7	.741
1941	Elmer Riddle, Cincinnati	19-4	.826	1977	John Candelaria, Pittsburgh	20-5	.800
1942	Larry French, Brooklyn	15-4	.789	1978	Gaylord Perry, San Diego	21-6	.778
1943	Mort Cooper, St. Louis	21-8	.724	1979	Tom Seaver, Cincinnati	16-6	.727
1944	Ted Wilks, St. Louis	17-4	.810	1980	Jim Bibby, Pittsburgh	19-6	.760
1945	Harry Brecheen, St. Louis	15-4	.789	1981	Tom Seaver, Cincinnati	14-2	.875
1946	Murray Dickson, St. Louis	15-6	.714	1982	Phil Niekro, Atlanta	17-4	.810
1947	Larry Jansen, New York	21-5	.808	1983	John Denny, Philadelphia	19-6	.760
1948	Harry Brecheen, St. Louis	20-7	.741	1984	Rick Sutcliffe, Chicago	16-1	.941
1949	Preacher Roe, Brooklyn	15-6	.714	1985	Orel Hershiser, Los Angeles	19-3	.864
1950	Sal Maglie, New York	18-4	.818	1986	Bob Ojeda, New York	18-5	.783
1951	Preacher Roe, Brooklyn	22-3	.880	1987	Dwight Gooden, New York	15-7	.682
1952	Hoyt Wilhelm, New York	15-3	.833	1988	David Cone, New York	20-3	.870
1953	Carl Erskine, Brooklyn	20-6	.769	1989	Scott Garrelts, San Francisco	14-5	.737
1954	Johnny Antonelli, New York	21-7	.750		& Sid Fernandez, New York	14-5	.737
1955	Don Newcombe, Brooklyn	20-5	.800	1990	Doug Drabek, Pittsburgh	22-6	.786
1956	Don Newcombe, Brooklyn	27-7	.794				

Note: In 1984, Sutcliffe was also 4-5 with Cle.(AL) for a combined record of 20-6 (.769).

American League

Multiple winners: Lefty Grove (5); Chief Bender and Whitey Ford (3); Johnny Allen, Eddie Cicotte, Roger Clemens, Mike Cuellar, Lefty Gomez, Catfish Hunter, Walter Johnson, Jim Palmer, Pete Vuckovich and Smokey Joe Wood (2).

Year		W-L	Pct	Year		W-L	Pct
1901	Clark Griffith, Chicago	24-7	.774	1922	Joe Bush, New York	26-7	.788
1902	Bill Bernhard, Phila-Cleve	18-5	.783	1923	Herb Pennock, New York	19-6	.760
1903	Cy Young, Boston	28-9	.757	1924	Walter Johnson, Washington	23-7	.767
1904	Jack Chesbro, New York	41-12	.774	1925	Stan Coveleski, Washington	20-5	.800
1905	Andy Coakley, Philadelphia	20-7	.741	1926	George Uhle, Cleveland	27-11	.711
1906	Eddie Plank, Philadelphia	19-6	.760	1927	Waite Hoyt, New York	22-7	.759
1907	Wild Bill Donovan, Detroit	25-4	.862	1928	General Crowder, St. Louis	21-5	.808
1908	Ed Walsh, Chicago	40-15	.727	1929	Lefty Grove, Philadelphia	20-6	.769
1909	George Mullin, Detroit	29-8	.784	1930	Lefty Grove, Philadelphia	28-5	.848
1910	Chief Bender, Philadelphia	23-5	.821	1931	Lefty Grove, Philadelphia	31-4	.886
1911	Chief Bender, Philadelphia	17-5	.773	1932	Johnny Allen, New York	17-4	.810
1912	Smokey Joe Wood, Boston	34-5	.872	1933	Lefty Grove, Philadelphia	24-8	.750
1913	Walter Johnson, Washington	36-7	.837	1934	Lefty Gomez, New York	26-5	.839
1914	Chief Bender, Philadelphia	17-3	.850	1935	Eldon Auker, Detroit	18-7	.720
1915	Smokey Joe Wood, Boston	15-5	.750	1936	Monte Pearson, New York	19-7	.731
1916	Eddie Cicotte, Chicago	15-7	.682	1937	Johnny Allen, Cleveland	15-1	.938
1917	Reb Russell, Chicago	15-5	.750	1938	Red Ruffing, New York	21-7	.750
1918	Sad Sam Jones, Boston	16-5	.762	1939	Lefty Grove, Boston	15-4	.789
1919	Eddie Cicotte, Chicago	29-7	.806	1940	Schoolboy Rowe, Detroit	16-3	.842
1920	Jim Bagby, Cleveland	31-12	.721	1941	Lefty Gomez, New York	15-5	.750
1921	Carl Mays, New York	27-9	.750	1942	Ernie Bonham, New York	21-5	.808

Year	W-L	Pct	Year	W-L	Pct
1943 Spud Chandler, New York	20-4	.833	1968 Denny McLain, Detroit	31-6	.838
1944 Tex Hughson, Boston	18-5	.783	1969 Jim Palmer, Baltimore	16-4	.800
1945 Hal Newhouser, Detroit	25-9	.735	1970 Mike Cuellar, Baltimore	24-8	.750
1946 Boo Ferriss, Boston	25-6	.806	1971 Dave McNally, Baltimore	21-5	.808
1947 Allie Reynolds, New York	19-8	.704	1972 Catfish Hunter, Oakland	21-7	.750
1948 Jack Kramer, Boston	18-5	.783	1973 Catfish Hunter, Oakland	21-5	.808
1949 Ellis Kinder, Boston	23-6	.793	1974 Mike Cuellar, Baltimore	22-10	.688
1950 Vic Raschi, New York	21-8	.724	1975 Mike Torrez, Baltimore	20-9	.690
1951 Bob Feller, Cleveland	22-8	.733	1976 Bill Campbell, Minnesota	17-5	.773
1952 Bobby Shantz, Philadelphia	24-7	.774	1977 Paul Splittorff, Kansas City	16-6	.727
1953 Ed Lopat, New York	16-4	.800	1978 Ron Guidry, New York	25-3	.893
1954 Sandy Consuegra, Chicago	16-3	.842	1979 Mike Caldwell, Milwaukee	16-6	.727
1955 Tommy Byrne, New York	16-5	.762	1980 Steve Stone, Baltimore	25-7	.781
1956 Whitey Ford, New York	19-6	.760	1981 Pete Vuckovich, Milwaukee	14-4	.778
1957 Dick Donovan, Chicago	16-6	.727	1982 Pete Vuckovich, Milwaukee	18-6	.750
& Tom Sturdivant, New York	16-6	.727	& Jim Palmer, Baltimore	15-3	.750
1958 Bob Turley, New York	21-7	.750	1983 Rich Dotson, Chicago	22-7	.759
1959 Bob Shaw, Chicago	18-6	.750	1984 Doyle Alexander, Toronto	17-6	.739
1960 Jim Perry, Cleveland	18-10	.643	1985 Ron Guidry, New York	22-6	.786
1961 Whitey Ford, New York	25-4	.862	1986 Roger Clemens, Boston	24-4	.857
1962 Ray Herbert, Chicago	20-9	.690	1987 Roger Clemens, Boston	20-9	.690
1963 Whitey Ford, New York	24-7	.774	1988 Frank Viola, Minnesota	24-7	.774
1964 Wally Bunker, Baltimore	19-5	.792	1989 Bret Saberhagen, Kansas City	23-6	.793
1965 Mudcat Grant, Minnesota	21-7	.750	1990 Bob Welch, Oakland	27-6	.818
1966 Sonny Siebert, Cleveland	16-8	.667			
1967 Joe Horlen, Chicago	19-7	.731			

Earned Run Average

Earned Run Averages were based on at least 10 complete games pitched (1900-50), at least 154 innings pitched (1950-60), and at least 162 innings pitched since 1961 in the AL and 1962 in the NL. In the strike year of 1981, qualifiers had to pitch at least as many innings as the total number of games their team played that season.

National League

Multiple winners: Grover Alexander, Sandy Koufax and Christy Mathewson (5); Carl Hubbell, Tom Seaver, Warren Spahn and Dazzy Vance (3); Bill Doak, Ray Kremer, Dolf Luque, Howie Pollett, Nolan Ryan, Bill Walker and Bucky Walters (2).

Year	ERA	Year	ERA	Year	ERA
1900 Rube Waddell, Pit	2.37	1930 Dazzy Vance, Bklyn	2.61	1960 Mike McCormick, SF	2.70
1901 Jesse Tannehill, Pit	2.18	1931 Bill Walker, NY	2.26	1961 Warren Spahn, Mil	3.01
1902 Jack Taylor, Chi	1.33	1932 Lon Warneke, Chi	2.37	1962 Sandy Koufax, LA	2.54
1903 Sam Leever, Pit	2.06	1933 Carl Hubbell, NY	1.66	1963 Sandy Koufax, LA	1.88
1904 Joe McGinnity, NY	1.61	1934 Carl Hubbell, NY	2.30	1964 Sandy Koufax, LA	1.74
1905 Christy Mathewson, NY	1.27	1935 Cy Blanton, Pit	2.59	1965 Sandy Koufax, LA	2.04
1906 Three Finger Brown, Chi	1.04	1936 Carl Hubbell, NY	2.31	1966 Sandy Koufax, LA	1.73
1907 Jack Pfiester, Chi	1.15	1937 Jim Turner, Bos	2.38	1967 Phil Niekro, Atl	1.87
1908 Christy Mathewson, NY	1.43	1938 Bill Lee, Chi	2.66	1968 Bob Gibson, St.L	1.12
1909 Christy Mathewson, NY	1.14	1939 Bucky Walters, Cin	2.29	1969 Juan Marichal, SF	2.10
1910 George McQuillan, Phi	1.60	1940 Bucky Walters, Cin	2.48	1970 Tom Seaver, NY	2.81
1911 Christy Mathewson, NY	1.99	1941 Elmer Riddle, Cin	2.24	1971 Tom Seaver, NY	1.76
1912 Jeff Tesreau, NY	1.96	1942 Mort Cooper, St.L	1.77	1972 Steve Carlton, Phi	1.98
1913 Christy Mathewson, NY	2.06	1943 Howie Pollet, St.L	1.75	1973 Tom Seaver, NY	2.08
1914 Bill Doak, St.L	1.72	1944 Ed Heusser, Cin	2.38	1974 Buzz Capra, Atl	2.28
1915 Grover Alexander, Phi	1.22	1945 Hank Borowy, Chi	2.14	1975 Randy Jones, SD	2.24
1916 Grover Alexander, Phi	1.55	1946 Howie Pollet, St.L	2.10	1976 John Denny, St.L	2.52
1917 Grover Alexander, Phi	1.86	1947 Warren Spahn, Bos	2.33	1977 John Candelaria, Pit	2.34
1918 Hippo Vaughn, Chi	1.74	1948 Harry Brecheen, St.L	2.24	1978 Craig Swan, NY	2.43
1919 Grover Alexander, Chi	1.72	1949 Dave Koslo, NY	2.50	1979 J.R. Richard, Hou	2.71
1920 Grover Alexander, Chi	1.91	1950 Jim Hearn, St.L-NY	2.49	1980 Don Sutton, LA	2.21
1921 Bill Doak, St.L	2.59	1951 Chet Nichols, Bos	2.88	1981 Nolan Ryan, Hou	1.69
1922 Rosy Ryan, NY	3.01	1952 Hoyt Wilhelm, NY	2.43	1982 Steve Rogers, Mon	2.40
1923 Dolf Luque, Cin	1.93	1953 Warren Spahn, Mil	2.10	1983 Atlee Hammaker, SF	2.25
1924 Dazzy Vance, Bklyn	2.16	1954 Johnny Antonelli, NY	2.29	1984 Alejandro Pena, LA	2.48
1925 Dolf Luque, Cin	2.63	1955 Bob Friend, Pit	2.84	1985 Dwight Gooden, NY	1.53
1926 Ray Kremer, Pit	2.61	1956 Lew Burdette, Mil	2.71	1986 Mike Scott, Hou	2.22
1927 Ray Kremer, Pit	2.47	1957 Johnny Podres, Bklyn	2.66	1987 Nolan Ryan, Hou	2.76
1928 Dazzy Vance, Bklyn	2.09	1958 Stu Miller, SF	2.47	1988 Joe Magrane, St.L	2.18
1929 Bill Walker, NY	3.08	1959 Sam Jones, SF	2.82	1989 Scott Garrelts, SF	2.28
				1990 Danny Darwin, Hou	2.21

Note: In 1945, Borowy had a 3.13 ERA in 18 games with New York (AL) for a combined ERA of 2.65.

Earned Run Average (Cont.)
American League

Multiple winners: Lefty Grove (9); Walter Johnson (5); Spud Chandler, Roger Clemens, Stan Coveleski, Red Faber, Whitey Ford, Lefty Gomez, Ron Guidry, Addie Joss, Hal Newhouser, Jim Palmer, Gary Peters, Luis Tiant and Ed Walsh (2).

Year		ERA	Year		ERA	Year		ERA
1901	Cy Young, Bos	1.62	1930	Lefty Grove, Phi	2.54	1960	Frank Baumann, Chi	2.67
1902	Ed Siever, Det	1.91	1931	Lefty Grove, Phi	2.06	1961	Dick Donovan, Wash	2.40
1903	Earl Moore, Cle	1.77	1932	Lefty Grove, Phi	2.84	1962	Hank Aguirre, Det	2.21
1904	Addie Joss, Cle	1.59	1933	Monte Pearson, Cle	2.33	1963	Gary Peters, Chi	2.33
1905	Rube Waddell, Phi	1.48	1934	Lefty Gomez, NY	2.33	1964	Dean Chance, LA	1.65
1906	Doc White, Chi	1.52	1935	Lefty Grove, Bos	2.70	1965	Sam McDowell, Cle	2.18
1907	Ed Walsh, Chi	1.60	1936	Lefty Grove, Bos	2.81	1966	Gary Peters, Chi	1.98
1908	Addie Joss, Cle	1.16	1937	Lefty Gomez, NY	2.33	1967	Joe Horlen, Chi	2.06
1909	Harry Krause, Phi	1.39	1938	Lefty Grove, Bos	3.08	1968	Luis Tiant, Cle	1.60
1910	Ed Walsh, Chi	1.27	1939	Lefty Grove, Bos	2.54	1969	Dick Bosman, Wash	2.19
1911	Vean Gregg, Cle	1.81	1940	Bob Feller, Cle	2.61	1970	Diego Segui, Oak	2.56
1912	Walter Johnson, Wash	1.39	1941	Thorton Lee, Chi	2.37	1971	Vida Blue, Oak	1.82
1913	Walter Johnson, Wash	1.09	1942	Ted Lyons, Chi	2.10	1972	Luis Tiant, Bos	1.91
1914	Dutch Leonard, Bos	1.01	1943	Spud Chandler, NY	1.64	1973	Jim Palmer, Bal	2.40
1915	Smokey Joe Wood, Bos	1.49	1944	Dizzy Trout, Det	2.12	1974	Catfish Hunter, Oak	2.49
1916	Babe Ruth, Bos	1.75	1945	Hal Newhouser, Det	1.81	1975	Jim Palmer, Bal	2.09
1917	Eddie Cicotte, Chi	1.53	1946	Hal Newhouser, Det	1.94	1976	Mark Fidrych, Det	2.34
1918	Walter Johnson, Wash	1.27	1947	Spud Chandler, NY	2.46	1977	Frank Tanana, Cal	2.54
1919	Walter Johnson, Wash	1.49	1948	Gene Bearden, Cle	2.43	1978	Ron Guidry, NY	1.74
1920	Bob Shawkey, NY	2.45	1949	Mel Parnell, Bos	2.77	1979	Ron Guidry, NY	2.78
1921	Red Faber, Chi	2.48	1950	Early Wynn, Cle	3.20	1980	Rudy May, NY	2.47
1922	Red Faber, Chi	2.80	1951	Saul Rogovin, Det-Chi	2.78	1981	Steve McCatty, Oak	2.32
1923	Stan Coveleski, Cle	2.76	1952	Allie Reynolds, NY	2.06	1982	Rick Sutcliffe, Cle	2.96
1924	Walter Johnson, Wash	2.72	1953	Ed Lopat, NY	2.42	1983	Rick Honeycutt, Tex	2.42
1925	Stan Coveleski, Wash	2.84	1954	Mike Garcia, Cle	2.64	1984	Mike Boddicker, Bal	2.79
1926	Lefty Grove, Phi	2.51	1955	Billy Pierce, Chi	1.97	1985	Dave Stieb, Tor	2.48
1927	Wilcy Moore, NY	2.28	1956	Whitey Ford, NY	2.47	1986	Roger Clemens, Bos	2.48
1928	Garland Braxton, Wash	2.51	1957	Bobby Shantz, NY	2.45	1987	Jimmy Key, Tor	2.76
1929	Lefty Grove, Phi	2.81	1958	Whitey Ford, NY	2.01	1988	Allen Anderson, Min	2.45
			1959	Hoyt Wilhelm, Bal	2.19	1989	Bret Saberhagen, KC	2.16
						1990	Roger Clemens, Bos	1.93

Note #1: In 1927, Moore pitched only six complete games, but led the league anyway with 213 innings pitched.
Note #2: In 1940, Ernie Bonham of NY had a 1.90 ERA and 10 complete games, but appeared in only a total of 12 games and 99 innings.

Strikeouts
National League

Multiple winners: Dazzy Vance (7); Grover Alexander (6); Steve Carlton, Christy Mathewson and Tom Seaver (5); Dizzy Dean, Sandy Koufax and Warren Spahn (4); Don Drysdale, Sam Jones and Johnny Vander Meer (3); Dwight Gooden, Bill Hallahan, J.R. Richard, Robin Roberts, Nolan Ryan and Hippo Vaughn (2).

Year		SO	Year		SO	Year		SO
1900	Rube Waddell, Pit	130	1920	Grover Alexander, Chi	173	1940	Kirby Higbe, Phi	137
1901	Noodles Hahn, Cinn	239	1921	Burleigh Grimes, Bklyn	136	1941	John Vander Meer, Cin	202
1902	Vic Willis, Bos	225	1922	Dazzy Vance, Bklyn	134	1942	John Vander Meer, Cin	186
1903	Christy Mathewson, NY	267	1923	Dazzy Vance, Bklyn	197	1943	John Vander Meer, Cin	174
1904	Christy Mathewson, NY	212	1924	Dazzy Vance, Bklyn	262	1944	Bill Voiselle, NY	161
1905	Christy Mathewson, NY	206	1925	Dazzy Vance, Bklyn	221	1945	Preacher Roe, Pitt	148
1906	Fred Beebe, Chi-St.L	171	1926	Dazzy Vance, Bklyn	140	1946	Johnny Schmitz, Chi	135
1907	Christy Mathewson, NY	178	1927	Dazzy Vance, Bklyn	184	1947	Ewell Blackwell, Cin	193
1908	Christy Mathewson, NY	259	1928	Dazzy Vance, Bklyn	200	1948	Harry Brecheen, St.L	149
1909	Orval Overall, Chi	205	1929	Pat Malone, Chi	166	1949	Warren Spahn, Bos	151
1910	Earl Moore, Phi	185	1930	Bill Hallahan, St.L	177	1950	Warren Spahn, Bos	191
1911	Rube Marquard, NY	237	1931	Bill Hallahan, St.L	159	1951	Don Newcombe, Bklyn	164
1912	Grover Alexander, Phi	195	1932	Dizzy Dean, St.L	191		& Warren Spahn, Bos	164
1913	Tom Seaton, Phi	168	1933	Dizzy Dean, St.L	199	1952	Warren Spahn, Bos	183
1914	Grover Alexander, Phi	214	1934	Dizzy Dean, St.L	195	1953	Robin Roberts, Phi	198
1915	Grover Alexander, Phi	241	1935	Dizzy Dean, St.L	182	1954	Robin Roberts, Phi	185
1916	Grover Alexander, Phi	167	1936	Van Lingle Mungo, Bklyn	238	1955	Sam Jones, Chi	198
1917	Grover Alexander, Phi	201	1937	Carl Hubbell, NY	159	1956	Sam Jones, Chi	176
1918	Hippo Vaughn, Chi	148	1938	Clay Bryant, Chi	135	1957	Jack Sanford, Phi	188
1919	Hippo Vaughn, Chi	141	1939	Claude Passeau, Phi-Chi	137	1958	Sam Jones, St.L	225
				& Bucky Walters, Cin	137	1959	Don Drysdale, LA	242

Year	SO	Year	SO	Year	SO
1960 Don Drysdale, LA	246	1970 Tom Seaver, NY	283	1980 Steve Carlton, Phi	286
1961 Sandy Koufax, LA	269	1971 Tom Seaver, NY	289	1981 F. Valenzuela,LA	180
1962 Don Drysdale, LA	232	1972 Steve Carlton, Phi	310	1982 Steve Carlton, Phi	286
1963 Sandy Koufax, LA	306	1973 Tom Seaver, NY	251	1983 Steve Carlton, Phi	275
1964 Bob Veale, Pit	250	1974 Steve Carlton, Phi	240	1984 Dwight Gooden, NY	276
1965 Sandy Koufax, LA	382	1975 Tom Seaver, NY	243	1985 Dwight Gooden, NY	268
1966 Sandy Koufax, LA	317	1976 Tom Seaver, NY	235	1986 Mike Scott, Hou	306
1967 Jim Bunning, Phi	253	1977 Phil Niekro, Atl	262	1987 Nolan Ryan, Hou	270
1968 Bob Gibson, St.L	268	1978 J.R. Richard, Hou	303	1988 Nolan Ryan, Hou	228
1969 Ferguson Jenkins, Chi	273	1979 J.R. Richard, Hou	313	1989 Jose DeLeon, St.L	201
				1990 David Cone, NY	233

American League

Multiple winners: Walter Johnson (12); Nolan Ryan (9); Bob Feller and Lefty Grove (7); Rube Waddell (6); Sam McDowell (5); Lefty Gomez, Camilo Pascual and Mark Langston (3); Len Barker, Tommy Bridges, Jim Bunning, Hal Newhouser, Allie Reynolds, Herb Score, Ed Walsh and Early Wynn (2).

Year	SO	Year	SO	Year	SO
1901 Cy Young, Bos	158	1931 Lefty Grove, Phi	175	1961 Camilo Pascual, Min	221
1902 Rube Waddell, Phi	210	1932 Red Ruffing, NY	190	1962 Camilo Pascual, Min	206
1903 Rube Waddell, Phi	302	1933 Lefty Gomez, NY	163	1963 Camilo Pascual, Min	202
1904 Rube Waddell, Phi	349	1934 Lefty Gomez, NY	158	1964 Al Downing, NY	217
1905 Rube Waddell, Phi	287	1935 Tommy Bridges, Det	163	1965 Sam McDowell, Cle	325
1906 Rube Waddell, Phi	196	1936 Tommy Bridges, Det	175	1966 Sam McDowell, Cle	225
1907 Rube Waddell, Phi	232	1937 Lefty Gomez, NY	194	1967 Jim Lonborg, Bos	246
1908 Ed Walsh, Chi	269	1938 Bob Feller, Cle	240	1968 Sam McDowell, Cle	283
1909 Frank Smith, Chi	177	1939 Bob Feller, Cle	246	1969 Sam McDowell, Cle	279
1910 Walter Johnson, Wash	313	1940 Bob Feller, Cle	261	1970 Sam McDowell, Cle	304
1911 Ed Walsh, Chi	255	1941 Bob Feller, Cle	260	1971 Mike Lolich, Det	308
1912 Walter Johnson, Wash	303	1942 Tex Hughson, Bos	113	1972 Nolan Ryan, Cal	329
1913 Walter Johnson, Wash	243	& Bobo Newsom,Wash.	113	1973 Nolan Ryan, Cal	383
1914 Walter Johnson, Wash	225	1943 Allie Reynolds, Cle	151	1974 Nolan Ryan, Cal	367
1915 Walter Johnson, Wash	203	1944 Hal Newhouser, Det	187	1975 Frank Tanana, Cal	269
1916 Walter Johnson, Wash	228	1945 Hal Newhouser, Det	212	1976 Nolan Ryan, Cal	327
1917 Walter Johnson, Wash	188	1946 Bob Feller, Cle	348	1977 Nolan Ryan, Cal	341
1918 Walter Johnson, Wash	162	1947 Bob Feller, Cle	196	1978 Nolan Ryan, Cal	260
1919 Walter Johnson, Wash	147	1948 Bob Feller, Cle	164	1979 Nolan Ryan, Cal	223
1920 Stan Coveleski, Cle	133	1949 Virgil Trucks, Det	153		
1921 Walter Johnson, Wash	143	1950 Bob Lemon, Cle	170	1980 Len Barker, Cle	187
1922 Urban Shocker, St.L	149	1951 Vic Raschi, NY	164	1981 Len Barker, Cle	127
1923 Walter Johnson, Wash	130	1952 Allie Reynolds, NY	160	1982 Floyd Bannister, Sea	209
1924 Walter Johnson, Wash	158	1953 Billy Pierce Chi	186	1983 Jack Morris, Det	232
1925 Lefty Grove, Phi	116	1954 Bob Turley, Bal	185	1984 Mark Langston, Sea	204
1926 Lefty Grove, Phi	194	1955 Herb Score, Cle	245	1985 Bert Blyleven,Cle-Min	206
1927 Lefty Grove, Phi	174	1956 Herb Score, Cle	263	1986 Mark Langston, Sea	245
1928 Lefty Grove, Phi	183	1957 Early Wynn, Cle	184	1987 Mark Langston, Sea	262
1929 Lefty Grove, Phi	170	1958 Early Wynn, Chi	179	1988 Roger Clemens, Bos	291
1930 Lefty Grove, Phi	209	1959 Jim Bunning, Det	201	1989 Nolan Ryan, Tex	301
		1960 Jim Bunning, Det	201	1990 Nolan Ryan, Tex	232

Perfect Games

Fourteen pitchers have thrown perfect games (27 up, 27 down) in major league history.

National League

Pitcher	Game	Date	Score
Lee Richmond	Wor.vs Cle.	6/12/1880	1-0
Monte Ward	Prov.vs Bos.	6/17/1880	5-0
Harvey Haddix	Pit.at Mil.	5/26/1959	0-1*
Jim Bunning	Phi.at NY	6/21/1964	6-0
Sandy Koufax	LA vs Chi.	9/9/1965	1-0
Tom Browning	Cin.vs LA	9/16/1988	1-0

*Haddix pitched 12 perfect innings before losing in the 13th. Braves' lead-off batter Felix Mantilla reached on a throwing error by Pirates 3B Don Hoak, Eddie Mathews sacrificed Mantilla to 2nd, Hank Aaron was walked intentionally, and Joe Adcock hit a 3-run HR. Adcock, however, passed Aaron on the bases and was only credited with a 1-run double.

American League

Pitcher	Game	Date	Score
Cy Young	Bos.vs Phi.	5/5/1904	3-0
Adrian Joss	Cle.vs Chi.	10/2/1908	1-0
Ernie Shore	Bos.vs Wash.	6/23/1917	4-0*
Charlie Robertson	Chi.at Det.	4/30/1922	2-0
Catfish Hunter	Oak.vs Min.	5/8/1968	4-0
Len Barker	Cle.vs Tor.	5/15/1981	3-0
Mike Witt	Cal.at Tex.	9/30/1984	1-0

*Babe Ruth started for Boston, walking Senators' lead-off batter Ray Morgan then getting thrown out of the game for punching umpire Brick Owens while arguing the call. Shore came on in relief. Morgan was caught stealing and Shore retired the next 26 batters in a row.

World Series

Pitcher	Game	Date	Score
Don Larson	NY vs Bklyn	10/8/1956	2-0

Major League All-Time Leaders

CAREER

Batting

Through the 1990 regular season. Players active in 1990 in **bold type**. Note that (*) indicates left-handed hitter and (†) indicates switch-hitter. Active player leaders are listed for batting average, hits, HRs and RBI.

Batting Avg.

	Yrs	AB	H	Avg
1 Ty Cobb*	24	11,429	4191	.367
2 Rogers Hornsby	23	8,137	2930	.358
3 Joe Jackson*	13	4,981	1774	.356
4 **Wade Boggs***	9	5,153	1784	.346
5 Ed Delahanty*	16	7,502	2591	.345
6 Ted Williams*	19	7,706	2654	.344
7 Tris Speaker*	22	10,208	3515	.344
8 Billy Hamilton*	14	6,284	2163	.344
9 Willie Keeler*	19	8,585	2947	.343
10 Dan Brouthers*	19	6,711	2296	.342
11 Babe Ruth*	22	8,399	2873	.342
12 Harry Heilmann	17	7,787	2660	.342
13 Pete Browning	13	4,820	1646	.341
14 Bill Terry*	14	6,428	2193	.341
15 George Sisler*	15	8,267	2812	.340
16 Lou Gehrig*	17	8,001	2721	.340
17 Jesse Burkett*	16	8,413	2853	.339
18 Nap Lajoie	21	9,592	3244	.338
19 Riggs Stephenson	14	4,508	1515	.336
20 Al Simmons	20	8,761	2927	.334
21 Paul Waner*	20	9,459	3152	.333
22 Eddie Collins*	25	9,949	3311	.333
23 Stan Musial*	22	10,972	3630	.331
24 Sam Thompson*	14	6,005	1986	.331
25 Heinie Manush*	17	7,653	2524	.330

Hits

	Yrs	AB	H	Avg
1 Pete Rose†	24	14,053	4256	.303
2 Ty Cobb*	24	11,429	4191	.367
3 Hank Aaron	23	12,364	3771	.305
4 Stan Musial*	22	10,972	3630	.331
5 Tris Speaker*	22	10,208	3515	.344
6 Carl Yastrzemski*	23	11,988	3419	.285
7 Honus Wagner	21	10,441	3418	.327
8 Eddie Collins*	25	9,949	3311	.333
9 Willie Mays	22	10,881	3283	.302
10 Nap Lajoie	21	9,592	3244	.338
11 Paul Waner*	20	9,459	3152	.333
12 Rod Carew*	19	9,315	3053	.328
13 Lou Brock*	19	10,332	3023	.293
14 Al Kaline	22	10,116	3007	.297
15 Cap Anson	22	9,108	3000	.329
16 Roberto Clemente	18	9,454	3000	.317
17 Sam Rice*	20	9,269	2987	.322
18 Sam Crawford*	19	9,580	2964	.309
19 Willie Keeler*	19	8,585	2947	.343
20 Frank Robinson	21	10,006	2943	.294
21 Jake Beckley*	20	9,527	2931	.308
22 Rogers Hornsby	23	8,173	2930	.358
23 Al Simmons	20	8,761	2927	.334
24 Zack Wheat*	19	9,106	2884	.317
25 Frankie Frisch	19	9,112	2880	.316

Players Active in 1990

	Yrs	AB	H	Avg
1 Wade Boggs*	9	5153	1784	.346
2 Tony Gwynn*	9	4651	1531	.329
3 Kirby Puckett	7	4395	1405	.320
4 Don Mattingly*	9	4416	1401	.317
5 George Brett*	18	8692	2707	.311
6 Pedro Guerrero	13	4819	1470	.305
7 Tim Raines	12	5305	1598	.301
8 Paul Molitor	13	6246	1870	.299
9 Ken Griffey,Sr	18	7144	2119	.297
10 Keith Hernandez	17	7370	2182	.296

Players Active in 1990

	Yrs	AB	H	Avg
1 Robin Yount	17	9494	2747	.289
2 Bill Buckner*	22	9397	2715	.289
3 George Brett*	18	8692	2707	.311
4 Dave Parker†	18	8856	2592	.293
5 Dave Winfield	17	8896	2548	.286
6 Dwight Evans	19	8726	2373	.272
7 Eddie Murray†	14	7997	2352	.294
8 Andre Dawson	15	7785	2201	.282
9 Carlton Fisk	21	8055	2192	.272
10 Keith Hernandez*	17	7370	2182	.296

Games Played

1 Pete Rose	3562
2 Carl Yastrzemski	3308
3 Hank Aaron	3298
4 Ty Cobb	3034
5 Stan Musial	3026
6 Willie Mays	2992
7 Rusty Staub	2951
8 Brooks Robinson	2896
9 Al Kaline	2834
10 Eddie Collins	2826
11 Reggie Jackson	2820
12 Frank Robinson	2808
13 Tris Speaker	2789
Honus Wagner	2789
15 Tony Perez	2777
16 Mel Ott	2734
17 Graig Nettles	2700
18 Darrell Evans	2687
19 Rabbit Maranville	2670
20 Joe Morgan	2649

At Bats

1 Pete Rose	14,053
2 Hank Aaron	12,364
3 Carl Yastrzemski	11,988
4 Ty Cobb	11,429
5 Stan Musial	10,972
6 Willie Mays	10,881
7 Brooke Robinson	10,654
8 Honus Wagner	10,441
9 Lou Brock	10,332
10 Luis Aparicio	10,230
11 Tris Speaker	10,208
12 Al Kaline	10,116
13 Rabbit Maranville	10,078
14 Frank Robinson	10,006
15 Eddie Collins	9,949
16 Reggie Jackson	9,864
17 Tony Perez	9,778
18 Rusty Staub	9,720
19 Vada Pinson	9,645
20 Nap Lajoie	9,592

Total Bases

1 Hank Aaron	6856
2 Stan Musial	6134
3 Willie Mays	6066
4 Ty Cobb	5863
5 Babe Ruth	5793
6 Pete Rose	5752
7 Carl Yastrzemski	5539
8 Frank Robinson	5373
9 Tris Speaker	5104
10 Lou Gehrig	5059
11 Mel Ott	5041
12 Jimmie Foxx	4956
13 Ted Williams	4884
14 Honus Wagner	4868
15 Al Kaline	4852
16 Reggie Jackson	4834
17 Rogers Hornsby	4712
18 Ernie Banks	4706
19 Al Simmons	4685
20 Billy Williams	4599

Home Runs

	Yrs	AB	HR	Pct
1 Hank Aaron	23	12,364	755	6.1
2 Babe Ruth*	22	8,399	714	8.5
3 Willie Mays	22	10,881	660	6.1
4 Frank Robinson	21	10,006	586	5.9
5 Harmon Killebrew	22	8,147	573	7.0
6 Reggie Jackson*	21	9,864	563	5.7
7 Mike Schmidt	18	8,352	548	6.6
8 Mickey Mantle†	18	8,102	536	6.6
9 Jimmie Foxx	20	8,134	534	6.6
10 Ted Williams*	19	7,706	521	6.8
Willie McCovey*	22	8,197	521	6.4
12 Eddie Mathews*	17	8,537	512	6.0
Ernie Banks	19	9,421	512	5.4
14 Mel Ott*	22	9,456	511	5.4
15 Lou Gehrig*	17	8,001	493	6.2
16 Willie Stargell*	21	7,927	475	6.0
Stan Musial*	22	10,972	475	4.3
18 Carl Yastrzemski*	23	11,988	452	3.8
19 Dave Kingman	16	6,677	442	6.6
20 Billy Williams*	18	9,350	426	4.6
21 Darrell Evans*	21	8,973	414	4.6
22 Duke Snider*	18	7,161	407	5.7
23 Al Kaline	22	10,116	399	3.9
24 Graig Nettles*	22	8,986	390	4.3
25 Johnny Bench	17	7,658	389	5.1

Players Active in 1990

	Yrs	AB	HR	Pct
1 Dwight Evans	19	8726	379	4.3
2 Eddie Murray†	14	7997	379	4.7
3 Dave Winfield	17	8896	378	4.2
4 Dale Murphy	15	7312	378	5.2
5 Carlton Fisk	21	8055	354	4.4
6 Andre Dawson	15	7785	346	4.4
7 Dave Parker*	18	8856	328	3.7
8 Gary Carter	17	7438	313	4.2
9 Jack Clark	16	6109	307	5.0
10 Fred Lynn*	17	6925	306	4.4
11 Lance Parrish	14	6066	285	4.7
12 George Brett*	18	8692	281	3.2

Runs Batted In

	Yrs	Gm	RBI	P/G
1 Hank Aaron	23	3298	2297	.70
2 Babe Ruth*	22	2503	2211	.88
3 Lou Gehrig*	17	2164	1990	.92
4 Ty Cobb*	24	3034	1961	.65
5 Stan Musial*	22	3026	1951	.64
6 Jimmie Foxx	20	2317	1921	.83
7 Willie Mays	22	2992	1903	.64
8 Mel Ott*	22	2732	1861	.68
9 Carl Yastrzemski*	23	3308	1844	.56
10 Ted Williams*	19	2292	1839	.80
11 Al Simmons	20	2215	1827	.82
12 Frank Robinson	21	2808	1812	.65
13 Honus Wagner	21	2786	1732	.62
14 Cap Anson	22	2276	1715	.75
15 Reggie Jackson*	21	2820	1702	.60
16 Tony Perez	23	2777	1652	.59
17 Ernie Banks	19	2528	1636	.65
18 Goose Goslin*	18	2287	1609	.70
19 Nap Lajoie	21	2475	1599	.65
20 Mike Schmidt	18	2404	1595	.66
21 Rogers Hornsby	23	2259	1584	.70
Harmon Killebrew	22	2435	1584	.65
23 Al Kaline	22	2834	1583	.56
24 Jake Beckley*	20	2386	1575	.66
25 Tris Speaker*	22	2789	1559	.56

Players Active in 1990

	Yrs	Gm	RBI	P/G
1 Dave Winfield	17	2401	1516	.63
2 Dave Parker*	18	2334	1434	.61
3 George Brett*	18	2279	1398	.61
4 Eddie Murray†	14	2135	1373	.64
5 Dwight Evans	19	2505	1346	.54
6 Andre Dawson	15	2018	1231	.61
Carlton Fisk	21	2278	1231	.54
8 Bill Buckner*	22	2517	1208	.48
9 Robin Yount*	17	2449	1201	.49
10 Dale Murphy	15	1983	1171	.59
11 Gary Carter	17	2100	1170	.56
12 Fred Lynn*	17	1969	1111	.56

Runs

1 Ty Cobb	2245
2 Babe Ruth	2174
Hank Aaron	2174
4 Pete Rose	2165
5 Willie Mays	2062
6 Stan Musial	1949
7 Lou Gehrig	1888
8 Tris Speaker	1881
9 Mel Ott	1859
10 Frank Robinson	1829
11 Eddie Collins	1818
12 Carl Yastrzemski	1816
13 Ted Williams	1798
14 Charlie Gehringer	1774
15 Jimmie Foxx	1751
16 Honus Wagner	1735
17 Willie Keeler	1727
18 Cap Anson	1719
19 Jesse Burkett	1718
20 Billy Hamilton	1692

Extra Base Hits

1 Hank Aaron	1477
2 Stan Musial	1377
3 Babe Ruth	1356
4 Willie Mays	1323
5 Lou Gehrig	1190
6 Frank Robinson	1186
7 Carl Yastrzemski	1157
8 Ty Cobb	1139
9 Tris Speaker	1132
10 Ted Williams	1117
Jimmie Foxx	1117
12 Reggie Jackson	1075
13 Mel Ott	1071
14 Pete Rose	1041
15 Mike Schmidt	1015
16 Rogers Hornsby	1011
17 Ernie Banks	1009
18 Honus Wagner	996
19 Al Simmons	995
20 Al Kaline	972

Slugging Avg.

1 Babe Ruth	.690
2 Ted Williams	.634
3 Lou Gehrig	.632
4 Jimmie Foxx	.609
5 Hank Greenberg	.605
6 Joe DiMaggio	.579
7 Rogers Hornsby	.577
8 Johnny Mize	.562
9 Stan Musial	.559
10 Willie Mays	.557
11 Mickey Mantle	.557
12 Hank Aaron	.555
13 Ralph Kiner	.548
14 Hack Wilson	.545
15 Chuck Klein	.543
16 Duke Snider	.540
17 Frank Robinson	.537
18 Al Simmons	.535
19 Dick Allen	.534
20 Earl Averill	.533

Major League All-Time Leaders (Cont.)

Stolen Bases		Bases on Balls		Strikeouts	
1 Lou Brock	938	1 Babe Ruth	2056	1 Reggie Jackson	2597
2 **Rickey Henderson**	936	2 Ted Williams	2019	2 Willie Stargell	1936
3 Billy Hamilton	915	3 Joe Morgan	1865	3 Mike Schmidt	1883
4 Ty Cobb	892	4 Carl Yastrzemski	1845	4 Tony Perez	1867
5 Eddie Collins	743	5 Mickey Mantle	1734	5 Dave Kingman	1816
6 Max Carey	738	6 Mel Ott	1708	6 Bobby Bonds	1757
7 Honus Wagner	703	7 Eddie Yost	1614	7 Lou Brock	1730
8 Joe Morgan	689	8 Darrell Evans	1605	8 Mickey Mantle	1710
9 Arlie Latham	679	9 Stan Musial	1599	9 Harmon Killebrew	1699
10 Bert Campaneris	649	10 Pete Rose	1566	10 **Dwight Evans**	1643
11 **Tim Raines**	634	11 Harmon Killebrew	1559	11 **Dale Murphy**	1627
12 Tom Brown	627	12 Lou Gehrig	1508	12 Lee May	1570
13 George Davis	615	13 Mike Schmidt	1507	13 Dick Allen	1556
14 **Willie Wilson**	612	14 Eddie Collins	1503	14 Willie McCovey	1550
15 Hugh Duffy	583	15 Willie Mays	1463	15 Frank Robinson	1532
16 Dummy Hoy	597	16 Jimmie Foxx	1452	16 Willie Mays	1526
17 Maury Wills	586	17 Eddie Mathews	1444	17 Rick Monday	1513
18 George Van Haltren	583	18 Frank Robinson	1420	18 Greg Luzinski	1495
19 Davey Lopes	557	19 Hank Aaron	1402	19 Eddie Mathews	1487
20 Cesar Cedeno	550	20 Tris Speaker	1381	20 Frank Howard	1460

Pitching

Through the 1990 regular season. Players active in 1990 in **bold type**. Note that (*) indicates left-handed pitcher. Active pitcher leaders are listed for wins, strikeouts and saves.

Wins

	Yrs	GS	W	L	Pct
1 Cy Young	22	815	511	315	.619
2 Walter Johnson	21	666	416	279	.599
3 Christy Mathewson	17	551	373	188	.665
Grover Alexander	20	598	373	208	.642
5 Warren Spahn*	21	665	363	245	.597
6 Kid Nichols	15	561	361	208	.634
Pud Galvin	14	682	361	308	.540
8 Tim Keefe	14	594	342	225	.603
9 Steve Carlton*	24	709	329	244	.574
10 Eddie Plank*	17	527	327	193	.629
11 John Clarkson	12	518	326	177	.648
12 Don Sutton	23	756	324	256	.559
13 Phil Niekro	24	716	318	274	.537
14 Gaylord Perry	22	690	314	265	.542
15 Old Hoss Radbourn	12	503	311	194	.616
Tom Seaver	20	647	311	205	.603
17 Mickey Welch	13	549	308	209	.596
18 **Nolan Ryan**	24	706	302	272	.526
19 Lefty Grove*	17	456	300	141	.680
Early Wynn	23	612	300	244	.551
21 Tommy John*	26	700	288	231	.555
22 Robin Roberts	19	609	286	245	.539
23 Tony Mullane	13	505	285	220	.564
24 Ferguson Jenkins	19	594	284	226	.557
25 Jim Kaat*	25	625	283	237	.544
26 Bert Blyleven	21	661	279	238	.540
27 Red Ruffing	22	536	273	225	.548
28 Burleigh Grimes	19	495	270	212	.560
29 Jim Palmer	19	521	268	152	.638
30 Bob Feller	18	484	266	162	.621

Strikeouts

	Yrs	IP	SO	P/9
1 **Nolan Ryan**	24	4991	5308	9.58
2 Steve Carlton*	24	5217	4136	7.13
3 Tom Seaver	20	4783	3640	6.85
4 **Bert Blyleven**	21	4837	3631	6.76
5 Don Sutton	23	5280	3574	6.09
6 Gaylord Perry	22	5351	3534	5.94
7 Walter Johnson	21	5924	3508	5.33
8 Phil Niekro	24	5403	3342	5.57
9 Ferguson Jenkins	19	4500	3192	6.38
10 Bob Gibson	17	3885	3117	7.22
11 Jim Bunning	17	3760	2855	6.83
12 Mickey Lolich*	16	3639	2832	7.00
13 Cy Young	22	7356	2796	3.42
14 Warren Spahn*	21	5244	2583	4.43
15 Bob Feller	18	3827	2581	6.07
16 Jerry Koosman*	19	3839	2556	5.99
17 Tim Keefe	14	5061	2527	4.50
18 Christy Mathewson	17	4782	2502	4.71
19 Don Drysdale	14	3432	2486	6.52
20 Jim Kaat*	25	4528	2461	4.89
25 **Frank Tanana***	18	3581	2459	6.18
21 Sam McDowell*	15	2493	2453	8.86
22 Luis Tiant	19	3486	2416	6.24
23 Sandy Koufax*	12	2324	2396	9.29
24 Robin Roberts	19	4689	2357	4.52
26 Early Wynn	23	4564	2334	4.60
27 Rube Waddell*	13	2961	2316	7.04
28 Juan Marichal	16	3509	2303	5.91
29 Lefty Grove*	17	3941	2266	5.17
30 Eddie Plank*	17	4505	2246	4.48

Pitchers Active in 1990

	Yrs	GS	W	L	Pct
1 Nolan Ryan	24	706	302	272	.526
2 Bert Blyleven	21	661	279	238	.540
3 Jerry Reuss*	22	547	220	191	.535
4 Rick Reuschel	18	528	214	189	.531
5 Frank Tanana*	18	520	207	196	.514
6 Jack Morris	14	408	198	150	.569
7 Charlie Hough	21	329	186	169	.524
8 Bob Welch	13	371	176	109	.618
9 John Candelaria*	16	356	174	113	.606
10 Dennis Eckersley	16	361	169	138	.550

Pitchers Active in 1990

	Yrs	IP	SO	P/9
1 Nolan Ryan	24	4991	5308	9.58
2 Bert Blyleven	21	4837	3631	6.76
3 Frank Tanana*	18	3581	2459	6.18
4 Rick Reuschel	18	3539	2011	5.12
5 Jerry Reuss*	22	3669	1907	4.67
6 Charlie Hough	21	3106	1988	5.76
7 Dennis Eckersley	16	2815	1938	6.19
8 Jack Morris	14	3043	1980	5.86
9 Fernando Valenzuela	11	2349	1759	6.74
10 Bob Welch	13	2512	1714	6.14

Note: Eckersley also has 146 saves (142 since 1987).

Winning Pct.

		Yrs	W-L	Pct
1	Bob Caruthers	9	218-97	.692
2	Dave Foutz	11	147-66	.690
3	Whitey Ford*	16	236-106	.690
4	Lefty Grove*	17	300-141	.680
5	Vic Raschi	10	132-66	.667
6	Christy Mathewson	17	373-188	.665
7	Larry Corcoran	8	177-90	.663
8	Sam Leever	13	194-101	.658
9	Sal Maglie	10	119-62	.657
10	Sandy Koufax*	12	165-87	.655
11	Johnny Allen	13	142-75	.654
12	Ron Guidry*	14	170-91	.651
13	Lefty Gomez*	14	189-102	.649
14	Three Finger Brown	14	239-129	.649
15	John Clarkson	12	326-177	.648
16	Dizzy Dean	12	150-83	.644
17	Grover Alexander	20	373-208	.642
18	Deacon Phillippe	13	189-107	.639
19	Jim Palmer	19	268-152	.638
20	Kid Nichols	15	361-208	.634

Losses

		Yrs	GS	W	L	Pct
1	Cy Young	22	815	511	313	.620
2	Pud Galvin	14	682	361	310	.538
3	Walter Johnson	21	666	416	279	.599
4	Phil Niekro	24	716	318	274	.537
5	Nolan Ryan	24	706	302	272	.526
6	Gaylord Perry	22	690	314	265	.542
7	Jack Powell	16	517	245	256	.489
	Don Sutton	23	756	324	256	.559
9	Eppa Rixey*	21	552	266	251	.515
10	Robin Roberts	19	609	286	245	.539
11	Warren Spahn*	21	665	363	245	.597
12	Early Wynn	23	612	300	244	.551
13	Steve Carlton*	24	709	329	244	.574
14	Bert Blyleven	21	661	279	238	.544
15	Jim Kaat	25	625	283	237	.544
16	Gus Weyhing	14	503	264	235	.529
17	Tommy John*	26	700	288	231	.555
18	Ted Lyons	21	484	260	230	.531
19	Bob Friend	16	497	197	230	.461
20	Ferguson Jenkins	19	594	284	226	.557

Games

1	Hoyt Wilhelm	1070
2	Kent Tekulve	1050
3	Lindy McDaniel	987
4	Rollie Fingers	944
5	Gene Garber	931
6	Cy Young	906
7	Sparky Lyle	899
8	Jim Kaat	898
9	Don McMahon	874
10	Phil Niekro	864
11	Goose Gossage	853
12	Roy Face	848
13	Tug McGraw	824
14	Walter Johnson	801
15	Gaylord Perry	777

Innings Pitched

1	Cy Young	7356
2	Pud Galvin	5941
3	Walter Johnson	5923
4	Phil Niekro	5403
5	Gaylord Perry	5351
6	Don Sutton	5280
7	Warren Spahn	5244
8	Steve Carlton	5217
9	Grover Alexander	5189
10	Kid Nichols	5084
11	Tim Keefe	5061
12	Nolan Ryan	4991
13	Bert Blyleven	4837
14	Mickey Welch	4802
15	Tom Seaver	4783

Earned Run Avg.

1	Ed Walsh	1.82
2	Addie Joss	1.88
3	Three Finger Brown	2.06
4	Monte Ward	2.10
5	Christy Mathewson	2.13
6	Rube Waddell	2.16
7	Walter Johnson	2.17
8	Orval Overall	2.24
9	Tommy Bond	2.25
10	Will White	2.28
11	Ed Reulbach	2.28
12	Jim Scott	2.32
13	Eddie Plank	2.34
14	Larry Corcoran	2.36
15	Eddie Cicotte	2.37

Shutouts

1	Walter Johnson	110
2	Grover Alexander	90
3	Christy Mathewson	80
4	Cy Young	76
5	Eddie Plank	69
6	Warren Spahn	63
7	Tom Seaver	61
8	Bert Blyleven	60
9	Nolan Ryan	59
10	Don Sutton	58
11	Three Finger Brown	57
	Pud Galvin	57
	Ed Walsh	57
14	Bob Gibson	56
15	Steve Carlton	55

Walks Allowed

1	Nolan Ryan	2614
2	Steve Carlton	1833
3	Phil Niekro	1809
4	Early Wynn	1775
5	Bob Feller	1764
6	Bobo Newsom	1732
7	Amos Rusie	1704
8	Gus Weyhing	1566
9	Red Ruffing	1541
10	Bump Hadley	1442
11	Warren Spahn	1434
12	Earl Whitehill	1431
13	Tony Mullane	1409
14	Sad Sam Jones	1396
15	Tom Seaver	1390

HRs Allowed

1	Robin Roberts	505
2	Ferguson Jenkins	484
3	Phil Niekro	482
4	Don Sutton	472
5	Warren Spahn	434
6	Steve Carlton	414
7	Garlord Perry	399
8	Bert Blyleven	413
9	Jim Kaat	395
10	Tom Seaver	380
11	Catfish Hunter	374
12	Jim Bunning	372
	Frank Tanana	372
14	Mickey Lolich	347
15	Luis Tiant	346

Saves

1	Rollie Fingers	341	8	Hoyt Wilhelm	227	14	Kent Tekulve	184	20 Tom Henke 154
2	Rich Gossage	307	9	Dave Righetti	224	15	John Franco	181	Stu Miller 154
3	Bruce Sutter	300	10	Gene Garber	218	16	Tug McGraw	180	22 Don McMahon 153
4	Jeff Reardon	287	11	Dave Smith	199	17	Ron Perranoski	179	23 Greg Minton 150
5	Lee Smith	261	12	Roy Face	193	18	Steve Bedrosian	178	24 Ted Abernathy 148
6	Dan Quisenberry	244	13	Mike Marshall	188	19	Lindy McDaniel	172	Bobby Thigpen 148
7	Sparky Lyle	238							

Relief Pitchers Active in 1990

1	Jeff Reardon	287	5	John Franco	181	9	Bobby Thigpen	148	13 Roger McDowell 125
2	Lee Smith	261	6	Steve Bedrosian	178	10	Dennis Eckersley	145	14 Dan Plesac 124
3	Dave Righetti	224	7	Tom Henke	154	11	Jay Howell	133	15 Doug Jones 121
4	Dave Smith	199	8	Greg Minton	150	12	Todd Worrell	126	Jesse Orosco 121

Major League All-Time Leaders (Cont.)

SINGLE SEASON

Batting

Through the 1990 regular season.

Batting Average

From 1900-49

	Year	AB	H	Avg
1 Rogers Hornsby, StL-NL	1924	536	227	.424
2 Nap Lajoie, Phi-AL	1901	543	229	.422
3 George Sisler, StL-AL	1922	586	246	.420
Ty Cobb, Det	1911	591	248	.420
5 Ty Cobb, Det	1912	533	227	.410
6 Joe Jackson, Cle	1911	571	233	.408
7 George Sisler, StL-AL	1920	631	257	.407
8 Ted Williams, Bos-AL	1941	456	185	.406
9 Rogers Hornsby, StL-NL	1925	504	203	.403
10 Harry Heilmann, Det	1923	524	211	.403

Since 1950

	Year	AB	H	Avg
1 George Brett, KC	1980	449	175	.390
2 Ted Williams, Bos	1957	420	163	.388
Rod Carew, Min	1977	616	239	.388
4 Tony Gwynn, SD	1987	589	218	.370
5 Wade Boggs, Bos	1985	653	240	.368
6 Wade Boggs, Bos	1988	584	214	.366
Rico Carty, Atl	1970	478	175	.366
8 Mickey Mantle, NY-AL	1957	474	173	.365
9 Rod Carew, Min	1974	599	218	.364
10 Joe Torre, St.L	1971	634	230	.363
Wade Boggs, Bos	1987	551	200	.363

Hits

	Year	AB	H	Avg
1 George Sisler, StL-AL	1920	631	257	.407
2 Bill Terry, NY-NL	1930	633	254	.401
Lefty O'Doul, Phi-NL	1929	638	254	.398
4 Al Simmons, Phi-AL	1925	658	253	.384
5 Rogers Hornsby, StL-NL	1922	623	250	.401
6 Chuck Klein, Phi-NL	1930	648	250	.386
7 Ty Cobb, Det	1911	591	248	.420
8 George Sisler, StL-AL	1922	586	246	.420
9 Babe Herman, Bklyn	1930	614	241	.393
Heinie Manush, StL-AL	1928	638	241	.378
11 Wade Boggs, Bos	1985	653	240	.368
12 Rod Carew, Min	1977	616	239	.388
13 Don Mattingly, NY-AL	1986	677	238	.352
14 Harry Heilmann, Det	1921	602	237	.394
Paul Waner, Pit	1927	623	237	.380
Joe Medwick, StL-NL	1937	633	237	.374
17 Jack Tobin, StL-AL	1921	671	236	.352
18 Rogers Hornsby, StL-NL	1921	592	235	.397

Home Runs

	Year	Gm	AB	HR
1 Roger Maris, NY-AL	1961	162	590	61
2 Babe Ruth, NY-AL	1927	151	540	60
3 Babe Ruth, NY-AL	1921	152	540	59
4 Hank Greenberg, Det	1938	155	556	58
Jimmie Foxx, Phi-AL	1932	154	585	58
6 Hack Wilson, Chi-NL	1930	155	585	56
7 Babe Ruth, NY-AL	1920	142	458	54
Mickey Mantle, NY-AL	1961	153	514	54
Babe Ruth, NY-AL	1928	154	536	54
Ralph Kiner, Pit	1949	152	549	54
11 Mickey Mantle, NY-AL	1956	150	533	52
Willie Mays, SF	1965	157	558	52
George Foster, Cin	1977	158	615	52
14 Ralph Kiner, Pit	1947	152	565	51
Cecil Fielder, Det	1990	159	573	51
Willie Mays, NY-NL	1955	152	580	51
Johnny Mize, NY-NL	1947	154	586	51
18 Jimmie Foxx, Bos-AL	1938	149	565	50

Runs Batted In

From 1900-49

	Year	Avg	HR	RBI
1 Hack Wilson, Chi-NL	1930	.356	56	190
2 Lou Gehrig, NY-AL	1931	.341	46	184
3 Hank Greenberg, Det	1937	.337	40	183
4 Lou Gehrig, NY-AL	1927	.373	47	175
Jimmie Foxx, Bos-AL	1938	.349	50	175
6 Lou Gehrig, NY-AL	1930	.379	41	174
7 Babe Ruth, NY-AL	1921	.378	59	171
8 Chuck Klein, Phi-NL	1930	.386	40	170
Hank Greenberg, Det	1935	.328	36	170
10 Jimmie Foxx, Phi-AL	1932	.364	58	169

Total Bases

From 1900-49

	Year	TB
1 Babe Ruth, New York-AL	1921	457
2 Rogers Hornsby, St.Louis-NL	1922	450
3 Lou Gehrig, New York-AL	1927	447
4 Chuck Klein, Philadelphia-NL	1930	445
5 Jimmie Foxx, Philadelphia-AL	1932	438
6 Stan Musial, St.Louis-NL	1948	429
7 Hack Wilson, Chicago-NL	1930	423
8 Chuck Klein, Philadelphia-NL	1932	420
9 Lou Gehrig, New York-AL	1930	419
10 Joe DiMaggio, New York-AL	1937	418

Since 1950

	Year	Avg	HR	RBI
1 Tommy Davis, LA-NL	1962	.346	27	153
2 George Foster, Cin	1977	.320	52	149
3 Johnny Bench, Cin	1970	.293	45	148
4 Al Rosen, Cle	1953	.336	43	145
Don Mattingly, NY-AL	1985	.324	35	145
6 Walt Dropo, Bos-AL	1950	.322	34	144
Vern Stephens, Bos-AL	1950	.295	30	144
8 Ernie Banks, Chi-NL	1959	.304	45	143
9 Roy Campanella, Bklyn	1953	.312	41	142
Orlando Cepeda, SF	1961	.311	46	142
Roger Maris, NY-AL	1961	.269	61	142

Since 1950

	Year	TB
1 Jim Rice, Boston	1978	406
2 Hank Aaron, Milwaukee	1959	400
3 George Foster, Cincinnati	1977	388
Don Mattingly, New York-AL	1986	388
5 Willie Mays, New York-NL	1955	382
Willie Mays, San Francisco	1962	382
Jim Rice, Boston	1977	382
8 Frank Robinson, Cincinnati	1962	380
9 Ernie Banks, Chicago-NL	1958	379
10 Duke Snider, Brooklyn	1954	378

Runs

	Year	Runs
1 Babe Ruth, New York-AL	1921	177
2 Lou Gehrig, New York-AL	1936	167
3 Babe Ruth, New York-AL	1928	163
Lou Gehrig, New York-AL	1931	163
5 Babe Ruth, New York-AL	1920	158
Babe Ruth, New York-AL	1927	158
Chuck Klein, Philadelphia-NL	1930	158
8 Rogers Hornsby, Chicago-NL	1929	156
9 Kiki Cuyler, Chicago-NL	1930	155
10 Lefty O'Doul, Philadelphia-NL	1929	152
Woody English, Chicago-NL	1930	152
Al Simmons, Philadelphia-AL	1930	152
Chuck Klein, Philadelphia-NL	1932	152
14 Babe Ruth, New York-AL	1923	151
Jimmie Foxx, Philadelphia-AL	1932	151
Joe DiMaggio, New York-AL	1937	151
17 Babe Ruth, New York-AL	1930	150
Ted Williams, Boston-AL	1940	150
19 Lou Gehrig, New York-AL	1927	149
Babe Ruth, New York-AL	1931	149

Stolen Bases

	Year	SB
1 Rickey Henderson, Oakland	1982	130
2 Lou Brock, St.Louis	1974	118
3 Vince Coleman, St.Louis	1985	110
4 Vince Coleman, St.Louis	1987	109
5 Rickey Henderson, Oakland	1983	108
6 Vince Coleman, St.LOuis	1986	107
7 Maury Wills, Los Angeles-NL	1962	104
8 Rickey Henderson, Oakland	1980	100
9 Ron LeFlore, Montreal	1980	97
10 Ty Cobb, Detroit	1915	96
11 Omar Moreno, Pittsburgh	1980	96
12 Maury Wills, Los Angeles	1965	94
13 Rickey Henderson, New York-AL	1988	93
14 Tim Raines, Montreal	1983	90
15 Clyde Milan, Washington	1912	88
16 Rickey Henderson, New York-AL	1986	87
17 Ty Cobb, Detroit	1911	83
Willie Wilson, Kansas City	1979	83
19 Bob Bescher, Cincinnati	1911	81
Eddie Collins, Philadelphia-AL	1910	81
Vince Coleman, St.Louis	1988	81

Bases on Balls

	Year	BB
1 Babe Ruth, New York-AL	1923	170
2 Ted Williams, Boston-AL	1947	162
Ted Williams, Boston-AL	1949	162
4 Ted Williams, Boston-AL	1946	156
5 Eddie Yost, Washington	1956	151
6 Eddie Joost, Philadelphia-AL	1949	149
7 Babe Ruth, New York-AL	1920	148
Eddie Stanky, Brooklyn	1945	148
Jimmy Wynn, Houston	1969	148
10 Jimmy Sheckard, Chicago-NL	1911	147
11 Mickey Mantle, New York-AL	1957	146
12 Ted Williams, Boston-AL	1941	145
Ted Williams, Boston-AL	1942	145
Harmon Killebrew, Minnesota	1969	145
15 Babe Ruth, New York-AL	1921	144

Strikeouts

	Year	SO
1 Bobby Bonds, San Francisco	1970	189
2 Bobby Bonds, San Francisco	1969	187
3 Rob Deer, Milwaukee	1987	186
4 Pete Incaviglia, Texas	1986	185
5 Cecil Fielder, Detroit	1990	182
6 Mike Schmidt, Philadelphia	1975	180
7 Rob Deer, Milwaukee	1986	179
8 Dave Nicholson, Chicago-AL	1963	175
Gorman Thomas, Milwaukee	1979	175
Jose Canseco, Oakland	1986	175
11 Jim Presley, Seattle	1986	172
Bo Jackson, Kansas City	1989	172
13 Reggie Jackson, Oakland	1968	171
14 Gorman Thomas, Milwaukee	1980	170
15 Andres Galarraga, Montreal	1990	169

Extra Base Hits

	Year	EBH
1 Babe Ruth, New York-AL	1921	119
2 Lou Gehrig, New York-AL	1927	117
3 Chuck Klein, Philadelphia-NL	1930	107
5 Chuck Klein, Philadelphia-NL	1932	103
Hank Greenberg, Detroit	1937	103
Stan Musial, St.Louis-NL	1948	103
7 Rogers Hornsby, St.Louis-NL	1922	102
8 Lou Gehrig, New York-AL	1930	100
Jimmie Foxx, Philadelphia	1933	100

Pinch Hits

Career pinch hits in parentheses.

	Year	PH	
1 Jose Morales, Mon	1976	25	(123)
2 Dave Philley, Bal	1961	24	(93)
Vic Davalillo, St.L	1970	24	(95)
Rusty Staub, NY-NL	1983	24	(100)
5 Wallace Johnson, Mon	1988	22	(78)
Peanuts Lowrey, St.L	1953	22	(62)
Sam Leslie, NY-NL	1932	22	(59)
Red Schoendienst, St.L	1962	22	(56)

Note: The All-Time career pinch hit leader is Manny Mota (150), followed by Smoky Burgess (145) an Greg Gross (143).

Slugging Average

From 1900-49

	Year	Avg
1 Babe Ruth, New York-AL	1920	.847
2 Babe Ruth, New York-AL	1921	.846
3 Babe Ruth, New York-AL	1927	.772
4 Lou Gehrig, New York-AL	1927	.765
5 Babe Ruth, New York-AL	1923	.764
6 Rogers Hornsby, St.Louis-NL	1925	.756
7 Jimmie Foxx, Philadelphia-AL	1932	.749
8 Babe Ruth, New York-AL	1924	.739
9 Babe Ruth, New York-AL	1926	.737
10 Ted Williams, Boston-AL	1941	.735

Since 1950

	Year	Avg
1 Ted Williams, Boston-AL	1957	.731
2 Mickey Mantle, New York-AL	1956	.705
3 Mickey Mantle, New York-AL	1961	.687
4 Hank Aaron, Atlanta	1971	.669
5 Willie Mays, New York-NL	1954	.667
6 Mickey Mantle, New York-AL	1957	.665
7 George Brett, Kansas City	1980	.664
8 Norm Cash, Detroit	1961	.662
9 Willie Mays, New York-NL	1955	.659
10 Willie McCovey, San Francisco	1969	.656

Major League All-Time Leaders (Cont.)

Pitching

Through the 1990 regular season.

Wins

From 1900-49

	Year	W	L	Pct
1 Jack Chesbro, NY-AL	1904	41	12	.774
2 Ed Walsh, Chi-AL	1908	40	15	.727
3 Christy Mathewson, NY-NL	1908	37	11	.771
4 Walter Johnson, Wash	1913	36	7	.837
5 Joe McGinnity, NY-NL	1904	35	8	.814
6 Smokey Joe Wood, Bos-AL	1912	34	5	.872
7 Cy Young, Bos-AL	1901	33	10	.767
Grover Alexander, Phi-NL	1916	33	12	.733
Christy Mathewson, NY-NL	1904	33	12	.733

Since 1950

	Year	W	L	Pct
1 Denny McLain, Det	1968	31	6	.838
2 Robin Roberts, Phi-NL	1952	28	7	.800
3 Bob Welch, Oak	1990	27	6	.818
4 Don Newcombe, Bklyn	1956	27	7	.794
Sandy Koufax, LA	1966	27	9	.750
6 Steve Carlton, Phi	1972	27	10	.730
7 Sandy Koufax, LA	1965	26	8	.765
Juan Marichal, SF	1968	26	9	.743

Note: 11 pitchers tied with 25 wins, including Marichal twice.

Earned Run Average

From 1900-1949

	Year	ShO	ERA
1 Dutch Leonard, Bos-AL	1914	7	1.01
2 Three Finger Brown,	1906	10	1.04
3 Walter Johnson, Wash	1913	11	1.09
4 Bob Gibson, St.L	1968	13	1.12
5 Christy Mathewson, NY-NL	1909	8	1.14
6 Jack Pfiester, Chi-NL	1907	3	1.15
7 Addie Joss, Cle	1908	9	1.16
8 Carl Lundgren, Chi-NL	1907	7	1.17
9 Grover Alexander, Phi-NL	1915	12	1.22
10 Cy Young, Bos-AL	1908	3	1.26

Since 1950

	Year	ShO	ERA
1 Bob Gibson, St.L	1968	13	1.12
2 Dwight Gooden, NY-NL	1985	8	1.53
3 Luis Tiant, Cle	1968	9	1.60
4 Dean Chance, LA-AL	1964	11	1.65
5 Nolan Ryan, Cal	1981	5	1.69
6 Sandy Koufax, LA	1966	5	1.73
7 Sandy Koufax, LA	1964	7	1.74
8 Ron Guidry, NY-AL	1978	9	1.74
9 Tom Seaver, NY-NL	1971	4	1.76
10 Sam McDowell, Cle	1968	3	1.81

Winning Pct.

	Year	W-L	Pct
1 Roy Face, Pit	1959	18-1	.947
2 Rick Sutcliffe, Chi-NL*	1984	16-1	.941
3 Johnny Allen, Cle	1937	15-1	.938
4 Ron Guidry, NY-AL	1978	25-3	.893
5 Freddie Fitzsimmons, Bklyn	1940	16-2	.889
6 Lefty Grove, Phi-AL	1931	31-4	.886
7 Bob Stanley, Bos	1978	15-2	.882
8 Preacher Roe, Bklyn	1951	22-3	.880
9 Tom Seaver, Cin	1981	14-2	.875
10 Smokey Joe Wood, Bos-AL	1912	34-5	.872

*Sutcliffe began 1984 with Cleveland and was 4-5 before being traded to the Cubs; his overall winning pct. was .769 (20-6).

Strikeouts

	Year	SO	P/G
1 Nolan Ryan, Cal	1973	383	10.57
2 Sandy Koufax, LA	1965	382	10.24
3 Nolan Ryan, Cal	1974	367	9.92
4 Rube Waddell, Phi-AL	1904	349	8.12
5 Bob Feller, Cle	1946	348	8.45
6 Nolan Ryan, Cal	1977	341	10.26
7 Nolan Ryan, Cal	1972	329	10.43
8 Nolan Ryan, Cal	1976	327	10.36
9 Sam McDowell, Cle	1965	325	10.71
10 Sandy Koufax, LA	1966	317	8.83

Games

	Year	Gm	Sv
1 Mike Marshall, LA	1974	106	21
2 Kent Tekulve, Pit	1979	94	31
3 Mike Marshall, LA	1973	92	31
4 Kent Tekulve, Pit	1978	91	31
5 Wayne Granger, Cin	1969	90	27
Mike Marshall, Min	1979	90	32
Kent Tekulve, Phi	1987	90	3

Saves

	Year	Gm	Sv
1 Bobby Thigpen, Chi-AL	1990	77	57
2 Dennis Eckersley, Oak	1990	63	48
3 Dave Righetti, NY-AL	1986	74	46
4 Dan Quisenberry, KC	1983	69	45
Bruce Sutter, St.L	1984	71	45
Dennis Eckersley, Oak	1988	60	45

Innings Pitched (since 1920)

	Year	IP	W-L
1 Wilbur Wood, Chi-AL	1972	377	24-17
2 Mickey Lolich, Det	1971	376	25-14
3 Bob Feller, Cle	1946	371	26-15
4 Grover Alexander, Chi-NL	1920	363	27-14
5 Wilbur Wood, Chi-AL	1973	359	24-20

Shutouts

	Year	ShO	ERA
1 Grover Alexander, Phi-NL	1916	16	1.55
2 Jack Coombs, Phi-AL	1910	13	1.30
Bob Gibson, St.L	1968	13	1.12
4 Christy Mathewson, NY-NL	1908	12	1.43
Grover Alexander, Phi-NL	1915	12	1.22

Walks Allowed

	Year	BB	SO
1 Bob Feller, Cle	1938	208	240
2 Nolan Ryan, Cal	1977	204	341
3 Nolan Ryan, Cal	1974	202	367
4 Bob Feller, Cle	1941	194	260
5 Bobo Newsom, St.L-AL	1938	192	226

Home Runs Allowed

	Year	HRs
1 Bert Blyleven, Minnesota	1986	50
2 Robin Roberts, Philadelphia	1956	46
Bert Blyleven, Minnesota	1987	46
4 Pedro Ramos, Washington	1957	43
5 Denny McLain, Detroit	1966	42

Triple Crown Winners

Batting

Players who led either league in Batting Average, Home Runs and Runs Batted In over a single season.

National League

	Year	Avg	HR	RBI
Paul Hines, Providence	1878	.358	4	50
Hugh Duffy, Boston	1894	.438	18	145
Heinie Zimmerman, Chicago	1912	.372	14	103
Rogers Hornsby, St.Louis	1922	.401	42	152
Rogers Hornsby, St.Louis	1925	.403	39	143
Chuck Klein, Philadelphia	1933	.368	28	120
Joe Medwick, St.Louis	1937	.374	31*	154

*Tied for league lead in HRs with Mel Ott, NY.

American League

	Year	Avg	HR	RBI
Nap Lajoie, Philadelphia	1901	.422	14	125
Ty Cobb, Detroit	1909	.377	9	115
Jimmie Foxx, Philadelphia	1933	.356	48	163
Lou Gehrig, New York	1934	.363	49	165
Ted Williams, Boston	1942	.356	36	137
Ted Williams, Boston	1947	.343	32	114
Mickey Mantle, New York	1956	.353	52	130
Frank Robinson, Baltimore	1966	.316	49	122
Carl Yastrzemski, Boston	1967	.326	44*	121

*Tied for league lead in HRs with Harmon Killebrew, Minn.

Pitching

Pitchers who led either league in Earned Run Average, Wins and Strikeouts over a single season.

National League

	Year	ERA	W-L	SO
Tommy Bond, Bos	1877	2.11	40-17	170
Hoss Radbourn, Prov	1884	1.38	60-12	441
Tim Keefe, NY	1888	1.74	35-12	333
John Clarkson, Bos	1889	2.73	49-19	284
Amos Rusie, NY	1894	2.78	36-13	195
Christy Mathewson, NY	1905	1.27	31-8	206
Christy Mathewson, NY	1908	1.43	37-11	259
Grover Alexander, Phi	1915	1.22	31-10	241
Grover Alexander, Phi	1916	1.55	33-12	167
Grover Alexander, Phi	1917	1.86	30-13	201
Hippo Vaugh, Chi	1918	1.74	22-10	148
Grover Alexander, Chi	1920	1.91	27-14	173
Dazzy Vance, Bklyn	1924	2.16	28-6	262
Bucky Walters, Cin	1939	2.29	27-11	137
Sandy Koufax, LA	1963	1.88	25-5	306
Sandy Koufax, LA	1965	2.04	26-8	382
Sandy Koufax, LA	1966	1.73	27-9	317
Steve Carlton, Phi	1972	1.97	27-10	310
Dwight Gooden, NY	1985	1.53	24-4	268

Ties: in 1894, Rusie tied for league lead in wins with Jouett Meekin, NY (36-10); in 1939, Walters tied for league lead in strikeouts with Claude Passeau, Phi-Chi; in 1963, Koufax tied for the league lead in wins with Juan Marichal, SF.

American League

	Year	ERA	W-L	SO
Cy Young, Bos	1901	1.62	33-10	158
Rube Waddell, Phi	1905	1.48	26-11	287
Walter Johnson, Wash	1913	1.09	36-7	243
Walter Johnson, Wash	1918	1.27	23-13	162
Walter Johnson, Wash	1924	2.72	23-7	158
Lefty Grove, Phi	1930	2.54	28-5	209
Lefty Grove, Phi	1931	2.06	31-4	175
Lefty Gomez, NY	1934	2.33	26-5	158
Lefty Gomez, NY	1937	2.33	21-11	194
Hal Newhouser, Det	1945	1.81	25-9	212

Consecutive Game Streaks

Games Played

Regular season games through 1990. Active streak in **bold type.**

		Games
1	Lou Gehrig	2130
2	**Cal Ripken**	**1411**
3	Everett Scott	1307
4	Steve Garvey	1207
5	Billy Williams	1117
6	Joe Sewell	1103
7	Stan Musial	895
8	Eddie Yost	829
9	Gus Suhr	822
10	Nellie Fox	798
11	Pete Rose	745
12	Dale Murphy	740
13	Richie Ashburn	730
14	Ernie Banks	717
15	Pete Rose	678
16	Earl Averill	673
17	Frank McCormick	652

Hitting

National League

	Gm	Year
Willie Keeler, Baltimore	44	1897
Pete Rose, Cincinnati	44	1978
Bill Dahlen, Chicago	42	1894
Tommy Holmes, Boston	37	1945
Billy Hamilton, Philadelphia	36	1894
Fred Clarke, Louisville	35	1895
George Davis, New York	33	1893
Rogers Hornsby, St.Louis	32	1922
Ed Delahanty, Philadelphia	31	1899
Rico Carty, Atlanta	31	1970

American League

	Gm	Year
Joe DiMaggio, New York	56	1941
George Sisler, St.Louis	41	1922
Ty Cobb, Detroit	40	1911
Paul Molitor, Milwaukee	39	1987
Ty Cobb, Detroit	35	1917
George Sisler, St.Louis	34	1925
John Stone, Detroit	34	1930
George McQuinn, St.Louis	34	1938
Dom DiMaggio, Boston	34	1949
Heinie Manush, Washington	33	1933
Sam Rice, Washington	31	1924
Ken Landreaux, Minnesota	31	1980

Four Home Runs in One Game

National League

	Date	H/A	Inn
Bobby Lowe, Boston	5/30/1894	H	9
Ed Delahanty, Philadelphia	7/13/96	A	9
Chuck Klein, Philadelphia	7/10/1936	A	10
Gil Hodges, Brooklyn	8/31/50	H	9
Joe Adcock, Milwaukee	7/31/54	A	9
Willie Mays, San Francisco	4/30/61	A	9
Mike Schmidt, Philadelphia	4/17/76	A	10
Bob Horner, Atlanta	7/6/86	H	9

American League

	Date	H/A	Inn
Lou Gehrig, New York	6/3/1932	A	9
Pat Seerey, Chicago	7/18/48	A	11
Rocky Colavito, Cleveland	6/10/59	A	9

The All-Star Game

Baseball's first All-Star Game was held on July 6, 1933, before 47,595 at Comiskey Park in Chicago. From that year on, the All-Star game has matched the best players in the American League against the best in the National. From 1959-62, two All-Star Games were played and in 1945, World War II travel restrictions made it necessary to call the All-Star Game off. The NL leads the series, 37-23-1.

In the chart below, the American League is listed in **bold type.**

Year Result	Host (Ballpark)	AL Manager	NL Manager
1933 **American,** 4-2	Chicago (Comiskey Park)	Connie Mack	John McGraw
1934 **American,** 9-7	New York (Polo Grounds)	Joe Cronin	Bill Terry
1935 **American,** 4-1	Cleveland (Cleveland Stadium)	Mickey Cochrane	Frankie Frisch
1936 National, 4-3	Boston (Braves Field)	Joe McCarthy	Charlie Grimm
1937 **American,** 8-3	Washington (Griffith Stadium)	Joe McCarthy	Bill Terry
1938 National, 4-1	Cincinnati (Crosley Field)	Joe McCarthy	Bill Terry
1939 **American,** 3-1	New York (Yankee Stadium)	Joe McCarthy	Gabby Hartnett
1940 National, 4-0	St.Louis (Sportsman's Park)	Joe Cronin	Bill McKechnie
1941 **American,** 7-5	Detroit (Briggs Stadium)	Del Baker	Bill McKechnie
1942 **American,** 3-1	New York (Polo Grounds)	Joe McCarthy	Leo Durocher
1943 **American,** 5-3	Philadelphia (Shibe Park)	Joe McCarthy	Billy Southworth
1944 National, 7-1	Pittsburgh (Forbes Field)	Joe McCarthy	Billy Southworth
1945 No Game			
1946 **American,** 12-0	Boston (Fenway Park)	Steve O'Neill	Charlie Grimm
1947 **American,** 2-1	Chicago (Wrigley Field)	Joe Cronin	Eddie Dyer
1948 **American,** 5-2	St.Louis (Sportsman's Park)	Bucky Harris	Leo Durocher
1949 **American,** 11-7	Brooklyn (Ebbets Field)	Lou Boudreau	Billy Southworth
1950 National, 4-3 (14)	Chicago (Comiskey Park)	Casey Stengel	Burt Shotton
1951 National, 8-3	Detroit (Briggs Stadium)	Casey Stengel	Eddie Sawyer
1952 National, 3-2	Philadelphia (Shibe Park)	Casey Stengel	Leo Durocher
1953 National, 5-1	Cincinnati (Crosley Field)	Casey Stengel	Charlie Dressen
1954 **American,** 11-9	Cleveland (Cleveland Stadium)	Casey Stengel	Walter Alston
1955 National, 6-5 (12)	Milwaukee (County Stadium)	Al Lopez	Leo Durocher
1956 National, 7-3	Washington (Griffith Stadium)	Casey Stengel	Walter Alston
1957 **American,** 6-5	St.Louis (Busch Stadium)	Casey Stengel	Walter Alston
1958 **American,** 4-3	Baltimore (Memorial Stadium)	Casey Stengel	Fred Haney
1959 National, 5-4	Pittsburgh (Forbes Field)	Casey Stengel	Fred Haney
American, 5-3	Los Angeles (Memorial Coliseum)	Casey Stengel	Fred Haney
1960 National, 5-3	Kansas City (Municipal Stadium)	Al Lopez	Walter Alston
National, 6-0	New York (Yankee Stadium)	Al Lopez	Walter Alston
1961 National, 5-4 (10)	San Francisco (Candlestick Park)	Paul Richards	Danny Murtaugh
TIE, 1-1 (9,rain)	Boston (Fenway Park)	Paul Richards	Danny Murtaugh
1962 National, 3-1	Washington (D.C.Stadium)	Ralph Houk	Fred Hutchinson
American, 9-4	Chicago (Wrigley Field)	Ralph Houk	Fred Hutchinson
1963 National, 5-3	Cleveland (Cleveland Stadium)	Ralph Houk	Al Dark
1964 National, 7-4	New York (Shea Stadium)	Al Lopez	Walter Alston
1965 National, 6-5	Minnesota (Metropolitan Stadium)	Al Lopez	Gene Mauch
1966 National, 2-1 (10)	St.Louis (Busch Memorial Stadium)	Sam Mele	Walter Alston
1967 National, 2-1 (15)	California (Anaheim Stadium)	Hank Bauer	Walter Alston
1968 National, 1-0	Houston (The Astrodome)	Dick Williams	Red Schoendienst
1969 National, 9-3	Washington (RFK Stadium)	Mayo Smith	Red Schoendienst
1970 National, 5-4	Cincinnati (Riverfront Stadium)	Earl Weaver	Gil Hodges
1971 **American,** 6-4	Detroit (Tiger Stadium)	Earl Weaver	Sparky Anderson
1972 National, 4-3	Atlanta (Atlanta Stadium)	Earl Weaver	Danny Murtaugh
1973 National, 7-1	Kansas City (Royals Stadium)	Dick Williams	Sparky Anderson
1974 National, 7-2	Pittsburgh (Three Rivers Stadium)	Dick Williams	Yogi Berra
1975 National, 6-3	Milwaukee (County Stadium)	Al Dark	Walter Alston
1976 National, 7-1	Philadelphia (Veterans Stadium)	Darrell Johnson	Sparky Anderson
1977 National, 7-5	New York (Yankee Stadium)	Billy Martin	Sparky Anderson
1978 National, 7-3	San Diego (San Diego Stadium)	Billy Martin	Tom Lasorda
1979 National, 7-6	Seattle (The Kingdome)	Bob Lemon	Tom Lasorda
1980 National, 4-2	Los Angeles (Dodger Stadium)	Earl Weaver	Chuck Tanner
1981 National, 5-4	Cleveland (Cleveland Stadium)	Jim Frey	Dallas Green
1982 National, 4-1	Montreal (Olympic Stadium)	Billy Martin	Tom Lasorda
1983 **American,** 13-3	Chicago (Comiskey Park)	Harvey Kuenn	Whitey Herzog
1984 National, 3-1	San Francisco (Candlestick Park)	Joe Altobelli	Paul Owens
1985 National, 6-1	Minnesota (HHH Metrodome)	Sparky Anderson	Dick Williams
1986 **American,** 3-2	Houston (The Astrodome)	Dick Howser	Whitey Herzog
1987 National, 2-0 (13)	Oakland (Oakland Coliseum)	John McNamara	Davey Johnson
1988 **American,** 2-1	Cincinnati (Riverfront Stadium)	Tom Kelly	Whitey Herzog
1989 **American,** 5-3	California (Anaheim Stadium)	Tony LaRussa	Tom Lasorda
1990 **American,** 2-0	Chicago (Wrigley Field)	Tony LaRussa	Roger Craig

Arch Ward Memorial Award

The All-Star Game MVP award is named after Arch Ward, the *Chicago Tribune* sports editor who founded the game in 1933. First given at the two All-Star games in 1962, the name of the award was changed to the Commissioner's Trophy in 1970 and back to the Ward Memorial Award in 1985.

Multiple winners: Gary Carter, Steve Garvey and Willie Mays (2).

Year		Year		Year	
1962-a	Maury Wills, LA (NL)	1972	Joe Morgan, Cin.	1982	Dave Concepcion, Cin.
1962-b	Leon Wagner, LA (AL)	1973	Bobby Bonds, SF	1983	Fred Lynn, Cal.
1963	Willie Mays, SF	1974	Steve Garvey, LA	1984	Gary Carter, Mon.
1964	Johnny Callison, Phi.	1975	Bill Madlock, Chi.(NL)	1985	LaMarr Hoyt, Chi.(AL)
1965	Juan Marichal, SF		& Jon Matlock, NY (NL)	1986	Roger Clemens, Bos.
1966	Brooks Robinson, Bal.	1976	George Foster, Cin.	1987	Tim Raines, Mon.
1967	Tony Perez, Cin.	1977	Don Sutton, LA	1988	Terry Steinbach, Oak.
1968	Willie Mays, SF	1978	Steve Garvey, LA	1989	Bo Jackson, KC
1969	Willie McCovey, SF	1979	Dave Parker, Pit		
				1990	Julio Franco, Tex.
1970	Carl Yastrzemski, Bos.	1980	Ken Griffey, Cin.		
1971	Frank Robinson, Bal.	1981	Gary Carter, Mon.		

All-Time Winningest Managers

Regular Season

Managers active in 1990 in **bold type**. Note that (1st) indicates number of pennants won.

		Yrs	Won	Lost	Pct	1st
1	Connie Mack	53	3731	3948	.486	9
2	John McGraw	33	2784	1959	.587	10
3	Bucky Harris	29	2157	2218	.493	3
4	Joe McCarthy	24	2125	1333	.615	9
5	Walter Alston	23	2040	1613	.558	7
6	Leo Durocher	24	2008	1709	.540	3
7	Casey Stengel	25	1905	1842	.508	10
8	Gene Mauch	26	1902	2037	.483	0
9	Bill McKechnie	25	1899	1724	.524	4
10	**Sparky Anderson**	21	1837	1446	.560	5
11	Ralph Houk	20	1619	1531	.514	3
12	Fred Clarke	19	1602	1181	.576	4
13	Dick Williams	21	1571	1451	.520	4
14	Clark Griffith	20	1491	1367	.522	1
15	Earl Weaver	17	1480	1060	.583	4

Note: McKechnie's one season (1915) as manager of Newark (NJ) in the Federal League is included in his record.

Where They Managed

Alston—Brooklyn/Los Angeles NL (1954-76); **Anderson**—Cincinnati NL (1970-78), Detroit AL (1979-   ); **Clarke**—Louisville NL (1897-99); Pittsburgh NL (1900-15); **Durocher**—Brooklyn NL (1939-46,48), New York NL (1948-55), Chicago NL (1966-72), Houston NL (1972-73); **Griffith**—Chicago AL (1901-02), New York AL (1903- 08), Cincinnati NL (1909-11), Washington AL (1912- 20); **Harris**—Washington AL (1924-28,35-42,50-54), Detroit AL (1929-33,55-56), Boston AL (1934), Philadelphia AL (1943), New York AL (1947-48); **Houk**—New York AL (1961-63,66-73), Detroit AL (1974-78), Boston AL (1900-15); **Mack**—Pittsburgh AL (1894-96), Philadelphia AL (1901-50); **Mauch**—Philadelphia NL (1960-68), Montreal NL (1969-75), Minnesota AL (1976-80), California AL (1981-82,85-87); **McCarthy**— Chicago NL (1926-30), New York AL (1931-46), Boston AL (1948-50); **McGraw**—Baltimore NL (1899), Baltimore AL (1901-02), New York NL (1902-32); **McKechnie**—Newark FL (1915), Pittsburgh NL (1922-26), St.Louis NL (1928-29), Boston NL (1930-37), Cincinnati NL (1938-46); **Stengel**—Brooklyn NL (1934-36), Boston NL (1938-43), New York AL (1949-60), NY Mets NL (1962-65); **Weaver**—Baltimore AL (1968-82,85-86); **Williams**—Boston AL (1967-69), Oakland AL (1971-73), California AL (1974-76), Montreal NL (1977-81), San Diego NL (1982-85), Seattle AL (1986-88).

World Series

Managers active in 1990 in **bold type**. Note that (1st) indicates world championships won.

		App	Gms	W	L	Pct	1st
1	Casey Stengel	10	63	37	26	.587	7
2	John McGraw	9	55	26	28	.589	2
3	Joe McCarthy	9	43	30	13	.698	7
	Connie Mack	8	43	24	19	.558	5
5	Walter Alston	7	40	20	20	500	4
6	Miller Huggins	6	34	18	15	.545	3
7	**Sparky Anderson**	5	28	16	12	.571	3
8	Dick Williams	4	26	12	14	.462	2
9	Earl Weaver	4	24	11	13	.458	1
10	**Tom Lasorda**	4	23	12	11	.522	2
11	Billy Southworth	4	22	11	11	.500	2
	Bill McKechnie	4	22	8	14	.364	2
13	Frank Chance	4	21	11	9	.550	2
	Bucky Harris	3	21	11	10	.524	2
	Whitey Herzog	3	21	10	11	.476	1
16	Charlie Grimm	3	17	5	12	.294	0
17	Ralph Houk	3	16	8	8	.500	2
	Bill Terry	3	16	7	9	.438	1
	Hughie Jennings	3	16	4	12	.250	0
20	Leo Durocher	3	15	7	8	.467	1
	Fred Clarke	2	15	7	8	.467	1

Note: McGraw won 10 pennants and Mack won nine, but there was no World Series in either 1902 (when Mack's Athletics won the AL) or 1904 (when McGraw's Giants won the NL).

Pennant Winners They Managed

Alston—Brooklyn/Los Angeles NL (1955-56,59,63, 65-66,74); **Anderson**—Cincinnati NL (1970,72,75-76), Detroit AL (1984); **Chance**—Chicago NL (1906-08,10); **Clarke**—Pittsburgh NL (1901-03,09); **Durocher**— Brooklyn NL (1941), New York NL (1951,54); **Grimm** —Chicago NL (1932,35,45); **Harris**—Washington AL (1924-25); New York AL (1947); **Herzog**—St. Louis NL (1982,85,87); **Houk**—New York AL (1961-63); **Huggins**—New York AL (1921-23,26-28); **Jennings**— Detroit AL (1907-09); **Lasorda**—Los Angeles NL (1977-78,81,88); **Mack**—Philadelphia AL (1905-10-11,13-14,29-31); **McCarthy**—Chicago NL (1929); New York AL (1932,36-39,41-43); **McGraw**—New York NL (1904-05,1911-13,17,21-24); **McKechnie**— Pittsburgh NL (1925); St.Louis NL (1928); Cincinnati NL (1939-40); **Southworth**—St.Louis NL (1942-44), Boston NL (1948); **Stengel**—New York AL (1949-53,55-58,60); **Terry**—New York NL (1933,36-37); **Weaver**— Baltimore AL (1969-71,79); **Williams**—Boston AL (1967), Oakland AL (1972-73), San Diego NL (1984).

Active Managers Records

Most Wins

Through the 1990 regular season.

American League

	Yrs	Won	Lost	Pct
1 Sparky Anderson, Det	21	1837	1446	.560
2 John McNamara, Cle	17	1125	1163	.492
3 Tony LaRussa, Oak	12	954	805	.542
4 Frank Robinson, Bal	10	667	727	.478
5 Bobby Valentine, Tex	6	451	487	.481
6 Tom Kelly, Min	5	342	329	.510
7 Tom Trebelhorn, Mil	5	339	318	.516
8 Doug Rader, Cal	6	327	354	.480
9 Jeff Torborg, Chi	5	320	361	.470
10 John Wathan, KC	4	272	248	.523
11 Joe Morgan, Bos	3	217	184	.541
12 Cito Gaston, Tor	2	163	125	.566
13 Jim Lefebvre, Sea	2	150	174	.463
14 Stump Merrill, NY	1	49	64	.434

National League

	Yrs	Won	Lost	Pct
1 Tom Lasorda, LA	15	1185	1033	.534
2 Don Zimmer, Chi	12	867	839	.508
3 Bobby Cox, Atl	9	661	672	.496
4 Buck Rodgers, Mon	9	624	572	.522
5 Roger Craig, SF	8	591	560	.513
6 Joe Torre, St.L	9	567	683	.454
7 Jim Leyland, Pit	5	398	410	.493
8 Lou Piniella, Cin	4	315	264	.544
9 Art Howe, Hou	2	161	163	.497
10 Nick Leyva, Phi	2	144	180	.444
11 Bud Harrelson, NY	1	71	49	.592
12 Greg Riddoch, SD	1	38	44	.463

Annual Awards

Manager of the Year

Given by *The Sporting News*. One award was presented from 1936-85. Two awards (one for each league) have been presented since 1986. Note than (*) indicates a league pennant (1936-68) or division championship (since 1969).

Multiple winners: Walter Alston, Leo Durocher, Joe McCarthy and Casey Stengel (3); Tony LaRussa, Bill McKechnie, Danny Murtaugh, Billy Southworth, Bill Virdon and Earl Weaver (2).

AL and NL Combined

Year	Improvement
1936 Joe McCarthy, NY (AL)	89-60 to 102-51*
1937 Bill McKechnie, Bos.(NL)	71-83 to 79-73
1938 Joe McCarthy, NY (AL)	102-52* to 99-53*
1939 Leo Durocher, Bklyn.(NL)	69-80 to 84-69
1940 Bill McKechnie, Cinn.	97-57* to 100-53*
1941 Billy Southworth, St.L.(NL)	84-69 to 97-56
1942 Billy Southworth, St.L.(NL)	97-56 to 106-48*
1943 Joe McCarthy, NY (AL)	103-51* to 98-56*
1944 Luke Sewell, St.L.(AL)	72-80 to 89-65*
1945 Ossie Bluege, Wash.	64-90 to 87-67
1946 Eddie Dyer, St.L.(NL)	95-59 to 98-58*
1947 Bucky Harris, NY (AL)	87-67 to 97-57*
1948 Bill Meyer, Pitt.	62-92 to 83-71
1949 Casey Stengel, NY (AL)	94-60 to 97-57*
1950 Red Rolfe, Detroit	87-67 to 95-59
1951 Leo Durocher, NY (NL)	86-68 to 98-59*
1952 Eddie Stanky, St.L.	81-73 to 88-66
1953 Casey Stengel, NY (AL)	95-59* to 99-52*
1954 Leo Durocher, NY (NL)	70-84 to 97-57*
1955 Walter Alston, Bklyn	92-62 to 98-55*
1956 Birdie Tebbetts, Cinn.	75-79 to 91-63
1957 Fred Hutchinson, St.L.	76-78 to 87-67
1958 Casey Stengel, NY (AL)	98-56* to 92-62*
1959 Walter Alston, LA	71-83 to 88-68*
1960 Danny Murtaugh, Pitt.	78-76 to 95-59*

Year	Improvement
1961 Ralph Houk, NY (AL)	97-57* to 109-53*
1962 Bill Rigney, LA (AL)	70-91 to 86-76
1963 Walter Alston, LA	102-63 to 99-63*
1964 Johnny Keane, St.L.	93-69 to 93-69*
1965 Sam Mele, Minnesota	79-83 to 102-60*
1966 Hank Bauer, Baltimore	94-68 to 97-63*
1967 Dick Williams, Boston	72-90 to 92-70*
1968 Mayo Smith, Detroit	91-71 to 103-59*
1969 Gil Hodges, New York (NL)	73-89 to 100-62*
1970 Danny Murtaugh, Pitts.	88-74 to 89-73*
1971 Charlie Fox, San Fran.	86-76 to 90-72*
1972 Chuck Tanner, Chicago (AL)	79-83 to 87-67
1973 Gene Mauch, Montreal	70-86 to 79-83
1974 Bill Virdon, New York (AL)	80-82 to 89-73
1975 Darrell Johnson, Bos.	84-78 to 95-65*
1976 Danny Ozark, Phila.	86-76 to 101-61*
1977 Earl Weaver, Balt.	88-74 to 97-64
1978 George Bamberger, Milw	67-95 to 93-69
1979 Earl Weaver, Balt.	90-71 to 102-57*
1980 Bill Virdon, Houston	89-73 to 93-70*
1981 Billy Martin, Oakland	83-79 to 64-45*
1982 Whitey Herzog, St.L.	59-43 to 92-70*
1983 Tony LaRussa, Chicago (AL)	87-75 to 99-63*
1984 Jim Frey, Chicago (NL)	71-91 to 96-75*
1985 Bobby Cox, Toronto	89-73 to 99-62*

Note: In 1981, both league seasons were reduced to 110 games or less due to a players' strike.

National League

Year	Improvement
1986 Hal Lanier, Houston	83-79 to 96-66*
1987 Buck Rodgers, Montreal	78-83 to 91-71
1988 Tom Lasorda, Los Angeles	73-89 to 94-67*
& Jim Leyland, Pittsburgh	80-82 to 85-75
1989 Don Zimmer, Chicago	77-85 to 93-69*

American League

Year	Improvement
1986 John McNamara, Boston	81-81 to 95-66*
1987 Sparky Anderson, Detroit	87-75 to 98-64*
1988 Tony LaRussa, Oakland	81-81 to 104-58*
1989 Frank Robinson, Bal	54-107 to 87-75

Most Valuable Player

There have been three different Most Valuable Player awards in baseball since 1911—the Chalmers Award (1911-14), presented by the Detroit-based automobile company; the League Award (1922-29), presented by the National and American Leagues; and the Baseball Writers' Award (since 1931), presented by the Baseball Writers' Association of America. Statistics for winning players are provided below. Stats for winning pitchers are listed separately.

Multiple winners: NL—Roy Campanella, Stan Musial and Mike Schmidt (3); Ernie Banks, Johnny Bench, Rogers Hornsby, Carl Hubbell, Willie Mays, Joe Morgan and Dale Murphy. **AL**—Yogi Berra, Joe DiMaggio, Jimmie Foxx and Mickey Mantle (3); Mickey Cochrane, Lou Gehrig, Hank Greenberg, Walter Johnson, Roger Maris, Hal Newhouser and Ted Williams. **NL & AL**—Frank Robinson (2).

Chalmers Award
Winning pitchers' statistics on next page.

National League					American League			
Year	Pos	HR	RBI	Avg	Year	Pos	HR	RBI	Avg
1911 Wildfire Schulte, Chi	OF	21	121	.300	1911 Ty Cobb, Det	OF	8	144	.420
1912 Larry Doyle, NY	2B	10	90	.330	1912 Tris Speaker, Bos	OF	10	98	.383
1913 Jake Daubert, Bklyn	1B	2	52	.350	1913 Walter Johnson, Wash	P			
1914 Johnny Evers, Bos	2B	1	40	.279	1914 Eddie Collins, Phi	2B	2	85	.344

League Award
Winning pitchers' statistics on next page.

National League					American League			
Year	Pos	HR	RBI	Avg	Year	Pos	HR	RBI	Avg
1922 No selection					1922 George Sisler, St.L	1B	8	105	.420
1923 No selection					1923 Babe Ruth, NY	OF	41	131	.393
1924 Dazzy Vance, Bklyn	P				1924 Walter Johnson, Wash	P			
1925 Rogers Hornsby, St.L	2B-Mgr	29	143	.403	1925 Roger Peckinpaugh, Wash	SS	4	64	.294
1926 Bob O'Farrell, St.L	C	7	68	.293	1926 George Burns, Cle	1B	4	114	.358
1927 Paul Waner, Pit	OF	9	131	.380	1927 Lou Gehrig, NY	1B	47	175	.373
1928 Jim Bottomley, St.L	1B	31	136	.325	1928 Mickey Cochrane, Phi	C	10	57	.293
1929 Rogers Hornsby, Chi	2B	39	149	.380	1929 No selection				

Baseball Writers' Award
Winning pitchers' statistics on next page.

National League					American League			
Year	Pos	HR	RBI	Avg	Year	Pos	HR	RBI	Avg
1930 Hack Wilson, Chi	OF	56	190	.356	1930 Joe Cronin, Wash	SS	13	126	.346
1931 Frankie Frisch, St.L	2B	4	82	.311	1931 Lefty Grove, Phi	P			
1932 Chuck Klein, Phi	OF	38	137	.348	1932 Jimmie Foxx, Phi	1B	58	169	.364
1933 Carl Hubbell, NY	P				1933 Jimmie Foxx, Phi	1B	48	163	.356
1934 Dizzy Dean, St.L	P				1934 Mickey Cochrane, Det	C-Mgr	2	76	.320
1935 Gabby Hartnett, Chi	C	13	91	.344	1935 Hank Greenberg, Det	1B	36	170	.328
1936 Carl Hubbell, NY	P				1936 Lou Gehrig, NY	1B	49	152	.354
1937 Joe Medwick, St.L	OF	31	154	.374	1937 Charlie Gehringer, Det	2B	14	96	.371
1938 Ernie Lombardi, Cin	C	19	95	.342	1938 Jimmie Foxx, Bos	1B	50	175	.349
1939 Bucky Walters, Cin	P				1939 Joe DiMaggio, NY	OF	30	126	.381
1940 Frank McCormick, Cin	1B	19	127	.309	1940 Hank Greenberg, Det	OF	41	150	.340
1941 Dolf Camilli, Bklyn	1B	34	120	.285	1941 Joe DiMaggio, NY	OF	30	125	.357
1942 Mort Cooper, St.L	P				1942 Joe Gordon, NY	2B	18	103	.322
1943 Stan Musial, St.L	OF	13	81	.357	1943 Spud Chandler, NY	P			
1944 Marty Marion, St.L	SS	6	63	.267	1944 Hal Newhouser, Det	P			
1945 Phil Cavarretta, Chi	1B	6	97	.355	1945 Hal Newhouser, Det	P			
1946 Stan Musial, St.L	1B-OF	16	103	.365	1946 Ted Williams, Bos	OF	38	123	.342
1947 Bob Elliott, Bos	3B	22	113	.317	1947 Joe DiMaggio, NY	OF	20	97	.315
1948 Stan Musial, St.L	OF	39	131	.376	1948 Lou Boudreau, Cle	SS-Mgr	18	106	.355
1949 Jackie Robinson, Bklyn	2B	16	124	.342	1949 Ted Williams, Bos	OF	43	159	.343
1950 Jim Konstanty, Phi	P				1950 Phil Rizzuto, NY	SS	7	66	.324
1951 Roy Campanella, Bklyn	C	33	108	.325	1951 Yogi Berra, NY	C	27	88	.294
1952 Hank Sauer, Chi	OF	37	121	.270	1952 Bobby Shantz, Phi	P			
1953 Roy Campanella, Bklyn	C	41	142	.312	1953 Al Rosen, Cle	3B	43	145	.336
1954 Willie Mays, NY	OF	41	110	.345	1954 Yogi Berra, NY	C	22	125	.307
1955 Roy Campanella, Bklyn	C	32	107	.318	1955 Yogi Berra, NY	C	27	108	.272
1956 Don Newcombe, Bklyn	P				1956 Mickey Mantle, NY	OF	52	130	.353
1957 Hank Aaron, Mil	OF	44	132	.322	1957 Mickey Mantle, NY	OF	34	94	.365
1958 Ernie Banks, Chi	SS	47	129	.313	1958 Jackie Jensen, Bos	OF	35	122	.286
1959 Ernie Banks, Chi	SS	45	143	.304	1959 Nellie Fox, Chi	2B	2	70	.306

Most Valuable Player Award (Cont.)

National League

Year		Pos	HR	RBI	Avg
1960	Dick Groat, Pit	SS	2	50	.325
1961	Frank Robinson, Cin	OF	37	124	.323
1962	Maury Wills, LA	SS	6	48	.299
1963	Sandy Koufax, LA	P			
1964	Ken Boyer, St.L	3B	24	119	.295
1965	Willie Mays, SF	OF	52	112	.317
1966	Roberto Clemente, Pit	OF	29	119	.317
1967	Orlando Cepeda, St.L	1B	25	111	.325
1968	Bob Gibson, St.L	P			
1969	Willie McCovey, SF	1B	45	126	.320
1970	Johnny Bench, Cin	C	45	148	.293
1971	Joe Torre, St.L	3B	24	137	.363
1972	Johnny Bench, Cin	C	40	125	.270
1973	Pete Rose, Cin	OF	5	64	.338
1974	Steve Garvey, LA	1B	21	111	.312
1975	Joe Morgan, Cin	2B	17	94	.327
1976	Joe Morgan, Cin	2B	27	111	.320
1977	George Foster, Cin	OF	52	149	.320
1978	Dave Parker, Pit	OF	30	117	.334
1979	Keith Hernandez, St.L	1B	11	105	.344
	& Willie Stargell, Pit	1B	32	82	.281
1980	Mike Schmidt, Phi	3B	48	121	.286
1981	Mike Schmidt, Phi	3B	31	91	.316
1982	Dale Murphy, Atl	OF	36	109	.281
1983	Dale Murphy, Atl	OF	36	121	.302
1984	Ryne Sandberg, Chi	2B	19	84	.314
1985	Willie McGee, St.L	OF	10	82	.353
1986	Mike Schmidt, Phi	3B	37	119	.290
1987	Andre Dawson, Chi	OF	49	137	.287
1988	Kirk Gibson, LA	OF	25	76	.290
1989	Kevin Mitchell, SF	OF	47	125	.291

American League

Year		Pos	HR	RBI	Avg
1960	Roger Maris, NY	OF	39	112	.283
1961	Roger Maris, NY	OF	61	142	.269
1962	Mickey Mantle, NY	OF	30	89	.321
1963	Elston Howard, NY	C	28	85	.287
1964	Brooks Robinson, Bal	3B	28	118	.317
1965	Zoilo Versalles, Min	SS	19	77	.273
1966	Frank Robinson, Bal	OF	49	122	.316
1967	Carl Yastrzemski, Bos	OF	44	121	.326
1968	Denny McLain, Det	P			
1969	Harmon Killebrew, Min.	3B-1B	49	140	.276
1970	Boog Powell, Bal	1B	35	114	.297
1971	Vida Blue, Oak	P			
1972	Dick Allen, Chi	1B	37	113	.308
1973	Reggie Jackson, Oak	OF	32	117	.293
1974	Jeff Burroughs, Tex	OF	25	118	.301
1975	Fred Lynn, Bos	OF	21	105	.331
1976	Thurman Munson, NY	C	17	105	.302
1977	Rod Carew, Min	1B	14	100	.388
1978	Jim Rice, Bos	OF-DH	46	139	.315
1979	Don Baylor, Cal	OF-DH	36	139	.296
1980	George Brett, KC	3B	24	118	.390
1981	Rollie Fingers, Mil	P			
1982	Robin Yount, Mil	SS	29	114	.331
1983	Cal Ripken, Bal	SS	27	102	.318
1984	Willie Hernandez, Det	P			
1985	Don Mattingly, NY	1B	35	145	.324
1986	Roger Clemens, Bos	P			
1987	George Bell, Tor	OF	47	134	.308
1988	Jose Canseco, Oak	OF	42	124	.307
1989	Robin Yount, Mil	OF	21	103	.318

MVP Pitchers' Statistics

Pitchers have been named Most Valuable Player on 22 occasions, 10 times in the NL and 12 in the AL. Three of them have been relief pitchers—Jim Konstanty, Rollie Fingers and Willie Hernandez.

National League

Year		Gm	W-L	SV	ERA
1924	Dazzy Vance, Bklyn	35	28-6	0	2.16
1933	Carl Hubbell, NY	45	23-12	5	1.66
1934	Dizzy Dean, St.L	50	30-7	7	2.65
1936	Carl Hubbell, NY	42	26-6	3	2.31
1939	Bucky Walters, Cin	39	27-11	0	2.29
1942	Mort Cooper, St.L	37	22-7	0	1.77
1950	Jim Konstanty, Phi	74	16-7	22	2.66
1956	Don Newcombe, Bklyn	38	27-7	0	3.06
1963	Sandy Koufax, LA	40	25-5	0	1.88
1968	Bob Gibson, St.L	34	22-9	0	1.12

American League

Year		Gm	W-L	SV	ERA
1913	Walter Johnson, Wash	47	36-7	2	1.09
1924	Walter Johnson, Wash	38	23-7	0	2.72
1931	Lefty Grove, Phi	41	31-4	5	2.05
1943	Spud Chandler, NY	30	20-4	0	1.64
1944	Hal Hewhouser, Det	47	29-9	2	2.22
1945	Hal Hewhouser, Det	40	25-9	2	1.81
1952	Bobby Shantz, Phi	33	24-7	0	2.48
1968	Denny McLain, Det	41	31-6	0	1.96
1971	Vida Blue, Oak	39	24-8	0	1.82
1981	Rollie Fingers, Mil	47	6-3	28	1.04
1984	Willie Hernandez, Det	80	9-3	32	1.92
1986	Roger Clemens, Bos	33	24-4	0	2.48

Cy Young Award

Voted on by the Baseball Writers Association of America. One award was presented from 1956-66, two since 1967. Pitchers who won the MVP and Cy Young awards in the same season are in **bold** type.

Multiple winners: NL—Steve Carlton (4); Sandy Koufax and Tom Seaver (3); Bob Gibson (2). **AL**—Jim Palmer (3); Roger Clemens and Denny McLain (2). **NL & AL**—Gaylord Perry (2).

Both Leagues Combined

Year	National League	Gm	W-L	SV	ERA
1956	**Don Newcombe**, Bklyn	38	27-7	0	3.06
1957	Warren Spahn, Mil	39	21-11	3	2.69
1960	Vernon Law, Pit	35	20-9	0	3.08
1962	Don Drysdale, LA	43	25-9	1	2.83
1963	**Sandy Koufax**, LA	40	25-5	0	1.88
1965	Sandy Koufax, LA	43	26-8	2	2.04
1966	Sandy Koufax, LA	41	27-9	0	1.73

Year	American League	Gm	W-L	SV	ERA
1958	Bob Turley, NY	33	21-7	1	2.97
1959	Early Wynn, Chi	37	22-10	0	3.17
1961	Whitey Ford, NY	39	25-4	0	3.21
1964	Dean Chance, LA	46	20-9	4	1.65

National League

Year		Gm	W-L	Sv	ERA
1967	Mike McCormick, SF	40	22-10	0	2.85
1968	**Bob Gibson**, St.L	34	22-9	0	1.12
1969	Tom Seaver, NY	36	25-7	0	2.21
1970	Bob Gibson, St.L	34	23-7	0	3.12
1971	Ferguson Jenkins, Chi	39	24-13	0	2.77
1972	Steve Carlton, Phi	41	27-10	0	1.97
1973	Tom Seaver, NY	36	19-10	0	2.08
1974	Mike Marshall, LA	106	15-12	21	2.42
1975	Tom Seaver, NY	36	22-9	0	2.38
1976	Randy Jones, SD	40	22-14	0	2.74
1977	Steve Carlton, Phi	36	23-10	0	2.64
1978	Gaylord Perry, SD	37	21-6	0	2.72
1979	Bruce Sutter, Chi	62	6-6	37	2.23
1980	Steve Carlton, Phi	38	24-9	0	2.34
1981	F. Valenzuela, LA	25	13-7	0	2.48
1982	Steve Carlton, Phi	38	23-11	0	3.10
1983	John Denny, Phi	36	19-6	0	2.37
1984	Rick Sutcliffe, Chi	20*	16-1	0	2.69
1985	Dwight Gooden, NY	35	24-4	0	1.53
1986	Mike Scott, Hou	37	18-10	0	2.22
1987	Steve Bedrosian, Phi	65	5-3	40	2.83
1988	Orel Hershiser, LA	35	23-8	1	2.26
1989	Mark Davis, SD	70	4-3	44	1.85

*NL games only, Sutcliffe pitched 15 games with Cleveland before being traded to the Cubs.

American League

Year		Gm	W-L	Sv	ERA
1967	Jim Lonborg, Bos	39	22-9	0	3.16
1968	**Denny McLain**, Det	41	31-6	0	1.96
1969	Denny McLain, Det	42	24-9	0	2.80
	& Mike Cuellar, Bal	39	23-11	0	2.38
1970	Jim Perry, Min	40	24-12	0	3.03
1971	Vida Blue, Oak	39	24-8	0	1.82
1972	Gaylord Perry, Cle	41	24-16	1	1.92
1973	Jim Palmer, Bal	38	22-9	1	2.40
1974	Catfish Hunter, Oak	41	25-12	0	2.49
1975	Jim Palmer, Bal	39	23-11	1	2.09
1976	Jim Palmer, Bal	40	22-13	0	2.51
1977	Sparky Lyle, NY	72	13-5	26	2.17
1978	Ron Guidry, NY	35	25-3	0	1.74
1979	Mike Flanagan, Bal	39	23-9	0	3.08
1980	Steve Stone, Bal	37	25-7	0	3.23
1981	**Rollie Fingers**, Mil	47	6-3	28	1.04
1982	Pete Vuckovich, Mil	30	18-6	0	3.34
1983	LaMarr Hoyt, Chi	36	24-10	0	3.66
1984	**Willie Hernandez**, Det	80	9-3	32	1.92
1985	Bret Saberhagen, KC	32	20-6	0	2.87
1986	**Roger Clemens**, Bos	33	24-4	0	2.48
1987	Roger Clemens, Bos	36	20-9	0	2.97
1988	Frank Viola, Min	35	24-7	0	2.64
1989	Bret Saberhagen, KC	36	23-6	0	2.16

Rookie of the Year

Voted on by the Baseball Writers Assn. of America. One award was presented from 1947-48. Two awards (one for each league) have been presented since 1949.

AL and NL Combined

Year		Pos	Year		Pos
1947	Jackie Robinson, Brooklyn	1B	1948	Al Dark, Boston, NL	SS

American League

Year		Pos
1949	Roy Sievers, St.L	OF
1950	Walt Dropo, Bos	1B
1951	Gil McDougald, NY	3B
1952	Harry Byrd, Phi	P
1953	Harvey Kuenn, Det	SS
1954	Bob Grim, NY	P
1955	Herb Score, Cle	P
1956	Luis Aparicio, Chi	SS
1957	Tony Kubek, NY	INF-OF
1958	Albie Pearson, Wash	OF
1959	Bob Allison, Wash	OF
1960	Ron Hansen, Bal	SS
1961	Don Schwall, Bos	P
1962	Tom Tresh, NY	SS-OF
1963	Gary Peters, Chi	P
1964	Tony Oliva, Min	OF
1965	Curt Blefary, Bal	OF
1966	Tommie Agee, Chi	OF
1967	Rod Carew, Min	2B
1968	Stan Bahnsen, NY	P
1969	Lou Piniella, KC	OF
1970	Thurman Munson, NY	C
1971	Chris Chambliss, Cle	1B
1972	Carlton Fisk, Bos	C
1973	Al Bumbry, Bal	OF
1974	Mike Hargrove, Tex	1B
1975	Fred Lynn, Bos	OF
1976	Mark Fidrych, Det	P
1977	Eddie Murray, Bal	DH-1B
1978	Lou Whitaker, Det	2B
1979	John Castino, Min	3B
	& Alfredo Griffin, Tor	SS
1980	J. Charboneau, Cle	OF-DH
1981	Dave Righetti, NY	P
1982	Cal Ripken, Bal	SS-3B
1983	Ron Kittle, Chi	OF
1984	Alvin Davis, Sea	1B
1985	Ozzie Guillen, Chi	SS
1986	Jose Canseco, Oak	OF
1987	Mark McGwire, Oak	1B
1988	Walt Weiss, Oak	SS
1989	Gregg Olson, Bal	P

National League

Year		Pos
1949	Don Newcombe, Brklyn	P
1950	Sam Jethroe, Bos	OF
1951	Willie Mays, NY	OF
1952	Joe Black, Brklyn	P
1953	Jim Gilliam, Brklyn	2B
1954	Wally Moon, St.L	OF
1955	Bill Virdon, Pit	OF
1956	Frank Robinson, Cin	OF
1957	Jack Sanford, Phi	P
1958	Orlando Cepeda, SF	1B
1959	Willie McCovey, SF	1B
1960	Frank Howard, LA	OF
1961	Billy Williams, Chi	OF
1962	Ken Hubbs, Chi	2B
1963	Pete Rose, Cin	2B
1964	Richie Allen, Phi	3B
1965	Jim Lefebvre, LA	2B
1966	Tommy Helms, Cin	3B
1967	Tom Seaver, NY	P
1968	Johnny Bench, Cin	C
1969	Ted Sizemore, LA	2B
1970	Carl Morton, Mon	P
1971	Earl Williams, Atl	C
1972	Jon Matlack, NY	P
1973	Gary Matthews, SF	OF
1974	Jake McBride, St.L	OF
1975	John Montefusco, SF	P
1976	Butch Metzger, SD	P
	& Pat Zachry, Cin	P
1977	Andre Dawson, Mon	OF
1978	Bob Horner, Atl	3B
1979	Rick Sutcliffe, LA	P
1980	Steve Howe, LA	P
1981	Fernando Valenzuela, LA	P
1982	Steve Sax, LA	2B
1983	Darryl Strawberry, NY	OF
1984	Dwight Gooden, NY	P
1985	Vince Coleman, St.L	OF
1986	Todd Warrell, St.L	P
1987	Benito Santiago, SD	C
1988	Chris Sabo, Cin	3B
1989	Jerome Walton, Chi	OF

College Baseball

1990 College World Series

Georgia won the College World Series for the first time on June 9, beating Oklahoma St., 2-1. The Bulldogs were the first team since Cal. State Fullerton in 1979 to win the CWS without ever before winning a game in Omaha (they were 0-2 in the only previous appearance in 1987). Georgia finished the nine-day, 14-game, double elimination series with a 4-1 record.

CWS results:

Game 1 Stanford 5 . . .(10 inn.) . . .Ga.Southern 4		**Game 8** Oklahoma St. 7 . . . . .LSU 1
Game 2 Georgia 3 . . . . .Mississippi St. 0		**Game 9** Stanford 6 . . . . .Mississippi St. 1
Game 3 LSU 8 . . . . .Citadel 2		**Game 10** LSU 6 .Citadel 1
Game 4 Oklahoma St. 14 . . . . . .Cal St.Fullerton 4		**Game 11** Stanford 4 . . . . .Georgia 2
Game 5 Mississippi St. 15 . . . . .Ga.Southern 1		**Game 12** Oklahoma St. 14 . . . . .LSU 3
Game 6 Georgia 16 . . . . .Stanford 2		**Game 13** Goergia 5 . . . . .Stanford 1
Game 7 Citadel 8 . . . .(12 inn.) . . . .CS-Fullerton 7		**Game 14** Georgia 2 . . . . .Oklahoma St. 1

Baseball America Top 25

Final Division I college rankings determined by the editors of *Baseball America*, following the College World Series. Final team records, including postseason games, are in parentheses.

1 Georgia (52-19)	8 Florida St. (57-15)	15 N.Carolina (51-14)	21 Houston (44-23)
2 Oklahoma St. (56-17)	9 CS-Fullerton (36-23)	16 Illinois (43-21)	22 Loyola Marymount
3 Stanford (59-12)	10 Texas (51-17)	17 San Diego St. (49-22)	(45-17)
4 LSU (54-19)	11 Ga. Southern (50-19)	18 Washington St. (48-19)	23 South Alabama (44-19)
5 Arizona St. (52-16)	12 Arkasas (47-15)	19 Wichita St. (45-19)	24 UCLA (41-26)
6 USC (40-22)	13 Miami-FL (52-13)	20 The Citadel (46-14)	25 Creighton (48-22)
7 Mississippi St. (50-21)	14 Southern Ill. (49-14)		

NCAA Division I Champions, 1947-90

Multiple winners: Southern Cal (11); Arizona St. (5); Texas (4); Arizona and Minnesota (3); Cal State Fullerton, California, Miami-FL, Michigan and Stanford (2).

Year	Winner	Coach	Score	Loser	Year	Winner	Coach	Score	Loser
1947	California	Clint Evans	8-7	Yale	1970	Southern Cal	Rod Dedeaux	2-1	Fla.St.
1948	Southern Cal	Sam Barry	9-2	Yale	1971	Southern Cal	Rod Dedeaux	7-2	So.Ill.
1949	Texas	Bibb Falk	10-3	W.Forest	1972	Southern Cal	Rod Dedeaux	1-0	Ariz.St.
1950	Texas	Bibb Falk	3-0	Wash.St.	1973	Southern Cal	Rod Dedeaux	4-3	Arizona
1951	Oklahoma	Jack Baer	3-2	Tennessee	1974	Southern Cal	Rod Dedeaux	7-3	Miami,FL
1952	Holy Cross	Jack Barry	8-4	Missouri	1975	Texas	Cliff Gustafson	5-1	S.Carolina
1953	Michigan	Ray Fisher	7-5	Texas	1976	Arizona	Jerry Kindall	7-1	E.Michigan
1954	Missouri	Hi Simmons	4-1	Rollins	1977	Arizona St.	Jim Brock	2-1	S.Carolina
1955	Wake Forest	Taylor Sanford	7-6	W.Mich.	1978	Southern Cal	Rod Dedeaux	10-3	Ariz.St.
1956	Minnesota	Dick Siebert	12-1	Arizona	1979	CS Fullerton	Augie Garrido	2-1	Arkansas
1957	California	Geo. Wolfman	1-0	Penn St.	1980	Arizona	Jerry Kindall	5-3	Hawaii
1958	Southern Cal	Rod Dedeaux	8-7	Missouri	1981	Arizona St.	Jim Brock	7-4	Okla.St.
1959	OklahomaSt.	Toby Greene	5-3	Arizona	1982	Miami,FL	Ron Fraser	9-3	Wichita St.
1960	Minnesota	Dick Siebert	2-1	USC	1983	Texas	Cliff Gustafson	4-3	Alabama
1961	Southern Cal	Rod Dedeaux	1-0	Okla.St.	1984	CS Fullerton	Augie Garrido	3-1	Texas
1962	Michigan	Don Lund	5-4	S.Clara	1985	Miami,FL	Ron Fraser	10-6	Texas
1963	Southern Cal	Rod Dedeaux	5-2	Arizona	1986	Arizona	Jerry Kindall	10-2	Fla.St.
1964	Minnesota	Dick Siebert	5-1	Missouri	1987	Stanford	M.Marquess	9-5	Okla.St.
1965	Arizona St.	Bobby Winkles	2-1	Ohio St.	1988	Stanford	M.Marquess	9-4	Ariz.St.
1966	Ohio St.	Marty Karow	8-2	Okla.St.	1989	Wichita St.	G.Stephenson	5-3	Texas
1967	Arizona St.	Bobby Winkles	11-2	Houston	1990	Georgia	Steve Webber	2-1	Okla.St.
1968	Southern Cal	Rod Dedeaux	4-3	So.Ill.					
1969	Arizona St.	Bobby Winkles	10-1	Tulsa					

Most Outstanding Players

A Most Outstanding Player has been selected every year of the College World Series since 1949. Winners who did not play for the CWS champion are listed in **bold type**. No player has won the award more than once.

Year		Year		Year	
1949	**Charles Teague**, W.Forest	1963	Bud Hollowell, USC	1978	Rod Boxberger, USC
1950	**Ray VanCleef**, Rutgers	1964	**Joe Ferris**, Maine	1979	Tony Hudson, CS-Full.
1951	**Sidney Hatfield**, Tenn.	1965	Sal Bando, Ariz.St.	1980	Terry Francona, Arizona
1952	James O'Neill, Holy Cross	1966	Steve Arlin, Ohio St.	1981	Stan Holmes, Ariz.St.
1953	**J.L. Smith**, Texas	1967	Ron Davini, Ariz.St.	1982	Dan Smith, Miami-FL
1954	**Tom Yewcic**, Mich.St.	1968	Bill Seinsoth, USC	1983	Calvin Schiraldi, Texas
1955	**Tom Borland**, Okla.St.	1969	John Dolinsek, Ariz.St.	1984	John Fishel, CS-Full.
1956	Jerry Thomas, Minn.	1970	**Gene Ammann**, Fla.St.	1985	Greg Ellena, Miami-FL
1957	**Cal Emery**, Penn St.	1971	**Jerry Tabb**, Tulsa	1986	Mike Senne, Arizona
1958	Bill Thom, USC	1972	Russ McQueen, USC	1987	Paul Carey, Stanford
1959	Jim Dobson, Okla.St.	1973	**Dave Winfield**, Minn.	1988	Lee Plemel, Stanford
1960	John Erickson, Minn.	1974	George Milke, USC	1989	Greg Brummett, Wich.St.
1961	**Littleton Flower**, Okla.St.	1975	Mickey Reichenbach, Tex.	1990	Mike Rebhan, Georgia
1962	**Bob Garibaldi**, S.Clara	1976	Steve Powers, Arizona		
		1977	Bob Horner, Ariz. St.		

Miami quarterback **Craig Erickson** makes his point after leading the Hurricanes to a 33-25 victory over Alabama in the Sugar Bowl. The win clinched the Canes' third national championship in seven years.

COLLEGE FOOTBALL

*Hurricanes blow away Notre Dame,
clinch No.1 for year & decade;
Ware throws his way to a Heisman;
Bo bows out and 38 juniors move on.*

COLLEGE FOOTBALL

1989 YEAR IN REVIEW

by Bill Connors

There was a predictable and traditional look to the 1989 college football picture. As projected, Notre Dame, the team of the century, and Miami, the team of the '80s, settled the national championship in a ballyhooed showdown. Miami prevailed, and one month later was crowned No. 1 for the third time in seven years.

Elsewhere, however, the landscape was rife with historic change, new stars, broken records, coaching turmoil, and hard times for Top Ten fixtures.

For the second straight season, an unheralded junior won the Heisman Trophy. Houston quarterback Andre Ware set 26 NCAA records, including most yards passing (4699), most completions (365) and most total yards (4661), and he overcame the stigma of his school's being on probation to win the Heisman.

Emmanual Hazard, Ware's favorite target, Terance Mathis of New Mexico and Duke's Clarkston Hines broke storied receiving records, while tailback Anthony Thompson of Indiana set marks in both rushing and scoring.

Meanwhile, Ware and 37 other juniors may have changed the game forever by taking advantage of a new NFL policy and making themselves available for the draft. Some of the game's leading coaches also departed, including Bo Schembechler, who retired, and Barry Switzer and Danny Ford, who resigned under pressure.

Next to Ware, the year's most-talked about player—cancer-stricken Colorado quarterback Sal Aunese—did not play a single down. Aunese died in September and the Buffaloes dedicated their season to him while rallying around his replacement Darian Hagan. In the process, they beat Oklahoma and Nebraska on consecutive weekends, won the Big Eight Conference outright and finished the regular season unbeaten and No.1 in the country.

Bill Connors is the Sports Editor of *The Tulsa (Okla.) World* and has been covering college football since 1952.

Oklahoma lost almost as many games (4) as it did in the four previous seasons combined and became the most celebrated power to fall from the national rankings, even when the sportswriters and broadcasters poll was expanded by the Associated Press to include the Top 25. Nebraska fell out of the Top Ten and UCLA had a losing (3-7-1) record. So did Texas (5-6) for the second straight year. But while some of the elite stumbled, SMU made history by scrambling back from a two-year suspension after being the first, and thus far only, recipient of the NCAA death penalty.

On the individual front, Ware proved television exposure was not a prerequisite for winning the Heisman (Houston's probation prevented the prolific Ware from performing on network or cable TV). But Ware's numbers could not be ignored. Nor did it hurt that he was accommodating to interviewers and came across as humble, grateful to his mother and generous in his praise of teammates.

Ware's story was much like the one 1988 Heisman recipient Barry Sanders wrote at Oklahoma State (with only one TV appearance). Like Sanders, Ware entered his junior season with minimal fanfare, despite setting a Southwest Conference record with 25 touchdown passes in 1988 as a part-time starter. As a junior, Ware blossomed in Houston's run-and-shoot offense.

Like Sanders, Ware said he would return to school for his final year of eligibility, only to change his mind and enter the NFL Draft (through a door that Sanders opened in 1989). As fate would have it, Ware was chosen by Sanders' team, the Detroit Lions.

Also like Sanders, Ware was an overlooked schoolboy who was recruited only by option teams or those who projected him as a defensive back. At the time, Houston used the Veer. But Ware's enrollment in 1986 was denied when he took the SAT on an unapproved date. He attended a junior college, but did not play football, and enrolled at Houston a year later just as Coach Jack Pardee arrived to junk the Veer and install the run-and-shoot.

"My mother's encouragement kept my confidence up through some hard times and Coach Pardee's offense and my teammates did the rest," Ware said.

Surrounded by Houston teammates after routing Rice, 64-0, on Dec. 2, record-breaking quarterback **Andre Ware** reacts to TV announcement that he has just won the Heisman Trophy.

Pardee, who left the Cougars before Ware did to move across town and coach the NFL Oilers, said Ware "was ideal for the run-and-shoot. He is a great athlete with a strong arm. Once he grasped the offense he played on a different level than everyone else."

A record-setting benefactor of Ware's heroics was Hazard. He set Divison I single season records with 142 receptions, 22 touchdown catches, TD catches in 10 different games and 19 TD catches from the same passer.

Mathis set Division I career marks with 263 receptions and 4254 yards. He also bettered the record of 34 career TD catches with 36, but Hines ended up with 38. Thompson, who was runner-up to Ware in the Heisman vote but winner of the Maxwell Trophy, set three Division I records: for a game by rushing for 377 yards against Wisconsin, and for a career by totaling 65 touchdowns and 394 points.

Although only 18 of the 38 juniors who declared for the draft were chosen by NFL teams, five of them were among the first seven players selected. Illinois quarterback Jeff George was the first pick and received a 6-year, $15 million contract from the Indianapolis Colts.

Alabama linebacker Keith McCants was selected fourth, linebacker Junior Seau and safety Mark Carrier of Southern Cal were the fifth and sixth picks, and Ware was picked seventh.

Reaction among college coaches to the NFL's new policy varied. Joe Paterno of Penn State predicted once it became obvious that only the most advanced of juniors had high-draft appeal the number of juniors leaving early would decline "and there won't be much of a problem."

But Southern Cal's Larry Smith feared agents would mislead large numbers of juniors to defect and predicted that the NFL's forthcoming World League of American Football would be drafting sophomores within five years. Smith called for his college peers to adopt defensive strategies to keep underclassmen in school.

Tom Osborne of Nebraska, whose program is built around redshirts, said, "This could change the way we structure our program. Before we redshirt a player, I would like to know if we can count on having him around. I would like to have some guidelines and advance information from the pros on what their plans are regarding our underclassmen."

Retaining underclassmen is no longer a problem for a number of familiar faces in the coaching ranks. Switzer, whose winning percentage of .837 through 1988 was the best of all active coaches, resigned at Oklahoma before the '89 season even began after five Sooner players were charged in criminal acts involving rape, drugs and a shooting.

Schembechler's announcement in December that he would retire after the Rose Bowl following 27 seasons and over 230 wins removed the dean of the class. Schembechler was head coach at Michigan for 21 years, leading the Wolverines to all or part of the Big Ten championship 13 times. He made it to the Rose Bowl for the 10th and final time in 1990, but lost his farewell game by a touchdown to USC. The defeat left Schembechler with a 2-8 record in Pasadena on New Year's.

Although only 60 years old, Schembechler had suffered a heart attack and undergone bypass surgery more than a decade ago. He said, "I could have continued, but the stress in coaching is awful

It all started with Lou Saban and Jim Kelly

When the 1980s began, some cynics wondered if a small private institution like the University of Miami, Fla. could sustain a competitive Division I-A football program. Ten years later, many doubted that any school, public or private, would ever match the success Miami enjoyed in the decade.

Three times the national champion and twice the No. 2 team in the country, the Hurricanes dominated the 1980s to take their rightful place in history alongside two other triple crown winners, Oklahoma (1950, 55-56), Alabama (1961, 64-65), and four-time champion Notre Dame (1943, 46-47, 49).

What separates Miami from the other three programs, however, is that while the Irish had Frank Leahy, the Sooners had Bud Wilkinson and the Tide had Bear Bryant, the Canes won their titles under three different head coaches—Howard Schnellenberger in 1983, Jimmy Johnson in 1987 and Dennis Erickson in 1989.

"The talent and tradition to win national championships were here when I arrived and that's why I came," said Erickson, who left Washington State for Coral Gables in 1989. "I think our staff did a fine job, but we know we inherited a great program that didn't need any tinkering."

Miami's fortunes began to turn around in 1977 when the much-traveled Lou Saban was hired to coach the team after several candidates turned down the job amid speculation that the school would soon drop football. Saban, who recruited quarterback Jim Kelly in 1978, left after two seasons and a 9-13 record but the foundation had been laid. By 1980, Kelly had led Schnellenberger's second team to a 9-3 record and Miami's first bowl appearence in 13 years—a 20-10 victory over Virginia Tech in the Peach.

Kelly was the first of five outstanding quarterbacks who would direct the pro style passing attack installed by Schnellenberger. The line of succession included Bernie Kosar, Vinny Testaverde, Steve Walsh and Craig Erickson.

Kosar led the Hurricanes to their first national championship in 1983 by upsetting No. 1 Nebraska, 31-30, in the Orange Bowl. Walsh guided UM's only undefeated team to the title in 1987 and Erickson presided in 1989. Testaverde didn't reach No. 1, but he did win the Heisman Trophy in 1986.

High school senior **Jim Kelly** shakes hands with head coach **Lou Saban** after agreeing to attend Miami in 1978.

When Schnellenberger left Miami for an ill-fated fling with the USFL in 1984, Oklahoma State head coach Jimmy Johnson was hired to take his place. Despite an 8-5 record, that first season was a long one for the defensive-minded Johnson, who watched in horror as the Canes lost to Maryland 42-40 after leading by 31 points and then fell to Boston College 47-45 on Doug Flutie's storied 48-yard, Hail Mary TD pass with time running out.

By 1986, Johnson's Hurricanes were perhaps the most talented and cocky team in college history, led by NFL first round draft choices like Testaverde, Alonzo Highsmith, Jerome Brown, Michael Irvin, and Bennie Blades. Heavily favored to win the Fiesta Bowl and the national championship, the Canes were upset by Penn State, 14-10.

Johnson won the title the following season when Miami, the underdog this time, defeated Oklahoma 20-14 in the Orange Bowl. The defeat was only the Sooners' third in three years—all to Miami.

The Canes also developed a fierce rivalry with Notre Dame during Johnson's tenure, highlighted by their 58-7 rout of the Irish in 1985 and Notre Dame's controversial 31-30 win that decided the national championship in 1988. In '89, Miami snapped ND's 23-game unbeaten streak, 21-6, and clinched the national title when the Irish defeated No.1 Colorado in the Orange Bowl.

Miami finished the '80s with a record of 99-20, trailing only Nebraska (103) and BYU (102) in overall wins. But it was the last four years that enabled the Hurricanes to lay claim to the decade. From 1986-89 they went 45-3 and ranked either No.1 or No.2 an unprecedented four consecutive seasons.

The Decade's Top 15

NCAA Division I-A football schools with the most victories from 1980-89.

	Overall Record	Bowls W-L-T	National Titles
Nebraska	103-20-0	4-6-0	None
BYU	102-27-0	5-5-0	1984
Miami, FL	99-20-0	5-3-0	1983,87,89
Oklahoma	91-26-2	4-4-0	1985
Michigan	90-29-2	5-5-0	None
Georgia	89-27-4	4-4-2	1980
Penn St	89-28-2	6-2-0	1982,86
Florida St	88-28-3	7-1-1	None
Clemson	87-25-4	5-1-0	1981
Auburn	86-31-2	5-2-1	None
Alabama	85-33-2	6-3-0	None
Arkansas	85-33-2	3-6-0	None
Washington	84-33-2	6-3-0	None
UCLA	82-30-6	7-1-0	None
Ohio State	82-35-2	5-3-0	None

Note: the only missing national champion from the above list is Notre Dame (1988). In the 1980s the Irish were 76-39-2 overall and 3-3 in bowl games.

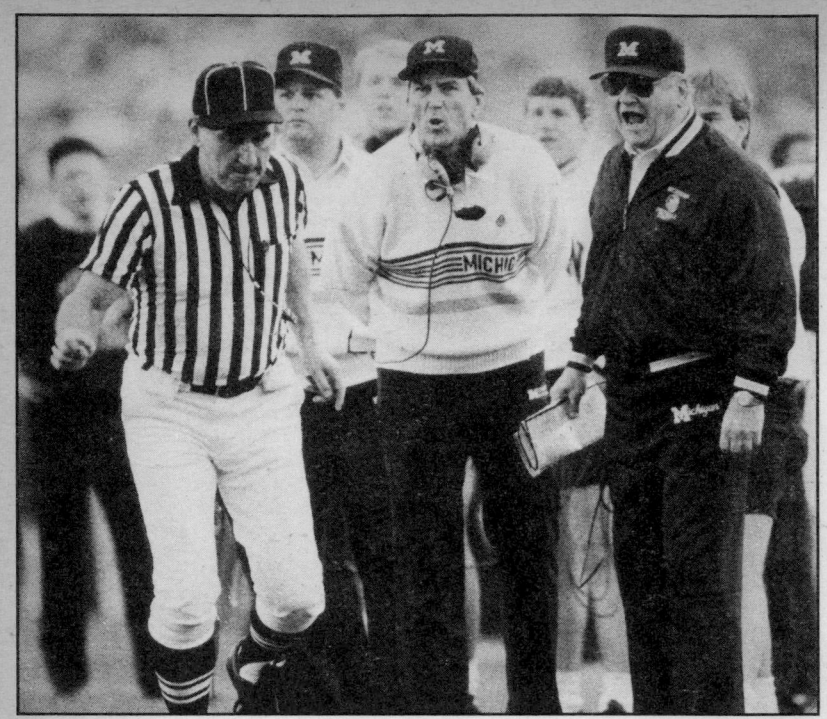

Wide World Photos

Michigan head coach **Bo Schembechler** (right) and heir apparent **Gary Moeller** voice their displeasure with an official during the Wolverines' 17-10 loss to Southern Cal in the Rose Bowl. Schembechler, 2-8 lifetime in Pasadena, retired following the game.

and I thought there was no sense taking any more chances."

Elsewhere, NCAA investigations prompted Florida to fire Galen Hall at midseason and Clemson to pressure Danny Ford into resigning once the season was over. And Bill Curry left Alabama, where fans apparently thought it was unacceptable for a Georgia Tech alumnus to coach at the Shrine of Bear Bryant and lose to Auburn.

Curry chose to escape Bryant's giant shadow by going to Kentucky, where Bryant coached in the early years of his legendary career (1946-53) and complained of being overshadowed by basketball coach Adolph Rupp. Curry replaced the retiring Jerry Claiborne, one of Bryant's favorite proteges.

Curry admitted his harrassing experience at Alabama "made it very difficult for my family." He made it clear he felt more comfortable at Kentucky where he said "everyone has a perspective on winning and education."

To replace Curry, Alabama hired Gene Stallings, who had not coached on the collegiate level since 1971 and had losing records in his only head coaching jobs at Texas A&M and in the NFL with the Phoenix Cardinals, each of whom fired him. But Stallings met Alabama's primary job requirement: he was one of Bear's boys, having played for Bryant at Texas A&M and coached for him at Alabama.

Ken Hatfield left Arkansas, his alma mater, to replace Ford at Clemson after differences with athletic director Frank Broyles, who six years earlier had given Hatfield the job Hatfield said "I always wanted." Meanwhile, Florida began the work of cleaning up its program by hiring Heisman Trophy alumnus Steve Spurrier from Duke.

Finally, three schools hired Notre Dame assistants. Wisconsin picked Barry Alvarez, UNLV Jim Strong, and Division I-AA Austin Peay hired John Palermo.

Those appointments followed a national championship race that entered Thanksgiving weekend as a contest between defending champion Notre Dame (11-0) and 1987 champ Miami (9-1), but which also included unbeatens Colorado (11-0) and Alabama (10-0).

Alabama was eliminated by losing a landmark finale to Auburn. The game was played at Auburn for the first time ever, and the hometown Tigers won 30-20. The loss did not keep the Tide from sharing the Southeastern Conference title (with Auburn and Tennessee) and going to the Sugar Bowl for the first time in 10 years, but it was Curry's 10th consecutive loss to Auburn. Even a Bryant man might not have survived that.

Colorado stayed in the race until the finish and was No. 1 after Miami beat Notre Dame, 27-10, in the season's most important game, Nov. 25 at the Orange Bowl. The Irish defeat snapped a school record 23-game winning streak.

Miami's earlier 24-10 loss to Florida State left Colorado the only 11-0 team. But on New Year's Day Notre Dame toppled Colorado, 21-6, in the Orange Bowl and Miami defeated Alabama, 33-25, in the Sugar Bowl to set the stage for the Hurricanes to be named the country's No.1 team for the third time in the 1980s (see box).

This came despite a lobbying effort by Notre Dame Coach Lou Holtz, who argued that the Irish deserved to be ranked first because they played the nation's most difficult schedule. Among the 12 teams that fell to Notre Dame in 1989 were four conference champions.

Holtz said, "We were No. 1 all year except for Nov. 25th. We played the toughest schedule and defeated the No. 1 ranked team in the Orange Bowl. I don't know what else we could do."

But voters were influenced by the position Holtz took in 1988 when the Irish defeated Miami, 31-30, with the help of a controversial goal line ruling against the Canes and despite being decisively out-gained. On the day it counted, Holtz reasoned back then, Notre Dame was best and voters agreed.

On the day it counted in 1989, Miami was best and the voters agreed. It wasn't close. Miami swept every national championship award.

One month after falling short in the polls, Notre Dame hit the jackpot when it signed a contract permitting NBC to televise all its home games through 1995 for $30 million. Notre Dame's announcement shocked the College Football Association, which had negotiated—with Notre Dame's help and on the assumption that the Irish would participate— a five-year, $210 million contract with ABC.

Charges of greed were hurled at Notre Dame. Paterno said, "Notre Dame went from the school of education to the school of banking." But the NBC contract seemed to be of small consolation to Holtz, who did one of his best coaching jobs and wanted to deny Miami the championship almost as much as he wanted it for Notre Dame.

In its first season under Dennis Erickson, Miami played the same defensive scheme and with the same intimidating style employed by Jimmy Johnson's powerhouses. The Hurricanes also unveiled their newest passing star, Craig Erickson (no relation to the coach), and peaked when the stakes were highest. Erickson was sidelined with an injury to his throwing hand when Miami lost to Florida State, 24-10.

Many thought FSU was the nation's best team when the dust cleared on Jan. 2. The Seminoles had plundered Nebraska, 41-17, in the Fiesta Bowl to finish at 10-2, but coach Bobby Bowden admitted his team forfeited its right to be No. 1 by losing its first two games to Southern Mississippi and Clemson.

"Maybe we were the best team at the end but we weren't the best for the season," Bowden said. "You can't lose two games like we did and be considered the best for the season."

Colorado had no argument to make for No. 1 after losing to Notre Dame in the Orange Bowl. But the Buffs had the most captivating season of any team.

It revolved around Aunese, who was stricken in the spring with terminal cancer and died on Sept. 23. In dedicating the season to him, the Buffs played with a passion and unity that they had not previously displayed.

The affection Colorado felt for Aunese was underscored at his funeral when coach Bill McCartney publicly acknowledged that Aunese was the father of his unmarried daughter's son and stressed how proud he was of his daughter, grandson and Aunese. Indeed, McCartney became an all-out participant in Aunese's glorification. His locker was retained, an empty chair at pre-game meals was a reminder of him, a seat on Colorado's team plane to Oklahoma was left vacant in his memory, and before and after every game his teammates raised their arms in unison in silent tribute.

But the loss of Aunese also enabled McCartney to elevate the more gifted Hagan to starter. Aunese was a first division quarterback. Hagan was a championship quarterback. He became only the sixth player in NCAA history to pass for 1000 yards and run for 1000 yards in the same season.

With Hagan making the decisive plays on offense, the Buffs beat Oklahoma and Nebraska back-to-back (20-3 and 27-21) and won their first outright Big Eight championship since 1961.

Aunese was gone, but Hagan was only a sophomore. □

Senior running back **J.J. Flannigan** spends an emotional moment at **Sal Aunese's** locker after Colorado beat Nebraska, 27-21, Nov. 4 in Boulder. Aunese's death in September served to inspire the Buffaloes to an undefeated regular season.

Cliff Grassmick/Boulder Daily Camera

THE 1991 INFORMATION PLEASE SPORTS ALMANAC

COLLEGE FOOTBALL
S T A T I S T I C S

THE SEASON IN REVIEW
1989-1990
TOP 25 • BOWLS • STANDINGS

SEC **A**

PAGE **101**

Final AP Top 25 Poll

Voted on by panel of 60 sportswriters & broadcasters following Jan.1, 1990 bowl games: first place votes in parentheses, records, total points (based on 25 for 1st, 24 for 2nd, etc.) bowl game result, head coach and career record, preseason rank and final regular season rank.

	Final Record	Points	Bowl Game	Head Coach (career record)	Aug.28 Rank	Dec.11 Rank
1 Miami,FL (39)	11–1–0	1474	Won Sugar	Dennis Erickson (8 yrs: 61-32-1)	4	2
2 Notre Dame (19)	12–1–0	1452	Won Orange	Lou Holtz (20 yrs: 153-76-5)	2	4
3 Florida St.(2)	10–2–0	1384	Won Fiesta	Bobby Bowden (24 yrs: 195-72-3)	6	5
4 Colorado	11–1–0	1320	Lost Orange	Bill McCartney (8 yrs: 46-45-1)	14	1
5 Tennessee	11–1–0	1228	Won Cotton	Johnny Majors (22 yrs: 150-97-8)	33	8
6 Auburn	10–2–0	1161	Won Hall/Fame	Pat Dye (16 yrs: 135-48-3)	8	9
7 Michigan	10–2–0	1091	Lost Rose	Bo Schembechler (27 yrs: 234-65-8)	1	3
8 Southern Cal	9–2–1	1067	Won Rose	Larry Smith (14 yrs: 93-63-4)	5	12
9 Alabama	10–2–0	1029	Lost Sugar	Bill Curry (10 yrs: 57-53-4)	16	7
10 Illinois	10–2–0	1019	Won Citrus	John Mackovic (5 yrs: 30-27-1)	22	11
11 Nebraska	10–2–0	860	Lost Fiesta	Tom Osborne (17 yrs: 168-38-2)	3	6
12 Clemson	10–2–0	820	Won Gator	Danny Ford (12 yrs: 96-29-4)	12	14
13 Arkansas	10–2–0	807	Lost Cotton	Ken Hatfield (11 yrs: 81-49-2)	10	10
14 Houston	9–2–0	748	On probation	Jack Pardee (3 yrs: 22-11-1)	21	13
15 Penn St	8–3–1	633	Won Holiday	Joe Paterno (24 yrs: 220-57-3)	11	18
16 Michigan St	8–4–0	507	Won Aloha	George Perles (7 yrs: 46-33-3)	29	22
17 Pittsburgh	8–3–1	478	Won Hancock	Mike Gottfried (12 yrs: 75-56-4)	20	23
18 Virginia	10–3–0	455	Lost Citrus	George Welsh (17 yrs: 105-86-3)	32	15
19 Texas Tech	9–3–0	451	Won All-Amer	Spike Dykes (3 yrs: 20-14-1)	—	24
20 Texas A&M	8–4–0	330	Lost Hancock	R.C.Slocum (1 yr: 8-4-0)	27	16
21 West Virginia	8–3–1	260	Lost Gator	Don Nehlen (19 yrs: 130-74-6)	17	17
22 BYU	10–3–0	231	Lost Holiday	LaVell Edwards (18 yrs: 165-56-1)	19	19
23 Washington	8–4–0	200	Won Freedom	Don James (19 yrs: 145-73-3)	28	27
24 Ohio St	8–4–0	154	Lost Hall/Fame	John Cooper (13 yrs: 93-51-3)	25	21
25 Arizona	8–4–0	77	Won Copper	Dick Tomey (13 yrs: 82-58-6)	18	28

Note: Pittsburgh fired Mike Gottfried as head coach on Dec.14. Pitt beat Texas A&M in John Hancock Bowl on Dec.30 for new coach Paul Hackett.

Other teams: 26. **Mississippi** (8-4, 69 points); 27. **Duke** (8-4, 59 pts); 28. **Syracuse** (8-4, 52 pts); 29. **Fresno St.** (11-1, 35 pts); 30. **Oregon** (8-4, 26 pts); 31. **Hawaii** (9-3, 11 pts); 32. **Florida** (7-5, 8 pts); 33. **Georgia Tech** (7-4, 2 pts) and **N.C.State** (7-5, 2 pts).

Bowl Games

Date		Result	Date		Result
12/09/89	California	Fresno St. 27, Ball St. 6	12/30/89	Gator	Clemson 27, West Va. 7
12/16/89	Indepen	Oregon 27, Tulsa 24	12/31/89	Copper	Arizona 17, N.C. State 10
12/25/89	Aloha	Mich.St. 33, Hawaii 13	1/1/90	Hall/Fame	Auburn 31, Ohio St. 14
12/28/89	All-Amer	Texas Tech 49, Duke 21	1/1/90	Fla.Citrus	Illinois 31, Virginia 21
12/28/89	Liberty	Ole Miss 42, Air Force 29	1/1/90	Cotton	Tennessee 31, Arkansas 27
12/29/89	Holiday	Penn St. 50, BYU 39	1/1/90	Fiesta	Fla.St. 41, Nebraska 17
12/30/89	J.Hancock	Pitt 31, Texas A&M 28	1/1/90	Rose	USC 17, Michigan 10
12/30/89	Freedom	Washington 34, Florida 7	1/1/90	Orange	N. Dame 21, Colorado 6
12/30/88	Peach	Syracuse 19, Georgia 18	1/1/90	Sugar	Miami, FL 33, Alabama 25

All-Star Bowl Games

Date		Result	Date		Result
12/25/89	Blue-Gray	Gray 28, Blue 10	1/20/90	Senior	North 41, South 0
1/13/90	Hula	West 21, East 13	1/21/90	Shrine	West 22, East 21
1/13/90	Japan	East 24, West 10			

NCAA Division I-A Final Standings

Atlantic Coast Conference

	Conference					Overall				
	W	L	T	PF	PA	W	L	T	PF	PA
Virginia*	6	1	0	251	117	10	3	0	371	272
Duke*	6	1	0	253	171	8	4	0	377	335
Clemson*	5	2	0	205	101	10	2	0	368	138
N.C.State* . . .	4	3	0	160	142	7	5	0	290	230
Ga. Tech	4	3	0	175	151	7	4	0	265	213
Maryland	2	5	0	148	170	3	7	1	215	238
Wake Forest . .	1	6	0	128	256	2	8	1	194	319
N.Carolina . . .	0	7	0	56	238	1	10	0	138	297

Note: Virginia beat Duke, 49-28 (Sep.23).
***Bowls:** Virginia (lost Citrus); Duke (lost All-American); Clemson (won Gator); N.C.State (lost Copper).

Big Eight Conference

	Conference					Overall				
	W	L	T	PF	PA	W	L	T	PF	PA
Colorado*	7	0	0	297	89	11	1	0	458	171
Nebraska* . . .	6	1	0	319	120	10	2	0	509	215
Oklahoma . . .	5	2	0	247	156	7	4	0	380	200
Iowa St	4	3	0	200	217	6	5	0	294	305
Okla.St	3	4	0	161	224	4	7	0	226	319
Kansas	2	5	0	148	266	4	7	0	248	383
Missouri	1	6	0	140	272	2	9	0	171	363
Kansas St	0	7	0	86	254	1	10	0	134	349

***Bowls:** Colorado (lost Orange); Nebraska (lost Fiesta).

Big Ten Conference

	Conference					Overall				
	W	L	T	PF	PA	W	L	T	PF	PA
Michigan*	8	0	0	241	99	10	2	0	335	184
Illinois*	7	1	0	239	108	10	2	0	332	182
Ohio St.*	6	2	0	251	182	8	4	0	339	297
Mich. St.*	6	2	0	241	103	8	4	0	356	163
Minnesota . . .	4	4	0	199	201	6	5	0	263	283
Indiana	3	5	0	219	226	5	6	0	289	262
Iowa	3	5	0	130	191	5	6	0	197	278
Purdue	2	6	0	129	193	3	8	0	172	281
Wisconsin . . .	1	7	0	132	260	2	9	0	172	341
Northwestern .	0	8	0	152	370	0	11	0	241	497

***Bowls:** Michigan (lost Rose); Illinois (won Citrus); Ohio St.(lost Hall of Fame); Michigan St. (won Aloha).

Big West Conference

	Conference					Overall				
	W	L	T	PF	PA	W	L	T	PF	PA
Fresno St.* . . .	7	0	0	253	92	11	1	0	441	220
CS-Fullerton . . .	5	2	0	208	150	6	4	1	307	279
San Jose St . . .	5	2	0	211	135	6	5	0	309	270
Utah St	4	3	0	159	166	4	7	0	191	355
UNLV	4	3	0	186	172	4	7	0	233	340
L.Beach St . . .	2	5	0	155	239	4	8	0	247	407
Pacific	2	5	0	129	206	2	10	0	179	406
N.Mexico St . .	0	7	0	106	247	0	11	0	162	428

***Bowl:** Fresno St.(won California).

Mid-American Conference

	Conference					Overall				
	W	L	T	PF	PA	W	L	T	PF	PA
Ball St.*	6	1	1	193	119	7	3	2	274	239
Eastern Mich . .	6	2	0	179	133	7	3	1	252	196
Toledo	6	2	0	206	178	6	5	0	255	272
Central Mich . .	5	2	1	179	103	5	5	1	228	182
Bowl.Green . .	5	3	0	193	195	5	6	0	233	319
Western Mich .	3	5	0	155	143	6	6	0	210	210
Miami,OH	2	5	1	98	156	2	8	1	122	262
Ohio Univ	1	6	1	172	209	1	9	1	191	348
Kent St	0	8	0	129	268	0	11	0	179	378

***Bowl:** Ball St.(lost California).

Pacific-10 Conference

	Conference					Overall				
	W	L	T	PF	PA	W	L	T	PF	PA
USC*	6	0	1	174	67	9	2	1	336	132
Arizona*	5	3	0	173	127	8	4	0	248	178
Oregon*	5	3	0	215	166	8	4	0	379	251
Washington* . .	5	3	0	213	158	8	4	0	332	225
Arizona St . . .	3	1	1	156	198	6	4	1	241	258
Oregon St	3	4	1	124	234	4	7	1	207	357
Wash. St	3	5	0	235	197	6	5	0	351	268
Stanford	3	5	0	113	164	3	8	0	187	258
UCLA	2	5	1	152	173	3	7	1	209	246
California	2	6	0	151	222	4	7	0	200	288

***Bowls:** USC (won Rose); Arizona (won Copper); Oregon (won Independence); Washington (won Freedom).

Southeastern Conference

	Conference					Overall				
	W	L	T	PF	PA	W	L	T	PF	PA
Alabama*	6	1	0	219	130	10	2	0	357	217
Tennessee* . . .	6	1	0	194	155	11	1	0	346	217
Auburn*	6	1	0	122	69	10	2	0	284	131
Florida*	4	3	0	145	103	7	5	0	268	202
Mississippi* . .	4	3	0	164	189	8	4	0	309	314
Georgia*	4	3	0	139	109	6	6	0	251	198
Kentucky	2	5	0	118	174	6	5	0	212	220
LSU	2	5	0	174	180	4	7	0	295	252
Miss.St	1	6	0	89	153	5	6	0	205	207
Vanderbilt	0	7	0	85	187	1	10	0	162	265

Note: Alabama, Tennessee and Auburn all went 1-1 in their three games against each other— Tennessee beat Auburn, 21-14 (Sep.30); Alabama beat Tennessee, 47-30 (Oct.21); and Auburn beat Alabama, 30-20 (Dec.2).
***Bowls:** Alabama (lost Sugar); Tennessee (won Cotton); Auburn (won Hall of Fame); Florida (lost Freedom); Mississippi (won Liberty); Georgia (lost Peach).

Southwest Conference

	Conference					Overall				
	W	L	T	PF	PA	W	L	T	PF	PA
Arkansas*	7	1	0	269	168	10	2	0	385	230
Houston	6	2	0	419	136	9	2	0	589	150
Texas A&M* . .	6	2	0	250	112	8	4	0	343	192
Texas Tech* . .	5	3	0	229	211	9	3	0	360	281
Baylor	4	4	0	189	139	5	6	0	245	190
Texas	4	4	0	174	222	5	6	0	220	289
TCU	2	6	0	127	261	4	7	0	183	301
Rice	2	6	0	136	258	2	8	1	175	313
SMU	0	8	0	115	401	2	9	0	187	499

***Bowls:** Arkansas (lost Cotton); Texas A&M (lost John Hancock); Texas Tech (won All-American).
Note: Houston was on NCAA probation and ineligible for postseason play.

Western Athletic Conference

	Conference				Overall				
	W	L	T	PF	PA	W	L	T	PF	PA
BYU*	8	0	0	330	212	10	3	0	523	369
Air Force*	5	1	1	298	207	8	3	1	440	323
Hawaii*	5	2	1	306	165	9	3	1	435	246
Wyoming	5	3	0	230	215	5	6	0	281	299
San Diego St	4	3	0	231	234	6	5	1	368	379
Colorado St	4	3	0	239	193	5	5	1	350	304
Utah	2	6	0	241	396	4	8	0	365	524
UTEP	1	7	0	169	302	2	10	0	238	412
New Mexico	0	7	0	134	254	2	10	0	298	378

Bowls: BYU (lost Holiday); Air Force (lost Liberty); Hawaii (lost Aloha).

Final UPI Top 20 Poll

Voted on by panel of 50 Division I-A head coaches: first place votes in parentheses with total points (based on 15 for 1st, 14 for 2nd, etc.).

	Pts		Pts
1 Miami (39)	707	11 Clemson	240
2 Florida St. (7)	661	12 Nebraska	214
3 N.Dame (6)	660	13 Arkansas	182
4 Colorado	626	14 Penn St.	85
5 Tennessee	499	15 Virginia	37
6 Auburn	415	16 Texas Tech	35
7 Alabama	378	Michigan St.	35
8 Michigan	373	18 BYU	17
9 USC	351	19 Pittsburgh	16
10 Illinois	313	20 Washington	8

Teams on probation (and ineligible to receive votes): Cincinnati, Houston, Oklahoma, Oklahoma St. and Memphis St.

Major Independents

	W	L	T	PF	PA
Notre Dame*	12	1	0	427	189
Miami,FL*	11	1	0	426	127
Florida St.*	10	2	0	424	199
Northern Illinois	9	2	0	344	269
West Virginia*	8	3	1	339	221
Penn St.*	8	3	1	259	169
Pittsburgh*	8	3	1	331	268
Syracuse*	8	4	0	286	243
SW Louisiana	7	4	0	241	232
Akron	6	4	1	283	264
South Carolina	6	4	1	228	250
Virginia Tech	6	4	1	203	180
Louisiana Tech	5	4	1	283	265
Army	6	5	0	316	212
Louisville	6	5	0	323	211
Tulsa*	6	5	0	302	271
East Carolina	5	5	1	301	286
Southern Miss	5	6	0	240	252
Tulane	4	8	0	247	337
Navy	3	8	0	145	272
Rutgers	2	7	2	245	319
Boston College	2	9	0	207	253
Memphis St	2	9	0	174	338
Cincinnati	1	9	1	111	379
Temple	1	10	0	141	387

Bowls: Notre Dame (won Orange); Miami,FL (won Sugar); Florida St. (won Fiesta); West Virginia (lost Gator); Penn St. (won Holiday); Pittsburgh (won John Hancock); Syracuse (won Peach); Tulsa (lost Independence).

50 Top Rivalries

Top Division I series records, including games through 1989 season. Note that Boston College and Holy Cross ended their series after the 1986 season. Florida and Miami, FL haven't played each other since 1987, but their series will resume with games in 1992 and '93, 1996-97, and 1999-2001.

	Games	Series Leader		Games	Series Leader
Air Force-Army	24	Air Force (12-11-1)	Kansas-Kansas St	87	Kansas (59-23-5)
Air Force-Navy	22	Air Force (14-8-0)	Kentucky-Tennessee	85	Tennessee (53-23-9)
Alabama-Auburn	54	Alabama (30-23-1)	Lafayette-Lehigh	130	Lafayette (69-51-10)
Alabama-Tennessee	72	Alabama (38-27-7)	LSU-Tulane	87	LSU (58-22-7)
Arizona-Arizona St.	63	Arizona (36-25-1)	Miami,FL-N.Dame	22	Notre Dame (14-7-1)
Arkansas-Texas	71	Texas (53-18-0)	Michigan-Mich.St.	82	Michigan (54-23-5)
Army-Navy	90	Navy (42-41-7)	Michigan-N.Dame	21	Micigan (13-8-0)
Auburn-Georgia	93	Auburn (44-42-7)	Michigan-Ohio St	86	Michigan (48-33-5)
Baylor-TCU	96	TCU (46-43-7)	Minnesota-Wisconsin	99	Minnesota (54-37-8)
BC-Holy Cross	79	BC (48-31-0)	Mississippi-Miss.St	86	Mississippi (50-30-6)
BYU-Utah	65	Utah (40-21-4)	Nebraska-Oklahoma	70	Oklahoma (38-29-3)
California-Stanford	92	Stanford (44-37-11)	N.Carolina-N.C.State	82	N.Carolina (52-21-6)
Cincinnati-Miami,OH	94	Miami (50-38-6)	Notre Dame-Purdue	61	Notre Dame (38-21-2)
Clemson-S.Carolina	87	Clemson (51-32-4)	Notre Dame-USC	61	Notre Dame (34-23-4)
Colorado-Colo.St.	66	Colorado (48-16-2)	Oklahoma-Okla.St	84	Oklahoma (66-12-6)
Duke-N.Carolina	75	N.Carolina (36-35-4)	Oklahoma-Texas	84	Texas (48-32-4)
Florida-Florida St	32	Florida (22-9-1)	Oregon-Oregon St	93	Oregon (45-38-10)
Florida-Miami,FL	49	Florida (25-24-0)	Penn St.-Pittsburgh	89	Penn St. (44-41-4)
Florida St.-Miami,FL	33	Miami (19-14-0)	Pittsburgh-West Va.	82	Pitt (54-24-3)
Georgia-Florida	67	Georgia (43-22-2)	Princeton-Yale	112	Yale (62-40-10)
Georgia-Ga.Tech	84	Georgia (45-34-5)	Richmond-Wm.&Mary	99	TIED (47-47-5)
Harvard-Yale	106	Yale (57-41-8)	Tennessee-Vanderbilt	83	Tennessee (52-26-5)
Indiana-Purdue	92	Purdue (57-29-6)	Texas-Texas A&M	96	Texas (63-28-5)
Iowa-Iowa St	37	Iowa (25-12-0)	UCLA-USC	59	USC (33-19-7)
Kansas-Missouri	98	Missouri (46-43-9)	Washington-Wash.St	82	Washington (52-24-6)

Major Award Winners

Heisman Trophy Vote

Presented since 1935 by the Downtown Athletic Club of New York City and named after former college coach and DAC athletic director John W.Heisman. Voting done by national media and former Heisman winners. Each ballot allows for three names (points based on 3 for 1st, 2 for 2nd and 1 for 3rd).

	Yr	Pos	Points
Andre Ware, Houston	Jr	QB	1073
Anthony Thompson, Indiana	Sr	RB	1003
Major Harris, West Va.	Jr	QB	709
Tony Rice, Notre Dame	Sr	QB	523
Darian Hagan, Colorado	So	QB	292
Dee Dowis, Air Force	Sr	QB	145
Emmitt Smith, Florida	Jr	RB	140
Percy Snow, Mich.St	Sr	LB	70
Ty Detmer, BYU	So	QB	49
Blair Thomas, Penn St	Sr	RB	48
Raghib Ismail, N.Dame	So	FL	48

First place votes: Ware (242), Thompson (185), Harris (115), Rice (72), Hagan (52), Dowis (15), Smith (13), Snow (7), Detmer (3), Thomas (4), Ismail (3).

Offensive Players of the Year

Maxwell Award (Top Player) .Anthony Thompson
Camp Award (Top Back) . . . . .Andre Ware
O'Brien Award (Top QB) . . . . .Andre Ware

Defensive Players of the Year

Rockne Award (Top Lineman)
. . . . .Chris Zorich, N.Dame, NT
Lombardi Award (Top Lineman) . . . . .Percy Snow
UPI Lineman of Year. . . . . .Chris Zorich
Outland Trophy (Interior Lineman)
. . . . .Mohammed Elewonibi, BYU
Butkus Award (Top LB) . . . . .Percy Snow
Thorpe Award (Top DB) . . . . . .Mark Carrier, USC

"Coaches Choice" Player of the Year
(Chosen by AFCA)

NCAA Div.I-A. . . . . .Anthony Thompson

Coaches of the Year

FWAA Div.I-A . . . . .Bill McCartney, Colorado
AFCA Div.I-A . . . . .Bill McCartney

Consensus All-America Team

NCAA Division I-A players cited most frequently by the following five: AFCA, AP, FWAA, UPI and Walter Camp Foundation. Unanimous selections in **bold type**.

Offense	Cl	Hgt	Wgt
WR—**Clarkston Hines**, Duke	Sr.	6-1	170
WR—Terance Mathis, New Mex	Sr.	5-9	162
TE—Mike Busch, Iowa St	Sr.	6-5	252
L—Mohammed Elewonibi, BYU	Sr.	6-4	305
L—Joe Garten, Colorado	Jr.	6-3	280
L—Bob Kula, Michigan St	Sr.	6-4	282
L—Jim Mabry, Arkansas	Sr.	6-4	262
L—**Eric Still**, Tennessee	Sr.	6-3	283
C—Jake Young, Nebraska	Sr.	6-4	270
QB—Andre Ware, Houston	Jr.	6-2	205
RB—**Emmitt Smith**, Florida	Jr.	5-10	201
RB—**Anthony Thompson**, Indiana	Sr.	6-0	209
K—Jason Hanson, Wash St	So.	6-0	165

Defense	Cl	Hgt	Wgt
L—**Moe Gardner**, Illinois	Jr.	6-2	242
L—Greg Mark, Miami,FL	Sr.	6-4	245
L—Tim Ryan, USC	Sr.	6-5	260
L—Chris Zorich, Notre Dame	Jr.	6-1	268
LB—**Keith McCants**, Alabama	Jr.	6-5	256
LB—**Percy Snow**, Michigan St	Sr.	6-3	240
LB—Alfred Williams, Colorado	Jr.	6-6	230
B—LeRoy Butler, Florida St	Sr.	6-0	194
B—**Mark Carrier**, USC	Jr.	6-1	185
B—**Todd Lyght**, Notre Dame	Jr.	6-1	181
B—**Tripp Welborne**, Michigan	Jr.	6-1	193
P—Tom Rouen, Colorado	Jr.	6-3	220

Juniors Selected in 1990 NFL Draft

First Round (8) — Drafted by
1. Jeff George, Illinois QB . . . . . . .Indianapolis
4. Keith McCants, Alabama LB . . . . .Tampa Bay
5. Junior Seau, USC LB . . . . .San Diego
6. Mark Carrier, USC DB . . . . .Chicago
7. Andre Ware, Houston QB . . . . .Detroit
15. Lamar Lathon, Houston LB . . . . . .Houston
17. Emmitt Smith, Florida RB . . . . .Dallas
24. Rodney Hampton, Georgia RB . . . .NY Giants

Second Round (3)
30. Reggie Cobb, Tennessee RB . . . . .Tampa Bay
33. Ron Cox, Fresno St. LB . . . . .Chicago
45. Leroy Hoard, Michigan RB. . . . . . .Cleveland

Third Round (1) — Drafted by
62. Marc Spindler, Pitt DT . . . . .Detroit

Fourth Round (1)
93. Scott Mitchell, Utah QB . . . . .Miami

Fifth Round (2)
128. Barry Foster, Arkansas RB . . . . . .Pittsburgh
132. Charles Wilson, Mem.St. WR . . . .Green Bay

Sixth Round (1)
149. Marcus Wilson, Virginia RB . . . . . .LA Raiders

Ninth Round (1)
241. Terry Allen, Clemson RB . . . . .Minnesota

Twelfth Round (1)
317. Major Harris, West Va. QB . . . . .LA Raiders

Juniors Left Undrafted (20)

Braxston Banks (RB), Notre Dame; Sean Barowski (RB), Syracuse; Dirk Borgognone (K), Pacific; Eugene Burkhalter (DB), Washington; Anthony Burnett (DB), UCLA; Danny Cash (T), Alabama; Michael Culberhouse (K), Lamar; Brad Gaines (RB), Vanderbilt; Thurman Geathers (RB), Oregon Tech; Octavius Gould (RB), Minnesota; Robert Hayes (RB), Greenville,IL; Jeff Klemp (K), Kansas; Chris Mongeau (G-T), AIC; John Mefford (DT), Carson-Newman; Leonard Morris (RB), Cal St-Hayward; Chuck Petitpas (K-P) McGill; Cornelius Price (DB), Houston; Bryan Tracy (RB), no college; John Tregellas (DE), Sacramento City JC; Tommy Woodward (DB), Murray St.

NCAA Division I-A Individual Leaders

REGULAR SEASON

Total Offense

		Rushing				Passing		Total Offense				
Player, School	Car	Gain	Loss	Net	Att	Yds	Plays	Yds	YdsPP	TDR	YdsPG
Andre Ware, Houston	50	177	215	−38	578	4699	628	4661	7.42	49	423.73
Ty Detmer, BYU	85	235	362	−127	412	4560	497	4433	8.92	38	369.42
Scott Mitchell, Utah	64	178	256	−78	444	3211	508	3133	6.17	33	313.30
Brian Mitchell, SW La	237	1463	152	+1311	312	1966	549	3277	5.97	25	297.91
Dan McGwire, S.Diego St	64	49	277	−228	440	3651	504	3423	6.79	18	285.25
Jeremy Leach, N.Mexico	79	152	362	−210	511	3573	590	3363	5.70	24	280.25
Peter Tom Willis, Fla.St	30	28	148	−120	346	3124	376	3004	7.99	22	273.09
Major Harris, West Va	144	1044	125	+919	224	1939	368	2858	7.77	22	259.82
Phil Barnhill, W.Forest	92	477	111	+366	377	2454	469	2820	6.01	20	256.36
Troy Taylor, Calif	87	271	225	+46	394	2738	481	2784	5.79	16	253.09

All Purpose Runners

Player, School	Gm	Rush	Rec	PR	KOR	Total Yds	YdsPG
Mike Pringle, CS-Fullerton	11	1727	249	0	714	2690	244.55
Sheldon Canley, San Jose St	11	1201	353	0	959	2513	228.45
Chuck Weatherspoon, Houston	11	1146	735	415	95	2391	217.36
Anthony Thompson, Indiana	11	1793	201	0	394	2388	217.09
Terance Mathis, New Mexico	12	38	1315	0	785	2138	178.17
Emmitt Smith, Florida	11	1599	207	0	0	1806	164.18
Steve Broussard, Wash.St	11	1237	326	0	227	1790	162.73
Andrew Greer, Ohio Univ	11	903	227	0	598	1728	157.09
Blaise Bryant, Iowa St	11	1516	202	0	0	1718	156.18
Emmanuel Hazard, Houston	11	0	1689	0	0	1689	153.55

Passing Efficiency
(Minimum 15 attempts per game)

Player, School	Gm	Att	Cmp	Cmp Pct	Int	Int Pct	Yds	Yds/ Att	TD	TD Pct	Rating Points
Ty Detmer, BYU	12	412	265	64.32	15	3.64	4560	11.07	32	7.77	175.6
David Brown, Drake	9	163	104	63.80	6	3.68	1479	9.07	14	8.59	161.0
Dan Speltz, CS-Fullerton	11	309	214	69.26	11	3.56	2671	8.64	20	6.47	156.1
Shawn Moore, Virginia	11	221	125	56.56	7	3.17	2078	9.40	18	8.14	156.1
Andre Ware, Houston	11	578	365	63.15	15	2.60	4699	8.13	46	7.96	152.5
Bill Scharr, Syracuse	11	169	107	63.31	8	4.73	1625	9.62	9	5.33	152.2
Peter Tom Willis, Fla. St.	11	346	211	60.98	9	2.60	3124	9.03	20	5.78	150.7
Major Harris, West Va	11	224	131	58.48	10	4.46	1939	8.66	16	7.14	145.8
Greg Frey, Ohio St	11	215	128	59.53	7	3.26	1900	8.84	12	5.58	145.7
Bret Oberg, Iowa St	11	245	152	62.04	9	3.67	2242	9.15	9	3.67	143.7

Abbreviation Key

Att—Attempted Passes; **Avg**—Average; **C**—Catches; **Car**—Carries; **Cmp**—Completions; **CPG**—Catches Per Game; **FG**—Field Goals; **FGA**—Field Goal Attempts; **FGPG**—Field Goals Per Game; **Gain**—Yards Gained; **Gm**—Games; **Int**—Interceptions; **IPG**—Interceptions Per Game; **KOR**—Kickoff Return Yards; **Loss**—Yards Lost; **Net**—Yards Gained minus Yards Lost; **No**—Number; **Pct**—Percentage; **Plays**—Plays from Scrimmage; **PR**—Punt Return Yards; **Pts**—Points; **PtsPG**—Points Per Game; **Rec**—Receiving Yards; **Rush**—Rushing Yards; **TD**—Touchdowns; **TDR**—Touchdowns Responsible For; **XP**—Extra Points; **Yds**—Yards; **Yds/Att**—Yards Per Attempt; **YdsPG**—Yards Per Game.

Scoring

Non-Kickers

Player, School	Gm	TD	Pts	PtsPG
Anthony Thompson, Ind.	11	25	154*	14.00
Emmanuel Hazard, Hou.	11	22	134*	12.18
James Gray, Texas Tech	11	20	120	10.91
Blaise Bryant, Iowa St	11	19	120*	10.91
Blake Ezor, Michigan St	9	16	96	10.67

*Note: Thompson also had 4 Extra Points, Hazard had 2 and Bryant had 6.

Kickers

Player, School	Gm	FG	XP	Pts	PtsPG
Roman Anderson, Hou	11	22	65	131	11.91
Carlos Huerta, Miami, FL	11	18	47	101	9.18
Gregg McCallum, Ore	11	22	34	100	9.09
Philip Doyle, Alabama	11	22	34	100	9.09
Jason Hanson, Wash. St	11	21	36	99	9.00
Chris Gardocki, Clem	11	20	38	98	8.91

NCAA Division I-A Individual Leaders (Cont.)

Rushing

Player, School	Car	Yds	TD	YdsPG
Anthony Thompson, Ind	358	1793	24	163.00
Mike Pringle, CS-Fullerton	296	1727	16	157.00
Emmitt Smith, Florida	284	1599	14	145.36
Blaise Bryant, Iowa St	299	1516	19	137.82
James Gray, Texas Tech	263	1509	18	137.18
Stacey Robinson, No.Ill	223	1443	19	131.18
Blake Ezor, Michigan St	226	1120	16	124.44
Derrick Douglas, La.Tech	281	1232	11	123.20
Jerry Mays, Ga.Tech	249	1349	8	122.64
Blair Thomas, Penn St	264	1341	5	121.91

Receiving

Player, School	C	Yds	TD	CPG
Emmanuel Hazard, Hous	142	1689	22	12.91
R.Buchanan, N'western	94	1115	9	8.55
Eric Henley, Rice	81	900	5	7.36
Terance Mathis, N.Mex	88	1315	13	7.33
Monty Gilbreath, S.Diego St	80	903	4	6.67
Dan Bitson, Tulsa	73	1425	16	6.64
Michael Smith, Kan.St	70	816	2	6.36
Rocky Palamara, CS-Full	69	1024	10	6.27
Brad Gaines, Vanderbilt	67	634	2	6.09
Dennis Smith, Utah	73	1089	18	6.08

Field Goals

Player, School	FGA	FG	Pct	FGPG
Philip Doyle, Alabama	25	22	.880	2.00
Gregg McCallum, Oregon	29	22	.759	2.00
Roman Anderson, Houston	36	22	.611	2.00
Mickey Thomas, Va.Tech	25	21	.840	1.91
Jason Hanson, Wash.St	27	21	.778	1.91
David Fuess, Tulsa	23	20	.870	1.82
Todd Wright, Arkansas	23	20	.870	1.82
Kevin Nicholl, C.Mich	24	20	.833	1.82
Chris Gardocki, Clemson	26	20	.769	1.82
Cary Blanchard, Okla.St	26	20	.769	1.82

Interceptions

Player,School	Int	Yds	TD	IPG
Cornelius Price, Houston	12	187	2	1.09
Bob Navarro, Eastern Mich	12	73	0	1.09
Ben Smith, Georgia	10	54	0	.91
Kevin Smith, Texas A&M	9	75	1	.82
Walter Briggs, Hawaii	9	116	1	.75

Punting
(At least 3.6 punts per game)

Player, School	No	Avg
Tom Rouen, Colorado	36	45.86
Kirk Maggio, UCLA	45	45.24
Rob Myers, Washington St	52	44.73
Shawn McCarthy, Purdue	69	44.57
Daren Parker, S.Carolina	49	44.29

Punt Returns

Player, School	No	Yds	TD	Avg
Larry Hargrove, Ohio U	17	309	2	15.24
Herb Jackson, Ball St	16	262	0	13.73
Dwight Pickens, Fresno St	30	470	1	13.43
Jeff Sydner, Hawaii	19	293	1	13.32
Tyrone Hughes, Nebraska	15	227	0	13.29

Kickoff Returns

Player,School	No	Yds	TD	Avg
Tony Smith, So.Miss	14	455	2	32.50
Mike Bellamy, Illinois	14	432	0	30.86
Chris Oldham, Oregon	14	402	0	28.71
Kelvin Means, Fresno St	18	509	0	28.28
Art Marshall, Georgia	16	445	0	27.81

NCAA Division I-A Team Leaders
REGULAR SEASON

Scoring Offense

	Gm	W-L-T	Pts	Avg
Houston	11	9-2-0	589	53.5
Nebraska	11	10-1-0	492	44.7
Colorado	11	11-0-0	452	41.1
BYU	12	10-2-0	484	40.3
Hawaii	12	9-2-1	457	38.1
Fresno St	11	11-1-0	414	37.6
Air Force	12	8-3-1	446	37.2
Miami,FL	11	10-1-0	393	35.7
Florida St	11	9-2-0	383	34.8
Oklahoma	11	7-4-0	380	34.5
Notre Dame	12	11-1-0	406	33.8

Scoring Defense

	Gm	W-L-T	Pts	Avg
Miami,FL	11	10-1-0	102	9.3
Auburn	11	9-2-0	117	10.6
Southern Cal	11	8-2-1	122	11.1
Penn St	11	7-3-1	130	11.8
Clemson	11	9-2-0	131	11.9
Michigan St	11	7-4-0	150	13.6
Colorado	11	11-0-0	150	13.6
Houston	11	9-2-0	150	13.6
Texas A&M	11	8-3-0	161	14.6
Illinois	11	9-2-0	161	14.6
Michigan	11	10-1-0	167	15.2

Total Offense

	Gm	Plays	Yds	Avg	TD	YdsPG
Houston	11	904	6874	7.6	70	624.91
BYU	12	852	6485	7.6	61	540.42
Nebraska	11	809	5646	7.0	63	513.27
Duke	11	866	5519	6.4	46	501.73
Air Force	12	886	5753	6.5	59	479.42
Colorado	11	768	5201	6.8	59	472.82
San Diego St	12	951	5610	5.9	46	467.50
Southern Cal	11	864	5029	5.8	39	457.18
Miami,FL	11	898	4995	5.6	46	454.09
Florida St	11	779	4965	6.4	46	451.36

Note: Touchdowns scored by rushing and passing only.

Total Defense

	Gm	Plays	Yds	Avg	TD	YdsPG
Miami,FL	11	709	2381	3.4	8	216.5
Southern Cal	11	635	2627	4.1	14	238.8
Florida	11	683	2661	3.9	18	241.9
Virginia Tech	11	705	2671	3.8	19	242.8
Clemson	11	690	2947	4.3	14	267.9
Auburn	11	686	2956	4.3	11	268.7
Eastern Mich	11	740	3014	4.1	20	274.0
Nebraska	11	727	3015	4.1	21	274.1
Baylor	11	749	3077	4.1	20	279.7
Illinois	11	721	3136	4.3	15	285.1
Michigan St	11	750	3137	4.2	19	285.2

Note: Touchdowns scored by rushing and passing only.

1989 NCAA DIVISION I-AA PLAYOFFS

| FIRST ROUND | QUARTER-FINALS | SEMI-FINALS | | SEMI-FINALS | QUARTER-FINALS | FIRST ROUND |

NCAA

Villanova 36 — Ga. Southern 45
Ga. Southern 52

Ga. Southern 45

Appalach. St. 21 — Mid. Tenn. St. 3
Mid. Tenn. St. 24

CHAMPIONSHIP GAME

Ga. Southern 45
S.F. Austin 21

Dec 16, 1989
at Statesboro, GA

Jackson St. 7 — Montana 25
Montana 48

Eastern Ill. 15

Eastern Ill. 38 — Eastern Ill. 19
Idaho 21

Seeded Teams
1. Ga. Southern 2. Furman 3. S.F. Austin 4. Idaho

Furman 42 — Furman 25 — Wm & Mary 10 / Furman 25

Furman 19

Youngstown St. 23 — Youngstown St. 28 / Eastern Ky. 24

S.F. Austin 21

SW Mo. St. 55 — Maine 35 / SW Mo. St. 38

S.F. Austin 25 — Grambling 56 / S.F. Austin 59

NCAA Division I-AA Final Standings

Big Sky Conference

	Conference				Overall				
	W	L	T	PF	PA	W	L	T	PF	PA
Idaho*	8	0	0	314	203	9	3	0	407	314
Montana*	7	1	0	255	124	11	3	0	451	283
Nevada-Reno	5	3	0	246	222	7	4	0	349	256
Boise St	5	3	0	194	179	6	5	0	261	245
East.Wash	4	4	0	198	175	4	6	0	255	264
Montana St	2	6	0	153	210	4	7	0	236	273
Idaho St	2	6	0	177	272	3	7	0	231	325
No.Ariz	2	6	0	193	244	3	8	0	258	317
Weber St	1	7	0	177	278	3	8	0	286	301

*Playoffs: Idaho (0-1,lost 1st Round); Montana (2-1,lost Semifinals).

Gateway Athletic Conference

	Conference				Overall				
	W	L	T	PF	PA	W	L	T	PF	PA
SW Mo.St.*	5	1	0	187	104	10	3	0	434	316
No.Iowa	4	2	0	149	142	8	3	0	302	211
E.Illinois*	4	2	0	127	91	9	4	0	278	180
Illinois St	4	2	0	118	105	5	6	0	190	240
Indiana St	2	4	0	99	122	4	7	0	222	240
W.Illinois	1	5	0	66	133	4	7	0	205	215
So.Illinois	1	5	0	107	156	2	9	0	222	290

*Playoffs: SW Missouri St.(1-1, lost Quarterfinals); Eastern Illinois (1-1, lost Quarterfinals).

Ivy League

	Conference				Overall				
	W	L	T	PF	PA	W	L	T	PF	PA
Yale	6	1	0	150	107	8	2	0	239	170
Princeton	6	1	0	168	80	7	2	1	237	177
Harvard	5	2	0	134	120	5	5	0	207	257
Dartmouth	4	3	0	115	82	5	5	0	170	178
Cornell	2	5	0	114	142	4	6	0	158	194
Penn	2	5	0	107	172	4	6	0	171	229
Brown	2	5	0	137	156	2	8	0	170	265
Columbia	1	6	0	104	170	1	9	0	130	287

Note: Yale beat Princeton, 14-7 (Nov.11).
*Playoffs: league does not play postseason games.

Mid-Eastern Athletic Conference

	Conference				Overall				
	W	L	T	PF	PA	W	L	T	PF	PA
Delaware St	5	1	0	138	78	7	4	0	244	202
Howard	4	2	0	91	58	8	3	0	205	116
Florida A&M	3	3	0	138	105	6	5	0	289	187
S.C.State	3	3	0	151	134	5	6	0	285	265
N.Car.A&T	2	4	0	93	135	5	6	0	200	214
Morgan St	2	4	0	76	140	4	6	1	183	269
Beth-Cook	2	4	0	80	117	4	6	0	178	199

*Playoffs: no teams from league qualified.

Ohio Valley Conference

	Conference				Overall				
	W	L	T	PF	PA	W	L	T	PF	PA
Mid.Tenn.St.*	6	0	0	196	54	9	4	0	318	225
E.Kentucky*	5	1	0	182	140	9	3	0	366	240
Murray St	3	3	0	174	171	6	4	1	284	258
Tenn.St	3	3	0	122	127	5	5	1	174	215
Morehead St	2	4	0	98	152	5	6	0	205	254
Tenn.Tech	2	4	0	88	115	4	6	0	191	230
Austin Peay	0	6	0	117	218	0	11	0	163	407

*Playoffs: Middle Tennessee St.(1-1, lost Quarterfinals); Eastern Kentucky (0-1, lost 1st Round).

Patriot League

	Conference				Overall				
	W	L	T	PF	PA	W	L	T	PF	PA
Holy Cross	4	0	0	144	49	10	1	0	396	161
Bucknell	2	2	0	103	147	5	5	0	253	260
Lafayette	2	2	0	128	131	5	5	0	319	249
Lehigh	1	3	0	119	143	5	6	0	371	360
Colgate	1	3	0	112	136	4	7	0	262	289
Fordham	—	—	—	—	—	2	6	0	119	253

Note: name changed from Colonial League to Patriot League on Dec.20, 1989.
Also: Fordham joined league in 1989 (replacing Davidson), but will not play a full league schedule until 1990 season (unofficially, the Rams lost to Colgate, Lehigh, Bucknell and Lafayette in '89).
*Playoffs: league does not play postseason games.

NCAA Division I-AA Final Standings (Cont.)

Southern Conference

	Conference				Overall			
	W	L	T	PF	PA	W	L	T	PF	PA
Furman*	7	0	0	227	74	12	2	0	430	189
Appalach.St.* .	5	2	0	173	102	9	3	0	306	177
Marshall	4	3	0	166	146	6	5	0	298	254
E.Tenn.St	4	3	0	161	178	4	7	0	218	325
Tenn-Chatt...	2	4	1	112	141	3	7	1	161	234
W.Carolina ...	1	4	1	104	155	3	7	1	190	261
VMI	1	4	1	66	145	2	8	1	151	306
Citadel	1	5	1	123	191	5	5	1	245	258

*Playoffs: Furman (2-1,lost Semifinals); Appalachian St.(0-1,lost 1st Round).

Southland Conference

	Conference				Overall			
	W	L	T	PF	PA	W	L	T	PF	PA
S.F.Austin St.* .	5	0	1	237	120	12	2	1	569	371
N'western St ..	3	1	2	113	95	4	5	2	204	197
SW Texas	3	3	0	117	111	5	6	0	245	198
NE Louisiana ..	2	3	1	129	161	4	6	1	201	257
McNeese St ...	2	4	0	116	129	5	6	0	254	221
North Texas ...	2	4	0	108	148	5	6	0	217	253
Sam Houston ..	2	4	0	74	130	3	8	0	133	272

*Playoffs: S.F.Austin St.(3-1,lost Final).

Southwestern Athletic Conference

	Conference				Overall			
	W	L	T	PF	PA	W	L	T	PF	PA
Grambling*...	7	0	0	304	103	9	3	0	464	215
Jackson St.* ..	5	2	0	242	88	8	4	0	364	205
Alcorn St	5	2	0	239	109	7	3	0	321	205
Southern-BR..	4	3	0	154	122	6	4	1	247	192
Tex.Southern ..	3	3	1	131	171	3	7	1	197	316
Alabama St...	2	4	1	154	136	4	5	1	203	174
Prairie View..	1	6	0	38	309	1	9	0	88	404
Miss.Valley ...	0	7	0	51	275	0	9	0	82	316

*Playoffs: Grambling (0-1,lost 1st Round); Jackson St.(0-1,lost 1st Round).

Yankee Conference

	Conference				Overall			
	W	L	T	PF	PA	W	L	T	PF	PA
Maine*	6	2	0	191	120	9	3	0	433	232
Villanova*	6	2	0	131	126	8	4	0	303	291
Connecticut ...	6	2	0	226	179	8	4	0	343	291
New Hamp ..	5	3	0	187	156	7	4	0	298	180
Delaware	3	0	0	246	207	6	5	0	313	257
Boston Univ...	4	4	0	175	175	7	4	0	319	229
UMass	3	5	0	180	215	4	7	0	230	285
Rhode Island .	1	7	0	118	178	4	7	0	161	261
Richmond	0	8	0	100	198	4	7	0	151	255

Note: Maine beat Villanova, 47-14 (Sep.16), and Connecticut, 30-8 (Oct.21); while Villanova beat UConn, 41-35 (Oct.7).
*Playoffs: Maine (0-1,lost 1st Round); Villanova (0-1,lost 1st Round).

Awards

Div. I-AA Player of the Year
Payton Award .... John Friesz, Idaho, QB
Div. II Player of the Year
Hill Trophy ..... Johnny Bailey, Texas A&I, RB
AFCA Coaches Choice Awards
NCAA Div. I-AA .... John Friesz
College Div. I .... Johnny Bailey
College Div. II ... Ricky Gales, Simpson, IA, RB
AFCA Coaches of the Year
NCAA Div. I-AA ... Erk Russell, Ga.Southern
NCAA Div. II ... John Williams, Mississippi Col.
NCAA Div. III .... Mike Kelly, Dayton

I-AA Independents

	W	L	T	PF	PA
Georgia Southern*	15	0	0	584	221
Youngstown St.*	9	4	0	372	245
William & Mary	8	3	1	286	261
Liberty	7	3	0	287	226
James Madison	5	4	1	267	159
Western Kentucky	6	5	0	279	238
Lamar	5	5	0	281	262
Arkansas St	5	6	0	261	265
Nicholls St	5	6	0	215	247
Samford	4	7	0	249	330
Northeastern	3	7	0	167	242
Towson St	2	8	0	162	279

Note: Lamar's board of regents voted Dec.14, 1989, to discontinue its football program.
*Playoffs: Georgia Southern (4-0,won Final); William & Mary (0-1,lost 1st Round); Youngstown St.(1-1,lost Quarterfinals).

NCAA Playoffs

Division II

First Round: St. Cloud St., MN 27, Augustana, SD 20; Mississippi College, Texas A&I 19; North Dakota St. 45, Edinboro, PA 32; Portland, St., OR 56, W. Chester, PA 50 (3 OT); Indiana, PA 34, Grand Valley St., MI 24; Angelo St., TX 28, UC-Davis, CA 23; Jacksonville St., AL 33, Alabama A&M 9.
Quarterfinals: Mississippi Col. 55, St. Cloud St. 24; Indiana, PA 17, Portland St. 0; Angelo St. 24, Pittsburg St. 21; Jacksonville St. 21, N. Dakota St. 17.
Semifinals: Mississippi Col. 26, Indiana, PA 14; Jacksonville St. 34, Angelo St. 16.
Championship Game (at Florence, AL): Mississippi Col. 3 (W-L 10-3), Jacksonville St. 0 (W-L: 13-1).

Division III

Regionals: Union, NY 42, Cortland St., NY 14; Montclair St., NJ 23, Hofstra, NY 6; Lycoming, PA 21, Dickinson, PA 0; Ferrum, VA 41, Wash. & Jefferson, PA 7; Dayton, OH 35, John Carroll, OH 10; Millikin, IL 21, Augustana, IL 12; Central, IA 55, St. Norbert, WI 7; St. John's, MN 42, Simpson, IA 35.
Quarterfinals: Union 45, Montclair St. 6; Ferrum 49, Lycoming 24; Dayton 28, Millikin 16; St.John's 27, Central 24.
Semifinals: Union 37, Ferrum 21; Dayton 28, St.John's 0.
Championship Game (Amos Alonzo Stagg Bowl Phenix City, AL): Dayton 17 (13-0-1), Union 7; (W-L: 13-1).

NAIA Playoffs

Division I

First Round: Adams St.,CO 30, NW Oklahoma St. 2; Central St.,OH 56, Moorhead St.,MN 7; Carson-Newman, TN 51, West Va.Tech 13; Emporia St.,KS 32, Harding,AR 9.
Semifinals: Carson-Newman 20, Central St. 17; Emporia St. 51, Adams St. 44.
Championship Game (at Jefferson City, TN): Carson-Newman 34 (W-L: 12-1), Emporia St. 20 (W-L: 10-3)

Division II

First Round: Wisc-La Crosse 30, Wisc-Stevens Pt. 20; Neb. Wesleyan 46, Chadron St.,NE 43 (2 OT); Baker, KS 30, Peru St.,NE 27; Missouri Valley 48, Hanover, IN 27; Central Wash. 51, Lewis & Clark,OR 0; Dickinson St.,ND 37, Carroll,MT 28; Westminster,PA 29, Georgetown,KY 9; Tarleton St.,TX 16, St.Mary/Plains, KS 6.
Quarterfinals: Wisc-La Crosse 29, Neb.Wesleyan 0; Baker 35, Missouri Valley 24; Central Wash. 49, Dickinson St. 7; Westminster 34, Tarleton St. 0.
Semifinals: Wisc-La Crosse 21, Baker 6; Westminster 21, Central Wash. 10.
Championship Game (at Canton, OH): Westminster 51 (W-L: 13-0), Wisc-La Crosse 30 (W-L: 12-2).

THE 1991 INFORMATION PLEASE SPORTS ALMANAC

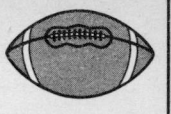

COLLEGE FOOTBALL
STATISTICS
THROUGH THE YEARS
1883-1990
BOWLS • ALL TIME LEADERS

SEC B

PAGE 109

National Champions, 1883–1989

Over the years, 23 different national selectors have chosen college football's Number One team by way of polls (12), mathematical rating systems (10) and historical research (1). The list below has been culled from four of those groups: the Helms Athletic Foundation (1883–1935), the Dickinson system (1924–40), the Associated Press (since 1936), United Press (1950–57) and United Press International (since 1958).

Bowl game results were counted in the Helms selections but not in the Dickinson picks. The final AP poll was taken after bowl games for the 1965 and '66 seasons and regularly since 1969. The final UPI poll has been taken after the bowls since the 1974 season.

In years where two champions are given, selectors' initials are noted.

Year		Record	Year		Record	Year		Record
1883	Yale	8–0–0	1889	Princeton	10–0–0	1895	Penn	14–0–0
1884	Yale	9–0–0	1890	Harvard	11–0–0	1896	Princeton	10–0–1
1885	Princeton	9–0–0	1891	Yale	13–0–0	1897	Penn	15–0–0
1886	Yale	9–0–1	1892	Yale	13–0–0	1898	Harvard	11–0–0
1887	Yale	9–0–0	1893	Princeton	11–0–0	1899	Harvard	10–0–1
1888	Yale	13–0–0	1894	Yale	16–0–0			

Year		Record	Bowl Game	Head Coach	Outstanding Player
1900	Yale	12–0–0	No bowl	Malcolm McBride	Perry Hale, HB
1901	Michigan	11–0–0	Won Rose	Hurry Up Yost	Willie Heston, HB
1902	Michigan	11–0–0	No bowl	Hurry Up Yost	Willie Heston, HB
1903	Princeton	11–0–0	No bowl	Art Hillebrand	John DeWitt, G
1904	Pennsylvania	12–0–0	No bowl	Carl Williams	Andy Smith, HB
1905	Chicago	11–0–0	No bowl	Amos Alonzo Stagg	Walter Eckersall, QB
1906	Princeton	9–0–1	No bowl	Bill Roper	Ed Dillon, HB
1907	Yale	9–0–1	No bowl	Bill Knox	T.A.D.Jones, HB
1908	Pennsylvania	11–0–1	No bowl	Sol Metzger	Hunter Scarlett, E
1909	Yale	10–0–0	No bowl	Howard Jones	Ted Coy, FB
1910	Harvard	8–0–1	No bowl	Percy Houghton	Percy Wendell, HB
1911	Princeton	8–0–2	No bowl	Bill Roper	Sanford White, E
1912	Harvard	9–0–0	No bowl	Percy Houghton	Charley Brickley, HB
1913	Harvard	9–0–0	No bowl	Percy Houghton	Eddie Mahan, FB
1914	Army	9–0–0	No bowl	Charley Daly	John McEwan, C
1915	Cornell	9–0–0	No bowl	Al Sharpe	Charley Barrett, HB
1916	Pittsburgh	8–0–0	No bowl	Pop Warner	Bob Peck, C
1917	Georgia Tech	9–0–0	No bowl	John Heisman	George Strupper, HB
1918	Pittsburgh	4–1–0	No bowl	Pop Warner	Tom Davies, HB
1919	Harvard	9–0–1	Won Rose	Bob Fisher	Ed Casey, HB
1920	California	9–0–0	Won Rose	Andy Smith	Brick Muller, E
1921	Cornell	8–0–0	No bowl	Gil Dobie	Eddie Kaw, HB
1922	Cornell	8–0–0	No bowl	Gil Dobie	George Pfann, QB
1923	Illinois	8–0–0	No bowl	Bob Zuppke	Red Grange, HB
1924	Notre Dame	10–0–0	Won Rose	Knute Rockne	"The Four Horsemen"*
1925	Alabama (H)	10–0–0	Won Rose	Wallace Wade	Johnny Mack Brown, HB
	Dartmouth (D)	8–0–0	No bowl	Jesse Hawley	Andy Oberlander, HB
1926	Alabama (H)	9–0–1	Tied Rose	Wallace Wade	Hoyt Winslett, E
	Stanford (D)	10–0–1	Tied Rose	Pop Warner	Ted Shipkey, E
1927	Illinois	7–0–1	No bowl	Bob Zuppke	Russ Crane, G
1928	Georgia Tech (H)	10–0–0	Won Rose	Bill Alexander	Pete Pund, C
	USC (D)	9–0–1	No bowl	Howard Jones	Lloyd Thomas, HB
1929	Notre Dame	9–0–0	No bowl	Knute Rockne	Frank Carideo, QB
1930	Notre Dame	10–0–0	No bowl	Knute Rockne	Frank Carideo, QB
1931	USC	10–1–0	Won Rose	Howard Jones	Ernie Pinckert, HB
1932	USC (H)	10–0–0	Won Rose	Howard Jones	Ernie Smith, T-K
	Michigan (D)	8–0–0	No bowl	Harry Kipke	Harry Newman, QB
1933	Michigan	7–0–1	No bowl	Harry Kipke	Frank Wistert, T

National Champions (Cont.)

Year		Record	Bowl Game	Head Coach	Outstanding Player
1934	Minnesota	8-0-0	No bowl	Bernie Bierman	Pug Lund
1935	Minnesota (H)	8-0-0	No bowl	Bernie Bierman	Dick Smith, T
	SMU	12-1-0	Lost Rose	Matty Bell	Bobby Wilson, HB
1936	Minnesota	7-1-0	No bowl	Bernie Bierman	Ed Widseth, T
1937	Pittsburgh	9-0-1	No bowl	Jock Sutherland	Marshall Goldberg, HB
1938	TCU	11-0-0	Won Sugar	Dutch Meyer	Davey O'Brien, QB
1939	Texas A&M	11-0-0	Won Sugar	Homer Norton	John Kimbrough
1940	Minnesota	8-0-0	No Bowl	Bernie Bierman	George Franck, FB
1941	Minnesota	8-0-0	No bowl	Bernie Bierman	Bruce Smith, HB
1942	Ohio St.	9-1-0	No bowl	Paul Brown	Gene Fekete, FB
1943	Notre Dame	9-1-0	No bowl	Frank Leahy	Angelo Bertelli, QB
1944	Army	9-0-0	No bowl	Red Blaik	Glenn Davis, HB
1945	Army	9-0-0	No bowl	Red Blaik	Doc Blanchard, FB
1946	Notre Dame	8-0-1	No bowl	Frank Leahy	Johnny Lujack, QB
1947	Notre Dame	9-0-0	No bowl	Frank Leahy	Johnny Lujack, QB
	Michigan†	10-0-0	Won Rose	Fritz Crisler	Bob Chappuis, HB
1948	Michigan	9-0-0	No bowl	Bennie Oosterbaan	Dick Rifenburg, E
1949	Notre Dame	10-0-0	No bowl	Frank Leahy	Leon Hart, E
1950	Oklahoma	10-1-0	Lost Sugar	Bud Wilkinson	Leon Heath, FB
1951	Tennessee	10-0-0	Lost Sugar	Bob Neyland	Hank Lauricella, QB
1952	Michigan St.	9-0-0	No bowl	Biggie Munn	Don McAuliffe, HB
1953	Maryland	10-1-0	Lost Orange	Jim Tatum	Bernie Faloney, QB
1954	Ohio St.	10-0-0	Won Rose	Woody Hayes	Howard Cassady, HB
	UCLA (UP)	9-0-0	No bowl	Red Sanders	Bob Davenport, FB
1955	Oklahoma	11-0-0	Won Orange	Bud Wilkinson	Jerry Tubbs, C
1956	Oklahoma	10-0-0	No bowl	Bud Wilkinson	Tommy McDonald, HB
1957	Auburn	10-0-0	No bowl	Shug Jordan	Jimmy Phillips, E
	Ohio St. (UP)	9-1-0	Won Rose	Woody Hayes	Bob White, FB
1958	LSU	11-0-0	Won Sugar	Paul Dietzel	Billy Cannon, HB
1959	Syracuse	11-0-0	Won Cotton	Ben Schwartzwalder	Ernie Davis, HB
1960	Minnesota	8-2-0	Lost Rose	Murray Warmath	Tom Brown, G
1961	Alabama	11-0-0	Won Sugar	Bear Bryant	Billy Neighbors, T
1962	Southern Cal	11-0-0	Won Rose	John McKay	Hal Bedsole, E
1963	Texas	11-0-0	Won Cotton	Darrell Royal	Scott Appleton, T
1964	Alabama	10-1-0	Lost Orange	Bear Bryant	Joe Namath, QB
1965	Alabama	9-1-1	Won Orange	Bear Bryant	Paul Crane, C
	Mich. St. (UPI)	10-1-0	Lost Rose	Duffy Daugherty	George Webster, DB
1966	Notre Dame	9-0-1	No bowl	Ara Parseghian	Jim Lynch, LB
1967	Southern Cal	10-1-0	Won Rose	John McKay	O.J. Simpson, HB
1968	Ohio St.	10-0-0	Won Rose	Woody Hayes	Rex Kern, QB
1969	Texas	11-0-0	Won Cotton	Darrell Royal	James Street, QB
1970	Nebraska	11-0-1	Won Orange	Bob Devaney	Jerry Tagge, QB
	Texas (UPI)	10-1-0	Lost Cotton	Darrell Royal	Steve Worster, RB
1971	Nebraska	13-0-0	Won Orange	Bob Devaney	Johnny Rodgers, WR
1972	Southern Cal	12-0-0	Won Rose	John McKay	Anthony Davis, RB
1973	Notre Dame	11-0-0	Won Sugar	Ara Parseghian	Mike Townsend, DB
	Alabama (UPI)	11-1-0	Lost Sugar	Bear Bryant	Buddy Brown, OT
1974	Oklahoma	11-0-0	No bowl	Barry Switzer	Joe Washington, RB
	Southern Cal (UPI)	10-1-1	Won Rose	John McKay	Anthony Davis, RB
1975	Oklahoma	11-1-0	Won Orange	Barry Switzer	Lee Roy Selmon, DT
1976	Pittsburgh	12-0-0	Won Sugar	Johnny Majors	Tony Dorsett, RB
1977	Notre Dame	11-1-0	Won Cotton	Dan Devine	Ross Browner, DE
1978	Alabama	11-1-0	Won Sugar	Bear Bryant	Marty Lyons, DT
	Southern Cal (UPI)	12-1-0	Won Rose	John Robinson	Charles White, RB
1979	Alabama	12-0-0	Won Sugar	Bear Bryant	Steadman Shealy, QB
1980	Georgia	12-0-0	Won Sugar	Vince Dooley	Herschel Walker, RB
1981	Clemson	12-0-0	Won Orange	Danny Ford	Jeff Davis, LB
1982	Penn St.	11-1-0	Won Sugar	Joe Paterno	Todd Blackledge, QB
1983	Miami, FL	11-1-0	Won Orange	H. Schnellenberger	Bernie Kosar, QB
1984	BYU	13-0-0	Won Holiday	LaVell Edwards	Robbie Bosco, QB
1985	Oklahoma	11-1-0	Won Orange	Barry Switzer	Brian Bosworth, LB
1986	Penn St.	12-0-0	Won Fiesta	Joe Paterno	D.J. Dozier, RB
1987	Miami, FL	12-0-0	Won Orange	Jimmy Johnson	Steve Walsh, QB
1988	Notre Dame	12-0-0	Won Fiesta	Lou Holtz	Tony Rice, QB
1989	Miami, FL	11-1-0	Won Sugar	Dennis Erickson	Craig Erickson, QB

*Notre Dame's **Four Horsemen** were Harry Stuhldreher (QB), Jim Crowley (HB), Don Miller (HB-P) and Elmer Layden (FB).

†Notre Dame won the final AP poll at the close of the 1947 regular season, but after Michigan trounced USC, 49-0, in the Rose Bowl there was a such an outcry for another vote that AP gave in. Michigan carried the unprecedented ballot, 226-119, but AP ruled that the earlier poll would be the vote of record.

Number 1 vs Number 2

Since the Associated Press writers poll started keeping track of such things in 1936, the No.1 and No.2 ranked teams in the country have met 25 times; 17 during the regular season and eight in bowl games. Since the first showdown in 1943, the No.1 team has beaten the No.2 team 15 times, lost eight and there have been two ties. Notre Dame (3–3–2) has been involved in eight of these games, two more than Oklahoma (1–5).

Each showdown is listed below with the date, the match-up, each team's record going into the game, the final score, the stadium and site.

Date	Match–up		Stadium
Oct. 9	#1 Notre Dame (2–0)	35	Michigan
1943	#2 Michigan (3–0)	12	(Ann Arbor)
Nov. 20	#1 Notre Dame (8–0)	14	Notre Dame
1943	#2 Iowa Pre-Flight (8–0)	...13	(South Bend)
Dec. 2	#1 Army (8–0)	23	Municipal
1944	#2 Navy (6–2)	7	(Baltimore)
Nov. 10	#1 Army (6–0)	48	Yankee
1945	#2 Notre Dame (5–0–1)	0	(New York)
Dec. 1	#1 Army (8–0)	32	Municipal
1945	#2 Navy (7–0–1)	13	(Phila.)
Nov. 9	#1 Army (7–0)	0	Yankee
1946	#2 Notre Dame (5–0)	0	(New York)

• • • •

Date	Match–up		Stadium
Jan. 1	#1 USC (10–0)	42	ROSE BOWL
1963	#2 Wisconsin (8–1)	37	(Pasadena)
Oct. 12	#2 Texas (3–0)	28	Cotton Bowl
1963	#1 Oklahoma (2–0)	7	(Dallas)
Jan. 1	#1 Texas (10–0)	28	COTTON BOWL
1964	#2 Navy (9–1)	6	(Dallas)
Nov. 19	#1 Notre Dame (8–0)	10	Spartan
1966	#2 Michigan St. (9–0)	10	(E. Lansing)
Sep. 28	#1 Purdue (1–0)	37	Notre Dame
1968	#2 Notre Dame (1–0)	22	(South Bend)
Jan. 1	#1 Ohio St. (9–0)	27	ROSE BOWL
1969	#2 USC (9–0–1)	16	(Pasadena)
Dec. 6	#1 Texas (9–0)	15	Razorback
1969	#2 Arkansas (9–0)	14	(Fayetteville)

Date	Match–up		Stadium
Nov. 25	#1 Nebraska (10–0)	35	Owen Field
1971	#2 Oklahoma (9–0)	31	(Norman)
Jan. 1	#1 Nebraska (12–0)	38	ORANGE BOWL
1972	#2 Alabama (11–0)	6	(Miami)
Jan. 1	#2 Alabama (10–1)	14	SUGAR BOWL
1979	#1 Penn St. (11–0)	7	(New Orleans)

• • • •

Date	Match–up		Stadium
Sep. 26	#1 USC (2–0)	28	Coliseum
1981	#2 Oklahoma (1–0)	24	(Los Angeles)
Jan. 1	#2 Penn St. (10–1)	27	SUGAR BOWL
1983	#1 Georgia (11–0)	23	(New Orleans)
Oct. 19	#1 Iowa (5–0)	12	Kinnick
1985	#2 Michigan (5–0)	10	(Iowa City)
Sep. 27	#2 Miami, FL (3–0)	28	Orange Bowl
1986	#1 Oklahoma (2–0)	16	(Miami)
Jan. 2	#2 Penn St. (11–0)	14	FIESTA BOWL
1987	#1 Miami, FL (11–0)	...10	(Tempe)
Nov. 21	#2 Oklahoma (10–0)	...17	Memorial
1987	#1 Nebraska (10–0)	7	(Lincoln)
Jan. 1	#2 Miami, FL (11–0)	...20	ORANGE BOWL
1988	#1 Oklahoma (11–0)	...14	(Miami)
Nov. 26	#1 Notre Dame (10–0)	..27	Coliseum
1988	#2 USC (10–0)	10	(Los Angeles)
Sep. 16	#2 Notre Dame (1–0)	...24	Michigan
1989	#1 Michigan (0–0)	19	(Ann Arbor)

Longest Division I Streaks

Winning Streaks
(Including bowl games)

No		Seasons	Spoiler	Score
47	Oklahoma	...1953–57	Notre Dame	7–0
39	Washington	..1908–14	Oregon St.	0–0
37	Yale	1890–93	Princeton	6–0
37	Yale	1887–89	Princeton	10–0
35	Toledo	1969–71	Tampa	21–0
34	Penn	1894–96	Lafayette	6–4
31	Oklahoma	..1948–50	Kentucky	13–7*
31	Pittsburgh	...1914–18	Cleve. Naval	10–9
31	Penn	1896–98	Harvard	10–0
30	Texas	1968–70	Notre Dame	24–11*
29	Michigan	1901–03	Minnesota	6–6
28	Alabama	1978–80	Miss.St.	6–3
28	Oklahoma	..1973–75	Kansas	23–3
28	Mich.St.	1950–53	Purdue	6–0
27	Nebraska	1901–04	Colorado	6–0
26	Cornell	1921–24	Williams	14–7
26	Michigan	1903–05	Chicago	2–0
25	BYU	1983–85	UCLA	27–24
25	Michigan	1946–49	Army	21–7
25	Army	1944–46	Notre Dame	0–0
25	USC	1931–33	Oregon St.	0–0

*Note: Kentucky beat Oklahoma in 1951 Sugar Bowl and Notre Dame beat Texas in 1971 Cotton Bowl.

Unbeaten Streaks
(Including bowl games)

No	W–T	Seasons	Spoiler	Score
63	59–4	Washington	.1907–17	California	27–0
56	55–1	Michigan	...1901–05	Chicago	2–0
50	46–4	California	...1920–25	Olympic	15–0
48	47–1	Oklahoma	..1953–57	N. Dame	7–0
48	47–1	Yale	1885–89	Princeton	10–0
47	42–5	Yale	1879–85	Princeton	6–5
44	42–2	Yale	1894–96	Princeton	24–6
42	39–3	Yale	1904–08	Harvard	4–0
39	37–2	N. Dame	...1946–50	Purdue	28–14
37	36–1	Oklahoma	..1972–75	Kansas	23–3
35	34–1	Minnesota	...1903–05	Wisc.	16–12

(W–T columns above: 63: 59–4; 56: 55–1; 50: 46–4; 48: 47–1; 48: 47–1; 47: 42–5; 44: 42–2; 42: 39–3; 39: 37–2; 37: 36–1; 35: 34–1)

Losing Streaks

No		Seasons	Victim	Score
44	Columbia	1983–88	Princeton	16–14
34	N'western	...1979–82	No.Illinois	31–6
28	Virginia	1958–60	Wm.&Mary	21–6*
22	Kansas St	1945–48	Arkansas St	37–6
27	E.Mich	1980–82	Kent St.	9–7

*Note: Virginia ended its streak in opening game of the 1961 season.

Winningest Division I-A Teams

All-Time Winning Pct.

Division I-A schools with best winning percentages through 1989 (including bowl games).

		Yrs	Games	W	L	T	Pct	Bowl Record
1	Notre Dame	101	926	683	203	40	.759	10–5–0
2	Michigan	110	969	703	233	33	.743	9–12–0
3	Alabama	95	922	651	228	43	.729	23–16–3
4	Oklahoma	95	905	628	227	50	.722	18–10–1
5	Texas	97	947	661	255	31	.714	16–15–2
6	Southern Cal.	97	887	605	232	50	.710	22–11–0
7	Ohio St.	100	929	626	253	50	.701	11–11–0
8	Penn St.	103	957	637	279	41	.687	16–8–2
9	Nebraska	100	955	635	281	39	.685	14–14–0
10	Tennessee	93	916	600	266	50	.682	16–14–0
11	Central Michigan	89	726	456	239	31	.649	0–0–0
12	Louisiana State	96	901	557	298	46	.644	11–16–1
13	Army	100	921	567	304	50	.643	2–1–0
14	Arizona State	77	679	422	233	24	.639	9–5–0
	Miami, Ohio	101	852	525	288	39	.639	5–2–1
16	Georgia	96	929	561	315	53	.632	13–13–3
17	Washington	100	874	524	301	49	.628	10–7–1
18	Auburn	97		529	301	49	.628	11–9–2
	Minnesota	106	913	541	329	43	.616	2–3–0
20	Michigan State	93	846	499	305	42	.615	4–5–0
21	Florida State	43	458	272	170	16	.611	9–7–2
22	Arkansas	96	906	533	335	38	.609	9–14–3
23	Pittsburgh	100	947	552	354	41	.605	8–10–0
24	UCLA	71	708	409	262	37	.604	9–7–1
25	Nevada-Las Vegas	22	244	145	95	4	.603	1–0–0
26	Tulsa	85	774	453	295	26	.602	3–7–0
27	Colorado	100	892	521	339	32	.602	4–10–0

Note: UNLV won the 1984 California Bowl, but had to forfeit the victory for using ineligible players.

All-Time Victories

Division I-A schools with most victories through 1989 (including bowl games).

	Wins			Wins			Wins
1 Michigan	703	15 Syracuse	550	28 California	500
2 Notre Dame	683	16 Minnesota	535	29 Michigan St	499
3 Texas	661	Navy	535	30 Missouri	494
4 Alabama	651	18 Arkansas	533	31 Clemson	493
5 Penn St.	637	19 West Virginia	531	32 Maryland	492
6 Nebraska	635	20 Auburn	529	33 Virginia Tech	491
7 Oklahoma	628	21 Georgia Tech	525	34 Vanderbilt	488
8 Ohio St	626	Miami, OH	525	35 Mississippi	485
9 Southern Cal	605	23 Washington	524	36 Kentucky	473
10 Tennessee	600	24 Colorado	521	37 Boston College	472
11 Army	567	25 North Carolina	516	38 Illinois	471
12 Georgia	561	26 Rutgers	510	39 Virginia	471
13 LSU	556	27 Texas A&M	508	40 Purdue	460
14 Pittsburgh	552				

Note: Division I-AA schools with over 600 wins through 1989: Yale (754), Harvard (686), Princeton (679), and Penn (672).

Most Bowl Appearances

Division I-A schools that have played in at least 20 postseason bowl games through 1989 season.

		Overall			Big Four					Bowls			Big Four		
	Bowls	W	L	T	W	L	T		Bowls	W	L	T	W	L	T
1 Alabama	42	23	16	3	17	12	1	9 Penn St	26	16	8	2	6	5	1
2 Southern Cal	33	22	11	0	19	8	0		Arkansas	26	9	14	3	4	10	1
	Texas	33	16	15	2	12	9	0	11 Georgia Tech	23	15	8	0	9	6	0
4 Tennessee	30	16	14	0	6	9	0		Mississippi	23	13	10	0	6	5	0
5 Oklahoma	29	18	10	1	15	6	0	13 Auburn	22	11	9	2	2	4	1
	Georgia	29	13	13	3	7	6	0		Ohio St	22	11	11	0	7	8	0
7 Nebraska	28	14	14	0	9	10	0	15 Michigan	21	9	12	0	6	10	0
	LSU	28	11	16	1	7	10	1								

Note: The Big Four bowls are the Rose, Orange, Sugar and Cotton. Only Alabama, Georgia, Georgia Tech and Notre Dame have won all four.

Bowl Games
JAN. 1, 1902 – JAN. 1, 1990
Rose Bowl

City: Pasadena, CA; **Stadium:** Rose Bowl; **Capacity:** 104,091; **Playing surface:** grass; **Automatic berths:** Pac-10 champion vs Big 10 champion (since 1947).

First year: 1902; **Playing sites:** Tournament Park (1902, 1916–22), Rose Bowl (1923–41), Duke Stadium, Durham, NC (1942); Rose Bowl (since 1943).

Year	Result	Year	Result	Year	Result
1902*	Michigan 49, Stanford 0	1940	USC 14, Tennessee 0	1965	Michigan 34, Oregon St. 7
1916	Washington St. 14, Brown 0	1941	Stanford 21, Nebraska 13	1966	UCLA 14, Michigan St. 12
1917	Oregon 14, Penn 0	1942	Oregon St. 20, Duke 16	1967	Purdue 14, USC 13
1918	Mare Island 19, Camp Lewis 7	1943	Georgia 9, UCLA 0	1968	USC 14, Indiana 3
1919	Great Lakes 17, Mare Is. 0	1944	USC 29, Washington 0	1969	Ohio St. 27, USC 16
1920	Harvard 7, Oregon 6	1945	USC 25, Tennessee 0		
1921	California 28, Ohio St. 0	1946	Alabama 34, USC 14	1970	USC 10, Michigan 3
1922	0–0, Calif. vs Wash.& Jeff.	1947	Illinois 45, UCLA 14	1971	Stanford 27, Ohio St. 17
1923	USC 14, Penn St. 0	1948	Michigan 49, USC 0	1972	Stanford 13, Michigan 12
1924	14–14, Navy vs Washington	1949	N'western 20, Calif. 14	1973	USC 42, Ohio St. 17
1925	Notre Dame 27, Stanford 10			1974	Ohio St. 42, USC 21
1926	Alabama 20, Washington 19	1950	Ohio St. 17, California 14	1975	USC 18, Ohio St. 17
1927	7–7, Alabama vs Stanford	1951	Michigan 14, California 6	1976	UCLA 23, Ohio St. 10
1928	Stanford 7, Pittsburgh 6	1952	Illinois 40, Stanford 7	1977	USC 14, Michigan 6
1929	Ga.Tech 8, California 7	1953	USC 7, Wisconsin 0	1978	Washington 27, Michigan 20
		1954	Michigan St. 28, UCLA 20	1979	USC 17, Michigan 10
1930	USC 47, Pittsburgh 14	1955	Ohio St. 20, USC 7		
1931	Alabama 24, Wash.St. 0	1956	Michigan St. 17, UCLA 14	1980	USC 17, Ohio St. 16
1932	USC 21, Tulane 12	1957	Iowa 35, Oregon St. 19	1981	Michigan 23, Washington 6
1933	USC 35, Pittsburgh 0	1958	Ohio St. 10, Oregon 7	1982	Washington 28, Iowa 0
1934	Columbia 7, Stanford 0	1959	Iowa 38, California 12	1983	UCLA 24, Michigan 14
1935	Alabama 29, Stanford 13			1984	UCLA 45, Illinois 9
1936	Stanford 7, SMU 0	1960	Washington 44, Wisconsin 8	1985	USC 20, Ohio St. 17
1937	Pitt 21, Washington 0	1961	Washington 17, Minnesota 7	1986	UCLA 45, Iowa 28
1938	California 13, Alabama 0	1962	Minnesota 21, UCLA 3	1987	Arizona St. 22, Michigan 15
1939	USC 7, Duke 3	1963	USC 42, Wisconsin 37 *	1988	Michigan St. 20, USC 17
		1964	Illinois 17, Washington 7	1989	Michigan 22, USC 14
				1990	USC 17, Michigan 10

*January game since 1902.

Orange Bowl

City: Miami, FL; **Stadium:** Orange Bowl; **Capacity:** 75,500; **Playing surface:** grass; **Automatic berths:** Big 8 champion (1954–64 and 1976–present).

First year: 1935; **Playing sites:** Orange Bowl (since 1935).

Year	Result	Year	Result	Year	Result
1935*	Bucknell 26, Miami,FL 0	1954	Oklahoma 7, Maryland 0	1973	Nebraska 40, Notre Dame 6
1936	Catholic U. 20, Mississippi 19	1955	Duke 34, Nebraska 7	1974	Penn St. 16, LSU 9
1937	Duquesne 13, Miss.St. 12	1956	Oklahoma 20, Maryland 6	1975	Notre Dame 13, Alabama 11
1938	Auburn 6, Michigan St. 0	1957	Colorado 27, Clemson 21	1976	Oklahoma 14, Michigan 6
1939	Tennessee 17, Oklahoma 0	1958	Oklahoma 48, Duke 21	1977	Ohio St. 27, Colorado 10
		1959	Oklahoma 21, Syracuse 6	1978	Arkansas 31, Oklahoma 6
1940	Georgia Tech 21, Missouri 7			1979	Oklahoma 31, Nebraska 24
1941	Miss.St. 14, Georgetown 7	1960	Georgia 14, Missouri 0		
1942	Georgia 40, TCU 26	1961	Missouri 21, Navy 14	1980	Oklahoma 24, Fla.St. 7
1943	Alabama 37, Boston Col. 21	1962	LSU 25, Colorado 7	1981	Oklahoma 18, Fla.St. 17
1944	LSU 19, Texas A&M 14	1963	Alabama 17, Oklahoma 0	1982	Clemson 22, Nebraska 15
1945	Tulsa 26, Georgia Tech 12	1964	Nebraska 13, Auburn 7	1983	Nebraska 21, LSU 20
1946	Miami,FL 13, Holy Cross 6	1965‡	Texas 21, Alabama 17	1984	Miami,FL 31, Nebraska 30
1947	Rice 8, Tennessee 0	1966	Alabama 39, Nebraska 28	1985	Washington 28, Oklahoma 17
1948	Georgia Tech 20, Kansas 14	1967	Florida 27, Ga.Tech 12	1986	Oklahoma 25, Penn St. 10
1949	Texas 41, Georgia 28	1968	Oklahoma 26, Tennessee 24	1987	Oklahoma 42, Arkansas 8
		1969	Penn St. 15, Kansas 14	1988	Miami,FL 20, Oklahoma 14
1950	Santa Clara 21, Kentucky 13			1989	Miami,FL 23, Nebraska 3
1951	Clemson 15, Miami,FL 14	1970	Penn St. 10, Missouri 3	1990	Notre Dame, 21, Colorado 6
1952	Georgia Tech 17, Baylor 14	1971	Nebraska 17, LSU 12		
1953	Alabama 61, Syracuse 6	1972	Nebraska 38, Alabama 6		

*January game since 1937.
‡Night game since 1965.

Bowl Games (Cont.)

Sugar Bowl

City: New Orleans, LA; **Stadium:** Louisiana Superdome; **Capacity:** 69,548; **Playing surface:** AstroTurf; **Automatic berths:** Southeastern Conference champion (since 1977).

First year: 1935; **Playing sites:** Tulane Stadium (1935–74), Superdome (since 1974).

Year	Result	Year	Result	Year	Result
1935*	Tulane 20, Temple 14	1954	Ga.Tech 42, West Va. 19	1972‡	Oklahoma 14, Penn St. 0
1936	TCU 3, LSU 2	1955	Navy 21, Mississippi 0	1973	Notre Dame 24, Alabama 23
1937	Santa Clara 21, LSU 14	1956	Ga.Tech 7, Pittsburgh 0	1974	Nebraska 13, Florida 10
1938	Santa Clara 6, LSU 0	1957	Baylor 13, Tennessee 7	1975	Alabama 13, Penn St. 6
1939	TCU 15, Carnegie Tech 7	1958	Mississippi 39, Texas 7	1977*	Pittsburgh 27, Georgia 3
		1959	LSU 7, Clemson 0	1978	Alabama 35, Ohio St. 6
1940	Texas A&M 14, Tulane 13			1979	Alabama 14, Penn St. 7
1941	Boston Col. 19, Tenn. 13	1960	Mississippi 21, LSU 0		
1942	Fordham 2, Missouri 0	1961	Mississippi 14, Rice 6	1980	Alabama 24, Arkansas 9
1943	Tennessee 14, Tulsa 7	1962	Alabama 10, Arkansas 3	1981	Georgia 17, Notre Dame 10
1944	Georgia Tech 20, Tulsa 18	1963	Mississippi 17, Arkansas 13	1982	Pittsburgh 24, Georgia 20
1945	Duke 29, Alabama 26	1964	Alabama 12, Mississippi 7	1983	Penn St. 27, Georgia 23
1946	Okla.A&M 33, St.Mary's 13	1965	LSU 13, Syracuse 10	1984	Auburn 9, Michigan 7
1947	Georgia 20, N.Carolina 10	1966	Missouri 20, Florida 18	1985	Nebraska 28, LSU 10
1948	Texas 27, Alabama 7	1967	Alabama 34, Nebraska 7	1986	Tennessee 35, Miami,FL 7
1949	Oklahoma 14, N.Carolina 6	1968	LSU 20, Wyoming 13	1987	Nebraska 30, LSU 15
		1969	Arkansas 16, Georgia 2	1988	16–16, Syracuse vs Auburn
1950	Oklahoma 35, LSU 0			1989	Florida St. 13, Auburn 7
1951	Kentucky 13, Oklahoma 7	1970	Mississippi 27, Arkansas 22	1990	Miami,FL 33, Alabama 25
1952	Maryland 28, Tennessee 13	1971	Tennessee 34, Air Force 13		
1953	Ga.Tech 24, Mississippi 7	1972	Oklahoma 40, Auburn 22		

*January game from 1935–72 and since 1977.
‡Game played on Dec. 31 from 1972–75.

Cotton Bowl

City: Dallas, TX; **Stadium:** Cotton Bowl; **Capacity:** 72,032; **Playing surface:** AstroTurf; **Automatic berths:** Southwest Athletic Conference champion (since 1942).

First year: 1937; **Playing sites:** Fair Park Stadium (1937); Cotton Bowl (since 1938).

Year	Result	Year	Result	Year	Result
1937*	TCU 16, Marquette 6	1955	Ga.Tech 14, Arkansas 6	1973	Texas 17, Alabama 13
1938	Rice 28, Colorado 14	1956	Mississippi 14, TCU 13	1974	Nebraska 19, Texas 3
1939	St.Mary's 20, Texas Tech 13	1957	TCU 28, Syracuse 17	1975	Penn St. 41, Baylor 20
		1958	Navy 20, Rice 7	1976	Arkansas 31, Georgia 10
1940	Clemson 6, Boston Col. 3	1959	0–0, TCU vs Air Force	1977	Houston 30, Maryland 21
1941	Texas A&M 13, Fordham 12			1978	Notre Dame 38, Texas 10
1942	Alabama 29, Texas A&M 21	1960	Syracuse 23, Texas 14	1979	Notre Dame 35, Houston 34
1943	Texas 14, Georgia Tech 7	1961	Duke 7, Arkansas 6		
1944	7–7, Texas vs Randolph Field	1962	Texas 12, Mississippi 7	1980	Houston 17, Nebraska 14
1945	Oklahoma A&M 34, TCU 0	1963	LSU 13, Texas 0	1981	Alabama 30, Baylor 2
1946	Texas 40, Missouri 27	1964	Texas 28, Navy 6	1982	Texas 14, Alabama 12
1947	0–0, Arkansas vs LSU	1965	Arkansas 10, Nebraska 7	1983	SMU 7, Pittsburgh 3
1948	13–13, SMU vs Penn St.	1966	LSU 14, Arkansas 7	1984	Georgia 10, Texas 9
1949	SMU 21, Oregon 13	1966‡	Georgia 24, SMU 9	1985	Boston Col. 45, Houston 28
		1968*	Texas A&M 20, Alabama 16	1986	Texas A&M 36, Auburn 16
1950	Rice 27, N.Carolina 13	1969	Texas 36, Tennessee 13	1987	Ohio St. 28, Texas A&M 12
1951	Tennessee 20, Texas 14			1988	Texas A&M 35, N.Dame 10
1952	Kentucky 20, TCU 7	1970	Texas 21, Notre Dame 17	1989	UCLA 17, Arkansas 3
1953	Texas 16, Tennessee 0	1971	Notre Dame 24, Texas 11	1990	Tennessee 31, Arkansas 27
1954	Rice 28, Alabama 6	1972	Penn St. 30, Texas 6		

*January game from 1937–66 and since 1968.
‡Game played on Dec. 31, 1966.

Fiesta Bowl

City: Tempe, AZ; **Stadium:** Sun Devil Stadium; **Capacity:** 74,000; **Playing surface:** grass; **Automatic berths:** none.

First year: 1971; **Playing sites:** Sun Devil Stadium (since 1971).

Year	Result	Year	Result	Year	Result
1971*	Ariz.St. 45, Florida St. 38	1978	10–10, Arkansas vs UCLA	1986	Michigan 27, Nebraska 23
1972	Ariz.St. 49, Missouri 35	1979	Pittsburgh 16, Arizona 10	1987	Penn St. 14, Miami,FL 10
1973	Ariz.St. 28, Pittsburgh 7	1980	Penn St. 31, Ohio St. 19	1988	Florida St. 31, Nebraska 28
1974	Oklahoma St. 16, BYU 6	1982‡	Penn St. 26, USC 10	1989	Notre Dame 34, West Va. 21
1975	Ariz.St. 17, Nebraska 14	1983	Ariz.St. 32, Oklahoma 21	1990	Florida St. 41, Nebraska 17
1976	Oklahoma 41, Wyoming 7	1984	Ohio St. 28, Pittsburgh 23		
1977	Penn St. 42, Ariz.St. 30	1985	UCLA 39, Miami,FL 37		

*December game from 1971–80.
‡January game since 1982.

Gator Bowl

City: Jacksonville, FL; **Stadium:** Gator Bowl; **Capacity:** 82,000; **Playing surface:** grass; **Automatic berths:** none.

First year: 1946; **Playing sites:** Gator Bowl (since 1946).

Year	Result	Year	Result	Year	Result
1946*	W.Forest 26, S.Carolina 14	1960‡	Florida 13, Baylor 12	1975	Maryland 13, Florida 0
1947	Oklahoma 34, N.C.State 13	1961	Penn St. 30, Ga.Tech 15	1976	Notre Dame 20, Penn St. 9
1948	20–20, Maryland vs Georgia	1962	Florida 17, Penn St. 7	1977	Pittsburgh 34, Clemson 3
1949	Clemson 24, Missouri 23	1963	N.Carolina 35, Air Force 0	1978	Clemson 17, Ohio St. 15
		1965*	Fla.St. 36, Oklahoma 19	1979	N.Carolina 17, Michigan 15
1950	Maryland 20, Missouri 7	1965‡	Ga.Tech 31, Texas Tech 21		
1951	Wyoming 20, Wash.& Lee 7	1966	Tennessee 18, Syracuse 12	1980	Pittsburgh 37, S.Carolina 9
1952	Miami,FL 14, Clemson 0	1967	17–17, Fla.St. vs Penn St.	1981	N.Carolina 31, Arkansas 27
1953	Florida 14, Tulsa 13	1968	Missouri 35, Alabama 10	1982	Florida St. 31, West Va. 12
1954	Texas Tech 35, Auburn 13	1969	Florida 14, Tennessee 13	1983	Florida 14, Iowa 6
1954‡	Auburn 33, Baylor 13			1984	Okla.St. 21, S.Carolina 14
1955	Vanderbilt 25, Auburn 13	1971*	Auburn 35, Mississippi 28	1985	Florida St. 34, Okla.St. 23
1956	Ga.Tech 21, Pittsburgh 14	1971‡	Georgia 7, N.Carolina 3	1986	Clemson 27, Stanford 21
1957	Tennessee 3, Texas A&M 0	1972	Auburn 24, Colorado 3	1987	LSU 30, S.Carolina 13
1958	Mississippi 7, Florida 3	1973	Texas Tech 28, Tennessee 19	1989*	Georgia 34, Michigan St. 27
		1974	Auburn 27, Texas 3	1989	Clemson 27, West Va. 7
1960*	Arkansas 14, Ga.Tech 7				

*January game from 1946–54, 1960, 1965, 1971 and in 1989.
‡December game from 1954–58, 1960–63, 1965–69 and 1971–88.

Florida Citrus Bowl

City: Orlando, FL; **Stadium:** Florida Citrus Bowl-Orlando; **Capacity:** 52,300; **Playing surface:** grass; **Automatic berths:** none.

First year: 1947; **Name change:** Tangerine Bowl (1947–82), Florida Citrus Bowl (since 1983); **Playing sites:** Tangerine Bowl (1947–72), Florida Field, Gainesville (1973), Tangerine Bowl (1974–82), Orlando Stadium (1983–85), Florida Citrus Bowl-Orlando (since 1986). The Tangerine Bowl, Orlando Stadium and Citrus Bowl are all the same stadium.

Note: No major college teams played in the Tangerine Bowl from 1947–61 or 1963–67.

Year	Result	Year	Result	Year	Result
1947*	Catawba 31, Maryville 6	1960*	Mid.Tenn. 21, Presbyterian 12	1975	Miami,OH 20, S.Carolina 7
1948	Catawba 7, Marshall 0	1960‡	Citadel 27, Tenn. Tech 0	1976	Oklahoma 49, BYU 21
1949	21–21, Murray St.	1961	Lamar 21, Middle Tenn. 14	1977	Fla.St. 40, Texas Tech 17
	vs. Sul Ross St.	1962	Houston 49, Miami,OH 21	1978	N.C.State 30, Pitt 17
		1963	West.Ky. 27, Coast Guard 0	1979	LSU 34, Wake Forest 10
1950	St.Vincent 7, Em.& Henry 6	1964	E.Carolina 14, Mass. 13		
1951	M.Harvey 35, Em.& Henry 14	1965	E.Carolina 31, Maine 0	1980	Florida 35, Maryland 20
1952	Stetson 35, Arkansas St. 20	1966	Morgan St. 14, W.Chester 6	1981	Missouri 19, So.Miss. 17
1953	E.Texas St. 33, Tenn. Tech 0	1967	Tenn.Martin 25, W.Chester 8	1982	Auburn 33, Boston Col. 26
1954	7–7, E.Texas St. vs Ark.St.	1968	Richmond 49, Ohio U. 42	1983	Tennessee 30, Maryland 23
1955	Neb.-Omaha 7, Eastern Ky. 6	1969	Toledo 56, Davidson 33	1984	17–17, Fla.St. vs Georgia
1956	6–6, Juniata vs Mo.Valley			1985	Ohio St. 10, BYU 7
1957	W.Texas St. 20, So.Miss. 13	1970	Toledo 40, Wm.& Mary 12	1987*	Auburn 16, USC 7
1958	E.Texas St. 10, So.Miss. 9	1971	Toledo 28, Richmond 3	1988	Clemson 35, Penn St. 10
1958‡	E.Texas St. 26, Mo.Valley 7	1972	Tampa 21, Kent St. 18	1989	Clemson 13, Oklahoma 6
		1973	Miami,OH 16, Florida 7		
		1974	Miami,OH 21, Georgia 10	1990	Illinois 31, Virginia 21

*January game from 1947–58, in 1960 and since 1987.
‡December game from 1958 and 1960–85.

Bowl Games (Cont.)

John Hancock Bowl

City: El Paso, TX; **Stadium:** Sun Bowl; **Capacity:** 52,000; **Playing surface:** AstroTurf; **Automatic berths:** none.

First year: 1936; **Name changes:** Sun Bowl (1936–86), John Hancock Sun Bowl (1987–88); John Hancock Bowl (since 1989); **Playing sites:** Kidd Field (1936–62), Sun Bowl (since 1963).

Year	Result	Year	Result	Year	Result
1936*	14–14, Hardin-Simmons vs New Mexico St.	1953	Pacific 26, So.Miss. 7	1970	Ga.Tech 17, Texas Tech 9
1937	Hardin-Simmons 34, Texas Mines 6	1954	Tex.Western 37, So.Miss. 14	1971	LSU 33, Iowa St. 15
		1955	Tex.Western 47, Fla.St. 20	1972	N.Carolina 32, Tex.Tech 28
1938	West Va. 7, Texas Tech 6	1956	Wyoming 21, Texas Tech 14	1973	Missouri 34, Auburn 17
1939	Utah 26, New Mexico 0	1957	Geo.Wash. 13, Tex.Western 0	1974	Miss.St. 26, N.Carolina 24
		1958	Louisville 34, Drake 20	1975	Pittsburgh 33, Kansas 19
1940	0–0, Catholic U. vs Ariz.St.	1958*	Wyoming 14, Hard.-Simmons 6	1977*	Texas A&M 37, Florida 14
1941	W.Reserve 26, Ariz.St. 13	1959	New Mex.St. 28, N.Texas 8	1977‡	Stanford 24, LSU 14
1942	Tulsa 6, Texas Tech 0			1978	Texas 42, Maryland 0
1943	2nd Air Force 13, Hardin Simmons 7	1960	New Mex.St. 20, Utah St. 13	1979	Washington 14, Texas 7
		1961	Villanova 17, Wichita 9		
1944	SW Texas 7, New Mexico 0	1962	West Texas 15, Ohio U. 14	1980	Nebraska 31, Miss.St. 17
1945	SW Texas 35, U.of Mexico 0	1963	Oregon 21, SMU 14	1981	Oklahoma 40, Houston 14
1946	New Mexico 34, Denver 24	1964	Georgia 7, Gergia Tech 0	1982	N.Carolina 26, Texas 10
1947	Cincinnati 18, Va.Tech 6	1965	Texas Western 13, TCU 12	1983	Alabama 28, SMU 7
1948	Miami,OH 13, Texas Tech 12	1966	Wyoming 28, Fla.St. 20	1984	Maryland 27, Tennessee 26
1949	West Va. 21, Texas Mines 12	1967	UTEP 14, Mississippi 7	1985	13–13, Georgia vs Arizona
		1968	Auburn 34, Arizona 10	1986	Alabama 28, Washington 6
1950	Tex.Western 33, Geo'town 20	1969	Nebraska 45, Georgia 6	1987	Okla.St. 35, West Va. 33
1951	West Texas 14, Cincinnati 13			1988	Alabama 29, Army 28
1952	Texas Tech 25, Pacific 14			1989	Pittsburgh 31, Texas A&M 28

*January game from 1936–58 and in 1977.   ‡December game from 1958–75 and since 1977.

Liberty Bowl

City: Memphis, TN; **Stadium:** Liberty Bowl Memorial Stadium; **Capacity:** 63,000; **Playing surface:** grass; **Automatic berths:** The winner of the Commander-in-Chief's Trophy (Army, Navy or Air Force)—if Air Force is also WAC champion, it is obligated to play in Holiday Bowl, in which case Liberty Bowl decides between Army and Navy.

First year: 1959; **Playing sites:** Philadelphia, PA (Municipal Stadium, 1959–63); Atlantic City, NJ (Convention Hall, 1964); Memphis (since 1965).

Year	Result	Year	Result	Year	Result
1959*	Penn St. 7, Alabama 0	1970	Tulane 17, Colorado 3	1980	Purdue 28, Missouri 25
		1971	Tennessee 14, Arkansas 13	1981	Ohio St. 31, Navy 28
1960	Penn St. 41, Oregon 12	1972	Ga.Tech 31, Iowa St. 30	1982	Alabama 21, Illinois 15
1961	Syracuse 15, Miami,FL 14	1973	N.C.State 31, Kansas 18	1983	N.Dame 19, Boston Col. 18
1962	Oregon St. 6, Villanova 0	1974	Tennessee 7, Maryland 3	1984	Auburn 21, Arkansas 15
1963	Miss.St. 16, N.C.State 12	1975	USC 20, Texas A&M 0	1985	Baylor 21, LSU 7
1964	Utah 32, West Virgina 6	1976	Alabama 36, UCLA 6	1986	Tennessee 21, Minnesota 14
1965	Mississippi 13, Auburn 7	1977	Nebraska 21, N.Carolina 17	1987	Georgia 20, Arkansas 17
1966	Miami,FL 14, Va.Tech 7	1978	Missouri 20, LSU 15	1988	Indiana 34, S.Carolina 10
1967	N.C.State 14, Georgia 7	1979	Penn St. 9, Tulane 6	1989	Mississippi 42, Air Force 29
1968	Mississippi 34, Va.Tech 17				
1969	Colorado 47, Alabama 33				

*December game since 1959.

Peach Bowl

City: Atlanta, GA; **Stadium:** Atlanta Fulton County Stadium; **Capacity:** 59,800; **Playing surface:** grass; **Automatic berths:** none.

First year: 1968; **Playing sites:** Grant Field (1968–70), Atlanta Stadium (since 1971).

Year	Result	Year	Result	Year	Result
1968*	LSU 31, Florida St. 27	1975	West Va. 13, N.C.State 10	1982	Iowa 28, Tennessee 22
1969	West Va. 14, S.Carolina 3	1976	Kentucky 21, N.Carolina 9	1983	Fla.St. 28, N.Carolina 3
		1977	N.C.State 24, Iowa St. 14	1984	Virginia 27, Purdue 24
1970	Ariz.St. 48, N.Carolina 26	1978	Purdue 41, Ga.Tech 21	1985	Army 31, Illinois 29
1971	Mississippi 41, Ga.Tech 18	1979	Baylor 24, Clemson 18	1986	Va.Tech 25, N.C.State 24
1972	N.C.State 49, West Va. 13			1988‡	Tennessee 27, Indiana 22
1973	Georgia 17, Maryland 16	*1981‡	Miami,FL 20, Va.Tech 10	1988*	N.C.State 28, Iowa 23
1974	6–6, Vanderbilt vs Tex.Tech	1981*	West Va. 26, Florida 6	1989	Syracuse 19, Georgia 18

*December game from 1968–79, 1981–86, and since 1988.   ‡January game in 1981 and 1988.

Independence Bowl

City: Shreveport, LA; **Stadium:** Independence Stadium; **Capacity:** 50,560; **Playing surface:** grass; **Automatic berths:** none.

First year: 1976; **Playing sites:** Independence Stadium (since 1976).

Year	Result	Year	Result	Year	Result
1976*	McNeese St. 20, Tulsa 16	1980	So.Miss 16, McNeese St. 14	1985	Minnesota 20, Clemson 13
1977	La.Tech 24, Louisville 14	1981	Texas A&M 33, Okla.St. 16	1986	Mississippi 20, Tex.Tech 17
1978	E.Carolina 35, La.Tech 13	1982	Wisconsin 14, Kansas St. 3	1987	Washington 24, Tulane 12
1979	Syracuse 31, McNeese St. 7	1983	Air Force 9, Mississippi 3	1988	So.Miss 38, UTEP 18
		1984	Air Force 23, Va.Tech 7	1989	Oregon 27, Tulsa 24

*December game since 1976.

All-American Bowl

City: Birmingham, AL; **Stadium:** Legion Field; **Capacity:** 75,808; **Playing surface:** AstroTurf; **Automatic berths:** none.

First year: 1977; **Name change:** Hall of Fame Classic (1977–84), All-American Bowl (since 1985); **Playing sites:** Legion Field (since 1977).

Year	Result	Year	Result	Year	Result
1977*	Maryland 17, Minnesota 7	1980	Arkansas 34, Tulane 15	1985	Ga.Tech 17, Mich.St. 14
1978	Texas A&M 28, Iowa St. 12	1981	Miss.St. 10, Kansas 0	1986	Florida St. 27, Indiana 13
1979	Missouri 24, S.Carolina 14	1982	Air Force 36, Vanderbilt 28	1987	Virginia 22, BYU 16
		1983	West Va. 20, Kentucky 16	1988	Florida 14, Illinois 10
		1984	Kentucky 20, Wisconsin 19	1989	Texas Tech 49, Duke 21

*December game since 1977.

Holiday Bowl

City: San Diego, CA; **Stadium:** San Diego Jack Murphy Stadium; **Capacity:** 60,750; **Playing surface:** grass; **Automatic berths:** Western Athletic Conference champion (except 1985).

First year: 1978; **Playing sites:** Jack Murphy Stadium (since 1978).

Year	Result	Year	Result	Year	Result
1978*	Navy 23, BYU 16	1981	BYU 38, Wash.St. 36	1985	Arkansas 18, Ariz.St. 17
1979	Indiana 38, BYU 37	1982	Ohio St. 47, BYU 17	1986	Iowa 39, S.Diego St. 38
		1983	BYU 21, Missouri 17	1987	Iowa 20, Wyoming 19
1980	BYU 46, SMU 45	1984	BYU 24, Michigan 17	1988	Okla.St. 62, Wyoming 14
				1989	Penn St. 50, BYU 39

*December game since 1978.

California Bowl

City: Fresno, CA; **Stadium:** Bulldog Stadium; **Capacity:** 30,000; **Playing surface:** grass; **Automatic berths:** Mid-American Conference and Big West champions (since 1981).

First year: 1981; **Playing sites:** Bulldog Stadium (since 1981).

Year	Result	Year	Result	Year	Result
1981*	Toledo 27, San Jose St. 25	1984	UNLV 30, Toledo 13	1987	E.Michigan 30, S.Jose St. 27
1982	Fresno St. 29, Bowl.Green 28	1985	Fresno St. 51, Bowl.Green 7	1988	Fresno St. 35, W.Michigan 30
1983	Northern Ill. 20, Cal St.-Fullerton 13	1986	San Jose St. 37, Miami,OH 7	1989	Fresno St. 27, Ball St. 6

*December game since 1981.
Note: Toledo ruled winner of 1984 game by forfeit when UNLV was found to have used ineligible players.

Aloha Bowl

City: Honolulu, HI; **Stadium:** Aloha Stadium; **Capacity:** 50,000; **Playing surface:** AstroTurf; **Automatic berths:** none.

First year: 1982; **Playing sites:** Aloha Stadium (since 1982).

Year	Result	Year	Result	Year	Result
1982*	Washington 21, Maryland 20	1985	Alabama 24, USC 3	1987	UCLA 20, Florida 16
1983	Penn St. 13, Washington 10	1986	Arizona 30, N.Carolina 21	1988	Wash.St. 24, Houston 22
1984	SMU 27, Notre Dame 20			1989	Michigan St. 33, Hawaii 13

*December game since 1982.

Bowl Games (Cont.)

Freedom Bowl

City: Anaheim, CA; **Stadium:** Anaheim Stadium; **Capacity:** 70,500; **Playing surface:** grass; **Automatic berths:** none.
First year: 1984; **Playing sites:** Anaheim Stadium (since 1984).

Year	Result	Year	Result	Year	Result
1984*	Iowa 55, Texas 17	1986	UCLA 31, BYU 10	1988	BYU 20, Colorado 17
1985	Washington 20, Colorado 17	1987	Ariz.St. 33, Air Force 28	1989	Washington 34, Florida 7

*December game since 1984.

Hall of Fame Bowl

City: Tampa, FL; **Stadium:** Tampa Stadium; **Capacity:** 74,315; **Playing surface:** grass; **Automatic berths:** none.
First year: 1986; **Playing sites:** Tampa Stadium (since 1986).

Year	Result	Year	Result	Year	Result
1986*	Boston Col. 27, Georgia 24	1989	Syracuse 23, LSU 10	1990	Auburn 31, Ohio St. 14
1988‡	Michigan 28, Alabama 24				

*December game in 1986.
‡January game since 1988.

Copper Bowl

City: Tucson, AZ; **Stadium:** Arizona; **Capacity:** 57,000; **Playing surface:** grass; **Automatic berths:** none.
First year: 1989; **Playing sites:** Arizona Stadium (since 1989).

Year	Result
1989*	Arizona 17, N.C.State 10

*December game since 1989.

Bowl Game Schedule for 1990–91

With the addition of the Blockbuster Bowl at Joe Robbie Stadium in Miami on Dec. 28, there are now 19 post-season bowl games certified by the NCAA. All starting times on the schedule below are Eastern Standard Time.

Date	Bowl	Time	Date	Bowl	Time	Date	All-Star Game	Time
Dec. 8	California	3:30 PM	Dec.31	John Hancock	12:30 PM	Dec.25	Blue Gray	12:00 PM
Dec.15	Independence	8:00 PM		Copper	5:00 PM	Jan.12	Japan	10:00 PM
Dec.25	Aloha	3:30 PM	Jan. 1	Gator	11:30 AM	Jan.19	Senior	12:00 PM
Dec.27	Liberty	8:00 PM		Hall of Fame	1:00 PM		Hula	3:30 PM
Dec.28	All-American	7:30 PM		Cotton	1:30 PM	Jan.26	Shrine	4:00 PM
	Blockbuster	8:00 PM		Fla.Citrus	1:30 PM			
Dec.29	Peach	12:30 PM		Fiesta	4:30 PM			
	Holiday	7:30 PM		Rose	5:00 PM			
	Freedom	8:00 PM		Orange	8.00 PM			
				Sugar	8:30 PM			

Bowls Discontinued in the 1980s

Bluebonnet (Houston)

Years: 1959–87; **Name change:** Astro-Bluebonnet Bowl (1968–76); **Playing sites:** Rice Stadium (1959–67, 1985–86), Astrodome (1968–84, 1987).

Year	Result	Year	Result	Year	Result
1959*	Clemson 23, TCU 7	1968	SMU 28, Oklahoma 27	1978	Stanford 25, Georgia 22
		1969	Houston 36, Auburn 7	1979	Purdue 27, Tennessee 22
1960	3–3, Texas vs Alabama	1970	24–24, Alabama vs Oklahoma		
1961	Kansas 33, Rice 7	1971	Colorado 29, Houston 17	1980	N.Carolina 16, Texas 7
1962	Missouri 14, Ga.Tech 10	1972	Tennessee 24, LSU 17	1981	Michigan 33, UCLA 14
1963	Baylor 14, LSU 7	1973	Houston 47, Tulane 7	1982	Arkansas 28, Florida 24
1964	Tulsa 14, Mississippi 7	1974	31–31, N.C.State vs Houston	1983	Okla.St. 24, Baylor 14
1965	Tennessee 27, Tulsa 6	1975	Texas 38, Colorado 21	1984	West Va. 31, TCU 14
1966	Texas 19, Mississippi 0	1976	Nebraska 27, Texas Tech 24	1985	Air Force 24, Texas 16
1967	Colorado 31, Miami,FL 21	1977	USC 47, Texas A&M 28	1986	Baylor 21, Colorado 9
				1987	Texas 32, Pittsburgh 27

*December game every year.

Cherry (Pontiac, MI)

Years: 1984–85; **Playing site:** Pontiac Silverdome (1984–85).

Year	Result
1984*	Army 10, Michigan St. 6
1985	Maryland 35, Syracuse 18

*December game both years.

Garden State (E.Rutherford, NJ)

Years: 1978–81; **Playing site:** Giants Stadium (1984–85).

Year*	Result	Year*	Result
1978*	Ariz.St. 34, Rutgers 18	1980	Houston 35, Navy 0
1979	Temple 28, California 17	1981	Tennessee 28, Wisconsin 21

*December game every year.

Major Conference Champions

Atlantic Coast Conference

Founded in 1953 when charter members all left Southern Conference to form ACC. **Charter members** (7): Clemson, Duke, Maryland, North Carolina, N.C.State, South Carolina, and Wake Forest. **Admitted later** (2): Virginia in 1953 (began play in '54), Ga.Tech in 1978 (began play in '83). **Withdrew later** (1): South Carolina in 1971. **Current playing membership** (8): Clemson, Duke, Ga.Tech, Maryland, North Carolina, N.C.State, Virginia and Wake Forest.

Year		Year		Year		Year	
1953	Duke (4-0) & Maryland (3-0)	1960	Duke (5-1)	1970	Wake Forest (5-1)	1980	N.Carolina (6-0)
1954	Duke (4-0)	1961	Duke (5-1)	1971	N.Carolina (6-0)	1981	Clemson (6-0)
1955	Maryland (4-0) & Duke (4-0)	1962	Duke (6-0)	1972	N.Carolina (6-0)	1982	Clemson (6-0)
		1963	N.Carolina (6-1) & N.C.State (6-1)	1973	N.C.State (6-0)	1983	Maryland (5-0)
1956	Clemson (4-0-1)			1974	Maryland (6-0)	1984	Maryland (5-0)
1957	N.C.State (5-0-1)	1964	N.C.State (5-2)	1975	Maryland (5-0)	1985	Maryland (6-0)
1958	Clemson (5-1)	1965	Clemson (5-2) & N.C.State (5-2)	1976	Maryland (5-0)	1986	Clemson (5-1-1)
1959	Clemson (6-1)			1977	N.Carolina (5-0-1)	1987	Clemson (6-1)
		1966	Clemson (6-1)	1978	Clemson (6-0)	1988	Clemson (6-1)
		1967	Clemson (6-0)	1979	N.C.State (5-1)	1989	Virginia (6-1) & Duke (6-1)
		1968	N.C.State (6-1)				
		1969	S.Carolina (6-0)				

Big Eight Conference

Originally founded in 1907 as Missouri Valley Intercollegiate Athletic Assn. **Charter members** (5): Iowa, Kansas, Missouri, Nebraska, and Washington Univ.of St.Louis. **Admitted later** (6): Drake and Iowa St.(then Ames College) in 1908; Kan.St. in 1913, Grinnell in 1919, Oklahoma in 1920 and Okla.A&M) in 1925. **Withdrew later** (1): Iowa in 1911. **Note:** Iowa belonged to both the MVIAA and Western Conference from 1907–10.
Big Six founded in 1928 when charter members left MVIAA. **Charter members** (6): Iowa St., Kansas, Kan.St., Missouri, Nebraska and Oklahoma. **Admitted later** (2): Colorado in 1947 (began play in '48), Okla.St. in 1957 (began play in '60). Renamed **Big Seven** in 1948 and **Big Eight** in 1958.
Current playing membership (8): Colorado, Iowa St., Kansas, Kansas St., Missouri, Nebraska, Oklahoma and Oklahoma St.

Year		Year		Year		Year	
1907	Iowa (1-0) & Nebraska (1-0)	1928	Nebraska (4-0)	1950	Oklahoma (6-0)	1973	Oklahoma (7-0)
1908	Kansas (4-0)	1929	Nebraska (3-0-2)	1951	Oklahoma (6-0)	1974	Oklahoma (7-0)
1909	Missouri (4-0-1)	1930	Kansas (4-1)	1952	Oklahoma (5-0-1)	1975	Nebraska (6-1) & Oklahoma (6-1)
1910	Nebraska (2-0)	1931	Nebraska (5-0)	1953	Oklahoma (6-0)		
1911	Iowa St. (2-0-1) & Nebraska (2-0-1)	1932	Nebraska (5-0)	1954	Oklahoma (6-0)	1976	Colorado (5-2), Oklahoma (5-2) & Okla.St.(5-2)
		1933	Nebraska (5-0)	1955	Oklahoma (6-0)		
1912	Iowa St. (2-0) & Nebraska (2-0)	1934	Kansas St.(5-0)	1956	Oklahoma (6-0)	1977	Oklahoma (7-0)
		1935	Nebraska (4-0-1)	1957	Oklahoma (6-0)	1978	Nebraska (6-1) & Oklahoma (6-1)
1913	Missouri (4-0) & Nebraska (3-0)	1936	Nebraska (5-0)	1958	Oklahoma (6-0)		
		1937	Nebraska (3-0-2)	1959	Oklahoma (5-1)	1979	Oklahoma (7-0)
1914	Nebraska (3-0)	1938	Oklahoma (5-0)			1980	Oklahoma (7-0)
1915	Nebraska (4-0)	1939	Missouri (5-0)	1960	Missouri (7-0)	1981	Nebraska (7-0)
1916	Nebraska (3-1)	1940	Nebraska (5-0)	1961	Colorado (7-0)	1982	Nebraska (7-0)
1917	Nebraska (2-0)	1941	Missouri (5-0)	1962	Oklahoma (7-0)	1983	Nebraska (7-0)
1918	Vacant (WWar I)	1942	Missouri (4-0-1)	1963	Nebraska (7-0)	1984	Oklahoma (6-1) & Nebraska (6-1)
1919	Missouri (4-0-1)	1943	Oklahoma (5-0)	1964	Nebraska (6-1)		
1920	Oklahoma (4-0-1)	1944	Oklahoma (4-0-1)	1965	Nebraska (7-0)	1985	Oklahoma (7-0)
1921	Nebraska (3-0)	1945	Missouri (5-0)	1966	Nebraska (6-1)	1986	Oklahoma (7-0)
1922	Nebraska (5-0)	1946	Oklahoma (4-1) & Kansas (4-1)	1967	Oklahoma (7-0)	1987	Oklahoma (7-0)
1923	Nebraska (3-0-2)			1968	Kansas (6-1) & Oklahoma (6-1)	1988	Nebraska (7-0)
1924	Missouri (5-1)	1947	Kansas (4-0-1) & Oklahoma (4-0-1)			1989	Colorado (7-0)
1925	Missouri (5-1)			1969	Missouri (6-1) & Nebraska (6-1)		
1926	Okla. A&M (3-0-1)	1948	Oklahoma (5-0)			*Oklahoma forfeited share of title in 1972.	
1927	Missouri (5-1)	1949	Oklahoma (5-0)	1970	Nebraska (7-0)		
				1971	Nebraska (7-0)		
				1972	Nebraska (5-1-1)*		

Major Conference Champions (Cont.)

Big Ten Conference

Originally founded in 1895 as the Intercollegiate Conference of Faculty Representatives, better known as the Western Conference. **Charter members** (7): Chicago, Illinois, Michigan, Minnesota, Northwestern, Purdue and Wisconsin. **Admitted later** (5): Indiana and Iowa in 1899, Ohio St. in 1912, Mich.St. in 1950 (began play in '53) and Penn St. in 1990 (won't begin play until mid-1990s). **Withdrew later** (2): Michigan in 1907 (rejoined in 1917), Chicago in 1940. **Note:** Iowa belonged to both the Missouri Valley and Western conferences from 1907–10.

Unofficially called **Big Ten** from 1912 until Chicago withdrew after 1939 season, then **Big Nine** from 1940 until Mich.St. began conference play in 1953. Formally renamed **Big Ten** in 1984.

Current playing membership (10): Illinois, Indiana, Iowa, Michigan, Mich.St., Minnesota, Northwestern, Ohio St., Purdue and Wisconsin.

Year		Year		Year		Year	
1896	Wisconsin (2-0-1)	1919	Illinois (6-1)	1943	Purdue (6-0)	1968	Ohio St. (7-0)
1897	Wisconsin (3-0)	1920	Ohio St. (5-0)		& Michigan (6-0)	1969	Ohio St. (6-1)
1898	Michigan (3-0)	1921	Iowa (5-0)	1944	Ohio St. (6-0)		& Michigan (6-1)
1899	Chicago (4-0)	1922	Iowa (5-0)	1945	Indiana (5-0-1)	1970	Ohio St. (7-0)
1900	Iowa (3-0-1)		& Michigan (4-0)	1946	Illinois (6-1)	1971	Michigan (8-0)
	& Minnesota (3-0-1)	1923	Illinois (5-0)	1947	Michigan (6-0)	1972	Ohio St. (8-0)
1901	Michigan (4-0)		& Michigan (4-0)	1948	Michigan (6-0)		& Michigan (7-1)
	& Wisconsin (2-0)	1924	Chicago (3-0-3)	1949	Ohio St. (4-1-1)	1973	Ohio St. (7-0-1)
1902	Michigan (5-0)	1925	Michigan (5-1)		& Michigan (4-1-1)		& Michigan (7-0-1)
1903	Michigan (3-0-1),	1926	Michigan (5-0)	1950	Michigan (4-1-1)	1974	Ohio St. (7-1)
	Minnesota (3-0-1)		& N'western (5-0)	1951	Illinois (5-0-1)		& Michigan (7-1)
	& N'western (1-0-2)	1927	Illinois (5-0)	1952	Wisconsin (4-1-1)	1975	Ohio St. (8-0)
1904	Minnesota (3-0)	1928	Illinois (4-1)		& Purdue (4-1-1)	1976	Michigan (7-1)
	& Michigan (2-0)	1929	Purdue (5-0)	1953	Michigan St. (5-1)		& Ohio St. (7-1)
1905	Chicago (7-0)	1930	Michigan (5-0)		& Illinois (5-1)	1977	Michigan (7-1)
1906	Wisconsin (3-0),		& N'western (5-0)	1954	Ohio St. (7-0)		& Ohio St. (7-1)
	Minnesota (2-0)	1931	Purdue (5-1),	1955	Ohio St. (6-0)	1978	Michigan (7-1)
	& Michigan (1-0)		Michigan (5-1)	1956	Iowa (5-1)		& Mich.St. (7-1)
1907	Chicago (4-0)		& N'western (5-1)	1957	Ohio St. (7-0)	1979	Ohio St. (8-0)
1908	Chicago (5-0)	1932	Michigan (6-0)	1958	Iowa (5-1)	1980	Michigan (8-0)
1909	Minnesota (3-0)	1933	Michigan (5-0-1)	1959	Wisconsin (5-2)	1981	Iowa (6-2)
1910	Illinois (4-0)	1934	Minnesota (5-0)	1960	Minnesota (5-1)		& Ohio St. (6-2)
	& Minnesota (2-0)	1935	Minnesota (5-0)		& Iowa (5-1)	1982	Michigan (8-1)
1911	Minnesota (3-0-1)		& Ohio St. (5-0)	1961	Ohio St. (6-0)	1983	Illinois (9-0)
1912	Wisconsin (6-0)	1936	Northwestern (6-0)	1962	Wisconsin (6-1)	1984	Ohio St. (7-2)
1913	Chicago (7-0)	1937	Minnesota (5-0)	1963	Illinois (5-1-1)	1985	Iowa (7-1)
1914	Illinois (6-0)	1938	Minnesota (4-1)	1964	Michigan (6-1)	1986	Michigan (7-1)
1915	Minnesota (3-0-1)	1939	Ohio St. (5-1)	1965	Michigan St. (7-0)		& Ohio St. (7-1)
	& Illinois (3-0-2)	1940	Minnesota (6-0)	1966	Michigan St. (7-0)	1987	Michigan St. (7-0-1)
1916	Ohio St. (4-0)	1941	Minnesota (5-0)	1967	Indiana (6-1),	1988	Michigan (7-0-1)
1917	Ohio St. (4-0)	1942	Ohio St. (5-1)		Purdue (6-1)	1989	Michigan (8-0)
1918	Illinois (4-0),				& Minnesota (6-1)		
	Michigan (2-0)						
	& Purdue (1-0)						

Big West Conference

Originally founded in 1969 as Pacific Coast Athletic Assn. **Charter members** (7): Cal-Santa Barbara, Cal St.-Los Angeles, Fresno St., Long Beach St., Pacific, San Diego St. and San Jose St. **Admitted later** (4): Cal St.-Fullerton in 1974, Utah St. in 1977 (began play in '78), Nevada-Las Vegas in 1982 and New Mexico St. in 1983 (began play in '84). **Withdrew later** (3): UC-Santa Barbara in 1972, CS-Los Angeles in 1974, San Diego St. in 1976. Renamed **Big West** in 1988.

Current playing membership (8): CS-Fullerton, Fresno St., Long Beach St., UNLV, New Mexico St., Pacific, San Jose St. and Utah St.

Year		Year		Year		Year	
1969	S.Diego St. (6-0)	1974	S.Diego St. (4-0)	1979	Utah St. (5-0)	1985	Fresno St. (7-0)
1970	L.Beach St. (5-1)	1975	San Jose St. (5-0)	1980	L.Beach St. (5-0)	1986	San Jose St. (7-0)
	& S.Diego St. (5-1)	1976	San Jose St. (4-0)	1981	San Jose St. (5-0)	1987	San Jose St. (7-0)
1971	L.Beach St. (5-1)	1977	Fresno St. (4-0)	1982	Fresno St. (6-0)	1988	Fresno St. (7-0)
1972	S.Diego St. (4-0)	1978	San Jose St. (4-1)	1983	CS-Fullerton (5-1)	1989	Fresno St. (7-0)
1973	S.Diego St. (3-0-1)		& Utah St. (4-1)	1984	CS-Fullerton (6-1)*		

*UNLV forfeited title in 1984.

Mid-American Conference

Founded in 1946. **Charter members** (6): Butler, Cincinnati, Miami of Ohio, Ohio Univ., Western Mich. and Western Reserve (Miami and W.Mich began play in '48). **Admitted later** (8): Kent State (now Kent) and Toledo in 1951 (Toledo began play in '52), Bowling Green in 1952, Marshall in 1954, Central Mich. and Eastern Mich. in 1972 (CMU began play in '75, EMU in '76), Ball St. and Northern Ill. in 1973 (both began play in '75). **Withdrew later** (5): Butler in 1950, Cincinnati in 1953, Western Reserve in 1955, Marshall in 1969, Northern Ill. in 1986.

Current playing membership (9): Ball St., Bowling Green, Central Mich., Eastern Mich., Kent, Miami, Ohio Univ., Toledo and Western Mich.

Year		Year		Year		Year	
1947	Cincinnati (3-1)	1958	Miami,OH (5-0)	1967	Toledo (5-1)	1978	Ball St. (8-0)
1948	Miami,OH (4-0)	1959	Bowl.Green (6-0)		& Ohio Univ. (5-1)	1979	Cent.Mich. (8-0-1)
1949	Cincinnati (4-0)	1960	Ohio Univ. (6-0)	1968	Ohio Univ. (6-0)	1980	Cent. Mich. (7-2)
1950	Miami,OH (4-0)	1961	Bowl.Green (5-1)	1969	Toledo (5-0)	1981	Toledo (8-1)
1951	Cincinnati (3-0)	1962	B.Green (5-0-1)	1970	Toledo (5-0)	1982	Bowl.Green (7-2)
1952	Cincinnati (3-0)	1963	Ohio Univ. (5-1)	1971	Toledo (5-0)	1983	Northern Ill. (8-1)
1953	Ohio Univ. (5-0-1)	1964	Bowl.Green (5-1)	1972	Kent St. (4-1)	1984	Toledo (7-1-1)
1954	Miami,OH (4-0)	1965	Bowl.Green (5-1)	1973	Miami,OH (5-0)	1985	Bowl.Green (9-0)
1955	Miami,OH (5-0)		& Miami,OH (5-1)	1974	Miami,OH (5-0)	1986	Miami,OH (6-2)
1956	B.Green (5-0-1)	1966	Miami,OH (5-1)	1975	Miami,OH (6-0)	1987	East.Mich. (7-1)
1957	Miami,OH (5-0)		& West.Mich. (5-1)	1976	Ball St. (4-1)	1988	West.Mich. (7-1)
				1977	Miami,OH (5-0)	1989	Ball St. (6-1-1)

Pac-10 Conference

Originally founded in 1915 as Pacific Coast Conference. **Charter members** (4): California, Oregon, Ore.St. and Washington. **Admitted later** (6): Wash.St. in 1917, Stanford in 1918, Southern Cal and Idaho in 1922, Montana in 1924, UCLA in 1928. **Withdrew later** (1): Montana in 1950.

The **PCC** dissolved in 1959 and the **AAWU** (Athletic Assn. of Western Universities) was founded. **Charter members** (5): California, Southern Cal, Stanford, UCLA and Washington. **Admitted later** (5): Wash.St. in 1962, Oregon and Ore.St. in 1964, Arizona and Ariz.St. in 1978. Conference renamed **Pac-8** in 1968 and **Pac-10** in 1978.

Current playing membership (10): Arizona, Arizona St., California, Oregon, Oregon St., Stanford, Southern Cal, UCLA, Washington and Washington St.

Year		Year		Year		Year	
1916	Wash. (3-0-1)	1935	California (4-1),	1952	USC (6-0)	1970	Stanford (6-1)
1917	Wash.St.(3-0)		Stanford (4-1)	1953	UCLA (6-1)	1971	Stanford (6-1)
1918	California (3-0)		& UCLA (4-1)	1954	UCLA (6-0)	1972	USC (7-0)
1919	Oregon (2-1)	1936	Wash. (6-0-1)	1955	UCLA (6-0)	1973	USC (7-0)
	& Washington (2-1)	1937	California (6-0-1)	1956	Oregon St.(6-1-1)	1974	USC (6-0-1)
1920	California (3-0)	1938	USC (6-1)	1957	Oregon (6-2)	1975	UCLA (6-1)
1921	California (5-0)		& California (6-1)		& Oregon St.(6-2)		& California (6-1)
1922	California (3-0)	1939	USC (5-0-2)	1958	California (6-1)	1976	USC (7-0)
1923	California (5-0)		& UCLA (5-0-3)	1959	Washington (3-1),	1977	Washington (6-1)
1924	Stanford (3-0-1)	1940	Stanford (7-0)		USC (3-1)	1978	USC (6-1)
1925	Washington (5-0)	1941	Oregon St.(7-2)		& UCLA (3-1)	1979	USC (6-0-1)
1926	Stanford (4-0)	1942	UCLA (6-1)	1960	Washington (4-0)	1980	Washington (6-1)
1927	USC (4-0-1)	1943	USC (4-0)	1961	UCLA (3-1)	1981	Washington (6-2)
	& Stanford (4-0-1)	1944	USC (3-0-2)	1962	USC (4-0)	1982	UCLA (5-1-1)
1928	USC (4-0-1)	1945	USC (5-1)	1963	Washington (4-1)	1983	UCLA (6-1-1)
1929	USC (6-1)	1946	UCLA (7-0)	1964	Oregon St.(3-1)	1984	USC (7-1)
1930	Wash.St.(6-0)	1947	USC (6-0)		& USC (3-1)	1985	UCLA (6-2)
1931	USC (7-0)	1948	California (6-0)	1965	UCLA (4-0)	1986	Arizona St.(5-1-1)
1932	USC (6-0)		& Oregon (6-0)	1966	USC (4-1)	1987	USC (7-1)
1933	Oregon (4-1)	1949	California (7-0)	1967	USC (6-1)		& UCLA (7-1)
	& Stanford (4-1)	1950	California (5-0-1)	1968	USC (6-0)	1988	USC (8-0)
1934	Stanford (5-0)	1951	Stanford (6-1)	1969	USC (6-0)	1989	USC (6-0-1)

Southeastern Conference

Founded in 1933 when charter members all left Southern Conference to form SEC. **Charter members** (13): Alabama, Auburn, Florida, Georgia, Ga.Tech, Kentucky, LSU, Mississippi, Miss.St., Sewanee, Tennessee, Tulane and Vanderbilt. **Withdrew later** (3): Sewanee in 1940, Ga.Tech in 1964, Tulane in 1966.

Current playing membership (10): Alabama, Auburn, Florida, Georgia, Kentucky, LSU, Mississippi, Mississippi St., Tennessee and Vanderbilt.

Year		Year		Year		Year	
1933	Alabama (5-0-1)	1939	Tennessee (6-0),	1944	Georgia Tech (4-0)	1950	Kentucky (5-1)
1934	Tulane (8-0)		Ga.Tech (6-0)	1945	Alabama (6-0)	1951	Georgia Tech (7-0)
	& Alabama (7-0)		& Tulane (5-0)	1946	Georgia (5-0)		& Tennessee (5-0)
1935	LSU (5-0)	1940	Tennessee (5-0)		& Tennessee (5-0)	1952	Georgia Tech (6-0)
1936	LSU (6-0)	1941	Miss.St.(4-0-1)	1947	Mississippi (6-1)	1953	Alabama (4-0-3)
1937	Alabama (6-0)	1942	Georgia (6-1)	1948	Georgia (6-0)	1954	Mississippi (5-1)
1938	Tennessee (7-0)	1943	Georgia Tech (3-0)	1949	Tulane (5-1)	1955	Mississippi (5-1)

Major Conference Champions (Cont.)
Southeastern Conference

Year		Year		Year		Year	
1956	Tennessee (6-0)	1966	Alabama (6-0)	1975	Alabama (6-0)	1982	Georgia (6-0)
1957	Auburn (7-0)		& Georgia (6-0)	1976	Georgia (5-1)	1983	Auburn (6-0)
1958	LSU (6-0)	1967	Tennessee (6-0)		& Kentucky (5-1)	1984	*Florida (5-0-1)
1959	Georgia (7-0)	1968	Georgia (5-0-1)	1977	Alabama (7-0)	1985	Tennessee (5-1)
1960	Mississippi (5-0-1)	1969	Tennessee (5-1)		& Kentucky (6-0)	1986	LSU (5-1)
1961	Alabama (7-0)	1970	LSU (5-0)	1978	Alabama (6-0)	1987	Auburn (5-0-1)
	& LSU (6-0)	1971	Alabama (7-0)	1979	Alabama (6-0)	1988	Auburn (6-1)
1962	Mississippi (6-0)	1972	Alabama (7-1)	1980	Georgia (6-0)		& LSU (6-1)
1963	Mississippi (5-0-1)	1973	Alabama (8-0)	1981	Georgia (6-0)	1989	Alabama (6-1),
1964	Alabama (8-0)	1974	Alabama (6-0)		& Alabama (6-0)		Tennessee (6-1)
1965	Alabama (6-1-1)						& Auburn (6-1)

*Title vacated

Southwest Conference

Founded in 1914 as Southwest Athletic Conference. **Charter members** (8): Arkansas, Baylor, Oklahoma, Okla.A&M, Rice, Southwestern, Texas, Texas A&M. **Admitted later** (5): SMU in 1918, Phillips in 1920, TCU in 1923, Texas Tech in 1956 (began play in 1960), Houston in 1971 (began play in 1976). **Withdrew later** (4): Southwestern in 1917, Oklahoma in 1920, Phillips in 1921, Okla.A&M in 1925.
   Current playing membership (9): Arkansas, Baylor, Houston, Rice, SMU, Texas, Texas A&M, TCU and Texas Tech.

Year		Year		Year		Year	
1914	No champion	1936	Arkansas (5-1)	1955	TCU (5-1)	1973	Texas (7-0)
1915	Oklahoma (3-0)	1937	Rice (4-1-1)	1956	Texas A&M (6-0)	1974	Baylor (6-1)
1916	No champion	1938	TCU (6-0)	1957	Rice (5-1)	1975	Arkansas (6-1),
1917	Texas A&M (2-0)	1939	Texas A&M (6-0)	1958	TCU (5-1)		Texas (6-1)
1918	No champion	1940	Texas A&M (5-1)	1959	Texas (5-1),		& Texas A&M (6-1)
1919	Texas A&M (4-0)		& SMU (5-1)		TCU (5-1)	1976	Houston (7-1)
1920	Texas (5-0)	1941	Texas A&M (5-1)		& Arkansas (5-1)		& Texas Tech (7-1)
1921	Texas A&M (3-0-2)	1942	Texas (5-1)	1960	Arkansas (6-1)	1977	Texas (8-0)
1922	Baylor (5-0)	1943	Texas (5-0)	1961	Texas (6-1)	1978	Houston (7-1)
1923	SMU (5-0)	1944	TCU (3-1-1)		& Arkansas (6-1)	1979	Houston (7-1)
1924	Baylor (4-0-1)	1945	Texas (5-1)	1962	Texas (6-0-1)		& Arkansas (7-1)
1925	Texas A&M (4-1)	1946	Rice (5-1)	1963	Texas (7-0)	1980	Baylor (8-0)
1926	SMU (5-0)		& Arkansas (5-1)	1964	Arkansas (7-0)	1981	†SMU (7-0-1)
1927	Texas A&M (4-0-1)	1947	SMU (5-0-1)	1965	Arkansas (7-0)	1982	SMU (7-0-1)
1928	Texas (5-1)	1948	SMU (5-0-1)	1966	SMU (6-1)	1983	Texas (8-0)
1929	TCU (4-0-1)	1949	Rice (6-0)	1967	Texas A&M (6-1)	1984	SMU (6-2)
1930	Texas (4-1)	1950	Texas (6-0)	1968	Arkansas (6-1)		& Houston (6-2)
1931	SMU (5-0-1)	1951	TCU (5-1)		& Texas (6-1)	1985	Texas A&M (7-1)
1932	TCU (6-0)	1952	Texas (6-0)	1969	Texas (7-0)	1986	Texas A&M (7-1)
1933	*Arkansas (4-1)	1953	Rice (5-1)	1970	Texas (7-0)	1987	Texas A&M (6-1)
1934	Rice (5-1)		& Texas (5-1)	1971	Texas (6-1)	1988	Arkansas (7-0)
1935	SMU (6-0)	1954	Arkansas (5-1)	1972	Texas (7-0)	1989	Arkansas (7-1)

*Title vacated.   †On probation, ineligible for Cotton Bowl.

Western Athletic Conference

Founded in 1962 when charter members left the Skyline and Border Conferences to form the WAC. **Charter members** (6): Arizona (an independent), Ariz.St. (from the Border), BYU, New Mexico, Utah and Wyoming (from the Skyline). **Added later** (5): Colo.St. and Texas-El Paso in 1967 (both began play in '68), San Diego St. in 1978, Hawaii in 1979, Air Force in 1980. **Withdrew later** (2): Arizona and Ariz.St. in 1978.
   Current playing membership (9): Air Force, BYU, Colorado St., Hawaii, New Mexico, San Diego St., UTEP, Utah and Wyoming.

Year		Year		Year		Year	
1962	New Mex. (2-1-1)	1969	Arizona St.(6-1)	1976	BYU (6-1)	1982	BYU (7-1)
1963	New Mexico (3-1)	1970	Arizona St.(7-0)		& Wyoming (6-1)	1983	BYU (7-0)
1964	Utah (3-1),	1971	Arizona St.(7-0)	1977	Arizona St.(6-1)	1984	BYU (8-0)
	New Mexico (3-1)	1972	Arizona St.(5-1)		& BYU (6-1)	1985	Air Force (7-1)
	& Arizona (3-1)	1973	Arizona St.(6-1)	1978	BYU (5-1)		& BYU (7-1)
1965	BYU (4-1)		& Arizona (6-1)	1979	BYU (7-0)	1986	San Diego St.(7-1)
1966	Wyoming (5-0)	1974	BYU (6-0-1)			1987	Wyoming (8-0)
1967	Wyoming (5-0)	1975	Arizona St.(7-0)	1980	BYU (6-1)	1988	Wyoming (8-0)
1968	Wyoming (6-1)			1981	BYU (7-1)	1989	BYU (8-0)

NCAA Division I-A All-Time Individual Leaders
CAREER

Total Offense

Yards Gained

	Years	Yards
Doug Flutie, Boston College	1981-84	11,317
Todd Santos, San Diego St	1984-87	10,513
Kevin Sweeney, Fresno St	1983-86	10,252
Brian McClure, Bowling Green	1982-85	9,774
Jim McMahon, BYU	1977-78,80-81	9,723

Yards Per Game

	Years	Yards	PerGm
Mike Perez, San Jose St	1986-87	6,182	309.1
Doug Gaynor, L.Beach St.	1984-85	6,710	305.0
Tony Eason, Illinois	1981-82	6,589	299.5
Steve Young, BYU	1981-83	8,817	284.4
Doug Flutie, Boston Col.	1981-84	11,317	269.5

Rushing

Yards Gained

	Years	Yards
Tony Dorsett, Pittsburgh	1973-76	6082
Charles White, USC	1976-79	5598
Herschel Walker, Georgia	1980-82	5259
Archie Griffin, Ohio St	1972-75	5177
Anthony Thompson, Indiana	1986-89	4965

Yards Per Game

	Years	Yards	PerGm
Ed Marinaro, Cornell	1969-71	4715	174.6
O.J. Simpson, USC	1967-68	3124	164.4
Herschel Walker, Georgia	1980-82	5259	159.4
Tony Dorsett, Pittsburgh	1973-76	6082	141.4
Mike Rozier, Nebraska	1981-83	4780	136.6

All-Purpose Running

Yards Gained

	Years	Yards
Napoleon McCallum, Navy	1981-85	7172
Darrin Nelson, Stanford	1977-78,80-81	6885
Terance Mathis, N.Mexico	1985-87,89	6691
Tony Dorsett, Pittsburgh	1973-76	6615
Paul Palmer, Temple	1983-86	6609

Yards Per Game

	Years	Yards	PerGm
Howard Stevens, L'ville	1971-72	3873	193.7
O.J.Simpson, USC	1967-68	3666	192.9
Ed Marinaro, Cornell	1969-71	4940	183.0
Herschel Walker, Georgia	1980-82	5749	174.2
Louie Giammona, Utah St	1973-75	5203	173.4

Passing
(Minimum 500 Completions)

Passing Efficiency

	Years	Rating
Jim McMahon, BYU	1977-78,80-81	156.9
Steve Young, BYU	1982,84-86	149.8
Troy Aikman, Okla-UCLA	1984-85,87-88	149.7
Robbie Bosco, BYU	1981-83	149.4
Chuck Hartlieb, Iowa	1985-88	148.9

Yards Gained

	Years	Yards
Todd Santos, San Diego St	1984-87	11,425
Kevin Sweeney, Fresno St	1983-86	10,623
Doug Flutie, Boston College	1981-84	10,579
Brian McClure, Bowling Green	1982-85	10,280
Ben Bennett, Duke	1980-83	9,614

Completions

	Years	No
Todd Santos, San Diego St	1984-87	910
Brian McClure, Bowling Green	1982-85	900
Ben Bennett, Duke	1980-83	820
John Elway, Stanford	1979-82	774
Jack Trudeau, Illinois	1981,83-85	736

Receiving

Catches

	Years	No
Terance Mathis, N.Mexico	1985-87,89	263
Mark Templeton, Long Beach St	1983-86	262
Howard Twilley, Tulsa	1963-65	261
David Williams, Illinois	1983-85	245
Marc Zeno, Tulane	1984-87	236

Catches Per Game

	Years	No	PerGm
Emmanuel Hazard, Houston	1989	142	12.9
Howard Twilley, Tulsa	1963-65	261	10.0
Jason Phillips, Houston	1987-88	207	9.4
Neal Sweeney, Tulsa	1965-66	134	7.4
David Williams, Illinois	1983-85	245	7.4

Yards Gained

	Years	No	Yards
Terance Mathis, N.Mex	1985-87,89	263	4254
Marc Zeno, Tulane	1984-87	236	3725
Ron Sellers, Florida St	1966-68	212	3598
Elmo Wright, Houston	1968-70	153	3347
Howard Twilley, Tulsa	1963-65	261	3343
Gerald Harp, W.Carolina	1977-80	197	3305

Scoring

Points (Kickers)

	Years	FG	XP	Pts
Derek Schmidt, Fla.St	1984-87	73	174	393
Luis Zendejas, Ariz.St	1981-84	78	134	368
Jeff Jaeger, Washington	1983-86	80	118	358
John Lee, UCLA	1982-85	79	116	353
Max Zendejas, Arizona	1982-85	77	122	353
Kevin Butler, Georgia	1981-84	77	122	353

Points (Non-Kickers)

	Years	TD	Xpt	FG	Pts
Anthony Thompson, Ind	1986-89	65	4	0	394
Tony Dorsett, Pitt	1973-76	59	2	0	356
Glenn Davis, Army	1943-46	59	0	0	354
Art Luppino, Arizona	1953-56	48	49	0	337
Steve Owens, Oklahoma	1967-69	56	0	0	336

Pts Per Gm (Non-Kickers)

	Years	Pts	PerGm
Emmanuel Hazard, Houston	1989	134	12.2
Bob Gaiters, N.Mexico St	1959-60	203	11.9
Ed Marinaro, Cornell	1969-71	318	11.8
Bill Burnett, Arkansas	1968-70	294	11.3
Steve Owens, Oklahoma	1967-69	336	11.2

Touchdowns Rushing

	Years	No
Steve Owens, Oklahoma	1967-69	56
Tony Dorsett, Pittsburgh	1973-76	55
Anthony Thompson, Indiana	1986-89	54
Ed Marinaro, Cornell	1969-71	50
Mike Rozier, Nebraska	1981-83	50

Touchdowns Passing

	Years	No
Jim McMahon, BYU	1977-78,80-81	84
Joe Adams, Tennessee St	1977-80	81
John Elway, Stanford	1979-82	77
Andre Ware, Houston	1987-89	75
Dan Marino, Pittsburgh	1979-82	74

Touchdown Catches

	Years	No
Clarkston Hines, Duke	1986-89	38
Terance Mathis, New Mexico	1985-87,89	36
Elmo Wright, Houston	1968-70	34
Howard Twilley, Tulsa	1963-65	32
Dan Bitson, Tulsa	1987-89	28

Field Goals

	Years	No
Jeff Jaeger, Washington	1983-86	80
John Lee, UCLA	1982-85	79
Luis Zendejas, Arizona St	1981-84	78
Kevin Butler, Georgia	1981-84	77
Max Zendejas, Arizona	1982-85	77

NCAA Division I-A All-Time Leaders (Cont.)

Miscellaneous

Interceptions	Years	No
Al Brosky, Illinois	1950-52	29
John Provost, Holy Cross	1972-74	27
Martin Bayless, Bowling Green	1980-83	27
Tom Curtis, Michigan	1967-69	25
Tony Thurman, Boston College	1981-84	25

Punting Average*	Years	Avg
Reggie Roby, Iowa	1979-82	45.6
Greg Montgomery, Michigan St	1985-87	45.4
Tom Tupa, Ohio St	1984-87	45.2
Barry Helton, Colorado	1984-87	44.9
Ray Guy, Southern Mississippi	1970-72	44.7

*At least 150 punts kicked

Punt Return Average*	Years	Avg
Jack Mitchell, Oklahoma	1946-48	23.6
Gene Gibson, Cincinnati	1949-50	20.5
Eddie Macon, Pacific	1949-51	18.9
Jackie Robinson, UCLA	1939-40	18.8
Mike Fuller, Auburn	1972-74	17.7
Bobby Dillon, Texas	1949-51	17.7

*At least 1.2 punt returns per game

Kickoff Return Average*	Years	Avg
Forrest Hall, San Francisco	1946-47	36.2
Anthony Davis, USC	1972-74	35.1
Overton Curtis, Utah St	1957-58	31.0
Altie Taylor, Utah St	1966-68	29.3
Raghib Ismail, Notre Dame	1988-89	29.2

*At least 1.2 kickoff returns per game

SINGLE SEASON

Total Offense

Yards Gained	Year	Gm	Plays	Yards
Andre Ware, Houston	1989	11	628	4661
Jim McMahon, BYU	1980	12	540	4627
Ty Detmer, BYU	1989	12	497	4433
Steve Young, BYU	1983	11	531	4346
Scott Mitchell, Utah	1988	11	589	4299

Yards Per Game	Year	Gm	Yards	YdsPG
Andre Ware, Houston	1989	11	4661	423.7
Steve Young, BYU	1983	11	4346	395.1
Scott Mitchell, Utah	1988	11	4299	390.8
Jim McMahon, BYU	1980	12	4627	385.6
Ty Detmer, BYU	1989	12	4433	369.4

Rushing

Yards Gained	Year	Gm	Car	Yards
Barry Sanders, Okla.St	1988	11	344	2628
Marcus Allen, USC	1981	11	403	2342
Mike Rozier, Nebraska	1983	12	275	2148
Tony Dorsett, Pittsburgh	1976	11	338	1948
Lorenzo White, Mich.St	1985	11	386	1908

Yards Per Game	Year	Gm	Yards	PerGm
Barry Sanders, Okla.St	1988	11	2628	238.9
Marcus Allen, USC	1981	11	2342	212.9
Ed Marinaro, Cornell	1971	9	1881	209.0
Charles White, USC	1979	10	1803	180.3
Mike Rozier, Nebraska	1983	12	2148	179.0

All-Purpose Running

Yards Per Game	Year	Yards
Barry Sanders, Oklahoma St	1988	3250
Paul Palmer, Temple	1986	2633
Marcus Allen, USC	1981	2559
Mike Rozier, Nebraska	1983	2486
Napoleon McCallum, Navy	1983	2385

Yards Per Game	Year	Yards	PerGm
Barry Sanders, Oklahoma St	1988	3250	295.5
Byron (Whizzer) White, Colo.	1937	1970	246.3
Mike Pringle, Fullerton St	1989	2690	244.6
Paul Palmer, Temple	1986	2633	239.4
Marcus Allen, USC	1981	2559	232.6

Passing
(Minimum 15 attempts Per Game)

Passing Efficiency	Year	Rating
Jim McMahon, BYU	1980	176.9
Ty Detmer, BYU	1989	175.6
Jerry Rhome, Tulsa	1964	172.6
Steve Young, BYU	1983	168.5
Vinny Testaverde, Miami,FL	1986	165.8
Brian Dowling, Yale	1968	165.8

Yards Gained	Year	Yards
Andre Ware, Houston	1989	4699
Jim McMahon, BYU	1980	4571
Ty Detmer, BYU	1989	4560
Scott Mitchell, Utah	1988	4322
Robbie Bosco, BYU	1985	4273

Completions	Year	Att	No
Andre Ware, Houston	1989	578	365
Robbie Bosco, BYU	1985	511	338
Scott Mitchell, Utah	1988	533	323
Doug Gaynor, Long Beach St	1985	452	321
Steve Young, BYU	1983	429	306
Todd Santos, San Diego St	1987	492	306

Receiving

	Year	Gm	No
Emmanuel Hazard, Houston	1989	11	142
Howard Twilley, Tulsa	1965	10	134
Jason Phillips, Houston	1988	11	108
James Dixon, Houston	1988	11	102
David Williams, Illinois	1984	11	101

Catches Per Game	Year	No	PerGm
Howard Twilley, Tulsa	1965	134	13.4
Emmanuel Hazard, Houston	1989	142	12.9
Jason Phillips, Houston	1988	108	9.8
Jerry Hendren, Idaho	1969	95	9.5
Howard Twilley, Tulsa	1964	95	9.5

Yards Gained	Year	No	Yards
Howard Twilley, Tulsa	1965	134	1779
Emmanuel Hazard, Houston	1989	142	1689
Chuck Hughes, UTEP*	1965	80	1519
Henry Ellard, Fresno St	1982	62	1510
Ron Sellers, Florida St	1968	86	1496

*UTEP was Texas Western in 1965.

Scoring

Points

	Year	TD	Xpt	FG	Pts
Barry Sanders, Okla.St	1988	39	0	0	234
Mike Rozier, Nebraska	1983	29	0	0	174
Lydell Mitchell, Penn St	1971	29	0	0	174
Art Luppino, Arizona	1954	24	22	0	166
Bobby Reynolds, Nebraska	1950	22	25	0	157

Points Per Game

	Year	Pts	PerGm
Barry Sanders, Okla.St	1988	234	21.3
Bobby Reynolds, Nebraska	1950	157	17.4
Art Luppino, Arizona	1954	166	16.6
Ed Marinaro, Cornell	1971	148	16.4
Lydell Mitchell, Penn St	1971	174	15.8

Touchdowns Rushing

	Year	No
Barry Sanders, Oklahoma St	1988	37
Mike Rozier, Nebraska	1983	29
Ed Marinaro, Cornell	1971	24
Anthony Thompson, Indiana	1988	24
Anthony Thompson, Indiana	1989	24

Touchdowns Passing

	Year	No
Jim McMahon, BYU	1980	47
Andre Ware, Houston	1989	46
Dennis Shaw, San Diego St	1969	39
Doug Williams, Grambling	1977	38
Steve Young, BYU	1983	33
Robbie Bosco, BYU	1984	33

Touchdown Catches

	Year	No
Emmanuel Hazard, Houston	1989	22
Tom Reynolds, San Diego St	1969	18
Dennis Smith, Utah	1989	18
Clarkston Hines, Duke	1989	17
Howard Twilley, Tulsa	1965	16
Dan Bitson, Tulsa	1989	16

Field Goals

	Year	No
John Lee, UCLA	1984	29
Paul Woodside, West Virginia	1982	28
Luis Zendejas, Arizona St	1983	28
Fuad Reveiz, Tennessee	1982	27

Three tied with 25 each.

Miscellaneous

Interceptions

	Year	No
Al Worley, Washington	1968	14
George Shaw, Oregon	1951	13

Seven tied with 12 each.

Punting Average*

	Year	Avg
Reggie Roby, Iowa	1981	49.8
Kirk Wilson, UCLA	1956	49.3
Zack Jordan, Colorado	1950	48.2
Ricky Anderson, Vanderbilt	1984	48.2
Marv Bateman, Utah	1971	48.1
Reggie Roby, Iowa	1982	48.1

*Qualifers for championship

Punt Return Average*

	Year	Avg
Bill Blackstock, Tennessee	1951	25.9
George Sims, Baylor	1948	25.0
Gene Derricotte, Michigan	1947	24.8
Erroll Tucker, Utah	1985	24.3
George Hoey, Michigan	1967	24.3

*At least 1.2 returns per game

Kickoff Return Average*

	Year	Avg
Forrest Hall, San Francisco	1946	38.2
Tony Ball, Tenn-Chattanooga	1977	36.4
Raghib Ismail, Notre Dame	1988	36.1
George Marinkov, N.Carolina St	1954	35.8
Bob Baker, Cornell	1964	35.1

*At least 1.2 kickoff returns per game

BEST GAMES

Total Offense

Yards Gained	Opponent	Year	Yds
Scott Mitchell, Utah	Air Force	1988	625
Virgil Carter, BYU	UTEP	1966	599
Jeremy Leach, N.Mexico	Utah	1989	594
Dave Wilson, Illinois	Ohio St.	1980	585
Marc Wilson, BYU	Utah	1977	582

Passing

Yards Gained	Opponent	Year	Yds
Scott Mitchell, Utah	Air Force	1988	631
Jeremy Leach, N.Mexico	Utah	1989	622
Dave Wilson, Illinois	Ohio St.	1980	621
Robbie Bosco, BYU	New Mex.	1985	585
Marc Wilson, BYU	Utah	1977	571

Completions	Opponent	Year	No
Sandy Schwab, N'western	Michigan	1982	45
Chuck Hartlieb, Iowa	Indiana	1988	44
Jim McMahon, BYU	Colo.St.	1981	44
Gary Schofield, W.Forest	Maryland	1981	43
Dave Wilson, Illinois	Ohio St.	1980	43
Rich Campbell, Cal	Florida	1980	43

Rushing

Yards Gained	Opponent	Year	Yds
Anthony Thompson, Ind	Wisconsin	1989	377
Rueben Mayes, Wash.St	Oregon	1984	357
Mike Pringle, CS-Fullerton	N.Mex.St	1989	357
Eddie Lee Ivery, Ga.Tech	Air Force	1978	356
Eric Allen, Michigan St	Purdue	1971	350

Receiving

Yards Gained	Opponent	Year	No
Jay Miller, BYU	N.Mexico	1973	22
Rick Eber, Tulsa	Idaho St.	1967	20
Howard Twilley, Tulsa	Colo.St.	1965	19
Ron Fair, Arizona St	Wash.St	1989	19
Emmanuel Hazard, Hou	TCU	1989	19
Emmanuel Hazard, Hou	Texas	1989	19

Yards Gained	Opponent	Year	Yds
Chuck Hughes, UTEP*	N.Tex.St.	1965	349
Rick Eber, Tulsa	Idaho St.	1967	322
Harry Wood, Tulsa	Idaho St.	1967	318
Jeff Evans, N.Mexico St	So.Ill.	1978	316
Tom Reynolds, S.Diego St	Utah St.	1971	290

*UTEP was Texas Western in 1965.

NCAA Division I-A All-Time Leaders (Cont.)

Scoring

Points

	Opponent	Year	Pts
Jim Brown, Syracuse	Colgate	1956	43
Showboat Boykin, Miss	Miss.St.	1951	42
Fred Wendt, UTEP*	N.Mex.St.	1948	42
Dick Bass, Pacific	S.Diego St.	1958	38
Jimmy Nutter, Wichita St.*	North.St.	1949	37

Note: Brown's 43 points (6 TDs, 7 extra points).
*UTEP was Texas Mines in 1948 and Wichita St. was Wichita Univ. in 1949.

Touchdowns Rushing

	Opponent	Year	No
Showboat Boykin, Miss	Miss.St.	1951	7

Note: Boykin's TD runs (21-14-12-14-85-1-5).

Touchdowns Passing

	Opponent	Year	No
Dennis Shaw, S.Diego St	N.Mex.St.	1969	9

Note: Shaw's TD passes (14-2-22-34-31-32-7-30-9).

Touchdown Catches

	Opponent	Year	No
Tim Delaney, S.Diego St	N.Mex.St.	1969	6

Note: Delaney TD catches (2-22-34-31-30-9).

Field Goals

	Opponent	Year	No
Dale Klein, Nebraska	Missouri	1985	7
Mike Prindle, W.Mich	Marshall	1984	7

Note: Klein (32-22-43-44-29-43-43); Prindle (32-44-42-23-48-41-27).

Extra Points (Kick)

	Opponent	Year	No
Terry Leiweke, Houston	Tulsa	1968	13

Extra Points (2-Pts)

	Opponent	Year	No
Jim Pilot, N.Mexico St	H-Simmons	1961	6

Longest Plays (since 1941)

Rushing

	Opponent	Year	Yds
Gale Sayers, Kansas	Nebraska	1963	99
Max Anderson, Ariz.St	Wyoming	1967	99
Ralph Thompson, W.Tex.St	Wich.St.	1970	99
Kelsey Finch, Tennessee	Florida	1977	99

Passing

	Opponent	Year	Yds
Fred Owens to Jack Ford, Portland	St.Mary's	1947	99
Bo Burris to Warren McVea, Houston	Wash.St.	1966	99
Colin Clapton to Eddie Jenkins, H.Cross	Boston U.	1970	99
Terry Peel to Robert Ford, Houston	Syracuse	1970	99
Terry Peel to Robert Ford, Houston	S.Diego St.	1972	99
Cris Collinsworth to Derrick Gaffney, Fla	Rice	1977	99
Scott Ankrom to James Maness, TCU	Rice	1984	99

Field Goals

	Opponent	Year	Yds
Steve Little, Arkansas	Texas	1977	67
Russell Erxleben, Texas	Rice	1977	67
Joe Williams, Wichita St	So.Ill.	1978	67

Punts

	Opponent	Year	Yds
Pat Brady, Nevada-Reno	Loyola,CA	1950	99
George O'Brien, Wisconsin	Iowa	1952	98

Punt Returns Opponent Year Yds
100-yd punt returns since 1941: 7 players.

Kickoff Returns Opponent Year Yds
100-yd kickoff returns since 1941: 160 players.

Annual Award Winners

Heisman Trophy

Originally presented in 1935 as the DAC Trophy by the Downtown Athletic Club of New York City to the best college football player east of the Mississippi. In 1936, players across the country were eligible and the award was renamed the Heisman Trophy following the death of former college coach and DAC athletic director John W.Heisman. Players listed in **bold type** helped lead their team to a national championship (according to AP).

Multiple winner: Archie Griffin (1974-75). **Winners in junior year:** Doc Blanchard (1945), Doak Walker (1948), Vic Janowicz (1950), Roger Staubach (1963), Griffin (1974), Billy Sims (1978), Herschel Walker (1982), Barry Sanders (1988), Andre Ware (1989).

Year
1935 Jay Berwanger, Chicago, HB
1936 Larry Kelley, Yale, E
1937 Clint Frank, Yale, HB
1938 **Davey O'Brien, TCU, QB**
1939 Nile Kinnick, Iowa, HB

1940 Tom Harmon, Michigan, HB
1941 **Bruce Smith, Minnesota, HB**
1942 Frank Sinkwich, Georgia, TB
1943 Angelo Bertelli, Notre Dame, QB
1944 Les Horvath, Ohio St., TB-QB
1945 **Doc Blanchard, Army, FB**
1946 Glenn Davis, Army, HB
1947 **Johnny Lujack, Notre Dame, QB**
1948 Doak Walker, SMU, HB
1949 **Leon Hart, Notre Dame, E**

1950 Vic Janowicz, Ohio St., HB
1951 Dick Kazmaier, Princeton, TB

Year
1952 Billy Vessels, Oklahoma, HB
1953 Johnny Lattner, Notre Dame, HB
1954 Alan Ameche, Wisconsin, FB
1955 Howard Cassady, Ohio St., HB
1956 Paul Hornung, Notre Dame, QB
1957 John David Crow, Texas A&M, HB
1958 Pete Dawkins, Army, HB
1959 Billy Cannon, LSU, HB

1960 Joe Bellino, Navy, HB
1961 Ernie Davis, Syracuse, HB
1962 Terry Baker, Oregon St., QB
1963 Roger Staubach, Navy, QB
1964 John Huarte, Notre Dame, QB
1965 Mike Garrett, USC, HB
1966 Steve Spurrier, Florida, QB
1967 Gary Beban, UCLA, QB
1968 O.J.Simpson, USC, HB
1969 Steve Owens, Oklahoma, HB

Year		Year	
1970	Jim Plunkett, Stanford, QB	1980	George Rogers, South Carolina, RB
1971	Pat Sullivan, Auburn, QB	1981	Marcus Allen, Southern Cal, RB
1972	Johnny Rodgers, Nebraska, FL	1982	Herschel Walker, Georgia, RB
1973	John Cappelletti, Penn St., RB	1983	Mike Rozier, Nebraska, RB
1974	Archie Griffin, Ohio St., RB	1984	Doug Flutie, Boston College, QB
1975	Archie Griffin, Ohio St., RB	1985	Bo Jackson, Auburn, RB
1976	**Tony Dorsett, Pittsburgh, RB**	1986	Vinny Testaverde, Miami, FL, QB
1977	Earl Campbell, Texas, RB	1987	Tim Brown, Notre Dame, WR
1978	Billy Sims, Oklahoma, RB	1988	Barry Sanders, Oklahoma St., RB
1979	Charles White, USC, RB	1989	Andre Ware, Houston, QB

Maxwell Award

First presented in 1937 by the Maxwell Memorial Football Club of Philadelphia, the award is named after Robert "Tiny" Maxwell, a Philadelphia native who was a standout lineman at the University of Chicago at the turn of the century.

Like the Heisman, the Maxwell is given to the outstanding college player in the nation. Both awards have gone to the same player in the same season 26 times. Those players are preceded by (#). Glenn Davis of Army and Doak Walker of SMU won both but in different years.

Multiple winner: Johnny Lattner (1952-53).

Year		Year	
1937	#Clint Frank, Yale, HB	1964	Glenn Ressler, Penn St., G
1938	#Davey O'Brien, TCU, QB	1965	Tommy Nobis, Texas, LB
1939	#Nile Kinnick, Iowa, HB	1966	Jim Lynch, Notre Dame, LB
1940	#Tom Harmon, Michigan, HB	1967	#Gary Beban, UCLA, QB
1941	Bill Dudley, Virginia, HB	1968	#O.J.Simpson, USC, HB
1942	Paul Governali, Columbia, QB	1969	Mike Reid, Penn St., DT
1943	Bob Odell, Pennsylvania, HB	1970	#Jim Plunkett, Stanford, QB
1944	Glenn Davis, Army, HB	1971	Ed Marinaro, Cornell, RB
1945	#Doc Blanchard, Army, FB	1972	Brad VanPelt, Michigan St., DB
1946	Charley Trippi, Georgia, HB	1973	#John Cappelletti, Penn St., RB
1947	Doak Walker, SMU, HB	1974	Steve Joachim, Temple, QB
1948	Chuck Bednarik, Penn, C	1975	#Archie Griffin, Ohio St., RB
1949	#Leon Hart, Notre Dame, E	1976	#Tony Dorsett, Pittsburgh, RB
1950	Reds Bagnell, Pennsylvania, HB	1977	Ross Browner, Notre Dame, DE
1951	#Dick Kazmaier, Princeton, TB	1978	Chuck Fusina, Penn St., QB
1952	Johnny Lattner, Notre Dame, HB	1979	#Charles White, USC, RB
1953	#Johnny Lattner, Notre Dame, HB	1980	Hugh Green, Pittsburgh, DE
1954	Ron Beagle, Navy, E	1981	#Marcus Allen, USC, RB
1955	#Howard Cassady, Ohio St., HB	1982	#Herschel Walker, Georgia, RB
1956	Tommy McDonald, Oklahoma, HB	1983	#Mike Rozier, Nebraska, RB
1957	Bob Reifsnyder, Navy, T	1984	#Doug Flutie, Boston College, QB
1958	#Pete Dawkins, Army, HB	1985	Chuck Long, Iowa, QB
1959	Rich Lucas, Penn St., QB	1986	#Vinny Testaverde, Miami, FL, QB
1960	#Joe Bellino, Navy, HB	1987	Don McPherson, Syracuse, QB
1961	Bob Ferguson, Ohio St., HB	1988	#Barry Sanders, Oklahoma St., RB
1962	#Terry Baker, Oregon St., QB	1989	Anthony Thompson, Indiana, RB
1963	#Roger Staubach, Navy, QB		

The Camp and Rockne Awards

Besides the Heisman Trophy and Maxwell Award, the Touchdown Club of Washington, DC, initiated two other player-of-the-year prizes in the late 1930s: the Walter Camp Award for the nation's best back, and the Knute Rockne Award for best lineman. The Camp Award, started in 1937, is named after the football innovator and college All-America Team originator. The Rockne Award, started in 1939, is named after the Notre Dame All-America end (1913) and football coach (1918-30).

Multiple winners: Camp—Ed Marinaro (1970-71); Rockne—Dick Butkus (1963-64).

Camp Award

Year		Year	
1937	Marshall Goldberg, Pittsburgh, HB	1947	Johnny Lujack, Notre Dame, QB
1938	Davey O'Brien, TCU, QB	1948	Charlie Justice, North Carolina, HB
1939	Nile Kinnick, Iowa, HB	1949	Emil Sitko, Notre Dame, HB
1940	Tom Harmon, Michigan, HB	1950	Babe Parilli, Kentucky, QB
1941	Bill Dudley, Virginia, HB	1951	Dick Kazmaier, Princeton, TB
1942	Frank Sinkwich, Georgia, HB	1952	Don McAuliffe, Michigan St., HB
1943	Angelo Bertelli, Notre Dame, QB	1953	Alan Ameche, Wisconsin, FB
1944	Glenn Davis, Army, HB		Bernie Faloney, Maryland, QB
1945	Doc Blanchard, Army, FB		Paul Giel, Minnesota, HB
1946	Charley Trippi, Georgia, HB		& Johnny Lattner, Notre Dame, HB

Annual Award Winners (Cont.)

Camp and Rockne Awards

Camp Award (Cont.)

Year		Year	
1954	Ralph Guglielmi, Notre Dame, QB	1972	Greg Pruitt, Oklahoma, RB
1955	Howard Cassady, Ohio St., HB	1973	John Cappelletti, Penn St., RB
1956	Paul Hornung, Notre Dame, QB	1974	Anthony Davis, USC, HB
1957	John David Crow, Texas A&M	1975	Chuck Muncie, California, RB
1958	Randy Duncan, Iowa, QB	1976	Tony Dorsett, Pittsburgh, RB
1959	Billy Cannon, LSU, HB	1977	Earl Campbell, Texas, RB
		1978	Chuck Fusina, Penn St., QB
1960	Joe Bellino, Navy, HB	1979	Charles White, USC, RB
1961	Ernie Davis, Syracuse, HB		
1962	Jerry Stovall, LSU, HB	1980	Herschel Walker, Georgia, RB
1963	Roger Staubach, Navy, QB	1981	Art Schlichter, Ohio St. QB
1964	Jerry Rhome, Tulsa, QB	1982	John Elway, Stanford, QB
1965	Jim Grabowski, Illinois, FB	1983	Mike Rozier, Nebraska, RB
1966	Steve Spurrier, Florida, QB	1984	Keith Byars, Ohio St., RB
1967	Gary Beban, UCLA, QB	1985	Lorenzo White, Michigan St., RB
1968	O.J.Simpson, USC, HB	1986	Paul Palmer, Temple, RB
1969	Archie Manning, LSU, QB	1987	Tim Brown, Notre Dame, WR
		1988	Barry Sanders, Oklahoma St., RB
1970	Ed Marinaro, Cornell, RB	1989	Andre Ware, Houston, QB
1971	Ed Marinaro, Cornell, RB		

Rockne Award

Year		Year	
1939	Ken Kavanaugh, LSU, E	1965	Tommy Nobis, Texas, LB
		1966	Jim Lynch, Notre Dame, LB
1940	Bob Suffridge, Tennessee, G	1967	Ron Yary, USC, OT
1941	Chub Peabody, Harvard, G	1968	Ted Hendricks, Miami,FL, DE
1942	Bob Dove, Notre Dame, E	1969	Mike Reid, Penn St., DT
1943	Cas Myslinski, Army, C		
1944	Don Whitmire, Navy, T	1970	Jim Stillwagon, Ohio St., MG
1945	Dick Duden, Navy, E	1971	Larry Jacobson, Nebraska, DT
1946	Burr Baldwin, UCLA, E	1972	John Hannah, Alabama, OG
1947	Chuck Bednarik, Penn, C	1973	Ed Jones, Tennessee St., DE
1948	Bill Fischer, Notre Dame, G	1974	Randy White, Maryland, DT
1949	Leon Hart, Notre Dame, E	1975	Lee Roy Selmon, Oklahoma, DT
		1976	Wilson Whitley, Houston, DT
1950	Bud McFadin, Texas, G	1977	Ken MacAfee, Notre Dame, TE
1951	Bob Ward, Maryland, G	1978	Greg Roberts, Oklahoma, OG
1952	Dick Modzelewski, Maryland, T	1979	Bruce Clark, Penn St., DT
1953	Stan Jones, Maryland, T		
1954	Max Boydston, Oklahoma, E	1980	Hugh Green, Pittsburgh, DE
1955	Bob Pellegrini, Maryland, C	1981	Kenneth Sims, Texas, DT
1956	Jerry Tubbs, Oklahoma, C	1982	Billy Ray Smith, Arkansas, DE
1957	Lou Michaels, Kentucky, T	1983	Bill Fralic, Pittsburgh, OT
1958	Bob Novogratz, Army, G	1984	Bruce Smith, Virginia Tech, DT
1959	Roger Davis, Syracuse, G	1985	Tony Casillas, Oklahoma, NG
		1986	Gordie Lockbaum, Holy Cross, E
1960	Tom Brown, Minnesota, G	1987	Chad Hennings, Air Force, DT
1961	Joe Romig, Colorado, G	1988	Tracy Rocker, Auburn, DT
1962	Pat Richter, Wisconsin, E	1989	Chris Zorich, Notre Dame, NT
1963	Dick Butkus, Illinois, C		
1964	Dick Butkus, Illinois, C		

Outland Trophy

First presented in 1946 by the Football Writers Association of America, honoring the nation's outstanding interior lineman. The award is named after its benefactor, Dr. John H. Outland (Kansas, Class of 1898).

Multiple winner: Dave Rimmington (1981-82).
Winners in junior year: Ross Browner (1976); Rimmington (1981).

Year		Year	
1946	George Connor, Notre Dame, T	1955	Calvin Jones, Iowa, G
1947	Joe Steffy, Army, G	1956	Jim Parker, Ohio St., G
1948	Bill Fischer, Notre Dame, G	1957	Alex Karras, Iowa, T
1949	Ed Bagdon, Michigan St., G	1958	Zeke Smith, Auburn, G
		1959	Mike McGee, Duke, T
1950	Bob Gain, Kentucky, T		
1951	Jim Weatherall, Oklahoma, T	1960	Tom Brown, Minnesota, G
1952	Dick Modzelewski, Maryland, T	1961	Merlin Olsen, Utah St., T
1953	J.D.Roberts, Oklahoma, G	1962	Bobby Bell, Minnesota, T
1954	Bill Brooks, Arkansas, G	1963	Scott Appleton, Texas, T

Year		Year	
1964	Steve DeLong, Tennessee, T	1977	Brad Shearer, Texas, DT
1965	Tommy Nobis, Texas, G	1978	Greg Roberts, Oklahoma, G
1966	Loyd Phillips, Arkansas, T	1979	Jim Richter, N.C.State, C
1967	Ron Yary, USC, T		
1968	Bill Stanfill, Georgia, T	1980	Mark May, Pittsburgh, T
1969	Mike Reid, Penn St., DT	1981	Dave Rimmington, Nebraska, C
		1982	Dave Rimmington, Nebraska, C
1970	Jim Stillwagon, Ohio St., MG	1983	Dean Steinkuhler, Nebraska, G
1971	Larry Jacobson, Nebraska, DT	1984	Bruce Smith, Virginia Tech, DT
1972	Rich Glover, Nebraska, MG	1985	Mike Ruth, Boston College, NG
1973	John Hicks, Ohio St., T	1986	Jason Buck, BYU, DT
1974	Randy White, Maryland, DT	1987	Chad Hennings, Air Force, DT
1975	Lee Roy Selmon, Oklahoma, DT	1988	Tracy Rocker, Auburn, DT
1976	Ross Browner, Notre Dame, DE	1989	Mohammed Elewonibi, BYU, G

Lombardi Award

First presented in 1970 by the Rotary Club of Houston, honoring the nation's best lineman. The award is named after pro football coach Vince Lombardi, who, as a guard, was a member of the famous "Seven Blocks of Granite" at Fordham in the 1930s.

The Lombardi and Outland awards have gone to the same player in the same year eight times. Those players are preceded by (#). Ross Browner of Notre Dame won both, but in different years.

Year		Year	
1970	#Jim Stillwagon, Ohio St., MG	1980	Hugh Green, Pittsburgh, DE
1971	Walt Patulski, Notre Dame, DE	1981	Kenneth Sims, Texas, DT
1972	#Rich Glover, Nebraska, MG	1982	#Dave Rimmington, Nebraska, C
1973	#John Hicks, Ohio St., OT	1983	#Dean Steinkuhler, Neb., OG
1974	#Randy White, Maryland, DT	1984	Tony Degrate, Texas, DT
1975	#Lee Roy Selmon, Okla., DT	1985	Tony Casillas, Oklahoma, NG
1976	Wilson Whitley, Houston, DT	1986	Cornelius Bennett, Alabama, LB
1977	Ross Browner, Notre Dame, DE	1987	Chris Spielman, Ohio St., LB
1978	Bruce Clark, Penn St., DT	1988	#Tracy Rocker, Auburn, DT
1979	Brad Budde, USC, OG	1989	Percy Snow, Michigan St., LB

O'Brien Quarterback Award

First presented in 1977 as the O'Brien Memorial Trophy, the award went to the outstanding player in the Southwest. In 1981, however, the Davey O'Brien Educational and Charitable Trust of Ft. Worth renamed the prize the O'Brien National Quarterback Award and now honors the nation's best quarterback.

The award is named after 1938 Heisman Trophy-winning QB Davey O'Brien of Texas Christian.

Multiple winner: Mike Singletary (1979-80).

Memorial Trophy

Year		Year	
1977	Earl Campbell, Texas, RB	1979	Mike Singletary, Baylor, LB
1978	Billy Sims, Oklahoma, RB	1980	Mike Singletary, Baylor, LB

Quarterback Award

Year		Year	
1981	Jim McMahon, BYU	1985	Chuck Long, Iowa
1982	Todd Blackledge, Penn St.	1986	Vinny Testaverde, Miami,FL
1983	Steve Young, BYU	1987	Don McPherson, Syracuse
1984	Doug Flutie, Boston College	1988	Troy Aikman, UCLA
		1989	Andre Ware, Houston

Butkus Award

First presented in 1985 by the Downtown Athletic Club of Orlando, Fla., to honor the nation's outstanding linebacker.

The award is named after Dick Butkus, two-time consensus All-America at Illinois and six-time All-Pro with the Chicago Bears.

Multiple winner: Brian Bosworth (1985-86).

Year	
1985	Brian Bosworth, Oklahoma
1986	Brian Bosworth, Oklahoma
1987	Paul McGowan, Florida St.
1988	Derrick Thomas, Alabama
1989	Percy Snow, Michigan St.

Thorpe Award

First presented in 1986 by the Jim Thorpe Athletic Club of Oklahoma City to honor the nation's outstanding defensive back.

The award is named after Jim Thorpe—Olympic champion, two-time consensus All-America HB at Carlisle, and pro football pioneer.

Year	
1986	Thomas Everett, Baylor
1987	Bennie Blades, Miami,FL
	Rickey Dixon, Oklahoma
1988	Deion Sanders, Florida St.
1989	Mike Carrier, USC

All-Time Winningest Division I-A Coaches

Minimum of 10 years in Division I-A through 1989 season. Regular season and bowl games included. Active coaches in **bold type.**

Top 25 Victories | | | | | | ### Top 25 Winning Pct. | | | |

	Yrs	W	L	T	Pct.		Yrs	W	L	T	Pct
Bear Bryant	38	323	85	17	.780	Knute Rockne	13	105	12	5	.881
Amos Alonzo Stagg	57	314	199	35	.605	Frank Leahy	13	107	13	9	.864
Pop Warner	44	313	106	32	.729	George Woodruff	12	142	25	2	.846
Woody Hayes	33	238	72	10	.759	Barry Switzer	16	157	29	4	.837
Bo Schembechler	27	234	65	8	.775	Percy Haughton	13	96	17	6	.832
Joe Paterno	24	220	57	3	.791	Bob Neyland	21	173	31	12	.829
Jess Neely	40	207	176	19	.539	Fielding Yost	29	196	36	12	.828
Warren Woodson	31	203	95	14	.673	Bud Wilkinson	17	145	29	4	.826
Vince Dooley	25	201	77	10	.715	**Tom Osborne**	17	168	38	2	.813
Eddie Anderson	39	201	128	15	.606	Jock Sutherland	20	144	28	14	.812
Dana X. Bible	33	198	72	23	.715	Bob Devaney	16	136	30	7	.806
Dan McGugin	30	197	55	19	.762	Frank Thomas	19	141	33	9	.795
Fielding Yost	29	196	36	12	.828	**Joe Paterno**	24	220	57	3	.791
Bobby Bowden	24	195	72	3	.728	Henry Williams	23	141	34	12	.786
Howard Jones	29	194	64	21	.733	Gil Dobie	33	180	45	15	.781
Johnny Vaught	25	190	61	12	.745	Bear Bryant	38	323	85	17	.780
John Heisman	36	185	70	17	.711	Fred Folsom	19	106	28	6	.779
Darrell Royal	23	184	60	5	.749	Bo Schembechler	27	234	65	8	.775
Gil Dobie	33	180	45	15	.781	Fritz Crisler	18	116	32	9	.768
Carl Snavely	32	180	96	16	.644	Charley Moran	18	122	33	12	.766
Jerry Claiborne	28	179	122	8	.592	Wallace Wade	24	171	49	10	.765
Ben Schwartzwalder	28	178	96	3	.648	Frank Kush	22	176	54	1	.764
Frank Kush	22	176	54	1	.764	Dan McGugin	30	197	55	19	.762
Shug Jordan	25	176	83	6	.675	Andy Smith	17	116	32	13	.761
Pappy Waldorf	31	174	100	22	.625	Jim Crowley	13	78	21	10	.761

Note: Eddie Robinson of Division I-AA Grambling (1941–42, 1945–present) is the all-time NCAA leader in coaching wins with a 358-125-15 record over 47 seasons.

Where They Coached

Anderson—Loras (1922-24), DePaul (1925-31), Holy Cross (1933-38), Iowa (1939-42), Holy Cross (1950-64); **Bible**—Miss.College (1913-15), LSU (1916), Texas A&M (1917 and 1919-28), Nebraska (1929-36), Texas (1937-46); **Bowden**—Samford (1959-62), West Va.(1970-75); **Florida St.(1976-present); Bryant**—Maryland (1945), Kentucky (1946-53), Texas A&M (1954-57), Alabama (1958-82); Claiborne—Va.Tech (1961-70), Maryland (1972-81), Kentucky (1982-89); **Crisler**—Minnesota (1930-31), Princeton (1932-37), Michigan (1938-47); **Crowley**—Michigan St.(1929-32), Fordham (1933-41); Devaney—Wyoming (1957-61), Nebraska (1962-72); **Dobie**—N.Dakota St.(1906-07), Washington (1908-16), Navy (1917-19), Cornell (1920-35), Boston Col.(1936-38). **Dooley**—Georgia (1964-88); **Folsom**—Colorado (1895-99,1901-02), Dartmouth (1903-06), Colorado (1908-15); **Haughton**—Cornell (1899-00), Harvard (1908-16), Columbia (1923-24); **Hayes**—Denison (1946-48), Miami-OH (1949-50), Ohio St.(1951-78); **Heisman**—Oberlin (1892,94), Akron (1893), Auburn (1895-99), Clemson (1900-03), Ga.Tech (1904-19), Penn (1920-22), Wash.& Jeff.(1923), Rice (1924-27); **Jones**—Syracuse (1908), Yale (1909), Ohio St.(1910), Yale (1913), Iowa (1916-23), Duke (1924), USC (1925-40); **Jordan**—Auburn (1951-75); **Kush**—Arizona St.(1958-79); **Leahy**—Boston Col.(1939-40), Notre Dame (1941-43,1946-53); **McGugin**—Vanderbilt (1904-17,1919-34); **Moran**—Texas A&M (1909-14), Centre (1919-23), Bucknell (1924-26), Catawba (1930-33).

Neely—Southwestern-TN (1924-27), Clemson (1931-39), Rice (1940-66); **Neyland**—Tennessee (1926-34,1936-40,1946-52); **Osborne**—Nebraska (1973-present); **Paterno**—Penn St. (1966-present); **Rockne**—Notre Dame (1918-30); **Royal**—Miss.St.(1954-55), Washington (1956), Texas (1957-76); **Schembechler**—Miami-OH (1963-68), Michigan (1969-89); **Schwartzwalder**—Muhlenberg (1946-48), Syracuse (1949-73); **Smith**—Penn (1909-12), Purdue (1913-15), California (1916-25); **Snavely**—Bucknell (1927-33), N.Carolina (1934-35), Cornell (1936-44), N.Carolina (1945-52), Washington-MO (1953-58); **Stagg**—Springfield-MA (1890-91), Chicago (1892-32), Pacific (1933-46); **Sutherland**—Lafayette (1919-23), Pittsburgh (1924-38); **Switzer**—Oklahoma (1973-88).

Thomas—Chattanooga (1925-28), Alabama (1931-42,1944-46); **Vaught**—Mississippi (1947-70,1973); **Wade**—Alabama (1923-30); **Duke (1931-41,1946-50); Waldorf**—Okla.City (1925-27), Okla.A&M (1929-33), Kansas St.(1934), Northwestern (1935-46), California (1947-56); **Warner**—Georgia (1895-96), Cornell (1897-98), Carlisle (1899-03), Cornell (1904-06), Carlisle (1907-14), Pittsburgh (1915-23), Stanford (1924-32), Temple (1933-38); **Wilkinson**—Oklahoma (1947-63); **Williams**—Army (1891), Minnesota (1900-21); **Woodruff**—Penn (1892-01), Illinois (1903), Carlisle (1905); **Woodson**—Conway St.(1935-40), Hardin-Simmons (1941-42,1946-51), Arizona (1952-56), N.Mexico St.(1958-67), Trinity-TX (1972-73); **Yost**—Ohio Wesleyan (1897), Nebraska (1898), Kansas (1899), Stanford (1900), Michigan (1901-23,1925-26).

All-Time Bowl Appearances
(Active coaches in **bold type**)

	Bowls	W	L	T	Pct
Bear Bryant	29	15	12	2	.552
Joe Paterno	20	13	6	1	.675
Vince Dooley	20	8	10	2	.450
Johnny Vaught	18	10	8	0	.556
Tom Osborne	17	8	9	0	.471
Bo Schembechler	17	5	12	0	.294
Darrell Royal	16	8	7	1	.531
Johnny Majors	14	8	6	0	.571
Lou Holtz	14	7	5	2	.571
LaVell Edwards	14	5	9	0	.357
Bobby Bowden	13	9	3	1	.731
Bobby Dodd	13	9	4	0	.692
Barry Switzer	13	8	5	0	.615
Charlie McClendon	13	7	6	0	.538
Don James	12	8	4	0	.667
Woody Hayes	12	6	6	0	.500
Shug Jordan	12	5	7	0	.417
Bill Yoeman	11	6	4	1	.591
Earle Bruce	11	6	5	0	.545
Hayden Fry	11	5	6	0	.455
Jerry Claiborne	11	3	8	0	.273

Active Coaches' Victories
(Minimum 5 years in Div. I-A)

	Yrs	W	L	T
Joe Paterno, Penn St	24	**220**	57	3
Bobby Bowden, Fla. St.	24	**195**	72	3
Hayden Fry, Iowa	28	**171**	135	8
Tom Osborne, Nebraska	17	**168**	38	2
LaVell Edwards, BYU	18	**165**	56	1
Lou Holtz, Notre Dame	20	**153**	76	5
Jim Sweeney, Fresno St.	25	**151**	121	2
Johnny Majors, Tennessee	22	**150**	97	8
Grant Teaff, Baylor	27	**149**	138	7
Bill Dooley, W.Forest	23	**147**	107	5
Don James, Washington	19	**145**	73	3
Earle Bruce, Colo.St.	18	**137**	71	2
Pat Dye, Auburn	16	**135**	48	3
Jim Wacker, TCU	19	**132**	81	3
Don Nehlen, West Va.	19	**130**	74	6
Bill Mallory, Indiana	20	**130**	89	2
Jim Young, Army	16	**114**	66	2
Terry Donahue, UCLA	14	**111**	45	8
Dick Crum, Kent St.	16	**111**	68	4
Fred Akers, Purdue	15	**106**	66	3

AFCA Coach of the Year

First presented in 1935 by the American Football Coaches Association.
Multiple winners: Joe Paterno (4); Bear Bryant (3); John McKay and Darrell Royal (2).

Year		Year		Year	
1935	Pappy Waldorf, N'western	1955	Duffy Daugherty, Mich.St.	1973	Bear Bryant
1936	Dick Harlow, Harvard	1956	Bowden Wyatt, Tennessee	1974	Grant Teaff, Baylor
1937	Hooks Mylin, Lafayette	1957	Woody Hayes, Ohio St.	1975	Frank Kush, Arizona St.
1938	Bill Kern, Carnegie Tech	1958	Paul Dietzel, LSU	1976	Johnny Majors, Pittsburgh
1939	Eddie Anderson, Iowa	1959	Ben Schwartzwalder, Syracuse	1977	Don James, Washington
1940	Clark Shaughnessy, Stanford	1960	Marray Warmath, Minnesota	1978	Joe Paterno, Penn St.
1941	Frank Leahy, Notre Dame	1961	Bear Bryant, Alabama	1979	Earle Bruce, Ohio St.
1942	Bill Alexander, Ga.Tech	1962	John McKay, Southern Cal	1980	Vince Dooley, Georgia
1943	Amos Alonzo Stagg, Pacific	1963	Darrell Royal, Texas	1981	Danny Ford, Clemson
1944	Carroll Widdoes, Ohio St.	1964	Frank Broyles, Arkansas	1982	Joe Paterno, Penn St.
1945	Bo McMillin, Indiana		& Ara Parseghian, N.Dame	1983	Ken Hatfield, Air Force
1946	Red Blaik, Army	1965	Tommy Prothro, UCLA	1984	LaVell Edwards, BYU
1947	Fritz Crisler, Michigan	1966	Tom Cahill, Army	1985	Fisher DeBerry, Air Force
1948	Bennie Oosterbaan, Michigan	1967	John Pont, Indiana	1986	Joe Paterno, Penn St.
1949	Bud Wilkinson, Oklahoma	1968	Joe Paterno, Penn St.	1987	Dick MacPherson, Syracuse
1950	Charlie Caldwell, Princeton	1969	Bo Schembechler, Michigan	1988	Don Nehlen, West Virginia
1951	Chuck Taylor, Stanford	1970	Charlie McClendon, LSU	1989	Bill McCartney, Colorado
1952	Biggie Munn, Michigan St.		& Darrell Royal, Texas		
1953	Jim Tatum, Maryland	1971	Bear Bryant		
1954	Red Sanders, UCLA	1972	John McKay		

FWAA Coach of the Year

First presented in 1957 by the Football Writers Association of America.
The FWAA and AFCA awards have both gone to the same coach in the same season 22 times. Those double winners are preceded by (#).
Multiple winners: Woody Hayes and Joe Paterno (3); Lou Holtz, Johnny Majors and John McKay (2).

Year		Year		Year	
1957	#Woody Hayes, Ohio St.	1968	Woody Hayes, Ohio St.	1980	#Vince Dooley, Georgia
1958	#Paul Dietzel, LSU	1969	#Bo Schembechler, Michigan	1981	#Danny Ford, Clemson
1959	#B.Schwatzwalder, Syracuse	1970	Alex Agase, Northwestern	1982	#Joe Paterno, Penn St.
1960	#Murray Warmath, Minnesota	1971	Bob Devaney, Nebraska	1983	H.Schnellenberger, Miami,FL
1961	Darrell Royal, Texas	1972	#John McKay, USC	1984	#LaVell Edwards, BYU
1962	#John McKay, Southern Cal	1973	Johnny Majors, Pittsburgh	1985	#Fisher DeBerry, Air Force
1963	#Darrell Royal, Texas	1974	#Grant Teaff, Baylor	1986	#Joe Paterno, Penn St.
1964	#Ara Parseghian, Notre Dame	1975	Woody Hayes, Ohio St.	1987	#Dick MacPherson, Syracuse
1965	Duffy Daugherty, Mich.St.	1976	#Johnny Majors, Pitt.	1988	Lou Holtz, Notre Dame
1966	#Tom Cahill, Army	1977	Lou Holtz, Arkansas	1989	#Bill McCartney, Colorado
1967	#John Pont, Indiana	1978	#Joe Paterno, Penn St.		
		1979	#Earle Bruce, Ohio St.		

Divisional Playoffs

The NCAA has decided its Division I-AA champion with a postseason playoff since 1978. Divisions II and III have had playoffs since 1973.

The NAIA has used playoffs since 1956 for Division I and since 1970 for Division II.

NCAA Divisional Champions

Division I-AA, 1978-89

Year	Winner	Score	Loser
1978	Florida A&M	35-28	Massachusetts
1979	Eastern Kentucky	30-7	Lehigh,PA
1980	Boise St.,ID	31-29	Eastern Kentucky
1981	Idaho St.	34-23	Eastern Kentucky
1982	Eastern Kentucky	17-14	Delaware
1983	Southern Illinois	43-7	Western Carolina
1984	Montana St.	19-6	Louisiana Tech
1985	Georgia Southern	44-42	Furman,SC
1986	Georgia Southern	48-21	Arkansas St.
1987	NE Louisiana	43-42	Marshall,WV
1988	Furman,SC	17-12	Georgia Southern
1989	Georgia Southern	37-34	S.F.Austin St.

Division II, 1973-89

Year	Winner	Score	Loser
1973	Louisiana Tech	34-0	Western Kentucky
1974	Central Michigan	54-14	Delaware
1975	Northern Michigan	16-14	Western Kentucky
1976	Montana St.	24-13	Akron,OH
1977	Lehigh,PA	33-0	Jacksonville,AL
1978	Eastern Illinois	10-9	Delaware
1979	Delaware	38-21	Youngstown St.,OH
1980	Cal Poly-SLO	21-13	Eastern Illinois
1981	SW Texas St.	42-13	North Dakota St.
1982	SW Texas St.	34-9	UC-Davis
1983	North Dakota St.	41-21	Central St.,OH
1984	Troy St.,AL	18-17	North Dakota St.
1985	North Dakota St.	35-7	North Alabama
1986	North Dakota St.	27-7	South Dakota
1987	Troy St.,AL	31-17	Portland St.,OR
1988	North Dakota St.	35-21	Portland St.,OR
1989	Mississippi Col.	3-0	Jacksonville St.

Division III, 1973-89

Year	Winner	Score	Loser
1973	Wittenberg,OH	41-0	Juniata,PA
1974	Central, IA	10-8	Ithaca,NY
1975	Wittenberg,OH	28-0	Ithaca,NY
1976	St.John's,MN	31-28	Towson St.,MD
1977	Widener,PA	39-36	Wabash,IN
1978	Baldwin-Wallace	24-10	Wittenberg,OH
1979	Ithaca,NY	14-10	Wittenberg,OH
1980	Dayton,OH	63-0	Ithaca,NY
1981	Widener,PA	17-10	Dayton,OH
1982	West Georgia	14-0	Augustana,IL
1983	Augustana,IL	21-17	Union,NY
1984	Augustana,IL	21-12	Central,IA
1985	Augustana,IL	20-7	Ithaca,NY
1986	Augustana,IL	31-3	Salisbury St.,MD
1987	Wagner,NY	19-3	Dayton,OH
1988	Ithaca,NY	39-24	Central,IA
1989	Dayton,OH	17-7	Union,NY

NAIA Divisional Champions

Division I, 1956-89

Year	Winner	Score	Loser
1956	Montana St. St.Joseph's,IN	0-0	—
1957	Pittsburg St.,KS	27-26	Hillsdale,MI
1958	NE Oklahoma	19-13	Northern Arizona
1959	Texas A&I	20-7	Lenoir-Rhyne,NC
1960	Lenoir-Rhyne,NC	15-14	Humboldt St.,CA
1961	Pittsburg St.,KS	12-7	Linfield,OR
1962	Central St.,OK	28-13	Lenoir-Rhyne,NC
1963	St.John's,MN	33-27	Prairie View,TX
1964	Concordia,MN Sam Houston,TX	7-7	—
1965	St.John's,MN	33-0	Linfield,OR
1966	Waynesburg,PA	42-21	Wisc-Whitewater
1967	Fairmont St.,WV	28-21	Eastern Wash.
1968	Troy St.,AL	43-35	Texas A&I
1969	Texas A&I	32-7	Concordia,MN
1970	Texas A&I	48-7	Wofford,SC
1971	Livingston,AL	14-12	Arkansas Tech
1972	East Texas St.	21-18	Car-Newman,TN
1973	Abilene Christian	42-14	Elon,NC
1974	Texas A&I	34-23	Henderson St.,AR
1975	Texas A&I	37-0	Salem, WV
1976	Texas A&I	26-0	Central Arkansas
1977	Abilene Christian	24-7	SW Oklahoma
1978	Angelo St.,TX	24-14	Elon,NC
1979	Texas A&I	20-14	Central St.,OK
1980	Elon,NC	17-10	NE Oklahoma
1981	Elon,NC	3-0	Pittsburg St.,KS
1982	Central St.,OK	14-11	Mesa,CO
1983	Car-Newman,TN	36-28	Mesa,CO
1984	Car-Newman,TN Central Arkansas	19-19	—
1985	Hillsdale,MI Central Arkansas	10-10	—
1986	Car-Newman,TN	17-0	Cameron,OK
1987	Cameron,OK	30-2	Car-Newman,TN
1988	Car-Newman,TN	56-21	Adams St.,CO
1989	Car-Newman,TN	34-20	Emporia St.,KS

Division II, 1970-89

Year	Winner	Score	Loser
1970	Westminster,PA	21-16	Anderson,IN
1971	Calif.Lutheran	30-14	Westminster,PA
1972	Missouri Southern	21-14	Northwestern,IA
1973	Northwestern,IA	10-3	Clenville St.,WV
1974	Texas Lutheran	42-0	Missouri Valley
1975	Texas Lutheran	34-8	Calif.Lutheran
1976	Westminster,PA	20-13	Redlands,CA
1977	Westminster,PA	27-9	Calif.Lutheran
1978	Concordia,MN	7-0	Findlay,OH
1979	Findlay,OH	51-6	Northwestern,IA
1981	Austin College,TX Concordia,MN	24-24	—
1982	Linfield,OR	33-15	Wm. Jewell, MO
1983	Northwestern,IA	25-21	Pacific Lutheran
1984	Linfield, OR	33-22	Northwestern,IA
1985	Wisc-La Crosse	24-7	Pacific Lutheran
1986	Linfield,OR	17-0	Baker,KS
1987	Pacific Lutheran Wisc-Stevens Pt.*	16-16	—
1988	Westminster,PA	21-14	Wisc-La Crosse
1989	Westminster,PA	51-30	Wisc-La Crosse

*Wisconsin-Stevens Point forfeited its entire 1987 schedule due to its use of an ineligible player.

Wide receiver **Jerry Rice** scoring the first of eight San Francisco touchdowns in the 49ers' 55-10 pounding of the Denver Broncos in Super Bowl XXIV. Rice caught three TD passes as the Niners won their fourth title of the decade.

PRO FOOTBALL

Forty-Niner juggernaut rolls unchecked through the Broncos and the '80s; Juniors come out and some cash in; Tagliabue eyes global NFL gridiron.

PRO FOOTBALL

1989 YEAR IN REVIEW

by Gary Myers

Junior Seau stood next to NFL commissioner Paul Tagliabue, joyously showing off the San Diego Chargers dark blue jersey with the No. 1 on front and back.

Moments before, Seau had been selected with the Chargers' first pick in the April 22nd draft. Now he was waving the jersey and pumping his fist. Seau, who calls himself a "mama's boy," was overcome with emotion after having been drafted by the Chargers. His family lives about 40 miles from San Diego.

And that will come in handy. Seau may be a linebacker, but after all, he's really just a kid, and he can probably still use some parental guidance and mama's cooking. Seau was one of 38 juniors who took advantage of Tagliabue's new eligibility rules this year that were designed to keep the NFL out of court. Tagliabue, who replaced Pete Rozelle on Oct. 26, 1989, is an accomplished attorney with a specialty in anti-trust law.

More than anybody, he knew it would take only one challenge and the league's seniors-only draft policy would be shot down in the courts.

So he relaxed the requirements and players like Seau came busting through the door. And why not? There is every indication that by the draft of 1991, the league and the players' union will reach an accord on a new collective bargaining agreement that will include a rookie wage scale. Consequently, this may have been the last year to cash in big. And there is always the fear of being one knee injury away from losing a career.

"I'm not trying to downgrade the educational system," said Seau, who was a Proposition 48 casualty and had to sit out his freshman year at Southern Cal, "but everybody wants to live the American dream."

Seau was born in American Samoa and didn't learn to speak English until his family moved to the mainland when he was seven years old. But he caught on quickly to the capitalist system. It didn't take him long to say "money." And he has parlayed his madman pass rush into big bucks. "Before, I had

Gary Myers is the national pro football columnist for the *New York Daily News* and a reporter on HBO's "Inside the NFL."

Happy he will be staying close to home, former USC linebacker **Junior Seau** (left) reacts to his selection by San Diego in the first round of the NFL Draft. The valet is league commissioner Paul Tagliabue.

to worry about having enough money to buy my girlfriend a hamburger," he said. "Now I'll have enough money to buy the place."

Juniors like Seau dominated the early portion of the draft. Illinois quarterback Jeff George went to the Indianapolis Colts, who traded Pro Bowl tackle Chris Hinton, wide receiver Andre Rison and a No.1 pick to Atlanta, for the first choice overall. George then signed a 6-year, $15 million contract, the most money ever thrown at a rookie and $4 million more than Troy Aikman got from the Cowboys in 1989. Five of the first seven players selected were underclassmen. Eight went in the 25-player first round, but only 10 were chosen in the last 11 rounds.

The NFL hopes that the plight of the 20 juniors who were not drafted at all makes an impression on impatient college players: Stay in school. League officials are also concerned about offending the colleges, which, after all, provide the pros with a free farm system.

"The colleges are the lifeline to our league and I hope they don't misconstrue the fact that because we drafted the juniors we're excited about them coming out," Tam-

pa Bay Buccaneers personnel director Jerry Angelo said.

New York Jets general manager Dick Steinberg, who took Penn State senior running back Blair Thomas with the second pick in the first round, added, "It'll be interesting to see if the thing everybody was afraid of with the juniors—lack of experience—was something that was worth being afraid of. If they don't do well, then I think some players may realize you better get all the experience you can get."

That a man of Tagliabue's stature was elected to succeed Rozelle would, at first blush, seem to indicate that NFL owners were pretty smart, too. Not a chance.

The league embarrassed itself over a prolonged seven-month search that centered around the younger, richer owners' desire to have more of a say in league matters. The old guard, led by Art Modell of Cleveland and the New York Giants' Wellington Mara, wanted to elect one of their own, New Orleans Saints president and general manager Jim Finks. The young turks, led by Norman Braman of Philadelphia, Pat Bowlen of Denver and Eddie DeBartolo of San Francisco, wanted somebody, anybody else. It was ironic that they latched on to Tagliabue, who for 20 years worked closely with Rozelle and for the last 10 was his chief advisor.

In the end, the old guard decided it could live with Tagliabue and he was elected unanimously on the 11th ballot. He said he wanted the $1 million-a-year job because it would be "fun." And, yes, negotiating the NFL's gigantic, new $3.65 billion network and cable TV contract was probably loads of fun—what with each of the league's 28 teams raking in an average of $32.6 million a year for four years (see "Business & Media"). But these days the commissioner's job is not what you would call a barrel of laughs.

In his first six months, Tagliabue broke the news to Dexter Manley, Earl Ferrell and Frank Warrent that they had flunked their drug tests for the third time and were gone for at least one year. He instituted six random steroid tests, trying to cut down on the use of the juice that is both a physical harm to the players using them and a potential danger to those going up against them—on and off the field. And he had to fight off a Super Bowl week report by a Washington TV station that three prominent quarterbacks had failed drug tests in the 1980s, but had never been punished.

Tagliabue did have some fun, however. He was at the Superdome in New Orleans to watch the San Francisco 49ers become the first team in 10 years to repeat as Super Bowl champion.

The 49ers, led by the marvelous Joe Montana, were the first team to put titles back-to-back since the 1978-79 Pittsburgh Steelers. "We want the three-peat," safety Ronnie Lott said moments after the 55-10 rout of the Denver Broncos. The Broncos' loss marked the third time in the last four years that they had defeated Cleveland in the AFC Championship Game only to suffer a Rocky Mountain Low in the Super Bowl. The three-game totals: NFC 136, Denver 40.

Of course, the 49ers' four Vince Lombardi Trophies made them a runaway choice as "Team of the '80s" (see box). Proving they could win without former head coach and resident genius, Bill Walsh, may have provided their greatest motivation. Walsh first kicked himself upstairs to team president, then quit altogether to take a job as a TV analyst with NBC. Former Walsh assistant George Seifert took over and the Niners never missed a beat.

Are the Niners the best ever?

You can talk all you want about the Green Bay Packers of the '60s, or the Pittsburgh Steelers of the '70s. But it would be hard to ignore the San Francisco 49ers of the '80s as the best pro football team of all time.

Since we will never know who would win the head-to-head battles, unless you believe in computer football, let's simply focus on how dominating the 49ers were winning four Super Bowls in the last decade, particularly the last two.

"It's always hard to compare teams," quarterback Joe Montana says. "But it's tough to say any team is better than this one."

Beginning with the 1988 playoffs, the 49ers have simply been unstoppable. Their 55-10 victory over Denver in Super Bowl XXIV in January was the icing on the decade. Consider some of these achievements:

► The Niners outscored the Vikings, Rams, and Broncos in the 1989 playoffs, 126-26. In the last six playoff games over the last two seasons, they outscored their opposition, 208-54, and in each game gave up only a field goal in the first half.

► In four Super Bowls, Montana has completed 83 of 122 passes for 1142 yards and 11 touchdowns and without an interception. Those marks plus a completion rate of 68% are all Super Bowl records.

► In last season's three playoff games, Montana was 65-of-83 (78.3%) for 800 yards with 11 TDs and no interceptions.

► In Super Bowl XXIV, they outgained Denver, 461 yards to 167, and kept the ball for 39:31. And remember, Denver gave up the fewest points in the NFL in 1989.

Now the question is, can the 49ers three-peat? The answer—why not? Montana, in his 12th season and third decade in the NFL, is only getting better with age and without Bill Walsh. Montana seemed to relish having his best season sans Genius, who often talked about Montana as nothing more than his puppet. As long as the 49ers offensive line continues to give him bulletproof protection and as long as Jerry Rice is around running slants, Montana seems capable of playing forever.

Rarely has a quarterback had so many weapons—Rice, the gazelle receiver; John Taylor, underpublicized but not unappreciated, playing opposite Rice; and a backfield of Roger Craig and Tom Rathman that can

Al Messerschmidt/Sports File

Jerry Rice holds Vince Lombardi's trophy and **Joe Montana** plugs Dwight Clark's restaurant following the 49ers latest Super Bowl triumph in New Orleans.

not only pound the ball inside and run outside, but are dangerous receivers as well. "I think they're playing as well as anybody ever has," Denver coach Dan Reeves said after watching his club get embarrassed in the Super Bowl. "They're playing at a level that's incredible."

How would the 49ers stack up against Vince Lombardi's Packers or the Steelers of the Terry Bradshaw, Franco Harris, Lynn Swan and Jack Lambert years? Who knows?

But consider this, nobody has ever won three Super Bowls in a row. Maybe that's what it will take to end all the arguments about the greatest team ever.

"I don't know if it's tri-peat or three-peat," says 49ers safety Ronnie Lott, "but I do know we want to do it again."

Two Decades, Two Dominant Teams

The Steelers of the '70s

Pittsburgh won four Super Bowls in four appearances, finished first in the AFC's Central Division seven times, and posted an overall record (regular season and playoffs) of 113-48-1 for a winning percentage of .701. (*) Denotes division title.

Year	Regular Season	Play-Offs	Comment
1970	5-9-0	None	7th losing year in row
1971	6-8-0	None	8th losing year in row
1972	11-3-0*	1-1	Lost AFC title game
1973	10-4-0	0-1	Lost AFC 1st round
1974	10-3-1*	3-0	**Won Super Bowl IX**
1975	12-2-0*	3-0	**Won Super Bowl X**
1976	10-4-0*	1-1	Lost AFC title game
1977	9-5-0*	0-1	Lost AFC 1st round
1978	14-2-0*	3-0	**Won Super Bowl XIII**
1979	12-4-0*	3-0	**Won Super Bowl XIV**
W-L	99-44-1	14-4	4 Super Bowl wins

The 49ers of the '80s

San Francisco won four Super Bowls in four appearances, finished first in the NFC's Western Division seven times, and posted an overall record (regular season and playoffs) of 117-51-1 for a winning percentage of .695. (*) Denotes division title.

Year	Regular Season	Play-Offs	Comment
1980	6-10-0	None	4th losing year in row
1981	13-3-0*	3-0	**Won Super Bowl XVI**
1982	3-6-0	None	Strike season
1983	10-6-0*	1-1	Lost NFC title game
1984	15-1-0*	3-0	**Won Super Bowl XIX**
1985	10-6-0	0-1	Lost NFC wildcard game
1986	10-5-1*	0-1	Lost NFC 2nd round
1987	13-2-0*	0-1	Lost NFC 2nd round
1988	10-6-0*	3-0	**Won Super Bowl XXIII**
1989	14-2-0*	3-0	**Won Super Bowl XXIV**
W-L	104-47-1	13-4	4 Super Bowl wins

It helped that Montana turned in an MVP year during the regular season, leading the 49ers to a 14-2 record with 26 touchdown passes and just eight interceptions. His completion percentage (70.2) and pass rating (112.4) were not only outstanding, but new NFL records.

Montana was clearly the year's best quarterback, but Green Bay's Don Majkowski may have been the most exciting—engineering five come-from-behind victories as the Pack improved its 4-12 record in 1988 to 10-6 in '89. Majkowski, who led the league in passing attempts (599), completions (353) and passing yardage (4318), also became the first Packer QB named to the Pro Bowl since Bart Starr in 1966.

And there were several other glittering performances during the season.

▶ Bo Jackson spent the summer slugging 32 homers, driving in 105 runs and walking off with the MVP award in baseball's All-Star Game. Come October, he exchanged his K.C. Royals No.16 for No.34 of the L.A. Raiders and rushed for 950 yards in 11 games.

▶ Detroit running back Barry Sanders, the 1988 Heisman Trophy winner who turned pro after his junior year at Oklahoma State, led the NFC in rushing with 1470 yards. Sanders' efforts were 10 yards behind NFL leader Christian Okoye of Kansas City, but more than enough to earn him Rookie of the Year.

▶ Minnesota's Rich Karlis kicked seven field goals against the L.A. Rams on Nov. 5, tying Jim Bakken's 22-year-old league record. Karlis, who also set a mark for most field goals in a game without missing, connected from 20, 24, 22, 25, 29, 36 and 40 yards out. The Vikings, who had trouble scoring touchdowns in 1989, won 23-21 with a safety in overtime.

▶ Wide receiver Willie (Flipper) Anderson of the L.A. Rams caught 15 Jim Everett passes for an NFL record 336 yards, Nov.26 in New Orleans. Anderson had two catches and drew a 35-yard pass interference call on the Rams' winning drive in overtime.

▶ And Seattle's incomparable Steve Largent retired after 14 seasons of catching passes and rewriting the NFL record book. Largent struggled through an injury-shortened 1989, but walked away as the all-time leader in receptions (819) yards gained (13,089) and touchdown catches (100). That 100th TD catch, a 10-yard toss from Dave Krieg on Dec.10 in Cincinnati, enabled Largent to finally move past Hall of Famer Don Hutson, whose record of 99 had been unapproached for 44 years.

Elsewhere, Cleveland tight end Ozzie Newsome, who indicated he was going to retire, decided to play another year. And who could blame him? Many players are simply making too much money to leave of their own volition. Just look at some of the mega-deals signed in the last year. Quarterbacks Bernie Kosar, who has never been to a Super Bowl; Randall Cunningham, who has never won a playoff game; and Jeff George, who had never even played in the NFL, all signed $15 million contracts.

Obviously, clubs are a bit concerned about what lies ahead in the free agent game and they're anxious to tie up their stars. That's why Buffalo QB Jim Kelly, who's been on the downside the last few years, was able to walk away with a new $20 million deal.

In this day of the big money, it's not surprising that contracts get outdated rather quickly. And that has led to some unhappy players. Miami's Dan Marino, in the middle of a 6-year, $9 million deal, has asked to be traded two years in a row. On the surface, his unhappiness can be traced to his deteriorating relationship with coach Don Shula. In reality, though, Marino just wants more money.

And since we're talking about unhappy players, how can we leave out Eric Dickerson, who holds NFL records for most yards gained in a season and most times wanting to be traded? Dickerson is not happy in Indianapolis, just as he wasn't happy with the Rams in L.A. Why? Money, what else?

The Dallas Cowboys, who used to make a habit of playing in January, finished up the decade with a 1-15 record under new coach Jimmy Johnson. Not many coaches get a chance to lose 15 games in one season. In fact, the 1980 Saints were the only other team to lose 15 in one year, but they went through a couple of coaches doing it. In Johnson's case, it helped that expectations were not high after taking over a club that was 3-13 in Tom Landry's final season. It helped even more that his best friend, Jerry Jones, owned the team and gave him a 10-year contract.

Johnson is building around Aikman, who one day, if his offensive line keeps him healthy, will be a franchise quarterback and one of the NFL stars of the '90s.

Another rookie, Hall of Famer Art Shell of the L.A. Raiders, became the NFL's first black head coach in the modern era. Shell replaced Mike Shanahan four games into the 1989 season, and although the 8-8 Raiders missed the playoffs for the fourth straight year, Shell seemed to have them headed in the right direction.

Al Davis hired Shell just prior to the end of Rozelle's regime, lending a nice twist to the stormy Davis-Rozelle relationship. One of the few drawbacks of Rozelle's 30-year run as commissioner was his inability to prod even one club into hiring a black head coach. Wasn't it nice of Davis, Rozelle's archenemy, to take him off the hook as the clock was winding down on his regime? In March, Davis announced he was accepting a $600 million offer to move the Raiders back to Oakland. When public criticism forced the city to restructure the deal, however, Davis backed off.

Part of Rozelle's legacy will be parity. In 1989, 17 teams were alive for the 10 playoff spots with one week to go in the regular season. Tagliabue's legacy could well be squeezing television and the public for every dollar out there. He's already expanded the playoffs to include two extra wild card teams in 1990 and stretched the 16-game regular season to 17 weeks, creating one off week per team. OK, fine, we'll accept that. The NFL has been slow to make changes and this should add some interest.

One thing that won't change, however, is the constant recycling of coaches. No sooner had Jerry Glanville lost his job in Houston than he talked his way into Atlanta. Joe Walton, much to the glee of the ''Joe Must Go,'' chanters in New York, was finally fired by the Jets after the team hired Steinberg as its first G.M. in nearly two decades. Walton, hired as Pittsburgh's offensive coordinator, was replaced in New York by Cincinnati offensive coordinator Bruce Coslet, who many feel was the brains behind Sam Wyche's no-huddle offense.

Joe Bugel, who conceived the Hogs' approach to offensive line play in Washington, was hired in Phoenix. Cards' owner Bill Bidwill ran off Gene Stallings, perhaps jealous of his popularity in a city turned off by Bidwill's bumbling. And when New England's Raymond Berry refused to revamp his coaching staff, he was told to leave and was quickly replaced by former assistant Rod Rust.

Wide World Photos

All-time NFL pass catching leader **Steve Largent** leaps to grab his 100th career touchdown reception Dec. 10 against Cincinnati.

Less than nine months after forcing the NFL to open its draft to junior undergraduates, **Barry Sanders** rushed out of the Detroit Lions backfield for 1470 yards and Rookie of the Year honors.

The hot name to look out for in the next year or so is 49ers offensive coordinator Mike Holmgren. He was the most talked about candidate for both the Jets and Cardinals jobs, but withdrew his name because he wanted to hang out with Montana for another year or so before going off on his own.

The 1990s will be an era of growth for the NFL. Tagliabue has announced that he wants to add four teams in the next few years, probably two at a time. Baltimore, the Carolinas, St. Louis, Jacksonville and Birmingham are the frontrunners. The new 12-team World League of American Football will begin play in the spring. The WLAF is sponsored by the NFL and run by Cowboys founding father Tex Schramm. The league will feature four European teams (Barcelona, Frankfurt, London and Milan) as well as franchises in Mexico City,

Montreal and six U.S. cities from New York to Sacramento.

Proving that TV feels the country's pigskin appetite is insatiable, ABC and USA cable network each gobbled up the new league's games.

But how will the public react? Games with second-line players will be a tough sell in New York on a beautiful spring day. How much of a draw will Barcelona be in Giants Stadium? And we all know that making it in New York is essential to the health of any league.

Tagliabue is deeply committed to the international concept. Preseason games were staged this past summer in Berlin, Tokyo, London and Montreal. There is talk next year of a game in Moscow. And don't look now, but Tagliabue predicts NFL teams will be stationed abroad by the year 2000. □

PRO FOOTBALL
S T A T I S T I C S

THE 1991 INFORMATION PLEASE SPORTS ALMANAC

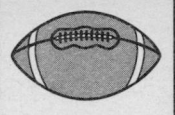

THE SEASON IN REVIEW
1989-1990
STANDINGS • PLAYOFFS • DRAFT

SEC **A**

PAGE **141**

Final NFL Standings

Division champions (*) and Wild Card playoff qualifiers (†) are noted. Number of seasons listed after each head coach refers to current tenure with club.

American Football Conference

Eastern Division

	W	L	T	Pct	PF	PA	vs Div
*Buffalo	9	7	0	.563	409	317	6-2-0
Indianapolis	8	8	0	.500	298	301	4-4-0
Miami	8	8	0	.500	331	379	4-4-0
New England	5	11	0	.313	297	391	4-4-0
NY Jets	4	12	0	.250	253	411	2-6-0

Head Coaches: Buf—Marv Levy (4th season); **Indy**—Ron Meyer (4th); **Mia**—Don Shula (20th); **NE**—Raymond Berry (6th); **NY**—Joe Walton (7th).

Central Division

	W	L	T	Pct	PF	PA	vs Div
*Cleveland	9	6	1	.594	334	254	3-3-0
†Houston	9	7	0	.563	365	412	3-3-0
†Pittsburgh	9	7	0	.563	265	326	1-5-0
Cincinnati	8	8	0	.500	404	285	5-1-0

Head Coaches: Clev—Bud Carson (1st season); **Hou**—Jerry Glanville (5th); **Pitt**—Chuck Noll (21st); **Cinn**—Sam Wyche (6th season).

Western Division

	W	L	T	Pct	PF	PA	vs Div
*Denver	11	5	0	.688	362	226	6-2-0
Kansas City	8	7	1	.531	318	286	3-5-0
LA Raiders	8	8	0	.500	315	297	3-5-0
Seattle	7	9	0	.438	241	327	4-4-0
San Diego	6	10	0	.375	266	290	4-4-0

Head Coaches: Den—Dan Reeves (8th season); **KC**—Marty Schottenheimer (1st); **LA**—replaced Mike Shanahan (2nd, 1-3) with assistant Art Shell (7-5) on Oct.3; **Sea**—Chuck Knox (7th); **SD**—Dan Henning (1st).

National Football Conference

Eastern Division

	W	L	T	Pct	PF	PA	vs Div
*NY Giants	12	4	0	.750	348	252	6-2-0
†Philadelphia	11	5	0	.688	342	274	7-1-0
Washington	10	4	0	.313	258	377	2-6-0
Phoenix	5	11	0	.313	258	377	2-6-0
Dallas	1	15	0	.063	204	393	1-7-0

Head Coaches: NY—Bill Parcells (7th season); **Phi**—Buddy Ryan (4th); **Wash**—Joe Gibbs (9th); **Pho**—replaced Gene Stallings (4th, 5-6) with assistant Hank Kuhlmann (0-5) on Nov.20; **Dal**—Jimmy Johnson (1st).

Central Division

	W	L	T	Pct	PF	PA	vs Div
*Minnesota	10	6	0	.625	351	275	6-2-0
Green Bay	10	6	0	.625	362	356	5-3-0
Detroit	7	9	0	.438	312	364	4-4-0
Chicago	6	10	0	.375	358	377	2-6-0
Tampa Bay	6	11	0	.313	320	393	3-5-0

Head Coaches: Minn—Jerry Burns (4th season); **GBay**—Lindy Infante (2nd); **Det**—Wayne Fontes (2nd); **Chi**—Mike Ditka (8th); **TBay**—Ray Perkins (3rd).

Western Division

	W	L	T	Pct	PF	PA	vs Div
*San Francisco	14	2	0	.875	442	253	5-1-0
†LA Rams	11	5	0	.688	426	344	4-2-0
New Orleans	9	7	0	.563	386	301	3-3-0
Atlanta	3	13	0	.188	279	437	0-6-0

Head Coaches: SF—George Seifert (1st season); **LA**—John Robinson (7th); **NO**—Jim Mora (4th); **Atl**—Marion Campbell (3rd, 3-9) retired on Nov.28 and was replaced by asst Jim Hanifan (0-4).

The World League of American Football

As of mid-October, 1990, the NFL's new 12-team international spring league was experiencing pronounced start-up difficulties. Scheduled to open its inaugural season Mar. 23, 1991, the WLAF has designated 11 of its 12 cities and signed contracts with ABC Sports and USA network to televise games. But independent owners have proven hard to find, and the league will probably have to operate several ownerless teams.

Of the 11 franchises granted so far, four are in European cities (Barcelona, Frankfurt, London and Milan), one in Montreal, one in Mexico City and five in the US (Birmingham, New York, Orlando, Sacramento and San Antonio).

On Oct. 10th, the WLAF's board of directors, chaired by Pittsburgh Steelers owner Dan Rooney, fired former Dallas Cowboys general manager Tex Schramm as president and named Minnesota Vikings GM Mike Lynn to take his place. Twenty-six of the 28 teams in the NFL have invested $200,000 in the WLAF. The two holdouts are Chicago and Phoenix.

NFL Individual Leaders

REGULAR SEASON

Passing Efficiency
(Minimum 192 attempts)

AFC	Att	Cmp	Cmp %	Yards	Rate	TD	TD %	Long	Int	Int %	Rating
Boomer Esiason, Cinn	455	258	56.7	3525	7.75	28	6.2	74-td	11	2.4	92.1
Warren Moon, Hou	464	280	60.3	3631	7.83	23	5.0	55	14	3.0	88.9
Jim Kelly, Buff	391	228	58.3	3130	8.01	25	6.4	78-td	18	4.6	86.2
Bernie Kosar, Clev	513	303	59.1	3533	6.89	18	3.5	97-td	14	2.7	80.3
Dan Marino, Miami	550	308	56.0	3997	7.27	24	4.4	78-td	22	4.0	76.9
Steve DeBerg, KC	324	196	60.5	2529	7.81	11	3.4	50	16	4.9	75.8
Dave Krieg, Sea	499	286	57.3	3309	6.63	21	4.2	60-td	20	4.0	74.8
Ken O'Brien, NY	477	288	60.4	3346	7.01	12	2.5	57	18	3.8	74.3
John Elway, Den	416	223	53.6	3051	7.33	18	4.3	69	18	4.3	73.7
Jim McMahon, SD	318	176	55.3	2132	6.70	10	3.1	69-td	10	3.1	73.5

NFC	Att	Cmp	Cmp %	Yards	Avg	TD	TD %	Long	Int	Int %	Rating
Joe Montana, SF	386	271	70.2	3521	9.12	26	6.7	95-td	8	2.1	112.4
Jim Everett, LA	518	304	58.7	4310	8.32	29	5.6	78-td	17	3.3	90.6
Mark Rypien, Wash	476	280	58.8	3768	7.92	22	4.6	80-td	13	2.7	88.1
Bobby Hebert, NO	353	222	62.9	2686	7.61	15	4.2	54-td	15	4.2	82.7
Don Majkowski, GB	599	353	58.9	4318	7.21	27	4.5	79-td	20	3.3	82.3
Phil Simms, NY	405	228	56.3	3061	7.56	14	3.5	62-td	14	3.5	77.6
Chris Miller, Atl	526	280	53.2	3459	6.58	16	3.0	72-td	10	1.9	76.1
Randall Cunningham, Phi	532	290	54.5	3400	6.39	21	3.9	66-td	15	2.8	75.5
Wade Wilson, Minn	362	194	53.6	2543	7.02	9	2.5	50	12	3.3	70.5
Gary Hogeboom, Pho	364	204	56.0	2591	7.12	14	3.8	59-td	19	5.2	69.5

Receiving

AFC	No	Yards	Avg	TD
Andre Reed, Buff	88	1312	14.9	9
Brian Blades, Sea	77	1063	13.8	5
Vance Johnson, Den	76	1095	14.4	7
John L.Williams, Sea	76	657	8.6	6
Anthony Miller, SD	75	1252	16.7	10
Drew Hill, Hou	66	938	14.2	8
Webster Slaughter, Clev	65	1236	19.0	6
Tim McGee, Cinn	65	1211	18.6	8
Mark Clayton, Miami	64	1011	15.8	9
Bill Brooks, Indy	63	919	14.6	4
Al Toon, NY	63	693	11.0	2

NFC	No	Yards	Avg	TD
Sterling Sharpe, GB	90	1423	15.8	12
Mark Carrier, TB	86	1422	16.5	9
Art Monk, Wash	86	1186	13.8	8
Jerry Rice, SF	82	1483	18.1	17
Ricky Sanders, Wash	80	1138	14.2	4
Gary Clark, Wash	79	1229	15.6	9
Tom Rathman, SF	73	616	8.4	1
Henry Ellard, LA	70	1382	19.7	8
Richard Johnson, Det	70	1091	15.6	8
Eric Martin, NO	68	1090	16.0	8
Keith Byars, Phila	68	721	10.6	0

Rushing

AFC	Att	Yards	Avg	TD
Christian Okoye, KC	370	1480	4.0	12
Eric Dickerson, Indy	314	1311	4.2	7
Thurman Thomas, Buff	298	1244	4.2	6
James Brooks, Cinn	221	1239	5.6	7
Bobby Humphrey, Den	294	1151	3.9	7
Bo Jackson, LA	173	950	5.5	4
John Stephens, NE	244	833	3.4	7
Tim Worley, Pitt	195	770	3.9	5
Johnny Hector, NY	177	702	4.0	3
Marion Butts, SD	170	683	4.0	9

NFC	Att	Yards	Avg	TD
Barry Sanders, Det	280	1470	5.3	14
Neal Anderson, Chi	274	1275	4.7	11
Dalton Hilliard, NO	344	1262	3.7	13
Greg Bell, LA	272	1137	4.2	15
Roger Craig, SF	271	1054	3.9	6
Ottis Anderson, NY	325	1023	3.1	14
Herschel Walker, Dal-Min	250	915	3.7	7
Gerald Riggs, Wash	201	834	4.1	4
Brent Fullwood, GB	204	821	4.0	5
John Settle, Atl	179	689	3.8	3

All Purpose Running

AFC	Rush	Rec	Ret	Total
Thurman Thomas, Buf	1244	669	0	1913
Anthony Miller, SD	21	1252	533	1806
Eric Metcalf, Cle	633	397	718	1748
JoJo Townsell, NY	0	787	952	1739
James Brooks, Cinn	1239	306	0	1545
Eric Dickerson, Indy	1311	211	0	1522
Christian Okoye, KC	1480	12	0	1492
Bobby Humphrey, Den	1151	156	86	1393
Andre Reed, Buf	31	1312	0	1343
Tim McGee, Cinn	36	1211	0	1247

NFC	Rush	Rec	Ret	Total
Barry Sanders, Det*	1470	282	118	1870
Dave Meggett, NY*	117	531	1159	1807
Dalton Hilliard, NO	1262	514	20	1796
Herschel Walker, Dal-Min	915	423	374	1712
Neal Anderson, Chi	1275	434	0	1709
Vai Sikahema, Pho	145	245	1307	1697
John Taylor, SF	6	1077	468	1551
Roger Craig, SF	1054	473	0	1527
Jerry Rice, SF	33	1483	0	1516
Sterling Sharpe, GB	25	1423	5	1453

Scoring

Kickers

AFC	PAT	FG	Long	Pts
David Treadwell, Den	39/40	27/33	46	120
Scott Norwood, Buff	46/47	23/30	48	115
Tony Zendejas, Hou	40/40	25/37	52	115
Nick Lowery, KC	34/35	24/33	50	106
Jeff Jaeger, LA	34/34	23/34	50	103
Pete Stoyanovich, Mia	38/39	19/26	59	95
Dean Biasucci, Indy	31/32	21/27	55	94
Gary Anderson, Pitt	28/28	21/30	49	91
Matt Bahr, Clev	40/40	16/24	50	88
Chris Bahr, SD	29/30	17/25	53	80

NFC	PAT	FG	Long	Pts
Mike Cofer, SF	49/51	29/36	47	136
Chip Lohmiller, Wash	41/41	29/40	48	128
Rich Karlis, Minn	27/28	31/39	51	120
Mike Lansford, LA	51/51	23/30	48	120
Chris Jacke, GB	42/42	22/28	52	108
Morten Andersen, NO	44/45	20/29	49	104
Donald Igwebuike, TB	33/35	22/28	53	99
Eddie Murray, Det	36/36	20/21	50	96
Greg Davis, NE-Atl	25/28	23/34	52	94
Kevin Butler, Chi	43/45	15/19	46	88

Touchdowns

AFC	TD	Rush	Rec	Ret	Pts
Christian Okoye, KC	12	12	0	0	72
Thurman Thomas, Buff	12	6	6	0	72
Anthony Miller, SD	11	0	10	1	66
Eric Metcalf, Clev	10	6	4	0	60
James Brooks, Cinn	9	7	2	0	54
Marion Butts, SD	9	9	0	0	54
Mark Clayton, Miami	9	0	9	0	54
Mervyn Fernandez, LA	9	0	9	0	54
Rodney Holman, Cinn	9	0	9	0	54
Andre Reed, Buff	9	0	9	0	54

NFC	TD	Rush	Rec	Ret	Pts
Dalton Hilliard, NO	18	13	5	0	108
Jerry Rice, SF	17	0	17	0	102
Neal Anderson, Chi	15	11	4	0	90
Greg Bell, LA	15	15	0	0	90
Ottis Anderson, NY	14	14	0	0	84
Barry Sanders, Det	14	14	0	0	84
Sterling Sharpe, GB	13	0	13	1	78
Cris Carter, Phila	11	0	11	0	66
Herschel Walker, Dal-Min	10	7	2	1	60
John Taylor, SF	10	0	10	0	60

Interceptions

AFC	No	Yds	Long	TD
Felix Wright, Clev	9	91	27-td	1
David Fulcher, Cinn	8	87	22	0
Keith Taylor, Indy	7	225	80-td	1
Gill Byrd, SD	7	38	22	0
Erik McMillan, NY	6	180	92-td	1
Tyrone Braxton, Den	6	103	34-td	1
Mark Kelso, Buff	6	101	43	0
Mike Prior, Indy	6	88	58-td	1

NFC	No	Yds	Long	TD
Eric Allen, Phila	8	38	18	0
Tim McDonald, Phoe	7	170	53-td	1

Six tied with 6 each.

Sacks

AFC	No
Lee Williams, San Diego	14
Bruce Smith, Buffalo	13
Leslie O'Neal, San Diego	12½
Simon Fletcher, Denver	12
Rufus Porter, Seattle	10½
Greg Townsend, Los Angeles	10½

NFC	No
Chris Doleman, Minnesota	20½
Tim Harris, Green Bay	19½
Keith Millard, Minnesota	18
Kevin Greene, Los Angeles	16½
Pat Swilling, New Orleans	16½

Punting

AFC	No	Yards	Lg	Avg	In.20
Greg Montgomery, Hou	56	2422	63	43.3	15
Rohn Stark, Indy	79	3392	64	42.9	14
Reggie Roby, Miami	58	2458	58	42.4	18
Harry Newsome, Pitt	82	3368	57	41.1	15
Jeff Gossett, LA	67	2711	60	40.5	12

NFC	No	Yards	Lg	Avg	In.20
Rich Camarillo, Phoe	76	3298	58	43.4	21
Jim Arnold, Det	82	3538	64	43.1	14
Sean Landeta, NY	70	3019	71	43.1	19
R.Mojsiejenko, Wash	62	2663	74	43.0	21
Scott Fulhage, Atl	84	3472	65	41.3	24

Punt Returns

AFC	No	Yds	Avg	TD
Clarence Verdin, Indy	23	296	12.9	1
Gerald McNeil, Clev	49	496	10.1	0
JoJo Townsell, NY	33	299	9.1	0
Mickey Sutton, Buff	31	273	8.8	0
Rod Woodson, Pitt	29	207	7.1	0

NFC	No	Yds	Avg	TD
Walter Stanley, Det	36	496	13.4	0
David Meggett, NY	46	582	12.7	1
Vai Sikahema, Phoe	37	433	11.7	0
John Taylor, SF	36	417	11.6	0
Deion Sanders, Atl	28	307	11.0	1
Willie Drewrey, TB	20	220	11.0	0

Kickoff Returns

AFC	No	Yds	Avg	TD	NFC	No	Yds	Avg	TD
Rod Woodson, Pit	36	982	27.2	1	Mel Gray, Det	24	640	26.7	0
Marc Logan, Mia	24	613	25.5	1	James Dixon, Dal	47	1181	25.1	1
Anthony Miller, SD	21	533	25.4	1	Joe Howard, Wash	21	522	24.9	1
Sammy Martin, NE	24	584	24.3	0	Dennis Gentry, Chi	28	667	23.8	0
James Jefferson, Sea	22	511	23.2	1	Dave Meggett, NY	27	577	21.4	0

NFL Team Leaders

REGULAR SEASON

Offense

AFC	Points For	Avg	Yardage Rush	Pass	Total	Avg
Cincinnati	404	25.3	2483	3618	6101	381.3
Buffalo	409	25.6	2264	3589	5853	365.8
Miami	331	20.7	1330	4216	5546	346.6
N.England	297	18.6	1749	3707	5456	341.0
Houston	365	22.8	1928	3499	5427	339.2
Kansas City ...	318	19.9	2227	3038	5265	329.1
Denver	362	22.6	2092	3001	5093	318.3
Cleveland	334	20.9	1609	3433	5042	315.1
New York	253	15.8	1596	3415	5011	313.2
Los Angeles ...	315	19.7	2038	2951	4989	311.8
San Diego	266	16.6	1873	3037	4910	306.9
Ind'polis	298	18.6	1853	2960	4813	300.8
Seattle	241	15.1	1392	3204	4596	287.3
Pittsburgh	265	16.6	1818	2178	3996	249.8

NFC	Points For	Avg	Yardage Rush	Pass	Total	Avg
San Fran	442	27.6	1966	4302	6268	391.8
Washington ...	386	24.1	1904	4349	6253	390.8
Los Angeles ...	426	26.6	1909	4133	6042	377.6
Green Bay	362	22.6	1732	4048	5780	361.3
Chicago	358	22.4	2287	3088	5375	335.9
N.Orleans	386	24.1	1948	3380	5328	333.0
Philadelphia ...	342	21.4	2208	3112	5320	332.5
Minnesota	351	21.9	2066	3189	5255	328.4
Detroit	312	19.5	2053	2939	4992	312.0
New York	348	21.8	1889	3074	4963	310.2
Tampa Bay ...	320	20.0	1507	3335	4842	302.6
Atlanta	279	17.4	1155	3514	4669	291.8
Phoenix	258	16.1	1361	3280	4641	290.1
Dallas	204	12.8	1409	2885	4294	268.4

Defense

AFC	Points Opp	Avg	Yardage Rush	Pass	Total	Avg
Kansas City ...	286	17.9	1766	2527	4293	268.3
Denver	226	14.1	1580	2827	4407	275.4
San Diego	290	18.1	1813	2951	4764	297.8
Cleveland	254	15.9	1670	3161	4831	301.9
Los Angeles...	297	18.6	1940	3063	5003	312.7
Buffalo	317	19.8	1840	3206	5046	315.4
Houston	412	25.8	1669	3542	5211	325.7
Seattle	327	20.4	2118	3097	5215	325.9
Cincinnati	285	17.8	2162	3135	5297	331.1
Pittsburgh	326	20.4	2008	3541	5549	346.8
Ind'polis	301	18.8	2077	3534	5611	350.7
N.England....	391	24.4	1978	3666	5644	352.8
Miami	379	23.7	2153	3543	5696	356.0
New York	411	25.7	2136	3858	5994	374.6

NFC	Points Opp	Avg	Yardage Rush	Pass	Total	Avg
Minnesota	275	17.2	1683	2501	4184	261.5
San Fran	253	15.8	1383	3235	4618	288.6
New York	252	15.8	1539	3125	4664	291.5
Philadelphia ..	274	17.1	1605	3289	4894	305.9
Washington ..	308	19.3	1344	3571	4915	307.2
N.Orleans	301	18.8	1326	3860	5186	324.1
Green Bay ...	356	22.3	2008	3339	5347	334.2
Tampa Bay ...	419	26.2	2023	3437	5460	341.3
Detroit	364	22.8	1621	3916	5537	346.1
Dallas	393	24.6	1991	3565	5556	347.3
Los Angeles ..	344	21.5	1543	4024	5567	347.9
Chicago	377	23.6	1897	3832	5729	358.1
Phoenix	377	23.6	2302	3575	5877	367.3
Atlanta	437	27.3	2471	3554	6025	376.6

Takeaways / Giveaways

AFC	Takeaways Int	Fum	Tot	Giveaways Int	Fum	Tot	Net Diff
Denver	21	22	43	20	12	32	+11
Pittsburgh	21	21	42	13	18	31	+11
Indianapolis	21	15	36	17	10	27	+9
Cleveland	27	11	38	15	15	30	+8
Cincinnati	21	16	37	13	19	32	+5
Houston	21	16	37	16	17	33	+4
Los Angeles	18	18	36	22	12	34	+2
San Diego	25	13	38	19	17	36	+2
Buffalo	23	13	36	20	21	41	−5
Kansas City	15	18	33	23	18	41	−8
New England.....	16	12	28	27	12	39	−11
Seattle	9	13	22	23	14	37	−15
New York	15	9	24	24	17	41	−17
Miami	15	8	23	25	16	41	−18

NFC	Takeaways Int	Fum	Tot	Giveaways Int	Fum	Tot	Net Diff
Philadelphia	30	26	56	16	16	32	+24
San Francisco	21	16	37	11	14	25	+12
Atlanta	20	12	32	12	11	23	+9
New Orleans	21	18	39	19	12	31	+8
New York	22	15	37	16	14	30	+7
Green Bay	25	15	40	20	13	33	+7
Los Angeles	21	15	36	18	11	29	+7
Washington	27	15	42	17	20	37	+5
Minnesota	18	18	36	19	14	33	+3
Tampa Bay	21	18	39	28	9	37	+2
Chicago	26	12	38	25	17	42	−4
Detroit	16	16	32	24	24	48	−16
Phoenix	16	11	27	30	14	44	−17
Dallas...........	7	10	17	27	15	42	−25

AFC Team by Team Statistics

Players who played with more than one team during the regular season are listed with their second club; (*) denotes rookies.

Buffalo Bills

QBs (10 Att)	Att	Cmp	Pct	Yds	TD	Rate
Frank Reich	87	53	60.9	701	7	103.7
Jim Kelly	391	228	58.3	3130	25	86.2

Interceptions: Kelly 18, Reich 2.

Top 5 Receivers	No	Yds	Avg	Long	TD
Andre Reed	88	1312	14.9	78-td	9
Thurman Thomas	60	669	11.2	74-td	6
Ronnie Harmon	29	363	12.5	42-td	4
Flip Johnson	25	303	12.1	36	1
Keith McKeller	20	341	17.1	39-td	2

Top 5 Rushers	Car	Yds	Avg	Long	TD
Thurman Thomas	298	1244	4.2	38	6
Larry Kinnebrew	131	533	4.1	25	6
Kenneth Davis	29	149	5.1	21	1
Jim Kelly	29	137	4.7	19	2
Ronnie Harmon	17	99	5.8	24	0

Top 5 Touchdowns	TD	Run	Rec	Ret	Pts
Thurman Thomas	12	6	6	0	72
Andre Reed	9	0	9	0	54
Larry Kinnebrew	6	6	0	0	36
Ronnie Harmon	4	0	4	0	24
Kenneth Davis	3	1	2	0	18
James Lofton	3	0	3	0	18

Acquired: Lofton signed (Sep.26).

Kicking	FG/Att	Lg	PAT/Att	Pts
Scott Norwood	19/26	59	38/39	95

Punts (10 or more)	No	Yds	Long	Avg	In.20
John Kidd	65	2564	60	39.4	15

Most Interceptions
Mark Kelso 6

Most Sacks
Bruce Smith 13

Cleveland Browns

QBs (10 Att)	Att	Cmp	Pct	Yds	TD	Rate
Bernie Kosar	513	303	59.1	3533	18	80.3
Mike Pagel	14	5	35.7	60	1	43.8

Interceptions: Kosar 14, Pagel 1.

Top 5 Receivers	No	Yds	Avg	Long	TD
Webster Slaughter	65	1236	19.0	97-td	6
Reggie Langhorne	60	749	12.5	62-td	2
Eric Metcalf*	54	397	7.4	68-td	4
Ozzie Newsome	29	324	11.2	31	1
Brian Brennan	28	289	10.3	38	0

Top 5 Rushers	Car	Yds	Avg	Long	TD
Eric Metcalf*	187	633	3.4	43-td	6
Tim Manoa	87	289	3.3	22	3
Barry Redden	40	180	4.5	38-td	1
Keith Jones	43	160	3.7	15	1
Kevin Mack	37	130	3.5	12	1

Top 5 Touchdowns	TD	Run	Rec	Ret	Pts
Eric Metcalf*	10	6	4	0	60
Webster Slaughter	6	0	6	0	36
Tim Manoa	5	3	2	0	30
Lawyer Tillman*	3	0	2	1	18

Three tied with 2 TDs each.

Kicking	FG/Att	Lg	PAT/Att	Pts
Matt Bahr	16/24	50	40/40	88

Punts (10 or more)	No	Yds	Long	Avg	In.20
Bryan Wagner	97	3817	60	39.4	32

Most Interceptions
Felix Wright 9

Most Sacks
Al Baker 7
Michael Dean Perry . . . 7

Cincinnati Bengals

QBs (10 Att)	Att	Cmp	Pct	Yds	TD	Rate
Boomer Esiason	455	258	56.7	3525	28	92.1
Erik Wilhelm*	56	30	53.6	425	4	87.3

Interceptions: Esiason 11, Wilhelm 2.

Top 5 Receivers	No	Yds	Avg	Long	TD
Tim McGee	65	1211	18.6	74-td	8
Eddie Brown	52	814	15.7	46	6
Rodney Holman	50	736	14.7	73-td	9
James Brooks	37	306	8.3	25	2
Ira Hillary	17	162	9.5	17	1

Top 5 Rushers	Car	Yds	Avg	Long	TD
James Brooks	221	1239	5.6	65-td	7
Eric Ball*	98	391	4.0	27	3
Stanford Jennings	83	293	3.5	17	2
Boomer Esiason	47	278	5.9	24	0
Craig Taylor	30	111	3.7	16	3

Top 5 Touchdowns	TD	Run	Rec	Ret	Pts
James Brooks	9	7	2	0	54
Rodney Holman	9	0	9	0	54
Tim McGee	8	0	8	0	48
Eddie Brown	6	0	6	0	36
Craig Taylor	5	3	2	0	30

Kicking	FG/Att	Lg	PAT/Att	Pts
Jim Breech	12/14	38	37/38	73

Punts (10 or more)	No	Yds	Long	Avg	In.20
Lee Johnson	61	2446	62	40.1	14

Most Interceptions
David Fulcher 8

Most Sacks
Jason Buck 6

Denver Broncos

QBs (10 Att)	Att	Cmp	Pct	Yds	TD	Rate
John Elway	416	223	53.6	3051	18	73.7
Gary Kubiak	55	32	58.2	284	2	69.1

Interceptions: Elway 18, Kubiak 2.

Top 5 Receivers	No	Yds	Avg	Long	TD
Vance Johnson	76	1095	14.4	69	7
Mark Jackson	28	446	15.9	49	2
Steve Sewell	25	416	16.6	56	3
Michael Young	22	402	18.3	47	2
Bobby Humphrey*	22	156	7.1	13	1

Top 5 Rushers	Car	Yds	Avg	Long	TD
Bobby Humphrey*	294	1151	3.9	40	7
Sammy Winder	110	351	3.2	16	2
John Elway	48	244	5.1	31	3
Jeff Alexander	45	146	3.2	11	2
Melvin Bratton*	30	108	3.6	9	1

Top 5 Touchdowns	TD	Run	Rec	Ret	Pts
Bobby Humphrey*	8	7	1	0	48
Vance Johnson	7	0	7	0	42
Mel Bratton*	4	1	3	0	24
John Elway	3	3	0	0	18
Steve Sewell	3	0	3	0	18

Kicking	FG/Att	Lg	PAT/Att	Pts
David Treadwell	27/33	46	39/40	120

Punts (10 or more)	No	Yds	Long	Avg	In.20
Mike Horan	77	3111	63	40.4	24

Most Interceptions
Tyrone Braxton 6

Most Sacks
Simon Fletcher 12

Houston Oilers

QBs (10 Att)	Att	Cmp	Pct	Yds	TD	Rate
Warren Moon	464	280	60.3	3631	23	88.9
Cody Carlson	31	15	48.4	155	0	49.8

Interceptions: Moon 14, Carlson 1.

Top 5 Receivers	No	Yds	Avg	Long	TD
Drew Hill	66	938	14.2	50	8
Ernest Givins	55	794	14.4	48	3
Haywood Jeffires	47	619	13.2	45-td	2
Curtis Duncan	43	613	14.3	55	5
Allen Pinkett	31	239	7.7	23	1

Top 5 Rushers	Car	Yds	Avg	Long	TD
Alonzo Highsmith	128	531	4.1	25	4
Allen Pinkett	94	449	4.8	60	1
Lorenzo White	104	349	3.4	33	5
Mike Rozier	88	301	3.4	17	2
Warren Moon	70	268	3.8	19	4

Top 5 Touchdowns	TD	Run	Rec	Ret	Pts
Drew Hill	8	0	8	0	48
Alonzo Highsmith	6	4	2	0	36
Curtis Duncan	5	0	5	0	30
Lorenzo White	5	5	0	0	30
Warren Moon	4	4	0	0	24

Kicking	FG/Att	Lg	PAT/Att	Pts
Tony Zendejas	25/37	52	40/40	115

Punts (10 or more)	No	Yds	Long	Avg	In.20
Greg Montgomery	56	2422	63	43.3	15

Most Interceptions		Most Sacks	
Steve Brown	5	Ray Childress	8½

Kansas City Chiefs

QBs (10 Att)	Att	Cmp	Pct	Yds	TD	Rate
Steve Pelluer	47	26	55.3	301	1	82.0
Steve DeBerg	324	196	60.5	2529	11	75.8
Ron Jaworski	61	36	59.0	385	2	54.3

Interceptions: DeBerg 16, Jaworski 5, Mike Elkins 1.
Acquired: Pelluer from Dallas (Oct.17).

Top 5 Receivers	No	Yds	Avg	Long	TD
Stephone Paige	44	759	17.3	50	2
Pete Mandley	35	476	13.6	44	1
Todd McNair*	34	372	10.9	24	1
Emile Harry	33	430	13.0	25	2
Herman Heard	25	246	9.8	27	1

Top 5 Rushers	Car	Yds	Avg	Long	TD
Christian Okoye	370	1480	4.0	59	12
James Saxon	58	233	4.0	19	3
Herman Heard	63	216	3.4	28	0
Steve Pelluer	17	143	8.4	27	2
Todd McNair*	23	121	5.3	25	0

Top 5 Touchdowns	TD	Run	Rec	Ret	Pts
Christian Okoye	12	12	0	0	72
James Saxon	3	3	0	0	18
Emile Harry	2	0	2	0	12
Jonathon Hayes	2	0	2	0	12
Stephone Paige	2	0	2	0	12
Steve Pelluer	2	2	0	0	12
Robb Thomas*	2	0	2	0	12

Kicking	FG/Att	Lg	PAT/Att	Pts
Nick Lowery	24/33	50	34/35	106

Punts (10 or more)	No	Yds	Long	Avg	In.20
Kelly Goodburn	67	2688	54	40.1	25

Most Interceptions		Most Sacks	
Albert Lewis	4	Derrick Thomas*	10
Kevin Ross	4		

Indianapolis Colts

QBs (10 Att)	Att	Cmp	Pct	Yds	TD	Rate
Jack Trudeau	362	190	52.5	2317	15	71.3
Tom Ramsey	50	24	48.0	280	1	63.8
Chris Chandler	80	39	48.8	537	2	63.4

Interceptions: Trudeau 13, Chandler 3, Ramsey 1.

Top 5 Receivers	No	Yds	Avg	Long	TD
Bill Brooks	63	919	14.6	55-td	4
Andre Rison*	52	820	15.8	61	4
Albert Bentley	52	525	10.1	61	3
Eric Dickerson	30	211	7.0	22	1
Clarence Verdin	20	381	19.1	82-td	1

Top 5 Rushers	Car	Yds	Avg	Long	TD
Eric Dickerson	314	1311	4.2	21-td	7
Albert Bentley	75	299	4.0	22	1
Jack Trudeau	35	91	2.6	17	2
Chris Chandler	7	57	8.1	23	1
Ivy Joe Hunter*	13	47	3.6	11	0

Top 5 Touchdowns	TD	Run	Rec	Ret	Pts
Eric Dickerson	8	7	1	0	48
Albert Bentley	5	1	3	1	30
Bill Brooks	4	0	4	0	24
Andre Rison*	4	0	4	0	24

Four tied with 2 each.

Kicking	FG/Att	Lg	PAT/Att	Pts
Dean Biasucci	21/27	55	31/32	94

Punts (10 or more)	No	Yds	Long	Avg	In.20
Rohn Stark	79	3392	64	42.9	14

Most Interceptions		Most Sacks	
Keith Taylor	7	Jon Hand	10

Los Angeles Raiders

QBs (10 Att)	Att	Cmp	Pct	Yds	TD	Rate
Steve Beuerlein	217	108	49.8	1677	13	78.4
Jay Schroeder	194	91	46.9	1550	8	60.3

Interceptions: Schroeder 13, Beuerlein 9.

Top 5 Receivers	No	Yds	Avg	Long	TD
Mervyn Fernandez	57	1069	18.8	75-td	9
Willie Gault	28	690	24.6	84-td	4
Mike Dyal*	27	499	18.5	67-td	2
Marcus Allen	20	191	9.6	26	0
Steve Smith	19	140	7.4	14	0

Top 5 Rushers	Car	Yds	Avg	Long	TD
Bo Jackson	173	950	5.5	92-td	4
Steve Smith	117	471	4.0	21	1
Marcus Allen	69	293	4.2	15	2
Vance Mueller	48	161	3.4	19	2
Kerry Porter	13	54	4.2	23	0

Top 5 Touchdowns	TD	Run	Rec	Ret	Pts
Mervyn Fernandez	9	0	9	0	54
Willie Gault	4	0	4	0	24
Bo Jackson	4	4	0	0	24
Vance Mueller	4	2	2	0	24

Five tied with 2 each.

Kicking	FG/Att	Lg	PAT/Att	Pts
Jeff Jaeger	23/34	50	34/34	103

Punts (10 or more)	No	Yds	Long	Avg	In.20
Jeff Gossett	67	2711	60	40.5	12

Most Interceptions		Most Sacks	
Eddie Anderson	5	Greg Townsend	10½

Miami Dolphins

QBs (10 Att)	Att	Cmp	Pct	Yds	TD	Rate
Dan Marino	550	308	56.0	3997	24	76.9
Scott Secules	50	22	44.0	286	1	44.3

Interceptions: Marino 22, Secules 3.

Top 5 Receivers	No	Yds	Avg	Long	TD
Mark Clayton	64	1011	15.8	78-td	9
Jim Jensen	61	557	9.1	20	6
Mark Duper	49	717	14.6	41	1
Ferrell Edmunds	32	382	11.9	30	3
Fred Banks	30	520	17.3	61	1

Top 5 Rushers	Car	Yds	Avg	Long	TD
Sammie Smith*	200	659	3.3	25	6
Troy Stradford	66	240	3.6	13	1
Marc Logan	57	201	3.5	14	0
Ron Davenport	14	56	4.0	9	1
Jim Jensen	8	50	6.3	4	1

Top 5 Touchdowns	TD	Run	Rec	Ret	Pts
Mark Clayton	9	0	9	0	54
Jim Jensen	6	0	6	0	36
Sammie Smith*	6	6	0	0	36
Andre Brown*	5	0	5	0	30
Ferrell Edmunds	3	0	3	0	18

Kicking	FG/Att	Lg	PAT/Att	Pts
Pete Stoyanovich*	19/26	59	38/39	95

Punts (10 or more)	No	Yds	Long	Avg	In.20
Reggie Roby	58	2458	58	42.4	18

Most Interceptions   **Most Sacks**
Louis Oliver 4   Jeff Cross 10

New York Jets

QBs (10 Att)	Att	Cmp	Pct	Yds	TD	Rate
Ken O'Brien	477	288	60.4	3346	12	74.3
Tony Eason	141	79	56.0	1016	4	70.5
NE	105	57	54.3	761	3	71.2
NYJ	36	22	61.1	255	1	68.6
Kyle Mackey	25	11	44.0	125	0	42.9
Pat Ryan	30	15	50.0	153	1	36.5

Interceptions: O'Brien 18, Eason 6 (4-2), Ryan 3, Mackey 1.

Acquired: Eason on waivers (Nov.7).

Top 5 Receivers	No	Yds	Avg	Long	TD
Al Toon	63	693	11.0	37-td	2
JoJo Townsell	45	787	17.5	63-td	5
Johnny Hector	38	330	8.7	32	2
Roger Vick	34	241	7.1	21	2
Freeman McNeil	31	310	10.0	25-td	1

Top 5 Rushers	Car	Yds	Avg	Long	TD
Johnny Hector	177	702	4.0	24	3
Roger Vick	112	434	3.9	39-td	5
Freeman McNeil	80	352	4.4	19-td	2
A.B.Brown	12	63	5.3	17	0
Ken O'Brien	9	18	2.0	5	0

Top 5 Touchdowns	TD	Run	Rec	Ret	Pts
Roger Vick	7	5	2	0	42
Johnny Hector	5	3	2	0	30
JoJo Townsell	5	0	5	0	30
Erik McMillan	3	0	0	3	18
Freeman McNeil	3	2	1	0	18

Kicking	FG/Att	Lg	PAT/Att	Pts
Pat Leahy	14/21	46	29/30	71

Punts (10 or more)	No	Yds	Long	Avg	In.20
Joe Prokop	87	3426	76	39.4	29

Most Intercepts   **Most Sacks**
Erik McMillan 6   Dennis Byrd* 7

New England Patriots

QBs (10 Att)	Att	Cmp	Pct	Yds	TD	Rate
Marc Wilson	150	75	50.0	1006	3	64.5
Steve Grogan	261	133	51.0	1697	9	60.8
Doug Flutie	91	36	39.6	493	2	46.6

Interceptions: Grogan 14, Wilson 5, Flutie 4.

Released: Tony Eason waived (Oct.31).

Top 5 Receivers	No	Yds	Avg	Long	TD
Eric Sievers	54	615	11.4	46	0
Hart Lee Dykes*	49	795	16.2	42	5
Cedric Jones	48	670	14.0	65-td	6
Irving Fryar	29	537	18.5	52	3
Robert Perryman	29	195	6.7	16	0

Top 5 Rushers	Car	Yds	Avg	Long	TD
John Stephens	244	833	3.4	35-td	7
Robert Perryman	150	562	3.7	18	2
Doug Flutie	16	87	5.4	22	0
Marvin Allen	11	51	4.6	18	1
Marc Wilson	7	42	6.0	11	0

Released: Reggie Dupard waived (Oct.24).

Top 5 Touchdowns	TD	Run	Rec	Ret	Pts
John Stephens	7	7	0	0	42
Cedric Jones	6	0	6	0	36
Hart Lee Dykes*	5	0	5	0	30
Irving Fryar	3	0	3	0	18
Stanley Morgan	3	0	3	0	18

Kicking	FG/Att	Lg	PAT/Att	Pts
Jason Staurovsky	14/17	50	14/14	56

Note: Greg Davis waived, Staurovsky signed (Nov.7).

Punts (10 or more)	No	Yds	Long	Avg	In.20
Jeff Feagles	63	2392	64	38.0	13

Most Interceptions   **Most Sacks**
Maurice Hurst* 5   Brent Williams 8

Pittsburgh Steelers

QBs (10 Att)	Att	Cmp	Pct	Yds	TD	Rate
Bubby Brister	342	187	54.7	2365	9	73.1
Todd Blackledge	60	22	36.7	282	1	36.9

Interceptions: Brister 10, Blackledge 3.

Top 5 Receivers	No	Yds	Avg	Long	TD
Louis Lipps	50	944	18.9	79-td	5
Rodney Carter	38	267	7.0	22-td	3
Merril Hoge	34	271	8.0	22	0
Derek Hill*	28	455	16.3	53	1
Mike Mularkey	22	326	14.8	34	1

Top 5 Rushers	Car	Yds	Avg	Long	TD
Tim Worley*	195	770	3.9	38	5
Merril Hoge	186	621	3.3	31	8
Louis Lipps	13	180	13.8	58-td	1
Warren Williams	37	131	3.5	13	1
Dwight Stone	10	53	5.3	32	0

Top 5 Touchdowns	TD	Run	Rec	Ret	Pts
Merril Hoge	8	8	0	0	48
Louis Lipps	6	1	5	0	36
Tim Worley*	5	5	0	0	30
Rodney Carter	4	1	3	0	24
Six tied with 1 each.					

Kicking	FG/Att	Lg	PAT/Att	Pts
Gary Anderson	21/30	49	28/28	91

Punts (10 or more)	No	Yds	Long	Avg	In.20
Harry Newsome	82	3368	57	41.1	15

Most Interceptions   **Most Sacks**
Dwayne Woodruff 4   Greg Lloyd 7

San Diego Chargers

QBs (10 Att)	Att	Cmp	Pct	Yds	TD	Rate
Jim McMahon	318	176	55.3	2132	10	73.5
B.J.Tolliver*	185	89	48.1	1097	5	57.9
David Archer	12	5	41.7	62	0	23.6

Interceptions: McMahon 10, Tolliver 8, Archer 1.

Top 3 Receivers	No	Yds	Avg	Long	TD
Anthony Miller	75	1252	16.7	69-td	10
Darrin Nelson	38	380	10.0	49	0
MIN	7	52	7.4	11	0
SD	31	328	10.6	49	0
Jamie Holland	26	336	12.9	37	0

Acquired: Nelson from Dallas (Oct.17).

Top 3 Rushers	Car	Yds	Avg	Long	TD
Marion Butts*	170	683	4.0	50-td	9
Tim Spencer	134	521	3.9	15	3
Darrin Nelson	67	321	4.8	28	0
MIN	31	124	4.0	24	0
SD	36	197	5.5	28	0

Acquired: Nelson from Dallas (Oct.17).

Top 3 Touchdowns	TD	Run	Rec	Ret	Pts
Anthony Miller	11	0	10	1	66
Marion Butts*	9	9	0	0	54
Tim Spencer	3	3	0	0	18

Kicking	FG/Att	Lg	PAT/Att	Pts
Chris Bahr	17/25	53	29/30	80

Punts (10 or more)	No	Yds	Long	Avg	In.20
Hank Ilesic	76	3049	64	40.1	11

Acquired: Ilesic on waivers (Sept.20).

Most Interceptions   **Most Sacks**
Gill Byrd 7   Lee Williams 14

Seattle Seahawks

QBs (10 Att)	Att	Cmp	Pct	Yds	TD	Rate
Dave Krieg	499	286	57.3	3309	21	74.8
Kelly Stouffer	59	29	49.2	270	0	40.9

Interceptions: Krieg 20, Stouffer 3.

Top 5 Receivers	No	Yds	Avg	Long	TD
Brian Blades	77	1063	13.8	60-td	5
John L.Wiliams	76	657	8.6	51-td	6
Paul Skansi	39	488	12.5	26	5
Steve Largent	28	403	14.4	33	3
Louis Clark	25	260	10.4	28	1

Top 5 Rushers	Car	Yds	Avg	Long	TD
Curt Warner	194	631	3.3	34	3
John L.Williams	146	499	3.4	21	1
Dave Krieg	40	160	4.0	18	0
Derrick Fenner*	11	41	3.7	9	1
Kevin Harmon	1	24	24.0	24	0

Top 5 Touchdowns	TD	Run	Rec	Ret	Pts
John L.Williams	7	1	6	0	42
Brian Blades	5	0	5	0	30
Paul Skansi	5	0	5	0	30
Curt Warner	4	3	1	0	24
Steve Largent	3	0	3	0	19

Note: Largent ran in a fumbled snap for a PAT.

Kicking	FG/Att	Lg	PAT/Att	Pts
Norm Johnson	15/25	50	27/27	72

Punts (10 or more)	No	Yds	Long	Avg	In.20
Ruben Rodriquez	75	2995	59	39.9	17

Most Interceptions   **Most Sacks**
Eugene Robinson 5   Rufus Porter 10½

NFC Team by Team Statistics

Players who played with more than one team during the regular season are listed with their second club; (*) denotes rookies.

Atlanta Falcons

QBs (10 Att)	Att	Cmp	Pct	Yds	TD	Rate
Hugh Millen	50	31	62.0	432	1	79.8
Chris Miller	526	280	53.2	3459	16	76.1

Interceptions: Miller 10, Millen 2.

Top 5 Receivers	No	Yds	Avg	Long	TD
Shawn Collins*	58	862	14.9	47	3
Keith Jones*	41	396	9.7	46	0
Michael Haynes	40	681	17.0	72-td	4
Gene Lang	39	436	11.2	32	1
John Settle	39	316	8.1	33	2

Top 5 Rushers	Car	Yds	Avg	Long	TD
John Settle	179	689	3.8	20	3
Keith Jones*	52	202	3.9	19	6
Gene Lang	47	176	3.7	22	1
Michael Haynes	4	35	8.8	21	0
Greg Paterra*	9	32	3.6	8	0

Top 5 Touchdowns	No	Yds	Avg	Ret	Pts
Keith Jones*	6	6	0	0	36
John Settle	5	3	2	0	30
Michael Haynes	4	0	4	0	24
Shawn Collins*	3	0	3	0	18
Gary Wilkins	3	0	3	0	18

Kicking	FG/Att	Lg	PAT/Att	Pts
Greg Davis	23/34	52	25/28	94
NE	16/23	52	13/16	61
ATL	7/11	46	12/12	33
Paul McFadden	15/20	54	18/18	63

Acquired: Davis on waivers (Nov.15).

Punts (10 or more)	No	Yds	Long	Avg	In.20
Scott Fulhage	84	3472	65	41.3	24

Most Interceptions   **Most Sacks**
Deion Sanders* 5   Marcus Cotton 9

Chicago Bears

QBs (10 Att)	Att	Cmp	Pct	Yds	TD	Rate
Jim Harbaugh	178	111	62.4	1204	5	70.5
Mike Tomczak	306	156	51.0	2058	16	68.2

Interceptions: Tomczak 16, Harbaugh 9.

Top 5 Receivers	No	Yds	Avg	Long	TD
Neal Anderson	50	434	8.7	49-td	4
Dennis Gentry	39	463	11.9	79-td	1
Brad Muster	32	259	8.1	25	3
Ron Morris	30	486	16.2	58-td	1
Dennis McKinnon	28	418	14.9	41	3

Top 5 Rushers	Car	Yds	Avg	Long	TD
Neal Anderson	274	1275	4.7	73	11
Brad Muster	82	327	4.0	20	5
Jim Harbaugh	45	276	6.1	26-td	3
Thomas Sanders	41	127	3.1	19	0
Dennis Gentry	17	106	6.2	29	0

Top 5 Touchdowns	TD	Run	Rec	Ret	Pts
Neal Anderson	15	11	4	0	90
Brad Muster	8	5	3	0	48
Wendell Davis	3	0	3	0	18
Jim Harbaugh	3	3	0	0	18
Dennis McKinnon	3	0	3	0	18
James Thornton	3	0	3	0	18

Kicking	FG/Att	Lg	PAT/Att	Pts
Kevin Butler	15/19	46	43/45	88

Punts (10 or more)	No	Yds	Long	Avg	In.20
Maury Buford	72	2844	60	39.5	21

Most Interceptions   **Most Sacks**
Lemuel Stinson 4   Richard Dent 9

Dallas Cowboys

QBs (10 Att)	Att	Cmp	Pct	Yds	TD	Rate
Steve Walsh*	219	110	50.2	1371	5	60.5
Troy Aikman*	292	155	53.1	1749	9	55.9

Interceptions: Aikman 18, Walsh 9.

Top 5 Receivers	No	Yds	Avg	Long	TD
Kelvin Martin	46	644	14.0	46	2
Steve Folsom	28	265	9.5	26	2
Michael Irvin	26	378	14.5	65-td	2
James Dixon	24	477	19.9	75-td	2
Derrick Shepard	20	304	15.2	37-td	1
NO	2	36	18.0	17	0
DAL	18	268	14.9	37-td	1

Acquired: Shepard signed (Oct.4).

Top 5 Rushers	Car	Yds	Avg	Long	TD
Paul Palmer	112	446	4.0	63-td	2
Troy Aikman*	38	302	7.9	25	0
Daryl Johnston*	67	212	3.2	13	0
Broderick Sargent	20	87	4.4	43	1
Darryl Clack	14	40	2.9	17	2

Acquired: Palmer from Detroit (Oct.17).

Top 5 Touchdowns	TD	Run	Rec	Ret	Pts
James Dixon	3	0	2	1	18
Daryl Johnston*	3	0	3	0	18

Six tied with 2 each.

Kicking	FG/Att	Lg	PAT/Att	Pts
Luis Zendejas	14/24	47	33/33	75
PHI	9/15	47	23/23	50
DAL	5/9	47	10/10	25
Roger Ruzek	5/11	43	14/15	29

Acquired: Zendejas signed (Nov.7).
Released: Ruzek waived (Nov.7).

Punts (10 or more)	No	Yds	Long	Avg	In.20
Mike Saxon	79	3233	56	40.9	18

Most Interceptions		Most Sacks	
Eugene Lockhart	2	Jim Jeffcoat	12

Detroit Lions

QBs (10 Att)	Att	Cmp	Pct	Yds	TD	Rate
Rodney Peete*	195	103	52.8	1479	5	67.0
Bob Gagliano	232	117	50.4	1671	6	61.2
Eric Hipple	18	7	38.9	90	0	15.7

Interceptions: Gagliano 12, Peete 9, Hipple 3.

Top 5 Receivers	No	Yds	Avg	Long	TD
Richard Johnson	70	1091	15.6	75-td	8
Robert Clark	41	748	18.2	69	2
Jason Phillips	30	352	11.7	55-td	1
Walter Stanley	24	304	12.7	37	0
Barry Sanders*	24	282	11.8	46	0

Acquired: Stanley signed (Sep.11).

Top 5 Rushers	Car	Yds	Avg	Long	TD
Barry Sanders*	280	1470	5.3	34	14
Bob Gagliano	41	192	4.7	19	4
Rodney Peete	33	148	4.5	14-td	4
Tony Paige	30	105	3.5	16	0
Carl Painter	15	64	4.3	9	0

Top 5 Touchdowns	TD	Run	Rec	Ret	Pts
Barry Sanders*	14	14	0	0	84
Richard Johnson	8	0	8	0	48
Bob Gagliano	4	4	0	0	24
Rodney Peete*	4	4	0	0	24
Robert Clark	2	0	2	0	12

Kicking	FG/Att	Lg	PAT/Att	Pts
Eddie Murray	20/21	50	36/36	96

Punts (10 or more)	No	Yds	Long	Avg	In.20
Jim Arnold	82	3538	64	43.1	14

Most Interceptions		Most Sacks	
Jerry Holmes	6	Jerry Ball	9
		Michael Cofer	9

Green Bay Packers

QBs (10 Att)	Att	Cmp	Pct	Yds	TD	Rate
Don Majkowski	599	353	58.9	4310	27	82.3

Interceptions: Majkowski 20.

Top 5 Receivers	No	Yds	Avg	Long	TD
Sterling Sharpe	90	1423	15.8	79-td	12
Keith Woodside	59	527	8.9	33	0
Perry Kemp	48	611	12.7	39	2
Herman Fontenot	40	372	9.3	38-td	3
Jeff Query*	23	350	15.2	45	2

Top 5 Rushers	Car	Yds	Avg	Long	TD
Brent Fullwood	204	821	4.0	38	5
Don Majkowski	75	358	4.8	20	5
Keith Woodside	46	273	5.9	68-td	1
Michael Haddix	44	135	3.1	10	0
Herman Fontenot	17	69	4.1	19	1

Top 5 Touchdowns	TD	Run	Rec	Ret	Pts
Sterling Sharpe	13	0	12	1	78
Brent Fullwood	5	5	0	0	30
Don Majkowski	5	5	0	0	30
Ed West	5	0	5	0	30
Herman Fontenot	4	1	3	0	24

Kicking	FG/Att	Lg	PAT/Att	Pts
Chris Jacke*	22/28	52	42/42	108

Punts (10 or more)	No	Yds	Long	Avg	In.20
Don Bracken	66	2682	63	40.6	17

Most Interceptions		Most Sacks	
Dave Brown	6	Tim Harris	19½

Los Angeles Rams

QBs (10 Att)	Att	Cmp	Pct	Yds	TD	Rate
Jim Everett	518	304	58.7	4310	29	90.6

Interceptions: Everett 17, Mark Herrmann 1.

Top 5 Receivers	No	Yds	Avg	Long	TD
Henry Ellard	70	1382	19.7	53	8
Pete Holohan	51	510	10.0	31	2
Flipper Anderson	44	1146	26.0	78-td	5
Buford McGee	37	303	8.2	25	4
Robert Delpino	34	334	9.8	25	1

Top 5 Rushers	Car	Yds	Avg	Long	TD
Greg Bell	272	1137	4.2	47	15
Robert Delpino	78	368	4.7	32-td	1
Cleveland Gary	37	163	4.4	18	1
Buford McGee	21	99	4.7	15	1
Gaston Green	26	73	2.8	9	0

Top 5 Touchdowns	TD	Run	Rec	Ret	Pts
Greg Bell	15	15	0	0	90
Henry Ellard	8	0	8	0	48
Flipper Anderson	5	0	5	0	30
Damone Johnson	5	0	5	0	30
Buford McGee	5	1	4	0	30

Kicking	FG/Att	Lg	PAT/Att	Pts
Mike Lansford	23/30	48	51/51	120

Punts (10 or more)	No	Yds	Long	Avg	In.20
Dale Hatcher	73	2834	54	38.8	15

Most Interceptions		Most Sacks	
Jerry Gray	6	Kevin Greene	16½

Minnesota Vikings

QBs (10 Att)	Att	Cmp	Pct	Yds	TD	Rate
Tommy Kramer	136	77	56.6	906	7	72.7
Wade Wilson	362	194	53.6	2543	9	70.5

Interceptions: Wilson 12, Kramer 7.

Top 5 Receivers	No	Yds	Avg	Long	TD
Anthony Carter	65	1066	16.4	50	4
Hassan Jones	42	694	16.5	50	1
Herschel Walker	40	423	10.6	52	2
DAL	22	261	11.9	52	1
MIN	18	162	9.0	24	1
Steve Jordan	35	506	14.5	34	3
Rick Fenney	30	254	8.5	26	2

Acquired: Walker from Dallas (Oct.12).

Top 5 Rushers	Car	Yds	Avg	Long	TD
Herschel Walker	250	915	3.7	47	7
DAL	81	246	3.0	20-td	2
MIN	169	669	4.0	47	5
Rick Fenney	151	588	3.9	25	4
D.J.Dozier	46	207	4.5	38	0
Alfred Anderson	52	189	3.6	14	2
Wade Wilson	32	132	4.1	23	1

Top 5 Touchdowns	TD	Run	Rec	Ret	Pts
Herschel Walker	10	7	2	1	60
DAL	3	2	1	0	18
MIN	7	5	1	1	42
Rick Fenney	6	4	2	0	36
Anthony Carter	4	0	4	0	24
Steve Jordan	3	0	3	0	18

Three tied with 2 each.

Kicking	FG/Att	Lg	PAT/Att	Pts
Rich Karlis	31/39	51	27/28	120

Punts (10 or more)	No	Yds	Long	Avg	In.20
Bucky Scribner	72	2864	55	39.8	16

Most Interceptions		Most Sacks	
Joey Browner	5	Chris Doleman	20½

New Orleans Saints

QBs (10 Att)	Att	Cmp	Pct	Yds	TD	Rate
John Fourcade	107	61	57.0	930	7	92.0
Bobby Hebert	353	222	62.9	2686	15	82.7

Interceptions: Hebert 15, Fourcade 4.

Top 5 Receivers	No	Yds	Avg	Long	TD
Eric Martin	68	1090	16.0	53-td	8
Dalton Hilliard	52	514	9.9	54-td	5
Lonzell Hill	48	636	13.3	46	4
Hoby Brenner	34	398	11.7	30-td	4
Floyd Turner*	22	279	12.7	54-td	1

Top 4 Rushers	Car	Yds	Avg	Long	TD
Dalton Hilliard	344	1262	3.7	40	13
Craig Heyward	49	183	3.7	15	1
Buford Jordan	38	179	4.7	32	3
Bobby Morse	2	43	21.5	39	0

Top 5 Touchdowns	TD	Run	Rec	Ret	Pts
Dalton Hilliard	18	13	5	0	108
Eric Martin	8	0	8	0	48
Hoby Brenner	4	0	4	0	24
Lonzell Hill	4	0	4	0	24
Buford Jordan	3	3	0	0	18

Kicking	FG/Att	Lg	PAT/Att	Pts
Morten Andersen	20/29	49	44/45	104

Punts (10 or more)	No	Yds	Long	Avg	In.20
Tommy Barnhardt	55	2179	56	39.6	16
George Winslow	16	595	50	37.2	4

Acquired: Barnhardt signed (Oct.11).
Released: Winslow waived (Oct.11).

Most Interceptions		Most Sacks	
Dave Waymer	6	Pat Swilling	16½

New York Giants

QBs (10 Att)	Att	Cmp	Pct	Yds	TD	Rate
Jeff Hostetler	39	20	51.3	294	3	80.5
Phil Simms	405	228	56.3	3061	14	77.6

Interceptions: Simms 14, Hostetler 2.

Top 5 Receivers	No	Yds	Avg	Long	TD
Odessa Turner	38	467	12.3	44	4
Dave Meggett*	34	531	15.6	62-td	4
Lionel Manuel	33	539	16.3	49	1
Ottis Anderson	28	268	9.6	26	0
Zeke Mowatt	27	288	10.7	31	0

Top 5 Rushers	Car	Yds	Avg	Long	TD
Ottis Anderson	325	1023	3.1	36-td	14
Lewis Tillman*	79	290	3.7	19	0
Maurice Carthon	57	153	2.7	18	0
Phil Simms	32	141	4.4	15	1
Dave Meggett*	28	117	4.2	18	0

Top 5 Touchdowns	TD	Run	Rec	Ret	Pts
Ottis Anderson	14	14	0	0	84
Dave Meggett*	5	0	4	1	30
Odessa Turner	4	0	4	0	24
Mark Bavaro	3	0	3	0	18
Stephen Baker	2	0	2	0	12
Jeff Hostetler	2	2	0	0	12

Kicking	FG/Att	Lg	PAT/Att	Pts
Raul Allegre	20/26	52	23/24	83
Bjorn Nittmo*	9/12	39	12/13	39

Punts (10 or more)	No	Yds	Long	Avg	In.20
Sean Landeta	70	3019	71	43.1	19

Most Interceptions		Most Sacks	
Terry Kinard	5	Lawrence Taylor	15

Philadelphia Eagles

QBs (10 Att)	Att	Cmp	Pct	Yds	TD	Rate
R.Cunningham	532	290	54.5	3400	21	75.5

Interceptions: Cunningham 15, Matt Cavanaugh 1.

Top 5 Receivers	No	Yds	Avg	Long	TD
Keith Byars	68	721	10.6	60	0
Keith Jackson	63	648	10.3	33	3
Cris Carter	45	605	13.4	42	11
Ron Johnson	20	295	14.8	34	1
Anthony Toney	19	124	6.5	15	0

Top 5 Rushers	Car	Yds	Avg	Long	TD
Randall Cunningham	104	621	6.0	51	4
Anthony Toney	172	582	3.4	44	3
Keith Byars	133	452	3.4	16-td	5
Mark Higgs	49	184	3.8	13	0
Heath Sherman*	40	177	4.4	37	2

Top 5 Touchdowns	TD	Run	Rec	Ret	Pts
Cris Carter	11	0	11	0	66
Keith Byars	5	5	0	0	30
Randall Cunningham	4	4	0	0	24
Keith Jackson	3	0	3	0	18
Anthony Toney	3	3	0	0	18

Kicking	FG/Att	Lg	PAT/Att	Pts
Roger Ruzek	13/22	46	28/29	67
DAL	5/11	43	14/15	29
PHI	8/11	46	14/14	38
Steve DeLine	3/7	49	3/3	12

Acquired: DeLine signed (Oct.22), Ruzek (Nov.22).
Released: Zendejas waived (Oct.30), DeLine (Nov.22).

Punts (10 or more)	No	Yds	Long	Avg	In.20
John Teltschik	57	2246	58	39.4	12
Max Runager	17	568	52	33.4	5

Most Interceptions		Most Sacks	
Eric Allen	8	Clyde Simmons	15½

Phoenix Cardinals

QBs (10 Att)	Att	Cmp	Pct	Yds	TD	Rate
Gary Hogeboom...	364	204	56.0	2591	14	69.5
Tom Tupa	134	65	48.5	973	3	52.2
Timm Rosenbach ..	22	9	40.9	95	0	35.2

Interceptions: Hogeboom 19, Tupa 9, Rosenbach 1.

Top 5 Receivers	No	Yds	Avg	Long	TD
J.T.Smith	62	778	12.5	31	5
Ernie Jones	45	838	18.6	72-td	3
Roy Green	44	703	16.0	59-td	7
Robert Awalt	33	360	10.9	28	0
Vai Sikahema	23	245	10.7	37	0
Jay Novacek	23	225	9.8	30	1

Top 5 Rushers	Car	Yds	Avg	Long	TD
Earl Ferrell	149	502	3.4	44-td	6
Tony Jordan	83	211	2.5	15	2
Stump Mitchell........	43	165	3.8	14	0
Vai Sikahema	38	145	3.8	27	0
Gary Hogeboom	27	89	3.3	15	1

Top 5 Touchdowns	TD	Run	Rec	Ret	Pts
Roy Green	7	0	7	0	42
Earl Ferrell	6	6	0	0	36
J.T.Smith	5	0	5	0	30
Ernie Jones	3	0	3	0	18
Tony Jordan	2	2	0	0	12

Kicking	FG/Att	Lg	PAT/Att	Pts
Al Del Greco	18/26	50	28/29	82

Punts (10 or more)	No	Yds	Long	Avg	In.20
Rich Camarillo.......	76	3298	58	43.4	21

Most Interceptions	Most Sacks
Tim McDonald 7	Ken Harvey 7

Tampa Bay Buccaneers

QBs (10 Att)	Att	Cmp	Pct	Yds	TD	Rate
Vinny Testaverde...	480	258	53.8	3133	20	68.9
Joe Ferguson	90	44	48.9	533	3	50.8

Interceptions: Testaverde 22, Ferguson 6.

Top 5 Receivers	No	Yds	Avg	Long	TD
Mark Carrier	86	1422	16.5	78-td	9
Bruce Hill	50	673	13.5	53	5
James Wilder	36	335	9.3	27	3
Ron Hall	30	331	11.0	32	2
William Howard	30	188	6.3	18	1

Top 5 Rushers	Car	Yds	Avg	Long	TD
Lars Tate	167	589	3.5	48	8
William Howard	108	357	3.3	15	1
James Wilder	70	244	3.5	14	0
Sylvester Stamps	29	141	4.9	21-td	1
Vinny Testaverde	25	139	5.6	16	0

Top 5 Touchdowns	TD	Run	Rec	Ret	Pts
Mark Carrier	9	0	9	0	54
Lars Tate	9	8	1	0	54
Bruce Hill	5	0	5	0	30
James Wilder	3	0	3	0	18
Three tied with 2 each.					

Kicking	FG/Att	Lg	PAT/Att	Pts
Donald Igwebuike........	22/28	53	33/35	99
Chris Mohr*	0/0	0	1/1	1

Punts (10 or more)	No	Yds	Long	Avg	In.20
Chris Mohr*	84	3311	58	39.4	10

Most Interceptions	Most Sacks
Harry Hamilton 6	Kevin Murphy 6
Mark Robinson 6	

San Francisco 49ers

QBs (10 Att)	Att	Cmp	Pct	Yds	TD	Rate
Steve Young	92	64	69.6	1001	8	120.8
Joe Montana	386	271	70.2	3521	26	112.4

Interceptions: Montana 8, Young 3.

Top 5 Receivers	No	Yds	Avg	Long	TD
Jerry Rice	82	1483	18.1	68-td	17
Tom Rathman	73	616	8.4	36	1
John Taylor	60	1077	18.0	95-td	10
Roger Craig	49	473	9.7	44	1
Brent Jones	40	500	12.5	36-td	4

Top 5 Rushers	Car	Yds	Avg	Long	TD
Roger Craig	271	1054	3.9	27	6
Tom Rathman	79	305	3.9	13	1
Joe Montana	49	227	4.6	19	3
Terrence Flagler ...	33	129	3.9	29-td	1
Steve Young	38	126	3.3	22	2

Top 5 Touchdowns	TD	Run	Rec	Ret	Pts
Jerry Rice	17	0	17	0	102
John Taylor	10	0	10	0	60
Roger Craig.......	7	6	1	0	42
Brent Jones	4	0	4	0	24
Joe Montana	3	3	0	0	18

Kicking	FG/Att	Lg	PAT/Att	Pts
Mike Cofer	29/36	47	49/51	136

Punts (10 or more)	No	Yds	Long	Avg	In.20
Barry Helton	55	2226	56	40.5	13

Most Interceptions	Most Sacks
Ronnie Lott 5	Charles Haley 10½
	Pierce Holt 10½

Washington Redskins

QBs (10 Att)	Att	Cmp	Pct	Yds	TD	Rate
Mark Rypien	476	280	58.8	3768	22	88.1
Stan Humphries....	10	5	50.0	91	1	75.4
Doug Williams ...	93	51	54.8	585	1	64.1

Interceptions: Rypien 13, Williams 3, Humphries 1.

Top 5 Receivers	No	Yds	Avg	Long	TD
Art Monk	86	1186	13.8	60-td	8
Ricky Sanders......	80	1138	14.2	68	4
Gary Clark	79	1229	15.6	80-td	9
Earnest Byner	54	458	8.5	27	2
Don Warren	15	167	11.1	25	1

Top 5 Rushers	Car	Yds	Avg	Long	TD
Gerald Riggs	201	834	4.1	58	4
Earnest Byner	134	580	4.3	24	7
Jamie Morris	124	336	2.7	12-td	2
Reggie Dupard	37	111	3.0	19	1
NE	25	63	2.5	10	1
WASH	12	48	4.0	19	0
Mark Rypien	26	56	2.2	15	1

Acquired: Dupard signed (Nov.8).

Top 5 Touchdowns	TD	Run	Rec	Ret	Pts
Earnest Byner	9	7	2	0	54
Gary Clark	9	0	9	0	54
Art Monk	8	0	8	0	48
Gerald Riggs	4	4	0	0	24
Ricky Sanders	4	0	4	0	24

Kicking	FG/Att	Lg	PAT/Att	Pts
Chip Lohmiller	29/40	48	41/41	128

Punts (10 or more)	No	Yds	Long	Avg	In.20
Ralf Mojsiejenko	62	2663	74	43.0	21

Most Interceptions	Most Sacks
Brian Davis 4	Charles Mann 10½
A.J. Johnson 4	
Alvin Walton 4	

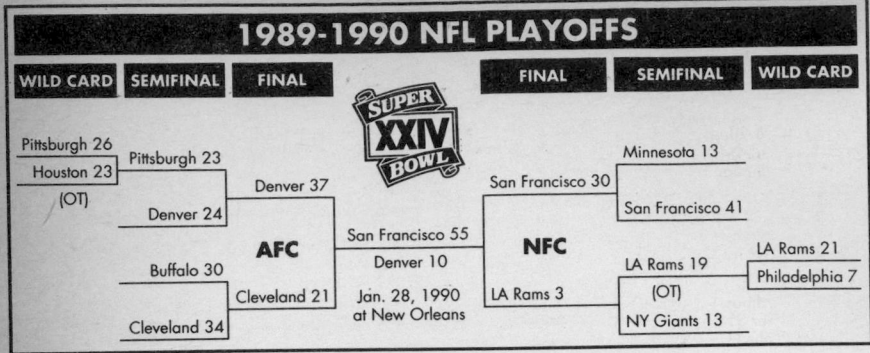

1989-1990 NFL PLAYOFFS

| WILD CARD | SEMIFINAL | FINAL | | FINAL | SEMIFINAL | WILD CARD |

SUPER XXIV BOWL

Pittsburgh 26
Houston 23 (OT)

Pittsburgh 23
Denver 24

Denver 37

AFC

San Francisco 55
Denver 10

San Francisco 30

NFC

LA Rams 3

Jan. 28, 1990
at New Orleans

Buffalo 30
Cleveland 21

Cleveland 34

Minnesota 13
San Francisco 41

LA Rams 19 (OT)
NY Giants 13

LA Rams 21
Philadelphia 7

Super Bowl Playoffs

AFC

Wildcard Game

	1	2	3	4	OT	F
Pittsburgh (10-7)	7	3	3	10	3	26
Houston (9-8)	0	6	3	14	0	23

Touchdowns: PIT (2)—Tim Worley 9-yd run; Merril Hoge 2-yd run. **HOU** (2)—Ernest Givens 18-yd pass from Warren Moon; Givens 9-yd pass from Moon.

Field Goals: PIT (4)—Gary Anderson (25, 30, 48, 50 yds, the last 3:26 into OT). **HOU** (3)—Tony Zendejas (26, 35, 26 yds).

Date—Dec. 31; **Att**—58,306; **Time**—3:55.

Semifinals

	1	2	3	4	F
Buffalo (9-8)	7	7	9	7	30
Cleveland (10-6-1)	3	14	14	3	34

Touchdowns: CLE (4)—Webster Slaughter 52-yd pass from Bernie Kosar; Ron Middleton 3-yd pass from Kosar; Slaughter 44-yd pass from Kosar: Eric Metcalf 90-yd kickoff return. **BUF** (4)—Andre Reed 72-yd pass from Jim Kelly; James Lofton 33-yd pass from Kelly; Thurman Thomas 6-yd pass from Kelly; Thomas 3-yd pass from Kelly.

Field Goals: CLE (2)—Matt Bahr (45, 47 yds). **BUF** (1)—Scott Norwood (30 yds).

Date—Jan. 6; **Att**—77,706; **Time**—3:42.

	1	2	3	4	F
Pittsburgh (10-8)	3	14	3	3	23
Denver (12-5)	0	10	7	7	24

Touchdowns: DEN (3)—Melvin Bratton 1-yd run; Vance Johnson 37-yd pass from John Elway; Bratton 1-yd run. **PIT** (2)—Merril Hoge 7-yd run; Louis Lipps 9-yd pass from Bubby Brister.

Field Goals: DEN (1)—David Treadwell (43 yds). **PIT** (3)—Gary Anderson (32, 35, 32 yds).

Date—Jan. 7; **Att**—75,868; **Time**—2:57.

Championship

	1	2	3	4	F
Cleveland (10-7-1)	0	0	21	0	21
Denver (13-5)	3	7	14	13	37

Touchdowns: DEN (4)—Michael Young 70-yd pass from John Elway; Orson Mobley 5-yd pass from Elway; Sammy Winder 7-yd run; Winder 39-yd pass from Elway; **CLE** (3)—Brian Brennan 27-yd pass from Bernie Kosar; Brennan 10-yd pass from Kosar; Tom Manoa 2-yd run.

Field Goals: DEN (3)—D.Treadwell (29, 34, 31 yds).

Date—Jan. 14; **Att**—77,706; **Time**—3:42.

NFC

Wildcard Game

	1	2	3	4	F
LA Rams (12-5)	14	0	0	7	21
Philadelphia (11-6)	0	0	0	7	7

Touchdowns: LA (3)—Henry Ellard 39-yd pass from Jim Everett; Damone Johnson 4-yd pass from Everett; Creg Bell 7-yd run. **PHI** (1)—Anthony Toney 1-yd run.

Date—Dec. 31; **Att**—57,869; **Time**—3:05.

Semifinals

	1	2	3	4	F
Minnesota (10-7)	3	0	3	7	13
San Francisco (15-2)	7	20	0	14	41

Touchdowns: SF (6)—Jerry Rice 72-yd pass from Joe Montana; Brent Jones 8-yd pass from Montana; John Taylor 8-yd pass from Montana; Rice 13-yd pass from Montana; Ronnie Lott 58-yd interception; Roger Craig 4-yd run. **MIN** (1)—Rick Fenney 3-yd run.

Field Goals: MIN (2)—Rich Karlis (38, 44 yds).

Date—Jan. 6; **Att**—64,585; **Time**—3:15.

	1	2	3	4	OT	F
LA Rams (13-5)	0	7	0	6	6	19
NY Giants (12-5)	6	0	7	0	0	13

Touchdowns: LA (2)—Flipper Anderson 20-yd pass from Jim Everett; Anderson 30-yd pass from Everett (1:06 into OT). **NY** (1)—Ottis Anderson 2-yd run.

Field Goals: LA (2)—Mike Lansford (31, 22 yds). **NY** (2)—Raul Allegre (35, 41 yds).

Date—Jan. 7; **Att**—76,325; **Time**—3:10.

Championship

	1	2	3	4	F
LA Rams (13-61)	3	0	0	0	3
San Francisco (16-2)	0	21	3	6	30

Touchdowns: SF (3)—Brent Jones 20-yd pass from Joe Montana; Roger Craig 1-yd run; John Taylor 18-yd pass from Montana.

Field Goals: SF (3)—Mike Cofer (28, 36, 25 yds). **LA** (1)—Mike Lansford (23 yds).

Date—Jan. 14; **Att**—64,769; **Time**—2:51.

Super Bowl XXIV

Sunday, Jan.28 at the Superdome, New Orleans

	1	2	3	4	F
San Francisco (17-2)	13	14	14	14	55
Denver (13-6)	3	0	7	0	10

1st Quarter

SF—Jerry Rice 20-yd pass from Joe Montana (Mike Cofer Kick), 4:54; Den—David Treadwell 42-yd FG, 8:13; SF—Brent Jones 7-yd pass from Montana (kick failed), 14:57.

2nd Quarter

SF—Tom Rathman 1-yd run (Cofer kick), 7:45; SF—Rice 38-yd pass from Montana (Cofer kick), 14:26.

3rd Quarter

SF—Rice 28-yd pass from Montana (Cofer kick), 2:12; SF—John Taylor 35-yd pass from Montana (Cofer kick), 5:16; Den—John Elway 3-yd run (Treadwell kick), 8:07.

4th Quarter

SF—Rathman 4-yd run (Cofer kick), 0:03; SF—Roger Craig 1-yd run (Cofer kick), 1:13.

Field: Astroturf
Weather: Indoors
Attendance: 72,919
Time: 3:21
Favorite: 49ers by 12½
TV Rating: 39.0 (CBS)
Shares: Winners $36,000 Losers $18,000

Team Statistics

	SF	DEN
First downs	28	12
Rushing	14	5
Passing	14	6
Penalties	0	1
3rd down efficiency	8-15	3-11
4th down efficiency	2-2	0-2
Time of possession	39:31	20:29
Total offense (net yards)	461	167
Plays	77	52
Average gain	6.0	3.2
Rushing attempts	44	17
net yards	144	64
Passing attempts	32	29
completions	24	11
net yards	317	103
Interceptions	0	2
Times sacked-yards lost	1-0	6-33
Fumbles-lost	0-0	3-2
Penalties-yards	4-38	0-0
Punts-Average	4-39.5	6-38.5
Punts blocks	0	0

Individual Statistics

San Francisco

Passing

	Att	Cmp	Pct.	Yds	TD	Int
Joe Montana	29	22	75.9	297	5	0
Steve Young	3	2	66.7	20	0	0
TOTAL	32	24	75.0	317	5	0

Receiving

	No	Yds	Avg	Lg	TD
Jerry Rice	7	148	21.1	38	3
Roger Craig	5	34	6.8	12	0
Tom Rathman	4	43	10.8	18	0
John Taylor	3	49	16.3	35	1
Mike Sherrard	1	13	13.0	13	0
Wesley Walls	1	9	9.0	9	0
Brent Jones	1	7	7.0	7	1
Harry Sydney	1	7	7.0	7	0
Jamie Williams	1	7	7.0	7	0
TOTAL	24	317	13.2	38	5

Rushing

	Car	Yds	Avg	Lg	TD
Roger Craig	20	69	3.5	18	1
Tom Rathman	11	38	3.5	18	2
Joe Montana	2	15	7.5	10	0
Terrence Flagler	6	14	2.3	10	0
Steve Young	4	6	1.5	11	0
Harry Sydney	1	2	2.0	2	0
TOTAL	44	144	3.3	18	3

Field Goals

	20-29	30-39	40-49	Total
Mike Cofer	0-0	0-0	0-0	0-0

Punting

	No	Yds	Long	Avg	In.20
Barry Helton	4	158	47	39.5	2

Punt Returns

	FC	Ret	Yds	Long	Avg	TD
John Taylor	2	3	38	17	12.7	0

Kickoff Returns

	No	Yds	Long	Avg	TD
Terrence Flagler	3	49	22	16.3	0

Interceptions

	No	Yds	Long	Avg	TD
Chet Brooks	1	38	38	38.0	0
Michael Walter	1	4	4	4.0	0
TOTAL	2	42	38	21.0	0

Denver

Passing

	Att	Cmp	Pct.	Yds	TD	Int
John Elway	26	10	38.5	108	0	2
Gary Kubiak	3	1	33.3	28	0	0
TOTAL	29	11	37.9	136	0	2

Receiving

	No	Yds	Avg	Lg	TD
Bobby Humphrey	3	38	12.7	27	0
Steve Sewell	2	22	11.0	12	0
Vance Johnson	2	21	10.5	13	0
Ricky Nattiel	1	28	28.0	28	0
Melvin Bratton	1	14	14.0	14	0
Sammy Winder	1	7	7.0	7	0
Clarence Kay	1	6	6.0	6	0
TOTAL	11	136	12.4	38	0

Rushing

	Car	Yds	Avg	Lg	TD
Bobby Humphrey	12	61	5.1	34	0
John Elway	4	8	2.0	3	1
Sammy Winder	1	−5	−5.0	−5	0
TOTAL	17	64	3.8	34	1

Field Goals

	20-29	30-39	40-49	Total
David Treadwell	0-0	0-0	1-1	1-1

Punting

	No	Yds	Long	Avg	In.20
Mike Horan	6	231	43	38.5	0

Punt Returns

	FC	Ret	Yds	Long	Avg	TD
Vance Johnson	1	2	11	7	5.5	0

Kickoff Returns

	No	Yds	Long	Avg	TD
Darren Carrington	9	146	39	24.3	0
Ken Bell	2	41	24	20.5	0
Melvin Bratton	1	9	9	9.0	0
TOTAL	12	196	39	21.8	0

Interceptions
None

Overall Playoff Statistics

San Francisco (3-0)

QBs	Att	Cmp	Pct	Yds	TD	Rate
Joe Montana	83	65	78.3	800	11	146.4
Steve Young	5	3	60.0	26	0	73.8
TOTAL	88	68	77.3	826	11	145.2

Interceptions: None.

Receivers	No	Yds	Avg	Long	TD
Jerry Rice	19	317	16.7	72	5
Tom Rathman	13	120	9.2	18	0
John Taylor	10	144	14.4	35	3
Brent Jones	8	77	9.6	20	3
Roger Craig	8	74	9.3	16	0
Mike Sherrard	3	34	11.3	15	0
Keith Henderson	2	24	12.0	15	0
Jamie Williams	2	13	6.5	7	0
Wesley Walls	1	9	9.0	9	0
Harry Sydney	1	7	7.0	7	0
Mike Wilson	1	7	7.0	7	0
TOTAL	68	826	12.1	72	11

Rushing	Car	Yds	Avg	Long	TD
Roger Craig	62	288	4.6	29	3
Tom Rathman	28	125	4.5	18	2
Terrence Flagler	19	46	2.4	12	0
Joe Montana	5	19	3.8	10	0
Steve Young	5	5	1.0	11	0
Harry Sydney	1	2	2.0	2	0
Keith Henderson	1	1	1.0	1	0
TOTAL	121	486	4.0	29	5

Touchdowns	TD	Run	Rec	Ret	Pts
Jerry Rice	5	0	5	0	30
Roger Craig	3	3	0	0	18
Brent Jones	3	0	3	0	18
John Taylor	3	0	3	0	18
Tom Rathman	2	2	0	0	12
Ronnie Lott	2	2	0	1	6
TOTALS	17	5	11	1	102

Kicking	FG/Att	Lg	PAT/Att	Pts
Mike Cofer	3/6	36	15/17	24

Punts	No	Yds	Long	Avg	In.20
Barry Helton	10	343	47	34.3	5

Interceptions		Sacks	
Chet Brooks	2	Kevin Fagan	3
Ronnie Lott	2	Danny Stubbs	3
Tim McKyer	2	Larry Roberts	2
Don Griffin	1	Don Griffin	1
Keena Turner	1	Charles Haley	1
Michael Walter	1	Pete Kugler	1
TOTAL	9	TOTAL	11

Denver (2-1)

QBs	Att	Cmp	Pct	Yds	TD	Rate
John Elway	82	42	51.2	732	4	83.0
Gary Kubiak	3	1	33.3	28	0	68.8
TOTAL	85	43	50.6	760	4	82.5

Interceptions: Elway (3).

Receivers	No	Yds	Avg	Long	TD
Vance Johnson	12	197	16.4	37	1
Mark Jackson	7	136	19.4	51	0
Steve Sewell	5	77	15.4	43	0
Bobby Humphrey	5	67	13.4	27	0
Michael Young	4	145	36.3	70	1
Sammy Winder	3	46	15.3	39	1
Melvin Bratton	2	21	10.5	14	0
Orson Mobley	2	22	11.0	17	1
Ricky Nattiel	2	43	21.5	28	0
Clarence Kay	1	6	6.0	6	0
TOTAL	43	760	17.7	70	4

Rushing	Car	Yds	Avg	Long	TD
Bobby Humphrey	38	169	4.4	34	0
John Elway	16	91	5.7	32	1
Sammy Winder	23	32	1.4	9	1
Steve Sewell	5	23	4.6	12	0
Melvin Bratton	5	7	1.4	4	2
TOTAL	87	322	3.7	34	4

Touchdowns	TD	Run	Rec	Ret	Pts
Melvin Bratton	2	2	0	0	12
Sammy Winder	2	1	1	0	12
John Elway	1	1	0	0	6
Vance Johnson	1	0	1	0	6
Orson Mobley	1	0	1	0	6
Michael Young	1	0	1	0	6
TOTALS	8	4	4	0	48

Kicking	FG/Att	Lg	PAT/Att	TD	Pts
David Treadwell	5/6	43	8/8	—	23

Punts	No	Yds	Long	Avg	In.20
Mike Horan	14	596	61	42.6	3
John Elway	1	17	17	17.0	1
TOTAL	15	613	61	40.9	4

Interceptions		Sacks	
Dennis Smith	2	Simon Fletcher	2
Kip Corrington	1	Tyrone Braxton	1
TOTAL	3	Alphonso Carreker	1
		Andre Townsend	1
		TOTAL	5

NFL Pro Bowl

40th NFL Pro Bowl Game. **Date:** Feb.4, 1990 at Aloha Stadium in Honolulu; **Coaches:** Bud Carson, Cleveland (AFC) and John Robinson, LA Rams (NFC); **MVP:** cornerback Jerry Gray, LA Rams (NFC), 6 solo tackles and 51-yd interception return for TD.

	1	2	3	4	Final
National	3	3	21	0	27
American	0	7	0	14	21

1st Quarter
NFC—Eddie Murray 23-yd FG, 6:30.

2nd Quarter
NFC—Murray 41-yd FG, 0:52; AFC—Christian Okoye 1-yd run (David Treadwell kick), 13:34.

3rd Quarter
NFC—Dave Meggett 11-yd pass from Cunningham (Murray kick), 4:43; NFC—Jerry Gray 51-yd interception (Murray kick), 10:30; NFC—Keith Millard 8-yd fumble return (Murray kick), 14:41.

4th Quarter
AFC—Ferrell Edmunds 5-yd pass from Dave Krieg (Treadwell kick), 6:52; AFC—Mike Johnson 22-yd interception (Treadwell kick), 8:00.
Att—50,445; **Time**—3:14.

STARTING LINE-UPS

National Conference

Offense	Defense
WR Jerry Rice, SF	LE Reggie White, Phi.
LT G.Zimmermann, Min.	NT Keith Millard, Min.
LG R.McDaniel, Min.	RE Chris Doleman, Min.
C Jay Hilgenberg, Chi.	LB Tim Harris, GB
RG Guy McIntyre, SF	LB Chris Spielman, Det.
RT Jackie Slater, LA	LB Mike Singletary, Chi.
TE Keith Jackson, Phi.	LB Lawrence Taylor, NY
WR Sterling Sharpe, GB	CB Carl Lee, Min.
QB R.Cunningham, Phi.	CB Jerry Gray, LA
RB Barry Sanders, Det.	SS Joey Browner, Min.
RB Ron Wolfley, Pho.	FS Ronnie Lott, SF
K Eddie Murray, Det.	P Rich Camarillo, Pho.

Substitutions

Offense: WR—Henry Ellard, LA and Mark Carrier, TB; **TE**—Steve Jordan, Min.; **T**—Luis Sharpe, Pho.; **G**—Bill Fralic, Atl.; **C**—Doug Smith, LA; **QB**—Mark Rypien, Wash.; **RB**—Dalton Hilliard, NO and Brent Fullwood, GB. **Defense: DE**—Charles Mann, Wash.; **NT**—Jerry Ball, Det.; **LB**—Kevin Greene, LA, Vaughan Johnson, NO and Pat Swilling, NO; **CB**—Eric Allen, Phi.; **S**—Tim McDonald, Pho. **Specialist: KR**—Dave Meggett, NY.

Did not play: RB Roger Craig, SF.

Replacements: QB Cunningham for Joe Montana, SF...QB Rypien for Don Majkowski, GB...RB Fullwood for Neal Anderson, Chi.

American Conference

Offense	Defense
WR Andre Reed, Buf.	LE Lee Williams, SD
LT Anthony Munoz, Cin.	NT M.D.Perry, Cle.
LG Mike Munchak, Hou.	RE Bruce Smith, Buf.
C Ray Donaldson, Ind.	LB Clay Matthews, Cle.
RG Bruce Matthews, Hou.	LB John Offerdahl, Mia.
RT Chris Hinton, Ind.	LB Shane Conlan, Buf.
TE Rodney Holman, Cin.	LB Derrick Thomas, KC
WR Webs.Slaughter, Cle.	CB Albert Lewis, KC
QB Warren Moon, Hou.	CB F.Minnifield, Cle.
RB James Brooks, Cin.	SS David Fulcher, Cin.
RB Christian Okoye, KC	FS Erik McMillan, NY
K David Treadwell, Den.	P Reggie Roby, Mia.

Substitutions

Offense: WR—Anthony Miller, SD and Brian Blades, Sea.; **TE**—Ferrell Edmunds, Mia; **T**—Tunch Ilkin, Pit.; **G**—Max Montoya, Cin.; **C**—Kent Hull, Buf.; **QB**—Dave Krieg, Sea.; **RB**—Eric Dickerson, Ind. and Thurman Thomas, Buf. **Defense: DE**—Howie Long, LA; **NT**—Greg Kragen, Den.; **LB**—Mike Johnson, Clev., Leslie O'Neal, SD and Johnny Rembert, NE; **CB**—Kevin Ross, KC; **S**—Dennis Smith, Den. **Specialists: KR**—Rod Woodson, Pit.; **Sp.Teams**—Rufus Porter, Sea.

Did not play: none.

Replacements: QB Krieg for John Elway, Den., who had been named to replace Boomer Esiason, Cin...LB Rembert for Karl Mecklenburg, Den.

Award Winners

The NFL does not sanction any postseason Player or Coach of the Year awards, but many are given out. Among the presenters are AP, UPI, The Sporting News and the Professional Football Writers of America. MVP awards are also given out by the Maxwell Club of Philadelphia (Bert Bell Award) and the Jim Thorpe Foundation of Oklahoma City (Jim Thorpe Trophy).

Most Valuable Player   **Selectors**
Joe Montana, San Francisco, QB...AP,PFWA,TSN, Maxwell,Thorpe

Offensive Players of the Year
NFL Joe Montana, San Francisco, QB ....AP
AFC Christian Okoye, Kansas City RB ....UPI
NFC Joe Montana, San Francisco, QB ....UPI

Defensive Players of the Year
NFL Keith Millard, Minnesota, DT ....AP
AFC Michael Dean Perry, Cleveland, NT......UPI
NFC Keith Millard, Minnesota, DT ....UPI

Rookies of the Year
NFL   Barry Sanders, Detroit, RB ....PFWA,TSN
Offense Barry Sanders, Detroit, RB ....AP,UPI
Defense Derrick Thomas, Kansas City, LB...AP,UPI

Coaches of the Year
NFL Lindy Infante, Green Bay ....AP,TSN

AFC Dan Reeves, Denver ....UPI
    Chuck Noll, Pittsburgh ....PFWA

NFC Lindy Infante, Green Bay ....PFWA,UPI

All-Pro Team

The 1989 NFL All-Pro Team, combining the selections of AP and the Professional Football Writers of America. Holdovers from the 1988 All-Pro Team are in **bold type**; (*) denotes rookies.

Offense

WR—**Jerry Rice**, San Francisco ....PFWA,AP
WR—Sterling Sharpe, Green Bay ....PFWA,AP
TE—**Keith Jackson**, Philadelphia .....PFWA,AP
T—**Anthony Munoz**, Cincinnati .....PFWA,AP
T—**Gary Zimmerman**, Minnesota ...PFWA
T—Jim Lachey, Washington..........AP
G—**Tom Newberry**, LA Rams ....PFWA,AP
G—Mike Munchak, Houston ....PFWA
G—**Bruce Matthews**, Houston ....AP
C—**Jay Hilgenberg**, Chicago ....PFWA,AP
QB—Joe Montana, San Francisco ....PFWA,AP
RB—Barry Sanders, Detroit* ....PFWA,AP
RB—Christian Okoye, Kansas City .....PFWA,AP
K—Eddie Murray, Detroit...........PFWA
K—Mike Cofer, San Francisco ....AP
KR—Rod Woodson, Pittsburgh ....PFWA,AP
PR—Dave Meggett, NY Giants* ....PFWA

Defense

DE—Chris Doleman, Minnesota ....PFWA,AP
DE—**Reggie White**, Philadelphia .....PFWA,AP
DT—**Keith Millard**, Minnesota .....PFWA,AP
NT—Michael Dean Perry, Cleveland ...PFWA,AP
OLB—Tim Harris, Green Bay ....PFWA,AP
OLB—**Lawrence Taylor**, NY Giants ....PFWA,AP
ILB—**Mike Singletary**, Chicago.......PFWA,AP
ILB—Karl Mecklenburg, Denver ....PFWA,AP
CB—Albert Lewis, Kansas City ....PFWA,AP
CB—Jerry Gray, LA Rams ....PFWA
CB—Eric Allen, Philadelphia..........AP
SS—David Fulcher, Cincinnati ....PFWA,AP
FS—Ronnie Lott, San Francisco ....PFWA,AP
P—Sean Landeta, BY Giants ....PFWA,AP

NFL Draft

First and second round picks at the 59th annual NFL Draft held April 22-23, 1990, in New York City. Juniors selected are noted in capital LETTERS.

First Round

Team		Pos
a-Indianapolis	JEFF GEORGE, Illinois	QB
NY Jets	Blair Thomas, Penn St.	RB
b-Seattle	Cortez Kennedy, Miami,FL	DT
Tampa Bay	KEITH McCANTS, Alabama	LB
San Diego	JUNIOR SEAU, USC	LB
Chicago	MARK CARRIER, USC	DB
Detroit	ANDRE WARE, Houston	QB
c-New England	Chris Singleton, Arizona	LB
Miami	Richmond Webb, Texas A&M	OT
d-New England	Ray Agnew, N.C.State	DL
LA Raiders	Anthony Smith, Arizona	DE
Cincinnati	James Francis, Baylor	LB
Kansas City	Percy Snow, Michigan St.	LB
New Orleans	Renaldo Turnbull, West Va.	DE
Houston	LAMAR LATHON, Houston	LB
Buffalo	James Williams, Fresno St.	DB
e-Dallas	EMMITT SMITH, Florida	RB
f-Green Bay	Tony Bennett, Mississippi	LB
Green Bay	Darrell Thompson, Minnesota	RB
g-Atlanta	Steve Broussard, Wash.St.	RB
h-Pittsburgh	Eric Green, Liberty	TE
Philadelphia	Ben Smith, Georgia	DB
LA Rams	Bern Brostek, Washington	C
NY Giants	RODNEY HAMPTON, Georgia	RB
San Francisco	Dexter Carter, Florida St.	RB

Note: Dallas (1st), Phoenix (4th) and Denver (27th) forfeited their 1990 first round selections by picking players in the 1989 Supplemental Draft. Dallas chose QB Steve Walsh of Miami,FL; Phoenix took Wash.St.QB Timm Rosenbach; and Denver took Alabama RB Bobby Humphrey.

Acquired picks: a—from Atlanta; **b**—from New England; **c**—from Seattle; **d**—from Indianapolis through Seattle; **e**—from Pittsburgh; **f**—from Cleveland; **g**—from Washington; **h**—from Minnesota through Dallas.

Second Round

Team		Pos
Dallas	Alexander Wright, Auburn	WR
Atlanta	Darion Connor, Jackson St.	LB
NY Jets	Reggie Rembert, West Va.	WR
i-Seattle	Terry Wooden, Syracuse	LB
Tampa Bay	REGGIE COBB, Tennessee	RB
Phoenix	Anthony Thompson, Indiana	RB
Chicago	Fred Washington, TCU	DL
j-Chicago	RON COX, Fresno St.	LB
Seattle	Robert Blackmon, Baylor	DB
Detroit	Dan Owens, USC	DL
Indianapolis	Anthony Johnson, N.Dame	RB
LA Raiders	Aaron Wallace, Texas A&M	LB
Cincinnati	Harold Green, S.Carolina	RB
Miami	Keith Sims, Iowa St.	OL
Kansas City	Tim Grunhard, Notre Dame	OL
Houston	Jeff Alm, Notre Dame	DL
Buffalo	Carwell Gardner, Louisville	RB
Pittsburgh	Kenny Davidson, LSU	DL
New Orleans	Vince Buck, Central St.	DB
Cleveland	LEROY HOARD, Michigan	RB
Washington	Andre Collins, Penn St.	LB
k-San Fran	Dennis Brown, Washington	DL
Green Bay	LeRoy Butler, Florida St.	DB
LA Rams	Pat Terrell, Notre Dame	DB
Philadelphia	Mike Bellamy, Illinois	WR
NY Giants	Mike Fox, West Virginia	DL
Denver	Alton Montgomery, Houston	DB
San Francisco	Eric Davis, Jack'ville St.	DB

Acquired picks: i—from New England; **j**—from San Diego; **k**—from Minnesota through Dallas.

Canadian Football League

Final 1989 Standings

Eastern Division

	W	L	T	Pts	PF	PA	vs Div
*Hamilton	12	6	0	24	519	517	9-1-0
†Toronto	7	11	0	14	369	428	5-5-0
†Winnipeg	7	11	0	14	408	462	3-7-0
Ottawa	4	14	0	8	426	630	3-7-0

Head Coaches: Ham—Al Bruno (7th season); **Tor**—Bob O'Billovich (8th); **Win**—Mike Riley (3rd); **Ott**—Steve Goldman (1st).

Western Division

	W	L	T	Pts	PF	PA	vs Div
*Edmonton	16	2	0	32	644	302	9-1-0
†Calgary	10	8	0	20	495	466	5-5-0
†Saskatchewan	9	9	0	18	547	567	3-7-0
Brit.Columbia	7	11	0	14	521	557	3-7-0

Head Coaches: Edm—Joe Faragalli (3rd season); **Calg**—Lary Kuharich (3rd); **Sask**—John Gregory (3rd); **BC**—Larry Donovan (3rd).

*Division champion.
†Playoff wild card.

Regular Season Award Winners

Player	Tracy Ham, QB, Edmonton
Canadian	Rocky DiPietro, SB, Hamilton
Off.Lineman	Rod Connop, C, Edmonton
Def.Player	Danny Bass, LB, Edmonton
Rookie	Stephen Jordan, DB, Hamilton
Coach	John Gregory, Saskatchewan

Regular Season Statistical Leaders

Points (TDs)	Tony Champion, Hamilton—90
Points (Kicking)	Paul Osbaldiston, Ham.—233
Yds (Rushing)	Reggie Taylor, Edm.—1503
Yds (from Scrim.)	Tim McCray, Sask.—2034
Pass Rating	Tracy Ham, Edmonton—85.2
Receptions	Tony Champion, Hamilton—95

1989 Playoffs

Division Semifinals

Eastern: Winnipeg 30 . . . . at Toronto 7
Western: Saskatchewan 33 . . . . at Calgary 26

Division Championships

Eastern: at Hamilton 14 . . . . Winnipeg 10
Western: Saskatchewan 32 . . . . . . at Edmonton 21

77th Grey Cup Championship
Nov.26 at SkyDome, Toronto

	1	2	3	4	F
Hamilton (13-7)	13	14	3	10	40
Saskatchewan (12-9)	1	21	12	9	43

Attendance: 54,088.

Players of the Game

Offense: Kent Austin, Saskatchewan QB (26-of-41, 474 yards, 3 TDs)
Defense: Charles Klingbeil, Saskatchewan, DT (2 sacks, 2 tackles)
Canadian: David Ridgway, Saskatchewan, K (4 FG, 4 converts, 16 points)

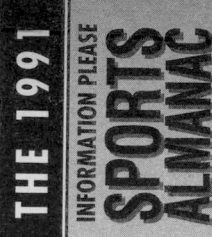

PRO FOOTBALL
STATISTICS

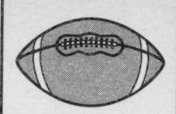

THROUGH THE YEARS
1920-1990

SUPERBOWLS • NFL LEADERS

SEC B

PAGE 157

The Super Bowl

The first AFL-NFL World Championship Game, as it was originally called, was played seven months after the two leagues agreed to merge in June of 1966. It became the Super Bowl (complete with roman numerals) by the third game in 1969. The Super Bowl winner has been presented the Vince Lombardi Trophy since 1971. Lombardi, whose Green Bay teams won the first two title games, died in 1970.

NFL champions (1966-69) and NFC champions (since 1970) are listed in capital LETTERS.

Season	Bowl	Winner	Head Coach	Score	Loser	Head Coach	Site
1966	I	GREEN BAY	Vince Lombardi	35-10	Kansas City	Hank Stram	Los Angeles
1967	II	GREEN BAY	Vince Lombardi	33-14	Oakland	John Rauch	Miami
1968	III	NY Jets	Weeb Ewbank	16- 7	BALTIMORE	Don Shula	Miami
1969	IV	Kansas City	Hank Stram	23- 7	MINNESOTA	Bud Grant	New Orleans
1970	V	Baltimore	Don McCafferty	16-13	DALLAS	Tom Landry	Miami
1971	VI	DALLAS	Tom Landry	24- 3	Miami	Don Shula	New Orleans
1972	VII	Miami	Don Shula	14- 7	WASHINGTON	George Allen	Los Angeles
1973	VIII	Miami	Don Shula	24- 7	MINNESOTA	Bud Grant	Houston
1974	IX	Pittsburgh	Chuck Noll	16- 6	MINNESOTA	Bud Grant	New Orleans
1975	X	Pittsburgh	Chuck Noll	21-17	DALLAS	Tom Landry	Miami
1976	XI	Oakland	John Madden	32-14	MINNESOTA	Bud Grant	Pasadena
1977	XII	DALLAS	Tom Landry	27-10	Denver	Red Miller	New Orleans
1978	XIII	Pittsburgh	Chuck Noll	35-31	DALLAS	Tom Landry	Miami
1979	XIV	Pittsburgh	Chuck Noll	31-19	LA RAMS	Ray Malavasi	Pasadena
1980	XV	Oakland	Tom Flores	27-10	PHILA.	Dick Vermeil	New Orleans
1981	XVI	SAN FRAN.	Bill Walsh	26-21	Cincinnati	Forrest Gregg	Pontiac, MI
1982	XVII	WASHINGTON	Joe Gibbs	27-17	Miami	Don Shula	Pasadena
1983	XVIII	LA Raiders	Tom Flores	38- 9	WASHINGTON	Joe Gibbs	Tampa
1984	XIX	SAN FRAN.	Bill Walsh	38-16	Miami	Don Shula	Stanford
1985	XX	CHICAGO	Mike Ditka	46-10	New England	Raymond Berry	New Orleans
1986	XXI	NY GIANTS	Bill Parcells	39-20	Denver	Dan Reeves	Pasadena
1987	XXII	WASHINGTON	Joe Gibbs	42-10	Denver	Dan Reeves	San Diego
1988	XXIII	SAN FRAN.	Bill Walsh	20-16	Cincinnati	Sam Wyche	Miami
1989	XXIV	SAN FRAN.	George Seifert	55-10	Denver	Dan Reeves	New Orleans

Super Bowl MVPs

Bowl	Date	Most Valuable Player	Bowl	Date	Most Valuable Player
I	1/15/67	QB Bart Starr, Green Bay	XIII	1/21/79	QB Terry Bradshaw, Pittsburgh
II	1/14/68	QB Bart Starr, Green Bay	XIV	1/20/80	QB Terry Bradshaw, Pittsburgh
III	1/12/69	QB Joe Namath, NY Jets	XV	1/25/81	QB Jim Plunkett, Oakland
IV	1/11/70	QB Len Dawson, Kansas City	XVI	1/24/82	QB Joe Montana, San Fran.
V	1/17/71	LB Chuck Howley, Dallas	XVII	1/30/83	RB John Riggins, Washington
VI	1/16/72	QB Roger Staubach, Dallas	XVIII	1/22/84	RB Marcus Allen, LA Raiders
VII	1/14/73	S Jake Scott, Miami	XIX	1/20/85	QB Joe Montana, San Fran.
VIII	1/13/74	RB Larry Csonka, Miami	XX	1/26/86	DE Richard Dent, Chicago
IX	1/12/75	RB Franco Harris, Pittsburgh	XXI	1/25/87	QB Phil Simms, NY Giants
X	1/18/76	WR Lynn Swann, Pittsburgh	XXII	1/31/88	QB Doug Williams, Wash.
XI	1/9/77	WR Fred Biletnikoff, Oakland	XXIII	1/22/89	WR Jerry Rice, San Fran.
XII	1/15/78	DE Harvey Martin, Dallas	XXIV	1/28/90	QB Joe Montana, San Fran.
		DT Randy White, Dallas			

All-Time Super Bowl Leaders
CAREER

Passing

Yardage	Gms	Att	Cmp	Pct	Yards
Joe Montana, SF	4	122	83	68.0	1142
Terry Bradshaw, Pit	4	84	49	58.3	932
Roger Staubach, Dal	4	98	61	62.2	734
John Elway, Den	3	101	46	45.5	669
Fran Tarkenton, Min	3	89	46	51.7	489
Bart Starr, GB	2	47	29	61.7	452
Jim Plunkett, Raiders	2	46	29	63.0	433
Joe Theismann, Wash	2	58	31	53.4	386
Len Dawson, KC	2	44	28	63.6	353
Doug Williams, Wash	1	29	18	62.1	340

Touchdown Passes	Gm	TD	Int
Joe Montana, San Francisco	4	11	0
Terry Bradshaw, Pittsburgh	4	9	4
Roger Staubach, Dallas	4	8	4
Jim Plunkett, LA Raiders	2	4	0
Doug Williams, Washington	1	4	1

Receiving

Catches	Gm	No	Yds	Avg	TD
Roger Craig, SF	3	20	212	10.6	3
Jerry Rice, SF	2	18	363	20.2	4
Lynn Swann, Pit	4	16	364	22.8	3
Chuck Foreman, Min	3	15	139	9.3	0
Cliff Branch, Raiders	3	14	181	12.9	3
Preston Pearson, Bal-Pit-Dal	5	12	105	8.8	0

Rushing

Yardage	Gm	Car	Yds	Avg	TD
Franco Harris, Pit	4	101	354	3.5	4
Larry Csonka, Mia	3	57	297	5.2	2
John Riggins, Wash	2	64	230	3.6	2
Timmy Smith, Wash	1	22	204	9.3	2
Roger Craig, SF	3	52	201	3.9	2
Marcus Allen, Raiders	1	20	191	9.5	2
Tony Dorsett, Dal	2	31	162	5.2	1
Mark van Eeghen, Raiders	2	37	153	4.1	0

All-Purpose Running

Yardage	Gm	Run	Rec	Ret	Total
Franco Harris, Pit	4	354	114	0	468
Roger Craig, SF	3	201	212	0	413
Lynn Swann, Pit	4	−7	364	34	391
Jerry Rice, SF	2	5	363	0	368
Larry Csonka, Mia	3	297	17	0	314

Scoring

Points	Gm	TD	FG	PAT	Pts
Roger Craig, SF	3	4	0	0	24
Franco Harris, Pit	4	4	0	0	24
Jerry Rice, SF	2	4	0	0	24
Ray Wersching, SF	2	0	5	7	22
Don Chandler, GB	2	0	4	8	20
Cliff Branch, Raiders	3	3	0	0	18
John Stallworth, Pit	4	3	0	0	18
Lynn Swann, Pit	4	3	0	0	18

SINGLE GAME
Passing

Yardage	Year	Att/Cmp	Yds
Joe Montana, SF vs Cin	1989	36/23	357
Doug Williams, Wash vs Den	1988	29/18	340
Joe Montana, SF vs Mia	1985	35/24	331
Terry Bradshaw, Pit vs Dal	1979	30/17	318
Dan Marino, Mia vs SF	1985	50/29	318
Terry Bradshaw, Pit vs Rams	1980	21/14	309
John Elway, Den vs NYG	1987	37/22	304
Ken Anderson, Cin vs SF	1982	34/25	300

Touchdown Passes	Year	TD	Int
Joe Montana, SF vs Den	1990	5	0
Terry Bradshaw, Pit vs Dal	1979	4	1
Doug Williams, Wash vs Den	1988	4	1
Roger Staubach, Dal vs Pit	1979	3	1
Jim Plunkett, Raid vs Phi	1981	3	0
Joe Montana, SF vs Mia	1985	3	0
Phil Simms, NYG vs Den	1987	3	0

Super Bowl Appearances

Through Super Bowl XXIV, 10 NFL teams have yet to play for the Vince Lombardi Trophy. In alphabetical order: Atlanta, Buffalo, Cleveland, Detroit, Houston, New Orleans, Phoenix, San Diego, Seattle and Tampa Bay. Of the 18 teams that have made it, Dallas and Miami have the most appearances (5), while Pittsburgh and San Francisco have the most Lombardi Trophies (4).

	No	W	L	Pct	PF	PA
Dallas Cowboys	5	2	3	.400	112	85
Miami Dolphins	5	2	3	.400	74	103
San Francisco 49ers	4	4	0	1.000	139	63
Pittsburgh Steelers	4	4	0	1.000	103	73
Oakland/LA Raiders	4	3	1	.750	111	66
Washington Redskins	4	2	2	.500	85	79
Minnesota Vikings	4	0	4	.000	34	95
Denver Broncos	4	0	4	.000	50	163
Green Bay Packers	2	2	0	1.000	68	24
Baltimore Colts	2	1	1	.500	23	29
Kansas City Chiefs	2	1	1	.500	33	42
Cincinnati Bengals	2	0	2	.000	37	46
Chicago Bears	1	1	0	1.000	46	10
New York Giants	1	1	0	1.000	39	20
New York Jets	1	1	0	1.000	16	7
Los Angeles Rams	1	0	1	.000	19	31
New England Patriots	1	0	1	.000	10	46
Philadelphia Eagles	1	0	1	.000	10	27

Receiving

Catches	Year	No	Yds	TD
Dan Ross, Cin vs SF	1982	11	104	2
Jerry Rice, SF vs Cin	1989	11	215	1
Ricky Sanders, Wash vs Den	1988	9	193	2
George Sauer, NYJ vs Bal	1969	8	133	0
Roger Craig, SF vs Cin	1989	8	101	0

Five players tied with 7 each.

Rushing

Yardage	Year	Car	Yds	TD
Timmy Smith, Wash vs Den	1988	22	204	2
Marcus Allen, Raid vs Wash	1984	20	191	2
John Riggins, Wash vs Mia	1983	38	166	1
Franco Harris, Pit vs Min	1975	34	158	1
Larry Csonka, Mia vs Min	1974	33	145	2
Clarence Davis, Raid vs Min	1977	16	137	0
Matt Snell, NYJ vs Bal	1969	30	121	1

Scoring

Points	Year	TD-FG-PAT	Pts
Roger Craig, SF vs Mia	1985	3-0-0	18
Jerry Rice, SF vs Den	1990	3-0-0	18
Don Chandler, GB vs Raid	1968	0-4-3	15
Ray Wersching, SF vs Cin	1982	0-4-2	14
Kevin Butler, Chi vs NE	1986	0-3-5	14

Touchdowns	Year	TD	Run	Rec
Roger Craig, SF vs Mia	1985	3	1	2
Jerry Rice, SF vs Den	1990	3	0	3

Thirteen players tied with 2 each.

Super Bowl Playoffs, 1966–88

The Super Bowl created pro football's first guaranteed multiple-game playoff format. Only four teams qualified for the playoffs in 1966, but by the time the 10 AFL teams joined the NFL in 1970, the field had doubled. Since 1978, 10 teams (out of 28) have made the postseason cut.

In the strike year of 1982, when the regular season was shortened to just nine games, playoff berths were extended to 16 teams and a 15-game tournament was played.

Throughout the following year-by-year playoff summary, home teams are noted in capital LETTERS and records of Super Bowl finalists include all games leading up to the Super Bowl.

1966 Season

NFL Playoffs
NFL Championship: Green Bay 34, DALLAS 27

AFL Playoffs
AFL Championship: Kansas City 31, BUFFALO 7

Super Bowl I
Memorial Coliseum, Los Angeles

Kansas City (12-2-1)	0	10	0	0-**10**
Green Bay (13-2)	7	7	14	7-**35**

MVP: Green Bay QB Bart Starr
(16 for 23, 250 yds, 2 TD, 1 Int)

1967 Season

NFL Playoffs
Eastern Conference: DALLAS 52, Cleveland 14
Western Conference: GREEN BAY 28, LA Rams 7
NFL Championship: GREEN BAY 21, Dallas 17

AFL Playoffs
AFL Championship: OAKLAND 40, Houston 7

Super Bowl II
Orange Bowl, Miami

Green Bay (11-4-1)	3	13	10	7-**33**
Oakland (14-1)	0	7	0	7-**14**

MVP: Green Bay QB Bart Starr
(13 for 24, 202 yds, 1 TD)

1968 Season

NFL Playoffs
Eastern Conference: CLEVELAND 31, Dallas 20
Western Conference: BALTIMORE 24, Minnesota 14
NFL Championship: Baltimore 34, CLEVELAND 0

AFL Playoffs
Western Division Tiebreaker: OAKLAND 41, Kan.City 6
AFL Championship: NY JETS 27, Oakland 23

Super Bowl III
Orange Bowl, Miami

NY Jets (12-3)	0	7	6	3-**16**
Baltimore (15-1)	0	0	0	7-**7**

MVP: NY Jets QB Joe Namath
(17 for 28, 206 yds)

1969 Season

NFL Playoffs
Eastern Conference: Cleveland 38, DALLAS 14
Western Conference: MINNESOTA 23, LA Rams 20
NFL Championship: MINNESOTA 27, Cleveland 7

AFL Playoffs
Divisional: Kansas City 13, NY JETS 6
OAKLAND 56, Houston 7
AFL Championship: Kansas City 17, OAKLAND 7

Super Bowl IV
Tulane Stadium, New Orleans

Minnesota (14-2)	0	0	7	0-**7**
Kansas City (13-3)	3	13	7	0-**23**

MVP: Kansas City QB Len Dawson
(12 for 17, 142 yds, 1 TD, 1 Int)

1970 Season

AFC Playoffs
(*denotes Wild Card qualifier)
Divisional: BALTIMORE 17, Cincinnati 0
OAKLAND 21, *Miami 14
AFC Championship: BALTIMORE 27, Oakland 17

NFC Playoffs
(*denotes Wild Card qualifier)
Divisional: DALLAS 5, *Detroit 0
San Francisco 17, MINNESOTA 14
NFC Championship: Dallas 17, SAN FRANCISCO 10

Super Bowl V
Orange Bowl, Miami

Baltimore (13-2-1)	0	6	0	10-**16**
Dallas (12-4)	3	10	0	0-**13**

MVP: Dallas LB Chuck Howley
(2 Interceptions for 22 yds)

1971 Season

AFC Playoffs
(*denotes Wild Card qualifier)
Divisional: Miami 27, KANSAS CITY 24 (OT)
*Baltimore 20, CLEVELAND 3
AFC Championship: MIAMI 21, Baltimore 0

NFC Playoffs
(*denotes Wild Card qualifier)
Divisional: Dallas 20, MINNESOTA 12
SAN FRANCISCO 24, *Washington 20
NFC Championship: DALLAS 14, San Francisco 3

Super Bowl VI
Tulane Stadium, New Orleans

Dallas (13-3-1)	3	7	7	7-**24**
Miami (12-3-1)	0	3	0	0-**3**

MVP: Dallas QB Roger Staubach
(12 for 19, 119 yds, 2 TD)

1972 Season

AFC Playoffs
(*denotes Wild Card qualifier)
Divisional: PITTSBURGH 13, Oakland 7
MIAMI 20, *Cleveland 14
AFC Championship: Miami 21, PITTSBURGH 17

NFC Playoffs
(*denotes Wild Card qualifier)
Divisional: *Dallas 30, SAN FRANCISCO 28
WASHINGTON 16, Green Bay 3
NFC Championship: WASHINGTON 26, Dallas 3

Super Bowl VII
Memorial Coliseum, Los Angeles

Miami (16-0)	7	7	0	0-**14**
Washington (13-3)	0	0	0	7- **7**

MVP: Miami safety Jake Scott
(2 Interceptions for 63 yds)

1973 Season

AFC Playoffs
(*denotes Wild Card qualifier)
Divisional: OAKLAND 33, *Pittsburgh 14
MIAMI 34, Cincinnati 16
AFC Championship: MIAMI 27, Oakland 10

NFC Playoffs
(*denotes Wild Card qualifier)
Divisional: MINNESOTA 27, *Washington 20
DALLAS 27, LA Rams 16
NFC Championship: Minnesota 27, DALLAS 10

Super Bowl VIII
Rice Stadium, Houston

Minnesota (14-2)	0	0	0	7- **7**
Miami (12-4)	14	3	7	0-**24**

MVP: Miami FB Larry Csonka
(33 carries, 145 yds, 2 TD)

1974 Season

AFC Playoffs
(*denotes Wild Card qualifier)
Divisional: OAKLAND 28, Miami 26
PITTSBURGH 32, *Buffalo 14
AFC Championship: Pittsburgh 24, OAKLAND 13

NFC Playoffs
(*denotes Wild Card qualifier)
Divisional: MINNESOTA 30, St.Louis 14
LA RAMS 19, *Washington 10
NFC Championship: MINNESOTA 14, LA Rams 10

Super Bowl IX
Tulane Stadium, New Orleans

Pittsburgh (12-3-1)	0	2	7	7-**16**
Minnesota (12-4)	0	0	0	6- **6**

MVP: Pittsburgh RB Franco Harris
(34 carries, 158 yds, 1 TD)

1975 Season

AFC Playoffs
(*denotes Wild Card qualifier)
Divisional: PITTSBURGH 28, Baltimore 10
OAKLAND 31, *Cincinnati 28
AFC Championship: PITTSBURGH 16, Oakland 10

NFC Playoffs
(*denotes Wild Card qualifier)
Divisional: LA RAMS 35, St.Louis 23
Dallas 17, MINNESOTA 14
NFC Championship: Dallas 37, LA RAMS 7

Super Bowl X
Orange Bowl, Miami

Dallas (12-4)	7	3	0	7-**17**
Pittsburgh (14-2)	7	0	0	14-**21**

MVP: Pittsburgh WR Lynn Swann
(4 catches, 161 yds, 1 TD)

1976 Season

AFC Playoffs
(*denotes Wild Card qualifier)
Divisional: OAKLAND 24, *New England 21
Pittsburgh 40, BALTIMORE 14
AFC Championship: OAKLAND 24, Pittsburgh 7

NFC Playoffs
(*denotes Wild Card qualifier)
Divisional: MINNESOTA 35, *Washington 20
LA Rams 14, DALLAS 12
NFC Championship: MINNESOTA 24, LA Rams 13

Super Bowl XI
Rose Bowl, Pasadena

Oakland (15-1)	0	16	3	13-**32**
Minnesota (13-2-1)	0	0	7	7-**14**

MVP: Oakland WR Fred Biletnikoff
(4 catches, 79 yds)

1977 Season

AFC Playoffs
(*denotes Wild Card qualifier)
Divisional: DENVER 34, Pittsburgh 21
*Oakland 37, BALTIMORE 31 (OT)
AFC Championship: DENVER 20, Oakland 17

NFC Playoffs
(*denotes Wild Card qualifier)
Divisional: DALLAS 37, *Chicago 7
Minnesota 14, LA RAMS 7
NFC Championship: DALLAS 23, Minnesota 6

Super Bowl XII
Louisiana Superdome, New Orleans

Dallas (14-2)	10	3	7	7-**27**
Denver (14-2)	0	0	10	0-**10**

MVP: Dallas DE Harvey Martin and DT Randy White
(Cowboys' defense forced 8 turnovers)

1978 Season

AFC Playoffs
Wild Cards: Houston 17, MIAMI 9
Divisional: Houston 31, NEW ENGLAND 14
PITTSBURGH 33, Denver 10
AFC Championship: PITTSBURGH 34, Houston 5

NFC Playoffs
Wild Cards: ATLANTA 14, Philadelphia 13
Divisional: DALLAS 27, Atlanta 20
LA RAMS 34, Minnesota 10
NFC Championship: Dallas 28, LA RAMS 0

Super Bowl XIII
Orange Bowl, Miami

Pittsburgh (16-2)	7	14	0	14-**35**
Dallas (14-4)	7	7	3	14-**31**

MVP: Pittsburgh QB Terry Bradshaw
(17 for 30, 318 yds, 4 TD, 1 Int)

1979 Season

AFC Playoffs
Wild Cards: HOUSTON 13, Denver 7
Divisional: Houston 17, SAN DIEGO 14
PITTSBURGH 34, Miami 14
AFC Championship: PITTSBURGH 27, Houston 13

NFC Playoffs
Wild Cards: PHILADELPHIA 27, Chicago 17
Divisional: TAMPA BAY 24, Philadelphia 17
LA Rams 21, DALLAS 19
NFC Championship: LA Rams 9, TAMPA BAY 0

Super Bowl XIV
Rose Bowl, Pasadena

LA Rams (11-7)	7	6	6	0-**19**
Pittsburgh (14-4)	3	7	7	14-**31**

MVP: Pittsburgh QB Terry Bradshaw
(14 for 21, 309 yds, 2 TD, 3 Int)

1980 Season

AFC Playoffs
Wild Cards: OAKLAND 27, Houston 7
Divisional: SAN DIEGO 20, Buffalo 14
Oakland 14, CLEVELAND 12
AFC Championship: Oakland 34, SAN DIEGO 27

NFC Playoffs
Wild Cards: DALLAS 34, LA Rams 13
Divisional: PHILADELPHIA 31, Minnesota 16
Dallas 30, ATLANTA 27
NFC Championship: PHILADELPHIA 20, Dallas 7

Super Bowl XV
Superdome, New Orleans

Oakland (14-5)	14	0	10	3-**27**
Philadelphia (14-4)	0	3	0	7-**10**

MVP: Oakland QB Jim Plunkett
(13 for 21, 261 yds, 3 TD)

1981 Season

AFC Playoffs
Wild Cards: Buffalo 31, NY JETS 27
Divisional: San Diego 41, MIAMI 38 (OT)
CINCINNATI 28, Buffalo 21
AFC Championship: CINCINNATI 27, San Diego 7

NFC Playoffs
Wild Cards: NY Giants 27, PHILADELPHIA 21
Divisional: DALLAS 38, Tampa Bay 0
FRANCISCO 38, NY Giants 24
NFC Championship: SAN FRANCISCO 28, Dallas 27

Super Bowl XVI
Pontiac Silverdome, Pontiac, MI

San Francisco (15-3)	7	13	0	6-**26**
Cincinnati (14-4)	0	0	7	14-**21**

MVP: San Francisco QB Joe Montana
(14 for 22, 157 yds, 1 TD;
6 carries, 18 yds, 1 TD)

1982 Season

A 57-day players' strike shortened the regular season from 16 games to nine. The playoff format was changed to a 16-team tournament open to the top eight teams in each conference.

AFC Playoffs
1st Round: LA RAIDERS 27, Cleveland 10
MIAMI 28, New England 3
NY Jets 44, CINCINNATI 17
San Diego 31, PITTSBURGH 28
2nd Round: NY Jets 17, LA RAIDERS 14
MIAMI 34, San Diego 13
AFC Championship: MIAMI 14, NY Jets 0

NFC Playoffs
1st Round: WASHINGTON 31, Detroit 7
DALLAS 30, Tampa Bay 17
GREEN BAY 41, St.Louis 16
MINNESOTA 30, Atlanta 24
2nd Round: WASHINGTON 21, Minnesota 7
DALLAS 37, Green Bay 26
NFC Championship: WASHINGTON 31, Dallas 17

Super Bowl XVII
Rose Bowl, Pasadena

Miami (10-2)	7	10	0	0-**17**
Washington (11-1)	0	10	3	14-**27**

MVP: Washington RB John Riggins
(38 carries, 166 yds, 1 TD; 1 catch, 15 yds)

1983 Season

AFC Playoffs
Wild Cards: SEATTLE 31, Denver 7
Divisional: Seattle 27, MIAMI 20
LA RAIDERS 38, Pittsburgh 10
AFC Championship: LA RAIDERS 30, Seattle 14

NFC Playoffs
Wild Cards: LA Rams 24, DALLAS 17
Divisional: SAN FRANCISCO 24, Detroit 23
WASHINGTON 51, LA Rams 7
NFC Championship: WASHINGTON 24,
San Francisco 21

Super Bowl XVIII
Tampa Stadium, Tampa

Washington (16-2)	0	3	6	0- **9**
LA Raiders (14-4)	7	14	14	3-**38**

MVP: LA Raiders RB Marcus Allen
(20 carries, 191 yds, 2 TD; 2 catches, 18 yds)

1984 Season

AFC Playoffs
Wild Cards: SEATTLE 13, LA Raiders 7
Divisional: MIAMI 31, Seattle 10
Pittsburgh 24, DENVER 17
AFC Championship: MIAMI 45, Pittsburgh 28

NFC Playoffs
Wild Cards: NY Giants 16, LA RAMS 13
Divisional: SAN FRANCISCO 21, NY Giants 10
Chicago 23, WASHINGTON 19
NFC Championship: SAN FRANCISCO 23, Chicago 0

Super Bowl XIX
Stanford Stadium, Stanford, CA

Miami (16-2)	10	6	0	0-**16**
San Francisco (17-1)	7	21	10	0-**38**

MVP: San Francisco QB Joe Montana
(24 for 35, 331 yds, 2 TD;
5 carries, 59 yards, 1 TD)

1985 Season

AFC Playoffs
Wild Cards: New England 26, NY JETS 14
Divisional: MIAMI 24, Cleveland 21
New England 27, LA RAIDERS 20
AFC Championship: New England 31, MIAMI 14

NFC Playoffs
Wild Cards: NY GIANTS 17, San Francisco 3
Divisional: LA RAMS 20, Dallas 0
CHICAGO 21, NY Giants 0
NFC Championship: CHICAGO 24, LA Rams 0

Super Bowl XX
Louisiana Superdome, New Orleans

Chicago Bears (17-1)	13	10	21	2-**46**
New England (14-5)	3	0	0	7-**10**

MVP: Chicago DE Richard Dent
(Bears defense: 7 sacks, 6 turnovers, 1 safety
and gave up just 123 total yards)

1986 Season

AFC Playoffs
Wild Cards: NY JETS 35, Kansas City 15
Divisional: CLEVELAND 23, NY Jets 20 (OT)
DENVER 22, New England 17
AFC Championship: Denver 23, CLEVELAND 20 (OT)

NFC Playoffs
Wild Cards: WASHINGTON 19, LA Rams 7
Divisional: Washington 27, CHICAGO 13
NY GIANTS 49, San Francisco 3
NFC Championship: NY GIANTS 17, Washington 0

Super Bowl XXI
Rose Bowl, Pasadena

Denver (13-5)	10	0	0	10-**20**
NY Giants (16-2)	7	2	17	13-**39**

MVP: NY Giants QB Phil Simms
(22 for 25, 268 yds, 3 TD; 3 carries, 25 yds)

1987 Season

A 24-day players' strike shortened the regular season
from 16 games to 15 with replacement teams playing
for three weeks. The playoffs proceeded as usual.

AFC Playoffs
Wild Cards: HOUSTON 23, Seattle 20 (OT)
Divisional: CLEVELAND 38, Indianapolis 21
DENVER 34, Houston 10
AFC Championship: DENVER 38, Cleveland 33

NFC Playoffs
Wild Cards: Minnesota 44, NEW ORLEANS 10
Divisional: Minnesota 36, SAN FRANCISCO 24
Washington 21, CHICAGO 17
NFC Championship: WASHINGTON 17, Minnesota 10

Super Bowl XXII
San Diego Jack Murphy Stadium

Washington (13-4)	0	35	0	7-**42**
Denver (12-4-1)	10	0	0	0-**10**

MVP: Washington QB Doug Williams
(18 for 29, 340 yds, 4 TD, 1 Int)

1988 Season

AFC Playoffs
Wild Cards: Houston 24, CLEVELAND 23
Divisional: BUFFALO 17, Houston 10
CINCINNATI 21, Seattle 13
AFC Championship: CINCINNATI 21, Buffalo 10

NFC Playoffs
Wild Cards: MINNESOTA 28, LA Rams 17
Divisional: SAN FRANCISCO 34, Minnesota 9
CHICAGO 20, Philadelphia 12
NFC Championship: San Francisco 28, CHICAGO 3

Super Bowl XXIII
Joe Robbie Stadium, Miami

Cincinnati (14-4)	0	3	10	3-**16**
San Francisco (12-6)	3	0	3	14-**20**

MVP: San Francisco WR Jerry Rice
(11 catches, 215 yds, 1 TD;
1 carry, 5 yds)

Before the Super Bowl

Time did not begin with the Super Bowl, it only seems that way. The first NFL champion was the Akron Pros in 1920, when the title went to the team with the best regular season record.

The first playoff game with the championship at stake came in 1932, followed by 33 championship games in the NFL and six in the AFL before Super Bowl I.

Finally, the NFL staged a consolation game between its conference runners-up from the 1960 season through 1969. Called the Bert Bell Benefit Bowl (after the late league commissioner) and referred to as the Playoff Bowl, it gave the winner of the game the bragging rights to third place in the NFL. All 10 Playoff Bowls were played in Miami.

Home teams in championship games are noted in capital LETTERS.

NFL Champions, 1920-31

Year	Champion	Head Coach, Pos.
1920	Akron (8-0-3)	Fritz Pollard, HB & Elgie Tobin, QB
1921	Chicago Staleys (9-1-1) (Renamed Bears in 1922)	George Halas, E
1922	Canton Bulldogs (10-0-2)	Guy Chamberlin, E
1923	Canton Bulldogs (11-0-1)	Guy Chamberlin, E
1924	Cleve.Bulldogs (7-1-1)	Guy Chamberlin, E
1925	Chi.Cardinals (11-2-1)	Norm Barry
1926	Frankford, PA (14-1-1)	Guy Chamberlin, E
1927	NY Giants (11-1-1)	Earl Potteiger, QB
1928	Providence, RI (8-2-1)	Jimmy Conzelman, HB
1929	Green Bay (12-0-1)	Curly Lambeau, QB
1930	Green Bay (10-3-1)	Curly Lambeau
1931	Green Bay (12-2)	Curly Lambeau

NFL Championship Game, 1932-65

Season	Tied for 1st place after regular season		Championship Game	Date	Winning Coach
1932	Portsmouth,OH (6-1-4) & Chicago Bears (6-1-6)		CHICAGO BEARS, 9-0	12/18/32	Ralph Jones

Season	Eastern Champion	Western Champion	Championship Game	Date	Winning Coach
1933	NY Giants (11-3)	Chicago Bears (10-2-1)	CHICAGO BEARS, 23-21	12/17/33	George Halas
1934	NY Giants (8-5)	Chicago Bears (13-0)	NY GIANTS, 30-13	12/9/34	Steve Owen
1935	NY Giants (9-3)	Detroit (7-3-2)	DETROIT, 26-7	12/15/35	Potsy Clark
1936	Bost. Redskins (7-5)	Green Bay (10-1-1)	Green Bay, 21-6 (Game played in New York)	12/13/36	Curly Lambeau
1937	Wash.Redskins (8-3)	Chicago Bears (9-1-1)	Washington, 28-21	12/12/37	Ray Flaherty
1938	NY Giants (8-2-1)	Green Bay (8-3)	NY GIANTS, 23-17	12/11/38	Steve Owen
1939	NY Giants (9-1-1)	Green Bay (9-2)	GREEN BAY, 27-0	12/10/39	Curly Lambeau
1940	Washington (9-2)	Chicago Bears (8-3)	Chicago Bears, 73-0	12/8/40	George Halas
1941	NY Giants (8-3)	Chicago Bears (11-1)*	CHICAGO BEARS, 37-9	12/21/41	George Halas
1942	Washington (10-1)	Chicago Bears (11-0)	WASHINGTON, 14-6	12/13/42	Ray Flaherty
1943	Washington (7-3-1)*	Chicago Bears (8-1-1)	CHICAGO BEARS, 41-21	12/26/43	Hunk Anderson & Luke Johnsos
1944	NY Giants (8-1-1)	Green Bay (8-2)	Green Bay, 14-7	12/17/44	Curly Lambeau
1945	Washington (8-2)	Cleveland Rams (9-1)	CLEVE.RAMS, 15-14	12/16/45	Adam Walsh
1946	NY Giants (7-3-1)	Chicago Bears (8-2-1)	Chicago Bears, 24-14	12/15/46	George Halas
1947	Philadelphia (9-4)*	Chicago Cards (9-3)	CHICAGO CARDS, 28-21	12/28/47	Jimmy Conzelman
1948	Philadelphia (9-2-1)	Chicago Cards (11-1)	PHILADELPHIA, 7-0	12/19/48	Greasy Neale
1949	Philadelphia (11-1)	LA Rams (8-2-2)	Philadelphia, 14-0	12/18/49	Greasy Neale

Season	American Conf.	National Conf.	Championship Game	Date	Winning Coach
1950	Cleveland (11-2)*	LA Rams (10-3)*	CLEVELAND, 30-28	12/24/50	Paul Brown
1951	Cleveland (11-1)	LA Rams (8-4)	LA RAMS, 24-17	12/23/51	Joe Stydahar
1952	Cleveland (8-4)	Detroit (10-3)*	Detroit, 17-7	12/28/52	Buddy Parke

Season	Eastern Conf.	Western Conf.	Championship Game	Date	Winning Coach
1953	Cleveland (11-1)	Detroit (10-2)	DETROIT, 17-16	12/27/53	Buddy Parker
1954	Cleveland (9-3)	Detroit (9-2-1)	CLEVELAND, 56-10	12/26/54	Paul Brown
1955	Cleveland (9-2-1)	LA Rams (8-3-1)	CLEVELAND, 38-14	12/26/55	Paul Brown
1956	NY Giants (8-3-1)	Chicago Bears (9-2-1)	NY GIANTS, 47-7	12/30/56	Jim Lee Howell
1957	Cleveland (9-2-1)	Detroit (9-4)*	DETROIT, 59-14	12/29/57	George Wilson
1958	NY Giants (10-3)*	Baltimore (9-3)	Baltimore, 23-17 (OT)	12/28/58	Weeb Ewbank
1959	NY Giants (10-2)	Baltimore (9-3)	BALTIMORE, 31-16	12/27/59	Weeb Ewbank
1960	Philadelphia (10-2)	Green Bay (8-4)	PHILADELPHIA, 17-13	12/26/60	Buck Shaw
1961	NY Giants (10-3-1)	Green Bay (11-3)	GREEN BAY, 37-0	12/31/61	Vince Lombardi
1962	NY Giants (12-2)	Green Bay (13-1)	Green Bay, 16-7	12/30/62	Vince Lombardi
1963	NY Giants (11-3)	Chicago Bears (11-1-2)	CHICAGO, 14-10	12/29/63	George Halas
1964	Cleveland (10-3-1)	Baltimore (12-2)	CLEVELAND, 27-0	12/27/64	Blanton Collier
1965	Cleveland (11-3)	Green Bay (11-3-1)*	GREEN BAY, 23-12	1/2/66	Vince Lombardi

Since 1965: see Super Bowl Playoffs.

*Divisional playoffs: 1941—Chi.Bears 33, Green Bay 14; 1943—Washington 28, NY Giants 0; 1947—Phila. 21, Pittsburgh 0; 1949—Cleveland 8, NY Giants 3 and LA Rams 24, Chicago Bears 14; 1952—Detroit 31, LA Rams 21; 1957—Detroit 31, San Fran. 27; 1958—NY Giants 10, Cleveland 0; 1965—Green Bay 13, Baltimore 10 (OT).

AFL Championship Game, 1960-65

Season	Eastern Conf.	Western Conf.	Championship Game	Date	Winning Coach
1960	Houston (10-4)	LA Chargers (10-4)	HOUSTON, 24-16	1/1/61	Lou Rymkus
1961	Houston (10-3-1)	SD Chargers (12-2)	Houston, 10-3	12/24/61	Wally Lemm
1962	Houston (11-3)	Dallas Texans (11-3)	Dallas, 20-17 (2 OT)	12/23/62	Hank Stram
1963	Boston (7-6-1)*	SD Chargers (11-3)	SD CHARGERS, 51-10	1/5/64	Sid Gillman
1964	Buffalo (12-2)	SD Chargers (8-5-1)	BUFFALO, 20-7	12/26/64	Lou Saban
1965	Buffalo (10-3-1)	SD Chargers (9-2-3)	Buffalo, 23-0	12/26/65	Lou Saban

From 1966-69: see Super Bowl Playoffs.

*Divisional playoffs: 1963—Boston 26, Buffalo 8.

NFL Playoff Bowl, 1961-70

Season	Eastern Runner-up	Western Runner-up	Consolation Game	Date	Winning Coach
1960	Cleveland (8-3-1)	Detroit (7-5)	Detroit, 17-16	1/7/61	George Wilson
1961	Philadelphia (10-4)	Detroit (8-5-1)	Detroit, 38-10	1/6/62	George Wilson
1962	Pittsburgh (9-5)	Detroit (11-3)	Detroit, 17-10	1/6/63	George Wilson
1963	Cleveland (10-4)	Green Bay (11-2-1)	Green Bay, 40-23	1/5/64	Vince Lombardi
1964	St.Louis (9-3-2)	Green Bay (8-5-1)	St.Louis, 24-17	1/3/65	Wally Lemm
1965	Dallas (7-7)	Baltimore (10-4-1)*	Baltimore, 35-3	1/9/66	Don Shula
1966	Philadelphia (9-5)	Baltimore (9-5)	Baltimore, 20-14	1/8/67	Don Shula
1967	Cleveland (9-6)**	LA Rams (11-2-2)**	LA Rams, 30-6	1/7/68	George Allen
1968	Dallas (12-3)**	Minnesota (8-7)**	Dallas, 17-13	1/5/69	Tom Landry
1969	Dallas (11-3-1)**	LA Rams (11-4)**	LA Rams, 31-0	1/3/70	George Allen

Discontinued after 1969 season.

*Qualified by losing divisional playoff game for first place.
**Qualified by losing Conference championship game.

Champions Of Leagues That Didn't Make It

No professional league in American sports has had to contend with more pretenders to the throne than the NFL. Seven times in as many decades a rival league has risen up to challenge the NFL and six of them went under in less than five seasons. Only the fourth American Football League (1960-69) succeeded, forcing the older league to sue for peace and a full partnership in 1966.

Of the six leagues that didn't make it, only the All-America Football Conference (1946-49) lives on—the Cleveland Browns and San Francisco 49ers joined the NFL after the AAFC folded in 1949.

The champions of leagues past are listed below. Home teams in championship games are noted in capital LETTERS.

American Football League I

Year	Champion	Head Coach
1926	Philadelphia Quakers	Bob Folwell

American Football League II

Year	Champion	Head Coach
1936	Boston Shamrocks	George Kennealy
1937	Los Angeles Bulldogs	Gus Henderson

American Football League III

Year	Champion	Head Coach
1940	Columbus Bullies	Phil Bucklew
1941	Columbus Bullies	Phil Bucklew

All-America Football Conference

Year	Champion	Head Coach
1946	CLEVELAND 14, NY Yankees 9	Paul Brown
1947	Cleve.Browns 14, NY YANKEES 3	Paul Brown
1948	CLEVELAND 49, Buffalo 7	Paul Brown
1949	CLEVELAND 21, S.F.49ers 7	Paul Brown

World Football League

Year	Champion	Head Coach
1974	BIRMINGHAM 22, Florida 21	Jack Gotta
1975	Folded mid-season	—

United States Football League

Year	Championship Game	Head Coach
1983	Michigan 24, Phila.Stars 22	Jim Stanley
1984	Phila.Stars 23. Arizona 3	Jim Mora
1985	Balt.Stars 28, Oakland 24	Jim Mora

USFL Championship Game sites: Denver (1983), Tampa (1984), East Rutherford, N.J. (1985).

NFL Franchise Origins

Here is what the current 28 teams in the National Football League have to show for the years they have put in as members of the American Professional Football Association (APFA), the NFL, the All-America Football Conference (AAFC) and the American Football League (AFL). League and Super Bowl titles are noted by season.

American Football Conference

	First Season		League Titles	Franchise Stops
Buffalo Bills	1960	(AFL)	2 AFL (1964-65)	Buffalo (1960-72) Orchard Park, NY (1973-)
Cincinnati Bengals	1968	(AFL)	None	Cincinnati (1968-)
Cleveland Browns	1946	(AAFC)	4 AAFC (1946-49) 4 NFL (1950,54-55,64)	Cleveland (1946-)
Denver Broncos	1960	(AFL)	None	Denver (1960-)
Houston Oilers	1960	(AFL)	2 AFL (1960-61)	Houston (1960-)
Indianapolis Colts	1953	(NFL)	3 NFL (1958-59,68) 1 Super Bowl (1970)	Baltimore (1953-83) Indianapolis (1984-)
Kansas City Chiefs	1960	(AFL)	3 AFL (1962,66,69) 1 Super Bowl (1969)	Dallas (1960-62) Kansas City (1963-)
Los Angeles Raiders	1960	(AFL)	1 AFL (1967) 3 Super Bowls (1976,80,83)	Oakland (1960-81) Los Angeles (1982-)
Miami Dolphins	1966	(AFL)	2 Super Bowls (1972-73)	Miami (1966-)
New England Patriots	1960	(AFL)	None	Boston (1960-70) Foxboro, MA (1971-)
New York Jets	1960	(AFL)	1 AFL (1968) 1 Super Bowl (1968)	New York (1960-83) E.Rutherford, NJ (1984-)
Pittsburgh Steelers	1933	(NFL)	4 Super Bowls (1974-75, 78-79)	Pittsburgh (1933-)
San Diego Chargers	1960	(AFL)	1 AFL (1963)	Los Angeles (1960) San Diego (1961-)
Seattle Seahawks	1976	(NFL)	None	Seattle (1976-)

National Football Conference

	First Season		League Titles	Franchise Stops
Atlanta Falcons	1966	(NFL)	None	Atlanta (1966-)
Chicago Bears	1920	(APFA)	7 NFL (1932-33,40-41,43,46,63) 1 Super Bowl (1985)	Decatur,IL (1920) Chicago (1921-)
Dallas Cowboys	1960	(NFL)	2 Super Bowls (1971,77)	Dallas (1960-70) Irving,TX (1971-)
Detroit Lions	1930	(NFL)	4 NFL (1935,52-53,57)	Portsmouth,OH (1930-33) Detroit (1934-74) Pontiac,MI (1975-)
Green Bay Packers	1921	(APFA)	8 NFL (1936,39,44,61-62,65-67) 2 Super Bowls (1966-67)	Green Bay (1921-)
Los Angeles Rams	1937	(NFL)	2 NFL (1945,51)	Cleveland (1937-45) Los Angeles (1946-79) Anaheim (1980-)
Minnesota Vikings	1961	(NFL)	1 NFL (1969)	Bloomington, MN (1961-81) Minneapolis,MN (1982-)
New Orleans Saints	1967	(NFL)	None	New Orleans (1967-)
New York Giants	1925	(NFL)	3 NFL (1934,38,56) 1 Super Bowl (1986)	New York (1925-73,75) New Haven,CT (1973-74) E.Rutherford,NJ (1976-)
Philadelphia Eagles	1933	(NFL)	3 NFL (1948-49,60)	Philadelphia (1933-)
Phoenix Cardinals	1920	(APFA)	1 NFL (1947)	Chicago (1920-59) St.Louis (1960-87) Phoenix (1988-)
San Francisco 49ers	1946	(AAFC)	4 Super Bowls (1981,84,88-89)	San Francisco (1946-)
Tampa Bay Buccaneers	1976	(NFL)	None	Tampa,FL (1976-)
Washington Redskins	1932	(NFL)	2 NFL (1937,42) 2 Super Bowls (1982,87)	Boston (1932-36) Washington,DC (1937-)

NFL All-Time Individual Leaders

Through 1989 regular season; players active in 1989 in **bold type.**

CAREER
Passing Efficiency

Ratings based on performance standards established for completion percentage, average gain, touchdown percentage, and interception percentage. Quarterbacks are allocated points according to how their statistics measure up to those standards. Minimum 1500 passing attempts.

	Yrs	Att	Comp	Comp %	Yards	Gain	TD	TD %	Int	Int %	Rating
Joe Montana	11	4059	2593	53.9	31,054	7.65	216	5.3	107	2.6	94.0
Dan Marino	7	3650	2174	59.6	27,853	7.63	220	6.0	125	3.4	89.3
Boomer Esiason	6	2285	1296	56.7	18,350	8.03	126	5.5	76	3.3	87.3
Dave Krieg	10	2843	1644	57.8	20,858	7.34	169	5.9	116	4.1	83.7
Bernie Kosar	5	1940	1134	58.4	13,888	7.16	75	3.9	47	2.4	83.4
Roger Staubach	11	2958	1685	57.0	22,700	7.67	153	5.2	109	3.7	83.4
Ken O'Brien	6	2467	1471	59.6	17,589	7.13	96	3.9	68	2.8	83.0
Jim Kelly	4	1742	1032	59.2	12,901	7.41	81	4.6	63	3.6	82.7
Neil Lomax	8	3153	1817	57.6	22,771	7.22	136	4.3	90	2.9	82.7
Sonny Jurgensen	18	4262	2433	57.1	32,224	7.56	255	6.0	189	4.4	82.6
Len Dawson	19	3741	2136	57.1	28,711	7.67	239	6.4	183	4.9	82.6
Ken Anderson	16	4475	2654	59.3	32,838	7.34	197	4.4	160	3.6	81.9
Danny White	13	2950	1761	59.7	21,959	7.44	155	5.3	132	4.5	81.7
Bart Starr	16	3149	1808	57.4	24,718	7.85	152	4.8	138	4.4	80.5
Fran Tarkenton	18	6467	3686	57.0	47,003	7.27	342	5.3	266	4.1	80.4
Tony Eason	7	1536	898	58.5	10,987	7.15	61	4.0	50	3.3	80.3
Dan Fouts	15	5604	3297	58.8	43,040	7.68	254	4.5	242	4.3	80.2
Jim McMahon	8	1831	1050	57.3	13,335	7.28	77	4.2	66	3.6	79.2
Bert Jones	10	2551	1430	56.1	18,190	7.13	124	4.9	101	4.0	78.2
Johnny Unitas	18	5186	2830	54.6	40,239	7.76	290	5.6	253	4.9	78.2
Otto Graham	6	1565	872	55.7	13,499	8.63	88	5.6	94	6.0	78.2
Frank Ryan	13	2133	1090	51.1	16,042	7.52	149	7.0	111	5.2	77.6
Joe Theismann	12	3602	2044	56.7	25,206	7.00	160	4.4	138	3.8	77.4

Note: The NFL does not recognize records from the All-American Football Conference (1946-49). If it did, Otto Graham would rank 4th (between Esiason and Krieg) with the following stats: 10 Yrs; 2626 Att; 1464 Comp; 55.8 Cmp %; 23,584 Yards; 8.98 Avg Gain; 174 TD; 6.6 TD %; 135 Int; 5.1 Int %; and an 86.6 Rating.

Passing Yardage

	Yrs	Att	Comp	Pct	Yards
Fran Tarkenton	18	6467	3686	57.0	47,003
Dan Fouts	15	5604	3297	58.8	43,040
Johnny Unitas	18	5186	2830	54.6	40,239
Jim Hart	19	5076	2593	51.1	34,665
John Hadl	16	4687	2363	50.4	33,513
Ken Anderson	16	4475	2654	59.3	32,838
Sonny Jurgensen	18	4262	2433	57.1	32,224
John Brodie	17	4491	2469	55.0	31,548
Joe Montana	11	4059	2593	63.9	31,054
Norm Snead	15	4311	2254	52.3	30,558
Joe Ferguson	17	4511	2367	52.5	29,796
Roman Gabriel	16	4498	2366	52.6	29,444
Len Dawson	19	3741	2136	57.1	28,711
Y.A. Tittle	15	3817	2118	55.5	28,339
Ron Jaworski	16	4117	2187	53.1	28,190
Terry Bradshaw	14	3901	2025	51.9	27,989
Ken Stabler	15	3793	2270	59.8	27,938
Craig Morton	18	3786	2053	54.2	27,908
Dan Marino	7	3650	2174	59.6	27,853
Joe Namath	13	3762	1886	50.1	27,663
George Blanda	26	4007	1911	47.7	26,920
Bobby Layne	15	3700	1814	49.0	26,768
Joe Theismann	12	3602	2044	56.7	25,206
Bob Griese	14	3429	1926	56.2	25,092
Bart Starr	16	3149	1808	57.4	24,718

Note: The NFL does not recognize records from the All-American Football Conference (1946-49). If it did, **Y.A. Tittle** would rank 6th (between Hadl and Anderson) with the following stats: 17 Yrs; 4395 Att; 2427 Comp; 55.2 Pct; and 33,070 Yards.

Touchdown Passes

	Yrs	TD	Int
Fran Tarkenton	18	342	266
Johnny Unitas	18	290	253
Sonny Jurgensen	18	255	189
Dan Fouts	15	254	242
John Hadl	16	244	268
Len Dawson	19	239	183
George Blanda	26	236	277
Dan Marino	7	220	125
Joe Montana	11	216	107
John Brodie	17	214	224
Terry Bradshaw	14	212	210
Y.A. Tittle	15	212	221
Jim Hart	19	209	247
Roman Gabriel	15	201	149
Ken Anderson	16	197	160
Norm Snead	15	196	253
Joe Ferguson	17	196	207
Bobby Layne	15	196	243
Ken Stabler	15	194	222
Bob Griese	14	192	172
Sammy Baugh	16	187	203
Craig Morton	18	183	187
Ron Jaworski	16	179	164
Norm Van Brocklin	12	173	178
Joe Namath	13	173	220

Note: The NFL does not recognize records from the All-American Football Conference (1946-49). If it did, **Y.A. Tittle** would rank 6th (between Hadl and Dawson) with the following stats: 17 Yrs; 242 TD; and 248 Int.

Receiving

	Yrs	No	Yards	Avg	TD		Yrs	No	Yards	Avg	TD
Steve Largent ...14	14	819	13,089	16.0	100	Harold Jackson ...16	16	579	10,372	17.9	76
Charlie Joiner 18	18	750	12,146	16.2	65	Lionel Taylor 10	10	567	7,195	12.7	45
Art Monk 10	10	662	9,165	13.8	47	Wes Chandler ...11	11	559	8,966	16.0	56
Charley Taylor ...13	13	649	9,110	14.0	79	Lance Alworth 11	11	542	10,266	18.9	85
Ozzie Newsome ..12	12	639	7,740	12.1	45	Kellen Winslow ...10	10	541	6,741	12.5	45
Don Maynard ...15	15	633	11,834	18.7	88	John Stallworth ...14	14	537	8,723	16.2	63
Raymond Berry ...13	13	631	9,275	14.7	68	Stanley Morgan .13	13	534	10,352	19.4	67
James Lofton ...12	12	607	11,251	18.5	57	J.T. Smith 12	12	526	6,749	12.8	33
Harold Carmichael 14	14	590	8,985	15.2	79	Bobby Mitchell ...11	11	521	7,954	15.3	65
Fred Biletnikoff ...14	14	589	8,974	15.2	76	Nat Moore 13	13	510	7,546	14.8	74

Running

Rushing Yardage

	Yrs	Car	Yards	Avg	TD
Walter Payton 13	13	3838	16,726	4.4	110
Tony Dorsett 12	12	2936	12,739	4.3	77
Jim Brown 9	9	2359	12,312	5.2	106
Franco Harris 13	13	2949	12,120	4.1	91
John Riggins 14	14	2916	11,352	3.9	104
O.J.Simpson 11	11	2404	11,236	4.7	61
Eric Dickerson 7	7	2450	11,226	4.6	82
Earl Campbell 8	8	2187	9,407	4.3	74
Ottis Anderson 12	12	2274	9,317	4.1	69
Jim Taylor 10	10	1941	8,597	4.4	83
Joe Perry 14	14	1737	8,378	4.8	53
Larry Csonka 11	11	1891	8,081	4.3	64
Gerald Riggs 8	8	1788	7,465	4.2	52
Mike Pruitt 11	11	1844	7,378	4.0	51
Marcus Allen 8	8	1781	7,275	4.1	63
Leroy Kelly 10	10	1727	7,274	4.2	74
George Rogers 7	7	1692	7,176	4.2	54
Freeman McNeil ...9	9	1605	7,146	4.5	30
John Henry Johnson .13	13	1571	6,803	4.3	48
Wilbert Montgomery...9	9	1540	6,789	4.4	45
Curt Warner........7	7	1649	6,705	4.1	55
Chuck Muncie 9	9	1561	6,702	4.3	71

Note: The NFL does not recognize records from the All-American Football Conference (1946-49). If it did, Joe Perry would rank 8th (between Dickerson and Campbell) with the following stats: 16 Yrs; 1,929 Att; 9,723 Yards; 5.0 Avg; and 71 TD.

All-Purpose Running

	Yrs	Rush	Rec	Ret	Total
Walter Payton ...13	13	16,726	4,538	539	21,803
Tony Dorsett ...12	12	12,739	3,554	33	16,326
Jim Brown 9	9	12,312	2,499	648	15,459
Franco Harris ...13	13	12,120	2,287	215	14,622
O.J.Simpson ...11	11	11,236	2,142	990	14,368
Bobby Mitchell ...11	11	2,735	7,954	3389	14,078
John Riggins ...14	14	11,352	2,090	-7	13,435
Steve Largent ...13	13	83	13,089	224	13,396
Greg Pruitt 12	12	5,672	3,069	4521	13,262
Ollie Matson ...14	14	5,173	3,285	4426	12,884
Eric Dickerson 7	7	11,226	1,633	0	12,859
Tim Brown 10	10	3,862	3,399	5423	12,684
Lenny Moore ...12	12	5,174	6,039	1238	12,451
Don Maynard ...15	15	70	11,834	475	12,379
Charlie Joyner ...18	18	22	12,146	199	12,367
Leroy Kelly 10	10	7,274	2,281	2775	12,330
Ottis Anderson .11	11	9,317	2,882	0	12,199
Floyd Little.......9	9	6,323	2,418	3432	12,173
Abner Haynes ...8	8	4,630	3,535	3900	12,065
Stump Mitchell .9	9	4,649	1,955	5431	12,035
Bruce Harper ...8	8	1,829	2,409	7191	11,429
Hugh McElhenny .13	13	5,281	3,247	2847	11,375
Roger Craig 7	7	6,625	4,241	32	10,898

Scoring

Overall Points

Points	Yrs	TD	FG	PAT	Points
George Blanda 26	26	9	335	943	2002
Jan Stenerud 19	19	0	373	580	1699
Jim Turner 16	16	1	304	521	1439
Mark Moseley 16	16	0	300	482	1382
Jim Bakken 17	17	0	282	534	1380
Fred Cox 15	15	0	282	519	1365
Lou Groza 17	17	1	234	641	1349
Pat Leahy 16	16	0	255	496	1261
Chris Bahr 14	14	0	241	490	1213
Gino Cappelletti 11	11	42	176	350	1130†
Ray Wersching 15	15	0	222	456	1122
Don Cockroft 13	13	0	216	432	1080
Garo Yepremian 14	14	0	210	444	1074
Bruce Gossett 11	11	0	219	374	1031
Nick Lowery 11	11	0	225	338	1013
Sam Baker 15	15	2	179	428	977
Jim Breech 11	11	0	184	418	970
Rafael Septien 10	10	0	180	420	960
Lou Michaels 13	13	1	187	386	955†
Eddie Murray 10	10	0	212	307	943
Roy Gerela 11	11	0	184	351	903

†Cappelletti's total includes four 2-point conversions, and Michaels' total includes one safety.

Note: The NFL does not recognize records from the All-American Football Conference (1946-49). If it did, Lou Groza would move up from 7th to 3rd (between Stenerud and Turner) with the following stats: 21 Yrs; 1 TD; 264 FG; 810 PAT; and 1,608 Points.

Touchdowns

	Yrs	Rush	Rec	Ret	Total
Jim Brown 9	9	106	20	0	126
Walter Payton 13	13	110	15	0	125
John Riggins 14	14	104	12	0	116
Lenny Moore 12	12	63	48	2	113
Don Hutson 11	11	3	99	3	105
Franco Harris 13	13	91	9	0	100
Steve Largent 14	14	1	100	0	101
Jim Taylor 10	10	83	10	0	93
Tony Dorsett 12	12	77	13	1	91
Bobby Mitchell..........11	11	18	65	8	91
Leroy Kelly 10	10	74	13	3	90
Charley Taylor 13	13	11	79	0	90
Don Maynard 15	15	0	88	0	88
Lance Alworth 11	11	2	85	0	87
Eric Dickerson 7	7	82	4	0	86
Paul Warfield 13	13	1	85	0	86
Tommy McDonald 12	12	0	84	1	85
Pete Johnson 8	8	76	6	0	82
Art Powell 10	10	0	81	0	82
Marcus Allen 8	8	63	16	1	80
Harold Carmichael ...14	14	0	79	0	79
Frank Gifford 12	12	34	43	1	78

NFL All-Time Individual Leaders (Cont.)

Miscellaneous

Interceptions

Players with at least 60 interceptions through 1989 regular season. Players active in 1989 in **bold type.**

	Yrs	No	Yards	TD
Paul Krause	16	81	1185	3
Emlen Tunnell	14	79	1282	4
Dick "Night Train" Lane	14	68	1207	5
Ken Riley	15	65	596	5
Dick LeBeau	13	62	762	3
Dave Brown	15	62	698	5

Punting Average

Top 5 punters with at least 300 punts through 1989 regular season. Players active in 1989 in **bold type.**

	Yrs	No	Yards	Avg
Sammy Baugh	16	338	15,245	45.1
Tommy Davis	11	511	22,833	44.7
Yale Lary	11	503	22,279	44.3
Rohn Stark	8	593	26,183	44.2
Horace Gillom	7	385	16,872	43.8
Jerry Norton	11	358	15,671	43.8

Kickoff Return Average

Top 5 kickoff returners with at least 75 returns through 1989 regular season. Players active in 1989 in **bold type.**

	Yrs	No	Yards	Avg	TD
Gale Sayers	7	91	2781	30.6	6
Lynn Chandnois	7	92	2720	29.6	3
Abe Woodson	9	193	5538	28.7	5
Buddy Young	6	90	2514	27.9	2
Travis Williams	5	102	2801	27.5	6

Punt Return Average

Top 5 punt returners with at least 75 returns through 1989 regular season. Players active in 1989 in **bold type.**

	Yrs	No	Yards	Avg	TD
George McAfee	8	112	1431	12.8	2
Jack Christiansen	8	85	1084	12.8	8
Claude Gibson	5	110	1381	12.6	3
Bill Dudley	9	124	1515	12.2	3
Rick Upchurch	9	248	3008	12.1	8
John Taylor	3	81	982	12.1	2

SINGLE SEASON

Scoring

Points

	Year	TD	PAT	FG	Pts
Paul Hornung, GB	1960	15	41	15	176
Mark Moseley, Wash	1983	0	62	33	161
Gino Cappelletti, Bos	1964	7	38	25	155
Gino Cappelletti, Bos	1961	8	48	17	147
Paul Hornung, GB	1961	10	41	15	146
Jim Turner, NY Jets	1968	0	43	34	145
John Riggins, Wash	1983	24	0	0	144
Kevin Butler, Chi	1985	0	51	31	144
Tony Franklin, NE	1986	0	44	32	140
Gary Anderson, Pitt	1985	0	40	33	139

Note: The NFL regular season schedule grew from 12 games (1947-60) to 14 (1961-77) to 16 (1978-present). The AFL regular season schedule was always 14 games (1960-69).

Field Goals

	Year	Att	No
Ali Haji-Sheikh, NY Giants*	1983	42	35
Jim Turner, NY Jets	1968	46	34
Chester Marcol, GB*	1972	48	33
Mark Moseley, Wash	1983	47	33
Gary Anderson, Pitt*	1985	42	33
Jim Turner, NY Jets	1969	47	32
Tony Franklin, NE*	1986	41	32
Scott Norwood, Buf*	1988	37	32
Morten Anderson, NO*	1985	35	31
Kevin Butler, Chicago*	1985	37	31
Rich Karlis, Minnesota*	1989	39	31

*Soccer-style kicker

Touchdowns

	Year	Rush	Rec	Ret	Tot
John Riggins, Wash	1983	24	0	0	24
O.J.Simpson, Buf	1975	16	7	0	23
Jerry Rice, SF	1987	1	22	0	23
Gale Sayers, Chi	1966	14	6	2	22
Chuck Foreman, Min	1975	13	9	0	22
Jim Brown, Clev	1965	17	4	0	21
Joe Morris, NY Giants	1985	21	0	0	21
Lenny Moore, Balt	1964	16	3	1	20
Leroy Kelly, Clev	1968	16	4	0	20
Eric Dickerson, LA Rams	1983	18	2	0	20

Touchdowns Rushing

	Year	No
John Riggins, Washington	1983	24
Joe Morris, NY Giants	1985	21
Jim Taylor, Green Bay	1962	19
Earl Campbell, Houston	1979	19
Chuck Muncie, San Diego	1981	19
Eric Dickerson, LA Rams	1983	18
George Rogers, Washington	1986	18
Jim Brown, Cleveland	1958	17
Jim Brown, Cleveland	1965	17

Touchdowns Passing

	Year	No
Dan Marino, Miami	1984	48
Dan Marino, Miami	1986	44
George Blanda, Houston	1961	36
Y.A.Tittle, NY Giants	1963	36
Y.A.Tittle, NY Giants	1962	33
Dan Fouts, San Diego	1981	33
Johnny Unitas, Baltimore	1959	32
Sonny Jurgensen, Philadelphia	1961	32
Lynn Dickey, Green Bay	1983	32

Touchdowns Receiving

	Year	No
Jerry Rice, San Francisco	1987	22
Mark Clayton, Miami	1984	18
Don Hutson, Green Bay	1942	17
Elroy "Crazylegs" Hirsch, LA Rams	1951	17
Bill Groman, Houston	1961	17
Jerry Rice, San Francisco	1989	17
Art Powell, Oakland	1963	16
Jerry Rice, San Francisco	1986	15

Passing

Yards Gained	Year	Att	Cmp	Pct	Yards
Dan Marino, Mia	1984	564	362	64.2	5084
Dan Fouts, SD	1981	609	360	59.1	4802
Dan Marino, Mia	1986	623	378	60.7	4746
Dan Fouts, SD	1980	589	348	59.1	4715
Neil Lomax, St.L	1984	560	345	61.6	4614
Lynn Dickey, GB	1983	484	289	59.7	4458
Dan Marino, Mia	1988	606	354	58.4	4434
Bill Kenney, KC	1983	603	346	57.4	4348
Don Majkowski, GB . .	1989	599	353	58.9	4318
Jim Everett, LARams . .	1989	518	304	58.7	4310

Rushing

Yards Gained	Year	Att	Yards	Avg
Eric Dickerson, LA Rams	1984	379	2105	5.6
O.J.Simpson, Buf	1973	332	2003	6.0
Earl Campbell, Hou	1980	373	1934	5.2
Jim Brown, Clev	1963	291	1883	6.4
Walter Payton, Chi	1977	339	1852	5.5
Eric Dickerson, LA Rams	1986	404	1821	4.5
O.J.Simpson, Buf	1975	329	1817	5.5
Eric Dickerson, LA Rams . . .	1983	390	1808	4.6
Marcus Allen, LA Raiders . . .	1985	390	1759	4.6
Gerald Riggs, Atl	1985	397	1719	4.3

Receiving

Catches	Year	No	Yards
Art Monk, Wash	1984	106	1372
Charley Hennigan, Hou	1964	101	1546
Lionel Taylor, Den	1961	100	1176
Todd Christensen, LA Raiders	1986	95	1153
Johnny Morris, Chi	1964	93	1200
Al Toon, NY Jets	1988	93	1067
Lionel Taylor, Den	1960	92	1235
Todd Christensen, LA Raiders	1983	92	1247
Roger Craig, SF	1985	92	1016
Art Monk, Wash	1985	91	1226
J.T.Smith, St.L	1987	91	1117

All-Purpose Running

	Year	Run	Rec	Ret	Total
Lionel James, SD . . .	1985	516	1027	992	2535
Terry Metcalf, St.L . .	1975	816	378	1268	2462
Mack Herron, NE . .	1974	824	474	1146	2444
Gale Sayers, Chi . . .	1966	1231	447	762	2440
Timmy Brown, Phi . .	1963	841	487	1100	2428
Tim Brown, Raiders .	1988	50	725	1542	2317
Marcus Allen, Raid . .	1985	1759	555	−6	2308
Timmy Brown, Phi . .	1962	545	849	912	2306
Gale Sayers, Chi . . .	1965	867	507	898	2272
Eric Dickerson, Rams	1984	2105	139	15	2259
O.J.Simpson, Buf . . .	1975	1817	426	0	2243

Miscellaneous

Interceptions	Year	No
Dick "Night Train" Lane, Detroit	1952	14
Dan Sandifer, Washington	1948	13
Spec Sanders, NY Yanks	1950	13
Lester Hayes, Oakland	1980	13

Punt Return Avg (qualifiers)	Year	Avg
Herb Rich, Baltimore	1950	23.0
Jack Christiansen, Detroit	1952	21.5
Dick Christy, NY Titans	1961	21.3
Bob Hayes, Dallas	1968	20.8

Punting Avg (qualifiers)	Year	Avg
Sammy Baugh, Washington	1940	51.4
Yale Lary, Detroit	1963	48.9
Sammy Baugh, Washington	1941	48.7
Yale Lary, Detroit	1961	48.4
Sammy Baugh, Washington	1942	48.2

Kickoff Return Avg (qualifiers)	Year	Avg
Travis Williams, Green Bay	1967	41.1
Gale Sayers, Chicago	1967	37.7
Ollie Matson, Chicago Cardinals	1958	35.5
Jim Duncan, Baltimore	1970	35.4
Lynn Chandnois, Pittsburgh	1952	35.2

BEST GAMES

Scoring

Points

	Date	Pts
Ernie Nevers, Cards vs Bears	11/28/29	40
Dub Jones, Clev. vs Chi.Bears	11/25/51	36
Gale Sayers, Chi.Bears vs SF	12/12/65	36
Paul Hornung, GB vs Balt	10/8/61	33
Bob Shaw, Chi.Cards vs Balt.	10/2/50	30
Jim Brown, Clev. vs Balt.	11/1/59	30
Abner Haynes, Dal.Texans vs Oak. . .	11/26/61	30
Billy Cannon, Hou. vs NY Titans	12/10/61	30
Cookie Gilchrist, Buf. vs NY Jets	12/8/63	30
Kellen Winslow, SD vs Oak	11/22/81	30

Note: Nevers celebrated Thanksgiving, 1929, by scoring all the Cardinals' points on six rushing TDs and four PATs. The Cards beat Red Grange and the Bears, 40-6.

Field Goals

	Date	No
Jim Bakken, St.Louis vs Pittsburgh . . .	9/24/67	7
Rich Karlis, Minn. vs LA Rams	11/5/89	7

Eight players tied with 6 FGs each.

Note: Bakken was 7-for-9, Karlis 7-for-7.

Touchdowns Rushing

	Date	No
Ernie Nevers, Cards vs Bears	11/28/29	6
Dub Jones, Clev. vs Chi.Bears	11/25/51	6
Gale Sayers, Chi.Bears vs SF	12/12/65	6

Seven players tied with 5 TDs each.

Touchdowns Passing

	Date	No
Sid Luckman, Chi.Bears vs NY G . . .	11/14/43	7
Adrian Burk, Phi. vs Wash	10/17/54	7
George Blanda, Hou. vs NY Titans .	11/19/61	7
Y.A.Tittle, NY Giants vs Wash.	10/28/62	7
Joe Kapp, Min. vs Balt.	9/28/69	7

Touchdown Catches

	Date	No
Bob Shaw, Chi.Cards vs Balt.	10/2/50	5
Kellen Winslow, SD vs Oak.	11/22/81	5

NFL All-Time Individual Leaders (Cont.)

BEST GAMES

Passing

Yards Gained	Date	Yds
Norm Van Brocklin, LA vs NY Yanks	.9/28/51	554
Dan Marino, Mia. vs NY Jets	10/23/88	521
Phil Simms, NY Giants vs Cin.	10/13/85	513
Vince Ferragamo, LA Rams vs Chi.	.12/26/82	509
Y.A.Tittle, NY Giants vs Wash.	10/28/62	505

Completions	Date	No
Richard Todd, NY Jets vs SF	.9/21/80	42
Ken Anderson, Cinn vs SD	12/20/82	40
Phil Simms, NY Giants vs Cin.	10/13/85	40
Dan Marino, Mia. vs Buf.	11/16/86	39
Tommy Kramer, Min. vs Clev.	12/14/80	38
Joe Ferguson, Buf. vs Mia. (OT)	10/9/83	38

Receiving

Catches	Date	No
Tom Fears, LA Rams vs GB	12/3/50	18
Clark Gaines, NY Jets vs SF	9/21/80	17
Sonny Randle, St.L vs NY Giants	11/4/62	16
Rickey Young, Min. vs NE	12/16/79	15
William Andrews, Atl. vs Pit.	11/15/81	15
Kellen Winslow, SD vs GB	10/7/84	15
Steve Largent, Sea. vs Det.	10/18/87	15
Flipper Anderson, LA Rams vs NO	11/26/89	15

Yards Gained	Date	Yds
Flipper Anderson, LA Rams vs NO	.11/26/89	336
Stephone Paige, KC vs SD	12/22/85	309
Jim Benton, Cle. vs Det.	11/22/45	303
Cloyce Box, Det. vs Balt.	12/3/50	302
John Taylor, SF vs LA Rams	12/11/89	286

Rushing

Yards Gained	Date	Yds
Walter Payton, Chi. vs Min.	11/20/77	275
O.J.Simpson, Buf. vs Det.	11/25/76	273
O.J.Simpson, Buf. vs NE	9/16/73	250
Willie Ellison, LA Rams vs NO	12/5/71	247
Cookie Gilchrist, Buf. vs NY Jets	12/8/63	243

All-Purpose Running

	Date	Yds
Billy Cannon, Hou. vs NY Titans	.12/10/61	373
Lionel James, SD vs LA Raiders*	.11/10/85	345
Timmy Brown, Phi. vs St.L	12/16/62	341
Gale Sayers, Chi. vs Min	12/18/66	339
Gale Sayers, Chi. vs SF	12/12/65	336
*Overtime.		

LONGEST PLAYS

Run from Scrimmage (all for TDs)	Date	Yds
Tony Dorsett, Dal. vs Min.	1/3/83	99
Andy Uram, GB vs Chi.Cards	10/8/39	97
Bob Gage, Pit. vs Chi.Bears	12/4/49	97

Passing (all for TDs)	Date	Yds
Frank Filchock to Andy Farkas, Wash. vs Pit.	10/15/39	99
George Izo to Bobby Mitchell, Wash. vs Clev.	9/15/63	99
Karl Sweetan to Pat Studstill, Det. vs Balt.	10/16/66	99
Sonny Jurgensen to Gerry Allen, Wash. vs Chi.	9/15/68	99
Jim Plunkett to Cliff Branch, LA Raiders vs Wash.	10/2/83	99
Ron Jaworski to Mike Quick, Phi. vs Atl.	11/10/85	99

Field Goals	Date	Yds
Tom Dempsey, NO vs Det.	11/8/70	63
Steve Cox, Clev. vs Cin.	10/21/84	60
Tony Franklin, Phi. vs Dal.	11/12/79	59

Punts	Date	Yds
Steve O'Neal, NY Jets vs Den.	9/21/69	98
Joe Lintzenich, Bears vs Giants	10/16/31	94
Randall Cunningham, Phi. vs Giants	12/3/89	91
Don Chandler, GBay vs SF	10/10/65	90

Punt Returns (all for TDs)	Date	Yds
Gil LeFebvre, Cin. vs Bklyn	12/3/33	98
Charlie West, Min. vs Wash.	11/3/68	98
Dennis Morgan, Dal. vs St.L	10/13/74	98

Kickoff Returns (all for TDs)	Date	Yds
Al Carmichael, GB vs Bears	10/7/56	106
Noland Smith, KC vs Den.	12/17/67	106
Roy Green, St.L vs Dal.	10/21/79	106
Seven players tied with 105-yd returns each.		

Interception Returns (all for TDs)	Date	Yds
Vencie Glenn, San Diego vs Denver	.11/29/87	103
Four players tied with 102-yd returns each.		

All Star Games

NFL Pro Bowl

A postseason All-Star game between the new league champion and a team of professional all-stars was added to the NFL schedule in 1939. In the first game at Wrigley Field in Los Angeles, the NY Giants beat a team made up of players from NFL teams and two independent clubs in L.A. (the LA Bulldogs and Hollywood Stars). An all-NFL All-Star team provided the opposition over the next four seasons, but the game was cancelled in 1943.
The Pro Bowl was revived in 1951 as a contest between conference all-star teams: American vs National (1951–53), Eastern vs Western (1954–70), and AFC vs NFC (since 1971).

Date	Winner	Score	Loser	Site	Year	Winner	Players of the Game
1/15/39	NY Giants	13–10	All-Stars	Los Ang.	1951	Amer, 28–27	Otto Graham, Cleveland
1/14/40	Green Bay	16–7	All-Stars	Los Ang.	1952	Natl, 30–13	Dan Towler, LA Rams
12/29/40	Chi.Bears	28–14	All-Stars	Los Ang.	1953	Natl, 27–7	Don Doll, Detroit
1/4/42	Chi.Bears	35–24	All-Stars	New York	1954	East, 20–9	Chuck Bednarik, Phila.
12/27/42	All-Stars	17–14	Washington	Phila.	1955	West, 26–19	Billy Wilson, San Fran.
1943–50	No game				1956	East, 31–30	Ollie Matson, Chi.Cards

Year	Winner	Players of the Game
1957	West, 19–10	Bert Rechichar, Balt. & Ernie Stautner, Pitt.
1958	West, 26–7	Hugh McElhenny, San Fran. & Gene Brito, Washington
1959	East, 28–21	Frank Gifford, NY Giants & Doug Aikins, Chi.Bears
1960	West, 38–21	Johnny Unitas, Baltimore & Big Daddy Lipscomb, Balt.
1961	West, 35–31	Johnny Unitas, Baltimore & Sam Huff, NY Giants
1962	West, 31–30	Jim Brown, Cleveland & Henry Jordan, Green Bay
1963	East, 30–20	Jim Brown, Cleveland & Big Daddy Lipscomb, Pitt.
1964	West, 31–17	Johnny Unitas, Baltimore & Gino Marchetti, Balt.
1965	West, 34–14	Fran Tarkenton, Minnesota & Terry Barr, Detroit
1966	East, 36–7	Jim Brown, Cleveland & Dale Meinert, St.Louis
1967	East, 20–10	Gale Sayers, Chicago & Floyd Peters, Phila.
1968	West, 38–20	Gale Sayers, Chicago & Dave Robinson, Green Bay
1969	West, 10–7	Roman Gabriel, LA Rams & Merline Olsen, LA Rams

Year	Winner	Players of the Game
1970	West, 16–13	Gale Sayers, Chicago & George Andrie, Dallas
1971	NFC, 27–6	Mel Renfro, Dallas & Fred Carr, Green Bay
1972	AFC, 26–13	Jan Stenerud, KC & Willie Lanier, KC
1973	AFC, 33–28	O.J.Simpson, Buffalo
1974	AFC, 15–13	Garo Yepremian, Miami
1975	NFC, 17–10	James Harris, LA Rams
1976	NFC, 23–20	Billy Johnson, Houston
1977	AFC, 24–14	Mel Blount, Pittsburgh
1978	NFC, 14–13	Walter Payton, Chicago
1979	NFC, 13–7	Ahmad Rashad, Minnesota
1980	NFC, 37–27	Chuck Muncie, New Orleans
1981	NFC, 21–7	Eddie Murray, Detroit
1982	AFC, 16–13	Kellen Winslow, San Diego & Lee Roy Selmon, Tampa Bay
1983	NFC, 20–19	Dan Fouts, San Diego & John Jefferson, Green Bay
1984	NFC, 45–3	Joe Theismann, Washington
1985	AFC, 22–14	Mark Gastineau, NY Jets
1986	NFC, 28–24	Phil Simms, NY Giants
1987	AFC, 10–6	Reggie White, Philadelphia
1988	AFC, 15–6	Bruce Smith, Buffalo
1989	NFC, 34–3	Randall Cunningham, Phila.
1990	NFC, 27–21	Jerry Gray, LA Rams

Playing Sites (1951–89)—Memorial Coliseum in Los Angeles (1951–72); Texas Stadium in Irving, TX (1973); Arrowhead Stadium in Kansas City (1974); Orange Bowl in Miami (1975); Superdome in New Orleans (1976); Kingdome in Seattle (1977); Tampa Stadium in Tampa, FL (1978); Memorial Coliseum in Los Angeles (1979); and Aloha Stadium in Honolulu (since 1980).

AFL All-Star Game

The AFL did not play an All-Star after its first season (1960), but did stage a January post-season contest from 1962–70. All-Star teams from the Eastern and Western Divisions played each other every year but 1966, when AFL champion Buffalo met an All-Star team made up of the league's other eight clubs.

Year	Winner	Players of the Game
1962	West, 47–27	Cotton Davidson, Oakland
1963	West, 21–14	Curtis McClinton, Dallas & Earl Faison, S.Diego
1964	West, 27–24	Keith Lincoln, San Diego & Archie Matsos, Oak.
1965	West, 38–14	Keith Lincoln, San Diego & Willie Brown, Denver
1966	All-Stars def. Buf., 30–19	Joe Namath, NY Jets & Frank Buncom, S.Diego

Year	Winner	Players of the Game
1967	East, 30–23	Babe Parilli, Boston & Verlon Biggs, NY Jets
1968	East, 25–24	Namath/Don Maynard, Jets & Speedy Duncan, S.Diego
1969	West, 38–25	Len Dawson, Kansas City & George Webster, Hous.
1970	West, 26–3	John Hadl, San Diego

Since 1970: see NFC vs AFC.

Playing Sites (1962–70)—Balboa Stadium in San Diego (1962–64); Jeppesen Stadium in Houston (1965); Rice Stadium in Houston (1966); Oakland Coliseum (1967); Gator Bowl in Jacksonville, FL (1968–69); and Astrodome in Houston (1970).

Chicago College All-Star Game

On Aug.31, 1934, a year after sponsoring Major League Baseball's first All-Star Game, the Chicago Tribune and sports editor Arch Ward presented the first Chicago College All-Star Game at Soldier Field. A crowd of 79,432 turned out to see an all-star team of graduated college seniors battle the 1933 NFL champion Chicago Bears to a scoreless tie. The preseason game was played annually at Soldier Field until it was cancelled in 1977.

Year	Result
1934	Chi.Bears 0, All-Stars 0
1935	Chi.Bears 5, All-Stars 0
1936	Detroit 7, All-Stars 0
1937	Chi.Bears 6, Green Bay 0
1938	All-Stars 28, Washington 16
1939	NY Giants 9, All-Stars 0
1940	Green Bay 45, All-Stars 28
1941	Chi.Bears 37, All-Stars 13
1942	Chi.Bears 21, All-Stars 0
1943	All-Stars 27, Washington 7
1944	Chi.Bears 24, All-Stars 21
1945	Green Bay 19, All-Stars 7
1946	All-Stars 16, LA Rams 0
1947	All-Stars 16, Chi.Bears 0
1948	Chi.Cards 28, All-Stars 0

Year	Result
1949	Philadelphia 38, All-Stars 0
1950	All-Stars 17, Philadelphia 7
1951	Cleveland 33, All-Stars 0
1952	LA Rams 10, All-Stars 7
1953	Detroit 24, All-Stars 10
1954	Detroit 31, All-Stars 6
1955	All-Stars 30, Cleveland 27
1956	Cleveland 26, All-Stars 0
1957	NY Giants 22, All-Stars 12
1958	All-Stars 35, Detroit 19
1959	Baltimore 29, All-Stars 0
1960	Baltimore 32, All-Stars 7
1961	Philadelphia 28, All-Stars 14
1962	Green Bay 42, All-Stars 20
1963	All-Stars 20, Green Bay 17

Year	Result
1964	Chi.Bears 28, All-Stars 17
1965	Cleveland 24, All-Stars 16
1966	Green Bay 38, All-Stars 0
1967	Green Bay 27, All-Stars 0
1968	Green Bay 34, All-Stars 17
1969	NY Jets 26, All-Stars 24
1970	Kansas City 24, All-Stars 3
1971	Baltimore 24, All-Stars 17
1972	Dallas 20, All-Stars 7
1973	Miami 14, All-Stars 3
1974	No Game (NFLPA Strike)
1975	Pittsburgh 21, All-Stars 14
1976	Pittsburgh 24, All-Stars 0*

*Downpour flooded field, game called with 1:22 left in 3rd quarter.

All-Time Winningest NFL Coaches

Minimum of 100 NFL victories through 1989 season. Regular season and playoffs included. Active coaches in **bold type**.

Top Winning Percentages

	Yrs	W	L	T	Pct	Playoff W-L
Vince Lombardi	10	106	36	6	.736	10-2
John Madden	10	112	39	7	.731	9-7
George Allen	12	120	54	5	.684	4-7
Don Shula	27	287	132	6	.682	18-13
Joe Gibbs	9	102	48	0	.680	11-3
George Halas	40	325	151	31	.672	6-3
Curly Lambeau	33	229	134	22	.623	3-2
Bill Walsh	10	102	64	1	.614	10-4
Paul Brown	21	170	109	6	.607	4-9
Bud Grant	18	168	109	5	.605	10-13
Tom Landry	29	271	180	6	.600	21-18
Chuck Knox	17	162	109	1	.597	7-11
Steve Owen	23	153	108	17	.581	2-8
Buddy Parker	15	107	76	9	.581	3-1
Chuck Noll	21	193	140	1	.579	16-8
Hank Stram	17	136	100	10	.573	5-3
Don Coryell	14	114	89	1	.561	3-6
Sid Gillman	18	123	104	7	.541	1-5
Weeb Ewbank	20	134	130	7	.507	4-1

Note: The NFL does not recognize records from the All-American Football Conference (1946-49). If it did, Brown (52-4-3 in four AAFC seasons) would rank 6th (between Halas and Lambeau) with the following stats: 25 Yrs; 222 Wins; 113 Losses; 9 Ties; .658 Pct; and a 9-9 playoff record.

Most Victories

	Wins		Wins
George Halas	325	Hank Stram	136
Don Shula	287	Weeb Ewbank	134
Tom Landry	271	Sid Gillman	123
Curly Lambeau	229	George Allen	120
Chuck Noll	193	Don Coryell	114
Paul Brown	170	John Madden	112
Bud Grant	168	Buddy Parker	107
Chuck Knox	162	Vince Lombardi	106
Steve Owen	153	**Joe Gibbs**	102
		Bill Walsh	102

Note: The following coaches had the following records in the often-forgotten Playoff Bowl: Lombardi (1-1), Shula (2-0), Allen (2-0), Brown (0-1), Grant (0-1) and Landry (1-2). The Playoff Bowl was contested by NFL conference runners-up from the 1960 season through 1969.

Active Coaches' Victories

Through 1989 season, including playoffs.

	Yrs	W	L	T	Pct
Don Shula, Miami	27	**287**	132	6	.682
Chuck Noll, Pittsburgh	21	**193**	140	1	.579
Chuck Knox, Seattle	17	**162**	109	1	.597
Joe Gibbs, Washington	9	**102**	48	0	.680
Dan Reeves, Denver	9	91	55	1	.622
Mike Ditka, Chicago	8	84	45	0	.651
John Robinson, LA Rams	7	71	50	0	.587
Bill Parcells, NY Giants	7	69	49	1	.580
Marv Levy, Buffalo	9	62	68	0	.477
Marty Schottenheimer, KC	6	54	38	1	.586
Sam Wyche, Cincinnati	6	51	47	0	.520
Ron Meyer, Indianapolis	7	47	38	0	.553
Jack Pardee, Houston	6	44	47	0	.484
Jerry Burns, Minnesota	4	41	28	0	.594
Jim Mora, New Orleans	4	38	26	0	.594
Ray Perkins, Tampa Bay	7	38	68	0	.358
Jerry Glanville, Atlanta	5	35	35	0	.500
Buddy Ryan, Philadelphia	4	33	31	1	.515
Dan Henning, San Diego	5	28	51	1	.356
George Seifert, San Fran.	1	17	2	0	.895
Lindy Infante, Green Bay	2	14	18	0	.438
Bud Carson, Cleveland	1	10	7	1	.583
Wayne Fontes, Detroit	2	9	12	0	.429
Art Shell, LA Raiders	1	7	5	0	.583
Jimmy Johnson, Dallas	1	1	15	0	.063
Joe Bugel, Phoenix	0	0	0	0	.000
Bruce Coslet, NY Jets	0	0	0	0	.000
Rod Rust, New England	0	0	0	0	.000

Where They Coached

Allen—LA Rams (1966-70), Washington (1971-77); **Brown**—Cleveland (1950-62), Cincinnati (1968-75); **Coryell**—St.Louis (1973-77), San Diego (1978-86); **Ewbank**—Baltimore (1954-62); NY Jets (1963-73); **Gibbs**—Washington (1981-); **Gillman**—LA Rams (1955-59), LA-SD Chargers (1960-69), Houston (1973-74). **Grant**—Minnesota (1967-83,85); **Halas**—Chicago Bears (1920-29,33-42,46-55,58-67); **Knox**—LA Rams (1973-77), Buffalo (1978-82), Seattle (1983-); **Lambeau**—Green Bay (1921-49), Chicago Cards (1950-51), Washington (1952-53); **Landry**—Dallas (1960-88); **Lombardi**—Green Bay (1959-67), Washington (1969). **Madden**—Oakland (1969-78); **Noll**—Pittsburgh (1969-); **Owen**—NY Giants (1931-53); **Parker**—Chicago Cards (1949), Detroit (1951-56), Pittsburgh (1957-64); **Shula**—Baltimore (1963-69), Miami (1970-); **Stram**—Dallas-Kansas City (1960-74), New Orleans (1976-77); **Walsh**—San Francisco (1979-88).

Annual Award Winners
NFL-NFC Coach of the Year

Presented by UPI to the top coach in the NFL (1955-69) and NFC (since 1970). Records indicate how much coach's team improved over one season.

Year		Improvement	Year		Improvement
1955	Joe Kuharich, Washington	3-9 to 8-4	1963	George Halas, Chicago	9-5 to 11-1-2
1956	Buddy Parker, Detroit	3-9 to 9-3	1964	Don Shula, Baltimore	8-6 to 12-2
1957	Paul Brown, Cleveland	5-7 to 9-2-1	1965	George Halas, Chicago	5-9 to 9-5
1958	Weeb Ewbank, Baltimore	7-5 to 9-3	1966	Tom Landry, Dallas	7-7 to 10-3-1
1959	Vince Lombardi, Green Bay	1-10-1 to 7-5	1967	George Allen, LA Rams	8-6 to 11-1-2
1960	Buck Shaw, Philadelphia	7-5 to 10-2	1968	Don Shula, Baltimore	11-1-2 to 13-1
1961	Allie Sherman, NY Giants	6-4-2 to 10-3-1	1969	Bud Grant, Minnesota	8-6 to 12-2
1962	Allie Sherman, NY Giants	10-3-1 to 12-2	1970	Alex Webster, NY Giants	6-8 to 9-5

NFL-NFC Coach of the Year

Year		Improvement	Year		Improvement
1971	George Allen, Washington	6-8 to 9-4-1	1980	Leeman Bennett, Atlanta	6-10 to 12-4
1972	Dan Devine, Green Bay	4-8-2 to 10-4	1981	Bill Walsh, San Francisco	6-10 to 13-3
1973	Chuck Knox, LA Rams	6-7-1 to 12-2	1982	Joe Gibbs, Washington	8-8 to 8-1
1974	Don Coryell, St.Louis	4-9-1 to 10-4	1983	John Robinson, LA Rams	2-7 to 9-7
1975	Tom Landry, Dallas	8-6 to 10-4	1984	Bill Walsh, San Francisco	10-6 to 15-1
1976	Jack Pardee, Chicago	4-10 to 7-7	1985	Mike Ditka, Chicago	10-6 to 15-1
1977	Leeman Bennett, Atlanta	4-10 to 7-7	1986	Bill Parcells, NY Giants	10-6 to 14-2
1978	Dick Vermeil, Philadelphia	5-9 to 9-7	1987	Jim Mora, New Orleans	7-9 to 12-3
1979	Jack Pardee, Washington	8-8 to 10-6	1988	Mike Ditka, Chicago	11-4 to 12-4
			1989	Lindy Infante, Green Bay	4-12 to 10-6

AFL-AFC Coach of the Year

Presented by UPI to the top coach in the AFL (1960-69) and AFC (since 1970). Records indicate how much coach's team improved over one season.

Year		Improvement	Year		Improvement
1960	Lou Rymkus, Houston	10-4	1975	Ted Marchibroda, Baltimore	2-12 to 10-4
1961	Wally Lemm, Houston	10-4 to 10-3-1	1976	Chuck Fairbanks, N.England	3-11 to 11-3
1962	Jack Faulkner, Denver	3-11 to 7-7	1977	Red Miller, Denver	9-5 to 12-2
1963	Al Davis, Oakland	1-13 to 10-4	1978	Walt Michaels, NY Jets	3-11 to 8-8
1964	Lou Saban, Buffalo	7-6-1 to 12-2	1979	Sam Rutigliano, Cleveland	8-8 to 9-7
1965	Lou Saban, Buffalo	12-2 to 10-3-1	1980	Sam Rutigliano, Cleveland	9-7 to 11-5
1966	Mike Holovak, Boston	4-8-2 to 8-4-2	1981	Forrest Gregg, Cincinnati	6-10 to 12-4
1967	John Rauch, Oakland	8-5-1 to 13-1	1982	Tom Flores, LA Raiders	7-9 to 8-1
1968	Hank Stram, Kansas City	9-5 to 12-2	1983	Chuck Knox, Seattle	4-5 to 9-7
1969	Paul Brown, Cincinnati	3-11 to 4-9-1	1984	Chuck Knox, Seattle	9-7 to 12-4
1970	Don Shula, Miami	3-10-1 to 10-4	1985	Raymond Berry, New England	9-7 to 11-5
1971	Don Shula, Miami	10-4 to 10-3-1	1986	Marty Schottenheimer, Cleve	8-8 to 12-4
1972	Chuck Noll, Pittsburgh	6-8 to 11-3	1987	Ron Meyer, Indianapolis	3-13 to 9-6
1973	John Ralston, Denver	5-9 to 7-5-2	1988	Marv Levy, Buffalo	7-8 to 12-4
1974	Sid Gillman, Houston	1-13 to 7-7	1989	Dan Reeves, Denver	8-8 to 11-5

NFL Player of the Year

Unlike the other major pro team sports, the NFL no longer sanctions a Most Valuable Player award. The league gave out the Joe F.Carr Trophy (Carr was NFL president from 1921-39) for nine years but discontinued it in 1947. Since then, four principal MVP awards have been given out: UPI (1953-69), AP (since 1957), the Maxwell Club of Philadelphia's Bert Bell Trophy (since 1959) and the Professional Football Writers Association (since 1976). UPI switched to AFC and NFC Player of the Year awards in 1970.

Year		Awards	Year		Awards
1938	Mel Hein, NY Giants, C	Carr	1965	Jim Brown, Cleveland, FB	UPI-AP
1939	Parker Hall, Cleveland Rams, HB	Carr		Pete Retzlaff, Philadelphia, TE	Bell
1940	Ace Parker, Brooklyn, HB	Carr	1966	Bart Starr, Green Bay, QB	UPI-AP
1941	Don Hutson, Green Bay, E	Carr		Don Meredith, Dallas, QB	Bell
1942	Don Hutson, Green Bay, E	Carr	1967	Johnny Unitas, Baltimore, QB	UPI-AP-Bell
1943	Sid Luckman, Chicago Bears, QB	Carr	1968	Earl Morrall, Baltimore, QB	UPI-AP
1944	Frank Sinkwich, Detroit, HB	Carr		Leroy Kelly, Cleveland, RB	Bell
1945	Bob Waterfield, Cleveland Rams, QB	Carr	1969	Roman Gabriel, LA Rams, QB	UPI-AP-Bell
1946	Bill Dudley, Pittsburgh, HB	Carr	1970	John Brodie, San Francisco, QB	AP
1947-52 No MVP chosen				George Blanda, Oakland, QB-K	Bell
1953	Otto Graham, Cleveland, QB	UPI	1971	Alan Page, Minnesota, DT	AP
1954	Joe Perry, San Francisco, FB	UPI		Roger Staubach, Dallas, QB	Bell
1955	Otto Graham, Cleveland, QB	UPI	1972	Larry Brown, Washington, RB	AP-Bell
1956	Frank Gifford, NY Giants, HB	UPI	1973	O.J.Simpson, Buffalo, RB	AP-Bell
1957	Y.A.Tittle, San Francisco, QB	UPI	1974	Ken Stabler, Oakland, QB	AP
	Jim Brown, Cleveland, FB	AP		Merlin Olsen, LA Rams, DT	Bell
1958	Jim Brown, Cleveland, FB	UPI	1975	Fran Tarkenton, Minnesota, QB	AP-Bell
	Gino Marchetti, Baltimore, DE	AP	1976	Bert Jones, Baltimore, QB	AP-PFWA
1959	Johnny Unitas, Baltimore, QB	UPI-Bell		Ken Stabler, Oakland, QB	Bell
	Charley Conerly, NY Giants, QB	AP	1977	Walter Payton, Chicago, RB	AP-PFWA
1960	Norm Van Brocklin, Phi., QB	UPI-AP(tie)-Bell		Bob Griese, Miami, QB	Bell
	Joe Schmidt, Detroit, LB	AP(tie)	1978	Terry Bradshaw, Pittsburgh, QB	AP-Bell
1961	Paul Hornung, Green Bay, HB	UPI-AP-Bell		Earl Campbell, Houston, RB	PFWA
1962	Y.A.Tittle, NY Giants, QB	UPI	1979	Earl Campbell, Houston, RB	AP-Bell-PFWA
	Jim Taylor, Green Bay, FB	AP	1980	Brian Sipe, Cleveland, QB	AP-PFWA
	Andy Robustelli, NY Giants, DE	Bell		Ron Jaworski, Philadelphia, QB	Bell
1963	Jim Brown, Cleveland, FB	UPI-Bell	1981	Ken Anderson, Cinn, QB	AP-Bell-PFWA
	Y.A.Tittle, NY Giants, QB	AP	1982	Mark Moseley, Washington, K	AP
1964	Johnny Unitas, Baltimore, QB	UPI-AP-Bell		Joe Theismann, Washington, QB	Bell
				Dan Fouts, San Diego, QB	PFWA

NFL Player of the Year (Cont.)

Year		Awards	Year		Awards
1983	Joe Theismann, Washington, QB	AP-PFWA	1987	John Elway, Denver, QB	AP
	John Riggins, Washington, RB	Bell		Jerry Rice, San Francisco, WR	Bell-PFWA
1984	Dan Marino, Miami, QB	AP-Bell-PFWA	1988	Boomer Esiason, Cinn, QB	AP-PFWA
1985	Marcus Allen, LA Raiders, RB	AP-PFWA		Randall Cunningham, Phila, QB	Bell
	Walter Payton, Chicago, RB	Bell	1989	Joe Montana, San Fran., QB	AP-Bell-PFWA
1986	Lawrence Taylor, Giants, LB	AP-Bell-PFWA			

NFC Player of the Year

Given out by UPI since 1970. Offensive and defensive players have been honored since 1983. Rookie winners are noted in **bold type**.

Year		Position	Year		Position
1970	John Brodie, San Francisco	QB	1983	**Off—Eric Dickerson,** LA Rams	RB
1971	Alan Page, Minnesota	DT		Def—Lionel Taylor, NY Giants	LB
1972	Larry Brown, Washington	RB	1984	**Off—Eric Dickerson,** LA Rams	RB
1973	John Hadl, LA Rams	QB		Def—Mike Singletary, Chicago	LB
1974	Jim Hart, St.Louis	QB	1985	Off—Walter Payton, Chicago	RB
1975	Fran Tarkenton, Minnesota	QB		Def—Mike Singletary, Chicago	LB
1976	Chuck Foreman, Minnesota	RB	1986	Off—Eric Dickerson, LA Rams	RB
1977	Walter Payton, Chicago	RB		Def—Lionel Taylor, NY Giants	LB
1978	Archie Manning, New Orleans	QB	1987	**Off—Jerry Rice,** San Fran	WR
1979	**Ottis Anderson,** St.Louis	RB		Def—Reggie White, Phila	DE
1980	Ron Jaworski, Philadelphia	QB	1988	Off—Roger Craig, San Fran	RB
1981	Tony Dorsett, Dallas	RB		Def—Mike Singletary, Chicago	LB
1982	Mark Moseley, Wshington	K	1989	Off—Joe Montana, San Fran	QB
				Def—Keith Millard, Minnesota	DT

AFL-AFC Player of the Year

Presented by UPI to the top player in the AFL (1960-69) and AFC (since 1970). Offensive and defensive players have been honored since 1983. Rookie winners are noted in **bold type**.

Year		Position	Year		Position
1960	**Abner Haynes,** Dallas Texans	HB	1980	Brian Sipe, Cleveland	QB
1961	George Blanda, Houston	QB	1981	Ken Anderson, Cincinnati	QB
1962	Cookie Gilchrist, Buffalo	FB	1982	Dan Fouts, San Diego	QB
1963	Lance Alworth, San Diego	FL	1983	**Off—Curt Warner,** Seattle	RB
1964	Gino Cappelletti, Boston	FL-K		Def—Rod Martin, LA Raiders	LB
1965	Paul Lowe, San Diego	HB	1984	Off—Dan Marino, Miami	QB
1966	Jim Nance, Boston	FB		Def—Mark Gastineau, NY Jets	DE
1967	Daryl Lamonica, Oakland	QB	1985	Off—Marcus Allen, LA Raiders	RB
1968	Joe Namath, NY Jets	QB		**Def—Andre Tippett,** New Eng	LB
1969	Daryl Lamonica, Oakland	QB	1986	Off—Curt Warner, Seattle	RB
1970	George Blanda, Oakland	QB-K		Def—Rulon Jones, Denver	DE
1971	Otis Taylor, Kansas City	WR	1987	Off—John Elway, Denver	QB
1972	O.J.Simpson, Buffalo	RB		**Def—Bruce Smith,** Buffalo	DE
1973	O.J.Simpson, Buffalo	RB	1988	Off—Boomer Esiason, Cinn	QB
1974	Ken Stabler, Oakland	QB		Def—Bruce Smith, Buffalo	DE
1975	O.J.Simpson, Buffalo	RB		& Cornelius Bennett, Buff	LB
1976	Bert Jones, Baltimore	QB	1989	Off—Christian Okoye, KC	RB
1977	Craig Morton, Denver	QB		Def—Michael Dean Perry, Clev	NT
1978	**Earl Campbell,** Houston	RB			
1979	Dan Fouts, San Diego	QB			

NFL-NFC Rookie of the Year

Presented by UPI to the top rookie in the NFL (1955-69) and NFC (since 1970).

Year		Position	Year		Position
1955	Alan Ameche, Baltimore	FB	1968	Earl McCullough, Detroit	FL
1956	Lenny Moore, Baltimore	HB	1969	Calvin Hill, Dallas	RB
1957	Jim Brown, Cleveland	FB	1970	Bruce Taylor, San Francisco	DB
1958	Jimmy Orr, Baltimore	FL	1971	John Brockington, Green Bay	RB
1959	Boyd Dowler, Green Bay	FL	1972	Chester Marcol, Green Bay	K
1960	Gail Cogdill, Detroit	FL	1973	Charle Young, Philadelphia	TE
1961	Mike Ditka, Chicago Bears	TE	1974	John Hicks, NY Giants	OG
1962	Ronnie Bull, Chicago Bears	FB	1975	Mike Thomas, Washington	RB
1963	Paul Flatley, Minnesota	FL	1976	Sammy White, Minnesota	WR
1964	Charley Taylor, Washington	HB	1977	Tony Dorsett, Dallas	RB
1965	Gale Sayers, Chicago	HB	1978	Bubba Baker, Detroit	DE
1966	Johnny Roland, St.Louis	HB	1979	Ottis Anderson, St.Louis	RB
1967	Mel Farr, Detroit	RB	1980	Billy Sims, Detroit	RB

NFL-NFC Rookie of the Year

Year		Position	Year		Position
1981	George Rogers, New Orleans	RB	1986	Reuben Mayes, New Orleans	RB
1982	Jim McMahon, Chicago	QB	1987	Robert Awalt, St.Louis	TE
1983	Eric Dickerson, LA Rams	RB	1988	Keith Jackson, Philadelphia	TE
1984	Paul McFadden, Philadelphia	PK	1989	Barry Sanders, Detroit	RB
1985	Jerry Rice, San Francisco	WR			

AFL-AFC Rookie of the Year

Presented by UPI to the top rookie in the AFL (1960-69) and AFC (since 1970).

Year		Position	Year		Position
1960	Abner Haynes, Dallas Texans	HB	1975	Robert Brazile, Houston	LB
1961	Earl Faison, San Diego	DE	1976	Mike Haynes, New England	DB
1962	Curtis McClinton, Dallas Texans	FB	1977	A.J.Duhe, Miami	DE
1963	Billy Joe, Denver	FB	1978	Earl Campbell, Houston	RB
1964	Matt Snell, NY Jets	FB	1979	Jerry Butler, Buffalo	WR
1965	Joe Namath, NY Jets	QB			
1966	Bobby Burnett, Buffalo	HB	1980	Joe Cribbs, Buffalo	RB
1967	George Webster, Houston	LB	1981	Joe Delaney, Kansas City	RB
1968	Paul Robinson, Cincinnati	RB	1982	Marcus Allen, LA Raiders	RB
1969	Greg Cook, Cincinnati	QB	1983	Curt Warner, Seattle	RB
			1984	Louis Lipps, Pittsburgh	WR
1970	Dennis Shaw, Buffalo	QB	1985	Kevin Mack, Cleveland	RB
1971	Jim Plunkett, New England	QB	1986	Leslie O'Neal, San Diego	DE
1972	Franco Harris, Pittsburgh	RB	1987	Shane Conlan, Buffalo	LB
1973	Boobie Clark, Cincinnati	RB	1988	John Stephens, New England	RB
1974	Don Woods, San Diego	RB	1989	Derrick Thomas, Kansas City	LB

Number One Draft Choices, 1936-90

In an effort to blunt the dominance of the Chicago Bears and New York Giants in the 1930s and distribute talent more evenly throughout the league, the NFL established the college draft in 1936.

The first player chosen in the first draft was Jay Berwanger, the first Heisman Trophy winner as college football's outstanding player. In all, 16 Heisman winners have also been a No.1 draft choice. They are noted in **bold type.**

The American Football League (formed in 1960) held its own draft from 1961-66 before agreeing to merge with the NFL.

Year	Team		Year	Team	
1936	Philadelphia	**Jay Berwanger**, HB, Chicago	1964	NFL San Fran	Dave Parks, E, Texas Tech
1937	Philadelphia	Sam Francis, FB, Nebraska		AFL Boston	Jack Concannon, QB, B.C.
1938	Cleve.Rams	Corbett Davis, FB, Indiana	1965	NFL Giants	Tucker Frederickson, HB, Auburn
1939	Chi.Cards	Ki Aldrich, C, TCU		AFL Houston	Lawrence Elkins, E, Baylor
1940	Chi.Cards	George Cafego, HB, Tennessee	1966	NFL Atlanta	Tommy Nobis, LB, Texas
1941	Chi.Bears	**Tom Harmon**, HB, Michigan		AFL Miami	Jim Grabowski, FB, Illinois
1942	Pittsburgh	Bill Dudley, HB, Viginia	1967	Baltimore	Bubba Smith, DT, Michigan St.
1943	Detroit	**Frank Sinkwich**, HB, Georgia	1968	Minnesota	Ron Yary, T, Southern Cal
1944	Boston Yanks	**Angelo Bertelli**, QB, N.Dame	1969	Buffalo (AFL)	**O.J.Simpson**, RB, Southern Cal
1945	Chi.Cards	Charley Trippi, HB, Georgia			
1946	Boston Yanks	Frank Dancewicz, QB, N.Dame	1970	Pittsburgh	Terry Bradshaw, QB, La.Tech
1947	Chi.Bears	Bob Fenimore, HB, Okla. A&M	1971	N.England	**Jim Plunkett**, QB, Stanford
1948	Washington	Harry Gilmer, QB, Alabama	1972	Buffalo	Walt Patulski, DE, Notre Dame
1949	Philadelphia	Chuck Bednarik, C, Penn	1973	Houston	John Matuszak, DE, Tampa
			1974	Dallas	Ed "Too Tall" Jones, Tenn.St.
1950	Detroit	**Leon Hart**, E, Notre Dame	1975	Atlanta	Steve Bartkowski, QB, Calif.
1951	NY Giants	Kyle Rote, HB, SMU	1976	Tampa Bay	Lee Roy Selmon, DE, Oklahoma
1952	LA Rams	Bill Wade, QB, Vanderbilt	1977	Tampa Bay	Ricky Bell, RB, Southern Cal
1953	San Fran.	Harry Babcock, E, Georgia	1978	Houston	**Earl Campbell**, RB, Texas
1954	Cleveland	Bobby Garrett, QB, Stanford	1979	Buffalo	Tom Cousineau, LB, Ohio St.
1955	Baltimore	George Shaw, QB, Oregon			
1956	Pittsburgh	Gary Glick, DB, Colo. A&M	1980	Detroit	**Billy Sims**, RB, Oklahoma
1957	Green Bay	**Paul Hornung**, QB, N.Dame	1981	New Orleans	**George Rogers**, RB, S.Carolina
1958	Chi.Cards	King Hill, QB, Rice	1982	New England	Kenneth Sims, DT, Texas
1959	Green Bay	Randy Duncan, QB, Iowa	1983	Baltimore	John Elway, QB, Stanford
			1984	New England	Irving Fryar, WR, Nebraska
1960	NFL LA Rams	**Billy Cannon**, HB, LSU	1985	Buffalo	Bruce Smith, DE, Va.Tech
	AFL No choice—		1986	Tampa Bay	**Bo Jackson**, RB, Auburn
1961	NFL Minn.	Tommy Mason, HB, Tulane	1987	Tampa Bay	**Vinny Testaverde**, QB, Miami,FL
	AFL Buffalo	Ken Rice, G, Auburn			
1962	NFL Wash.	**Ernie Davis**, HB, Syracuse	1988	Atlanta	Aundray Bruce, LB, Auburn
	AFL Oakland	Roman Gabriel, QB, N.C.State	1989	Dallas	Troy Aikman, QB, UCLA
1963	NFL LA RAms	**Terry Backer**, QB, Oregon St.	1990	Indianapolis	Jeff George, QB, Illinois
	AFL Kan.City	Buck Buchanan, DT, Grambling			

Canadian Football League
Grey Cup Champions, 1909–89

Earl Grey, the Governor-General of Canada (1904–11) donated a trophy in 1909 for the Rugby Football Championship of Canada. The trophy, which later became known as the Grey Cup, was originally open to competition for teams registered with the Canada Rugby Union. Since 1954, the Cup has gone to the champion of the Canadian Football League (CFL).

In 1940, the Grey Cup winner was determined in a two-game, total points format that was discontinued in 1941.

Year	Winner	Score	Loser
1909	Univ.of Toronto	26–6	Toronto Parkdale
1910	Univ.of Toronto	16–7	Hamilton Tigers
1911	Univ.of Toronto	14–7	Toronto Argonauts
1912	Hamilton Alerts	11–4	Toronto Argonauts
1913	Hamilton Tigers	44–2	Toronto Parkdale
1914	Toronto Argonauts	14–2	Univ.of Toronto
1915	Hamilton Tigers	13–7	Toronto Rowing
1916	No Game (WW I)		
1917	No Game (WW I)		
1918	No Game (WW I)		
1919	No Game (WW I)		
1920	Univ.of Toronto	16–3	Toronto Argonauts
1921	Toronto Argonauts	23–0	Edmonton Eskimos
1922	Queen's University	13–1	Edmonton Elks
1923	Queen's University	54–0	Regina Roughriders
1924	Queen's University	11–3	Tor.Balmy Beach
1925	Ottawa Senators	24–1	Winnipeg Tigers
1926	Ottawa Senators	10–7	Univ.of Toronto
1927	Tor.Balmy Beach	9–6	Hamilton Tigers
1928	Hamilton Tigers	30–0	Regina Roughriders
1929	Hamilton Tigers	14–3	Regina Roughriders
1930	Tor.Balmy Beach	11–6	Regina Roughriders
1931	Montreal AAA	22–0	Regina Roughriders
1932	Hamilton Tigers	25–6	Regina Roughriders
1933	Toronto Argonauts	4–3	Sarnia Imperials
1934	Sarnia Imperials	20–12	Regina Roughriders
1935	Winn.Winnipegs	18–12	Hamilton Tigers
1936	Sarnia Imperials	26–20	Ot'wa Rough Riders
1937	Toronto Argonauts	4–3	Winn.Blue Bombers
1938	Toronto Argonauts	30–7	Winn.Blue Bombers
1939	Winn.Blue Bombers	8–7	Ot'wa Rough Riders
1940	Ot'wa Rough Riders	8–2	Tor.Balmy Beach
	Ot'wa Rough Riders	12–5	Tor.Balmy Beach
1941	Winn.Blue Bombers	18–16	Ot'wa Rough Riders
1942	Toronto RACF	8–5	Winnipeg RACF
1943	Hamilton Wildcats	23–14	Winnipeg RACF
1944	Montreal HMCS	7–6	Hamilton Wildcats
1945	Toronto Argonauts	35–0	Winn.Blue Bombers
1946	Toronto Argonauts	28–6	Winn.Blue Bombers
1947	Toronto Argonauts	10–9	Winn.Blue Bombers
1948	Calg. Stampeders	12–7	Ot'wa Rough Riders
1949	Montreal Alouettes	28–15	Calg. Stampeders

Year	Winner	Score	Loser
1950	Toronto Argonauts	13–0	Winn.Blue Bombers
1951	Ot'wa Rough Riders	21–14	Saskatchewan
1952	Toronto Argonauts	21–11	Edmonton Eskimos
1953	Hamilton Tiger Cats	12–6	Winn.Blue Bombers

*The first Rough Riders vs Roughriders Grey Cup final. Regina Roughriders became Saskatchewan Roughriders in 1946.

Year	Grey Cup Game (CFL)	Winning Coach
1954	Edmonton 26, Montreal 25	Pop Ivy
1955	Edmonton 34, Montreal 19	Pop Ivy
1956	Edmonton 50, Montreal 27	Pop Ivy
1957	Hamilton 32, Winnipeg 7	Jim Trimble
1958	Winnipeg 35, Hamilton 28	Bud Grant
1959	Winnipeg 21, Hamilton 7	Bud Grant
1960	Ottawa 16, Edmonton 6	Frank Clair
1961	Winn. 21, Hamilton 14 (OT)	Bud Grant
1962	Winnipeg 28, Hamilton 27	Bud Grant
1963	Hamilton 21, BC Lions 10	Ralph Sazio
1964	BC Lions 34, Hamilton 24	Dave Skrien
1965	Hamilton 22, Winnipeg 16	Ralph Sazio
1966	Saskatchewan 29, Ottawa 14	Eagle Keys
1967	Hamilton 24, Saskat. 1	Ralph Sazio
1968	Ottawa 24, Calgary 21	Frank Clair
1969	Ottawa 29, Saskatchewan 11	Frank Clair
1970	Montreal 23, Calgary 10	Sam Etcheverry
1971	Calgary 14, Toronto 11	Jim Duncan
1972	Hamilton 13, Saskat. 10	Jerry Williams
1973	Ottawa 22, Edmonton 18	Jack Gotta
1974	Montreal 20, Edmonton 7	Marv Levy
1975	Edmonton 9, Montreal 8	Ray Jauch
1976	Ottawa 23, Saskatchewan 20	George Brancato
1977	Montreal 41, Edmonton	Marv Levy
1978	Edmonton 20, Montreal 13	Hugh Campbell
1979	Edmonton 17, Montreal 9	Hugh Campbell
1980	Edmonton 48, Hamilton 10	Hugh Campbell
1981	Edmonton 26, Ottawa 23	Hugh Campbell
1982	Edmonton 32, Toronto 16	Hugh Campbell
1983	Toronto 18, B.C.Lions 17	Bob O'Billovich
1984	Winnipeg 47, Hamilton 17	Cal Murphy
1985	BC Lions 37, Hamilton 24	Don Matthews
1986	Hamilton 39, Edmonton 15	Al Bruno
1987	Edmonton 38, Toronto 36	Joe Faragalli
1988	Winnipeg 22, BC Lions 21	Mike Riley
1989	**Saskatch. 43, Hamilton 40**	**John Gregory**

CFL Player of the Year
CFL regular season Player of the Year from 1953–89.

Year	Player of the Year
1953	Billy Vessels, Edm., RB
1954	Sam Etcheverry, Mon., RB
1955	Pat Abbruzzi, Mon., RB
1956	Hal Patterson, Mon., E-DB
1957	Jackie Parker, Edm., RB
1958	Jackie Parker, Edm., QB
1959	Johnny Bright, Edm., RB
1960	Jackie Parker, Edm., QB
1961	Bernie Faloney, Ham., QB
1962	George Dixon, Mon., RB
1963	Russ Jackson, Ott., QB
1964	Lovell Coleman, Calg., RB
1965	George Reed, Sask., RB

Year	Player of the Year
1966	Russ Jackson, Ott., QB
1967	Peter Liske, Calg., QB
1968	Bill Symons, Tor., RB
1969	Russ Jackson, Ott., QB
1970	Ron Lancaster, Sask., QB
1971	Don Jonas, Win., QB
1972	Garney Henley, Ham., WR
1973	George McGowan, Edm., WR
1974	Tom Wilkinson, Edm., QB
1975	Willie Burden, Calg., RB
1976	Ron Lancaster, Sask., QB
1977	Jimmy Edwards, Ham., RB
1978	Tony Gabriel, Ott., TE

Year	
1979	David Green, Mon., RB
1980	Dieter Brock, Win., QB
1981	Dieter Brock, Win., QB
1982	Condredge Holloway, Tor., QB
1983	Warren Moon, Edm., QB
1984	Willard Reaves, Win., RB
1985	Merv Fernandez, BC, WR
1986	James Murphy, Win., WR
1987	Tom Clements, Win., QB
1988	David Williams, BC, WR
1989	Tracy Ham, Edm., QB

Nevada-Las Vegas head coach **Jerry Tarkanian** says a few words to the assembled in Denver as his Rebels revel following their 103-73 rout of Duke in the NCAA Final.

COLLEGE BASKETBALL

*Tarkanian's Rebels rule NCAA roost,
Duke subdued in Denver, 103-73;
Gathers' death inspires Loyola Marymount;
N.C. State mess sends Valvano packing.*

1989 YEAR IN REVIEW

by Billy Reed

Nobody except Jerry Tarkanian knows what he was really thinking on the night of April 2, sitting there on the Las Vegas bench in Denver's McNichols Arena, hands clasped behind his bald head as he watched his team dismantle Duke, 103-73, in the NCAA championship game. It wasn't even close after an 18-0 Vegas bombshell early in the second half, meaning that Tarkanian didn't have to go to the trademark wet towel that he likes to chew in moments of duress. What ended as the biggest blowout in championship game history also was a sort of tribute to Tarkanian, whose trials and tribulations with the NCAA go all the way back to 1972, when he was at Long Beach State.

But if Tarkanian felt any sense of vindication at the idea of having the NCAA finally hand him its most coveted trophy, he didn't show it. To the contrary, he was gracious and humble in the postgame ceremonies,

thanking the team's fans for their loyal support. "This isn't sweet revenge," he said. "It's just sweet, that's all." Even as he spoke, of course, UNLV was under investigation—again—for alleged rules violations. During what was to be his championship season, Tarkanian had to deal with 11 visits by NCAA investigators, not to mention such distractions as a brawl with Utah State, various player suspensions, and academic problems. Just the usual stuff, in other words, that has made Vegas one of the nation's most notorious programs, year after year. Amazingly, it has also managed to remain one of the best.

It was ironic, but also fitting in a perverse sort of way, that Duke would be the Rebels' final victim. Under Mike Krzyzewski, the Blue Devils have come to represent sugar and spice and everything nice. Good kids, good students, good school. Yet the Blue Devils are also 0-4 in Final Four appearances during the Krzyzewski era, pushing their all-time record to 0-for-8, worst in NCAA history. Whatever else it is, the Final Four isn't a morality play. Or, as UNLV's Stacey Augmon puckishly put it

Billy Reed, who has covered the last 23 Final Fours, is a sports columnist for the *Lexington (Ky.) Herald-Leader* and a senior writer at *Sports Illustrated*.

when asked if the title game was a case of Good vs. Bad, ''Oh, I don't think Duke is so bad.''

Augmon, a 6-6 junior who was a member of the United States' 1988 silver medal Olympic team, was magnificent in the title game, scoring 12 points and notching seven assists in only 26 minutes. Even at that, he was overshadowed by 6-7 classmate and consensus first team All-America Larry Johnson, a junior college transfer with a physique that brought to mind the young George McGinnis. Johnson had 22 points, 11 rebounds, and four steals in only 26 minutes—an outstanding performance, but not the most outstanding. That honor went to 6-1 sophomore guard Anderson Hunt, whose 29 points were forged mainly on 12-of-14 shooting from the field. Earlier in the season, Hunt had been suspended for a game for being delinquent in payments on his student loan, one of the lesser problems with which Tarkanian had to deal.

Afterward, a shell-shocked Krzyzewski said, ''This wasn't a game of X's and O's. . .it was a complete domination.'' He was correct, of course, which was sort of surprising. Although the Rebels became the first team since North Carolina in 1982 to win the title after being ranked No. 1 in the preseason by the Associated Press, they never really broke away from the pack until the final game of the tournament.

Indeed, after being upset by Kansas in the preseason NIT, Vegas sort of moved aside and made way for the Big Eight, which hogged the No. 1 ranking through most of the regular season. The trouble was, Kansas, Missouri, and Oklahoma all took so much out of each other during the season and the conference tournament they had nothing left when it was time for the Big Show. None of the three even made it to a regional.

As has been the case in recent years, college basketball continued to get more popular, entertaining, and competitive in 1989-90, mostly because of the up-tempo style created by the three-point shot and the 45-second clock. These innovations are the legacy of rules maker Edward Steitz, who died of a heart attack on May 21 at age 69.

However, the game's success on the floor is too often overshadowed by its failure off the court. A book released during the season, **Raw Recruits**, written by **Sports Illustrated**'s Alexander Wolff and Armen Keteyian of ABC News, exposed the game's soft underbelly in such graphic fashion that not even the game's most ardent cheerleaders—TV analysts Billy Packer and Dick Vitale—have enough whitewash or clout to make a convincing argument that everything is really OK, despite what you might read in the newspapers.

The sorriest story of the season happened at North Carolina State, home of two NCAA championships and one of the game's proudest traditions, dating back to the days of Everett Case in the 1940s. Already on NCAA probation at the start of the season, coach Jim Valvano's program was rocked by even more revelations, the most serious of which indicated that Valvano had paid scant attention to his players' academic progress.

After resigning as athletic director in December, Valvano ultimately quit as coach after the Atlantic Coast Conference tournament. The final straw was a story that one of his former players had been involved in point-shaving. Sadly, Valvano attempted to justify himself and hold out for a big sever-

N.C. State head coach **Jim Valvano** with junior guard **Chris Corchiani** after the Wolfpack's final regular season game, a loss to Wake Forest.

ance check instead of just walking quietly away. When he finally quit and was replaced by Les Robinson, a former Wolfpack player who had recently enjoyed success as the coach at East Tennessee State, another grim chapter in the game's history was closed.

While many viewed Valvano's departure as good riddance—Indiana coach Bob Knight said that Valvano seemed to become consumed by making money after winning the 1983 NCAA title—the departure of others was mourned, particularly Virginia's Terry Holland and Oklahoma City's Abe Lemons. Holland, one of the game's class acts and a two-time NCAA semifinalist, stepped down to become athletic director at Davidson. Lemons, a 599-game winner over 34 seasons in the NCAA and NAIA, made sure the game maintained a sense of humor even as it grew into a big, grim business capable of commanding an incredible $1 billion TV contract from CBS for seven years' worth of tournament rights.

The Valvano of 1988-89, Eddie Sutton, didn't come off looking so hot in *Raw Recruits.* Neither did his former assistant, Leonard Hamilton. Yet when Hamilton left Oklahoma State in April to take the Miami (Fla.) job, doggone if OSU didn't turn to Sutton, an alumnus who played for Hank Iba in the 1950s. In taking the Oklahoma State job, Sutton indicated that the problems that led to his leaving Kentucky were beyond his control. Another of his former assistants, Dwayne Casey, lost an appeal of the NCAA's decision to keep him out of coaching for five years. Go figure.

Among the other depressing stories to emerge during the season were Don DeVoe's inability to restore order and integrity at Florida, where the program came unraveled when star players Dwayne Schintzius and Livingston Chatman quit in protest of DeVoe's discipline. . .a scary, gym-clearing brawl in a game between traditional black powers North Carolina A&T and North Carolina Central. . .allegations of major NCAA rules violations at Missouri and Illinois, two of the sport's premier programs under longtime coaches Norm Stewart and Lou Henson, respectively. . .and, of course, the collapse and death of Loyola Marymount star Hank Gathers during a Big West tournament game on March 4 (see box).

But for all that, and more, the game's success stories somehow managed to prevail,

Wide World Photos

Hank Gathers
1967–1990

The image won't quickly be erased from the memories of anyone who loves college basketball. One moment, Hank Gathers of Loyola Marymount was a picture of strength and joy, slamming home one of the dunks he dearly loved. The next he was lying on the floor, life ebbing from his 6-7 body as his teammates and fans stood helpless, the shock evident on their horror-stricken faces. Taken to a hospital, Gathers died on the night of Sunday, March 4, from apparent heart failure.

The tragedy happened in a West Coast Conference tournament game against Portland on Loyola's home floor in Los Angeles. The rest of the tournament was canceled, but the NCAA still extended the Lions a bid which they accepted, vowing to play the tournament as a tribute to their fallen leader. Said Bo Kimble, who grew up with Gathers in Philadelphia and came west with him to play ball, "It was hard on everyone, but we knew Hank would have wanted us to play in the NCAAs. At the memorial service, I looked over and saw his coffin was in the paint. I knew then we would have to find a way to win for him."

The paint, of course, is where Gathers worked during games. He and Kimble initially signed to play with Southern Cal, but transferred to Loyola after George Raveling replaced Stan Morrison as the Trojans' coach. It turned out to be a fortuitous move. They liked Loyola coach Paul Westhead not only because he had a Philly background, but also because he utilized a style so up-

"Basketball is the easy part."

tempo that his rivals couldn't believe it, much less keep up. As a junior, Gathers became only the second player in NCAA history to lead the nation in both scoring and rebounding (the first was Xavier McDaniels of Wichita State in 1985). As a senior, Gathers hoped to improve on his averages of 32.7 points and 13.7 rebounds. His only deficiency was free-throw shooting, which was so erratic that he decided to shoot them left-handed.

The first sign of trouble came on Dec. 9, when Gathers mysteriously collapsed during a game against UC Santa Barbara. He was diagnosed as having an irregular heartbeat and put on medication. After missing only two regular-season games and one exhibition, he returned to the Lions and went on to average 29 points and 10.8 rebounds. And yet Gathers complained that the medication made him feel so sluggish and fatigued that he eventually persuaded his cardiologist to reduce the dosage.

Heading into the tournament, he told friends that he felt stronger and better than he had all season. Then came the tragedy against Portland. "Words are hard right now," said Westhead in a written statement released shortly after Gathers' death. "This is the hardest thing I've experienced. To be so close to a player and see him fall and for it to be over. I feel a deep hurt for his family."

The Lions were seeded only 11th in the West Regional and assigned to play New Mexico State in Long Beach. The game was tied at halftime, but Kimble had four fouls. Amazingly, however, the Lions exploded at the start of the second half and rolled to an 111-92 victory in which Kimble scored 45 points and grabbed 13 rebounds. The most touching moment of the game came when Kimble shot his first free throw left-handed, in tribute to Gathers. It swished, causing the arena to erupt in emotion. "When Bo got up there and shot left-handed," said Loyola reserve Greg Walker, "it just brought back the whole season, why we're here, why we're playing."

Only two days later, the Lions crushed Michigan, the defending national champion. Their 149-115 victory shattered the tournament record for points scored by a team (the previous mark was the 127 scored by St. Joseph's in a four-overtime game in 1961). At this point, the Lions were looking

like a team of destiny, a team on a mission, and fans everywhere were beginning to wonder if they might be able to go all the way.

"Basketball is the easy part," Westhead said, seeking perspective. "We all know, when this is over we are going to have to face Hank's death again—and there won't be the games to fall back on."

In the West Regional semifinals, the Lions beat Alabama, but just barely, 62-60. In the final, playing against a UNLV team that had beaten them 102-91 earlier in the season, the end finally came. Las Vegas won, 131-101, yet nobody felt that Gathers' memory had been disgraced. The Lions just got beat at their own game by the eventual national champion. "Without them having Hank," said UNLV's Stacey Augmon, "it seemed very weird out there. Like something was missing."

Bo Kimble
Left-handed for Hank.

Wide World Photos

giving rise to the hope that big-time college basketball is worth saving—and savoring—regardless of its excesses and problems.

Some examples:

► Kentucky, staggered by a two-year NCAA probation for rules violations and expecting one of the worst seasons in its glorious history, rebounded to a 14-14 record under new coach Rick Pitino, formerly of the New York Knicks. The fans so loved Pitino's emphasis on fullcourt pressure and three-point bombing that they turned out in record numbers for the home games. Pitino and his boss, athletic director C.M. Newton, former head coach at Transylvania, Alabama, and Vanderbilt, swear the Wildcats will be back sooner than anybody expects, but completely within the framework of the NCAA rules.

► Lionel "L-Train" Simmons of La Salle, who grew up playing with and against Gathers in Philadelphia, was the consensus Player of the Year. A splendid 6-7 forward, he wound up as the game's No. 3 all-time scorer, behind LSU's Pete Maravich and Freeman Williams of Portland State.

► Clarence "Bighouse" Gaines of Winston-Salem became only the second coach ever to win as many as 800 games. However, Gaines expressed less than a whole-hearted respect for the other member of the 800 Club, former Kentucky coach Adolph Rupp. As Gaines put it, Rupp beat up on weaker teams in an era when basketball was still growing and had racist tendencies, besides. "He wouldn't even let a black dog in his house," Gaines said.

► Alec Kessler of Georgia proved that the ideal of the student-athlete was alive and well in Athens. The 6-11, 230-lb senior was among the Southeastern Conference leaders in scoring, rebounding and grade point average. A 3.91 student majoring in microbiology, Kessler was admitted to several medical schools, including Johns Hopkins, but decided to defer his graduate studies until after he sees what he can do in the NBA.

► The year's surprise team was Connecticut. Off the radar screen before the season began—69 other teams received at least one vote in the first AP Poll—the Huskies wound up at No.3 in the final regular season vote, thanks in no small part to Nadav Henefeld, a 21-year-old freshman forward and former Israeli soldier whose quick hands turned the UConn defense into a holy terror. In the East Regional, the Huskies defeated Clemson on an improbable shot by

Wide World Photos

La Salle's **Lionel Simmons**, the consensus Player of the Year, also became the game's third all-time leading scorer.

Tate George in the very last tenth of a second, but then were denied a trip to the Final Four by another buzzer-beater in the East final, this one by Duke's Christian Laettner.

► DePaul finally got around to retiring No. 99, which was worn by all-time great George Mikan in the late 1940s, and Duke retired the No. 25 worn by Art Heyman, its 1963 Player of the Year. At UCLA, the numbers worn by Kareem Abdul-Jabbar (33), Bill Walton (32) and Ann Meyers (15) were also raised to the rafters.

Speaking of Meyers, the women's game also had another good year. Stanford (32-1) won the NCAA championship in its first trip to the Final Four, beating Auburn, 88-81, before 20,023 in Knoxville, Tenn. Stanford's senior guard Jennifer Azzi of nearby Oak Ridge was voted the tournament's Most Outstanding Player, although teammate Katy Steding led the Cardinal in scoring with 36 points.

Auburn, which has now reached the finals three straight years and lost each time, knocked off unbeaten Louisiana Tech (32-1) in the semifinals. Virginia fell to Stanford in the other semifinal, after upsetting top-seeded Tennessee in the East Regional championship game.

Stanford's **Jennifer Azzi** gives herself a lift after leading the Cardinal to its first NCAA women's championship.

Azzi, the only repeat member of the Kodak All-America team, shared Player of the Year honors with Louisiana Tech center Venus Lacy. Azzi won the Naismith and Wade awards while Lacy was the coaches' pick. Elsewhere, a major uproar developed when Oklahoma announced it was eliminating its women's team. However, the Sooners quickly reversed their field, as befits a football school.

As usual, the men's season revolved around the quest to identify the best team in the nation. For the longest while, it looked as if Kansas, Missouri or Oklahoma was destined to give the Big Eight its second national

title in three years. One of the three schools was ranked No. 1 in the AP Top 25 every week from Jan. 8 through the final regular season poll on March 12. In fact, for five of those 10 weeks, the Big Eight ranked 1-2.

Kansas and Missouri alternated at the top until Oklahoma gained the upper hand late in the season, routing both the Tigers (107-90) and Jayhawks (100-78) within 48 hours, Feb. 25-27. Missouri and Kansas were each ranked No. 1 when Oklahoma beat them and when the dust settled, the Sooners had taken over.

Meanwhile, lurking in the background all the way was Michigan, which seemed to have the talent necessary to become the first back-to-back champion since UCLA's run of seven straight titles from 1967-73. Yet Rumeal Robinson, Loy Vaught & Co. never completely adapted to the loss of Glen Rice, the hot-shooting forward who gunned the Wolverines to the 1989 title.

When the NCAA tournament committee announced its 64-team field and pairings on March 11, the Big Ten had a record seven entrants. Yet, as the tournament unfolded, the favorites and the big names took a horrible beating. Only two Big Ten teams—Michigan State and Minnesota—reached the Sweet Sixteen.

Heading into the Final Four, seven games had been decided by a point, 10 by two points, and six by three points—a total of 23 games by three points or less (see page 187). It was marvelous theater, and a perfect—if bittersweet—way for ESPN, Vitale, and the NCAA to end the 10-year relationship of early-round action that had enhanced the reputations of all three. Beginning in 1991, CBS will do the entire tournament employing, no doubt, the format it learned from ESPN.

Of all the buzzer-beaters, the most significant one came in Georgia Tech's victory over Michigan State in the semifinals of the Southeast Regional in New Orleans. The Yellow Jackets got the break of the tournament when the officials allowed a desperation, game-tying jumper by freshman sensation Kenny Anderson, even though it was clearly put up after regulation time had expired. Taking full advantage of that reprieve, Tech pulled out an 81-80 victory in overtime to advance to the regional final, then beat Minnesota, 93-91, to earn a trip to Denver and a date with UNLV.

Las Vegas won the West Regional by barely surviving Ball State and then finally ending Loyola Marymount's emotional, Win-It-for Hank run. The Final Four was rounded out by East champion Duke, making its fourth appearance in five years, and Arkansas, which had to dispatch North Carolina and arch-rival Texas to win the Midwest.

The Final Four was held in a "traditional" arena, meaning that fewer than 18,000 seats were available. This led to a field day for ticket scalpers, who were commanding as much as $1500 per ticket. In the semifinals on Saturday, March 31, Duke trailed Arkansas by seven points midway through the second half, but rallied to win easily, 97-84. In the second game, Georgia Tech built up a 53-46 lead at the half, but Las Vegas came back to win by nine, 90-81.

After that the biggest story took place off the court when CBS informed Brent Musburger late Saturday night that it wouldn't renew his $2-million-a-year contract. When word began to seep out on Sunday morning, April 1, the media initially assumed that it was an April Fool's joke, considering how long Musburger had been the preeminent player at CBS Sports. Later that day, however, the network confirmed that Musburger, indeed, was gone, although he would do the championship game with Packer, his longtime sidekick.

The Musburger flap detracted from the championship game to an extent, but not as much as had been feared. The Vegas-Duke matchup was so delicious, such a great contrast in image and philosophy, that the media doted on it. Tarkanian and Krzyzewski, on the other hand, emphasized that their programs were a lot more alike than anyone may have imagined, at least in the way they approached the game defensively. "Las Vegas plays the same kind of aggressive man-to-man that we do," Krzyzewski said. "It will be a good defensive game," added Tarkanian, "but not a low-scoring one."

So much for Tark the Shark as a Las Vegas sharpie. His team played a tremendous defensive game and the game was high-scoring, albeit one-sided. The Blue Devils at least kept it respectable for a while, trailing by only 10 at halftime. But then came that amazing 18-0 run in which Hunt made two treys and three other baskets. It was an awesome display and a couple of the best tributes came from Duke players. "We

Wide World Photos

The Big Three of the Big Eight—Kansas, Oklahoma and Missouri—dominated the voting for No. 1 all winter. Here **Mark Randall** of the Jayhawks and **William Davis** of the Sooners collide in pursuit of a rebound.

couldn't get the ball past the hash marks," said Laettner. Added center Alaa Abdelnaby, "They engulfed us."

The Vegas players were keenly aware of what the title meant to Tarkanian. Or, as Johnson had said after the semifinals, "We want to win this championship bad, so that the NCAA guys will have to stare at the trophy on Coach's desk while they ask all those questions during the next investigation." After the title game, the players donned T-shirts that bore the inscription, "Shark Takes His Bite."

He did, finally, and now it will be up to history to judge whether Jerry Tarkanian was really Don Quixote, chewing on a towel and tilting at windmills, or Don Shark, boss of college basketball's netherworld. □

THE 1991 INFORMATION PLEASE SPORTS ALMANAC

COLLEGE BASKETBALL
S T A T I S T I C S

THE SEASON IN REVIEW
1989-1990

TOP 25 • NCAA'S • STANDINGS

SEC **A**

PAGE **185**

Final AP Top 25 Poll
Taken before start of NCAA tournament.

The sportswriters & broadcasters poll: first place votes in parentheses; records through March 11; total points (based on 25 for 1st, 24 for 2nd, etc.); record in NCAA tourney and team lost to; head coach (career years and record, including NCAA tourney), and preseason ranking. Teams in **bold type** went on to reach NCAA Final Four.

		Mar.11 Record	Points	NCAA Recap	Head Coach	Preseason Rank
1	Oklahoma	(57) 26-4	1590	1-1 (N.Carolina)	Billy Tubbs (16th year: 363-153)	16
2	**UNLV**	(3) 29-5	1472	6-0	Jerry Tarkanian (22nd: 565-119)	1
3	Connecticut	 28-5	1436	3-1 (Duke)	Jim Calhoun (18th: 326-189)	—
4	Michigan St.	(3) 26-5	1411	2-1 (Ga.Tech)	Jed Heathcote (19th: 322-221)	42
5	Kansas	 29-4	1276	1-1 (UCLA)	Roy Williams (2nd: 49-17)	38
6	Syracuse	 24-6	1186	2-1 (Minnesota)	Jim Boeheim (14th: 343-108)	3
7	**Arkansas**	 26-4	1120	4-1 (Duke)	Nolan Richardson (10th: 226-88)	9
8	Georgetown	 23-6	1064	1-1 (Xavier)	John Thompson (18th: 423-142)	5
9	**Georgia Tech**	 24-6	1046	4-1 (UNLV)	Bobby Cremins (15th: 281-169)	22
10	Purdue	 21-7	971	1-1 (Texas)	Gene Keady (12th: 253-112)	68
11	Missouri	 26-5	940	0-1 (No.Iowa)	Norm Stewart (29th: 552-273)	11
12	La Salle	(1) 29-1	908	1-1 (Clemson)	Speedy Morris (4th: 100-31)	34
13	Michigan	 22-7	881	1-1 (Loyola Mmt)	Steve Fisher (2nd: 29-8)	4
14	Arizona	 24-6	854	1-1 (Alabama)	Lute Olsen (17th: 353-155)	6
15	**Duke**	 24-8	791	5-1 (UNLV)	Mike Krzyzewski (15th: 304-160)	10
16	Louisville	 26-7	654	1-1 (Ball St.)	Denny Crum (19th: 463-156)	12
17	Clemson	 24-8	509	2-1 (UConn)	Cliff Ellis (15th: 290-153)	28
18	Illinois	 21-7	482	0-1 (Dayton)	Lou Henson (28th: 556-257)	8
19	LSU	 22-8	384	1-1 (Ga.Tech)	Dale Brown (18th: 340-202)	2
20	Minnesota	 20-8	327	3-1 (Ga.Tech)	Clem Haskins (10th: 162-131)	20
21	Loyola Marymount	...23-5	303	3-1 (UNLV)	Paul Westhead (14th: 247-153)	31
22	Oregon St	 22-6	230	0-1 (Ball St.)	Jim Anderson (1st: 22-7)	37
23	Alabama	 24-8	186	2-1 (Loyola-Mmt)	Wimp Sanderson (10th: 216-99)	36
24	New Mexico St	 26-4	167	0-1 (Loyola-Mmt)	Neil McCarthy (15th: 296-157)	—
25	Xavier,OH	 26-4	112	2-1 (Texas)	Pete Gillen (5th: 119-39)	39

Others receiving votes: 26. Houston (23-6,103 pts); **27.** Georgia (20-8,96); **28.** Virginia (19-11,56); **29.** East Tenn.St.(27-6,49); **30.** St.John's (23-9,25); **31.** Ohio St.(16-12,24); **32.** UTEP (21-10,23); **33.** Dayton (21-9,19), UCLA (20-10,19); **35.** Princeton (20-6,13); **36.** Ball St.(24-6,12); **37.** Texas (21-8,9); **38.** Illinois St.(18-12,8), Southern Ill.(26-7,8); **40.** Kansas St.(17-14,6); **41.** Long Beach St.(22-8,5), North Carolina (19-12,5); **43.** Ark-Little Rock (20-9,4); **44.** Colorado St.(21-8,3), Temple (20-10,3); **46.** Indiana (18-10,2), Wright St.(21-7,2); **48.** Ala-Birmingham (22-8,1); Coastal Carolina (23-6,1); Maryland (18-13,1); Richmond (22-9,1); Robert Morris (22-7,1); UC-Santa Barbara (20-8,1).

NCAA Division I Tournament Seeds

EAST	MIDWEST	SOUTHEAST	WEST
1. Connecticut (28-5)	1. Oklahoma (26-4)	1. Michigan St.(26-5)	1. **UNLV** (29-5)
2. Kansas (29-4)	2. Purdue (21-7)	2. Syracuse (24-6)	2. Arizona (24-6)
3. **Duke** (24-8)	3. Georgetown (23-6)	3. Missouri (26-5)	3. Michigan (22-7)
4. La Salle (29-1)	4. **Arkansas** (26-4)	4. **Georgia Tech** (24-6)	4. Louisville (26-7)
5. Clemson (24-8)	5. Illinois (21-7)	5. LSU (22-8)	5. Oregon St. (22-6)
6. St.John's (23-9)	6. Xavier,OH (26-4)	6. Minnesota (20-8)	6. N.Mexico St.(26-4)
7. UCLA (20-10)	7. Georgia (20-8)	7. Virginia (19-11)	7. Alabama (24-8)
8. Indiana (18-10)	8. N.Carolina (19-12)	8. Houston (23-6)	8. Ohio St.(16-12)
9. California (21-9)	9. SW Missouri St.(22-6)	9. UC-S.Barbara (20-8)	9. Providence (17-11)
10. Ala-Birm. (22-8)	10. Texas (21-8)	10. Notre Dame (16-12)	10. Colorado St.(21-8)
11. Temple (20-10)	11. Kansas St.(17-14)	11. UTEP (21-10)	11. Loyola-Mmt. (23-5)
12. BYU (21-8)	12. Dayton (21-9)	12. Villanova (18-14)	12. Ball St. (24-6)
13. South.Miss.(20-11)	13. Princeton (20-6)	13. East Tenn.St.(27-6)	13. Idaho (25-5)
14. Richmond (22-9)	14. Tex.Southern (19-11)	14. Northern Iowa (22-8)	14. Illinois St.(18-12)
15. Robert Morris (22-7)	15. NE Louisiana (22-7)	15. Coppin St.(26-6)	15. South Florida (20-10)
16. Boston Univ.(18-11)	16. Towson St.(18-12)	16. Murray St.(21-8)	16. Ark-Little Rock (20-9)

1990 NCAA BASKETBALL MEN'S DIVISION I

NCAA FINAL FOUR 1990

NATIONAL CHAMPIONSHIP
DENVER, CO — April 2

UNLV 103
Duke 73

National Semifinals — DENVER, CO — March 31

- Georgia Tech 81
- UNLV 90
- Duke 97
- Arkansas 83

SOUTHEAST

1st ROUND March 15-16	2nd ROUND March 17-18	REGIONALS March 23 & 25 (NEW ORLEANS, LA)
1 Michigan State 75		
16 Murray State 71	Michigan St. 62	
8 Houston 66		Michigan St 80
9 UC-Santa Barbara 70	UC-Santa Barbara 58	
5 LSU 70		
12 Villanova 63	LSU 91	
4 Georgia Tech 99		Georgia Tech 81
13 E. Tenn State 83	Georgia Tech 94	
6 Minnesota 64		
11 UTEP 61	Minnesota 81	
3 Missouri 71		Minnesota 82
14 N. Iowa 74	No. Iowa 78	
7 Virginia 75		
10 Notre Dame 67	Virginia 61	
2 Syracuse 70		Syracuse 75
15 Coppin State 48	Syracuse 63	

Georgia Tech 93 / Minnesota 91 → Georgia Tech 81

WEST

1st ROUND March 15-16	2nd ROUND March 17-18	REGIONALS March 23 & 25 (OAKLAND, CA)
1 UNLV 102		
16 Ark. Little Rock 72	UNLV 76	
8 Ohio State 84		UNLV 69
9 Providence 83	Ohio State 65	
5 Oregon State 53		
12 Ball State 54	Ball State 62	
4 Louisville 78		Ball St. 67
13 Idaho 59	Louisville 60	
6 New Mexico St. 92		
11 Loyola-Marymount 111	Loyola Mmt 149	
3 Michigan 76		Loyola Mmt 101
14 Illinois State 70	Michigan 115	
7 Alabama 71		
10 Colorado State 54	Alabama 77	
2 Arizona 79		Alabama 60
15 S. Florida 67	Arizona 55	

UNLV 131 / Loyola Mmt → UNLV 90

EAST

1st ROUND March 15-16	2nd ROUND March 17-18	REGIONALS March 22 & 24 (E. RUTHERFORD, NJ)
1 Connecticut 76		
16 Boston Univ 52	Connecticut 74	
8 Indiana 63		Connecticut 71
9 California 65	California 54	
5 Clemson 49		
12 Brigham Young 47	Clemson 79	
4 La Salle 79		Clemson 70
13 So. Mississippi 63	La Salle 75	
6 St. John's 81		
11 Temple 65	St. John's 72	
3 Duke 81		Duke 90
14 Richmond 46	Duke 76	
7 UCLA 68		
10 UAB 56	UCLA 71	
2 Kansas 79		UCLA 81
15 Robert Morris 71	Kansas 70	

Connecticut 78 / Duke 70 → Duke 97

MIDWEST

1st ROUND March 15-16	2nd ROUND March 17-18	REGIONALS March 22 & 24 (DALLAS, TX)
1 Oklahoma 77		
16 Towson St. 68	Oklahoma 77	
8 N. Carolina 83		N. Carolina 73
9 SW Missouri 70	N. Carolina 79	
5 Illinois 86		
12 Dayton 88	Dayton 84	
4 Arkansas 68		Arkansas 96
13 Princeton 64	Arkansas 86	
6 Xavier, OH 87		
11 Kansas St. 79	Xavier 74	
3 Georgetown 70		Xavier 89
14 Texas South 52	Georgetown 71	
7 Georgia 88		
10 Texas 100	Texas 73	
2 Purdue 75		Texas 102
15 NE Louisiana 63	Purdue 72	

Arkansas 88 / Texas 85 → Arkansas 83

Championship Game
UNLV 103, Duke 73

Duke	Min	FB M-A	FT M-A	Pts	Rb	A	F
Robert Brickey	24	2-4	0-2	4	3	2	2
Christian Laettner	29	5-12	5-6	15	9	5	4
Alaa Abdelnaby	24	5-7	4-6	14	7	0	3
Phil Henderson	32	9-20	2-2	21	2	0	2
Bobby Hurley	32	0-3	2-2	2	0	3	3
Brian Davis	21	2-5	2-3	6	1	0	1
Greg Koubek	14	1-4	0-0	2	2	0	0
Thomas Hill	8	0-2	0-0	0	3	1	0
Bill McCaffrey	9	1-3	2-2	4	2	0	1
Clay Buckley	3	0-0	0-0	0	1	0	0
Crawford Palmer	2	0-0	3-4	3	3	0	0
Joe Cook	2	1-1	0-0	2	0	0	0
TOTALS	200	26-61	20-27	73	33	11	16

Three-point FG: 1-11 (Henderson 1-8, Hurley 0-2, Koubek 0-1); **Team Rebounds:** 6 (not listed above); **Blocked Shots:** 3 (Abdelnaby 2, Davis); **Turnovers:** 23 (Henderson 6, Hurley 5, Laettner 3, Brickey 2, McCaffrey 2, Abdelnaby, Buckley, Cook, Hill, Koubek); **Steals:** 5 (Davis, Henderson, Hill, Hurley, Laettner). **Team FG Pct:** .462 (1st half); .400 (2nd Half); .426 (Game). **Team FT Pct:** .688 (1st Half); .818 (2nd Half); .741 (Game).

UNLV	Min	FB M-A	FT M-A	Pts	Rb	A	F
Larry Johnson	30	8-12	4-4	22	11	2	3
Stacey Augmon	26	6-7	0-1	12	4	7	5
David Butler	27	1-4	2-2	4	3	3	3
Anderson Hunt	31	12-16	1-2	29	2	2	0
Greg Anthony	30	5-11	3-4	13	1	6	3
Moses Scurry	12	2-5	1-2	5	6	0	2
Travis Bice	9	0-1	0-0	0	0	2	2
Barry Young	12	2-2	0-0	5	0	0	1
James Jones	8	4-5	0-0	8	2	0	2
Stacey Cvijanovich	10	1-2	2-2	5	1	2	2
Chris Jeter	3	0-0	0-0	0	0	0	0
Dave Rice	2	0-2	0-0	0	1	0	0
TOTALS	200	41-67	13-17	103	31	24	23

Three-point FG: 8-14 (Hunt 4-7, Johnson 2-2, Cvijanovich 1-1, Young 1-1, Anthony 0-1, Bice 0-1, Rice 0-1); **Team Rebounds:** 2 (not listed above); **Blocked Shots:** 3 (Augmon 2, Johnson); **Turnovers:** 17 (Anthony 3, Augmon 3, Bice 3, Johnson 3, Scurry 3, Hunt, Jeter, Young); **Steals:** 16 (Anthony 5, Johnson 4, Augmon 2, Cvijanovich 2, Bice, Butler, Scurry). **Team FG Pct:** .559 (1st half); .667 (2nd half); .612 (Game). **Team FT Pct:** .778 (1st half); .750 (2nd half); .765 (Game).

Duke (ACC)		35 38—	73
UNLV (Big West)		47 56—	103

Technical Fouls: none. **Officials:** Ed Hightower, Tim Higgins and Richard Ballesteros. **Attendance:** 17,765. **TV Rating:** 20.0/31 share (CBS).

THE FINAL FOUR
McNichols Sports Arena, Denver
Semifinals

Duke 97 . . . . Arkansas 83
UNLV 90 . . . . Georgia Tech 81

Championship

UNLV 103 . . . . Duke 73

Final records: UNLV (35-5), Duke (29-9), Arkansas (30-5), Georgia Tech (28-7).

Most Outstanding Player: Anderson Hunt, UNLV, guard (Semifinal—20 points, 7 assists; Final— 29 pts).

All-Tournament Team: Hunt, Larry Johnson and Stacey Augmon, UNLV; Phil Henderson, Duke; Dennis Scott, Ga.Tech.

Close Games

Twenty-three games in the 1990 NCAA Division I tournament were decided by three points or less.

First Round

1-pt	Ball St. 54 . . . . OT . . . . Oregon St. 53	
	Ohio St. 84 . . . . . . OT . . . . . . Providence 83	
2-pt	California 65 . . . . Indiana 63	
	Clemson 49 . . . . BYU 47	
	Dayton 88 . . . . Illinois 86	
3-pt	Minnesota 64 . . . . OT . . . . UTEP 61	
	No.Iowa 74 . . . . Missouri 71	

Second Round

1-pt	UCLA 71 . . . . Kansas 70	
	Texas 73 . . . . Purdue 72	
2-pt	Arkansas 86 . . . . Dayton 84	
	Ball St. 62 . . . . Louisville 60	
	N.Carolina 79 . . . . Oklahoma 77	
	Syracuse 63 . . . . Virginia 61	
3-pt	Ga.Tech 94 . . . . LSU 91	
	Minnesota 81 . . . . No.Iowa 78	
	Xavier 74 . . . . Georgetown 71	

Regional Semifinals

1-pt	Connecticut 71 . . . . Clemson 70	
	Ga.Tech 81 . . . . . . OT . . . . Mich.St. 80	
2-pt	Loyola Mmt. 62 . . . . Alabama 60	
	UNLV 69 . . . . Ball St. 67	

Regional Finals

1-pt	Duke 79 . . . . OT . . . . . . Connecticut 78	
2-pt	Ga.Tech 93 . . . . Minnesota 91	
3-pt	Arkansas 88 . . . . Texas 85	

National Invitation Tournament

The 53rd annual National Invitational Tournament had a 32-team field. First three rounds played on home court of higher seeded teams. Semifinal, Third Place and Championship games played March 26 and 28 at Madison Square Garden in New York.

First Round—Penn. St. 57, Marquette 54; New Orleans 78, J. Madison 74; Tennessee 73, Memphis St. 71; Fordham 106, Southern Univ. 80; Maryland 91, Massachusetts 81; Hawaii 69, Stanford 57; Miss.St. 84, Baylor 75; Oklahoma ST.83, Tulsa 74; Vanderbilt 98, La.Tech 90 (OT); Wisc-Green Bay 73, Southern Ill. 60; Rutgers 87, Holy Cross 75; Cincinnati 75, Bowling Green 60; St.Louis 85, Kent St.74; DePaul 89, Creighton 72; New Mexico 89, Oregon 78; Long Beach St. 86, Arizona St.71.

Second Round—Vanderbilt 89, Tennessee 85; Penn. St. 80, Maryland 78; Rugters 81, Fordham 74; New Orleans 65, Miss.St.60; St. Louis 58, Wisc.-Green Bay 54; DePaul 61, Cincinnati 59; New Mexico 90, Oklahoma St.88; Hawaii 84, Long Beach St. 79. **Quarterfinals**—Penn St. 58, Rutgers 55; Vanderbilt 88, New Orleans 65; St. Louis 54, DePaul 47; New Mexico 80, Hawaii 58. **Semifinals**—Vanderbilt 75, Penn St.62; St. Louis 80, New Mexico 73. **Third Place**—Penn St. 83, New Mexico 81. **Championship**— Vanderbilt 74, St.Louis 72. **MVP:** Scott Draud, Vanderbilt.

NCAA Men's Division I Leaders
Including games through NCAA tournament.

INDIVIDUAL

Scoring

	Cl	Gm	Pts	Avg
Bo Kimble, Loyola,CA	Sr	32	1131	35.3
Kevin Bradshaw, U.S.Int'l	Jr	28	875	31.3
Dave Jamerson, Ohio U	Sr	28	874	31.2
Alphonzo Ford, Miss.Valley	Fr	27	808	29.9
Steve Rogers, Alabama St.	So	28	831	29.7
Hank Gathers, Loyola,CA	Sr	26	754	29.0
Darryl Brooks, Tenn.St	Jr	24	690	28.8
Chris Jackson, LSU	So	32	889	27.8
Dennis Scott, Ga.Tech	Jr	35	970	27.7
Mark Stevenson, Duquesne	Sr	29	788	27.2
Lionel Simmons, La Salle	Sr	32	847	26.5
Keith Gailes, Loyola,IL	Jr	29	762	26.3
Kurk Lee, Towson St	Sr	31	805	26.0
Gary Payton, Oregon St	Sr	29	746	25.7
Bailey Alston, Liberty	Sr	28	714	25.5
Sydney Grider, SW La	Sr	29	739	25.5

Rebounding

	Cl	Gm	Reb	Avg
Anthony Bonner, St.Louis	Sr	33	456	13.8
Eric McArthur, UC-S.Barb	Sr	29	377	13.0
Tyrone Hill, Xavier,OH	Sr	32	402	12.6
Lee Campbell, SW Mo.St	Sr	29	363	12.5
Cedric Ceballos, CS-Full	Sr	29	362	12.5
Hakim Shahid, S.Florida	Sr	31	383	12.4
Ron Draper, American	Sr	29	354	12.2
Derrick Coleman, Syracuse	Sr	33	398	12.1
Shaquille O'Neal, LSU	Fr	32	385	12.0
Clarence Weatherspoon, S.Miss	So	32	371	11.6

Blocked Shots

	Cl	Gm	BS	Avg
Kenny Green, Rhode Island	Sr	26	124	4.8
Dikembe Mutombo, G'town	Jr	31	128	4.1
Kevin Roberson, Vermont	So	30	114	3.8
Lorenzo Williams, Stetson	Jr	32	121	3.8
Omar Roland, Marshall	Sr	28	101	3.6
Shaquille O'Neal, LSU	Fr	32	115	3.6
Steve Stevenson, Prairie Vw	Jr	27	97	3.6
David Harris, Texas A&M	Jr	31	108	3.5
Luc Longley, New Mexico	Jr	34	117	3.4
Walter Palmer, Dartmouth	Sr	25	85	3.4

Assists

	Cl	Gm	Ast	Avg
Todd Lehman, Drexel	Sr	28	260	9.3
Aaron Mitchell, SW La	Sr	29	264	9.1
Keith Jennings, E.Tenn.St	Jr	34	297	8.7
Otis Livingston, Idaho	Sr	31	262	8.5
Kenny Anderson, Ga.Tech	Fr	35	285	8.1
Gary Payton, Oregon St	Sr	29	235	8.1
Tony Edmond, TCU	Sr	29	234	8.1
Chris Corchiani, N.C.State	Jr	30	238	7.9
Darelle Porter, Pittsburgh	Jr	29	229	7.9
Lamar Holt, Prairie View	Sr	27	213	7.9

Steals

	Cl	Gm	Stl	Avg
Ronn McMahon, E.Wash	Sr	29	130	4.5
Robert Dowdell, C.Caro	Jr	29	109	3.8
Nadav Henefeld, UConn	Fr	37	138	3.7
Larry Robinson, Centenary	Sr	30	104	3.5
Gary Payton, Oregon St	Sr	28	100	3.5

Field Goal Percentage

	Cl	Gm	FG	FGA	Pct
Lee Campbell, SW Mo.St	Sr	29	192	275	.6982
Stephen Scheffler, Purdue	Sr	30	173	248	.6976
Felton Spencer, L'ville	Sr	35	188	276	.681
Brian Parker, Cleve.St	Sr	26	155	236	.657
Brian Hill, Evansville	Sr	32	180	278	.647

Free Throw Percentage

	Cl	Gm	FT	FTA	Pct
Rob Robbins, N.Mexico	Jr	34	101	108	.935
Mike Joseph, Bucknell	Sr	29	144	155	.929
Chris Jackson, LSU	So	32	191	210	.910
Andy Kennedy, UAB	Jr	31	111	123	.902
Steve Henson, Kan.St	Sr	32	101	112	.902

3-Pt Field Goal Percentage

	Cl	Gm	FG	FGA	Pct
Matt Lapin, Princeton	Sr	27	71	133	.534
Mike Iuzzolino, St.Fran,PA	Jr	27	79	153	.516
Dan Oberbrunner, WGB	Sr	31	47	93	.505
Lee Mayberry, Arkansas	So	35	65	129	.504
Dwight Pernell, H.Cross	Sr	30	81	161	.503

3-Pt Field Goals Per Game

	Cl	Gm	FG	Avg
Dave Jamerson, Ohio U	Sr	28	131	4.7
Sydney Grider, SW La	Sr	29	131	4.5
Mark Alberts, Akron	So	28	122	4.4
Jeff Fryer, Loyola,CA	Sr	28	121	4.3
Darryl Brooks, Tenn.St	Jr	24	95	4.0

TEAM

Scoring Offense

	Gm	W-L	Pts	Avg
Loyola Marymount	32	26-6	3918	122.4
Oklahoma	32	27-5	3243	101.3
Southern-Baton Rouge	31	25-6	3078	99.3
U.S.International	28	12-16	2738	97.8
Centenary	30	22-8	2877	95.9
Arkansas	35	30-5	3345	95.6
Texas	33	24-9	3091	93.7
UNLV	40	35-5	3739	93.5
Kansas	35	30-5	3223	92.1
LSU	32	23-9	2921	91.3

Scoring Defense

	Gm	W-L	Pts	Avg
Princeton	27	20-7	1378	51.0
Ball St	33	26-7	1935	58.6
Colorado St	30	21-9	1778	59.3
Wisconsin-Green Bay	32	24-8	1913	59.8
Northern Illinois	28	17-11	1710	61.1
Yale	26	19-7	1588	61.1
Alabama	35	26-9	2151	61.5
Boise St	27	12-15	1683	62.3
Monmouth	29	17-12	1818	62.7
Fairfield	29	10-19	1833	63.2

Scoring Margin

	Off	Def	Margin
Oklahoma	101.3	80.4	21.0
Kansas	92.1	72.3	19.7
Georgetown	81.5	64.8	16.7
Arkansas	95.6	79.8	15.8
Southern-Baton Rouge	99.3	83.1	15.2
UNLV	93.5	78.4	15.0

Final NCAA Men's Division I Standings

Conference records include regular season games only. Overall records include all post-season tournament games.

American South Conference

	Conference			Overall		
	W	L	Pct	W	L	Pct
†New Orleans	8	2	.800	21	11	.656
†Louisiana Tech	8	2	.800	20	8	.714
Texas-Pan American	7	3	.700	21	9	.700
SW Louisiana	4	6	.400	20	9	.690
Arkansas St	2	8	.200	15	13·	.536
Lamar	1	9	.100	7	21	.250

Note: New Orleans was 1st seed in Conf.Tourney.
Conf.Tourney Final: New Orleans 48, Texas-Pan Am 44.
†NIT Tournament (2-2): New Orleans (2-1); La.Tech (0-1).

Association of Mid-Continent Universities

	Conference			Overall		
	W	L	Pct	W	L	Pct
*SW Missouri St	11	1	.917	22	7	.759
†Wisconsin-Green Bay	9	3	.750	24	8	.750
*Northern Iowa	6	6	.500	23	9	.719
Illinois-Chicago	6	6	.500	16	12	.571
Western Illinois	6	6	.500	16	13	.552
Eastern Illinois	3	9	.250	10	18	.357
Valparaiso	1	11	.083	4	24	.143
Cleveland St	—	—	—	15	13	.536

Note: Cleveland St. on probation, ineligible for AMCU regular season and tournament, and NCAA tournament.
Conf.Tourney Final: Northern Iowa 53, Wisc-Green Bay 45.
NCAA Tournament (1-2): Northern Iowa (1-1); SW Missouri St.(0-1).
†NIT Tournament (1-1): Wisc-Green Bay (1-1).

Atlantic Coast Conference

	Conference			Overall		
	W	L	Pct	W	L	Pct
*Clemson	10	4	.714	26	9	.743
*Duke	9	5	.643	29	9	.763
*Georgia Tech	8	6	.571	28	7	.800
*North Carolina	8	6	.571	21	13	.618
*Virginia	6	8	.429	20	12	.625
North Carolina St	6	8	.429	18	12	.600
†Maryland	6	8	.429	19	14	.576
Wake Forest	3	11	.214	12	16	.429

Note: N.C.State on probation, ineligible for NCAA tournament.
Conf.Tourney Final: Georgia Tech 70, Virginia 61.
NCAA Tournament (14-5): Duke (5-1); Ga.Tech (4-1); Clemson (2-1); N.Carolina (2-1); Virginia (1-1).
†NIT Tournament (1-1): Maryland (1-1).

Atlantic 10 Conference

	Conference			Overall		
	W	L	Pct	W	L	Pct
*Temple	15	3	.833	20	11	.645
†Penn St	13	5	.722	25	9	.735
West Virginia	11	7	.611	16	12	.571
Rhode Island	11	7	.611	15	13	.536
†Rutgers	11	7	.611	18	17	.514
†Massachusetts	10	8	.556	17	14	.548
George Washington	6	12	.333	14	17	.452
St.Joseph's,PA	5	13	.278	7	21	.250
Duquesne	5	13	.278	7	22	.241
St.Bonaventure	3	15	.167	8	20	.286

Conf.Tourney Final: Temple 53, Massachusetts 51.
NCAA Tournament (0-1): Temple (0-1).
†NIT Tournament (6-3): Penn St.(4-1); Rutgers (2-1); UMass (0-1).

Big East Conference

	Conference			Overall		
	W	L	Pct	W	L	Pct
*Syracuse	12	4	.750	26	7	.788
*Connecticut	12	4	.750	31	6	.838
*Georgetown	11	5	.688	24	7	.774
*St.John's	10	6	.625	24	10	.706
*Providence	8	8	.500	17	12	.586
*Villanova	8	8	.500	18	15	.545
Seton Hall	5	11	.313	12	16	.429
Pittsburgh	5	11	.313	12	17	.414
Boston College	1	15	.063	8	20	.286

Conf.Tourney Final: Connecticut 78, Syracuse 75.
NCAA Tournament (7-6): UConn (3-1); Syracuse (2-1); Georgetown (1-1); St.John's (1-1); Providence (0-1); Villanova (0-1).

Big Eight Conference

	Conference			Overall		
	W	L	Pct	W	L	Pct
*Missouri	12	2	.857	26	6	.813
*Kansas	11	3	.786	30	5	.857
*Oklahoma	11	3	.786	27	5	.844
*Kansas St	7	7	.500	17	15	.531
†Oklahoma St	6	8	.429	17	14	.548
Iowa St	4	10	.286	10	18	.357
Nebraska	3	11	.214	10	18	.357
Colorado	2	12	.143	12	18	.400

Conf.Tourney Final: Oklahoma 92, Colorado 80.
NCAA Tournament (2-4): Oklahoma (1-1); Kansas (1-1); Missouri (0-1); Kansas St.(0-1).
†NIT Tournament (1-1): Oklahoma St.(1-1).

Big Sky Conference

	Conference			Overall		
	W	L	Pct	W	L	Pct
*Idaho	13	3	.813	25	6	.806
Eastern Washington	11	5	.688	18	11	.621
Montana	10	6	.625	18	11	.621
Nevada-Reno	9	7	.563	15	13	.536
Montana St	8	8	.500	17	12	.586
Weber St	8	8	.500	14	15	.483
Boise St	7	9	.438	12	15	.444
Northern Arizona	3	13	.188	8	20	.286
Idaho St	3	13	.188	6	21	.222

Conf.Tourney Final: Idaho 65, E.Washington 62.
NCAA Tournament (0-1): Idaho (0-1).

Big South Conference

	Conference			Overall		
	W	L	Pct	W	L	Pct
Coastal Carolina	11	1	.917	23	6	.793
NC-Asheville	7	5	.583	18	12	.600
Campbell	7	5	.583	15	13	.536
Winthrop	6	6	.500	19	10	.655
Baptist College	4	8	.333	9	19	.321
Augusta	4	8	.333	8	20	.286
Radford	3	9	.250	7	22	.241

Conf.Tourney Final: Coast.Carolina 76, NC-Asheville 73.

Final NCAA Men's Division I Standings (Cont.)

Big Ten Conference

	Conference			Overall		
	W	L	Pct	W	L	Pct
*Michigan St	15	3	.833	28	6	.824
*Purdue	13	5	.722	22	8	.733
*Michigan	12	6	.667	23	8	.742
*Illinois	11	7	.611	21	8	.724
*Minnesota	11	7	.611	23	9	.719
*Ohio St	10	8	.556	17	13	.567
*Indiana	8	10	.444	18	11	.621
Wisconsin	4	14	.222	14	17	.452
Iowa	4	14	.222	12	16	.429
Northwestern	2	16	.111	9	19	.321

Conf.Tourney Final: Big Ten has no tournament.
***NCAA Tournament (8-7):** Minnesota (3-1); Mich.St.(2-1); Purdue (1-1); Michigan (1-1); Ohio St.(1-1); Illinois (0-1); Indiana (0-1).

Big West Conference

	Conference			Overall		
	W	L	Pct	W	L	Pct
*New Mexico St	16	2	.889	26	5	.839
*UNLV	16	2	.889	35	5	.875
*UC Santa Barbara	13	5	.722	21	9	.700
†Long Beach St	12	6	.667	23	9	.719
Utah St	8	10	.444	14	16	.467
Pacific	7	11	.389	15	14	.517
CS-Fullerton	6	12	.333	13	16	.448
San Jose St	5	13	.278	8	20	.286
Fresno St	4	14	.222	10	19	.345
UC Irvine	3	15	.167	5	23	.179

Conf.Tourney Final: UNLV 92, Long Beach St.74.
***NCAA Tournament (7-2):** UNLV (6-0); UC Santa Barbara (1-1); New Mexico St.(0-1)
†NIT Tournament (1-1): Long Beach St.(1-1).

Colonial Athletic Association

	Conference			Overall		
	W	L	Pct	W	L	Pct
†James Madison	11	3	.786	20	11	.645
*Richmond	10	4	.714	22	10	.688
American	10	4	.714	20	9	.690
George Mason	10	4	.714	20	12	.625
East Carolina	6	8	.429	13	18	.419
Navy	4	10	.286	5	23	.179
NC-Wilmington	3	11	.214	8	20	.286
William & Mary	2	12	.143	6	22	.214

Conf.Tourney Final: Richmond 77, James Madison 72.
***NCAA Tournament (0-1):** Richmond (0-1).
†NIT Tournament (0-1): James Madison (0-1).

East Coast Conference

	Conference			Overall		
	W	L	Pct	W	L	Pct
*Towson St	8	6	.571	18	13	.581
Lehigh	8	6	.571	18	12	.600
Hofstra	8	6	.571	13	15	.464
Delaware	7	7	.500	16	13	.552
Lafayette	7	7	.500	15	13	.536
Drexel	7	7	.500	13	15	.464
Bucknell	6	8	.429	15	14	.517
Rider	5	9	.357	10	18	.357

Conf.Tourney Final: Towson St.73, Lehigh 60.
***NCAA Tournament (0-1):** Towson St.(0-1).

Ivy League

	Conference			Overall		
	W	L	Pct	W	L	Pct
*Princeton	11	3	.786	20	7	.741
Yale	10	4	.714	19	7	.731
Dartmouth	7	7	.500	12	14	.462
Harvard	7	7	.500	12	14	.462
Pennsylvania	7	7	.500	12	14	.462
Brown	7	7	.500	10	16	.385
Cornell	5	9	.357	12	17	.414
Columbia	1	13	.071	4	22	.154

Conf.Tourney Final: The Ivy League has no tournament.
***NCAA Tournament (0-1):** Princeton (0-1).

Metro Conference

	Conference			Overall		
	W	L	Pct	W	L	Pct
*Louisville	12	2	.857	27	8	.771
*Southern Miss	9	5	.643	20	12	.625
†Cincinnati	9	5	.643	20	14	.588
†Memphis St	8	6	.571	18	12	.600
Florida St	6	8	.429	16	15	.516
South Carolina	6	8	.429	14	14	.500
Virginia Tech	5	9	.357	13	18	.419
Tulane	1	13	.071	4	24	.143

Conf.Tourney Final: Louisville 83, Southern Miss 80.
***NCAA Tournament (1-2):** Louisville (1-1); Southern Miss.(0-1).
†NIT Tournament (1-2): Cincinnati (1-1); Memphis St.(0-1).

Metro Atlantic Conference

	Conference			Overall		
North	W	L	Pct	W	L	Pct
†Holy Cross	14	2	.875	24	6	.800
Siena	11	5	.688	16	13	.552
†Fordham	10	6	.625	20	13	.606
Canisius	5	11	.313	11	18	.379
Army	5	11	.313	9	19	.345
Niagara	5	11	.313	6	22	.214
South	W	L	Pct	W	L	Pct
*La Salle	16	0	1.000	30	2	.938
Iona	8	8	.500	13	15	.464
St.Peter's	7	9	.438	14	14	.500
Manhattan	7	9	.438	11	17	.393
Fairfield	6	10	.375	10	19	.345
Loyola,MD	2	14	.125	4	24	.143

Conf.Tourney Final: La Salle 71, Fordham 61.
***NCAA Tournament (1-1):** La Salle (1-1).
†NIT Tournament (1-2): Fordham (1-1); Holy Cross (0-1).

Mid-American Conference

	Conference			Overall		
	W	L	Pct	W	L	Pct
*Ball St	13	3	.813	26	7	.743
†Kent St	12	4	.750	21	8	.724
†Bowling Green	9	7	.563	18	11	.621
Miami,OH	9	7	.563	14	15	.483
Eastern Michigan	8	8	.500	19	13	.594
Toledo	7	9	.438	12	16	.429
Central Michigan	6	10	.375	13	17	.433
Ohio University	5	11	.313	12	16	.429
Western Michigan	3	13	.188	9	18	.333

Conf.Tourney Final: Ball St.78, Central Michigan 56.
***NCAA Tournament (2-1):** Ball St.(2-1).
†NIT Tournament (0-2): Kent St.(0-1); Bowling Green (0-1).

Mid-Eastern Athletic Conference

	Conference			Overall		
	W	L	Pct	W	L	Pct
*Coppin St	15	1	.938	26	7	.788
Florida A&M	13	3	.813	18	11	.621
Delaware St	9	7	.563	14	14	.500
South Carolina St	8	8	.500	13	16	.448
Bethune-Cookman	8	8	.500	10	18	.357
North Carolina A&T	6	10	.375	13	16	.448
Howard	5	11	.313	8	20	.286
Maryland-East.Shore	4	12	.250	10	17	.370
Morgan St	4	12	.250	8	20	.286

Conf.Tourney Final: Coppin St.54, N.Carolina A&T 50.
*NCAA Tournament (0-1): Coppin St.(0-1).

Midwestern Collegiate Conference

	Conference			Overall		
	W	L	Pct	W	L	Pct
*Xavier,OH	12	2	.857	28	5	.848
†Dayton	10	4	.714	22	10	.688
†St.Louis	9	5	.643	21	12	.636
†Marquette	9	5	.643	15	14	.517
Evansville	8	6	.571	17	15	.531
Detroit	3	11	.214	10	18	.357
Loyola,IL	3	11	.214	7	22	.241
Butler	2	12	.143	6	22	.214

Conf.Tourney Final: Dayton 98, Xavier 89.
*NCAA Tournament (3-2): Xavier (2-1); Dayton (1-1).
†NIT Tournament (4-2): St.Louis (4-1); Marquette (0-1).

Missouri Valley Conference

	Conference			Overall		
	W	L	Pct	W	L	Pct
†Southern Illinois	10	4	.714	26	8	.765
†Creighton	9	5	.643	21	12	.636
*Illinois St	9	5	.643	18	13	.581
†Tulsa	9	5	.643	17	13	.567
Bradley	6	8	.429	11	20	.355
Wichita St	6	8	.429	10	19	.345
Drake	5	9	.357	13	18	.419
Indiana St	2	12	.143	8	20	.286

Conf.Tourney Final: Illinois St.81, Southern Ill.78.
*NCAA Tournament (0-1): Illinois St.(0-1).
†NIT Tournament (0-3): Southern Ill.(0-1); Creighton (0-1); Tulsa (0-1).

North Atlantic Conference

	Conference			Overall		
	W	L	Pct	W	L	Pct
Northeastern	9	3	.750	16	12	.571
*Boston Univ	9	3	.750	18	12	.600
Hartford	8	4	.667	17	11	.607
Maine	6	6	.500	11	17	.393
Vermont	4	8	.333	13	17	.433
Colgate	3	9	.250	8	21	.276
New Hampshire	3	9	.250	5	23	.179

Conf.Tourney Final: Boston Univ.75, Vermont 57.
*NCAA Tournament (0-1): Boston Univ.(0-1).

Northeast Conference

	Conference			Overall		
	W	L	Pct	W	L	Pct
*Robert Morris	12	4	.750	22	8	.733
Monmouth	11	5	.688	17	12	.586
Marist	10	6	.625	17	11	.607
St.Francis,PA	10	6	.625	17	11	.607
Mt.St.Mary's	10	6	.625	16	12	.571
Fairleigh Dickinson	8	8	.500	16	13	.552
Wagner	6	10	.375	11	17	.393
St.Francis,NY	4	12	.250	9	18	.333
Long Island	1	15	.063	3	23	.115

Conf.Tourney Final: Robt.Morris 71, Monmouth 66.
*NCAA Tournament (0-1): Robert Morris (0-1).

Ohio Valley Conference

	Conference			Overall		
	W	L	Pct	W	L	Pct
*Murray St	10	2	.833	21	9	.700
Tennessee Tech	9	3	.750	19	9	.679
Morehead St	7	5	.583	16	13	.552
Eastern Kentucky	7	5	.583	13	17	.433
Middle Tennessee	5	7	.417	12	16	.429
Austin Peay	2	10	.167	10	19	.345
Tennessee St	2	10	.167	7	21	.250

Conf.Tourney Final: Murray St.64, Eastern Ky.57.
*NCAA Tournament (0-1): Murray St.(0-1).

Pacific-10 Conference

	Conference			Overall		
	W	L	Pct	W	L	Pct
*Oregon St	15	3	.833	22	7	.759
*Arizona	15	3	.833	25	7	.781
*California	12	6	.667	22	10	.688
*UCLA	11	7	.611	22	11	.667
†Oregon	10	8	.556	15	14	.517
†Stanford	9	9	.500	18	12	.600
†Arizona St	6	12	.333	15	16	.484
Southern Cal	6	12	.333	12	16	.429
Washington	5	13	.278	12	17	.414
Washington St	1	17	.056	6	22	.214

Conf.Tourney Final: Arizona 94, UCLA 78.
*NCAA Tournament (4-4): UCLA (2-1); Arizona (1-1); California (1-1); Oregon St.(0-1).
†NIT Tournament (0-3): Oregon (0-1); Stanford (0-1); Arizona St.(0-1).

Southeastern Conference

	Conference			Overall		
	W	L	Pct	W	L	Pct
*Georgia	13	5	.722	20	9	.690
*Alabama	12	6	.667	26	9	.743
*LSU	12	6	.667	23	9	.719
†Tennessee	10	8	.556	16	14	.533
Kentucky	10	8	.556	14	14	.500
Mississippi	8	10	.444	13	17	.433
Auburn	8	10	.444	13	18	.419
†Mississippi St	7	11	.389	16	14	.533
†Vanderbilt	7	11	.389	21	14	.600
Florida	3	15	.167	7	21	.250

Note: Kentucky on probation, ineligible for SEC and NCAA tournaments.
Conf.Tournament Final: Alabama 70, Mississippi 51.
*NCAA Tournament (3-3): Alabama (2-1); LSU (1-1); Georgia (0-1).
†NIT Tournament (7-2): Vanderbilt (5-0, won tourney); Tennessee (1-1); Miss.St.(1-1).

Final NCAA Men's Division I Standings (Cont.)

Southern Conference

	Conference			Overall		
	W	L	Pct	W	L	Pct
*East Tennessee St	12	2	.857	27	7	.794
Marshall	9	5	.643	15	13	.536
Appalachian St	8	6	.571	19	11	.633
Tenn-Chattanooga	7	7	.500	14	14	.500
VMI	7	7	.500	14	15	.483
Furman	5	9	.357	15	16	.484
Citadel	5	9	.357	12	16	.429
Western Carolina	3	11	.214	10	18	.357

Conf.Tourney Final: E.Tenn.St. 96, Appalachian St. 75.
*NCAA Tournament (0-1):** E.Tennessee St.(0-1).

Southland Conference

	Conference			Overall		
	W	L	Pct	W	L	Pct
*NE Louisiana	13	1	.929	22	8	.733
McNeese St	11	3	.786	14	13	.519
SW Texas St	9	5	.643	13	15	.464
Sam Houston St	8	6	.571	10	18	.357
Texas-Arlington	6	8	.429	13	16	.448
Northwestern LA	5	9	.357	10	19	.345
North Texas	3	11	.214	5	25	.167
Stephen F.Austin	1	13	.071	2	25	.074

Conf.Tourney Final: NE Louisiana 84, North Texas 68.
*NCAA Tournament (0-1):** NE Louisiana (0-1).

Southwest Conference

	Conference			Overall		
	W	L	Pct	W	L	Pct
*Arkansas	14	2	.875	30	5	.857
*Houston	13	3	.813	25	8	.758
*Texas	12	4	.750	24	9	.727
TCU	9	7	.563	16	13	.552
†Baylor	7	9	.438	16	14	.533
Texas A&M	7	9	.438	14	17	.452
Rice	5	11	.313	11	17	.393
SMU	5	11	.313	10	18	.357
Texas Tech	0	16	.000	5	22	.185

Conf.Tourney Final: Arkansas 96, Houston 84.
*NCAA Tournament (7-3):** Arkansas (4-1); Texas (3-1); Houston (0-1).
†NIT Tournament (0-1):** Baylor (0-1).

Southwestern Athletic Conference

	Conference			Overall		
	W	L	Pct	W	L	Pct
†Southern University	12	2	.857	25	6	.806
*Texas Southern	10	4	.714	19	12	.613
Alabama St	7	7	.500	15	13	.536
Mississippi Valley St	7	7	.500	11	18	.379
Alcorn St	6	8	.429	7	22	.241
Prairie View A&M	5	9	.357	9	18	.333
Grambling St	5	9	.357	9	19	.321
Jackson St	4	10	.286	9	19	.321

Conf.Tourney Final: Texas Southern 94, Southern Univ. 89.
*NCAA Tournament (0-1):** Texas Southern (0-1).
†NIT Tournament (0-1):** Southern Univ.(0-1).

Sun Belt Conference

	Conference			Overall		
	W	L	Pct	W	L	Pct
*Alabama-Birmingham	12	2	.857	22	9	.710
*South Florida	9	5	.643	20	11	.645
Old Dominion	7	7	.500	14	14	.500
Western Kentucky	7	7	.500	13	17	.433
NC-Charlotte	6	8	.429	16	14	.533
Jacksonville	5	9	.357	13	16	.448
South Alabama	5	9	.357	11	17	.393
Va.Commonwealth	5	9	.357	11	17	.393

Conf.Tourney Final: South Florida 81, NC-Charlotte 74.
*NCAA Tournament (0-2):** Ala-Birmingham (0-1); South Florida (0-1).

Trans America Athletic Conference

	Conference			Overall		
	W	L	Pct	W	L	Pct
Centenary	14	2	.875	22	8	.733
Texas-San Antonio	13	3	.813	22	7	.759
*Arkansas-Little Rock	12	4	.750	20	10	.667
Georgia Southern	11	5	.688	17	11	.607
Stetson	8	8	.500	15	17	.469
Hardin-Simmons	5	11	.313	9	19	.321
Samford	4	12	.250	6	22	.214
Georgia St	3	13	.188	5	22	.185
Mercer	2	14	.125	7	20	.259

Note: Hardin-Simmons quit league and dropped from Div.I to Div.III after completion of season.
Conf.Tourney Final: Ark-Little Rock 105, Centenary 95.
*NCAA Tournament (0-1):** Ark-Little Rock (0-1).

West Coast Athletic Conference

	Conference			Overall		
	W	L	Pct	W	L	Pct
*Loyola Marymount	13	1	.929	26	6	.813
Pepperdine	10	4	.714	17	11	.607
San Diego	9	5	.643	16	12	.571
Portland	7	7	.500	11	17	.393
Santa Clara	6	8	.429	9	19	.321
San Francisco	4	10	.286	8	20	.286
St.Mary's	4	10	.286	7	20	.259
Gonzaga	3	11	.214	8	20	.286

Conf.Tourney Final: Loyola Marymount declared winner after 1st round following death of player Hank Gathers.
*NCAA Tournament (3-1):** Loyola Marymount (3-1).

Western Athletic Conference

	Conference			Overall		
	W	L	Pct	W	L	Pct
*Colorado St	11	5	.688	21	9	.700
*BYU	11	5	.688	21	9	.700
†Hawaii	10	6	.625	25	10	.714
*UTEP	10	6	.625	21	11	.656
†New Mexico	9	7	.563	20	14	.588
Utah	7	9	.438	16	14	.533
Wyoming	7	9	.438	15	14	.517
San Diego St	4	12	.250	13	18	.419
Air Force	3	13	.188	12	20	.375

Conf.Tourney Final: UTEP 75, Hawaii 58.
*NCAA Tournament (0-3):** Colorado St.(0-1); BYU (0-1); UTEP (0-1).
†NIT Tournament (5-3):** New Mexico (3-2); Hawaii (2-1).

Division I Independents

	Overall		
	W	L	Pct
Wright St	21	7	.750
Northern Illinois	17	11	.607
†DePaul	20	15	.571
Akron	16	12	.571
*Notre Dame	16	13	.552
Miami,FL	13	15	.464
Missouri-Kansas City	13	15	.464
Southern Utah	13	15	.464
Maryland-Baltimore County	12	16	.429
U.S.International	12	16	.429
Liberty	11	17	.393
Youngstown St	8	20	.286
Brooklyn	7	21	.250
Central Florida	7	21	.250
Florida International	7	21	.250
Chicago St	6	22	.214
Central Connecticut	5	22	.185
Nicholls St	4	23	.148
Davidson	4	24	.143

*NCAA Tournament (0-1): Notre Dame (0-1).
†NIT Tournament (2-1): DePaul (2-1).

Final UPI Top 20 Poll

Final Board of Coaches vote through games of March 11 and before NCAA tournament: first place votes in parentheses with total points (based on 15 for 1st, 14 for 2nd, etc.).

	Pts		Pts
1 Oklahoma (34)	586	11 Missouri	215
2 UNLV (3)	520	12 Arizona	177
3 Connecticut	510	13 La Salle (1)	138
4 Mich.St. (1)	457	14 Duke	135
5 Kansas	368	15 Michigan	113
6 Syracuse (1)	340	16 Louisville	47
7 Ga.Tech	296	17 Clemson	31
8 Arkansas	282	18 Illinois	26
9 Georgetown	264	19 Alabama	13
10 Purdue	222	20 N.Mexico St	11

Other teams receiving votes (in alphabetical order): Georgia, Houston, LSU, Loyola-Marymount, Minnesota, N.Carolina, Oregon St., UC-Santa Barbara, St.John's, UTEP, Virginia and Xavier.

Teams on probation (and ineligible to receive votes): Cleveland St. and Kentucky.

Consensus All-America

The NCAA Division I players cited most frequently by the following All-America selectors: AP, US Basketball Writers, National Assn. of Basketball Coaches, and UPI.

First Team

	Class	Hgt	Pos
Derrick Coleman, Syracuse	Sr.	6-10	F/C
Gary Payton, Oregon St	Sr.	6-4	G
Lionel Simmons, La Salle	Sr.	6-7	F
Chris Jackson, LSU	So.	6-1	G
Larry Johnson, UNLV	Jr.	6-7	F

Second Team

	Class	Hgt	Pos
Rumeal Robinson, Michigan	Sr.	6-2	G
Doug Smith, Missouri	Jr.	6-10	C
Alonzo Mourning, Georgetown	So.	6-10	C/F
Dennis Scott, GeorgiaTech	Jr.	6-8	F
Bo Kimble, Loyola Marymount	Sr.	6-5	F
Kendall Gill, Illinois	Sr.	6-4	G

Awards

Player of the Year

Lionel Simmons, La Salle . . . . . . AP,NABC,Naismith, UPI,USBWA and Wooden

Coaches of the Year

Jim Calhoun, Connecticut . . . . AP,UPI
Bobby Cremins, Ga.Tech . . . . Naismith
Jud Heathcote, Mich.St . . . . NABC
Roy Williams, Kansas . . . . USBWA

Other Men's Tournaments

NCAA Division II

After eight regionals, the 1990 Div.II Quarterfinal pairings were as follows: SE Missouri St.(26-4) vs Kentucky Wesleyan (28-2); North Dakota (26-6) vs Jacksonville St.,AL (24-4); Bridgeport,CT (24-8) vs CS-Bakersfield (27-4); Gannon,PA (24-7) vs Morehouse,GA (25-5). The Final Eight played March 24-26 in Springfield, MA.

Quarterfinals

Ky.Wesleyan 91 . . . . OT . . . . SE Mo.St. 90
North Dakota 89 . . . . Jacksonville St. 67
CS-Bakersfield 87 . . . . Bridgeport 72
Morehouse 75 . . . . Gannon 69

Semifinals

Ky.Wesleyan 101 . . . . North Dakota 92
CS-Bakerfield 85 . . . . Morehouse 60

Third Place

North Dakota 98 . . . . Morehouse 77

Championship

Ky.Wesleyan 93 . . . . CS-Bakersfield 79

NCAA Division III

After four regionals, the 1990 Div.III Semifinal pairings were as follows: Calvin,MI (29-1) vs DePauw,IN (23-6); Rochester,NY (24-5) vs Washington,MD (24-5). The Final Four played March 16-17 in Springfield, OH.

Semifinals

DePauw 82 . . . . Calvin 79
Rochester 86 . . . . Washington 70

Third Place

Washington 87 . . . . Calvin 86

Championship

Rochester 43 . . . . DePauw 42

NAIA

After two rounds in the Men's 32-team tournament March 13-19 at Kemper Arena in Kansas City, the Quarterfinal pairings were as follows: David Lipscomb,TN (40-4) vs Pfeiffer,NC (22-10); SC-Spartanburg (29-2) vs Birmingham-Southern,AL (28-3); Oral Roberts,OK (36-5) vs Georgetown,KY (28-6); Central Washington (31- 4) vs Wisconsin-Eau Claire (28-3).

Quarterfinals

David Lipscomb 125 . . . . Pfeiffer 83
Birm-Southern 87 . . . . Spartanburg 80
Georgetown 80 . . . . Oral Roberts 78
Wisc-Eau Claire 84 . . . . Central Wash. 57

Semifinals

Birm-Southern 98 . . . . David Lipscomb 96
Wisc-Eau Claire 76 . . . . Georgetown 65

Championship

Birm-Southern 88 . . . . Wisc-Eau Claire 80

Final Women's Top 25 Poll
Taken before start of NCAA tournament.

The **Philadelphia Inquirer** coaches' poll, compiled by Mel Greenberg: first place votes in parentheses; records through March 11; total points (based on 25 for 1st, 24 for 2nd, etc.); record in NCAA tourney and team lost to; head coach (career years and record, including NCAA tourney), and preseason ranking. Teams in **bold type** went on to reach NCAA Final Four.

	Mar.11 Record	Points	NCAA Recap	Head Coach	Preseason Rank
1 **Louisiana Tech** (56)	29-0	1494	3-1 (Auburn)	Leon Barmore (8th year: 243-24)	2
2 **Stanford** (3)	27-1	1437	5-0	Tara VanDerveer (12th: 266-89)	3
3 Washington	26-2	1324	2-1 (Auburn)	Chris Gobrecht (11th: 207-123)	16
4 Tennessee	25-5	1301	2-1 (Virginia)	Pat Summitt (16th: 412-113)	1
5 UNLV (1)	28-2	1237	0-1 (Ole Miss)	Jim Bolla (8th: 196-53)	10
6 S.F.Austin	25-2	1166	1-1 (Arkansas)	Gary Blair (5th: 128-30)	12
7 Georgia	25-4	1080	0-1 (Arkansas)	Andy Landers (11th: 286-75)	4
8 Texas	25-4	1052	2-1 (La.Tech)	Jody Conradt (21st: 556-126)	5
9 **Auburn**	24-6	1013	4-1 (Stanford)	Joe Ciampi (13th: 329-79)	7
10 Iowa	23-5	962	0-1 (Vanderbilt)	Vivian Stringer (18th: 415-94)	11
11 N.C.State	24-5	925	1-1 (Texas)	Kay Yow (19th: 397-137)	6
12 **Virginia**	26-5	886	3-1 (Stanford)	Debbie Ryan (13th: 270-119)	15
13 Northwestern	24-4	734	0-1 (S.Carolina)	Don Perrelli (13th: 275-141)	46
14 Long Beach St	24-8	685	1-1 (S.F.Austin)	Joan Bonvicini (11th: 301-62)	9
15 Purdue	22-6	615	1-1 (La.Tech)	Lin Dunn (19th: 309-212)	8
16 Hawaii	25-3	586	1-1 (Stanford)	Vince Goo (3rd: 60-28)	36
17 Northern Illinois	25-4	546	1-1 (Purdue)	Jane Albright (6th: 97-74)	32
18 Providence	26-4	432	1-1 (Virgina)	Bob Foley (5th: 109-46)	53
19 South Carolina	22-8	370	2-1 (Wash.)	Nancy Wilson (14th: 318-124)	19
20 Southern Miss	26-4	332	1-1 (La.Tech)	Kay James (18th: 323-148)	40
21 Tennessee Tech	25-4	299	1-1 (Auburn)	Bill Worrell (4th: 91-30)	20
22 Arkansas	22-4	295	3-1 (Stanford)	John Sutherland (6th: 122-56)	46
23 LSU	21-8	106	0-1 (So.Miss.)	Sue Gunter (20th: 434-155)	13
24 Mississippi	20-9	102	2-1 (Stanford)	Van Chancellor (12th: 292-93)	14
25 St.Joseph's,PA	24-6	99	0-1 (Old Dom.)	Jim Foster (12th: 230-114)	21

Others receiving votes: 26. Penn St.(24-6,88 pts); **27.** Connecticut (25-5,71); **28.** Montana (27-2,48); **29.** Clemson (20-9,46); **30.** Maryland (18-10,35); **31.** Oklahoma St.(20-10,32); **32.** Vanderbilt (21-10,25); **33.** DePaul (21-9,15); **34.** Texas Tech (19-10,12); **35.** Southern Ill.(21-9,11); **36.** Bowling Green (22-8,7); **37.** Maine (22-5,6), Ohio St.(17-11,6); **39.** Richmond (25-4,5); **40.** Michigan (19-9,4), Old Dominion (20-9,4); **42.** Florida St.(21-8,3), UCLA (17-11,3); **44.** Missouri (20-8,2), Notre Dame (22-6,2); **46.** Dartmouth (23-3,1), Fairfield (21-8,1), Kansas St.(20-10,1), Manhattan (18-12,1).

NCAA Women's Division I

Individual Leaders
Includes games through NCAA tournament.

Scoring

	Cl	Gm	Pts	Avg
Kim Perrot, SW Louisiana	Sr	28	839	30.0
Pam Hudson, NW Louisiana	Sr	29	829	28.6
Dale Hodges, St.Joe's,PA	Sr	31	855	27.6
Adrian Vickers, S.Alabama	Sr	30	795	26.5
Lisa McMullen, Alabama St	So	28	735	26.3
Judy Mosley, Hawaii	Sr	30	772	25.7
Tonya Grant, St.Peter's	Sr	28	716	25.6
Wendy Scholtens, Vanderbilt	Jr	34	855	25.1
Rachel Bouchard, Maine	Jr	29	724	25.0
Kelly Lyons, Old Dominion	Sr	31	764	24.6
Carmen Jones, Tulane	Sr	28	690	24.6

Rebounding

	Cl	Gm	Reb	Avg
Pam Hudson, NW Louisiana	Sr	29	438	15.1
Judy Mosley, Hawaii	Sr	30	431	14.4
Sonya Dixon, Tex-Southern	Sr	29	411	14.2
Jeanette Saunds, LIU	Sr	27	369	13.7
Tarcha Hollis, Grambling	Jr	27	361	13.4

Assists

	Cl	Gm	Ast	Avg
Tine Freil, Pacific	Fr	29	321	11.1
Shanya Evans, Providence	Jr	30	287	9.6
Camille Ratledge, Florida	Sr	27	228	8.4
Anja Bordt, St.Mary's,CA	Jr	28	225	8.0

Tournament Seeds

EAST
1. Tennessee (25-5)
2. Virginia (26-5)
3. Providence (26-4)
4. Connecticut (25-5)
5. Clemson (20-9)
6. Maryland (18-10)
7. Penn St.(24-6)
8. Old Dominion (20-9)
9. St.Joseph's,PA (24-6)
10. Florida St.(21-8)
11. Appalachian St.(20-8)
12. Manhattan (18-12)

WEST
1. **Stanford** (27-1)
2. Georgia (25-4)
3. S.F.Austin St.(27-2)
4. UNLV (28-2)
5. Mississippi (20-9)
6. Long Beach St.(24-8)
7. Arkansas (22-4)
8. Montana (27-2)
9. Hawaii (25-3)
10. UCLA (17-11)
11. California (17-11)
12. Utah (20-9)

MIDEAST
1. Washington (26-2)
2. **Auburn** (24-6)
3. Iowa (23-5)
4. Northwestern (24-4)
5. South Carolina (22-8)
6. Vanderbilt (21-10)
7. Tenn.Tech (25-4)
8. DePaul (21-9)
9. Western Ky.(17-11)
10. Richmond (25-4)
11. Rutgers (20-9)
12. Bowling Green (22-8)

MIDWEST
1. **Louisiana Tech** (29-0)
2. N.Carolina St.(24-5)
3. Texas (25-4)
4. Purdue (22-6)
5. Northern Ill.(25-4)
6. Ohio St.(17-11)
7. Oklahoma St. (20-10)
8. Southern Miss. (26-4)
9. LSU (21-8)
10. Michigan (19-9)
11. Southern Ill. (21-9)
12. Texas Tech (19-10)

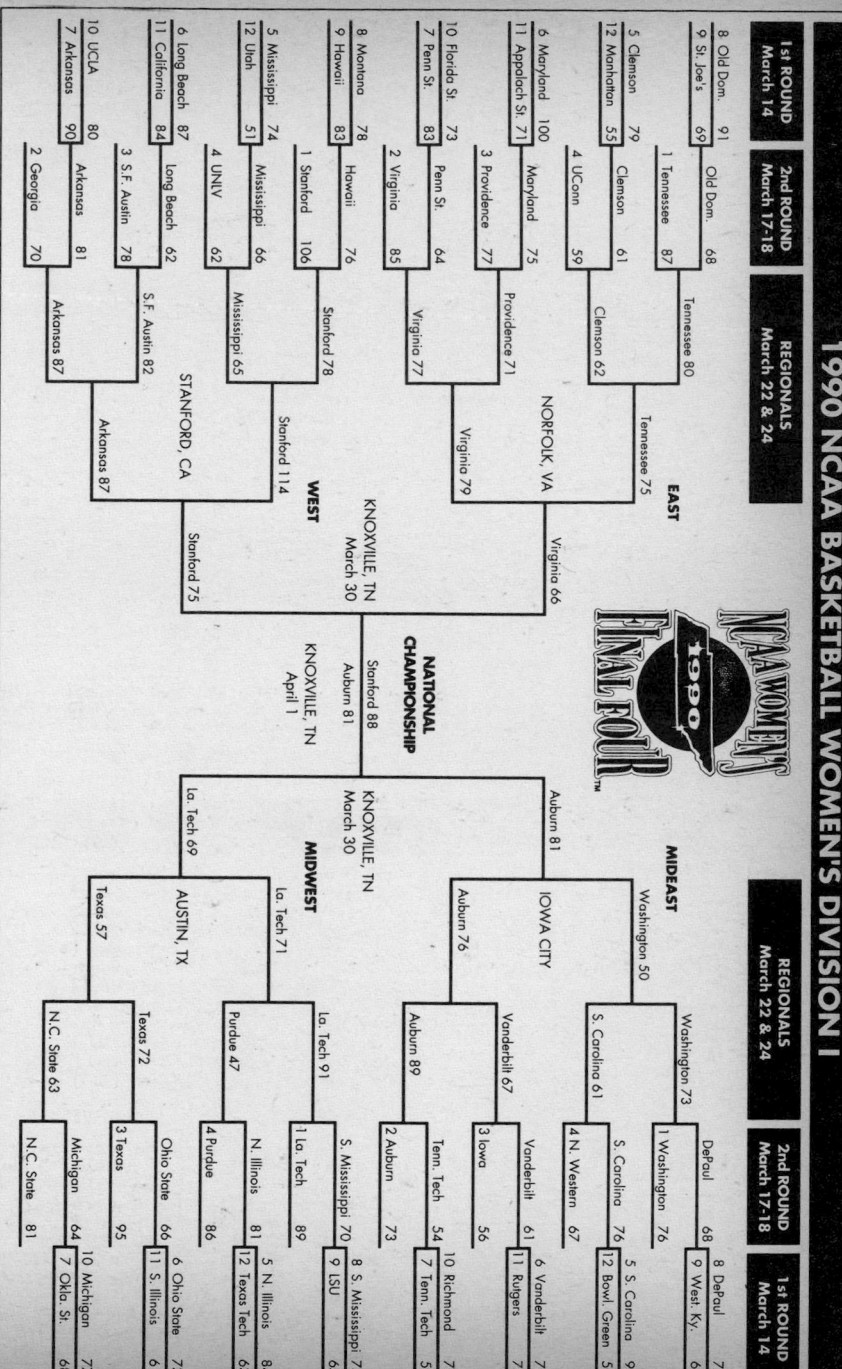

NCAA Women's Division I (Cont.)

Championship Game
Stanford 88, Auburn 81

Auburn	Min	FG M-A	FT M-A	Pts	Rb	A	F
Evelyn Thompson	31	3-11	2-2	10	2	1	5
Kendall Mago	25	2-6	0-2	4	5	0	3
C.C.Hayden	31	6-8	3-6	15	5	0	3
Chantel Tremitiere	40	7-9	1-2	17	5	5	1
Carolyn Jones	36	7-17	8-9	24	9	2	4
Linda Godby	22	4-10	1-3	9	4	0	5
Lynn Stevenson	13	1-2	0-0	2	3	3	3
Lauretta Freeman	2	0-0	0-0	0	1	0	1
TOTALS	200	30-63	15-24	81	34	11	25

Three-point FG: 6-12 (Thompson 2, Tremitiere 2-2, Jones 2-6, Godby 0-1, Stevenson 0-1); **Team Rebounds:** 5 (not included above); **Blocked Shots:** 3 (Jones 2, Godby); **Turnovers:** 9 (Thompson 3, Stevenson 2, Tremitiere 2, Hayden, Jones); **Steals:** 4 (Tremitiere 2, Jones, Thompson). **Team FG Pct:** .476; **Team FT Pct:** .625.

Stanford	Min	FG M-A	FT M-A	Pts	Rb	A	F
Kacy Steding	34	6-18	0-0	18	7	5	3
Julie Zeilstra	30	2-8	5-5	9	6	2	2
Trisha Stevens	28	6-13	4-5	16	10	1	4
Jennifer Azzi	39	5-10	3-5	17	4	5	5
Sonja Henning	39	6-11	8-11	21	9	1	0
Val Whiting	24	3-6	1-5	7	4	0	1
Martha Richards	5	0-0	0-0	0	0	0	1
Stacy Parson	1	0-0	0-0	0	0	0	0
TOTALS	200	28-66	21-31	88	40	14	16

Three-point FG: 11-26 (Steding 6-15, Azzi 4-8, Henning 1-3); **Team Rebounds:** 11 (not included above); **Blocked Shots:** 2 (Steding, Whiting); **Turnovers:** 13 (Whiting 3, Zeilstra 3, Azzi 2, Henning 2, Stevens 2, Richards); **Steals:** 5 (Henning, Steding, Stevens, Whiting, Zeilstra). **Team FG Pct:** .424; **Team FT Pct:** .677.

Auburn (SEC)	41	40—81
Stanford (Pac-10)	41	47—88

Technical Fouls: none. **Officials:** Art Bomengen, Sally Bell. **Attendance:** 16,595. **TV Rating:** 3.7/11 share (CBS).

THE FINAL FOUR
Thompson-Boling Arena, Knoxville, TN

Semifinals
Stanford 75 . . . . Virginia 66
Auburn 81 . . . . La.Tech 69

Championship
Sanford 88 . . . . Auburn 81

Final records: Stanford (32-1), Auburn (28-7), Louisiana Tech (32-1), Virginia (29-6).

Most Outstanding Player: Jennifer Azzi, Stanford guard (Semifinal—15 points; Final—17 pts).

All-Tournament Team: Azzi and Katy Steding, Stanford; Carolyn Jones and Chantel Tremitiere, Auburn; Venus Lacy, La.Tech.

Consensus All-America

The NCAA Division I players cited most frequently by the following All-America selectors: US Basketball Writers and National Assn. of Basketball Coaches.

	Class	Hgt	Pos
Jennifer Azzi, Stanford	Sr.	5-8	G
Portia Hill, SF Austin	Sr.	6-3	C
Dale Hodges, St.Joe's,PA	Sr.	6-1	C
Venus Lacy, La.Tech	Sr.	6-4	C
Andrea Stinson, NC State	Jr.	5-10	G

Awards
Players of the Year
Jennifer Azzi, Stanford . . . . Naismith and Wade
Venus Lacy, La.Tech . . . . USBWA and WBCA
Note: Broderick Award will be announced in Fall.

Coaches of the Year
Leon Barmore, La.Tech . . . . USBWA
Tara VanDerveer, Stanford . . . . Naismith
Kay Yow, N.C.State . . . . WBCA

Other Women's Tournaments

NCAA Division II
After eight regionals, the 1990 Div.II Quarterfinal pairings were as follows: Bentley,MA (29-3) vs Bellarmine, KY (25-5); Central Missouri St.(29-2) vs Oakland,MI (26-4); Lock Haven,PA (26-6) vs Delta St.,MS (29-1); North Dakota (27-3) vs Cal Poly Pomona (27-3). **Quarterfinals**—Bentley 74, Bellarmine 69; Oakland 66, Central Mo.St.61; Delta St.90, Lock Haven 59; Cal Poly Pomona 67, North Dakota 64. **Final Four** (March 23-24, at Pomona,CA): **Semifinals**—Bentley 72, Oakland 68; Delta St.67, Cal Poly Pomona 53. **Third Place**—Cal Poly Pomona 87, Oakland 68. **Championship**—Delta St.77, Bentley 43.

NCAA Division III
After eight regionals, the 1990 Div.III Quarterfinal pairings were as follows: St.John Fisher,NY (29-1) vs Scranton,PA (26-4); Southern Maine (25-4) vs Heidelberg, OH (25-5); Concordia-Moorhead,MN (24-4) vs Centre, KY (21-6); Buena Vista,IA (23-5) vs Hope,MI (21-2). **Quarterfinals**—St.John Fisher 66, Scranton 60; Heidelberg 71, Southern Maine 64; Centre 70, Concordia-Moorhead 65; Hope 85, Buena Vista 79 (OT). **Final Four** (March 16-17, at Holland,MI): **Semifinals**—Hope 75, Centre 62; St.John Fisher 77, Heidelberg 54. **Third Place**—Heidelberg 71, Centre 60. **Championship**—Hope 65, St.John Fisher 63.

NIT
Div.I tournament played March 22-24, in Amarillo,TX. Pairings of eight-team field as follows: Miami,FL (24-4) vs Illinois St.(20-9); N.Carolina-Charlotte (22-7) vs Fresno St.(19-11); Toledo (23-6) vs Wyoming (24-5); Kentucky (20-8) vs Maine (22-5). **First Round**—Miami,FL 85, Illinois St.83; NC-Charlotte 70, Fresno St.67; Toledo 76, Wyoming 58; Kentucky 76, Maine 66. **Semifinals**—Toledo 77, NC-Charlotte 66; Kentucky 80, Miami,FL 68. **Third Place**—NC-Charlotte 80, Miami,FL 80. **Championship**—Kentucky 85, Toledo 76.

NAIA
After two rounds in the Women's 16-team tournament March 16-20 in Jackson, the Quarterfinal pairings were as follows: St.Ambrose,IA (33-0) vs Central St.,OH. (26-5) Claflin,SC (32-3) vs Simon Fraser of Brit.Columbia (28-6); Arkansas-Monticello (32-2) vs Wayland Baptist,TX (31-10); Southwestern Oklahoma (27-4) vs Western New Mexico (25-5). **Quarterfinals**—St.Ambrose 81, Central St.73; Claflin 104, Simon Fraser 98 (OT); Ark-Monticello 105, Wayland Baptist 67; SW Oklahoma 76, W.New Mexico 42. **Semifinals**—SW Oklahoma 83, St.Ambrose 76; Ark-Monticello 93, Claflin 86. **Championship**—SW Oklahoma 82, Ark-Monticello 75.

THE 1991
INFORMATION PLEASE SPORTS ALMANAC

COLLEGE BASKETBALL
S T A T I S T I C S

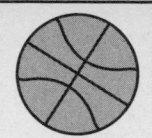

THROUGH THE YEARS
1901-1990
NCAA'S • ALL TIME LEADERS

SEC
B

PAGE
197

National Champions, 1901–90

The Helms Foundation of Los Angeles, under the direction of founder Bill Schroeder, selected national college basketball champions from 1942-82 and researched retroactive picks from 1901-41. The first NIT tournament and then the NCAA tournament have settled the national championship since 1938, but there are four years (1939,'40,'44 and '54) where the Helms selections differ.

Year	Champion	Record	Head Coach	Outstanding Player
1901	Yale	10-4	No coach	G.M.Clark, F
1902	Minnesota	11-0	Louis Cooke	W.C.Deering, F
1903	Yale	15-1	W.H.Murphy	R.B.Hyatt, F
1904	Columbia	17-1	No coach	Harry Fisher, F
1905	Columbia	19-1	No coach	Harry Fisher, F
1906	Dartmouth	16-2	No coach	George Grebenstein, F
1907	Chicago	22-2	Joseph Raycroft	John Schommer, C
1908	Chicago	21-2	Joseph Raycroft	John Schommer, C
1909	Chicago	12-0	Joseph Raycroft	John Schommer, C
1910	Columbia	11-1	Harry Fisher	Ted Kiendl, F
1911	St.John's,NY	14-0	Claude Allen	John Keenan, F-C
1912	Wisconsin	15-0	Doc Meanwell	Otto Stangel, F
1913	Navy	9-0	Louis Wenzell	Laurence Wild, F
1914	Wisconsin	15-0	Doc Meanwell	Gene Van Gent, C
1915	Illinois	16-0	Ralph Jones	Ray Woods, G
1916	Wisconsin	20-1	Doc Meanwell	George Levis, F
1917	Washington St	25-1	Doc Bohler	Roy Bohler, G
1918	Syracuse	16-1	Edmund Dollard	Joe Schwarzer, G
1919	Minnesota	13-0	Louis Cooke	Arnold Oss, F
1920	Pennsylvania	22-1	Lon Jourdet	George Sweeney, F
1921	Pennsylvania	21-2	Edward McNichol	Danny McNichol, G
1922	Kansas	16-2	Phog Allen	Paul Endacott, G
1923	Kansas	17-1	Phog Allen	Paul Endacott, G
1924	North Carolina	25-0	Bo Shepard	Jack Cobb, F
1925	Princeton	21-2	Al Wittmer	Art Loeb, G
1926	Syracuse	19-1	Lew Andreas	Vic Hanson, F
1927	Notre Dame	19-1	George Keogan	John Nyikos, C
1928	Pittsburgh	21-0	Doc Carlson	Chuck Hyatt, F
1929	Montana St	36-2	Schubert Dyche	John (Cat) Thompson, F
1930	Pittsburgh	23-2	Doc Carlson	Chuck Hyatt, F
1931	Northwestern	16-1	Dutch Lonborg	Joe Reiff, C
1932	Purdue	17-1	Piggy Lambert	John Wooden, G
1933	Kentucky	20-3	Adolph Rupp	Forest Sale, F
1934	Wyoming	26-3	Dutch Witte	Les Witte, G
1935	NYU	18-1	Howard Cann	Sid Gross, F
1936	Notre Dame	22-2-1	George Keogan	John Moir, F
1937	Stanford	25-2	John Bunn	Hank Luisetti, F

Year	Champion	Record	Winner	Head Coach	Outstanding Player
1938	Temple	23-2	NIT	James Usilton	Meyer Bloom, G
1939	Oregon	29-5	NCAA	Howard Hobson	Slim Wintermute, C
	LIU (Helms)	24-0	NIT	Clair Bee	Irv Torgoff, F
1940	Indiana	20-3	NCAA	Branch McCracken	Marv Huffman, G
	USC (Helms)	20-3	*	Sam Barry	Ralph Vaughn, F
1941	Wisconsin	20-3	NCAA	Bud Foster	Gene Englund, F
1942	Stanford	28-4	NCAA	Everett Dean	Jim Pollard, F

National Champions (Cont.)

Year	Champion	Record	Winner	Head Coach	Outstanding Player
1943	Wyoming	31-2	NCAA	Everett Shelton	Kenny Sailors, G
1944	Utah	22-4	NCAA	Vadal Peterson	Arnie Ferrin, F
	Army (Helms)	15-0	**	Ed Kelleher	Dale Hall, F
1945	Oklahoma A&M	27-4	NCAA	Hank Iba	Bob Kurland, C
1946	Oklahoma A&M	31-2	NCAA	Hank Iba	Bob Kurland, C
1947	Holy Cross	27-3	NCAA	Doggie Julian	George Kaftan, F
1948	Kentucky	36-3	NCAA	Adolph Rupp	Ralph Beard, G
1949	Kentucky	32-2	NCAA	Adolph Rupp	Alex Groza, C
1950	CCNY	24-5	NCAA/NIT	Nat Holman	Irwin Dambrot, G
1951	Kentucky	32-2	NCAA	Adolph Rupp	Bill Spivey, C
1952	Kansas	28-3	NCAA	Phog Allen	Clyde Lovellette, C
1953	Indiana	23-3	NCAA	Branch McCracken	Don Schlundt, C
1954	La Salle	26-4	NCAA	Ken Loeffler	Tom Gola, F
	Kentucky (Helms)	25-0	***	Adolph Rupp	Cliff Hagan, G
1955	San Francisco	28-1	NCAA	Phil Woolpert	Bill Russell, C
1956	San Francisco	29-0	NCAA	Phil Woolpert	Bill Russell, C
1957	North Carolina	32-0	NCAA	Frank McGuire	Lennie Rosenbluth, F
1958	Kentucky	23-6	NCAA	Adolph Rupp	Vern Hatton, G
1959	California	25-4	NCAA	Pete Newell	Darrall Imhoff, C
1960	Ohio St	25-3	NCAA	Fred Taylor	Jerry Lucas, C
1961	Cincinnati	27-3	NCAA	Ed Jucker	Bob Wiesenhahn, F
1962	Cincinnati	29-2	NCAA	Ed Jucker	Paul Hogue, C
1963	Loyola, IL	29-2	NCAA	George Ireland	Jerry Harkness, F
1964	UCLA	30-0	NCAA	John Wooden	Walt Hazzard, G
1965	UCLA	28-2	NCAA	John Wooden	Gail Goodrich, G
1966	Texas Western	28-1	NCAA	Don Haskins	Bobby Joe Hill, G
1967	UCLA	30-0	NCAA	John Wooden	Lew Alcindor, C
1968	UCLA	29-1	NCAA	John Wooden	Lew Alcindor, C
1969	UCLA	29-1	NCAA	John Wooden	Lew Alcindor, C
1970	UCLA	28-2	NCAA	John Wooden	Sidney Wicks, F
1971	UCLA	29-1	NCAA	John Wooden	Sidney Wicks, F
1972	UCLA	30-0	NCAA	John Wooden	Bill Walton, C
1973	UCLA	30-0	NCAA	John Wooden	Bill Walton, C
1974	N.C. State	30-1	NCAA	Norm Sloan	David Thompson, F
1975	UCLA	28-3	NCAA	John Wooden	Dave Meyers, F
1976	Indiana	32-0	NCAA	Bob Knight	Scott May, F
1977	Marquette	25-7	NCAA	Al McGuire	Butch Lee, G
1978	Kentucky	30-2	NCAA	Joe B. Hall	Jack Givens, F
1979	Michigan St	26-6	NCAA	Jud Heathcote	Magic Johnson, G
1980	Louisville	33-3	NCAA	Denny Crum	Darrell Griffith, G
1981	Indiana	26-9	NCAA	Bob Knight	Isiah Thomas, G
1982	North Carolina	32-2	NCAA	Dean Smith	James Worthy, F
1983	N.C. State	28-8	NCAA	Jim Valvano	Sidney Lowe, G
1984	Georgetown	34-3	NCAA	John Thompson	Patrick Ewing, C
1985	Villanova	25-10	NCAA	Rollie Massimino	Ed Pinckney, C
1986	Louisville	32-7	NCAA	Denny Crum	Pervis Ellison, C
1987	Indiana	30-4	NCAA	Bob Knight	Steve Alford, G
1988	Kansas	27-11	NCAA	Larry Brown	Danny Manning, C
1989	Michigan	30-7	NCAA	Steve Fisher	Glen Rice, F
1990	UNLV	35-5	NCAA	Jerry Tarkanian	Larry Johnson, F

*Southern Cal was beaten by Kansas in the West Regional final of the NCAA tournament.

**Army did not lift its own policy against postseason play until accepting a bid to the 1961 NIT.

***Unbeaten Kentucky turned down a bid to the NCAA tournament after NCAA declared seniors Cliff Hagan, Frank Ramsey and Lou Tsioropoulos ineligible for postseason play.

The Red Cross Benefit Games
1943-45

For three seasons during World War II, the NCAA and NIT champions met in a benefit game at Madison Square Garden to raise money for the Red Cross. The NCAA champion won all three games.

Year	Winner	Score	Loser
1943	Wyoming (NCAA)	52-47	St. John's (NIT)
1944	Utah (NCAA)	43-36	St. John's (NIT)
1945	Okla. A&M (NCAA)	52-44	DePaul (NIT)

NCAA Final Four, 1939-90

The NCAA basketball championship began in 1939 under the sponsorship of the National Association of Basketball Coaches, but was taken over by the NCAA in 1940.

From 1939-51, the winners of the Eastern and Western Regionals played for the national championship, while regional runners-up shared third place. The concept of a Final Four originated in 1952 when four teams qualified for the first national semifinals. Consolation games to determine overall third place were held between regional finalists from 1946-51 and then national semifinalists from 1952-81.

Multiple winners: UCLA (10); Indiana and Kentucky (5); Cincinnati, Kansas, Louisville, North Carolina, N.C.State, Oklahoma A&M (now Okla.St.) and San Francisco (2).

Year Champion	Runner-up	Score	Final Two	Third Place	
1939 Oregon	Ohio St.	46-33	@ Evanston,IL	Oklahoma	Villanova
1940 Indiana	Kansas	60-42	@ Kansas City	Duquesne	USC
1941 Wisconsin	Washington St.	39-34	@ Kansas City	Arkansas	Pittsburgh
1942 Stanford	Dartmouth	53-38	@ Kansas City	Colorado	Kentucky
1943 Wyoming	Georgetown	46-34	@ New York	DePaul	Texas
1944 Utah	Dartmouth	42-40	@ New York	Iowa St.	Ohio St.
1945 Oklahoma A&M	NYU	49-45	@ New York	Arkansas	Ohio St.

Year Champion	Runner-up	Score	Final Two	Third Place	Fourth Place
1946 Oklahoma A&M	North Carolina	43-40 (OT)	@ New York	Ohio St.	California
1947 Holy Cross	Oklahoma	58-47	@ New York	Texas	CCNY
1948 Kentucky	Baylor	58-42	@ New York	Holy Cross	Kansas St.
1949 Kentucky	Oklahoma A&M	46-36	@ Seattle	Illinois	Oregon St.
1950 CCNY	Bradley	71-68	@ New York	N.C.State	Baylor
1951 Kentucky	Kansas St.	68-58	@ Minneapolis	Illinois	Oklahoma A&M

Year Champion	Runner-Up	Score	Third Place	Fourth Place	Final Four
1952 Kansas	St.John's	80-63	Illinois	Santa Clara	@ Seattle
1953 Indiana	Kansas	69-68	Washington	LSU	@ Kansas City
1954 La Salle	Bradley	92-76	Penn St.	USC	@ Kansas City
1955 San Francisco	La Salle	77-63	Colorado	Iowa	@ Kansas City
1956 San Francisco	Iowa	83-71	Temple	SMU	@ Evanston,IL
1957 North Carolina	Kansas	54-53 (3 OT)	San Francisco	Michigan St.	@ Kansas City
1958 Kentucky	Seattle	84-72	Temple	Kansas St.	@ Louisville
1959 California	West Virginia	71-70	Cincinnati	Louisville	@ Louisville
1960 Ohio St.	California	75-55	Cincinnati	NYU	@ San Fran.
1961 Cincinnati	Ohio St.	70-65 (OT)	St.Joe's,PA	Utah	@ Kansas City
1962 Cincinnati	Ohio St.	71-59	Wake Forest	UCLA	@ Louisville
1963 Loyola,IL	Cincinnati	60-58 (OT)	Duke	Oregon St.	@ Louisville
1964 UCLA	Duke	98-83	Michigan	Kansas St.	@ Kansas City
1965 UCLA	Michigan	91-80	Princeton	Wichita St.	@ Portland,OR
1966 Texas Western	Kentucky	72-65	Duke	Utah	@ Col.Park,MD
1967 UCLA	Dayton	79-64	Houston	N.Carolina	@ Louisville
1968 UCLA	North Carolina	78-55	Ohio St.	Houston	@ Los Angeles
1969 UCLA	Purdue	92-72	Drake	N.Carolina	@ Louisville
1970 UCLA	Jacksonville	80-69	N.Mexico St.	St.Bonaventure	@ Col.Park,MD
1971 UCLA	Villanova	68-62	Western Ky.	Kansas	@ Houston
1972 UCLA	Florida St.	81-76	N.Carolina	Louisville	@ Los Angeles
1973 UCLA	Memphis St.	87-66	Indiana	Providence	@ St.Louis
1974 N.C.State	Marquette	76-64	UCLA	Kansas	@ Greensboro,NC
1975 UCLA	Kentucky	92-85	Louisville	Syracuse	@ San Diego
1976 Indiana	Michigan	86-68	UCLA	Rutgers	@ Philadelphia
1977 Marquette	North Carolina	67-59	UNLV	NC-Charlotte	@ Atlanta
1978 Kentucky	Duke	94-88	Arkansas	Notre Dame	@ St.Louis
1979 Michigan St.	Indiana St.	75-64	DePaul	Penn	@ S.Lake City
1980 Louisville	UCLA	59-54	Purdue	Iowa	@ Indianapolis
1981 Indiana	North Carolina	63-50	Virginia	LSU	@ Philadelphia

Year Champion	Runner-Up	Score	Third Place		Final Four
1982 North Carolina	Georgetown	63-62	Houston	Louisville	@ New Orleans
1983 N.C.State	Houston	54-52	Georgia	Louisville	@ Albuquerque
1984 Georgetown	Houston	84-75	Kentucky	Virginia	@ Seattle
1985 Villanova	Georgetown	66-64	Memphis St.	St.John's	@ Lexington
1986 Louisville	Duke	72-69	Kansas	LSU	@ Dallas
1987 Indiana	Syracuse	74-73	Providence	UNLV	@ New Orleans
1988 Kansas	Oklahoma	83-79	Arizona	Duke	@ Kansas City
1989 Michigan	Seton Hall	80-79 (OT)	Duke	Illinois	@ Seattle
1990 UNLV	Duke	103-73	Arkansas	Georgia Tech	@ Denver

Note: Five teams have had their standing in the Final Four vacated for using ineligible players: **1961**—St.Joseph's,PA (3rd place); **1971**—Villanova (Runner-up) and Western Kentucky (3rd place); **1980**—UCLA (Runner-up); **1985**—Memphis St. (3rd place).

Most Outstanding Player

A Most Outstanding Player has been selected every year of the NCAA tournament. Winners who did not play for the tournament champion are listed in **bold type**.
Multiple winners: Lew Alcindor (3); Alex Groza, Bob Kurland, Jerry Lucas and Bill Walton (2).

Year		Year		Year	
1939	**Jimmy Hull,** Ohio St.	1956	**Hal Lear,** Temple	1973	Bill Walton, UCLA
1940	Marv Huffman, Indiana	1957	**Wilt Chamberlain,** Kansas	1974	David Thompson, N.C.State
1941	John Kotz, Wisconsin	1958	**Elgin Baylor,** Seattle	1975	Richard Washington, UCLA
1942	Howie Dallmar, Stanford	1959	**Jerry West,** West Va.	1976	Kent Benson, Indiana
1943	Kenny Sailors, Wyoming			1977	Butch Lee, Marquette
1944	Arnie Ferrin, Utah	1960	Jerry Lucas, Ohio St.	1978	Jack Givens, Kentucky
1945	Bob Kurland, Okla.A&M	1961	**Jerry Lucas,** Ohio St.	1979	Magic Johnson, Mich.St.
1946	Bob Kurland, Okla.A&M	1962	Paul Hogue, Cincinnati		
1947	George Kaftan, H.Cross	1963	**Art Heyman,** Duke	1980	Darrell Griffith, Louisville
1948	Alex Groza, Kentucky	1964	Walt Hazzard, UCLA	1981	Isiah Thomas, Indiana
1949	Alex Groza, Kentucky	1965	**Bill Bradley,** Princeton	1982	James Worthy, N.Carolina
		1966	**Jerry Chambers,** Utah	1983	**Akeem Olajuwon,** Houston
1950	Irwin Dambrot, CCNY	1967	Lew Alcindor, UCLA	1984	Patrick Ewing, Georgetown
1951	Bill Spivey, Kentucky	1968	Lew Alcindor, UCLA	1985	Ed Pinckney, Villanova
1952	Clyde Lovelette, Kansas	1969	Lew Alcindor, UCLA	1986	Pervis Ellison, Louisville
1953	**B.H.Born,** Kansas			1987	Keith Smart, Indiana
1954	Tom Gola, La Salle	1970	Sidney Wicks, UCLA	1988	Danny Manning, Kansas
1955	Bill Russell, San Fran.	1971	**Howard Porter,** Villanova	1989	Glen Rice, Michigan
		1972	Bill Walton, UCLA		
				1990	Anderson Hunt, UNLV

Note: Howard Porter (1971) was declared ineligible by the NCAA after the tournament and his award was vacated.

NIT Finals, 1938-90

The National Invitation Tournament began under the sponsorship of the Metropolitan New York Basketball Writers Assn. in 1938. The NIT is now administered by the Metropolitan Intercollegiate Basketball Assn. All championship games have been played at Madison Square Garden.

Year	Winner	Score	Loser	Year	Winner	Score	Loser
1938	Temple	60-36	Colorado	1977	St.Bonaventure	94-91	Houston
1939	Long Island U.	44-32	Loyola,IL	1978	Texas	101-93	N.C.State
1940	Colorado	51-40	Duquesne	1979	Indiana	53-52	Purdue
1941	Long Island U.	56-42	Ohio Univ.	1980	Virginia	58-55	Minnesota
1942	West Virginia	47-45	Western Ky.	1981	Tulsa	86-84*	Syracuse
1943	St.John's,NY	48-27	Toledo	1982	Bradley	67-58	Purdue
1944	St.John's,NY	47-39	DePaul	1983	Fresno St.	69-60	DePaul
1945	DePaul	71-54	Bowling Green	1984	Michigan	83-63	Notre Dame
1946	Kentucky	46-45	Rhode Island	1985	UCLA	65-62	Indiana
1947	Utah	49-45	Kentucky	1986	Ohio St.	73-63	Wyoming
1948	St.Louis	65-52	NYU	1987	Southern Miss.	84-80	La Salle
1949	San Francisco	48-47	Loyola,IL	1988	Connecticut	72-67	Ohio St.
1950	CCNY	69-61	Bradley	1989	St.John's,NY	73-65	St.Louis
1951	BYU	62-43	Dayton	1990	Vanderbilt	74-72	St.Louis
1952	La Salle	75-64	Dayton	*Overtime			
1953	Seton Hall	58-46	St.John's,NY				
1954	Holy Cross	71-62	Duquesne				
1955	Duquesne	70-58	Dayton				
1956	Louisville	93-80	Dayton				
1957	Bradley	84-83	Memphis St.				
1958	Xavier,OH	78-74*	Dayton				
1959	St.John's,NY	76-71*	Bradley				
1960	Bradley	88-72	Providence				
1961	Providence	62-59	St.Louis				
1962	Dayton	73-67	St.John's,NY				
1963	Providence	81-66	Canisius				
1964	Bradley	86-54	New Mexico				
1965	St.John's,NY	55-51	Villanova				
1966	BYU	97-84	NYU				
1967	So.Illinois	71-56	Marquette				
1968	Dayton	61-48	Kansas				
1969	Temple	89-76	Boston College				
1970	Marquette	65-53	St.John's,NY				
1971	North Carolina	84-66	Georgia Tech				
1972	Maryland	100-69	Niagara				
1973	Virginia Tech	92-91*	Notre Dame				
1974	Purdue	97-81	Utah				
1975	Princeton	80-69	Providence				
1976	Kentucky	71-67	NC-Charlotte				

Teams in both NCAA and NIT

Fourteen teams played in both the NCAA and NIT tournaments from 1940-52. Colorado (1940), Utah (1944), Kentucky (1949) and BYU (1951) won one of the titles, while CCNY won two in 1950, beating Bradley in both championship games.

Year		NIT	NCAA
1940	Colorado	**Won Final**	Lost 1st Rd
	Duquesne	Lost Final	Lost 2nd Rd
1944	Utah	Lost 1st Rd	**Won Final**
1949	Kentucky	Lost 2nd Rd	**Won Final**
1950	CCNY	**Won Final**	**Won Final**
	Bradley	Lost Final	Lost Final
1951	BYU	**Won Final**	Lost 2nd Rd
	St.John's	Lost 3rd Rd	Lost 2nd Rd
	N.C.State	Lost 2nd Rd	Lost 2nd Rd
	Arizona	Lost 2nd Rd	Lost 1st Rd
1952	St.John's	Lost Final	Lost 2nd Rd
	Dayton	Lost 1st Rd	Lost Final
	Duquesne	Lost 2nd Rd	Lost 2nd Rd
	St.Louis	Lost 2nd Rd	Lost 2nd Rd

NCAA and NIT Tournament Fields

Older than the NCAA tournament by one year, the NIT has grown from six teams to 32 since 1938 while the NCAA has gone from eight teams to 64. The fields, year-by-year:

Year	NCAA	NIT	Year	NCAA	NIT	Year	NCAA	NIT	Year	NCAA	NIT
1938	—	6	1951	16	12	1965	23	14	1979	40	24
1939	8	6	1952	16	12	1966	22	14	1980	48	32
1940	8	6	1953	22	12	1967	23	14	1981	48	32
1941	8	8	1954	24	12	1968	23	16	1982	48	32
1942	8	8	1955	24	12	1969	25	16	1983	52	32
1943	8	8	1956	25	12	1970	25	16	1984	53	32
1944	8	8	1957	23	12	1971	25	16	1985	64	32
1945	8	8	1958	24	12	1972	25	16	1986	64	32
1946	8	8	1959	23	12	1973	25	16	1987	64	32
1947	8	8	1960	25	12	1974	25	16	1988	64	32
1948	8	8	1961	24	12	1975	32	16	1989	64	32
1949	8	12	1962	25	12	1976	32	12	1990	64	32
1950	8	12	1963	25	12	1977	32	16			
			1964	25	12	1978	32	16			

Winningest Division I Teams

Through 1989-90; regular season and tournament games included.

All-Time Winning Pct.

		Yrs	Won	Lost	Tied	Pct
1	Kentucky	87	1479	489	1	.751
2	North Carolina	80	1479	544	0	.731
3	St.John's	83	1421	604	0	.708
4	UCLA	71	1221	552	0	.687
5	Kansas	92	1432	669	0	.682
6	Western Ky	71	1223	574	0	.681
7	Syracuse	89	1292	619	0	.676
8	DePaul	67	1078	524	0	.673
9	Notre Dame	85	1323	648	1	.671
10	Duke	85	1345	686	0	.662
11	Louisville	76	1174	618	0	.655
12	Weber St	28	516	272	0	.655
13	La Salle	60	990	524	0	.654
14	N.C.State	78	1214	652	0	.651
15	Temple	94	1332	725	0	.648
16	Illinois	85	1192	652	0	.646
17	Houston	45	803	441	0	.645
18	Villanova	70	1122	619	0	.644
19	Indiana	90	1242	695	0	.641
20	Purdue	92	1204	683	0	.638

All-Time Victories

		Yrs	Wins
1	North Carolina	80	1479
2	Kentucky	87	1479
3	Kansas	92	1432
4	St.John's	83	1421
5	Oregon St	88	1373
6	Duke	85	1345
7	Temple	94	1332
8	Notre Dame	85	1323
9	Pennsylvania	89	1315
10	Syracuse	89	1292
11	Washington	88	1280
12	Indiana	90	1242
13	Western Kentucky	71	1223
14	UCLA	71	1221
15	Princeton	90	1218
16	Fordham	87	1217
17	North Carolina St	78	1214
18	Bradley	86	1210
19	West Virginia	81	1208
20	Purdue	92	1204

Most NCAA Tournaments

Through 1990; listed are number of appearances, overall tournament record, times reaching Final Four, and number of NCAA titles.

App		W-L	F4	Championships	App		W-L	F4	Championships
33	Kentucky	55-30	9	5 (1948-49,51,58,78)	18	Syracuse	26-19	2	None
26	UCLA	64-20	14	10 (1964-65,67-73,75)	18	DePaul	20-21	2	None
24	N.Carolina	50-25	9	2 (1957,82)	17	Marquette	25-18	2	1 (1977)
24	N.Dame	25-28	1	None	17	Houston	26-22	5	None
21	Louisville	38-23	7	2 (1980,86)	16	N.C.State	26-15	3	2 (1974,83)
20	Villanova	34-20	3	1 (1985)	16	West Va	11-16	1	None
20	Kansas St	27-24	4	None	16	Ohio St	26-15	8	1 (1960)
20	St.John's	19-22	2	None	16	Arkansas	18-17	4	None
19	Indiana	39-14	6	5 (1940,53,76,81,87)	16	Oregon St	12-19	2	None
19	Kansas	37-19	8	2 (1952,88)	16	Princeton	11-20	1	None

All-Time Division I Winning Streaks

Full Season

No	Team	Seasons	Broken by	Score
88	UCLA	1971-74	Notre Dame	71-70
60	San Francisco	1955-57	Illinois	62-33
47	UCLA	1966-68	Houston	71-69
44	Texas	1913-17	Rice	24-18
43	Seton Hall	1939-41	LIU-Brooklyn	49-26
43	LIU-Brooklyn	1935-37	Stanford	45-31
41	UCLA	1968-69	Southern Cal	46-44

Regular Season

No	Team	Seasons	Broken by	Score
77	UCLA	1971-74	Notre Dame	71-70
57	Indiana	1975-77	Toledo	59-57
56	Marquette	1970-72	Detroit	70-49
54	Kentucky	1952-55	Ga.Tech	59-58
51	San Francisco	1955-57	Illinois	62-33
48	Pennsylvania	1970-72	Temple	57-52
47	Ohio St	1960-62	Wisconsin	86-87

NCAA Division I All-Time Individual Leaders
CAREER
Scoring

Points	Years	Gm	Total	Average	Years	Pts	Avg
Pete Maravich, LSU	1968-70	83	3667	Pete Maravich, LSU	1968-70	3667	44.2
Freeman Williams, Port.St.	1975-78	106	3249	Austin Carr, Notre Dame	1969-71	2560	34.6
Lionel Simmons, La Salle	1987-90	131	3217	Oscar Robertson, Cincinnati	1958-60	2973	33.8
Harry Kelly, Texas Southern	1980-83	110	3066	Calvin Murphy, Niagara	1968-70	2548	33.1
Hersey Hawkins, Bradley	1985-88	125	3008	Dwight Lamar, SW La.	1972-73	1862	32.7
Oscar Robertson, Cincinnati	1958-60	88	2973	Frank Selvy, Furman	1952-54	2538	32.5
Danny Manning, Kansas	1985-88	147	2951	Rick Mount, Purdue	1968-70	2323	32.3
Alfredrick Hughes, Loyola-IL	1982-85	120	2914	Darrell Floyd, Furman	1954-56	2281	32.1
Elvin Hayes, Houston	1966-68	93	2884	Nick Werkman, Seton Hall	1962-64	2273	32.0
Larry Bird, Indiana St	1977-79	94	2850	Willie Humes, Ohio St	1970-71	1510	31.5

Field Goal Pct.	Years	FG	FGA	Pct	Free Throw Pct.	Years	FT	FTA	Pct
Stephen Scheffler, Pur	1987-90	408	596	68.5	Greg Starrick, Ky/So.Ill	1969-72	341	375	90.9
Steve Johnson, Ore.St	1978-81	828	1222	67.8	Jack Moore, Nebraska	1979-82	446	495	90.1
Murray Brown, Fla.St	1977-80	566	847	66.8	Steve Henson, Kan.St	1987-90	361	401	90.0
Lee Campbell, SW Mo.St	1987-90	411	618	66.5	Steve Alford, Indiana	1984-87	535	596	89.8
Joe Senser, W.Chester	1976-79	476	719	66.2	Bob Lloyd, Rutgers	1965-67	543	605	89.8

Note: Minimum 400 FGs scored. Note: Minimum 250 FTs scored.

2000 Points/1000 Rebounds

Players with at least 2000 points and 1000 rebounds in their careers who have 4000 or more points and rebounds combined.

	Gm	Pts	Reb	Total		Gm	Pts	Reb	Total
Tom Gola, La Salle	118	2462	2201	4663	Harry Kelly, Texas So	110	3066	1085	4151
Lionel Simmons, LaSalle	131	3217	1429	4646	Danny Manning, Kansas	147	2951	1187	4138
Elvin Hayes, Houston	93	2884	1602	4486	Larry Bird, Indiana St	94	2850	1247	4097
Dickie Hemric, W.Forest	104	2587	1802	4389	Elgin Baylor, Col.Idaho				
Oscar Robertson, Cinn	88	2973	1338	4311	& Seattle	80	2500	1559	4059
Joe Holup, Geo.Wash.	104	2226	2030	4256	Michael Brooks, LaSalle	114	2628	1372	4000

Years Played—Gola (1952-55); Simmons (1987-90); Hayes (1966-68); Hemric (1952-55); Robertson (1958-60); Holup (1953-56); Kelly (1980-83); Manning (1985-88); Bird (1977-79); Baylor (1956-58); Brooks (1977-80).

Rebounding

Rebounds (before 1973)	Years	Gm	Total	Rebounds (since 1973)	Years	Gm	Total
Tom Gola, La Salle	1952-55	118	2201	Derrick Coleman, Syracuse	1987-90	143	1537
Joe Holup, G.Washington	1953-56	104	2030	Ralph Sampson, Virginia	1980-83	132	1511
Charlie Slack, Marshall	1953-56	88	1916	Pete Padgett, Nev-Reno	1973-76	104	1464
Ed Conlin, Fordham	1951-55	102	1884	Lionel Simmons, La Salle	1987-90	131	1429
Dickie Hemric, W.Forest	1952-55	104	1802	Anthony Bonner, St.Louis	1987-90	133	1424

Assists
(Recorded since 1984)

Assists	Years	Gm	Total	Average	Years	Gm	Avg
Sherman Douglas, Syracuse	1986-89	138	960	Avery Johnson, Cameron			
Gary Payton, Oregon St	1987-90	120	938	& Southern-BR	1986-88	838	8.9
Andre LaFleur, N'eastern	1984-87	128	894	Mark Wade, Okla.& UNLV	1985-87	693	8.8
Jim Les, Bradley	1983-86	118	884	Taurence Chisholm, Del.	1985-88	877	8.0
Frank Smith, Old Dominion	1985-88	120	883	Anthony Manuel, Bradley	1986-89	855	7.9
				Gary Payton, Oregon St	1987-90	938	7.8

Note: Minimum 550 assists.

SINGLE SEASON
Scoring

Points	Year	Gm	Total	Average	Year	Pts	Avg
Pete Maravich, LSU	1970	31	1381	Pete Maravich, LSU	1970	1381	44.5
Elvin Hayes, Houston	1968	33	1214	Pete Maravich, LSU	1969	1148	44.2
Frank Selvy, Furman	1954	29	1209	Pete Maravich, LSU	1968	1138	43.8
Pete Maravich, LSU	1969	26	1148	Frank Selvy, Furman	1954	1209	41.7
Pete Maravich, LSU	1968	26	1138	Johnny Neumann, Mississippi	1971	923	40.1
Bo Kimble, Loyola Mmt	1990	32	1131	Freeman Williams, Port.St	1977	1010	38.8
Hersey Hawkins, Bradley	1988	31	1125	Billy McGill, Utah	1962	1009	38.8
Austin Carr, Notre Dame	1970	29	1106	Calvin Murphy, Niagara	1968	916	38.2
Austin Carr, Notre Dame	1971	29	1101	Austin Carr, Notre Dame	1970	1106	38.1
Otis Birdsong, Houston	1977	36	1090	Austin Carr, Notre Dame	1971	1101	38.0

Field Goal Pct.

Field Goal Pct.	Year	FG	FGA	Pct
Steve Johnson, Ore.St.	1981	235	315	74.6
Dwayne Davis, Florida	1989	179	248	72.2
Keith Walker, Utica,NY	1985	154	216	71.3
Steve Johnson, Ore.St.	1980	211	297	71.0
Alan Williams, Princeton	1987	163	232	70.3
Mark McNamara, Calif.	1982	231	329	70.2

3-Pt Field Goal Pct	Year	FG	FGA	Pct
Glenn Tropf, Holy Cross	1988	52	82	63.4
Dave Calloway, Monmouth	1989	48	82	58.5
Steve Kerr, Arizona	1988	114	199	57.3
Reginald Jones, Prairie	1987	64	112	57.1
Joel Tribelhorn, Colo.St.	1989	76	135	56.3
Mike Joseph, Bucknell	1988	65	116	56.0

Free Throw Pct.

Free Throw Pct.	Year	FT	FTA	Pct
Craig Collins, Penn St	1985	94	98	95.9
Rod Foster, UCLA	1982	95	100	95.0
Carlos Gibson, Marshall	1978	84	89	94.4
Jim Barton, Dartmouth	1986	65	69	94.2
Jack Moore, Nebraska	1982	123	131	93.9

Assists

Average	Year	Gm	No	Avg
Avery Johnson, Southern	1988	30	399	13.3
Anthony Manuel, Bradley	1988	31	373	12.0
Avery Johnson, Southern	1987	31	333	10.7
Mark Wade, UNLV	1987	38	406	10.7
Glenn Williams, H.Cross	1989	28	278	9.9

Rebounding

Rebounds	Year	Gm	Total
Walter Dukes, Seton Hall	1953	33	734
Leroy Wright, Pacific	1959	26	652
Tom Gola, La Salle	1954	30	652
Charlie Tyra, Louisville	1956	29	645
Paul Silas, Creighton	1964	29	631

Average (before 1973)	Year	Rebs	Avg
Charlie Slack, Marshall	1955	538	25.6
Leroy Wright, Pacific	1959	652	25.1
Art Quimby, Connecticut	1955	611	24.4

Average (since 1973)	Year	Rebs	Avg
Kermit Washington, Amer.	1973	439	20.0
Marvin Barnes, Providence	1973	571	19.0
Marvin Barnes, Providence	1974	597	18.7

Blocked Shots

Average	Year	Gm	No	Avg
David Robinson, Navy	1986	35	207	5.9
Alonzo Mourning, G'town	1989	34	169	5.0
Kenny Green, Rhode Island	1990	26	124	4.8
David Robinson, Navy	1987	32	144	4.5
Derrick Lewis, Maryland	1987	26	114	4.4

Steals

Average	Year	Gm	No	Avg
Darron Bittman, Chicago St	1986	28	139	5.0
Aldwin Ware, Florida A&M	1988	29	142	4.9
Ronn McMahon, East.Was	1990	29	130	4.5
Jim Paguaga, St.Francis,NY	1986	28	120	4.3
Marty Johnson, Towson St	1988	30	124	4.1
Tony Fairly, Baptist	1987	28	114	4.1

BEST GAMES

Scoring

Points vs Div.I Team	Year	Pts
Pete Maravich, LSU vs Alabama	1970	69
Calvin Murphy, Niagara vs Syracuse	1969	68
Jay Handlan, Wash.& Lee vs Furman	1951	66
Pete Maravich, LSU vs Tulane	1969	66
Anthony Roberts, O.Rbts. vs N.C.A&T	1977	66
Scott Haffner, Evansville vs Dayton	1989	65
Anthony Roberts, O.Rbts. vs Oregon	1977	65
Pete Maravich, LSU vs Kentucky	1970	64
Hersey Hawkins, Bradley vs Detroit	1988	63
Johnny Neumann, Mississippi vs LSU	1971	63

Points vs Non-Div.I Team	Year	Pts
Frank Selvy, Furman vs Newberry	1954	100
Paul Arizin, Villanova vs Phila.NAMC	1949	85
Freeman Williams, Port.St.vs Rocky Mt	1978	81
Bill Mlkvy, Temple vs Wilkes	1951	73
Freeman Williams, Port.St.vs So.Ore.	1977	71

Rebounding

Rebounds (before 1973)	Year	No
Bill Chambers, Wm.& Mary vs Virginia	1953	51
Charlie Slack, Marshall vs M.Harvey	1954	43
Tom Heinsohn, Holy Cross vs BC	1955	42
Art Quimby, Connecticut vs BU	1955	40
Maurice Stokes, St.Francis vs J.Carroll	1955	39
Dave DeBusschere, Detroit vs C.Mich.	1960	39
Keith Swagerty, Pacific vs UCSB	1965	39

Rebounds (since 1973)	Year	No
David Vaughn, Oral Rbts. vs Brandeis	1973	34
Robert Parish, Centenary vs So.Miss	1973	33
Jim Bradley, No.Ill vs Wisc-Milwaukee	1973	31
Calvin Natt, NE La. vs Ga.Southern	1976	31
Eddie Woods, Oral Roberts vs Lamar	1972	30
Eddie Woods, Oral Roberts vs La.Tech	1972	30
Brad Robinson, Kent St.vs C.Mich.	1974	30

NCAA Division I All-Time Team Leaders

SINGLE SEASON

Scoring

	Year	Gm	Pts	Avg
Loyola Marymount	1990	32	3918	122.4
Loyola Marymount	1989	31	3486	122.5
UNLV	1976	31	3426	110.5
Loyola Marymount	1988	32	3528	110.3
UNLV	1977	32	3426	107.1
Oral Roberts	1972	28	2943	105.1
Oklahoma	1988	39	4012	102.9
Oklahoma	1989	36	3680	102.2
Oklahoma	1990	32	3243	101.3
Jacksonville	1970	28	2809	100.3

BEST GAMES

Scoring

	Score	Date
Loyola Mmt	181-150, vs US Int'l	1/31/89
UNLV	164-111, vs Hawaii-Hilo	2/19/76
Loyola Mmt	164-138, vs Azusa-Pacific	11/28/88
Loyola Mmt	162-144, vs US Unt'l	1/7/89
Oral Roberts	155-113, vs Union, TN	2/24/72
Jacksonville	152-106, vs St. Peter's	12/3/70
Oklahoma	152-84, vs Centenary	12/12/87
Oklahoma	152-122, vs Oral Rbts.	12/10/88
Loyola Mmt	151-107, vs US Int'l	1/11/86
Oklahoma	151-99, vs Dayton	12/24/87

NCAA Division I Tournament All-Time Individual Leaders

CAREER

Scoring

Points	Years	Gm	Total
Elvin Hayes, Houston	1966-68	13	358
Danny Manning, Kansas	1985-88	16	328
Oscar Robertson, Cincinnati	1958-60	10	324
Glen Rice, Michigan	1986-89	13	308
Lew Alcindor, UCLA	1967-69	12	304

Average	Years	Pts	Avg
Austin Carr, Notre Dame	1969-71	289	41.3
Bill Bradley, Princeton	1963-65	303	33.7
Oscar Robertson, Cincinnati	1958-60	324	32.4
Jerry West, W.Virginia	1958-60	275	30.6
Len Chappell, Wake Forest	1961-62	221	27.6

Rebounding

Rebounds	Years	Gm	Tot	Avg
Elvin Hayes, Houston	1966-68	13	222	17.1
Lew Alcindor, UCLA	1967-69	12	201	16.8
Jerry Lucas, Ohio St	1960-62	12	197	16.4
Bill Walton, UCLA	1972-74	12	159	13.3
Sam Lacey, N.Mex.St	1968-70	11	157	14.3

Average	Years	Gm	Tot	Avg
Johnny Green, Mich.St	1957-59	6	118	19.7
Artis Gilmore, J'ville	1970-71	6	115	19.2
Paul Silas, Creighton	1962-64	6	111	18.5
Elvin Hayes, Houston	1966-68	13	222	17.1
Lew Alcindor, UCLA	1967-69	12	201	16.8

SINGLE TOURNAMENT

Scoring

Points	Year	Gm	Total
Glen Rice, Michigan	1989	6	184
Bill Bradley, Princeton	1965	5	177
Elvin Hayes, Houston	1968	5	167
Danny Manning, Kansas	1988	6	163
Hal Lear, Temple	1956	5	160
Jerry West, West Virginia	1959	6	160

Average	Year	Gm	Pts	Avg
Austin Carr, Notre Dame	1970	3	158	52.7
Austin Carr, Notre Dame	1971	3	125	41.7
Jerry Chambers, Utah	1966	4	143	35.8
Bill Bradley, Princeton	1965	5	177	35.4
Clyde Lovellette, Kansas	1952	4	141	35.3
Jerry West, West Virginia	1960	3	105	35.0

Rebounding

Rebounds	Year	Gm	Tot	Avg
Elvin Hayes, Houston	1968	5	97	19.4
Artis Gilmore, Jack'ville	1970	5	93	18.6
Elgin Baylor, Seattle	1958	5	91	18.2
Sam Lacey, N.Mex.St	1970	5	90	18.0
Clarence Glover, W.Ky	1971	5	89	17.8

BEST GAMES

Scoring

Points	Year	Pts
Austin Carr, N.Dame vs Ohio U	1970	61
Bill Bradley, Princeton vs Wich.St	1965	58
Oscar Robertson, Cinn. vs Arkansas	1958	56
Austin Carr, N.Dame vs Ky.	1970	52
Austin Carr, N.Dame vs TCU	1971	52
David Robinson, Navy vs Michigan	1987	50
Elvin Hayes, Hou. vs Loyola-IL	1968	49
Hal Lear, Temple vs SMU	1956	48
Austin Carr, N.Dame vs Houston	1971	47
Dave Corzine, DePaul vs L'ville	1978	46
Bob Houbregs, Wash. vs Sea.	1956	45
Austin Carr, N.Dame vs Iowa	1970	45
Bo Kimble, Loy.Mmt vs N.Mex.St.	1990	45

Rebounding

Rebounds	Year	Tot
Nate Thurmond, B.Green vs Miss. St	1963	31
Jerry Lucas, Ohio St. vs Kentucky	1961	30
Toby Kimball, Conn. vs St.Joe-PA	1965	29
Elvin Hayes, Houston vs Pacific	1966	28

Three players tied with 27 each.

Player of the Year Awards

UPI picked the first national Division I Player of the Year in 1955. Since then, The U.S.Basketball Writers Assn.(1959), the Commonwealth Athletic Club of Kentucky's Adolph Rupp Trophy (1961), the Atlanta Tip-Off Club (1969), the National Assn. of Basketball Coaches (1975), and the LA Athletic Club's John Wooden Award (1977) have joined in.

Since 1977, the first year all six awards were given out, the same player has won all of them in the same season seven times: Marques Johnson in 1977, Larry Bird in 1979, Ralph Sampson in both 1982 and '83, Michael Jordan in 1984, David Robinson in 1987 and Lionel Simmons in 1990.

United Press International

Voted on by a panel of UPI college basketball writers and first presented in 1955.
Multiple winners: Oscar Robertson, Ralph Sampson and Bill Walton (3); Lew Alcindor and Jerry Lucas (2).

Year		Year		Year	
1955	Tom Gola, La Salle	1967	Lew Alcindor, UCLA	1980	Mark Aguirre, DePaul
1956	Bill Russell, San Francisco	1968	Elvin Hayes, Houston	1981	Ralph Sampson, Virginia
1957	Chet Forte, Columbia	1969	Lew Alcindor, UCLA	1982	Ralph Sampson, Virginia
1958	Oscar Robertson, Cincinnati	1970	Pete Maravich, LSU	1983	Ralph Sampson, Virginia
1959	Oscar Robertson, Cinn.	1971	Austin Carr, Notre Dame	1984	Michael Jordan, N.Carolina
1960	Oscar Robertson, Cinn.	1972	Bill Walton, UCLA	1985	Chris Mullin, St.John's
1961	Jerry Lucas, Ohio St.	1973	Bill Walton, UCLA	1986	Walter Berry St.John's
1962	Jerry Lucas, Ohio St.	1974	Bill Walton, UCLA	1987	David Robinson, Navy
1963	Art Heyman, Duke	1975	David Thompson, N.C.State	1988	Hersey Hawkins, Bradley
1964	Gary Bradds, Ohio St.	1976	Scott May, Indiana	1989	Danny Ferry, Duke
1965	Bill Bradley, Princeton	1977	Marques Johnson, UCLA	1990	Lionel Simmons, La Salle
1966	Cazzie Russell, Michigan	1978	Butch Lee, Marquette		
		1979	Larry Bird, Indiana St.		

U.S. Basketball Writers Association

Voted on by the USBWA and first presented in 1959.
Multiple winners: Ralph Sampson and Bill Walton (3); Lew Alcindor, Jerry Lucas, Oscar Robertson (2).

Year	Year	Year
1959 Oscar Robertson, Cincinnati	1970 Pete Maravich, LSU	1980 Mark Aguirre, DePaul
1960 Oscar Robertson, Cinn.	1971 Sidney Wicks, UCLA	1981 Ralph Sampson, Virginia
1961 Jerry Lucas, Ohio St.	1972 Bill Walton, UCLA	1982 Ralph Sampson, Virginia
1962 Jerry Lucas, Ohio St.	1973 Bill Walton, UCLA	1983 Ralph Sampson, Virginia
1963 Art Heyman, Duke	1974 Bill Walton, UCLA	1984 Michael Jordan, N.Carolina
1964 Walt Hazzard, UCLA	1975 David Thompson, N.C.State	1985 Chris Mullin, St.John's
1965 Bill Bradley, Princeton	1976 Adrian Dantley, Notre Dame	1986 Walter Berry St.John's
1966 Cazzie Russell, Michigan	1977 Marques Johnson, UCLA	1987 David Robinson, Navy
1967 Lew Alcindor, UCLA	1978 Phil Ford, North Carolina	1988 Hersey Hawkins, Bradley
1968 Elvin Hayes, Houston	1979 Larry Bird, Indiana St	1989 Danny Ferry, Duke
1969 Lew Alcindor, UCLA		1990 Lionel Simmons, La Salle

Rupp Trophy (AP)

Voted on by AP sportswriters and broadcasters and first presented in 1961 by the Commonwealth Athletic Club of Kentucky in the name of former Univ.of Kentucky coach Adolph Rupp.
Multiple winners: Ralph Sampson (3); Lew Alcindor, Jerry Lucas, David Thompson and Bill Walton (2).

Year	Year	Year
1961 Jerry Lucas, Ohio St.	1970 Pete Maravich, LSU	1980 Mark Aguirre, DePaul
1962 Jerry Lucas, Ohio St.	1971 Austin Carr, Notre Dame	1981 Ralph Sampson, Virginia
1963 Art Heyman, Duke	1972 Bill Walton, UCLA	1982 Ralph Sampson, Virginia
1964 Gary Bradds, Ohio St.	1973 Bill Walton, UCLA	1983 Ralph Sampson, Virginia
1965 Bill Bradley, Princeton	1974 David Thompson, N.C.State	1984 Michael Jordan, N.Carolina
1966 Cazzie Russell, Michigan	1975 David Thompson, N.C.St.	1985 Patrick Ewing, Georgetown
1967 Lew Alcindor, UCLA	1976 Scott May, Indiana	1986 Walter Berry, St.John's
1968 Elvin Hayes, Houston	1977 Marques Johnson, UCLA	1987 David Robinson, Navy
1969 Lew Alcindor, UCLA	1978 Butch Lee, Marquette	1988 Hersey Hawkins, Bradley
	1979 Larry Bird, Indiana St.	1989 Sean Elliott, Arizona
		1990 Lionel Simmons, La Salle

Naismith Award

Voted on by a panel of coaches, sportswriters and broadcasters and first presented in 1969 by the Atlanta Tip-Off Club in 1969 in the name of the inventor of basketball, Dr.James Naismith.
Multiple winners: Ralph Sampson and Bill Walton (2).

Year	Year	Year
1969 Lew Alcindor, UCLA	1976 Scott May, Indiana	1983 Ralph Sampson, Virginia
1970 Pete Maravich, LSU	1977 Marques Johnson, UCLA	1984 Michael Jordan, N.Carolina
1971 Austin Carr, Notre Dame	1978 Butch Lee, Marquette	1985 Patrick Ewing, Georgetown
1972 Bill Walton, UCLA	1979 Larry Bird, Indiana St.	1986 Johnny Dawkins, Duke
1973 Bill Walton, UCLA	1980 Mark Aguirre, DePaul	1987 David Robinson, Navy
1974 Bill Walton, UCLA	1981 Ralph Sampson, Virginia	1988 Danny Manning, Kansas
1975 David Thompson, N.C.State	1982 Ralph Sampson, Virginia	1989 Danny Ferry, Duke
		1990 Lionel Simmons, La Salle

National Association of Basketball Coaches

Voted on by the NABC and first presented by the Eastman Kodak Co. in 1975.
Multiple winner: Ralph Sampson (2).

Year	Year	Year
1975 David Thompson, N.C.State	1980 Michael Brooks, La Salle	1986 Walter Berry St.John's
1976 Scott May, Indiana	1981 Danny Ainge, BYU	1987 David Robinson, Navy
1977 Marques Johnson, UCLA	1982 Ralph Sampson, Virginia	1988 Danny Manning, Kansas
1978 Phil Ford, North Carolina	1983 Ralph Sampson, Virginia	1989 Sean Elliott, Arizona
1979 Larry Bird, Indiana St.	1984 Michael Jordan, N.Carolina	1990 Lionel Simmons, La Salle
	1985 Patrick Ewing, Georgetown	

Wooden Award

Voted on by a panel of coaches, sportswriters and broadcasters and first presented in 1977 by the Los Angeles Athletic Club in the name of former Purdue All-America and UCLA coach John Wooden.
Multiple winner: Ralph Sampson (2).

Year	Year	Year
1977 Marques Johnson, UCLA	1981 Danny Ainge, BYU	1986 Walter Berry St.John's
1978 Phil Ford, North Carolina	1982 Ralph Sampson, Virginia	1987 David Robinson, Navy
1979 Larry Bird, Indiana St.	1983 Ralph Sampson, Virginia	1988 Danny Manning, Kansas
1980 Darrell Griffith, Louisville	1984 Michael Jordan, N.Carolina	1989 Sean Elliott, Arizona
	1985 Chris Mullin, St.John's	1990 Lionel Simmons, La Salle

All-Time Winningest Division I Coaches

Minimum 10 seasons as Division I head coach; regular season and tournament games included; coaches active during 1989-90 in **bold type**.

Top 20 Victories

	Yrs	W	L	Pct
Adolph Rupp	41	**875**	190	.822
Hank Iba	41	**767**	338	.694
Ed Diddle	42	**759**	302	.715
Phog Allen	48	**746**	264	.739
Ray Meyer	42	**724**	354	.672
Dean Smith	29	**688**	203	.772
John Wooden	29	**664**	162	.804
Ralph Miller	38	**657**	382	.632
Marv Harshman	40	**642**	448	.589
Norm Sloan	37	**627**	395	.614
Cam Henderson	36	**611**	245	.714
Abe Lemons	34	**599**	343	.636
Slats Gill	36	**599**	392	.604
Guy Lewis	30	**592**	279	.680
Jerry Tarkanian	22	**565**	119	.826
Don Haskins	29	**563**	243	.699
Lefty Driesell	28	**560**	249	.692
Tony Hinkle	41	**560**	392	.588
Lou Henson	28	**556**	257	.684
Frank McGuire	30	**550**	235	.701

Top 20 Winning Pct.

	Yrs	Won	Lost	Pct
Clair Bee	21	410	86	.827
Jerry Tarkanian	22	565	119	.826
Adolph Rupp	41	875	190	.822
John Wooden	29	664	162	.804
Dean Smith	29	688	203	.772
George Keogan	24	385	117	.767
Jack Ramsay	11	231	71	.765
Frank Keaney	28	403	124	.765
Vic Bubas	10	213	67	.761
Jim Boeheim	14	343	108	.761
Chick Davies	21	314	106	.748
John Thompson	18	423	142	.749
Denny Crum	19	463	156	.748
Ray Mears	21	399	135	.747
Phog Allen	48	746	264	.739
Al McGuire	20	405	143	.739
Everett Case	18	376	133	.739
Lou Carnesecca	22	484	180	.729
Bob Knight	25	532	198	.729
Lew Andreas	25	355	134	.726

Note: Clarence "Bighouse" Gaines of Division II Winston Salem (1947-present) is No.2 on the all-time NCAA list of all coaches regardless of division. His record is 806-396 over 44 seasons.

Where They Coached

Allen—Baker (1906-08), Haskell (1909), Central Mo.St.(1913-19), Kansas (1908-09, 20-56); **Andreas**—Syracuse (1925-43; 45-50); **Bee**—Rider (1929-31), LIU-Brooklyn (1932-45, 46-51); **Boeheim**—Syracuse (1977—); **Bubas**—Duke (1960-69); **Carnesecca**—St.John's (1966-70, 74—); **Case**—N.C.State (1947-64); **Crum**—Louisville (1972—); **Davies**—Duquesne (1925-43, 47-48); **Diddle**—Western Ky.(1923-64); **Driesell**—Davidson (1961-69), Maryland (1970-86), J.Madison (1989—).

Gill—Oregon St.(1929-64); **Harshman**—Pacific Lutheran (1946-58), Wash.St.(1959-71), Washington (1972-85); **Haskins**—UTEP (1962—); **Henderson**—Muskingum (1920-22), Davis & Elkins (1923-35), Marshall (1936-55); **Henson**—Hardin-Simmons (1963-66), N.Mexico St.(1967-75), Illinois (1976—); **Hinkle**—Butler (1927-42, 46-70); **Iba**—NW Missouri St.(1930-33), Colorado (1934), Oklahoma St.(1935-70).

Keaney—Rhode Island (1921-48); **Knight**—Army (1966-71), Indiana (1972—); **Koegan**—St.Louis (1916), Allegheny (1919), Valparaiso (1920-21), Notre Dame (1924-43); **Lemons**—Okla.City (1956-73), Pan American (1974-76), Texas (1977-82), Okla.City (1984-90); **Lewis**—Houston (1957-86); **A.McGuire**—Belmont Abbey (1958-64), Marquette (1965-77); **F.McGuire**—St.John's (1948-52), North Carolina (1953-61), South Carolina (1965-80); **Mears**—Wittenberg (1957-62), Tennessee (1963-77); **R.Meyer**—DePaul (1943-84); **Miller**—Wichita St.(1952-64), Iowa (1965-70), Oregon St.(1971-89).

Ramsay—St.Joseph's PA (1956-66); **Rupp**—Kentucky (1931-72); **Sloan**—Presbyterian (1952-55), Citadel (1957-60), Florida (1961-66), N.C.State (1967-80), Florida (1981-89); **Smith**—North Carolina (1962—); **Tarkanian**—Long Beach St.(1969-73), UNLV (1974—); **Thompson**—Georgetown (1973—); **Wooden**—Indiana St.(1947-48), UCLA (1949-75).

Most NCAA Tournaments

Division I coaches with most appearances in the NCAA tournament through 1990. Listed are number of appearances, overall tournament record, times reaching Final Four, and number of NCAA titles. Coaches active during 1989-90 in **bold type**.

App		W-L	F4	Championships
20	**Dean Smith**	43-21	7	1 (1982)
20	Adolph Rupp	30-18	6	4 (1948-49, 51,58)
16	John Wooden	47-10	12	10 (1964-65, 67-73,75)
16	**Lou Carnesecca**	14-18	1	None
15	**Jerry Tarkanian**	33-15	3	1 (1990)
15	**Denny Crum**	32-15	6	2 (1980,86)
15	**Lou Henson**	18-16	2	None
15	**Digger Phelps**	17-17	1	None
14	**Bob Knight**	29-11	4	3 (1976,81,87)
14	**John Thompson**	26-13	3	1 (1984)
14	Guy Lewis	26-18	5	None
13	Eddie Sutton	17-13	1	None
13	**Don Haskins**	12-12	1	1 (1966)
13	Ray Meyer	14-16	2	None

Active Coaches' Victories

Minimum 5 seasons in Division I.

	Yrs	Wins
Dean Smith, N.Carolina	29	**688**
Jerry Tarkanian, UNLV	22	**565**
Don Haskins, UTEP	29	**563**
Lefty Driesell, James Madison	28	**560**
Lou Henson, Illinois	28	**556**
Norm Stewart, Missouri	29	**552**
Gene Bartow, Ala-Birmingham	28	**536**
Bob Knight, Indiana	25	**532**
Glenn Wilkes, Stetson	33	**512**
Tom Young, Old Dominion	30	**510**
Lou Carnesecca, St.John's	22	**484**
Eldon Miller, Northern Iowa	28	**469**
Denny Crum, Louisville	19	**463**
Hugh Durham, Georgia	24	**448**
Bill Foster, Northwestern	30	**445**
Butch van Breda Kolff, Hofstra	24	**430**
Eddie Sutton, Oklahoma St	20	**430**
John Thompson, Georgetown	18	**423**
John Chaney, Temple	18	**417**
Pete Carril, Princeton	24	**408**
Digger Phelps, Notre Dame	20	**407**

Coach of the Year Awards

UPI picked the first national Division I Coach of the Year in 1955. Since then, The U.S.Basketball Writers Assn. (1959), AP (1967), the National Assn. of Basketball Coaches (1969), and the Atlanta Tip-Off Club (1987) have joined in.

Since 1969, the first year all four awards were given out, the same coach has won all of them in the same season five times: John Wooden of UCLA in 1970 and '72, Bob (then Bobby) Knight of Indiana in 1975, Ralph Miller of Oregon St. in 1981 and John Chaney of Temple in 1988.

United Press International

Voted on by a panel of UPI college basketball writers and first presented in 1955.
Multiple winners: John Wooden (6); Bob Knight, Ray Meyer, Adolph Rupp, Fred Taylor and Phil Woopert (2).

Year	Year	Year
1955 Phil Woolpert, San Francisco	1967 John Wooden, UCLA	1979 Bill Hodges, Indiana St.
1956 Phil Woolpert, San Fran	1968 Guy Lewis, Houston	1980 Ray Meyer, DePaul
1957 Frank McGuire, N.Carolina	1969 John Wooden, UCLA	1981 Ralph Miller, Oregon St.
1958 Tex Winter, Kansas St.		1982 Norm Stewart, Missouri
1959 Adolph Rupp, Kentucky	1970 John Wooden, UCLA	1983 Jerry Tarkanian, UNLV
	1971 Al McGuire, Marquette	1984 Ray Meyer, DePaul
1960 Pete Newell, California	1972 John Wooden, UCLA	1985 Lou Carnesecca, St.John's
1961 Fred Taylor, Ohio St.	1973 John Wooden, UCLA	1986 Mike Krzyzewski, Duke
1962 Fred Taylor, Ohio St.	1974 Digger Phelps, Notre Dame	1987 John Thompson, Georgetown
1963 Ed Jucker, Cincinnati	1975 Bobby Knight, Indiana	1988 John Chaney, Temple
1964 John Wooden, UCLA	1976 Tom Young, Rutgers	1989 Bob Knight, Indiana
1965 Dave Strack, Michigan	1977 Bob Gaillard, San Francisco	
1966 Adolph Rupp, Kentucky	1978 Eddie Sutton, Arkansas	1990 Jim Calhoun, Connecticut

U.S. Basketball Writers Assn.

Voted on by the USBWA and first presented in 1959.
Multiple winners: John Wooden (5); Bob Knight (3); Guy Lewis, Ray Meyer and Ralph Miller (2).

Year	Year	Year
1959 Eddie Hickey, Marquette	1970 John Wooden, UCLA	1980 Ray Meyer, DePaul
	1971 Al McGuire, Marquette	1981 Ralph Miller, Oregon St.
1960 Pete Newell, California	1972 John Wooden, UCLA (4)	1982 Ralph Miller, Oregon St.
1961 Fred Taylor, Ohio St.	1973 John Wooden, UCLA (5)	1983 Guy Lewis, Houston
1962 Fred Taylor, Ohio St.	1974 Norm Sloan, N.C.State	1984 Ray Meyer, DePaul
1963 Ed Jucker, Cincinnati	1975 Bobby Knight, Indiana	1985 Bill Frieder, Michigan
1964 John Wooden, UCLA	1976 Bobby Knight, Indiana	1986 Eddie Sutton, Kentucky
1965 B.van Breda Kolff, Princeton	1977 Bob Gaillard, San Francisco	1987 Tom Davis, Iowa
1966 Adolph Rupp, Kentucky	1978 Eddie Sutton, Arkansas	1988 John Chaney, Temple
1967 John Wooden, UCLA	1979 Bill Hodges, Indiana St.	1989 Bob Knight, Indiana
1968 Guy Lewis, Houston		
1969 Maury John, Drake		1990 Roy Williams, Kansas

Associated Press

Voted on by AP sportswriters and broadcasters and first presented in 1967.
Multiple winners: John Wooden (5); Bob Knight (3); Guy Lewis, Ray Meter, Ralph Mille and Eddie Sutton (2).

Year	Year	Year
1967 John Wooden, UCLA	1975 Bobby Knight, Indiana	1983 Guy Lewis, Houston
1968 Guy Lewis, Houston	1976 Bobby Knight, Indiana	1984 Ray Meyer, DePaul
1969 John Wooden, UCLA	1977 Bob Gailliard, San Francisco	1985 Bill Frieder, Michigan
	1978 Eddie Sutton, Arkansas	1986 Eddie Sutton, Kentucky
1970 John Wooden, UCLA	1979 Bill Hodges, Indiana St.	1987 Tom Davis, Iowa
1971 Al McGuire, Marquette		1988 John Chaney, Temple
1972 John Wooden, UCLA	1980 Ray Meyer, DePaul	1989 Bob Knight, Indiana
1973 John Wooden, UCLA	1981 Ralph Miller, Oregon St.	
1974 Norm Sloan, N.C.State	1982 Ralph Miller, Oregon St.	1990 Jim Calhoun, Connecticut

National Association of Basketball Coaches

Voted on by NABC and first presented in 1969.
Multiple winner: John Wooden (3).

Year	Year	Year
1969 John Wooden, UCLA	1977 Dean Smith, N.Carolina	1983 Lou Carnesecca, St.John's
	1978 Bill Foster, Duke	1984 Marv Harshman, Washington
1970 John Wooden, UCLA	& Abe Lemons, Texas	1985 John Thompson, Georgetown
1971 Jack Kraft, Villanova	1979 Ray Meyer, DePaul	1986 Eddie Sutton, Kentucky
1972 John Wooden, UCLA		1987 Rick Pitino, Providence
1973 Gene Bartow, Memphis St.	1980 Lute Olson, Iowa	1988 John Chaney, Temple
1974 Al McGuire, Marquette	1981 Ralph Miller, Oregon St.	1989 P.J.Carlesimo, Seton Hall
1975 Bobby Knight, Indiana	& Jack Hartman, Kansas St.	
1976 Johnny Orr, Michigan	1982 Don Monson, Idaho	1990 Jud Heathcote, Mich.St.

Coach of the Year Awards (Cont.)
Naismith Award

Voted on by a panel of coaches, sportswriters and broadcasters and first presented by the Atlanta Tip-Off Club in 1987.

Year		Year		Year	
1987	Bob Knight, Indiana	1989	Mike Krzyzewski, Duke	1990	Bobby Cremins, Ga.Tech.
1988	Larry Brown, Kansas				

Other Men's Champions

NCAA Div.II Finals, 1957-90

Year	Winner	Score	Loser
1957	Wheaton,IL	89-65	Ky.Wesleyan
1958	South Dakota	75-53	St.Michaels,VT
1959	Evansville,IN	83-67	SW Missouri St.
1960	Evansville,IN	90-69	Chapman,CA
1961	Wittenberg,OH	42-38	SE Missouri St.
1962	Mt.St.Mary's, MD	58-57*	CS-Sacramento
1963	South Dakota St.	42-40	Wittenberg,OH
1964	Evansville,IN	72-59	Akron,OH
1965	Evansville,IN	85-82*	Southern Illinois
1966	Ky.Wesleyan	54-51	Southern Illinois
1967	Winston-Salem,NC	77-74	SW Missouri St.
1968	Ky.Wesleyan	63-52	Indiana St.
1969	Ky.Wesleyan	75-71	SW Missouri St.
1970	Phila.Textile	76-65	Tennessee St.
1971	Evansville,IN	97-82	Old Dominion,VA
1972	Roanoke,VA	84-72	Akron,OH
1973	Ky.Wesleyan	78-76*	Tennessee St.
1974	Morgan St.,MD	67-52	SW Missouri St.
1975	Old Dominion,VA	76-74	New Orleans,LA
1976	Puget Sound, WA	83-74	Tennessee-Chatt.
1977	Tennessee-Chatt.	71-62	Randolph-Macon
1978	Cheyney,PA	47-40	Wisc-Green Bay
1979	North Alabama	64-50	Wisc-Green Bay
1980	Virginia Union	80-74	New York Tech
1981	Florida Southern	73-68	Mt.St.Mary's,MD
1982	Dist.of Columbia	73-63	Florida Southern
1983	Wright St.,OH	92-73	Dist.of Columbia
1984	Central Mo.St.	81-77	St.Augustine's,NC
1985	Jacksonville St.	74-73	South Dakota St.
1986	Sacred Heart,CT	93-87	SE Missouri St.
1987	Ky.Wesleyan	92-74	Gannon,PA
1988	Lowell,MA	75-72	Alaska-Anchorage
1989	N.C.Central	73-46	SE Missouri St.
1990	Ky.Wesleyan	93-79	CS-Bakersfield

*Overtime

NCAA Div.III Finals, 1975-90

Year	Winner	Score	Loser
1975	LeMoyne-Owen,TN	57-54	Glassboro St.,NJ
1976	Scranton,PA	60-57	Wittenberg,OH
1977	Wittenberg,OH	79-66	Oneonta St.,NY
1978	North Park,IL	69-57	Widener,PA
1979	North Park,IL	66-62	Potsdam St.,NY
1980	North Park,IL	83-76	Upsala,NJ
1981	Potsdam St.,NY	67-65*	Augustana,IL
1982	Wabash,IN	83-62	Potsdam St.,NY
1983	Scranton,PA	64-63	Wittenberg,OH
1984	Wisc-Whitewater	103-86	Clark,MA
1985	North Park,IL	72-71	Potsdam St.,NY
1986	Potsdam St.,NY	76-73	LeMoyne-Owen,TN
1987	North Park,IL	106-100	Clark,MA
1988	Ohio Wesleyan	92-70	Scranton,PA
1989	Wisc-Whitewater	94-86	Trenton St.,NJ
1990	Rochester	43-42	DePauw

*Overtime

NAIA Finals, 1937-90

NAIA tournament held in Kansas City at Municipal Auditorium (1937-74) and Kemper Arena (since 1975).

Year	Winner	Score	Loser
1937	Central Missouri	35-24	Morningside,IA
1938	Central Missouri	45-30	Roanoke,VA
1939	Southwestern,KS	32-31	San Diego St.
1940	Tarkio,MO	52-31	San Diego St.
1941	San Diego St.	36-32	Murray St.,KY
1942	Hamline,MN	33-31	S'eastern Okla.
1943	SE Missouri St.	34-32	NW Missouri St.
1944	No tournament held		
1945	Loyola,LA	49-36	Pepperdine,CA
1946	Southern Illinois	49-40	Indiana St.
1947	Marshall,WV	73-59	Mankato St.,MN
1948	Louisville,KY	82-70	Indiana St.
1949	Hamline,MN	57-46	Regis,CO
1950	Indiana St.	61-47	East Central,OK
1951	Hamline,MN	69-61	Millikin,IL
1952	SW Missouri St.	73-64	Murray St.,KY
1953	SW Missouri St.	79-71	Hamline,MN
1954	St.Benedict's,KS	62-56	Western Illinois
1955	East Texas St.	71-54	S'eastern Okla.
1956	McNeese St.,LA	60-55	Texas Southern
1957	Tennessee St.	92-73	S'eastern Okla.
1958	Tennessee St.	85-73	Western Illinois
1959	Tennessee St.	97-87	Pacific-Luth., WA
1960	SW Texas St.	66-44	Westminster,PA
1961	Grambling,LA	95-75	Georgetown,KY
1962	Prairie View,TX	62-53	Westminster,PA
1963	Pan American,TX	73-62	Western Carolina
1964	Rockhurst,MO	66-56	Pan American,TX
1965	Central St.,OH	85-51	Oklahoma Baptist
1966	Oklahoma Baptist	88-59	Georgia Southern
1967	St.Benedict's,KS	71-65	Oklahoma Baptist
1968	Central St.,OH	51-48	Fairmont St.,WV
1969	Eastern N.Mexico	99-76	MD-Eastern Shore
1970	Kentucky St.	79-71	Central Wash.
1971	Kentucky St.	102-82	Eastern Michigan
1972	Kentucky St.	71-62	Wisc-Eau Claire
1973	Guilford,NC	99-96	MD-Eastern Shore
1974	West Georgia	97-79	Alcorn St.,MS
1975	Grand Canyon,AZ	65-54	M'western St.,TX
1976	Coppin St.,MD	96-91	Henderson St.,AR
1977	Texas Southern	71-44	Campbell,NC
1978	Grand Canyon,AZ	79-75	Kearney St.,NE
1979	Drury,MO	60-54	Henderson St.,AR
1980	Cameron,OK	84-77	Alabama St.
1981	Beth.Nazarene,OK	86-85*	Ala-Huntsville
1982	USC-Spartanburg	51-38	Biola,CA
1983	C.of Charleston,SC	57-53	West Va.Wesleyan
1984	Fort Hays St.,KS	48-46*	Wisc-Stevens Pt.
1985	Fort Hays St.,KS	82-80*	Wayland Bapt.,TX
1986	David Lipscomb,TN	67-54	Ark-Monticello
1987	Washburn,KS	79-77	West Va.St.
1988	Grand Canyon,AZ	88-86*	Auburn-Montg,AL
1989	St.Mary's,TX	61-58	East Central,OK
1990	Birm-Southern,AL	88-80	Wisc-Eau Claire

*Overtime

Women's Basketball

NCAA Final Four, 1982-90

Replaced the Association of Intercollegiate Athletics for Women (AIAW) tournament in 1982 as the official playoff for the national championship.

Multiple winners: Louisiana Tech, Southern Cal and Tennessee (2).

Year	Champion	Head Coach	Score	Runner-up	Third Place	
1982	Louisiana Tech	Sonya Hogg	76-62	Cheyney	Maryland	Tennessee
1983	Southern Cal	Linda Sharp	69-67	Louisiana Tech	Georgia	Old Dominion
1984	Southern Cal	Linda Sharp	72-61	Tennessee	Cheyney	Louisiana Tech
1985	Old Dominion	Marianne Stanley	70-65	Georgia	NE Louisiana	Western Ky.
1986	Texas	Jody Conradt	97-81	Southern Cal	Tennessee	Western Ky.
1987	Tennessee	Pat Summitt	67-44	Louisiana Tech	Long Beach St.	Texas
1988	Louisiana Tech	Leon Barmore	56-54	Auburn	Long Beach St.	Tennessee
1989	Tennessee	Pat Summitt	76-60	Auburn	Louisiana Tech	Maryland
1990	Stanford	Tara VanDerveer	88-81	Auburn	Louisiana Tech	Virginia

Most Outstanding Player

A Most Outstanding Player has been selected every year of the NCAA tournament.

Multiple winner: Cheryl Miller (2).

Year		Year		Year	
1982	Janice Lawrence, La.Tech	1985	Tracy Claxton, ODU	1988	Erica Westbrooks, La.Tech
1983	Cheryl Miller, USC	1986	Clarissa Davis, Texas	1989	Bridgette Gordon, Tenn
1984	Cheryl Miller, USC	1987	Tonya Edwards, Tennessee	1990	Jennifer Azzi, Stanford

Player of the Year Awards

The Broderick Award was first given out to the Women's Division I or Large School Player of the Year in 1977. Since then, the National Assn. for Girls and Women in Sports (1978), the Women's Basketball Coaches Assn. (1983) and the Atlanta Tip-Off Club (1983) have joined in.

Since 1983, the first year all four awards were given out, the same player has won all of them in the same season once: Cheryl Miller of Southern Cal in 1985.

Broderick Award

Voted on by a national panel of women's collegiate athletic directors and first presented by the late Thomas Broderick, an athletic outfitter who created the award in 1976. Honda has presented the award since 1987. Basketball Player of the Year is one of 10 nominated for Collegiate Woman Athlete of the Year; (*) indicates player also won Athlete of the Year.

Multiple winners: Nancy Lieberman and Cheryl Miller (2).

Year		Year		Year	
1977	Lucy Harris, Delta St.*	1981	Lynette Woodward, Kansas	1986	Kamie Ethridge, Texas*
1978	Anne Meyers, UCLA*	1982	Pam Kelly, La.Tech.	1987	Katrina McClain, Georgia
1979	Nancy Lieberman, ODU*	1983	Anne Donovan, ODU	1988	T.Weatherspoon, La.Tech*
1980	Nancy Lieberman, ODU*	1984	Cheryl Miller, USC*	1989	Bridgette Gordon, Tennessee
		1985	Cheryl Miller, USC	1990	TBA in Fall

Wade Trophy

Voted on by the National Assn. for Girls and Women in Sports (NAGWS) and first presented in 1978 in the name of former Delta St. coach Margaret Wade.

Multiple winner: Nancy Lieberman (2).

Year		Year		Year	
1978	Carol Blazejowski, Mont.St.	1982	Pam Kelly, La.Tech.	1987	Shelly Pennefather, V'nova
1979	Nancy Lieberman, ODU	1983	LaTaunya Pollard, L.Beach St.	1988	T.Weatherspoon, La.Tech.
1980	Nancy Lieberman, ODU	1984	Janice Lawrence, La.Tech.	1989	Clarissa Davis, Texas
1981	Lynette Woodward, Kansas	1985	Cheryl Miller, USC	1990	Jennifer Azzi, Stanford
		1986	Kamie Ethridge, Texas		

Naismith Trophy

Voted on by a panel of coaches, sportwriters and broadcasters and first presented in 1983 by the Atlanta Tip-Off Club in the name of the inventor of basketball, Dr. James Naismith.

Multiple winners: Cheryl Miller (3); Clarissa Davis (2).

Year		Year		Year	
1983	Anne Donovan, ODU	1986	Cheryl Miller, USC	1989	Clarissa Davis, Texas
1984	Cheryl Miller, USC	1987	Clarissa Davis, Texas	1990	Jennifer Azzi, Stanford
1985	Cheryl Miller, USC	1988	Sue Wicks, Rutgers		

WBCA Player of the Year

Voted on by the WBCA and first presented by Champion athletic outfitters in 1983.

Multiple winner: Cheryl Miller (2).

Year		Year		Year	
1983	Anne Donovan, ODU	1986	Cheryl Miller, USC	1989	Clarissa Davis, Texas
1984	Janice Lawrence, La.Tech.	1987	Katrina McClain, Georgia	1990	Venus Lacey, La.Tech
1985	Cheryl Miller, USC	1988	Michelle Edwards, Iowa		

Coach of the Year Award

Voted on by the Women's Basketball Coaches Assn. and first presented by Converse athletic outfitters in 1983.
Multiple winner: Jody Conradt (2).

Year		Year		Year	
1983	Pat Summitt, Tennessee	1986	Jody Conradt, Texas	1989	Tara VanDerveer, Stanford
1984	Jody Conradt, Texas	1987	Theresa Grentz, Rutgers	1990	Kay Yow, N.C.State
1985	Jim Foster, St. Joe's, PA	1988	Vivian Stringer, Iowa		

Other Women's Champions

AIAW Finals, 1972-82

The Association of Intercollegiate Athletics for Women Large College tournament determined the women's national champion for 10 years until supplanted by the NCAA. In 1982, most Division I teams entered the first NCAA tournament rather than the last one staged by the AIAW.

Year	Winner	Score	Loser
1972	Immaculata,PA	52-48	West Chester,PA
1973	Immaculata,PA	59-52	Queens College,NY
1974	Immaculata,PA	68-53	Mississippi Col.
1975	Delta St.,MS	90-81	Immaculata,PA
1976	Delta St.,MS	69-64	Immaculata,PA
1977	Delta St.,MS	68-55	LSU
1978	UCLA	90-74	Maryland
1979	Old Dominion	75-65	Louisiana Tech
1980	Old Dominion	68-53	Tennessee
1981	Louisiana Tech	79-59	Tennessee
1982	Rutgers	83-77	Texas

NCAA Div.III Finals, 1982-90

Division III Finals held in Elizabethtown,PA (1982); Worcester,MA (1983); Scranton,PA (1984,87); DePere,WI (1985); Salem,MA (1986); Moorhead,MN (1988); Danville,KY (1989); Holland,MI (1990).

Year	Winner	Score	Loser
1982	Elizabethtown,PA	67-66*	NC-Greensboro
1983	North Central,IL	83-71	Elizabethtown,PA
1984	Rust College,MS	51-49	Elizabethtown,PA
1985	Scranton,PA	68-59	New Rochelle,NY
1986	Salem St.,MA	89-85	Bishop,TX
1987	Wisc-Stevens Pt.	81-74	Concordia,MN
1988	Concordia,MN	65-57	St.John Fisher,NY
1989	Elizabethtown,PA	66-65	CS-Stanislaus
1990	Hope	65-63	St.John Fisher

*Overtime
Note: Concordia,MN is Concordia College in Moorhead,MN, not Concordia College in St.Paul,MN.

NCAA Div.II Finals, 1982-90

Division II Finals held in Springfield,MA (1982-87); Fargo,ND (1988); Cleveland,MS (1989); Pomona,CA (1990).

Year	Winner	Score	Loser
1982	Cal Poly Pomona	93-74	Tuskegee,AL
1983	Virginia Union	73-60	Cal Poly Pomona
1984	Central Mo.St.	80-73	Virginia Union
1985	Cal Poly Pomona	80-69	Central Mo.St.
1986	Cal Poly Pomona	70-63	North Dakota St.
1987	New Haven,CT	77-75	Cal Poly Pomona
1988	Hampton,VA	65-48	West Texas St.
1989	Delta St.,MS	88-58	Cal Poly Pomona
1990	Delta St.,MS	77-43	Bentley

NAIA Finals, 1981-90

NAIA tournament held in Kansas City,MO (1981- 83, and since 1987); and Cedar Rapids,IA (1984-86).

Year	Winner	Score	Loser
1981	Kentucky St.	73-67	Texas Southern
1982	S'western Okla.	80-45	Mo.Southern
1983	S'western Okla.	80-68	Ala-Huntsville
1984	NC-Asheville	72-70*	Portland,OR
1985	S'western Okla.	55-54	Saginaw Val.,MI
1986	Francis Marion,SC	75-65	Wayland Bapt.,TX
1987	S'western Okla.	60-58	North Georgia
1988	Oklahoma City	113-95	Claflin,SC
1989	So.Nazarene	98-96	Claflin,SC
1990	SW Oklahoma	82-75	Ark-Monticello

*Overtime

Half of the 10 NCAA titles won by UCLA coach **John Wooden** between 1967-75 were anchored by Kareem Abdul Jabbar (then Lew Alcindor) and Bill Walton. Both players had their numbers retired in 1990.

COLLEGE BASKETBALL
YEAR BY YEAR

From the First NIT to the NCAA Final Four

Last year, **The Sports Almanac** ran a special chapter on college football that chronicled the game, year by year, from 1936 (the first season of the Associated Press poll) through 1988. This year, the **Almanac** gives college basketball the same treatment, from 1938 (the year of the first major postseason tournament) through 1989.

This chapter provides a brief summary of the season, complete NIT and NCAA tournament results, major conference champions, Player and Coach of the Year winners, and the consensus All-America teams. From 1938-48, the head coaches, regular season records and final records of the tournament teams are given. Starting in 1949, the first year of the AP basketball poll, coaches and records are given for the teams listed on the final regular season Top 20.

Background

James Naismith, a 30-year-old Canadian physical education instructor attending the YMCA training school in Springfield, Mass., invented basketball in December, 1891. But it was Ned Irish, a 29-year-old sportswriter-turned-promoter who invented big time college basketball when he staged the sport's first intersectional doubleheader at Madison Square Garden in New York on Dec. 19, 1934.

An overflow crowd of 16,188 attended that first Garden twin bill as NYU beat Notre Dame, 25-18, and Westminster College of Pennsylvania beat St.John's, 37-33. In the midst of the Great Depression college basketball had arrived.

Two years later, it was was ready for its first Game of the Century. On Dec. 30, 1936 at the Garden (where else, by now every kid who could dribble a ball was dreaming of playing there) Long Island University, winners of 43 straight, played Stanford, the Pacific Coast Conference champion. Eastern establishment vs. Western mavericks. Legendary coach—Clair Bee of LIU—vs. the game's first superstar—Hank Luisetti of Stanford.

Stanford won the game, 43-31, but the next day it wasn't the upset fans were talking about—it was the revolutionary way in which the Indians had gone about mopping the Garden floor with the mighty Blackbirds. Until that game, the slow, deliberate, style of play practiced by LIU and other Eastern powers was the accepted and successful way to go. Two-hand set shots on offense and man-to-man on defense.

But Stanford didn't play Eastern style. The Indians ran with the ball, switched on defense and most remarkable of all, this guy Luisetti shot one-handed and on the move. To Eastern coaches the one-hander was blasphemy, a low percentage shot that smacked of showing off. But Luisetti was averaging 20 points a game. Besides, crowds loved him and Stanford was winning.

"No doubt about it," said Howie Dallmar, the former Stanford All-America and coach. "Hank simply revolutionized basketball. He was at least 20 years ahead of his time."

In Luisetti's wake, basketball became much more than just a game that was played between the football and baseball seasons. It developed a national following and with it the need for a tournament to decide a national champion. Promoter Irish and the New York sportswriters stepped into the void in 1938 with the National Invitation Tournament at the Garden. A year later, the National Association of Basketball Coaches organized a tournament of their own and held it at Northwestern. The NABC asked the NCAA to take over running the tournament in 1940.

For three years during World War II (1943-45), the NIT and NCAA champions met in an unofficial national championship game in New York for the benefit of the Red Cross. The NCAA champs won all three games, including a 1945 showdown between big men Bob Kurland of Oklahoma A&M and George Mikan of DePaul.

While the NIT conducted its entire tournament at Madison Square Garden, only the two regional champions made it to the NCAA championship site, which, from 1943-48, was also the Garden. The Final Two changed somewhat in 1946 when both regional runners-up were invited to the championship site, but they could only play for third place. The Final Four was really born in 1952 when the NCAAs expanded to four regional sites and the four winners advanced to Seattle to play for the title.

By the time San Francisco, with Bill Russell and K.C.Jones, was putting together back-to-back national titles in 1955-56, the NCAA tournament had overtaken the NIT as the true playoff for the national championship. By then, the NCAAs had automatic berths for all major conference champions and had expanded from eight to 25 teams while the NIT was still inviting only 12.

A third postseason playoff—the Collegiate Commissioners' Assn. Tournament—sprang up in 1974 and further diluted the NIT field by inviting all eight major conference runner-ups. In 1975, the NCAAs expanded to 32 teams and allowed conference runner-ups to accept at-large bids. That spelled the end for the CAA and it discontinued play after only two years.

As the NCAA tournament became more popular, it kept expanding—to 40 teams in 1979, 48 in 1980, 52 in 1983 and finally, the present 64-team field in 1985. Network television also became a major player in 1969 when NBC Sports paid over $500,000 to broadcast the championship game between UCLA and Purdue. Ten years later, Michigan State and Indiana State played for the title and that meeting between Magic Johnson and Larry Bird set a ratings record that still stands.

Ten years after that, CBS agreed to pay the NCAA $1 billion over seven years for exclusive rights to the entire tournament. That exclusivity meant the end of cable network ESPN's 10-year run of early round coverage, which did much to popularize the tournament.

Highest-Rated NCAA Championship Games

The 15 highest-rated NCAA championship games since the first year the championship was decided on network television in 1969. Listed below are the finalists (winning team first), date of game, TV network, and TV rating/audience share.

	Teams	Date	Net	Rtg/Shr
1	Mich.St.-Indiana St.	3/26/79	NBC	24.1/38
2	Georgetown-Villanova	4/1/85	CBS	23.3/33
3	N.C.State-Houston	4/4/83	CBS	22.3/32
4	N.Carolina-G'town	3/29/82	CBS	21.6/31
5	UCLA-Kentucky	3/31/75	NBC	21.3/33
	Michigan-Seton Hall	4/3/89	CBS	21.3/33
7	Louisville-Duke	3/31/86	CBS	20.7/31
8	Indiana-N.Carolina	3/30/81	NBC	20.7/29
9	UCLA-Memphis St.	3/26/73	NBC	20.5/32
10	Indiana-Michigan	3/29/76	NBC	20.4/31
11	UNLV-Duke	4/2/90	CBS	20.0/31
12	Kentucky-Duke	3/27/78	NBC	19.9/31
13	N.C.State-Marquette	3/25/74	NBC	19.9/30
14	Louisville-UCLA	3/24/80	NBC	19.8/30
15	Georgetown-Houston	4/2/84	CBS	19.7/29

NCAA Division I Scoring Leaders, 1948-89

The NCAA did not begin keeping individual scoring records until the 1947-48 season. All averages include postseason games where applicable. Fourteen underclassmen have won the scoring title; sophomores are indicated by (#) and juniors by (*).

Year		Gm	Pts	Avg	Year		Gm	Pts	Avg
1948	Murray Wier, Iowa	19	399	21.0	1970	Pete Maravich, LSU	31	1381	44.5
1949	Tony Lavelli, Yale	30	671	22.4	1971	Johnny Neumann, Miss.#	23	923	40.1
1950	Paul Arizin, Villanova	29	735	25.3	1972	Dwight Lamar, SW La.*	29	1054	36.3
1951	Bill Mlkvy, Temple	25	731	29.2	1973	William Averitt, Pepperdine	25	848	33.9
1952	Clyde Lovellette, Kansas	28	795	28.4	1974	Larry Fogle, Canisius#	25	835	33.4
1953	Frank Selvy, Furman*	25	738	29.5	1975	Bob McCurdy, Richmond	26	855	32.9
1954	Frank Selvy, Furman	29	1209	41.7	1976	Marshall Rodgers, Pan Am	25	919	36.8
1955	Darrell Floyd, Furman*	25	897	35.9	1977	Freeman Williams, Port.St.*	26	1010	38.8
1956	Darrell Floyd, Furman	28	946	33.8	1978	Freeman Williams, Port.St	27	969	35.9
1957	Grady Wallace, S.Carolina	29	906	31.2	1979	Lawrence Butler, Idaho St	27	812	30.1
1958	Oscar Robertson, Cinn#	28	984	35.1	1980	Tony Murphy, Southern-BR	29	932	32.1
1959	Oscar Robertson, Cinn*	30	978	32.6	1981	Zam Fredrick, S.Carolina	27	781	28.9
1960	Oscar Robertson, Cinn	30	1011	33.7	1982	Harry Kelly, TX-Southern*	29	862	29.7
1961	Frank Burgess, Gonzaga	26	842	32.4	1983	Harry Kelly, TX-Southern	29	835	28.8
1962	Billy McGill, Utah	26	1009	38.8	1984	Joe Jakubick, Akron	27	814	30.1
1963	Nick Werkman, Seton Hall*	22	650	29.5	1985	Xavier McDaniel, Wichita St	31	844	27.2
1964	Howie Komives, B.Green	23	844	36.7	1986	Terrance Bailey, Wagner*	29	854	29.4
1965	Rick Barry, Miami,FL	26	973	37.4	1987	Kevin Houston, Army	29	953	32.9
1966	Dave Schellhase, Purdue	24	781	32.5	1988	Hersey Hawkins, Bradley	31	1125	36.3
1967	Jimmy Walker, Providence	28	851	30.4	1989	Hank Gathers, Loyola-Mmt.*	31	1015	32.7
1968	Pete Maravich, LSU#	26	1138	43.8					
1969	Pete Maravich, LSU*	26	1148	44.2					

1938

The season began with the elimination of the center jump after each basket and ended with Temple winning the first National Invitation Tournament at Madison Square Garden in New York.

In between, Hank Luisetti closed out his sensational four-year career at Stanford with a season that featured an unheard of 50-point game against Duquesne and a third straight Pacific Coast Conference championship. After a 9-18 record his freshman year, Luisetti and Stanford went 68-12 over the next three seasons under coach John Bunn.

The Indians were 21-3 in 1938, but did not play in the inaugural NIT. Temple, at 20-2 the top team in the East, did play and trounced all three Midwestern teams in the tournament—Bradley, Oklahoma A&M and Colorado—to win the title.

One of the Colorado starters was football hero and future Supreme Court Justice Byron "Whizzer" White, who had led the nation in scoring and total offense in the fall. He joined the basketball team in January after taking the football team to the Cotton Bowl.

Player of the Year

Hank Luisetti, Stanford..................Helms

Consensus All-America Team
(In alphabetical order)

Meyer Bloom, Temple; Hank Luisetti, Stanford; John Moir, Notre Dame; Paul Nowak, Notre Dame; Fred Pralle, Kansas; Jewell Young, Purdue.

Major Conference Champions

Conference	Regular Season	Tournament
Big 6	Kansas (9-1)	—
Big 7	Colorado/Utah (10-2)	—
Big 10	Purdue (10-2)	—
Ivy	Dartmouth (8-4)	—
Mo.Valley	Oklahoma A&M (13-1)	—
New Eng.	Rhode Island St.(8-0)	—
PCC North	Oregon (14-6)	—
South	Stanford (10-2)*	—
SEC	Kentucky (6-0)	Ga. Tech
Southern	N.Carolina (13-3)	Duke
SWC	Arkansas (11-1)	—

*Won playoff for league championship.

NIT Tournament Teams
(In alphabetical order)

	Before NIT	Head Coach	Final Record
Bradley	18-1	Alfred Robertson	18-2
Colorado	14-5	Frosty Cox	15-6
LIU	23-3	Clair Bee	23-4
NYU	15-6	Howard Cann	16-8
Okla. A&M	24-2	Hank Iba	25-3
Temple	20-2	James Usilton	23-2

Note: Temple won the NIT.

NIT Tournament (6 teams)
All games at Madison Sq.Garden, New York

Quarterfinals—Temple 53, Bradley 40; NYU 39, LIU 37.
Semifinals—Temple 54, Oklahoma A&M 44; Colorado 48, NYU 47. **Third Place**—Oklahoma A&M 37, NYU 24. **Championship**—Temple 60, Colorado 36.
Most Valuable Player—Don Shields, Temple.

1939

Long Island University and Loyola of Chicago, both 20-0 during the regular season, met in the final of the second NIT tournament in New York. LIU, paced by All-America forward Irv Torgoff's 12 points, won easily and extended its two-year win streak to 26. The tournament's most valuable player, however, was Bill Lloyd of St.John's, who scored 31 against Roanoke in the quarterfinals.

Back in Evanston, Ill., PCC champion Oregon faced Big 10 champ Ohio State in the title game of the first NCAA tournament, played at Patten Gymnasium on the campus of Northwestern. The "Tall Firs" of Eugene, featuring 6'8" All-America center Slim Wintermute, won easily. Ohio State's lone consolation was that its All-America forward Jimmy Hull was named the tournament's outstanding player with 58 points in three games.

Turnout for the Final Two was disappointing, so the National Assn.of Basketball Coaches turned operation of the tournament over to the NCAA.

New England Conference champion Rhode Island State was 17-4, averaged 70 points a game and had the country's top player in forward Chet Jaworski. Unfortunately, the Rams didn't participate in either tournament.

Major Conference Champions

Conference	Regular Season	Tournament
Big 6	Missouri/Oklahoma (7-3)	—
Big 7	Colorado (10-2)	—
Big 10	Ohio St. (10-2)	—
Ivy	Dartmouth (10-2)	—
Mo.Valley	Okla.A&M/Drake (11-3)	—
New Eng.	Rhode Island St.(7-1)	—
PCC North	Oregon (14-2)*	—
South	California (10-3)	—
SEC	Alabama (13-4)	Kentucky
Southern	Wake Forest (15-3)	Clemson
SWC	Texas (10-2)	—
*Won playoff for league championship.

NCAA & NIT Tournament Teams
(In alphabetical order)

	Before Tourns	Head Coach	Final Record
Bradley	18-2	Al Robertson	19-3
Brown	17-3	George Allen	17-4
LIU	20-0	Clair Bee	23-0
Loyola,IL	20-0	Leonard Sachs	21-1
New Mex.A&M	16-2	Jerry Hines	16-3
Ohio St.	14-6	Harold Olsen	16-7
Oklahoma	11-8	Bruce Drake	12-9
Oregon	26-5	Howard Hobson	29-5
Roanoke	21-2	Pop White	21-3
St.John's	17-2	Joe Lapchick	18-4
Texas	19-4	Jack Gray	19-6
Utah St.	16-6	Dick Romney	17-7
Villanova	19-4	Al Severance	20-5
Wake Forest	18-5	Murray Greason	18-6
Note: Long Island Univ. won the NIT and Oregon won the NCAAs.

NCAA Tournament (8 teams)
East Regional
Semifinals—Villanova 42, Brown 30; Ohio St. 64, Wake Forest 52. **Third Place**—No game. **Final**—Ohio St.53, Villanova 36.

West Regional
Semifinals—Oklahoma 50, Utah St.39; Oregon 56, Texas 41. **Third Place**—Utah St. 51, Texas 49. **Final**—Oregon 55, Oklahoma 37.

FINAL TWO
at Patten Gymnasium, Evanston, IL
Championship—Oregon 46, Ohio St. 33.
Most Outstanding Player—Jimmy Hull, Ohio St. **All-Tournament**—Not selected.

NIT Tournament (6 teams)
All games at Madison Sq.Garden, New York

Quarterfinals—LIU 52, New Mexico A&M 45; St.John's 71, Roanoke 47.
Semifinals—LIU 36, Bradley 32; Loyola-IL 51, St.John's 46. **Third Place**—Bradley 40, St.John's 35.
Championship—LIU 44, Loyola-IL 32.
Most Valuable Player—Bill Lloyd, St.John's.

Player of the Year
Chet Jaworski, Rhode Island St . . . . Helms

Consensus All-America
(In alphabetical order)
First Team
Ernie Andres, Indiana; Jimmy Hull, Ohio St.; Chet Jaworski, Rhode Island St.; Irv Torgoff, LIU; Slim Wintermute, Oregon.

Second Team
Bob Anet, Oregon; Bob Calihan, Detroit; Bob Hassmiller, Fordham; Mike Novak, Loyola (IL); Bernie Opper, Kentucky.

1940

One era passed and another began during the 1939-40 season.

Dr. James Naismith died on Nov. 28, 1939, nearly 50 years after inventing the game and three years after seeing it gain worldwide acceptance as an Olympic sport at the 1936 Summer Games in Berlin.

Exactly three months later, on Feb. 28, 1940, college basketball appeared on television for the first time when experimental station W2XBS in New York televised a Pitt-Fordham and Georgetown-NYU doubleheader at Madison Square Garden.

Indiana finished second to Purdue in the Big Ten, but district officials sent the Hoosiers to the NCAA tournament because of their two regular season wins against the Boilermakers. Good choice. Indiana, led by All-America guard Marv Huffman, won the eight-team tournament, beating Big Six representative Kansas by 18 in the final. NCAA moved the Final Two to Kansas City in search of more exposure.

Colorado and Duquesne, both early round losers in the NCAAs, went to New York and ended up meeting in the NIT final. The Buffaloes won, 51-40.

Major Conference Champions

Conference	Regular Season	Tournament
Big 6	Kansas/Missouri/ Oklahoma (8-2)	—
Big 7	Colorado (11-1)	—
Big 10	Purdue (10-2)	—
Ivy	Dartmouth (11-1)	—
Mo. Valley	Oklahoma A&M (12-0)	—
New Eng.	Rhode Island St.(8-0)	—
PCC North	Oregon St.(12-4)	—
South	USC (10-2)*	—
SEC	Alabama (14-4)	Kentucky
Southern	Duke (13-2)	N.Carolina
SWC	Rice (10-2)	—

*Won playoff for league championship.
Note: Big 10 selected 2nd place Indiana (9-3) to go to NCAAs because the Hoosiers beat Purdue twice during regular season.

NCAA & NIT Tournament Teams
(In alphabetical order)

	Before Tourns	Head Coach	Final Record
Colorado	15-2	Frosty Cox	17-4
DePaul	21-4	Tom Haggerty	22-6
Duquesne	17-1	Chick Davies	20-3
Indiana	17-3	Branch McCracken	20-3
Kansas	17-5	Phog Allen	19-6
LIU	19-3	Clair Bee	19-4
Okla. A&M	25-2	Hank Iba	26-3
Rice	21-2	Buster Brannon	22-3
St.John's	15-3	Joe Lapchick	15-4
USC	19-2	Sam Barry	20-3
Springfield	16-2	Ed Hickox	16-3
Western Ky.	24-5	Ed Diddle	24-6

Note: Colorado won the NIT and Indiana won the NCAAs. Colorado and Duquesne played in both tourneys.

NCAA Tournament
East Regional
Semifinals—Duquesne 30, Western Ky.29; Indiana 48, Springfield- MA 24. **Third Place**—No game. **Final**—Indiana 39, Duquesne 30.

West Regional
Semifinals—Kansas 50, Rice 44; USC 38, Colorado 32. **Third Place**—Rice 60, Colorado 56 (OT). **Final**—Kansas 43, USC 42.

FINAL TWO
at Municipal Auditorium, Kansas City

Championship—Indiana 60, Kansas 42.
Most Outstanding Player: Marv Huffman, Indiana.
All-Tournament—Huffman, Jay McCreary and Bill Menke, Indiana; Howard Engleman and Bob Allen, Kansas.

NIT Tournament
All games at Madison Sq.Garden, New York

Quarterfinals—DePaul 45, LIU 38; Duquesne 38, St.John's 31.
Semifinals—Colorado 52, DePaul 37; Duquesne 34, Oklahoma A&M 30. **Third Place**—Oklahoma A&M 23, DePaul 22. **Championship**—Colorado 51, Duquesne 40.
Most Valuable Player—Bob Doll, Colorado.

Player of the Year
George Glamack, North Carolina ....Helms

Consensus All-America
(In alphabetical order)
First Team
Gus Broberg, Dartmouth; John Dick, Oregon; George Glamack, North Carolina; Bill Hapac, Illinois; Ralph Vaughn, USC.

Second Team
Jack Harvey, Colorado; Marv Huffman, Indiana; Jim McNatt, Oklahoma; Jesse Renick, Oklahoma A&M.

1941

Seton Hall entered the NIT on a 42-game winning streak, two behind the national record of 44 set by Texas from 1913-17 and one less than Long Island's 43-game skein of 1935-37. After beating Rhode Island in the quarterfinals, the Pirates ran up against LIU in the semifinals. It wasn't close. LIU won by 23, ending the Hall's streak on the same floor Stanford had humbled the Blackbirds four years before.

LIU went on to post its second tournament championship in four years, beating Ohio U. in the final, 56-42.

Wisconsin came out of nowhere to win the NCAA championship in basketball's 50th anniversary season. In 1940, the Badgers finished one rung from the bottom of the Big Ten standings with a 3-9 record. A year later they were conference champs and entered the postseason on a 12-game winning streak. Led by All-America center Gene Englund and sophomore guard Johnny Kotz, Wisconsin hosted and won the East Regional then beat Washington State, 39-34, in Kansas City for the title.

Jackie Robinson of UCLA, who would break major league baseball's color line in 1947, led the PCC in scoring (11.1) for the second straight season.

Major Conference Champions

Conference	Regular Season	Tournament
Big 6	Iowa St./Kansas (7-3)	—
Big 7	Wyoming (10-2)	—
Big 10	Wisconsin (11-1)	—
Ivy	Dartmouth (10-2)	—
Mo.Valley	Creighton (9-3)	—
New Eng.	Rhode Is.St./Conn.(7-1)	—
PCC North	Washington St.(13-3)*	—
South	Stanford (10-2)	—
SEC	Kentucky (8-1)	Tennessee
Southern	North Carolina (14-1)	Duke
SWC	Arkansas (12-0)	—

*Won playoff for league championship.

NCAA & NIT Tournament Teams
(In alphabetical order)

	Before Tourns	Head Coach	Final Record
Arkansas	19-2	Glen Rose	20-3
CCNY	15-4	Nat Holman	17-5
Creighton	17-6	Eddie Hickey	18-7
Dartmouth	18-4	Ozzie Cowles	19-5
Duquesne	17-2	Chick Davies	17-3
LIU	22-2	Clair Bee	25-2
N.Carolina	15-6	Bill Lange	15-8
Ohio Univ.	16-3	Bill Trautwein	18-4
Pittsburgh	12-5	Doc Carlson	13-6
R.Island St.	21-3	Frank Keaney	21-4
Seton Hall	19-0	Honey Russell	20-2
Virginia	16-4	Gus Tebell	16-5
Wash.St.	24-5	Jack Friel	26-6
Westminster	20-1	Grover Washabaugh	20-2
Wisconsin	17-3	Bud Foster	20-3
Wyoming	13-4	Everett Shelton	13-6

Note: Long Island Univ. won the NIT and Wisconsin won the NCAAs.

NCAA Tournament

East Regional

Semifinals—Pittsburgh 26, North Carolina 20; Wisconsin 51, Dartmouth 50. **Third Place**—Dartmouth 60, North Carolina 59. **Final**—Wisconsin 36, Pittsburgh 30.

West Regional

Semifinals—Arkansas 52, Wyoming 40; Washington St. 48, Creighton 39. **Third Place**—Creighton 45, Wyoming 44. **Final**—Washington St. 64, Arkansas 53.

FINAL TWO
at Municipal Auditorium, Kansas City

Championship—Wisconsin 39, Washington St. 34. **Most Outstanding Player:** John Kotz, Wisconsin. **All-Tournament**—Not selected.

NIT Tournament
All games at Madison Sq.Garden, New York

Quarterfinals—CCNY 64, Virginia 35; Ohio Univ. 55, Duquesne 40; Seton Hall 70, Rhode Island St. 54; LIU 48, Westminster-MO 36. **Semifinals**—LIU 49, Seton Hall 26; Ohio Univ. 45, CCNY 43. **Third Place**—CCNY 42, Seton Hall 27. **Championship**—LIU 56, Ohio Univ. 42. **Most Valuable Player**—Frank Baumholtz, Ohio Univ.

Player of the Year

George Glamack, North Carolina . . . . Helms

Consensus All-America
(In alphabetical order)

First Team

John Adams, Arkansas; Gus Broberg, Dartmouth; Howard Engleman, Kansas; Gene Englund, Wisconsin; George Glamack, North Carolina.

Second Team

Frank Baumholtz, Ohio Univ.; Bob Kinney, Rice; Paul Lindeman, Washington St.; Stan Modzelewski, Rhode Island St.; Oscar Schectman, LIU.

1942

The 1941-42 season had barely gotten under way when the Japanese attacked Pearl Harbor on Dec. 7 and pulled the United States into World War II. Over the next four years the game would take on a leaner, younger look as older players left for the service, travel was restricted and many schools, unable to field a squad, would be forced to cancel schedules.

Long Island, 24-3 during the regular season, was heavily favored to win its third NIT in five years, but the Blackbirds were ousted in the first round by West Virginia. The Mountaineers, 19-4 coming into the tourney, beat LIU in overtime, then knocked off Toledo and nipped Western Kentucky in the last 20 seconds to win the title. Rudy Baric scored 17 in the final for WVU and was named MVP.

There were Indians everywhere you looked in the NCAA championship game, as Stanford took on Dartmouth in Kansas City. Both teams had to win conference playoffs to qualify for the tournament. Stanford, led by Howie Dallmar's 15 points, won the NCAA title, 53-38.

Speaking of Stanford, Hank Luisetti's career scoring record of 1596 points was eclipsed during the season by Rhode Island State's Stan Modzelewski.

Major Conference Champions

Conference	Regular Season	Tournament
Big 6	Kansas/Okla.(8-2)	—
Big 7	Colorado (11-1)	—
Big 10	Illinois (13-2)	—
Ivy	Dartmouth (11-2)	—
Mo.Valley	Creighton (9-1)	—
PCC North	Oregon St.(11-5)	—
South	Stanford (11-1)*	—
SEC	Tennessee (7-1)	Kentucky
Southern	Duke (15-1)	Duke
SWC	Rice/Arkansas (10-2)	—

*Won playoff for league championship.

NCAA & NIT Tournament Teams
(In alphabetical order)

	Before Tourns	Head Coach	Final Record
CCNY	16-2	Nat Holman	16-3
Colorado	15-1	Frosty Cox	16-2
Creighton	17-4	Eddie Hickey	19-5
Dartmouth	20-3	Ozzie Cowles	22-4
Illinois	18-3	Doug Mills	18-5
Kansas	16-4	Phog Allen	17-5
Kentucky	18-5	Adolph Rupp	19-6
LIU	24-3	Clair Bee	24-4
Penn St.	17-2	John Lawther	18-3
R.Island St.	18-3	Frank Keaney	18-4
Rice	22-3	Buster Brannon	22-5
Stanford	24-4	Everett Dean	27-4
Toledo	22-3	Harold Anderson	23-5
West Texas	28-2	Al Baggett	28-3
Western Ky.	27-4	Ed Diddle	29-5
West Va.	16-4	Dyke Raese	19-4

Note: Stanford won the NCAAs and West Virginia won the NIT.

NCAA Tournament (8 teams)
East Regional

Semifinals—Dartmouth 44, Penn St.39; Kentucky 46, Illinois 44. **Third Place**—Penn St.41, Illinois 34. **Final**—Dartmouth 47, Kentucky 28.

West Regional

Semifinals—Colorado 46, Kansas 44; Stanford 53, Rice 47. **Third Place**—Kansas 55, Rice 53. **Final**—Stanford 46, Colorado 35.

FINAL TWO
at Municipal Auditorium, Kansas City

Championship—Stanford 53, Dartmouth 38.
Most Outstanding Player—Howie Dallmar, Stanford.
All-Tournament—Not selected.

NIT Tournament (8 teams)
All games at Madison Sq.Garden, New York

Quarterfinals—West Virginia 58, LIU 49; Creighton 59, West Texas St. 58; Western Ky.49, CCNY 46; Toledo 82, Rhode Island St. 71.
Semifinals—West Virginia 51, Toledo 39; Western Ky.49, Creighton 36. **Third Place**—Creighton 48, Toledo 46. **Championship**—West Virginia 47, Western Ky.45.
Most Valuable Player: Rudy Baric, West Virginia.

Player of the Year

Stan Modzelewski, Rhode Island St . . . . Helms

Consensus All-America
(In alphabetical order)
First Team

Price Brookfield, West Texas St.; Bob Davies, Seton Hall; Bob Kinney, Rice; John Kotz, Wisconsin; Andy Phillip, Illinois.

Second Team

Don Burness, Stanford; Wilfred Doerner, Evansville; Bob Doll, Colorado; John Mandic, Oregon St.; Stan Modzelewski, Rhode Island St.; George Munroe, Dartmouth.

1943

College basketball's first true national championship game was played at Madison Square Garden when a special Red Cross benefit game was arranged between NIT champion St. John's and NCAA champion Wyoming.

Travel restrictions weren't a problem because the NCAA had moved its Final Two to the Garden. The NIT-NCAA showdown gave New York basketball fans a chance to get another look at Wyoming's All-America guard Kenny Sailors, whose dribbling wizardry and innovative jump shot made him the sensation of the season.

Sailors had scored 16 to lead the Cowboys to a come-from-behind win over Georgetown in the NCAA final. St. John's, meanwhile, had beaten Toledo by 21 to win the NIT crown. Wyoming won the Red Cross game, 52-47.

The best team in the country, however, was probably Big Ten champion Illinois (17-1), which declined invites to both tourneys. The Illini were paced by the Whiz Kids—20 year-old All-America forward Andy Phillip and teenagers Ken Menke, Gene Vance, Jack Smiley and Art Mathisen. They so dominated the Big Ten, that only Northwestern's Otto Graham could crack the all-conference team.

Major Conference Champions

Conference	Regular Season	Tournament
Big 6	Kansas (10-0)	—
Big 7 East	BYU (7-1)	—
West	Wyoming (4-0)*	—
Big 10	Illinois (12-0)	—
Ivy	Dartmouth (11-1)	—
Mo.Valley	Creighton (10-0)	—
New Eng.	Rhode Island St.(7-1)	—
PCC North	Washington (12-4)*	—
South	Southern Cal (7-1)	—
SEC	Kentucky (8-1)	Tennessee
Southern	Duke (12-1)	Geo.Wash.
SWC	Texas/Rice (9-3)	—

*Won playoff for league championship.
Note: Because of travel restrictions and a reduction in active teams to five, the Big 7 split into two divisions in 1942–43.

NCAA & NIT Tournament Teams
(In alphabetical order)

	Before Tourns	Head Coach	Final Record
Creighton	18-1	Eddie Hickey	19-2
Dartmouth	19-2	Ozzie Cowles	20-3
DePaul	18-4	Ray Meyer	19-5
Fordham	15-4	Ed Kelleher	16-6
Georgetown	20-4	Elmer Ripley	22-5
Manhattan	18-2	Joe Daher	18-3
NYU	16-4	Howard Cann	16-6
Oklahoma	17-8	Bruce Drake	18-9
Rice	17-5	Joe Davis	17-6
St. John's	18-3	Joe Lapchick	21-3
Texas	18-6	Bully Gilstrap	19-7
Toledo	20-3	Berle Friddle	22-4
Washington	24-5	Hec Edmundson	24-7
Wash.& Jeff.	16-4	Adam Sanders	18-5
Western Ky.	24-2	Ed Diddle	24-3
Wyoming	28-2	Everett Shelton	31-2

Note: St. John's won NIT and Wyoming won NCAAs.

NCAA Tournament (8 teams)
East Regional
Semifinals—Georgetown 55, NYU 36; DePaul 46, Dartmouth 35. **Third Place**—Dartmouth 51, NYU 49. **Final**—Georgetown 53, DePaul 49.

West Regional
Semifinals—Wyoming 53, Oklahoma 50; Texas 59, Washington 55. **Third Place**—Oklahoma 48, Washington 43. **Final**—Wyoming 58, Texas 54.

FINAL TWO
at Madison Square Garden, New York

Championship—Wyoming 46, Georgetown 34. **Most Outstanding Player:** Kenny Sailors, Wyoming. **All-Tournament**—Not selected.

NIT Tournament (8 teams)
All games at Madison Sq.Garden, New York

Quarterfinals—St.John's 51, Rice 49; Fordham 60, Western Ky.58; Toledo 54, Manhattan 47; Wash.& Jefferson 43, Creighton 42. **Semifinals**—Toledo 46, Wash.& Jefferson 39; St.John's 69, Fordham 43. **Third Place**—Wash.& Jefferson 39, Fordham 34. **Championship**—St.John's 48, Toledo 27.

Most Valuable Player—Harry Boykoff, St,John's.

Red Cross World War II Benefit Game
(NCAA Champion vs NIT Champion)
at Madison Square Garden, New York
Wyoming 52, St.John's 47

Player of the Year
George Senesky, St.Joseph's,PA . . . . Helms

Consensus All-America
(In alphabetical order)

First Team
Ed Beisser, Creighton; Charley Black, Kansas; Harry Boykoff, St.John's; Bill Closs, Rice; Andy Phillip, Illinois; Kenny Sailors, Wyoming; George Senesky, St.Joseph's (PA).

Second Team
Gale Bishop, Washington St.; Otto Graham, Northwestern; John Kotz, Wisconsin; Bob Rensberger, Notre Dame; Gene Rock, USC; Gerry Tucker, Oklahoma.

1944

This was the year of Utah's Blitz Kids—Arnie Ferrin, Wat Misaka, Fred Sheffield, Herb Wilkinson, Dick Smuin and Bob Lewis. Average age: 18½.

While the Whiz Kids of Illinois had stayed home in 1943, the Blitz Kids of Utah didn't even have a home in '44. The Skyline Conference had suspended play and the Army had taken over the Utes' fieldhouse in Salt Lake City, so coach Vadal Peterson was obliged to play mostly service teams in church gyms.

Utah went 18-3 and was invited to both NIT and NCAA tournaments. Peterson took the NIT offer because it included travel expenses, but the Utes were knocked out in the first round by Kentucky. Meanwhile, when Arkansas was forced to pull out of the NCAAs after a car accident injured several starters, the West Regional berth was offered to Utah. This time the Utes accepted and ended up back in New York for the Final Two. There, the Blitz Kids beat a transfer-laden Dartmouth team (including St.John's star Dick McGuire) 42-40, on a Wilkinson buzzer-beater in overtime.

The Utes met NIT champion St.John's in the second Red Cross Benefit game a few nights later before 18,125 at the Garden. St.John's had beaten George Mikan and DePaul in the NIT final, but Ferrin (17 points) and the rest of the Kids had finally found a home and won easily, 43-36.

Major Conference Champions

Conference	Regular Season	Tournament
Big 6	Iowa St./Okla.(9-1)	—
Big 7	No competition	
Big 10	Ohio St.(10-2)	—
Ivy	Dartmouth (8-0)	—
Mo.Valley	Oklahoma A&M	
New Eng.	No competition	
PCC North	Washington (15-1)*	—
South	California (4-0)*	
SEC	Tulane (4-0)	Kentucky
Southern	North Carolina (9-1)	Duke
SWC	Arkansas/Rice (11-1)	—

*Co-champions, no PCC playoff held (travel restrictions).
Note: Oklahoma A&M awarded Missouri Valley championship after going 27-6 overall during regular season.

NCAA/NIT Tournament Teams
(In alphabetical order)

	Before Tourns	Head Coach	Final Record
Bowling Green	22-3	Harold Anderson	22-4
Canisius	15-5	Allie Seelbach	15-6
Catholic	17-5	John Long	17-7
Dartmouth	17-1	Earl Brown	19-2
DePaul	20-3	Ray Meyer	22-4
Iowa St.	13-3	Lou Menze	14-4
Kentucky	17-1	Adolph Rupp	19-2
Missouri	9-8	George Edwards	10-9
Muhlenberg	19-5	Doggie Julian	19-6
Ohio St.	13-6	Harold Olsen	14-7
Oklahoma A&M	26-4	Hank Iba	27-6
Pepperdine	21-11	Wade Ruby	21-13
St.John's	15-5	Joe Lapchick	18-5
Temple	13-8	Josh Cody	14-9
Utah	18-3	Vadal Peterson	21-4

Note: St.John's won the NIT and Utah won the NCAAs. Utah also played in both tourneys.

NCAA Tournament (8 teams)

East Regional

Semifinals—Dartmouth 63, Catholic 38; Ohio St.57, Temple 47. **Third Place**—Temple 55, Catholic 35. **Final**—Dartmouth 60, Ohio St.53.

West Regional

Semifinals—Iowa St.44, Pepperdine 39; Utah 45, Missouri 35. **Third Place**—Missouri 61, Pepperdine 46. **Final**—Utah 40, Iowa St.31.

FINAL TWO
at Madison Square Garden, New York

Championship—Utah 42, Dartmouth 40 (OT). **Most Outstanding Player:** Arnie Ferrin, Utah. **All-Tournament**—Not selected.

NIT Tournament (8 teams)
All games at Madison Sq.Garden, New York

Quarterfinals—Oklahoma A&M 43, Canisius 29; Kentucky 46, Utah 38; St.John's 44, Bowling Green 40; DePaul 68, Muhlenberg 45. **Semifinals**—St.John's 48, Kentucky 45; DePaul 41, Oklahoma A&M 38. **Third Place**—Kentucky 45, Oklahoma A&M 29. **Championship**—St.John's 47, DePaul 39. **Most Valuable Player**—Bill Kotsores, St.John's.

Red Cross World War II Benefit Game
(NCAA Champion vs NIT Champion)
at Madison Square Garden, New York

Utah 43, St.John's 36

Player of the Year
George Mikan, DePaul . . . . .Helms

Consensus All-America
(In alphabetical order)

First Team

Bob Brannum, Kentucky; Audley Brindley, Dartmouth; Otto Graham, Northwestern; Leo Klier, Notre Dame; Bob Kurland, Oklahoma A&M; George Mikan, DePaul; Alva Paine, Oklahoma.

Second Team

Bob Dille, Valparaiso; Arnie Ferrin, Utah; Don Grate, Ohio St.; Dale Hall, Army; Bill Henry, Rice; Dick Triptow, DePaul.

1945

The biggest stars of the mid-40s were also the biggest players: 6-10 George Mikan of DePaul and 7-0 Bob Kurland of Oklahoma A&M.

Many officials thought All-Americas Mikan and Kurland were too big and introduced the goaltending rule to nullify their shot-swatting prowess around the hoop. Forced to develop other skills, Mikan and Kurland actually got better and led their teams to NIT and NCAA titles.

Mikan, the country's leading scorer, threw down 120 points in three games (53 against Rhode Island alone) as DePaul rolled to the NIT championship, while Kurland led the more deliberate A&M attack to victory in the NCAA.

For the third and final year the NCAA and NIT champs met in the Red Cross Benefit Game in New York. Mikan and Kurland filled the Garden to the rafters, but the ballyhooed battle of big men never materialized. Mikan fouled out in the first half with only nine points, Kurland scored 14 and the Aggies won 52-44.

Big Ten champion Iowa (17-1) and Notre Dame (15-5), two teams that could have made their presence felt in the postseason, both declined tournament invitations.

Major Conference Champions

Conference	Regular Season	Tournament
Big 6	Iowa St.(8-2)	—
Big 7	Utah (8-0)	—
Big 10	Iowa (11-1)	—
Ivy	Pennsylvania (5-1)	—
Mo.Valley	Oklahoma A&M	—
New Eng.	No competition	
PCC North	Oregon (13-6)*	—
South	UCLA (3-1)*	—
SEC	Tennessee (8-2)	Kentucky
Southern	South Carolina (9-0)	N.Carolina
SWC	Rice (12-0)	—

*Co-champions, no PCC playoff held (travel restrictions).
Note: Oklahoma A&M awarded Missouri Valley championship after going 27-4 overall during regular season.

NCAA/NIT Tournament Teams
(In alphabetical order)

	Before Tourns	Head Coach	Final Record
Arkansas	16-8	Eugene Lambert	17-9
Bowling Green	22-3	Harold Anderson	24-4
DePaul	18-3	Ray Meyer	21-3
Kentucky	21-3	Adolph Rupp	22-4
Muhlenberg	24-3	Doggie Julian	24-4
NYU	12-6	Howard Cann	14-7
Ohio St.	14-4	Harold Olsen	15-5
Okla. A&M	24-4	Hank Iba	27-4
Oregon	29-12	Howard Hobson	30-13
RPI	13-0	Ed Donald	13-1
R.Island St.	19-3	Frank Keaney	20-5
St.John's	19-2	Joe Lapchick	21-3
Tennessee	18-4	John Mauer	18-5
Tufts	10-6	Richard Cochran	10-8
Utah	17-2	Vadal Peterson	17-4
West Va.	12-5	John Brickels	12-6

Note: DePaul won the NIT and Oklahoma A&M won the NCAAs.

NCAA Tournament (8 teams)

East Regional

Semifinals—NYU 59, Tufts 44; Ohio St.45, Kentucky 37. **Third Place**—Kentucky 66, Tufts 56. **Final**—NYU 70, Ohio St.65 (OT).

West Regional

Semifinals—Arkansas 79, Oregon 76; Oklahoma A&M 62, Utah 37. **Third Place**—Oregon 69, Utah 66. **Final**—Oklahoma A&M 68, Arkansas 41.

FINAL TWO
at Madison Sq.Garden, New York

Championship—Oklahoma A&M 49, NYU 45. **Most Outstanding Player:** Bob Kurland, Oklahoma A&M. **All-Tournament**—Not selected.

NIT Tournament (8 teams)
All games at Madison Sq.Garden, New York

Quarterfinals—Rhode Island St.51, Tennessee 44; Bowling Green 60, RPI 45; DePaul 76, West Virginia 52; St.John's 34, Muhlenberg 33.
Semifinals—DePaul 97, Rhode Island St.53; Bowling Green 57, St.John's 44. **Third Place**—St.John's 64, Rhode Island St. 57. **Championship**—DePaul 71, Bowling Green 54.
Most Valuable Player—George Mikan, DePaul.

Red Cross World War II Benefit Game
(NCAA Champion vs NIT Champion)
at Madison Square Garden, New York

Oklahoma A&M 52, DePaul 44

Player of the Year
George Mikan, DePaul . . . . .Helms

Consensus All-America
(In alphabetical order)

First Team

Howie Dallmar, Penn; Arnie Ferrin, Utah; Wyndol Gray, Bowling Green; Bob Kurland, Oklahoma A&M; Walton Kirk, Illinois; Billy Hassett, Notre Dame; Bill Henry, Rice; George Mikan, DePaul.

Second Team

Don Grate, Ohio St.; Dale Hall, Army; Vince Hanson, Washington St.; Richard Ives, Iowa; Max Morris, Northwestern; Herb Wilkinson, Iowa.

1946

With the war over, soldier-athletes came back to campuses around the country to find coach Hank Iba's Oklahoma A&M team at the top of the heap in college basketball and determined to stay there.

Big Bob Kurland, who had led A&M to an NCAA championship in '45, was back for his senior year and the Aggies, once known for their deliberate style of play, were now scoring points with a very unIba-like abandon. Paced by Kurland, who led the country in scoring (58 points in his final home game against St.Louis), A&M went 12-0 in the Missouri Valley, 28-2 in the regular season and 3-0 in the NCAAs. They beat North Carolina in the final, 43-40, as Kurland, winning his second straight MVP award, outscored the Tar Heels' Bones McKinney, 23-5.

Southeastern Conference champion Kentucky won the NIT when freshman guard Ralph Beard sank a free throw in the final seconds of the championship game to beat Rhode Island, 46-45.

Like Kurland, George Mikan (a 5th year eligible) returned in '46. Mikan was an All-America again, but the 19-5 Demons didn't play in either tourney.

Major Conference Champions

Conference	Regular Season	Tournament
Big 6	Kansas (10-0)	—
Big 7	Wyoming (10-2)	—
Big 10	Ohio St.(10-2)	—
Ivy	Dartmouth (7-1)	—
Mo.Valley	Oklahoma A&M (12-0)	—
PCC North	Idaho (11-5)	
South	California (11-1)*	—
SEC	LSU (8-0)/Ky.(6-0)	Kentucky
Southern	North Carolina (13-1)	Duke
SWC	Baylor (11-1)	—

*Won playoff for league championship.

NCAA & NIT Tournament Teams
(In alphabetical order)

	Before Tourns	Head Coach	Final Record
Arizona	25-4	Fred Enke	25-5
Baylor	24-3	Bill Henderson	24-5
Bowling Green	27-4	Harold Anderson	27-5
California	29-4	Nibs Price	30-6
Colorado	11-5	Frosty Cox	12-6
Harvard	19-1	Floyd Stahl	19-3
Kentucky	25-2	Adolph Rupp	28-2
Muhlenberg	22-3	Lee Coker	23-5
NYU	18-2	Howard Cann	19-3
N.Carolina	27-4	Ben Carnevale	29-5
Ohio St.	14-4	Harold Olsen	16-5
Okla. A&M	28-2	Hank Iba	31-2
R.Island St.	20-2	Frank Keaney	22-3
St.John's	17-5	Joe Lapchick	17-6
Syracuse	23-3	Lew Andreas	23-4
West Va.	22-2	Lee Patton	24-3

Note: Kentucky won the NIT and Oklahoma A&M won the NCAAs.

NCAA Tournament (8 teams)
East Regional
Semifinals—Ohio St.46, Harvard 38; North Carolina 57, NYU 49. **Third Place**—NYU 67, Harvard 61. **Final**—North Carolina 60, Ohio St.57 (OT).

West Regional
Semifinals—Oklahoma A&M 44, Baylor 29; California 50, Colorado 44. **Third Place**—Colorado 59, Baylor 44. **Final**—Oklahoma A&M 68, California 52-35.

FINAL FOUR
at Madison Square Garden, New York
Third Place—Ohio St.63, California 45. **Championship**—Oklahoma A&M 43, North Carolina 40. **Most Outstanding Player:** Bob Kurland, Oklahoma A&M. **All-Tournament**—Not selected.

NIT Tournament (8 teams)
All games at Madison Sq.Garden, New York
Quarterfinals—Rhode Island St.82, Bowling Green 79 (OT); West Virginia 70, St.John's 58; Kentucky 77, Arizona 53; Muhlenberg 47, Syracuse 41. **Semifinals**—Rhode Island St.59, Muhlenberg 49; Kentucky 59, West Virginia 51. **Third Place**—West Virginia 65, Muhlenberg 40. **Championship**—Kentucky 46, Rhode Island St.45.
Most Valuable Player—Ernie Calverley, Rhode Island St.

Player of the Year
Bob Kurland, Oklahoma A&M . . . . Helms

Consensus All-America
(In alphabetical order)
First Team
Bob Kurland, Oklahoma A&M; Leo Klier, Notre Dame; George Mikan, DePaul; Max Morris, Northwestern; Sid Tanenbaum, NYU.

Second Team
Charley Black, Kansas; John Dillon, North Carolina; Billy Hassett, Notre Dame; Tony Lavelli, Yale; Jack Parkinson, Kentucky; Kenny Sailors, Wyoming.

1947

Arnie Ferrin and little Wat Misaka, two of the Blitz Kids of '44, mustered out of the service and back to Utah for the 1946-47 season to lead the Utes to another championship—this time the NIT. In the process, they became the first two collegians ever to play for NCAA and NIT-winning teams.

In wasn't easy. Employing the deliberate playing style that yielded a 16-5 regular season record, Utah came to New York and squeezed out wins over Duquesne (by 1), West Virginia (by 2) and defending NIT champ Kentucky (by 4) in the title game. Ferrin and MVP Vern Gardner each scored 15 against UK, but it was Misaka's handcuffing of the Wildcats' Ralph Beard (1 point) that did the trick. Kentucky had come into the final with 34 wins and an average winning score of 73-37.

In the NCAAs, Holy Cross borrowed a page from the 1944 Utah playbook and won the championship as orphans. With no place large enough to play in Worcester, Mass., coach Doggie Julian's Crusaders went 24-3 on the road and came into the tournament on a 20-game win streak. At the Final Two in New York, Holy Cross, led by 18 year-old sophomore forward George Kaftan, beat Gerry Tucker and Oklahoma, 58-47. That NCAA title is still the only one ever won by a New England school.

Major Conference Champions

Conference	Regular Season	Tournament
Big 6	Oklahoma (8-2)	—
Big 7	Wyoming (11-1)	—
Big 10	Wisconsin (9-3)	—
Ivy	Columbia (11-1)	—
Mo.Valley	St.Louis (11-1)	—
PCC North	Oregon St.(13-3)*	—
South	UCLA (9-3)	—
SEC	Kentucky (11-0)	Kentucky
Southern	N.C.State (11-2)	N.C.State
SWC	Texas (12-0)	—

*Won playoff for league championship.

NCAA & NIT Tournament Teams
(In alphabetical order)

	Before Tourns	Head Coach	Final Record
Bradley	25-6	Al Robertson	25-7
CCNY	15-4	Nat Holman	16-6
Duquesne	20-1	Chick Davies	20-2
Holy Cross	24-3	Doggie Julian	27-3
Kentucky	32-2	Adolph Rupp	34-3
LIU	17-3	Clair Bee	17-4
Navy	16-1	Ben Carnevale	16-3
N.C.State	24-4	Everett Case	26-5
Oklahoma	22-6	Bruce Drake	24-7
Oregon St.	27-4	Slats Gill	28-5
St.John's	16-6	Joe Lapchick	16-7
Texas	24-1	Jack Gray	26-2
Utah	16-5	Vadal Peterson	19-5
West Va.	18-1	Lee Patton	19-3
Wisconsin	15-5	Bud Foster	16-6
Wyoming	22-4	Everett Shelton	22-6

Note: Holy Cross won the NCAAs and Utah won the NIT.

NCAA Tournament (8 teams)

East Regional

Semifinals—Holy Cross 55, Navy 47; CCNY 70, Wisconsin 56. **Third Place**—Wisconsin 50, Navy 49. **Final**—Holy Cross 60, CCNY 45.

West Regional

Semifinals—Texas 42, Wyoming 40; Oklahoma 56, Oregon St.54. Third Place—Oregon St.63, Wyoming 46. **Final**—Oklahoma 55, Texas 54.

FINAL FOUR
at Madison Square Garden, New York

Third Place—Texas 54, CCNY 50. **Championship**—Holy Cross 58, Oklahoma 47. **Most Outstanding Player:** George Kaftan, Holy Cross. **All-Tournament**—Not selected.

NIT Tournament (8 teams)
All games at Madison Sq.Garden, New York

Quarterfinals—Utah 45, Duquesne 44; Kentucky 66, LIU 62; N.C.State 61, St.John's 55; West Virginia 69, Bradley 60.

Semifinals—Utah 64, West Virginia 62; Kentucky 60, N.C.State 42. **Third Place**—N.C.State 64, West Virginia 52. **Championship**—Utah 49, Kentucky 45. **Most Valuable Player**—Vern Gardner, Utah.

Player of the Year

Gerry Tucker, Oklahoma . . . . .Helms

Consensus All-America
(In alphabetical order)

First Team

Ralph Beard, Kentucky; Alex Groza, Kentucky; Ralph Hamilton, Indiana; Sid Tanenbaum, NYU; Gerry Tucker, Oklahoma.

Second Team

Don Barksdale, UCLA; Arnie Ferrin, Utah; Vern Gardner, Utah; John Hargis, Texas; George Kaftan, Holy Cross; Ed Koffenberger, Duke; Andy Phillip, Illinois.

1948

Upset in the NIT final the year before, Kentucky went back to New York a year later and brought home the NCAA championship.

This time coach Adolph Rupp had a new starting line-up, the Fabulous Five—center Alex Groza, forwards Wah Wah Jones and Cliff Barker, and guards Ralph Beard and Kenny Rollins.

After winning a fifth straight SEC title, Kentucky came into the NCAAs with a record of 33-3 and met defending NCAA titlist Holy Cross in the East Regional final. The Crusaders were 26-2 and riding an 18-game winning streak. They also had George Kaftan back and a sophomore ballhandling whiz named Bob Cousy in the backcourt.

Rupp assigned Rollins to guard Cousy in the game's key match-up, and with Rollins holding Cousy to just one point, Kentucky won, 60-52. Three days later, UK beat West Regional winner Baylor by 16 for the title.

Dolph Schayes and NYU went into the NIT final on a 19-game win streak, but lost to Easy Ed Macauley and St.Louis, 65-52.

Major Conference Champions

Conference	Regular Season	Tournament
Big 7	Kansas St.(9-3)	—
Big 10	Michigan (10-2)	—
Ivy	Columbia (11-1)	—
Mo. Valley	Oklahoma A&M (10-0)	—
PCC North	Washington (11-6)*	—
South	California (11-1)	—
Skyline 6	BYU (8-2)	—
SEC	Kentucky (9-0)	Kentucky
Southern	N.C.State (12-0)	N.C.State
SWC	Baylor (11-0)	—

*Won playoff for league championship.
Note: Colorado left the Big 7 (Mountain States A.C.) for the Big 6 in 1947, making the Big 6 the new Big 7 and the old Big 7 the new Skyline 6.

NCAA & NIT Tournament Teams
(In alphabetical order)

	Before Tourns	Head Coach	Final Record
Baylor	22-7	Bill Henderson	24-8
Bowling Green	27-5	Harold Anderson	27-6
Columbia	21-1	Gordon Ridings	21-3
DePaul	21-6	Ray Meyer	22-8
Holy Cross	25-2	Doggie Julian	27-3
Kansas St.	21-4	Jack Gardner	22-6
Kentucky	33-3	Adolph Rupp	36-3
La Salle	20-3	Charles McGlone	20-4
Michigan	14-5	Ozzie Cowles	15-6
NYU	20-3	Howard Cann	22-4
N.C.State	29-2	Everett Case	29-3
St.Louis	21-3	Eddie Hickey	24-3
Texas	20-4	Jack Gray	20-5
Washington	22-10	Art McLarney	23-11
Western Ky.	26-1	Ed Diddle	28-2
Wyoming	18-7	Everett Shelton	18-9

Note: Kentucky won the NCAAs and St.Louis won the NIT.

NCAA Tournament (8 teams)
East Regional
Semifinals—Holy Cross 63, Michigan 45; Kentucky 76, Columbia 53. **Third Place**—Michigan 66, Columbia 49. **Final**—Kentucky 60, Holy Cross 52.

West Regional
Semifinals—Kansas St.58, Wyoming 48; Baylor 64, Washington 62. **Third Place**—Washington 57, Wyoming 47. **Final**—Baylor 60, Kansas St.52.

FINAL FOUR
at Madison Square Garden, New York

Third Place—Holy Cross 60, Kansas St.54. **Championship**—Kentucky 58, Baylor 42.
Most Outstanding Player: Alex Groza, Kentucky.
All-Tournament—Not selected.

NIT Tournament (8 teams)
at Madison Square Garden, New York

Quarterfinals—Western Ky. 68, La Salle 61; St.Louis 69, Bowling Green 53; NYU 45, Texas 43; DePaul 75, N.C.State 64.
Semifinals—NYU 72, DePaul 59; St.Louis 60, Western Ky. 53. **Third Place**—Western Ky. 61, DePaul 59.
Championship—St.Louis 65, NYU 52.
Most Valuable Player—Ed Macauley, St.Louis.

Player of the Year
Ed Macauley, St.Louis .... Helms

Consensus All-America
(In alphabetical order)
First Team
Ralph Beard, Kentucky; Ed Macauley, St.Louis; Jim McIntyre, Minnesota; Kevin O'Shea, Notre Dame; Murray Wier, Iowa;

Second Team
Dick Dickey, N.C.State; Arnie Ferrin, Utah; Alex Groza, Kentucky; Harold Haskins, Hamline; George Kaftan, Holy Cross; Duane Klueh, Indiana St.; Tony Lavelli, Yale; Jack Nichols, Washington; Andy Wolfe, California.

1949

With four-fifths of the Fabulous Five back (Alex Groza, Wah Wah Jones, Cliff Barker, and Ralph Beard), a regular season record of 29-1, and the No.1 ranking in the new AP Top 10, Kentucky coach Adolph Rupp set out to do what no other team had ever done: win both the NIT and the NCAA tournaments in the same year.

Rupp's plan hit an immediate snag, however, when the top-seeded Wildcats came up against Loyola of Chicago in the quarterfinals of the NIT. No stiff at 23-5, Loyola upset UK, 61-56, as Rambler center Jack Kerris played the game of his life and outscored Groza, 23-12. This was the year of the Manhattan Massacre at the NIT, when all four seeded teams (Kentucky, St.Louis, Utah and Western Kentucky) and all four New York City teams (CCNY, Manhattan, NYU and St.John's) lost their opening games. Loyola reached the final but lost to San Francisco, 47-46.

A chastened Kentucky entered the NCAAs determined to become only the second team in the 11-year history of the tourney to win back-to-back championships. The first? Oklahoma A&M. And it was the No.2-ranked Aggies who awaited the Wildcats at the final in Seattle. Kentucky won by 10 as Groza redeemed himself with 25 points and a second straight MVP award.

Rule change of the year: coaches were now allowed to talk to their players during timeouts.

Final AP Top 10
Writers' poll taken before tournament.

		Before Tourns	Head Coach	Final Record
1	Kentucky	29-1	Adolph Rupp	32-2
2	Okla.A&M	21-4	Hank Iba	23-5
3	St.Louis	22-3	Eddie Hickey	22-4
4	Illinois	19-3	Harry Combes	21-4
5	Western Ky.	25-3	Ed Diddle	25-4
6	Minnesota	18-3	Ozzie Cowles	same
7	Bradley	25-6	Forddy Anderson	27-8
8	San Fran.	21-5	Pete Newell	25-5
9	Tulane	24-4	Cliff Wells	same
10	Bowl.Green	21-6	Harold Anderson	24-7

Note: Kentucky won the NCAAs and San Francisco won the NIT. Kentucky also played in both tourneys.

Other NCAA & NIT Tournament Teams
(In alphabetical order)

	Before Tourns	Head Coach	Final Record
Arkansas	14-10	Eugene Lambert	15-11
CCNY	17-7	Nat Holman	17-8
Loyola-IL	22-5	Tom Haggerty	25-6
Manhattan	18-7	Ken Norton	18-8
NYU	12-7	Howard Cann	12-8
Oregon St.	23-10	Slats Gill	24-12
St.John's	16-8	Frank McGuire	16-9
Utah	24-7	Vadal Peterson	24-8
Villanova	22-3	Al Severance	23-4
Wyoming	25-8	Everett Shelton	25-10
Yale	22-6	Howard Hobson	22-8

Major Conference Champions

Conference	Regular Season	Tournament
Big 7	Nebraska/Okla.(9-3)	—
Big 10	Illinois (10-2)	—
Ivy	Yale (9-3)	—
Mo.Valley	Oklahoma A&M (9-1)	—
PCC North	Oregon St.(12-4)*	—
South	UCLA (11-1)	—
Skyline 6	Wyoming (15-5)	—
SEC	Kentucky (13-0)	Kentucky
Southern	N.C.State (14-1)	N.C.State
SWC	Ark./Baylor/Rice (9-3)	—

*Won playoff for league championship.

NCAA Tournament (8 teams)

East Regional
Semifinals—Kentucky 85, Villanova 72; Illinois 71, Yale 67. **Third Place**—Villanova 78, Yale 67. **Final**—Kentucky 76, Illinois 47.

West Regional
Semifinals—Oklahoma A&M 40, Wyoming 39; Oregon St.56, Arkansas 38. **Third Place**—Arkansas 61, Wyoming 48. **Final**—Oklahoma A&M 55, Oregon St.30.

FINAL FOUR
at Edmundson Pavilion, Seattle

Third Place—Illinois 57, Oregon St.53. **Championship**—Kentucky 46, Oklahoma A&M 36.
Most Outstanding Player: Alex Groza, Kentucky.
All-Tournament—Not selected.

NIT Tournament (12 teams)
All games at Madison Sq.Garden, New York

First Round—Bowling Green 77, St.John's 64; San Francisco 68, Manhattan 43; Bradley 89, NYU 67; Loyola-IL 62, CCNY 47. **Quarterfinals**—Loyola-IL 61, Kentucky 56; Bradley 95, Western Ky.86; San Francisco 64, Utah 63; Bowling Green 80, St.Louis 74. **Semifinals**—San Francisco 49, Bowling Green 39; Loyola-IL 55, Bradley 50. **Third Place**—Bowling Green 82, Bradley 77. **Championship**—San Francisco 48, Loyola-IL 47.
Most Valuable Player—Don Lofgan, San Francisco.

Player of the Year
Tony Lavelli, Yale . . . . Helms

Consensus All-America
(In alphabetical order)

First Team
Ralph Beard, Kentucky; Vince Boryla, Denver; Alex Groza, Kentucky; Tony Lavelli, Yale; Ed Macauley, St.Louis.

Second Team
Bill Erickson, Illinois; Vern Gardner, Utah; Wallace Jones, Kentucky; Jim McIntyre, Minnesota; Ernie Vandeweghe, Colgate.

1950

The NIT-NCAA double that Kentucky coach Adolph Rupp had envisioned for his team in 1949 became a reality a year later, but for a very unlikely squad from City College of New York.

CCNY, made up of mostly sophomores and coached by Original Celtic Nat Holman, posted a 17-5 record during the regular season, but failed to attract any support in the final AP Top 20. The Beavers didn't land a single player on anybody's All-America team, either.

Yet, once the tournaments got underway, CCNY—led by Irwin Dambrot and Ed Warner—went on a 7-0 tear and beat all comers: defending NIT champion San Francisco (by 19 points), defending NCAA champ Kentucky (by 39, the worst defeat ever for a Rupp-coached team), No.6 Duquesne (by 10), No.5 North Carolina State (by 5), No.2 Ohio State (by 1), and top-ranked Bradley twice (by 8 and by 3).

Kentucky, the SEC champ for the seventh year in a row, lost to CCNY in the NIT. The Wildcats were also denied a shot at defending their NCAA title when N.C.State was awarded the district berth.

Meanwhile, CCNY's two wins over Bradley came in the two championship games—69-61 in the NIT and 71-68 in the NCAA. Both titles were won in the friendly confines of Madison Square Garden, but the "Allaga-roo-garoo-gara" cheers that saluted the hometown team's unique double were short-lived. There were dark clouds on the horizon.

Final AP Top 20
Writers' poll taken before major tournaments.

	Before Tours	Head Coach	Final Record
1 Bradley	28-3	Forddy Anderson	32-5
2 Ohio St.	21-3	Tippy Dye	22-4
3 Kentucky	25-4	Adolph Rupp	25-5
4 Holy Cross	27-2	Buster Sheary	27-4
5 N.C.State	25-5	Everett Case	27-6
6 Duquesne	22-5	Dudey Moore	23-6
7 UCLA	24-5	John Wooden	24-7
8 Western Ky.	24-5	Ed Diddle	25-6
9 St.John's	23-4	Frank McGuire	24-5
10 La Salle	20-3	Ken Loeffler	21-4
11 Villanova	25-4	Al Severance	same
12 San Fran.	19-6	Pete Newell	19-7
13 LIU	20-4	Clair Bee	20-5
14 Kansas St.	17-7	Jack Gardner	same
15 Arizona	26-4	Fred Enke	26-5
16 Wisconsin	17-5	Bud Foster	same
17 San Jose St.	21-7	Walter McPherson	same
18 Wash.St.	19-13	Jack Friel	same
19 Kansas	14-11	Phog Allen	same
20 Indiana	17-5	Branch McCracken	same

Note: Unranked CCNY (17-5, Nat Holman, 24-5) won both the NCAAs and NIT. Bradley was runner-up in both finals.

Major Conference Champions

Conference	Regular Season	Tournament
Big 7	Kan./Kan.St./Neb.(8-4)	—
Big 10	Ohio St.(11-1)	—
Ivy	Princeton (11-1)	—
Mo.Valley	Bradley (11-1)	—
PCC North:	Washington St.(11-5)	—
South:	UCLA (10-2)*	—
SEC	Kentucky (11-2)	Kentucky
Southern	N.C.State (12-2)	N.C.State
SWC	Baylor/Ark.(8-4)	—

*Won playoff for league championship.

NCAA Tournament (8 teams)

Eastern Regional

First Round—CCNY 56, Ohio St.55; N.C.State 87, Holy Cross 74. **Third Place**—Ohio St.72, Holy Cross 52. **Final**—CCNY 78, N.C.State 73.

Western Regional

First Round—Baylor 56, BYU 55; Bradley 73, UCLA 59. **Third Place**—BYU 83, UCLA 62. **Final**—Bradley 68, Baylor 66.

FINAL FOUR
at Madison Square Garden, New York

Third Place—N.Carolina St.53, Baylor 41. **Championship**—CCNY 71, Bradley 68.
Most Outstanding Player: Irwin Dambrot, CCNY.
All-Tournament: No team chosen, 1941-51.

NIT Tournament (12 teams)
All games at Madison Sq.Garden, New York

First Round—Western Ky.79, Niagara 72; CCNY 65, San Francisco 46; Syracuse 80, Long Island 52; La Salle 72, Arizona 66. **Quarterfinals**—St.John's 69, Western Ky.60; Bradley 78, Syracuse 66; Duquesne 49, La Salle 47; CCNY 89, Kentucky 50.
Semifinals—Bradley 83, St.John's 72; CCNY 62, Duquesne 52. **Third Place**—St.John's 69, Duquesne 67 (OT). **Championship**—CCNY 69, Bradley 61.
Most Valuable Player—Ed Warner, CCNY.

Player of the Year

Paul Arizin, Villanova . . . . Helms

Consensus All-America
(In alphabetical order)

First Team

Paul Arizin, Villanova; Bob Cousy, Holy Cross; Dick Schnittker, Ohio St.; Bill Sharman, Southern Cal; Paul Unruh, Bradley.

Second Team

Chuck Cooper, Duquesne; Don Lofgran, San Francisco; Kevin O'Shea, Notre Dame; Don Rehfeldt, Wisconsin; Sherman White, LIU.

1951

Fix. Dump. Point shaving. Call it what you like, but spell it S-C-A-N-D-A-L. The biggest in sports since the Black Sox threw the 1919 World Series.

Less than a year after CCNY won both the NIT and NCAA tournaments, seven members of the team and 11 from other colleges were arrested for taking money from gamblers to fix games. Investigations by the New York District Attorney's office would eventually show that between 1947-51, 86 games had been fixed in 23 cities in 17 states by 32 players from seven colleges. CCNY had company: LIU, NYU, Manhattan, Toledo, Bradley, even Kentucky. In addition, the New York City Board of Higher Education, which was also looking into the CCNY program, reported that the high school records of 14 players had been tampered with to make them eligible for admission.

Kentucky's involvement in the point-shaving mess was still to be uncovered when the No.1-ranked Wildcats arrived in Minneapolis in search of their third NCAA championship in four years. There they met No.4 Kansas State, the champion of the Big Seven. Led by 7-foot junior All-America Bill Spivey and sophomore Cliff Hagan, the Cats won, 68-58, and coach Rupp had his third title.

The celebration didn't last long. Shortly after winning the title, the point-shaving scandal breaking in New York overtook Kentucky.

"The gamblers couldn't touch my boys with a 10-foot pole," Rupp had said. But five of his players, including Alex Groza, Ralph Beard and Spivey were implicated. Groza and Beard, stars of the 1948 U.S. Olympic basketball team and now professionals, were thrown out of the NBA. Spivey fought the charges, but never played another game in college or the pros.

Finally, BYU, a second round loser to Kansas State in the NCAAs, rebounded in the NIT. Paced by Roland (the Cat) Minson's 28 points, the Cougars beat Dayton by 19 for the title.

Final AP Top 20

Writers' poll taken before major tournaments.

	Before Tourns	Head Coach	Final Record
1 **Kentucky**	28-2	Adolph Rupp	32-2
2 Okla.A&M	27-4	Hank Iba	29-6
3 Columbia	22-0	Lou Rossini	22-1
4 Kansas St.	22-3	Jack Gardner	25-4
5 Illinois	19-4	Harry Combes	22-5
6 Bradley	32-6	Forddy Anderson	same
7 Indiana	19-3	Branch McCracken	same
8 N.C.State	29-4	Everett Case	30-7
9 St.John's	22-3	Frank McGuire	26-5
10 St.Louis	21-7	Eddie Hickey	22-8
11 **BYU**	22-8	Stan Watts	26-10
12 Arizona	24-4	Fred Enke	24-6
13 Dayton	24-4	Tom Blackburn	27-5
14 Toledo	23-8	Jerry Bush	same
15 Washington	22-5	Tippy Dye	24-6
16 Murray St.	21-6	Harlan Hodges	same
17 Cincinnati	18-3	John Wiethe	18-4
18 Siena	19-8	Dan Cunha	same
19 USC	21-6	Forrest Twogood	same
20 Villanova	25-6	Al Severance	25-7

Note: Kentucky won the NCAAs and Brigham Young won the NIT. Arizona, BYU, N.C.State and St.John's all played in both tourneys.

Major Conference Champions

Conference	Regular Season	Tournament
Big 8	Kansas St.(11-1)	—
Big 10	Illinois (13-1)	—
Ivy	Columbia (12-0)	—
Mo.Valley	Oklahoma A&M (12-2)	—
PCC North:	Washington (11-5)	—
South:	UCLA**/USC (8-4)	—
SEC	Kentucky (14-0)	Vanderbilt
Southern	N.C.State (13-1)	N.C.State
SWC	Tex.A&M*/ TCU/Texas (8-4)	—

*Won playoff for league championship.
**Won playoffs for division and league titles.

NCAA Tournament (16 teams)
East Regional

First Round—Illinois 79, Columbia 71; N.C.State 67, Villanova 62; Kentucky 79, Louisville 68; St.John's 63, Connecticut 52. **Semifinals**—Illinois 84, N.C.State 70; Kentucky 59, St.John's 43. **Third Place**—St.John's 71, N.C.State 59. **Final**—Kentucky 76, Illinois 74.

West Regional

First Round—Washington 62, Texas A&M 40; Oklahoma A&M 50, Montana 46; BYU 68, San Jose St.61; Kansas St.61, Arizona 59. **Semifinals**—Oklahoma A&M 61, Washington 57; Kansas St.64, BYU 54. **Third Place**—Washington 80, BYU 67. **Final**—Kansas St.68, Oklahoma A&M 44.

FINAL FOUR
at Williams Arena, Minneapolis

Third Place—Illinois 61, Oklahoma St.46. **Championship**—Kentucky 68, Kansas St.58.
Most Outstanding Player—Bill Spivey, Kentucky. **All-Tournament**—no team chosen, 1941-51.

NIT Tournament (12 teams)
All games at Madison Sq.Garden, New York

First Round—Dayton 77, Lawrence Tech 71; Seton Hall 71, Beloit 57; St.Louis 73, La Salle 61; St.Bonaventure 70, Cincinnati 67 (2 OT). **Quarterfinals**—BYU 75, St.Louis 58; St.John's 60, St.Bonaventure 58; Dayton 74, Arizona 68; Seton Hall 71, N.C.State 59. **Semifinals**—Dayton 69, St.John's 62 (OT); BYU 69, Seton Hall 59. **Third Place**—St.John's 70, Seton Hall 68 (2 OT). **Championship**—BYU 62, Dayton 43. **Most Valuable Player**—Roland Minson, BYU.

Player of the Year

Dick Groat, Duke . . . . Helms

Consensus All-America
(In alphabetical order)
First Team

Clyde Lovellette, Kansas; Gene Melchiorre, Bradley; Bill Mlkvy, Temple; Sam Ranzino, N.C.State.; Bill Spivey, Kentucky.

Second Team

Ernie Barrett, Kansas St.; Bill Garrett, Indiana; Dick Groat, Duke; Mel Hutchins, BYU; Gale McArthur, Oklahoma A&M.

1952

Despite the involvement of five players in the point-shaving scandal brought to light in 1951, Kentucky kept on winning. Led by forwards Cliff Hagan and Frank Ramsey, the Wildcats went 28-2 and entered the NCAA tourney ranked No.1 by AP. The Cats' march to a fourth title was halted in the East Regional final, however, when St.John's beat them, 64-57.

St.John's advanced to the first full-fledged Final Four in Seattle, March 25-26. From 1946-51, four teams had gone to the site of the championship, but only the two regional champions contended for the title. The two regional runners-up played for third place. Now the tournament had four regionals (two in the East and two in the West) and four contenders: the Redmen, Illinois, Kansas and Santa Clara.

Kansas, led by 6-9 All-America center Clyde Lovellette, easily won the playoff, beating Santa Clara by 19 and then St.John's by 17. It would be KU coach Phog Allen's only NCAA crown.

This was also Duke All-America Dick Groat's final season. By 1960, he would be the MVP-winning short-stop for the world champion Pittsburgh Pirates.

Final AP Top 20
Writers' poll taken before major tournaments.

	Before Tourns	Head Coach	Final Record
1 Kentucky	28-2	Adolph Rupp	29-3
2 Illinois	19-3	Harry Combes	22-4
3 Kansas St.	19-5	Jack Gardner	same
4 Duquesne	21-1	Dudey Moore	23-4
5 St.Louis	22-6	Eddie Hickey	23-8
6 Washington	25-6	Tippy Dye	same
7 Iowa	19-3	Bucky O'Connor	same
8 Kansas	24-3	Phog Allen	28-3
9 West Va.	23-4	Red Brown	same
10 St.John's	22-3	Frank McGuire	25-5
11 Dayton	24-3	Tom Blackburn	28-5
12 Duke	24-6	Harold Bradley	same
13 Holy Cross	23-3	Buster Sheary	24-4
14 Seton Hall	25-2	Honey Russell	25-3
15 St.Bona.	19-5	Ed Melvin	21-6
16 Wyoming	27-6	Everett Shelton	28-7
17 Louisville	20-5	Peck Hickman	20-6
18 Seattle	29-7	Al Brightman	29-8
19 UCLA	19-10	John Wooden	19-12
20 SW Tex.St.	30-1	Milton Jowers	same

Note: Kansas won the NCAAs and unranked La Salle (21-7, Ken Loeffler, 25-7) won the NIT. Dayton, Duquesne, St.John's and St.Louis all played in both tourneys.

Major Conference Champions

Conference	Regular Season	Tournament
Big 8	Kansas (11-1)	—
Big 10	Illinois (12-2)	—
Ivy	Princeton (10-2)	—
Mo.Valley	St.Louis (9-1)	—
PCC North:	Washington 10-2)	—
South:	UCLA (8-4)*	—
SEC	Kentucky (14-0)	Kentucky
Southern	West Virginia (15-1)	N.C.State
SWC	TCU (11-1)	—

*Won playoff for league championship.

NCAA Tournament (16 teams)
East Regionals
Bracket A
Semifinals—Kentucky 82, Penn St.54; St.John's 60, N.C.State 49. **Third Place**—N.C.State 69, Penn St.60. **Final**—St.John's 64, Kentucky 57.

Bracket B
Semifinals—Illinois 80, Dayton 61; Duquesne 60, Princeton 49. **Third Place**—Dayton 77, Princeton 61. **Final**—Illinois 74, Duquesne 68.

West Regionals
Bracket A
Semifinals—Kansas 68, TCU 64; St.Louis 62, New Mexico St.53. **Third Place**—TCU 61, New Mexico St.44. **Final**—Kansas 74, St.Louis 55.

Bracket B
Semifinals—Santa Clara 68, UCLA 59; Wyoming 54, Oklahoma City 48. **Third Place**—Oklahoma City 55, UCLA 53. **Final**—Santa Clara 56, Wyoming 53.

FINAL FOUR
at Edmundson Pavilion, Seattle
Semifinals—St.John's 61, Illinois 59; Kansas 74, Santa Clara 59. **Third Place**—Illinois 67, Santa Clara 64. **Championship**—Kansas 80, St.John's 63. **Most Outstanding Player**—Clyde Lovellette, Kansas. **All-Tournament**—Lovellette and Dean Kelley, Kansas; Ron MacGilvray and Bob Zawoluk, St.John's; John Kerr, Illinois.

NIT Tournament (12 teams)
All games at Madison Sq.Garden, New York

First Round—Dayton 81, NYU 66; Western Ky.62, Louisville 59; La Salle 80, Seton Hall 76; Holy Cross 77, Seattle 72. **Quarterfinals**—St.Bonaventure 70, Western Ky.69; La Salle 51, St.John's 45; Duquesne 78, Holy Cross 68; Dayton 68, St.Louis 58. **Semifinals**—La Salle 59, Duquesne 46; Dayton 69, St.Bonaventure 62. **Third Place**—St.Bonaventure 48, Duquesne 34. **Championship**—La Salle 75, Dayton 64. **Most Valuable Players**—Tom Gola and Norm Grekin, La Salle.

Player of the Year
Clyde Lovellette, Kansas . . . . Helms

Consensus All-America
(In alphabetical order)
First Team
Chuck Darling, Iowa; Rod Fletcher, Illinois; Dick Groat, Duke; Cliff Hagan, Kentucky; Clyde Lovellette, Kansas.

Second Team
Bob Houbregs, Washington; Don Meineke, Dayton; Johnny O'Brien, Seattle; Mark Workman, West Va.; Bob Zawoluk, St.John's.

1953

Both the NCAA and SEC put Kentucky's basketball program on the shelf for the entire 1952-53 season, grounding Rupp and the Wildcats not for any involvement with gamblers, but for recruiting violations.

Meanwhile, Indiana (19-3) rose to No.1 in the final AP Top 20 and wound up meeting third-ranked Kansas (back despite the graduation of Clyde Lovellette and three other starters) in the NCAA final at Kansas City. The Hoosiers won, but needed a Bob Leonard free throw with 27 seconds left. Indiana's 6-10 center Don Schlundt had 30 points in the final, but Kansas' 6-9 center B.H. Born was named the outstanding player of the tournament with 28 points against Washington in the semifinals and 26 more against Indiana.

Back in New York, the 12-team NIT field narrowed to a Seton Hall-St.John's final with the Hall, led by 6-10 center Walter Dukes, winning 58-46.

The one-and-one free throw was introduced and both team and individual scoring averages soared. Frank Selvy of Furman led the nation in scoring with a record 29.5 points a game (he would hit 41.7 in 1954) while the Paladins averaged over 90 points an outing. Another rule change ended the option of waiving free throws in favor of taking the ball out of bounds.

Final AP Top 20

Writers' poll taken before major tournaments.

	Before Tourns	Head Coach	Final Record
1 **Indiana**	19-3	Branch McCracken	23-3
2 **Seton Hall**	28-2	Honey Russell	31-2
3 Kansas	16-5	Phog Allen	19-6
4 Washington	27-2	Tippy Dye	30-3
5 LSU	22-1	Harry Rabenhorst	24-3
6 La Salle	25-2	Ken Loeffler	25-3
7 St.John's	14-5	Al DeStefano	17-6
8 Okla.A&M	22-6	Hank Iba	23-7
9 Duquesne	18-7	Dudey Moore	21-8
10 Notre Dame	17-4	John Jordan	19-5
11 Illinois	18-4	Harry Combes	same
12 Kansas St.	17-4	Jack Gardner	same
13 Holy Cross	18-5	Buster Sheary	20-6
14 Seattle	27-3	Al Brightman	29-4
15 Wake Forest	21-6	Murray Greason	22-7
16 Santa Clara	18-6	Bob Feerick	20-7
17 Western Ky.	25-5	Ed Diddle	25-6
18 N.C.State	26-6	Everett Case	same
19 DePaul	18-7	Ray Meyer	19-9
20 SW Mo.St.	19-4	Bob Vanatta	24-4

Note: Indiana won the NCAAs, Seton Hall won the NIT and SW Missouri St. won the NAIAs.

Major Conference Champions

Conference	Regular Season	Tournament
Big 8	Kansas (10-2)	—
Big 10	Indiana (17-1)	—
Ivy	Penn (10-2)	—
Mo.Valley	Oklahoma A&M (8-2)	—
PCC North:	Washington (15-1)*	—
South:	California (9-3)	—
SEC	LSU (13-0)	—
Southern	N.C.State (13-3)	Wake Forest
SWC	TCU (9-3)	—

*Won playoff for league championship.
Note: SEC did not hold tournament from 1953-78.

NCAA Tournament (22 teams)

East Regionals

Bracket A

First Round—Holy Cross 87, Navy 74; Lebanon Valley 80, Fordham 67. **Semifinals**—Holy Cross 79, Wake Forest 71; LSU 89, Lebanon Valley 76. **Third Place**—Wake Forest 91, Lebanon Valley 71; **Final**—LSU 81, Holy Cross 73.

Bracket B

First Round—Notre Dame 72, Eastern Ky. 57; DePaul 74, Miami-OH 72. **Semifinals**—Notre Dame 69, Penn 57; Indiana 82, DePaul 80. **Third Place**—Penn 90, DePaul 70. **Final**—Indiana 79, Notre Dame 66.

West Regionals

Bracket A

First Round—Seattle 88, Idaho St. 77; Santa Clara 81, Hardin-Simmons 56. **Semifinals**—Washington 92, Seattle 70; Santa Clara 67, Wyoming 52. **Third Place**—Seattle 80, Wyoming 64. **Final**—Washington 74, Santa Clara 62.

Bracket B

First Round—No games. **Semifinals**—Kansas 73, Oklahoma City 65; Oklahoma A&M 71, TCU 54. **Third Place**—TCU 58, Oklahoma City 56. **Final**—Kansas 61, Oklahoma A&M 55.

FINAL FOUR

at Municipal Auditorium, Kansas City

Semifinals—Indiana 80, LSU 67; Kansas 79, Washington 53. **Third Place**—Washington 88, LSU 69. **Championship**—Indiana 69, Kansas 68. **Most Outstanding Player**—B.H.Born, Kansas. **All-Tournament**—Born and Dean Kelley, Kansas; Bob Leonard and Don Schlundt, Indiana; Bob Houbregs, Washington.

NIT Tournament (12 teams)

All games at Madison Sq.Garden, New York

First Round—Duquesne 88, Tulsa 69; Louisville 92, Georgetown 79; St.John's 81, St.Louis 64; Niagara 82, BYU 76 (OT). **Quarterfinals**—St.John's 75, La Salle 74; Manhattan 79, Louisville 66; Seton Hall 79, Niagara 74; Duquesne 69, Western Ky. 61. **Semifinals**—Seton Hall 74, Manhattan 56; St.John's 64, Duquesne 55. **Third Place**—Duquesne 81, Manhattan 67. **Championship**—Seton Hall 58, St.John's 46. **Most Valuable Player**—Walter Dukes, Seton Hall.

Player of the Year

Bob Houbregs, Washington . . . . .Helms

Consensus All-America

(In alphabetical order)

First Team

Ernie Beck, Penn; Walt Dukes, Seton Hall; Tom Gola, La Salle; Bob Houbregs, Washington; Johnny O'Brien, Seattle.

Second Team

Dick Knostman, Kansas St.; Bob Pettit, LSU; Joe Richey, BYU; Don Schlundt, Indiana; Frank Selvy, Furman.

1954

Kentucky returned from forced exile to win all 25 of its regular season games and reclaim the No.1 spot in the AP poll.

Despite a cancelled 1952-53 schedule, the Wildcats had stayed together and practiced regularly during their year off. No Rupp team was ever hungrier for an NCAA title. Tying LSU for the SEC championship (they didn't play during the regular season), the Cats beat the Tigers in a playoff to determine the NCAA qualifier. The NCAA, however, ruled that UK seniors Cliff Hagan, Frank Ramsey and Lou Tsioropoulos all had enough credits to graduate (which technically made them graduate students) and were ineligible to compete in postseason play.

Rupp cursed his fate (and the NCAA) and refused the berth.

Second-ranked La Salle (21-4), 1953's NIT champion, stepped up to the NCAA title with a 16-point victory over No.7 Bradley in the tournament's first nationally televised final. Tom Gola paced the Explorers with 114 points in five games and won his second MVP award in two tourneys.

Another Eastern independent, No.3 Holy Cross, beat No.5 Duquesne for the NIT title.

Final AP Top 20
Writers' poll taken before major tournaments.

	Before Tourns	Head Coach	Final Record
1 Kentucky	25-0	Adolph Rupp	same
2 **La Salle**	21-4	Ken Loeffler	26-4
3 **Holy Cross**	23-2	Buster Sheary	26-2
4 Indiana	19-3	Branch McCracken	20-4
5 Duquesne	24-2	Dudey Moore	26-3
6 Notre Dame	20-2	John Jordan	22-3
7 Bradley	15-12	Forddy Anderson	19-13
8 Western Ky.	28-1	Ed Diddle	29-3
9 Penn St.	14-5	Elmer Gross	18-6
10 Okla.A&M	23-4	Hank Iba	24-5
11 USC	17-12	Forrest Twogood	19-14
12 Geo.Wash.	23-2	Bill Reinhart	23-3
13 Iowa	17-5	Bucky O'Connor	same
14 LSU	21-3	Harry Rabenhorst	21-5
15 Duke	22-6	Harold Bradley	same
16 Niagara	22-5	Taps Gallagher	24-6
17 Seattle	26-1	Al Brightman	26-2
18 Kansas	16-5	Phog Allen	same
19 Illinois	17-5	Harry Combes	17-5
20 Maryland	23-7	Bud Millikan	same

Note: La Salle won the NCAAs and Holy Cross won the NIT.

Major Conference Champions

Conference	Regular Season	Tournament
ACC	Duke (9-1)	N.C.State
Big 8	Kansas/Colorado (10-2)	—
Big 10	Indiana (12-2)	—
Ivy	Cornell*/Prin.(11-3)	—
Mo.Valley	Oklahoma A&M (9-1)	—
PCC North:	Oregon St.(11-5)*	—
South:	USC (8-4)*	—
SEC	Kentucky*/LSU (14-0)	—
Southern	Geo.Washington (10-0)	Geo.Wash.
SWC	Rice*/Texas (9-3)	—

*Won playoff for league championship.
Note: Kentucky and LSU did not play during the regular season. Kentucky won a playoff to determine NCAA tournament entry, then turned down the bid to protest NCAA's cancelling Wildcats' entire 1953 schedule due to academic and recruiting violations.

NCAA Tournament (24 teams)

East Regionals

Bracket A
First Round—Penn St. 62, Toledo 50; Notre Dame 80, Loyola-LA 70. **Semifinals**—Penn St. 78, LSU 70; Notre Dame 65, Indiana 64. **Third Place**—Indiana 73, LSU 62. **Final**—Penn St. 71, Notre Dame 63.

Bracket B
First Round—Navy 85, Connecticut 80; La Salle 76, Fordham 74; N.C.State 75, Geo.Washington 73. **Semifinals**—Navy 69, Cornell 67; La Salle 88, N.C.State 81. **Third Place**—N.C.State 65, Cornell 54. **Final**—La Salle 64, Navy 48.

West Regionals

Bracket A
First Round—Bradley 61, Oklahoma City 55. **Semifinals**—Bradley 76, Colorado 64; Oklahoma A&M 51, Rice 45. **Third Place**—Rice 78, Colorado 55. **Final**—Bradley 71, Oklahoma A&M 57.

Bracket B
First Round—Idaho St. 77, Seattle 75 (OT); Santa Clara 73, Texas Tech 64. **Semifinals**—USC 73, Idaho St. 59; Santa Clara 73, Colorado St. 50. **Third Place**—Idaho St. 62, Colorado St. 57. **Final**—USC 66, Santa Clara 65 (2OT).

FINAL FOUR
at Municipal Auditorium, Kansas City

Semifinals—La Salle 69, Penn St. 54; Bradley 74, USC 72. **Third Place**—Penn St. 70, USC 61. **Championship**—La Salle 92, Bradley 76. **Most Outstanding Player**—Tom Gola, La Salle. **All-Tournament**—Gola and Chuck Singley, La Salle; Bob Carney, Bradley; Jesse Arnelle, Penn St.; Roy Irvin, USC.

NIT Tournament (12 teams)
All games at Madison Sq.Garden, New York

First Round—St.Francis-NY 60, Louisville 55; Dayton 90, Manhattan 79; Bowling Green 88, Wichita 84; St.Francis-PA 81; BYU 68. **Quarterfinals**—Western Ky. 95, Bowling Green 81; Niagara 77, Dayton 74; Duquesne 69, St. Francis-PA 63; Holy Cross 93, St.Francis-NY 69.

Semifinals—Duquesne 66, Niagara 51; Holy Cross 75, Western Ky. 69. **Third Place**—Niagara 71, Western Ky. 65. **Championship**—Holy Cross 71, Duquesne 62. **Most Valuable Player**—Togo Palazzi, Holy Cross.

Player of the Year
Tom Gola, La Salle . . . . Helms

Consensus All-America
(In alphabetical order)

First Team
Tom Gola, La Salle; Cliff Hagan, Kentucky; Bob Pettit, LSU; Don Schlundt, Indiana; Frank Selvy, Furman.

Second Team
Bob Leonard, Indiana; Tom Marshall, Western Ky.; Bob Mattick, Oklahoma A&M; Frank Ramsey, Kentucky; Dick Ricketts, Duquesne.

1955

After opening the 1954-55 campaign with two quick wins, San Francisco lost its third game to UCLA (47-40, in Westwood) before running off 21 consecutive victories to finish the regular season first in the AP poll.

Led by guard K.C.Jones and center Bill Russell, the Dons edged PCC champ Oregon State, 57-56, in the West Regional final at Corvallis, Ore., then went on to meet Tom Gola and defending champion La Salle in the NCAA championship game in Kansas City. In a surprise move, USF coach Phil Woolpert assigned the 6-1 Jones to cover the 6-7 Gola and K.C. outscored UPI's first Player of the Year, 24-16. Russell, meanwhile, scored 23 and pulled down 25 rebounds as the Dons beat the third-ranked Explorers easily, 77-63, to end the year at 28-1.

No.2 Kentucky entered the NCAA tournament at 22-2, but was an eight point loser to Marquette in the semifinals of the East Regional. ACC champ North Carolina State, 28-4 and fourth in the final AP poll, was on probation for a year (recruiting violations) and ineligible for the NCAAs.

Sixth-ranked Duquesne, paced by first team All-Americas Si Green and Dick Ricketts, captured its first NIT in eight tries.

Final AP Top 20
Writers' poll taken before major tournaments.

	Before Tourns	Head Coach	Final Record
1 **San Fran.**	23-1	Phil Woolpert	28-1
2 Kentucky	22-2	Adolph Rupp	23-3
3 La Salle	22-4	Ken Loeffler	26-5
4 N.C.State	28-4	Everett Case	same
5 Iowa	17-5	Bucky O'Connor	19-7
6 **Duquesne**	19-4	Dudey Moore	22-4
7 Utah	23-3	Jack Gardner	24-4
8 Marquette	22-2	Jack Nagle	24-3
9 Dayton	23-3	Tom Blackburn	25-4
10 Oregon St.	21-7	Slats Gill	22-8
11 Minnesota	15-7	Ozzie Cowles	same
12 Alabama	19-5	Johnny Dee	same
13 UCLA	21-5	John Wooden	same
14 Geo.Wash.	24-6	Bill Reinhart	same
15 Colorado	16-5	Bebe Lee	19-6
16 Tulsa	20-6	Clarence Iba	21-7
17 Vanderbilt	16-6	Bob Polk	same
18 Illinois	17-5	Harry Combes	same
19 West Va.	19-10	Fred Schaus	19-11
20 St.Louis	19-7	Eddie Hickey	20-8

Note: San Francisco won the NCAAs and Duquesne won the NIT.

Major Conference Champions

Conference	Regular Season	Tournament
ACC	N.C.State (12-2)	N.C.State
Big 8	Colorado (11-1)	—
Big 10	Iowa (11-3)	—
Ivy	Princeton*/Colum.(10-4)	—
Mo.Valley	Tulsa/St.Louis (8-2)	—
PCC North:	Oregon St.(15-1)*	—
South:	UCLA (11-1)	—
SEC	Kentucky (12-2)	—
Southern	West Virginia (9-1)	West Va.
SWC	SMU (9-3)	—

*Won playoff for league championship.

NCAA Tournament (24 teams)
East Regionals
Bracket A
First Round—Marquette 90, Miami-OH 79; Penn St. 59, Memphis 55. **Semifinals**—Marquette 79, Kentucky 71; Iowa 82, Penn St. 53. **Third Place**—Kentucky 84, Penn St. 59. **Final**—Iowa 86, Marquette 81.

Bracket B
First Round—La Salle 95, West Va. 61; Canisius 73, Williams 60; Villanova 74, Duke 73. **Semifinals**—La Salle 73, Princeton 46; Canisius 73, Villanova 71. **Third Place**—Villanova 65, Princeton 57. **Final**—La Salle 99, Canisius 64.

West Regionals
Bracket A
First Round—Bradley 69, Oklahoma City, 65. **Semifinals**—Bradley 81, SMU 79; Colorado 69, Tulsa 59. **Third Place**—Tulsa 68, SMU 67. **Final**—Colorado 93, Bradley 81.

Bracket B
First Round—Seattle 80, Idaho St. 63; San Francisco 89, West Texas St. 66. **Semifinals**—Oregon St. 83, Seattle 71; San Francisco 78, Utah 59. **Third Place**—Utah 108, Seattle 85. **Final**—San Francisco 57, Oregon St. 56.

FINAL FOUR
at Municipal Auditorium, Kansas City

Semifinals—La Salle 76, Iowa 73; San Francisco 62, Colorado 50. **Third Place**—Colorado 75, Iowa 74. **Championship**—San Francisco 77, La Salle 63. **Most Outstanding Player**—Bill Russell, San Francisco. **All-Tournament**—Russell and K.C.Jones, San Francisco; Tom Gola, La Salle; Jim Ranglos, Colorado; Carl Cain, Iowa.

NIT Tournament (12 teams)
All games at Madison Sq.Garden, New York

First Round—Louisville 91, Manhattan 86; Niagara 83, Lafayette 70; St.Francis-PA 89, Seton Hall 78; St. Louis 110, Connecticut 103. **Quarterfinals**—Duquesne 74, Louisville 66; Cincinnati 85, Niagara 83 (2 OT); St. Francis-PA 68, Holy Cross 64; Dayton 97, St.Louis 81. **Semifinals**—Dayton 79, St.Francis-PA 73 (OT); Duquesne 65, Cincinnati 51. **Third Place**—Cincinnati 96, St.Francis-PA 91 (OT). **Championship**—Duquesne 70, Dayton 58.

Most Valuable Player—Maurice Stokes, St.Francis-PA.

Players of the Year
Tom Gola, La Salle . . . . UPI
Bill Russell, San Francisco . . . . Helms

Coach of the Year
Phil Woolpert, San Francisco . . . . UPI

Consensus All-America
(In alphabetical order)
First Team
Dick Garmaker, Minnesota; Tom Gola, La Salle; Si Green, Duquesne; Dick Ricketts, Duquesne; Bill Russell, San Francisco.

Second Team
Darrell Floyd, Furman; Robin Freeman, Ohio St.; Dickie Hemric, Wake Forest; Don Schlundt, Indiana; Ron Shavik, N.C.State.

1956

Defending national champion San Francisco staked its claim as the best college basketball team ever in 1955-56. The Dons entered the season on a 26-game winning streak and exited with a record 55 in a row by becoming the first undefeated team (29-0) ever to win the NCAA title.

All four of USF's tourney opponents were ranked—No.8 UCLA, No.18 Utah, No.7 SMU and No.4 Iowa—and the Dons beat them all by at least 11 points. Iowa, the Big Ten champ for the second straight year, came into the NCAA final on a 17-game win streak of its own before losing, 83-71.

USF center Bill Russell might have cinched his second tournament Most Outstanding Player award if Temple's 5-11 Hal Lear hadn't scored 160 points in five games. But the defensive-minded Russell was everybody's Player of the Year and established such an intimidating court presence that following the season, the NCAA passed the so-called ''Russell Rule,'' extending the foul lane from six to 12 feet.

Second-ranked N.C.State (24-3) was expected to challenge USF for the NCAA title, until unranked Canisius upset them in the opening round in four overtimes.

Finally, Kansas coach Phog Allen retired with a 48-year record of 746-264.

Final AP Top 20
Writers' poll taken before major tournaments.

	Before Tourns	Head Coach	Final Record
1 San Fran.	25-0	Phil Woolpert	29-0
2 N.C.State	24-3	Everett Case	24-4
3 Dayton	23-3	Tom Blackburn	25-4
4 Iowa	17-5	Bucky O'Connor	20-6
5 Alabama	21-3	Johnny Dee	same
6 Louisville	23-3	Peck Hickman	26-3
7 SMU	22-2	Doc Hayes	25-4
8 UCLA	21-5	John Wooden	22-6
9 Kentucky	19-5	Adolph Rupp	20-6
10 Illinois	18-4	Harry Combes	same
11 Okla.City	18-6	Abe Lemons	20-7
12 Vanderbilt	19-4	Bob Polk	same
13 N.Carolina	18-5	Frank McGuire	same
14 Holy Cross	22-4	Roy Leenig	22-5
15 Temple	23-3	Harry Litwack	27-4
16 W.Forest	19-9	Murray Greason	same
17 Duke	19-7	Harold Bradley	same
18 Utah	21-5	Jack Gardner	22-6
19 Okla.A&M	18-8	Hank Iba	18-9
20 West Va.	21-8	Fred Schaus	21-9

Note: San Francisco won the NCAAs and Louisville won the NIT.

Major Conference Champions

Conference	Regular Season	Tournament
ACC	N.C.St./N.Caro.(11-3)	N.C.State
Big 8	Kansas St.(9-3)	—
Big 10	Iowa (13-1)	—
Ivy	Dartmouth (10-4)	—
Mo.Valley	Houston (9-3)	—
PCC	UCLA (16-0)	—
SEC	Alabama (14-0)	—
Southern	G.Wash./West Va.(10-2)	West.Va.
SWC	SMU (12-0)	—

Note: PCC realigned into one division.

NCAA Tournament (25 teams)

East Regional
First Round—Connecticut 84, Manhattan 75; Temple 74, Holy Cross 72; Dartmouth 61, West Va. 59 (OT); Canisius 79, N.C.State 78 (4 OT). **Semifinals**—Temple 65, Connecticut 59; Canisius 66, Dartmouth 58. **Third Place**—Dartmouth 85, Connecticut 64. **Final**—Temple 60, Canisius 58.

Midwest Regional
First Round—Morehead St. 107, Marshall 92; Wayne St. 72, DePaul 63. **Semifinals**—Iowa 97, Morehead St. 83; Kentucky 84, Wayne St. 64. **Third Place**—Morehead St. 95, Wayne St. 84. **Final**—Iowa 89, Kentucky 77.

West Regional
First Round—SMU 68, Texas Tech 67; Oklahoma City 97, Memphis St. 81. **Semifinals**—SMU 89, Houston 74; Oklahoma City 97, Kansas St. 93. **Third Place**—Kansas St. 89, Houston 70. **Final**—SMU 84, Oklahoma City 63.

Far West Regional
First Round—Seattle 68, Idaho St. 66. **Semifinals**—Utah 81, Seattle 72; San Francisco 72, UCLA 61. **Third Place**—UCLA 94, Seattle 70. **Final**—San Francisco 92, Utah 77.

FINAL FOUR
at McGaw Hall, Evanston,IL

Semifinals—Iowa 83, Temple 76; San Francisco 76, SMU 68. **Third Place**—Temple 90, SMU 81. **Championship**—San Francisco 83, Iowa 71. **Most Outstanding Player**—Hal Lear, Temple. **All-Tournament**—Lear, Temple; Hal Perry and Bill Russell, San Francisco; Carl Cain and Bill Logan, Iowa.

NIT Tournament (12 teams)
All games at Madison Sq.Garden, New York

First Round—St.Francis-NY 85, Lafayette 74; Duquesne 69, Oklahoma A&M 61; Seton Hall 74, Marquette 78; Xavier-OH 84, St.Louis 80. **Quarterfinals**—Louisville 84, Duquesne 72; St.Francis-NY 74, Niagara 72; St.Joseph's-PA 74, Seton Hall 65; Dayton 72, Xavier-OH 68.
Semifinals—Dayton 89, St.Francis-NY 58; Louisville 89, St.Joseph's-PA 79. **Third Place**—St.Joseph's-PA 93, St.Francis-NY 82. **Championship**—Louisville 93, Dayton 80.
Most Valuable Player—Charlie Tyra, Louisville.

Player of the Year
Bill Russell, San Francisco . . . . UPI,Helms

Coach of the Year
Phil Woolpert, San Francisco . . . . UPI

Consensus All-America
(In alphabetical order)
First Team
Robin Freeman, Ohio St.; Si Green, Duquesne; Tom Heinsohn, Holy Cross; Bill Russell, San Francisco; Ron Shavik, N.C.State.

Second Team
Bob Burrow, Kentucky; Darrell Floyd, Furman; Rod Hundley, West Virginia; K.C.Jones, San Francisco; Willie Naulls, UCLA; Bill Uhl, Dayton.

1957

North Carolina became the first team from the Old South to win the NCAA tournament, but the Tar Heels did it with a roster full of Irish Catholic Yankees (and one Jew) from coach Frank McGuire's hometown of New York City.

They also did it by winning two triple overtime games in less than 24 hours at the Final Four and beating Wilt Chamberlain in the title game.

Paced by All-America forward Lennie Rosenbluth and guard Pete Brennan, the top-ranked Heels had to outlast Michigan State, 74-70, in three extra periods on March 22 and then do battle with Chamberlain and No.2 Kansas on March 23.

The first No.1 vs No.2 championship game since 1949 reached halftime with Carolina in front 29-22, but Kansas rallied in the second half to lead 44-41 with 1:45 left. Despite losing Rosenbluth on fouls, the Tar Heels came back to tie the score (46-46) in regulation and force the first title game overtime in tourney history. The Heels finally won it in the third extra period when Joe Quigg sank two foul shots with six seconds left. Chamberlain, a sophomore, led all scorers with 23 points and was named MVP.

Elsewhere, San Francisco had its three-season win streak snapped at 60 by Illinois (62-33), but made it back to the Final Four and placed third.

Final AP Top 20

Writers' poll taken before major tournaments.

	Before Tourns	Head Coach	Final Record
1 N.Carolina	27-0	Frank McGuire	32-0
2 Kansas	21-2	Dick Harp	24-3
3 Kentucky	22-4	Adolph Rupp	23-5
4 SMU	21-3	Doc Hayes	22-4
5 Seattle	24-2	John Castellani	24-3
6 Louisville	21-5	Peck Hickman	same
7 West Va.	25-4	Fred Schaus	25-5
8 Vanderbilt	17-5	Bob Polk	same
9 Okla.City	17-8	Abe Lemons	19-9
10 St. Louis	19-7	Eddie Hickey	19-9
11 Mich.St.	14-8	Forddy Anderson	16-10
12 Memphis St.	21-5	Bob Vanatta	24-6
13 California	20-4	Pete Newell	21-5
14 UCLA	22-4	John Wooden	same
15 Miss.St.	17-8	Babe McCarthy	same
16 Idaho St.	24-2	John Grayson	25-4
17 Notre Dame	18-7	John Jordan	20-8
18 W.Forest	19-9	Murray Greason	same
19 Canisius	20-5	Joe Curran	22-6
Okla.A&M	17-9	Hank Iba	same

Note: North Carolina won the NCAAs and unranked Bradley (19-7, Chuck Orsborn, 22-7) won the NIT.

Major Conference Champions

Conference	Regular Season	Tournament
ACC	North Carolina (14-0)	N.Carolina
Big 8	Kansas (11-1)	—
Big 10	Indiana/Mich.St.(10-4)	—
Ivy	Yale (12-2)	—
Mo.Valley	St.Louis (12-2)	—
PCC	California (14-2)	—
SEC	Kentucky (12-2)	—
Southern	West Virginia (12-0)	West Va.
SWC	SMU (11-1)	—

NCAA Tournament (23 teams)

East Regional

First Round—Syracuse 82, Connecticut 76; Canisius 64, West Virginia 56; North Carolina 90, Yale 74. **Semifinals**— Syracuse 75, Lafayette 71; North Carolina 87, Canisius 75. **Third Place**—Canisius 82, Lafayette 76. **Final**—North Carolina 67, Syracuse 58.

Mideast Regional

First Round—Pittsburgh 86, Morehead St. 85; Notre Dame 89, Miami-OH 77. **Semifinals**—Kentucky 98, Pittsburgh 92; Michigan St. 85, Notre Dame 83. **Third Place**—Notre Dame 86, Pittsburgh 85. **Final**—Michigan St. **80, Kentucky 68.**

Midwest Regional

First Round—Oklahoma City 76, Loyola-LA 55. **Semifinals**—Oklahoma City 75, St.Louis 66; Kansas 73, SMU 65 (OT). **Third Place**—SMU 78, St.Louis 68. **Final**—Kansas 81, Oklahoma City 61.

West Regional

First Round—Idaho St. 68, Hardin-Simmons 57. **Semifinals**—San Francisco 66, Idaho St. 51; California 86, BYU 59. **Third Place**—BYU 65, Idaho St. 54. **Final**—San Francisco 50, California 46.

FINAL FOUR

at Municipal Auditorium, Kansas City

Semifinals—North Carolina 74, Michigan St. 70 (3 OT); Kansas 80, San Francisco 56. **Third Place**—San Francisco 67, Michigan St. 60. **Championship**—North Carolina 54, Kansas 53 (3 OT).

Most Outstanding Player—Wilt Chamberlain, Kansas. **All-Tournament**—Chamberlain, Kansas; Pete Brennan and Lennie Rosenbluth, North Carolina; Gene Brown, San Francisco; Johnny Green, Michigan St.

NIT Tournament (12 teams)

All games at Madison Sq.Garden, New York

First Round—Memphis St. 77, Utah 75; Xavier-OH 85, Seton Hall 79; Dayton 79, St.Peter's 71; St.Bonaventure 90, Cincinnati 72. **Quarterfinals**—Memphis St. 85, Manhattan 73; St.Bonaventure 85, Seattle 68; Bradley 116, Xavier-OH 81; Temple 77, Dayton 66. **Semifinals**—Memphis St. 80, St.Bonaventure 78; Bradley 78, Temple 66. **Third Place**—Temple 67, St.Bonaventure 50. **Championship**—Bradley 84, Memphis St. 83.

Most Valuable Player—Win Wilfong, Memphis St.

Players of the Year

Chet Forte, Columbia . . . . UPI
Lennie Rosenbluth, North Carolina . . . . Helms

Coach of the Year

Frank McGuire, North Carolina . . . . UPI

Consensus All-America

(In alphabetical order)

First Team

Wilt Chamberlain, Kansas; Chet Forte, Columbia; Rod Hundley, West Virginia; Jim Krebs, SMU; Lennie Rosenbluth, North Carolina; Charlie Tyra, Louisville.

Second Team

Elgin Baylor, Seattle; Frank Howard, Ohio St.; Guy Rodgers, Temple; Gary Thompson, Iowa St.; Grady Wallace, South Carolina.

1958

Sophomores Jerry West of West Virginia and Oscar Robertson of Cincinnati burst on the scene in 1957-58 and led their teams to the top of the final AP Top 25.

West and the Mountaineers were 26-1 through the regular season, winning their fourth straight Southern Conference title. Cincinnati was 24-2 and conference champ in its first year as a member of the Missouri Valley, while Robertson became the first soph ever to lead the nation in scoring (35.1) and gain Player of the Year honors. Come the NCAAs, however, both teams lost their opening games—West Virginia to unranked Manhattan and Cincinnati to No.3 Kansas State.

The eventual national champion turned out to be ninth-ranked Kentucky, giving coach Adolph Rupp four NCAA titles. The Wildcats reached the Final Four in Louisville, then proceeded to slip past Temple, 61-60, in the semifinals and beat Elgin Baylor and Seattle by 12 for the championship.

Wilt Chamberlain and Kansas, NCAA finalists in 1957, lost the Big Eight crown to Kansas State and didn't make it back for the '58 tournament. Wilt then decided not to return for the 1958-59 season and signed with the Harlem Globetrotters for $65,000.

In the NIT, unranked Xavier of Ohio, which entered the tourney just four games over .500, upset defending champion and No. 14 Bradley in the quarterfinals and did the same to No. 11 Dayton in the finals—winning 78-74 in overtime.

Final AP Top 20
Writers' poll taken before major tournaments.

	Before Tourns	Head Coach	Final Record
1 West Va.	26-1	Fred Schaus	26-2
2 Cincinnati	24-2	George Smith	25-3
3 Kansas St.	20-3	Tex Winter	22-5
4 San Fran.	24-1	Phil Woolpert	25-2
5 Temple	24-2	Harry Litwack	27-3
6 Maryland	20-6	Bud Millikan	22-7
7 Kansas	18-5	Dick Harp	same
8 Notre Dame	22-4	John Jordan	24-5
9 **Kentucky**	19-6	Adolph Rupp	23-6
10 Duke	18-7	Harold Bradley	same
11 Dayton	23-3	Tom Blackburn	25-4
12 Indiana	12-10	Branch McCracken	13-11
13 N.Carolina	19-7	Frank McGuire	same
14 Bradley	20-6	Chuck Orsborn	20-7
15 Miss.St.	20-5	Babe McCarthy	same
16 Auburn	16-6	Joel Eaves	same
17 Mich.St.	16-6	Forddy Anderson	same
18 Seattle	20-6	John Castellani	24-7
19 Okla.St.	19-7	Hank Iba	21-8
20 N.C.State	18-6	Everett Case	same

Note: Kentucky won the NCAAs and unranked Xavier (15-11, Jim McCafferty, 19-11) won the NIT.

Major Conference Champions

Conference	Regular Season	Tournament
ACC	Duke (11-3)	Maryland
Big 8	Kansas St.(10-2)	—
Big 10	Indiana (10-4)	—
Ivy	Dartmouth (11-3)	—
Mo.Valley	Cincinnati (13-1)	—
PCC	Oregon St./Calif.(12-4)	—
SEC	Kentucky (12-2)	—
Southern	West Virginia (12-0)	West Va.
SWC	Arkansas*/SMU (9-5)	—

*Won playoff for league championship.

NCAA Tournament (24 teams)

East Regional
First Round—Maryland 86, Boston College 63; Manhattan 89, West Va. 84; Dartmouth 75, Connecticut 64. **Semifinals**—Temple 71, Maryland 67; Dartmouth 79, Manhattan 62. **Third Place**—Maryland 59, Manhattan 55. **Final**—Temple 69, Dartmouth 50.

Mideast Regional
First Round—Miami-OH 82, Pittsburgh 77; Notre Dame 94, Tennessee Tech 61. **Semifinals**—Kentucky 94, Miami-OH 70; Notre Dame 94, Indiana 87. **Third Place**—Indiana 98, Miami-OH 91. **Final**—Kentucky 89, Notre Dame 56.

Midwest Regional
First Round—Oklahoma A&M 59, Loyola-LA 42. **Semifinals**—Oklahoma A&M 65, Arkansas 40; Kansas St. 83, Cincinnati 80 (OT). **Third Place**—Cincinnati 97, Arkansas 62. **Final**—Kansas St. 69, Oklahoma A&M 57.

West Regional
First Round—Seattle 88, Wyoming 51; Idaho St. 72, Arizona St. 68. **Semifinals**—Seattle 69, San Francisco 67; California 54, Idaho St. 43. **Third Place**—San Francisco 57, Idaho St. 51. **Final**—Seattle 66, California 62 (OT).

FINAL FOUR
at Freedom Hall, Louisville

Semifinals—Kentucky 61, Temple 60; Seattle 73, Kansas St. 51. **Third Place**—Temple 67, Kansas St. 57. **Championship**—Kentucky 84, Seattle 72. **Most Outstanding Player**—Elgin Baylor, Seattle. **All-Tournament**—Baylor and Charley Brown, Seattle; John Cox and Vern Hatton, Kentucky; Guy Rodgers, Temple.

NIT Tournament (12 teams)
All games at Madison Sq.Garden, New York

First Round—St.John's 79, Butler 69; St.Joseph's-PA 83, St.Peter's 76; Xavier-OH 95, Niagara 86; Fordham 83, St.Francis-PA 59. **Quarterfinals**—St.John's 71, Utah 70; St.Bonaventure 79, St. Joseph's-PA 75; Xavier-OH 95, Niagara 86; Fordham 83, St.Francis-PA 59. **Semifinals**—Dayton 80, St.John's 56; Xavier-OH 72, St.Bonaventure 53. **Third Place**—St.Bonaventure 84, St.John's 69. **Championship**—Xavier-OH 78, Dayton 74 (OT). **Most Valuable Player**—Hank Stein, Xavier-OH.

Players of the Year

Oscar Robertson, Cincinnati . . . . UPI
Elgin Baylor, Seattle . . . . Helms

Coach of the Year

Tex Winter, Kansas St . . . . UPI

Consensus All-America
(In alphabetical order)

First Team
Elgin Baylor, Seattle; Bob Boozer, Kansas St.; Wilt Chamberlain, Kansas; Don Hennon, Pittsburgh; Oscar Robertson, Cincinnati; Guy Rodgers, Temple.

Second Team
Pete Brennan, North Carolina; Archie Dees, Indiana; Dave Gambee, Oregon St.; Mike Farmer, San Francisco; Bailey Howell, Mississippi St.

1959

Ten years after leading an unheralded San Francisco team to the NIT championship, coach Pete Newell did the same thing in the NCAAs, this time with California.

Newell's defensive-minded Golden Bears, led by 6-10 Darrall Imhoff and 6-5 Bill McClintock, went 20-4 during the regular season, held the opposition to 51 points a game, and were ranked No.11 by AP. At the Final Four in Louisville, they had to play Oscar Robertson and Jerry West on consecutive nights.

Cal beat Cincinnati in the semfinals, 64-58, holding Robertson and the Bearcats 26 points below their per game average. In the final, West scored 28, but the Bears won 71-70.

West was named tournament MVP, the fourth straight year the honor went to a member of a losing team. The other three were Hal Lear of Temple and two future L.A. Lakers teammates of West's—Wilt Chamberlain and Elgin Baylor.

The country's top two teams at the end of the regular season, Kansas State and Kentucky, were knocked out of the NCAA tournament in the regionals—No.1 K-State by Cincinnati in the Midwest final and UK by cross-state rival Louisville in the Mideast semifinals.

Finally, No.3 Mississippi State (24-1), the SEC champion, refused an invitation to the NCAAs because it was an integrated event.

Final AP Top 20

Writers' poll taken before major tournaments.

	Before Tourns	Head Coach	Final Record
1 Kansas St.	24-1	Tex Winter	25-2
2 Kentucky	23-2	Adolph Rupp	24-3
3 Miss.St.	24-1	Babe McCarthy	same*
4 Bradley	23-3	Chuck Orsborn	25-4
5 Cincinnati	23-3	George Smith	26-4
6 N.C.State	22-4	Everett Case	same
7 Mich.St.	18-3	Forddy Anderson	19-4
8 Auburn	20-2	Joel Eaves	same
9 N.Carolina	20-4	Frank McGuire	20-5
10 West Va.	25-4	Fred Schaus	29-5
11 **California**	20-4	Pete Newell	24-4
12 St. Louis	20-5	John Benington	20-6
13 Seattle	23-6	Vince Cazzetta	same
14 St.Joe's,PA	22-3	Jack Ramsay	22-5
15 St.Mary's,CA	18-5	Jim Weaver	19-6
16 TCU	19-5	Buster Brannon	20-6
17 Okla.City	20-6	Abe Lemons	20-7
18 Utah	21-5	Jack Gardner	21-7
19 St.Bona.	20-2	Eddie Donovan	20-3
20 Marquette	22-4	Eddie Hickey	23-6

Note: California won the NCAAs and unranked St.John's (16-6, Joe Lapchick, 20-6) won the NIT.

Major Conference Champions

Conference	Regular Season	Tournament
AAWU	California (14-2)	—
ACC	N.C.St./N.Caro.(12-2)	N.C.State
Big 8	Kansas St.(14-0)	—
Big 10	Michigan St.(12-2)	—
Ivy	Dartmouth*/Prince.(13-1)	—
Mo.Valley	Cincinnati (13-1)	—
SEC	Mississippi St.(13-1)	—
Southern	West Virginia (11-0)	West Va.
SWC	TCU (12-2)	—

*Won playoff for league championship.
Note: PCC dissolved and reformed as the Athletic Assn. of Western Universities (AAWU).

NCAA Tournament (23 teams)

East Regional

First Round—West Virginia 82, Dartmouth 68; Boston Univ. 60, Connecticut 58; Navy 76, North Carolina 63. **Semifinals**—West Virginia 95, St. Joseph's-PA 92; Boston Univ. 62, Navy 55. **Third Place**—Navy 70, St. Joseph's-PA 56. **Final**—West Virginia 86, Boston Univ. 82.

Mideast Regional

First Round—Louisville 77, Eastern Ky. 63; Marquette 89, Bowling Green 71. **Semifinals**—Louisville 76, Kentucky 61; Michigan St. 74, Marquette 69. **Third Place**—Kentucky 98, Marquette 69. **Final**—Louisville 88, Michigan St. 81.

Midwest Regional

First Round—DePaul 57, Portland 56. **Semifinals**—Kansas St. 102, DePaul 70; Cincinnati 77, TCU 73. **Third Place**—TCU 71, DePaul 65. **Final**—Cincinnati 85, Kansas St. 75.

West Regional

First Round—Idaho St. 62, New Mexico St. 61. **Semifinals**—St.Mary's-CA 80, Idaho St. 71; California 71, Utah 53. **Third Place**—Idaho St. 71, Utah 65. **Final**—California 66, St.Mary's-CA 46.

FINAL FOUR
at Freedom Hall, Louisville

Semifinals—West Virginia 94, Louisville 79; California 64, Cincinnati 58. **Third Place**—Cincinnati 98, Louisville 85. **Championship**—California 71, West Virginia 70.

Most Outstanding Player—Jerry West, W.Virginia. **All-Tournament**—West, W.Virginia; Denny Fitzpatrick and Darrall Imhoff, California; Oscar Robertson, Cincinnati; Don Goldstein, Louisville.

NIT Tournament (12 teams)
All games at Madison Sq.Garden, New York

First Round—Butler 94, Fordham 80; NYU 90, Denver 81; Providence 68, Manhattan 66; St.John's 75, Villanova 67. **Quarterfinals**—Bradley 83, Butler 77; NYU 63, Oklahoma 48; Providence 75, St.Louis 72 (2 OT); St.John's 82, St.Bonaventure 74. **Semifinals**—Bradley 59, NYU 57; St.John's 76, Providence 55. **Third Place**—NYU 71, Providence 57. **Championship**—St.John's 76, Bradley 71 (OT). **Most Valuable Player**—Tony Jackson, St.John's.

Player of the Year

Oscar Robertson, Cincinnati . . . . UPI,USBWA,Helms

Coaches of the Year

Adolph Rupp, Kentucky . . . . .UPI
Eddie Hickey, Marquette . . . . .USBWA

Consensus All-America
(In alphabetical order)

First Team
Bob Boozer, Kansas St.; Johnny Cox, Kentucky; Bailey Howell, Mississippi St.; Oscar Robertson, Cincinnati; Jerry West, West Virginia.

Second Team
Leo Byrd, Marshall; Johnny Green, Michigan St.; Tom Hawkins, Notre Dame; Don Hennon, Pittsburgh; Alan Seiden, St.John's.

1960

For the second straight year, Oscar Robertson and Cincinnati ran into California in the Final Four semifinals and lost. This time, they were both No.1 when they met—Cincy in the AP poll, Cal according to UPI. The Golden Bears beat the Bearcats, 77-69, and the Big O ended his college career with three scoring titles, three Player of the Year awards, and no NCAA title.

Cal, now in position to join Oklahoma A&M, Kentucky and San Francisco as the NCAA's only repeat champions, advanced to the championship game against No.3 Ohio State. It shaped up as a classic final: OSU's No.1 offense (90.5 ppg) vs Cal's No.1 defense (49.5 ppg). All-America sophomore Jerry Lucas of the Buckeyes vs. All-America senior Darrall Imhoff of the Bears in the pivot.

Ohio State shot 68.4 from the field and won basketball's version of the Rose Bowl (Big 10 vs AAWU) by 20 points. The Buckeyes' sophomore center Jerry Lucas was named the outstanding player in the tournament, the first time since 1956 that the MVP award went to a member of the championship team.

In New York, No.4 Bradley won its second NIT title, beating 14th-ranked Providence, 88-72 in the final. The losing Friars did have the tourney MVP, however, in guard Lenny Wilkens.

And for the second year in a row, Mississippi State won the SEC championship and declined to play in the integrated NCAA tournament.

Final AP Top 20

Writers' poll taken before major tournaments.

	Before Tourns	Head Coach	Final Record
1 Cincinnati	25-1	George Smith	28-2
2 California	24-1	Pete Newell	28-2
3 Ohio St.	21-3	Fred Taylor	25-3
4 Bradley	24-2	Chuck Orsborn	27-2
5 W.Virginia	24-4	Fred Schaus	26-5
6 Utah	24-2	Jack Gardner	26-3
7 Indiana	20-4	Branch McCracken	same
8 Utah St.	22-4	Cecil Baker	24-5
9 St.Bona.	19-3	Eddie Donovan	21-5
10 Miami,FL	23-3	Bruce Hale	23-4
11 Auburn	19-3	Joel Eaves	same
12 NYU	19-4	Lou Rossini	22-5
13 Ga.Tech	21-5	Whack Hyder	22-6
14 Providence	21-4	Joe Mullaney	24-5
15 St.Louis	19-7	John Benington	19-8
16 Holy Cross	20-5	Roy Leenig	20-6
17 Villanova	19-5	Al Severance	20-6
18 Duke	15-10	Vic Bubas	17-11
19 W.Forest	21-7	Bones McKinney	same
20 St.John's	17-7	Joe Lapchick	17-8

Note: Ohio St. won the NCAAs and Bradley won the NIT.

Major Conference Champions

Conference	Regular Season	Tournament
AAWU	California (11-1)	—
ACC	W.Forest/N.Caro.(12-2)	Duke
Big 8	Kansas/Kan.St.(10-4)	—
Big 10	Ohio St.(13-1)	—
Ivy	Princeton (11-3)	—
Mo.Valley	Cincinnati (13-1)	—
SEC	Auburn (12-2)	—
Southern	Va.Tech (12-1)	W.Virginia
SWC	Texas (11-3)	—

NCAA Tournament (25 teams)

East Regional

First Round—Duke 84, Princeton 60; West Virginia 94, Navy 86; NYU 78, Connecticut 59. **Semifinals**—Duke 58, St.Joseph's-PA 56; NYU 82, West Virginia 81. **Third Place**—West Virginia 106, St.Joseph's-PA 100. **Final**—NYU 74, Duke 59.

Mideast Regional

First Round—Ohio Univ. 74, Notre Dame 66; Western Ky. 107, Miami-FL 84. **Semifinals**— Georgia Tech 57, Ohio Univ. 54; Ohio St. 98, Western Ky. 79. **Third Place**—Western Ky. 97, Ohio Univ. 87. **Final**—Ohio St. 86, Georgia Tech 69.

Midwest Regional

First Round—DePaul 69, Air Force 63. **Semifinals**—Cincinnati 99, DePaul 59; Kansas 90, Texas 81. **Third Place**—DePaul 67, Texas 61. **Final**—Cincinnati 82, Kansas 71.

West Regional

First Round—California 71, Idaho St. 44; Oregon 68, New Mexico St. 60; Utah 80, USC 73. **Semifinals**—California 69, Santa Clara 49; Oregon 65, Utah 54. **Third Place**—Utah 89, Santa Clara 81. **Final**—California 70, Oregon 49.

FINAL FOUR

at the Cow Palace, San Francisco

Semifinals—Ohio St.76, NYU 54; California 77, Cincinnati 69. **Third Place**—Cincinnati 95, NYU 71. **Championship**—Ohio St.75, California 55. **Most Outstanding Player:** Jerry Lucas, Ohio St. **All-Tournament:** Lucas and Mel Nowell, Ohio St.; Darrall Imhoff, California; Oscar Robertson, Cincinnati; Tom (Satch) Sanders, NYU.

NIT Tournament (12 teams)

All games at Madison Sq.Garden, New York

First Round—Villanova 88, Detroit 86; Providence 71, Memphis St. 70; St.Bonaventure 94, Holy Cross 81; Dayton 72, Temple 51. **Quarterfinals**—Utah St. 73, Villanova 72 (OT); Providence 64, St.Louis 53; Bradley 78, Dayton 64; St.Bonaventure 106, St.John's 71. **Semifinals**—Bradley 82, St.Bonaventure 71; Providence 68, Utah St.62. **Third Place**—Utah St.99, St.Bonaventure 93. **Championship**—Bradley 88, Providence 72.

Most Valuable Player—Lenny Wilkens, Providence.

Player of the Year

Oscar Robertson, Cincinnati . . . . UPI,USBWA,Helms

Coach of the Year

Pete Newell, California . . . . UPI,USBWA

Consensus All-America

(By position, in alphabetical order)

First Team

Darrall Imhoff, California; Jerry Lucas, Ohio St.; Oscar Robertson, Cincinnati; Tom Stith, St.Bonaventure; Jerry West, W.Virginia.

Second Team

Terry Dischinger, Purdue; Tony Jackson, St.John's; Roger Kaiser, Georgia Tech; Lee Shaffer, North Carolina; Lenny Wilkens, Providence.

1961

The NCAA title that eluded Oscar Robertson for three years was brought home by Cincinnati in 1961 on one of the most memorable evenings in Final Four history.

On the last night of the season in Kansas City, two teams from the same state (Cincy and defending champ Ohio State) met in the championship game, the Buckeyes were ranked No.1 and the Bearcats No.2, and both the title and consolation games went into overtime. The preliminary for third place actually went four OT periods before St.Joseph's beat Utah, 127-120.

In the Final, a layup by Ohio State's Bobby Knight sent the game into OT, tied at 61. Cincy, led by Paul Hogue and Bob Wiesenhahn, took it from there, winning 70-65. Jerry Lucas scored 27 points for the losers and was named MVP for the second straight year.

Ohio State reached the Final unbeaten (some said "unbeatable") in 27 games. Lucas, a junior, was everybody's pick for Player of the Year, while Buckeyes' coach Fred Taylor was the unanimous choice for Coach of the Year.

At the NIT, Providence, a finalist in 1960, won the title with a 62-59 victory over St. Louis.

Elsewhere, 10 years after the point-shaving scandals of the '50s, the New York District Attorney's office uncovered another one, this time involving 37 players on 22 teams from Connecticut to Detroit to Mississippi St.

Final AP Top 20

Writers' poll taken before major tournaments.

	Before Tourns	Head Coach	Final Record
1 Ohio St.	24-0	Fred Taylor	27-1
2 **Cincinnati**	23-3	Ed Jucker	27-3
3 St.Bona.	22-3	Eddie Donovan	24-4
4 Kansas St.	22-3	Tex Winter	23-4
5 N.Carolina	19-4	Frank McGuire	same
6 Bradley	21-5	Chuck Orsborn	same
7 USC	20-6	Forrest Twogood	21-8
8 Iowa	18-6	Sharm Scheuerman	same
9 W.Virginia	23-4	George King	same
10 Duke	22-6	Vic Bubas	same
11 Utah	21-6	Jack Gardner	23-8
12 Texas Tech	14-9	Polk Robison	15-10
13 Niagara	16-4	Taps Gallagher	16-5
14 Memphis St.	20-2	Bob Vanatta	20-3
15 W.Forest	17-10	Bones McKinney	19-11
16 St.John's	20-4	Joe Lapchick	20-5
17 St.Joe's,PA	22-4	Jack Ramsay	25-5
18 Drake	19-7	Maury John	same
19 Holy Cross	19-4	Roy Leenig	22-5
20 Kentucky	18-8	Adolph Rupp	19-9

Note: Cincinnati won the NCAAs and unranked Providence (20-5, Joe Mullaney, 24-5) won the NIT.

Major Conference Champions

Conference	Regular Season	Tournament
AAWU	USC (9-3)	—
ACC	North Carolina (12-2)	Wake Forest
Big 8	Kansas St.(13-1)	—
Big 10	Ohio St.(14-0)	—
Ivy	Princeton (11-3)	—
Mo.Valley	Cincinnati (10-2)	—
SEC	Mississippi St.(11-3)	—
Southern	West Virginia (11-1)	Geo.Wash.
SWC	Texas Tech (11-3)	—

NCAA Tournament (24 teams)

East Regional

First Round—Princeton 84, Geo.Washington 67; St.Bonaventure 86, Rhode Island 76; Wake Forest 97, St.John's 74. **Semifinals**—St.Joseph's-PA 72, Princeton 67; Wake Forest 78, St.Bonaventure 73. **Third Place**—St.Bonaventure 85, Princeton 67. **Final**—St. Joseph's-PA 96, Wake Forest 86.

Mideast Regional

First Round—Louisville 76, Ohio Univ. 70; Morehead St. 71, Xavier-OH 66. **Semifinals**—Ohio St. 56, Louisville 55; Kentucky 71, Morehead St. 64. **Third Place**—Louisville 83, Morehead St. 61. **Final**—Ohio St. 87, Kentucky 74.

Midwest Regional

First Round—Houston 77, Marquette 61. **Semifinals**—Kansas St. 75, Houston 64; Cincinnati 78, Texas Tech 55. **Third Place**—Texas Tech 69, Houston 67. **Final**—Cincinnati 69, Kansas St. 64.

West Regional

First Round—Arizona St. 72, Seattle 70; USC 81, Oregon 79. **Semifinals**—Arizona St. 86, USC 71; Utah 91, Loyola-CA 75. **Third Place**—Loyola-CA 69, USC 67. **Final**—Utah 88, Arizona 80.

FINAL FOUR
at Municipal Auditorium, Kansas City

Semifinals—Ohio St. 95, St. Joseph's- PA 69; Cincinnati 82, Utah 67. **Third Place**—St. Joseph's-PA 127, Utah 120 (4 OT). **Championship**—Cincinnati 70, Ohio St. 65 (OT).

Most Outstanding Player—Jerry Lucas, Ohio St. **All-Tournament**—Lucas and Larry Siegfried, Ohio St.; Carl Bouldin and Bob Wiesenhahn, Cincinnati; Jack Egan, St.Joseph's-PA.

NIT Tournament (12 teams)
All games at Madison Sq.Garden, New York

First Round—St.Louis 58, Miami-FL 56; Holy Cross 86, Detroit 82; Temple 79, Army 66; Providence 73, DePaul 67. **Quarterfinals**—St.Louis 59, Colorado St. 53; Holy Cross 81, Memphis St. 69; Dayton 62, Temple 60; Providence 71, Niagara 68. **Semifinals**—St.Louis 67, Dayton 60; Providence 90, Holy Cross 83 (OT). **Third Place**—Holy Cross 85, Dayton 67. **Championship**—Providence 62, St.Louis 59.

Most Valuable Player—Vin Ernst, Providence.

Player of the Year

Jerry Lucas, Ohio St . . . . UPI,USBWA,AP,Helms

Coach of the Year

Fred Taylor, Ohio St . . . . UPI,USBWA

Consensus All-America
(By position, in alphabetical order)

First Team
Terry Dischinger, Purdue; Roger Kaiser, Georgia Tech; Jerry Lucas, Ohio St.; Tom Stith, St.Bonaventure; Chet Walker, Bradley;

Second Team
Walt Bellamy, Indiana; Frank Burgess, Gonzaga; Tony Jackson, St. John's; Billy McGill, Utah; Larry Siegfried, Ohio St.

1962

Cincinnati and Ohio State, again ranked 1-2 at the end of the regular season, became the first teams to play each other in two consecutive NCAA championship games. Each had something to prove in Louisville—the Bearcats that their 1961 title was not a fluke, the Buckeyes that it was.

Unlike a year ago, this game was not close. Cincy led by eight at the half and won by 12 as Paul Hogue and Tom Thacker led the way with 22 and 21 points, respectively. When it was over, the Bearcats' second year coach Ed Jucker had a pair of NCAA titles in two tries.

Ohio State's chances took a bad turn in the semifinal against Billy Packer and Wake Forest when consensus Player of the Year Jerry Lucas injured his left knee.

Wake Forest won the consolation game, beating UCLA by two points. It was the Bruins' first trip to the Final Four and John Wooden would be back.

In New York, Dayton finally won the NIT. The Flyers had reached the finals five times in the 1950s and lost them all. But that was then and this was now. Final score: Dayton 73, St. John's 67. The MVP award went to the Flyers' 6-10 center Bill Chmielewski.

The nation's leading scorer was Utah All-America Billy McGill, who averaged 38.8 points a game. The seventh-ranked Utes won the Skyline Conference, but were ineligible for tournament play.

Final AP Top 20

Writers' poll taken before major tournaments.

	Before Tours	Head Coach	Final Record
1 Ohio St.	23-1	Fred Taylor	26-2
2 **Cincinnati**	25-2	Ed Jucker	29-2
3 Kentucky	22-2	Adolph Rupp	23-3
4 Miss.St.	19-6	Babe McCarthy	same
5 Bradley	21-6	Chuck Orsborn	21-7
6 Kansas St.	22-3	Tex Winter	same
7 Utah	23-3	Jack Gardner	same
8 Bowl.Green	21-3	Harold Anderson	same
9 Colorado	18-6	Sox Walseth	19-7
10 Duke	20-5	Vic Bubas	same
11 Loyola,IL	21-3	George Ireland	23-4
12 St.John's	19-4	Joe Lapchick	21-5
13 W.Forest	18-8	Bones McKinney	22-9
14 Oregon St.	22-4	Slats Gill	24-5
15 W.Virginia	24-5	George King	24-6
16 Arizona St.	23-3	Ned Wulk	23-4
17 Duquesne	20-5	Red Manning	22-7
18 Utah St.	21-5	Ladell Andersen	22-7
19 UCLA	16-9	John Wooden	18-11
20 Villanova	19-6	Jack Kraft	21-7

Note: Cincinnati won the NCAAs and unranked Dayton (20-6, Tom Blackburn, 24-6) won the NIT.

Major Conference Champions

Conference	Regular Season	Tournament
AAWU	UCLA (10-2)	—
ACC	Wake Forest (12-2)	Wake Forest
Big 8	Colorado (13-1)	—
Big 10	Ohio St.(13-1)	—
Ivy	Yale (13-1)	—
Mo.Valley	Cinn./Bradley (10-2)	—
SEC	Kentucky/Miss.St.(13-1)	—
Southern	West Virginia (12-1)	West Va.
SWC	Texas Tech*/SMU (11-3)	—

*Won playoff for league championship.

NCAA Tournament (25 teams)

East Regional

First Round—Wake Forest 92, Yale 82 (OT); NYU 70, Massachusetts 50; Villanova 90, West Virginia 75. **Semifinals**—Wake Forest 96, St.Joseph's-PA 85; Villanova 79, NYU 76. **Third Place**—NYU 94, St. Joseph's-PA 85. **Final**—Wake Forest 79, Villanova 69.

Mideast Regional

First Round—Butler 56, Bowling Green 55; Western Ky. 90, Detroit 81. **Semifinals**—Kentucky 81, Butler 60; Ohio St. 93, Western Ky. 73. **Third Place**—Butler 87, Western Ky. 86 (OT). **Final**—Ohio St. 74, Kentucky 64.

Midwest Regional

First Round—Texas Tech 68, Air Force 66; Creighton 87, Memphis St. 83. **Semifinals**—Colorado 67, Texas Tech 60; Cincinnati 66, Creighton 46. **Third Place**—Creighton 63, Texas Tech 61. **Final**—Cincinnati 73, Colorado 46.

West Regional

First Round—Oregon St. 69, Seattle 65 (OT); Utah St. 78, Arizona St. 73. **Semifinals**—Oregon St. 69, Pepperdine 67; UCLA 73, Utah St. 62. **Third Place**—Pepperdine 75, Utah St. 71. **Final**—UCLA 88, Oregon St. 69.

FINAL FOUR

at Freedom Hall, Louisville

Semifinals—Ohio St. 84, Wake Forest 68; Cincinnati 72, UCLA 70. **Third Place**—Wake Forest 82, UCLA 80. **Championship**—Cincinnati 71, Ohio St. 59. **Most Outstanding Player**—Paul Hogue, Cincinnati. **All-Tournament**—Hogue and Tom Thacker, Cincinnati; John Havlicek and Jerry Lucas, Ohio St.; Len Chappell, Wake Forest.

NIT Tournament (12 teams)

All games at Madison Sq.Garden, New York

First Round—Dayton 79, Wichita 71; Temple 80, Providence 78; Holy Cross 71, Colorado St. 71; Duquesne 70, Navy 58. **Quarterfinals**—Dayton 94, Houston 77; Loyola-IL 75, Temple 64; Duquesne 88, Bradley 85; St.John's 80, Holy Cross 74. **Semifinals**—Dayton 98, Loyola-IL 82; St.John's 76, Duquesne 65. **Third Place**—Loyola-IL 75, Duquesne 84. **Championship**—Dayton 73, St.John's 67. **Most Valuable Player**—Bill Chmielewski, Dayton.

Players of the Year

Jerry Lucas, Ohio St . . . . UPI,USBWA,AP
Paul Hogue, Cincinnati . . . . Helms

Coach of the Year

Fred Taylor, Ohio St . . . . UPI,USBWA

Consensus All-America

(By position, in alphabetical order)

First Team

Len Chappell, Wake Forest; Terry Dischinger, Purdue; Jerry Lucas, Ohio St.; Billy McGill, Utah; Chet Walker, Bradley.

Second Team

Jack Foley, Holy Cross; John Havlicek, Ohio St.; Art Heyman, Duke; Cotton Nash, Kentucky; John Rudometkin, USC; Rod Thorn, W.Virginia.

1963

Since the beginning of the NCAA tournament in 1939, no team had won three straight titles. In fact, no team had reached three straight championship games. Until Cincinnati.

The Bearcats were on as impressive a roll as any college team had ever been. Over the last six years, they had won the tough Missouri Valley Conference six times, finished the regular season ranked either No.1 or No.2 five times, and reached the Final Four five years running.

Too bad they had to play Cinderella for the title in 1963.

Despite its No.3 ranking and a scoring average of 91.8, nobody expected Loyola of Chicago to beat Cincinnati, especially when the Ramblers fell behind by 15 in the second half. But Loyola rallied to send the game into OT and won the title on a last second rebound and basket by Vic Rouse.

A footnote: SEC champ Mississippi State finally agreed to play in the integrated NCAA tourney and lost its opening game to Loyola, the first nationally prominent college team to start four black players.

Final AP Top 10
Writers' poll taken before major tournaments. From 1962-63 through 1967-68, AP ranked only 10 teams.

	Before Tourns	Head Coach	Final Record
1 Cincinnati	23-1	Ed Jucker	26-2
2 Duke	24-2	Vic Bubas	27-3
3 Loyola,IL	24-2	George Ireland	29-2
4 Arizona St.	24-2	Ned Wulk	26-3
5 Wichita	19-7	Ralph Miller	19-8
6 Miss.St.	21-5	Babe McCarthy	22-6
7 Ohio St.	20-4	Fred Taylor	same
8 Illinois	19-5	Harry Combes	20-6
9 NYU	17-3	Lou Rossini	18-5
10 Colorado	18-6	Sox Walseth	19-7

Note: Loyola,IL won the NCAAs.

Second 10
Taken from final UPI coaches' poll.

11 Stanford	16-9	Howie Dallmar	same
12 Texas	18-6	Harold Bradley	20-7
13 Providence	21-4	Joe Mullaney	24-4
14 Oregon St.	19-7	Slats Gill	22-9
15 UCLA	20-7	John Wooden	20-9
16 St.Joe's,PA	21-4	Jack Ramsay	23-5
W.Virginia	21-7	George King	23-8
18 Bowl.Green	18-6	Harold Anderson	19-8
19 Kansas St.	16-9	Tex Winter	same
Seattle	21-5	Vince Cazzetta & Clair Markey	21-6

Note: Providence won the NIT.

Major Conference Champions

Conference	Regular Season	Tournament
AAWU	UCLA/Stanford (7-5)	—
ACC	Duke (14-0)	Duke
Big 8	Colorado/Kan.St.(11-3)	—
Big 10	Ohio St./Illinois (11-3)	—
Ivy	Princeton*/Yale (11-3)	—
Mo.Valley	Cincinnati (11-1)	—
SEC	Mississippi St.(12-2)	—
Southern	West Virginia (11-2)	West Va.
SWC	Texas (13-1)	—
WAC	Arizona St.(9-1)	—

*Won playoff for league championship.

NCAA Tournament (25 teams)
East Regional
First Round—NYU 93, Pittsburgh 83; West Virginia 77, Connecticut 71; St.Joseph's-PA 82, Princeton 81. **Semifinals**—Duke 81, NYU 76; St.Joseph's-PA 97; West Virginia 88. **Third Place**—West Virginia 83, NYU 73. **Final**—Duke 73, St.Joseph's-PA 59.

Mideast Regional
First Round—Bowling Green 77, Notre Dame 72; Loyola-IL 111, Tennessee Tech 42. **Semifinals**—Illinois 70, Bowling Green 67; Loyola-IL 61, Mississippi St. 51. **Third Place**—Mississippi St. 65, Bowling Green 60. **Final**—Loyola-IL 79, Illinois 64.

Midwest Regional
First Round—Oklahoma City 70, Colorado St. 67; Texas 65, Texas Western 47. **Semifinals**—Colorado 78, Oklahoma City 72; Cincinnati 73, Texas 68. **Third Place**—Texas 90, Oklahoma City 83. **Final**—Cincinnati 67, Colorado 60.

West Regional
First Round—Arizona St. 79, Utah St. 75; Oregon St. 70, Seattle 66. **Semifinals**—Arizona St. 93, UCLA 79; Oregon St. 65, San Francisco 61. **Third Place**—San Francisco 76, UCLA 75. **Final**—Oregon St. 83, Arizona St. 65.

FINAL FOUR
at Freedom Hall, Louisville
Semifinals—Loyola-IL 94, Duke 75; Cincinnati 80, Oregon St. 46. **Third Place**—Duke 85, Oregon St. 63. **Championship**—Loyola-IL 60, Cincinnati 58 (OT). **Most Outstanding Player**—Art Heyman, Duke. **All-Tournament**—Heyman, Duke; Les Hunter, Loyola-IL; Ron Bonham, Tom Thacker and George Wilson, Cincinnati.

NIT Tournament (12 teams)
All games at Madison Sq.Garden, New York

First Round—Villanova 63, DePaul 51; Memphis St. 70, Fordham 49; St.Louis 63, La Salle 61; Miami-FL 71, St.Francis-NY 70. **Quarterfinals**—Villanova 54, Wichita 53; Canisius 76, Memphis St. 67; Marquette 84, St.Louis 49; Providence 106, Miami-FL 96. **Semifinals**—Providence 70, Marquette 64; Canisius 61, Villanova 46. **Third Place**—Marquette 66, Villanova 58. **Championship**—Providence 81, Canisius 66. **Most Valuable Player**—Ray Flynn, Providence.

Player of the Year
Art Heyman, Duke .... UPI,USBWA,AP,Helms

Coach of the Year
Ed Jucker, Cincinnati .... UPI,USBWA

Consensus All-America
(By position, in alphabetical order)

First Team
Ron Bonham, Cincinnati; Jerry Harkness, Loyola; Art Heyman, Duke; Barry Kramer, NYU; Tom Thacker, Cincinnati.

Second Team
Gary Bradds, Ohio St.; Bill Green, Colorado St.; Cotton Nash, Kentucky; Rod Thorn, W.Virginia; Nate Thurmond, Bowling Green.

1964

UCLA made its first trip to the Final Four in 1962 and finished fourth. Two years later, the Bruins returned and won it all. Little did anyone know that John Wooden & Co. would win 9 more titles in the next 11 years.

Led by the backcourt of Walt Hazzard and Gail Goodrich, UCLA was undefeated during the regular season and entered the NCAAs ranked No.1. At the Final Four in Kansas City, the Bruins beat local favorite Kansas State in the semifinals, snapping the Wildcats' 13-game win streak in the process. No.3 Duke beat No.2 Michigan in the other semifinal.

In the championship game, UCLA—with no players over 6-5—beat the taller and slower Blue Devils by 15 to give coach Wooden his first championship.

Unranked Bradley won the NIT for the third time in eight years, routing No.14 New Mexico by 32 in the final.

Seven players averaged better than 30 points a game in 1964, led by Bowling Green's Howie Komives, who averaged 36.7.

Final AP Top 10

Writers' poll taken before major tournaments. From 1962-63 through 1967-68, AP ranked only 10 teams.

		Before Tourns	Head Coach	Final Record
1	UCLA	26-0	John Wooden	30-0
2	Michigan	20-4	Dave Strack	23-5
3	Duke	23-4	Vic Bubas	26-5
4	Kentucky	21-4	Adolph Rupp	21-6
5	Wichita St.	22-5	Ralph Miller	23-6
6	Oregon St.	25-3	Slats Gill	25-4
7	Villanova	22-3	Jack Kraft	24-4
8	Loyola,IL	20-5	George Ireland	22-6
9	DePaul	21-3	Ray Meyer	21-4
10	Davidson	22-4	Lefty Driesell	same

Note: UCLA won the NCAAs.

Second 10

Taken from final UPI coaches' poll.

11	TX Western	23-2	Don Haskins	25-3
12	Kansas St.	20-5	Tex Winter	22-7
13	Drake	20-6	Maury John	21-7
	San Fran.	22-4	Peter Peletta	23-5
15	Utah St.	20-6	Ladell Andersen	21-8
16	Ohio St.	16-8	Fred Taylor	same
	New Mexico	21-5	Bob King	23-6
18	Texas A&M	18-6	Shelby Metcalf	18-7
19	Arizona St.	16-10	Ned Wulk	16-11
	Providence	20-5	Joe Mullaney	20-6

Note: Unranked Bradley (20-6, Chuck Orsborn, 23-6) won the NIT.

Major Conference Champions

Conference	Regular Season	Tournament
AAWU	UCLA (15-0)	—
ACC	Duke (13-1)	Duke
Big 8	Kansas St.(12-2)	—
Big 10	Michigan/Ohio St.(11-3)	—
Ivy	Princeton (12-2)	—
Mo.Valley	Wichita St./Drake (10-2)	—
SEC	Kentucky (11-3)	—
Southern	Davidson (9-2)	VMI
SWC	Texas A&M (13-1)	—
WAC	N.Mexico/Ariz.St.(7-3)	—

NCAA Tournament (25 teams)

East Regional

First Round—Villanova 77, Providence 66; Connecticut 53, Temple 48; Princeton 86, VMI 60. **Semifinals**—Duke 87, Villanova 73; Connecticut 52, Princeton 50. **Third Place**—Villanova 74, Princeton 62. **Final**—Duke 101, Connecticut 54.

Mideast Regional

First Round—Ohio Univ. 71, Louisville 69; Loyola-IL 101, Murray St. 91. **Semifinals**—Ohio Univ. 85, Kentucky 69; Michigan 84, Loyola-IL 80. **Third Place**—Loyola-IL 100, Kentucky 91. **Final**—Michigan 69, Ohio Univ. 57.

Midwest Regional

First Round—Creighton 89, Oklahoma City 78; Texas Western 68, Texas A&M 62. **Semifinals**—Wichita St. 84, Creighton 68; Kansas St. 64, Texas Western 60. **Third Place**—Texas Western 63, Creighton 52. **Final**—Kansas St. 94, Wichita St. 86.

West Regional

First Round—Seattle 61, Oregon St. 57; Utah St. 92, Arizona St. 90. **Semifinals**—UCLA 95, Seattle 90; San Francisco 64, Utah St. 58. **Third Place**—Seattle 88, Utah St. 78. **Final**—UCLA 76, San Francisco 72.

FINAL FOUR

at Municipal Auditorium, Kansas City

Semifinals—Duke 91, Michigan 80; UCLA 90, Kansas St. 84. **Third Place**—Michigan 100, Kansas St. 90. **Championship**—UCLA 98, Duke 83. **Most Outstanding Player**—Walt Hazzard, UCLA. **All-Tournament**—Hazzard and Gail Goodrich, UCLA; Jeff Mullins, Duke; Bill Buntin, Michigan; Willie Murrell, Kansas St.

NIT Tournament (12 teams)

All games at Madison Sq.Garden, New York

First Round—St.Joseph's-PA 86, Miami-FL 76; NYU 77, Syracuse 68; Army 64, St.Bonaventure 62; Drake 87, Pittsburgh 82. **Quarterfinals**—Bradley 83, St.Joseph's-PA 81; NYU 79, DePaul 66; New Mexico 65, Drake 60; Army 67, Duquesne 65 (OT). **Semifinals**—New Mexico 72, NYU 65; Bradley 67, Army 52. **Third Place**—Army 60, NYU 59. **Championship**—Bradley 86, New Mexico 54. **Most Valuable Player**—Lavern Tart, Bradley.

Players of the Year

Gary Bradds, Ohio St .... UPI,AP
Walt Hazzard, UCLA .... USBWA,Helms

Coach of the Year

John Wooden, UCLA .... UPI,USBWA

Consensus All-America

(By position, in alphabetical order)

First Team

Gary Bradds, Ohio St.; Bill Bradley, Princeton; Walt Hazzard, UCLA; Cotton Nash, Kentucky; Dave Stallworth, Wichita St.

Second Team

Ron Bonham, Cincinnati; Mel Counts, Oregon St.; Fred Hetzel, Davidson; Jeff Mullins, Duke; Cazzie Russell, Michigan.

1965

The Game of the Year came on Dec.30, 1964, when Cazzie Russell and Michigan beat Bill Bradley and Princeton by two points in the finals of the Holiday Festival at Madison Square Garden.

Bradley fouled out with less than five minutes to go after scoring 41 points to give the Tigers a 12-point lead over the No.1 Wolverines. The ovation Bradley received as he left the game rocked the Garden and has stayed with fans who were there long after the final score has faded from memory.

The two teams met again in the NCAA semifinals in Portland, but this time Michigan won easily, 93-76. Player of the Year and tourney MVP Bradley said goodbye to college ball with 58 points in the consolation game, which overshadowed defending champ UCLA's nine-point victory over Michigan in the title game.

Unranked St.John's upset No.8 Villanova by four to win the NIT, a retirement gift to coach and basketball legend Joe Lapchick.

Final AP Top 10
Writers' poll taken before major tournaments. From 1962-63 through 1967-68, AP ranked only 10 teams.

	Before Turns	Head Coach	Final Record
1 Michigan	21-3	Dave Strack	24-4
2 UCLA	24-2	John Wooden	28-2
3 St.Joe's,PA	25-1	Jack Ramsay	26-3
4 Providence	22-1	Joe Mullaney	24-2
5 Vanderbilt	23-3	Roy Skinner	24-4
6 Davidson	24-2	Lefty Driesell	same
7 Minnesota	19-5	John Kundla	same
8 Villanova	21-4	Jack Kraft	23-5
9 BYU	21-5	Stan Watts	21-7
10 Duke	20-5	Vic Bubas	same

Note: UCLA won the NCAAs.

Second 10
Taken from final UPI coaches' poll.

11 San Fran.	23-4	Peter Peletta	24-5
12 N.C.State	20-4	Press Maravich	21-5
13 Okla. St.	19-6	Hank Iba	20-7
14 Wichita St.	19-7	Gary Thompson	21-9
15 Connecticut	23-2	Fred Shabel	23-3
16 Illinois	18-6	Harry Combes	same
17 Tennessee	20-5	Ray Mears	same
18 Indiana	19-5	Branch McCracken	same
19 Miami,FL	22-4	Bruce Hale	same
20 Dayton	20-6	Don Donoher	22-7

Note: Unranked St.John's (17-8, Joe Lapchick, 21-8) won the NIT.

Major Conference Champions

Conference	Regular Season	Tournament
AAWU	UCLA (14-0)	—
ACC	Duke (11-3)	N.C.State
Big 8	Oklahoma St.(12-2)	—
Big 10	Michigan (13-1)	—
Ivy	Princeton (13-1)	—
Mo.Valley	Wichita St.(11-3)	—
SEC	Vanderbilt (15-1)	—
Southern	Davidson (12-0)	West Va.
SWC	SMU*/Texas (10-4)	—
WAC	BYU (8-2)	—

*Won playoff for league championship.

NCAA Tournament (23 teams)
East Regional
First Round—Princeton 60, Penn St. 58; St.Joseph's-PA 67, Connecticut 61; Providence 91, West Virginia 67. **Semifinals**—Princeton 66, N.C.State 48; Providence 81, St.Joseph's-PA 73 (OT). **Third Place**—N.C.State 103, St.Joseph's-PA 81. **Final**—Princeton 109, Providence 69.

Mideast Regional
First Round—Dayton 66, Ohio Univ. 65; DePaul 99, Eastern Ky. 52. **Semifinals**—Michigan 98, Dayton 71; Vanderbilt 83, DePaul 78 (OT). **Third Place**—Dayton 74, DePaul 69. **Final**—Michigan 87, Vanderbilt 85.

Midwest Regional
First Round—Houston 99, Notre Dame 98. **Semifinals**—Oklahoma St. 75, Houston 60; Wichita St. 86, SMU 87. **Third Place**—SMU 89, Houston 87. **Final**—Wichita St. 54, Oklahoma St. 46.

West Regional
First Round—Oklahoma City 70, Colorado St. 68. **Semifinals**—San Francisco 91, Oklahoma City 67; UCLA 100, BYU 76. **Third Place**—Oklahoma City 112, BYU 93. **Final**—UCLA 101, San Francisco 93.

FINAL FOUR
at Memorial Coliseum, Portland,OR
Semifinals—Michigan 93, Princeton 76; UCLA 108, Wichita St. 89. **Third Place**—Princeton 118, Wichita St. 82. **Championship**—UCLA 91, Michigan 80. **Most Outstanding Player**—Bill Bradley, Princeton. **All-Tournament**—Bradley, Princeton; Gail Goodrich, Edgar Lacey and Kenny Washington, UCLA; Cazzie Russell, Michigan.

NIT Tournament (14 teams)
All games at Madison Sq.Garden, New York
First Round—St.John's 114, Boston College 92; Manhattan 71, Texas Western 53; Western Ky. 57, Fordham 53; Army 70, St.Louis 66; NYU 71, Bradley 70; Detroit 93, La Salle 86. **Quarterfinals**—St.John's 61, New Mexico 54; Villanova 73, Manhattan 71; NYU 87, Detroit 76; Army 58, Western Ky 54. **Semifinals**—Villanova 91, NYU 69; St.John's 67, Army 60. **Third Place**—Army 75, NYU 74. **Championship**—St.John's 55, Villanova 51.
Most Valuable Player—Ken McIntyre, St.John's.

Players of the Year
Bill Bradley, Princeton . . . UPI,USBWA,AP,Helms(tie)
Gail Goodrich, UCLA . . . . Helms(tie)

Coaches of the Year
Dave Strack, Michigan . . . . UPI
Butch vanBreda Kolff, Princeton . . . . USBWA

Consensus All-America
(By position, in alphabetical order)
First Team
Rick Barry, Miami (FL); Bill Bradley, Princeton; Gail Goodrich, UCLA; Fred Hetzel, Davidson; Cazzie Russell, Michigan
Second Team
Bill Buntin, Michigan; Wayne Estes, Utah St.; Clyde Lee, Vanderbilt; Dave Schellhase, Purdue; Dave Stallworth, Wichita St.

1966

UCLA lost the AAWU (now Pac-10) title to Oregon State in 1965-66 and couldn't defend its NCAA crown. That opened the door for Texas Western (now UTEP) to emerge from the western half of the tournament draw and meet top-ranked Kentucky for the championship.

Kentucky, NCAA champions four times under Adolph Rupp, came to College Park, Md., looking to give its legendary coach an unprecedented fifth national title.

It wasn't to be. Kentucky, with five white starters, was upset by Texas Western, which started five blacks, 72-65. The Miners, led by Bobby Joe Hill and center Dave "Big Daddy" Lattin, won the game at the foul line with 28 points.

It was a watershed game for black players. Afterward, all colleges started recruiting blacks. Three years later, even Rupp had broken the color line.

Meanwhile, Player of the Year Cazzie Russell led No.9 Michigan to its third straight Big Ten title, but the Wolverines lost to Kentucky in the Mideast final.

Final AP Top 10

Writers' poll taken before major tournaments. From 1962-63 through 1967-68, AP ranked only 10 teams.

	Before Tourns	Head Coach	Final Record
1 Kentucky	24-1	Adolph Rupp	27-2
2 Duke	23-3	Vic Bubas	26-4
3 TX Western	23-1	Don Haskins	28-1
4 Kansas	22-3	Ted Owens	23-4
5 St.Joe's,PA	22-4	Jack Ramsay	24-5
6 Loyola,IL	22-2	George Ireland	22-3
7 Cincinnati	21-5	Tay Baker	21-7
8 Vanderbilt	22-4	Roy Skinner	same
9 Michigan	17-7	Dave Strack	18-8
10 Western Ky.	23-2	Johnny Oldham	25-3

Note: Texas Western won the NCAAs.

Second 10
Taken from final UPI coaches' poll.

11 Providence	22-4	Joe Mullaney	22-5
12 Nebraska	20-5	Joe Cipriano	same
13 Utah	21-6	Jack Gardner	23-8
14 Okla.City	24-3	Abe Lemons	24-4
15 Houston	21-5	Guy Lewis	23-6
16 Oregon St.	20-6	Paul Valenti	21-7
17 Syracuse	21-5	Fred Lewis	22-6
18 Pacific	22-4	Dick Edwards	22-6
19 Davidson	20-5	Lefty Driesell	21-7
20 BYU	17-5	Stan Watts	20-5
Dayton	22-4	Don Donoher	23-6

Note: Brigham Young won the NIT.

Major Conference Champions

Conference	Regular Season	Tournament
AAWU	Oregon St.(12-2)	—
ACC	Duke (12-2)	Duke
Big 8	Kansas (13-1)	—
Big 10	Michigan (11-3)	—
Ivy	Penn (12-2)	—
Mo.Valley	Cincinnati (10-4)	—
SEC	Kentucky (15-1)	—
Southern	Davidson (11-1)	Davidson
SWC	SMU (11-3)	—
WAC	Utah (7-3)	—

NCAA Tournament (22 teams)

East Regional

First Round—St.Joseph's-PA 65, Providence 48; Davidson 95, Rhode Island 65. **Semifinals**—Duke 76, St.Joseph's-PA 74; Syracuse 94, Davidson 78. **Third Place**—St.Joseph's-PA 92, Davidson 76. **Final**—Duke 91, Syracuse 81.

Mideast Regional

First Round—Dayton 58, Miami-OH 51; Western Ky. 105, Loyola-IL 86. **Semifinals**—Kentucky 86, Dayton 79; Michigan 80, Western Ky. 79. **Third Place**—Western Ky. 82, Dayton 62. **Final**—Kentucky 84, Michigan 77.

Midwest Regional

First Round—Texas Western 89, Oklahoma City 74. **Semifinals**—Texas Western 78, Cincinnati 76 (OT); Kansas 76, SMU 70. **Third Place**—SMU 89, Cincinnati 84. **Final**—

West Regional

First Round—Houston 82, Colorado St. 76. **Semifinals**—Oregon St. 63, Houston 60; Utah 83, Pacific 74. **Third Place**—Houston 102, Pacific 91. **Final**—Utah 70, Oregon St. 64.

FINAL FOUR
at Cole Fieldhouse, College Park,MD

Semifinals—Kentucky 83, Duke 79; Texas Western 85, Utah 78. **Third Place**—Duke 79, Utah 77. **Championship**—Texas Western 72, Kentucky 65. **Most Outstanding Player**—Jerry Chambers, Utah. **All-Tournament**—Chambers, Utah; Bobby Joe Hill, Texas Western; Louie Dampier and Pat Riley, Kentucky; Jack Marin, Duke.

NIT Tournament (14 teams)
All games at Madison Sq.Garden, New York

First Round—Temple 88, Virginia Tech 73; NYU 68, DePaul 65; San Francisco 89, Penn St. 77; Villanova 63, St.John's 61; Army 71, Manhattan 66; Boston College 96, Louisville 90 (3 OT). **Quarterfinals**—BYU 90, Temple 78; NYU 90, Wichita St. 84 (OT); Army 80, San Francisco 63; Villanova 86, Boston College 85. **Semifinals**—BYU 96, Army 60; NYU 69, Villanova 63. **Third Place**—Villanova 76, Army 65. **Championship**—BYU 97, NYU 84. **Most Valuable Player**— Bill Melchionni, Villanova.

Player of the Year

Cazzie Russell, Michigan . . . . UPI,USBWA,AP,Helms

Coach of the Year

Adolph Rupp, Kentucky . . . . UPI,USBWA

Consensus All-America
(By position, in alphabetical order)

First Team
Dave Bing, Syracuse; Clyde Lee, Vanderbilt; Cazzie Russell, Michigan; Dave Schellhase, Purdue; Jimmy Walker, Providence.

Second Team
Louie Dampier, Kentucky, Matt Guokas, St.Joseph's-PA; Jack Marin, Duke; Dick Snyder, Davidson; Bob Verga, Duke; Walt Wesley, Kansas.

1967

Enter Lew Alcindor.

In 1966, UCLA was the defending NCAA champion but while the Bruins may have been No.1 in the country, they were No.2 on campus. The freshman team was better and beat the varsity 75-60 to prove it. A year later, those frosh were sophomores and they beat everyone in sight. Thirty and oh. At the NCAA tourney in Louisville, they won by margins of 49, 16, 15 and 15—the last against Dayton in the title game.

Alcindor, the 7-foot New Yorker who would later become one of the greatest pro basketball players ever as his future pro colleagues Bill Russell and Wilt Chamberlain had done. He was easily the best player of the year and the tournament.

Back in New York, the NIT said goodbye to the only home it had ever known—the old Madison Square Garden on 50th Street. Future N.Y. Knick guard Walt Frazier and Southern Illinois won the finale, beating ex-Knick Al McGuire and his Marquette five, 71-56. The NIT would open shop at the new Garden on 33rd Street in 1968.

Final AP Top 10

Writers' poll taken before major tournaments. From 1962-63 through 1967-68, AP ranked only 10 teams.

		Before Tourns	Head Coach	Final Record
1	UCLA	26-0	John Wooden	30-0
2	Louisville	23-3	Peck Hickman	23-5
3	Kansas	22-3	Ted Owens	23-4
4	N.Carolina	24-4	Dean Smith	26-6
5	Princeton	23-2	B.vanBreda Kolff	25-3
6	Western Ky.	23-2	Johnny Oldham	23-3
7	Houston	23-3	Guy Lewis	27-4
8	Tennessee	21-5	Ray Mears	21-7
9	Boston Col.	19-2	Bob Cousy	21-3
10	TX Western	20-5	Don Haskins	22-6

Note: UCLA won the NCAAs.

Second 10

Taken from final UPI coaches' poll.

11	Toledo	23-1	Bob Nichols	23-2
12	St.John's	22-3	Lou Carnesecca	23-5
13	Tulsa	19-7	Joe Swank	19-8
14	Vanderbilt	21-5	Roy Skinner	same
	Utah St.	20-5	Ladell Andersen	20-6
16	Pacific	23-3	Dick Edwards	24-4
17	Providence	20-6	Joe Mullaney	21-7
18	New Mexico	18-7	Bob King	19-8
19	Duke	18-8	Vic Bubas	18-9
20	Florida	21-4	Tommy Bartlett	same

Note: Unranked Southern Illinois (20-2, Jack Hartman, 24-2) won the NIT.

Major Conference Champions

Conference	Regular Season	Tournament
AAWU	UCLA (14-0)	—
ACC	North Carolina (12-2)	N.Carolina
Big 8	Kansas (13-1)	—
Big 10	Indiana/Mich.St.(10-4)	—
Ivy	Princeton (13-1)	—
Mo.Valley	Louisville (12-2)	—
SEC	Tennessee (15-3)	—
Southern	West Virginia (9-1)	West Va.
SWC	SMU (12-2)	—
WAC	Wyoming/BYU (8-2)	—

NCAA Tournament (23 teams)

East Regional

First Round—Princeton 68, West Virginia 57; St.John's 57, Temple 53; Boston College 48, Connecticut 42. **Semifinals**—North Carolina 78, Princeton 70 (OT); Boston College 63, St.John's 62. **Third Place**—Princeton 78, St.John's 58. **Final**—North Carolina 96, Boston College 80.

Mideast Regional

First Round—Dayton 69, Western Ky. 67 (OT); Virginia Tech 82, Toledo 76. **Semifinals**—Dayton 53, Tennessee 52; Virginia Tech 79, Indiana 70. **Third Place**—Indiana 51, Tennessee 44. **Final**—Dayton 71, Virginia Tech 66 (OT).

Midwest Regional

First Round—Houston 59, New Mexico St. 58. **Semifinals**—Houston 66, Kansas 53; SMU 83, Louisville 81. **Third Place**—Kansas 70, Louisville 68. **Final**—Houston 83, SMU 75.

West Regional

First Round—Texas Western 62, Seattle 54. **Semifinals**—Pacific 72, Texas Western 63; UCLA 109, Wyoming 60. **Third Place**—Texas Western 69, Wyoming 67. **Final**—UCLA 80, Pacific 64.

FINAL FOUR
at Freedom Hall, Louisville

Semifinals—Dayton 76, North Carolina 62; UCLA 73, Houston 58. **Third Place**—Houston 84, North Carolina 62. **Championship**—UCLA 79, Dayton 64. **Most Outstanding Player**—Lew Alcindor, UCLA. **All-Tournament**—Alcindor, Lucius Allen and Mike Warren, UCLA; Don May, Dayton; Elvin Hayes, Houston.

NIT Tournament (14 teams)

All games at Madison Sq.Garden, New York

First Round—Marshall 70, Villanova 68 (OT); So.Illinois 103, St.Peter's 58; Providence 77, Memphis St. 68; New Mexico 66, Syracuse 64; Marquette 64, Tulsa 60; Rutgers 78, Utah St. 76. **Quarterfinals**—So.Illinois 72, Duke 63; Marshall 119, Nebraska 88; Rutgers 65, New Mexico 60; Marquette 81, Providence 80 (OT). **Semifinals**—Marquette 83, Marshall 78; Southern Illinois 79, Rutgers 70. **Third Place**—Rutgers 93, Marshall 76. **Championship**—So.Illinois 71, Marquette 56. **Most Valuable Player**—Walt Frazier, So.Illinois.

Player of the Year

Lew Alcindor, UCLA . . . . UPI,USBWA,AP,Helms

Coach of the Year

John Wooden, UCLA . . . . UPI,USBWA,AP

Consensus All-America

(By position, in alphabetical order)

First Team

Lew Alcindor, UCLA; Clem Haskins, Western Ky.; Elvin Hayes, Houston; Bob Lloyd, Rutgers; Wes Unseld, Louisville; Bob Verga, Duke; Jimmy Walker, Providence.

Second Team

Louie Dampier, Kentucky; Mel Daniels, New Mexico; Sonny Dove, St.John's; Don May, Dayton; Larry Miller, North Carolina.

1968

The biggest basketball crowd in NCAA history (52,693) packed the Astrodome on Jan.20 to watch local hero Elvin Hayes and No.2 Houston take on Lew Alcindor and No.1 UCLA.

Hayes had the game of his life, scoring 39 points, pulling down 15 rebounds and tossing in the deciding free throws for a dramatic 71-69 Cougar victory. Alcindor had only 15 points, but played with a scratched left eyeball.

Two months later they met again, this time at the L.A. Sports Arena in the NCAA semifinals. No contest. UCLA crushed Houston 101-69. The Bruins then routed North Carolina by 23 for the title.

This was also the first season that the dunk shot was outlawed during games and pregame warm-ups. Aimed at moderating the dominance of big men like Alcindor, the rule remained in effect through the 1976-77 season.

Meanwhile sophomores Pete Maravich of LSU and Calvin Murphy of Niagara led the country in scoring with 43.8 and 38.2 averages, respectively.

Final AP Top 10

Writers' poll taken before major tournaments. From 1962-63 through 1967-68, AP ranked only 10 teams.

		Before Tourns	Head Coach	Final Record
1	Houston	28-0	Guy Lewis	31-2
2	**UCLA**	25-1	John Wooden	29-1
3	St.Bona.	22-0	Larry Weise	23-2
4	N.Carolina	25-3	Dean Smith	28-4
5	Kentucky	21-4	Adolph Rupp	22-5
6	New Mexico	23-3	Bob King	23-5
7	Columbia	21-4	Jack Rohan	23-5
8	Davidson	22-4	Lefty Driesell	24-5
9	Louisville	20-6	John Dromo	21-7
10	Duke	21-5	Vic Bubas	22-6

Note: UCLA won the NCAAs.

Second 10

Taken from final UPI coaches' poll.

11	Marquette	21-5	Al McGuire	23-6
12	N.Mexico St.	21-5	Lou Henson	23-6
13	Vanderbilt	20-6	Roy Skinner	same
14	Kansas St.	19-7	Tex Winter	19-9
15	Princeton	20-6	Pete Carril	same
16	Army	20-4	Bobby Knight	20-5
17	Santa Clara	21-3	Dick Garibaldi	22-4
18	Utah	17-9	Jack Gardner	same
19	Bradley	19-8	Joe Stowell	19-9
20	Iowa	16-9	Ralph Miller	same

Note: Unranked Dayton (17-9, Don Donoher, 21-9) won the NIT.

Major Conference Champions

Conference	Regular Season	Tournament
ACC	North Carolina (12-2)	N.Carolina
Big 8	Kansas St.(11-3)	—
Big 10	Ohio St./Iowa (10-4)	—
Ivy	Columbia*/Prince.(12-2)	—
Mo.Valley	Louisville (14-2)	—
Pac-8	UCLA (14-0)	—
SEC	Kentucky (15-3)	—
Southern	Davidson (9-1)	Davidson
SWC	TCU (9-5)	—
WAC	New Mexico (8-2)	—

*Won playoff for league championship.

NCAA Tournament (23 teams)

East Regional

First Round—St.Bonaventure 102, Boston College 93; Davidson 79, St.John's 70; Columbia 83, La Salle 69. **Semifinal**—North Carolina 91, St.Bonaventure 72; Davidson 61, Columbia 59 (OT). **Third Place**—Columbia 95, St.Bonaventure 75. **Final**—North Carolina 70, Davidson 66.

Mideast Regional

First Round—East Tenn.St. 79, Florida St. 69; Marquette 72, Bowling Green 71. **Semifinal**—Ohio St. 79, East Tenn.St. 72; Kentucky 107, Marquette 89. **Third Place**—Marquette 69, East Tenn.St. 57. **Final**—Ohio St. 82, Kentucky 81.

Midwest Regional

First Round—Houston 94, Loyola-IL 76. **Semifinal**—Houston 91, Louisville 75; TCU 77, Kansas St. 72. **Third Place**—Louisville 93, Kansas St. 63. **Final**—Houston 103, TCU 68.

West Regional

First Round—New Mexico St. 68, Weber St. 57. **Semifinal**—UCLA 58, New Mexico St. 49; Santa Clara 86, New Mexico 73. **Third Place**—New Mexico St. 62, New Mexico 58. **Final**—UCLA 87, Santa Clara 66.

FINAL FOUR

at the Sports Arena, Los Angeles

Semifinals—North Carolina 80, Ohio St. 66; UCLA 101, Houston 69. **Third Place**—Ohio St. 89, Houston 85. **Championship**—UCLA 78, North Carolina 55. **Most Outstanding Player**—Lew Alcindor, UCLA. **All-Tournament**—Alcindor, Lucius Allen, Lynn Shackleford and Mike Warren, UCLA; Larry Miller, North Carolina.

NIT Tournament (16 teams)

All games at Madison Sq.Garden, New York

First Round—St.Peter's 102, Marshall 93 (2 OT); Duke 97, Oklahoma City 81; Kansas 82, Temple 76; Villanova 77, Wyoming 66; Notre Dame 62, Army 58; LIU 80, Bradley 77; Fordham 69, Duquesne 60; Dayton 87, West Virginia 68. **Quarterfinals**—Kansas 55, Villanova 49; St.Peter's 100, Duke 71; Dayton 61, Fordham 60; Notre Dame 62, LIU 60. **Semifinals**—Dayton 76, Notre Dame 74 (OT); Kansas 58, St.Peter's 46. **Third Place**—Notre Dame 81, St.Peter's 78. **Championship**—Dayton 61, Kansas 48. **Most Valuable Player**—Don May, Dayton.

Players of the Year

Elvin Hayes, Houston . . . . .UPI,USBWA,AP
Lew Alcindor, UCLA .Helms

Coach of the Year

Guy Lewis, Houston . . . . .UPI,USBWA,AP

Consensus All-America

(By position, in alphabetical order)

First Team

Lew Alcindor, UCLA; Elvin Hayes, Houston; Pete Maravich, LSU; Larry Miller, North Carolina; Wes Unseld, Louisville.

Second Team

Lucius Allen, UCLA; Bob Lanier, St.Bonaventure; Don May, Dayton; Calvin Murphy, Niagara; JoJo White, Kansas.

1969

The Lew Alcindor Era came to an unprecedented close as UCLA became the first team to win three straight NCAA championships and Alcindor became the tournament's first three-time Most Outstanding Player.

The victory in the finals gave Alcindor an overall record of 88-2 in three seasons, the only losses coming to Houston in 1968 and Southern Cal this year—a 46-44 freeze-o-rama in the final Pac-8 game of the season that broke the Uclans' 85-game winning streak at home.

Any thought that UCLA might be ripe for the picking in the NCAAs vanished when No.3 Santa Clara (26-1) met the Bruins in the West Regional final and was trashed, 90-52. UCLA had a lot of trouble with Drake in the semifinals before winning by three, then drubbed Purdue by 20 in the title game as Alcindor bowed out with 37 points.

La Salle, 23-1 and ranked second in the country, was ineligible for the tournament due to academic and recruiting violations that occurred before Tom Gola took over the program in 1968.

Maravich won the scoring title again, breaking his single season record with an average of 44.2. And University of Detroit sophomore Spencer Haywood, the hero of the 1968 U.S. Olympic team, was the nation's rebounding leader with 21.5 boards a game. Haywood turned pro before the year was out and led Denver to an ABA championship in 1970 while being named Rookie of the Year and MVP.

Final AP Top 20
Writers' poll taken before major tournaments.

	Before Tourns	Head Coach	Final Record
1 UCLA	25-1	John Wooden	29-1
2 La Salle	23-1	Tom Gola	same*
3 Santa Clara	26-1	Dick Garibaldi	27-2
4 N.Carolina	25-3	Dean Smith	27-5
5 Davidson	24-2	Lefty Driesell	26-3
6 Purdue	20-4	George King	23-5
7 Kentucky	22-4	Adolph Rupp	23-5
8 St.John's	22-4	Lou Carnesecca	23-6
9 Duquesne	19-4	Red Manning	21-5
10 Villanova	21-4	Jack Kraft	21-5
11 Drake	23-4	Maury John	26-5
12 N.Mexico St.	22-3	Lou Henson	24-5
13 S.Carolina	20-6	Frank McGuire	21-7
14 Marquette	22-4	Al McGuire	24-5
15 Louisville	20-5	John Dromo	21-6
16 Boston Col.	21-3	Bob Cousy	24-4
17 Notre Dame	20-6	Johnny Dee	20-7
18 Colorado	20-6	Sox Walseth	21-7
19 Kansas	20-6	Ted Owens	20-7
20 Illinois	19-5	Harvey Schmidt	same

Note: UCLA won NCAAs and Temple (18-8, Harry Litwack, 22-8) won the NIT.

Major Conference Champions

Conference	Regular Season	Tournament
ACC	North Carolina (12-2)	N.Carolina
Big 8	Colorado (10-4)	—
Big 10	Purdue (13-1)	—
Ivy	Princeton (14-0)	—
Mo.Valley	Drake/L'ville (13-3)	—
Pac-8	UCLA (13-1)	—
SEC	Kentucky (16-2)	—
Southern	Davidson (9-0)	Davidson
SWC	Texas A&M (12-2)	—
WAC	BYU/Wyoming (6-4)	—

NCAA Tournament (25 teams)
East Regional
First Round—Duquesne 74, St.Joseph's-PA 52; Davidson 75, Villanova 61; St.John's 72, Princeton 63. **Semifinals**—North Carolina 79, Duquesne 78; Davidson 79, St.John's 69. **Third Place**—Duquesne 75, St.John's 72. **Final**—North Carolina 87, Davidson 85.

Mideast Regional
First Round—Miami-OH 63, Notre Dame 60; Marquette 82, Murray St. 62. **Semifinals**—Purdue 91, Miami-OH 71; Marquette 81, Kentucky 74. **Third Place**—Kentucky 72, Miami-OH 71. **Final**—Purdue 75, Marquette 73 (OT).

Midwest Regional
First Round—Texas A&M 81, Trinity-TX 66; Colorado St. 52, Dayton 50. **Semifinals**—Drake 81, Texas A&M 63; Colorado St. 64, Colorado 56. **Third Place**—Colorado 97, Texas A&M 82. **Final**—Drake 84, Colorado St. 77.

West Regional
First Round—New Mexico St. 74, BYU 62; Weber St. 75, Seattle 73. **Semifinals**—UCLA 53, New Mexico St. 38; Santa Clara 63, Weber St. 59. **Third Place**—Weber St. 58, New Mexico St. 56. **Final**—UCLA 90, Santa Clara 52.

FINAL FOUR
at Freedom Hall, Louisville

Semifinals—Purdue 92, North Carolina 65; UCLA 85, Drake 82. **Third Place**—Drake 104, North Carolina 84. **Championship**—UCLA 92, Purdue 72. **Most Outstanding Player**—Lew Alcindor, UCLA. **All-Tournament**—Alcindor and John Vallely, UCLA; Rick Mount, Purdue; Willie McCarter, Drake; Charlie Scott, North Carolina.

NIT Tournament (16 teams)
All games at Madison Sq.Garden, New York

First Round—Temple 82, Florida 66; St.Peter's 75, Tulsa 71; Ohio Univ. 82, West Texas St. 80; Tennessee 67, Rutgers 51; Army 51, Wyoming 49; South Carolina 72, So.Illinois 63; Boston College 78, Kansas 62; Louisville 73, Fordham 70. **Quarterfinals**—Temple 94, St.Peter's 78; Tennessee 75, Ohio Univ. 64; Army 59, South Carolina 45; Boston College 88, Louisville 83. **Semifinals**—Temple 63, Tennessee 58; Boston College 73, Army 61. **Third Place**—Tennessee 64, Army 52. **Championship**—Temple 89, Boston College 76. **Most Valuable Player**—Terry Driscoll, Boston College.

Player of the Year
Lew Alcindor, UCLA . . . . . . UPI,USBWA,AP,Helms

Coaches of the Year
John Wooden, UCLA . . . . UPI,AP,NABC
Maury John, Drake . . . . USBWA

Consensus All-America
(In alphabetical order)
First Team
Lew Alcindor, UCLA; Spencer Haywood, Detroit; Pete Maravich, LSU; Rick Mount, Purdue; Calvin Murphy, Niagara.

Second Team
Dan Issel, Kentucky; Mike Maloy, Davidson; Bud Ogden, Santa Clara; Charlie Scott, North Carolina; JoJo White, Kansas.

1970

Pete Maravich may have been the greatest college basketball player since Hank Luisetti never to play in the NCAA tournament. The 1970 Player of the Year was certainly the most exciting player to miss the Big Dance.

In the three years Maravich played varsity ball at LSU, the Tigers were only 49-35 and never won the SEC, but "Pistol Pete" led the nation in scoring each year—averaging 43.8 as a sophomore, 44.2 as a junior and 44.5 as a senior. He was the college game's all-time scoring machine, throwing in 3667 points in just 83 games for a career average of 44.2 points a game—10 points better than anyone else—ever.

Meanwhile, back at the NCAAs, UCLA became the first team to win four consecutive titles. Lew Alcindor was gone, but John Wooden dusted off the zone press and the Bruins wrapped up the season beating 7-2 Artis Gilmore and high-scoring Jacksonville (100.3 ppg), 80-69.

No.3 St.Bonaventure reached the Final Four for the first time, but when star Bob Lanier tore up his right knee in the East Regional final the Bonnies' chances went down with him.

No.8 Marquette and No.9 Notre Dame made their presence felt in the postseason. The Warriors passed up an NCAA bid for the NIT and won the tournament for the first time, beating St.John's by 12 in the final. And Austin Carr of the Irish scored 61 points against Ohio U. in the first round of the NCAAs to break Bill Bradley's single game record of 58.

Final AP Top 20
Writers' poll taken before tournament.

			Before Tourns	Head Coach	Final Record
1	Kentucky		25-1	Adolph Rupp	26-2
2	**UCLA**		24-2	John Wooden	28-2
3	St.Bona.		22-1	Larry Weise	25-3
4	Jacksonville		23-1	Joe Williams	27-2
5	N.Mexico.St.		23-2	Lou Henson	27-3
6	S.Carolina		25-3	Frank McGuire	25-3
7	Iowa		19-4	Ralph Miller	20-5
8	**Marquette**		22-3	Al McGuire	26-3
9	Notre Dame		20-6	Johnny Dee	21-8
10	N.C.State		22-6	Norm Sloan	23-7
11	Florida St.		23-3	Hugh Durham	23-3
12	Houston		24-3	Guy Lewis	25-5
13	Penn		25-1	Dick Harter	25-2
14	Drake		21-6	Maury John	22-7
15	Davidson		22-4	Terry Holland	22-5
16	Utah St.		20-6	Ladell Andersen	22-7
17	Niagara		21-5	Frank Layden	22-7
18	Western Ky.		22-2	John Oldham	22-3
19	L.Beach St.		23-3	Jerry Tarkanian	24-5
20	USC		18-8	Bob Boyd	18-8

Note: UCLA won the NCAAs and Marquette won the NIT.

Major Conference Champions

Conference	Regular Season	Tournament
ACC	S.Carolina (14-0)	N.C.State
Big 8	Kansas St.(10-4)	—
Big 10	Iowa (14-0)	—
Ivy	Penn (14-0)	—
Mo.Valley	Drake (14-2)	—
Pac-8	UCLA (12-2)	—
SEC	Kentucky (17-1)	—
SWC	Rice (10-4)	—
WAC	UTEP (10-4)	—

NCAA Tournament (25 teams)
East Regional
First Round—St.Bonaventure 85, Davidson 72; Niagara 79, Penn 69; Villanova 77, Temple 69. **Semifinals**—St.Bonaventure 80, N.C.State 68; Villanova 98, Niagara 73. **Third Place**—N.C.State 108, Niagara 88. **Final**—St.Bonaventure 97, Villanova 74.

Mideast Regional
First Round—Notre Dame 112, Ohio Univ.82; Jacksonville 109, Western Ky.96. **Semifinals**—Kentucky 109, Notre Dame 99; Jacksonville 104, Iowa 103. **Third Place**—Iowa 121, Notre Dame 106. **Final**—Jacksonville 106, Kentucky 100.

Midwest Regional
First Round—Houston 71, Dayton 64; N.Mexico St. 101, Rice 77. **Semifinals**—Drake 92, Houston 87; N.Mexico St.70, Kansas St.66. **Third Place**—Kansas St.107, Houston 98. **Final**—N.Mexico St.87, Drake 78.

West Regional
First Round—Long Beach St.92, Weber St.73; Utah St.91, UTEP 81. **Semifinals**—UCLA 88, L.Beach St.65; Utah St.69, Santa Clara 68. **Third Place**—Santa Clara 89, L.Beach St.86. **Final**—UCLA 101, Utah St.79.

FINAL FOUR
at Cole Fieldhouse, College Park,MD

Semifinals—Jacksonville 91, St.Bonaventure 83; UCLA 93, New Mexico St.77. **Third Place**—N.Mexico St.79, St.Bonaventure 73. **Championship**—UCLA 80, Jacksonville 69.

Most Outstanding Player: Sidney Wicks, UCLA. **All-Tournament:** Wicks, Curtis Rowe and John Vallely, UCLA; Artis Gilmore, Jacksonville; Jimmy Collins, N. Mexico St.

NIT Tournament (16 teams)
All games at Madison Sq.Garden, New York

First Round—Ga.Tech 78, Duquesne 68; St.John's 70, Miami,OH 57; Manhattan 95, N.Carolina 90; Army 72, Cincinnati 69; Utah 78, Duke 75; Marquette 62, Massachusetts 55; LSU 83, Georgetown 82; Oklahoma 74, Louisville 73.
Quarterfinals—St.John's 56, Ga.Tech 55; Army 77, Manhattan 72; Marquette 83, Utah 63; LSU 97, Oklahoma 94.
Semifinals—St.John's 60, Army 59; Marquette 101, LSU 79. **Third Place**—Army 75, LSU 68. **Championship**—Marquette 65, St.John's 53.
MVP—Dean Meminger, Marquette.

Players of the Year

Pete Maravich, LSU . . . . UPI,AP,USBWA, Naismith,Helms(tie)
Sidney Wicks, UCLA . . . . .Helms(tie)

Coach of the Year
John Wooden, UCLA . . . . . .UPI,AP,USBWA,NABC

Consensus All-America
(In alphabetical order)

First Team—Dan Issel, Kentucky; Bob Lanier, St.Bonventure; Pete Maravich, LSU; Rick Mount, Purdue and Calvin Murphy, Niagara.

Second Team—Austin Carr, Notre Dame; Jimmy Collins, N.Mexico St.; John Roche, S.Carolina; Charlie Scott, N.Carolina and Sidney Wicks, UCLA.

1971

UCLA lost one game during the 1970-71 season, to Notre Dame in South Bend. Austin Carr scored 48 points and the Irish won, 89-82.

Everybody else who played the Bruins lost. All 29. At the NCAAs, Long Beach State gave the Uclans a scare in the West Regional final but were eventually beaten back, 57-55.

At the Final Four in Houston, Villanova beat Western Kentucky, in a double overtime semifinal, then lost to UCLA by six when the Bruins' Steve Patterson outscored Howard Porter of the Wildcats, 29-25. Porter was named MVP, but when it was disclosed later that he had signed a pro contract before the tourney, the NCAA voided both the award and Villanova's records.

Otherwise, No.2 Marquette and No.3 Penn, both undefeated during the regular season, were beaten in their second tournament games—Marquette by Ohio State and Penn by Big Five rival Villanova. And South Carolina won the ACC tournament in its final year as a conference member.

Hard luck team of the year? How about No.5 Southern Cal. USC had a 24-2 record, but finished second to you-know-who in the Pac- 8 and didn't make the NCAAs.

North Carolina won the ACC regular season title, lost the league tournament final to South Carolina, then bounced back to win the NIT with an 84-66 victory over another ACC rival—Georgia Tech. Bill Chamberlain led the Tar Heels with 35 points and was named MVP.

Final AP Top 20
Writers' poll taken before tournament.

	Before Tourns	Head Coach	Final Record
1 **UCLA**	25-1	John Wooden	29-1
2 Marquette	26-0	Al McGuire	28-1
3 Penn	26-0	Dick Harter	28-1
4 Kansas	25-1	Ted Owens	27-3
5 USC	24-2	Bob Boyd	same
6 S.Carolina	23-4	Frank McGuire	23-6
7 Western Ky.	20-5	John Oldham	24-6
8 Kentucky	22-4	Adolph Rupp	22-6
9 Fordham	25-1	Digger Phelps	23-3
10 Ohio St.	19-5	Fred Taylor	20-6
11 Jacksonville	22-3	Tom Wasdin	22-4
12 Notre Dame	19-7	Johnny Dee	20-9
13 **N.Carolina**	22-6	Dean Smith	26-6
14 Houston	20-6	Guy Lewis	22-7
15 Duquesne	21-3	Red Manning	21-4
16 L.Beach St.	21-4	Jerry Tarkanian	23-5
17 Tennessee	20-6	Ray Mears	21-7
18 Villanova	19-5	Jack Kraft	23-6
19 Drake	20-7	Maury John	21-8
20 BYU	18-9	Stan Watts	18-11

Note: UCLA won the NCAAs and North Carolina won the NIT.

Major Conference Champions

Conference	Regular Season	Tournament
ACC	N.Carolina (11-3)	S.Carolina
Big 8	Kansas (14-0)	—
Big 10	Ohio St.(13-1)	—
Ivy	Penn (14-0)	—
Mo.Valley	Drake/Louisville/ St.Louis (9-5)	—
Pac-8	UCLA (14-0)	—
SEC	Kentucky (16-2)	—
SWC	TCU (11-3)	—
WAC	BYU (10-4)	—

NCAA Tournament (25 teams)
East Regional
First Round—Penn 70, Duquesne 65; Villanova 93, St. Joseph's,PA 75; Fordham 105, Furman 74. **Semifinals** —Penn 79, S.Carolina 64; Villanova 85, Fordham 75. **Third Place**—Fordham 100, S.Carolina 90. **Final**—Villanova 90, Penn 47.

Mideast Regional
First Round—Western Ky.74, Jacksonville 72; Marquette 62, Miami,OH 47. **Semifinals**—Western Ky. 107, Kentucky 83; Ohio St.60, Marquette 59. **Third Place**—Marquette 91, Kentucky 74. **Final**—Western Ky.81, Ohio St.78 (OT).

Midwest Regional
First Round—Notre Dame 102, TCU 94; Houston 72, N.Mexico St. 69. **Semifinals**—Drake 79, Notre Dame 72 (OT); Kansas 78, Houston 77. **Third Place**— Houston 119, Notre Dame 106. **Final**—Kansas 73, Drake 71.

West Regional
First Round—BYU 91, Utah St. 82; Long Beach St. 77, Weber St. 66. **Semifinals**—UCLA 91, BYU 73; L.Beach St. 78, Pacific 65. **Third Place**—Pacific 84, BYU 81. **Final**—UCLA 57, L.Beach St.55.

FINAL FOUR
at The Astrodome, Houston,TX
Semifinals—Villanova 92, Western Ky.89 (2 OT); UCLA 68, Kansas 60. **Third Place**—Western Ky.77, Kansas 75. **Championship**—UCLA 68, Villanova 62. **Most Outstanding Player**—Howard Porter, Villanova. **All-Tournament**—Porter, Hank Siemiontkowski, Villanova; Steve Patterson, Sidney Wicks, UCLA; and Jim McDaniels, Western Ky.

Note: Porter, Siemiontkowski and McDaniels were all declared ineligible subsequent to tournament. Their records and their teams' records have been deleted by the NCAA.

NIT Tournament (16 teams)
All games at Madison Sq.Garden, New York
First Round—N.Carolina 94, Massachusetts 49; Duke 68, Dayton 60; Providence 64, Louisville 58; Tennessee 84, St.John's 83 (2 OT); Ga.Tech 70, La Salle 67; Michigan 86, Syracuse 76; St.Bonaventure 94, Purdue 79; Hawaii 87, Oklahoma 86 (2 OT).
Quarterfinals—N.Carolina 86, Providence 79; Duke 78, Tennessee 64; Ga.Tech 78, Michigan 70; St.Bonaventure 73, Hawaii 64.
Semifinals—N.Carolina 73, Duke 69; Ga.Tech 76, St. Bonaventure 71 (2 OT). **Third Place**—St.Bonaventure 92, Duke 88 (OT). **Championship**—N.Carolina 84, Ga.Tech 66.
MVP—Bill Chamberlain, N.Carolina.

Players of the Year
Austin Carr, N.Dame . . . UPI,AP,Naismith,Helms(tie)
Sidney Wicks, UCLA . . . . USBWA,Helms(tie)

Coaches of the Year
Al McGuire, Marquette . . . . UPI,AP,USBWA
Jack Kraft, Villanova . . . . NABC

Consensus All-America
(In alphabetical order)

First Team—Austin Carr, Notre Dame; Artis Gilmore, Jacksonville; Dean Meminger, Marquette; Jim McDaniels, Western Ky.; Sidney Wicks, UCLA.

Second Team—Ken Durrett, La Salle; Johnny Neumann, Mississippi; Howard Porter, Villanova; John Roche, S.Carolina; Curtis Rowe, UCLA.

1972

Only one man has been inducted into the Basketball Hall of Fame twice—John Wooden.

He was enshrined the first time in 1960 when he was cited for his accomplishments as a star guard at Purdue from 1930-32. Wooden captained the Boilermakers his junior and senior years and was Player of the Year in 1932, the school's only national championship season.

In 1972 he was honored again, this time for his coaching achievements at UCLA. Ordinarily, Halls of Fame wait until an all-time great has retired before they hand him a plaque, but Wooden's eight NCAA championships were anything but ordinary, so they elevated the Wizard of Westwood now.

And he wasn't finished yet. Not with the arrival of Bill Walton. In '72, UCLA went 30-0 and posted an average winning margin of 33 points. Both Walton and Wooden were everybody's picks for Player and Coach of the Year.

Meanwhile in Kentucky, Adolph Rupp, the only other coach to win as many as four NCAA titles, retired after 41 years and 875 wins.

The low point of the year in amateur basketball came during the Summer Olympics in Munich, West Germany, where the unbeaten United States team (62-0) lost for the first time ever in a controversial gold medal final against the Soviet Union. The Russians were given three chances to win the game in the final seconds and finally won, 51-50. The Americans refused to accept the silver medal.

Final AP Top 20
Writers' poll taken before tournament.

	Before Tours	Head Coach	Final Record
1 UCLA	26-0	John Wooden	30-0
2 N.Carolina	23-4	Dean Smith	26-5
3 Penn	23-2	Chuck Daly	25-3
4 Louisville	23-4	Denny Crum	26-5
5 L.Beach St.	23-3	Jerry Tarkanian	25-4
6 S.Carolina	22-4	Frank McGuire	24-5
7 Marquette	24-2	Al McGuire	25-4
8 SW La.	23-3	Beryl Shipley	25-4
9 BYU	21-4	St.an Watts	21-5
10 Florida St.	23-5	Hugh Durham	27-6
11 Minnesota	17-6	Bill Musselman	18-7
12 Marshall	23-3	Carl Tacy	23-4
13 Memphis St.	21-6	Gene Bartow	21-7
14 Maryland	23-5	Lefty Driesell	27-5
15 Villanova	19-6	Jack Kraft	20-8
16 Oral Robts.	25-1	Ken Trickey	26-2
17 Indiana	17-7	Bobby Knight	17-8
18 Kentucky	20-6	Adolph Rupp	21-7
19 Ohio St.	18-6	Fred Taylor	same
20 Virginia	21-6	Bill Gibson	21-7

Note: UCLA won the NCAAs and Maryland won the NIT.

Major Conference Champions

Conference	Regular Season	Tournament
ACC	N.Carolina (9-3)	N.Carolina
Big 8	Kansas St.(12-2)	—
Big 10	Minnesota (11-3)	—
Ivy	Penn (13-1)	—
Mo.Valley	L'ville/Memp.St.(12-2)	—
Pac-8	UCLA (14-0)	—
SEC	Kentucky/Tenn.(14-4)	—
SWC	Texas*/SMU (10-4)	—
WAC	BYU (12-2)	—

*Won playoff for league championship.

NCAA Tournament (25 teams)
East Regional
First Round—S.Carolina 53, Temple 51; Villanova 85, E.Carolina 70; Penn 76, Providence 60. Semifinals—N.Carolina 92, S.Carolina 69; Penn 78, Villanova 67. Third Place—S.Carolina 90, Villanova 78. Final—N.Carolina 73, Penn 59.

Mideast Regional
First Round—Marquette 73, Ohio Univ.49; Florida St.83, Eastern Ky.81. Semifinals—Kentucky 85, Marquette 69; Florida St.70, Minnesota 56. Third Place—Minnesota 77, Marquette 72. Final—Florida St.73, Kentucky 54.

Midwest Regional
First Round—SW Louisiana 112, Marshall 101; Texas 85, Houston 74. Semifinals—Louisville 88, SW Louisiana 84; Kansas St.66, Texas 55. Third Place—SW Louisiana 100, Texas 70. Final—Louisville 72, Kansas St.65.

West Regional
First Round—Weber St.91, Hawaii 64; Long Beach St.95, BYU 90 (OT). Semifinals—UCLA 90, Weber St. 58; L.Beach St.75, San Francisco 55. Third Place—San Fran. 74, Weber St. 64. Final—UCLA 73, L.Beach St. 57.

FINAL FOUR
at the Sports Arena, Los Angeles

Semifinals—Florida St.79, N.Carolina 75; UCLA 96, Louisville 77. Third Place—N.Carolina 105, Louisville 91. Championship—UCLA 81, Florida St.76. Most Outstanding Player—Bill Walton, UCLA. All-Tournament—Walton, Keith Wilkes, UCLA; Ron King, Florida St.; Bob McAdoo, N.Carolina; Jim Price, Louisville.

NIT Tournament (16 teams)
All games at Madison Sq.Garden, New York

First Round—Lafayette 72, Virginia 71; Jacksonville 94, Fordham 75; Syracuse 81, Davidson 77; Maryland 67, St. Joseph's,PA 55; Oral Roberts 94, Memphis St.74; St.John's 82, Missouri 81 (OT); Princeton 68, Indiana 60; Niagara 76, UTEP 57. Quarterfinals—Jacksonville 87, Lafayette 76; Maryland 71, Syracuse 65; St.John's 94, Oral Roberts 78; Niagara 65, Princeton 60. Semifinals—Maryland 91, Jacksonville 77; Niagara 69, St.John's 67. Third Place—Jacksonville 83, St.John's 80. Championship—Maryland 100, Niagara 69.

MVP—Tom McMillen, Maryland.

Player of the Year
Bill Walton, UCLA . . . . UPI,AP,USBWA, Naismith,Helms

Coach of the Year
John Wooden, UCLA . . . . . UPI,AP,USBWA, NABC

Consensus All-America
(In alphabetical order)

First Team—Henry Bibby, UCLA; Jim Chones, Marquette; Dwight Lamar, Southwestern La.; Bob McAdoo, N.Carolina; Ed Ratleff, L.Beach St.; Tom Riker, S.Carolina; Bill Walton, UCLA.

Second Team—Richard Fuque, Oral Roberts; Barry Parkhill, Virginia; Jim Price, Louisville; Bud Stallworth, Kansas; Henry Wilmore, Michigan.

1973

Freshmen became eligible to play varsity ball for the 1972-73 season. It was becoming a young man's game, all right. The year before, the pros had grabbed undergrads like Julius Erving, George McGinnis, Johnny Neumann and Jim Chones. The ABA's N.Y. Nets had snatched Chones from Marquette just as the unbeaten Warriors were preparing for the NCAAs (they went nowhere without him).

Now the colleges were restless to recruit youngsters. North Carolina State was so excited about landing freshman David Thompson that the NCAA put the Wolfpack on probation for using unapproved recruiting methods. With Thompson in the line-up, N.C.State went 27-0 and finished the regular season ranked No.2, but couldn't go to the NCAAs.

UCLA? The Bruins went 30-0, stretched their winning streak to a record 75 straight, won their seventh straight NCAA title in a breeze, and Bill Walton and John Wooden were everybody's Player and Coach of the Year again. Walton even became the first basketball player since Bill Bradley to win the Sullivan Award as the nation's best amateur athlete.

No.4 Providence, led by Ernie DiGregorio, became the first New England team to reach the Final Four since Holy Cross (and Bob Cousy) did it in 1948. The Friars placed fourth.

Final AP Top 20
Writers' poll taken before tournament.

	Before Tourns	Head Coach	Final Record
1 **UCLA**	26-0	John Wooden	30-0
2 N.C.State	27-0	Norm Sloan	same*
3 L.Beach St.	24-2	Jerry Tarkanian	26-3
4 Providence	24-2	Dave Gavitt	27-4
5 Marquette	23-3	Al McGuire	25-4
6 Indiana	19-5	Bobby Knight	22-6
7 SW La.	23-2	Beryl Shipley	24-5
8 Maryland	22-6	Lefty Driesell	23-7
9 Kansas St.	22-4	Jack Hartman	23-5
10 Minnesota	20-4	Bill Musselman	21-5
11 N.Carolina	22-7	Dean Smith	25-8
12 Memphis St.	21-5	Gene Bartow	24-6
13 Houston	23-3	Guy Lewis	23-4
14 Syracuse	22-4	Roy Danforth	24-5
15 Missouri	21-5	Norm Stewart	21-6
16 Ariz.St.	18-7	Ned Wulk	19-9
17 Kentucky	19-7	Joe B.Hall	20-8
18 Penn	20-5	Chuck Daly	21-7
19 Aust.Peay	21-5	Lake Kelly	22-7
20 San Fran.	22-4	Bob Gaillard	23-5

*N.C.State ineligible for NCAA tournament for improper methods used in recruiting David Thompson.
Note: UCLA won the NCAAs and unranked Virginia Tech (18-5, Don DeVoe, 22-5) won the NIT.

Major Conference Champions

Conference	Regular Season	Tournament
ACC	N.C.State (12-0)	N.C.State
Big 8	Kansas St.(12-2)	—
Big 10	Indiana (11-3)	—
Mo.Valley	Memphis St.(12-2)	—
Ivy	Penn (12-2)	—
Pac-8	UCLA (14-0)	—
SEC	Kentucky (14-4)	—
SWC	Texas Tech (12-2)	—
WAC	Arizona St.(10-4)	—

NCAA Tournament (25 teams)
East Regional
First Round—Syracuse 83, Furman 82; Penn 62, St. John's 61; Providence 89, St.Joseph's,PA 76. **Semifinals**—Maryland 91, Syracuse 75; Providence 87, Penn 65. **Third Place**—Syracuse 69, Penn 68. **Final**—Providence 103, Maryland 89.

Midwest Regional
First Round—S.Carolina 78, Texas Tech 70; SW Louisiana 102, Houston 89. **Semifinals**—Memphis St.90, S. Carolina 76; Kansas St.66, SW Louisiana 63. **Third Place**—S.Carolina 90, SW.Louisiana 85. **Final**—Memphis St.92, Kansas St.72.

Mideast Regional
First Round—Marquette 77, Miami,OH 62; Austin Peay 77, Jacksonville 75. **Semifinals**—Indiana 75, Marquette 69; Kentucky 106, Austin Peay 100 (OT). **Third Place**—Marquette 88, Austin Peay 73. **Final**—Indiana 72, Kentucky 65.

West Regional
First Round—Long Beach St.88, Weber St.75; Arizona St.103, Oklahoma City 78. **Semifinals**—San Francisco 77, L.Beach St.67; UCLA 98, Arizona St.81. **Third Place**—L.Beach St.84, Arizona St.80. **Final**—UCLA 54, San Fran.39.

FINAL FOUR
at The Arena, St.Louis

Semifinals—Memphis St.98, Providence 85; UCLA 70, Indiana 59. **Third Place**—Indiana 97, Providence 79. **Championship**—UCLA 87, Memphis St. 66. **Most Outstanding Player**—Bill Walton, UCLA. **All-Tournament**—Walton; Larry Finch and Larry Kenon, Memphis St.; Steve Downing, Indiana; Ernie DiGregorio, Providence.

NIT Tournament (16 teams)
All games at Madison Sq.Garden, New York

First Round—Notre Dame 69, Southern Cal 65; Louisville 97, American 84; N.Carolina 82, Oral Roberts 65; Massachusetts 78, Missouri 71; Fairfield 80, Marshall 76; Va.Tech 65, New Mexico 63; Minnesota 68, Rutgers 59; Alabama 87, Manhattan 86. **Quarterfinals**—N.Carolina 73, UMass 63; Notre Dame 79, Louisville 71; Va.Tech 77, Fairfield 76; Alabama 69, Minnesota 65. **Semifinals**—Va.Tech 74, Alabama 73; Notre Dame 78, N.Carolina 71. **Third Place**—N.Carolina 88, Alabama 69. **Championship**—Va.Tech 92, Notre Dame 91 (OT).

MVP—John Shumate, Notre Dame.

Player of the Year
Bill Walton, UCLA . . . . UPI,AP,USBWA, Naismith,Helms

Coaches of the Year
John Wooden, UCLA . . . . UPI,AP,USBWA
Gene Bartow, Memphis St . . . . NABC

Consensus All-America
(In alphabetical order)

First Team—Doug Collins, Illinois St.; Ernie DiGregorio, Providence; Dwight Lamar, Southwestern La.; Ed Ratleff, L.Beach St.; David Thompson, N.C.State; Bill Walton, UCLA; Keith Wilkes, UCLA.

Second Team—Jim Brewer, Minnesota; Tom Burleson, N.C.State; Larry Finch, Memphis St.; Kevin Joyce, S.Carolina; Tom McMillen, Maryland; Kermit Washington, American.

1974

UCLA's two big streaks were finally broken in 1974.
On Jan.19 in South Bend, Notre Dame handed the No.1 Bruins their first defeat in four years, 71-70, coming from behind to halt UCLA's all-time NCAA winning streak at 88. Notre Dame was also the victor the last time UCLA lost a game in 1971.

On March 23 in Greensboro, N.C., David Thompson and N.C. State ended UCLA's run of seven straight NCAA championships, beating Bill Walton and Co., 80-77 in double overtime in the NCAA semifinals. The Wolfpack then beat Marquette for their first title. Walton and Thompson shared Player of the Year honors, but Thompson was tournament MVP.

Final AP Top 20
Writers' poll taken before tournament.

	Before Tourns	Head Coach	Final Record
1 **N.C.State**	26-1	Norm Sloan	30-1
2 UCLA	24-2	John Wooden	26-4
3 Marquette	22-4	Al McGuire	26-5
4 Maryland	23-5	Lefty Driesell	same
5 Notre Dame	24-2	Digger Phelps	26-3
6 Michigan	21-4	Johnny Orr	22-5
7 Kansas	21-5	Ted Owens	23-7
8 Providence	26-3	Dave Gavitt	28-4
9 **Indiana**	20-5	Bobby Knight	23-5
10 L.Beach St.	24-2	Lute Olson	same
11 **Purdue**	18-8	Fred Schaus	22-8
12 N.Carolina	22-5	Dean Smith	22-6
13 Vanderbilt	23-3	Roy Skinner	23-5
14 Alabama	22-4	C.M.Newton	same
15 Utah	19-7	Bill Foster	22-8
16 Pittsburgh	23-3	Buzz Ridl	25-4
17 USC	22-4	Bob Boyd	24-5
18 Oral Robts.	21-5	Ken Trickey	23-6
19 S.Carolina	22-4	Frank McGuire	22-5
20 Dayton	19-7	Don Donoher	20-9

Note: N.C.State won the NCAAs, Indiana won the CCA and Purdue won the NIT.

Major Conference Champions

Conference	Regular Season	Tournament
ACC	N.C. State (12-0)	N.C.State
Big 8	Kansas (13-1)	—
Big 10	Mich./Indiana (12-2)	—
Ivy	Penn (13-1)	—
Mo.Valley	Louisville (11-1)	—
Pac-8	UCLA (12-2)	—
SEC	Vanderbilt/Alabama (15-3)	—
SWC	Texas (11-3)	—
WAC	New Mexico (10-4)	—

NCAA Tournament (25 teams)

East Regional
First Round—Providence 84, Penn 69; Pittsburgh 54, St. Joseph's,PA 42; Furman 75, S.Carolina 67. **Semifinals**—N.C.State 92, Providence 78; Pittsburgh 81, Furman 78. **Third Place**—Providence 95, Furman 83. **Final**—N.C.State 100, Pittsburgh 72.

West Regional
First Round—New Mexico 73, Idaho St.65; Dayton 88, Cal St-Los Angeles 80. **Semifinals**—San Francisco 64, New Mexico 61; UCLA 111, Dayton 100 (3 OT). **Third Place**—New Mexico 66, Dayton 61. **Final**—UCLA 83, San Fran.60.

Mideast Regional
First Round—Notre Dame 108, Austin Peay 66; Marquette 85, Ohio Univ.59. **Semifinals**—Michigan 77, Notre Dame 68; Marquette 69, Vanderbilt 61. **Third Place**—Notre Dame 118, Vanderbilt 88. **Final**—Marquette 72, Michigan 70.

Midwest Regional
First Round—Oral Roberts 86, Syracuse 82 (OT); Creighton 77, Texas 61. **Semifinals**—Oral Roberts 96, Louisville 93; Kansas 55, Creighton 54. **Third Place**—Creighton 80, Louisville 71. **Final**—Kansas 93, Oral Roberts 90 (OT).

FINAL FOUR
at Greensboro (NC) Coliseum

Semifinals—N.C.State 80, UCLA 77 (2 OT); Marquette 64, Kansas 51. **Third Place**—UCLA 78, Kansas 61. **Championship**—N.C.State 76, Marquette 64. **Most Outstanding Player**—David Thompson, N.C.State. **All-Tournament**—Thompson, Tom Burleson and Monte Towe, N.C.State; Maurice Lucas, Marquette; Bill Walton, UCLA.

Collegiate Commissioners Assn. Tournament (8 teams)
at The Arena, St.Louis

First Round—Toledo 81, Arizona St.74; Indiana 73, Tennessee 71; Bradley 68, Kansas St.64; USC 82, SMU 70.

Semifinals—Indiana 73, Toledo 72; USC 74, Bradley 73. **Championship**—Indiana 85, USC 60. **Most Outstanding Player**—Kent Benson, Indiana.

NIT Tournament (16 teams)
All games at Madison Sq.Garden, New York

First Round—MD-East.Shore 84, Manhattan 81; Jacksonville 73, Massachusetts 69; Hawaii 66, Fairfield 65; Purdue 82, N.Carolina 71; Memphis St.73, Seton Hall 72; Utah 102, Rutgers 89; Connecticut 82, St.John's 70; Boston Col.63, Cincinnati 62. **Quarterfinals**—Jacksonville 85, MD-East.Shore 83; Purdue 85, Hawaii 72; Utah 92, Memphis State 78; Boston Col.76, UConn 75. **Semifinals**—Purdue 78, Jacksonville 63; Utah 117, Boston Col.93. **Third Place**—Boston Col.87, Jacksonville 77. **Championship**—Purdue 87, Utah 81. **MVP**—Mike Sojourner, Utah.

Players of the Year
Bill Walton, UCLA . . . . UPI, USBWA,Naismith, Helms(tie)
David Thompson . . . . AP,Helms(tie)

Coaches of the Year
Norm Sloan, N.C.State. . . . . AP,USBWA
Al McGuire, Marquette . . . . NABC
Digger Phelps, Notre Dame . . . . UPI

Consensus All-America
(In alphabetical order)

First Team—Marvin Barnes, Providence; John Shumate, Notre Dame; David Thompson, N.C.State; Bill Walton, UCLA; Keith Wilkes, UCLA.

Second Team—Len Elmore, Maryland; Bobby Jones, N.Carolina; Bill Knight, Pittsburgh; Larry Fogle, Canisius; Campy Russell, Michigan.

1975

John Wooden finally called it a career in 1975, but not before taking one last NCAA title into retirement with him.

The timing of his announcement was exquisite, coming immediately after UCLA's 75-74 overtime win against Louisville in the NCAA semifinal at San Diego. That was March 29. Two nights later, the Bruins won one more championship for the Wizard—beating Kentucky, 92-85, as Richard Washington and David Meyers combined for 52 points.

Wooden walked away with 10 NCAA titles, an overall record of 664-162, an NCAA tournament record of 47-10, and 19 different Coach of the Year awards over 29 seasons.

UCLA (AP) and Indiana (UPI) shared No.1 honors during the regular season, but the Hoosiers missed a trip to the Final Four when they lost to Kentucky in the Mideast Regional final.

Final AP Top 20

Writers' poll taken before tournament.

	Before Tourns	Head Coach	Final Record
1 UCLA	23-3	John Wooden	28-3
2 Kentucky	22-4	Joe B.Hall	26-5
3 Indiana	29-0	Bobby Knight	31-1
4 Louisville	24-2	Denny Crum	28-3
5 Maryland	22-4	Lefty Driesell	24-5
6 Syracuse	20-7	Roy Danforth	23-9
7 N.C.State	22-6	Norm Sloan	22-6
8 Ariz.St.	23-3	Ned Wulk	25-4
9 N.Carolina	21-7	Dean Smith	23-8
10 Alabama	22-4	C.M.Newton	22-5
11 Marquette	23-3	Al McGuire	23-4
12 Princeton	18-8	Pete Carril	22-8
13 Cincinnati	21-5	Gale Catlett	23-6
14 Notre Dame	18-8	Digger Phelps	19-10
15 Kansas St.	18-8	Jack Hartman	20-9
16 Drake	16-10	Bob Ortegel	19-10
17 UNLV	22-4	Jerry Tarkanian	24-5
18 Oregon St.	18-10	Ralph Miller	19-12
19 Michigan	19-7	Johnny Orr	19-8
20 Penn	23-4	Chuck Daly	23-5

Note: UCLA won the NCAAs, Princeton won the NIT and Drake won CCA.

Major Conference Champions

Conference	Regular Season	Tournament
ACC	Maryland (10-2)	N.Carolina
Big 8	Kansas (11-3)	—
Big 10	Indiana (18-0)	—
Ivy	Penn (13-1)	—
Mo.Valley	Louisville (12-2)	—
Pac-8	UCLA (12-2)	—
SEC	Kentucky/Alabama (15-3)	—
SWC	Texas A&M (12-2)	—
WAC	Arizona St.(12-2)	—

NCAA Tournament (32 teams)

East Regional

First Round—Syracuse 87, La Salle 83 (OT); N.Carolina 93, N.Mexico St.69; Boston Col.82, Furman 76; Kansas St.69, Penn 62. **Semifinals**—Syracuse 78, N.Carolina 76; Kansas St.74, Boston Col.65. **Third Place**—N.Carolina 110, Boston Col.90. **Final**—Syracuse 95, Kansas St.87 (OT).

Mideast Regional

First Round—Central Mich.77, Georgetown 75; Kentucky 76, Marquette 54; Indiana 78, UTEP 53; Oregon St.78, Middle Tenn.St. 67. **Semifinals**—Kentucky 90, Central Mich. 73; Indiana 81, Oregon St. 71. **Third Place**—Central Mich 88, Oregon St. 87. **Final**—Kentucky 92, Indiana 90.

Midwest Regional

First Round—Cincinnati 87, Texas A&M 79; Louisville 91, Rutgers 78; Maryland 83, Creighton 79; Notre Dame 77, Kansas 71. **Semifinals**—Louisville 78, Cincinnati 63; Maryland 83, Notre Dame 71. **Third Place**—Cincinnati 95, Notre Dame 87 (OT). **Final**—Louisville 96, Maryland 82.

West Regional

First Round—Arizona St. 97, Alabama 94; UNLV 90, San Diego St. 80; UCLA 103, Michigan 91 (OT); Montana 69, Utah St. 63. **Semifinals**—Arizona St. 84, UNLV 81; UCLA 67, Montana 64. **Third Place**—UNLV 75, Montana 67. **Final**—UCLA 89, Arizona St.75.

FINAL FOUR

at San Diego Sports Arena

Semifinals—Kentucky 95, Syracuse 79; UCLA 75, Louisville 74 (OT). **Third Place**—Louisville 96, Syracuse 88 (OT). **Championship**—UCLA 92, Kentucky 85. **Most Outstanding Player**—Richard Washington, UCLA. **All-Tournament**—Washington and David Meyers, UCLA; Kevin Grevey, Kentucky; Allen Murphy, Louisville; Jim Lee, Syracuse.

Collegiate Commissioners Assn. Tournament (8 teams)

at Freedom Hall, Louisville

First Round—Arizona 94, E.Carolina 78; Purdue 87, Missouri 74; Bowling Green 67, Tennessee 58; Drake 80, USC 70. **Semifinals**—Arizona 102, Purdue 96; Drake 78, Bowling Green 65. **Championship**—Drake 83, Arizona 76. **Most Outstanding Player**—Bob Elliott, Arizona.

NIT Tournament (16 teams)

All games at Madison Sq.Garden, New York

First Round—Manhattan 68, Massachusetts 51; Providence 91, Clemson 84; Pittsburgh 70, Southern Ill.65; St.John's 94, Lafayette 76; S.Carolina 71, Connecticut 61; Princeton 84, Holy Cross 63; Oral Roberts 97, Memphis St.95; Oregon 85, St.Peter's 79. **Quarterfinals**—Providence 101, Pittsburgh 80; St.John's 57, Manhattan 56; Oregon 68, Oral Roberts 59; Princeton 87, S.Carolina 67. **Semifinals**—Providence 85, St.John's 72; Princeton 58, Oregon 57. **Third Place**—Oregon 80, St.John's 76 (OT). **Championship**—Princeton 80, Providence 69. **MVP**—Ron Lee, Oregon.

Players of the Year

David Thompson, N.C.State . . . . . . AP,UPI,USBWA, Naismith,NABC

Kevin Grevey, Kentucky . . . . Helms(tie)
David Meyers, UCLA . . . . Helms(tie)

Coach of the Year

Bobby Knight, Indiana . . . . AP,UPI, USBWA, NABC

Consensus All-America

(In alphabetical order)

First Team—Adrian Dantley, Notre Dame; John Lucas, Maryland; Scott May, Indiana; David Meyers, UCLA; David Thompson, N.C.State.

1976

"And the winners are. . . Indiana, 86-68."

Actor and basketball fan Elliott Gould ripped open the envelope and made that announcement at the Academy Awards just as he was supposed to name the winner of the Oscar for Best Film Editing, Monday night, March 29.

Then the world knew what Bobby Knight and his unbeaten Hoosiers had wrought.

Indiana, 31-1 in 1975, came back a year later to go 32-0, routing Michigan in the first NCAA final between members of the same conference. Kent Benson was the tourney MVP, but the Hoosiers also had Player of the Year Scott May, Quinn Buckner and Bobby Wilkerson— all of whom would eventually be first round picks in the NBA draft.

Memphis State coach Gene Bartow replaced John Wooden at UCLA and led the Bruins to their 13th Final Four in the last 15 years. They lost to Indiana in the semifinals, but beat Rutgers in the consolation game.

Bobby Knight's college coach, Fred Taylor of Ohio State, retired at the end of the regular season after 18 years. Taylor, who was 35 when the Buckeyes won their only NCAA title in 1960, led OSU to seven Big Ten titles and three straight NCAA finals (1960-62).

By the way, the Best Film Editing Oscar went to Vera Fields for "Jaws."

Final AP Top 20
Writers' poll taken before tournament.

	Before Tourns	Head Coach	Final Record
1 **Indiana**	27-0	Bobby Knight	32-0
2 Marquette	25-1	Al McGuire	27-2
3 UNLV	28-1	Jerry Tarkanian	29-2
4 Rutgers	28-0	Tom Young	31-2
5 UCLA	24-3	Gene Bartow	28-4
6 Alabama	22-4	C.M.Newton	23-5
7 Notre Dame	22-5	Digger Phelps	23-6
8 N.Carolina	25-3	Dean Smith	25-4
9 Michigan	21-6	Johnny Orr	25-7
10 W.Michigan	24-2	Eldon Miller	25-3
11 Maryland	22-6	Lefty Driesell	same
12 Cincinnati	25-5	Gale Catlett	25-6
13 Tennessee	21-5	Ray Mears	21-6
14 Missouri	24-4	Norm Stewart	26-5
15 Arizona	22-8	Fred Snowden	24-9
16 Texas Tech	24-5	Gerald Myers	25-6
17 DePaul	19-8	Ray Meyer	20-9
18 Virginia	18-11	Terry Holland	18-12
19 Centenary	22-5	Larry Little	same
20 Pepperdine	21-5	Gary Colson	22-6

Note: Indiana won the NCAAs and unranked Kentucky (22-4, Joe B.Hall, 26-4) won the NIT.

Major Conference Champions

Conference	Regular Season	Tournament
ACC	N.Carolina (11-1)	Virginia
Big 8	Missouri (12-2)	—
Big 10	Indiana (18-0)	—
Ivy	Princeton (14-0)	—
Metro	No champion	Cincinnati
Mo.Valley	Wichita St.(10-2)	—
Pac-8	UCLA (12-2)	—
SEC	Alabama (12-2)	—
SWC	Texas A&M (14-2)	Texas Tech
WAC	Arizona (11-3)	—

NCAA Tournament (32 teams)
East Regional
First Round—DePaul 69, Virginia 60; VMI 81, Tennessee 75; Rutgers 54, Princeton 53; Connecticut 80, Hofstra 78 (OT). **Semifinals**—VMI 71, DePaul 66; Rutgers 93, UConn 79. **Final**—Rutgers 91, VMI 75.

Midwest Regional
First Round—Michigan 74, Wichita St. 73; Notre Dame 79, Cincinnati 78; Missouri 69, Washington 67; Texas Tech 69, Syracuse 56. **Semifinals**—Missouri 86, Texas Tech 75; Michigan 80, Notre Dame 76. **Final**—Michigan 95, Missouri 88.

Mideast Regional
First Round—Alabama 79, N.Carolina 64; Indiana 90, St.John's 70; Marquette 79, Western Ky.60; Western Mich.77, Va.Tech 67 (OT). **Semifinals**—Indiana 74, Alabama 69; Marquette 62, Western Mich. 57. **Final**—Indiana 65, Marquette 56.

West Regional
First Round—Pepperdine 87, Memphis St.77; UCLA 74, San Diego St.64; Arizona 83, Georgetown 76; UNLV 103, Boise St.78. **Semifinals**—UCLA 70, Pepperdine 61; Arizona 114, UNLV 109 (OT). **Final**—UCLA 82, Arizona 66.

FINAL FOUR
at The Spectrum, Philadelphia

Semifinals—Michigan 86, Rutgers 70; Indiana 65, UCLA 51. **Third Place**—UCLA 106, Rutgers 92. **Championship**—Indiana 86, Michigan 68. **Most Outstanding Player**—Kent Benson, Indiana. **All-Tournament**—Benson, Scott May and Tom Abernethy, Indiana; Rickey Green, Michigan; Marques Johnson, UCLA.

NIT Tournament (12 teams)
All games at Madison Sq.Garden, New York

First Round—NC-Charlotte 79, San Francisco 74; Holy Cross 84, St.Peter's 78; Kentucky 67, Niagara 61; Providence 84, N.Carolina A&T 68.
Quarterfinals—NC-Charlotte 79, Oregon 72; N.C.State 78, Holy Cross 68; Kentucky 81, Kansas St.78; Providence 73, Louisville 67.
Semifinals—NC-Charlotte 80, N.C.State 79; Kentucky 79, Providence 78. **Third Place**—N.C.State 74, Providence 69. **Championship**—Kentucky 71, NC-Charlotte 67.
MVP—Cedric Maxwell, NC-Charlotte.

Players of the Year
Scott May, Indiana . . . . UPI,AP,Naismith, NABC,Helms(tie)
Kent Benson, Indiana . . . . Helms(tie)
Adrian Dantley, Notre Dame . . . . USBWA

Coaches of the Year
Bobby Knight, Indiana . . . . AP,USBWA
Johnny Orr, Michigan . . . . NABC
Tom Young, Rutgers . . . . UPI

Consensus All-America
(In alphabetical order)

First Team—Kent Benson, Indiana; Adrian Dantley, Notre Dame; John Lucas, Maryland; Scott May, Indiana; Richard Washington, UCLA

Second Team—Phil Ford, N.Carolina; Bernard King, Tennessee; Mitch Kupchak, N.Carolina; Phil Sellers, Rutgers; Earl Tatum, Marquette.

1977

Three years after playing and losing its first NCAA Final to North Carolina State, Marquette returned to the championship game in 1977 and beat North Carolina for the title.

The Warriors (25-7) ended the season with more losses than any previous NCAA champion, but they won the title knowing their biggest loss would come after their last game. Coach Al McGuire was retiring after 13 seasons at the Milwaukee school.

The colorful McGuire was as New York City as you could be—a native who played for both St.John's and the Knicks—but North Carolina had a huge influence on his career. His only other college head coaching job had been a seven-year stint at Belmont Abbey in Belmont, N.C.

Still another North Carolina school, N.C.-Charlotte, almost beat McGuire in the semifinals, but Butch Lee and Jerome Whitehead saved the day. With three seconds left, Lee heaved a court-length pass to Whitehead (off the fingertips of UNCC's Cornbread Maxwell) for the dunk and a 51-49 win.

The championship game was somewhat easier on McGuire's heart. More in control of his emotions than in the 1974 Final (when he picked up two technical fouls) McGuire kept his cool until the last minute when he broke down and wept as Marquette claimed the title by nine points.

Final AP Top 20
Writers' poll taken before tournament.

	Before Tourns	Head Coach	Final Record
1 Michigan	24-3	Johnny Orr	26-4
2 UCLA	24-3	Gene Bartow	25-4
3 Kentucky	24-3	Joe B.Hall	26-4
4 UNLV	25-2	Jerry Tarkanian	29-3
5 N.Carolina	24-4	Dean Smith	28-5
6 Syracuse	25-3	Jim Boeheim	26-4
7 **Marquette**	20-7	Al McGuire	25-7
8 San.Fran.	29-1	Bob Gaillard	29-2
9 W.Forest	20-7	Carl Tacy	22-8
10 Notre Dame	21-6	Digger Phelps	22-7
11 Alabama	23-4	C.M.Newton	25-6
12 Detroit	24-3	Dick Vitale	25-4
13 Minnesota	24-3	Jim Dutcher	same
14 Utah	22-6	Jerry Pimm	23-7
15 Tennessee	22-5	Ray Mears	22-6
16 Kansas St.	23-6	Jack Hartman	24-7
17 UNCC	25-3	Lee Rose	28-5
18 Arkansas	26-1	Eddie Sutton	26-2
19 Louisville	21-6	Denny Crum	21-7
20 VMI	25-3	Charlie Schmaus	26-4

Note: Marquette won the NCAAs and unranked St.Bonaventure (20-6, Jim Satalin, 24-6) won the NIT.

Major Conference Champions

Conference	Regular Season	Tournament
ACC	N.Carolina (9-3)	N.Carolina
Big 8	Kansas St.(11-3)	—
Big 10	Michigan (16-2)	—
Ivy	Princeton (13-1)	—
Metro	Louisville (6-1)	Cincinnati
Mo.Valley	So.Ill./N.Mex.St.(8-4)	So.Ill.
Pac-8	UCLA (11-3)	—
SEC	Tenn./Kentucky (16-2)	—
SWC	Arkansas (16-0)	Arkansas
WAC	Utah (11-3)	—

NCAA Tournament (32 teams)
East Regional
First Round—VMI 73, Duquesne 66; Kentucky 72, Princeton 58; Notre Dame 90, Hofstra 83; N.Carolina 69, Purdue 66. **Semifinals**—Kentucky 93, VMI 78; N.Carolina 79, Notre Dame 77. **Final**—N.Carolina 79, Kentucky 72.

West Regional
First Round—UCLA 87, Louisville 79; Idaho St.83, Long Beach St. 72; Utah 72, St.John's 68; UNLV 121, San Francisco 95. **Semifinals**—Idaho St.76, UCLA 75; UNLV 88, Utah 83. **Final**—UNLV 107, Idaho St.90.

Mideast Regional
First Round—Michigan 92, Holy Cross 81; Detroit 93, Middle Tenn.St.76; NC-Charlotte 91, Central Mich.86 (OT); Syracuse 93, Tennessee 88 (OT). **Semifinals**—Michigan 86, Detroit 81; NC-Charlotte 81, Syracuse 59. **Final**—NC-Charlotte 75, Michigan 68;

Midwest Regional
First Round—Marquette 66, Cincinnati 51; Kansas St.87, Providence 80; Wake Forest 86, Arkansas 80; Southern Ill. 81, Arizona 77. **Semifinals**—Marquette 67, Kansas St.66; Wake Forest 86, Southern Ill.81. **Final**—Marquette 82, Wake Forest 68.

FINAL FOUR
at The Omni, Atlanta

Semifinals—Marquette 51, NC-Charlotte, 49; N.Carolina 84, UNLV 83. **Third Place**—UNLV 106, NC-Charlotte 94. **Championship**—Marquette 67, N.Carolina 59.

Most Outstanding Player—Butch Lee, Marquette. **All-Tournament**—Lee, Bo Ellis and Jerome Whitehead, Marquette; Mike O'Koren and Walter Davis, N. Carolina; Cedric Maxwell, NC-Charlotte.

NIT Tournament (16 teams)
at Madison Square Garden, New York
First Round—Alabama 86, Memphis St.63; Va.Tech 83, Georgetown 79; Illinois St.65, Creighton 58; Houston 83, Indiana St.82; Villanova 71, Old Dominion 68 (OT); Massachusetts 86, Seton Hall 85; Oregon 90, Oral Roberts 89; St.Bonaventure 79, Rutgers 77. **Quarterfinals**—Alabama 79, Va.Tech 72; Houston 91, Illinois St.90; Villanova 81, UMass 71; St.Bonaventure 79, Rutgers 77. **Semifinals**—Houston 82, Alabama 76; St.Bonaventure 86, Villanova 82. **Third Place**—Villanova 102, Alabama 89. **Championship**—St.Bonaventure 94, Houston 91.

MVP—Greg Sanders, St.Bonaventure.

Player of the Year
Marques Johnson, UCLA . . . . UPI,AP USBWA, Naismith,NABC,Wooden,Helms

Coaches of the Year
Bob Gaillard, San Francisco . . . . UPI,AP
Eddie Sutton, Arkansas . . . . USBWA
Dean Smith, North Carolina . . . . NABC

Consensus All-America
(In alphabetical order)
First Team—Otis Birdsong, Houston; Kent Benson, Indiana; Phil Ford, N.Carolina; Rickey Green, Michigan; Marques Johnson, UCLA; Bernard King, Tennessee.

Second Team—Greg Ballard, Oregon; Bill Cartwright, San Francisco; Rod Griffin, Wake Forest; Ernie Grunfeld, Tennessee; Phil Hubbard, Michigan; Butch Lee, Marquette; Mychal Thompson, Minnesota.

1978

The 1977-78 season was just beginning when Adolph Rupp died on Dec.10. Three and a half months later, Kentucky won its fifth NCAA championship. It was the Wildcats' first title in 20 years.

Coached by Joe B. Hall, who succeeded Rupp in 1972, the Wildcats were favored to win it all right from the start and the pressure to live up to that prediction and break the 20-year dry spell was intense.

Kentucky came into the tournament ranked No.1 and with a record of 25-2. In the Mideast Regional, the Wildcats played three conference champions (Florida St., Miami of Ohio and Michigan St.) and beat them all. At the Final Four in St.Louis, they defeated two more champions, Arkansas in the semifinals and Duke in the Final to win the title and end their misery.

Forward Jack Givens scored 41 points against Duke to win MVP honors.

Fifth-ranked Arkansas and No.6 Notre Dame both made it to the Final Four for the first time ever. In St.Louis, however, they each lost their semifinal games— the Razorbacks to Kentucky and the Irish to Duke. Arkansas won the consolation game at the buzzer, 71-69.

Texas shared the Southwest Conference title with Arkansas and coaches Eddie Sutton and Abe Lemons were two of the Coaches of the Year. Lemons and Texas had to settle for a bid to the NIT where the Longhorns met North Carolina State in the final and won by eight.

Final AP Top 20
Writers' poll taken before tournament.

	Before Tourns	Head Coach	Final Record
1 **Kentucky**	25-2	Joe B.Hall	30-2
2 UCLA	24-2	Gary Cunningham	25-3
3 DePaul	25-2	Ray Meyer	27-3
4 Mich.St.	23-4	Jud Heathcote	25-5
5 Arkansas	28-3	Eddie Sutton	32-3
6 Notre Dame	20-6	Digger Phelps	23-8
7 Duke	23-6	Bill Foster	27-7
8 Marquette	24-3	Hank Raymonds	24-4
9 Louisville	22-6	Denny Crum	23-7
10 Kansas	24-4	Ted Owens	24-5
11 San Fran.	22-5	Bob Gaillard	23-6
12 New Mexico	24-3	Norm Ellenberger	24-4
13 Indiana	20-7	Bobby Knight	21-8
14 Utah	22-5	Jerry Pimm	23-6
15 Florida St.	23-5	Hugh Durham	23-6
16 N.Carolina	23-7	Dean Smith	23-8
17 **Texas**	22-5	Abe Lemons	26-5
18 Detroit	24-3	Dave Gaines	25-4
19 Miami,OH	18-8	Darrell Hedric	19-9
20 Penn	19-7	Bob Weinhauer	20-8

Note: Kentucky won the NCAAs and Texas won the NIT.

Major Conference Champions

Conference	Regular Season	Tournament
ACC	N.Carolina (9-3)	Duke
Big 8	Kansas (13-1)	—
Big 10	Michigan St.(15-3)	—
Ivy	Penn (12-2)	—
Metro	Florida St.(11-1)	Louisville
Mo.Valley	Creighton (12-4)	Creighton
Pac-8	UCLA (14-0)	—
SEC	Kentucky (16-2)	—
SWC	Texas/Arkansas (14-2)	Houston
WAC	New Mexico (13-1)	—

NCAA Tournament (32 teams)

East Regional
First Round—Duke 63, Rhode Is. 62; Penn 92, St. Bona. 83; Indiana 63, Furman 62; Villanova 103, La Salle 97. **Semifinals**—Duke 84, Penn 80; Villanova 61, Indiana 60. **Final**—Duke 90, Villanova 72.

Midwest Regional
First Round—Utah 86, Missouri 79 (2 OT); Notre Dame 100, Houston 77; DePaul 80, Creighton 78; Louisville 76, St.John's 68. **Semifinals**—Notre Dame 69, Utah 56; DePaul 90, Louisville 89 (2 OT). **Final**—Notre Dame 84, DePaul 64.

Mideast Regional
First Round—Michigan St.77, Providence 63; Western Ky.87, Syracuse 86 (OT); Miami,OH 84, Marquette 81 (OT); Kentucky 85, Florida St.76. **Semifinals**—Michigan St.90, Western Ky.69; Kentucky 91, Miami,OH 69. **Final**—Kentucky 52, Michigan St.49.

West Regional
First Round—UCLA 83, Kansas 76; Arkansas 73, Weber St.52; San Francisco 68, N.Carolina 64; Cal St-Fullerton 90, New Mexico 85. **Semifinals**—Arkansas 74, UCLA 70; Cal St-Fullerton 75, San Fran.72. **Final**—Arkansas 61, Cal St-Fullerton 58.

FINAL FOUR
at The Checkerdome, St.Louis
Semifinals—Kentucky 64, Arkansas 59; Duke 90, Notre Dame 86. **Third Place**—Arkansas 71, Notre Dame 69. **Championship**—Kentucky 94, Duke 88. **Most Outstanding Player**—Jack Givens, Kentucky. **All-Tournament**—Givens and Rick Robey, Kentucky; Mike Gminski and Jim Spanarkel, Duke; Ron Brewer, Arkansas.

NIT Tournament (16 teams)
at Madison Square Garden, New York

First Round—Georgetown 70, Virginia 68; Nebraska 67, Utah St.66; Texas 72, Temple 58; Rutgers 72, Army 70; Indiana 73, Illinois St.71; N.C.State 82, S.Carolina 70; Detroit 94, VCU 86; Dayton 108, Fairfield 93. **Quarterfinals**—Georgetown 71, Dayton 62; Texas 67, Nebraska 48; Rutgers 57, Indiana St.56; N.C.State 84, Detroit 77. **Semifinals**—Texas 96, Rutgers 76; N.C.State 86, Georgetown 85. **Third Place**—Rutgers 85, Georgetown 72. **Championship**—Texas 101, N.C.State 93. **MVPs**—Ron Baxter and Jim Krivacs, Texas.

Players of the Year

Phil Ford, N.Carolina . . . . . USBWA, NABC,Wooden
Butch Lee, Marquette . . . . UPI,AP,Naismith
Jack Givens, Kentucky . . . . Helms

Coaches of the Year

Eddie Sutton, Arkansas . . . . .UPI,AP
Bill Foster, Duke . . . . NABC (tie)
Abe Lemons, Texas . . . . NABC (tie)
Ray Meyer, DePaul . . . . .USBWA

Consensus All-America
(In alphabetical order)

First Team—Larry Bird, Indiana St.; Phil Ford, N.Carolina; David Greenwood, UCLA; Butch Lee, Marquette; Mychal Thompson, Minnesota.

Second Team—Ron Brewer, Arkansas; Jack Givens, Kentucky; Rod Griffin, Wake Forest; Rick Robey, Kentucky; Freeman Williams, Portland St.

1979

The NCAA tournament, which began the decade with a 25-team field, had expanded to include 40 teams by 1979. In the process, the Final Four had become an annual rite of Spring, right up there with the Masters and Opening Day of the baseball season. But it wasn't a national obsession. Yet.

Then Indiana State played Michigan State for the NCAA championship in Salt Lake City.

And Larry Bird met Magic Johnson. It was a showdown made in TV heaven. Bird of the unbeaten Sycamores (fifth-year senior, Player of the Year and already a first round draft pick of the Boston Celtics) vs Magic of the Spartans (only a sophomore, but a 6-9 point guard who was every bit the ball wizard Bird was).

Michigan St. won the game by 11 as Magic outscored Bird, 24-19, but the numbers that really counted were these: NBC-TV pulled a 24.1 rating and a 38 share that are still NCAA tournament records.

A year later, Bird was Rookie the Year in the NBA and Magic, who entered the '79 draft as an underclassman, helped lead the L.A. Lakers to the world championship.

No.6 DePaul upset third-ranked UCLA, 95-91, in the West Regional championship game, giving Blue Demons' coach Ray Meyer his first (and only) ticket to the Final Four. After a two-point loss to Indiana State in the semifinal, DePaul beat Penn for third place.

Final AP Top 20
Writers' poll taken before tournament.

	Before Tourns	Head Coach	Final Record
1 Indiana St.	29-0	Bill Hodges	33-1
2 UCLA	23-4	Gary Cunningham	25-5
3 **Mich.St.**	21-6	Jud Heathcote	26-6
4 Notre Dame	22-5	Digger Phelps	24-6
5 Arkansas	23-4	Eddie Sutton	25-5
6 DePaul	22-5	Ray Meyer	26-6
7 LSU	22-5	Dale Brown	23-6
8 Syracuse	25-3	Jim Boeheim	26-4
9 N.Carolina	23-5	Dean Smith	23-6
10 Marquette	21-6	Hank Raymonds	22-7
11 Duke	22-7	Bill Foster	22-8
12 San Fran.	21-6	Dan Belluomini	22-7
13 Louisville	23-7	Denny Crum	24-8
14 Penn	21-5	Bob Weinhauer	25-7
15 Purdue	23-7	Lee Rose	27-8
16 Oklahoma	20-9	Dave Bliss	21-10
17 St.John's	18-10	Lou Carnesecca	21-11
18 Rutgers	21-8	Tom Young	22-9
19 Toledo	21-6	Bob Nichols	22-7
20 Iowa	20-7	Lute Olson	20-8

Note: Michigan St.won the NCAAs and unranked Indiana (17-12, Bobby Knight, 22-12) won the NIT.

Major Conference Champions

Conference	Regular Season	Tournament
ACC	Duke/N.Carolina (9-3)	N.Carolina
Big 8	Oklahoma (10-4)	—
Big 10	Mich.St./Purdue/ Iowa (13-5)	—
Ivy	Penn (13-1)	—
Metro	Louisville (9-1)	Va.Tech
Mo.Valley	Indiana St.(16-0)	Indiana St.
Pac-10	UCLA (15-3)	—
SEC	LSU (14-4)	Tennessee
SWC	Texas/Arkansas (13-3)	Arkansas
WAC	BYU (10-2)	—

NCAA Tournament (40 teams)
East Regional
First Round—St.John's 75, Temple 70; Penn 73, Iona 69. **Second Round**—St.John's 80, Duke 78; Rutgers 64, Georgetown 58; Penn 72, N.Carolina 71; Syracuse 89, Connecticut 81. **Semifinals**—St.John's 67, Rutgers 65; Penn 84, Syracuse 76. **Final**—Penn 64, St.John's 62.

Mideast Regional
First Round—Lamar 95, Detroit 87; Tennessee 97, Eastern Ky.81. **Second Round**—Michigan St. 95, Lamar 64; LSU 71, Appalachian St. 57; Notre Dame 73, Tennessee 67; Toledo 74, Iowa 72. **Semifinals**—Michigan St.87, LSU 71; Notre Dame 79, Toledo 71. **Final**—Michigan St.80, Notre Dame 68.

West Regional
First Round—Southern Cal 86, Utah St. 67; Pepperdine 92, Utah 88 (OT). **Second Round**—DePaul 89, Southern Cal 78; Marquette 73, Pacific 48; UCLA 76, Pepperdine 71; San Francisco 86, BYU 63. **Semifinals**—DePaul 62, Marquette 56; UCLA 99, San Fran.81. **Final**—DePaul 95, UCLA 91.

Midwest Regional
First Round—Weber St.81, N.Mexico St.78 (OT); Va. Tech 70, Jacksonville 53. **Second Round**—Arkansas 74, Weber St.63; Louisville 69, S.Alabama 66; Indiana St. 86, Va.Tech 69; Oklahoma 70, Texas 76. **Semifinals**—Arkansas 73, Louisville 62; Indiana St.93, Oklahoma 72. **Final**—Indiana St.73, Arkansas 71.

FINAL FOUR
at Special Events Center, Salt Lake City.
Semifinals—Michigan St. 101, Penn 67; Indiana St.76, DePaul 74. **Third Place**—DePaul 96, Penn 93. **Championship**—Michigan St.75, Indiana St.64.
Most Outstanding Player—Magic Johnson, Michigan St. **All-Tournament**—Johnson and Greg Kelser, Michigan St.; Larry Bird, Indiana St.; Mark Aguirre and Gary Garland, DePaul.

NIT Tournament (24 teams)
at Madison Square Garden, New York
Field—Alabama, Alcorn St., Central Mich., Clemson, Dayton, Holy Cross, Indiana, Kentucky, Maryland, Miss.St., Nevada-Reno, N.Mexico, NE La., ODU, Ohio St., Ore.St., Purdue, Rhode Is., St.Bona., St.Joe's-PA, Texas A&M, Texas Tech, Virginia, Wagner. **Semifinals**—Indiana 64, Ohio St.55; Purdue 87, Alabama 68. **Third Place**—Alabama 96, Ohio St.86. **Championship**—Indiana 53, Purdue 52. **MVPs**—Clarence Carter and Ray Tolbert, Indiana.

Player of the Year
Larry Bird, Indiana St . . . . UPI,AP,USBWA
Naismith,NABC,Wooden,Helms

Coaches of the Year
Bill Hodges, Indiana St . . . . UPI,AP
Ray Meyer, DePaul . . . . NABC
Dean Smith, North Carolina . . . . USBWA

Consensus All-America
(In alphabetical order)
First Team—Larry Bird, Indiana St; Mike Gminski, Duke; David Greenwood, UCLA; Magic Johnson, Michigan St.; Sidney Moncrief, Arkansas

Second Team—Bill Cartwright, San Francisco; Calvin Natt, NE Louisiana; Kelly Tripucka, Notre Dame; Mike O'Koren, N.Carolina; Jim Spanarkel, Duke; Jim Paxson, Dayton; Sly Williams, Rhode Island.

1980

Denny Crum played for John Wooden at UCLA in the late 1950s and served as the Wizard's top assistant and chief recruiter from 1967-70. Then, after four NCAA championships, Crum left to coach Louisville in 1970-71.

In 1972 and again in '75, Crum got the Cardinals into the Final Four and both times lost to Wooden and the Bruins in the semifinals. In 1980, Crum & Co. returned to the Big Dance, beat Iowa in the semifinals and met UCLA (who else?) for the championship.

But Larry Brown was coaching the Bruins now. So with Wooden gone and Darrell Griffith (23 points) and Rodney McCray (11 boards) leading Louisville's Doctors of Dunk, Crum won his first NCAA title as head man.

Player of the Year Mark Aguirre and No.1 DePaul were eliminated by UCLA in the second round of the West Regional.

The NCAA tournament field, which expanded from 32 to 40 teams in 1979, grew to 48 in 1980 (24 automatic qualifiers and 24 at-large teams). The NIT, meanwhile, kept pace, adding 16 teams for a total of 32. In other words, 80 Division I teams now had a shot at a postseason tournament—double the number of berths available just 10 years ago.

Final AP Top 20

Writers' poll taken before tournament.

			Before NCAAs	Head Coach	Final Record
1	DePaul		26-1	Ray Meyer	26-2
2	**Louisville**		28-3	Denny Crum	33-3
3	LSU		24-5	Dale Brown	26-6
4	Kentucky		28-5	Joe B.Hall	29-6
5	Oregon St.		26-3	Ralph Miller	26-4
6	Syracuse		25-3	Jim Boeheim	26-4
7	Indiana		20-7	Bob Knight	21-8
8	Maryland		23-6	Lefty Driesell	24-7
9	Notre Dame		20-7	Digger Phelps	20-8
10	Ohio St.		24-5	Eldon Miller	21-8
11	Georgetown		24-5	John Thompson	26-6
12	BYU		24-4	Frank Arnold	24-5
13	St.John's		24-4	Lou Carnesecca	24-5
14	Duke		22-8	Bill Foster	24-9
15	N.Carolina		21-7	Dean Smith	21-8
16	Missouri		23-5	Norm Stewart	25-6
17	Weber St.		26-2	Neil McCarthy	26-3
18	Arizona St.		21-6	Ned Wulk	22-7
19	Iona		28-4	Jim Valvano	29-5
20	Purdue		19-9	Lee Rose	23-10

Note: Louisville won the NCAAs.

Major Conference Champions

Conference	Regular Season	Tournament
ACC	Maryland (11-3)	Duke
Big East	Syracuse/Georgetown/	
	St.John's (5-1)	Georgetown
Big 8	Missouri (11-3)	Kansas St.
Big 10	Indiana (13-5)	
Metro	Louisville (12-0)	Louisville
Mo.Valley	Bradley (13-3)	Bradley
Pac-10	Oregon St.(16-2)	
PCAA	Utah St.(11-2)	San Jose St.
SEC	Kentucky (15-3)	LSU
SWC	Texas A&M (14-2)	Texas A&M
WAC	BYU (13-1)	—

NCAA Tournament (48 teams)

East Regional

First Round—Villanova 77, Marquette 59; Iowa 86, Va.Comm.72; Iona 84, Holy Cross 78; Tennessee 80, Furman 69. **Second Round**—Syracuse 97, Villanova 83; Iowa 77, N.C.State 64; Georgetown 74, Iona 71; Maryland 86, Tennessee 75. **Semifinals**—Iowa 88, Syracuse 77; Georgetown 74, Maryland 68. **Final**—Iowa 81, Georgetown 80.

Midwest Regional

First Round—Alcorn St.70, South Ala.62; Missouri 61, San Jose St.51; Texas A&M 55, Bradley 53; Kansas St. 71 Arkansas 53. **Second Round**—LSU 98, Alcorn St. 88; Missouri 87, Notre Dame 84; Texas A&M 78, N. Carolina 61 (2 OT); Louisville 71, Kansas St.69 (OT). **Semifinals**—LSU 68, Missouri 63; Louisville 66, Texas A&M 55 (OT). **Final**—Louisville 86, LSU 66.

Mideast Regional

First Round—Fla.St.94, Toledo 91; Penn 62, Wash.St. 55; Purdue 90, La Salle 82; Va.Tech 89, Western Ky.85. **Second Round**—Kentucky 97, Fla.St.78; Duke 52, Penn 42; Purdue 87, St.John's 72; Indiana 68, Va.Tech 59. **Semifinals**—Duke 55, Kentucky 54; Purdue 76, Indiana 69. **Final**—Purdue 68, Duke 60.

West Regional

First Round—UCLA 87, Old Dom.74; Ariz.St.99, Loyola-CA 71; Clemson 76, Utah St.73; Lamar 87, Weber St.86. **Second Round**—UCLA 77, DePaul 71; Ohio St.89, Ariz.St.75; Clemson 71, BYU 66; Lamar 81, Ore. St. 77. **Semifinals**—UCLA 72, Ohio St.68; Clemson 74, Lamar 66. **Final**—UCLA 67, Purdue 62.

FINAL FOUR

at Market Square Arena, Indianapolis
Semifinals—Louisville 80, Iowa 72; UCLA 67, Purdue 62; **Championship**—Louisville 59, UCLA 54. **Outstanding Player:** Darrell Griffith, Louisville. **All-Tournament:** Griffith and Rodney McCray, Louisville; Rod Foster and Kiki Vandeweghe, UCLA; Joe Barry Carroll, Purdue.

NIT Tournament (32 teams)

Final Four at Madison Sq.Garden, New York
Field—Alabama, Ala-Birm., Boston Col., Boston U., Bowl.Green, UConn, Duquesne, Grambling, Illinois, Ill. St., Jacksonville, Lafayette, L.Beach St., Loyola-IL, Michigan, Minnesota, Mississippi, Murray St., Nebraska, UNLV, Penn St., Pepperdine, Pitt, St.Joe's-PA, St. Peter's, SW La., Texas, UTEP, Virginia, Washington, W.Texas St., Wichita St.
Semifinals—Virginia 90, UNLV 71; Minnesota 65, Illinois 63. **Third Place**—Illinois 84, UNLV 74. **Championship**—Virginia 58, Minnesota 55.
MVP—Ralph Sampson, Virginia.

Players of the Year

Mark Aguirre, DePaul . . .UPI,AP,USBWA, Naismith
Michael Brooks, La Salle . . . .
Darrell Griffith, Louisville. . . . . .Wooden

Coaches of the Year

Ray Meyer, DePaul . . . . .UPI,AP,USBWA
Lute Olson, Iowa . . . . .NABC

Consensus All-America

(In alphabetical order)
First Team—Mark Aguirre, DePaul; Michael Brooks, LaSalle; Joe Barry Carroll, Purdue; Darrell Griffith, Louisville; Kyle Macy, Kentucky.
Second Team—Mike Gminski, Duke; Albert King, Maryland; Mike O'Koren, N.Carolina; Kelvin Ransey, Ohio St.; Sam Worthen, Marquette.

1981

Ray Meyer took over the basketball program at DePaul in 1943 and for his first four years got to coach George Mikan.

With the 6-10 Mikan in the pivot, DePaul finished third in the 1943 NCAA tournament, second in the 1944 NIT and then won the NIT in 1945.

After Mikan graduated and went off to the pros, Meyer and DePaul avoided the glare of public attention until the late 1970s when the Blue Demons, ranked No.3 after the regular season in 1978, finished third in the NCAAs in 1979 and entered the postseason ranked No.1 in both 1980 and '81.

Both of those No.1 DePaul clubs were upset in the first round by unranked teams—in 1980 by UCLA (77-71) and in 1981 by St. Joseph's of Pa. (49-48). In fact, '81 was a big year for watching the mighty fall. No.2 Oregon State lost to Kansas State (50-48) while No.3 Arizona State was routed by Kansas (88-71).

With the tournament suddenly wide open, No.9 Indiana, led by sophomore guard Isiah Thomas, came out of the Mideast Regional to win the title. The Hoosiers defeated North Carolina by 13 in the final. Thomas, the tournament MVP, turned pro after the season and was the first round draft pick of the Detroit Pistons.

Final AP Top 20
Writers' poll taken before tournament.

	Before NCAAs	Head Coach	Final Record
1 DePaul	27-1	Ray Meyer	27-2
2 Oregon St.	26-1	Ralph Miller	26-2
3 Ariz.St.	24-3	Ned Wulk	24-4
4 LSU	28-3	Dale Brown	31-5
5 Virginia	25-3	Terry Holland	29-4
6 N.Carolina	25-7	Dean Smith	29-8
7 Notre Dame	22-5	Digger Phelps	23-6
8 Kentucky	22-5	Joe B.Hall	22-6
9 **Indiana**	21-9	Bob Knight	26-9
10 UCLA	20-6	Larry Brown	20-7
11 W.Forest	22-6	Carl Tacy	22-7
12 Louisville	21-8	Denny Crum	21-9
13 Iowa	21-6	Lute Olson	21-7
14 Utah	24-4	Jerry Pimm	25-5
15 Tennessee	20-7	Don DeVoe	21-8
16 BYU	22-6	Frank Arnold	25-7
17 Wyoming	23-5	Jim Brandenburg	24-6
18 Maryland	20-9	Lefty Driesell	21-10
19 Illinois	20-7	Lou Henson	21-8
20 Arkansas	22-7	Eddie Sutton	24-8

Note: Indiana won the NCAAs.

Major Conference Champions

Conference	Regular Season	Tournament
ACC	Virginia (13-1)	N.Carolina
Big East	Boston College (10-4)	Syracuse
Big 8	Missouri (10-4)	Kansas
Big 10	Indiana (14-4)	—
Metro	Louisville (11-1)	Louisville
Mo.Valley	Wichita St.(12-4)	Creighton
Pac-10	Oregon St.(17-1)	—
PCAA	Fresno St.(12-2)	Fresno St.
SEC	LSU (17-1)	Mississippi
SWC	Arkansas (13-3)	Houston
WAC	Utah/Wyoming (13-3)	—

NCAA Tournament (48 teams)

East Regional
First Round—Villanova 90, Houston 72; Va.Comm.85, LIU 69; BYU 60, Princeton 51; J.Madison 61, Georgetown 55. **Second Round**—Virginia 54, Villanova 50; Tennessee 58, Va.Comm.56 (OT); BYU 78, UCLA 55; Notre Dame 54, J.Madison 45. **Semifinals**—Virginia 62, Tennessee 48; BYU 51, Notre Dame 50. **Final**—Virginia 74, BYU 60.

West Regional
First Round—Kansas St.64, San Fran.60; Wyoming 78, Howard 43; N'eastern 55, Fresno St.53; Pitt 70, Idaho 69. **Second Round**—Kansas St.50, Ore.St.48; Illinois 67, Wyoming 65; Utah 94, N'eastern 69; N.Car. 74, Pitt 57. **Semifinals**—Kansas St.57, Illinois 52; N.Car. 61, Utah 56. **Final**—N.Carolina 82, Kansas St. 68.

Midwest Regional
First Round—Lamar 71, Missouri 67; Arkansas 73, Mercer 67; Wichita St.95, Southern-BR 70; Kansas 69, Mississippi 66. **Second Round**—LSU 100, Lamar 78; Arkansas 74, Louisville 73; Wichita St.60, Iowa 56; Kansas 88, Ariz.St.71. **Semifinals**—LSU 72, Arkansas 56; Wich.St.66, Kansas 65. **Final**—LSU 96, Wichita St.85.

Mideast Regional
First Round—St.Joe's-PA 59, Creighton 57; Boston Col.93, Ball St.90; Maryland 81, Tenn-Chatt.69; Ala-Birm.93, Western Ky.68. **Second Round**—St.Joe's 49, DePaul 48; Boston Col.67, Wake Forest 64; Indiana 99, Maryland 64; Ala-Birm.69, Kentucky 62. **Semifinals**—St.Joe's 42, Boston Col.41; Indiana 87, Ala-Birm.72. **Final**—Indiana 78, St.Joe's 46.

FINAL FOUR
at The Spectrum, Philadelphia
Semifinals—N.Carolina 78, Virginia 65; Indiana 67, LSU 49. **Third Place**—Virginia 78, LSU 74. **Championship**—Indiana 63, N.Carolina 50. **Outstanding Player**—Isiah Thomas, Indiana. **All-Tournament**—I.Thomas, Jim Thomas and Landon Turner, Indiana; Al Wood, N.Carolina; Jeff Lamp, Virginia.

NIT Tournament (32 teams)
Final Four at Madison Sq.Garden, New York
Field—Alabama, American, Clemson, UConn, Dayton, Drake, Duke, Duquesne, Fordham, Georgia, Holy Cross, Marquette, Michigan, Minnesota, N.Car.A&T, Old Dom., Pan Amer., Penn, Purdue, Rhode Island, St. John's, San Jose St., South Ala., South Fla., So.Miss., Syracuse, Temple, TX-Arlington, UTEP, Toledo, Tulsa, West Va.
Semifinals—Tulsa 89, West Va.87; Syracuse 70, Purdue 63. **Third Place**—Purdue 75, West Va.72 (OT). **Championship**—Tulsa 86, Syracuse 84.
MVP—Greg Stewart, Tulsa.

Players of the Year
Ralph Sampson, Virginia . . UPI,AP,USBWA,Naismith
Danny Ainge, BYU . . . . NABC,Wooden

Coaches of the Year
Ralph Miller, Oregon St . UPI,AP,USBWA,NABC(tie)
Jack Hartman, Kansas St . . . . NABC(tie)

Consensus All-America
(In alphabetical order)
First Team—Mark Aguirre, DePaul; Danny Ainge, BYU; Steve Johnson, Oregon St.; Ralph Sampson, Virginia; Isiah Thomas, Indiana.
Second Team—Sam Bowie, Kentucky; Jeff Lamp, Virginia; Durand Macklin, LSU; Kelly Tripucka, Notre Dame; Danny Vranes, Utah; Al Wood, N.Carolina.

1982

Junior James Worthy and freshman Michael Jordan led North Carolina to the ACC championship, the regular season No.1 ranking, and the Tar Heels' first NCAA championship in 25 years.

In the title game against Georgetown in the Superdome, Worthy scored 28 points while Jordan hit the winning jump shot as the Tar Heels edged the Hoyas, 62-61. Worthy, who was named tourney MVP, also received an errant pass in the waning seconds from Georgetown's Fred Brown to ice the victory.

The last Carolina title came in 1957 in the famous triple OT win over Wilt Chamberlain and Kansas. Dean Smith rode the bench as a member of the Jayhawks that night. He became head coach at North Carolina in 1961 and after guiding the Heels to six Final Fours finally won the title on his seventh trip.

Not long after returning from New Orleans, Worthy declared for the NBA Draft and went to the Lakers as the first overall pick.

Two traditional staples were eliminated or nearly eliminated from the Division I diet in 1982—the Final Four consolation game and the jump ball. While the consolation game was discontinued, the jump ball—a constant since the sport's peach basket days—was largely replaced by the alternating possession arrow (except for the start of games and overtime periods).

Final AP Top 20
Writers' poll taken before tournament.

		Before NCAAs	Head Coach	Final Record
1	N.Carolina	27-2	Dean Smith	32-2
2	DePaul	26-1	Ray Meyer	26-2
3	Virginia	29-3	Terry Holland	30-4
4	Oregon St.	23-4	Ralph Miller	25-5
5	Missouri	26-3	Norm Stewart	27-4
6	Georgetown	26-6	John Thompson	30-7
7	Minnesota	22-5	Jim Dutcher	23-6
8	Idaho	26-2	Don Monson	27-3
9	Memphis St.	23-4	Dana Kirk	24-5
10	Tulsa	24-5	Nolan Richardson	24-6
11	Fresno St.	26-2	Boyd Grant	27-3
12	Arkansas	23-5	Eddie Sutton	23-6
13	Alabama	23-6	Wimp Sanderson	24-7
14	West Va.	26-3	Gale Catlett	27-4
15	Kentucky	22-7	Joe B.Hall	22-8
16	Iowa	20-7	Lute Olson	21-8
17	Ala-Birm	23-5	Gene Bartow	25-6
18	W.Forest	20-8	Carl Tacy	21-9
19	UCLA	21-6	Larry Farmer	21-6
20	Louisville	20-9	Denny Crum	23-10

Note: North Carolina won the NCAAs.

Major Conference Champions

Conference	Regular Season	Tournament
ACC	N.Car./Virginia (12-2)	N.Carolina
Big East	Villanova (11-3)	Georgetown
Big 8	Missouri (12-2)	Missouri
Big 10	Minnesota (14-4)	—
Metro	Memphis St.(10-2)	Memphis St.
Mo.Valley	Bradley (13-3)	Tulsa
Pac-10	Oregon St.(16-2)	—
PCAA	Fresno St.(13-1)	Fresno St.
SEC	Kentucky/Tenn.(13-5)	Alabama
SWC	Arkansas (12-4)	Arkansas
WAC	Wyoming (14-2)	—

NCAA Tournament (48 teams)
East Regional
First Round—J.Madison 55, Ohio St.48; St.John's 66, Penn 56; N'eastern 63, St.Joe's-PA 62; Wake Forest 74, Old Dom.57. **Second Round**—N.Carolina 52, J.Madison 50; Alabama 69, St.John's 68; Villanova 76, N'eastern 72 (3 OT); Memphis St. **56, Wake Forest 55.** **Semifinals**—N.Carolina 74, Alabama 69; Villanova 70, Memphis St.66. **Final**—N.Carolina 70, Villanova 60.

Midwest Regional
First Round—Boston Col.70, San Fran.66; Kansas St. 77, No.Ill.68; Houston 94, Alcorn St.84; Marquette 67, Evansville 62. **Second Round**—BC 82, DePaul 75; Kansas St.65, Arkansas 64; Houston 78, Tulsa 74; Missouri 73, Marquette 69. **Semifinals**—BC 69, Kansas St.65; Houston 79, Missouri 78. **Final**—Houston 99, BC 92.

Mideast Regional
First Round—Tennessee 61, SW La.57; Indiana 94, R. Morris 62; Mid.Tenn.St.50, Kentucky 44; Tenn-Chatt. 58, N.C.State 51. **Second Round**—Virginia 54, Tennessee 51; Ala-Birm.80, Indiana 70; Louisville 81, Mid.Tenn.St.56; Minnesota 62, Tenn-Chatt.61. **Semifinals**—Ala-Birm.68, Virginia 66; Louisville 67, Minnesota 61. **Final**—Louisville 75, Ala-Birm.68.

West Regional
First Round—Wyoming 61, Southern Cal 58; West Va. 102, N.Car.A&T 57; Iowa 70, NE La.63; Pepperdine 99, Pitt 88. **Second Round**—Georgetown 51, Wyoming 43; Fresno St.50, West Va.46; Idaho 69, Iowa 67 (OT); Ore.St.70, Pepperdine 51. **Semifinals**—Georgetown 50, Fresno St.40; Ore.St.60, Idaho 42. **Final**—Georgetown 69, Ore.St.45.

FINAL FOUR
at The Superdome, New Orleans
Semifinals—N.Carolina 68, Houston 63; Georgetown 50, Louisville 46. **Championship**—N.Carolina 63, Georgetown 62.
Outstanding Player—James Worthy, N.Carolina. **All-Tournament**—Worthy, Michael Jordan and Sam Perkins, N.Carolina; Patrick Ewing and Sleepy Floyd, Georgetown.

NIT Tournament (32 teams)
Final Four at Madison Sq.Garden, New York
Field—American, Bradley, BYU, Cal-Irvine, UConn, Clemson, Dayton, Fordham, Georgia, Illinois, Iona, Lamar, LIU, LSU, Maryland, Mississippi, Murray St., Oklahoma, Oral Robts, Purdue, Richmond, Rutgers, S.Diego St., St.Peter's, Syracuse, Temple, Texas A&M, Tulane, UNLV, Va.Tech, Washington, Western Ky.
Semifinals—Bradley 84, Oklahoma 68; Purdue 61, Georgia 60. **Championship**—Bradley 67, Purdue 58.
MVP—Mitchell Anderson, Bradley.

Player of the Year
Ralph Sampson, Virginia . . . . UPI,AP,USBWA, Naismith, NABC,Wooden

Coaches of the Year
Norm Stewart, Missouri .UPI
Ralph Miller, Oregon St . . . . .AP
John Thompson, Georgetown . . . . .USBWA
Don Monson, Idaho .NABC

Consensus All-America
(In alphabetical order)
First Team—Terry Cummings, DePaul; Quintin Dailey, San Fran.; Eric (Sleepy) Floyd, Georgetown; Ralph Sampson, Virginia; James Worthy, N.Carolina.
Second Team—Dale Ellis, Tennessee; Kevin Magee, Cal-Irvine; John Paxson, Notre Dame; Sam Perkins, N.Carolina, Paul Pressey, Tulsa.

1983

Ralph Sampson of Virginia was the consensus Player of the Year for the third season in a row, but this was North Carolina State's year.

N.C.State's year? Wait a minute, wasn't the Wolfpack 17-10 going into the ACC tournament? True, but then they won nine straight games.

NCSU played Sampson and Virginia twice during that streak and won by a combined four points—first in the ACC tournament final (81-78) and then in the NCAA West Regional final (63-62).

Good luck followed coach Jim Valvano's squad to the Final Four in Albuquerque where No.1 Houston and No.2 Louisville faced off in one semifinal and the Wolfpack met No.18 Georgia in the other.

The eventual Houston-N.C.State title game was a slow-paced contest that came down to one shot: a desperation jumper by Dereck Whittenburg in the last seconds that Lorenzo Charles picked off and dunked at the buzzer for the 54-52 upset.

Houston center Akeem Olajuwon was named the tournament's outstanding player, making him the 12th member of a losing team to receive the honor in 45 years.

The tournament expanded by four teams to 52. One of the 48 teams that didn't make it to Albuquerque was No.3 St.John's, which went 28-4 before losing to Georgia in the East Regional semifinals.

Final AP Top 20
Writers' poll taken before tournament.

	Before NCAAs	Head Coach	Final Record
1 Houston	27-2	Guy Lewis	31-3
2 Louisville	29-3	Denny Crum	32-4
3 St.John's	27-4	Lou Carnesecca	28-5
4 Virginia	27-4	Terry Holland	29-5
5 Indiana	23-5	Bob Knight	24-6
6 UNLV	28-2	Jerry Tarkanian	28-3
7 UCLA	23-5	Larry Farmer	23-6
8 N.Carolina	26-7	Dean Smith	28-8
9 Arkansas	25-3	Eddie Sutton	26-4
10 Missouri	26-7	Norm Stewart	26-8
11 Boston Col.	24-6	Gary Williams	25-7
12 Kentucky	22-7	Joe B.Hall	23-8
13 Villanova	22-7	Rollie Massimino	24-8
14 Wichita St.	25-3	Gene Smithson	same
15 Tenn-Chatt	26-3	Murray Arnold	26-4
16 N.C.State	20-10	Jim Valvano	26-10
17 Memphis St.	22-7	Dana Kirk	23-8
18 Georgia	21-9	Hugh Durham	24-10
19 Okla.St.	24-6	Paul Hansen	24-7
20 Georgetown	21-9	John Thompson	22-10

Note: N.C.State won the NCAAs.

Major Conference Champions

Conference	Regular Season	Tournament
ACC	N.Car./Virginia (12-2)	N.C.State
Big East	Boston Col./Villanova/ St.John's (12-4)	St.John's
Big 8	Missouri (12-2)	Okla St.
Big 10	Indiana (13-5)	—
Metro	Louisville (12-0)	Louisville
Mo.Valley	Wichita St.(17-1)	Illinois St.
Pac-10	UCLA (15-3)	—
PCAA	UNLV (15-1)	UNLV
SEC	Kentucky (13-5)	Georgia
SWC	Houston (16-0)	Houston
WAC	UTEP/Utah/BYU (11-5)	—

NCAA Tournament (52 teams)
East Regional
First Round—Rutgers 60, SW La.53; Va.Comm.76, La Salle 67; Syracuse 74, Morehead St.59; J.Madison 57, West Va.50. **Second Round**—St. John's 66, Rutgers 55; Georgia 56, Va.Comm.54; Ohio St.79, Syracuse 74; N.Carolina 68, J.Madison 49. **Semifinals** — Georgia 70, St.John's 67; N.Carolina 64, Ohio St. 51. **Final**—Georgia 82, N.Carolina 77.

West Regional
First Round—Wash.St.62, Weber St.52; Princeton 56, Okla.St.53; N.C.State 69, Pepperdine 67 (2 OT); Utah 52, Illinois 49. **Second Round**—Virginia 54, Wash.St. 49; Boston Col.51, Princeton 42; N.C.State 71, UNLV 70; Utah 67, UCLA 61. **Semifinals**—Virginia 95, BC 92; N.C.State 75, Utah 56. **Final**—N.C.State 63, Virginia 62.

Midwest Regional
First Round—Maryland 52, Tenn-Chatt.51; Georgetown 68, Alcorn St.63; Lamar 73, Alabama 50; Iowa 64, Utah St.59. **Second Round**—Houston 60, Maryland 50; Memphis St.66, Georgetown 57; Villanova 60, Lamar 58; Iowa 77, Missouri 63. **Semifinals**—Houston 70, Memphis St.63; Villanova 55, Iowa 54. **Final**—Houston 89, Villanova 71.

Mideast Regional
First Round—Tennessee 57, Marquette 56; Purdue 55, R.Morris 53; Ohio U.51, Ill.St.49; Oklahoma 71, Ala-Birm.63. **Second Round**—Louisville 70, Tennessee 57; Arkansas 78, Purdue 68; Kentucky 57, Ohio U.40; Indiana 63, Oklahoma 49. **Semifinals**—Louisville 65, Arkansas 63; Kentucky 64, Indiana 59. **Final**—Louisville 80, Kentucky 68 (OT).

FINAL FOUR
at The Pit, Albuquerque,NM
Semifinals—N.C.State 67, Georgia 60; Houston 94, Louisville 81. **Championship**—N.C.State 54, Houston 52.
Outstanding Player—Akeem Olajuwon, Houston.
All-Tournament—Olajuwon, Houston; Thurl Bailey, Sidney Lowe and Dereck Whittenburg, N.C.State; Milt Wagner, Louisville.

NIT Tournament (32 teams)
Final Four at Madison Sq.Garden, New York
Field—Ala.St., Ariz.St., Bowl.Green, CS-Full, De Paul, East Tenn.St., Fordham, Fresno St., Idaho, Iona, LSU, Mich.St., Minn, Miss, Murray St., Nebraska, New Orleans, N'western, Notre Dame, Old Dom., Ore.St., St.Bona., S.Carolina, South Fla., TCU, Tulane, Tulsa, UTEP, Vanderbilt, Va.Tech, Wake Forest, Wm.& Mary. **Semifinals**—Fresno St.86, Wake Forest 62; DePaul 68, Nebraska 58. **Championship**—Fresno St.69, DePaul 60. **MVP**—Ron Anderson, Fresno St.

Player of the Year
Ralph Sampson, Virginia . . . . UPI,AP,USBWA, Naismith,NABC,Wooden

Coaches of the Year
Lou Carnesecca, St.John's . . . . USBWA,NABC
Guy Lewis, Houston . . . . AP
Jerry Tarkanian, UNLV . . . . UPI

Consensus All-America
(In alphabetical order)
First Team—Dale Ellis, Tennessee; Patrick Ewing, Georgetown; Michael Jordan, N.Carolina; Keith Lee, Memphis St.; Sam Perkins, N.Carolina; Ralph Sampson, Virginia; Wayman Tisdale, Oklahoma.
Second Team—Clyde Drexler, Houston; Sidney Green, UNLV; John Paxson, Notre Dame; Steve Stipanovich, Missouri; Jon Sundvold, Missouri; Darrell Walker, Arkansas; Randy Wittman, Indiana.

1984

Led by Player of the Year Michael Jordan, North Carolina (27-2) entered the NCAA tournament as the Number One team in the country. But any thought of bringing the national championship back to Chapel Hill after loaning it to Raleigh for a year died in the semifinals of the East Regional. That's where unranked Indiana upset the Tar Heels, 72-68.

Indiana fell to unranked and Ralph Sampson-less (he was in the NBA now) Virginia in the East final. The Cavaliers joined No.2 Georgetown, No.3 Kentucky and No.6 Houston in Seattle for the Final Four.

Georgetown and Houston, the losing teams in the last two NCAA title games, met for the title and the Hoyas, led by tourney MVP Patrick Ewing, beat the Cougars and last year's MVP Akeem Olajuwon, 84-75.

Jordan, meanwhile, left Carolina and declared for the NBA Draft with a year of eligibility remaining but no collegiate worlds left to conquer. He was the third player chosen in the first round, behind the 7-0 Olajuwon (by Houston) and 7-1 Kentucky center Sam Bowie (by Portland). Jordan was taken by the Chicago Bulls and was Rookie of the Year in 1985.

Finally, the NIT had a great football match-up for its 47th championship game, as Michigan beat Notre Dame, 83-63.

Final AP Top 20
Writers' poll taken before tournament.

	Before NCAAs	Head Coach	Final Record
1 N.Carolina	27-2	Dean Smith	28-3
2 Georgetown	29-3	John Thompson	34-3
3 Kentucky	26-4	Joe B.Hall	29-5
4 DePaul	26-2	Ray Meyer	27-3
5 Houston	28-4	Guy Lewis	32-5
6 Illinois	24-4	Lou Henson	26-5
7 Oklahoma	29-4	Billy Tubbs	29-5
8 Arkansas	25-6	Eddie Sutton	25-7
9 UTEP	27-3	Don Haskins	27-4
10 Purdue	22-6	Gene Keady	22-7
11 Maryland	23-7	Lefty Driesell	24-8
12 Tulsa	27-3	Nolan Richardson	27-4
13 UNLV	27-5	Jerry Tarkanian	29-6
14 Duke	24-9	Mike Krzyzewski	24-10
15 Washington	22-6	Marv Harshman	24-7
16 Memphis St.	24-6	Dana Kirk	26-7
17 Oregon St.	22-6	Ralph Miller	22-7
18 Syracuse	22-8	Jim Boeheim	23-9
19 W.Forest	21-8	Carl Tacy	23-9
20 Temple	25-4	John Chaney	26-5

Note: Georgetown won the NCAAs.

Major Conference Champions

Conference	Regular Season	Tournament
ACC	N.Carolina (14-0)	Maryland
Big East	Georgetown (14-2)	Georgetown
Big 8	Oklahoma (13-1)	Kansas
Big 10	Illinois/Purdue (15-3)	—
Metro	L'ville/Memp.St.(11-3)	Memphis St.
Mo.Valley	Ill.St./Tulsa (13-3)	Tulsa
Pac-10	Wash./Ore.St.(15-3)	—
PCAA	UNLV (16-2)	Fresno St.
SEC	Kentucky (14-4)	Kentucky
SWC	Houston (15-1)	Houston
WAC	UTEP (13-3)	UTEP

NCAA Tournament (53 teams)
East Regional
First Round—Temple 65, St.John's 63; Richmond 72, Auburn 71; Va.Comm.70, N'eastern 69; Virginia 58, Iona 57. **Second Round**—N.Carolina 77, Temple 66; Indiana 75, Richmond 67; Syracuse 78, Va.Comm.63; Virginia 53, Arkansas 51 (OT). **Semifinals**—Indiana 72, N.Carolina 68; Virginia 63, Syracuse 55. **Final**—Virginia 50, Indiana 48.

Midwest Regional
First Round—Ill.St.49, Alabama 48; Kansas 57, Alcorn St.56; Memphis St.92, Oral Robts 83; La.Tech 66, Fresno St.56. **Second Round**—DePaul 75, Ill.St.61; Wake Forest 69, Kansas 59; Memphis St.66, Purdue 48; Houston 77, La.Tech 56. **Semifinals**—Wake Forest 73, DePaul 71 (OT); Houston 78, Memphis St.71. **Final**—Houston 68, Wake Forest 63.

Mideast Regional
First Round—BYU 84, Ala-Birm.68; Louisville 72, Morehead St.59; West Va.64, Ore.St.62; Villanova 84, Marshall 72. **Second Round**—Kentucky 93, BYU 68; Louisville 69, Tulsa 67; Maryland 102, West Va.77; Illinois 64, Villanova 56. **Semifinals**—Kentucky 72, Louisville 67; Illinois 72, Maryland 70. **Final**—Kentucky 54, Illinois 51.

West Regional
First Round—SMU 83, Miami-OH 69; UNLV 68, Princeton 56; Washington 64, Nev-Reno 54; Dayton 74, LSU 66. **Second Round**—Georgetown 37, SMU 36; UNLV 73, UTEP 60; Washington 80, Duke 78; Dayton 89, Oklahoma 85. **Semifinals**—Georgetown 62, UNLV 48; Dayton 64, Washington 58. **Final**—Georgetown 61, Dayton 49.

FINAL FOUR
at The Kingdome, Seattle
Semifinals—Houston 49, Virginia 47 (OT); Georgetown 53, Kentucky 40. **Championship**—Georgetown 84, Houston 75.
Outstanding Player—Patrick Ewing, Georgetown.
All-Tournament—Ewing and Michael Graham, Georgetown; Alvin Franklin, Akeem Olajuwon and Michael Young, Houston.

NIT Tournament (32 teams)
Final Four at Madison Sq.Garden, New York
Field—Bos. Col., Creighton, Florida, Fla.St., Fordham, Georgia, Ga.Tech, IowaSt., Lamar, LaSalle, Marquette, Michigan, Nebraska, N.Mexico, N.C.St., Notre Dame, Ohio St., Old Dom., Oregon, Pitt, S.Clara, South Ala., SW La., St.Joe's-PA, St. Peter's, Tennessee, Tenn-Chatt., Utah St., Va.Tech, Weber St., Wichita St., Xavier.
Semifinals—Michigan 78, Va.Tech 75; Notre Dame 65, SW La.59. **Third Place**—Va.Tech 71, SW La.70. **Championship**—Michigan 83, Notre Dame 63.
MVP—Tim McCormick, Michigan.

Player of the Year
Michael Jordan, N.Carolina . . . . . . UPI,AP,USBWA, Naismith,NABC,Wooden

Coaches of the Year
Ray Meyer, DePaul . . . . UPI,AP
Marv Harshman, Washington . . . . NABC
Gene Keady, Purdue . . . . USBWA

Consensus All-America
(In alphabetical order)
First Team—Patrick Ewing, Georgetown; Michael Jordan, N. Carolina; Akeem Olajuwon, Houston; Sam Perkins, N.Carolina; Wayman Tisdale, Oklahoma.
Second Team—Michael Cage, San Diego St. Devin Durrant, BYU; Keith Lee, Memphis St.; Chris Mullin, St.John's; Mel Turpin, Kentucky; Leon Wood, CS-Fullerton.

1985

The NCAA championship game was scheduled for April Fools night and promised to be a laugher.

Georgetown, after all, was the defending champion, the No.1 team in the country and started Co-Player of the Year Patrick Ewing at center. Villanova, on the other hand, wasn't even ranked and had lost to the Hoyas both times the two teams met in Big East play.

Nevertheless, the underdog Wildcats shot 78.6 percent (22 for 28) and won, 66-64. Some joke.

Meanwhile, the NCAA tourney field was increased to 64 teams.

Final AP Top 20
Writers' poll taken before tournament.

	Before NCAAs	Head Coach	Final Record
1 Georgetown	30-2	John Thompson	35-3
2 Michigan	25-3	Bill Frieder	26-4
3 St.John's	27-3	Lou Carnesecca	31-4
4 Oklahoma	28-5	Billy Tubbs	31-6
5 Memphis St.	27-3	Dana Kirk	31-4
6 Ga.Tech.	24-7	Bobby Cremins	27-8
7 N.Carolina	24-8	Dean Smith	27-9
8 La.Tech.	27-2	Andy Russo	29-3
9 UNLV	27-3	Jerry Tarkanian	28-4
10 Duke	22-7	Mike Krzyzewski	23-8
11 Va.Comm.	25-5	J.D.Barnett	26-6
12 Illinois	24-8	Lou Henson	26-9
13 Kansas	25-7	Larry Brown	26-8
14 Loyola,IL	25-5	Gene Sullivan	27-6
15 Syracuse	21-8	Jim Boeheim	22-9
16 N.C.State	20-9	Jim Valvano	23-10
17 Texas Tech.	23-7	Gerald Myers	23-8
18 Tulsa	23-7	Nolan Richardson	23-8
19 Georgia	21-8	Hugh Durham	22-9
20 LSU	19-9	Dale Brown	19-10

Note: Unranked Villanova (19-10, Rollie Massimino, 25-10) won the NCAAs.

Major Conference Champions

Conference	Regular Season	Tournament
ACC	Ga.Tech/N.Carolina/ N.C.State (9-5)	Ga.Tech
Big East	St.John's (15-1)	Georgetown
Big 8	Oklahoma (13-1)	Oklahoma
Big 10	Michigan (16-2)	—
Metro	Memphis St.(13-1)	Memphis St.
Mo.Valley	Tulsa (12-4)	Wichita St.
Pac-10	USC/Washington (13-5)	—
PCAA	UNLV (17-1)	UNLV
SEC	LSU (13-5)	Auburn
SWC	Texas Tech (12-4)	Texas Tech
WAC	UTEP (12-4)	San Diego St.

NCAA Tournament (64 teams)
East Regional
First Round—Georgetown 68, Lehigh 43; Temple 60, Va.Tech 57; SMU 85, Old Dom.68; Loyola-IL 59, Iona 58; Georgia 67, Wichita St.59; Illinois 76, N'eastern 57; Syracuse 70, DePaul 65; Ga.Tech 65, Mercer 58. **Second Round**—Georgetown 63, Temple 46; Loyola-IL 70, SMU 57; Illinois 74, Georgia 58; Ga.Tech 70, Syracuse 53. **Semifinals**—Georgetown 65, Loyola,IL 53; Ga.Tech 61, Illinois 53. **Final**—Georgetown 60, Ga. Tech 54.

West Regional
First Round—St.John's 83, Southern-BR 59; Arkansas 63, Iona 54; Kentucky 66, Washington 58; UNLV 85, S.Diego St. 80; UTEP 79, Tulsa 75; N.C.State 65, Nev-Reno 56; Alabama 50, Arizona 41; Va.Comm.81, Marshall 65. **Second Round**—St.John's 68, Arkansas 65; Kentucky 64, UNLV 61; N.C.State 86, UTEP 73; Alabama 63, Va.Comm.59. **Semifinals**—St.John's 86, Kentucky 70; N.C.State 61, Alabama 55. **Final**—St. John's 69, N.C.State 60.

Midwest Regional
First Round—Oklahoma 96, N.Car.A&T 83; Ill.St.58, Southern Cal 55; La.Tech 78, Pitt 54; Ohio St.75, Iowa St.64; Boston Col.55, Texas Tech 53; Duke 75, Pepperdine 62; Ala-Birm.70, Mich.St.68; Memphis St.67, Penn 55. **Second Round**—Oklahoma 75, Ill.St.69; La.Tech 79, Ohio St.67; BC 74, Duke 73; Memphis St.67, Ala-Birm.66 (OT). **Semifinals**—Oklahoma 86, La.Tech 84 (OT); Memphis St.59, BC 57. **Final**—Memphis St.63, Oklahoma 61.

Southeast Regional
First Round—Michigan 59, FDU-Teaneck 55; Villanova 51, Dayton 49; Maryland 69, Miami-OH 68; Navy 78, LSU 55; Auburn 59, Purdue 58; Kansas 49, Ohio U. 38; Notre Dame 79, Ore.St.70; N.Carolina 76, Mid. Tenn.St.57. **Second Round**—Villanova 59, Michigan 55; Maryland 64, Navy 59; Auburn 66, Kansas 64; N. Carolina 60, Notre Dame 58. **Semifinals**—Villanova 46, Maryland 43; N.Carolina 62, Auburn 56. **Final**—Villanova 56, N.Carolina 44.

FINAL FOUR
at Rupp Arena, Lexington,KY
Semifinals—Georgetown 77, St.John's 59; Villanova 52, Memphis St.45. **Championship**—Villanova 66, Georgetown 64.
Outstanding Player—Ed Pinckney, Villanova. **All-Tournament**—Pinckney, Harold Jensen, Dwayne McClain and Gary McLain, Villanova; Patrick Ewing, Georgetown.

NIT Tournament (32 teams)
Final Four at Madison Sq.Garden, New York
Field—Alcorn St., Bradley, Butler, Canisius, Cincinnati, Clemson, Florida, Fordham, Fresno St., Houston, Indiana, Kent St., Lamar, Louisville, Marquette, Missouri, Montana, Nebraska, New Mexico, Richmond, St.Joe's-PA, Santa Clara, South Fla., SW La., Tennessee, Tenn-Chatt., Tenn.Tech, Texas A&M, UCLA, Virginia, W.Forest, West Va.
Semifinals—UCLA 75, Louisville 66; Indiana 74, Tennessee 67. **Third Place**—Tennessee 100, Louisville 84. **Championship**—UCLA 65, Indiana 62.
MVP—Reggie Miller, UCLA.

Players of the Year
Chris Mullin, St.John's . . . . . . UPI,USBWA,Wooden
Patrick Ewing, Georgetown . . . . AP,NABC,Naismith

Coaches of the Year
Lou Carnesecca, St.John's . . . . UPI,USBWA
Bill Frieder, Michigan . . . . AP
John Thompson, Georgetown . . . . NABC

Consensus All-America
(In alphabetical order)
First Team—Johnny Dawkins, Duke; Patrick Ewing, Georgetown; Keith Lee, Memphis St.; Xavier McDaniel, Wichita St.; Chris Mullin, St.John's; Wayman Tisdale, Oklahoma.
Second Team—Len Bias, Maryland; Jon Koncak, SMU; Mark Price, Ga.Tech; Kenny Walker, Kentucky; Dwayne Washington, Syracuse.

1986

"Never Nervous" Pervis Ellison scored 25 points and grabbed 11 rebounds to lead No.7 Louisville to a 72-69 victory over top-ranked Duke in the NCAA Final. The title was the Cardinals' second of the decade. As tourney MVP, Ellison was the first freshman to win the honor since Utah's Arnie Ferrin in 1944.

No.3 St.John's had the Player of the Year for the second straight season (last year Chris Mullin, this year Walter Berry), but exited the NCAAs in the second round.

This was also the year the NCAA adopted the 45-second clock and started awarding two shots and possession of the ball for an intentional foul.

Final AP Top 20
Writers' poll taken before tournament.

	Before NCAAs	Head Coach	Final Record
1 Duke	32-2	Mike Krzyzewski	37-3
2 Kansas	31-3	Larry Brown	35-4
3 Kentucky	29-3	Eddie Sutton	32-4
4 St.John's	30-4	Lou Carnesecca	31-5
5 Michigan	27-4	Bill Frieder	28-5
6 Ga.Tech.	25-6	Bobby Cremins	27-7
7 **Louisville**	26-7	Denny Crum	32-7
8 N.Carolina	26-5	Dean Smith	28-6
9 Syracuse	25-5	Jim Boeheim	26-6
10 Notre Dame	23-5	Digger Phelps	23-6
11 UNLV	31-4	Jerry Tarkanian	33-5
12 Memphis St.	27-5	Dana Kirk	28-6
13 Georgetown	23-7	John Thompson	24-8
14 Bradley	31-2	Dick Versace	32-3
15 Oklahoma	25-8	Billy Tubbs	26-9
16 Indiana	21-7	Bob Knight	21-8
17 Navy	27-4	Paul Evans	30-5
18 Mich.St.	21-7	Jud Heathcote	23-8
19 Illinois	21-9	Lou Henson	22-10
20 UTEP	27-5	Don Haskins	27-6

Note: Louisville won the NCAAs.

Major Conference Champions

Conference	Regular Season	Tournament
ACC	Duke (12-2)	Duke
Big East	St.J's/Syracuse (14-2)	St.John's
Big 8	Kansas (13-1)	Kansas
Big 10	Michigan (14-4)	—
Metro	Louisville (10-2)	Louisville
Mo.Valley	Bradley (16-0)	Tulsa
Pac-10	Arizona (14-4)	—
PCAA	UNLV (16-2)	UNLV
SEC	Kentucky (17-1)	Kentucky
SWC	TCU/Texas/ Texas A&M (12-4)	Texas Tech
WAC	Wy./UTEP/Utah (12-4)	UTEP

NCAA Tournament (64 teams)
East Regional
First Round—Duke 85, Miss.Valley 78; Old Dom.72, West Va.64; DePaul 72, Virginia 68; Oklahoma 80, N' eastern 74; St.Joe's-PA 60, Richmond 59; Cleve.St.83, Indiana 79; Navy 87, Tulsa 68; Syracuse 101, Brown 52. **Second Round**—Duke 89, Old Dom.61; DePaul 74, Oklahoma 69; Cleve.St.75, St.Joe's-PA 69; Navy 97, Syracuse 85. **Semifinals**—Duke 74, DePaul 67; Navy 71, Cleve.St.70. **Final**—Duke 71, Navy 50.

Midwest Regional
First Round—Kansas 71, N.Car.A&T 46; Temple 61, Jacksonville 50 (OT); Mich.St.71, Washington 70; Georgetown 70, Texas Tech 64; N.C.State 66, Iowa 64; Ark-LR 90, Notre Dame 83; Iowa St.81, Miami-OH 79 (OT); Michigan 70, Akron 64. **Second Round**—Kansas 65, Temple 43; Mich.St.80, Georgetown 68; N.C.State 80, Ark-LR 66 (2 OT); Iowa St. 72, Michigan 69. **Semifinals**—Kansas 96, Mich.St.86 (OT); N.C.State 70, Iowa St.66. **Final**—Kansas 75, N.C.State 67.

Southeast Regional
First Round—Kentucky 75, Davidson 55; Western Ky. 67, Nebraska 59; Alabama 97, Xavier 80; Illinois 75, Fairfield 51; LSU 94, Purdue 87 (2 OT); Memphis St.95, Ball St.63; Villanova 71, Va.Tech 62; Ga.Tech 68, Marist 53. **Second Round**—Kentucky 71, Western Ky.64; Alabama 58, Illinois 56; LSU 83, Memphis St.81; Ga. Tech 66, Villanova 61. **Semifinals**—Kentucky 68, Alabama 63; LSU 70, Ga.Tech 64. **Final**—LSU 59, Kentucky 57.

West Regional
First Round—St.John's 83, Montana St.74; Auburn 73, Arizona 63; Maryland 69, Pepperdine 64; UNLV 74, NE La.51; Ala-Birm.66, Missouri 64; N.Carolina 84, Utah 72; Bradley 83, UTEP 65; Louisville 93, Drexel 73. **Second Round**—Auburn 81, St.John's 65; UNLV 70, Maryland 64; N.Carolina 77, Ala-Birm.59; Louisville 82, Bradley 68. **Semifinals**—Auburn 70, UNLV 63; Louisville 94, N.Carolina 79. **Final**—Louisville 84, Auburn 76.

FINAL FOUR
at Reunion Arena, Dallas

Semifinals—Duke 71, Kansas 67; Louisville 88, LSU 77.
Championship—Louisville 72, Duke 69.
Outstanding Player—Pervis Ellison, Louisville. **All-Tournament**—Ellison and Billy Thompson, Louisville; Mark Alarie, Tommy Amaker and Johnny Dawkins, Duke.

NIT Tournament (32 teams)
Final Four at Madison Sq.Garden, New York
Field—Boston U., BYU, California, Cal-Irvine, Clemson, Dayton, Drake, Florida, Georgia, G.Mason, Lamar, La.Tech, Loyola-CA, Marquette, McNeese St., Mid.Tenn.St., Montana, New Mexico, No.Ariz., Ohio St., Ohio U., Pitt, Providence, SMU, So.Miss., SW Mo.St., Tenn-Chatt., Texas, Texas A&M, TCU, UCLA, Wyoming.
Semifinals—Ohio St.79, La.Tech 66; Wyoming 67, Florida 58. **Third Place**—La.Tech 67, Florida 62. **Championship**—Ohio St.73, Wyoming 63.
MVP—Brad Sellers, Ohio St.

Players of the Year
Walter Berry, St.John's ....UPI,AP,USBWA, NABC,Wooden
Johnny Dawkins, Duke ....Naismith

Coaches of the Year
Eddie Sutton, Kentucky ....AP,NABC
Mike Krzyzewski, Duke ....UPI
Dick Versace, Bradley...................USBWA

Consensus All-America
(In alphabetical order)
First Team—Steve Alford, Indiana; Walter Berry, St.John's; Len Bias, Maryland; Johnny Dawkins, Duke; Kenny Walker, Kentucky.
Second Team—Dell Curry, Va.Tech; Brad Daugherty, N.Carolina; Ron Harper, Miami,OH; Danny Manning, Kansas; David Robinson, Navy; Scott Skiles, Michigan St.

1987

The NCAA embraced the three-point field goal, drawing the firing line at 19-feet, nine inches.

Providence played "bombs away" better than most and made it all the way to the Final Four. There the Friars went cold and lost to Big East rival Syracuse while No.3 Indiana beat No.1 UNLV.

The title game was held on Oscar night and while the nominated "Hoosiers" didn't win in Hollywood, Bob Knight's Hoosiers did in New Orleans. Keith Smart hit the winning jumper (a deuce not a trey) for the 74-73 win.

Final AP Top 20
Writers' poll taken before tournament.

	Before NCAAs	Head Coach	Final Record
1 UNLV	33-1	Jerry Tarkanian	37-2
2 N.Carolina	29-3	Dean Smith	32-4
3 Indiana	24-4	Bob Knight	30-4
4 Georgetown	26-4	John Thompson	29-5
5 DePaul	26-2	Joey Meyer	28-3
6 Iowa	27-4	Tom Davis	30-5
7 Purdue	24-4	Gene Keady	25-5
8 Temple	31-3	John Chaney	32-4
9 Alabama	26-4	Wimp Sanderson	28-5
10 Syracuse	26-6	Jim Boeheim	31-7
11 Illinois	23-7	Lou Henson	23-8
12 Pittsburgh	24-7	Paul Evans	25-8
13 Clemson	25-5	Cliff Ellis	25-6
14 Missouri	24-9	Norm Stewart	24-10
15 UCLA	24-6	Walt Hazzard	25-7
16 N.Orleans	25-3	Benny Dees	26-4
17 Duke	22-8	Mike Krzyzewski	24-9
18 Notre Dame	22-7	Digger Phelps	24-8
19 TCU	23-6	Jim Killingsworth	24-7
20 Kansas	23-10	Larry Brown	25-11

Note: Indiana won the NCAAs.

Major Conference Champions

Conference	Regular Season	Tournament
ACC	N.Carolina (14-0)	N.C.State
Big East	Syracuse/Georgetown/ Pittsburgh (12-4)	Georgetown
Big 8	Missouri (11-3)	Missouri
Big 10	Indiana/Purdue (15-3)	—
Metro	Louisville (9-3)	Memphis St.
Mo.Valley	Tulsa (11-3)	Wichita St.
Pac-10	UCLA (14-4)	UCLA
PCAA	UNLV (18-0)	UNLV
SEC	Alabama (16-2)	Alabama
SWC	TCU (14-2)	Texas A&M
WAC	UTEP (13-3)	Wyoming

NCAA Tournament (64 teams)
East Regional
First Round—N.Carolina 113, Penn 82; Michigan 97, Navy 82; Notre Dame 84, Mid.Tenn.St.71; TCU 76, Marshall 61; Florida 82, N.C.State 70; Purdue 104, N'eastern 95; Western Ky.64, West Va.62; Syracuse 79, Ga.Southern 73. **Second Round**—N.Carolina 109, Michigan 97; Notre Dame 58, TCU 57; Florida 85, Purdue 66; Syracuse 104, Western Ky.86. **Semifinals**—N.Carolina 74, Notre Dame 68; Syracuse 87, Florida 81. **Final**—Syracuse 79, N.Carolina 75.

Southeast Regional
First Round—Georgetown 75, Bucknell 53; Ohio St.91, Kentucky 77; Kansas 66, Houston 55; SW Mo.St.65, Clemson 60; Providence 90, Ala-Birm.68; Austin Peay 68, Illinois 67; New Orleans 83, BYU 79; Alabama 88, N.Car.A&T 71. **Second Round**—Georgetown 82, Ohio St.79; Kansas 67, SW Mo.St.63; Providence 90, Austin Peay 87 (OT); Alabama 101, New Orleans 76. **Semifinals**—Georgetown 70, Kansas 57; Providence 103, Alabama 82. **Final**—Providence 88, Georgetown 73.

Midwest Regional
First Round—Indiana 92, Fairfield 58; Auburn 62, San Diego 61; Duke 58, Texas A&M 51; Xavier 70, Missouri 69; St.John's 57, Wichita St.55; DePaul 76, La.Tech 62; LSU 85, Ga.Tech 79; Temple 75, Southern-BR 56. **Second Round**—Indiana 107, Auburn 90; Duke 65, Xavier 60; DePaul 83, St.John's 75 (OT); LSU 72, Temple 62. **Semifinals**—Indiana 88, Duke 82; LSU 63, DePaul 58. **Final**—Indiana 77, LSU 76.

West Regional
First Round—UNLV 95, Idaho St.70; Kansas St.82, Georgia 79 (OT); Wyoming 64, Virginia 60; UCLA 92, Cent.Mich.73; Oklahoma 74, Tulsa 69; Pitt 93, Marist 68; UTEP 98, Arizona 91; Iowa 99, Santa Clara 76. **Second Round**—UNLV 80, Kansas St.61; Wyoming 78, UCLA 68; Oklahoma 96, Pitt 93; Iowa 84, UTEP 82. **Semifinals**—UNLV 92, Wyoming 78; Iowa 93, Oklahoma 91 (OT). **Final**—UNLV 84, Iowa 81.

FINAL FOUR
at The Superdome, New Orleans
Semifinals—Syracuse 77, Providence 63; Indiana 97, UNLV 93. **Championship**—Indiana 74, Syracuse 73. **Outstanding Player**—Keith Smart, Indiana. **All-Tournament**—Smart and Steve Alford, Indiana; Derrick Coleman and Sherman Douglas, Syracuse; Armon Gilliam, UNLV.

NIT Tournament (32 teams)
at Madison Square Garden, New York
Field—Akron, Arkansas, Ark-LR, Ark.St., Baylor, Boise St., California, CS-Fullerton, Cleve.St., Fla.St., Ill.St., Jacksonville, J.Madison, La Salle, Marquette, Mississippi, Montana St., Nebraska, New Mexico, Niagara, Ore.St., Rhode Island, St.Louis, St.Peter's, Seton Hall, So.Miss., S.F.Austin, Tenn- Chatt., Utah, Vanderbilt, Villanova, Washington.
Semifinals—So.Miss.82, Nebraska 75; La Salle 92, Ark-LR 73. **Third Place**—Nebraska 76, Ark-LR 67. **Championship**—So.Miss.84, La Salle 80. **MVP**—Randolph Keys, So.Miss.

Player of the Year
David Robinson, Navy .... UPI,AP,USBWA, Naismith,NABC,Wooden

Coaches of the Year
John Chaney, Temple .... USBWA
Tom Davis, Iowa .... AP
Bob Knight, Indiana .... Naismith
Rick Pitino, Providence .... NABC
John Thompson, Georgetown .... UPI

Consensus All-America
(In alphabetical order)
First Team—Steve Alford, Indiana; Danny Manning, Kansas; David Robinson, Navy; Kenny Smith, N.Carolina; Reggie Williams, Georgetown.
Second Team—Armon Gilliam, UNLV; Dennis Hopson, Ohio St.; Mark Jackson, St. John's; Ken Norman, Illinois; Horace Grant, Clemson.

1988

Did someone say "parity"? For the third time in six years, a decided underdog won the NCAA championship.

Unranked Kansas, entering the tournament with 11 losses, beat Big Eight rival and third-ranked Oklahoma, 83-79. Danny Manning scored 31 points to lead the Jayhawks to their first national title since 1952.

In November, however, Kansas was put on probation for recruiting violations and became the first champion to be barred from defending its title.

Final AP Top 20
Writers' poll taken before tournament.

	Before NCAAs	Head Coach	Final Record
1 Temple	29-1	John Chaney	32-2
2 Arizona	31-2	Lute Olson	35-3
3 Purdue	27-3	Gene Keady	29-4
4 Oklahoma	30-3	Billy Tubbs	35-4
5 Duke	24-6	Mike Krzyzewski	28-7
6 Kentucky	25-5	Eddie Sutton	27-6
7 N.Carolina	24-6	Dean Smith	27-7
8 Pittsburgh	23-6	Paul Evans	24-7
9 Syracuse	25-8	Jim Boeheim	26-9
10 Michigan	24-7	Bill Frieder	26-8
11 Bradley	26-4	Stan Albeck	26-5
12 UNLV	27-5	Jerry Tarkanian	28-6
13 Wyoming	26-5	Benny Dees	26-6
14 N.C.State	24-7	Jim Valvano	24-8
15 Loyola,CA	27-3	Paul Westhead	28-4
16 Illinois	22-9	Lou Henson	23-10
17 Iowa	22-9	Tom Davis	24-10
18 Xavier,OH	26-3	Pete Gillen	26-4
19 BYU	25-5	Ladell Andersen	26-6
20 Kansas St.	22-8	Lon Kruger	25-9

Note: Unranked Kansas (21-11, Larry Brown, 27-11) won the NCAAs.

Major Conference Champions

Conference	Regular Season	Tournament
ACC	N.Carolina (11-3)	Duke
Big East	Pittsburgh (12-4)	Syracuse
Big 8	Oklahoma (12-2)	Oklahoma
Big 10	Purdue (16-2)	—
Metro	Louisville (9-3)	Louisville
Mo.Valley	Bradley (12-2)	Bradley
Pac-10	Arizona (17-1)	Arizona
PCAA	UNLV (15-3)	Utah St.
SEC	Kentucky (13-5)*	Kentucky*
SWC	SMU (12-4)	SMU
WAC	BYU (13-3)	Wyoming

*Both SEC titles were vacated in 1989.

NCAA Tournament (64 teams)
East Regional
First Round—Temple 87, Lehigh 73; Georgetown 66, LSU 63; Ga.Tech 90, Iowa St.78; Richmond 72, Indiana 69; Rhode Island 87, Missouri 80; Syracuse 69, N.Car. A&T 55; SMU 83, Notre Dame 75; Duke 85, Boston U.69. **Second Round**—Temple 74, Georgetown 53; Richmond 59, Ga.Tech 55; Rhode Island 97, Syracuse 94; Duke 94, SMU 79. **Semifinals**—Temple 69, Richmond 47; Duke 73, Rhode Island 72. **Final**—Duke 63, Temple 53.

Midwest Regional
First Round—Purdue 94, FDU-Teaneck 79; Memphis St.75, Baylor 60; DePaul 83, Wichita St.62; Kansas St.66, La Salle 53; Kansas 85, Xavier 72; Murray St.78, N.C.State 75; Vanderbilt 80, Utah St.77; Pitt 108, East.Mich.90. **Second Round**—Purdue 100, Memphis St.73; Kansas St.66, DePaul 58; Kansas 61, Murray St.58; Vanderbilt 80, Pitt 74 (OT). **Semifinals**—Kansas St.73, Purdue 70; Kansas 77, Vanderbilt 64. **Final**—Kansas 71, Kansas St.58.

Southeast Regional
First Round—Oklahoma 94, Tenn-Chatt.66; Auburn 90, Bradley 86; Louisville 70, Ore.St. 61; BYU 98, NC-Charlotte 92 (OT); Villanova 82, Arkansas 74; Illinois 81, TX-San Antonio 72; Maryland 92, UC-Santa Barb. 82; Kentucky 99, Southern-BR 84. **Second Round**—Oklahoma 107, Auburn 87; Louisville 97, BYU 76; Villanova 66, Illinois 63; Kentucky 90, Maryland 81. **Semifinal**—Oklahoma 108, Louisville 98; Villanova 80, Kentucky 74. **Final**—Oklahoma 78, Villanova 59.

West Regional
First Round—Arizona 90, Cornell 50; Seton Hall 80, UTEP 64; Iowa 102, Fla.St.98; UNLV 54, SW Mo.St.50; Florida 62, St.John's 59; Michigan 63, Boise St.58; Loyola-CA 119, Wyoming 115; N.Carolina 83, North Texas 65. **Second Round**—Arizona 84, Seton Hall 55; Iowa 104, UNLV 86; Michigan 108, Florida 85; N.Carolina 123, Loyola-CA 97. **Semifinal**—Arizona 99, Iowa 79; N.Carolina 78, Michigan 69. **Final**—Arizona 70, N.Carolina 52.

FINAL FOUR
at Kemper Arena, Kansas City,MO
Semifinals—Kansas 66, Duke 59; Oklahoma 86, Arizona 78. **Championship**—Kansas 83, Oklahoma 79.
Outstanding Player—Danny Manning, Kansas. **All-Tournament**—Manning and Milt Newton, Kansas; Stacey King and Dave Sieger, Oklahoma; Sean Elliott, Arizona.

NIT Tournament (32 teams)
at Madison Square Garden, New York
Field—Ark-LR, Ark.St., Boston Col., Clemson, Cleve.St., UConn, Colo.St., Evansville, Fordham, Georgia, Ga. Southern, Houston, Ill.St., L.Beach St., La.Tech, Marshall, Mid.Tenn.St., New Mexico, New Orleans, NE La., Ohio St., Old Dom., Oregon, Pepperdine, Santa Clara, Siena, So.Miss., Stanford, Tennessee, Utah, Va.Comm., West Va.
Semifinals—UConn 73, BC 67; Ohio St.64, Colo.St.62; **Third Place**—Colo.St.58, BC 57. **Championship**—UConn 72, Ohio St.67.
MVP—Phil Gamble, UConn.

Players of the Year
Hersey Hawkins, Bradley . . . . UPI,AP,USBWA
Danny Manning, Kansas . . Naismith,NABC,Wooden

Coaches of the Year
John Chaney, Temple . . . . . . UPI,AP,USBWA,NABC
Larry Brown, Kansas . . . . Naismith

Consensus All-America
(In alphabetical order)
First Team—Sean Elliott, Arizona; Gary Grant, Michigan; Hersey Hawkins, Bradley; Danny Manning, Kansas; J.R.Reid, N.Carolina.
Second Team—Danny Ferry, Duke; Jerome Lane, Pittsburgh; Mark Macon, Temple; Mitch Richmond, Kansas St.; Rony Seikaly, Syracuse; Michael Smith, BYU.

1989

The decade came to a fitting climax on April 3, when the NCAA title game between Michigan and Seton Hall went into overtime for the first time in 26 years.

Rumeal Robinson's two free throws with three seconds left in OT won the game and the title (their first) for the Wolverines, who were playing under an interim coach with no tournament experience.

The final score of 80-79 marked the third time in the decade that the championship game was decided by one point. The average margin of victory in title games through the 1980s was four points.

Final AP Top 20
Writers' poll taken before tournament.

	Before NCAAs	Head Coach	Final Record
1 Arizona	27-3	Lute Olson	29-4
2 Georgetown	26-4	John Thompson	29-5
3 Illinois	27-4	Lou Henson	31-5
4 Oklahoma	28-5	Billy Tubbs	30-6
5 N.Carolina	27-7	Dean Smith	29-8
6 Missouri	27-7	Norm Stewart & Rich Daly	29-8
7 Syracuse	27-7	Jim Boeheim	30-8
8 Indiana	25-7	Bob Knight	27-8
9 Duke	24-7	Mike Krzyzewski	28-8
10 **Michigan**	24-7	Bill Frieder & Steve Fisher	30-7
11 Seton Hall	26-6	P.J.Carlesimo	31-7
12 Louisville	22-8	Denny Crum	24-9
13 Stanford	26-6	Mike Montgomery	26-7
14 Iowa	22-9	Tom Davis	23-10
15 UNLV	26-7	Jerry Tarkanian	29-8
16 Florida St.	22-7	Pat Kennedy	22-8
17 West Va.	25-4	Gale Catlett	26-5
18 Ball St.	28-2	Rick Majerus	29-3
19 N.C.State	20-8	Jim Valvano	22-9
20 Alabama	23-7	Wimp Sanderson	23-8

Note: Michigan won the NCAAs.

Major Conference Champions

Conference	Regular Season	Tournament
ACC	N.C.State (10-4)	N.Carolina
Big East	Georgetown (13-3)	Georgetown
Big 8	Oklahoma (12-2)	Missouri
Big 10	Indiana (15-3)	—
Big West	UNLV (16-2)	UNLV
Metro	Florida St.(9-3)	Louisville
Mo.Valley	Creighton (11-3)	Creighton
Pac-10	Arizona (17-1)	Arizona
SEC	Florida (13-5)	Alabama
SWC	Arkansas (13-3)	Arkansas
WAC	Colorado St.(12-4)	UTEP

NCAA Tournament (64 teams)
East Regional
First Round—Georgetown 50, Princeton 49; Notre Dame 81, Vanderbilt 65; N.C.State 81, S.Carolina 66; Iowa 87, Rutgers 73; Minnesota 86, Kansas St.75; Siena 80, Stanford 78; West Va.84, Tennessee 68; Duke 90, S.C.State 69. **Second Round**—Georgetown 81, Notre Dame 74; N.C.State 102, Iowa 96 (2 OT); Minnesota 80, Siena 67; Duke 104, West Va.63. **Semifinals**—Georgetown 69, N.C.State 61; Duke 87, Minnesota 70. **Final**—Duke 85, Georgetown 77.

West Regional
First Round—Arizona 94, R.Morris 60; Clemson 83, St.Mary's-CA 70; DePaul 66, Memphis St.63; UNLV 68, Idaho 56; Evansville 94, Ore.St.90 (OT); Seton Hall 60, SW Mo.St.51; UTEP 85, LSU 74; Indiana 99, G.Mason 85. **Second Round**—Arizona 94, Clemson 68; UNLV 85, DePaul 70; Seton Hall 87, Evansville 73; Indiana 91, UTEP 69. **Semifinals**—UNLV 68, Arizona 67; Seton Hall 78, Indiana 65. **Final**—Seton Hall 84, UNLV 61.

Midwest Regional
First Round—Illinois 77, McNeese St.71; Ball St.68, Pitt 64; Arkansas 120, Loyola-CA 101; Louisville 76, Ark-LR 71; Texas 76, Ga.Tech 70; Missouri 85, Creighton 69; Colo.St.68, Florida 46; Syracuse 104, Bucknell 81. **Second Round**—Illinois 72, Ball St.60; Louisville 93, Arkansas 84; Missouri 108, Texas 89; Syracuse 65, Colo. St.50. **Semifinals**—Illinois 83, Louisville 69; Syracuse 83, Missouri 80. **Final**—Illinois 89, Syracuse 86.

Southeast Regional
First Round—Oklahoma 72, East Tenn.St.71; La.Tech 83, La Salle 74; Virginia 100, Providence 97; Mid.Tenn. St.97, Fla.St.83; South Ala. 86, Alabama 84; Michigan 92, Xavier 87; UCLA 84, Iowa St.74; N.Carolina 93, Southern-BR 79. **Second Round**—Oklahoma 124, La.Tech 81; Virginia 104, Mid.Tenn.St.88; Michigan 91, South Ala.82; N.Carolina 88, UCLA 81. **Semifinals**—Virginia 86, Oklahoma 80; Michigan 92, N.Carolina 87. **Final**—Michigan 102, Virginia 65.

FINAL FOUR
at The Kingdome, Seattle
Semifinals—Seton Hall 95, Duke 78; Michigan 83, Illinois 81. **Championship**—Michigan 80, Seton Hall 79 (OT).

Outstanding Player—Glen Rice, Michigan. **All-Tournament**—Rice and Rumeal Robinson, Michigan; Gerald Greene and John Morton, Seton Hall; Danny Ferry, Duke.

NIT Tournament (32 teams)
at Madison Square Garden, New York
Field—Akron, Ala-Birm., Ark.St., Boise St., California, UConn, Ga.Southern, Hawaii, Kent St., Mich.St., Mississippi, Murray St., Nebraska, New Mexico, N.Mex.St., New Orleans, NC-Charlotte, Ohio St., Okla.St., Penn St., Pepperdine, Richmond, St.John's, St.Louis, St. Peter's, UC-Santa Barb., Santa Clara, So.Ill., Temple, Villanova, Wichita St., Wisconsin.
Semifinals—St.John's 76, Ala-Birm.65; St.Louis 74, Mich.St.64. **Third Place**—Ala-Birm.78, Mich.St.76. **Championship**—St.John's 73, St.Louis 65. **MVP**—Jayson Williams, St.John's.

Players of the Year
Sean Elliott, Arizona . . . . AP,NABC,Wooden
Danny Ferry, Duke . . . . UPI,USBWA,Naismith

Coaches of the Year
Bob Knight, Indiana . . . . UPI,AP,USBWA
P.J.Carlesimo, Seton Hall . . . . NABC
Mike Krzyzewski, Duke . . . . Naismith

Consensus All-America
(In alphabetical order)
First Team—Sean Elliott, Arizona; Pervis Ellison, Louisville; Danny Ferry, Duke; Chris Jackson, LSU; Stacey King, Oklahoma.
Second Team—Mookie Blaylock, Oklahoma; Sherman Douglas, Syracuse; Jay Edwards, Indiana; Todd Lichti, Stanford; Glen Rice, Michigan; Lionel Simmons, La Salle.

John Discher

Detroit's **John Salley** gets a grip on **Michael Jordan** of Chicago during Game 7 of the Eastern Conference finals. The Pistons won the game and went on to repeat as NBA champion.

PRO BASKETBALL

Determined Pistons remove all doubt with second straight NBA title; Magic edges Barkley for MVP; Ensign Robinson buoys Spurs.

PRO BASKETBALL

1989-90 YEAR IN REVIEW

by Bob Ryan

Let the debate begin. Is Detroit a team for the ages, or merely the best available team?

By winning their second straight NBA championship, the 1989-90 Pistons joined the Lakers and Celtics as the only teams in league history to win consecutive titles. Greatness, however, demands longevity and there the Pistons have a way to go before they draw favorable comparisons with the George Mikan Lakers of 1949-54 (five titles in six years), the Bill Russell Celtics of 1957-69 (11 titles in 13 years) and the Kareem-Magic Lakers of 1980-88 (four titles in nine years).

A year ago, Detroit swept a battered Lakers team from the Finals to win the first championship in the 41-year history of franchise. But because the Lakers had been hurting, the respect the Pistons felt they deserved was not immediately forthcoming this season.

Bob Ryan is a columnist for *The Boston Globe* and has covered the NBA for 16 years. He wrote the 1990 best seller, *Drive: The Story of My Life*, with Larry Bird.

"We kept hearing too much about how our championship was a fluke last year, how we only won because of injuries," said center Bill Laimbeer. "Well, that ticked us off. We paid our dues to win that title. And when we finally reached the top, people tried to knock us down."

Not this year. Led by Isiah Thomas, who earned MVP honors in the Finals by averaging 27.6 points, 5.2 rebounds and seven assists per game, the Pistons successfully defended their title by blowing away a strong Portland team in five games, capping it off by merely accomplishing the impossible—beating the Trail Blazers three straight at Memorial Coliseum. Anyone doubting the superiority of this powerful team had to be convinced of their greatness after witnessing *that*.

As usual, Detroit was short on individual accomplishments (Thomas and Joe Dumars tied for last among vote-getters in the regular season MVP vote) and long on collective achievement, particularly on defense. During the regular season the Pistons held the opposition to 98.3 points per game on .447 shooting, each league lows by a wide margin. The Pistons themselves failed to break 100 points on 32 occasions, but that hardly mattered since they kept foes under three figures a whopping 44 times.

During the playoffs, Detroit kept opponents under 100 in 13 out of 20 games. On six occasions, the other team could not break 90. Even Michael Jordan and the Chicago Bulls were embarrassed in two games when they were unable to get out of the 70s (77 and 74). Small wonder many knowledgeable NBA observers are starting to think that the Pistons are the best defensive team the league has ever seen.

As the playoffs approached, many assumed that the Pistons and Lakers would reach the Finals for the third year in a row, and indeed that seemed likely when the Lakers won their ninth straight Pacific Division pennant with the best record in the league (63-19) and Pat Riley, everybody's Coach of the '80s, finally won his first Coach of the Year award.

There was no indication that a collapse was imminent, yet once the playoffs started, it was obvious the Lakers were not themselves. They struggled to get past a mediocre Houston club in the first round then were rudely bounced from the second round in five games by Phoenix, marking their earliest exit from the playoffs since 1986. A month later, Riley, the all-time leader in NBA playoff victories with 102, retired from coaching (with, some said, a healthy shove from management) and headed for a desk job at NBC Sports, the NBA's new TV network. NBC also wanted Detroit coach Chuck Daly (see box), but Daly passed up the analyst's chair to remain on the Pistons' bench.

The Pistons aside, the balance of power in the NBA shifted to the West in 1989-90. It can be argued that four of the best five teams in the league are Western Conference aggregations. In addition to conference champion Portland and Laker-killer Phoenix, Utah and San Antonio also had strong clubs.

Portland was able to improve its regular season record by 20 games and reach the Finals mainly because they acquired Buck Williams, one of the league's premier power forwards, to play along-

Kevin Geil/San Antonio Express-News

Unanimous Rookie of the Year pick **David Robinson** of San Antonio rejects an offering by Utah's **Thurl Bailey.**

side Clyde Drexler and Terry Porter. A strengthened bench helped, too, thanks to the addition of Yugoslav guard Drazen Petrovic and rookie forward Cliff Robinson. The Blazers also responded well to the guidance of coach Rick Adelman, a long-time assistant working his first full year as the head man.

Big things had been expected of Phoenix, but the Suns got off to a so-so start. The problem was that not only did sparkplug Kevin Johnson have a nagging leg injury but the team was missing a certain intangible. Johnson eventually healed and that missing intangible materialized when owner-president-GM Jerry Colangelo traded for veteran Kurt Rambis. "We need," Colangelo explained, "somebody to give us 20 hard minutes a game." Rambis did.

Utah got monster seasons from Karl Malone (31 points, 11.1 boards) and John Stockton (14.5 assists and 2.65 steals). Both get better every year—Malone had a 61-point game against Milwaukee and Stockton's assist average set a league record—but the Jazz were a player or two short come the playoffs and fell to Phoenix in the first round.

San Antonio was unquestionably the league's most improved team. A year ago, the Spurs were adrift in the Midwest Division with a won-loss record 40 games below the waterline. But that changed in a hurry when Ensign David Robinson was piped aboard and proved to be worth the wait and the bundle ($26 million over eight years) that general manager Bob Bass had signed him for as the top pick in the 1987 NBA Draft. Along with veteran Terry Cummings, who was acquired from Milwaukee during the off-season, and irrepressible second-year coach Larry Brown, the Spurs won the division with a dazzling 56-26 record. The 35-victory improvement in the course of one season is an NBA record, topping the Boston Celtics' 32-game advance when Larry Bird arrived in 1979-80.

"What happened is that, in one season, this has become David's team," said Brown going into the playoffs. "He is the heart and soul. I'm not sure he realizes that yet because everything happened so fast." Golden State coach Don Nelson was also impressed. "I've waited 20 years to mention someone in the same breath as Bill Russell," said Nelson, who played with Russell for four years in Boston. "Now I can."

The 7-1 Robinson led the Spurs in scoring (24.3) and rebounding (12.0) and was the unanimous choice for Rookie of the Year. Any other season and he might have joined Wilt Chamberlain and Wes Unseld as the only rookies ever to be named Most Valuable Player. But this was a season unusually rich in MVP candidates with three veterans—Magic Johnson of the Lakers, Charles Barkley of Philadelphia and Jordan—finishing within 65 votes of each other in the balloting for the Maurice Podoloff Award.

Detroit's Daly dose of defense

It was the 1982 NBA Annual Meeting, taking place in Los Angeles. One of the staples of all Annual Meetings, in all sports, is the presence of job seekers, out-of-work coaches, scouts and broadcasters who know enough to be where the action is.

One such jobless person this particular year was a recently deposed NBA head coach. He struck up a conversation with a writer in the hotel lobby, behind, of all things, a potted palm.

"I'm over 50 years old," he said. "It's a little scary. What's going to happen to me if I don't get a job?"

The unemployed coach was Chuck Daly.

He didn't land a coaching job at those '82 meetings, but after a year as a color commentator in Philadelphia, Daly was hired by Detroit Pistons' general manager Jack McCloskey. Keep in mind that by 1983 the Pistons had been around for 35 years and had never won an NBA championship. Not only that, they had never put together consecutive winning seasons. They'd seen plenty of coaches, though—19, and none of them lasting as many as four full seasons.

Seven years later, the Pistons are two-time NBA champs and Chuck Daly is the most sought after coach in the league. Courted by NBC Sports, which wanted him as an analyst, and by Denver and Philadelphia, who wanted him as a general manager, Daly ended speculation on July 10, when he re-signed with the Pistons for $650,000 a year and a shot at three titles in a row.

"I really don't know anything else," he said at the news conference announcing his decision to stay. "This is what I've always done. I'm a basketball coach."

The dapper, 60 year-old Daly has the face of a clothes salesman, which he is eminently qualified to be, but looks can be deceiving. This is a very tough guy.

When he arrived in Detroit in 1983, the Pistons were a sieve. They could score, yes, but so could you, if you happened to be their opponent on any given night and needed a basket at a key moment

Pistons' coach **Chuck Daly** (left) and assistant **Brendan Suhr** discuss strategy with the reigning NBA champions.

of the game. Daly decided this nonsense had to stop.

He has always been a defensive coach. Offense, he reasons, comes and goes, but defense can be a constant. You want fireworks, hire Paul Westhead or Billy Tubbs. When Daly coached college ball at Penn, he was criticized for holding back his players. That was considered to be a sin, even in the Ivy League. Now his concept of team defense is considered a virtue.

"Detroit has created a defensive mind-set around the league and teams copy success," says former colleague Pat Riley. "In the early '80s, transition defense was nonexistent. When a team was running, a coach would just say, 'Get back.' Chuck made defense sophisticated."

Dennis Rodman, the NBA's Defensive Player of the Year, lives to get back and play some D. "My defense is more important than anything," says Rodman. "I don't like scoring because to me it's not exciting."

Daly has taken incomplete players like Rodman and John Salley and allowed them to flourish as defensive specialists. He has learned to live with a center, Bill Laimbeer, who never ventures into the paint on offense, preferring to shoot three-pointers. But Laimbeer also likes to rebound and stick his nose in on defense, so Daly can live with his eccentricities.

Daly has carefully nurtured a gentle soul named Joe Dumars—not rushing him prematurely, but allowing him to thrive at his own pace. He has also gotten maximum mileage out of Mark Aguirre, James Edwards, and Vinnie (the Microwave) Johnson. But most of all, he has worked to bring out the best in the immensely gifted Isiah Thomas, the MVP of the 1990 playoffs, whose immaturity frustrated Daly's predecessor, Scotty Robertson.

Chuck Daly has an ego. No man dresses as consistently top-drawer as he does unless he cares very much what the outside world thinks. He also understands the necessity of checking that ego at the locker room door. If he has a secret it's in the way he has of letting his players think what they want about him while persuading them to do precisely what he wants them to do.

"Chuck is our coach, but he's really our manager," says Laimbeer. "He manages us. We do the playing, but he keeps us going. He manages all these personalities and brings out the best in us."

Wide World Photos

Charles Barkley led Philadelphia to 1st place, but lost the closest MVP vote ever.

Although Barkley gathered more first place votes than Johnson and Jordan (38 to 27 to 21), Magic won the closest MVP vote on record, edging Barkley by 22 points. While leading the Lakers to the best record in the NBA, Johnson paced his club in scoring, assists and steals and was second in rebounds. He also topped the league in triple doubles with 11. "The bottom line," said coach Riley, "is that we lost the greatest player in history, Kareem Abdul-Jabbar, and we were better. That's testimony to Earvin Johnson."

Magic was also named MVP of the All-Star Game in Miami, Feb.11, leading all scorers with 22 points, but the Western Conference lost to the East, 130-113. Adding his first All-Star award to his three regular season and three playoff awards, Johnson trails only Abdul-Jabbar in career MVPs, 8-7.

Jordan, meanwhile, continued to im-prove and amaze audiences from coast to coast. Pro sports' most merchandised player led the league in scoring (33.6) for the fourth year in a row, three short of Chamberlain's seven-year streak set from 1960-66. He also got great support from Chicago teammate Scottie Pippen, who made the All-Star Game for the first time and established himself as one of the finest all-around forwards in the game. But improvement in other areas was slight (center, for instance), and the Bulls remain just outside the inner circle of NBA teams. They did push Detroit to the brink in the Eastern Conference finals, but Game 7 turned out to be a huge disappointment when Jordan's supporting cast only shot 24 percent and the Bulls lost, 93-74.

Houston center Akeem Olajuwon was not only the league leader in both rebounds (14.0) and blocked shots (4.59), but on March 29 he became just the third player in NBA history to record a quadruple double when he registered 18 points, 16 rebounds, 11 blocks and 10 assists against Milwaukee. Alvin Robertson (1986) and Nate Thurmond (1974) have the other two quads.

Larry Bird, back in uniform for Boston after missing nearly all of last season recovering from foot surgery, made a run at Calvin Murphy's consecutive free throw record of 78. He crested Feb. 13 in Houston at 71 straight, but led the league from the line with a .930 percentage. At the other end of the scale, Chris Dudley of New Jersey missed a staggering 124 of 182 foul shots for a percentage of .319.

Boston, a 42-game winner in 1988-89, welcomed Bird back by winning 52, despite losing starting point guard Brian Shaw to the Italian League. The proud but elderly Celtics—the frontcourt of Bird, Robert Parish and Kevin McHale averaged 34 years-old—stayed competitive, at least until New York (down 0-2) eliminated them in the first round of the playoffs.

The Celtics were gone by May 6. By June 12, the most storied franchise in the league had undergone a surprising reorganization that resulted in the firing of coach Jimmy Rodgers, the hiring of Big East commissioner Dave Gavitt as CEO and general manager, the unsuccessful

Wide World Photos

Former Big East commissioner **Dave Gavitt** (left) shares a laugh with Boston Celtics' president **Red Auerbach** after being named head of basketball operations on May 30.

(and humiliating) pursuit of Duke coach Mike Krzyzewski, and the eventual naming of Chris Ford (seven years a Celtic assistant) as coach.

Four other coaching positions opened up after the regular season. Riley (Lakers) and Mike Fratello (Atlanta) quit and went to work for NBC; Bernie Bickerstaff (Seattle) accepted the Denver GM position that Georgetown's John Thompson turned down; and the L.A. Clippers dismissed Don Casey. The replacements included Mike Dunleavy (Lakers), Bob Weiss (Atlanta), K.C. Jones (Seattle) and Mike Schuler (Clippers).

Prior to that changing of the guard, three coaches had been replaced during the regular season: John MacLeod by Richie Adubato in Dallas, Dick Harter by Gene Littles in Charlotte, and Jerry Reynolds by Dick Motta in Sacramento.

New Jersey coach Bill Fitch, whose woeful Nets had the distinction of winning fewer games (17) than both expansion teams, got a consolation prize in Syracuse center Derrick Coleman, the overall first round pick in the 1990 Draft. Motta and the Kings traded Pervis Ellison

(1989's overall No.1) and Rodney McCray then drafted a record four players in the first round, including college Player of the Year Lionel Simmons of La Salle. These are lean years for Fitch and Motta, who have won a combined 1708 games in 38 NBA seasons.

Otherwise, while the other professional leagues talked about expansion, the NBA added two new teams for the second year in a row and, once again, the newcomers were boffo at the box office. The Orlando Magic came within a body or two of selling out each game (playing to 99.9 percent of capacity) and the Minnesota Timberwolves did even better at the gate—establishing a new one-season NBA home attendance record of 1,072,572 playing in the spacious Metrodome (25,810 seats). The Wolves, who brought the NBA back to Minneapolis 30 years after the Lakers moved to L.A., surprised everyone by winning 22 games.

Just how booming these times are for the NBA was made obvious the first week of the season when NBC outbid CBS for TV broadcast rights, agreeing to pay

$600 million over four years—a hefty 350 percent increase. The escalation in TV cable rights was equally impressive as TNT swallowed hard and went from a two-year, $50 million deal to one costing $275 million over four years.

No wonder grateful NBA owners voted at the All-Star break to give commissioner David Stern a new five-year contract worth $3.5 million a year. Stern, 47, succeeded Larry O'Brien as league boss in 1984.

One of the stars that NBC and TNT are counting on to attract viewers is the quoteable and pugnacious Barkley of Philadelphia, who, according to 76er stat mavin Harvey Pollack, rang up a record $38,050 in fines during the season. Among Barkley's transgressions was a fight with Detroit's Bill Laimbeer in April (cost: $20,000) and the revelation that he and New York's Mark Jackson had a running $500 side bet on who could win the most Sixer-Knick games with a last second shot (cost: $5000).

Asked about the hole this activity put in his $2.6 million salary, an unconcerned Barkley said, ''I'll write it off my income tax.'' In July, the IRS announced that yes, indeed, he could deduct the fines as ''an ordinary expense.''

The 76ers were the surprise of the Atlantic Division, winning the championship by one game over Boston. Led by Barkley, but sparked in large measure by a dynamic young backcourt, the Sixers assumed control of the race with a midseason 12-game winning streak. The pro game is becoming more and more a contest of speed and quickness in the backcourt and the 76ers were well-served by Johnny Dawkins and Hersey Hawkins. Dawkins arrived from San Antonio in a trade for esteemed veteran Maurice Cheeks and answered doubters with a solid season, while Hawkins shook off a disastrous 1989 playoff to average 18 points a game.

New York, the defending Atlantic champs, followed a disappointing regular season with a dramatic comeback win over hated Boston in a first-round playoff series. Leading the division race for almost three months, the Knicks unraveled during the second half of the season, falling behind both Philadelphia and Boston. Along the way, young playmaker Rod Strickland was traded to the Spurs for Cheeks, who had never been able to adapt to his new surroundings in San Antonio after a decade in Philadelphia. The one constant presence for New York was center Patrick Ewing, who finished fifth in rebounding, third in scoring, second in blocks and first in aggressive springs from end-to-end among all NBA centers.

On Jan. 15, the Knicks' Trent Tucker beat Chicago on a desperation three-pointer with only 1/10th of a second left in the game. Tucker somehow caught an inbounds pass, wheeled and got off a 26-footer in that fraction of a second. Despite vigorous objections from the visiting Bulls, the Knicks' 109-106 victory was allowed to stand.

Another last second prayer that went in —this one by Portland's Danny Young in Game 4 of the Finals—was not allowed. The call was made by referee Earl Strom officiating his final game after 32 seasons in the NBA and ABA. Strom ruled that Young's shot came after the final horn. As usual, the TV replay backed him up.

''I can't tell you how much I hate to see Earl go,'' said one league official, who for obvious reasons must remain anonymous. ''He's 61 and he's still our best referee.''

Earlier in the year, four numbers were retired by three different teams. In Los Angeles, the Lakers hung up Kareem Abdul-Jabbar's #33; in Milwaukee, it was Sidney Moncrief's #4; and in New York, Dick Barnett's #12 and Red Holtzman's #613 (the number of regular season wins as Knicks' coach). Joe Barry Carroll, traded from New Jersey to Denver on Feb. 21, asked the Nuggets if he could wear #44, which used to belong to Dan Issel and hangs from the rafters of McNichols Arena. Hearing about it, Issel said, ''Tell him if he wants that number, he's going to have to jump up and get it.'' Carroll was issued #11.

And finally, Don Nelson of Golden State and Doug Moe of Denver became the ninth and tenth head coaches to reach 600 regular season wins—Nelson on Jan. 21 with a victory over the Celtics at Boston Garden and Moe on March 13 at home against Houston.

Said Moe on his arrival to the 600 Club: ''I think the other nine guys have just been dishonored.'' □

PRO BASKETBALL
STATISTICS

THE SEASON IN REVIEW
1989-1990
STANDINGS • PLAYOFFS • DRAFT

SEC **A**

PAGE **273**

Final NBA Standings

Number of seasons listed after each head coach refers to current tenure with club.

Eastern Conference

Atlantic Division

	W	L	Pct	GB	For	Opp
Philadelphia	53	29	.646	—	110.2	105.2
Boston	52	30	.634	1	110.0	106.0
New York	45	37	.549	8	108.3	106.9
Washington	31	51	.378	22	107.7	109.9
Miami	18	64	.220	35	100.6	110.3
New Jersey	17	65	.207	36	100.1	108.0

Head Coaches: Phi—Jim Lynam (3rd season); **Bos**—Jimmy Rodgers (2nd); **NY**—Stu Jackson (1st); **Was**—Wes Unseld (3rd); **Mia**—Ron Rothstein (2nd); **NJ**—Bill Fitch (1st).

Central Division

	W	L	Pct	GB	For	Opp
Detroit	59	23	.720	—	104.3	98.3
Chicago	55	27	.671	4	109.5	106.2
Milwaukee	44	38	.537	15	106.0	106.8
Cleveland	42	40	.512	17	102.6	102.9
Indiana	42	40	.512	17	109.3	109.1
Atlanta	41	41	.500	18	108.5	107.5
Orlando	18	64	.220	41	110.9	119.8

Head Coaches: Det—Chuck Daly (7th season); **Chi**—Phil Jackson (1st); **Mil**—Del Harris (3rd); **Ind**—Dick Versace (2nd); **Cle**—Lenny Wilkens (4th); **Atl**—Mike Fratello (7th); **Orl**—Matt Guokas (1st).

Western Conference

Midwest Division

	W	L	Pct	GB	For	Opp
San Antonio	56	26	.683	—	106.3	102.8
Utah	55	27	.671	1	106.8	102.0
Dallas	47	35	.573	9	102.2	102.2
Denver	43	39	.524	13	114.6	113.2
Houston	41	41	.500	15	106.7	105.3
Minnesota	22	60	.268	34	95.2	99.4
Charlotte	19	63	.232	37	100.4	108.2

Head Coaches: Utah—Jerry Sloan (2nd season); **SA**—Larry Brown (2nd); **Dal**—replaced John MacLeod (3rd, 5-6) with Richie Adubato (42-29) on Nov.29; **Den**—Doug Moe (10th); **Hou**—Don Chaney (2nd); **Min**—Bill Musselman (1st); **Char**—replaced Dick Harter (2nd, 8-32) with Gene Littles (11-31) on Jan.31.

Pacific Division

	W	L	Pct	GB	For	Opp
LA Lakers	63	19	.768	—	110.7	103.9
Portland	59	23	.720	4	114.2	107.9
Phoenix	54	28	.659	9	114.9	107.8
Seattle	41	41	.500	22	106.9	105.9
Golden St	37	45	.451	26	116.3	119.4
LA Clippers	30	52	.366	33	103.8	107.2
Sacramento	23	59	.280	40	101.7	106.8

Head Coaches: LAL—Pat Riley (9th season); **Port**—Rick Adelman (2nd); **Pho**—Cotton Fitzsimmons (2nd); **Sea**—Bernie Bickerstaff (5th); **GS**—Don Nelson (2nd); **LAC**—Don Casey (2nd); **Sac**—promoted Jerry Reynolds (4th, 7-20) to GM and named Dick Motta (16-39) on Jan.4.

Overall Conference Standings

Sixteen teams—8 from each conference—qualify for the NBA Playoffs. In each conference, the two regular season division champions get automatic berths and the top two seeds with the remaining spots going to the teams with the six next best records. (*) denotes division champions.

Eastern Conference

	W	L	Home	Away	Conf
1. Detroit*	59	23	35-6	24-17	40-14
2. Philadelphia*	53	29	34-7	19-22	37-17
3. Chicago	55	27	36-5	19-22	37-17
4. Boston	52	30	30-11	22-19	36-18
5. New York	45	37	29-12	16-25	30-24
6. Milwaukee	44	38	27-14	17-24	28-26
7. Cleveland	42	40	27-14	15-26	30-24
8. Indiana	42	40	28-13	14-27	30-24
Atlanta	41	41	25-16	16-25	27-27
Washington	31	51	20-21	11-30	20-34
Orlando	18	64	12-29	6-35	12-42
Miami	18	64	11-30	7-34	11-43
New Jersey	17	65	13-28	4-37	13-41

Western Conference

	W	L	Home	Away	Conf
1. LA Lakers*	63	19	37-4	26-15	44-12
2. Utah*	55	27	36-5	19-22	38-18
3. Portland	59	23	35-6	24-17	41-15
4. San Antonio	56	26	34-7	22-19	40-16
5. Phoenix	54	28	32-9	22-19	38-18
6. Dallas	47	35	30-11	17-24	29-27
7. Denver	43	39	28-13	15-26	28-20
8. Houston	41	41	31-10	10-31	28-28
Seattle	41	41	30-11	11-30	26-30
Golden St	37	45	27-14	10-31	24-32
LA Clippers	30	52	20-21	10-31	17-39
Sacramento	23	59	16-25	7-34	14-42
Minnesota	22	60	17-24	5-36	12-44
Charlotte	19	63	13-28	6-35	13-43

NBA Individual Leaders

Scoring
(Minimum 70 games or 1400 points)

	GP	FG	FT	Pts	Avg
Michael Jordan, Chi	82	1034	593	2753	33.6
Karl Malone, Utah	82	914	696	2540	31.0
Patrick Ewing, NY	80	922	502	2347	28.6
Tom Chambers, Pho	81	810	557	2201	27.2
Dominique Wilkins, Atl	80	810	459	2138	26.7
Charles Barkley, Phi	79	706	557	1989	25.2
Chris Mullin, GS	78	682	505	1956	25.1
Reggie Miller, Ind	82	661	544	2016	24.6
Akeem Olajuwon, Hou	82	806	382	1995	24.3
David Robinson, SA*	82	690	613	1993	24.3
Larry Bird, Bos	75	718	319	1820	24.3
Jeff Malone, Wash	75	781	257	1820	24.3
Clyde Drexler, Port	73	670	333	1703	23.3
Tony Campbell, Min	82	723	448	1903	23.2
Kevin Johnson, Pho	74	578	501	1665	22.5
Terry Cummings, SA	81	728	343	1818	22.4
Bernard King, Wash	82	711	412	1837	22.4
Magic Johnson, LAL	79	546	567	1765	22.3
Wayman Tisdale, Sac	79	726	306	1758	22.3
Mitch Richmond, GS	78	640	406	1720	22.1
Charles Smith, LAC	78	595	454	1645	21.1
James Worthy, LAL	80	711	248	1685	21.1
Kevin McHale, Bos	82	648	393	1712	20.9
Chuck Person, Ind	77	605	211	1515	19.7
Mark Price, Cle	73	489	300	1430	19.6

Rebounds

	Avg
Olajuwon, Hou	14.0
Robinson, SA	11.5
Barkley, Phi	11.5
Malone, Utah	11.1
Ewing, NY	10.9
Seikaly, Mia	10.4
Parish, Bos	10.1
Malone, Atl	10.0
Cage, Sea	10.0
Williams, Port	9.8

Assists

	Avg
Stockton, Utah	14.5
Johnson, LAL	11.5
K.Johnson, Pho	11.4
Bogues, Char	10.7
Grant, LAC	10.0
Thomas, Det	9.4
Price, Cle	9.1
Porter, Port	9.1
Hardaway, GS	8.7
Walker, Wash	8.0

Field Goal Pct.

	Pct
West, Pho	.625
Barkley, Phi	.600
Parish, Bos	.580
Malone, Utah	.562
Woolridge, LAL	.556

Free Throw Pct.

	Pct
Bird, Bos	.930
E.Johnson, Pho	.917
Davis, Den	.912
Dumars, Det	.900
McHale, Bos	.893

Blocked Shots

	Avg
Olajuwon, Hou	4.59
Ewing, NY	3.99
Robinson, SA	3.89
Bol, GS	3.17
Benjamin, LAC	2.63

Steals

	Avg
Jordan, Chi	2.77
Stockton, Utah	2.65
Pippen, Chi	2.57
Robertson, Mil	2.56
Harper, Dal	2.28

3-Pt FG Pct

	Pct
Kerr, Cle	.507
Hodges, Chi	.481
Petrovic, Port	.459
Sundvold, Mia	.440
Scott, LAL	.423

Triple Doubles

Johnson, LAL	11
Bird, Bos	10
Walker, Wash	9
Lever, Den	5
Olajuwon, Hou	4

Note: Olajuwon also had the season's only Quadruple Double (18 pt, 16 reb, 11 blk, 10 ast) vs Mil., Mar.29, 1990.

1990 NBA All-Star Game
East 130, West 113

40th NBA All-Star Game. **Date:** Feb.11, at Miami Arena; **Coaches:** Chuck Daly, Detroit (East) and Pat Riley, LA Lakers (West); **MVP:** Magic Johnson, LA Lakers (West), 22 pts.

Western Conference

Starters	Min	FG M/A	Pts	Rb	A
Magic Johnson, LAL	25	9/15	22	6	4
Akeem Olajuwon, Hou	31	2/14	8	16	2
John Stockton, Utah	15	1/4	2	0	6
James Worthy, LAL	19	1/11	2	4	0
A.C. Green, LAL	12	0/3	0	3	1
Bench					
Tom Chambers, Pho	21	8/12	21	3	1
Lafayette Lever, Den	22	7/13	16	3	2
Rolando Blackman, Dal	21	7/9	15	2	2
David Robinson, SA	25	7/12	15	10	1
Clyde Drexler, Port	19	2/6	7	4	2
Chris Mullin, GS	16	1/5	3	3	1
Kevin Johnson, Pho	14	1/1	2	0	4
Totals	240	46/105	113	54	26

Three-Pointers M/A—M.Johnson 4/6, Drexler 1/1, Stockton 0-1, Chambers 0-1, Lever 0-2; **Free Throws M/A**—Chambers 5/7, Olajuwon 4/10, Drexler 2/2, Lever 2/2, Blackman 1/1, Robinson 1/2, Mullin 1/2; **Percentages**—2-Pt FG (41/94 =.436), 3-Pt FG (5/11 =.455), Combined FG (46/105 =.438), Free Throws (16/26 =.615); **Turnovers (23)**—Olajuwon 4, Chambers 3, K. Johnson 3, M.Johnson 3, Stockton 3, Blackman 2, Drexler, Green, Mullin, Robinson, Worthy; **Steals (13)**—Blackman 2, Lever 2, Mullin 2, Robinson 2, Chambers, Drexler, Olajuwon, Stockton, Worthy; **Blocked Shots (7)**—Drexler, Green, M.Johnson, Mullin, Olajuwon, Robinson, Stockton; **Fouls (10)**—K.Johnson 2, Blackman, Drexler, Green, M.Johnson, Olajuwon, Robinson, Stockton, Worthy.

Eastern Conference

Starters	Min	FG M/A	Pts	Rb	A
Charles Barkley, Phi	22	7/12	17	4	0
Michael Jordan, Chi	29	8/17	17	5	2
Isiah Thomas, Det	27	7/12	15	4	9
Patrick Ewing, NY	27	5/9	12	10	1
Larry Bird, Bos	23	3/8	8	8	3
Bench					
Robert Parish, Bos	21	7/11	14	4	2
Kevin McHale, Bos	20	6/11	13	8	1
Dominique Wilkins, Atl	16	5/10	13	0	4
Joe Dumars, Det	18	3/4	9	1	5
Reggie Miller, Ind	14	2/3	4	1	4
Dennis Rodman, Det	11	2/4	4	4	1
Scottie Pippen, Chi	12	2/4	4	1	0
Totals	240	57/105	130	50	31

Three-Pointers M/A—Dumars 2/2, Barkley 1/1, McHale 1/1, Jordan 1/1, Thomas 1/1, Wilkins 1-1, Bird 0/1, Miller 0/1, Pippen 0/1; **Free Throws M/A**—Bird 2/2, Ewing 2/2, Wilkins 2/2, Barkley 2/3, Dumars 1/2, Parish 0-1; **Percentages**—2-Pt FG (50/95 =.526), 3-Pt FG (7/10 =.700), Combined FG (57/105 = .543), Free Throws (9/12 =.750); **Turnovers (23)**—Ewing 5, Jordan 5, Bird 3, Dumars 3, Barkley 2, Rodman 2, Parish, Pippen, Thomas; **Steals (16)**—Jordan 5, Bird 3, Thomas 3, Barkley, Ewing, Miller, Pippen, Wilkins; **Blocked Shots (10)**—Ewing 5, Barkley, Jordan, Parish, Pippen, Rodman; **Fouls (20)**—Ewing 5, McHale 4, Parish 4, Barkley, Bird, Jordan, Miller, Pippen, Rodman, Wilkins.

	1	2	3	4	Final
West	23	29	31	30	113
East	40	25	35	30	130

Halftime—East, 65-52; **Technical Fouls**—None; **Officials**—Earl Strom, Bill Oakes, Paul Mihalak; **Attendance**—14,810; **Time**—2:05.

Team by Team Statistics

At least 25 games played. Players who played with more than one team during the regular season are listed with their final clubs; (*) denotes rookies.

Atlanta Hawks

	GP	FG%	TPts	Pts	Reb	Ast
				—Per Game—		
Dominique Wilkins .80	.484	2138	26.7	6.5	2.5
Moses Malone 81	.480	1528	18.9	10.0	1.6
Doc Rivers 48	.454	598	12.5	4.2	5.5
Kevin Willis 81	.519	1006	12.4	8.0	0.7
Kenny Smith 79	.466	943	11.9	2.0	5.6
SAC..........46	.461	688	15.0	2.6	6.6
ATL..........33	.480	255	7.7	1.1	4.3
John Battle 60	.506	654	10.9	1.7	2.6
Spud Webb 82	.477	751	9.2	2.5	5.8
John Long 48	.453	404	8.4	1.7	1.8
Cliff Levingston ..75	.509	516	6.9	4.3	1.1
Alexander Volkov .72	.482	357	5.0	1.7	1.2
Jon Koncak.......54	.614	198	3.7	4.2	0.4

Triple Doubles: None.
Acquired: Smith from Sac.(Feb.13).

Boston Celtics

	GP	FG%	TPts	Pts	Reb	Ast
				—Per Game—		
Larry Bird 75	.473	1820	24.3	9.5	7.5
Kevin McHale.....82	.549	1712	20.9	8.3	2.1
Reggie Lewis 79	.496	1340	17.0	4.4	2.8
Robert Parish 79	.580	1243	15.7	10.1	1.3
Dennis Johnson ..75	.434	531	7.1	2.7	6.5
Jim Paxson 72	.453	460	6.4	1.1	1.9
Joe Kleine........81	.480	435	5.4	4.4	0.6
Kevin Gamble ...71	.455	362	5.1	1.6	1.7
Michael Smith*....65	.476	327	5.0	1.5	1.2
Ed Pinckney 77	.542	362	4.7	2.9	0.9
John Bagley 54	.459	230	4.3	1.6	5.5
Charles Smith* 60	.444	171	2.9	1.2	1.7

Triple Doubles: Bird (10).

Charlotte Hornets

	GP	FG%	TPts	Pts	Reb	Ast
				—Per Game—		
Rex Chapman 54	.408	945	17.5	3.3	2.4
Armon Gilliam ...76	.515	1271	16.7	7.9	1.3
PHO 16	.430	143	8.9	4.4	0.5
CHAR 60	.527	1128	18.8	8.8	1.5
Dell Curry 67	.466	1070	16.0	2.5	2.4
Kelly Tripucka ...79	.430	1232	15.6	4.1	2.8
J.R.Reid*........82	.440	908	11.1	8.4	1.2
Muggsy Bogues ..81	.491	763	9.4	2.6	10.7
Randolph Keys ..80	.432	701	8.8	3.2	1.1
CLEV 48	.421	365	7.6	2.9	0.8
CHAR 32	.445	336	10.5	3.6	1.5
Kenny Gattison ..63	.550	372	5.9	3.1	0.6
Robert Reid......72	.391	414	5.8	2.1	1.3
PORT 12	.391	31	2.6	0.7	0.7
CHAR 60	.391	383	6.4	2.4	1.4
Michael Williams .28	.504	156	5.6	1.1	2.9
PHO 6	.200	5	0.8	0.2	0.7
DAL			Did not play		
CHAR 22	.532	151	6.9	1.4	3.5
Brian Rowsom ...44	.436	225	5.1	3.0	0.5
Richard Anderson .54	.417	231	4.3	2.4	1.0

Triple Doubles: None.
Acquired: Gilliam from Pho.(Dec.13); Keyes from Cle.(Feb.22).
Signed: R.Reid (Dec.13) after he was waived by Port.(Dec.6); Williams (Mar. 13) after he was waived by Pho.(Dec.12) then by Dal.(Dec.26).

Chicago Bulls

	GP	FG%	TPts	Pts	Reb	Ast
				—Per Game—		
Michael Jordan ...82	.526	2753	33.6	6.9	6.3
Scottie Pippen ...82	.489	1351	16.5	6.7	5.4
Horace Grant....80	.523	1071	13.4	7.9	2.8
Bill Cartwright ...71	.488	811	11.4	6.5	2.0
John Paxson 82	.516	819	10.0	1.5	4.1
Stacey King* 82	.504	728	8.9	4.7	1.1
Craig Hodges ...82	.438	407	6.5	0.8	1.7
B.J.Armstrong* ...81	.485	452	5.6	1.3	2.5
Will Perdue 77	.414	294	3.8	2.8	0.6
Charles Davis ...53	.367	130	2.5	1.5	0.3
Ed Nealy........46	.529	104	2.3	3.0	0.6
Jeff Sanders* 31	.325	28	0.9	1.3	0.3

Triple Doubles: Jordan (1).

Cleveland Cavaliers

	GP	FG%	TPts	Pts	Reb	Ast
				—Per Game—		
Mark Price 73	.459	1430	19.6	3.4	9.1
John Williams.....82	.493	1381	16.8	8.1	2.0
Brad Daugherty ...41	.479	690	16.8	9.1	3.2
Larry Nance 62	.511	1011	16.3	8.3	2.6
Craig Ehlo 81	.464	1102	13.6	5.4	4.6
Chucky Brown* ...75	.470	545	7.3	3.1	0.7
Steve Kerr 78	.444	520	6.7	1.3	3.2
Winston Bennett* ..55	.479	338	6.1	3.4	1.0
Derrick Chievous ..55	.477	293	5.3	1.6	0.6
HOU..........41	.506	244	6.0	1.8	0.7
CLE 14	.357	49	3.5	1.1	0.3
Paul Mokeski 38	.420	151	4.0	2.6	0.4
John Morton* 37	.298	146	3.9	0.9	1.8
Tree Rollins 48	.456	125	2.6	3.2	0.5

Triple Doubles: Price (1).
Acquired: Chievous from Hou.(Feb.21).

Dallas Mavericks

	GP	FG%	TPts	Pts	Reb	Ast
				—Per Game—		
Rolando Blackman .80	.498	1552	19.4	3.5	3.6
Derek Harper 82	.488	1473	18.0	3.0	7.4
Roy Tarpley 45	.451	758	16.8	13.1	1.5
Sam Perkins 76	.493	1206	15.9	7.5	2.3
Adrian Dantley ...45	.477	662	14.7	3.8	1.8
James Donaldson ..73	.539	665	9.1	8.6	0.8
Herb Williams 81	.444	700	8.6	4.8	1.5
Brad Davis 73	.490	470	6.4	1.3	3.3
Bill Wennington ..60	.449	270	4.5	3.3	0.7
Randy White* 55	.369	237	4.3	3.1	0.4
Steve Alford 41	.457	168	4.1	0.6	1.0
Anthony Jones ...66	.371	195	3.0	1.2	0.4

Triple Doubles: None.

Team by Team Statistics (Cont.)

Denver Nuggets

	GP	FG%	TPts	Pts	Reb	Ast
				—Per Game—		
Fat Lever	79	.443	1443	18.3	9.3	6.5
Alex English	80	.491	1433	17.9	3.6	2.8
Walter Davis	69	.481	1207	17.5	2.6	2.2
Michael Adams	79	.402	1221	15.5	2.8	6.3
Blair Rasmussen	81	.497	1001	12.4	7.3	1.0
Dan Schayes	53	.494	551	10.4	6.5	1.2
Joe Barry Carroll	76	.411	761	10.0	5.8	1.3
NJ	46	.393	403	8.8	5.4	0.9
DEN	30	.432	358	11.9	6.4	1.8
Todd Lichti*	79	.486	630	8.0	1.9	1.5
Bill Hanzlik	81	.452	500	6.2	2.6	2.3
Tim Kempton	71	.490	383	5.4	3.1	1.7
Jerome Lane	67	.469	334	5.0	5.4	1.6
Eddie Hughes	60	.411	209	3.5	1.2	1.9
T.R.Dunn	65	.454	114	1.8	2.1	0.7

Triple Doubles: Lever (5).
Acquired: Carroll from NJ (Feb.21).

Houston Rockets

	GP	FG%	TPts	Pts	Reb	Ast
				—Per Game—		
Akeem Olajuwon	82	.501	1995	24.3	14.0	2.9
Otis Thorpe	82	.548	1401	17.1	9.0	3.2
Mitchell Wiggins	66	.488	1024	15.5	4.3	1.6
Buck Johnson	82	.495	1215	14.8	4.6	3.1
Sleepy Floyd	82	.451	1000	12.2	4.7	7.3
Vernon Maxwell	79	.439	714	9.0	2.9	3.7
SA	49	.435	340	6.9	2.9	3.0
HOU	30	.442	374	12.5	2.9	5.0
Mike Woodson	61	.395	394	6.5	1.4	1.1
John Lucas	49	.375	286	5.8	1.8	4.9
Anthony Bowie	66	.406	284	4.3	1.8	1.5
Byron Dinkins*	33	.404	115	3.5	1.2	2.3
Larry Smith	74	.474	222	3.0	6.1	0.9
Adrian Caldwell*	51	.553	97	1.9	2.1	0.1

Triple Doubles: Olajuwon (4, including one Quadruple Double).
Acquired: Maxwell from SA (Feb.21).

Detroit Pistons

	GP	FG%	TPts	Pts	Reb	Ast
				—Per Game—		
Isiah Thomas	81	.438	1492	18.4	3.8	9.4
Joe Dumars	75	.480	1335	17.8	2.8	4.9
James Edwards	82	.498	1189	14.5	4.2	0.8
Mark Aguirre	78	.488	1099	14.1	3.9	1.9
Bill Laimbeer	81	.484	981	12.1	9.6	2.1
Vinnie Johnson	82	.431	804	9.8	3.1	3.1
Dennis Rodman	82	.581	719	8.8	9.7	0.9
John Salley	82	.512	593	7.2	5.4	0.8
William Bedford	42	.432	118	2.8	1.4	0.1
Gerald Henderson	57	.486	135	2.4	0.8	1.3
MIL	11	.423	27	2.5	1.1	1.2
DET	46	.506	108	2.3	0.7	1.3
David Greenwood	37	.423	60	1.6	2.1	0.3
Scott Hastings	40	.303	42	1.1	0.8	0.2

Triple Doubles: None.
Signed: Henderson (Dec.6) after he was waived by Mil.(Nov.27).

Indiana Pacers

	GP	FG%	TPts	Pts	Reb	Ast
				—Per Game—		
Reggie Miller	82	.514	2016	24.6	3.6	3.8
Chuck Person	77	.487	1515	19.7	5.8	3.0
Detlef Schrempf	78	.516	1267	16.2	7.9	3.2
Rik Smits	82	.533	1271	15.5	6.2	1.7
Vern Fleming	82	.508	1176	14.3	3.9	7.4
LaSalle Thompson	82	.473	554	6.8	7.7	1.3
Mike Sanders	82	.470	510	6.2	2.8	1.1
Rickey Green	69	.433	244	3.5	0.8	2.6
George McCloud*	44	.313	118	2.7	1.0	1.0
Randy Wittman	61	.508	130	2.1	0.5	0.6
Greg Dreiling	49	.377	65	1.3	1.8	0.2

Triple Doubles: None.

Golden State Warriors

	GP	FG%	TPts	Pts	Reb	Ast
				—Per Game—		
Chris Mullin	78	.536	1956	25.1	5.9	4.1
Mitch Richmond	78	.497	1720	22.1	4.6	2.9
Terry Teagle	82	.480	1323	16.1	4.5	1.9
Tim Hardaway*	79	.471	1162	14.7	3.9	8.7
S.Marciulionis*	75	.519	905	12.1	2.9	1.6
Rod Higgins	82	.481	909	11.1	5.1	1.6
Tom Tolbert	70	.493	616	8.8	5.2	0.8
Jim Petersen	43	.426	172	4.0	3.7	0.5
Kelvin Upshaw	40	.438	160	4.0	1.0	1.4
BOS	14	.308	30	2.1	0.9	2.0
DAL	3	.333	2	0.7	0.0	0.0
GS	23	.490	128	5.6	1.2	1.1
Chris Welp	27	.377	65	2.4	1.8	0.3
SA	13	.304	15	1.2	0.9	0.4
GS	14	.421	50	3.6	2.6	0.3
Manute Bol	75	.331	146	1.9	3.7	0.5

Triple Doubles: Hardaway (3).
Acquired: Welp from SA (Feb.22).
Signed: Upshaw (Feb.28) after he was waived by Bos.(Dec.26) and Dal.(Jan.22).

Los Angeles Clippers

	GP	FG%	TPts	Pts	Reb	Ast
				—Per Game—		
Ron Harper	35	.473	798	22.8	5.9	5.2
CLE	7	.442	154	22.0	6.9	7.0
LAC	28	.481	644	23.0	5.6	4.8
Charles Smith	78	.520	1645	21.1	6.7	1.5
Danny Manning	71	.533	1154	16.3	5.9	2.6
Ken Norman	70	.510	1128	16.1	6.7	2.3
Benoit Benjamin	71	.526	959	13.5	9.3	2.2
Gary Grant	44	.466	575	13.1	4.4	10.0
Winston Garland	79	.401	574	7.3	2.7	3.8
GS	51	.375	270	5.3	2.2	3.1
LAC	28	.428	304	10.9	3.7	5.2
Tom Garrick	73	.494	508	7.0	2.2	4.0
Jeff Martin*	69	.411	433	6.3	2.3	0.6
Michael Young	45	.474	219	4.9	1.9	0.5
Joe Wolf	77	.395	370	4.8	3.0	0.8
David Rivers	52	.406	219	4.2	1.6	3.0
Ken Bannister	52	.478	206	4.0	2.2	0.3

Triple Doubles: Grant (1).
Acquired: Harper from Cle.(Nov.16); Garland from GS (Feb.22).

Los Angeles Lakers

	GP	FG%	TPts	Pts	Reb	Ast
Magic Johnson 79		.480	1765	22.3	6.6	11.5
James Worthy.....80		.548	1685	21.1	6.0	3.6
Byron Scott 77		.470	1197	15.5	3.1	3.6
A.C.Green.......82		.478	1061	12.9	8.7	1.1
Orlando Woolridge .62		.556	788	12.7	3.0	1.5
Mychal Thompson ..70		.500	706	10.1	6.8	0.6
Vlade Divac*.....82		.499	701	8.5	6.2	0.9
Michael Cooper ...80		.387	515	6.4	2.8	2.7
Larry Drew 80		.444	418	5.2	1.2	2.7
Jay Vincent 41		.490	214	5.2	1.5	0.4
PHI 17		.429	124	7.3	2.1	0.5
LAL 24		.526	90	3.8	1.1	0.4
Mark McNamara ..33		.442	102	3.1	1.9	0.1

Triple Doubles: Johnson (11).
Signed: Vincent (Dec.24) after he was waived by Phi.(Dec.13).

Minnesota Timberwolves

	GP	FG%	TPts	Pts	Reb	Ast
Tony Campbell 82		.457	1903	23.2	5.5	2.6
Tyrone Corbin 82		.481	1203	14.7	7.4	2.6
Sam Mitchell*....80		.446	1012	12.7	5.8	1.1
Pooh Richardson*..82		.461	938	11.4	2.6	6.8
Randy Breuer 81		.428	722	8.9	5.1	1.2
MIL 30		.462	204	6.8	4.2	0.8
MIN 51		.416	518	10.2	5.7	1.7
Tod Murphy 82		.471	680	8.3	6.9	1.3
Scott Roth 71		.379	486	6.8	1.6	1.6
Donald Royal*....66		.459	387	5.9	2.1	0.7
Brad Sellers 59		.406	264	4.5	1.5	0.6
SEA 45		.424	217	4.8	1.6	0.7
MIN 14		.339	47	3.4	1.4	0.1
Doug West*......52		.393	135	2.6	1.3	0.3
Sidney Lowe 80		.319	187	2.3	2.0	4.2

Triple Doubles: None.
Acquired: Breuer from Mil.(Jan.4); Sellers from Sea.(Feb.22).

Miami Heat

	GP	FG%	TPts	Pts	Reb	Ast
Rony Seikaly......74		.502	1228	16.6	10.4	1.1
Sherman Douglas* .81		.494	1155	14.3	2.5	7.6
Glen Rice* 77		.439	1048	13.6	4.6	1.8
Kevin Edwards 78		.412	938	12.0	3.6	3.2
Billy Thompson 79		.516	867	11.0	7.0	2.1
Tellis Frank 77		.448	735	9.5	5.0	1.1
Grant Long 81		.483	686	8.5	5.0	1.2
Jon Sundvold 63		.408	384	6.1	1.1	1.6
Rory Sparrow 82		.412	487	5.9	1.7	3.6
Terry Davis*......63		.466	298	4.7	3.6	0.4
Pat Cummings 37		.484	175	4.7	2.5	0.4
Scott Haffner*....43		.406	196	4.6	1.2	1.9

Triple Doubles: None.

New Jersey Nets

	GP	FG%	TPts	Pts	Reb	Ast
Dennis Hopson 79		.434	1251	15.8	3.5	1.9
Roy Hinson.......25		.507	376	15.0	6.9	0.9
Chris Morris 80		.422	1187	14.8	5.3	1.8
Sam Bowie 68		.416	998	14.7	10.1	1.3
Purvis Short 82		.455	1072	13.1	3.0	1.8
Mookie Blaylock*..50		.371	505	10.1	2.8	4.2
Chas.Shackleford ..70		.462	573	8.2	6.8	0.8
Lester Conner 82		.414	648	7.9	3.2	4.7
Chris Dudley......64		.411	350	5.5	6.6	0.6
CLE 37		.389	184	5.0	5.5	0.5
NJ 27		.441	166	6.1	8.1	0.7
Jack Haley 67		.398	361	5.4	4.5	0.4
CHI 11		.450	25	2.3	1.6	0.4
NJ 56		.394	336	6.0	5.0	0.4
Pete Myers 52		.396	244	4.7	1.8	2.6
NY 24		.333	46	1.9	1.2	1.5
NJ 28		.411	198	7.1	2.4	3.6
Jaren Jackson*....28		.362	67	2.4	0.9	0.5
Leon Wood 28		.327	50	1.8	0.4	1.7

Triple Doubles: None.
Acquired: Dudley from Cle.(Feb.21).
Signed: Haley (Dec.20) after he was waived by Chi.(Dec.18); Myers (Feb.27) after he was waived by NY (Feb.23).

Milwaukee Bucks

	GP	FG%	TPts	Pts	Reb	Ast
Ricky Pierce 59		.510	1359	23.0	2.8	2.3
Jay Humphries 81		.494	1237	15.3	3.3	5.8
Alvin Robertson ...81		.503	1153	14.2	6.9	5.5
Jack Sikma 71		.416	986	13.9	6.9	3.2
Paul Pressey......57		.472	628	11.0	3.0	4.3
Fred Roberts 82		.495	857	10.5	3.8	1.8
Brad Lohaus 80		.460	732	9.2	5.0	2.1
MIN 28		.465	210	7.5	3.9	2.2
MIL 52		.458	522	10.0	5.5	2.0
Greg Anderson ...60		.507	529	8.8	6.2	0.4
Jeff Grayer......71		.460	548	7.7	3.1	1.5
Ben Coleman 22		.474	126	5.7	4.0	0.5
Tony Brown 61		.427	219	3.6	1.2	0.7
Jerry Sichting 35		.400	121	3.5	0.5	2.7
CHAR 34		.420	118	3.5	0.6	2.7
MIL 1		.000	3	3.0	0.0	2.0
Frank Kornet* ...57		.368	113	2.0	1.2	0.4
Tito Horford 35		.290	51	1.5	1.7	0.1

Triple Doubles: Robertson (2).
Acquired: Lohaus from Min.(Jan.4).
Signed: Sichting (Feb.27) after he was waived by Char.(Feb.22).

New York Knicks

	GP	FG%	TPts	Pts	Reb	Ast
Patrick Ewing 82		.551	2347	28.6	10.9	2.2
Charles Oakley ...61		.524	889	14.6	11.9	2.4
Gerald Wilkins 82		.457	1191	14.5	4.5	4.0
Johnny Newman ..80		.476	1032	12.9	2.4	2.3
Mark Jackson 82		.437	809	9.9	3.9	7.4
Maurice Cheeks ...81		.504	789	9.7	3.0	5.6
SA 50		.478	545	10.9	3.3	6.0
NY 31		.579	244	7.9	2.4	4.9
Trent Tucker 81		.417	667	8.2	2.1	2.1
Kenny Walker 68		.531	535	7.9	5.0	0.7
Eddie Lee Wilkins .79		.455	371	4.7	3.4	0.2
Stuart Gray 58		.424	116	2.0	2.5	0.3
CHAR 39		.463	101	2.6	3.4	0.4
NY 19		.235	15	0.8	0.7	0.1
Brian Quinnett* ..31		.328	40	1.3	0.9	0.4

Triple Doubles: None.
Acquired: Cheeks from SA (Feb.21); Gray from Char.(Feb.22).

Team by Team Statistics (Cont.)

Orlando Magic

	GP	FG%	TPts	—Per Game— Pts	Reb	Ast
Terry Catledge 74	.474	1435	19.4	7.6	1.0
Reggie Theus 76	.439	1438	18.9	2.9	5.4
Otis Smith 65	.492	875	13.5	4.6	2.3
Jerry Reynolds 67	.417	858	12.8	4.8	2.7
Nick Anderson* . . .81	.494	931	11.5	3.9	1.5
Sam Vincent 63	.457	705	11.2	3.1	5.6
Sidney Green 73	.468	761	10.4	8.1	1.4
Michael Ansley* . . .72	.497	626	8.7	5.0	0.6
Scott Skiles 70	.409	536	7.7	2.3	4.8
Morlon Wiley 40	.442	229	5.7	1.3	2.9
Jeff Turner 60	.429	308	5.1	3.8	0.9
Mark Acres 80	.484	362	4.5	5.4	0.8

Triple Doubles: Vincent (1); Skiles (1).

Philadelphia 76ers

	GP	FG%	TPts	—Per Game— Pts	Reb	Ast
Charles Barkley . . .79	.600	1989	25.2	11.5	3.9
Hersey Hawkins . . .82	.460	1515	18.5	3.7	3.2
Johnny Dawkins . . .81	.489	1162	14.3	3.0	7.4
Mike Gminski 81	.457	1112	13.7	8.5	1.6
Ron Anderson 78	.451	926	11.9	3.8	1.8
Rick Mahorn 75	.497	811	10.8	7.6	1.3
Derek Smith 75	.508	668	8.9	2.3	1.5
Scott Brooks 72	.431	319	4.4	0.9	2.9
Kenny Payne* 35	.435	114	3.3	0.7	0.3
Kurt Nimphius 38	.418	90	2.4	1.6	0.2
Bob Thornton 56	.429	123	2.2	2.4	0.3

Triple Doubles: Barkley (2).

Phoenix Suns

	GP	FG%	TPts	—Per Game— Pts	Reb	Ast
Tom Chambers . . .81	.501	2201	27.2	7.0	2.3
Kevin Johnson 74	.499	1665	22.5	3.6	11.4
Jeff Hornacek 67	.536	1179	17.6	4.7	5.0
Eddie Johnson 64	.453	1080	16.9	3.8	1.7
Dan Majerle 73	.424	809	11.1	5.9	2.6
Mark West 82	.625	861	10.5	8.9	0.5
Kurt Rambis 74	.509	462	6.2	7.1	1.8
CHAR 16	.500	146	9.1	7.5	1.8
PHO 58	.514	316	5.4	7.0	1.8
Tim Perry 60	.513	254	4.2	2.5	0.3
Ken Battle* 59	.547	242	4.1	2.1	0.6
Andrew Lang 74	.557	258	3.5	3.7	0.3
Greg Grant* 67	.384	208	3.1	0.9	2.5
Mike Morrison* . . .36	.338	72	2.0	0.6	0.3

Triple Doubles: K.Johnson (3); Hornacek (1).
Acquired: Rambis from Char.(Dec.13).

Portland Trail Blazers

	GP	FG%	TPts	—Per Game— Pts	Reb	Ast
Clyde Drexler 73	.494	1703	23.3	6.9	5.9
Terry Porter 80	.462	1406	17.6	3.4	9.1
Kevin Duckworth . .82	.478	1327	16.2	6.2	1.1
Jerome Kersey 82	.478	1310	16.0	8.4	2.3
Buck Williams 82	.548	1114	13.6	9.8	1.4
Cliff Robinson* 82	.397	746	9.1	3.8	0.9
Drazen Petrovic* . .77	.485	583	7.6	1.4	1.5
Byron Irvin* 50	.473	258	5.2	1.5	0.9
Danny Young 82	.421	383	4.7	1.5	2.8
Wayne Cooper 79	.454	301	3.8	4.3	0.6
Mark Bryant 58	.458	168	2.9	2.5	0.2

Triple Doubles: Drexler (1).

Sacramento Kings

	GP	FG%	TPts	—Per Game— Pts	Reb	Ast
Wayman Tisdale . .79	.525	1758	22.3	7.5	1.4
Danny Ainge 75	.438	1342	17.9	4.3	6.0
Rodney McCray . . .82	.515	1358	16.6	8.2	4.6
Antoine Carr 77	.494	949	12.3	4.2	1.5
ATL 44	.516	335	7.6	3.4	1.2
SAC 33	.482	614	18.6	5.2	2.0
Vinny Del Negro . .76	.462	739	9.7	2.6	3.3
Harold Pressley . . .72	.424	636	8.8	4.3	2.1
Pervis Ellison* 34	.442	271	8.0	5.8	1.9
Henry Turner* 36	.475	156	4.3	1.4	0.6
Ralph Sampson . . .26	.372	109	4.2	3.2	1.1
Sedric Toney 64	.348	264	4.1	0.9	2.7
ATL 32	.417	88	2.8	0.4	1.6
SAC 32	.320	176	5.5	1.4	3.8
Randy Allen 63	.444	235	3.7	2.2	0.4
Greg Kite 71	.432	230	3.2	5.3	1.1

Triple Doubles: Ainge (1).
Acquired: Carr and Toney from Atl.(Feb.13).

San Antonio Spurs

	GP	FG%	TPts	—Per Game— Pts	Reb	Ast
David Robinson* . .82	.531	1993	24.3	12.0	2.0
Terry Cummings . .81	.475	1818	22.4	8.4	2.7
Willie Anderson . . .82	.492	1288	15.7	4.5	4.4
Rod Strickland 82	.454	868	10.6	3.2	5.7
NY 51	.440	429	8.4	2.5	4.3
SA 31	.468	439	14.2	4.3	8.0
Sean Elliott* 81	.481	810	10.0	3.7	1.9
Reggie Williams . . .47	.388	320	6.8	1.8	1.1
LAC 5	.368	60	12.0	3.0	2.0
CLE 32	.381	218	6.8	1.9	1.2
SA 10	.452	42	4.2	0.8	0.5
David Wingate 78	.448	527	6.8	2.5	2.7
Frank Brickowski . .78	.545	517	6.6	4.2	1.3
Zarko Paspalj* 28	.342	72	2.6	1.1	0.4
Caldwell Jones 72	.465	173	2.4	3.2	0.3
Johnny Moore 53	.373	118	2.2	1.0	1.5
Uwe Blab 47	.398	98	2.1	2.3	0.5
GS 40	.379	83	2.1	2.5	0.6
SA 7	.545	15	2.1	1.3	0.1

Triple Doubles: Robinson (3).
Acquired: Strickland from NY (Feb.21); Blab from GS (Feb.22).
Signed: Williams (Mar.5) after he was traded by LAC (Nov.16) then waived by Cle.(Feb.24).

Seattle SuperSonics

	GP	FG%	TPts	—Per Game— Pts	Reb	Ast
Dale Ellis 55	.497	1293	23.5	4.3	2.0
Xavier McDaniel . .69	.496	1471	21.3	6.5	2.5
Derrick McKey 80	.493	1254	15.7	6.1	2.3
Sedale Threatt 65	.506	744	11.4	1.8	3.3
Michael Cage 82	.504	798	9.7	10.0	0.9
Dana Barros* 81	.405	782	9.7	1.6	2.5
Quintin Dailey 30	.404	247	8.2	1.7	1.1
Shawn Kemp* 81	.479	525	6.5	4.3	0.3
Jim Farmer 38	.438	243	6.4	1.1	0.7
Nate McMillan 82	.473	523	6.4	4.9	0.3
Steve Johnson 25	.522	117	4.7	2.1	0.7
MIN 4	.000	0	0.0	0.8	0.3
SEA 21	.533	117	5.6	2.4	0.8
Olden Polynice 79	.540	360	4.6	3.8	0.2
Avery Johnson 53	.387	140	2.6	0.8	3.1
Scott Meents* 26	.432	55	2.1	1.2	0.3

Triple Doubles: McMillan (1).
Acquired: S.Johnson from Min.(Feb.22).

Utah Jazz

	GP	FG%	TPts	Pts	Reb	Ast
Karl Malone	82	.562	2540	31.0	11.1	2.8
John Stockton	78	.514	1345	17.2	2.6	14.5
Thurl Bailey	82	.481	1162	14.2	5.0	1.7
Darrell Griffith	82	.464	733	8.9	2.0	0.8
Blue Edwards*	82	.507	727	8.9	3.1	1.8
Robert Hansen	81	.467	617	7.6	2.8	1.8
Mike Brown	82	.515	512	6.2	4.5	0.6
Mark Eaton	82	.527	395	4.8	7.3	0.5
Eric Leckner	77	.563	331	4.3	2.5	0.2
Delaney Rudd	77	.429	273	3.5	0.7	2.3
Eric Johnson*	48	.238	54	1.1	0.6	1.3

Triple Doubles: None.

Washington Bullets

	GP	FG%	TPts	Pts	Reb	Ast
Jeff Malone	75	.491	1820	24.3	2.7	3.2
Bernard King	82	.487	1837	22.4	4.9	4.6
Ledell Eackles	78	.439	1055	13.5	2.2	2.3
Mark Alarie	82	.473	860	10.5	4.6	1.7
Darrell Walker	81	.454	772	9.5	8.8	8.0
Harvey Grant	81	.473	664	8.2	4.2	1.6
Tom Hammonds*	61	.437	321	5.3	2.8	0.8
Steve Colter	73	.478	361	4.9	2.4	2.0
Mel Turpin	59	.526	276	4.7	3.7	0.5
Ed Horton*	45	.494	202	4.5	2.4	0.4
Charles Jones	81	.508	256	3.2	6.2	1.7
Doug Roth*	42	.430	81	1.9	2.9	0.5

Triple Doubles: Walker (9).

Award Winners

Podoloff Trophy

For Most Valuable Player, voting by 92-member panel of local and national pro basketball writers and broadcasters. Voters each pick five, points awarded on 10-7-5-3-1 basis.

	1st	2nd	3rd	4th	5th	Pts
Magic Johnson, LAL	27	38	15	7	4	636
Chas. Barkley, Phi	38	15	16	14	7	614
Michael Jordan, Chi	21	25	30	8	5	571
Karl Malone, Utah	2	8	10	23	19	214
Patrick Ewing, NY	1	1	11	22	24	162
David Robinson, SA	2	4	4	7	13	102
Akeem Olajuwon, Hou	1	0	4	7	13	64
Tom Chambers, Pho	0	1	1	0	0	12
John Stockton, Utah	0	0	1	1	1	9
Larry Bird, Bos	0	0	0	1	2	5
Buck Williams, Port	0	0	0	1	2	5
Clyde Drexler, Port	0	0	0	1	0	3
Joe Dumars, Det	0	0	0	0	1	1
Isiah Thomas, Det	0	0	0	0	1	1

Gottlieb Trophy

For Rookie of the Year, voting by 92-member panel of local and national pro basketball writers and broadcasters.

Unanimous	Votes
David Robinson, San Antonio	92

Auerbach Trophy

For Coach of the Year, voting by 92-member panel of local and national pro basketball writers and broadcasters.

Top 5	Votes
Pat Riley, LA Lakers	52
Jim Lynam, Philadelphia	14½
Rick Adelman, Portland	12½
Chuck Daly, Detroit	5
Larry Brown, San Antonio	4

Other Awards

Defensive Player of the Year—Dennis Rodman, Detroit; **Most Improved Player**—Rony Seikaly, Miami; **Sixth Man Award**—Ricky Pierce, Milwaukee; **Schick Award** (for contributing most to team's success)— David Robinson, S. Antonio; **Good Hands Award** (for ball handling)—Darrell Walker, Washington; **Kennedy Citizenship Award**—Doc Rivers, Atlanta.

All-NBA

Voting by 92-member panel of local and national pro basketball writers and broadcasters.

First Team	Pos	1st	Pts
Magic Johnson, LA Lakers	G	91	458
Charles Barkley, Philadelphia	F	91	456
Karl Malone, Utah	F	90	456
Michael Jordan, Chicago	G	90	453
Patrick Ewing, New York	C	44	344

Second Team	Pos	1st	Pts
Akeem Olajuwon, Houston	C	42	326
John Stockton, Utah	G	2	241
Tom Chambers, Phoenix	F	1	234
Larry Bird, Boston	F	1	209
Kevin Johnson, Phoenix	G	0	177

Third Team	Pos	1st	Pts
David Robinson, San Antonio	C	7	160
Clyde Drexler, Portland	G	0	113
Joe Dumars, Detroit	G	0	94
James Worthy, LA Lakers	F	0	85
Chris Mullin, Golden St	F	0	60

All-Defense

Voting by NBA head coaches.

First Team	Pos	1st	Pts
Dennis Rodman, Detroit	F	24	49
Joe Dumars, Detroit	G	19	41
Akeem Olajuwon, Houston	C	17	39
Michael Jordan, Chicago	G	17	37
Buck Williams, Portland	F	6	20

Second Team	Pos	1st	Pts
Alvin Robertson, Milwaukee	G	4	22
Rick Mahorn, Philadelphia	F	6	18
David Robinson, San Antonio	C	4	17
Derek Harper, Dallas	G	4	16
Kevin McHale, Boston	F	6	15

All-Rookie

Voting by NBA head coaches.

First Team	College	Pts
David Robinson, San Antonio	Navy	52
Tim Hardaway, Golden St	UTEP	52
Vlade Divac, LA Lakers	Yugoslavia	40
Sherman Douglas, Miami	Syracuse	39
Pooh Richardson, Minnesota	UCLA	33

Second Team	College	Pts
J.R. Reid, Charlotte	N. Carolina	28
Sean Elliott, San Antonio	Arizona	26
Stacey King, Chicago	Oklahoma	23
Blue Edwards, Utah	E. Carolina	20½
Glen Rice, Miami	Michigan	20

NBA Playoffs
Eastern Conference
FIRST ROUND (Best of 5)

	W	L	Avg	Leading Scorer
Detroit	3	0	104.0	Thomas (18.7)
Indiana	0	3	91.7	Miller (20.7)

Date	Winner	Home Court
Apr.26	Detroit, 104-92	at Detroit
Apr.28	Detroit, 100-87	at Detroit
May 1	Detroit, 108-96	at Indiana

	W	L	Avg	Leading Scorer
Philadelphia	3	2	104.4	Hawkins (27.2)
Cleveland	2	3	106.8	Daugherty (22.8)

Date	Winner	Home Court
Apr.26	Philadelphia, 111-106	at Phila.
Apr.29	Philadelphia, 107-101	at Phila.
May 1	Cleveland, 122-95	at Cleveland
May 3	Cleveland, 108-96	at Cleveland
May 5	Philadelphia, 113-97	at Phila.

	W	L	Avg	Leading Scorer
New York	3	2	118.2	Ewing (31.6)
Boston	2	3	118.8	Bird (24.4)

Date	Winner	Home Court
Apr.26	Boston, 116-105	at Boston
Apr.28	Boston, 157-128	at Boston
May 2	New York, 102-99	at New York
May 4	New York, 135-108	at New York
May 6	New York, 121-114	at Boston

	W	L	Avg	Leading Scorer
Chicago	3	1	110.5	Jordan (36.8)
Milwaukee	1	3	101.0	Robertson (23.5)

Date	Winner	Home Court
Apr.27	Chicago, 111-97	at Chicago
Apr.29	Chicago, 109-102	at Chicago
May 1	Milwaukee, 119-112	at Milwaukee
May 3	Chicago, 110-86	at Milwaukee

SEMIFINALS (Best of 7)

	W	L	Avg	Leading Scorer
Detroit	4	1	103.2	Edwards (19.4)
New York	1	4	91.8	Ewing (27.2)

Date	Winner	Home Court
May 8	Detroit, 112-77	at Detroit
May 10	Detroit, 104-97	at Detroit
May 12	New York, 111-103	at New York
May 13	Detroit, 102-90	at New York
May 15	Detroit, 95-84	at Detroit

	W	L	Avg	Leading Scorer
Chicago	4	1	107.4	Jordan (43.0)
Philadelphia	1	4	99.8	Barkley (23.8)

Date	Winner	Home Court
May 7	Chicago, 96-85	at Chicago
May 9	Chicago, 101-96	at Chicago
May 11	Philadelphia, 118-112	at Phila.
May 13	Chicago, 111-101	at Phila.
May 16	Chicago, 117-99	at Chicago

CHAMPIONSHIP (Best of 7)

	W	L	Avg	Leading Scorer
Detroit	4	3	96.0	Dumars (20.0)
Chicago	3	4	93.0	Jordan (32.1)

Date	Winner	Home Court	Date	Winner	Home Court
May 20	Detroit, 86-77	at Detroit	May 30	Detroit, 97-83	at Detroit
May 22	Detroit, 102-93	at Detroit	Jun. 1	Chicago, 109-91	at Chicago
May 26	Chicago, 109-102	at Chicago	Jun. 3	Detroit, 93-74	at Detroit
May 28	Chicago, 108-101	at Chicago			

Western Conference

FIRST ROUND (Best of 5)

	W	L	Avg	Leading Scorer
LA Lakers	3	1	105.5	Worthy (28.0)
Houston	1	3	97.8	Thorpe (20.0)

Date	Winner	Home Court
Apr.27	LA Lakers, 101-89	at L.Angeles
Apr.29	LA Lakers, 104-100	at L.Angeles
May 1	Houston, 114-108	at Houston
May 3	LA Lakers, 109-88	at Houston

	W	L	Avg	Leading Scorer
San Antonio	3	0	126.3	Robinson (27.7)
Denver	0	3	114.3	English (19.7)

Date	Winner	Home Court
Apr.26	San Antonio, 119-103	at S.Antonio
Apr.28	San Antonio, 129-120	at S.Antonio
May 1	San Antonio, 131-120	at Denver

	W	L	Avg	Leading Scorer
Phoenix	3	2	103.8	Chambers (20.0)
Utah	2	3	102.4	Malone (25.2)

Date	Winner	Home Court
Apr.27	Utah, 113-96	at Utah
Apr.29	Phoenix, 105-87	at Utah
May 2	Phoenix, 120-105	at Phoenix
May 4	Utah, 105-94	at Phoenix
May 6	Phoenix, 104-102	at Utah

	W	L	Avg	Leading Scorer
Portland	3	0	109.7	Porter (21.0)
Dallas	0	3	100.3	Blackman (20.0)

Date	Winner	Home Court
Apr.26	Portland, 109-102	at Portland
Apr.28	Portland, 114-107	at Portland
May 2	Portland, 106-92	at Dallas

SEMIFINALS (Best of 7)

	W	L	Avg	Leading Scorer
Phoenix	4	1	108.2	K.Johnson (22.0)
LA Lakers	1	4	106.6	M.Johnson (30.2)

Date	Winner	Home Court
May 8	Phoenix, 104-102	at L.Angeles
May 10	LA Lakers, 124-100	at L.Angeles
May 12	Phoenix, 117-103	at Phoenix
May 13	Phoenix, 114-101	at Phoenix
May 15	Phoenix, 106-103	at L.Angeles

	W	L	Avg	Leading Scorer
Portland	4	3	110.7	Porter (23.4)
San Antonio	3	4	113.0	Cummings (25.9)

Date	Winner	Home Court
May 5	Portland, 107-94	at Portland
May 8	Portland, 122-112	at Portland
May 10	San Antonio, 121-98	at S.Antonio
May 12	San Antonio, 115-105	at S.Antonio
May 15	Portland, 138-132 (2 OT)	at Portland
May 17	San Antonio, 112-97	at S.Antonio
May 19	Portland, 108-105 (OT)	at Portland

CHAMPIONSHIP
(Best of 7)

	W	L	Avg	Leading Scorer
Portland	4	2	106.0	Kersey (21.5)
Phoenix	2	4	111.7	Chambers (24.5)

Date	Winner	Home Court
May 21	Portland, 100-98	at Portland
May 23	Portland, 108-107	at Portland
May 25	Phoenix, 123-89	at Phoenix
May 27	Phoenix, 119-107	at Phoenix
May 29	Portland, 120-114	at Portland
May 31	Portland, 112-109	at Phoenix

NBA FINALS

	W	L	Avg	Leading Scorer
Detroit	4	1	107.0	Thomas (27.6)
Portland	1	4	102.0	Drexler (26.4)

Date	Winner	Home Court
Jun. 5	Detroit, 105-99	at Detroit
Jun. 7	Portland, 106-105 (OT)	at Detroit
Jun.10	Detroit, 121-106	at Portland
Jun.12	Detroit, 112-109	at Portland
Jun.14	Detroit, 92-90	at Portland

Most Valuable Player
Isiah Thomas, Detroit

Final Playoff Scoring

At least four games played.

	GP	FG	FT	Pts	Avg
Michael Jordan, Chi	16	219	133	587	36.7
Patrick Ewing, NY	10	114	65	294	29.4
Magic Johnson, LAL	9	76	70	227	25.2
Karl Malone, Utah	5	46	34	126	25.2
Terry Cummings, SA	10	103	42	249	24.9
Charles Barkley, Phi	10	88	65	247	24.7
David Robinson, SA	10	89	65	243	24.3
Larry Bird, Bos	5	44	29	122	24.4
James Worthy, LAL	9	90	36	218	24.2
Hersey Hawkins, Phi	10	81	59	235	23.5
Alvin Robertson, Mil	4	35	24	94	23.5
Brad Daugherty, Cle	5	41	32	114	22.8
Ricky Pierce, Mil	4	28	28	89	22.3
Tom Chambers, Pho	16	117	116	355	22.2
Kevin McHale, Bos	5	42	25	110	22.0

Final Playoff Standings

	GP	W	L	Pct	Per Game For	Per Game Opp
Detroit	20	15	5	.750	101.8	94.8
Portland	21	12	9	.571	107.1	109.4
Chicago	16	10	6	.625	101.9	98.4
Phoenix	16	9	7	.563	108.1	105.1
San Antonio	10	6	4	.600	117.0	111.8
LA Lakers	9	4	5	.444	106.1	103.6
Philadelphia	10	4	6	.400	102.1	107.1
New York	10	4	6	.400	105.0	111.0
Cleveland	5	2	3	.400	106.8	104.4
Boston	5	2	3	.400	118.8	118.2
Utah	5	2	3	.400	102.4	103.8
Houston	4	1	3	.250	97.8	105.5
Milwaukee	4	1	3	.250	101.0	110.5
Dallas	3	0	3	.000	100.3	109.7
Denver	3	0	3	.000	114.3	126.3
Indiana	3	0	3	.000	91.7	104.0

Playoff Composite Box Scores

NBA FINALS

Detroit Pistons

	GP	FG%	TPts	Pts	Reb	Ast
Isiah Thomas	5	.542	138	27.6	5.2	7.0
Joe Dumars	5	.415	103	20.6	2.8	5.6
James Edwards	5	.446	72	14.4	3.8	0.8
Bill Laimbeer	5	.444	66	13.2	13.4	2.4
Vinnie Johnson	5	.543	61	12.2	2.0	1.2
Mark Aguirre	5	.333	48	9.6	3.6	0.8
John Salley	5	.375	33	6.6	6.4	0.4
Dennis Rodman	4	.444	9	2.3	5.5	0.8
David Greenwood	3	.333	3	1.0	3.0	0.0
Gerald Henderson	2	1.000	2	1.0	0.0	0.0
Scott Hastings	2	.000	0	0.0	0.0	0.0
PISTONS	5	.454	535	107.0	43.4	18.8
TRAIL BLAZERS	5	.456	510	102.0	40.4	20.6

Three-pointers: Thomas (11 for 16), Laimbeer (8-22), Aguirre (4-8), Dumars (2-7), Edwards (0-1), Hastings (0-1), Johnson (0-1).

Portland Trail Blazers

	GP	FG%	TPts	Pts	Reb	Ast
Clyde Drexler	5	.543	132	26.4	7.8	6.2
Jerome Kersey	5	.473	95	19.0	7.0	1.2
Terry Porter	5	.393	95	19.0	2.6	8.4
Kevin Duckworth	5	.523	78	15.6	5.6	0.0
Buck Williams	5	.465	56	11.2	9.0	1.8
Cliff Robinson	5	.250	19	3.8	2.4	0.8
Danny Young	5	.400	15	3.0	1.4	1.6
Drazen Petrovic	4	.357	10	2.5	0.3	0.5
Wayne Cooper	5	.333	9	1.8	4.0	0.0
Mark Bryant	2	—	1	0.5	0.4	0.0
TRAIL BLAZERS	5	.456	510	102.0	40.4	20.6
PISTONS	5	.454	535	107.0	43.4	18.8

Three-pointers: Porter (7 for 25), Drexler (2-12), Young (2-6), Kersey (0-2), Petrovic (0-1), Robinson (0-1).

NBA Draft

First and second round picks at the 44th annual NBA Draft held June 27, 1990 in New York City. Juniors selected are noted in capital LETTERS.

First Round

	Team	Player Selected
1	New Jersey	Derrick Coleman, Syracuse, F
2	Seattle	Gary Payton, Oregon St., G
3	a-Denver	CHRIS JACKSON, LSU, G
4	Orlando	DENNIS SCOTT, Ga.Tech, F
5	Charlotte	Kendall Gill, Illinois, G
6	Minnesota	Felton Spencer, L'ville, C
7	Sacramento	Lionel Simmons, La Salle, F
8	LA Clippers	Bo Kimble, Loyola-CA, G
9	b-Miami	Willie Burton, Minnesota, F
10	c-Atlanta	Rumeal Robinson, Michigan, G
11	d-Golden St	Tyrone Hill, Xavier, F
12	Houston*	Alec Kessler, Georgia, F
13	e-LA Clippers	Loy Vaught, Michigan, F
14	f-Sacramento	Travis Mays, Texas, G
15	g-Miami	Dave Jamerson, Ohio U., G
16	Milwaukee	Terry Mills, Michigan, F
17	New York	JERROD MUSTAF, Maryland, F
18	h-Sacramento	Duane Causwell, Temple, C
19	Boston	Dee Brown, Jacksonville, G
20	i-Minnesota	Gerald Glass, Ole Miss, G
21	Phoenix	Jayson Williams, St.John's, F
22	j-New Jersey	Tate George, Connecticut, G
23	k-Sacramento	Anthony Bonner, St.Louis, F
24	San Antonio	Dwayne Schintzius, Fla., C
25	Portland	Alaa Abdelnaby, Duke, F
26	Detroit	Lance Blanks, Texas, G
27	LA Lakers	Elden Campbell, Clemson, F

Note: Houston traded Kessler to Miami for Jamerson and No.30 pick.

Second Round

	Team	Player Selected
28	l-Golden St	Les Jepsen, Iowa, C
29	m-Chicago	Toni Kukoc, Yugoslavia, F
30	Miami	CARLOS HERRERA, Houston, F
31	n-Phoenix	Negele Knight, Dayton, G
32	o-Phila	Bryan Oliver, Ga.Tech, G
33	p-Utah	Walter Palmer, Dartmouth, C
34	q-Golden St	Kevin Pritchard, Kansas, G
35	Washington	Greg Foster, UTEP, C
36	r-Atlanta	Trevor Wilson, UCLA, F
37	s-Washington	A.J.English, Va.Tech, F
38	Seattle*	Jud Buechler, Arizona, F
39	t-Charlotte	Steve Scheffler, Purdue, F
40	u-Sacramento	Bimbo Coles, Va.Tech, G
41	v-Atlanta	Stephen Bardo, Illinois, G
42	Denver	MARCUS LIBERTY, Illinois, F
43	w-S.Antonio	Tony Massenburg, Maryland, F
44	x-Milwaukee	Steve Henson, Kansas St., G
45	y-Indiana	Antonio Davis, UTEP, F
46	z-Indiana	KEN WILLIAMS, Eliz.Cty,St.,F
47	Philadelphia	Derek Strong, Xavier, F
48	Phoenix	Cedric Ceballos, CS-Full., F
49	aa-Dallas	Phil Henderson, Duke, G
50	bb-Phoenix	Milos Babic, Tenn.Tech, C
51	cc-LA Lakers	Tony Smith, Marquette, G
52	dd-Cleve.	Stefano Rusconi, Italy, C
53	ee-Seattle	Abdul Shamsid-Deen, Prov., C
54	ff-S.Antonio	SEAN HIGGINS, Michigan, G

Note: Seattle gave rights to Buechler to New Jersey for not drafting Dennis Scott; Sacramento traded rights to Coles to Miami for Rory Sparrow.

Underclassmen Not Drafted

Kelvin Ardister, Pensacola JC; Herb Barthol, Cleveland St.; Gabe Estaba, South Alabama; David Shon Henderson, Idaho; Ken Miller, Loyola-IL; Jesse Spinner, Grambling and Per Sumer, Loyola-CA.

Acquired Picks

First Round: a—from Miami; b—from Denver via Dallas via Washington; c—from Atlanta; d—from Golden St.; e—from Cleveland; f—from Dallas via Indiana; g—from Denver; h—from Dallas; i—from Philadelphia; j—from Chicago; k—from Utah.

Second Round: l—from Atlanta via New Jersey; m—from Orlando; n—from Charlotte; o—from Minnesota; p—from Sacramento; q—from LA Clippers; r—from Golden St.; s—from Atlanta; t—from Houston; u—from Indiana; v—from Golden St.through Cleveland via Miami; w—from Milwaukee; x—from New York via Seattle; y—from Dallas; z—from Boston; aa—from Sacramento via Utah; bb—from Chicago (rights traded to Cle. for Rusconi); cc—from San Antonio; dd—from Detroit via Phila.; ee—from Portland; ff—from LA Lakers.

THE 1991 INFORMATION PLEASE SPORTS ALMANAC

PRO BASKETBALL STATISTICS

THROUGH THE YEARS
1946-1990
CHAMPIONS • NBA LEADERS

SEC B

PAGE 283

NBA Finals, 1947-90

Although the National Basketball Association traces its first championship back to the 1946-47 season, the league was then called the Basketball Association of America (BAA). It did not become the NBA until after the 1948-49 season when the BAA and the National Basketball League (NBL) agreed to merge.

In the chart below, the Eastern finalists (representing the NBA Eastern Division from 1947-70, and the NBA Eastern Conference since 1971) are listed in capital LETTERS. Also, each NBA champion's wins and losses are noted in parentheses after the series score.

Year	Winner	Head Coach	Series	Loser	Head Coach
1947	PHILA.WARRIORS	Eddie Gottlieb	4-1 (WWWLW)	Chicago Stags	Harold Olsen
1948	Balt.Bullets	Buddy Jeannette	4-2 (LWWWLW)	PHILA.WARRIORS	Eddie Gottlieb
1949	Minn.Lakers	John Kundla	4-2 (WWLLWW)	WASH.CAPITOLS	Red Auerbach
1950	Minn.Lakers	John Kundla	4-2 (WLWWLW)	SYRACUSE	Al Cervi
1951	Rochester	Les Harrison	4-3 (WWWLLLW)	NEW YORK	Joe Lapchick
1952	Minn.Lakers	John Kundla	4-3 (WLWLWLW)	NEW YORK	Joe Lapchick
1953	Minn.Lakers	John Kundla	4-1 (LWWWW)	NEW YORK	Joe Lapchick
1954	Minn.Lakers	John Kundla	4-3 (WLWLWLW)	SYRACUSE	Al Cervi
1955	SYRACUSE	Al Cervi	4-3 (WWLLLWW)	Ft.Wayne Pistons	Charles Eckman
1956	PHILA.WARRIORS	George Senesky	4-1 (WLWWW)	Ft.Wayne Pistons	Charles Eckman
1957	BOSTON	Red Auerbach	4-3 (LWLWWLW)	St.Louis Hawks	Alex Hannum
1958	St.Louis Hawks	Alex Hannum	4-2 (WLWLWW)	BOSTON	Red Auerbach
1959	BOSTON	Red Auerbach	4-0	Minn.Lakers	John Kundla
1960	BOSTON	Red Auerbach	4-3 (WLWLWLW)	St.Louis Hawks	Ed Macauley
1961	BOSTON	Red Auerbach	4-1 (WWLWW)	St.Louis Hawks	Paul Seymour
1962	BOSTON	Red Auerbach	4-3 (WLLWLWW)	LA Lakers	Fred Schaus
1963	BOSTON	Red Auerbach	4-2 (WWLWLW)	LA Lakers	Fred Schaus
1964	BOSTON	Red Auerbach	4-1 (WWLWW)	SF Warriors	Alex Hannum
1965	BOSTON	Red Auerbach	4-1 (WWLWW)	LA Lakers	Fred Schaus
1966	BOSTON	Red Auerbach	4-3 (LWWWLLW)	LA Lakers	Fred Schaus
1967	PHILA.76ERS	Alex Hannum	4-2 (WWWLWW)	SF Warriors	Bill Sharman
1968	BOSTON	Bill Russell	4-2 (WLWLWW)	LA Lakers	B.van Breda Kolff
1969	BOSTON	Bill Russell	4-3 (LLWWLWW)	LA Lakers	B.van Breda Kolff
1970	NEW YORK	Red Holzman	4-3 (WLWLWLW)	LA Lakers	Joe Mullaney
1971	Milwaukee	Larry Costello	4-0	BALT.BULLETS	Gene Shue
1972	LA Lakers	Bill Sharman	4-1 (LWWWW)	NEW YORK	Red Holzman
1973	NEW YORK	Red Holzman	4-1 (LWWWW)	LA Lakers	Bill Sharman
1974	BOSTON	Tommy Heinsohn	4-3 (WLWLWLW)	Milwaukee	Larry Costello
1975	Gold.St.Warriors	Al Attles	4-0	WASH.BULLETS	K.C. Jones
1976	BOSTON	Tommy Heinsohn	4-2 (WWLLWW)	Phoenix	John MacLeod
1977	Portland	Jack Ramsay	4-2 (LLWWWW)	PHILA.76ERS	Gene Shue
1978	WASH.BULLETS	Dick Motta	4-3 (LWLWLWW)	Seattle	Lenny Wilkens
1979	Seattle	Lenny Wilkens	4-1 (LWWWW)	WASH.BULLETS	Dick Motta
1980	LA Lakers	Paul Westhead	4-2 (WLWLWW)	PHILA.76ERS	Billy Cunningham
1981	BOSTON	Bill Fitch	4-2 (WLWLWW)	Houston	Del Harris
1982	LA Lakers	Pat Riley	4-2 (WLWLW)	PHILA 76ERS	Billy Cunningham
1983	PHILA.76ERS	Billy Cunningham	4-0	LA Lakers	Pat Riley
1984	BOSTON	K.C. Jones	4-3 (LWLWWLW)	LA Lakers	Pat Riley
1985	LA Lakers	Pat Riley	4-2 (LWWWLW)	BOSTON	K.C. Jones
1986	BOSTON	K.C. Jones	4-2 (WWLWLW)	Houston	Bill Fitch
1987	LA Lakers	Pat Riley	4-2 (WWLWLW)	BOSTON	K.C. Jones
1988	LA Lakers	Pat Riley	4-3 (LWWLLWW)	DETROIT PISTONS	Chuck Daly
1989	DETROIT PISTONS	Chuck Daly	4-0	LA Lakers	Pat Riley
1990	DETROIT	Chuck Daly	4-1 (WLWWW)	Portland	Rick Adelman

Note: Four Finalists were led by player-coaches: **1948**—Buddy Jeannette (guard) of Baltimore; **1950**—Al Cervi (guard) of Syracuse; **1968**—Bill Russell (center) of Boston; **1969**—Bill Russell (center) of Boston.

NBA Playoff MVPs

Selected by an 11-member media panel and presented since 1969 by Sport Magazine. Winners who did not play for the NBA champion are **bold type**.

Multiple winners: Magic Johnson (3); Kareem Abdul-Jabbar and Larry Bird (2).

Year	Most Valuable Player	Year	Most Valuable Player
1969	**Jerry West**, LA Lakers, G	1980	Magic Johnson, LA Lakers, G/C
		1981	Cedric Maxwell, Boston, F
1970	Willis Reed, New York, C	1982	Magic Johnson, LA Lakers, G
1971	Kareem Abdul-Jabbar, Milwaukee, C	1983	Moses Malone, Philadelphia, C
1972	Wilt Chamberlain, LA Lakers, C	1984	Larry Bird, Boston, F
1973	Willis Reed, New York, C	1985	Kareem Abdul-Jabbar, LA Lakers, C
1974	John Havlicek, Boston, F	1986	Larry Bird, Boston, F
1975	Rick Barry, Golden State, F	1987	Magic Johnson, LA Lakers, G
1976	Jo Jo White, Boston, G	1988	James Worthy, LA Lakers, F
1977	Bill Walton, Portland, C	1989	Joe Dumars, Detroit, G
1978	Wes Unseld, Washington, C		
1979	Dennis Johnson, Seattle, G	1990	Isiah Thomas, Detroit, G

NBA All-Time Playoff Leaders
CAREER

NBA Playoff leaders through 1990. Years listed indicate number of playoff appearances. Players active in 1990 playoffs in **bold type**.

Points

	Yrs	Gms	Points	Avg
Kareem Abdul-Jabbar	18	237	5762	24.3
Jerry West	13	153	4457	29.1
John Havlicek	13	172	3776	22.0
Larry Bird	10	150	3681	24.5
Elgin Baylor	12	134	3623	27.0
Wilt Chamberlain	13	160	3607	22.5
Magic Johnson	11	167	3226	19.3
Dennis Johnson	13	180	3116	17.3
Julius Erving	11	141	3088	21.9
Sam Jones	12	154	2909	18.9
Kevin McHale	10	144	2713	18.8
Bill Russell	13	165	2673	16.2
Robert Parish	11	154	2458	16.0
James Worthy	7	120	2574	21.5
Bob Pettit	9	88	2240	25.5
Elvin Hayes	10	96	2194	22.9
George Mikan	9	91	2141	23.5
Tom Heinsohn	9	104	2058	19.8
Moses Malone	11	89	2056	23.1
Bob Cousy	13	109	2018	18.5
Isiah Thomas	7	93	2015	21.7

Scoring Average

Minimum of 25 games or 700 points.

	Yrs	Gms	Points	Avg
Michael Jordan	6	53	1896	35.8
Jerry West	13	153	4457	29.1
Elgin Baylor	12	134	3623	27.0
George Gervin	9	59	1592	27.0
Akeem Olajuwon	6	47	1260	26.8
Dominique Wilkins	6	43	1151	26.8
Bob Pettit	9	88	2240	25.5
Rick Barry	7	74	1833	24.8
Larry Bird	10	150	3681	24.5
Alex English	10	68	1661	24.4
Kareem Abdul-Jabbar	18	237	5762	24.3
Paul Arizin	8	49	1186	24.2
George Mikan	9	91	2141	23.5
Moses Malone	11	89	2056	23.1
Elvin Hayes	10	96	2194	22.9
Bob Love	6	47	1076	22.9
Terry Cummings	6	54	1232	22.8
Wilt Chamberlain	13	160	3607	22.5

Field Goals

	Yrs	FGA	FGM	Pct
Kareem Abdul-Jabbar	18	4422	2356	.533
Jerry West	13	3460	1622	.469
John Havlicek	13	3329	1451	.436
Wilt Chamberlain	13	2728	1425	.522
Elgin Baylor	12	3161	1388	.439
Larry Bird	10	2896	1375	.475

Free Throws

	Yrs	FTA	FTM	Pct
Jerry West	13	1507	1213	.805
Kareem Abdul-Jabbar	18	1452	1077	.742
Magic Johnson	11	1063	883	.831
John Havlicek	13	1046	874	.836
Elgin Baylor	12	1101	847	.769
Larry Bird	10	957	854	.892

Assists

	Yrs	Gms	Ast	Avg
Magic Johnson	11	167	2080	12.5
Dennis Johnson	13	180	1006	5.6
Jerry West	13	153	970	6.3
Bob Cousy	13	109	937	8.6
Larry Bird	10	150	976	6.5
Maurice Cheeks	11	125	892	7.1

Rebounds

	Yrs	Gms	Reb	Avg
Bill Russell	13	165	4104	24.9
Wilt Chamberlain	13	160	3913	24.5
Kareem Abdul-Jabbar	18	237	2481	10.5
Wes Unseld	12	119	1777	14.9
Elgin Baylor	12	134	1725	12.9

Personal Fouls

	Yrs	Gms	Fouls	DQ
Kareem Abdul-Jabbar	18	237	797	7
Dennis Johnson	13	180	575	8
Bill Russell	13	165	546	8
Robert Parish	11	154	543	15
Tom Sanders	11	130	508	26
Kevin McHale	10	144	489	8
Paul Silas	14	163	469	7

Most Years Played

	Yrs		Yrs
K.Abdul-Jabbar	18	John Havlicek	13
Dolph Schayes	15	**Dennis Johnson**	13
Paul Silas	14	Bill Russell	13
Wilt Chamberlain	13	Chet Walker	13
Bob Cousy	13	Jerry West	13
Hal Greer	13		

Games Played

	Gms		Gms
K.Abdul-Jabbar	237	Wilt Chamberlain	160
Dennis Johnson	180	Sam Jones	154
John Havlicek	172	**Robert Parish**	154
Michael Cooper	168	Jerry West	153
Magic Johnson	167	**Larry Bird**	150
Bill Russell	165	Don Nelson	150
Paul Silas	163		

BEST GAMES

Points

	Date	FG-FT—Pts
Michael Jordan, Chi.at Bos.*	4/20/86	22-19— 63
Elgin Baylor, LA at Bos	4/14/62	22-17— 61
Wilt Chamberlain, Phi.vs Syr	3/22/62	22-12— 56
Rick Barry, SF vs Phi	4/18/67	22-11— 55
Michael Jordan, Chi.vs Cle	5/1/88	24- 7— 55

*Double overtime.

Field Goals

	Date	FGA	FGM
Wilt Chamberlain, Phi.vs Syr	3/14/60	42	24
John Havlicek, Bos.vs Atl	4/1/73	36	24
Michael Jordan, Chi.vs Cle	5/1/88	45	24

Seven players tied with 22 each.

Free Throws

	Date	FTA	FTM
Bob Cousy, Bos.vs Syr.†	3/21/53	32	30
Michael Jordan, Chi.vs NY	5/14/89	28	23
Oscar Robertson, Cin.at Bos	4/10/63	22	21
Bob Cousy, Bos.vs Syr.*	3/17/54	25	20
Jerry West, LA at Det	4/3/62	23	20
Jerry West, LA vs Balt	4/5/65	21	20

†Four overtimes.   *One overtime.

3-Pt Field Goals

	Date	No
Michael Cooper, LA Lakers vs Bos	6/4/87	6
Michael Adams, Den.at Pho	4/30/89	6
Eddie Johnson, Pho.vs Utah	5/4/90	6
Bill Laimbeer, Det.vs Port.*	6/7/90	6

Five players tied with 5 each.

*One overtime.

Assists

	Date	No
Magic Johnson, LA vs Pho	5/15/84	24
John Stockton, Utah at LA Lakers	5/17/88	24
Magic Johnson, LA Lakers at Port	5/3/85	23
Doc Rivers, Atl.vs Bos	5/16/88	22
Magic Johnson, LA vs Bos	6/3/84	21

Rebounds

	Date	No
Wilt Chamberlain, Phi.vs Bos	4/5/67	41
Bill Russell, Bos.vs Phi	3/23/58	40
Bill Russell, Bos.vs St.L	3/29/60	40
Bill Russell, Bos.vs LA*	4/18/62	40

Three players tied with 39 each.

*One overtime.

Blocked Shots

	Date	No
Mark Eaton, Utah vs Hou	4/26/85	10
Akeem Olajuwon, Hou.at LA Lakers	4/29/90	10
Kareem Abdul-Jabbar, LA vs G.St	4/22/77	9
Manute Bol, Wash.at Phi	4/18/86	9

13 players tied with 8 each.

Steals

	Date	No
Rick Barry, G.St.vs Sea	4/14/75	8
Lionel Hollins, Port.at LA	5/8/77	8
Maurice Cheeks, Phi.vs NJ	4/11/79	8
Craig Hodges, Mil.at Phi	5/9/86	8

Nine players tied with 7 each.

BEST NBA FINALS

Points

Series		Year	Pts
4-Gm	Rick Barry, G.St.vs Wash	1975	118
5-Gm	Jerry West, LA vs Bos	1965	169
6-Gm	Rick Barry, SF vs Phi	1967	245
7-Gm	Elgin Baylor, LA vs Bos	1962	284

Field Goals

Series		Year	No
4-Gm	K.Abdul-Jabbar, Mil.vs Bal	1971	46
5-Gm	Wilt Chamberlain, SF vs Bos	1964	62
6-Gm	Rick Barry, SF vs Phi	1967	94
7-Gm	Elgin Baylor, LA vs Bos	1962	101

Assists

Series		Year	No
4-Gm	Bob Cousy, Bos.vs Mpls	1959	51
5-Gm	Bob Cousy, Bos.vs St.L	1961	53
6-Gm	Magic Johnson, LA vs Bos	1985	84
7-Gm	Magic Johnson, LA vs Bos	1984	95

Rebounds

Series		Year	No
4-Gm	Bill Russell, Bos.vs Mpls	1959	118
5-Gm	Bill Russell, Bos.vs St.L	1961	144
6-Gm	Wilt Chamberlain, Phi.vs SF	1967	171
7-Gm	Bill Russell, Bos.vs LA	1962	189

Appearances in NBA Finals

Standings of all teams that have reached the NBA Finals. Based on number of appearances.

	App	Titles	Last Won
LA Lakers	23	11	1988
Boston Celtics	19	16	1986
Philadelphia 76ers	8	3	1983
Golden St.Warriors	6	3	1975
New York Knicks	6	2	1973
Detroit Pistons	4	1	1990
Atlanta Hawks	4	1	1958
Washington Bullets	4	1	1978
Milwaukee Bucks	2	1	1971
Seattle SuperSonics	2	1	1979
Houston Rockets	2	0	—
Balt.Bullets (folded)	1	1	1948
Sacramento Kings	1	1	1951
Chicago Stags (folded)	1	0	—
Wash.Capitols (folded)	1	0	—

NBA Franchise Origins

Here is what the current 27 teams in the National Basketball Association have to show for the years they have put in as members of the National Basketball League (NBL), Basketball Association of America (BAA), the NBA, and the American Basketball Association (ABA). League titles are noted by year won.

Eastern Conference

	First Season	League Titles	Franchise Stops
Atlanta Hawks	1946-47 (NBL)	1 NBA (1958)	Tri-Cities (1946-51)
			Milwaukee (1951-55)
			St.Louis (1955-68)
			Atlanta (1968-)
Boston Celtics	1946-47 (BAA)	16 NBA (1957,59-66,68-69 74,76,81,84,86)	Boston (1946-)
Chicago Bulls	1966-67 (NBA)	None	Chicago (1966-)
Cleveland Cavaliers	1970-71 (NBA)	None	Cleveland (1970-74)
Detroit Pistons	1941-42 (NBL)	2 NBL (1944-45) 2 NBA (1989-90)	Ft.Wayne,IN (1941-57)
			Detroit (1957-78)
			Pontiac,MI (1978-88)
			Auburn Hills,MI (1988-)
Indiana Pacers	1967-68 (ABA)	3 ABA (1970,72-73)	Indianapolis (1967-)
Miami Heat	1988-89 (NBA)	None	Miami (1988-)
Milwaukee Bucks	1968-69 (NBA)	1 NBA (1971)	Milwaukee (1968-)
New Jersey Nets	1967-68 (ABA)	2 ABA (1974,76)	Paramus,NJ (1967-68)
			Commack,NY (1968-69)
			W.Hempstead,NY (1969-71)
			Uniondale,NY (1971-77)
			Piscataway,NJ (1977-81)
			E.Rutherford,NJ (1981-)
New York Knicks	1946-47 (BAA)	2 NBA (1970,73)	New York (1946-)
Orlando Magic	1989-90 (NBA)	None	Orlando,FL (1989-)
Philadelphia 76ers	1949-50 (NBL)	3 NBA (1955,67,83)	Syracuse,NY (1949-63)
			Philadelphia (1963-)
Washington Bullets	1961-62 (NBA)	1 NBA (1978)	Chicago (1961-63)
			Baltimore (1963-73)
			Landover,MD (1973-)

Note: The Tri-Cities Blackhawks represented Moline and Rock Island, Ill., and Davenport, Iowa.

Western Conference

	First Season	League Titles	Franchise Stops
Charlotte Hornets	1988-89 (NBA)	None	Charlotte (1988-)
Dallas Mavericks	1980-81 (NBA)	None	Dallas (1980-)
Denver Nuggets	1967-68 (ABA)	None	Denver (1967-)
Golden St. Warriors	1946-47 (BAA)	1 BAA (1947) 2 NBA (1956,75)	Philadelphia (1946-62)
			San Francisco (1962-71)
			Oakland (1971-)
Houston Rockets	1967-68 (NBA)	None	San Diego (1967-71)
			Houston (1971-)
LA Clippers	1970-71 (NBA)	None	Buffalo (1970-78)
			San Diego (1978-84)
			Los Angeles (1984-)
LA Lakers	1947-48 (NBL)	1 NBL (1947) 1 BAA (1949) 10 NBA (1950,52-54,72, 80,82,85,87-88)	Minneapolis (1947-60)
			Los Angeles (1960-67)
			Inglewood,CA (1967-)
Minn. Timberwolves	1989-90 (NBA)	None	Minneapolis (1989-)
Phoenix Suns	1968-69 (NBA)	None	Phoenix (1968-)
Portland Trail Blazers	1970-71 (NBA)	1 NBA (1977)	Portland (1970-)
Sacramento Kings	1945-46 (NBL)	1 NBL (1946) 1 NBA (1951)	Rochester,NY (1945-58)
			Cincinnati (1958-72)
			KC-Omaha (1972-75)
			Kansas City (1975-85)
			Sacramento (1985-)
San Antonio Spurs	1967-68 (ABA)	None	Dallas (1967-73)
			San Antonio (1973-)
Seattle SuperSonics	1967-68 (NBA)	1 NBA (1979)	Seattle (1967-)
Utah Jazz	1974-75 (NBA)	None	New Orleans (1974-79)
			Salt Lake City (1979-)

NBA All-Time Individual Leaders
CAREER
Through 1989-90 regular season; players active in 1989-90 in **bold type.**

Points

	Yrs	Gms	Points	Avg
Kareem Abdul-Jabbar	20	1560	38,387	24.6
Wilt Chamberlain	14	1045	31,419	30.1
Elvin Hayes	16	1303	27,313	21.0
Oscar Robertson	14	1040	26,710	25.7
John Havlicek	16	1270	26,395	20.8
Jerry West	14	932	25,192	27.0
Moses Malone	14	1082	24,868	23.0
Alex English	14	1114	24,850	22.3
Elgin Baylor	14	846	23,149	27.4
Adrian Dantley	14	945	23,120	24.5
Hal Greer	15	1122	21,586	19.2
Walt Bellamy	14	1043	20,941	20.1
Bob Pettit	11	792	20,880	26.4
George Gervin	10	791	20,708	26.2
Larry Bird	11	792	19,719	24.9
Dolph Schayes	16	1059	19,249	18.2
Bob Lanier	14	959	19,248	20.1
Gail Goodrich	14	1031	19,181	18.6
Chet Walker	13	1032	18,831	18.2
Bob McAdoo	14	852	18,787	22.1
Rick Barry	10	794	18,395	23.2
Julius Erving	11	836	18,364	22.0
Dave Bing	12	901	18,327	20.3
Robert Parish	14	1100	18,312	16.6
Walter Davis	13	916	18,140	19.8

Combined NBA-ABA Leaders
Points
All-time scoring list for NBA players with ABA (1968-76) service added.

	Yrs	Gms	Points	Avg
Kareem Abdul-Jabbar	20	1560	38,387	24.6
Wilt Chamberlain	14	1045	31,419	30.1
Julius Erving*	16	1243	30,026	24.2
Dan Issel*	15	1218	27,482	22.6
Elvin Hayes	16	1303	27,313	21.0
Moses Malone*	16	1208	27,039	22.4
Oscar Robertson	14	1040	26,710	25.7
George Gervin*	14	1060	26,595	25.1
John Havlicek	16	1270	26,395	20.8
Rick Barry*	14	1020	25,279	24.8
Jerry West	14	932	25,192	27.0
Artis Gilmore*	17	1329	24,941	18.8
Alex English	14	1114	24,850	22.3
Elgin Baylor	14	846	23,149	27.4
Adrian Dantley	14	945	23,120	24.5
Hal Greer	15	1122	21,586	19.2
Walt Bellamy	14	1043	20,941	20.1
Bob Pettit	11	792	20,880	26.4
Larry Bird	11	792	19,719	24.9
Dolph Schayes	16	1059	19,249	18.2
Bob Lanier	14	959	19,248	20.1
Gail Goodrich	14	1031	19,181	18.6
Chet Walker	13	1032	18,831	18.2
Bob McAdoo	14	852	18,787	22.1
Dave Bing	12	901	18,327	20.3

ABA Totals: Erving (5 yrs, 407 gms, 11,662 pts, 28.7 avg); **Issel** (6 yrs, 500 gms, 12,823 pts, 25.6 avg); **Gervin** (4 yrs, 269 gms, 5887 pts, 21.9 avg); **Malone** (2 yrs, 126 gms, 2171 pts, 17.2 avg); **Barry** (4 yrs, 226 gms, 6884 pts, 30.5 avg); **Gilmore** (5 yrs, 420 gms, 9362 pts, 22.3 avg).

Scoring Average
Minimum of 400 games or 10,000 points.

	Yrs	Gms	Points	Avg
Michael Jordan	6	427	14,016	32.8
Wilt Chamberlain	14	1045	31,419	30.1
Elgin Baylor	14	846	23,149	27.4
Jerry West	14	932	25,192	27.0
Bob Pettit	11	792	20,880	26.4
George Gervin	10	791	20,708	26.2
Dominique Wilkins	8	639	16,695	26.1
Oscar Robertson	14	1040	26,710	25.7
Larry Bird	11	792	19,719	24.9
Karl Malone	5	407	10,116	24.9
Kareem Abdul-Jabbar	20	1560	38,387	24.6
Adrian Dantley	14	945	23,120	24.5
Pete Maravich	10	658	15,948	24.2
Rick Barry	10	794	18,395	23.2
Akeem Olajuwon	6	468	10,878	23.2
Moses Malone	14	1082	24,868	23.0
Mark Aguirre	9	680	15,587	22.9
Paul Arizin	10	713	16,266	22.8
Charles Barkley	6	468	10,605	22.7
Bernard King	12	778	17,615	22.6
George Mikan	9	520	11,764	22.6
Kiki Vandeweghe	10	627	14,033	22.4
Alex English	14	1114	24,850	22.3
Terry Cummings	8	631	13,977	22.2
Bob McAdoo	14	852	18,787	22.1
David Thompson	8	509	11,264	22.1

Field Goals

	Yrs	FGA	FGM	Pct
Kareem Abdul-Jabbar	20	28,307	15,837	.559
Wilt Chamberlain	14	23,497	12,681	.540
Elvin Hayes	16	24,272	10,976	.452
John Havlicek	16	23,900	10,513	.440
Alex English	14	20,302	10,337	.509
Oscar Robertson	14	19,620	9,508	.485
Jerry West	14	19,032	9,016	.474
Elgin Baylor	14	20,171	8,693	.431
Moses Malone	14	17,389	8,587	.494
Hal Greer	15	18,811	8,504	.452

Note: If field goals made in the ABA are included, consider these totals: Julius Erving (11,818), Dan Issel (10,431), George Gervin (10,368), Rick Barry (9,695), Moses Malone (9,429) and Artis Gilmore (9,403).

Free Throws

	Yrs	FTA	FTM	Pct
Oscar Robertson	14	9,185	7694	.838
Moses Malone	14	10,034	7690	.766
Jerry West	14	8,801	7160	.814
Dolph Schayes	16	8,273	6979	.844
Adrian Dantley	14	8,325	6814	.818
Kareem Abdul-Jabbar	20	9,304	6712	.721
Bob Pettit	11	8,119	6182	.761
Wilt Chamberlain	14	11,862	6057	.511
Elgin Baylor	14	7,391	5763	.780
Lenny Wilkens	15	6,973	5394	.774

Note: If free throws made in the ABA are included, consider these totals: Moses Malone (8177), Dan Issel (6591), Julius Erving (6256), and Artis Gilmore (6132).

NBA All-Time Individual Leaders (Cont.)

Assists

	Yrs	Gms	Asts	Avg
Oscar Robertson	14	1040	9887	9.5
Magic Johnson	11	795	8932	11.2
Lenny Wilkens	15	1077	7211	6.7
Isiah Thomas	9	716	6985	9.8
Bob Cousy	14	924	6955	7.5
Guy Rodgers	12	892	6917	7.8
Maurice Cheeks	12	934	6665	7.1
Nate Archibald	13	876	6476	7.4
John Lucas	14	928	6454	7.0
Norm Nixon	10	768	6386	8.3

Rebounds

	Yrs	Gms	Reb	Avg
Wilt Chamberlain	14	1045	23,924	22.9
Bill Russell	13	963	21,620	22.5
Kareem Abdul-Jabbar	20	1560	17,440	11.2
Elvin Hayes	16	1303	16,279	12.5
Nate Thurmond	14	964	14,464	15.0
Walt Bellamy	14	1043	14,241	13.7
Wes Unseld	13	984	13,769	14.0
Moses Malone	14	1082	14,483	13.4
Jerry Lucas	11	829	12,942	15.6
Bob Petit	11	792	12,849	16.2

Note: If rebounds pulled down in the ABA are included, consider the following totals: Artis Gilmore (16,330), Moses Malone (15,293).

Personal Fouls

	Yrs	Gms	Fouls	DQ
Kareem Abdul-Jabbar	20	1560	4657	48
Elvin Hayes	16	1303	4193	53
Hal Greer	15	1122	3855	72
Dolph Schayes	16	1059	3664	90
Jack Sikma	13	1030	3661	76

Note: If ABA records are included, consider the following personal foul totals: Artis Gilmore (4,529), Caldwell Jones (4,436), and Dan Issel (3,504).

Disqualifications

	Yrs	Gms	DQ
Vern Mikkelsen	10	699	127
Walter Dukes	8	553	121
Charlie Share	8	555	105
Paul Arizin	10	713	104
Darryl Dawkins	14	726	100

Years Played

	Yrs	Career	Gms
Kareem Abdul-Jabbar	20	1970-89	1560
Dolph Schayes	16	1949-64	1059
John Havlicek	16	1963-78	1270
Paul Silas	16	1965-80	1254
Elvin Hayes	16	1969-84	1303
Hal Greer	15	1959-73	1122
Lenny Wilkens	15	1961-75	1077

Note: If ABA records are included, consider the following year totals: Artis Gilmore (17, 1972-88); Caldwell Jones (17, 1974—); Julius Erving (16, 1972-87); Moses Malone (16, 1975—); Dan Issel (15, 1971-85); Billy Paultz (15, 1971-85).

Games Played

	Yrs	Career	Gms
Kareem Abdul-Jabbar	20	1970-89	1560
Elvin Hayes	16	1969-84	1303
John Havlicek	16	1963-78	1270
Paul Silas	16	1965-80	1254
Hal Greer	15	1959-73	1122
Lenny Wilkens	15	1961-75	1077

Note: If ABA records are included, consider the following game totals: Artis Gilmore (1329); Caldwell Jones (1299); Julius Erving (1243); Dan Issel (1218); Moses Malone (1208); Billy Paultz (1124).

SINGLE SEASON

Scoring Average

	Season	Avg
Wilt Chamberlain, Phi	1961-62	50.4
Wilt Chamberlain, SF	1962-63	44.8
Wilt Chamberlain, Phi	1960-61	38.4
Elgin Baylor, LA	1961-62	38.3
Wilt Chamberlain, Phi	1959-60	37.6
Michael Jordan, Chi	1986-87	37.1
Wilt Chamberlain, SF	1963-64	36.9
Rick Barry, SF	1966-67	35.6
Michael Jordan, Chi	1987-88	35.0
Elgin Baylor, LA	1960-61	34.8
Kareem Abdul-Jabbar, Mil	1971-72	34.8
Wilt Chamberlain, SF-Phi	1964-65	34.7

Assists

	Season	Avg
John Stockton, Utah	1989-90	14.5
Isiah Thomas, Det	1984-85	13.9
John Stockton, Utah	1987-88	13.8
John Stockton, Utah	1988-89	13.6
Kevin Porter, Det	1978-79	13.4
Magic Johnson, LAL	1983-84	13.1
Magic Johnson, LAL	1988-89	12.8
Magic Johnson, LAL	1984-85	12.6
Magic Johnson, LAL	1985-86	12.6

3-Pt Field Goal Pct

	Season	Pct
Jon Sundvold, Mia	1988-89	.522
Steve Kerr, Cle	1989-90	.507
Craig Hodges, Mil-Pho	1987-88	.491
Mark Price, Cle	1987-88	.486
Kiki Vandeweghe, Port	1986-87	.481
Craig Hodges, Chi	1989-90	.481

Rebounds

	Season	Avg
Wilt Chamberlain, Phi	1960-61	27.2
Wilt Chamberlain, Phi	1959-60	27.0
Wilt Chamberlain, Phi	1961-62	25.7
Bill Russell, Bos	1963-64	24.7
Wilt Chamberlain, Phi	1965-66	24.6
Wilt Chamberlain, SF	1962-63	24.2
Wilt Chamberlain, Phi	1966-67	24.2
Bill Russell, Bos	1964-65	24.1
Bill Russell, Bos	1959-60	24.0

Field Goal Pct

	Season	Pct
Wilt Chamberlain, LA	1972-73	.727
Wilt Chamberlain, SF	1966-67	.683
Artis Gilmore, Chi	1980-81	.670
Artis Gilmore, Chi	1981-82	.652
Wilt Chamberlain, LA	1971-72	.649

Free Throw Pct

	Season	Pct
Calvin Murphy, Hou	1980-81	.958
Rick Barry, Hou	1978-79	.947
Ernie DiGregorio, Buf	1976-77	.945
Ricky Sobers, Chi	1980-81	.935
Rick Barry, Hou	1979-80	.935

Blocked Shots

	Season	Avg
Mark Eaton, Utah	1984-85	5.56
Manute Bol, Wash	1985-86	4.96
Elmore Smith, LA	1973-74	4.85
Mark Eaton, Utah	1985-86	4.61
Akeem Olajuwon, Hou	1989-90	4.59

Steals

	Season	Avg
Alvin Robertson, SA	1985-86	3.67
Don Buse, Ind	1976-77	3.47
Magic Johnson, LA	1980-81	3.43
Michael Ray Richardson, NY	1979-80	3.23
Alvin Robertson, SA	1986-87	3.21

BEST GAMES

Points

	Date	—Pts
Wilt Chamberlain, Phi.vs NY	3/2/62	—100
Wilt Chamberlain, Phi.vs LA†	12/8/61	— 78
Wilt Chamberlain, Phi.vs Chi	1/13/62	— 73
Wilt Chamberlain, SF at NY	11/16/62	— 73
David Thompson, Den.at Det	4/9/78	— 73
Wilt Chamberlain, SF at LA	11/3/62	— 72
Elgin Baylor, LA at NY	11/15/60	— 71
Wilt Chamberlain, SF at Syr	3/10/63	— 70

*Overtime.   †Triple overtime.
Note: Chamberlain's 100-point game vs New York was played at Hershey, PA.

Blocked Shots

	Date	No
Elmore Smith, LA vs Port	10/28/73	17
Manute Bol, Wash.vs Atl	1/25/86	15
Manute Bol, Wash.vs Ind	2/26/87	15
Four players tied with 14 each.		

Steals

	Date	No
Larry Kenon, San Antonio vs KC	2/9/80	11

11 players tied with 10 each, including Alvin Robertson of San Antonio (3 times).

Field Goals

	Date	FGA	FGM
Wilt Chamberlain, Phi.vs NY	3/2/62	63	36
Wilt Chamberlain, Phi.vs LA†	12/8/61	62	31
Wilt Chamberlain, Phi.at Chi	12/16/67	40	30
Rick Barry, G.St.vs Port	2/26/74	45	30
Four players tied with 29 each.			

†Triple overtime.

Free Throws

	Date	FGA	FGM
Wilt Chamberlain, Phi.vs NY	3/2/62	32	28
Adrian Dantley, Utah vs Hou	1/4/84	29	28
Adrian Dantley, Utah vs Den	11/25/83	31	27
Adrian Dantley, Utah vs Dal	10/21/80	29	26
Michael Jordan, Chi.vs NJ	2/26/87	27	26

3-Pt Field Goals

	Date	No
Dale Ellis, Sea.vs LA Clippers	4/20/90	9
Rick Barry, Hou.vs Utah	2/9/80	8
John Roche, Den.vs Seattle	1/9/82	8
Michael Adams, Den.vs Mil	1/21/89	8
Four players tied with 7 each.		

Assists

	Date	No
Kevin Porter, NJ vs Hou	2/24/78	29
Bob Cousy, Bos.vs Mpls	2/27/59	28
Guy Rodgers, SF vs St.L	3/14/63	28
Geoff Huston, Cle.vs G.St	1/27/82	27
John Stockton, Utah at NY	12/19/89	27

Rebounds

	Date	No
Wilt Chamberlain, Phi.vs Bos	11/24/60	55
Bill Russell, Bos.vs Syr	2/5/60	51
Bill Russell, Bos.vs Phi	11/16/57	49
Bill Russell, Bos.vs Det	3/11/65	49
Wilt Chamberlain, Phi.vs Syr	2/6/60	45
Wilt Chamberlain, Phi.vs LA	1/21/61	45

Wilt Chamberlain's 100-Point Game

March 2, 1962 at Hershey, PA

Final Score:
Philadelphia Warriors, 169
New York Knicks, 147

New York	FGA	FGM	FTA	FTM	Pts
Willie Naulls	22	9	15	13	31
Johnny Green	7	3	0	0	6
Darrall Imhoff	7	3	1	1	7
Richie Guerin	29	13	17	13	39
Al Butler	13	4	0	0	8
Cleveland Butler	26	16	1	1	33
Dave Budd	8	6	1	1	13
Donnie Butcher	6	3	6	4	10
TOTALS	118	57	41	33	147

FG Pct.: .483, FT Pct.: .805.

Philadelphia	FGA	FGM	FTA	FTM	Pts
Paul Arizin	18	7	2	2	16
Tom Meschery	12	7	2	2	16
Wilt Chamberlain	63	36	32	28	100
Guy Rodgers	4	1	12	9	11
Al Attles	8	8	1	1	17
York Larese	5	4	1	1	9
Ed Conlin	4	0	0	0	0
Joe Ruklick	1	0	2	0	0
Ted Luckenbill	0	0	0	0	0
TOTALS	115	63	52	43	169

FG Pct.: .548, FT Pct.: .827.

Score by Periods	1	2	3	4	Final
New York	26	42	38	41	147
Philadelphia	42	37	46	44	169

Officials: Willie Smith and Pete D'Ambrosio.
Attendance: 4,124.

NBA Scoring Champions, 1947–90

The NBA scoring championship was decided by total points from 1947-69, and per game average since then.
Multiple winners: Wilt Chamberlain (7); Michael Jordan (4); Neil Johnston, George Gervin, Bob McAdoo, and George Mikan (3); Kareem Abdul-Jabbar, Paul Arizin, Adrian Dantley and Bob Pettit (2).

Year		Gms	Pts	Avg	Year		Gms	Pts	Avg
1947	Joe Fulks, Phi	60	1389	23.2	1970	Jerry West, LA	74	2309	31.2
1948	Max Zaslofsky, Chi	48	1007	21.0	1971	Lew Alcindor†, Mil	82	2596	31.7
1949	George Mikan, Mpls	60	1698	28.3	1972	Kareem Abdul-Jabbar, Mil	81	2822	34.8
					1973	Nate Archibald, KC-Oma	80	2719	34.0
1950	George Mikan, Mpls	68	1865	27.4	1974	Bob McAdoo, Buf	74	2261	30.6
1951	George Mikan, Mpls	68	1932	28.4	1975	Bob McAdoo, Buf	82	2831	34.5
1952	Paul Arizin, Phi	66	1674	25.4	1976	Bob McAdoo, Buf	78	2427	31.1
1953	Neil Johnston, Phi	70	1564	22.3	1977	Pete Maravich, NO	73	2273	31.1
1954	Neil Johnston, Phi	72	1759	24.4	1978	George Gervin, SA	82	2232	27.2
1955	Neil Johnston, Phi	72	1631	22.7	1979	George Gervin, SA	80	2365	29.6
1956	Bob Pettit, St.L	72	1849	25.7					
1957	Paul Arizin, Phi	71	1817	25.6	1980	George Gervin, SA	78	2585	33.1
1958	George Yardley, Det	72	2001	27.8	1981	Adrian Dantley, Utah	80	2452	30.7
1959	Bob Pettit, St.L	72	2105	29.2	1982	George Gervin, SA	79	2551	32.3
					1983	Alex English, Den	82	2326	28.4
1960	Wilt Chamberlain, Phi	72	2707	37.6	1984	Adrian Dantley, Utah	79	2418	30.6
1961	Wilt Chamberlain, Phi	79	3033	38.4	1985	Bernard King, NY	55	1809	32.9
1962	Wilt Chamberlain, Phi	80	4029	50.4	1986	Dominique Wilkins, Atl	78	2366	30.3
1963	Wilt Chamberlain, SF	80	3586	44.8	1987	Michael Jordan, Chi	82	3041	37.1
1964	Wilt Chamberlain, SF	80	2948	36.9	1988	Michael Jordan, Chi	82	2868	35.0
1965	Wilt Chamberlain, SF-Phi	73	2534	34.7	1989	Michael Jordan, Chi	81	2633	32.5
1966	Wilt Chamberlain, Phi	79	2649	33.5	1990	Michael Jordan, Chi	82	2753	33.6
1967	Rick Barry, SF	78	2775	35.6					
1968	Dave Bing, Det	79	2142	27.1					
1969	Elvin Hayes, SD	82	2327	28.4					

†Alcindor changed his name to Kareem Abdul-Jabbar after the 1970-71 season.

NBA All-Star Game, 1951-90

The NBA staged its first All-Star Game before 10,094 at Boston Garden on March 2, 1951. From that year on, the All-Star game has matched the best players in the East against the best in the West. Winning coaches are listed first.
Series: East leads, 26-14.
Multiple MVP winners: Bob Pettit (4); Oscar Roberston (3); Bob Cousy, Julius Erving and Isiah Thomas (2).

Year	Result	Host	Coaches	Most Valuable Player
1951	East 111, West 94	Boston	Joe Lapchick, John Kundla	Ed Macauley, Boston
1952	East 108, West 91	Boston	Al Cervi, John Kundla	Paul Arizin, Phila.
1953	West 79, East 75	Ft.Wayne	John Kundla, Joe Lapchick	George Mikan, Minn.
1954	East 98, West 93 (OT)	New York	Joe Lapchick, John Kundla	Bob Cousy, Boston
1955	East 100, West 91	New York	Al Cervi, Charley Eckman	Bill Sharman, Boston
1956	West 108, East 94	Rochester	Charley Eckman, George Senesky	Bob Pettit, St.Louis
1957	East 109, West 97	Boston	Red Auerbach, Bobby Wanzer	Bob Cousy, Boston
1958	East 130, West 118	St.Louis	Red Auerbach, Alex Hannum	Bob Pettit, St.Louis
1959	West 124, East 108	Detroit	Ed Macauley, Red Auerbach	Bob Pettit, St.Louis & Elgin Baylor, Minn.
1960	East 125, West 115	Philadelphia	Red Auerbach, Ed Macauley	Wilt Chamberlain, Phila.
1961	West 153, East 131	Syracuse	Paul Seymour, Red Auerbach	Oscar Robertson, Cinn.
1962	West 150, East 130	St.Louis	Fred Schaus, Red Auerbach	Bob Pettit, St.Louis
1963	East 115, West 108	Los Angeles	Red Auerbach, Fred Schaus	Bill Russell, Boston
1964	East 111, West 107	Boston	Red Auerbach, Fred Schaus	Oscar Robertson, Cinn.
1965	East 124, West 123	St.Louis	Red Auerbach, Alex Hannum	Jerry Lucas, Cinn.
1966	East 137, West 94	Cincinnati	Red Auerbach, Fred Schaus	Adrian Smith, Cinn.
1967	West 135, East 120	San Francisco	Fred Schaus, Red Auerbach	Rick Barry, San Fran.
1968	East 144, West 124	New York	Alex Hannum, Bill Sharman	Hal Greer, Phila.
1969	East 123, West 112	Baltimore	Gene Shue, Richie Guerin	Oscar Robertson, Cinn.
1970	East 142, West 135	Philadelphia	Red Holzman, Richie Guerin	Willis Reed, New York
1971	West 108, East 107	San Diego	Larry Costello, Red Holzman	Lenny Wilkens, Seattle
1972	West 112, East 110	Los Angeles	Bill Sharman, Tom Heinsohn	Jerry West, Los Ang.
1973	East 104, West 84	Chicago	Tom Heinsohn, Bill Sharman	Dave Cowens, Boston
1974	West 134, East 123	Seattle	Larry Costello, Tom Heinsohn	Bob Lanier, Detroit
1975	East 108, West 102	Phoenix	K.C.Jones, Al Attles	Walt Frazier, New York
1976	East 123, West 109	Philadelphia	Tom Heinsohn, Al Attles	Dave Bing, Washington
1977	West 125, East 124	Milwaukee	Larry Brown, Gene Shue	Julius Erving, Phila.
1978	East 133, West 125	Atlanta	Billy Cunningham, Jack Ramsay	Randy Smith, Buffalo
1979	West 134, East 129	Detroit	Lenny Wilkens, Dick Motta	David Thompson, Denver
1980	East 144, West 135 (OT)	Washington	Billy Cunningham, Len Wilkens	George Gervin, S.Ant.
1981	East 123, West 120	Cleveland	Billy Cunningham, John MacLeod	Nate Archibald, Bost.
1982	East 120, West 118	New Jersey	Bill Fitch, Pat Riley	Larry Bird, Boston

Year	Result	Host	Coaches	Most Valuable Player
1983	East 132, West 123	Los Angeles	Billy Cunningham, Pat Riley	Julius Erving, Phila.
1984	East 154, West 145 (OT)	Denver	K.C.Jones, Frank Layden	Isiah Thomas, Detroit
1985	West 140, East 129	Indiana	Pat Riley, K.C.Jones	Ralph Sampson, Houston
1986	East 139, West 132	Dallas	K.C.Jones, Pat Riley	Isiah Thomas, Detroit
1987	West 154, East 149 (OT)	Seattle	Pat Riley, K.C.Jones	Tom Chambers, Seattle
1988	East 138, West 133	Chicago	Mike Fratello, Pat Riley	Michael Jordan, Chicago
1989	West 143, East 134	Houston	Pat Riley, Lenny Wilkens	Karl Malone, Utah
1990	East 130, West 113	Miami	Chuck Daly, Pat Riley	Magic Johnson, LA Lakers

All-Time Winningest NBA Coaches

Minimum of 400 NBA victories through 1989-90 season. Regular season and playoffs included. Active coaches in **bold type**.

Top Winning Percentages

	Yrs	W	L	Pct	Playoff W-L
Pat Riley	9	635	241	.725	102-47
Billy Cunningham	8	520	235	.689	66-39
K.C.Jones	8	542	247	.687	79-54
Red Auerbach	20	1037	479	.662	99-69
Chuck Daly	8	440	268	.621	62-31
Tommy Heinsohn	9	474	296	.616	47-33
Larry Costello	10	467	323	.591	37-23
Don Nelson	13	666	478	.582	46-50
John Kundla	11	483	337	.589	60-35
Doug Moe	13	642	542	.542	33-50
Red Holzman	18	754	651	.537	58-47
Alex Hannum	12	516	446	.536	45-34
Lenny Wilkens	17	768	688	.527	43-41
Jack Ramsay	21	908	841	.519	44-58
John MacLeod	17	722	673	.518	47-51
Al Attles	14	588	548	.518	31-30
Dick Motta	20	880	859	.506	56-70
Bill Fitch	19	828	822	.502	49-43
Cotton Fitzsimmons	17	726	728	.499	29-39
Gene Shue	22	814	908	.473	30-47

Note: The NBA does not recognize ABA coaching records, so the overall ABA record of **Hannum** (194-164 in 4 years) is not included above. Also, **Larry Brown's** overall ABA coaching record was 249-129 in four years.

Where They Coached

Attles—Golden St.(1970-80,80-83); **Auerbach**—Washington (1946- 49); Tri-Cities (1949-50); Boston (1950-66); **Costello**—Milwaukee (1968-72), Chicago (1978-79); **Cunningham**—Philadelphia (1977-85); **Daly**—Cleveland (1981-82), Detroit (1983—); **Fitch**—Cleveland (1970-79), Boston (1979-83), Houston (1983-88), New Jersey (1989—); **Fitzsimmons**—Phoenix (1970-72), Atlanta (1972-76), Buffalo (1977-78), Kansas City (1978-84), San Antonio (1984-86), Phoenix (1988—); **Hannum**—St.Louis (1957-58), Syracuse (1960-63), San Francisco (1963-66), Philadelphia (1966-68), Houston (1970-71); **Heinsohn**—Boston (1969-77); **Holzman**—Milwaukee-St.Louis (1954-57), NY Knicks (1968-77,78-82).

Jones—Washington (1973-76), Boston (1983-88), Seattle (1990—); **Kundla**—Minneapolis (1948-57,58-59); **MacLeod**—Phoenix (1973- 87), Dallas (1987-89); **Moe**—San Antonio (1976-80), Denver (1981-90); **Motta**—Chicago (1968-76), Washington (1976-80), Dallas (1980-87), Sacramento (1990—); **Nelson**—Milwaukee (1976-87), Golden St.(1988—); **Ramsay**—Philadelphia (1968-72), Buffalo (1972-76), Portland (1976-86), Indiana (1986-88); **Riley**—LA Lakers (1981-90); **Shue**—Baltimore (1967-73), Philadelphia (1973-77), San Diego (1978-80), Washington (1980-86), LA Clippers (1987-89); **Wilkens**—Seattle (1969-72), Portland (1974-76), Seattle (1977-85), Cleveland (1986—).

Most Victories

	Regular Season	Playoffs	Total
Red Auerbach	938	99	1037
Jack Ramsay	864	44	908
Dick Motta	824	56	880
Bill Fitch	779	49	828
Gene Shue	784	30	814
Lenny Wilkens	725	43	768
Red Holzman	696	58	754
Cotton Fitzsimmons	697	29	726
John MacLeod	675	47	722
Don Nelson	620	46	666
Doug Moe	609	33	642
Pat Riley	533	102	635
Al Attles	557	31	588
K.C.Jones	463	79	542
Billy Cunningham	454	66	520
Alex Hannum	471	45	516

Note: The NBA does not recognize ABA coaching records, so the ABA victories of **Hannum** (178 + 16 = 194) and **Larry Brown** (229 + 20 = 249) are not included above.

Active Coaches' Victories

Through 1989-90 season, including playoffs.

	Yrs	W	L	Pct
Dick Motta, Sacramento	20	880	859	.506
Bill Fitch, New Jersey	18	828	822	.502
Lenny Wilkens, Cleveland	17	768	688	.527
Cotton Fitzsimmons, Phoenix	17	726	728	.499
Don Nelson, Golden St	13	666	478	.582
K.C.Jones, Seattle	8	542	247	.687
Chuck Daly, Detroit	8	440	268	.621
Larry Brown, San Antonio	7	308	262	.540
Del Harris, Milwaukee	7	297	327	.476
Jerry Sloan, Utah	5	193	183	.513
Jim Lynam, Philadelphia	6	171	188	.476
Paul Westhead, Denver	4	152	110	.580
Matt Guokas, Orlando	4	145	161	.474
Don Chaney, Houston	5	141	216	.395
Mike Schuler, LA Clippers	3	129	90	.589
Wes Unseld, Washington	3	103	121	.460
Rick Adelman, Portland	2	85	56	.603
Phil Jackson, Chicago	1	65	33	.663
Dick Versace, Indiana	2	64	76	.457
Bob Weiss, Atlanta	2	59	108	.353
Stu Jackson, New York	1	49	43	.533
Bill Musselman, Minnesota	3	49	127	.278
Richie Adubato, Dallas	1	42	32	.568
Ron Rothstein, Miami	2	33	131	.201
Gene Littles, Charlotte	1	11	31	.262
Mike Dunleavy, LA Lakers	0	0	0	.000
Chris Ford, Boston	0	0	0	.000

Note: The NBA does not recognize ABA coaching records, so **Brown's** overall ABA record of (249-129 in 4 years) is not included above.

Annual Award Winners
Maurice Podoloff Trophy

Awarded to the most valuable player for the regular season and named after the first commissioner of the NBA. Winners first selected by the NBA players (1956-80) then a national panel of pro basketball writers and broadcasters (since 1981). Winners' scoring averages are provided; (*) denotes led league.

Multiple winners: Kareem Abdul-Jabbar (6); Bill Russell (5); Wilt Chamberlain (4); Larry Bird, Magic Johnson and Moses Malone (3); Bob Pettit (2).

Year		Pts	Year		Pts
1956	Bob Pettit, St.L, F	25.7*	1974	Kareem Abdul-Jabbar, LA, C	27.0
1957	Bob Cousy, Bos., G	20.6	1975	Bob McAdoo, Buf., F	34.5*
1958	Bill Russell, Bos., C	16.6	1976	Kareem Abdul-Jabbar, LA, C	27.7
1959	Bob Pettit, St.Louis, F	29.2*	1977	Kareem Abdul-Jabbar, LA, C	26.2
1960	Wilt Chamberlain, Phi., C	37.6*	1978	Bill Walton, Port., C	18.9
1961	Bill Russell, Bos, C	16.9	1979	Moses Malone, Hou., C	24.8
1962	Bill Russell, Bos., C	18.9	1980	Kareem Abdul-Jabbar, LA, C	24.8
1963	Bill Russell, Bos., C	16.8	1981	Julius Erving, Phi., F	24.6
1964	Oscar Robertson, Cinn, G	31.4	1982	Moses Malone, Hou., C	31.1
1965	Bill Russell, Bos., C	14.1	1983	Moses Malone, Phi., C	24.5
1966	Wilt Chamberlain, Phi., C	33.5*	1984	Larry Bird, Bos., F	24.2
1967	Wilt Chamberlain, Phi., C	24.1	1985	Larry Bird, Bos., F	28.7
1968	Wilt Chamberlain, Phi., C	24.3	1986	Larry Bird, Bos., F	25.8
1969	Wes Unseld, Balt., C	13.8	1987	Magic Johnson, LA Lakers, G	23.9
1970	Willis Reed, NY, C	21.7	1988	Michael Jordan, Chi., G	35.0*
1971	Lew Alcindor$, Mil., C	31.7*	1989	Magic Johnson, LA Lakers, G	22.5
1972	Kareem Abdul-Jabbar, Mil., C	34.8*	1990	Magic Johnson, LA Lakers, G	22.3
1973	Dave Cowens, Bos., C	20.5			

*Alcindor changed his name to Kareem Abdul-Jabbar after the 1970-71 season.

Eddie Gottlieb Trophy

Awarded to the outstanding rookie of the regular season and named after the pro basketball pioneer and owner-coach of the first NBA champion Philadelphia Warriors. Winners selected by a national panel of pro basketball writers and broadcasters. Winners' scoring averages provided; (*) denotes led league.

Year		Pts	Year		Pts
1953	Don Meineke, Ft.Wayne, F	10.8	1973	Bob McAdoo, Buf., C/F	18.0
1954	Ray Felix, Balt., C	17.6	1974	Ernie DiGregorio, Buf., G	15.2
1955	Bob Pettit, Mil., F	20.4	1975	Keith Wilkes, G.St., F	14.2
1956	Maurice Stokes, Roch., F/C	16.8	1976	Alvan Adams, Pho., C	19.0
1957	Tommy Heinsohn, Bos., F	16.2	1977	Adrian Dantley, Buf., F	20.3
1958	Woody Sauldsberry, Phi., F/C	12.8	1978	Walter Davis, Pho., G	24.2
1959	Elgin Baylor, Mpls., F	24.9	1979	Phil Ford, KC, G	15.9
1960	Wilt Chamberlain, Phi., C#	37.6*	1980	Larry Bird, Bos., F	21.3
1961	Oscar Robertson, Cinn., G	30.5	1981	Darrell Griffith, Utah, G	20.6
1962	Walt Bellamy, Chi., C	31.6	1982	Buck Williams, NJ, F	15.5
1963	Terry Dischinger, Chi., F	25.5	1983	Terry Cummings, SD, F	23.7
1964	Jerry Lucas, Cinn., F/C	17.7	1984	Ralph Sampson, Hou., C	21.0
1965	Willis Reed, NY, C	19.5	1985	Michael Jordan, Chi., G	28.2
1966	Rick Barry, SF, F	25.7	1986	Patrick Ewing, NY, C	20.0
1967	Dave Bing, Det., G	20.0	1987	Chuck Person, Ind., F	18.8
1968	Earl Monroe, Balt., G	24.3	1988	Mark Jackson, NY, G	13.6
1969	Wes Unseld, Balt., C#	13.8	1989	Mitch Richmond, G.St., G	22.0
1970	Lew Alcindor‡, Mil., C	28.8	1990	David Robinson, SA, C	24.3
1971	Dave Cowens, Bos., C	17.0			
	& Geoff Petrie, Port., F	24.8			
1972	Sidney Wicks, POrt., F	24.5			

#Chamberlain and Unseld are the only players to be named Rookie of the Year and MVP in the same season.
‡Alcindor changed his name to Kareem Abdul-Jabbar after the 1970-71 season.

Red Auerbach Trophy

Awarded to the outstanding coach of the year and renamed in 1967 for the former Boston coach who led the Celtics to nine NBA titles. Winners selected by a national panel of pro basketball writers and broadcasters. Previous season and winning season records are provided; (*) denotes division title.

Multiple winners: Bill Fitch, Cotton Fitzsimmons, Don Nelson and Gene Shue (2).

Year		Improvement		Year		Improvement	
1963	Harry Gallatin, St.L	29-51	to 48-32	1970	Red Holzman, NY	54-28	to 60-22*
1964	Alex Hannum, SF	31-49	to 48-32*	1971	Dick Motta, Chi	39-43	to 51-31
1965	Red Auerbach, Box	59-21*	to 61-18*	1972	Bill Sharman, LA	48-34*	to 69-13*
1966	Dolph Schayes, Phi	40-40	to 55-25*	1973	Tommy Heinsohn, Bos	56-26*	to 68-14*
1967	Johnny Kerr, Chi	Expan.	to 33-48	1974	Ray Scott, Det	40-42	to 52-30
1968	Richie Guerin, St.L	39-42	to 56-26*	1975	Phil Johnson, KC-Oma	33-49	to 44-38
1969	Gene Shue, Balt	36-46	to 57-25*	1976	Bill Fitch, Cle	40-42	to 49-33*

Year	Improvement
1977 Tom Nissalke, Hou	40-42 to 49-33*
1978 Hubie Brown, Atl	31-51 to 41-41
1979 Cotton Fitzsimmons, KC	31-51 to 48-34*
1980 Bill Fitch, Bos	29-53 to 61-21*
1981 Jack McKinney, Ind	37-45 to 44-38
1982 Gene Shue, Wash	39-43 to 43-39
1983 Don Nelson, Mil	55-27* to 51-31*

Year	Improvement
1984 Frank Layden, Utah	30-52 to 45-37*
1985 Don Nelson, Milw	50-32* to 59-23*
1986 Mike Fratello, Atl	34-48 to 50-32
1987 Mike Schuler, Port	40-42 to 49-33
1988 Doug Moe, Den	37-45 to 54-28*
1989 Cotton Fitzsimmons, Pho	28-54 to 55-27
1990 Pat Riley, LA Lakers	57-25* to 63-19*

Repeat Champions in NBA

Only three NBA franchises—the Lakers, Celtics and Pistons—have ever won back-to-back league championships. The Lakers have had three consecutive streaks (1949-50, 1952-54 and 1987-88), the Celtics two (1959-66 and 1968-69) and the Pistons one (1989-90).

Minneapolis Lakers
1948—Member of the National Basketball League
1949—**NBA Champs;** beat Washington, 4-2
1950—**NBA Champs;** beat Syracuse, 4-2
1951—lost Western Final to Rochester, 3-1
1952—**NBA Champs;** beat New York, 4-3
1953—**NBA Champs;** beat New York, 4-1
1954—**NBA Champs;** beat Syracuse, 4-3
1955—lost Western Final to Ft.Wayne, 3-1

Boston Celtics
1956—lost Eastern Semi to Syracuse, 2-1
1957—**NBA Champs;** beat St. Louis, 4-3
1958—lost NBA Final to St.Louis, 4-2
1959—**NBA Champs;** beat Mpls Lakers, 4-0
1960—**NBA Champs;** beat St.Louis, 4-3
1961—**NBA Champs;** beat St.Louis, 4-1
1962—**NBA Champs;** beat L.A. Lakers, 4-3
1963—**NBA Champs;** beat L.A. Lakers, 4-2
1964—**NBA Champs;** beat S.F. Warriors, 4-1
1965—**NBA Champs;** beat L.A. Lakers, 4-1
1966—**NBA Champs;** beat L.A. Lakers, 4-3

1967—lost Eastern Final to Philadelphia, 4-1
1968—**NBA Champs;** beat L.A. Lakers, 4-2
1969—**NBA Champs;** beat L.A. Lakers, 4-3
1970—did not qualify for playoffs

Los Angeles Lakers
1979—lost Western Semifinal to Seattle, 4-1
1980—**NBA Champs;** beat Philadelphia, 4-2
1981—lost Western 1st Round to Houston, 2-1
1982—**NBA Champs;** beat Philadelphia, 4-2
1983—lost NBA Final to Philadelphia, 4-0
1984—lost NBA Final to Boston, 4-3
1985—**NBA Champs;** beat boston, 4-2
1986—lost Western Final to Houston, 4-1
1987—**NBA Champs;** beat Boston, 4-2
1988—**NBA Champs;** beat Detroit, 4-3
1989—lost NBA Final to Detroit, 4-0

Detroit Pistons
1987—lost Eastern Final to Boston, 4-3
1988—lost NBA Final to L.A. Lakers, 4-3
1989—**NBA Champs;** beat L.A. Lakers, 4-0
1990—**NBA Champs;** beat Portland, 4-1

Number One Draft Choices, 1966-90

Overall first choices in the NBA Draft since the abolition of the Territorial Draft in 1966. Players who became Rookie of the Year in **bold type.**

Year Team	Overall 1st Pick
1966 New York	Cazzie Russell, Michigan
1967 Detroit	Jimmy Walker, Providence
1968 Houston	Elvin Hayes, Houston
1969 Milwaukee	**Lew Alcindor,** UCLA*
1970 Detroit	Bob Lanier, St.Bonaventure
1971 Cleveland	Austin Carr, Notre Dame
1972 Portland	LaRue Martin, Loyola-Chicago
1973 Philadelphia	Doug Collins, Illinois St.
1974 Portland	Bill Walton, UCLA
1975 Atlanta	David Thompson, N.C.State (signed with Denver of ABA)
1976 Houston	John Lucas, Maryland
1977 Milwaukee	Kent Benson, Indiana
1978 Portland	Mychal Thompson, Minnesota
1979 LA Lakers	Magic Johnson, Michigan St.

Year Team	Overall 1st Pick
1980 Golden St	Joe Barry Carroll, Purdue
1981 Dallas	Mark Aguirre, DePaul
1982 LA Lakers	James Worthy, N.Carolina
1983 Houston	**Ralph Sampson,** Virginia
1984 Houston	Akeem Olajuwon, Houston
1985 New York	Patrick Ewing, Georgetown
1986 Cleveland	Brad Daugherty, N.Carolina
1987 San Antonio	**David Robinson,** Navy†
1988 LA Clippers	Danny Manning, Kansas
1989 Sacramento	Pervis Ellison, Louisville
1990 New Jersey	Derrick Coleman, Syracuse

*Alcindor changed his name to Kareem Abdul-Jabbar after the 1970-71 season.
†Robinson joined NBA for 1989-90 season after fulfilling military obligation.

American Basketball Association
ABA Finals, 1968-76

The American Basketball Assn. began play in 1967-68 as a 10-team rival of the 21 year-old NBA. The ABA, which introduced the three-point basket, a multi-colored ball and the All-Star Game Slam Dunk Contest, lasted nine seasons before folding following the 1975-76 season. Four ABA teams—Denver, Indiana, New York and San Antonio—survived to enter the NBA in 1976-77. The NBA also adopted the 3-pt basket (in 1979-80) and the All-Star Game Slam Dunk Contest. The older league, however, refused to take in the ABA ball.

In the chart below, each ABA champion's wins and losses are noted in parentheses after the series score.

Year	Winner	Head Coach	Seres	Loser	Head Coach
1968	Pittsburgh Pipers	Vince Cazetta	4-2 (WLLWLWW)	New Orleans Bucs	Babe McCarthy
1969	Oakland Oaks	Alex Hannum	4-1 (WLWWW)	Indiana Pacers	Bob Leonard
1970	Indiana Pacers	Bob Leonard	4-2 (WWLWLW)	Los Angeles Stars	Bill Sharman
1971	Utah Stars	Bill Sharman	4-3 (WWLLWLW)	Kentucky Colonels	Frank Ramsey
1972	Indiana Pacers	Bob Leonard	4-2 (WLWLWW)	New York Nets	Lou Carnesecca
1973	Indiana Pacers	Bob Leonard	4-3 (WLLWWLW)	Kentucky Colonels	Joe Mullaney
1974	New York Nets	Kevin Loughery	4-1 (WWWLW)	Utah Stars	Joe Mullaney
1975	Kentucky Colonels	Hubie Brown	4-1 (WWWLW)	Indiana Pacers	Bob Leonard
1976	New York Nets	Kevin Loughery	4-2 (WLWWLW)	Denver Nuggets	Larry Brown

Most Valuable Player

Winners scoring averages are provided; (*) denotes led league.

Multiple winners: Julius Erving (3); Mel Daniels (2).

Year		Pts
1968	Connie Hawkins, Pit., C	26.8*
1969	Mel Daniels, Ind., C	24.0
1970	Spencer Haywood, Den., C	30.0*
1971	Mel Daniels, Ind., C	21.0
1972	Artis Gilmore, Ky., C	23.8
1973	Billy Cunningham, Caro., F	24.1
1974	Julius Erving, NY, F	27.4*
1975	(Tie) George McGinnis, Ind., F	29.8*
	Julius Erving, NY, F	27.9
1976	Julius Erving, NY, F	29.3*

Rookie of the Year

Winners' scoring averages provided; (*) denotes led league.

Year		Pts
1968	Mel Daniels, Min., C	22.2
1969	Warren Armstrong†, Oak., G	21.5
1970	Spencer Haywood, Den., C	30.0*
1971	(Tie) Dan Issel, Ky., C	29.8*
	Charlie Scott, Vir., G	27.1
1972	Artis Gilmore, Ky., C	23.8
1973	Brian Taylor, NY, G	15.3
1974	Swen Nater, Vir-SA, C	14.1
1975	Marvin Barnes, St.L., C	24.0
1976	David Thompson, Den., F	26.0

†Armstrong changed his name to Warren Jabali after the 1970-71 season.

Coach of the Year

Previous season and winning season records are provided; (*) denotes division title.

Multiple winners: Larry Brown (3).

Year		Improvement		
1968	Vince Cazetta, Pit	—	to	54-24*
1969	Alex Hannum, Oak	22-56	to	60-18*
1970	Joe Belmont, Den	44-34	to	51-33*
	& Bill Sharman, LA	33-45	to	43-41
1971	Al Bianchi, Vir	44-40	to	55-29*
1972	Tom Nissalke, Dal	30-54	to	42-42
1973	Larry Brown, Caro	35-49	to	57-27*
1974	Babe McCarthy, Ky	56-28	to	53-31
	& Joe Mullaney, Utah	55-29*	to	51-33*
1975	Larry Brown, Den	37-47	to	65-19*
1976	Larry Brown, Den	65-19*	to	60-24*

Scoring Leaders

Multiple winners: Julius Erving (3).

Year		Gms	Pts	Avg
1968	Connie Hawkins, Pit	70	1875	26.8
1969	Rick Barry, Oak	35	1190	34.0
1970	Spencer Haywood, Den	84	2519	30.0
1971	Dan Issel, Ky	83	2480	29.8
1972	Charlie Scott, Vir	73	2524	34.6
1973	Julius Erving, Vir	71	2268	31.9
1974	Julius Erving, NY	84	2299	27.4
1975	George McGinnis, Ind	79	2353	29.8
1976	Julius Erving, NY	84	2462	29.3

ABA All-Star Game, 1968-76

The ABA All-Star Game was an Eastern Division vs Western Division contest from 1968-75. League membership had dropped to seven teams by 1976, the ABA's last season, so the team in first place at the break (Denver) played an All-Star team made up from the other six clubs.

Series: East won 5, West 3 and Denver 1.

Year	Result	Host	Coaches	Most Valuable Player
1968	East 126, West 120	Indiana	Jim Pollard, Babe McCarthy	Larry Brown, NO
1969	West 133, East 127	Louisville	Alex Hannum, Gene Rhodes	John Beasley, Dal.
1970	West 128, East 98	Indiana	Babe McCarthy, Bob Leonard	Spencer Haywood, Den.
1971	East 126, West 122	Carolina	Al Bianchi, Bill Sharman	Mel Daniels, Ind.
1972	East 142, West 115	Louisville	Joe Mullaney, Ladell Andersen	Dan Issel, Ky.
1973	West 123, East 111	Utah	Ladell Andersen, Larry Brown	Warren Jabali, Den.
1974	East 128, West 112	Virginia	Babe McCarthy, Joe Mullaney	Artis Gilmore, Ky.
1975	East 151, West 124	San Antonio	Kevin Loughery, Larry Brown	Freddie Lewis, St.L.
1976	Denver 144, ABA 138	Denver	Larry Brown, Kevin Loughery	David Thompson, Den.

Edmonton captain **Mark Messier** hoists the Oilers' fifth Stanley Cup after beating Boston four games to one.

HOCKEY

Edmonton recaptures Stanley Cup two years after Gretzky trade; Messier breaks Bourque's Hart; Parity everywhere but Quebec.

PRO HOCKEY

1989-90 YEAR IN REVIEW

by Eric Duhatschek

Wayne Who? No, it never really came to that. On the May 24th night that the Edmonton Oilers won their fifth Stanley Cup in seven years, the ghost of Wayne Gretzky cast a long shadow over the proceedings. Few people thought the Oilers could win without Gretzky, but here they were steamrolling over the Boston Bruins 4-1 in the fifth game of the final and winning the series by the same 4-1 margin.

The Oilers received a first-round scare from the Winnipeg Jets—they were down 3 games to 1 before winning in seven—and then breezed through the next three playoff rounds. They lost only three games and established once again that, as far as the NHL is concerned, the West remains the best. In six of the past seven years, the Stanley Cup has summered in the province of Alberta.

Imagine the Lakers trading Magic Johnson and you get a pretty good idea what the Oilers went through less than 20 months before—on Aug. 9, 1988—when Edmonton owner Peter Pocklington sent Gretzky to Los Angeles for a Kings' ransom in players and draft choices. Oilers' defenseman Kevin Lowe likened the trade to a "death in the family" and the team spent the next season grieving and stumbling. It took a full season and a first-round loss to Los Angeles in the '89 playoffs before the Oilers collectively shed their black armbands. "Part of it," said coach John Muckler, "was seeing how happy Wayne was to beat us last year."

The other part was general manager Glenn Sather's shrewd dealings. Only three games into the season, center Jimmy Carson, the principal player acquired in the Gretzky deal, walked out on the Oilers. Unhappy in Edmonton and disturbed by the constant pressure to live up to Gretzky's name, Carson sat out a month before getting his wish. Sather traded him to Detroit for four young

Eric Duhatschek has covered the Flames, the NHL and international hockey for the *Calgary Herald* since 1980. He is also a correspondent for *The Hockey News*.

Oilers' goalie **Bill Ranford** took over for Grant Fuhr and walked off with the Conn Smythe Trophy.

players: Joe Murphy, Adam Graves, Petr Klima, and Jeff Sharples. Sharples didn't play a game in Edmonton and Klima spent all but a handful of playoff minutes tied to the bench, but Murphy, Graves and Martin Gelinas, acquired from L.A. in the Gretzky deal, gave the Oilers a decent third line, one to supplement the team's veteran core of Mark Messier, Jari Kurri, Glenn Anderson and Lowe.

Messier played with a blend of skill and aggression in 1989–90 that no other NHL player could duplicate. Gradually, Messier stamped his mark on the Oilers' team, imbuing them with his deep-seated will-to-win and righting a franchise that looked to be on a downward slide. The numbers tell you only a little about Messier's impact, but the numbers were there too: 129 regular-season points (second only to Gretzky's 142) and 31 post-season points (tying him with linemate

Craig Simpson atop the playoff scoring list). Messier capped the year by winning his first-ever Hart Trophy as the league's most valuable player.

Perhaps just as improbable was the emergence of goalie Bill Ranford as the playoff MVP. Grant Fuhr, a constant source of strength in goal for the Oilers' four previous Cup-winning teams, suffered through a second injury-filled year that climaxed with his getting hurt again in the final week of the season. While Messier had a year to overcome the burden of replacing Gretzky, Ranford had only a week to shrug off Fuhr's mystique. Things looked bleak following an erratic playoff opener against Winnipeg when he stumbled through a 7-2 loss. From that low point, he picked up his play dramatically and in a delicious subplot to the story, outplayed the man he'd been traded for, Andy Moog, in the Stanley Cup finals. "I took a lot of flak," said Ranford, "but my teammates told me winning was the way for me to get back at everyone who jumped on me."

Gretzky made his most tangible contribution to the Oilers' cause by leading the Kings to a 4 games to 2 win over the Calgary Flames. Gretzky missed the first two games of the series because of a back injury, but played the final four, and picked up 10 points as the Kings eliminated the reigning Stanley Cup champion for the second consecutive year.

In the next round, Los Angeles fell to Edmonton in four consecutive games. Gretzky watched the last one from the press box, his back acting up again. He saw the Oilers win the Cup on television and cheerfully rooted them on. "The biggest disease in the world is jealousy," said Gretzky. "The guys on that club know I don't have that disease." No arguments there. Messier and Lowe decided on the final day to win one for Wayne. "He was a big part of our lives and we felt that would be the best way to show him how much we missed him," said Messier.

Gretzky, who earlier in the season surpassed Gordie Howe as the NHL's all-time scoring leader, consoled himself with another scoring championship. He won because the Pittsburgh Penguins' Mario Lemieux missed the final quarter of the regular season (21 games), also because of a back problem. Under healthier circumstances in January, Lemieux outscored Gretzky 4-0 at the All-Star Game in Pittsburgh and the Wales Conference routed the Campbells, 12-7. Still, the prevalence of injuries proved to be a major concern to the NHL brass. Too many impact players were lost for too many games because of back problems. Team chiropractors became as important as team coaches.

Part of the problem could be traced to a subtle shift in the way teams played in the late 1980s. Since the introduction of Megg nets—the easy-to-dislodge goals that were adopted to keep injuries down—players changed the way they broke for the front of the net. The result? More injuries than ever to goalies. Three of the best—Fuhr, Philadelphia's Ron Hextall and Calgary's Mike Vernon—missed big chunks of the season because of assorted hurts. Just as the National Football League adopted a rule to protect its quarterbacks, the NHL was left to ponder how to stop the assault on goaltenders. "It's a joke, it really is," said Hextall. "It's ruining the game."

Despite their loss to Edmonton in the finals, the Bruins proved to be one of the year's most engaging stories. General manager Harry Sinden, seeing that his best player, defenseman Ray Bourque, was about to join the thirtysomething generation, made a conscious decision to go for the Stanley Cup midway through the year. He brought in three players with a cumulative 28 years of experience—Dave Poulin and Brian Propp from Philadelphia and Dave Christian from Washington—to bolster a lineup that thinned out around the 10th man.

Coach Mike Milbury molded the disparate group into the NHL's only 100-point team and the Bruins took home the President's Trophy, awarded to the league's overall regular season champion. Bourque won the Norris Trophy as the league's top defenseman for the third time in four years. Perhaps the only reason he didn't win the Hart, too—Bourque came up two votes short in a controversial vote that saw him left off six ballots—was because of teammate Cam Neely. Neely scored 55 goals for a team that finished in the middle of the NHL pack in scoring and thus left voters wondering if the Bruins had one MVP or two.

They came, they saw, they bombed.

The scene played like something out of an O.Henry short story, dripping with irony. There was the Soviet Union's Viacheslav Fetisov, holding court for reporters in Bern, Switzerland's Allemand Stadium, scene of the 1990 World Hockey Championships.

Along came his coach, Viktor Tikhonov, a man Fetisov had warred with for years and not spoken to since rejoining the Soviet team from the New Jersey Devils. Tikhonov saw the crowd, peered into its middle and when he spotted Fetisov, gave him a brisk salute. A broad smile crossed his face as Tikhonov—clearly feeling vindicated about something—strolled out of the arena.

Some background may be in order here. Fetisov helped to precipitate one of the National Hockey League's most compelling stories of the 1989-90 season—the Soviet invasion—by staging a revolt against Tikhonov's draconian coaching practices. He and the three members of the Soviets' fabulous Green Line—Sergei Makarov, Igor Larionov and Vladimir Krutov—lobbied long and hard for permission to play in the NHL. Ultimately, they secured their releases, despite Tikhonov's bitter opposition.

The presence of nine Soviet players on NHL rosters was supposed to signal a new ice age. As the league moved into the 1990s, it seemed like the NHL was truly becoming a little global village. As it turned out, the Soviet invasion was all hype. With only a couple of exceptions—Calgary's Sergei Makarov and the Devils' Alexei Kasatonov, who signed on at midseason— the Soviet players coming to the NHL did not live up to their advance notices.

The reasons were many and varied. Denied a chance to train with their former teams and perhaps seduced by their new freedoms, the players did not show up in the same physical condition associated with the Tikhonov regime.

Their unfamiliarity with the NHL game —smaller ice surface, longer schedule— also worked against them. The 31-year-

Wide World Photos

Soviet coach **Viktor Tikhonov** hugs player **Pavel Bure** during final moments of Russia's 5-0 win over Czechoslovakia to capture the World Championship in May.

old Makarov proved to be the most notable exception. He won the Calder Trophy as the NHL's rookie of the year, the result of 86 regular-season points and a mercurial playing style that, from night to night, could be either dazzling or disappointing.

Then came the World Championships. With Makarov, Flames' teammate Sergei Priakin and Fetisov in the lineup—although playing only bit parts—the Soviets retained their world title and struck a blow for Tikhonov's approach, however inhumane it might be.

Perhaps Pittsburgh coach Bob Johnson, watching Makarov struggle overseas, said it best: "He's not the same player he was. He used to dominate. Now he's on the fourth line."

These days, the Soviets' dominating players are named Viacheslav Bykov, Andrei Khomutov and Valeri Kamenski. Bykov and Khomutov are headed for Switzerland next season. "And when they come back, they won't be the same either," predicted Johnson. "They miss that training regimen."

For his part, Tikhonov used the world championships as a forum to defend himself against his critics. Commenting on the fact that the NHL stripped him of his five best players, Tikhonov said: "We approach things differently. We grow our talent ourselves. We do not buy it."

There were signs, however, that the NHL's insatiable appetite for talent will gobble up ever more Soviet players. In June, 14 of the best young Soviet players were taken in the annual entry draft, including center Viacheslav Kozlov by Detroit in the third round, the earliest a Soviet player has ever been picked.

Even Makarov predicted that his countrymen would have a greater impact the second time around.

"Soviet players are good players, this we know," said Makarov the night he won the Calder Trophy. "The first year you come to a strange country and play a full NHL season, there's a period of adaptation. Next year, I can tell you, all of us will perform better."

Calgary produced a season that has become increasingly familiar to their supporters—following a strong regular season with a do-nothing playoff. Apart from the 1989 Stanley Cup victory, the Flames have lost playoff series in three of the past four years to teams that finished well below them in the standings. The most prominent casualty? Coach Terry Crisp. In his three years behind the bench, Crisp's teams won almost seven out of every 10 games they played, logging a record of 144-63-33 and a winning percentage of .669. His playoff failures, fueled by a player revolt against his Captain Queeg-like tactics, eventually cost him his job.

Crisp went down fighting, however. Against the Kings, the final game was decided in double overtime just after 3 A.M. EST when L.A.'s Mike Krushelnyski scored a goal lying flat on his back in front of the Calgary goal. One overtime period earlier, the Flames' Doug Gilmour had apparently scored the winning goal, only to have it disallowed by referee Denis Morel. Crisp bleated in characteristic fashion, but it did no good. The Flames were out on April 15 and 24 days later, so was he.

The beginnings of a hockey renaissance in New York came when the Rangers won the Patrick Division—the first time since 1942 they had won anything. Following the trade-a-week philosophy of ousted GM Phil Esposito, the Rangers chose a different path. They hired one of hockey's bright young men, 35-year-old Neil Smith, as their general manager and he brought in Roger Neilson as coach. Under Smith, the Rangers made two of the most controversial deals of the season—adding center Bernie Nicholls from Los Angeles and Mike Gartner from Minnesota—to punch up the team's popgun attack. Nicholls gave the Rangers a strong center-ice presence and was not afraid to say so. "Don't make me sound cocky or arrogant, but I think I've done for this team what Wayne did for L.A. last year," said Nicholls, immodestly. Maybe in time, but not in 1990. The Rangers exited in the second playoff round, losing to Washington.

Two of the league's most welcome goals, parity and purity, were both achieved in a single season. For the second consecutive year, fighting majors were reduced and that one-time symbol of the NHL—the goon, the player who dresses only to fight—looked to be going the way of the dinosaur.

Apart from one truly awful team, the Quebec Nordiques, the NHL completed its most competitive season since the 1967 expansion doubled the size of the league from six teams to 12. The Nordiques won only 12 games and their 31-point total was the league's lowest since the expansion Washington Capitals managed only 21 in 1974-75. Heads inevitably rolled. The Nords, borrowing a page from the Rangers' book, made a daring move by hiring coach Pierre Page away from Minnesota and installing him as their general manager. Page's unspoken mandate will be to finish last overall one more time so that Quebec can draft Eric Lindros, considered the new Lemieux, in the 1991 entry draft.

Exclude the Nordiques and only 35 points separated the Bruins from 20th-place Vancouver. That closeness carried over into the first playoff round. One division champion, Calgary, fell, while two others, Boston and Chicago, were stretched to seven games by fourth-place teams.

Parity added a certain mystery to postseason play, but it also led to a significant debate within NHL circles. Does it mean competitiveness or mediocrity? There was a school of thought that said the league needed a dominant team—an NHL version of the NFL's San Francisco 49ers—to establish a benchmark for the rest of the pack.

The Montreal Canadiens used to set that standard, having won an unprecedented 23 Stanley Cups. But even there coach Pat Burns predicted the age of NHL dynasties was over. "The teams are too close now," said Burns. "When you're on top, you can get vertigo. You look down and your head starts to spin."

For a change, the NHL's coaching merry-go-round saw only six men thrown off the carousel (and one of them got back on). Apart from Crisp and Quebec's Michel Bergeron, three Patrick Division teams made changes in midseason: New Jersey replaced Jim Schoenfeld with John Cunniff, Craig Patrick took over from Gene Ubriaco in Pittsburgh, and in

Washington Bryan Murray's job was given to his brother Terry. Patrick, whose grandfather Lester is the man the division is named after, later replaced himself with Bob Johnson, the ex-Calgary coach and executive director of USA Hockey, the governing body of amateur hockey in the U.S. The sixth coach to lose his job was Jacques Demers, who was fired by Detroit after taking the Red Wings from first place to last in the Norris Division. His replacement was Bryan Murray.

Three general managers were also fired, Bobby Clarke in Philadelphia; Tony Esposito in Pittsburgh; and Martin Madden in Quebec. It took Clarke less than two months to resurface, however, accepting the Minnesota GM position from the team's new ownership triumvirate of Norman Green, Howard Baldwin and Morris Belzberg. The trio purchased the North Stars from George and Gordon Gund, who were in turn granted an expansion franchise for the San Francisco Bay area, to begin operations for the 1991-92 season. Shortly after setting up shop in Minnesota, Clarke signed former Montreal captain Bob Gainey as the team's new coach.

The NHL took an unexpectedly bold step in December, unveiling a long-range plan that could see seven expansion teams added to its fraternity by the turn of the century. Two more teams are to be added by the 1992-93 season and over 50 applicants have expressed interest in shelling out a whopping $50 million for the right to join the league. In the last expansion 10 years ago, franchises went for $16 million apiece.

The season also marked the first time NHL players allowed their salaries to be published. Unlike players from the three other major professional team sports, NHL players had kept their salary structure a closely guarded secret, one that ultimately kept their pay relatively low. All that changed in January when the NHL Players Association made its salary figures public.

The highest paid player turned out to be Lemieux, who topped Gretzky's annual salary $2 million to $1.72 million (a shortfall the Kings remedied two days later by signing their captain to an eight-year, $29.7 million contract extension that will make him hockey's first $4 million

Wide World Photos

All-Star back ailments sidelined **Wayne Gretzky** (left) during the playoffs and **Mario Lemieux** for much of the regular season.

player by 1996-97). The league's best bargain? Easy: Brett Hull of St. Louis, who, for $125,000 a year, scored 72 goals during the regular season, a record for right wingers. Even Hull's father Bobby, the storied Golden Jet, never scored more than 58 in a season. The Golden Brett moved into Lemieux's financial district in June by signing a three-year deal worth $6 million. He also won the Lady Byng Trophy for sportsmanship, presented to him following the season by his father, who won the award in 1965.

Hull's contract was one of the last negotiated by player agent Bob Goodenow, who was named in January to replace Alan Eagleson as the head of the NHLPA. Eagleson will serve until the end of 1991, meaning he will be in charge of the next collective bargaining negotiations with NHL owners.

The league lost a legendary defenseman and one of its most colorful curmudgeons during the season when seven-time Norris Trophy winner Doug Harvey died in December at age 65 and Harold Ballard, the crusty 86-year-old owner of

St. Louis right wing **Brett Hull** (right) celebrates his 50th goal of the season with his Hall of Fame father **Bobby** on Feb. 7.

the Toronto Maple Leafs, died in April. Both deaths came after long illnesses.

Harvey played 14 of his 21 seasons with Montreal and helped lead the Canadiens to six Stanley Cups. Ballard, on the other hand, presided over the worst years in the history of the Toronto franchise, from 1971 to 1989. Still, the Leafs' lack of success, never got in the way of their owner's acerbic tongue. To Ballard, NHL president John Ziegler was "a know-nothing shrimp." "Women," he said, were most useful "on their backs." Television evangelism was a "racket," but he wouldn't mind getting in on it. Well, you get the idea.

Ballard spent his last days in Toronto, drifting in and out of consciousness, so it was unclear if he was sound enough to see the strides made by his hockey club. The Leafs won as many games as they lost for the first time since 1978 and were finally making a push towards respectability.

So too was the Detroit Red Wings' Bob Probert. Probert watched much of the 1989-90 season from the lounge of a state prison in Rochester, Minn., while he served a 90-day sentence for cocaine possession. Upon his release and after a review by Ziegler, he was reinstated by the league on March 9. Probert actually returned to the Red Wings lineup for the final four games of the season and made an immediate impact, scoring three times. His primary goal, however, was to stay clean and sober. "My life was totally out of hand," he said. "I'm lucky I didn't hurt anybody, kill anybody driving or something...."

Despite Probert's return, Detroit missed the playoffs for the first time in four years. The Wings watched as Chicago won the improving Norris Division for the second year in a row and then fell to the Oilers in the conference finals.

Since entering the league as a refugee from the WHA in 1979, it seems like Edmonton is always there at the end. Only two franchises in the 73-year history of the NHL—Montreal and Toronto—have won more Stanley Cups than the Oilers have in just 11 seasons. Of the seven Oilers whose names appear on the Cup five times, Lowe is the oldest at 30. Messier is only 29. Lowe bumped into Canadiens' legend, Henri Richard, during the playoffs and remembered that Richard played on 11 Cup winners. Said Lowe: "That's my goal now."

Five down, six to go. □

THE 1991 INFORMATION PLEASE SPORTS ALMANAC

HOCKEY STATISTICS

THE SEASON IN REVIEW
1989-1990
NHL • WORLD • U.S. COLLEGES

SEC A

PAGE 303

Final NHL Standings

Division champions (*) and playoff qualifiers (†) are noted. Number of seasons listed after each head coach refers to current tenure with club.

Wales Conference

Adams Division

	W	L	T	Pts	Goals For	Goals Opp	+/−
*Boston	46	25	9	**101**	289	232	+57
†Buffalo	45	27	8	**98**	286	248	+38
†Montreal	41	28	11	**93**	288	234	+54
†Hartford	38	33	9	**85**	275	268	+7
Quebec	12	61	7	**31**	240	407	−167

Head Coaches: Bos—Mike Milbury (1st season) **Buf**—Rick Dudley (1st); **Mon**—Pat Burns (2nd); **Hart**—Rick Ley (1st); **Que**—Michel Bergeron (1st).

Patrick Division

	W	L	T	Pts	Goals For	Goals Opp	+/−
*NY Rangers	36	31	13	**85**	279	267	+12
†New Jersey	37	34	9	**83**	295	288	+7
†Washington	36	38	6	**78**	284	275	+9
†NY Islanders	31	38	11	**73**	281	288	−7
Pittsburgh	32	40	8	**72**	318	359	−41
Philadelphia	30	39	11	**71**	290	297	−7

Head Coaches: NYR—Roger Neilson (1st season); **NJ**—replaced Jim Schoenfeld (3rd, 6-6-2) with assistant John Cunniff on Nov.6; **Wash**—replaced Bryan Murray (9th, 18-24-4) with brother Terry Murray on Jan.15; **NYI**—Al Arbour (2nd); **Pit**—replaced Gene Ubriaco (2nd, 10-14-2) with Craig Patrick on Dec.5; **Phi**—Paul Holmgren (2nd).

Campbell Conference

Norris Division

	W	L	T	Pts	Goals For	Goals Opp	+/−
*Chicago	41	33	6	**88**	316	294	+22
†St.Louis	37	34	9	**83**	295	279	+16
†Toronto	38	38	4	**80**	337	358	−21
†Minnesota	36	40	4	**76**	284	290	−6
Detroit	28	38	14	**70**	288	323	−35

Head Coaches: Chi—Mike Keenan (2nd season); **StL**—Brian Sutter (2nd); **Tor**—Doug Carpenter (1st); **Min**—Pierre Page (2nd); **Det**—Jacques Demers (4th).

Smythe Division

	W	L	T	Pts	Goals For	Goals Opp	+/−
*Calgary	42	23	15	**99**	348	265	+83
†Edmonton	38	28	14	**90**	315	283	+32
†Winnipeg	37	32	11	**85**	298	290	+8
†Los Angeles	34	39	7	**75**	338	337	+1
Vancouver	25	41	14	**64**	245	306	−61

Head Coaches: Calg—Terry Crisp (3rd season); **Edm**—John Muckler (1st); **Win**—Bob Murdoch (1st); **LA**—Tom Webster (1st); **Van**—Bob McCammon (3rd).

Home & Away, Division Records

Team-by-team records (wins-losses-ties) for games at home, away and within the division. Teams are ranked by overall points.

Wales Conference

	Pts	Home	Away	Div
Boston	101	23-13-4	23-12-5	18-10-4
Buffalo	98	27-11-2	18-16-6	20-9-3
Montreal	93	26- 8-6	15-20-5	17-12-3
Hartford	85	17-18-5	21-15-4	14-16-3
NY Rangers	85	20-11-9	16-20-4	15-16-4
New Jersey	83	22-15-3	15-19-6	18-12-5
Washington	78	19-18-3	17-20-3	17-16-1
NY Islanders	73	15-17-8	16-21-3	10-16-8
Pittsburgh	72	22-15-3	10-25-5	18-14-3
Philadelphia	71	17-19-4	12-21-7	13-18-4
Quebec	31	8-26-6	4-35-1	3-26-3

Campbell Conference

	Pts	Home	Away	Div
Calgary	99	28- 7- 5	14-16-10	16-12-4
Edmonton	90	23-11- 6	15-17- 8	18-10-4
Chicago	88	25-13- 2	16-20- 4	14-15-2
Winnipeg	85	22-13- 5	15-19- 6	15-12-4
St.Louis	83	20-15- 5	17-19- 4	14-16-2
Toronto	80	24-14- 2	14-24- 2	16-15-1
Minnesota	76	26-12- 2	10-28- 2	17-14-1
Los Angeles	75	21-16- 3	13-23- 4	11-14-6
Detroit	70	20-14- 6	8-24- 8	14-15-2
Vancouver	64	13-16-11	12-25- 3	6-18-8

NHL Individual Leaders
Scoring

	Pos	GP	G	A	Pts	PM
Wayne Gretzky, LA	C	73	40	102	142	42
Mark Messier, Edm	C	79	45	84	129	79
Steve Yzerman, Det	C	79	62	65	127	79
Mario Lemieux, Pit	C	59	45	78	123	78
Brett Hull, St.L	R	80	72	41	113	24
Bernie Nicholls, LA-NYR	C	79	39	73	112	86
Pierre Turgeon, Buf	C	80	40	66	106	29
Pat LaFontaine, NYI	C	74	54	51	105	38
Paul Coffey, Pit	D	80	29	74	103	95
Joe Sakic, Que	C	80	39	63	102	27
Adam Oates, St.L	C	80	23	79	102	30
Luc Robitaille, LA	L	80	52	49	101	38
Ron Francis, Hart	C	80	32	69	101	73
Brian Bellows, Min	L	80	55	44	99	72
Rick Tocchet, Phi	R	75	37	59	96	196

Goals

B.Hull, StL	72
Yzerman, Det	62
Neely, Bos	55
Bellows, Min	55
LaFontaine, NYI	54
Robitaille, LA	52
Leeman, Tor	51
Richer, Mon	51

Assists

Gretzky, LA	102
Messier, Edm	84
Oates, Montreal	79
M.Lemieux, Pit	78
Coffey, Pit	74
Nicholls, LA-NYR	73
Francis, Hart	69
Gilmour, Calg	67

Power Play Goals

B.Hull, StL	27
Neely, Bos	25
Bellows, Min	21
Gartner, Min-NYR	21
Robitaille, LA	20

Short-Handed Goals

Yzerman, Det	7
McLlwain, Win	7
Messier, Edm	6
MacTavish, Edm	6
Five tied with 4	

Plus/Minus

P.Cavallini, StL	+38
Richer, Mon	+35
Macoun, Calg	+34
Corson, Mon	+33
Makarov, Calg	+33

Penalty Minutes

McRae, Min	351
May, Wash	339
McSorley, LA	322
Mallette, NYR	305
Van Dorp, Chi	303

Goaltending
(Minimum 25 games)

	GP	Min	GA	SO	Avg
Mike Liut, Hart-Wash	37	2161	91	4	2.526
Patrick Roy, Mon	54	3173	134	3	2.534
Reggie Lemelin, Bos	43	2310	108	2	2.81
Andy Moog, Bos	46	2536	122	3	2.886
Daren Puppa, Buf	56	3241	156	1	2.889
Jacques Cloutier, Chi	43	2178	112	2	3.09
Mike Vernon, Calg	47	2795	146	0	3.13
Bob Essensa, Win	36	2035	107	1	3.15
Bill Ranford, Edm	56	3107	165	1	3.19
Don Beaupre, Was	48	2793	150	2	3.222
Jon Casey, Min	61	3407	183	3	3.223

Wins

	W- L -T
Roy, Mon	31-16-5
Puppa, Buf	31-16-6
Casey, Min	31-22-4
Moog, Bos	24-10-7
Ranford, Edm	24-16-9

Shutouts

Liut, Hart-Wash	4
Roy, Mon	3
Moog, Bos	3
Casey, Min	3
Fitzpatrick, NYI	3

Save Pct.

Roy, Mon	.912
Liut, Hart-Wash	.905
Puppa, Buf	.903
Malarchuk, Buf	.903
Fitzpatrick, NYI	.898

Losses

	W- L -T
McLean, Van	21-30-10
Tugnutt, Que	5-24- 3
Wregget, Phi	22-24- 3
Burke, NJ	22-22- 6
Casey, Min	31-22- 4

NHL All-Star Game
Wales 12, Campbell 7

Date: Jan.21, at Pittsburgh Civic Arena; **Coaches:** Pat Burns, Montreal (Wales), Terry Crisp, Calgary (Campbell); **MVP:** Mario Lemieux, Pittsburgh (Wales), 4 goals.

Wales Conference

Starters	G	A	Pts	PM
Mario Lemieux, Pittsburgh, C	4	0	4	0
Cam Neely, Boston, RW	1	2	3	2
Paul Coffey, Pittsburgh, D	0	2	2	0
Brian Propp, Philadelphia, LW	0	1	1	0
Ray Bourque, Boston, D	0	1	1	0
Patrick Roy, Montreal, G	0	0	0	2
Bench				
Kirk Muller, New Jersey, LW	2	1	3	0
Pierre Turgeon, Buffalo, RW	2	0	2	0
Dave Andreychuk, Buffalo, LW	1	1	2	0
Rick Tocchet, Philadelphia, RW	1	1	2	0
Ron Francis, Hartford, C	0	2	2	0
Joe Sakic, Quebec, C	0	2	2	0
Shayne Corson, Montreal, LW	1	0	1	0
Kevin Hatcher, Washington, D	0	1	1	0
Phil Housley, Buffalo, D	0	1	1	0
Pat LaFontaine, NY Islanders, C	0	1	1	0
Chris Chelios, Montreal, D	0	0	0	0
Brian Leetch, NY Rangers, D	0	0	0	0
Daren Puppa, Buffalo, G	0	0	0	0
Stephane Richer, Montreal, RW	0	0	0	0
TOTALS	12	16	28	4

Goaltenders	Mins	Shots	Saves	GA
Patrick Roy, Montreal	29:14	11	8	3
Daren Puppa, Buffalo	30:46	31	27	4
TOTALS	60:00	42	35	7

Campbell Conference

Starters	G	A	Pts	PM
Brett Hull, St.Louis, RW	0	3	3	0
Luc Robitaille, Los Angeles, LW	2	0	2	0
Al MacInnis, Calgary, D	1	0	1	0
Kevin Lowe, Edmonton, D	0	1	1	0
Wayne Gretzky, Los Angeles, C	0	0	0	0
Mike Vernon, Calgary, G	0	0	0	0
Bench				
Steve Yzerman, Detroit, C	1	2	3	0
Joe Mullen, Calgary, RW	1	1	2	0
Doug Smail, Winnipeg, LW	1	1	2	2
Mark Messier, Edmonton, LW	1	0	1	0
Bernie Nicholls, LA-NYR, C	0	1	1	0
Joe Nieuwendyk, Calgary, LW	0	1	1	0
Paul Cavallini, St.Louis, D	0	0	0	0
Steve Duchesne, Los Angeles, D	0	0	0	0
Mike Gartner, Minnesota, RW	0	0	0	0
Al Iafrate, Toronto, D	0	0	0	2
Jari Kurri, Edmonton, RW	0	0	0	0
Kirk McLean, Vancouver, G	0	0	0	0
Doug Wilson, Chicago, D	0	0	0	0
TOTALS	7	10	17	4

Goaltenders	Mins	Shots	Saves	GA
Mike Vernon, Calgary	29:14	21	13	8
Kirk McLean, Vancouver	30:46	24	20	4
TOTALS	60:00	45	33	12

Score by Periods

	1	2	3	Final
Campbell (West)	2	2	3—	7
Wales (East)	7	2	3—	12

Power plays—CAMPBELL (1 for 2), WALES (0 for 2). **Officials**—Kerry Fraser (Referee), Bob Hodges and Dan McCourt (Linesmen). **Attendance**—16,235.

Team by Team Statistics

At least 14 points scored for skaters and five games played for goaltenders. Players who played with more than one team during the regular season are listed with their final club; (*) denotes rookies.

Boston Bruins

Top Scorers	Pos	GP	G	A	Pts	+/−	PM
Cam Neely	R	76	55	37	92	+10	117
Ray Bourque	D	76	19	65	84	+31	50
Craig Janney	C	55	24	38	62	+3	4
Bob Carpenter	L	80	25	31	56	−3	97
Bob Sweeney	C	70	22	24	46	+2	93
Dave Poulin	C	60	15	27	42	+16	24
PHI		28	9	8	17	+5	12
BOS		32	6	19	25	+11	12
Brian Propp	L	54	16	24	40	+5	41
PHI		40	13	15	28	+3	31
BOS		14	3	9	12	+2	10
Dave Christian	R	78	15	25	40	−8	12
WAS		28	3	8	11	−12	4
BOS		50	12	17	29	+4	8
Andy Brickley	L	43	12	28	40	+11	8
John Carter	L	76	17	22	39	+17	26
Greg Hawgood	C	77	11	27	38	+12	76
Glen Wesley	D	78	9	27	36	+6	48
Garry Galley	D	71	8	27	35	+2	75
Randy Burridge	L	63	17	15	32	+9	47
Bob Gould	R	77	8	17	25	−3	92
Jim Wiemer	D	61	5	14	19	+11	63
Rob Cimetta*	L	47	8	9	17	+4	33
Brian Lawton	L	35	7	7	14	−15	30
MIN		13	2	1	3	−2	6
QUE		14	5	6	11	−9	10
BOS		8	0	0	0	−4	14

Acquired: Christian from Wash.(Dec.13); Poulin from Phila.(Jan.16); Lawton as free agent (Feb.6); Propp from Phila.(Mar.2).

Goaltending	GP	Min	Avg	SO	Record
Reggie Lemelin	43	2310	2.81	2	22-15-2
Andy Moog	46	2536	2.89	3	24-10-7
BOSTON	80	4856	2.87	5	46-25-9

Assists: Moog (3). **PM:** Lemelin (32), Moog (18).

Buffalo Sabres

Top Scorers	Pos	GP	G	A	Pts	+/−	PM
Pierre Turgeon	C	80	40	66	106	+10	29
Dave Andreychuk	L	73	40	42	82	+6	42
Phil Housley	D	80	21	60	81	+11	32
Christian Ruuttu	C	75	19	41	60	+9	66
Rick Vaive	R	70	29	19	48	+9	74
Doug Bodger	D	71	12	36	48	E	64
Alexander Mogilny*	L	65	15	28	43	+8	16
Mike Foligno	R	61	15	25	40	+13	99
Scott Arniel	L	79	18	14	32	+4	77
Dave Snuggerud*	R	80	14	16	30	+8	41
Mike Ramsey	D	73	4	21	25	+21	47
Uwe Krupp	D	74	3	20	23	+15	85
Mike Hartman	L	60	11	10	21	−10	211
Jay Wells	D	60	3	17	20	+5	129
PHI		59	3	16	19	+4	129
BUF		1	0	1	1	+1	0
Benoit Hogue	C	45	11	7	18	E	79
Grant Ledyard	D	67	2	13	15	+2	37
Ken Priestlay	C	35	7	7	14	−1	14
Dean Kennedy	D	80	2	12	14	−12	53

Acquired: Wells from Phi.(Mar.6).

Goaltending	GP	Min	Avg	SO	Record
Daren Puppa	56	3241	2.89	1	31-16-6
Clint Malarchuk	29	1596	3.35	0	14-11-2
BUFFALO	80	4850	3.07	1	45-27-8

Assists: Puppa (4), Malarchuk (2). **PM:** Malarchuk (14), Puppa (4).

Calgary Flames

Top Scorers	Pos	GP	G	A	Pts	+/−	PM
Joe Nieuwendyk	C	79	45	50	95	+32	40
Doug Gilmour	C	78	24	67	91	+20	54
Al MacInnis	D	79	28	62	90	+20	82
Sergei Makarov*	R	80	24	62	86	+33	55
Gary Suter	D	76	16	60	76	+4	97
Gary Roberts	L	78	39	33	72	+31	222
Joey Mullen	R	78	36	33	69	+6	24
Theo Fleury	C	80	31	35	66	+22	157
Paul Ranheim*	L	80	26	28	54	+27	23
Brian MacLellan	L	65	20	18	38	−3	26
Jamie Macoun	D	78	8	27	35	+34	70
Joel Otto	C	75	13	20	33	+4	116
Jiri Hrdina	R	64	12	18	30	+10	31
Dana Murzyn	D	78	7	13	20	+19	140
Brad McCrimmon	D	79	4	15	19	+18	78
Ric Nattress	D	49	1	14	15	+14	26

Goaltending	GP	Min	Avg	SO	Record
Mike Vernon	47	2795	3.13	0	23-14- 9
Rick Wamsley	36	1969	3.26	2	18- 8- 6
CALGARY	80	4895	3.25	2	42-23-15

Assists: Vernon (3). **PM:** Vernon (21), Wamsley (4), Steve Guenette (2).

Chicago Blackhawks

Top Scorers	Pos	GP	G	A	Pts	+/−	PM
Steve Larmer	R	80	31	59	90	+25	40
Denis Savard	C	60	27	53	80	+8	56
Doug Wilson	D	70	23	50	73	+13	40
Steve Thomas	L	76	40	30	70	−3	91
Adam Creighton	C	80	34	36	70	+4	224
Jeremy Roenick*	C	78	26	40	66	+2	54
Troy Murray	C	68	17	38	55	−2	86
Dirk Graham	R	73	22	32	54	+1	102
Michel Goulet	L	65	20	30	50	−32	51
QUE		57	16	29	45	−33	42
CHI		8	4	1	5	+1	9
Greg Gilbert	L	70	12	25	37	+27	54
Dave Manson	D	59	5	23	28	+4	301
Jocelyn Lemieux	R	73	14	13	27	−1	108
MON		34	4	2	6	−1	61
CHI		39	10	11	21	E	47
Keith Brown	D	67	5	20	25	+26	87
Bob Murray	D	49	5	19	24	+3	45
Al Secord	L	43	14	7	21	+5	131
Mike Hudson	C	49	9	12	21	−3	56
Trent Yawney	D	70	5	15	20	−6	82
Duane Sutter	R	72	4	14	18	−2	156
Steve Konroyd	D	75	3	14	17	+6	34

Acquired: Lemieux from Mon.(Jan.5); Goulet from Que.(Mar.5).

Goaltending	GP	Min	Avg	SO	Record
Jacques Cloutier	43	2178	3.09	2	18-15-2
Greg Millen	49	2900	3.89	1	19-25-5
STL	21	1245	2.94	1	11- 7-3
QUE	18	1080	5.28	0	3-14-1
CHI	10	575	3.34	0	5- 4-1
CHICAGO	80	4835	3.65	2	41-33-6

Assists: Millen (1); **PM:** Cloutier (8).
Acquired: Millen from Que.(Mar.5).
Note: Alain Chevrier traded to Pit.(Mar.6).

Team by Team Statistics (Cont.)

Detroit Red Wings

Top Scorers	Pos	GP	G	A	Pts	+/−	PM
Steve Yzerman	C	79	62	65	127	−5	79
Gerard Gallant	L	69	36	44	80	−6	254
Bernie Federko	C	73	17	40	57	−8	24
Shawn Burr	L	76	24	32	56	+14	82
John Chabot	C	69	9	40	49	+5	24
Steve Chiasson	....D	67	14	28	42	−16	114
Jimmy Carson	C	48	21	18	39	−7	8
EDM		4	1	2	3	−2	0
DET		44	20	16	36	−5	8
Joey Kocur	......R	71	16	20	36	−5	268
Dave Barr	......R	62	10	25	35	+4	45
Marc Habscheid	...R	66	15	11	26	+1	33
Rick Zombo	......D	77	5	20	25	+13	95
Daniel Shank*	....R	57	11	13	24	+1	143
Lee Norwood	.....D	64	8	14	22	+15	95
Borje Salming	....D	49	2	17	19	+20	52
Mike O'Connell	..D	66	4	14	18	−11	22
Greg C.Adams	....D	35	4	10	14	−2	33
QUE		7	1	3	4	−2	17
DET		28	3	7	10	E	16

Acquired: Carson from Edm.(Nov.2); Adams from Que. (Dec.4).

Goaltending	GP	Min	Avg	SO	Record
Sam St.Laurent	14	607	3.76	0	2- 6- 1
Tim Cheveldae*	...28	1600	3.79	0	10- 9- 8
Greg Stefan	7	359	4.01	0	1- 5- 0
Glen Hanlon	45	2290	4.03	1	15-18- 5
DETROIT	80	4880	3.97	1	28-38-14

Assists: Hanlon (3), Cheveldae (1), Stefan (1); **PM:** Hanlon (24), Stefan (4), Cheveldae (2), St.Laurent (2).

Edmonton Oilers

Top Scorers	Pos	GP	G	A	Pts	+/−	PM
Mark Messier	C	79	45	84	129	+19	79
Jari Kurri	.........R	78	33	60	93	+18	48
Glenn Anderson	...R	73	34	38	72	−1	107
Petr Klima	L	76	30	33	63	−9	72
DET		13	5	5	10	−8	6
EDM		63	25	28	53	−1	66
Esa Tikkanen	L	79	30	33	63	+17	161
Craig Simpson	L	80	29	32	61	−2	180
Craig MacTavish	..C	80	21	22	43	+13	89
Steve Smith	......D	75	7	34	41	+6	171
Kevin Lowe	.......D	78	7	26	33	+18	140
Joe Murphy	C	71	10	19	29	+5	60
DET		9	3	1	4	+4	4
EDM		62	7	18	25	+1	56
Mark Lamb	C	58	12	16	28	+10	42
Martin Gelinas*	...L	46	17	8	25	E	30
Randy Gregg	....D	48	4	20	24	+24	42
Charlie Huddy	.....D	70	1	23	24	−13	56
Adam Graves	L	76	9	13	22	E	136
DET		13	0	1	1	−5	13
EDM		63	9	12	21	+5	123
Vladimir Ruzicka*	.C	25	11	6	17	−21	10
Craig Muni	......D	71	5	12	17	+22	81
Geoff Smith*	......D	74	4	11	15	+13	52
Reijo Ruotsalainen	.D	41	3	12	15	−5	20
NJ		31	2	5	7	−4	14
EDM		10	1	7	8	−1	6

Acquired: Klima, Murphy and Graves from Det.(Nov.2); Ruotsalainen from NJ (Mar.6).

Goaltending	GP	Min	Avg	SO	Record
Pokey Reddick	11	604	3.08	0	5- 4- 2
Bill Radford	56	3107	3.19	1	24-16- 9
Grant Fuhr	21	1081	3.89	1	9- 7- 3
EDMONTON	80	4882	3.48	2	38-28-14

Assists: Ranford (2), Mike Greenlay (1); **PM:** Ranford (18), Fehr (2).

Hartford Whalers

Top Scorers	Pos	GP	G	A	Pts	+/−	PM
Ron Francis	C	80	32	69	101	+13	73
Pat Verbeek	.......R	80	44	45	89	+1	228
Kevin Dineen	......R	67	25	41	66	+7	164
Scott Young	.......R	80	24	40	64	−24	47
Ray Ferraro	C	79	25	29	54	−15	109
Dean Evason	.......R	78	18	25	43	+7	138
Dave Babych	......D	72	6	37	43	−16	62
Mikael Andersson	..L	50	13	24	37	E	6
Brad Shaw*	......D	64	3	32	35	+2	41
Todd Krygier*	C	58	18	12	30	+4	52
Randy Cunneyworth.L		71	14	15	29	−11	75
WIN		28	5	6	11	−7	34
HAR		43	9	9	18	−4	41
Dave Tippett	L	66	8	19	27	E	32
Mike Tomlak*	C	70	7	14	21	+5	48
Yvon Corriveau	L	63	13	7	20	+2	72
WAS		50	9	6	15	−1	50
HAR		13	4	1	5	+3	22
Jody Hull	........R	38	7	10	17	−6	21
Randy Ladouceur	..D	71	3	12	15	−6	143

Acquired: Cunneyworth from Win.(Dec.13); Corriveau from Wash.(Mar.5).

Goaltending	GP	Min	Avg	SO	Record
Kay Whitmore	9	442	3.53	0	4- 2- 1
Peter Sidorkiewicz	..46	2703	3.57	1	19-19-7
HARTFORD	80	4843	3.32	4	38-33-9

Assists: Sidorkiewicz (1), Whitmore (1); **PM:** Sidorkiewicz (4), Whitmore (4).
Note: Mike Liut traded to Wash.(Mar.5).

Los Angeles Kings

Top Scorers	Pos	GP	G	A	Pts	+/−	PM
Wayne Gretzky	...C	73	40	102	142	+8	42
Luc Robitaille	L	80	52	49	101	+8	38
Tomas Sandstrom	..R	76	32	39	71	−11	128
NYR		48	19	19	38	−10	100
LA		28	13	20	33	−1	28
John Tonelli	L	73	31	37	68	−8	62
Steve Duchesne	...D	79	20	42	62	−3	36
Steve Kasper	C	77	17	28	45	+4	27
Mike Krushelnyski	.L	63	16	25	41	+7	50
Dave Taylor*	.....R	58	15	26	41	+17	96
Larry Robinson	...D	64	7	32	39	+7	34
Robert Kudelski	...R	62	23	13	36	−7	49
Marty McSorley	...D	75	15	21	36	+2	322
Tony Granato	.....R	56	12	24	36	−1	122
NYR		37	7	18	25	+1	77
LA		19	5	6	11	−2	45
Todd Elik*	C	48	10	23	33	+4	41
Mikko Makela	....R	65	9	17	26	−14	18
NYI		20	2	3	5	−10	2
LA		45	7	14	21	−4	16
Brian Benning	....D	55	6	19	25	−2	106
STL		7	1	1	2	−3	2
LA		48	5	18	23	+1	104
Keith Crowder	....R	55	6	13	17	+2	93

Acquired: Benning from StL.(Nov.10); Makela from NYI (Nov.29); Sandstrom and Granato from NYR (Jan.20).

Goaltending	GP	Min	Avg	SO	Record
Ron Scott*	12	654	3.67	0	5- 6-0
Mario Gosselin	...26	1226	3.87	0	7-11-1
Kelly Hrudey	52	2860	4.07	2	22-21-6
LOS ANGELES	...80	4846	4.17	2	34-39-7

Assists: None; **PM:** Hrudey (18), Scott (2).

Minnesota North Stars

Top Scorers

Top Scorers	Pos	GP	G	A	Pts	+/−	PM
Brian Bellows	L	80	55	44	99	−3	72
Neal Broten	C	80	23	62	85	−16	45
Dave Gagner	C	79	40	38	78	−1	54
Mike Modano*	C	80	29	46	75	−7	63
Larry Murphy	D	77	10	58	68	−13	44
Ulf Dahlen	R	76	20	22	42	−3	30
NYR		63	18	18	36	−4	30
MIN		13	2	4	6	+1	0
Aaron Broten	C	77	19	17	36	−23	58
NJ		42	10	8	18	−15	36
MIN		35	9	9	18	−8	22
Don Barber*	R	45	15	19	34	+4	32
Basil McRae	L	66	9	17	26	−5	351
Shawn Chambers	D	78	8	18	26	−2	81
Stewart Gavin	L	80	12	13	25	+9	76
Gaetan Duchesne	L	72	12	8	20	+5	33
Perry Berezan	C	64	3	12	15	−4	31
Ville Siren	D	53	1	13	14	+1	60

Acquired: A.Broten from NJ (Jan.5); Dahlen from NYR (Mar.6).

Goaltending

Goaltending	GP	Min	Avg	SO	Record
Jon Casey	61	3407	3.22	3	31-22-4
Daniel Berthiaume	29	1627	3.69	1	11-14-3
WIN	24	1387	3.72	1	10-11-3
MIN	5	240	3.50	0	1- 3-0
Kari Takko	21	1012	4.03	0	4-12-0
MINNESOTA	80	4833	3.61	3	36-40-4

Assists: Casey (3), Berthiaume (1), Takko (1); **PM:** Casey (18), Berthiaume (8), Takko (2).
Acquired: Berthiaume from Win.(Jan.22).

New Jersey Devils

Top Scorers

Top Scorers	Pos	GP	G	A	Pts	+/−	PM
Kirk Muller	C	80	30	56	86	−1	74
John MacLean	R	80	41	38	79	+17	80
Patrik Sundstrom	L	74	27	49	76	+15	34
Peter Stastny	C	74	29	44	73	−46	40
QUE		62	24	38	62	−45	24
NJ		12	5	6	11	−1	16
Brendan Shanahan	R	73	30	42	72	+15	137
Bruce Driver	D	75	7	46	53	+6	63
Sylvain Turgeon	C	72	30	17	47	−8	81
Mark Johnson	C	63	16	29	45	−8	12
Viacheslav Fetisov*	D	72	8	34	42	+9	52
Doug Brown	R	69	14	20	34	+7	16
Janne Ojanen*	C	64	17	13	30	−5	12
Tommy Albelin	D	68	6	23	29	−1	63
Bob Brooke	C	73	12	14	26	−2	63
MIN		38	4	4	8	−5	33
NJ		35	8	10	18	+3	30
David Maley	L	67	8	17	25	−2	160
Alexei Kasatonov*	D	39	6	15	21	+15	16
Ken Daneyko	D	74	6	15	21	+15	216
Walt Poddubny	L	33	4	10	14	−4	28

Acquired: Brooke from Min.(Jan.5); Stastny from Que.(Mar.6).

Goaltending

Goaltending	GP	Min	Avg	SO	Record
Chris Terreri	35	1931	3.42	0	15-12-3
Sean Burke	52	2914	3.60	0	22-22-6
NEW JERSEY	80	4864	3.55	0	37-34-9

Assists: Burke (1); **PM:** Burke (38).

Montreal Canadiens

Top Scorers

Top Scorers	Pos	GP	G	A	Pts	+/−	PM
Stephane Richer	R	75	51	40	91	+35	46
Shayne Corson	C	76	31	44	75	+33	144
Russ Courtnall	R	80	27	32	59	+14	27
Guy Carbonneau	C	68	19	36	55	+21	37
Brian Skrudland	C	59	11	31	42	+21	56
Mike McPhee	L	56	23	18	41	+28	47
Mats Naslund	L	72	21	20	41	+3	19
Petr Svoboda	D	60	5	31	36	+20	98
Stephan Lebeau*	C	57	15	20	35	+13	11
Chris Chelios	D	53	9	22	31	+20	136
Bobby Smith	C	53	12	14	26	−4	35
Brent Gilchrist	C	57	9	15	24	+3	28
Mike Keane	R	74	9	15	24	E	78
Ryan Walter	L	70	8	16	24	+4	59
Mathieu Schneider*	D	44	7	14	21	+2	25
Claude Lemieux	R	39	8	10	18	−8	106
Eric Desjardins	D	55	3	13	16	+1	51
Craig Ludwig	D	73	1	15	16	+24	108

Goaltending

Goaltending	GP	Min	Avg	SO	Record
Patrick Roy	54	3173	2.53	3	31-16- 5
Brian Hayward	29	1674	3.37	1	10-12- 6
MONTREAL	80	4870	2.88	4	41-28-11

Assists: Roy (5); **PM:** Hayward (4).

New York Islanders

Top Scorers

Top Scorers	Pos	GP	G	A	Pts	+/−	PM
Pat LaFontaine	C	74	54	51	105	−13	38
Brent Sutter	C	67	33	35	68	+9	65
Doug Crossman	D	80	15	44	59	+3	54
Jeff Norton	D	60	4	49	53	−9	65
Patrick Flatley	R	62	17	32	49	+10	101
Randy Wood	L	74	24	24	48	−10	39
Don Maloney	L	79	16	27	43	+6	47
Derek King	L	46	13	27	40	+2	20
David Volek	L	80	17	22	39	−2	41
Hubie McDonough	C	76	21	15	36	+14	36
LA		22	3	4	7	+4	10
NYI		54	18	11	29	+10	26
Alan Kerr	R	75	15	20	35	−1	129
Gary Nylund	D	64	4	21	25	+8	144
Bryan Trottier	C	59	13	11	24	−11	29
Brad Lauer	L	63	6	18	24	+5	19
Gerald Diduck	D	76	3	17	20	+2	163
Dave Chyzowski*	L	34	8	6	14	−4	45

Acquired: McDonough from LA (Nov.29).

Goaltending

Goaltending	GP	Min	Avg	SO	Record
Mark Fitzpatrick	47	2653	3.39	3	19-19- 5
Glenn Healy	39	2197	3.50	2	12-19- 6
NY ISLANDERS	80	4872	3.55	5	31-38-11

Assists: Fitzpatrick (2), Healy (1); **PM:** Fitzpatrick (18), Healy (7).

Team by Team Statistics (Cont.)

New York Rangers

Top Scorers	Pos	GP	G	A	Pts	+/−	PM
Bernie Nicholls	C	79	39	73	112	−9	86
LA		47	27	48	75	−6	66
NYR		32	12	25	37	−3	20
Mike Gartner	R	79	45	41	86	−4	38
MIN		67	34	36	70	−8	32
NYR		12	11	5	16	+4	6
John Ogrodnick	L	80	43	31	74	+11	44
Brian Mullen	R	76	27	41	68	+7	42
Darren Turcotte*	R	76	32	34	66	+3	32
Kelly Kisio	C	68	22	44	66	+11	105
James Patrick	D	73	14	43	57	+4	50
Brian Leetch	D	72	11	45	56	−18	26
Troy Mallette*	L	79	13	16	29	−8	305
Carey Wilson	C	41	9	17	26	+4	57
Mark Hardy	D	54	0	15	15	+4	94
Miloslav Horava	D	45	4	10	14	+10	26

Acquired: Nicholls from LA (Jan.20); Gartner from Min. (Mar.6).

Goaltending	GP	Min	Avg	SO	Record
Mike Richter*	23	1320	3.00	0	12- 5- 5
Bob Froese	15	812	3.33	0	5- 7- 1
John Vanbiesbrouck	47	2734	3.38	1	19-19- 7
NY RANGERS	80	4878	3.28	1	36-31-13

Assists: Richter (3), Vanbiesbrouck (2); **PM:** Vanbiesbrouck (24).

Pittsburgh Penguins

Top Scorers	Pos	GP	G	A	Pts	+/−	PM
Mario Lemieux	C	59	45	78	123	−18	78
Paul Coffey	D	80	29	74	103	−25	95
John Cullen	C	72	32	60	92	−13	138
Rob Brown	R	80	33	47	80	−10	102
Kevin Stevens	L	76	29	41	70	−13	171
Mark Recchi*	R	74	30	37	67	+6	44
Tony Tanti	R	78	28	36	64	−10	72
VAN		41	14	18	32	+1	50
PIT		37	14	18	32	−11	22
Phil Bourque	L	76	22	17	39	−7	108
Bob Errey	L	78	20	19	39	+3	109
Zarley Zalapski	D	51	6	25	31	−14	37
Barry Pederson	C	54	6	25	31	−13	39
VAN		16	2	7	9	−3	10
PIT		38	4	18	22	−10	29
Troy Loney	L	67	11	16	27	−9	168
Randy Gilhen	C	61	5	11	16	−8	54
Jim Johnson	D	75	3	13	16	−20	154
Randy Hillier	D	61	3	12	15	+11	71
Chris Dahlquist	D	62	4	10	14	−2	56

Acquired: Tanti and Pederson from Van.(Jan.8).

Goaltending	GP	Min	Avg	SO	Record
Wendell Young	43	2318	4.17	1	16-20-3
Alain Chevrier	42	2060	4.25	0	17-16-3
CHI	39	1894	4.18	0	16-14-3
PIT	3	166	5.06	0	1- 2-0
Frank Pietrangelo	21	1066	4.33	0	8- 6-2
Tom Barrasso	24	1294	4.68	0	7-12-3
PITTSBURGH	80	4856	4.44	1	32-40-8

Assists: Young (4), Chevrier (3); **PM:** Barrasso (8), Chevrier (8), Young (8), Pietrangelo (2).
Acquired: Chevrier from Chi.(Mar.6).

Philadelphia Flyers

Top Scorers	Pos	GP	G	A	Pts	+/−	PM
Rick Tocchet	R	75	37	59	96	+4	196
Murray Craven	L	76	25	50	75	+2	42
Mike Bullard	C	70	27	37	64	E	67
Pelle Eklund	C	70	23	39	62	+7	16
Tim Kerr	R	40	24	24	48	−3	34
Ron Sutter	C	75	22	26	48	+2	104
Ilkka Sinisalo	R	59	23	23	46	+6	26
Gord Murphy	D	75	14	27	41	−7	95
Ken Linseman	C	61	11	25	36	+5	96
BOS		32	6	16	22	+12	66
PHI		29	5	9	14	−7	30
Mark Howe	D	40	7	21	28	+22	24
Keith Acton	C	69	13	14	27	−2	80
Scott Mellanby	R	57	6	17	23	−4	77
Kjell Samuelsson	D	66	5	17	22	+20	91
Terry Carkner	D	63	4	18	22	−8	167
Jiri Latal*	D	32	6	13	19	+4	6
Craig Berube	L	74	4	14	18	−7	291
Kevin Maguire	R	66	7	9	16	−4	121
BUF		61	6	9	15	−3	115
PHI		5	1	0	1	−1	6

Acquired: Linseman from Bos.(Jan.16); Maguire from Buf.(Mar.6).

Goaltending	GP	Min	Avg	SO	Record
Ken Wregget	51	2961	3.42	0	22-24- 3
Bruce Hoffort*	7	329	3.65	0	3- 0- 2
Pete Peeters	24	1140	3.74	1	1-13- 5
Ron Hextall	8	419	4.15	0	4- 2- 1
PHILADELPHIA	80	4870	3.66	1	30-39-11

Assists: Wregget (2), Peeters (1); **PM:** Wregget (12), Hextall (14), Hoffort (2), Peeters (2).

Quebec Nordiques

Top Scorers	Pos	GP	G	A	Pts	+/−	PM
Joe Sakic	C	80	39	63	102	−40	27
Michel Petit	D	63	12	24	36	−38	215
Guy Lafleur	R	39	12	22	34	−15	4
Tony McKegney	L	62	18	12	30	−29	53
DET		14	2	1	3	+2	8
QUE		48	16	11	27	−31	45
Marc Fortier	C	59	13	17	30	−16	28
Tony Hrkac	C	50	9	20	29	−4	10
STL		28	5	12	17	+1	8
QUE		22	4	8	12	−5	2
Mike Hough	L	43	13	13	26	−24	84
Claude Loiselle	C	72	11	14	25	−27	104
Paul Gillis	C	71	8	14	22	−24	234
Jeff Jackson	L	65	8	12	20	−21	71
Iiro Jarvi	L	41	7	13	20	−11	18
Joe Cirella	D	56	4	14	18	−14	67
Mario Marois	D	67	3	15	18	−45	104
Lucien DeBlois	C	70	9	8	17	−29	45
Ken McRae	C	66	7	8	15	−38	191
Bryan Fogarty*	D	45	4	10	14	−47	31

Acquired: McKegney from Det.(Dec.3); Hrkac from St.L (Dec.13).

Goaltending	GP	Min	Avg	SO	Record
Mario Brunetta	6	191	4.08	0	1- 2-0
Ron Tugnutt	35	1978	4.61	0	5-24-3
Sergei Mylnikov	10	568	4.96	0	1- 7-2
Scott Gordon*	10	597	5.33	0	2- 8-0
Stephane Fiset*	6	342	5.96	0	0- 5-1
QUEBEC	80	4836	5.05	0	12-61-7

Assists: None; **PM:** Tugnutt (2).
Note: Greg Millen acquired from St.L (Dec.13), traded to Chi.(Mar.5).

St. Louis Blues

Top Scorers	Pos	GP	G	A	Pts	+/−	PM
Brett Hull	R	80	72	41	113	−1	24
Adam Oates	C	80	23	79	102	+9	30
Peter Zezel	C	73	25	47	72	−9	30
Paul MacLean	R	78	34	33	67	+2	100
Rod Brind'Amour*	C	79	26	35	61	+23	46
Sergio Momesso ..	L	79	24	32	56	−15	199
Jeff Brown	D	77	16	38	54	−26	55
QUE		29	6	10	16	−14	18
STL		48	10	28	38	−12	37
Paul Cavallini	D	80	8	39	47	+38	106
Gino Cavallini ...	L	80	15	15	30	−8	77
Dave Lowry	L	78	19	6	25	+1	75
Rick Meagher	C	76	8	17	25	+4	47
Steve Tuttle	R	71	12	10	22	−6	4
Rich Sutter	R	74	11	9	20	−3	155
VAN		62	9	9	18	−1	133
STL		12	2	0	2	−2	22
Ron Wilson	L	33	3	17	20	+5	23
Gordie Roberts ...	D	75	3	14	17	−12	140
Mike Lalor	D	78	0	16	16	−6	81

Acquired: Brown from Que.(Dec.13); Sutter from Van.(Mar.6).

Goaltending	GP	Min	Avg	SO	Record
Curtis Joseph*	15	852	3.38	0	9- 5-1
Vincent Riendeau	43	2551	3.50	1	17-19-5
ST.LOUIS	80	4861	3.44	2	37-34-9

Assists: Joseph (1); **PM:** Riendeau (6).
Note: Greg Millen traded to Que.(Dec.13).

Toronto Maple Leafs

Top Scorers	Pos	GP	G	A	Pts	+/−	PM
Gary Leeman	R	80	51	44	95	+4	63
Vincent Damphousse	L	80	33	61	94	+2	56
Ed Olczyk	C	79	32	56	88	E	78
Daniel Marois	R	68	39	37	76	+1	82
Mark Osborne	L	78	23	50	73	+2	91
Al Iafrate	D	75	21	42	63	−4	135
Tom Kurvers	D	71	15	37	52	−9	29
NJ		1	0	0	0	−1	0
TOR		70	15	37	52	−8	29
Rob Ramage	D	80	8	41	49	−1	202
Tom Fergus	C	54	19	26	45	−18	62
Lou Franceschetti ..	R	80	21	15	36	−12	127
Dave Reid	L	70	9	19	28	−8	9
Wendel Clark	L	38	18	8	26	+2	116
Gilles Thibaudeau ...	C	41	11	15	26	+8	30
NYI		20	4	4	8	+2	17
TOR		21	7	11	18	+6	13
Dan Daoust	C	65	7	11	18	+1	89
Luke Richardson ...	D	67	4	14	18	−1	122
John McIntyre*	C	59	5	12	17	−12	117
Dave Hannan	C	39	6	9	15	−12	55
Scott Pearson*	L	41	5	10	15	−7	90
Todd Gill	D	48	1	14	15	−8	92
Brad Marsh	D	79	1	13	14	+14	95

Acquired: Kurvers from NJ (Oct.16); Thibaudeau from NYI (Dec.20).

Goaltending	GP	Min	Avg	SO	Record
Mark LaForest	27	1343	3.89	0	9-14-0
Jeff Reese*	21	1101	4.41	0	9- 6-3
Allan Bester	42	2206	4.49	0	20-16-0
TORONTO	80	4842	4.44	0	38-38-4

Assists: Bester (2), LaForest (1), Reese (1); **PM:** LaForest (23), Reese (10), Bester (4).

Vancouver Canucks

Top Scorers	Pos	GP	G	A	Pts	+/−	PM
Dan Quinn	C	78	25	38	63	−17	49
PIT		41	9	20	29	−15	22
VAN		37	16	18	34	−2	27
Paul Reinhart	D	67	17	40	57	+2	30
Trevor Linden	R	73	21	30	51	−17	43
Greg Adams	L	65	30	20	50	−8	18
Brian Bradley	C	67	19	29	48	+5	65
Petri Skriko	L	77	15	33	48	−21	36
Igor Larionov*	C	74	17	27	44	−5	20
Doug Lidster	D	80	8	28	36	−16	36
Vladimir Krutov* ...	L	61	11	23	34	−5	20
Jyrki Lumme*	C	65	4	26	30	+17	49
MON		54	1	19	20	+17	41
VAN		11	3	7	10	E	8
Jim Sandlak	R	70	15	8	23	−15	104
Steve Bozek	L	58	14	9	23	−3	32
Andrew McBain	R	67	9	14	23	−11	73
PIT		41	5	9	14	−8	51
VAN		26	4	5	9	−3	22
Garth Butcher	D	80	6	14	20	−10	205
Stan Smyl	R	47	1	15	16	−14	71

Acquired: Quinn and McBain from Pit.(Jan.8); Lumme from Mont.(Mar.6).

Goaltending	GP	Min	Avg	SO	Record
Kirk McLean	63	3739	3.47	0	21-30-10
Steve Weeks	21	1142	4.15	0	4-11- 4
VANCOUVER	80	4892	3.75	0	25-41-14

Assists: McLean (3); **PM:** McLean (6).

Washington Capitals

Top Scorers	Pos	GP	G	A	Pts	+/−	PM
Dino Ciccarelli	R	80	41	38	79	−5	122
Geoff Courtnall	L	80	35	39	74	+27	104
Mike Ridley	C	74	30	43	73	E	27
Michal Pivonka	C	77	25	39	64	−7	54
Dale Hunter	C	80	23	39	62	+17	233
Kevin Hatcher	D	80	13	41	54	+4	102
Kelly Miller	L	80	18	22	40	−2	49
Scott Stevens	D	56	11	29	40	+1	154
Calle Johansson	D	70	8	31	39	+7	25
Steve Leach	R	70	18	14	32	+10	104
John Tucker	C	46	10	21	31	+8	12
BUF		8	1	2	3	−3	2
WASH		38	9	19	28	+11	10
Bob Rouse	D	70	4	16	20	−2	123
Alan May*	R	77	7	10	17	−1	339
Bob Joyce	D	47	6	10	16	−6	26
BOS		23	1	2	3	−8	22
WASH		24	5	8	13	+2	4

Acquired: Joyce from Bos.(Dec.13); Tucker from Buf.(Jan.4).

Goaltending	GP	Min	Avg	SO	Record
Mike Liut	37	2161	2.53	4	19-16-1
HART	29	1683	2.64	3	15-12-1
WASH	8	478	2.13	1	4- 4-0
Don Beaupre	48	2793	3.22	2	23-18-5
Bob Mason	16	822	3.50	0	4- 9-1
Jim Hrivnak*	11	609	3.55	0	5- 5-0
WASHINGTON	80	4837	3.14	3	36-38-6

Assists: Beaupre (1), Hrivnak (1); **PM:** Beaupre (24), Mason (4).
Acquired: Liut from Hart.(Mar.5).

Team by Team Statistics (Cont.)

Winnipeg Jets

Top Scorers	Pos	GP	G	A	Pts	+/−	PM
Dale Hawerchuk	C	79	26	55	81	−11	60
Pat Elynuik	R	80	32	42	74	+2	83
Thomas Steen	C	53	18	48	66	+2	35
Brent Ashton	L	79	22	34	56	+4	37
Fredrik Olausson	D	77	9	46	55	−1	32
Dave McLlwain	C	80	25	26	51	−1	60
Paul Fenton	L	80	32	18	50	+2	40
Doug Smail	L	79	25	24	49	+15	63
Greg Paslawski	R	71	18	30	48	−4	14
Dave Ellett	D	77	17	29	46	−15	96
Teppo Numminen	D	79	11	32	43	−4	20
Paul MacDermid	R	73	13	22	35	+5	169
HART		29	6	12	18	+1	69
WIN		44	7	10	17	+4	100
Moe Mantha	D	73	2	26	28	+8	28
Laurie Boschman	C	66	10	17	27	−11	103
Doug Evans	L	30	10	8	18	+7	33
STL		3	0	0	0	E	0
WIN		27	10	8	18	+7	33
Randy Carlyle	D	53	3	15	18	+8	50
Mark Kumpel	R	56	8	9	17	−5	21
Phil Sykes	L	48	9	6	15	−8	26

Acquired: MacDermid from Hart.(Dec.13); Evans from St.L.(Jan.22).

Goaltending	GP	Min	Avg	SO	Record
Bob Essensa*	36	2035	3.15	1	18- 9- 5
Steph. Beauregard*	19	1079	3.28	0	7- 8- 3
Tom Draper*	6	359	4.35	0	2- 4- 0
WINNIPEG	80	4873	3.57	2	37-32-11

Assists: Essensa (2); **PM:** Beauregard (4).
Note: Daniel Berthiaume traded to Min.(Jan.22).

All-NHL

Voting done by Pro Hockey Writers' Assn.

First Team		1st	Pts
G	Patrick Roy, Montreal	59	304
D	Ray Bourque, Boston	62	315
D	Al MacInnis, Calgary	0	257
C	Mark Messier, Edmonton	54	287
R	Brett Hull, St.Louis	56	298
L	Luc Robitaille, Los Angeles	29	214

Second Team		1st	Pts
G	Daren Puppa, Buffalo	1	136
D	Paul Coffey, Pittsburgh	1	138
D	Doug Wilson, Chicago	0	128
C	Wayne Gretzky, Los Angeles	9	173
R	Cam Neely, Boston	7	183
L	Brian Bellows, Minnesota	26	194

All-Rookie Team

Voting done by Pro Hockey Writers' Assn. Vote not released.

G Bob Essensa, Winnipeg
D Brad Shaw, Hartford
D Geoff Smith, Edmonton
C Mike Modano, Minnesota
R Sergei Makarov, Calgary
L Rod Brind'Amour, St.Louis

Note: Makarov, 32, won the Calder Trophy as Rookie of the Year. In the future, all candidates must be 25 years old or younger.

Award Winners

Voting on all awards, except the Vezina Trophy and Adams Award, done by the Professional Hockey Writers Association. Vezina Trophy voting is done by NHL general managers and the Adams Award is voted on by the NHL broadcasters.

Hart Trophy

For Most Valuable Player.

Top 5	1st	2nd	3rd	—	Pts
Mark Messier, Edm., C	29	24	10	—	227
Ray Bourque, Bos., D	29	26	2	—	225
Brett Hull, St.L., RW	4	9	23	—	80
Wayne Gretzky, LA, C	1	2	5	—	16
Pat LaFontaine, NYI, C	0	1	5	—	8
Patrick Roy, Mon., G	0	1	5	—	8

Calder Trophy

For Rookie of the Year.

Top 5	1st	2nd	3rd	—	Pts
Sergei Makarov, Calg., RW	37	5	5	—	204
Mike Modano, Min., C	12	17	9	—	120
Jeremy Roenick, Chi., C	7	9	9	—	71
Rod Brind'Amour, St.L., C	3	12	7	—	58
Mark Recchi, Pit., RW	2	11	10	—	53

Norris Trophy

For Best Defenseman.

Top 5	1st	2nd	3rd	—	Pts
Ray Bourque, Boston	63	0	0	—	315
Al MacInnis, Calgary	0	38	13	—	127
Doug Wilson, Chicago	0	7	19	—	40
Paul Coffey, Pittsburgh	0	7	12	—	33
Phil Housley, Buffalo	0	7	11	—	32

Vezina Trophy

For Outstanding Goaltender.

Top 5	1st	2nd	3rd	—	Pts
Patrick Roy, Montreal	15	5	1	—	91
Daren Puppa, Buffalo	3	13	5	—	58
Andy Moog, Boston	2	2	10	—	26
Reggie Lemelin, Boston	1	0	1	—	7
Mike Liut, Hart-Wash.	0	1	1	—	4

Adams Award

For Coach of the Year.

Top 5	1st	2nd	3rd	—	Pts
Bob Murdoch, Winnipeg	16	14	6	—	128
Mike Milbury, Boston	15	14	6	—	123
Roger Neilson, NY Rangers	4	1	5	—	28
Rick Dudley, Buffalo	1	5	8	—	28
Brian Sutter, St.Louis	2	3	6	—	25

Other Awards

Lady Byng Trophy (for gentlemanly play and ability)—Brett Hull, St.Louis; **Selke Trophy** (best defensive forward)—Rick Meagher, St.Louis. **Lester Pearson Award** (NHL Players Assn.MVP)—Mark Messier, Edmonton; **Jennings Trophy** (fewest team goals against)—Andy Moog and Reggie Lemelin, Boston; **Masterton Trophy** (for perseverance and dedication to hockey)—Gord Kluzak, Boston; **King Clancy Trophy** (for leadership and community service)—Kevin Lowe, Edmonton; **NHL Man of the Year** (positive role model)—Kevin Lowe, Edmonton.

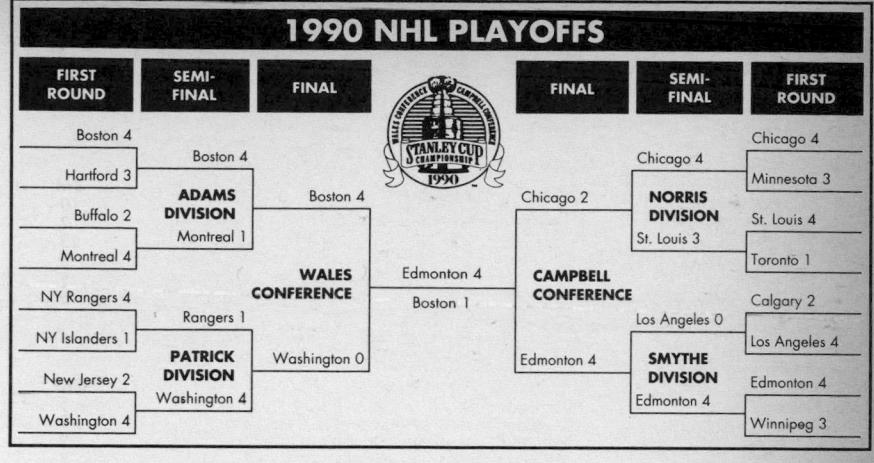

1990 NHL PLAYOFFS

FIRST ROUND	SEMI-FINAL	FINAL		FINAL	SEMI-FINAL	FIRST ROUND
Boston 4						Chicago 4
Hartford 3	Boston 4				Chicago 4	Minnesota 3
Buffalo 2	**ADAMS DIVISION**	Boston 4		Chicago 2	**NORRIS DIVISION**	St. Louis 4
Montreal 4	Montreal 1				St. Louis 3	Toronto 1
NY Rangers 4	**WALES CONFERENCE**	Edmonton 4	**CAMPBELL CONFERENCE**			Calgary 2
NY Islanders 1	Rangers 1	Boston 1			Los Angeles 0	Los Angeles 4
New Jersey 2	**PATRICK DIVISION**	Washington 0		Edmonton 4	**SMYTHE DIVISION**	Edmonton 4
Washington 4	Washington 4				Edmonton 4	Winnipeg 3

Stanley Cup Playoffs

All series Best-of-7 games.

Wales Conference

ADAMS DIVISION

Semifinals

	W-L	GF	Leading Scorer
Boston	4-3	23	Neely (4-6—10)
Hartford	3-4	21	Shaw (2-5—7)

Date	Winner	Home Ice
Apr. 5	Hartford, 4-3	at Boston
Apr. 7	Boston, 3-1	at Boston
Apr. 9	Hartford, 5-3	at Hartford
Apr.11	Boston, 6-5	at Hartford
Apr.13	Boston, 3-2	at Boston
Apr.15	Hartford, 3-2 (OT)	at Hartford
Apr.17	Boston, 3-1	at Boston

	W-L	GF	Leading Scorer
Montreal	4-2	17	Richer (5-2—7)
Buffalo	2-4	13	Andreychuk (2-5—7)

Date	Winner	Home Ice
Apr. 5	Buffalo, 4-1	at Buffalo
Apr. 7	Montreal, 3-0*	at Buffalo
Apr. 9	Montreal, 2-1 (OT)	at Montreal
Apr.11	Buffalo, 4-2	at Montreal
Apr.13	Montreal,4-2	at Buffalo
Apr.15	Montreal, 5-2	at Montreal

*Shutout: Roy (26 saves).

Final

	W-L	GF	Leading Scorer
Boston	4-1	16	Bourque (1-5—6) & Janney (0-6—6)
Montreal	1-4	12	Corson (1-3—4)

Date	Winner	Home Ice
Apr.19	Boston, 1-0*	at Boston
Apr.21	Boston, 5-4 (OT)	at Boston
Apr.23	Boston, 6-3	at Montreal
Apr.25	Montreal, 4-1	at Montreal
Apr.27	Boston, 3-1	at Boston

*Shutout: Moog (20 saves).

PATRICK DIVISION

Semifinals

	W-L	GF	Leading Scorer
NY Rangers	4-1	22	J.Patrick (2-5—7) & Kisio (1-6—7)
NY Islanders	1-4	13	B.Sutter (2-3—5) & Volek (1-4—5)

Date	Winner	Home Ice
Apr. 5	Rangers, 2-1	at Rangers
Apr. 7	Rangers, 5-2	at Rangers
Apr. 9	Islanders, 4-3 (2 OT)	at Islanders
Apr.11	Rangers, 6-1	at Islanders
Apr.13	Rangers, 6-5	at Rangers

	W-L	GF	Leading Scorer
Washington	4-2	21	Ciccarelli (8-3—11)
New Jersey	2-4	18	Shanahan (3-3—6) & Driver (1-5—6)

Date	Winner	Home Ice
Apr. 5	Washington, 5-4 (OT)	at N.Jersey
Apr. 7	New Jersey, 6-5	at N.Jersey
Apr. 9	New Jersey, 2-1	at Washington
Apr.11	Washington, 3-1	at Washington
Apr.13	Washington, 4-3	at N.Jersey
Apr.15	Washington, 3-2	at Washington

Final

	W-L	GF	Leading Scorer
Washington	4-1	22	Druce (9-2—11)
NY Rangers	1-4	15	Nicholls (4-4—8)

Date	Winner	Home Ice
Apr.19	NY Rangers, 7-3	at New York
Apr.21	Washington, 6-3	at New York
Apr.23	Washington, 7-1	at Washington
Apr.25	Washington, 4-3 (OT)	at Washington
Apr.27	Washington, 2-1 (OT)	at New York

1990 Stanley Cup Playoffs (Cont.)

WALES CONFERENCE FINAL

	W-L	GF	Leading Scorer
Boston	4-0	15	Neely (5-4—9)
Washington	0-4	6	Druce (2-1—3)

Date	Winner	Home Ice	Date	Winner	Home Ice
May 3	Boston, 5-3	at Boston	May 7	Boston, 4-1	at Washington
May 5	Boston, 3-0*	at Boston	May 9	Boston, 3-2	at Washington

*Shutout: Moog (28 saves).

Campbell Conference

NORRIS DIVISION

Semifinals

	W-L	GF	Leading Scorer
Chicago	4-3	21	Larmer (2-5—7)
			& Thomas (2-5—7)
Minnesota	3-4	18	Bellows (4-3—7)

Date	Winner	Home Ice
Apr. 4	Minnesota, 2-1	at Chicago
Apr. 6	Chicago, 5-3	at Chicago
Apr. 8	Chicago, 2-1	at Minnesota
Apr.10	Minnesota, 4-0*	at Minnesota
Apr.12	Chicago, 5-1	at Chicago
Apr.14	Minnesota, 5-3	at Minnesota
Apr.16	Chicago, 5-2	at Chicago

*Shutout: Casey (29 saves).

	W-L	GF	Leading Scorer
St.Louis	4-1	20	Hull (5-5—10)
Toronto	1-4	16	Leeman (3-3—6)

Date	Winner	Home Ice
Apr. 4	St.Louis, 4-2	at St.Louis
Apr. 6	St.Louis, 4-2	at St.Louis
Apr. 8	St.Louis, 6-5 (OT)	at Toronto
Apr.10	Toronto, 4-2	at Toronto
Apr.12	St.Louis, 4-3	at St.Louis

Final

	W-L	GF	Leading Scorer
Chicago	4-3	28	Larmer (4-6—10)
St.Louis	3-4	22	Hull (8-3—11)

Date	Winner	Home Ice
Apr.18	St.Louis, 4-3	at Chicago
Apr.20	Chicago, 5-3	at Chicago
Apr.22	St.Louis, 5-4	at St.Louis
Apr.24	Chicago, 3-2	at St.Louis
Apr.26	Chicago, 3-2	at Chicago
Apr.28	St.Louis, 4-2	at St.Louis
Apr.30	Chicago, 8-2	at Chicago

CAMPBELL CONFERENCE FINAL

	W-L	GF	Leading Scorer
Edmonton	4-2	25	Messier (4-7—11)
Chicago	2-4	20	Savard (3-7—10)

Date	Winner	Home Ice
May 2	Edmonton, 5-2	at Edmonton
May 4	Chicago, 4-3	at Edmonton
May 6	Chicago, 5-1	at Chicago
May 8	Edmonton, 4-2	at Chicago
May 10	Edmonton, 4-3	at Edmonton
May 12	Edmonton, 8-4	at Chicago

SMYTHE DIVISION

Semifinals

	W-L	GF	Leading Scorer
Los Angeles	4-2	29	Gretzky (2-7—9)
Calgary	2-4	24	Nieuwendyk (4-6—10)

Date	Winner	Home Ice
Apr. 4	Los Angeles, 5-3	at Calgary
Apr. 6	Calgary, 8-5	at Calgary
Apr. 8	Los Angeles, 2-1 (OT)	at L.Angeles
Apr.10	Los Angeles, 12-4	at L.Angeles
Apr.12	Calgary, 5-1,	at Calgary
Apr.14	Los Angeles, 4-3 (2 OT)	at L.Angeles

	W-L	GF	Leading Scorer
Edmonton	4-3	24	Kurri (3-7—10)
Winnipeg	3-4	22	Hawerchuk (3-5—8)

Date	Winner	Home Ice
Apr. 4	Winnipeg, 7-5	at Edmonton
Apr. 6	Edmonton, 3-2 (OT)	at Edmonton
Apr. 8	Winnipeg, 2-1	at Winnipeg
Apr.10	Winnipeg, 4-3 (2 OT)	at Winnipeg
Apr.12	Edmonton, 4-3	at Edmonton
Apr.14	Edmonton, 4-3	at Winnipeg
Apr.15	Edmonton, 4-1	at Edmonton

Final

	W-L	GF	Leading Scorer
Edmonton	4-0	24	Simpson (4-5—9)
Los Angeles	0-4	10	Elik (1-3—4)

Date	Winner	Home Ice
Apr.18	Edmonton, 7-0*	at Edmonton
Apr.20	Edmonton, 6-1	at Edmonton
Apr.22	Edmonton, 5-4	at L.Angeles
Apr.24	Edmonton, 6-5 (OT)	at L.Angeles

*Shutout: Ranford (25 saves).

STANLEY CUP CHAMPIONSHIP

	W-L	GF	Leading Scorer
Edmonton	4-1	20	Simpson (4-4—8)
			& Kurri (3-5—8)
Boston	1-4	8	Bourque (3-2—5)

Date	Winner	Home Ice
May 18	Edmonton, 3-2 (3 OT)	at Boston
May 20	Edmonton, 7-2	at Boston
May 22	Boston, 2-1	at Edmonton
May 24	Edmonton, 5-1	at Edmonton
May 26	Edmonton, 4-1	at Boston

Conn Smythe Trophy (MVP)
Bill Ranford, Edmonton

Stanley Cup Playoff Statistics

Scoring

	GP	G	A	Pts	+/−	PM
Craig Simpson, Edm	22	16	15	31	+11	8
Mark Messier, Edm	22	9	22	31	+5	20
Cam Neely, Bos	21	12	16	28	+7	51
Jari Kurri, Edm	22	10	15	25	+13	18
Esa Tikkanen, Edm	22	13	11	24	+12	26
Glenn Anderson, Edm	22	10	12	22	+12	20
Steve Larmer, Chi	20	7	15	22	+2	12
Denis Savard, Chi	20	7	15	22	E	41
Craig Janney, Bos	18	3	19	22	+3	2
Brett Hull, St.L	12	13	8	21	+1	17
Jeremy Roenick, Chi*	20	11	7	18	−1	8
John Druce, Wash	15	14	3	17	−2	23
Mark Lamb, Edm	22	6	11	17	+12	2
Ray Bourque, Bos	17	5	12	17	+11	16
Wayne Presley, Chi	19	9	6	15	+8	29

Goaltending
(Minimum 5 games)

	GP	Min	GA	SO	Avg
Andy Moog, Bos	20	1195	44	2	2.21
Patrick Roy, Mon	11	641	26	1	2.43
Daren Puppa, Buf	6	370	15	0	2.43
Ed Belfour, Chi*	9	409	17	0	2.49
Bill Ranford, Edm	22	1401	59	1	2.53
Don Beaupre, Wash	8	401	18	0	2.69
J. Vanbiesbrouck, NYR	6	298	15	0	3.02
Jon Casey, Min	7	415	21	1	3.04
P. Sidorkiewicz, Hart	7	429	23	0	3.22
Curtis Joseph, St.L*	6	327	18	0	3.30

Goals

Simpson, Edm	16	Messier, Edm	22
Druce, Wash	14	Janney, Bos	19
Hull, St.L	13	Neely, Bos	16
Tikkanen, Edm	13	Larmer, Chi	15
Neely, Bos	12	Kurri, Edm	15
Roenick, Chi	12	Savard, Chi	15
		Simpson, Edm	15

Assists
(see above)

Wins

	W-L		
Ranford, Edm	16-6		
Moog, Bos	13-7		
Millen, Chi	6-6		
Roy, Mon	5-6		
Five tied with 4.			

Save Pct

Puppa, Buf	.921
Belfour, Chi	.915
Ranford, Edm	.912
Roy, Mon	.911
Moog, Bos	.909

Power Play Goals

Druce, Wash	8
Hull, St.L	7
Kurri, Edm	6
Simpson, Edm	6
Five tied with 4.	

Short-Handed Goals

Larmer, Chi	2
Tikkanen, Edm	2
Twenty tied with 1.	

Final Standings

	GP	W	L	Pts	For	Opp	Dif
Edmonton	22	16	6	32	93	60	+33
Boston	21	13	8	26	62	59	+3
Chicago	20	10	10	20	69	65	+4
Washington	15	8	7	16	49	48	+1
St.Louis	12	7	5	14	42	44	−2
NY Rangers	10	5	5	10	35	38	−3
Montreal	11	5	6	10	29	29	E
Los Angeles	10	4	6	8	39	48	−9
Winnipeg	7	3	4	6	22	24	−2
Hartford	7	3	4	6	21	23	−2
Minnesota	7	3	4	6	18	21	−3
Calgary	6	2	4	4	24	29	−5
New Jersey	6	2	4	4	18	21	−3
Buffalo	6	2	4	4	13	17	−4
Toronto	5	1	4	2	16	20	−4
NY Islanders	5	1	4	2	13	22	−9

Plus/Minus

S.Smith, Edm	+15
Kurri, Edm	+13
Ruotsalainen, Edm	+13
Three tied with 12.	

Penalty Minutes

Sheehy, Wash	91
Mallette, NYR	81
Momesso, St.L	63
D.Hunter, Wash	61
Creighton, Chi	59

Finalists' Composite Box Score

Boston Bruins

Scoring	Pos	GP	G	A	Pts	+/−	PM
Cam Neely	R	21	12	16	28	+7	51
Craig Janney	C	18	3	19	22	+3	2
Ray Bourque	D	17	5	12	17	+11	16
Randy Burridge	L	21	4	11	15	+2	14
Dave Poulin	C	18	8	5	13	+1	8
Brian Propp	L	20	4	9	13	+5	2
Bob Carpenter	L	21	4	6	10	−3	39
John Carter	L	21	6	3	9	E	45
Glen Wesley	D	21	2	6	8	+6	36
Garry Galley	D	21	3	3	6	−8	34
Don Sweeney	D	21	1	5	6	−10	18
Dave Christian	R	21	4	1	5	−6	4
Greg Hawgood	C	15	1	3	4	−9	12
John Byce*	C	8	2	0	2	+2	4
Bob Beers*	L	14	1	1	2	+1	18
Bob Sweeney	C	20	0	2	2	−7	30
Greg Johnston	R	5	1	0	1	−1	4
Lyndon Byers	R	17	1	0	1	−4	12
Peter Douris	R	8	0	1	1	E	5
Jim Wiemer	D	8	0	1	1	−4	4

Goaltending	GP	Min	GA	Avg	SO	Record
Andy Moog	20	1195	44	2.21	2	13-7
Reggie Lemelin	3	135	13	5.78	0	0-1
BOSTON	21	1331	59	2.66	2	13-8

Empty Net Goals: 2.
Assists: None. **PM:** Moog (6).

Edmonton Oilers

Scoring	Pos	GP	G	A	Pts	+/−	PM
Craig Simpson	L	22	16	15	31	+11	8
Mark Messier	C	22	9	22	31	+5	20
Jari Kurri	R	22	10	15	25	+13	18
Esa Tikkanen	L	22	13	11	24	+12	26
Glenn Anderson	R	22	10	12	22	+12	20
Mark Lamb	C	22	6	11	17	+12	2
Steve Smith	D	22	5	10	15	+15	37
Joe Murphy	C	21	6	8	14	+1	16
Reijo Ruotsalainen	D	22	2	11	13	+13	12
Adam Graves	L	22	5	6	11	+1	17
Randy Gregg	D	20	2	6	8	+1	16
Craig MacTavish	C	22	2	6	8	+6	29
Charlie Huddy	D	22	0	6	6	+11	10
Petr Klima	L	21	5	0	5	−2	8
Martin Gelinas*	L	20	2	3	5	E	6
Kelly Buchberger	L	19	0	5	5	+2	13
Craig Muni	D	22	0	3	3	+7	16
Kevin Lowe	D	20	0	2	2	+3	10

Goaltending	GP	Min	GA	Avg	SO	Record
Pokey Reddick	1	2	0	0.00	0	0-0
Bill Radford	22	1401	59	2.53	1	16-6
EDMONTON	22	1405	60	2.56	1	16-6

Empty net goals: 1.
Assists: Ranford (2); **PM:** Ranford (4).

NHL Draft

First and second round picks at the 28th annual NHL Draft held June 16, 1990 in Vancouver.

First Round

Team	Player Selected
1 Quebec	Owen Nolan, Cornwall, RW
2 Vancouver	Petr Nedved, Seattle, C
3 Detroit	Keith Primeau, Niagara Falls, C
4 Phila	Mike Ricci, Peterborough, C
5 Pittsburgh	Jaromir Jagr, Czech., LW
6 NY Isles	Scott Scissons, Saskatoon, C
7 Los Angeles	Darryl Sydor, Kamloops, D
8 Minnesota	Derian Hatcher, North Bay, D
9 Washington	John Slaney, Cornwall, D
10 Toronto	Drake Berehowsky, Kingston, D
11 a-Calgary	Trevor Kidd, Brandon, G
12 b-Montreal	Turner Stevenson, Seattle, R
13 NY Rangers	Michael Stewart, Mich.St., D
14 c-Buffalo	Brad May, Niagara Falls, L
15 Hartford	Mark Greig, Lethbridge, R
16 Chicago	Karl Dykhuis, Hull, D
17 Edmonton	Scott Allison, Prin.Albert, C
18 d-Vancouver	Shawn Antoski, North Bay, L
19 e-Winnipeg	Keith Tkachuk, Malden HS, RW
20 f-N.Jersey	Martin Brodeur, St.Hyacin., G
21 Boston	Bryan Smolinski, Mich.St., C

Acquired picks: a—from New Jersey; **b**—from St.Louis; **c**—from Winnipeg; **d**—from Montreal; **e**—from Buffalo; **f**—from Calgary.

Second Round

Team	Player Selected
22 Quebec	Ryan Hughes, Cornell, C
23 Vancouver	Jiri Slegr, Czech., D
24 g-N.Jersey	David Harlock, Michigan, D
25 Phila	Chris Simon, Ottawa, LW
26 h-Calgary	Nick Perreault, Hawkesbury, D
27 NY Isles	Chris Taylor, London, C
28 Los Angeles	Randy Semchuk, Team Canada, RW
29 i-N.Jersey	Chris Gotziaman, Roseau HS, RW
30 Washington	Rod Pasma, Cornwall, D
31 Toronto	Felix Potvin, Chicoutimi, G
32 j-Calgary	Vesa Viitakoski, Finland, LW
33 St.Louis	Craig Johnson, Hill-Murray HS, C
34 NY Rangers	Doug Weight, L.Superior St., C
35 Winnipeg	Mike Muller, Wayzata HS, D
36 Hartford	Geoff Sanderson, S.Current, C
37 Chicago	Ivan Droppa, Czech., D
38 Edmonton	Alex.Legault, Boston Univ., D
39 Montreal	Ryan Kuwabara, Ottawa, RW
40 k-Phila	Mikael Renberg, Sweden, F
41 Calgary	Etienne Belzile, Cornell, D
42 l-Phila	Terran Sandwith, Tri-Cities, D

Acquired picks: g—from Detroit via Calgary; **h**—from Pittsburgh; **i**—from Minnesota; **j**—from N.Jersey; **k**—from Buffalo; **l**—from Boston.

Affiliations: OHL (Ontario Hockey League)—Cornwall, Kingston, London, Niagara Falls, North Bay, Ottawa, Peterborough; **WHL (Western Hockey League)**—Brandon, Kamloops, Lethbridge, Prince Albert, Saskatoon, Seattle, Swift Current, Tri-Cities; **QMJHL** (Quebec Major Jr.Hockey League)—Chicoutimi, Hull, St-Hyacinthe; **Tier II**—Hawkesbury; **US Colleges**—Boston Univ.(Hockey East), Cornell (ECAC), Lake Superior St.(CCHA), Michigan (CCHA), Michigan St.(CCHA); **US High Schools**—Hill-Murray (MN), Malden Catholic (MA), Roseau (MN), Wayzata (MN); **National Teams**—Canada, Czechoslovakia, Finland, Sweden.

World Hockey Championship

The 43rd World Hockey Championships, held in Bern, Switzerland, Apr.16-May 2, 1990. Eight teams participate in preliminary round-robin with top four teams advancing to the medal round and the bottom four teams playing a consolation. Rosters for Canada and USA were limited to players not participating in Stanley Cup playoffs.

Final Standings

MEDAL GROUP

Top four teams after preliminary round-robin. Only Medal Round games count in standings, overall tournament record in parentheses.

	W	L	T	Pts	GF	GA
Soviet Union (8-1-1)	3	0	0	6	15	1
Sweden (7-2-1)	1	1	1	3	11	12
Czechoslovakia (5-4-1)	1	1	1	3	8	12
Canada (6-3-1)	0	3	0	0	7	16

Round One—Soviet Union 3, Sweden 0; Czech.3, Canada 2. **Round Two**—Soviet Union 7, Canada 1; Sweden 5, Czech.5. **Round Three**—Soviet Union 5, Czech. 0; Sweden 6, Canada 4.

CONSOLATION GROUP

Bottom four teams after preliminary round-robin. All tournament games count in standings, Consolation Group record in parentheses.

	W	L	T	Pts	GF	GA
USA (3-0-0)	6	4	0	12	35	43
Finland (1-1-1)	2	6	2	6	29	32
W.Germany (1-1-1)	1	8	1	3	19	42
Norway (0-3-0)	1	8	1	3	21	61

Round One—USA 5, W.Germany 3; Finland 8, Norway 1. **Round Two**—USA 4, Norway 1; Finland 1, W.Germany 1. **Round Three**—USA 3, Finland 2; W.Germany 4, Norway 0.

Note: Norway drops to World B Group and will be replaced by B Group champion Switzerland in 1991.

Leading Scorers

	GP	G	A	Pts
Steve Yzerman, Canada	10	9	10	19
Andrei Khomoutov, USSR	10	11	5	16
Kent Nilsson, Sweden	10	10	2	12
Robert Reichel, Czech	10	5	6	11
Theo Fleury, Canada	9	4	7	11
Hakan Loob, Sweden	10	4	7	11
Thomas Rundkvist, Sweden	10	3	8	11
Mikhail Tatarinov, USSR	10	3	8	11
Gerhard Truntschka, W.Ger	10	4	6	10
Viacheslav Fetisov, USSR	8	2	8	10

All-Tournament Teams

First Team

Goal—Dominik Hasek, Czech. **Defense**—Mikhail Tatarinov, USSR; Viacheslav Fetisov, USSR. **Forwards**—Steve Yzerman, Canada; Andrei Khomoutov, USSR; Robert Reichel, Czech.

Second Team

Goal—Artur Irbe, USSR. **Defense**—Paul Coffey, Canada; Anders Eldebrink, Sweden. **Forwards**—Pavel Bure, USSR; Kent Nilsson, Sweden; Valeri Kamenski, USSR.

U.S. College Hockey
NCAA Division I

Regular season standings. Overall records, including NCAA tournament games, in parentheses.

Western Collegiate Hockey Assn.(WCHA)

	W	L	T	Pts	GF	FA
*Wisconsin (36-9-1)	19	8	1	39	147	111
*Minnesota (28-16-2)	17	9	2	36	147	124
*N.Dakota (27-13-4)	15	10	3	33	149	114
N.Michigan (22-19-1)	15	12	1	31	130	129
Denver (18-24-0)	13	15	0	26	130	139
Minn-Duluth (20-19-1)	13	15	0	26	114	112
Colorado Col.(18-20-2)	10	17	1	21	97	129
Mich.Tech (10-30-0)	6	22	0	12	112	168

Conf.Tourney Final: Wisconsin 7, Minnesota 1
*NCAA Tournament: Wisconsin (4-0); Minnesota (3-2); N.Dakota (1-2).

Central Collegiate Hockey Assn. (CCHA)

	W	L	T	Pts	GF	FA
*Michigan St.(35-7-3)	26	3	3	55	190	93
*L.Super.St.(33-10-3)	24	6	2	50	169	91
*Bowl.Green (25-17-2)	20	10	2	42	153	142
Michigan (24-12-6)	16	11	5	37	148	125
W.Michigan (14-24-2)	12	18	2	26	145	162
Ohio St.(11-24-5)	11	17	4	26	138	164
Miami,OH (12-24-4)	8	21	3	19	138	175
Ferris St.(11-23-6)	6	20	6	18	106	162
IL-Chicago (10-27-1)	7	24	1	15	104	177

Conf.Tourney Final: Michigan St.4, Lake Superior St.3.
*NCAA Tournament: Lake Superior St.(2-2); Michigan St.(1-2); Bowling Green (0-2).

Eastern Collegiate Athletic Assn.(ECAC)

	W	L	T	Pts	GF	FA
*Colgate (31-6-1)	18	3	1	37	101	62
RPI (20-14-0)	14	8	0	28	131	107
Cornell (16-10-3)	12	7	3	27	86	69
*Clarkson (21-9-3)	12	7	3	27	91	77
St.Lawrence (13-15-4)	12	8	2	26	87	74
Harvard (13-14-1)	12	9	1	25	110	77
Princeton (12-14-1)	11	10	1	23	95	91
Brown (10-16-3)	8	11	3	19	78	94
Vermont (9-20-2)	7	13	2	16	71	96
Yale (8-20-1)	6	15	1	13	75	105
Dartmouth (4-18-4)	4	14	4	12	58	98
Army (10-16-4)	4	15	3	11	58	91

Conf.Tourney Final: Colgate 5, RPI 4.
*NCAA Tournament: Colgate (3-1); Clarkson (0-2).

Hockey East

	W	L	T	Pts	GF	FA
*Boston Col.(28-13-1)	15	6	0	30	101	69
*Maine (31-9-2)	14	6	1	29	88	57
*Boston Univ.(15-12-2)	12	7	2	26	88	63
Providence (22-10-3)	11	7	3	25	90	69
Northeastern (16-19-2)	9	10	2	20	96	100
New Hamp.(17-17-5)	8	9	4	20	86	86
Lowell (13-20-2)	5	14	2	12	65	106
Merrimack (9-22-1)	3	18	0	6	64	128

Conf.Tourney Final: Boston College 4, Maine 3.
*NCAA Tournament: Boston Univ.(4-3); Boston Col.(2-2); Maine (2-2).

NCAA Top 15
Final Regular Season Poll

Final regular season poll taken Feb.26,1990. Records do not include postseason games.

		League	W	L	T	Pts
1	Michigan St.	CCHA	30	5	3	60
2	Wisconsin	WCHA	28	9	1	55
3	Boston College	ECAC	22	9	1	52
4	Lake Superior St.	CCHA	28	7	3	48
5	Maine	H.East	28	8	2	44
6	Colgate	ECAC	24	5	1	41
7	North Dakota	WCHA	24	10	4	36
8	Providence	H.East	21	8	3	30
9	Boston Univ	H.East	18	12	2	26
	Minnesota	WCHA	22	13	2	26
11	Bowling Green	CCHA	23	13	2	22
12	Michigan	CCHA	21	11	6	15
13	Clarkson	ECAC	19	8	3	9
	RPI	ECAC	17	13	0	9
15	N.Michigan	WCHA	20	17	1	5

Leading Scorers

West	Yr	Pos	GP	G	A	Pts
Kip Miller, Mich.St.	Sr.	C	45	48	53	101
Jim Dowd, LSS	Jr.	C	46	25	67	92
Pat Murray, Mich.St.	Jr.	L	45	24	60	84
Nelson Emerson, BG	Sr.	C	44	30	52	82
Gary Shuchuk, Wisc	Sr.	C	45	41	39	80
Lee Davidson, N.Dak	Sr.	C	45	26	49	75
Dave Shields, Denver	Sr.	C	42	31	43	74
Chris Tancill, Wisc	Sr.	R	45	39	32	71
Jeff Jablonski, LSS	Sr.	L	46	38	33	71
John Byce, Wisc	Sr.	L	46	27	44	71
Dixon Ward, N.Dak	So.	W	45	35	34	69
Doug Weight, LSS	Fr.	C	46	21	48	69

East	Yr	Pos	GP	G	A	Pts
David Emma, BC	Jr.	C	42	38	34	72
Joey Juneau, RPI	Jr.	C	34	18	52	70
Jean-Yves Roy, Maine	Fr.	R	46	39	26	65
Steve Heinze, BC	So.	R	40	27	36	63
Joel Gardner, Colgate	Sr.	C	38	26	36	62
Harry Mews, N'eastern	Sr.	C	36	20	39	59
Tony Amonte, BU	Fr.	W	41	25	33	58
Shawn MacEachern, BU	So.	C	43	25	31	56
Marty McInnis, BC	Sr.	C	41	24	29	53
Bruce Coles, RPI	Jr.	R	34	28	24	52
Joe Sacco, BU	Jr.	W	44	28	24	52
Marc Dupere, Colgate	Sr.	R	38	23	29	52

Leading Goaltenders

West	Yr	Record	GA	Avg
Darrin Madeley, LSS	Fr.	21-7-1	68	2.42
Mike Gilmore, Mich.St.	So.	9-1-0	29	2.73
Jason Muzzatti, Mich.St.	Jr.	26-4-3	99	3.01
Warren Sharples, Mich	Sr.	20-10-6	117	3.24
Duane Derksen, Wisc	So.	31-8-1	133	3.40

East	Yr	Record	GA	Avg
Matt Merten, Prov	Sr.	8-4-2	38	2.51
Jim Crozier, Cornell	Jr.	10-3-1	38	2.63
Scott King, Maine	Sr.	17-7-2	67	2.63
Scott LeGrand, BC	Fr.	17-4-0	57	2.70
Dave Gagnon, Colgate	Jr.	28-4-1	93	2.81

U.S. College Hockey (Cont.)

Award Winners

Hobey Baker Award

For College Player of the Year. National coaches' vote determines 10 finalists. Winner then selected by 12-member panel of writers, broadcasters, coaches and pro scouts. First presented in 1981 by the Decathlon Athletic Club of Bloomington,MN, in the name of the late Princeton collegiate hockey and football star.

Top Vote Getters
Vote totals not released.

		Pos	Class
1	Kip Miller, Michigan St	C	Sr.
2	Greg Brown, Boston College	D	Jr

Other Finalists—Rick Bennett, Providence, Sr., LW; Bob Blake, Bowling Green, Jr., D; Nelson Emerson, Bowling Green, Sr., C; Dave Emma, Boston College, Jr., C; Dave Gagnon, Colgate, Jr., G; Joe Juneau, RPI, Jr., C; Russ Parent, North Dakota, Sr., D; Dave Shields, Denver, Sr., C.

Division I All-America

East Team

Pos		Yr	Hgt	Wgt
G	Dave Gagnon, Colgate	Jr.	6-0	190
D	Dave Brown, Boston College	Jr.	6-1	190
D	Rob Cowie, Northeastern	Jr.	6-0	185
F	Joe Juneau, RPI	Jr.	6-0	185
F	Steve Heinze, Boston College	So.	6-0	190
F	Dave Emma, Boston College	Jr.	5-9	175

West Team

		Yr	Hgt	Wgt
G	Chad Erickson, Minn-Duluth	So.	5-10	170
D	Russ Parent, North Dakota	Sr.	5-9	188
D	Rob Blake, Bowling Green	Jr.	6-3	215
F	Kip Miller, Michigan St	Sr.	5-10	190
F	Nelson Emerson, Bowling Green	Sr.	5-10	175
F	Gary Shuchuk, Wisconsin	Sr.	5-10	180

NCAA Division I Tournament

Tournament Seeds

EAST
1. Boston Col.(26-11-1)   4. Boston Univ.(21-14-2)
2. **Colgate** (28-5-1)   5. Clarkson (21-9-3)
3. Maine (31-9-2)   6. AK-Anchorage (17-9-3)

WEST
1. Michigan St.(34-5-3)   4. Minnesota (25-14-2)
2. **Wisconsin** (32-9-1)   5. North Dakota (27-11-4)
3. L.Superior St.(31-8-3)   6. Bowling Green (25-15-2)

First Round (Best of 3)
LAKE SUPERIOR ST. over Alaska-Anchorage, 2 games to none (6-2,10-3); MAINE over Bowling Green, 2 games to none (8-4,5-2); MINNESOTA over Clarkson, 2 games to none (6-1,5-1); BOSTON UNIV. over North Dakota, 2 games to 1 (5-8,5-3,5-0).

Quarterfinals (Best of 3)
BOSTON UNIV.over Michigan St., 2 games to 1 (3-6,5-3,5-3); BOSTON COLLEGE over Minnesota, 2 games to 1 (4-2,1-2,6-1); WISCONSIN over Maine, 2 games to none (7-3,4-3 OT); COLGATE over Lake Superior St., 2 games to none (3-2,2-1).

Final Four (Single Games)
at Joe Louis Arena, Detroit
Semifinals: COLGATE 3, Boston Univ. 2; WISCONSIN 2, Boston College 1.
Championship: WISCONSIN 7, Colgate 3.
Final records: Wisconsin (36-9-1), Colgate (31-6-1), Boston College (28-13-1), Boston Univ.(25-17-2)
Outstanding Player: Chris Tancill, F, Wisconsin (Semifinal—2 goals; Final—1 goal).
All-Tournament Team: F—Tancill and John Byce of Wisconsin, Joel Gardner of Colgate; D—Rob Andringa and Mark Oiecki of Wisconsin; G—Duane Derksen, Wisconsin.

Championship Game

Wisconsin 7, Colgate 3
Sunday, April 1, 1990
at Joe Louis Arena, Detroit (15,034)

Colgate (31-6-1) . . . . 1 1 1—3
Wisconsin (36-9-1) . . . . 4 2 1—7

Scoring
1st Period: WIS—John Byce (Sean Hill, Rob Andringa), power play, 0:37; WIS—Byce 2 (Rob Mendel), short-handed, 3:23; COL—Joel Gardner (Marc Dupere, Steve Spott), power play, 4:58; WIS—Chris Tancill (Andringa, Hill), power play, 7:33; WIS—Andringa (Hill, Doug MacDonald), power play, 14:53.
2nd Period: WIS—Dennis Snedden (Brett Kurtz, Mark Osiecki), 5:03; COL—Steve Poapst (Gardner), power play, 9:42; WIS—Gary Shuchuk (Barry Richter, Steve Rohlik), power play, 13:09.
3rd Period: COL—Jamie Cooke (Craig Woodcroft, Shawn Lillie), power play, 9:34; WIS—Byce 3 (unassisted), empty net, 19:18.

Goaltenders
Saves: COL—Dave Gagnon 6-5-2—13; WIS—Duane Derksen 4-4-13—21, Jon Michelizzi x-x-0—0.

NCAA Division III Tournament

All rounds are decided in two games with mini-game (one 20-minute period), if necessary. There is no NCAA Division II tournament.

First Round
BABSON over Geneseo St in 3 games (3-3,1-1,1-0); PLATTSBURGH ST. over Elmira in 3 games (2-5,4-2,1-0); MANKATO ST. over Gustavus Adolphus in 2 games (4-1,2-2); WISCONSIN-STEVENS POINT over St.Thomas,MN in 2 games (4-4,3-0)

Semifinals
PLATTSBURGH ST. over Babson in 3 games (4-4,4-4,2-1); WISC-STEVENS PT. over Mankato St. in 2 games (5-4,3-3).

Championship
(Mar.23-24, at Wisc-Stevens Pt.)
WISC-STEVENS PT. over Plattsburgh St. in 3 games (10-1,3-6,1-0).

The Stanley Cup

The Stanley Cup was originally donated to the Canadian Amateur Hockey Assn. by Sir Frederick Arthur Stanley, Lord Stanley of Preston and 16th Earl of Derby, who had become interested in the sport while Governor General of Canada from 1888 to 1893. Stanley wanted the trophy to be a challenge cup, contested for each year by the best amateur hockey teams in Canada.

In 1893, the Cup was presented without a challenge to the AHA champion Montreal Amateur Athletic Assn. team. Every year since, however, there has been a playoff. In 1914, Cup trustees limited the field challenging for the trophy to the champion of the eastern professional National Hockey Assn.(NHA, organized in 1910) and the western professional Pacific Coast Hockey Assn.(PCHA, organized in 1912).

The NHA became the National Hockey League (NHL) in November, 1917. From 1918 to 1926, the NHL and PCHL champions played for the Cup with the Western Canada Hockey League (WCHL) champion joining in a three-way challenge in 1923 and '24. The PCHA disbanded after the 1925-26 season and the NHL playoffs have decided the winner of the Stanley Cup ever since.

Stanley Cup Champions, 1893-1917

Year	Champion	Year	Champion	Year	Champion
1893	Montreal A.A.A.	1901	Winnipeg Victorias	1909	Ottawa Senators
1894	Montreal A.A.A.	1902	Montreal A.A.A.	1910	Montreal Wanderers
1895	Montreal Victorias	1903	Ottawa Silver Seven	1911	Ottawa Senators
1896	(Feb.) Winn.Victorias	1904	Ottawa Silver Seven	1912	Quebec Bulldogs
	(Dec.) Mont.Victorias	1905	Ottawa Silver Seven	1913	Quebec Bulldogs
1897	Montreal Victorias	1906	Montreal Wanderers	1914	Toronto Blueshirts (NHA)
1898	Montreal Victorias	1907	(Jan.) Kenora Thistles	1915	Vancouver Millionaires (PCHA)
1899	Montreal Shamrocks		(Mar.) Mon.Wanderers	1916	Montreal Canadiens (NHA)
1900	Montreal Shamrocks	1908	Montreal Wanderers	1917	Seattle Metropolitans (PCHA)

Stanley Cup Champions, 1918-90

Year	Winner	Head Coach	Series	Loser	Head Coach
1918	Toronto Arenas	Dick Carroll	3-2 (WLWLW)	Vancouver (PCHA)	Frank Patrick
1919	No Decision: (see below).				
1920	Ottawa	Pete Green	3-2 (WWLLW)	Seattle (PCHA)	Pete Muldoon
1921	Ottawa	Pete Green	3-2 (LWWLW)	Vancouver (PCHA)	Frank Patrick
1922	Toronto St.Pats	Eddie Powers	3-2 (LWLWW)	Vancouver (PCHA)	Frank Patrick
1923	Ottawa	Pete Green	3-1 (WLWW)	Vancouver (PCHA)	Frank Patrick
			2-0	Edmonton (WCHL)	K.C.McKenzie
1924	Montreal	Leo Dandurand	2-0	Vancouver (PCHA)	Frank Patrick
			2-0	Calgary (WCHL)	Eddie Oatman
1925	Victoria (PCHA)	Lester Patrick	3-1 (WWLW)	Montreal	Leo Dandurand
1926	Montreal Maroons	Eddie Gerard	3-1 (WWLW)	Victoria (PCHA)	Lester Patrick
1927	Ottawa	Dave Gil	2-0 (TWTW)	Boston	Art Ross
1928	NY Rangers	Lester Patrick	3-2 (LWLWW)	Montreal	Cecil Hart
1929	Boston	Art Ross	2-0	NY Rangers	Lester Patrick
1930	Montreal	Cecil Hart	2-0	Boston	Art Ross
1931	Montreal	Cecil Hart	3-2 (WLLWW)	Chicago	Art Duncan
1932	Toronto	Dick Irvin	3-0	NY Rangers	Lester Patrick
1933	NY Rangers	Lester Patrick	3-1 (WWLW)	Toronto	Dick Irvin
1934	Chicago	Tommy Gorman	3-1 (WWLW)	Detroit	Jack Adams
1935	Montreal Maroons	Lionel Conacher	3-0	Toronto	Dick Irvin
1936	Detroit	Jack Adams	3-1 (WWLW)	Toronto	Dick Irvin
1937	Detroit	Jack Adams	3-2 (LWLWW)	NY Rangers	Lester Patrick
1938	Chicago	Bill Stewart	3-1 (WLWW)	Toronto	Dick Irvin
1939	Boston	Art Ross	4-1 (WLWWW)	Toronto	Dick Irvin
1940	NY Rangers	Frank Boucher	4-2 (WWLLWW)	Toronto	Dick Irvin
1941	Boston	Cooney Weiland	4-0	Detroit	Jack Adams
1942	Toronto	Hap Day	4-3 (LLLWWWW)	Detroit	Jack Adams

Stanley Cup Champions, 1918-90 (Cont.)

Year	Winner	Head Coach	Series	Loser	Head Coach
1943	Detroit	Ebbie Goodfellow	4-0	Boston	Art Ross
1944	Montreal	Dick Irvin	4-0	Chicago	Paul Thompson
1945	Toronto	Hap Day	4-3 (WWWLLLW)	Detroit	Jack Adams
1946	Montreal	Dick Irvin	4-1 (WWWLW)	Boston	Dit Clapper
1947	Toronto	Hap Day	4-2 (LWWWLW)	Montreal	Dick Irvin
1948	Toronto	Hap Day	4-0	Detroit	Tommy Ivan
1949	Toronto	Hap Day	4-0	Detroit	Tommy Ivan
1950	Detroit	Tommy Ivan	4-3 (WLWLLWW)	NY Rangers	Lynn Patrick
1951	Toronto	Joe Primeau	4-1 (WLWWW)	Montreal	Dick Irvin
1952	Detroit	Tommy Ivan	4-0	Montreal	Dick Irvin
1953	Montreal	Dick Irvin	4-1 (WLWWW)	Boston	Lynn Patrick
1954	Detroit	Tommy Ivan	4-3 (WLWWLLW)	Montreal	Dick Irvin
1955	Detroit	Jimmy Skinner	4-3 (WWLLWLW)	Montreal	Dick Irvin
1956	Montreal	Toe Blake	4-1 (WWLWW)	Detroit	Jimmy Skinner
1957	Montreal	Toe Blake	4-1 (WWWLW)	Boston	Milt Schmidt
1958	Montreal	Toe Blake	4-2 (WLWLWW)	Boston	Milt Schmidt
1959	Montreal	Toe Blake	4-1 (WWLWW)	Toronto	Punch Imlach
1960	Montreal	Toe Blake	4-0	Toronto	Punch Imlach
1961	Chicago	Rudy Pilous	4-2 (WLWLWW)	Detroit	Sid Abel
1962	Toronto	Punch Imlach	4-2 (WWLLWW)	Chicago	Rudy Pilous
1963	Toronto	Punch Imlach	4-1 (WWLWW)	Detroit	Sid Abel
1964	Toronto	Punch Imlach	4-3 (WLLWLWW)	Detroit	Sid Abel
1965	Montreal	Toe Blake	4-3 (WWLWLW)	Chicago	Billy Reay
1966	Montreal	Toe Blake	4-2 (LLWWWW)	Detroit	Sid Abel
1967	Toronto	Punch Imlach	4-2 (LWWLWW)	Montreal	Toe Blake
1968	Montreal	Toe Blake	4-0	St. Louis	Scotty Bowman
1969	Montreal	Claude Ruel	4-0	St. Louis	Scotty Bowman
1970	Boston	Harry Sinden	4-0	St. Louis	Scotty Bowman
1971	Montreal	Al MacNeil	4-3 (LLWWWLWW)	Chicago	Billy Reay
1972	Boston	Tom Johnson	4-2 (WWLWLW)	NY Rangers	Emile Francis
1973	Montreal	Scotty Bowman	4-2 (WWLWLW)	Chicago	Billy Reay
1974	Philadelphia	Fred Shero	4-2 (LWWWLW)	Boston	Bep Guidolin
1975	Philadelphia	Fred Shero	4-2 (WWLLWW)	Buffalo	Floyd Smith
1976	Montreal	Scotty Bowman	4-0	Philadelphia	Fred Shero
1977	Montreal	Scotty Bowman	4-0	Boston	Don Cherry
1978	Montreal	Scotty Bowman	4-2 (WWLLWW)	Boston	Don Cherry
1979	Montreal	Scotty Bowman	4-1 (LWWWW)	NY Rangers	Fred Shero
1980	NY Islanders	Al Arbour	4-2 (WLWWLW)	Philadelphia	Pat Quinn
1981	NY Islanders	Al Arbour	4-1 (WWWLW)	Minnesota	Glen Sonmor
1982	NY Islanders	Al Arbour	4-0	Vancouver	Roger Neilson
1983	NY Islanders	Al Arbour	4-0	Edmonton	Glen Sather
1984	Edmonton	Glen Sather	4-1 (WLWWW)	NY Islanders	Al Arbour
1985	Edmonton	Glen Sather	4-1 (LWWWW)	Philadelphia	Mike Keenan
1986	Montreal	Jean Perron	4-1 (LWWWW)	Calgary	Bob Johnson
1987	Edmonton	Glen Sather	4-3 (WWLWLLW)	Philadelphia	Mike Keenan
1988	Edmonton	Glen Sather	4-0	Boston	Terry O'Reilly
1989	Calgary	Terry Crisp	4-2 (WLLWWW)	Montreal	Pat Burns
1990	Edmonton	John Muckler	4-1 (WWLWW)	Boston	Mike Milbury

Note: The 1919 Finals were cancelled after five games due to an influenza epidemic with Montreal and Seattle tied at 2-2-1.

Conn Smythe Trophy

The Most Valuable Player of the Stanley Cup Playoffs, as selected by the Pro Hockey Writers Assn. Presented since 1965 by Maple Leaf Gardens Limited in the name of the former Toronto coach, GM and owner, Conn Smythe. Winners who did not play for the Cup champion are in **bold type**.
   Multiple winners: Wayne Gretzky, Bobby Orr, Bernie Parent (2).

Year		Year		Year	
1965	Jean Beliveau, Mon., C	1975	Bernie Parent, Phil., G	1985	Wayne Gretzky, Edm., C
1966	**Roger Crozier,** Det., G	1976	**Reggie Leach,** Phil., RW	1986	Patrick Roy, Mon., G
1967	Dave Keon, Tor., C	1977	Guy Lafleur, Mon., RW	1987	**Ron Hextall,** Phil., G
1968	**Glenn Hall,** St.L., G	1978	Larry Robinson, Mon., D	1988	Wayne Gretzky, Edm., C
1969	Serge Savard, Mon., D	1979	Bob Gainey, Mon., LW	1989	Al MacInnis, Cal., D
1970	Bobby Orr, Bos., D	1980	Bryan Trottier, NY Isles, C	1990	Bill Ranford, Edm., G
1971	Ken Dryden, Mon., G	1981	Butch Goring, NY Isles, C		
1972	Bobby Orr, Bos., D	1982	Mike Bossy, NY Isles, RW		
1973	Yvan Cournoyer, Mon., RW	1983	Billy Smith, NY Isles, G		
1974	Bernie Parent, Phil, G	1984	Mark Messier, Edm., LW		

Note: Ken Dryden (1971) and Patrick Roy (1986) are the only players to win the Smythe Trophy as rookies.

All-Time Stanley Cup Playoff Leaders
CAREER

Stanley Cup Playoff leaders through 1990. Years listed indicate number of playoff appearances. Players active in 1990 playoffs in **bold type**.

Scoring

Points

	Yrs	Gm	G	A	Pts
Wayne Gretzky	11	138	89	195	284
Jari Kurri	10	146	92	110	202
Mark Messier	11	148	76	124	200
Jean Beliveau	17	162	79	97	176
Glenn Anderson	10	146	75	95	170
Bryan Trottier	14	175	64	106	170
Denis Potvin	14	185	56	108	164
Mike Bossy	10	129	85	75	160
Gordie Howe	20	157	68	92	160
Stan Mikita	18	155	59	91	150
Jacques Lemaire	11	145	61	78	139
Bobby Smith	11	154	55	84	139
Larry Robinson	18	213	27	112	139
Phil Esposito	15	130	61	76	137
Guy Lafleur	14	128	58	76	134
Bobby Hull	14	119	62	67	129
Henri Richard	18	180	49	80	129
Yvan Cornoyer	12	147	64	63	127
Maurice Richard	15	133	82	44	126
Brian Propp	12	136	56	69	125
Brad Park	17	162	35	90	125

Goals

	Yrs	Gm	G
Jari Kurri	10	146	92
Wayne Gretzky	11	138	89
Mike Bossy	10	129	85
Maurice Richard	17	133	82
Jean Beliveau	17	162	79
Mark Messier	11	148	76
Glenn Anderson	10	146	75
Gordie Howe	20	157	68
Yvon Cournoyer	12	147	64
Bryan Trottier	14	175	64

Assists

	Yrs	Gm	A
Wayne Gretzky	11	138	195
Mark Messier	11	148	124
Larry Robinson	18	213	112
Jari Kurri	10	146	110
Denis Potvin	13	185	108
Bryan Trottier	14	175	106
Jean Beliveau	17	162	97
Glenn Anderson	10	146	95
Gordie Howe	20	157	92
Stan Mikita	18	155	91

Goaltending

Wins

	Gm	Mins	W-L	ShO	Avg
Billy Smith	132	7645	88-36	5	2.73
Ken Dryden	112	6841	80-32	10	2.40
Jacques Plante	112	6651	71-37	15	2.17
Grant Fuhr	94	5509	66-25	2	3.04
Turk Broda	102	6406	58-42	13	1.99
Terry Sawchuk	106	6291	54-48	12	2.64
Glenn Hall	115	6899	49-65	6	2.79
Gerry Cheevers	88	5396	47-35	8	3.30
Gump Worsley	70	4080	41-25	5	2.82
Bernie Parent	71	4302	38-33	6	2.43

Shutouts

	Gm	ShO
Clint Benedict	48	15
Jacques Plante	112	15
Turk Broda	102	13
Terry Sawchuck	106	12
Ken Dryden	112	10

Goals Against Avg.
At least 50 games played.

	Gm	Mins	GA	Avg
George Hainsworth	52	3486	112	1.93
Turk Broda	101	6348	211	1.98
Jacques Plante	112	6651	241	2.17
Ken Dryden	112	6841	274	2.40
Bernie Parent	71	4302	174	2.43

Note: Clint Benedict had an average of 1.88, but played in only 48 games.

Stanley Cup Final Appearances

Standings of all teams that have reached the Stanley Cup finals, beginning in 1918.

	App	Cups	Last Cup
Montreal Canadiens	30	22*	1986
Toronto Maple Leafs	21	13†	1967
Detroit Red Wings	18	7	1955
Boston Bruins	17	5	1972
Chicago Blackhawks	9	3	1961
New York Rangers	9	3	1940
Edmonton Oilers	6	5	1990
Philadelphia Flyers	6	2	1975
New York Islanders	5	4	1983
Vanc. Millionaires (PCHA)	5	0	—
Ottawa Senators	4	4	1927
Montreal Maroons	3	2	1935
St. Louis Blues	3	0	—
Calgary Flames	2	1	1989
Victoria Cougars (PCHA)	1	1	1925
Buffalo Sabres	1	0	—
Calgary Tigers (WCHL)	1	0	—
Edmonton Eskimos (WCHL)	1	0	—
Minnesota North Stars	1	0	—
Seattle Metropolitans (PCHA)	1	0	—
Vancouver Canucks	1	0	—

*Montreal also won Cup in 1916.

†Toronto won Cup under three nicknames—Arenas (1), St.Pats (1) and Maple Leafs (11);

Teams now defunct (6): Calgary Tigers, Edmonton Eskimos, Montreal Maroons, Ottawa, Seattle, Vancouver Millionaires and Victoria.

Note: Vancouver (1918,1921-24) and Seattle (1919-20) played the Cup out of the Pacific Coast Hockey Assn. Seattle's final with Montreal was cancelled in 1919 due to an influenza epidemic.

All-Time Stanley Cup Playoff Leaders (Cont.)
Miscellaneous

Championships

	Yrs	Cups
Henri Richard, Montreal	18	11
Jean Beliveau, Montreal	17	10
Yvan Cournoyer, Montreal	15	10
Claude Provost, Montreal	14	9
Maurice Richard, Montreal	17	8
Red Kelly, Detroit-Toronto	19	8
Jacques Lemaire, Montreal	11	8

Years in Playoffs

	Yrs	Gm
Gordie Howe, Detroit-Hartford	20	157
Red Kelly, Detroit-Toronto	19	164
Stan Mikita, Chicago	18	155
Henri Richard, Montreal	18	180
Larry Robinson, Montreal-LA	18	213

Games Played

	Yrs	Gm
Larry Robinson, Los Angeles	18	213
Denis Potvin, NY Islanders	15	185
Bob Gainey, Montreal	16	182
Henri Richard, Montreal	18	180
Bryan Trottier, NY Islanders	14	175

Games Played in Goal

	Yrs	Gm
Billy Smith, NY Islanders	13	132
Glenn Hall, Det-Chi-StL	17	115
Jacques Plante, Mon-StL-Tor-Bos	16	112
Ken Dryden, Montreal	8	112
Terry Sawchuk, Det-Tor-LA-NYR	15	106

Penalty Minutes

	Yrs	Gm	PM
Dale Hunter, Que-Wash	10	102	507
Willi Plett, Atl-Calg-Min-Bos	10	83	466
Chris Nilan, Mon-NYR	10	85	464
Dave Williams, Tor-Van-LA	12	83	455
Dave Schultz, Phi-LA-Buf	6	73	412

SINGLE SEASON PLAYOFF YEAR

Scoring

Points

	Year	Gm	G	A	Pts
Wayne Gretzky, Edm	1985	18	17	30	47
Wayne Gretzky, Edm	1988	19	12	31	43
Wayne Gretzky, Edm	1983	16	12	26	38
Paul Coffey, Edm	1985	18	12	25	37
Mike Bossy, NYI	1981	18	17	18	35
Wayne Gretzky, Edm	1984	19	13	22	35
Mark Messier, Edm	1988	19	11	23	35
Wayne Gretzky, Edm	1987	21	5	29	34
Rick Middleton, Bos	1983	17	11	22	33
Barry Pederson, Bos	1983	17	14	18	32

Goals

	Year	Gm	G
Reggie Leach, Phi	1976	16	19
Jari Kurri, Edm	1985	18	19
Mike Bossy, NYI	1981	18	17
Wayne Gretzky, Edm	1985	18	17
Steve Payne, Minn	1981	19	17
Mike Bossy, NYI	1982	19	17
Mike Bossy, NYI	1983	19	17

Assists

	Year	Gm	A
Wayne Gretzky, Edm	1988	19	31
Wayne Gretzky, Edm	1985	18	30
Wayne Gretzky, Edm	1987	21	29
Wayne Gretzky, Edm	1983	16	26
Paul Coffey, Edm	1985	18	25

Goaltending

Wins

	Year	Gm	Mins	W-L
Grant Fuhr, Edm	1988	19	1136	16- 2
Mike Vernon, Calg	1989	22	1381	16- 5
Bill Ranford, Edm	1990	22	1401	16- 6
Billy Smith, NYI	1982	18	1120	15- 3
Grant Fuhr, Edm	1985	18	1064	15- 3
Billy Smith, NYI	1980	20	1198	15- 4
Patrick Roy, Mon	1986	20	1218	15- 5
Ron Hextall, Phi	1987	26	1540	15-11
Billy Smith, NYI	1981	17	994	14- 3
Grant Fuhr, Edm	1987	19	1148	14- 5

Shutouts

	Year	Gm	ShO
Clint Benedict, M.Maroons	1928	9	4
Dave Kerr, NYR	1937	9	4
Frank McCool, Tor	1945	13	4
Terry Sawchuck, Det	1952	8	4
Bernie Parent, Phi	1975	17	4
Ken Dryden, Mon	1977	14	4

Goals Against Avg.
At least eight games played.

	Year	Gm	Min	GA	Avg
Terry Sawchuk, Det	1952	8	480	5	0.63
Turk Broda, Tor	1951	9	509	9	1.06
Dave Kerr, NYR	1937	9	553	10	1.08
Jacques Plante, Mon	1960	8	488	11	1.35
Jacques Plante, StL	1969	10	589	14	1.43

SINGLE GAME
Scoring

Points

	Date	G	A	Pts
Patrik Sundstrom, NJ vs Wash	4/22/88	3	5	8
Mario Lemieux, Pit.vs Phi	4/25/89	5	3	8
Wayne Gretzky, Edm.at Calg	4/17/83	4	3	7
Wayne Gretzky, Edm.at Win	4/25/85	3	4	7
Wayne Gretzky, Edm.vs LA	4/9/87	1	6	7

Goals

	Date	G
Maurice Richard, Mon.vs Tor	3/23/44	5
Darryl Sittler, Tor.vs Phi	4/22/76	5
Reggie Leach, Phi.vs Bos	5/6/76	5
Mario Lemieux, Pit.vs Phi	4/25/89	5

NHL Franchise Origins

Here is what the current 21 teams in the National Hockey League have to show for the years they have put in as members of the NHL and World Hockey Association (WHA). League titles are noted by year won.

Prince of Wales Conference

	First Season	League Titles	Franchise Stops
Boston Bruins	1924-25 (NHL)	5 NHL (1929,39,41,70,72)	Boston (1924-)
Buffalo Sabres	1970-71 (NHL)	None	Buffalo (1970-)
Hartford Whalers	1972-73 (WHA)	1 WHA (1973)	Boston (1972-74)
			W.Springfield,MA (1974-75)
			Hartford,CT (1975-78)
			Springfield,MA (1978-80)
			Hartford (1980-)
Montreal Canadiens	1917-18 (NHL)	22 NHL (1924,30-31,44,46,53, 56-60,65-66,68-69, 71,73,76-79,86)	Montreal (1917-)
New Jersey Devils	1974-75 (NHL)	None	Kansas City (1974-76)
			Denver (1976-82)
			E.Rutherford,NJ (1982-)
New York Islanders	1972-73 (NHL)	4 NHL (1980-83)	Uniondale,NY (1972-)
New York Rangers	1926-27 (NHL)	3 NHL (1928,33,40)	New York (1926-)
Philadelphia Flyers	1967-68 (NHL)	2 NHL (1974-75)	Philadelphia (1967-)
Pittsburgh Penguins	1967-68 (NHL)	None	Pittsburgh (1967-)
Quebec Nordiques	1972-73 (WHA)	1 WHA (1977)	Quebec City (1972-)
Washington Capitals	1974-75 (NHL)	None	Landover,MD (1974-)

Note: The Hartford Civic Center roof caved in Jan,1978, forcing the Whalers to move home games to the Springfield,MA Civic Center for two years.

Clarence Campbell Conference

	First Season	League Titles	Franchise Stops
Calgary Flames	1972-73 (NHL)	1 NHL (1989)	Atlanta (1972-80)
			Calgary (1980-)
Chicago Blackhawks	1926-27 (NHL)	3 NHL (1934,38,61)	Chicago (1926-)
Detroit Red Wings	1926-27 (NHL)	7 NHL (1936-37,43,50, 52,54-55)	Detroit (1926-)
Edmonton Oilers	1973-74 (WHA)	5 NHL (1984-85,87-88, 90)	Edmonton (1972-)
Los Angeles Kings	1967-68 (NHL)	None	Los Angeles (1967-)
Minn.North Stars	1967-68 (NHL)	None	Bloomington,MN (1967-)
St.Louis Blues	1967-68 (NHL)	None	St.Louis (1967-)
Toronto Maple Leafs	1917-18 (NHL)	13 NHL (1918,22,32,42,45, 47-49,51,62-64,67)	Toronto (1917-)
Vancouver Canucks	1970-71 (NHL)	None	Vancouver (1970-)
Winnipeg Jets	1972-73 (WHA)	3 WHA (1976,78-79)	Winnipeg (1972-)

Combined All-Time NHL-WHA Leaders

All-Time scoring and wins leaders for NHL skaters and goaltenders with WHA (1972-79) service added. Players active during 1989-90 in **bold type**; (*) indicates WHA players.

Points

	Yrs	Gm	G	A	Pts
Gordie Howe*	32	2186	975	1383	2358
Wayne Gretzky*	12	907	723	1366	2089
Bobby Hull*	23	1474	913	895	1808
Marcel Dionne	18	1348	731	1040	1771
Phil Esposito	18	1282	717	873	1590
Stan Mikita	22	1394	541	926	1467
John Bucyk	23	1540	556	813	1369
Norm Ullman*	22	1554	537	822	1359
Bryan Trottier	15	1123	500	853	1353
Frank Mahovlich*	22	1418	622	713	1335
Gilbert Perreault	17	1191	512	814	1326
Guy Lafleur	16	1067	548	777	1325
Alex Delvecchio	24	1549	456	825	1281
Dave Keon*	22	1597	498	779	1277
Jean Ratelle	21	1281	491	776	1267

*WHA Totals: Howe (6 yrs, 419 gms, 174-334—508); Gretzky (1 yr, 60 gms, 46-64-110); Hull (7 yrs, 411 gms, 303-335—638); Ullman (2 yrs, 144 gms, 47-83—130); Mahovlich (4 yrs, 237 gms, 89-143—232); Keon (4 yrs, 301 gms, 102-189—291); Tardif (6 yrs, 446 gms, 316-350—666).

Wins

	Yrs	Gm	W	L	T	Pct
Jacques Plante*	19	868	449	260	138	.597
Terry Sawchuk	21	971	435	337	188	.545
Tony Esposito	16	886	423	307	151	.563
Glenn Hall	18	906	407	327	165	.540
Rogie Vachon	16	795	355	291	115	.519
Gump Worsley	21	862	335	353	150	.476
Harry Lumley	16	804	332	324	143	.502
Gerry Cheevers*	16	609	329	172	83	.608
Bernie Parent*	14	671	303	225	121	.542
Turk Broda	12	629	302	224	101	.560
Billy Smith	18	680	301	216	100	.516
Mike Liut*	13	689	301	287	73	.490
Ed Giacomin	13	610	289	206	97	.553
Dan Bouchard	14	655	286	232	113	.523
Tiny Thompson	12	553	284	194	75	.581

*WHA Totals: Plante (1 yr, 31 gms, 15-14-1); Cheevers (4 yrs, 191 gms, 99-78-9); Parent (1 yr, 63 gms, 33-28-0); Liut (2 yrs, 81 gms, 31-39-4).

NHL All-Time Individual Leaders
CAREER
Through 1989-90 regular season; players active during1989-90 in **bold type**.

Points

	Yrs	Gm	G	A	Pts
Wayne Gretzky	11	847	677	1302	1979
Gordie Howe	26	1767	801	1049	1850
Marcel Dionne	18	1348	731	1040	1771
Phil Esposito	18	1282	717	873	1590
Stan Mikita	22	1394	541	926	1467
John Bucyk	23	1540	556	813	1369
Bryan Trottier	15	1123	500	853	1353
Gilbert Perreault	17	1191	512	814	1326
Guy Lafleur	16	1067	548	777	1325
Alex Delvecchio	24	1549	456	825	1281
Jean Ratelle	21	1281	491	776	1267
Norm Ullman	20	1410	490	739	1229
Jean Beliveau	20	1125	507	712	1219
Bobby Clarke	15	1144	358	852	1210
Bobby Hull	16	1063	610	560	1170
Bernie Federko	14	1000	369	761	1130
Mike Bossy	10	752	573	553	1126
Darryl Sittler	15	1096	484	637	1121
Frank Mahovlich	18	1181	533	570	1103
Peter Stastny	10	749	385	674	1059
Denis Potvin	15	1060	310	742	1052
Henri Richard	20	1256	358	688	1046
Jari Kurri	10	754	474	569	1043
Rod Gilbert	18	1065	406	615	1021
Denis Savard	10	736	351	662	1013

Goals

	Yrs	Gm	Goals
Gordie Howe	26	1767	801
Marcel Dionne	18	1348	731
Phil Esposito	18	1282	717
Wayne Gretzky	11	847	677
Bobby Hull	16	1063	610
Mike Bossy	10	752	573
John Bucyk	23	1540	556
Guy Lafleur	16	1067	548
Maurice Richard	18	978	544
Stan Mikita	22	1394	541
Frank Mahovlich	18	1181	533
Gilbert Perreault	17	1191	512
Jean Beliveau	18	1125	507
Lanny McDonald	16	1111	500
Bryan Trottier	15	1123	500
Jean Ratelle	21	1281	491
Norm Ullman	20	1410	490
Darryl Sittler	15	1096	484
Jari Kurri	10	754	474
Michel Goulet	11	821	460
Alex Delvecchio	24	1549	456
Mike Gartner	11	850	449
Rick Middleton	14	1005	448
Yvan Cournoyer	16	968	428
Steve Shutt	13	930	424

Assists

	Yrs	Gm	Assists
Wayne Gretzky	11	847	1302
Gordie Howe	26	1767	1049
Marcel Dionne	18	1348	1040
Stan Mikita	22	1394	926
Phil Esposito	18	1281	873
Bryan Trottier	15	1123	853
Bobby Clarke	15	1144	852
Alex Delvecchio	24	1549	825
Gilbert Perreault	17	1191	814
John Bucyk	23	1540	813
Guy Lafleur	16	1067	777
Jean Ratelle	21	1281	776
Bernie Federko	14	1000	761
Denis Potvin	15	1060	742
Norm Ullman	20	1410	739
Larry Robinson	18	1266	718
Jean Beliveau	20	1125	712
Henri Richard	20	1256	688
Brad Park	17	1113	683
Peter Stastny	10	749	674
Paul Coffey	10	733	669
Denis Savard	10	736	662
Bobby Orr	12	657	645
Darryl Sittler	15	1096	637
Borje Salming	17	1148	637

Penalty Minutes

	Yrs	Gm	PMin
Dave Williams	13	962	3966
Willi Plett	12	834	2572
Chris Nilan	11	591	2506
Dave Schultz	9	535	2294
Dale Hunter	10	762	2237
Bryan Watson	16	878	2212
Terry O'Reilly	14	891	2095
Tim Hunter	8	481	2095
Al Secord	11	766	2093
Phil Russell	15	1016	2038
Andre Dupont	13	810	1986
Laurie Boschman	11	786	1964
Harold Snepsts	16	979	1959
Garry Howatt	12	720	1836
Rob Ramage	11	835	1822
Carol Vadnais	17	1087	1813
Larry Playfair	12	688	1812
Ted Lindsay	17	1068	1808
Brian Sutter	12	779	1786
Jay Wells	11	731	1759
Mike Foligno	11	819	1755
Torrie Robertson	9	442	1751
Jim Korn	10	597	1750
Wilf Paiement	13	923	1718
Gordie Howe	26	1767	1685

Years Played

	Yrs
Gordie Howe	26
Alex Delvecchio	24
Tim Horton	24
John Bucyk	23
Stan Mikita	22
Doug Mohns	22
Dean Prentice	22
Harry Howell	21
Eric Nesterenko	21
Jean Ratelle	21
Terry Sawchuk	21
Allan Stanley	21
Ron Stewart	21
Gump Worsley	21
George Armstrong	20
Jean Beliveau	20
Dit Clapper	20
Bill Gadsby	20
Red Kelly	20
Marcel Pronovost	20
Henri Richard	20
Norm Ullman	20

Note: Combined NHL-WHA years played: Howe (32); Howell (24); Nesterenko and Bobby Hull (23); Ullman, Frank Mahovlich and Dave Keon (22).

Games Played

	Gms
Gordie Howe	1767
Alex Delvecchio	1549
John Bucyk	1540
Tim Horton	1446
Harry Howell	1411
Norm Ullman	1410
Stan Mikita	1394
Doug Mohns	1390
Dean Prentice	1378
Ron Stewart	1353
Marcel Dionne	1348
Red Kelly	1316
Dave Keon	1296
Phil Esposito	1282
Jean Ratelle	1281
Larry Robinson	1266
Henri Richard	1256
Bill Gadsby	1248
Allan Stanley	1244
Ed Westfall	1227
Eric Nesterenko	1219
Marcel Pronovost	1206

Note: Combined NHL-WHA games played: Howe (2,186), Keon (1597), Howell (1581), Ullman (1554), Hull (1474), Mahovlich (1418) and Nesterenko (1248).

Goaltending

Wins

	Yrs	Gm	W	L	T	Pct
Terry Sawchuk	21	971	435	337	188	.545
Jacques Plante	18	837	434	246	137	.600
Tony Esposito	16	886	423	307	151	.563
Glenn Hall	18	906	407	327	165	.540
Rogie Vachon	16	795	355	291	115	.519
Gump Worsley	21	862	335	353	150	.476
Harry Lumley	16	804	332	324	143	.502
Turk Broda	12	629	302	224	101	.560
Billy Smith	18	680	301	216	100	.516
Ed Giacomin	13	610	289	206	97	.553
Dan Bouchard	14	655	286	232	113	.523
Tiny Thompson	12	553	284	194	75	.581
Bernie Parent	13	608	270	197	121	.544
Mike Liut	11	607	270	248	69	.502
Gilles Meloche	18	761	262	342	126	.427
Ken Dryden	8	397	258	57	74	.743
Frank Brimsek	10	514	252	182	80	.568
Johnny Bower	15	549	251	196	90	.539
George Hainsworth	11	465	247	146	74	.611
Pete Peeters	11	463	237	148	50	.566
Eddie Johnston	16	592	236	256	87	.472
Chico Resch	14	571	231	224	82	.476
Gerry Cheevers	13	418	230	94	74	.671
Grant Fuhr	9	410	220	113	51	.599

Shutouts

	Yrs	Gm	ShO
Terry Sawchuk	21	971	103
George Hainsworth	11	465	94
Glenn Hall	18	906	84
Jacques Plante	18	837	82
Tiny Thompson	12	552	81
Alex Connell	12	416	80
Tony Esposito	16	886	76
Lorne Chabot	11	412	73
Harry Lumley	16	803	71
Roy Worters	12	488	66
Turk Broda	12	628	62
Clint Benedict	13	360	58
John Roach	14	492	58
Bernie Parent	13	608	55
Ed Giacomin	13	610	54
Dave Kerr	11	427	51
Rogie Vachon	16	795	51
Ken Dryden	8	397	46
Gump Worsley	21	860	43
Chuck Gardiner	7	316	42
Frank Brimsek	10	515	40
Johnny Bower	15	552	37
Bill Durnan	7	383	34
Eddie Johnston	16	592	32

Goals Against Average

Minimum of 300 games played.

Careers Ending Before 1950

	Gm	Mins	GA	Avg
George Hainsworth	465	29,415	937	1.91
Alex Connell	416	26,030	837	2.01
Chuck Gardiner	316	19,687	664	2.02
Lorne Chabot	412	25,309	861	2.04
Tiny Thompson	552	34,174	1183	2.08
Dave Kerr	426	26,519	960	2.17
Roy Worters	484	30,175	1143	2.27
Clint Benedict	362	22,321	863	2.32
Bill Durnan	383	22,945	901	2.36
John Roach	491	30,423	1246	2.46

Careers Ending Since 1950

	Gm	Mins	GA	Avg
Ken Dryden	397	23,352	870	2.24
Jacques Plante	837	49,633	1965	2.38
Glenn Hall	906	53,484	2239	2.51
Terry Sawchuk	971	57,205	2401	2.52
Johnny Bower	552	32,077	1347	2.52
Bernie Parent	608	35,136	1493	2.55
Turk Broda	628	37,680	1605	2.56
Frank Brimsek	515	31,210	1404	2.70
Charlie Hodge	358	20,593	927	2.70
Harry Lumley	803	48,107	2210	2.76

NHL All-Time Individual Leaders (Cont.)

SINGLE SEASON

Scoring

Points

	Season	G	A	Pts
Wayne Gretzky, Edm	1985-86	52	163	215
Wayne Gretzky, Edm	1981-82	92	120	212
Wayne Gretzky, Edm	1984-85	73	135	208
Wayne Gretzky, Edm	1983-84	87	118	205
Mario Lemieux, Pit	1988-89	85	114	199
Wayne Gretzky, Edm	1982-83	71	125	196
Wayne Gretzky, Edm	1986-87	62	121	183
Mario Lemieux, Pit	1987-88	70	98	168
Wayne Gretzky, LA	1988-89	54	114	168
Wayne Gretzky, Edm	1980-81	55	109	164
Phil Esposito, Bos	1970-71	76	76	152

WHA 150 points or more: 154—Marc Tardif, Que.(1977-78).

Goals

	Season	Gm	G
Wayne Gretzky, Edm	1981-82	80	92
Wayne Gretzky, Edm	1983-84	74	87
Mario Lemieux, Pit	1988-89	76	85
Phil Esposito, Bos	1970-71	78	76
Wayne Gretzky, Edm	1984-85	80	73
Brett Hull, St.L	1989-90	80	72
Jari Kurri, Edm	1984-85	73	71
Wayne Gretzky, Edm	1982-83	80	71
Mario Lemieux, Pit	1987-88	77	70
Bernie Nicholls, LA	1988-89	79	70
Mike Bossy, NYI	1978-79	80	69
Phil Esposito, Bos	1973-74	78	68
Jari Kurri, Edm	1985-86	78	68
Mike Bossy, NYI	1980-81	79	68
Phil Esposito, Bos	1971-72	76	66
Lanny McDonald, Calg	1982-83	80	66
Steve Yzerman, Det	1988-89	80	65

WHA 65 goals or more: 77—Bobby Hull, Win.(1974-75); **75**—Real Cloutier, Que.(1978-79); **71**—Marc Tardif, Que.(1975-76); **70**—Anders Hedberg, Win.(1976-77); **66**—Real Cloutier, Que.(1976-77); **65**—Marc Tardif, Que.(1977-78) and Morris Lukowich, Win.(1978-79).

Assists

	Season	Gm	A
Wayne Gretzky, Edm	1985-86	80	163
Wayne Gretzky, Edm	1984-85	80	135
Wayne Gretzky, Edm	1982-83	80	125
Wayne Gretzky, Edm	1986-87	79	121
Wayne Gretzky, Edm	1981-82	80	120
Wayne Gretzky, Edm	1983-84	74	118
Mario Lemieux, Pit	1988-89	76	114
Wayne Gretzky, LA	1988-89	78	114
Wayne Gretzky, Edm	1987-88	64	109
Wayne Gretzky, Edm	1980-81	80	109
Wayne Gretzky, LA	1989-90	73	102
Bobby Orr, Bos	1970-71	78	102
Mario Lemieux, Pit	1987-88	77	98
Mario Lemieux, Pit	1985-86	79	93
Peter Stastny, Que	1981-82	80	93
Bobby Orr, Bos	1973-74	74	90
Paul Coffey, Edm	1985-86	79	90
Steve Yzerman, Det	1988-89	80	90

WHA 90 assists or more: 106—Andre Lacroix, S.Diego (1974-75); **94**—Ulf Nilsson, Win.(1974-75).

Goaltending

Wins

	Season	W	L	T
Bernie Parent, Phi	1973-74	47	13	12
Bernie Parent, Phi	1974-75	44	14	9
Terry Sawchuk, Det	1950-51	44	13	13
Terry Sawchuk, Det	1951-52	44	14	12
Jacques Plante, Mon	1955-56	42	12	10
Jacques Plante, Mon	1961-62	42	14	14
Ken Dryden, Mon	1975-76	42	10	8

WHA 40 wins or more: 44—Richard Brodeur, Que.(1975-76); **41**—Joe Daley, Win.(1975-76) and Dave Dryden, Edm.(1978-79).

Losses

	Season	W	L	T
Gary Smith, Cal	1970-71	19	48	4
Al Rollins, Chi	1953-54	12	47	7
Harry Lumley, Chi	1951-52	17	44	9
Harry Lumley, Chi	1950-51	12	41	10
Eddie Johnston, Bos	1963-64	18	40	12

Most WHA losses in one season: 36—Don McLeod, Van.(1974-75) and Andy Brown, Ind.(1974-75).

Shutouts

	Season	Gm	ShO
George Hainsworth, Mon	1928-29	44	22
Alex Connell, Ottawa	1925-26	36	15
Alex Connell, Ottawa	1927-28	44	15
Hal Winkler, Bos	1927-28	44	15
Tony Esposito, Chi	1969-70	63	15
George Hainsworth, Mon	1926-27	44	14

Most WHA shutouts in one season: 5—Gerry Cheevers, Cle.(1972-73) and Joe Daly, Win.(1975-76).

Goals Against Average

Before 1950

	Season	Gm	Avg
George Hainsworth, Mon	1928-29	44	0.98
George Hainsworth, Mon	1927-28	44	1.09
Alex Connell, Ottawa	1925-26	36	1.17
Tiny Thompson, Bos	1928-29	44	1.18
Roy Worters, NY Amer	1928-29	38	1.21

Since 1950

	Season	Gm	Avg
Al Rollins, Tor	1950-51	40	1.77
Tony Esposito, Chi	1971-72	48	1.77
Harry Lumley, Tor	1953-54	69	1.86
Jacques Plante, Mon	1955-56	64	1.86
Jacques Plante, Tor	1970-71	40	1.88

Penalty Minutes

	Season	PM
Dave Schultz, Phi	1974-75	472
Paul Baxter, Pit	1981-82	407
Dave Schultz, LA	1977-78	405
Basil McRae, Min	1987-88	382
Tim Hunter, Calg	1988-89	375

WHA 350 minutes or more: 365—Curt Brackenbury, Min-Que.(1975-76); **351**—Kim Clackson, Ind.(1975-76)

SINGLE GAME
Scoring

Points

	Date	G	A	Pts
Darryl Sittler, Tor. vs Bos	2/7/76	6	4	10
Maurice Richard, Mon. vs Det	12/28/44	5	3	8
Bert Olmstead, Mon. vs Chi	1/9/54	4	4	8
Tom Bladon, Phi. vs Cle	12/11/77	4	4	8
Bryan Trottier, NYI vs NYR	12/23/78	5	3	8
Peter Stastny, Que. at Wash	2/22/81	4	4	8
Anton Stastny, Que. at Wash	2/22/81	3	5	8
Wayne Gretzky, Edm. vs NJ	11/19/83	3	5	8
Wayne Gretzky, Edm. vs Minn	1/4/84	4	4	8
Paul Coffey, Edm. vs Det	3/14/86	2	6	8
Mario Lemieux, Pit. vs StL	10/15/88	2	6	8
Bernie Nicholls, LA vs Tor	12/1/88	2	6	8
Mario Lemieux, Pit. vs NJ	12/31/88	5	3	8

Goals

	Date	G
Joe Malone, Que. vs Tor	1/31/20	7
Newsy Lalonde, Mon. vs Tor	1/10/20	6
Joe Malone, Que. vs Ott	3/10/20	6
Corb Denneny, Tor. vs Ham	1/26/21	6
Cy Denneny, Ott. vs Ham	3/7/21	6
Syd Howe, Det. vs NYR	2/3/44	6
Red Berenson, St.L. at Phi	11/7/68	6
Darryl Sittler, Tor. vs Bos	2/7/76	6

Assists

	Date	A
Billy Taylor, Det. at Chi	3/16/47	7
Wayne Gretzky, Edm. vs Wash	2/15/80	7
Wayne Gretzky, Edm. at Chi	12/11/85	7
Wayne Gretzky, Edm. vs Que	2/14/86	7

NHL All-Star Game, 1947-90

The NHL All-Star Game began at the start of the 1947-48 season as an exhibition contest between the defending league champion and a squad of star players from the other five teams. Two All-Star teams played each other in 1951 and '52, but 1953 saw a return to the original format. The game moved to mid-season in 1967, became an East Division vs West Division contest in 1969, and finally a Wales Conference vs Campbell Conference contest in 1975. Winning coaches are listed first.

Year	Result	Host	Coaches	Most Valuable Player
1947	All-Stars 4, Toronto 3	Toronto	Dick Irvin, Hap Day	No award
1948	All-Stars 3, Toronto 1	Chicago	Tommy Ivan, Hap Day	No award
1949	All-Stars 3, Toronto 1	Toronto	Tommy Ivan, Hap Day	No award
1950	Detroit 7, All-Stars 1	Detroit	Tommy Ivan, Lynn Patrick	No award
1951	1st Team 2, 2nd Team 2	Toronto	Joe Primeau, Hap Day	No award
1952	1st Team 1, 2nd Team 1	Detroit	Tommy Ivan, Dick Irvin	No award
1953	All-Stars 3, Montreal 1	Montreal	Lynn Patrick, Dick Irvin	No award
1954	All-Stars 2, Detroit 2	Detroit	King Clancy, Jim Skinner	No award
1955	Detroit 3, All-Stars 1	Detroit	Jim Skinner, Dick Irvin	No award
1956	All-Stars 1, Montreal 1	Montreal	Jim Skinner, Toe Blake	No award
1957	All-Stars 5, Montreal 3	Montreal	Milt Schmidt, Toe Blake	No award
1958	Montreal 6, All-Stars 3	Montreal	Toe Blake, Milt Schmidt	No award
1959	Montreal 6, All-Stars 1	Montreal	Toe Blake, Punch Imlach	No award
1960	All-Stars 2, Montreal 1	Montreal	Punch Imlach, Toe Blake	No award
1961	All-Stars 3, Chicago 1	Chicago	Sid Abel, Rudy Pilous	No award
1962	Toronto 4, All-Stars 1	Toronto	Punch Imlach, Rudy Pilous	Eddie Shack, Toronto
1963	All-Stars 3, Toronto 3	Toronto	Sid Abel, Punch Imlach	Frank Mahovlich, Tor.
1964	All-Stars 3, Toronto 2	Toronto	Sid Abel, Punch Imlach	Jean Beliveau, Mont.
1965	All-Stars 5, Montreal 2	Montreal	Billy Reay, Toe Blake	Gordie Howe, Detroit
1966	No Game (see below)			
1967	Montreal 3, All-Stars 0	Montreal	Toe Blake, Sid Abel	Henri Richard, Mont.
1968	Toronto 4, All-Stars 3	Toronto	Punch Imlach, Toe Blake	Bruce Gamble, Tor.
1969	West 3, East 3	Montreal	Scotty Bowman, Toe Blake	Frank Mahovlich, Det.
1970	East 4, West 1	St.Louis	Claude Ruel, Scotty Bowman	Bobby Hull, Chicago
1971	West 2, East 1	Boston	Scotty Bowman, Harry Sinden	Bobby Hull, Chicago
1972	East 3, West 2	Minnesota	Al MacNeil, Billy Reay	Bobby Orr, Boston
1973	East 5, West 4	NY Rangers	Tom Johnson, Billy Reay	Greg Polis, Pitt.
1974	West 6, East 4	Chicago	Billy Reay, Scotty Bowman	Garry Unger, St.L.
1975	Wales 7, Campbell 1	Montreal	Bep Guidolin, Fred Shero	Syl Apps, Jr., Pitt.
1976	Wales 7, Campbell 5	Philadelphia	Floyd Smith, Fred Shero	Peter Mahovlich, Mont.
1977	Wales 4, Campbell 3	Vancouver	Scotty Bowman, Fred Shero	Rick Martin, Buffalo
1978	Wales 3, Campbell 2 (OT)	Buffalo	Scotty Bowman, Fred Shero	Billy Smith, NYI
1979	No Game (see below)			
1980	Wales 6, Campbell 3	Detroit	Scotty Bowman, Al Arbour	Reggie Leach, Phila.
1981	Campbell 4, Wales 1	Los Angeles	Pat Quinn, Scotty Bowman	Mike Liut, St.Louis
1982	Wales 4, Campbell 2	Washington	Al Arbour, Glen Sonmor	Mike Bossy, NYI
1983	Campbell 9, Wales 3	NY Islanders	Roger Neilson, Al Arbour	Wayne Gretzky, Edm.
1984	Wales 7, Campbell 6	New Jersey	Al Arbour, Glen Sather	Don Maloney, NYR

NHL All-Star Game, 1947-90 (Cont.)

Year	Result	Host	Coaches	Most Valuable Player
1985	Wales 6, Campbell 4	Calgary	Al Arbour, Glen Sather	Mario Lemieux, Pitt.
1986	Wales 4, Campbell 3 (OT)	Hartford	Mike Keenan, Glen Sather	Grant Fuhr, Edm.
1987	No Game (see below)			
1988	Wales 6, Campbell 5 (OT)	St.Louis	Mike Keenan, Glen Sather	Mario Lemieux, Pitt.
1989	Campbell 9, Wales 5	Edmonton	Glen Sather, Terry O'Reilly	Wayne Gretzky, LA
1990	Wales 12, Campbell 7	Pittsburgh	Pat Burns, Terry Crisp	Mario Lemieux, Pit.

No All-Star Game: in 1966 (moved from start of season to mid-season); in 1979 (replaced by Challenge Cup series with USSR); in 1987 (replaced by Rendez-Vous'87 series with USSR). See ''International Series'' for outcome.

All-Time Winningest NHL Coaches

Minimum of 300 NHL victories through 1989-90 season. Regular season and playoffs included. Active coaches in **bold type**.

Top Winning Percentages

	Yrs	Gms	W	L	T	Pct
Scotty Bowman	17	1462	853	399	210	**.655**
Toe Blake	13	1033	582	292	159	**.640**
Glen Sather	10	926	535	287	104	**.634**
Fred Shero	10	842	451	272	119	**.606**
Al Arbour	18	1465	760	497	208	**.590**
Tommy Ivan	9	677	338	227	112	**.582**
Mike Keenan	6	573	309	218	46	**.579**
Bryan Murray	9	725	367	275	83	**.563**
Billy Reay	16	1219	599	445	175	**.563**
Emile Francis	11	871	433	326	112	**.561**
Hap Day	10	626	308	237	81	**.557**
Dick Irvin	26	1627	790	609	228	**.556**
Art Ross	16	798	393	310	95	**.552**
Lester Patrick	13	669	312	242	115	**.552**
Punch Imlach	15	1051	467	421	163	**.522**
Jack Adams	17	1069	465	442	164	**.512**
Bob Pulford	14	838	364	344	130	**.512**
Bob Berry	9	721	315	306	100	**.506**
Michel Bergeron	10	860	369	387	104	**.490**
Jacques Demers	8	711	304	321	86	**.488**
Sid Abel	15	1039	414	470	155	**.473**
Red Kelly	10	804	302	368	134	**.459**

Note: The NHL does not recognize WHA coaching records, so the overall WHA records of **Sather** (103-91-7 in three years) and **Demers** (155-164-22 in four years) are not included above.

Most Victories

	Regular Season	Playoffs	Total
Scotty Bowman	739	114	**853**
Dick Irvin	690	100	**790**
Al Arbour	646	114	**760**
Billy Reay	542	57	**599**
Toe Blake	500	82	**582**
Glen Sather	446	89	**535**
Punch Imlach	423	44	**467**
Jack Adams	413	52	**465**
Fred Shero	390	61	**451**
Emile Francis	393	40	**433**
Sid Abel	382	32	**414**
Art Ross	361	32	**393**
Michel Bergeron	338	31	**369**
Bryan Murray	343	24	**367**
Bob Pulford	336	28	**364**
Tommy Ivan	302	36	**338**
Bob Berry	311	4	**315**
Lester Patrick	281	31	**312**
Mike Keenan	258	51	**309**
Hap Day	259	49	**308**
Jacques Demers	268	36	**304**
Red Kelly	278	24	**302**

Note: The NHL does not recognize WHA coaching records, so the WHA victories of **Sather** (95 + 8 = 103) and **Demers** (147 + 8 = 155) are not included above.

Where They Coached

Abel—Chicago (1952-54), Detroit (1957-68,69-70), St.Louis (1971-72), Kansas City (1975-76); **Adams**—Detroit (1927-44); **Arbour**—St.Louis (1970-73), NY Islanders (1973-86,88—); **Bergeron**—Quebec (1980-87), NY Rangers (1987-89), Quebec (1989-90); **Berry**—Los Angeles (1978-81), Montreal (1981-84), Pittsburgh (1984-87); **Blake**—Montreal (1955-68); **Bowman**—St.Louis (1967-71), Montreal (1971-79), Buffalo (1979-87); **Day**—Toronto (1940-50); **Demers**—St.Louis (1983-86), Detroit (1986—); **Francis**—NY Rangers (1965-75), St.Louis (1976-77,81-83).

Imlach—Toronto (1958-69), Buffalo (1970-72), Toronto (1979-81); **Irvin**—Chicago (1930-31,55-56), Toronto (1931-40), Montreal (1940-55); **Ivan**—Detroit (1947-54), Chicago (1956-58); **Keenan**—Philadelphia (1984-88), Chicago (1988—); **Kelly**—Los Angeles (1967-69), Pittsburgh (1969-73), Toronto (1973-77); **Murray**—Washington (1982-90); **Patrick**—NY Rangers (1926-39); **Pulford**—Los Angeles (1972-77), Chicago (1977-79,81-82,85-87); **Reay**—Toronto (1957-59), Chicago (1963-77); **Ross**—Boston (1924-28,29-34,36-39,41-45); **Sather**—Edmonton (1979-89); **Shero**—Philadelphia (1971-78), NY Rangers (1978-81).

Active Coaches' Victories

Through 1989-90 season, including playoffs.

	Yrs	W	L	T	Pct
Al Arbour, NY Isles	18	760	497	208	.590
Bryan Murray, Detroit	9	367	275	83	.563
Mike Keenan, Chicago	6	309	218	46	.579
Roger Neilson, NY Rangers	8	252	226	87	.523
Bob Johnson, Pittsburgh	5	218	182	52	.540
Bob McCammon, Vanc.	7	206	207	62	.499
Doug Carpenter, Toronto	5	139	208	28	.408
Pat Burns, Montreal	2	113	59	20	.641
Brian Sutter, St.Louis	2	82	79	21	.508
Paul Holmgren, Phila.	2	76	84	19	.478
Bob Murdoch, Winnipeg	2	71	81	20	.471
John Muckler, Edmonton	2	60	57	20	.511
Mike Milbury, Boston	1	59	33	9	.629
Rick Dudley, Buffalo	1	47	31	8	.593
Tom Webster, Los Ang	2	43	52	9	.457
Rick Ley, Hartford	1	41	37	9	.523
John Cunniff, New Jersey	1	33	32	7	.507
Terry Murray, Washington	1	26	21	2	.551
Dave Chambers, Quebec	0	0	0	0	.000
Bob Gainey, Minnesota	0	0	0	0	.000
Doug Risebrough, Calgary	0	0	0	0	.000

Annual Award Winners

Hart Memorial Trophy

Awarded to the player "adjudged to be the most valuable to his team" and named after Cecil Hart, the former manager-coach of the Montreal Canadiens. Winners selected by Pro Hockey Writers Assn. (PHWA). Winners' scoring statistics or goaltender W-L records & goals against average are provided; (*) denotes led league in scoring.

Multiple winners: Wayne Gretzky (9); Gordie Howe (6); Eddie Shore (4); Bobby Clarke, Howie Morenz and Bobby Orr (3); Jean Beliveau, Bill Cowley, Phil Esposito, Bobby Hull, Guy Lafleur, Stan Mikita, and Nels Stewart (2).

Year		G	A	Pts	Year		G	A	Pts
1924	Frank Nighbor, Ottawa., C	10	3	13	1958	Gordie Howe, Det., RW	33	44	77
1925	Billy Burch, Hamilton, C	20	4	24	1959	Andy Bathgate, NRY, RW	40	48	88
1926	Nels Stewart, Maroons, C	34	8	42*	1960	Gordie Howe, Det., RW	28	45	73
1927	Herb Gardiner, Mon., D	6	6	12	1961	Bernie Geoffrion, Mon., RW	50	45	95*
1928	Howie Morenz, Mon, C	33	18	51*	1962	Jacques Plante, Mon., G	42-14-14; 2.37*		
1929	Roy Worters, NYA, G	16-13-9; 1.21			1963	Gordie Howe, Det., RW	38	48	86*
1930	Nels Stewart, Maroons, C	39	16	55	1964	Jean Beliveau, Mon., C	28	50	78
1931	Howie Morenz, Mon., C	28	23	51*	1965	Bobby Hull, Chi., LW	39	32	71
1932	Howie Morenz, Mon., C	24	25	49	1966	Bobby Hull, Chi., LW	54	43	97*
1933	Eddie Shore, Bos, D	8	27	35	1967	Stan Mikita, Chi., C	35	62	97*
1934	Aurel Joliat, Mon., LW	22	15	37	1968	Stan Mikita, Chi., C	40	47	87*
1935	Eddie Shore, Bos., D	7	26	33	1969	Phil Esposito, Bos., C	49	77	126*
1936	Eddie Shore, Bos., D	3	16	19	1970	Bobby Orr, Bos., D	33	87	120*
1937	Babe Siebert, Mon., D	8	20	28	1971	Bobby Orr, Bos., D	37	102	139
1938	Eddie Shore, Bos., D	3	14	17	1972	Bobby Orr, Bos., D	37	80	117
1939	Toe Blake, Mon., LW	24	23	47*	1973	Bobby Clarke, Phi., C	37	67	104
1940	Ebbie Goodfellow, Det.,D	11	17	28	1974	Phil Esposito, Bos., C	68	77	145*
1941	Bill Cowley, Bos., C	17	45	62*	1975	Bobby Clarke, Phi., C	27	89	116
1942	Tommy Anderson, NYA., D	12	29	41	1976	Bobby Clarke, Phi., C	30	89	119
1943	Bill Cowley, Bos, C	27	45	72	1977	Guy Lafleur, Mon., RW	56	80	136*
1944	Babe Pratt, Tor., D	17	40	57	1978	Guy Lafleur, Mon., RW	60	72	132*
1945	Elmer Lach, Mon., C	26	54	80*	1979	Bryan Trottier, NYI., C	47	87	134*
1946	Max Bentley, Chi., C	31	30	61*	1980	Wayne Gretzky, Edm., C	51	86	137
1947	Maurice Richard, Mon., RW	45	26	71	1981	Wayne Gretzky, Edm., C	55	109	164*
1948	Buddy O'Connor, NYR, C	24	36	60	1982	Wayne Gretzky, Edm., C	92	120	212*
1949	Sid Abel, Det., C	28	26	54	1983	Wayne Gretzky, Edm., C	71	125	196*
1950	Chuck Rayner, NYR, G	28-30-11; 2.62			1984	Wayne Gretzky, Edm., C	87	118	205*
1951	Milt Schmidt, Bos., C	22	39	61	1985	Wayne Gretzky, Edm., C	73	135	208*
1952	Gordie Howe, Det., RW	47	39	86*	1986	Wayne Gretzky, Edm., C	52	163	215*
1953	Gordie Howe, Det., RW	49	46	95*	1987	Wayne Gretzky, Edm., C	62	121	183*
1954	Al Rollins, Chi., G	12-47-7; 3.23			1988	Mario Lemieux, Pit., C	70	98	168*
1955	Ted Kennedy, Tor., C	10	42	52	1989	Wayne Gretzky, LA, C	54	114	168
1956	Jean Beliveau, Mon., C	47	41	88*	1990	Mark Messier, Edm., C	45	84	129
1957	Gordie Howe, Det., RW	44	45	89*					

Art Ross Trophy

Given to the player who leads the league in points scored and named after the former Boston Bruins general manager-coach. First presented in 1947, names of prior leading scorers have been added retroactively. A tie for the scoring championship is broken three ways: 1. total goals; 2. fewest games played; 3. first goal scored.

Multiple winners: Wayne Gretzky (8); Gordie Howe (6); Phil Esposito (5); Stan Mikita (4); Guy Lafleur (3); Max Bentley, Charlie Conacher, Bill Cook, Babe Dye, Bernie Geoffrion, Bobby Hull, Elmer Lach, Newsy Lalonde, Mario Lemieux, Joe Malone, Dickie Moore, Howie Morenz, Bobby Orr and Sweeney Schriner (2).

Year		Gm	G	A	Pts	Year		Gm	G	A	Pts
1918	Joe Malone, Mon	20	44	n.a.	44	1937	Sweeney Schriner, NYA	48	21	25	46
1919	Newsy Lalonde, Mon	17	23	9	32	1938	Gordie Drillon, Tor	48	26	26	52
1920	Joe Malone, Que	24	39	6	45	1939	Toe Blake, Mon	48	24	23	47
1921	Newsy Lalonde, Mon	24	33	8	41	1940	Milt Schmidt, Bos	48	22	30	52
1922	Punch Broadbent, Ott	24	32	14	46	1941	Bill Cowley, Bos	46	17	45	62
1923	Babe Dye, Tor	22	26	11	37	1942	Bryan Hextall, NYR	48	24	32	56
1924	Cy Denneny, Ott	21	22	1	23	1943	Doug Bentley, Chi	50	33	40	73
1925	Babe Dye, Tor	29	38	6	44	1944	Herbie Cain, Bos	48	36	46	82
1926	Nels Stewart, Maroons	36	34	8	42	1945	Elmer Lach, Mon	50	26	54	80
1927	Bill Cook, NYR	44	33	4	37	1946	Max Bentley, Chi	47	31	30	61
1928	Howie Morenz, Mon	43	33	18	51	1947	Max Bentley, Chi	60	29	43	72
1929	Ace Bailey, Tor	44	22	10	32	1948	Elmer Lach, Mon	60	30	31	61
1930	Cooney Weiland, Bos	44	43	30	73	1949	Roy Conacher, Chi	60	26	42	68
1931	Howie Morenz, Mon	39	28	23	51	1950	Ted Lindsay, Det	69	23	55	78
1932	Busher Jackson, Tor	48	28	25	53	1951	Gordie Howe, Det	70	43	43	86
1933	Bill Cook, NYR	48	28	22	50	1952	Gordie Howe, Det	70	47	39	86
1934	Charlie Conacher, Tor	42	32	20	52	1953	Gordie Howe, Det	70	49	46	95
1935	Charlie Conacher, Tor	47	36	21	57	1954	Gordie Howe, Det	70	33	48	81
1936	Sweeney Schriner, NYA	48	19	26	45						

Annual Award Winners (Cont.)

Art Ross Trophy (Cont.)

Year		Gm	G	A	Pts	Year		Gm	G	A	Pts
1955	Bernie Geoffrion, Mon	70	38	37	75	1973	Phil Esposito, Bos	78	55	75	130
1956	Jean Beliveau, Mon	70	47	41	88	1974	Phil Esposito, Bos	78	68	77	145
1957	Gordie Howe, Det	70	44	45	89	1975	Bobby Orr, Bos	80	46	89	135
1958	Dickie Moore, Mon	70	36	48	84	1976	Guy Lafleur, Mon	80	56	59	125
1959	Dickie Moore, Mon	70	41	55	96	1977	Guy Lafleur, Mon	80	56	80	136
						1978	Guy Lafleur, Mon	79	60	72	132
1960	Bobby Hull, Chi	70	39	42	81	1979	Bryan Trottier, NYI	76	47	87	134
1961	Bernie Geoffrion, Mon	64	50	45	95						
1962	Bobby Hull, Chi.*	70	50	34	84	1980	Marcel Dionne, LA*	80	53	84	137
1963	Gordie Howe, Det	70	38	48	86	1981	Wayne Gretzky, Edm	80	55	109	164
1964	Stan Mikita, Chi	70	39	50	89	1982	Wayne Gretzky, Edm	80	92	120	212
1965	Stan Mikita, Chi	70	28	59	87	1983	Wayne Gretzky, Edm	80	71	125	196
1966	Bobby Hull, Chi	65	54	43	97	1984	Wayne Gretzky, Edm	74	87	118	205
1967	Stan Mikita, Chi	70	35	62	97	1985	Wayne Gretzky, Edm	80	73	135	208
1968	Stan Mikita, Chi	72	40	47	87	1986	Wayne Gretzky, Edm	80	52	163	215
1969	Phil Esposito, Bos	74	49	77	126	1987	Wayne Gretzky, Edm	79	62	121	183
						1988	Mario Lemieux, Pit	77	70	98	168
1970	Bobby Orr, Bos	76	33	87	120	1989	Mario Lemieux, Pit	76	85	114	199
1971	Phil Esposito, Bos	78	76	76	152						
1972	Phil Esposito, Bos	76	66	67	133	1990	Wayne Gretzky, LA	73	40	102	142

*Note: The two times players have tied for total points in one season the player with more goals has won the trophy. In 1961-62, Hull outscored Andy Bathgate of NY Rangers, 50 goals to 28. In 1979-80, Dionne outscored Wayne Gretzky of Edmonton, 53-51.

Lady Byng Memorial Trophy

Awarded to the player "adjudged to have exhibited the best type of sportsmanship and gentlemanly conduct combined with a high standard of playing ability" and named after the wife of former Canadian Governor General (1921-26) Baron Byng of Vinny. Winners selected by PHWA.

Multiple winners: Frank Boucher (7); Red Kelly (4); Bobby Bauer, Mike Bossy and Alex Delvecchio (3); Johnny Bucyk, Marcel Dionne, Dave Keon, Stan Mikita, Joey Mullen, Frank Nighbor, Jean Ratelle, Clint Smith and Sid Smith (2).

Year		Year		Year	
1925	Frank Nighbor, Ott., C	1947	Bobby Bauer, Bos., RW	1969	Alex Delvecchio, Det., LW
1926	Frank Nighbor, Ott., C	1948	Buddy O'Connor, NYR, C	1970	Phil Goyette, St.L., C
1927	Billy Burch, NYA, C	1949	Bill Quackenbush, Det., D	1971	Johnny Bucyk, Bos., LW
1928	Frank Boucher, NYR, C	1950	Edgar Laprade, NYR,	1972	Jean Ratelle, NYR, C
1929	Frank Boucher, NYR, C	1951	Red Kelly, Det., D	1973	Gilbert Perreault, Buf., C
1930	Frank Boucher, NYR, C	1952	Sid Smith, Tor., LW	1974	Johnny Bucyk, Bos., LW
1931	Frank Boucher, NYR, C	1953	Red Kelly, Det., D	1975	Marcel Dionne, Det., C
1932	Joe Primeau, Tor., C	1954	Red Kelly, Det., D	1976	Jean Ratelle, NY-Bos., C
1933	Frank Boucher, NYR, C	1955	Sid Smith, Tor., LW	1977	Marcel Dionne, LA, C
1934	Frank Boucher, NYR, C	1956	Earl Reibel, Det., C	1978	Butch Goring, LA, C
1935	Frank Boucher, NYR, C	1957	Andy Hebenton, NYR, RW	1979	Bob MacMillan, Atl., RW
1936	Doc Romnes, Chi., F	1958	Camille Henry, NYR, LW	1980	Wayne Gretzky, Edm., C
1937	Marty Barry, Det., C	1959	Alex Delvecchio, Det., LW	1981	Rick Kehoe, Pit., RW
1938	Gordie Drillon, Tor., RW	1960	Don McKenney, Bos., C	1982	Rick Middleton, Bos., RW
1939	Clint Smith, NYR, C	1961	Red Kelly, Tor., D	1983	Mike Bossy, NYI, RW
1940	Bobby Bauer, Bos., RW	1962	Dave Keon, Tor., C	1984	Mike Bossy, NYI, RW
1941	Bobby Bauer, Bos., RW	1963	Dave Keon, Tor., C	1985	Jari Kurri, Edm., RW
1942	Syl Apps, Tor., C	1964	Ken Wharram, Chi., RW	1986	Mike Bossy, NYI, RW
1943	Max Bentley, Chi., C	1965	Bobby Hull, Chi., LW	1987	Joey Mullen, Calg., RW
1944	Clint Smith, Chi., C	1966	Alex Delvecchio, Det., LW	1988	Mats Naslund, Mon., LW
1945	Bill Mosienko, Chi., RW	1967	Stan Mikita, Chi., C	1989	Joey Mullen, Calg., RW
1946	Toe Blake, Mon., LW	1968	Stan Mikita, Chi., C	1990	Brett Hull, St.L., RW

Note: Quackenbush and Kelly are the only defensemen to win the Lady Byng.

Lester Pearson Award

Awarded to the season's most outstanding player and named after the former diplomat, Nobel Peace Prize winner and Canadian prime minister. Winners selected by the NHL Players Assn.

Multiple winners: Wayne Gretzky (5); Guy Lafleur (3); Marcel Dionne, Phil Esposito and Mario Lemieux (2).

Year		Year		Year	
1971	Phil Esposito, Bos., C	1979	Marcel Dionne, LA, C	1986	Mario Lemieux, Pit., C
1972	Jean Ratelle, NY R, C	1980	Marcel Dionne, LA, C	1987	Wayne Gretzky, Edm., C
1973	Phil Esposito, Bos., C	1981	Mike Liut, St. L., G	1988	Mario Lemieux, Pit., C
1974	Bobby Clarke, Phila., C	1982	Wayne Gretzky, Edm., C	1989	Steve Yzerman, Det., C
1975	Bobby Orr, Bos., D	1983	Wayne Gretzky, Edm., C	1990	Mark Messier, Edm., C
1976	Guy Lafleur, Mon., RW	1984	Wayne Gretzky, Edm., C		
1977	Guy Lafleur, Mon., RW	1985	Wayne Gretzky, Edm., C		
1978	Guy Lafleur, Mon., RW				

Vezina Trophy

From 1926-80, given to the principal goaltender(s) on the team allowing the fewest goals during the regular season and named after 1920's goalie Georges Vezina of the Montreal Canadiens, who died of tuberculosis in 1926.

Since the 1980-81 season, the trophy has been awarded to the most outstanding goaltender of the year as selected by the league's general managers.

Multiple winners: Jacques Plante (7, one of them shared); Bill Durnan (6); Ken Dryden (5, three shared); Bunny Larocque (4, all shared); Tiny Thompson (4); Terry Sawchuk (4, one shared); Tony Esposito (3, one shared); George Hainsworth (3); Glenn Hall (3, two shared); Frank Brimsek (2); Turk Broda (2); Johnny Bower (2, one shared); Chuck Gardiner (2); Charlie Hodge (2, one shared); Bernie Parent (2); Patrick Roy (2); Gump Worsley (2, both shared).

Year		Record	Avg
1927	George Hainesworth, Mon	28-14-2	1.52
1928	George Hainesworth, Mon	26-11-7	1.09
1929	George Hainesworth, Mon	22-7-15	0.98
1930	Tiny Thompson, Bos	38-5-1	2.23
1931	Roy Worters, NYA	18-16-10	1.68
1932	Chuck Gardiner, Chi	18-19-11	2.10
1933	Tiny Thompson, Bos	25-15-8	1.83
1934	Chuck Gardiner, Chi	20-17-11	1.73
1935	Lorne Chabot, Chi	26-17-5	1.83
1936	Tiny Thompson, Bos	22-20-6	1.73
1937	Norm Smith, Det	25-14-9	2.13
1938	Tiny Thompson, Bos	30-11-7	1.85
1939	Frank Brimsek, Bos	33-9-1	1.59
1940	Dave Kerr, NYR	27-11-10	1.60
1941	Turk Broda, Tor	28-14-6	2.06
1942	Frank Brimsek, Bos	24-17-6	2.44
1943	Johnny Mowers, Det	25-14-11	2.48
1944	Bill Durnan, Mon	38-5-7	2.18
1945	Bill Durnan, Mon	38-8-4	2.42
1946	Bill Durnan, Mon	24-11-5	2.60
1947	Bill Durnan, Mon	34-16-10	2.30
1948	Turk Broda, Tor	32-15-13	2.38
1949	Bill Durnan, Mon	28-23-9	2.10
1950	Bill Durnan, Mon	26-21-17	2.20
1951	Al Rollins, Tor	27-5-8	1.75
1952	Terry Sawchuk, Det	44-14-12	1.90
1953	Terry Sawchuk, Det	32-15-16	1.90
1954	Harry Lumley, Tor	32-24-13	1.85
1955	Terry Sawchuk, Det	40-17-11	1.94
1956	Jacques Plante, Mon	42-12-10	1.86
1957	Jacques Plante, Mon	31-18-12	2.02
1958	Jacques Plante, Mon	34-14-8	2.11
1959	Jacques Plante, Mon	38-16-13	2.18
1960	Jacques Plante, Mon	40-17-12	2.54
1961	Johnny Bower, Tor	33-15-10	2.50
1962	Jacques Plante, Mon	42-14-14	2.37
1963	Glenn Hall, Chi	30-20-16	2.51
1964	Charlie Hodge, Mon	33-18-11	2.26
1965	Johnny Bower, Tor	13-13-8	2.38
	& Terry Sawchuk, Tor	17-13-6	2.56

Year		Record	Avg
1966	Gump Worsley, Mon	29-14-6	2.36
	& Charlie Hodge, Mon	12-7-2	2.58
1967	Glenn Hall, Chi	19-5-5	2.38
	& Denis Dejordy, Chi	22-12-7	2.46
1968	Gump Worsley, Mon	19-9-8	1.98
	& Rogie Vachon, Mon	23-13-2	2.48
1969	Jacques Plante, St.L	18-12-6	1.96
	& Glenn Hall, St.L	19-12-8	2.17
1970	Tony Esposito, Chi	38-17-8	2.17
1971	Ed Giacomin, NYR	27-10-7	2.16
	& Gilles Villemure, NYR	22-8-4	2.30
1972	Tony Esposito, Chi	31-10-6	1.77
	& Gary Smith, Chi	14-5-6	2.42
1973	Ken Dryden, Mon	33-7-13	2.26
1974	(Tie) Bernie Parent, Phi	47-13-12	1.89
	Tony Esposito, Chi	34-14-21	2.04
1975	Bernie Parent, Phi	44-14-10	2.03
1976	Ken Dryden, Mon	42-10-8	2.03
1977	Ken Dryden, Mon	41-6-8	2.14
	& Bunny Larocque, Mon	19-2-4	2.09
1978	Ken Dryden, Mon	37-7-7	2.05
	& Bunny Larocque	22-3-4	2.67
1979	Ken Dryden, Mon	30-10-7	2.30
	& Bunny Larocque	22-7-4	2.84
1980	Bob Sauve, Buf	20-8-4	2.36
	& Don Edwards	27-9-12	2.57
1981	Richard Sevigny, Mon	20-4-3	2.40
	Denis Herron, Mon	6-9-6	3.50
	& Bunny Larocque	16-9-3	3.03
1982	Billy Smith, NYI	32-9-4	2.97
1983	Pete Peeters, Bos	40-11-9	2.36
1984	Tom Barrasso, Buf	26-12-3	2.84
1985	Pelle Lindbergh, Phi	40-17-7	3.02
1986	John Vanbiesbrouck, NYR	31-21-5	3.32
1987	Ron Hextall, Phi	37-21-6	3.00
1988	Grant Fuhr, Edm	40-24-9	3.43
1989	Patrick Roy, Mon	33-5-6	2.47
1990	Patrick Roy, Mon	31-16-5	2.53

Norris Memorial Trophy

Awarded to the most outstanding defenseman of the year and named after James Norris, the late Detroit Red Wings owner-president. Winners selected by PHWA.

Multiple winners: Bobby Orr (8); Doug Harvey (7); Ray Bourque and Pierre Pilote and Denis Potvin (3); Paul Coffey, Rod Langway and Larry Robinson (2).

Year		Year		Year	
1954	Red Kelly, Detroit	1967	Harry Howell, NY Rangers	1980	Larry Robinson, Montreal
1955	Doug Harvey, Montreal	1968	Bobby Orr, Boston	1981	Randy Carlyle, Pittsburgh
1956	Doug Harvey, Montreal	1969	Bobby Orr, Boston	1982	Doug Wilson, Chicago
1957	Doug Harvey, Montreal	1970	Bobby Orr, Boston	1983	Rod Langway, Washington
1958	Doug Harvey, Montreal	1971	Bobby Orr, Boston	1984	Rod Langway, Washington
1959	Tom Johnson, Montreal	1972	Bobby Orr, Boston	1985	Paul Coffey, Edmonton
1960	Doug Harvey, Montreal	1973	Bobby Orr, Boston	1986	Paul Coffey, Edmonton
1961	Doug Harvey, Montreal	1974	Bobby Orr, Boston	1987	Ray Bourque, Boston
1962	Doug Harvey, NY Rangers	1975	Bobby Orr, Boston	1988	Ray Bourque, Boston
1963	Pierre Pilote, Chicago	1976	Denis Potvin, NY Islanders	1989	Chris Chelios, Montreal
1964	Pierre Pilote, Chicago	1977	Larry Robinson, Montreal	1990	Ray Bourque, Boston
1965	Pierre Pilote, Chicago	1978	Denis Potvin, NY Islanders		
1966	Jacques Laperriere, Mon.	1979	Denis Potvin, NY Islanders		

Annual Award Winners (Cont.)

Calder Memorial Trophy

Awarded to the most outstanding rookie of the year and named after Frank Calder, the late NHL president (1917-43). Winners selected by PHWA. Winners' scoring statistics or goaltender W-L record & goals against average are provided.

Year		G	A	Pts	Year		G	A	Pts
1933	Carl Voss, NYR-Det., C	8	15	23	1962	Bobby Rousseau, Mon., RW	21	24	45
1934	Russ Blinco, M.Maroons, C	14	9	23	1963	Kent Douglas, Tor., D	7	15	22
1935	Sweeney Schriner, NYA., LW	18	22	40	1964	Jacques Laperriere, Mon., D	2	28	30
1936	Mike Karakas, Chi., G	21-19-8;	1.92		1965	Roger Crozier, Det., G	40-23-7;	2.42	
1937	Syl Apps, Tor., C	16	29	45	1966	Brit Selby, Tor., LW	14	13	27
1938	Cully Dahlstrom, Chi., C	10	9	19	1967	Bobby Orr, Bos., D	13	28	41
1939	Frank Brimsek, Bos., G	33-9-1;	1.58		1968	Derek Sanderson, Bos., C	24	25	49
					1969	Danny Grant, Min., LW	34	31	65
1940	Kilby MacDonald, NYR, LW	15	13	28					
1941	John Quilty, Mon., C	18	16	34	1970	Tony Esposito, Chi., G	38-17-8;	2.17	
1942	Knobby Warwick, NYR, RW	16	17	33	1971	Gilbert Perreault, Buf., C	38	34	72
1943	Gaye Stewart, Tor., LW	24	23	47	1972	Ken Dryden, Mon., G	39-8-15;	2.24	
1944	Gus Bodnar, Tor., C	22	40	62	1973	Steve Vickers, NYR, LW	30	23	53
1945	Frank McCool, Tor., G	24-22-2;	3.22		1974	Denis Potvin, NYI, D	17	37	54
1946	Edgar Laprade, NYR, C	15	19	34	1975	Eric Vail, Atl., LW	39	21	60
1947	Howie Meeker, Tor., RW	27	18	45	1976	Bryan Trottier, NYI, C	32	63	95
1948	Jim McFadden, Det., C	24	24	48	1977	Willi Plett, Atl., RW	33	23	56
1949	Penny Lund, NYR, RW	14	16	30	1978	Mike Bossy, NYI, RW	53	38	91
					1979	Bobby Smith, Min., C	30	44	74
1950	Jack Gelineau, Bos., G	22-30-15;	3.28						
1951	Terry Sawchuck, Det., G	44-13-13;	1.99		1980	Ray Bourque, Bos., D	17	48	65
1952	Bernie Geoffrion, Mon., RW	30	24	54	1981	Peter Stastny, Que., C	39	70	109
1953	Gump Worsley, NYR, G	13-29-13,	3.06		1982	Dale Hawerchuk, Win., C	45	58	103
1954	Camille Henry, NYR, LW	24	15	39	1983	Steve Larmer, Chi., RW	43	47	90
1955	Ed Litzenberger, Mon-Chi., RW	16	24	40	1984	Tom Barrasso, Buf., G	26-12-3;	2.84	
1956	Glenn Hall, Det., G	30-24-16;	2.11		1985	Mario Lemieux, Pit., C	43-57	100	
1957	Larry Regan, Bos., RW	14	19	33	1986	Gary Suter, Calg., D	18-50	68	
1958	Frank Mahovlich, Tor., LW	20	16	36	1987	Luc Robitaille, LA, LW	45-39	84	
1959	Ralph Backstrom, Mon., C	18	22	40	1988	Joe Nieuwendyk, Calg., C	51-41	92	
					1989	Brian Leetch, NYR, D	23-48	71	
1960	Billy Hay, Chi., C	18-37	55						
1961	Dave Keon, Tor., C	20-25	45		1990	Sergei Makarov, Calg., RW	24-62	86	

Bill Masterton Memorial Trophy

Awarded to the player who "best exemplifies the qualities of perseverance, sportsmanship and dedication to hockey" and named after the 29-year-old rookie center of the Minnesota North Stars who died of a head injury sustained in a 1968 NHL game. Presented by the PHWA.

Year	Year	Year
1968 Claude Provost, Mon., RW	1976 Rod Gilbert, NYR, RW	1984 Brad Park, Det., D
1969 Ted Hampson, Oak., C	1977 Ed Westfall, NYI, RW	1985 Anders Hedberg, NYR, RW
	1978 Butch Goring, LA, C	1986 Charlie Simmer, Bos., LW
1970 Pit Martin, Chi., C	1979 Serge Savard, Mon., D	1987 Doug Jarvis, Hart., C
1971 Jean Ratelle, NYR, C		1988 Bob Bourne, LA, C
1972 Bobby Clarke, Phi., C	1980 Al MacAdam, Min., RW	1989 Tim Kerr, Phi., C
1973 Lowell MacDonald, Pit.,RW	1981 Blake Dunlop, St.L., C	
1974 Henri Richard, Mon., C	1982 Chico Resch, Colo., G	1990 Gord Kluzak, Bos., D
1975 Don Luce, Buf., C	1983 Lanny McDonald, Calg., RW	

Jack Adams Award

Awarded to the coach "adjudged to have contributed the most to his team's success" and named after the late Detroit Red Wings coach and general manager. Winners selected by NHL Broadcasters' Assn; (*) indicates division champion.

Multiple winner: Jacques Demers (2).

Year		Improvement		Year		Improvement	
1974	Fred Shero, Phi	37-30-11	to 50-16-12*	1983	Orval Tessier, Chi	30-38-12	to 47-23-10*
1975	Bob Pulford, Chi	41-14-23	to 37-35- 8	1984	Bryan Murray, Wash	39-25-16	to 48-27- 5
1976	Don Cherry, Bos	40-26-14	to 48-15-17*	1985	Mike Keenan, Phi	44-26-10	to 53-20- 7*
1977	Scotty Bowman, Mon	58-11-11*	to 60- 8-12*	1986	Glen Sather, Edm	49-20-11*	to 56-17- 7*
1978	Bobby Kromm, Det	16-55- 9	to 32-34-14	1987	Jacques Demers, Det	17-57- 6	to 34-36-10
1979	Al Arbour, NYI	48-17-15*	to 51-15-14*	1988	Jacques Demers, Det	34-36-10	to 41-28-11*
				1989	Pat Burns, Mon	45-22-13	to 53-18- 9*
1980	Pat Quinn, Phi	40-25-15	to 48-12-20*	1990	Bob Murdoch, Win	26-42-12	to 37-32-11
1981	Red Berenson, StL	34-34-12	to 45-18-17*				
1982	Tom Watt, Win	9-57-14	to 33-33-14				

World Hockey Association

WHA Finals, 1973-79

The World Hockey Association began play in 1972-73 as a 12-team rival of the 56-year-old NHL. The WHA played for the Avco World Trophy in its seven playoff finals (Avco Financial Services underwrote the playoffs).

Year	Winner	Head Coach	Series	Loser	Head Coach
1973	NE Whalers	Jack Kelley	4-1 (WWLWW)	Winnipeg Jets	Bobby Hull
1974	Houston Aeros	Bill Dineen	4-0	Chicago Cougars	Pat Stapleton
1975	Houston Aeros	Bill Dineen	4-0	Que.Nordiques	Jean-Guy Gendron
1976	Winnipeg Jets	Bobby Kromm	4-0	Houston Aeros	Bill Dineen
1977	Que.Nordiques	Marc Boileau	4-3 (LWLWWLW)	Winnipeg Jets	Bobby Kromm
1978	Winnipeg Jets	Larry Hillman	4-0	NE Whalers	Harry Neale
1979	Winnipeg Jets	Larry Hillman	4-2 (WWLWLW)	Edmonton Oilers	Glen Sather

Playoff MVPs, 1973-79

1973—No award; **1974**—No award; **1975**—Ron Grahame, Houston, G; **1976**—Ulf Nilsson, Winnipeg, C; **1977**—Serg Bernier, Quebec, C; **1978**—Bobby Guindon, Winnipeg, C; **1979**—Rich Preston, Winnipeg, RW.

Annual Awards

Most Valuable Player
(Gordie Howe Trophy, 1976-79)

Year		G	A	Pts
1973	Bobby Hull, Win., LW	51	52	103
1974	Gordie Howe, Hou., RW	31	69	100
1975	Bobby Hull, Win., LW	77	65	142
1976	Marc Tardif, Que., LW	71	77	148
1977	Robbie Ftorek, Pho., C	46	71	117
1978	Marc Tardif, Que., LW	65	89	154
1979	Dave Dryden, Edm., G	41-17-2; 2.89		

Scoring Leaders

Year		Gm	G	A	Pts
1973	Andre Lacroix, Phi	78	50	74	124
1974	Mike Walton, Min	78	57	60	117
1975	Andre Lacroix, S.Diego	78	41	106	147
1976	Marc Tardif, Que	81	71	77	148
1977	Real Cloutier, Que	76	66	75	141
1978	Marc Tardif, Que	78	65	89	154
1979	Real Cloutier, Que	77	75	54	129

Note: In 1979, 18 year-old Rookie of the Year Wayne Gretzky finished third in scoring (46-64—110).

Rookie of the Year

Year		G	A	Pts
1973	Terry Caffery, N.Eng., C	39	41	100
1974	Mark Howe, Hou., LW	38	41	79
1975	Anders Hedberg, Win., RW	53	47	100
1976	Mark Napier, Tor., RW	43	50	93
1977	George Lyle, N.Eng., LW	39	33	72
1978	Kent Nilsson, Win., C	42	65	107
1979	Wayne Gretzky, Edm., C	46	64	110

Best Goaltender

Year		Record	Avg
1973	Gerry Cheevers, Cle	32-20-0	2.84
1974	Don MacLeod, Hou	33-13-3	2.56
1975	Ron Grahame, Hou	33-10-0	3.03
1976	Michel Dion, Indy	14-15-1	2.74
1977	Ron Grahame, Hou	27-10-2	2.74
1978	Al Smith, N.Eng	30-20-3	3.22
1979	Dave Dryden, Edm	41-17-2	2.89

Best Defenseman

Year	
1973	J.C.Tremblay, Quebec
1974	Pat Stapleton, Chicago
1975	J.C.Tremblay, Quebec
1976	Paul Shmyr, Cleveland
1977	Ron Plumb, Cincinnati
1978	Lars-Erik Sjoberg, Winnipeg
1979	Rick Ley, New England

Coach of the Year

Year		Improvement		
1973	Jack Kelley, N.Eng	—	to	46-30-2*
1974	Billy Harris, Tor	35-39-4	to	41-33-4
1975	Sandy Hucul, Pho	—	to	39-31-8
1976	Bobby Kromm, Win	38-35-5	to	52-27-2*
1977	Bill Dineen, Hou	53-27-0*	to	50-24-6*
1978	Bill Dineen, Hou	50-24-6*	to	42-34-4
1979	John Brophy, Birm	36-41-3	to	32-42-6

*Won Division.

WHA All-Star Game, 1973-79

The WHA All-Star Game was an Eastern Division vs Western Division contest from 1973-75. In 1976, the league's five Canadian-based teams played the nine teams in the US. Over the final three seasons—East played West in 1977; AVCO Cup champion Quebec played a WHA All-Star team in 1978; and in 1979, a full WHA All-Star team played a three-game series with Moscow Dynamo of the Soviet Union.

Year	Result	Host	Coaches	Most Valuable Player
1973	East 6, West 2	Quebec	Jack Kelley, Bobby Hull	Wayne Carleton, Ottawa
1974	East 8, West 4	St.Paul,MN	Jack Kelley, Bobby Hull	Mike Walton, Minnesota
1975	West 6, East 4	Edmonton	Bill Dineen, Ron Ryan	Rejean Houle, Quebec
1976	Canada 6, USA 1	Cleveland	Jean-Guy Gendron, Bill Dineen	Can—Real Cloutier, Que. USA—Paul Shmyr, Cleve.
1977	East 4, West 2	Hartford	Jacques Demers, Bobby Kromm	East—L.Levasseur, Min. West—W.Lindstrom, Win.
1978	Quebec 5, WHA 4	Quebec	Marc Boileau, Bill Dineen	Quebec—Marc Tardif WHA—Mark Howe, NE
1979	WHA 4, Moscow Dynamo 2	Edmonton	Larry Hillman, P.Iburtovich	No awards
	WHA 4, Moscow Dynamo 2	Edmonton		
	WHA 4, Moscow Dynamo 3	Edmonton		

International Hockey

World Championships, 1920-90

World and Olympic champions from 1920 to the present. Olympic years and winners are indicated in **bold type**. There were no tournaments during World War II (1940-45) and 1946.

Year	Winner	Year	Winner	Year	Winner	Year	Winner
1920	**Canada**	1943	No tournament	**1960**	**United States**	**1976**	**Olym: USSR**
1924	**Canada**	1944	No tournament	1961	Canada		World: Czech.
1928	**Canada**	1945	No tournament	1962	Sweden	1977	Czechoslovakia
		1946	No tournament	1963	Soviet Union	1978	Soviet Union
1930	Canada	1947	Czechoslovakia	**1964**	**Soviet Union**	1979	Soviet Union
1931	Canada	**1948**	**Canada**	1965	Soviet Union		
1932	**Canada**	1949	Czechoslovakia	1966	Soviet Union	**1980**	**United States**
1933	United States			1967	Soviet Union	1981	Soviet Union
1934	Canada	1950	Canada	**1968**	**Soviet Union**	1982	Soviet Union
1935	Canada	1951	Canada	1969	Soviet Union	1983	Soviet Union
1936	**Great Britain**	**1952**	**Canada**			**1984**	**Soviet Union**
1937	Canada	1953	Sweden	1970	Soviet Union	1985	Czechoslovakia
1938	Canada	1954	Soviet Union	1971	Soviet Union	1986	Soviet Union
1939	Canada	1955	Canada	**1972**	**Olym: USSR**	1987	Sweden
		1956	**Soviet Union**		World: Czech.	**1988**	**Soviet Union**
1940	No tournament	1957	Sweden	1973	Soviet Union	1989	Soviet Union
1941	No tournament	1958	Canada	1974	Soviet Union		
1942	No tournament	1959	Canada	1975	Soviet Union	1990	Soviet Union

Canada vs USSR Summits

The first competition between the Soviet National Team and the NHL took place Sept.2-28, 1972. A team of NHL All-Stars emerged as the winner of the heralded 8-game series, but just barely—winning with a record of 4-3-1 after trailing 1-3-1.

Two years later a WHA All-Star team played the Soviet Nationals and could win only one game and tie three others in eight contests. Two other Canada vs USSR series took place during NHL All-Star breaks: the three-game Challenge Cup at New York in 1979, and the two-game Rendez-Vous '87 in Quebec City in 1987.

The NHL All-Stars played the USSR in a three-game Challenge Cup series in 1979.

1972 Team Canada vs USSR

NHL All-Stars vs Soviet National Team.

Date	City	Result	Goaltenders
9/2	Montreal	USSR, 7-3	Tretiak/Dryden
9/4	Toronto	Canada, 4-1	Esposito/Tretiak
9/6	Winnipeg	Tie, 4-4	Tretiak/Esposito
9/8	Vancouver	USSR, 5-4	Tretiak/Dryden
9/22	Moscow	USSR, 5-4	Tretiak/Esposito
9/24	Moscow	Canada, 3-2	Dryden/Tretiak
9/26	Moscow	Canada, 4-3	Esposito/Tretiak
9/28	Moscow	Canada, 6-5	Dryden/Tretiak

Standings

	W	L	T	Pts	GF	GA
Team Canada (NHL)	4	3	1	8	32	32
Soviet Union	3	4	1	8	32	32

Leading Scorers

1. Phil Esposito, Canada, (7-6—13); **2.** Aleksandr Yakushev, USSR (7-4—11); **3.** Paul Henderson, Canada (7-2—9); **4.** Boris Shadrin, USSR (3-5—8); **5.** Valeri Kharlamov, USSR (3-4—7) and Vladimir Petrov, USSR (3-4—7); **7.** Bobby Clarke, Canada (2-4—6).

1974 Team Canada vs USSR

WHA All-Stars vs Soviet National Team.

Date	City	Result	Goaltenders
9/17	Quebec	Tie, 3-3	Tretiak/Cheevers
9/19	Toronto	Canada, 4-1	Cheevers/Tretiak
9/21	Winnipeg	USSR, 8-5	Tretiak/McLeod
9/23	Vancouver	Tie, 5-5	Tretiak/Cheevers
10/1	Moscow	USSR, 3-2	Tretiak/Cheevers
10/3	Moscow	USSR, 5-2	Tretiak/Cheevers
10/5	Moscow	Tie, 4-4	Cheevers/Tretiak
10/6	Moscow	USSR, 3-2	Sdn'kov/Cheevers

Standings

	W	L	T	Pts	GF	GA
Soviet Union	4	1	3	11	32	27
Team Canada (WHA)	1	4	3	5	27	32

Leading Scorers

1. Bobby Hull, Canada (7-2—9); **2.** Aleksandr Yakushev, USSR (6-2—8), Ralph Backstrom, Canada (4-4—8) and Valeri Kharlamov, USSR (2-6—8); **5.** Gordie Howe, Canada (3-4—7), Andre Lacroix, Canada (1-6—7) and Vladimir Petrov, USSR (1-6—7).

1979 Challenge Cup Series

NHL All-Stars vs Soviet National Team

Date	City	Result	Goaltenders
2/8	New York	NHL, 4-2	K.Dryden/Tretiak
2/10	New York	USSR, 5-4	Tretiak/K.Dryden
2/11	New York	USSR, 6-0	Myshkin/Cheevers

Rendez-Vous '87

NHL All-Stars vs Soviet National Team

Date	City	Result	Goaltenders
2/11	Quebec	NHL, 4-3	Fuhr/Belosheykhin
2/13	Quebec	USSR, 5-3	Belosheykhin/Fuhr

The Canada Cup

After organizing the historic 8-game Team Canada-Soviet Union series of 1972, NHL Players Association executive director Alan Eagleson and the NHL created the Canada Cup in 1976. For the first time, the best players from the world's six major hockey powers—Canada, Czechoslovakia, Finland, Russia, Sweden and the USA competed together in one tournament.

1976
Round Robin Standings

	W	L	T	Pts	GF	GA
Canada	4	1	0	8	22	6
Czechoslovakia	3	1	1	7	19	9
Soviet Union	2	2	1	5	23	14
Sweden	2	2	1	5	16	18
United States	1	3	1	3	14	21
Finland	1	4	0	2	16	42

Finals (Best of 3 Games)

Date	City	Score
9/13	Toronto	Canada 6, Czechoslovakia 0
9/15	Montreal	Canada 5, Czechoslovakia 4 (OT)

Note: Darryl Sittler scored the winning goal for Canada at 11:33 in overtime to clinch the Cup, 2 games to none.

Team MVPs

Canada—Rogie Vachon   Sweden—Borje Salming
Czech.—Milan Novy   USA—Robbie Ftorek
USSR—Alexandr Maltsev Finland—Matti Hagman
Tournament MVP—Bobby Orr, Canada

1984
Round Robin Standings

	W	L	T	Pts	GF	GA
Soviet Union	5	0	0	10	22	7
United States	3	1	1	7	21	13
Sweden	3	2	0	6	15	16
Canada	2	2	1	5	23	18
West Germany	0	4	1	1	13	29
Czechoslovakia	0	4	1	1	10	21

Semifinals

Date	City	Score
9/12	Edmonton	Sweden 9, United States 2
9/15	Montreal	Canada 3, USSR 2 (OT)

Note: Mike Bossy scored the winning goal for Canada at 12:29 in overtime.

Finals (Best of 3 Games)

Date	City	Score
9/16	Calgary	Canada 5, Sweden 2
9/18	Edmonton	Canada 6, Sweden 5

Leading Scorers

1. Wayne Gretzky, Canada (5-7—12); **2.** Michel Goulet, Canada (5-6—11), Kent Nilsson, Sweden (3-8—11), Paul Coffey, Canada (3-8—11); **5.** Hakan Loob, Sweden (6-4—10).

All-Star Team

Goal—Vladimir Myshkin, USSR; **Defense**—Paul Coffey, Canada and Rod Langway, USA; **Forwards**—Wayne Gretzky, Canada, John Tonelli, Canada, and Sergei Makarov, USSR. **Tournament MVP**—Tonelli.

1981
Round Robin Standings

	W	L	T	Pts	GF	GA
Canada	4	0	1	9	32	13
Soviet Union	3	1	1	7	20	13
Czechoslovakia	2	1	2	6	21	13
United States	2	2	1	5	17	19
Sweden	1	4	0	2	13	20
Finland	0	4	1	1	6	31

Semifinals

Date	City	Score
9/11	Ottawa	USSR 4, Czechoslovakia 1
9/15	Montreal	Canada 4, United States 1

Finals

Date	City	Score
9/13	Montreal	USSR 8, Canada 1

Leading Scorers

1. Wayne Gretzky, Canada (5-7—12); **2.** Mike Bossy, Canada (8-3—11), Bryan Trottier, Canada (3-8--11), Guy Lafleur, Canada (2-9—11), Alexei Kasatonov, USSR (1-10—11).

All-Star Team

Goal—Vladislav Tretiak, USSR; **Defense**—Arnold Kadlec, Czech. and Alexei Kasatonov, USSR; **Forwards**—Mike Bossy, Canada, Gil Perreault, Canada, and Sergei Shepelev, USSR. **Tournament MVP**—Tretiak.

1987
Round Robin Standings

	W	L	T	Pts	GF	GA
Canada	3	0	2	8	19	13
Soviet Union	3	1	1	7	22	13
Sweden	3	2	0	6	17	14
Czechoslovakia	2	2	1	5	12	15
United States	2	3	0	4	13	14
Finland	0	5	0	0	9	23

Semifinals

Date	City	Score
9/8	Hamilton	USSR 4, Sweden 2
9/9	Montreal	Canada 5, Czechoslovakia 3

Finals (Best of 3 Games)

Date	City	Score
9/11	Montreal	USSR 6, Canada 5 (OT)
9/13	Hamilton	Canada 6, USSR 5 (2 OT)
9/15	Hamilton	Canada 6, USSR 5

Note: In Game 1, Alexander Semak of USSR scored at 5:33 in overtime. In Game 2, Mario Lemieux of Canada scored at 10:07 in the second overtime period. Lemieux also won Game 3 on a goal with 1:26 left in regulation time.

Leading Scorers

1. Wayne Gretzky, Canada (3-18—21); **2.** Mario Lemieux, Canada (11-7—18); **3.** Sergei Makarov, USSR (7-8—15); **4.** Vladimir Krutov, USSR (7-7—14); **5.** Viacheslav Bykov, USSR (2-7—9); **6.** Ray Bourque, Canada (2-6—8).

All-Star Team

Goal—Grant Fuhr, Canada; **Defense**—Ray Bourque, Canada and Viacheslav Fetisov, USSR; **Forwards**—Wayne Gretzky, Canada, Mario Lemieux, Canada, and Vladimir Krutov, USSR. **Tournament MVP**—Gretzky.

U.S. College Hockey

NCAA Division I Finals, 1948-90

Year	Winner	Score	Loser	Year	Winner	Score	Loser
1948	Michigan	8-4	Dartmouth	1970	Cornell	6-4	Clarkson
1949	Boston College	4-3	Dartmouth	1971	Boston Univ.	4-2	Minnesota
				1972	Boston Univ.	4-0	Cornell
1950	Colorado College	13-4	Boston Univ.	1973	Wisconsin	4-2	Denver
1951	Michigan	7-1	Brown	1974	Minnesota	4-2	Michigan Tech
1952	Michigan	4-1	Colorado College	1975	Michigan Tech	6-1	Minnesota
1953	Michigan	7-3	Minnesota	1976	Minnesota	6-4	Michigan Tech
1954	RPI	5-4 OT	Minnesota	1977	Wisconsin	6-5 OT	Michigan
1955	Michigan	5-3	Colorado College	1978	Boston Univ.	5-3	Boston College
1956	Michigan	7-5	Michigan Tech	1979	North Dakota	4-3	North Dakota
1957	Colorado College	13-6	Michigan				
1958	Denver	6-2	North Dakota	1980	North Dakota	5-2	Northern Mich.
1959	North Dakota	4-3 OT	Michigan St.	1981	Wisconsin	6-3	Minnesota
				1982	North Dakota	5-2	Wisconsin
1960	Denver	5-3	Michigan Tech	1983	Wisconsin	6-2	Harvard
1961	Denver	12-2	St.Lawrence	1984	Bowling Green	5-4 OT	Minn.-Duluth
1962	Michigan Tech	7-1	Clarkson	1985	RPI	2-1	Providence
1963	North Dakota	6-5	Denver	1986	Michigan St.	6-5	Harvard
1964	Michigan	6-3	Denver	1987	North Dakota	5-3	Michigan St.
1965	Michigan Tech	8-2	Boston College	1988	Lake Superior St.	4-3 OT	St.Lawrence
1966	Michigan St.	6-1	Clarkson	1989	Harvard	4-3 OT	Minnesota
1967	Cornell	4-1	Boston Univ.				
1968	Denver	4-0	North Dakota	1990	Wisconsin	7-3	Colgate
1969	Denver	4-3	Cornell				

Overtime Goals: 1954—1:54; **1959**—4:22; **1977**—0:23; **1984**—7:11 in 4th OT; **1988**—4:46; **1989**—4:16.

Most Outstanding Player

The Most Outstanding Players of each NCAA Div.I tournament since 1948. Winners of the award who did not play for the tournament champion are in **bold type**. In 1960, three players, none on the winning team, shared the award.

Year		Year		Year	
1948	**Joe Riley,** Dartmouth, F	1962	Lou Angotti, Mich. Tech., F	1978	Jack O'Callahan, Boston U., F
1949	**Dick Desmond,** Dart., G	1963	Al McLean, N.Dakota, F	1979	Steve Janaszak, Minn., G
1950	**Ralph Bevins,** Boston U., G	1964	Bob Gray, Michigan, G	1980	Doug Smail, N.Dakota, F
1951	**Ed Whiston,** Brown, G	1965	Gary Milroy, Mich. Tech, F	1981	Marc Behrend, Wisc., G
1952	**Ken Kinsley,** Colo. Col., G	1966	Gaye Cooley, Mich. St., G	1982	Phil Sykes, N.Dakota, F
1953	John Matchefts, Mich., F	1967	Walt Stanowski, Cornell, D	1983	Marc Behrend, Wisc., G
1954	Abbie Moore, RPI, F	1968	Gerry Powers, Denver, G	1984	Gary Kruzich, Bowl.Green, G
1955	**Phil Hilton,** Colo. Col., D	1969	Keith Magnuson, Denver, D	1985	**Chris Terreri,** Prov., G
1956	Lorne Howes, Mich., G	1970	Dan Lodboa, Cornell, D	1986	Mike Donnelly, Mich.St., F
1957	Bob McCusker, Colo.Col., F	1971	Dan Brady, Boston, U., G	1987	Tony Hrkac, N.Dakota, F
1958	Murray Massier, Denver, F	1972	Tim Regan, Boston, U., G	1988	Bruce Hoffort, Lk.Superior, G
1959	Reg Morelli, N.Dakota, F	1973	Dean Talafous, Wisc., F	1989	Ted Donato, Harvard, F
1960	**Lou Angotti,** Mich.Tech, F; **Bob Marquis,** Boston U., F; **& Barry Urbanski,** Bos.U., G	1974	Brad Shelstad, Minn., G	1990	Chris Tancill, Wisconsin, F
		1975	Jim Warden, Mich. Tech, G		
		1976	Tom Vanelli, Minn., F		
1961	Bill Masterton, Denver, F	1977	Julian Baretta, Wisc., G		

Hobey Baker Award

College hockey's Player of the Year award; voted on by a national panel of sportswriters, broadcasters, college coaches and pro scouts. First presented in 1981 by the Decathlon Athletic Club of Bloomington, MN, in the name of the late Princeton collegiate hockey and football star.

Year		Class	Year		Class
1981	Neal Broten, Minnesota, F	So.	1987	Tony Hrkac, North Dakota, F	So.
1982	George McPhee, Bowling Green, F	Sr.	1988	Robb Stauber, Minnesota, G	So.
1983	Mark Fusco, Harvard, D	Sr.	1989	Lane MacDonald, Harvard, F	Sr.
1984	Tom Kurvers, Minnesota-Duluth, D	Sr.	1990	Kip Miller, Michigan St., F	Sr.
1985	Bill Watson, Minnesota-Duluth, F	Jr.			
1986	Scott Fusco, Harvard, F	Sr.			

The NCAA finally caught up with **Jerry Tarkanian** on July 20, ending a 13-year battle with the UNLV basketball coach by banning his national champions from the 1991 postseason.

COLLEGE SPORTS

*Probation stuns UNLV basketball—
Champions unable to defend;
NCAA serious about reform
Conferences play musical chairs.*

COLLEGE SPORTS

1989 YEAR IN REVIEW

by Caulton Tudor

Probation for UNLV. Some dubbed it "Jaws: This Time the Shark Really Gets It!" Veteran observers knew, however, that the running battle between Nevada-Las Vegas basketball coach Jerry Tarkanian and the National Collegiate Athletic Association was not over. Not after a mere decade or two.

Over or not—appeals were pending as the summer ended—the NCAA sent out a clear message on July 20: Sharks can swim, but they can't hide. After 13 years, the governing body finally harpooned the UNLV program for recruiting violations committed in the mid-1970s. The resulting one-year probation will keep the national champion Runnin' Rebels from defending their title in Indianapolis.

It was the second time in three years that the national champion had been put on probation and barred from the following year's tournament. Kansas, the 1988

winner, was also grounded for recruiting violations.

That was one of several messages delivered to high-profile institutions by the reform-minded NCAA in 1989-90. North Carolina State was another. But even as the NCAA exercised some control over its subjects, there were also significant demonstrations of independence from the rank and file.

Two announcements early in the year particularly shook the Division I landscape. First, on Dec. 19, 1989, the Big Ten announced that it was admitting longtime football independent Penn State. Then, less than two months later, on Feb. 5, Notre Dame broke with sacred tradition and signed its own five-year home-games-only TV football contract with NBC for $38 million.

Expansion and TV money were suddenly the talk of Division I-A football schools. Change was in the wind.

"What the leagues will look like five years from now is something no one can envision at this point," said NCAA executive director Dick Schultz.

Caulton Tudor is the assistant sports editor of the Raleigh (N.C.) *News and Observer*, and has covered ACC basketball and football since 1968.

Penn State football coach **Joe Paterno** (center) accepts congratulations from Illinois president **Stanley Eikenberry** (right) and Big Ten commissioner **Jim Delaney** after the Nittany Lions officially joined the conference Dec. 19.

''We could have super-conferences. We could have playoffs in football. Almost anything is possible. On the other hand, there's a possibility everything could be just as it is right now.''

Not if the Southeastern Conference has anything to say about it. By late spring, the SEC was busy trying to pry Arkansas loose from the Southwest Conference, where the Razorbacks were the defending champion in both football and basketball. What the SEC was offering Arkansas athletic director Frank Broyles was hard to ignore: superior competition, a bigger TV market and a much larger share of pooled conference revenue— $1.6 million per member per year as opposed to the SWC's annual payout of $700,000.

To no one's surprise, Arkansas officially accepted the offer on Aug. 1, agreeing to compete in all SEC sports except football beginning in 1991-92, and playing an SEC football schedule in 1992 after a transition year as an independent.

With SEC and Big Ten membership now at 11 teams each, there is no doubt that each will add at least one more school. Potential Big Ten candidates range from Eastern independents Pittsburgh, Rutgers and Syracuse to Nebraska of the Big

Eight, while the SEC is said to be eyeing three teams—Texas and Texas A&M of the SWC and independent Florida State.

Meanwhile, the SWC, determined to keep Texas and Texas A&M in the fold, might go after Oklahoma of the Big Eight, a possibility that moved Big Eight commissioner Carl James to suggest that the two conferences merge in a ploy to ward off raiders from the south and west.

Earlier in the year, the Metro Conference commissioned Raycom, Inc., the independent television packager, to draw up expansion plans and got back a proposal that called for doubling the size of the eight-team basketball league and making it a football league as well. The addition of eight Eastern independents for football, said Raycom, would give the Metro 35.2 percent of U.S. television households, almost double that of the Big Ten.

Elsewhere, the Atlantic Coast Conference, 38 years old and never with a membership greater than eight schools, earnestly began inspecting independents like Miami, Florida State and Rutgers as possible recruits. The ACC's rationale was the same as the Metro's—access to bigger TV markets.

All this expansion panic was rooted in

Wide World Photos

Led by athletic director **Frank Broyles,** Arkansas switched conferences on Aug. 1, leaving the SWC for the SEC.

the conferences' anxiety about the future of the College Football Association, a loose affiliation of Division I-A football schools not in the Big Ten or Pacific-10 conferences.

The CFA, which has negotiated national TV contracts for its members since 1985, faced pressure on two fronts. The loss of Notre Dame home games meant that recently signed five-year contracts with ABC and ESPN (for a combined $335 million) had to be renegotiated—for $35 million less. Then there was the Federal Trade Commission threat to take the CFA to court for violating anti-trust laws. Resolution of the case, should it ever go to trial, probably wouldn't come until after the current TV contracts have expired in 1995.

"It's 1995 and beyond that has everyone so jumpy," said ACC Commissioner Gene Corrigan, formerly the athletic director at Notre Dame.

"If there was some guarantee that the CFA could remain strong and viable and successful in what it does, there would be no rush for expansion. But there are no guarantees. It could be that every league or every school, in the cases of the independents, are on their own."

Indeed, the pending departure of Penn State and the immediate defection of Notre Dame as a TV factor added to the uncertainty of an organization already without the lucrative Midwestern and West Coast markets held by the Big Ten and Pac-10.

"You have to wonder what the CFA is going to be left with in terms of traditional top draws on TV," said Miami of Florida athletic director Sam Jankovich.

As the 1990 football season began, Jankovich's program was the CFA's prized possession. Three times national champion in the 1980s, the Hurricanes were more popular on television than even Notre Dame.

But after Miami, the CFA's national appeal was limited to schools like Florida State, Auburn, Nebraska, Alabama and Oklahoma, if the Sooners can get it going again under tougher academic entrance requirements. As TV markets go, the next most popular group included Clemson, Texas, Georgia Tech, LSU, Syracuse, Pittsburgh and Texas A&M.

"Overall TV market balance is a concern for CFA members," Corrigan said. "It has to be."

Such balance is not a major concern in college basketball, where the NCAA negotiates for all Division I schools. On Nov. 21, 1989, the NCAA signed a seven-year, $1 billion deal with CBS for exclusive TV rights to its year-end tournament.

On July 12, the organization's budget committee approved measures that would end direct monetary payouts to tournament participants and allow all Division I schools to share in the revenue. In the 1990 tournament, teams made $286,500 for each game played and Final Four participants were guaranteed at least $1.4 million each. Now the money will be shared according to a formula that rewards schools with broad-based athletic programs that sponsor a variety of sports and provide scholarships for a large number of athletes.

The NCAA's decision to put Nevada-Las Vegas on probation will not affect regular season TV coverage for 1990-91. UNLV will be allowed to play on TV until the postseason, when it won't be allowed to play at all.

UNLV's punishment stemmed from a two-year probation for recruiting violations handed down by the NCAA in 1977; a ruling that also included an unprecedented directive that Las Vegas also remove Tarkanian as coach for two years. UNLV served the probation, but backed Tarkanian in his successful fight to get a court injunction prohibiting the school from suspending him.

On December 12, 1988, the United States Supreme Court ruled that the NCAA did not violate Tark's constitutional rights by ordering the suspension. Eighteen months later, the NCAA in effect waived the two-year suspension, but would not grant total clemency.

The NCAA verdict was rendered by a special panel that consisted of three law professors, a history teacher, a conference commissioner and a school administrator.

"It makes you wonder if I'll ever be treated fairly," said Tarkanian afterward.

UNLV president Robert Maxson was more emphatic. "I think it's a miscarriage of justice," he said. "We're being penalized twice for the same offense and that violates one of the basic principles of justice."

Only days after the announcement, attorney Stephan Stein said he might represent several UNLV players in a law suit of their own. "The players," Stein said, "feel they shouldn't be penalized for something that happened when they were six or seven years old."

The decision to expel the Runnin' Rebels from the 1991 tournament was imposed as another investigation into UNLV's recruiting policies continued. This inquiry involved the pursuit of 1987 high school star Lloyd Daniels.

UNLV was the centerpiece of widespread NCAA action during the school year and into the summer. Meanwhile, Florida, Illinois and Missouri braced for the possibility of even more sentencing.

The 1989-90 school year saw the NCAA issue a stern message to collegiate athletic administrations: Reform now.

That message came from several different sources, but none higher or more powerful than the deeply pragmatic Schultz. "The scope or even the existence of the problem no longer is relevant," Schultz told his organization's membership. "The fact is that the public perceives college athletics to be in serious trouble. Perception has become reality in our case. We must do something to change the perception."

Schultz, formerly the director of athletics at the University of Virginia, did not have to look beyond the backyards of his old neighborhood to find evidence that this perception was largely based upon fact. Atlantic Coast Conference basketball, which essentially had dodged scandal for most of its 37 years, went through a double wringer—at North Carolina State and at Maryland, where the 1986 narcotics-related death of All-American Len Bias first raised pressing questions about the lifestyles of young athletes.

At N.C. State, a nine-year trend of academic abuse and careless player supervision was uncovered in the basketball program (see box). NCSU's chancellor, Bruce R. Poulton, and the Wolfpack's high-profile athletic director and head basketball coach, Jim Valvano, both faced significant degrees of pressure and embarrassment, and eventually abdicated their positions.

Maryland, which had undergone a similar administrative house-cleaning only two years earlier, was called on the carpet again when it was discovered that former Terrapin coach Bob Wade had taken illegal recruiting liberties and then misrepresented the school's intentions during an ensuing investigation.

The NCAA put both programs on probation. On Dec.12, N.C.State was given two years with no postseason play in 1990. Then on Aug.3, Maryland began serving a three-year sentence that prohibited live TV for one year and postseason play for two years.

At both N.C. State and Maryland, the NCAA found that players knowingly had sold game tickets. In additon, NCSU players had sold factory-provided tennis shoes, in street-vendor manner, to customers of all ages.

In fact, athletic footwear became a hot topic unto itself as the year progressed. A fascinating book, **Raw Recruits**, which was published almost in conjunction with the NCAA Tournament in March, told of virtual mayhem at the most basic development levels of basketball. The book, co-authored by nationally prominent reporters Alexander Wolff and Armen Keteyian, dealt in part with a sports shoe sub-culture that is devoted to, reliant upon, and generally supervised by a corporate segment with questionable merchandising motives.

What *Raw Recruits* could boast in journalistic expertise, Peter Golenbock's *Personal Fouls*, a scathing account of Valvano's N.C. State program, generally lacked. It was the Golenbock effort, however, though widely flawed and loosely edited, that created more national impact and served as a rallying point for an expanding group of critics who felt that big-time college athletics had sped past too many caution signals.

Among the first to call for action were William C. Friday, president emeritus of the University of North Carolina System, and the Rev. Theodore M. Hesburgh, president emeritus of the University of Notre Dame. Backed by a $2 million funding grant from the Knight-Ridder Newspapers chain, Friday and Hesburgh were given the charge to form a 22-member commission that would take on what Knight Foundation president Creed Black called a sometime hopeless 60-year-old battle to clean up college sports.

The Knight Commission, formed in January, had what Friday called one overriding purpose: "To restore academic integrity to college sports.

"There are other areas of pressing concern, to be sure," Friday said. "But until this one problem can be isolated and conquered, I'm not certain that the rest can be reasonably approached."

Though purely an advisory and fact-finding body, the Knight Commission quickly enjoined eminent allies, one of whom was Schultz, who said the Friday-Hesburgh group and the NCAA shared important common ground.

"The executive officers—chancellors and presidents—have to be put back in control of athletics at their schools," Schultz said. "Hopefully this can be done in concert with the athletic directors, who are supposed to be experts in all facets of the athletic operation."

No Fast Break for Classroom at N.C. State

On the morning of Jan. 7, 1989, Jim Valvano picked up the local newspaper and read a front-page banner headline that would change his life: "Book alleges wrongdoing in NCSU basketball program."

On the morning of April 7, 1990, Valvano, in exchange for a $213,000 contract buyout, stepped aside as basketball coach at the school he had taken to the 1983 NCAA championship.

What happened in between the bombshell set off by Peter Golenbock's book *Personal Fouls* and Valvano's forced resignation 15 months later may be remembered as a landmark development in the area of coaching responsibility. In the long run, Valvano's employers determined that the coach not only was responsible, but also accountable, for the actions of his players at all times and under all circumstances.

To be certain, Valvano's downfall as one of America's most popular, successful and entertaining coaches began with his own actions. He recruited an abnormally high number of academically irresponsible and unprepared prospects. The university, in turn, admitted them (Chris Washburn, for instance, was admitted in 1984 despite a combined 470 on the Scholastic Aptitude Test). The recruits, predictably enough, accumulated perfectly lousy grades.

That Valvano would be dismissed as coach became inevitable on Aug. 22, 1989, the day Bruce Poulton, the last line of defense against an admissions policy gone haywire, was forced to resign as NCSU's chancellor. Two months later, Valvano was forced to step down as athletic director and seven months after that he was gone altogether.

Valvano departed a popular man, particularly among rank-and-file Wolfpack fans. And to almost no one's surprise, the 44 year-old former coach and businessman (he had capitalized on his celebrity by building a small financial empire) landed on his wallet—signing a three-year, $900,000 deal as a commentator with ABC Sports.

Bob Jordan/Raleigh News and Observer

Ex-Wolfpack basketball coach **Jim Valvano** faces the press on April 7 following his agreement with school officials to leave N.C.State after 10 years.

Ironically, it was ABC News that delivered the final blow to Valvano's hopes to hang on as coach. Four months before, the network had produced an unidentified man who claimed to be a former Wolfpack player. On camera, but with his face and features distorted, the individual said he had evidence of point-shaving during the 1987-88 season. Former Wolfpack star Charles Shackleford and three unspecified teammates were alleged to have committed the crime.

Investigations were immediately launched in North Carolina and New Jersey after Shackleford admitted to having accepted $65,000 in loans from New Jersey businessman Robert Kramer prior to the completion of the player's final season at NCSU.

The New Jersey probe ended just over a month after its beginning. No charges were pressed. The N.C. Bureau of Investigation continued its mission late into 1990

without commenting on its findings.

The school did not escape unscathed, however. On Dec. 12, 1989, the NCAA hit the basketball program with a two-year probation, including a ban on 1990 postseason play, after a seven-month probe found that former Wolfpack players had sold game tickets and athletic shoes.

Finally in late April, following Valvano's resignation and the hiring of former N.C. State player Les Robinson as the new coach, the NCAA levied a $405,756 fine from 1988 tournament winnings—the result of Shackleford's accepting a $6000 loan from a booster.

Valvano was not cited for wrongdoing in the NCAA findings, nor for any illegal action in separate investigations by the NCSBI, the school and the N.C. university governing body.

But an unmistakable pattern of academic abuse and careless supervision was evident. Through the 1988 season, only 11 of 41 Valvano recruits had maintained a C average minimum. The five-year graduation rate, though not indecently behind the NCSU average, was far from good.

"I'm concerned that many people have missed a very crucial point in this academic issue," Valvano said. "And that is, what responsibility does the university have? What responsibility do the professors have? What responsibility do advisers have? What responsibility do tutors have? It's an oversimplification to state a graduation rate and simply associate it with the coach."

But in the final analysis, the school said it was his fault, making Valvano the first major college coach to be fired because the majority of his players did not achieve passing grades.

The most sensational charges first leveled in **Personal Fouls** were proved inaccurate. There were no million dollar player payoffs, no grade-fixing, no illegal recruiting, no players treated unethically and no drug distribution.

"It was a circus," said Wolfpack guard Chris Corchiani when it was all over. "It was a circus about everything, but it all came down to a circus about players who didn't have enough pride in themselves to take advantage of the educational opportunity they were given."

Wayne O. Davis

NCAA executive director **Dick Schultz** (left) with NFL commissioner **Paul Tagliabue** (center) and Dallas Cowboys' coach **Jimmy Johnson** at NCAA headquarters in June.

Another flashpoint of concern for Schultz (and the American Football Coaches Association) was the National Football League. In the NCAA and AFCA's view, the NFL's decision to draft juniors in 1990 and its disruptive practice of subjecting draft picks to multiple workouts and minicamps in the off-season prevented too many players from finishing their education.

After meeting with Schultz and the AFCA in June, NFL commissioner Paul Tagliabue announced on Aug.2 that any player wishing to forego his senior intercollegiate year must declare himself by Feb.1. All potential draft picks will then be able to attend the annual NFL Scouting Combine workouts. In addition, all rookies will be limited to one three-day minicamp until the academic year is completed.

The NCAA Presidents Commission, which earlier in the school year had acted to curtail spring football practice time and the length of basketball schedules, made a historic move in late June by meeting with a student-athlete advisory panel in Chicago. Thirty-eight of the 44 members of the commission, including chairman Dr. Martin Massengale of the University of Nebraska, attended the closed meetings. It was the first time in the 80-year history of the NCAA that

formal representation was allowed the athletes.

A two-day reform agenda session included suggestions from the student group on how to provide contestants with what they said was most needed—more time for their private lives. The NCAA athletes were represented by 16 of their cohorts on the panel, who were promised floor time to address the time reduction issue at the January, 1991 NCAA Convention in Nashville, Tenn.

A 1989 survey by the Presidents Commission found the biggest complaint from athletes was that practices, conditioning schedules and travel to contests took a great toll on time for social and academic pursuits.

The Presidents departed the summit vowing to present legislation at Nashville that would limit athletes' participation to 20 hours weekly.

Well-intentioned as such a recommendation would be, it could translate into fewer Olympic medals for the United States. Angry that they would be punished for the sins of big-time college football and basketball programs, athletes like Stanford swimmer Janet Evans, the Olympic gold-medalist and 1989 Sullivan Award winner, said they might have to leave school if limits were put on practice time. ☐

1989-90 NCAA Team Champions

Stanford and **Texas** each won three NCAA Division I team championships during the 1989-90 school year. The Cardinal won Women's Basketball in the winter and swept both Men's and Women's Tennis for the fourth time in the last five years in the spring. Texas won all three of its titles in the winter, taking both Men's and Women's Swimming & Diving championships as well as Women's Indoor Track.

Double winners in Division I included **Arizona State** (Men's and Women's Golf), **LSU** (Men's and Women's Outdoor Track), and **North Carolina** (Women's Field Hockey and Soccer).

In Division II, **Cal Poly-San Luis Obispo** and **Cal State-Bakersfield** were both three-time champions. Cal Poly-SLO brought home trophies for Women's Cross Country and Outdoor Track and Men's Tennis, while CS-Bakersfield won Women's Volleyball, Men's Swimming & Diving, and Women's Softball. The lone double winner in Division II was **St.Augustine's College** of Raleigh, NC (Men's Indoor and Outdoor Track).

There were no triples in Division III, but three schools won twice: **Eastern Connecticut State** (Baseball and Softball), **Kenyon College** (sweeping Men's and Women's Swimming & Diving for the seventh straight year), **Lincoln University** (Men's Indoor and Outdoor Track), and **Wisconsin-Oshkosh** (Men's Cross Country and Women's Outdoor Track).

As usual, California schools combined for the most team titles, winning 16 of the year's 77 NCAA championships in the three divisions. Pennsylvania followed with eight, New York and North Carolina with five each, Texas and Wisconsin with four each and Ohio with three.

FALL

Cross Country

Men's Division I . . . . Iowa St.
    Division II . . . . South Dakota St.
    Division III . . . . Wisconsin-Oshkosh

Women's Division I . . . . Villanova
    Division II . . . . Cal Poly-SLO
    Division III . . . . Cortland St., NY

Field Hockey

Women's Division I . . . . North Carolina
    Division II . . . . No competition
    Division III . . . . Lock Haven, PA

Football

Men's Division I-A . . . . Miami, FL*
    Division I-AA . . . . Georgia Southern
    Division II . . . . Mississippi Col.
    Division III . . . . Dayton
*There is no official NCAA Div.I-A playoff.

Soccer

Men's Division I . . . . Santa Clara, CA
                      & Virginia*
    Division II . . . . New Hampshire Col.
    Division III . . . . Elizabethtown, PA
*Co-champions, title game ended in 1-1 tie after two scoreless overtimes.

Women's Division I . . . . North Carolina
    Division II . . . . Barry Univ., FL
    Division III . . . . Cal-San Diego

Volleyball

Women's Division I . . . . Cal St.-Long Beach
    Division II . . . . Cal St.-Bakersfield
    Division III . . . . Washington, MO

Water Polo

Men's Champion . . . . Cal-Irvine

WINTER

Basketball

Men's Division I . . . . Nevada-Las Vegas
    Division II . . . . Kentucky Wesleyan
    Division III . . . . Rochester, NY

Women's Division I . . . . Stanford
    Division II . . . . Delta St., MS
    Division III . . . . Hope College, MI

Fencing

Men/Women Combined . . . . Penn St.

Gymnastics

Men's Champion . . . . Nebraska
Women's Champion . . . . Utah

Ice Hockey

Men's Division I . . . . Wisconsin
    Division II . . . . No competition
    Division III . . . . Wisconsin-Stevens Pt.

Rifle

Men/Women Combined . . . . West Virginia

Skiing

Men/Women Combined . . . . Vermont

Swimming & Diving

Men's Division I . . . . Texas
    Division II . . . . Cal St-Bakersfield
    Division III . . . . Kenyon, OH

Women's Division I . . . . Texas
    Division II . . . . Oakland, MI
    Division III . . . . Kenyon, OH

Indoor Track

Men's Division I . . . . Arkansas
    Division II . . . . St.Augustine's, NC
    Division III . . . . Lincoln, PA

Women's Division I . . . . Texas
    Division II . . . . Abilene Christian, TX
    Division III . . . . Christopher Newport, VA

Wrestling

Men's Division I . . . . Oklahoma St.
    Division II . . . . Portland St., OR
    Division III . . . . Ithaca, NY

SPRING

Baseball

Men's Division I . . . . Georgia
Division II . . . . Jacksonville St., AL
Division III . . . . Eastern Conn. St.

Golf

Men's Division I . . . . Arizona St.
Division II . . . . Florida Southern
Division III . . . . Methodist College, NC

Women's Champion . . . . Arizona St.

Lacrosse

Men's Division I . . . . Syracuse
Division II . . . . No competition
Division III . . . . Hobart, NY

Women's Division I . . . . Harvard
Division II . . . . No competition
Division III . . . . Ursinus, PA

Softball

Women's Division I . . . . UCLA
Division II . . . . Cal St-Bakersfield
Division III . . . . Eastern Conn. St.

Tennis

Men's Division I . . . . Stanford
Division II . . . . Cal Poly-SLO
Division III . . . . Swarthmore, PA

Women's Division I . . . . Stanford
Division II . . . . Cal-Davis
Division III . . . . . Gustavus Adolphus, MN

Outdoor Track

Men's Division I . . . . LSU
Division II . . . . St.Augustine's, NC
Division III . . . . Lincoln, PA

Women's Division I . . . . LSU
Division II . . . . Cal Poly-SLO
Division III . . . . Wisconsin-Oshkosh

Volleyball

Men's Champion . . . . Southern Cal

1989-90 NAIA Team Champions

Adams State College of Colorado won four of the NAIA's 21 team championships during the year, the only member school to win more than once. The Indians took home titles in Men's and Women's Cross Country, Men's Indoor Track, and Wrestling.

FALL

Cross Country

Men's . . . . Adams St.,CO
Women's . . . . Adams St.,CO

Football

Men's Division I . . . . Carson-Newman,TN
Division II . . . . Westminster,PA

Soccer

Men's . . . . West Va.Wesleyan
Women's . . . . Pacific Lutheran,WA

Volleyball

Women's . . . . Fresno Pacific,CA

WINTER

Basketball

Men's . . . . Birmingham-Southern,AL
Women's . . . . SW Oklahoma St.

Swimming & Diving

Men's . . . . Drury,MO
Women's . . . . Puget Sound,WA

Indoor Track

Men's . . . . Adams St.,CO
Women's . . . . Simon Fraser,BC

Wrestling

Men's . . . . Adams St.,CO

SPRING

Baseball

Men's . . . . Lewis Clark St.,ID

Golf

Men's . . . . Texas Wesleyan

Softball

Women's . . . . Kearney St.,NE

Tennis

Men's . . . . Elon,NC
Women's . . . . Flagler,FL

Outdoor Track

Men's . . . . Oklahoma Baptist
Women's . . . . Prairie View A&M,TX

NCAA Schools on Probation

(as of Aug. 3, 1990)

School (Division)	Sport	Yrs	Penalty To End
Alabama A&M (I) ...	Soccer	1½	Indef.
Minnesota (I)	Basketball	2	Indef.
SMU (I-A)	Football	3	9/1/90
Texas A&M (I)	Football	2	9/20/90
Arizona St.(I)	M&W Track	2	11/10/90
Cleveland St.(I)	Basketball	3	4/21/91
Clemson (I-A)	Football	1	6/1/91
Grambling (I)	Basketball	2	8/15/91
Kansas (I)	Basketball	3	11/1/91
Cincinnati (I)	Football	3	11/3/91
	& Basketball	3	11/3/91
Oklahoma (I-A)	Football	3	12/27/91
Houston (I-A)	Football	3	12/31/91
N.C.State (I)	Basketball	2	1/2/92
W.Texas St.(II)	Basketball	3	1/6/92
S.Carolina (I)	Basketball	2	2/15/92
Marshall (I)	Basketball	2	3/12/92
Platts.St.(III)	Ice Hockey	2	4/13/92
Kentucky (I)	Basketball	3	5/19/92
Robert Morris (I) ...	Basketball	2	5/31/92
Florida A&M (I)	W.Tennis	2	6/14/92
Adelphi (II)	Basketball	3	7/21/92
Memphis St.(I-A)	Football	3	8/7/92
Okla.St.(I-A)	Football	4	1/9/93
Houston Bapt.(I)....	Gymnastics	3	4/2/93
Maryland (I)	Basketball	3	8/3/93
SE Louisiana (I)	Basketball	5	10/2/94

Sanctions Imposed

Adelphi—No postseason 1989-90; only those receiving grants-in-aid in 1988-89 may receive them in 1990-91 with the exception of those the university is committed to aid for 1989-90; forfeiture of all wins in 1986-87; recertification of all sports programs; submit written reports on compliance.

Alabama A&M—No postseason indefinite; grant-in-aid restrictions 1986-87.

Arizona St.—No postseason 1988-89; no expense-paid visits 1988-89; no off-campus recruiting for 1988-89; no initial grants-in-aid 1989-90; only home track meets for 1988-89 (meets shall not exceed number of home meets in 1987-88); submit written reports on compliance.

Cincinnati—No postseason 1988-89 for football and basketball; no more than 11 total grants in 1989-90 for basketball; no more than 12 total grants-in-aid in 1990-91 for basketball; initial grants limited to 19 in 1989-90, 21 in 1990-91 and 22 in 1991-92 in football.

Clemson—Disassociate one representative from program; submit written reports on compliance.

Cleveland St.—No postseason 1988-89 and 1989-90; no TV 1988-89; expense-paid visits cut from 15 to 10 for 1988-89; only one coach (rather than 3) permitted to recruit off-campus.

Florida A&M—No postseason 1990-91; no new financial aid until 8/1/92; disassociate one representative from program; recertification of all sports programs.

Grambling—Only 15 expense-paid visits for 1989-90; only 13 grants-in-aid for each 1989-90 and 1990-91.

Houston—No postseason 1989-90 and 1990-91; no TV 1989-90; no more than 15 new grants-in-aid 1989-90; expense-paid visits limited to 50 for 1989-90; submit written reports on compliance.

Houston Baptist—No postseason 1990-91 and 1991-92; no new grants-in-aid 1990-91 and 1991-92; no increase in percentage of aid 1990-91 and 1991-92; no participation in or support for participation in out-side club competition; head coach prohibited from all coaching and athletically related responsibilities; all team and individual records vacated for 1987,88 and 89 NCAA tournaments.

Kansas—No postseason 1988-89; no expense-paid visits 1989; only 12 grants-in-aid for 1989-90; submit written reports on compliance as well as on summer jobs program and summer camp salaries to student athletes.

Kentucky—No postseason 1989-90 and 1990-91; no TV 1989-90; only 2 new grants-in-aid plus one already committed for 1989-90; only 3 new grants for 1990-91; disassociate one representative from program; return receipts from participation in 1988 NCAA tournament.

Marshall—No postseason 1990-91; three expense-paid visits cut for both 1989-90 and 1990-91; one grant-in-aid cut for 1990-91 and 2 grants cut for 1991-92; disassociate 8 representatives from program; return receipts from participation in 1987 NCAA tournament; student-athletes must live in university housing; submit written reports on compliance.

Maryland—No postseason 1990-91 and 1991-92; no TV 1990-91; must return receipts from participation in 1988 tournament; committee adopted university grant-in-aid restrictions of two grant cuts each for 1990-91 and 1991-92; submit written reports on compliance.

Memphis St.—No postseason 1989-90; no TV 1990; four grants-in-aid cut for 1990-91; only 55 expense-paid visits for 1989-90; submit written reports on compliance.

Minnesota—No postseason 1987-88; only 2 full-time coaches (rather than 3) can recruit off campus from 7/1/88 to 6/30/89; school must submit annual audits at conclusion of 1987-88, 1988-89 and 1989-90 basketball seasons. Also, football program reprimanded and required to implement compliance program; school's actions adopted requiring one assistant football coach (on probation for 1 year and salary frozen for 1988-89). Note that football program is not on probation.

N.C.State—No postseason 1989-90; three grants-in-aid cut for 1990-91 and 1991-92; no off-campus recruiting for 1989-90; no expense-paid visits for 1989-90; coaching staff limitations for 1989-90 and 1990-91. Unrelated to this probation, N.C.State instructed to return receipts from participation in 1988 NCAA tournament.

Oklahoma—No postseason in 1989-90 and 1990-91; no TV in 1989-90; no more than 50 expense-paid visits for 1988-89 and 1989-90; only 8 coaches (2 fewer than maximum permitted) may recruit off campus in 1989-90; only 18 new grants-in-aid for each 1989-90 and 1990-91; disassociate one representative from program; submit written reports on compliance.

Oklahoma St.—No postseason 1989-90, 1990-91 and 1991-92; no TV 1989-90 and 1990-91; only 20 initial grants each year for 1989-90, 1990-91 and 1991-92; only 50 official paid visits for each 1988-89 and 1989-90; disassociate 14 representatives from program; submit written reports regarding compliance.

Plattsburgh St.—No postseason 1990-91; no expense-paid visits by representatives of school's athletic interests; disassociate 8 representatives from program; self-imposed restrictions regarding off-campus housing; submit written reports on compliance.

Robert Morris—No postseason 1990-91; no TV 1990-91; only 2 new grants-in-aid for 1991-92; return receipts from participation in 1989 NCAA tournament; submit written reports on compliance.

South Carolina—No postseason 1987-88.

NCAA Schools on Probation (Cont.)

SMU—No outside competition 1987-88; no practice 1987-88; no more than 7 games or scrimmages 1988-89 (none shall be a home game); no more than one head coach and 5 full-time assistant coaches until 8/1/89; no off-campus recruiting until 8/1/88; no expense-paid visits until 1988-89; no more than 45 expense-paid visits during 1988-89; no scholarships for 1987-88; 15 athletically related grants and 15 'recruited walk-ons' with no unearned aid permitted for 1988-89.

SW Louisiana— University must prepare a self-study with emphasis on athletics philosophy; university suspended men's basketball program; if team is reinstated before 1990-91 season committee will impose further penalties; submit written reports on compliance.

Texas A&M—No postseason 1988-89; a reduction of 5 new grants-in-aid for 1989-90; 10 expense-paid visits cut for 1988-89; no more than 8 full-time coaches may recruit off campus; head coach placed on administrative probation; submit written reports on probation.

W.Texas St.—No postseason 1988-89; no expense-paid visits 1989-90; no more than 10 full grants for 1989-90 and 1990-91; submit written reports on compliance.

Coaching Changes

Division I-A Football

Twenty head coaching changes have been made at Division I-A football schools since the end of the 1989 season. New head coaches announced before Aug. 1, 1990 are listed below.

School	Old Coach	New Coach
Alabama	Bill Curry	Gene Stallings
Arkansas	Ken Hatfield	Jack Crowe
Clemson	Danny Ford	Ken Hatfield
Duke	Steve Spurrier	Barry Wilson
Florida	Galen Hall & Gary Darnell*	Steve Spurrier
Houston	Jack Pardee	John Jenkins
Kentucky	Jerry Claiborne	Bill Curry
L.Beach St	Larry Reisbig	George Allen
Michigan	Bo Schembechler	Gary Moeller
Miami,OH	Tim Rose	Randy Walker
Navy	Elliot Uzelac	George Chaump
N.Mex.St.	Mike Knoll	Jim Hess
Ohio U	Cleve Bryant	Tom Lichtenberg
Pittsburgh	Mike Gottfried	Paul Hackett
Rutgers	Dick Anderson	Doug Graber
San Jose St	Claude Gilbert	Terry Shea
Toledo	Dan Simrell	Nick Saban
UNLV	Wayne Nunnely	Jim Strong
Utah	Jim Fassel	Ron McBride
Wisconsin	Don Morton	Barry Alvarez

*Interim coach in 1989.

Quit one head job for another (6)—Chaump (Marshall to Navy), Curry (Alabama to Kentucky), Hatfield (Arkansas to Clemson), Pardee (Houston of SWC to Houston of NFL), Spurrier (Duke to Florida).
Promoted to head job (5)—Crowe (Arkansas), Hackett (Pitt), Jenkins (Houston), Moeller (Michigan), Wilson (Duke).

Fired (10)—Anderson (Rutgers), Bryant (Ohio U.), Fassel (Utah), Gilbert (San Jose St), Gottfried (Pitt), Knoll (N.Mexico St.), Morton (Wisconsin), Rose (Miami, OH), Simrell (Toledo), Uzelac (Navy). **Resigned** (4)—Ford (Clemson), Hall (Florida), Nunnely (UNLV), Reisbig (L.Beach St.). **Retired** (2)—Claiborne (Ky.), Schembechler (Mich.).

Division I Basketball

Thirty-seven head coaching changes have been made at Division I basketball schools since the end of the 1989-90 season. New head coaches announced before Aug. 1, 1990 are listed below.

School	Old Coach	New Coach
American	Ed Tapscott	Chris Knoche
Ark-L.Rock	Mike Newell	Jim Platt
Army	Les Wothke	Tom Miller
Austin Peay	Lake Kelly	Dave Loos
Boston U	Mike Jarvis	Bob Brown
Brooklyn	Mark Reiner	Ron Kestenbaum
Cleve.St.	Kevin Mackey	Vacant
Colorado	Tom Miller	Joe Harrington
Columbia	Wally Halas	Jack Rohan
Drake	Tom Abatemarco & Eddie Fields*	Rudy Washington
E.Tenn.St	Les Robinson	Alan LeForce
East.Wash	Bob Hofman	John H.Wade II
Florida	Don DeVoe	Lon Kruger
Fla.Int'l	Rich Walker	Bob Weltlich
Fresno St	Ron Adams	Gary Colson
Geo.Wash.	John Kuester	Mike Jarvis
Howard	A.B.Williamson	Butch Beard
Idaho	Kermit Davis,Jr.	Larry Eustachy
Idaho St	Jim Boutin	Herb Williams
Kansas St	Lon Kruger	Dana Altman
Lamar	Tony Branch	Mike Newell
L.Beach St	Joe Harrington	Seth Greenberg
Marshall	Dana Altman	Dwight Freeman
MD-E.Shore	Steve Williams	Bob Hopkins
Miami,FL	Bill Foster	Leonard Hamilton
Montana St	Stu Starner	Mick Durham
Morgan St	Nat Frazier	Michael Holmes
Nicholls St	Gordon Stauffer	Rickey Broussard
N.C.State	Jim Valvano	Les Robinson
NC-Wilm	Robt.McPherson	Kevin Eastman
No.Ariz	Pat Raftery	Harold Merritt
Okla.St	Leonard Hamilton	Eddie Sutton
St.Joe's,PA	Jim Boyle	John Griffin
S.F.Austin	Mike Martin & Andrew Prince*	Ned Fowler
Texas A&M	Shelby Metcalf & John Thornton*	Kermit Davis Jr.
TX-San Ant	Ken Burmeister	Stu Starner
Virginia	Terry Holland	Jeff Jones
Western Ky	Murray Arnold	Ralph Willard

*Interim coach in 1989-90.

Quit one head job for another (9)—Altman (Marshall to Kansas St.), Brown (So.Maine to BU), Davis (Idaho to Texas A&M), Hamilton (Okla.St. to Miami,FL), Harrington (L.Beach St. to Colorado), Jarvis (BU to Geo.Wash.), Kruger (Kansas St. to Florida), Newell (Ark-LR to Lamar), Robinson (E.Tenn St. to N.C.State), Starner (Montana St. to Texas-San Antonio). **Quit head job for an assistant's job** (1)—Walker (Fla. Int'l to Iowa St.). **Promoted to head job** (7)—Durham (Montana St.), Freeman (Marshall), Greenberg (L.Beach St.), Jones (Virginia), Knoche (American), LeForce (E.Tenn.St.), Merritt (No.Ariz.).

Fired (9)—Branch (Lamar), Frazier (Morgan St.), Kuester (Geo.Wash.), Mackey (Cleve.St.), Martin (S.F.Austin), Metcalf (Texas A&M), Miller (Colorado), Valvano (N.C.State), Williamson (Howard). **Reassigned** (1)—Abatemarco (Drake). **Resigned** (14)—Adams (Fresno St.), Arnold (Western Ky.), Boutin (Idaho St.), Boyle (St.Joe's,PA), Halas (Columbia), Hofman (Eastern Wash.), Kelly (A.Peay), Mc Pherson (NC-Wilmington), Rafferty (No.Arizona), Reiner (Brooklyn), Stauffer (Nicholls St.), Tapscott (American), S.Williams (MD-Eastern Shore), Wothke (Army). **Retired** (2)—Foster (Miami,FL), Holland (Virginia).

NCAA Division I Basketball Schools

(Conferences and Coaches as of Aug. 1, 1990.)

New conference: Patriot League. **Conference name change:** ECAC North now North Atlantic.

Switching conferences: Army, Fordham, and Holy Cross from Metro Atlantic to Patriot League; Colgate from North Atlantic to Patriot; Bucknell, Lafayette and Lehigh from East Coast to Patriot; SW Missouri St. from Mid-Continent to Missouri Valley. **Leaving conference and division:** Hardin-Simmons from Trans America to Division III. **Switching conferences in future:** Penn State has officially joined the Big Ten, but will remain an Atlantic 10 member for at least one more season; Arkansas from SWC to SEC in 1991-92; Navy from Colonial to Patriot in 1991-92; Old Dominion from Sun Belt to Colonial in 1991-92; Texas-San Antonio from Trans America to Southland in 1991-92.

Independents joining conferences: Akron to Mid-Continent; Central Connecticut St. to East Coast; Central Florida to American South; Davidson to Big South; Maryland-Baltimore County to East Coast; Northern Illinois to Mid-Continent. **New Independent:** Missouri-Kansas City. **Independents joining conferences in future:** Florida International to Trans America in 1991-92; Nicholls St. to Southland in 1991-92.

School	Nickname	Conference	Head Coach	Location	Colors
Air Force	Falcons	WAC	Reggie Minton	Colo.Springs,CO	Blue/Silver
Akron	Zips	Mid-Cont.	Coleman Crawford	Akron,OH	Blue/Gold
Alabama	Crimson Tide	SEC	Wimp Sanderson	Tuscaloosa,AL	Crimson/White
Alabama St	Hornets	S'western	James Oliver	Montgomery,AL	Black/Gold
Ala-Birm	Blazers	Sun Belt	Gene Bartow	Birmingham,AL	Green/Gold
Alcorn St	Braves	S'western	Lonnie Walker	Lorman,MS	Purple/Gold
American	Eagles	Colonial	Chris Knoche	Washington,DC	Red/White/Blue
Appalach.St	Mountaineers	Southern	Tom Apke	Boone,NC	Black/Gold
Arizona	Wildcats	Pac-10	Lute Olson	Tucson,AZ	Cardinal/Navy
Arizona St	Sun Devils	Pac-10	Bill Frieder	Tempe,AZ	Maroon/Gold
Arkansas	Razorbacks	SWC	Nolan Richardson	Fayetteville,AR	Cardinal/White
Arkansas St	Indians	Am.South	Nelson Catalina	State Univ.,AR	Scarlet/Black
Ark-L.Rock	Trojans	Trans Am.	Jim Platt	Little Rock,AR	Maroon/White
Army	Cadets	Patriot	Tom Miller	West Point,NY	Black/Gold/Gray
Auburn	Tigers	SEC	Tommy Joe Eagles	Auburn,AL	Orange/Blue
Augusta	Jaguars	Big South	Clint Bryant	Augusta,GA	Blue/White
Austin Peay	Governors	Ohio Valley	Dave Loos	Clarksville,TN	Red/White
Ball St	Cardinals	MAC	Dick Hunsaker	Muncie,IN	Cardinal/White
Baptist	Buccaneers	Big South	Gary Edwards	Charleston,SC	Blue/Gold
Baylor	Bears	SWC	Gene Iba	Waco,TX	Green/Gold
Beth-Cook	Wildcats	Mid-Eastern	Jack McLairen	Daytona Beach,FL	Maroon/Gold
Boise St	Broncos	Big Sky	Bobby Dye	Boise,ID	Orange/Blue
Boston Coll	Eagles	Big East	Jim O'Brien	Chestnut Hill,MA	Maroon/Gold
Boston Univ	Terriers	North Atl.	Bob Brown	Boston,MA	Scarlet/White
Bowl.Green	Falcons	MAC	Jim Larranaga	Bowl.Green,OH	Orange/Brown
Bradley	Braves	Mo.Valley	Stan Albeck	Peoria,IL	Red/White
BYU	Cougars	WAC	Roger Reid	Provo,UT	Blue/White
Brooklyn	Kingsmen	Indep.	Ron Kestenbaum	Brooklyn,NY	Maroon/Gold
Brown	Bruins	Ivy	Mike Cingiser	Providence,RI	Brown/Red/White
Bucknell	Bison	Patriot	Charlie Woollum	Lewisburg,PA	Orange/Blue
Butler	Bulldogs	Midwestern	Barry Collier	Indianapolis,IN	Blue/White
California	Golden Bears	Pac-10	Lou Campanelli	Berkeley,CA	Blue/Gold
CS-Fullerton	Titans	Big West	John Sneed	Fullerton,CA	Orange/Blue/White
Campbell	Fighting Camels	Big South	Billy Lee	Buies Creek,NC	Orange/Black
Canisius	Golden Griffins	Metro Atl.	Marty Marbach	Buffalo,NY	Blue/Gold
Centenary	Gentlemen	Trans Am.	Tom Canterbury	Shreveport,LA	Maroon/White
Central Conn	Blue Devils	East Coast	Mike Brown	New Britain,CT	Blue/White
Central Fla	Knights	Am.South	Joe Dean Jr.	Orlando,FL	Black/Gold
Central Mich	Chippewas	MAC	Charlie Coles	Mt.Pleasant,MI	Maroon/Gold
Chicago St	Cougars	Indep.	Tommy Suitts	Chicago,IL	Green/White
Cincinnati	Bearcats	Metro	Bob Huggins	Cincinnati,OH	Red/Black
The Citadel	Bulldogs	Southern	Randy Nesbit	Charleston,SC	Blue/White
Clemson	Tigers	ACC	Cliff Ellis	Clemson,SC	Purple/Orange
Cleveland St	Vikings	Mid-Cont.	Vacant	Cleveland,OH	Green/White
Coastal Caro	Chanticleers	Big South	Russ Bergman	Conway,SC	Red/White/Black
Colgate	Red Raiders	Patriot	Jack Bruen	Hamilton,NY	Maroon/White
Colorado	Buffaloes	Big 8	Joe Harrington	Boulder,CO	Silver/Gold/Black
Colorado St	Rams	WAC	Boyd Grant	Ft.Collins,CO	Green/Gold
Columbia	Lions	Ivy	Jack Rohan	New York,NY	Lt.Blue/White
Connecticut	Huskies	Big East	Jim Calhoun	Storrs,CT	Blue/White
Coppin St	Eagles	Mid-Eastern	Ron Mitchell	Baltimore,MD	Blue/Gold
Cornell	Big Red	Ivy	Mike Dement	Ithaca,NY	Red/White
Creighton	Bluejays	Mo.Valley	Tony Barone	Omaha,NE	Blue/White

NCAA Division I Basketball Schools (Cont.)

School	Nickname	Conference	Head Coach	Location	Colors
Dartmouth	Big Green	Ivy	Paul Cormier	Hanover,NH	Green/White
Davidson	Wildcats	Big South	Bob McKillop	Davidson,NC	Red/Black
Dayton	Flyers	Midwestern	Jim O'Brien	Dayton,OH	Red/Blue
DePaul	Blue Demons	Indep.	Joey Meyer	Chicago,IL	Scarlet/Blue
Delaware	Blue Hens	East Coast	Steve Steinwedel	Newark,DE	Blue/Gold
Delaware St	Hornets	Mid-Eastern	Jeff Jones	Dover,DE	Red/Blue
Detroit	Titans	Midwestern	Ricky Byrdsong	Detroit,MI	Cardinal/White
Drake	Bulldogs	Mo.Valley	Rudy Washington	Des Moines,IA	Blue/White
Drexel	Dragons	East Coast	Ed Burke	Philadelphia,PA	Navy/Gold
Duke	Blue Devils	ACC	Mike Krzyzewski	Durham,NC	Royal Blue/White
Duquesne	Dukes	Atlantic 10	John Carroll	Pittsburgh,PA	Red/Blue
East Carolina	Pirates	Colonial	Mike Steele	Greenville,NC	Purple/Gold
East Tenn.St	Buccaneers	Southern	Alan LeForce	Johnson City,TN	Blue/Gold
Eastern Ill	Panthers	Mid-Cont.	Rick Samuels	Charleston,IL	Blue/Gray
Eastern Ky	Colonels	Ohio Valley	Mike Pollio	Richmond,KY	Maroon/White
Eastern Mich	Hurons	MAC	Ben Braun	Ypsilanti,MI	Green/White
Eastern Wash	Eagles	Big Sky	John H.Wade II	Cheney,WA	Red/White
Evansville	Purple Aces	Midwestern	Jim Crews	Evansville,IN	Purple/White
Fairfield	Stags	Metro Atl.	Mitch Buonaguro	Fairfield,CT	Cardinal Red
FDU-Teaneck	Knights	Northeast	Tom Green	Teaneck,NJ	Maroon/White/Blue
Florida	Gators	SEC	Lon Kruger	Gainesville,FL	Orange/Blue
Florida A&M	Rattlers	Mid-Eastern	Willie Booker	Tallahassee,FL	Orange/Green
Florida Int'l	Golden Panthers	Indep.	Bob Weltlich	Miami,FL	Blue/Gold
Florida St	Seminoles	Metro	Pat Kennedy	Tallahassee,FL	Garnet/Gold
Fordham	Rams	Patriot	Nick Macarchuk	Bronx,NY	Maroon/White
Fresno St	Bulldogs	Big West	Ron Adams	Fresno,CA	Cardinal/Blue
Furman	Paladins	Southern	Butch Estes	Greenville, SC	Purple/White
Geo.Mason	Patriots	Colonial	Ernie Nestor	Fairfax,VA	Green/Gold
Geo.Wash	Colonials	Atlantic 10	Mike Jarvis	Washington,DC	Buff/Blue
Georgetown	Hoyas	Big East	John Thompson	Washington,DC	Blue/Gray
Georgia	Bulldogs,'Dawgs	SEC	Hugh Durham	Athens,GA	Red/Black
Ga.Southern	Eagles	Trans Am.	Frank Kerns	Statesboro,GA	Blue/White
Georgia St	Crimson Panthers	Trans Am.	Bob Reinhart	Atlanta,GA	Royal Blue/Crimson
Georgia Tech	Yellow Jackets	ACC	Bobby Cremins	Atlanta,GA	Old Gold/White
Gonzaga	Bulldogs,Zags	West Coast	Dan Fitzgerald	Spokane,WA	Blue/White/Red
Grambling	Tigers	S'western	Robert Hopkins	Grambling,LA	Black/Gold
Hartford	Hawks	North Atl.	Jack Phelan	W.Hartford,CT	Scarlet/White
Harvard	Crimson	Ivy	Peter Roby	Cambridge,MA	Crimson/Black/White
Hawaii	Rainbows	WAC	Riley Wallace	Honolulu,HI	Green/White
Hofstra	Flying Dutchmen	East Coast	B.vanBreda Kolff	Hempstead,NY	Blue/White/Gold
Holy Cross	Crusaders	Patriot	George Blaney	Worcester,MA	Royal Purple
Houston	Cougars	SWC	Pat Foster	Houston,TX	Cougar Red/White
Howard	Bison	Mid-Eastern	Butch Beard	Washington,DC	Blue/White
Idaho	Vandals	Big Sky	Larry Eustachy	Moscow,ID	Silver/Gold
Idaho St	Bengals	Big Sky	Herb Williams	Pocatello,ID	Orange/Black
Illinois	Fighting Illini	Big 10	Lou Henson	Champaign,IL	Orange/Blue
Ill-Chicago	Flames	Mid-Cont.	Bob Hallberg	Chicago,IL	Indigo/Flame
Illinois St	Redbirds	Mo.Valley	Bob Bender	Normal,IL	Red/White
Indiana	Hoosiers	Big 10	Bob Knight	Bloomington,IN	Cream/Crimson
Indiana St	Sycamores	Mo.Valley	Tates Locke	Terre Haute,IN	Blue/White
Iona	Gaels	Metro Atl.	Gary Brokaw	New Rochelle,NY	Maroon/Gold
Iowa	Hawkeyes	Big 10	Tom Davis	Iowa City,IA	Old Gold/Black
Iowa St	Cyclones	Big 8	Johnny Orr	Ames,IA	Cardinal/Gold
Jackson St	Tigers	S'western	John Prince	Jackson,MS	Blue/White
Jacksonville	Dolphins	Sun Belt	Rich Haddad	Jacksonville,FL	Green/Gold
J.Madison	Dukes	Colonial	Lefty Driesell	Harrisonburg,VA	Purple/Gold
Kansas	Jayhawks	Big 8	Roy Williams	Lawrence,KS	Crimson/Blue
Kansas St	Wildcats	Big 8	Dana Altman	Manhattan,KS	Purple/White
Kent	Golden Flashes	MAC	Jim McDonald	Kent,OH	Navy Blue/Gold
Kentucky	Wildcats	SEC	Rick Pitino	Lexington,KY	Blue/White

School	Nickname	Conference	Head Coach	Location	Colors
La Salle	Explorers	Metro Atl.	Bill Morris	Philadelphia, PA	Blue/Gold
Lafayette	Leopards	Patriot	John Leone	Easton, PA	Maroon/White
Lamar	Cardinals	Am.South	Mike Newell	Beaumont, TX	Red/White
Lehigh	Engineers	Patriot	Dave Duke	Bethlehem, PA	Brown/White
Liberty	Flames	Indep.	Jeff Meyer	Lynchburg, VA	Red/White/Blue
Long Beach St	49ers	Big West	Seth Greenberg	Long Beach, CA	Brown/Gold
LIU-Brooklyn	Blackbirds	Northeast	Paul Lizzo	Brooklyn, NY	Blue/White
LSU	Fighting Tigers	SEC	Dale Brown	Baton Rouge, LA	Purple/Gold
Louisiana Tech	Bulldogs	Am.South	Jerry Loyd	Ruston, LA	Red/Blue
Louisville	Cardinals	Metro	Denny Crum	Louisville, KY	Red/Black/White
Loyola, CA	Lions	West Coast	Paul Westhead	Los Angeles, CA	Crimson/Gray/Lt.Blue
Loyola, IL	Ramblers	Midwestern	Will Rey	Chicago, IL	Maroon/Gold
Loyola, MD	Greyhounds	Metro Atl.	Tom Schneider	Baltimore, MD	Green/Gray
Maine	Black Bears	North Atl.	Rudy Keeling	Orono. ME	Blue/White
Manhattan	Jaspers	Metro Atl.	Steve Lappas	Riverdale, NY	Green/White
Marist	Red Foxes	Northeast	Dave Magarity	Poughkeepsie, NY	Red/White
Marquette	Warriors	Midwestern	Kevin O'Neill	Milwaukee, WI	Blue/Gold
Marshall	Thundering Herd	Southern	Dwight Freeman	Huntington, WV	Green/White
Maryland	Terrapins	ACC	Gary Williams	College Park, MD	Red/White/Black/Gold
Md-Balt.Cty	Retrievers	East Coast	Earl Hawkins	Baltimore, MD	Black/Old Gold
Md-E.Shore	Hawks	Mid-Eastern	Bob Hopkins	Princess Anne, MD	Maroon/Gray
Massachusetts	Minutemen	Atlantic 10	John Calipari	Amherst, MA	Maroon/White
McNeese St	Cowboys	Southland	Steve Welch	Lake Charles, LA	Blue/Gold
Memphis St	Tigers	Metro	Larry Finch	Memphis, TN	Blue/Gray
Mercer	Bears	Trans Am.	Bill Bibb	Macon, GA	Orange/Black
Miami, FL	Hurricanes	Indep.	Leonard Hamilton	Miami, FL	Orange/Green/White
Miami, OH	Redskins	MAC	Jerry Peirson	Oxford, OH	Red/White
Michigan	Wolverines	Big 10	Steve Fisher	Ann Arbor, MI	Maize/Blue
Michigan St	Spartans	Big 10	Jud Heathcote	East Lansing, MI	Green/White
Mid.Tenn.St	Blue Raiders	Ohio Valley	Bruce Stewart	Murfreesboro, TN	Blue/White
Minnesota	Golden Gophers	Big 10	Clem Haskins	Minneapolis, MN	Maroon/White
Mississippi	Rebels, Ole Miss	SEC	Ed Murphy	Oxford, MS	Red/Blue
Miss.St	Bulldogs	SEC	Richard Williams	Starkville, MS	Maroon/White
Miss.Valley	Delta Devils	S'western	Lafayette Stribling	Itta Bena, MS	Green/White
Missouri	Tigers	Big 8	Norm Stewart	Columbia, MO	Old Gold/Black
Missouri-KC	Kangaroos	Indep.	Lee Hunt	Kansas City, MO	Blue/Gold
Monmouth	Hawks	Northeast	Terry Glasgow	W.Lg.Branch, NJ	Royal Blue/White
Montana	Grizzlies	Big Sky	Stew Morrill	Missoula, MT	Copper/Silver/Gold
Montana St	Bobcats	Big Sky	Mick Durham	Bozeman, MT	Blue/Gold
Morehead St	Eagles	Ohio Valley	Tommy Gaither	Morehead, KY	Blue/Gold
Morgan St	Bears	Mid-Eastern	Michael Holmes	Baltimore, MD	Blue/Orange
Mt.St.Mary's	Mountaineers	Northeast	Joe McGuinness	Emmitsburg, MD	Navy Blue/Old Gold
Murray St	Racers	Ohio Valley	Steve Newton	Murray, KY	Blue/Gold
Navy	Midshipmen	Colonial	Pete Herrmann	Annapolis, MD	Navy Blue/Gold
Nebraska	Cornhuskers	Big 8	Danny Nee	Lincoln, NE	Scarlet/Cream
Nevada-Reno	Wolf Pack	Big Sky	Len Stevens	Reno, NV	Silver/Blue
New Hamp	Wildcats	North Atl.	Jim Boylan	Durham, NH	Blue/White
New Mexico	Lobos	WAC	Dave Bliss	Albuquerque, NM	Cherry/Silver
N.Mexico St	Aggies	Big West	Neil McCarthy	Las Cruces, NM	Crimson/White
New Orleans	Privateers	Am.South	Tim Floyd	New Orleans, LA	Royal Blue/Silver
Niagara	Purple Eagles	Metro Atl.	Andy Walker	Niagara U., NY	Purple/White/Gold
Nicholls St	Colonels	Indep.	Rickey Broussard	Thibodaux, LA	Red/Gray
N.Carolina	Tar Heels	ACC	Dean Smith	Chapel Hill, NC	Carolina Blue/White
N.Car.A&T	Aggies	Mid-Eastern	Don Corbett	Greensboro, NC	Blue/Gold
N.C.State	Wolfpack	ACC	Les Robinson	Raleigh, NC	Red/White
NC-Asheville	Bulldogs	Big South	Don Doucette	Asheville, NC	Royal Blue/White
NC-Charlotte	49ers	Sun Belt	Jeff Mullins	Charlotte, NC	Green/White
NC-Wilm.	Seahawks	Colonial	Kevin Eastman	Wilmington, NC	Green/Gold
North Texas	Mean Green	Southland	Jimmy Gales	Denton, TX	Green/White
NE Louisiana	Indians	Southland	Mike Vining	Monroe, LA	Maroon/Gold
Northeastern	Huskies	North Atl.	Karl Fogel	Boston, MA	Red/Black
No.Arizona	Lumberjacks	Big Sky	Harold Merritt	Flagstaff, AZ	Blue/Gold
No.Illinois	Huskies	Mid-Cont.	Jim Molinari	De Kalb, IL	Cardinal/Black
No.Iowa	Panthers	Mid-Cont.	Eldon Miller	Cedar Falls, IA	Purple/Old Gold
Northwestern	Wildcats	Big 10	Bill Foster	Evanston, IL	Purple/White
N'western La	Demons	Southland	Dan Bell	Natchitoches, LA	Burnt Orange/Purple
Notre Dame	Fighting Irish	Indep.	Digger Phelps	South Bend, IN	Gold/Blue

NCAA Division I Basketball Schools (Cont.)

School	Nickname	Conference	Head Coach	Location	Colors
Ohio Univ	Bobcats	MAC	Larry Hunter	Athens,OH	Kelly Green/White
Ohio St	Buckeyes	Big 10	Randy Ayers	Columbus,OH	Scarlet/Gray
Oklahoma	Sooners	Big 8	Billy Tubbs	Norman,OK	Crimson/Cream
Oklahoma St	Cowboys	Big 8	Eddie Sutton	Stillwater,OK	Orange/Black
Old Dominion	Monarchs	Sun Belt	Tom Young	Norfolk,VA	Slate Blue/Silver
Oregon	Ducks	Pac-10	Don Monson	Eugene,OR	Green/Yellow
Oregon St	Beavers	Pac-10	Jim Anderson	Corvallis,OR	Orange/Black
Pacific	Tigers	Big West	Bob Thomason	Stockton,CA	Orange/Black
Pan American	Broncs	Am.South	Kevin Wall	Edinburg,TX	Green/White
Penn St	Nittany Lions	Atlantic 10	Bruce Parkhill	Univ.Park,PA	Blue/White
Pennsylvania	Quakers	Ivy	Fran Dunphy	Philadelphia,PA	Red/Blue
Pepperdine	Waves	West Coast	Tom Asbury	Malibu,CA	Blue/Orange
Pittsburgh	Panthers	Big East	Paul Evans	Pittsburgh,PA	Gold/Blue
Portland	Pilots	West Coast	Larry Steele	Portland,OR	Purple/White
Prairie View	Panthers	S'western	Jim Duplantier	Prairie View,TX	Purple/Gold
Princeton	Tigers	Ivy	Pete Carril	Princeton,NJ	Orange/Black
Providence	Friars	Big East	Rick Barnes	Providence,RI	Black/White
Purdue	Boilermakers	Big 10	Gene Keady	W.Lafayette,IN	Old Gold/Black
Radford	Highlanders	Big South	Oliver Purnell	Radford,VA	Blue/Red/Green
Rhode Island	Rams	Atlantic 10	Al Skinner	Kingston,RI	Blue/White
Rice	Owls	SWC	Scott Thompson	Houston,TX	Blue/Gray
Richmond	Spiders	Colonial	Dick Tarrant	Richmond,VA	Red/Blue
Rider	Broncs	East Coast	Kevin Bannon	Lawrenceville,NJ	Purple/Gold
Robert Morris	Colonials	Northeast	Jarrett Durham	Coraopolis,PA	Blue/White
Rutgers	Scarlet Knights	Atlantic 10	Bob Wenzel	N.Brunswick,NJ	Scarlet
St.Bonaventure	Bonnies	Atlantic 10	Tom Chapman	St.Bona.,NY	Brown/White
St.Francis, NY	Terriers	Northeast	Rich Zvosec	Brooklyn,NY	Red/Blue
St.Francis, PA	Red Flash	Northeast	Jim Baron	Loretto,PA	Red/White
St.John's	Redmen	Big East	Lou Carnesecca	Jamaica,NY	Red/White
St.Joe's, PA	Hawks	Atlantic 10	John Griffin	Philadelphia,PA	Crimson/Gray
St.Louis	Billikens	Midwestern	Rich Grawer	St.Louis,MO	Blue/White
St.Mary's, CA	Gaels	West Coast	Paul Landreaux	Moraga,CA	Red/Blue
St.Peter's	Peacocks	Metro Atl.	Ted Fiore	Jersey City,NJ	Blue/White
Sam Hous.St	Bearkats	Southland	Larry Brown	Huntsville,TX	Orange/White
Samford	Bulldogs	Trans Am.	Ed McLean	Birmingham,AL	Crimson/Blue
San Diego	Toreros	West Coast	Hank Egan	San Diego,CA	Lt.Blue/Navy/White
San Diego St	Aztecs	WAC	Jim Brandenburg	San Diego,CA	Scarlet/Black
San Francisco	Dons	West Coast	Jim Brovelli	San Francisco,CA	Green/Gold
San Jose St	Spartans	Big West	Stan Morrison	San Jose,CA	Gold/White/Blue
Santa Clara	Broncos	West Coast	Carroll Williams	Santa Clara,CA	Bronco Red/White
Seton Hall	Pirates	Big East	P.J.Carlesimo	South Orange,NJ	Blue/White
Siena	Saints	Metro Atl.	Mike Deane	Loudonville,NY	Green/Gold
S.Alabama	Jaguars	Sun Belt	Ronnie Arrow	Mobile,AL	Red/White/Blue
S.Carolina	Gamecocks	Metro	George Felton	Columbia,SC	Garnet/Black
S.Carolina St	Bulldogs	Mid-Eastern	Cy Alexander	Orangeburg,SC	Garnet/Blue
S.Florida	Bulls	Sun Belt	Bobby Paschal	Tampa,FL	Green/Gold
Southern Cal	Trojans	Pac-10	George Raveling	Los Angeles,CA	Cardinal/Gold
So.Illinois	Salukis	Mo.Valley	Rich Herrin	Carbondale,IL	Maroon/White
SMU	Mustangs	Southwest	John Shumate	Dallas,TX	Red/Blue
Southern Miss	Golden Eagles	Metro	M.K.Turk	Hattiesburg,MS	Black/Gold
So.Utah St	Thunderbirds	Indep.	Neil Roberts	Cedar City,UT	Scarlet/Royal Blue
Southern-BR	Jaguars	S'western	Ben Jobe	Baton Rouge,LA	Blue/Gold
SW Mo.St	Bears	Mo.Valley	Charlie Spoonhour	Springfield,MO	Maroon/White
SW Texas St	Bobcats	Southern	Harry Larrabee	San Marcos, TX	Maroon/Gold
SW Louisiana	Ragin' Cajuns	Am.South	Marty Fletcher	Lafayette,LA	Vermilion/White
Stanford	Cardinal	Pac 10	Mike Montgomery	Palo Alto,CA	Cardinal/White
S.F.Austin St	Lumberjacks	Southern	Ned Fowler	Nacogdoches,TX	Purple/White
Stetson	Hatters	Trans Am.	Glenn Wilkes	DeLand,FL	Green/White
Syracuse	Orangemen	Big East	Jim Boeheim	Syracuse,NY	Orange
Temple	Owls	Atlantic 10	John Chaney	Philadelphia,PA	Cherry/White
Tennessee	Volunteers	SEC	Wade Houston	Knoxville,TN	Orange/White
Tenn-Chatt.	Moccasins	Southern	Mack McCarthy		
Tennessee St	Tigers	Ohio Valley	Ron Abernathy	Nashville,TN	Blue/White
Tenn Tech	Golden Eagles	Ohio Valley	Tom Deaton	Cookeville,TN	Purple/Gold
Texas	Longhorns	SWC	Tom Penders	Chattanooga,TN	Navy Blue/Gold

School	Nickname	Conference	Head Coach	Location	Colors
Texas A&M	Aggies	SWC	Kermit Davis Jr.	Austin,TX	Burnt Orange/White
TCU	Horned Frogs	SWC	Moe Iba	Coll.Station,TX	Maroon/White
Tex.Southern	Tigers	S'western	Robt.Moreland	Ft.Worth,TX	Purple/White
Texas Tech	Red Raiders	SWC	Gerald Myers	Houston,TX	Maroon/Gray
TX-Arlington	Mavericks	Southland	Mark Nixon	Lubbock,TX	Scarlet/Black
TX-S.Antonio	Roadrunners	Trans Am.	Stu Starner	Arlington,TX	Royal Blue/White
Toledo	Rockets	MAC	Jay Eck	San Antonio,TX	Orange/Navy Blue
Towson St	Tigers	East Coast	Terry Truax	Toledo,OH	Blue/Gold
Tulane	Green Wave	Metro	Perry Clark	Towson,MD	Gold/White/Black
Tulsa	Golden Hurricane	Mo.Valley	J.D.Barnett	Tulsa,OK	Blue/Red/Gold
US Int'l	Gulls	Indep.	Gary Zarkecky	San Diego,CA	Lt.Blue/Sun Gold
UC-Irvine	Anteaters	Big West	Bill Mulligan	Irvine,CA	Blue/Gold
UCLA	Bruins	Pac-10	Jim Harrick	Los Angeles,CA	Blue/Gold
UC-S.Barbara	Gauchos	Big West	Jerry Pimm	Santa Barb.,CA	Blue/Gold
UNLV	Runnin' Rebels	Big West	Jerry Tarkanian	Las Vegas,NV	Scarlet/Gray
Utah	Utes	WAC	Rick Majerus	Salt Lake City,UT	Crimson/White
Utah St	Aggies	Big West	Kohn Smith	Logan,UT	Navy Blue/White
UTEP	Miners	WAC	Don Haskins	El Paso,TX	Orange/White/Blue
Valparaiso	Crusaders	Mid-Cont.	Homer Drew	Valparaiso,IN	Brown/Gold
Vanderbilt	Commodores	SEC	Eddie Fogler	Nashville,TN	Black/Gold
Vermont	Catamounts	North Atl.	Tom Brennan	Burlington,VT	Green/Gold
Villanova	Wildcats	Big East	Rollie Massimino	Villanova,PA	Blue/White
Virginia	Cavaliers	ACC	Jeff Jones	Charlottesville,VA	Orange/Blue
VCU	Rams	Sun Belt	Sonny Smith	Richmond,VA	Black/Gold
VMI	Keydets	Southern	Joe Cantafio	Lexington,VA	Red/White/Yellow
Virginia Tech	Hokies,Gobblers	Metro	Frankie Allen	Blacksburg,VA	Orange/Maroon
Wagner	Seahawks	Northeast	Tim Capstraw	Staten Island,NY	Green/White
Wake Forest	Demon Deacons	ACC	Dave Odom	W.-Salem,NC	Old Gold/Black
Washington	Huskies	Pac-10	Lynn Nance	Seattle,WA	Purple/Gold
Wash.St	Cougars	Pac-10	Kelvin Sampson	Pullman,WA	Crimson/Gray
Weber St	Wildcats	Big Sky	Denny Huston	Ogden,UT	Royal Purple/White
West Va	Mountaineers	Atlantic 10	Gale Catlett	Morgantown,WV	Old Gold/Blue
Western Caro	Catamounts	Southern	Greg Blatt	Cullowhee,NC	Purple/Gold
Western Ill	Leathernecks	Mid-Cont.	Jack Margenthaler	Macomb,IL	Purple/Gold
Western Ky	Hilltoppers	Sun Belt	Ralph Willard	Bowl.Green,KY	Red/White
Western Mich	Broncos	MAC	Bob Donewald	Kalamazoo,MI	Brown/Gold
Wichita St	Shockers	Mo.Valley	Mike Cohen	Wichita,KS	Yellow/Black
Wm.& Mary	Indians	Colonial	Chuck Swenson	Williamsburg,VA	Green/Gold/Silver
Winthrop	Eagles	Big South	Steve Vacendak	Rock Hill,SC	Garnet/Gold
Wisconsin	Badgers	Big 10	Steve Yoder	Madison,WI	Cardinal/White
Wisc-G.Bay	Phoenix	Mid-Cont.	Dick Bennett	Green Bay,WI	Cardinal/Green
Wright St	Raiders	Indep.	Ralph Underhill	Dayton,OH	Green/Gold
Wyoming	Cowboys	WAC	Benny Dees	Laramie,WY	Brown/Yellow
Xavier	Muskateers	Midwestern	Pete Gillen	Cincinnati,OH	Blue/White
Yale	Bulldogs,Elis	Ivy	Dick Kuchen	New Haven,CT	Yale Blue/White
Yngstown St	Penguins	Indep.	Jim Cleamons	Youngstown,OH	Scarlet/White

NCAA Division I-A Football Schools
(Conferences and Coaches as of Aug. 1, 1990)

Switching conference in future: Arkansas has officially joined the SEC, but will remain in the SWC for 1990 season then play as an independent in 1991 before competing in the SEC. **Independent joining conference in future:** Penn State has officially joined the Big Ten, but will not compete for conference championship until mid-1990s.

School	Nickname	Conference	Head Coach	Location	Colors
Air Force	Falcons	WAC	Fisher DeBerry	Colo.Springs,CO	Blue/Silver
Akron	Zips	Indep.	Gerry Faust	Akron,OH	Blue/Gold
Alabama	Crimson Tide	SEC	Gene Stallings	Tuscaloosa,AL	Crimson/White
Arizona	Wildcats	Pac-10	Dick Tomey	Tucson,AZ	Cardinal/Navy
Arizona St	Sun Devils	Pac-10	Larry Marmie	Tempe,AZ	Maroon/Gold
Arkansas	Razorbacks	SWC	Jack Crowe	Fayetteville,AR	Cardinal/White
Army	Cadets	Indep.	Jim Young	West Point,NY	Black/Gold/Gray
Auburn	Tigers	SEC	Pat Dye	Auburn,AL	Orange/Blue
Ball St	Cardinals	MAC	Paul Schudel	Muncie,IN	Cardinal/White
Baylor	Bears	SWC	Grant Teaff	Waco,TX	Green/Gold
Boston Coll.	Eagles	Indep.	Jack Bicknell	Chestnut Hill,MA	Maroon/Gold
Bowl.Green	Falcons	MAC	Moe Ankney	Bowl. Green,OH	Orange/Brown
BYU	Cougars	WAC	LaVell Edwards	Provo,UT	Blue/White

NCAA Division I-A Football Schools (Cont.)

School	Nickname	Conference	Head Coach	Location	Colors
California	Golden Bears	Pac-10	Bruce Snyder	Berkeley,CA	Blue/Gold
CS-Fullerton	Titans	Big West	Gene Murphy	Fullerton,CA	Orange/Blue/White
Central Mich	Chippewas	MAC	Herb Deromedi	Mt.Pleasant,MI	Maroon/Gold
Cincinnati	Bearcats	Indep.	Tim Murphy	Cincinnati,OH	Red/Black
Clemson	Tigers	ACC	Ken Hatfield	Clemson,SC	Purple/Orange
Colorado	Buffaloes	Big 8	Bill McCartney	Boulder,CO	Silver/Gold/Black
Colorado St	Rams	WAC	Earle Bruce	Ft.Collins,CO	Green/Gold
Duke	Blue Devils	ACC	Barry Wilson	Durham,NC	Royal Blue/White
East Carolina	Pirates	Indep.	Bill Lewis	Greenville,NC	Purple/Gold
Eastern Mich	Hurons	MAC	Jim Harkema	Ypsilanti,MI	Green/White
Florida	Gators	SEC	Steve Spurrier	Gainesville,FL	Orange/Blue
Florida St	Seminoles	Indep.	Bobby Bowden	Tallahassee,FL	Garnet/Gold
Fresno St	Bulldogs	Big West	Jim Sweeney	Fresno,CA	Cardinal/Blue
Georgia	Bulldogs,'Dawgs	SEC	Ray Goff	Athens,GA	Red/Black
Georgia Tech	Yellow Jackets	ACC	Bobby Ross	Atlanta,GA	Old Gold/White
Hawaii	Rainbows	WAC	Bob Wagner	Honolulu,HI	Green/White
Houston	Cougars	SWC	John Jenkins	Houston,TX	Cougar Red/White
Illinois	Fighting Illini	Big 10	John Mackovic	Champaign,IL	Orange/Blue
Indiana	Hoosiers	Big 10	Bill Mallory	Bloomington,IN	Cream/Crimson
Iowa	Hawkeyes	Big 10	Hayden Fry	Iowa City,IA	Old Gold/Black
Iowa St	Cyclones	Big 8	Jim Walden	Ames,IA	Cardinal/Gold
Kansas	Jayhawks	Big 8	Glen Mason	Lawrence,KS	Crimson/Blue
Kansas St	Wildcats	Big 8	Bill Snyder	Manhattan,KS	Purple/White
Kent	Golden Flashes	MAC	Dick Crum	Kent,OH	Navy Blue/Gold
Kentucky	Wildcats	SEC	Bill Curry	Lexington,KY	Blue/White
Long Beach St	49ers	Big West	George Allen	Long Beach,CA	Brown/Gold
LSU	Fighting Tigers	SEC	Mike Archer	Baton Rouge,LA	Purple/Gold
Louisville	Cardinals	Indep.	H.Schnellenberger	Louisville,KY	Red/Black/White
Maryland	Terrapins,Terps	ACC	Joe Krivak	Coll.Park,MD	Red/White/Black/Gold
Memphis St	Tigers	Indep.	Chuck Stobart	Memphis,TN	Blue/Gray
Miami, FL	Hurricanes	Indep.	Dennis Erickson	Miami,FL	Orange/Green/White
Miami, OH	Redskins	MAC	Randy Walker	Oxford,OH	Red/White
Michigan	Wolverines	Big 10	Gary Moeller	Ann Arbor,MI	Maize/Blue
Michigan St	Spartans	Big 10	George Perles	East Lansing,MI	Green/White
Minnesota	Golden Gophers	Big 10	John Gutekunst	Minneapolis,MN	Maroon/Gold
Mississippi	Rebels,Ole Miss	SEC	Billy Brewer	Oxford, MS	Card.Red/Navy Blue
Miss.St	Bulldogs	SEC	Rockey Felker	Starkville, MS	Maroon/White
Missouri	Tigers	Big 8	Bob Stull	Columbia,MO	Old Gold/White
Navy	Midshipmen	Indep.	George Chaump	Annapolis,MD	Navy Blue/Gold
Nebraska	Cornhuskers	Big 8	Tom Osborne	Lincoln,NE	Scarlet/Cream
New Mexico	Lobos	WAC	Mike Sheppard	Albuquerque,NM	Cherry/Silver
N.Mexico St	Aggies	Big West	Jim Hess	Las Cruces,NM	Crimson/White
N.Carolina	Tar Heels	ACC	Mack Brown	Chapel Hill,NC	Carolina Blue/White
N.C.State	Wolfpack	ACC	Dick Sheridan	Raleigh,NC	Red/White
No.Illinois	Huskies	Indep.	Jerry Pettibone	De Kalb,IL	Cardinal/Black
Northwestern	Wildcats	Big 10	Francis Peay	Evanston,IL	Purple/White
Notre Dame	Fighting Irish	Indep.	Lou Holtz	South Bend,IN	Gold/Blue
Ohio Univ	Bobcats	MAC	Tom Lichtenberg	Athens,OH	Kelly Green/White
Ohio St	Buckeyes	Big 10	John Cooper	Columbus,OH	Scarlet/Gray
Oklahoma	Sooners	Big 8	Gary Gibbs	Norman,OK	Crimson/Cream
Oklahoma St	Cowboys	Big 8	Pat Jones	Stillwater,OK	Orange/Black
Oregon	Ducks	Pac-10	Rich Brooks	Eugene,OR	Green/Yellow
Oregon St	Beavers	Pac-10	Dave Kragthorpe	Corvallis,OR	Orange/Black
Pacific	Tigers	Big West	Walt Harris	Stockton,CA	Orange/Black
Penn St	Nittany Lions	Indep.	Joe Paterno	Univ.Park,PA	Blue/White
Pittsburgh	Panthers	Indep.	Paul Hackett	Pittsburgh,PA	Blue/Gold
Purdue	Boilermakers	Big 10	Fred Akers	W.Lafayette,IN	Old Gold/Black
Rice	Owls	SWC	Fred Goldsmith	Houston,TX	Blue/Gray
Rutgers	Scarlet Knights	Indep.	Doug Graber	N.Brunswick,NJ	Scarlet

School	Nickname	Conference	Head Coach	Location	Colors
San Diego St	Aztecs	WAC	Al Luginbill	San Diego,CA	Scarlet/Black
San Jose St	Spartans	Big West	Terry Shea	San Jose,CA	Gold/White Blue
S.Carolina	Gamecocks	Indep.	Sparky Woods	Columbia,SC	Garnet/Black
Southern Cal	Trojans	Pac-10	Larry Smith	Los Angeles,CA	Cardinal/Gold
SMU	Mustangs	SWC	Forrest Gregg	Dallas,TX	Red/Blue
Southern Miss	Golden Eagles	Indep.	Curley Hallman	Hattiesburg,MS	Black/Gold
SW Louisiana	Ragin' Cajuns	Indep.	Nelson Stokley	Lafayette,LA	Vermilion/White
Stanford	Cardinal	Pac-10	Dennis Green	Palo Alto,CA	Cardinal/White
Syracuse	Orangemen	Indep.	Dick MacPherson	Syracuse,NY	Orange
Temple	Owls	Indep.	Jerry Berndt	Philadelphia,PA	Cherry/White
Tennessee	Volunteers	SEC	Johnny Majors	Knoxville,TN	Orange/White
Texas	Longhorns	SWC	Dave McWilliams	Austin,TX	Burnt Orange/White
Texas A&M	Aggies	SWC	R.C.Slocum	Coll.Station,TX	Maroon/White
TCU	Horned Frogs	SWC	Jim Wacker	Ft.Worth,TX	Purple/White
Texas Tech	Red Raiders	SWC	Spike Dykes	Lubbock,TX	Scarlet/Black
Toledo	Rockets	MAC	Nick Saban	Toledo,OH	Blue/Gold
Tulane	Green Wave	Indep.	Greg Davis	New Orleans,LA	Olive Green/Sky Blue
Tulsa	Golden Hurricane	Indep.	David Rader	Tulsa,OK	Blue/Gold
UCLA	Bruins	Pac-10	Terry Donahue	Los Angeles,CA	Blue/Gold
UNLV	Runnin' Rebels	Big West	Jim Strong	Las Vegas,NV	Scarlet/Gray
Utah	Utes	WAC	Ron McBride	Salt Lake City,UT	Crimson/White
Utah St	Aggies	Big West	Chuck Shelton	Logan,UT	Navy Blue/White
UTEP	Miners	WAC	David Lee	El Paso,TX	Orange/White/Blue
Vanderbilt	Commodores	SEC	Watson Brown	Nashville,TN	Black/Gold
Virginia	Cavaliers	ACC	George Welsh	Charlottesville,VA	Orange/Blue
Virginia Tech	Hokies,Gobblers	Indep.	Frank Beamer	Blacksburg,VA	Orange/Maroon
Wake Forest	Demon Deacons	ACC	Bill Dooley	W.-Salem,NC	Old Gold/Black
Washington	Huskies	Pac-10	Don James	Seattle,WA	Purple/Gold
Wash.St	Cougars	Pac-10	Mike Price	Pullman,WA	Crimson/Gray
West Va	Mountaineers	Indep.	Don Nehlen	Morgantown,WV	Old Gold/Blue
Western Mich	Broncos	MAC	Al Molde	Kalamazoo,MI	Brown/Gold
Wisconsin	Badgers	Big 10	Barry Alvarez	Madison,WI	Cardinal/White
Wyoming	Cowboys	WAC	Paul Roach	Laramie,WY	Brown/Yellow

NCAA Division I-AA Football Schools

(Conferences and Coaches as of Aug. 1, 1990)

Conference name change: Colonial League renamed Patriot League. **Discontinued programs:** Lamar, Prairie View A&M

School	Nickname	Conference	Head Coach	Location	Colors
Alabama St	Hornets	S'western	Houston Markham	Montgomery,AL	Black/Gold
Alcorn St	Braves	S'western	Theo Danzy	Lorman,MS	Purple/Gold
Appalach.St	Mountaineers	Southern	Jerry Moore	Boone,NC	Black/Gold
Arkansas St	Indians	Indep.	Al Kincaid	State Univ.,AR	Scarlet/Black
Austin Peay	Governors	Ohio Valley	John Palermo	Clarksville,TN	Red/White
Beth-Cookman	Wildcats	Mid-Eastern	Larry Little	Daytona Beach,FL	Maroon/Gold
Boise St	Broncos	Big Sky	Skip Hall	Boise,ID	Orange/Blue
Boston Univ	Terriers	Yankee	Dan Allen	Boston,MA	Scarlet/White
Brown	Bruins	Ivy	Mickey Kwiatkowski	Providence,RI	Brown/Red/White
Bucknell	Bison	Patriot	Lou Maranzana	Lewisburg,PA	Orange/Blue
Central Fla	Knights	Indep.	Gene McDowell	Orlando,FL	Black/Gold
The Citadel	Bulldogs	Southern	Charlie Taaffe	Charleston,SC	Blue/White
Colgate	Red Raiders	Patriot	Mike Foley	Hamilton,NY	Maroon/White
Columbia	Lions	Ivy	Ray Tellier	New York,NY	Lt.Blue/White
Connecticut	Huskies	Yankee	Tom Jackson	Storrs,CT	Blue/White
Cornell	Big Red	Ivy	Jim Hofher	Ithaca,NY	Red/White
Dartmouth	Big Green	Ivy	Buddy Teevens	Hanover,NH	Green/White
Davidson	Wildcats	Indep.	Dave Fogg	Davidson,NC	Red/Black
Delaware	Blue Hens	Yankee	Tubby Raymond	Newark,DE	Blue/Gold
Delaware St	Hornets	Mid-Eastern	William Collick	Dover,DE	Red/Blue
East Tenn.St	Buccaneers	Southern	Don Riley	Johnson City,TN	Blue/Gold
Eastern Ill	Panthers	Gateway	Bob Spoo	Charleston,IL	Blue/Gold
Eastern Ky	Colonels	Ohio Valley	Roy Kidd	Richmond,KY	Maroon/White
Eastern Wash	Eagles	Big Sky	Dick Zornes	Cheney,WA	Red/White
Florida A&M	Rattlers	Mid-Eastern	Ken Riley	Tallahassee,FL	Orange/Green
Fordham	Rams	Patriot	Larry Glueck	New York,NY	Maroon/White
Furman	Paladins	Southern	Jim Satterfield	Greenville, SC	Purple/White

NCAA Division I-AA Football Schools (Cont.)

School	Nickname	Conference	Head Coach	Location	Colors
Ga.Southern	Eagles	Indep.	Tim Stowers	Statesboro,GA	Blue/White
Grambling	Tigers	S'western	Eddie Robinson	Grambling,LA	Black/Gold
Harvard	Crimson	Ivy	Joe Restic	Cambridge,MA	Crimson/Black/White
Holy Cross	Crusaders	Patriot	Mark Duffner	Worcester,MA	Royal Purple
Howard	Bison	Mid-Eastern	Steve Wilson	Washington,DC	Blue/White
Idaho	Vandals	Big Sky	John L. Smith	Moscow,ID	Silver/Gold
Idaho St	Bengals	Big Sky	Garth Hall	Pocatello,ID	Orange/Black
Illinois St	Redbirds	Gateway	Jim Heacock	Normal,IL	Red/White
Indiana St	Sycamores	Gateway	Dennis Raetz	Terre Haute,IN	Blue/White
Jackson St	Tigers	S'western	W.C.Gorden	Jackson,MS	Blue/White
J.Madison	Dukes	Indep.	Joe Purzycki	Harrisonburg,VA	Purple/Gold
Lafayette	Leopards	Patriot	Bill Russo	Bethlehem,PA	Brown/White
Lehigh	Brown & White	Patriot	Hank Small		
Liberty	Flames	Indep.	Sam Rutigliano	Lynchburg,VA	Red/White/Blue
La.Tech	Bulldogs	Indep.	Joe Raymond Peace	Ruston,LA	Red/Blue
Maine	Black Bears	Yankee	Kirk Ferentz	Orono.ME	Blue/White
Marshall	Thundering Herd	Southern	Jim Donnan	Huntington,WV	Green/White
Massachusetts	Minutemen	Yankee	Jim Reid	Amherst,MA	Maroon/White
McNeese St	Cowboys	Southland	Bobby Keasler	Lake Charles,LA	Blue/Gold
Mid.Tenn.St	Blue Raiders	Ohio Valley	Boots Donnelly	Murfreesboro,TN	Blue/White
Miss.Valley	Delta Devils	S'western	Larry Dorsey	Itta Bena,MS	Green/White
Montana	Grizzlies	Big Sky	Don Read	Missoula,MT	Copper/Silver/Gold
Montana St	Bobcats	Big Sky	Earle Solomonson	Bozeman,MT	Blue/Gold
Morehead St	Eagles	Ohio Valley	Cole Proctor	Morehead,KY	Blue/Gold
Morgan St	Bears	Mid-Eastern	Ed Wyche	Baltimore,MD	Blue/Orange
Murray St	Racers	Ohio Valley	Mike Mahoney	Murray,KY	Blue/Gold
Nevada-Reno	Wolf Pack	Big Sky	Chris Ault	Reno,NV	Silver/Blue
New Hamp	Wildcats	Yankee	Bill Bowes	Durham,NH	Blue/White
Nicholls St	Colonels	Indep.	Phil Greco	Thibodaux,LA	Red/Gray
N.Car.A&T	Aggies	Mid-Eastern	Bill Hayes	Greensboro,NC	Blue/Gold
North Texas	Mean Green	Southland	Corky Nelson	Denton,TX	Green/White
NE Louisiana	Indians	Southland	Dave Roberts	Monroe,LA	Maroon/Gold
Northeastern	Huskies	Indep.	Paul Pawlak	Boston,MA	Red/Black
No.Ariz	Lumberjacks	Big Sky	Steve Akman	Flagstaff,AZ	Blue/Gold
No.Iowa	Panthers	Gateway	Terry Allen	Cedar Falls,IA	Purple/Old Gold
N'western St	Demons	Southland	Sam Goodwin	Natchitoches,LA	Purple/White
Penn	Quakers	Ivy	Gary Steele	Philadelphia,PA	Red/Blue
Princeton	Tigers	Ivy	Steve Tosches	Princeton,NJ	Orange/Black
Rhode Is	Rams	Yankee	Bob Griffin	Kingston,RI	Blue/White
Richmond	Spiders	Yankee	Jim Marshall	Richmond,VA	Red/Blue
Sam Hous.St	Bearkats	Southland	Ron Randleman	Huntsville,TX	Orange/White/Blue
Samford	Bulldogs	Indep.	Terry Bowden	Birmingham,AL	Crimson/Blue
S.Car.St	Bulldogs	Mid Eastern	Willie Jeffries	Orangeburg,SC	Garnet/Blue
Southern Ill	Salukis	Gateway	Bob Smith	Carbondale,IL	Maroon/White
Southern-BR	Jaguars	SWAC	Gerald Kimble	Baton Rouge,LA	Blue/Gold
SW Mo.St	Bears	Gateway	Jesse Branch	Springfield,MO	Maroon/White
SW Texas St	Bobcats	Southland	Dennis Franchione	San Marcos, TX	Maroon/Gold
S.F.Austin St	Lumberjacks	Southland	Lynn Graves	Nacogdoches,TX	Purple/White
Tenn-Chatt	Moccasins	Southern	Buddy Nix	Chattanooga,TN	Navy Blue/Gold
Tenn.St	Tigers	Ohio Valley	Joe Gilliam, Sr.	Nashville,TN	Blue/White
Tenn Tech	Golden Eagles	Ohio Valley	Jim Ragland	Cookeville,TN	Purple/Gold
Tex.Southern	Tigers	SWAC	Walt Highsmith	Houston,TX	Maroon/Gray
Towson St	Tigers	Indep.	Phil Albert	Towson,MD	Gold/White
Villanova	Wildcats	Yankee	Andy Talley	Villanova,PA	Blue/White
VMI	Keydets	Southern	Jim Shuck	Lexington,VA	Red/White/Yellow
Weber St	Wildcats	Big Sky	Dave Arslanian	Ogden,UT	Purple/White
Western Car	Catamounts	Southern	Steve Hodgin	Cullowhee,NC	Purple/Gold
Western Ill	Leathernecks	Gateway	Randy Ball	Macomb,IL	Purple/Gold
Western Ky	Hilltoppers	Indep.	Jack Harbaugh	Bowl.Green,KY	Red/White
Wm.& Mary	Indians	Indep.	Jimmye Laycock	Williamsburg,VA	Green/Gold
Yale	Bulldogs,Elis	Ivy	Carmen Cozza	New Haven,CT	Yale Blue/White
Yngstown St	Penguins	Indep.	Jim Tressel	Youngstown,OH	Scarlet/White

Among the charter members of the International Boxing Hall of Fame inducted June 10 in Canastota, N.Y. were (clockwise): **Jersey Joe Walcott, Muhammad Ali, Emile Griffith, Kid Gavilan,** and **Ike Williams.**

HALLS OF FAME & AWARDS

Auto Racing Halls of Fame

Indianapolis Motor Speedway Hall of Fame

Originally the Auto Racing Hall of Fame. Established by the American Automobile Association Contest Board in 1952, disbanded in 1955, and revived by the Indianapolis Speedway Foundation in 1962. **Address:** 4790 West 16th Street, Indianapolis, IN, 46222. **Telephone:** 317-248-6747.

Eligibility: candidates cannot be nominated until at least 20 years after the date of first active participation in auto racing. Voting done by 100-member panel made up of racing officials, Hall of Fame members and media representatives.

Class of 1990: promoter and car owner **J.C. Agajanian** and driver **Bobby Unser.**

Members are listed with year of induction; (+) indicates deceased members.

Drivers

+Aitken, Johnny 1981	Foyt, A.J 1978	+Murphy, Jimmy 1964
+Anderson, Gil 1983	+Frame, Fred 1984	Nalon, Dennis (Duke) 1983
Andretti, Mario 1986	+Goux, Jules 1989	+Oldfield, Barney 1952
+Baker, Cannonball 1981	+Grant, Harry...........1982	+Parsons, Johnnie 1986
Banks, Henry............1985	Gurney, Dan 1988	+Resta, Dario 1953-54
+Bergere, Cliff 1976	Hanks, Sam 1981	+Rickenbacker, Eddie 1954
+Bettenhausen, Tony 1968	+Harroun, Ray 1952	+Roberts, Floyd 1985
+Boyer, Joe 1985	+Hartz, Harry 1963	+Rose, Mauri 1967
+Bruce-Brown, David 1980	+Hearne, Eddie 1964	Rutherford, Johnny 1987
+Burman, Bob 1953-54	+Hepburn, Ralph 1970	+Shaw, Wilbur 1963
+Bryan, Jimmy 1973	+Horn, Ted 1964	+Snyder, Jimmy 1981
+Chevrolet, Gaston 1964	Jones, Parnelli 1985	+Stevens, Myron 1983
+Chevrolet, Louis 1952	+Keech, Ray 1984	+Strang, Lewis 1982
+Clark, Jimmy 1988	+Lockhart, Frank 1965	Unser, Al...............1986
+Cooper, Earl 1953-54	+Mays, Rex 1963	Unser, Bobby 1990
+Cummings, Bill..........1970	+McGrath, Jack..........1987	+Vukovich, Bill 1972
+Dawson, Joe 1976	Meyer, Louis 1963	Ward, Roger 1981
+DePalma, Ralph 1953-54	+Milton, Tommy 1953-54	+Wilcox, Howard 1963
+DePaolo, Peter 1963	+Moore, Lou 1969	
+Durant, Cliff 1983	+Mulford, Ralph.......1953-54	
+Fengler, Harlan 1983		

Contributors

+Agajanian, J.C. 1990	+Firestone, Harvey, Sr 1952	+Offenhauser, Fred.......1982
+Allison, James A 1964	+Fisher, Carl 1952	+Pillsbury, Art 1981
Bignotti, George 1975	+Ford, Henry 1952	+Ricker, Chester 1989
+Brawner, Clint 1984	+Gilmore, Earl 1987	+Robertson, George 1980
+Christie, Walter 1980	+Goossen, Leo 1978	+Sparks, Art 1987
+Cloutier, Joe 1989	+Henning, Harry (Cotton)..1969	+Stutz, Henry 1963
+Dingley, Bert 1952	+Hulman, Tony 1967	+Vanderbilt, William K 1952
+Duesenberg, Augie 1963	+Kurtis, Frank 1983	+Wagner, Fred 1952
+Duesenberg, Fred 1962	+Marcenac, Jean 1968	Watson, A.J 1981
+Edenburn, Eddie 1986	+Miller, Harry 1963	+Welch, Lew 1986
	+Myers, T.E.(Pop) 1952	+Winfield, Ed 1983

International Motor Sports Hall of Fame

Established in 1990 by the International Motor Sports Hall of Fame Commission. **Address:** P.O. Box 1018, Talladega, AL, 35160. **Telephone:** 205-362-5002.

Eligibility: nominees must be retired from original active participation in motor sports for five years. Voting done by 150-member panel made up of worldwide auto racing media.

Class of 1990: 20 charter members (see below).

Members are listed with year of induction; (+) indicates deceased members.

Formula One Drivers

Brabham, Jack 1990	
+Clark, Jim 1990	
+Juan Manuel Fangio 1990	
+Hill, Graham 1990	
Moss, Stirling 1990	
Stewart, Jackie 1990	

Indy Car Drivers

+Donahue, Mark.......................1990
Gurney, Dan 1990
Jones, Parnelli........................1990
+Oldfield, Barney 1990
Unser, Bobby 1990

NASCAR Drivers

Baker, Buck 1990
Johnson, Junior 1990
Petty, Lee............................1990
Roberts, Fireball 1990

World Record Holder

+Campbell, Sir Malcolm 1990

Driver-Builders

+Thompson, Mickey....................1990
Yunick, Smokey 1990

Contributors

France, Bill, Sr 1990
+Hulman, Tony 1990

Motorsports Hall of Fame of America

Established in 1989. **Address:** P.O.Box 194, Novi, MI 48050. **Telephone:** 313-349-7223.

Eligibility: nominees must be retired at least three years or engaged in their area of motor sports for at least 20 years. Areas include: open wheel, stock car, dragster, sports car, motorcycle, power boat and air racing.

Class of 1990: Auto drivers **Mario Andretti, Jim Clark, Mark Donahue,** drag racer **Shirley Muldowney,** power boat racer **Gar Wood,** motorcyclist **Kenny Roberts;** aviator **Glenn Curtis;** driver-builder **Mickey Thompson** and NASCAR founder **Bill France, Sr.**

Members are listed with year of induction; (+) indicates deceased members.

Andretti, Mario 1990	Foyt, A.J 1989	Petty, Richard 1989
+Baker, Cannonball 1989	Garlits, Don 1989	Roberts, Kenny 1990
+Clark, Jim 1990	Hill, Phil 1989	+Thompson, Mickey 1990
+Curtiss, Glenn 1990	Muldowney, Shirley 1990	+Wood, Gar 1990
+Donahue, Mark 1990	Muncy, Bill 1989	**Contributor**
Doolittle, Jimmy 1989	+Oldfield, Barney 1989	France, Bill, Sr. 1990

National Baseball Hall of Fame

Established in 1935 by Major League Baseball to celebrate the game's 100th anniversary. **Address:** P.O.Box 590, Cooperstown, NY 13326. **Telephone:** 607-547-9988.

Eligibility: nominated players must have played at least part of 10 seasons in the Major Leagues and be retired for five years. Voting done by Baseball Writers Association of America.

Class of 1990: second baseman **Joe Morgan,** Houston (1963-71), Cincinnati (1972-79), Houston (1980), San Francisco (1981-82), Philadelphia (1983), Oakland (1984); and pitcher **Jim Palmer,** Baltimore (1965-67,69-84).

Top 10 vote-getters (333 votes to elect): **Palmer** (411), **Morgan** (363), Gaylord Perry (320), Ferguson Jenkins (296), Jim Bunning (257), Orlando Cepeda (211), Tony Oliva (142), Bill Mazeroski (131), Harvey Kuenn (107) and Ron Santo (96).

Elected first year on ballot (21): Hank Aaron, Ernie Banks, Johnny Bench, Lou Brock, Bob Feller, Bob Gibson, Al Kaline, Sandy Koufax, Mickey Mantle, Willie Mays, Willie McCovey, **Joe Morgan,** Stan Musial, **Jim Palmer,** Brooks Robinson, Frank Robinson, Jackie Robinson, Warren Spahn, Willie Stargell, Ted Williams and Carl Yastrzemski.

Members are listed with year of induction; (+) indicates deceased members.

1st Basemen

+Anson, Cap 1939	+Connor, Roger 1976	Killebrew, Harmon 1984
+Beckley, Jake 1971	+Foxx, Jimmie 1951	McCovey, Willie 1986
+Bottomley, Jim 1974	+Gehrig, Lou 1939	Mize, Johnny 1981
+Brouthers, Dan 1945	+Greenberg, Hank 1956	+Sisler, George 1939
+Chance, Frank 1946	+Kelly, George 1973	Stargell, Willie 1988
		+Terry, Bill 1954

2nd Basemen

+Collins, Eddie 1939	+Frisch, Frankie 1947	+Lajoie, Nap 1937
Doerr, Bobby 1986	Gehringer, Charlie 1949	Morgan, Joe 1990
+Evers, Johnny 1946	Herman, Billy 1975	+Robinson, Jackie 1962
	+Hornsby, Rogers 1942	Schoendienst, Red 1989

Shortstops

Aparicio, Luis 1984	+Cronin, Joe 1956	+Sewell, Joe 1977
Appling, Luke 1964	+Jackson, Travis 1982	+Tinker, Joe 1946
+Bancroft, Dave 1971	+Jennings, Hugh 1945	+Vaughan, Arky 1985
Banks, Ernie 1977	+Maranville, Rabbit 1954	+Wagner, Honus 1936
Boudreau, Lou 1970	Reese, Pee Wee 1984	+Wallace, Bobby 1953
		+Ward, Monte 1964

3rd Basemen

+Baker, Frank 1955	Kell, George 1983	Mathews, Eddie 1978
+Collins, Jimmy 1945	+Lindstrom, Fred 1976	Robinson, Brooks 1983
		+Traynor, Pie 1948

Left Fielders

Brock, Lou 1985	+Hafey, Chick 1971	+O'Rourke, Jim 1945
+Burkett, Jesse 1946	+Kelley, Joe 1971	+Simmons, Al 1953
+Clarke, Fred 1945	Kiner, Ralph 1975	+Wheat, Zack 1959
+Delahanty, Ed 1945	+Manush, Heinie 1964	Williams, Billy 1987
+Goslin, Goose 1968	+Medwick, Joe 1968	Williams, Ted 1966
	Musial, Stan 1969	Yastrzemski, Carl 1989

Center Fielders

+Averill, Earl 1975	DiMaggio, Joe 1955	+Roush, Edd 1962
+Carey, Max 1961	+Duffy, Hugh 1945	Snider, Duke 1980
+Cobb, Ty 1936	+Hamilton, Billy 1961	+Speaker, Tris 1937
+Combs, Earle 1970	Mantle, Mickey 1974	+Waner, Lloyd 1967
	Mays, Willie 1979	+Wilson, Hack 1979

National Baseball Hall of Fame (Cont.)

Right Fielders

Aaron, Hank 1982
+Clemente, Roberto 1973
+Crawford, Sam 1957
+Cuyler, Kiki 1968
+Flick, Elmer 1963
+Heilmann, Harry 1952

+Hooper, Harry 1971
Kaline, Al 1980
+Keeler, Willie 1939
+Kelly, King 1945
+Klein, Chuck 1980
+McCarthy, Tommy 1946
+Ott, Mel 1951

+Rice, Sam 1963
Robinson, Frank 1982
+Ruth, Babe 1936
Slaughter, Enos 1985
+Thompson, Sam 1974
+Waner, Paul 1952
+Youngs, Ross 1972

Catchers

Bench, Johnny 1989
Berra, Yogi 1972
+Bresnahan, Roger 1945

Campanella, Roy 1969
+Cochrane, Mickey 1947
Dickey, Bill 1954
+Ewing, Buck 1939

Ferrell, Rick 1984
+Hartnett, Gabby 1955
+Lombardi, Ernie 1986
+Schalk, Ray 1955

Pitchers

+Alexander, Grover 1938
+Bender, Chief 1953
+Brown, Mordecai 1949
+Chesbro, Jack 1946
+Clarkson, John 1963
+Coveleski, Stan 1969
+Dean, Dizzy 1953
Drysdale, Don 1984
+Faber, Red 1964
Feller, Bob 1962
Ford, Whitey 1974
+Galvin, Pud 1965
Gibson, Bob 1981
+Gomez, Lefty 1972
+Grimes, Burleigh 1964

+Grove, Lefty 1947
+Haines, Jess 1970
+Hoyt, Waite 1969
+Hubbell, Carl 1947
Hunter, Catfish 1987
+Johnson, Walter 1936
+Joss, Addie 1978
+Keefe, Tim 1964
Koufax, Sandy 1972
Lemon, Bob 1976
+Lyons, Ted 1955
Marichal, Juan 1983
+Marquard, Rube 1971
+Mathewson, Christy 1936
+McGinnity, Joe 1946
+Nichols, Kid 1949

Palmer, Jim 1990
+Pennock, Herb 1948
+Plank, Eddie 1946
+Radbourne, Old Hoss . . .1939
+Rixey, Eppa 1963
Roberts, Robin 1976
+Ruffing, Red 1967
+Rusie, Amos 1977
Spahn, Warren 1973
+Vance, Dazzy 1955
+Waddell, Rube 1946
+Walsh, Ed 1946
+Welch, Mickey 1973
Wilhelm, Hoyt 1985
Wynn, Early 1972
+Young, Cy 1937

From Negro Leagues

Bell, Cool Papa (OF) 1974
+Charleston, Oscar (1B-OF) 1976
Dandridge, Ray (3B) 1987

+Dihigo, Martin (P-OF) 1977
+Foster, Rube (P-Mgr) 1981
+Gibson, Josh (C) 1972
Irvin, Monte (OF) 1973

+Johnson, Judy (3B) 1975
Leonard, Buck (1B) 1972
+Lloyd, Pop (SS) 1977
+Paige, Satchel (P) 1971

Managers

+Alston, Walter 1983
+Harris, Bucky 1975
+Huggins, Miller 1964

Lopez, Al 1977
+Mack, Connie 1937
+McCarthy, Joe 1957

+McGraw, John 1937
+McKechnie, Bill 1962
+Robinson, Wilbert 1945
+Stengel, Casey 1966

Umpires

Barlick, Al 1989
+Conlan, Jocko 1974

+Connolly, Tom 1953
+Evans, Billy 1973

+Hubbard, Cal 1976
+Klem, Bill 1953

Pioneers and Executives

+Barrow, Ed 1953
+Bulkeley, Morgan 1937
+Cartwright, Alexander . . .1938
+Chadwick, Henry 1938
Chandler, Happy 1982
+Comiskey, Charles 1939

+Cummings, Candy 1939
+Frick, Ford 1970
+Giles, Warren 1979
+Griffith, Clark 1946
+Harridge, Will 1972
+Johnson, Ban 1937
+Landis, Kenesaw 1944

+MacPhail, Larry 1978
+Rickey, Branch 1967
+Spalding, Al 1939
+Weiss, George 1971
+Wright, George 1937
+Wright, Harry 1953
+Yawkey, Tom 1980

J.G.Taylor Spink Award

First presented in 1962 by the Baseball Writers Association of America for meritorious contributions by members of the BBWAA. Named in honor of the late publisher of *The Sporting News*, the Spink Award does not constitute induction into the Hall of Fame. Winners are honored in the year following their selection.

Year
1962 J.G.Taylor Spink
1963 Ring Lardner
1964 Hugh Fullerton
1965 Charley Dryden
1966 Grantland Rice
1967 Damon Runyon
1968 H.G.Salsinger
1969 Sid Mercer
1970 Heywood Broun
1971 Frank Graham
1972 Dan Daniel, Fred Lieb
    & J.Roy Stockton

Year
1973 Warren Brown,
    John Drebinger
    & John Kieran
1974 John Carmichael
    & James Isaminger
1975 Tom Meaney
    & Shirley Povich
1976 Harold Kaese
    & Red Smith
1977 Gordon Cobbledick
    & Edgar Munzel
1978 Tim Murnane
    & Dick Young

Year
1979 Bob Broeg & Tommy Holmes
1980 Joe Reichler & Milt Richman
1981 Bob Addie & Allen Lewis
1982 Si Burick
1983 Ken Smith
1984 Joe McGuff
1985 Earl Lawson
1986 Jack Lang
1987 Jim Murray
1988 Bob Hunter & Ray Kelly
1989 Jerome Holtzman

Ford Frick Award

First presented in 1978 by Hall of Fame for meritorious contributions by baseball broadcasters. Named in honor of the late broadcaster, National League president and commissioner, the Frick Award does not constitute induction into the Hall of Fame.

Year		Year		Year	
1978	Mel Allen & Red Barber	1982	Vin Scully	1987	Jack Buck
1979	Bob Elson	1983	Jack Brickhouse	1988	Lindsey Nelson
1980	Russ Hodges	1984	Curt Gowdy	1989	Harry Caray
1981	Ernie Harwell	1985	Buck Canel	1990	Byrum Saam
		1986	Bob Prince		

Naismith Memorial Basketball Hall of Fame

Established in 1949 by the National Association of Basketball Coaches in memory of the sport's inventor, Dr. James Naismith. First Hall opened in 1968 and current Hall in 1985. **Address:** 1150 West Columbus Ave., Springfield, MA 01105. **Telephone:** 413-781-6500.

Eligibility: nominated players and referees must be retired for five years, coaches must have coached 25 years or be retired for five, and contributors must have already completed their noteworthy service to the game. Voting done by 24-member honors committee made up of media representatives, Hall of Fame members and trustees.

Class of 1990: guard **Dave Bing**—Syracuse (1964-66), NBA (Det-Wash-Bos, 1966-78); forward **Elvin Hayes**—Houston (1966-68), NBA (SD-Hou-Bal-Wash-Hou, 1968-84); forward **Neil Johnston**—Ohio St.(1949-51), NBA (Phila, 1951-59); and guard **Earl Monroe**—Winston-Salem St.(1965-67), NBA (Bal-NY, 1967-80).

Members are listed with year of induction; (+) indicates deceased members.

Players

Arizin, Paul	1977	+Gruenig, Robert	1963	Murphy, Charles (Stretch)	1960
+Barlow, Thomas (Babe)	1980	Hagan, Cliff	1977	+Page, Harlan (Pat)	1962
Barry, Rick	1987	+Hanson, Victor	1960	Pettit, Bob	1970
Baylor, Elgin	1976	Havlicek, John	1983	Phillip, Andy	1961
+Beckman, John	1972	Hayes, Elvin	1990	Pollard, Jim	1977
Bing, Dave	1990	Heinsohn, Tom	1986	Ramsey, Frank	1981
+Borgmann, Benny	1961	Holman, Nat	1964	Reed, Willis	1981
Bradley, Bill	1982	Houbregs, Bob	1987	Robertson, Oscar	1979
+Brennan, Joe	1974	+Hyatt, Chuck	1959	+Roosma, John	1961
Cervi, Al	1984	+Johnson, Bill (Skinny)	1976	+Russell, John (Honey)	1964
Chamberlain, Wilt	1978	+Johnston, Neil	1990	Russell, Bill	1974
+Cooper, Charles (Tarzan)	1976	Jones, K. C	1989	Schayes, Dolph	1972
Cousy, Bob	1970	Jones, Sam	1983	+Schmidt, Ernest J	1973
Cunningham, Billy	1986	Krause, Edward (Moose)	1975	+Schommer, John	1959
+Davies, Bob	1969	Kurland, Bob	1961	+Sedran, Barney	1962
+DeBernardi, Forrest	1961	+Lapchick, Joe	1966	Sharman, Bill	1975
DeBusschere, Dave	1982	Lovellette, Clyde	1988	+Steinmetz, Christian	1961
+Dehnert, Dutch	1968	Lucas, Jerry	1979	Thompson, John (Cat)	1962
Endacott, Paul	1971	Luisetti, Hank	1959	Thurmond, Nate	1984
Foster, Bud	1964	Macauley, Ed	1960	Twyman, Jack	1982
Frazier, Walt	1987	+Maravich, Pete	1987	Unseld, Wes	1988
+Friedman, Marty	1971	Martin, Slater	1981	+Vandivier, Robert (Fuzzy)	1974
+Fulks, Joe	1977	+McCracken, Branch	1960	+Wachter, Ed	1961
Gale, Laddie	1976	+McCracken, Jack	1962	Wanzer, Bobby	1987
Gates, William (Pop)	1989	McDermott, Bobby	1988	West, Jerry	1979
Gola, Tom	1975	Mikan, George	1959	Wilkens, Lenny	1989
Greer, Hal	1981	Monroe, Earl	1990	Wooden, John	1960

Coaches

+Anderson, Harold (Andy)	1984	+Gill, Amory (Slats)	1967	McCutchan, Arad	1980
Auerbach, Red	1968	Harshman, Marv	1984	McGuire, Frank	1976
+Barry, Sam	1978	+Hickey, Eddie	1978	+Meanwell, Walter (Doc)	1959
+Blood, Ernest (Prof)	1960	Hobson, Howard (Hobby)	1965	Meyer, Ray	1978
Cann, Howard	1967	Holzman, Red	1986	Miller, Ralph	1988
+Carlson, Henry (Doc)	1959	Iba, Henry	1968	+Rupp, Adolph	1968
Carnevale, Ben	1969	+Julian, Alvin (Doggie)	1967	+Sachs, Leonard	1961
+Case, Everett	1981	+Keaney, Frank	1960	+Shelton, Everett	1979
Dean, Everett	1966	+Keogan, George	1961	Smith, Dean	1982
+Diddle, Ed	1971	+Lambert, Ward (Piggy)	1960	Taylor, Fred	1985
+Drake, Bruce	1972	Litwack, Harry	1975	Wade, Margaret	1984
Gaines, Clarence	1981	+Loeffler, Ken	1964	Watts, Stan	1985
Gardner, Jack	1983	+Lonborg, Dutch	1972	Wooden, John	1972

Referees

+Enright, Jim	1978	+Kennedy, Pat	1959	+Quigley, Ernest (Quig)	1961
+Hepbron, George	1960	+Leith, Lloyd	1982	Shirley, J. Dallas	1979
+Hoyt, George	1961	Mihalik, Red	1986	Tobey, Dave	1961
		Nucatola, John	1977	+Walsh, David	1961

Naismith Memorial Basketball Hall of Fame (Cont.)

Teams

Buffalo Germans 1961	New York Renaissance 1963
First Team 1959	Original Celtics 1959

Contributors

+Abbott, Senda Berenson ..1984	Hinkle, Tony 1965	+Porter, Henry (H.V.) 1960
+Allen, Forrest (Phog) 1959	+Irish, Ned 1964	+Reid, William A 1963
+Bee, Clair 1967	+Jones, R. William 1964	+Ripley, Elmer 1972
+Brown, Walter A 1965	+Kennedy, Walter 1980	+St. John, Lynn W 1962
+Bunn, John 1964	+Liston, Emil (Liz) 1974	+Saperstein, Abe 1970
+Douglas, Bob 1971	McLendon, John 1978	+Schabinger, Arthur 1961
+Duer, Al 1981	+Mokray, Bill 1965	+Stagg, Amos Alonzo 1959
Fagen, Clifford B 1983	+Morgan, Ralph 1959	+Steitz, Ed 1983
+Fisher, Harry 1973	+Morgenweck, Frank (Pop).1962	+Taylor, Chuck 1968
+Gottlieb, Eddie 1971	+Naismith, James 1959	Teague, Bertha 1984
+Gulick, Luther 1959	Newell, Pete 1978	+Tower, Oswald 1959
Harrison, Les 1979	+O'Brien, John J. (Jack) ...1961	+Trester, Ather (A.L.) 1961
+Hepp, Ferenc 1980	+Olsen, Harold G 1959	+Wells, Cliff 1971
+Hickcox, Ed 1959	+Podoloff, Maurice 1973	+Wilke, Lou 1982

National Bowling Hall of Fame

The National Bowling Hall is one museum with separate wings for honorees of the American Bowling Congress (ABC), the Professional Bowlers' Association (PBA) and Women's International Bowling Congress (WIBC). **Address:** 111 Stadium Plaza, St.Louis, MO 63102. **Telephone:** 314-231-6340.

American Bowling Congress

Established in 1941 and open to professional and amateur bowlers. **Eligibility:** nominated bowlers must have competed in at least 20 years of ABC Tournaments. Voting done by 150-member panel made up of Hall of Fame members, ABC officials and media representatives.

Class of 1990: Performance—**Dave Davis, Jim Schroeder** and **Rich Wonders.**
Members are listed with year of induction; (+) indicates deceased members.

Performance

Allison, Glenn 1979	Godman, Jim 1987	Norris, Joe 1954
Anthony, Earl 1986	Golembiewski, Billy 1979	O'Donnell, Chuck 1968
+Asplund, Harold 1978	Guenther, Johnny 1988	Pappas, George 1989
Baer, Gordy 1987	Hardwick, Billy 1985	+Patterson, Pat 1974
Benkovic, Frank 1958	Hennessey, Tom 1976	Ritger, Dick 1984
Billick, George 1982	Hoover, Dick..........1974	Salvino, Carmen 1979
+Blouin, Jimmy 1953	Howard, George.......1986	Schroeder, Jim 1990
Bluth, Ray 1973	Jackson, Eddie 1988	+Schwoegler, Connie 1968
+Bodis, Joe 1941	Johnson, Don 1982	+Sielaff, Lou 1968
+Bomar, Buddy 1966	Johnson,Earl 1987	+Sinke, Joe 1977
+Brandt, Allie 1960	+Joseph, Joe 1969	+Sixty, Billy 1961
+Brosius, Eddie 1976	+Jouglard, Lee 1979	Smith, Harry 1978
+Bujack, Fred 1967	+Kartheiser, Frank.......1967	+Smith, Jimmy 1941
Bunetta, Bill 1968	+Kawolics, Ed 1968	Soutar, Dave 1985
Burton, Nelson, Sr.......1964	+Kissoff, Joe 1976	+Sparando, Tony 1968
Burton, Nelson, Jr........1981	Klares, John 1982	Spinella, Barney 1968
+Campi, Lou 1968	+Knox, Billy 1954	+Steers, Harry 1941
+Carlson, Adolph 1941	+Koster, John 1941	Stefanich, Jim 1983
Carter, Don 1970	+Krems, Eddie 1973	+Stein, Otto, Jr 1971
+Caruana, Frank 1977	Kristof, Joe 1968	Strampe, Bob 1977
+Cassio, Marty 1972	+Krumske, Paul 1968	+Thoma, Sykes 1971
+Castellano, Graz 1976	+Lange, Herb 1941	Tountas, Pete 1989
+Clause, Frank 1980	Lauman, Hank 1976	Tucker, Bill 1988
Cohn, Alfred 1985	Lillard, Bill 1972	+Varipapa, Andy 1957
Crimmins, John 1962	Lindenmann, Tony 1979	+Ward, Walter 1959
Davis, Dave...........1990	+Lindsey, Mort 1941	Weber, Dick 1970
+Daw, Charlie 1941	Lippe, Henry 1989	+Welu, Billy 1975
+Day, Ned 1952	Lubanski, Ed 1971	+Wilman, Joe 1951
+Easter, Sarge 1963	Lucci, Vince, Sr 1978	+Wolf, Phil 1961
Ellis, Don 1981	+Marino, Hank 1941	Wonders, Rich 1990
+Falcaro, Joe 1968	+Martino, John 1969	+Young, George 1959
Faragalli, Lindy 1968	+McMahon, Junie 1967	Zahn, Wayne 1980
Fazio, Buzz 1963	+Mercurio, Skang 1967	Zikes, Les 1983
+Gersonde, Russ 1968	+Meyers, Norm 1984	+Zunker, Gil 1941
+Gibson, Therm.........1965	+Nagy, Steve 1963	

Meritorious Service

+Allen, Harold 1966	+Baumgarten, Elmer 1963	+Bensinger, Bob 1969
Baker, Frank 1975	+Bellisimo, Lou 1986	+Chase, LeRoy 1972

+ Coker, John 1980
+ Collier, Chuck 1963
+ Cruchon, Steve 1983
+ Ditzen, Walt 1973
+ Doehrman, Bill 1968
  Elias, Eddie 1985
+ Hagerty, Jack 1963
+ Hattstrom, H.A.(Doc) 1980
+ Hermann, Cone 1968
+ Howley, Pete 1941

+ Kennedy, Bob 1981
+ Langtry, Abe 1963
+ Levine, Sam 1971
+ Luby, David 1969
  Luby, Mort, Jr. 1988
+ Luby, Mort, Sr. 1974
+ McCullough, Howard 1971
+ Patterson, Morehead 1985
+ Petersen, Louie 1963
  Pezzano, Chuck 1982

  Pluckhahn, Bruce 1989
  Raymer, Milt 1972
+ Reed, Elmer 1978
  Rudo, Milt 1984
  Schenkel, Chris 1988
+ Sweeney, Dennis 1974
+ Thum, Joe 1980
  Weinstein, Sam 1970
+ Whitney, Eli 1975
  Wolf, Fred 1976

Professional Bowlers Association

Established in 1975. **Eligibility:** nominees must be at least 35 years old. Voting done by 50-member panel that includes writers who have covered bowling for at least 12 years.

Class of 1990: Performance—**Joe Berardi** and **Marshall Holman.** Veterans—**Andy Marzich.**

Members are listed with year of induction; (+) indicates deceased members.

Performance

Allen, Bill 1983
Anthony, Earl 1986
Berardi, Joe 1990
Bluth, Ray 1975
Burton, Nelson, Jr. 1979
Carter, Don 1975
Davis, Dave 1978
Dickinson, Gary 1988
Durbin, Mike 1984

Fazio, Buzz 1976
Godman, Jim 1987
Hardwick, Billy 1977
Holman, Marshall 1990
Hudson, Tommy 1989
Johnson, Don 1977
Laub, Larry 1985
Pappas, George 1986
Petraglia, John 1982

Ritger, Dick 1978
Roth, Mark 1987
Salvino, Carmen 1975
Smith, Harry 1975
Soutar, Dave 1979
Stefanich, Jim 1980
Weber, Dick 1975
+ Welu, Billy 1975
Zahn, Wayne 1981

Veterans

Allison, Glenn 1984
Asher, Barry 1988
Guenther, Johnny 1986

+ Joseph, Joe 1985
Marzich, Andy 1990
McGrath, Mike 1988

+ St.John, Jim 1989
Strampe, Bob 1987

Meritorious Service

Archibald, John 1989
Elias, Eddie 1976
Esposito, Frank 1975
Evans, Dick 1986
Firestone, Raymond 1987

Fisher, E.A.(Bud) 1984
Frantz, Lou 1978
Golden, Harry 1983
Hoffman, Ted, Jr 1985
Jowdy, John 1988
Kelley, Joe 1989

+ Nagy, Steve 1977
Pezzano, Chuck 1975
+ Richards, Joe 1976
Schenkel, Chris 1976
Stitzlein, Lorraine 1980

Women's International Bowling Congress

Established in 1953. **Eligibility:** nominees must have competed in at least 15 years of WIBC Tournaments and won at least one WIBC Queens title or one international title. Voting done by 12-member committee made up of Hall of Fame members, WIBC officials and media representatives.

Class of 1990: Performance—**Pam Buckner** and **Dorothy Wilkinson.** Meritorious Service—**Gertrude Finke.**

Members are listed with year of induction; (+) indicates deceased members.

Performance

Abel, Joy 1984
Bolt, Mae 1978
Bouvia, Gloria 1987
Boxberger, Loa 1984
Buckner, Pam 1990
Cantaline, Anita 1979
Carter, LaVerne 1977
Coburn, Doris 1976
Costello, Pat 1986
Costello, Patty 1989
Dryer, Pat 1978
Duval, Helen 1970
Fothergill, Dotty 1980

Garms, Shirley 1971
Graham, Mary Lou 1989
Harman, Janet 1985
Havlish, Jean 1987
Hoffman, Martha 1979
Holm, Joan 1974
+ Humphreys, Birdie 1979
Jacobson, D.D. 1981
Kelly, Annesse 1985
+ Knechtges, Doris 1983
Kuczynski, Betty 1981
Ladewig, Marion 1964
Martin, Sylvia Wene 1966

Martorella, Millie 1975
Merrick, Marge 1980
+ Mikiel, Val 1979
Morris, Betty 1983
Nichols, Lorrie 1989
Norton, Virginia 1988
Notaro, Phyllis 1979
Ortner, Bev 1972
+ Sablatnik, Ethel 1979
Soutar, Judy 1976
Wilkinson, Dorothy 1990
Zimmerman, Donna 1982

Stars of Yesteryear

Bohlen, Philena 1955
Burling, Catherine 1958
Burns, Nina Van Camp . . .1977
+ Chapman, Emily 1957
Duffy, Agnes 1987
Fellmeth, Catherine 1970
+ Fritz, Deane 1966
Gloor, Olga 1976
+ Greenwald, Goldie 1953
Hartrick, Stella 1972

+ Hatch, Grayce 1953
+ Hochstadter, Bee 1967
+ Jaeger, Emma 1953
+ Matthews, Merle 1974
+ McCutcheon, Floretta . . .1956
+ Miller, Dorothy 1954
+ Mraz, Jo 1959
Powers, Connie 1973
+ Robinson, Leona 1969
+ Rump, Anita 1962
+ Ruschmeyer, Addie 1961

+ Ryan, Esther 1963
+ Schulte, Myrtle 1965
Shablis, Helen 1977
+ Simon, Violet (Billy) 1960
Small, Tess 1971
+ Smith, Grace 1968
+ Stockdale, Louise 1953
Toepfer, Elvira 1976
+ Twyford, Sally 1964
+ Warmbier, Marie 1953
+ Winandy, Cecelia 1975

Women's International Bowling Congress (Cont.)

Meritorious Service

Baetz, Helen 1977	Higley, Margaret 1969	Porter, Cora 1986
Baker, Helen 1989	+Kay, Nora 1964	+Quinn, Zoe 1979
Berger, Winifred 1976	+Kelly, Ellen............1979	+Rishling, Gertrude 1972
Borschuk, Lo 1988	Kelone, Theresa 1978	Sloan, Catherine 1985
Botkin, Freda 1986	+Knepprath, Jeannette ...1963	+Speck, Birdie 1966
+Crowe, Alberta 1982	+Lasher, Iolia 1967	+Spring, Alma 1979
+Dornblaser, Gertrude 1979	Marrs, Mabel 1979	+Switzer, Pearl 1973
Duffy, Agnes 1987	+McBride, Bertha 1968	+Veatch, Georgia 1974
Finke, Gertrude 1990	+Menne, Catherine 1979	White, Mildred 1975
+Fisk, Rae 1983	+Phaler, Emma 1965	+Wood, Ann 1970
+Haas, Dorothy.........1977		

International Boxing Hall of Fame

Established in 1989 and opened in 1990. **Address:** 1 Hall of Fame Drive, Canastota, NY, 13032. **Telephone:** 315-697-7095.

Eligibility: all nominees must be retired for five years. Voting done by 115-member panel made up of Boxing Writers' Association members and world-wide boxing historians.

Class of 1990: 52 charter members (see below).

Members are listed with year of induction; (+) indicates deceased members.

Modern Era

Ali, Muhammad.........1990	Gavilan, Kid 1990	Napoles, Jose 1990
+Armstrong, Henry 1990	Griffith, Emile 1990	Pep, Willie............1990
Basilio, Carmen 1990	LaMotta, Jake 1990	+Robinson, Sugar Ray 1990
Charles, Ezzard 1990	+Louis, Joe 1990	Saddler, Sandy 1990
Conn, Billy 1990	+Marciano, Rocky 1990	Walcott, Jersey Joe 1990
Foster, Bob 1990	Monzon, Carlos 1990	Williams, Ike 1990
Frazier, Joe 1990	Moore, Archie 1990	

Old-Timers

+Attell, Abe.............1990	+Fitzsimmons, Bob 1990	+Langford, Sam.........1990
+Britton, Jack 1990	+Gans, Joe 1990	+Leonard, Benny 1990
+Canzoneri, Tony 1990	+Greb, Harry 1990	+McGovern, Terry 1990
+Corbett, James J 1990	+Jackson, Peter 1990	+Ross, Barney 1990
+Dempsey, Jack 1990	+Jeffries, James J 1990	+Tunney, Gene 1990
+Dixon, George 1990	+Johnson, Jack 1990	+Walker, Mickey 1990
+Driscoll, Jim 1990	+Ketchel, Stanley 1990	+Wilde, Jimmy 1990

Pioneers

+Broughton, Jack 1990	+Mendoza, Daniel.......1990	+Sullivan, John L 1990
+Mace, Jem.............1990	+Sayers, Tom 1990	

Contributors

+Chambers, John Graham .1990	+Kearns, Jack (Doc) 1990	+Queensberry, Marquis of .1990
+Fleischer, Nat 1990	+Lonsdale, Lord 1990	+Rickard, Tex 1990
+Jacobs, Mike 1990		

College Football Hall of Fame

Established in 1955 by the National Football Foundation. **Current Address:** 5440 Kings Island Drive, Kings Island, OH 45034. **Future Address:** moving to One Auction Avenue, Memphis, TN, 38103, in June of 1991. **Current Telephone:** 513-398-5410.

Eligibility: nominated players must be out of college 10 years and a first team All-America pick by a major selector during career; coaches must be retired three years. Voting done by 12-member panel made up of athletic directors, conference and bowl officials and media representatives.

Class of 1990: Players—FB **Don Bosseler**, Miami, FL (1953-56); HB **Ron Burton**, Northwestern (1957-59); RB **Earl Campbell**, Texas (1974-77); FB **Jack Cloud**, Wm.& Mary (1946-48); LB **Jack Ham**, Penn St.(1968-70); HB **Leroy Keyes**, Purdue (1966-68); center **Vaughn Mancha**, Alabama (1944-47); guard **Mike McGee**, Duke (1957-59); end **Wayne Millner**, Notre Dame (1933-35); guard **Ed Molinski**, Tennessee (1938-40); QB **Jim Plunkett**, Stanford (1968-70); guard **Max Staroevich**, Washington (1934-36); and center **John Tavener**, Indiana (1941-44). Coaches—**Harry Baujan**, Dayton (1923-42,46); **Dick Colman**, Princeton (1957-68) and **Ray Graves**, Florida (1960-69).

Member players are listed with final year they played in college and member coaches are listed with year of induction; (+) indicates deceased members.

Players

+Abell, Earl–Colgate......1915	Alworth, Lance–Arkansas .1961	Bacon, Everett–Wesleyan .1912
Agase, Alex–Purdue/III ...1946	+Ames, Knowlton–Princeton 1889	Bagnall, Reds–Penn 1950
+Agganis, Harry–Boston U .1952	Ameche, Alan–Wisconsin .1954	+Baker, Hobey–Princeton ..1913
Albert, Frank–Stanford ...1941	Amling, Warren–Ohio St .1946	+Baker, John–USC 1931
+Aldrich, Ki–TCU 1938	Anderson, Donny–Tex.Tech 1966	+Baker, Moon–N'western ..1926
Aldrich, Malcolm–Yale ...1921	+Anderson, Hunk–N.Dame .1921	Baker, Terry–Oregon St ..1962
+Alexander, Joe–Syracuse .1920	Atkins, Doug–Tennessee ..1952	+Ballin, Harold–Princeton ..1914

College Football Hall of Fame (Cont.)

Pro Football Hall of Fame

Established in 1963 by National Football League to commemorate the sport's professional origins. **Address:** 2121 George Halas Drive NW, Canton, OH 44708. **Telephone:** 216-456-8207.

Eligibility: nominated players must be retired five years and coaches must be retired. Voting done by panel made up of media representatives from all 28 NFL cities.

Class of 1990: Players—DT **Buck Buchanan**, Kansas City (1963-75); QB **Bob Griese**, Miami (1967-80); RB **Franco Harris**, Pittsburgh (1972-83), Seattle (1984); LB **Ted Hendricks**, Baltimore (1969-73), Green Bay (1974), Oakland-LA Raiders (1975-83); LB **Jack Lambert**, Pittsburgh (1974-84); and tackle **Bob St.Clair**, San Francisco (1953-63). Coach—**Tom Landry**, Dallas (1960-88).

1990 Finalists (nominated, but not selected): Players—Dan Dierdorf, Larry Little, John Mackey, Ken Stabler, Lynn Swann, Ron Yary and Jack Youngblood. Coach-contributor—Al Davis.

Members are listed with year of induction; (+) indicates deceased members.

Players

Adderley, Herb 1980	Harris, Franco 1990	+Nevers, Ernie 1963
Alworth, Lance 1978	+Healey, Ed 1964	Nitschke, Ray 1978
Atkins, Doug 1982	Hein, Mel 1963	Nomellini, Leo 1969
	Hendricks, Ted 1990	
Badgro, Red 1981	+Henry, Pete 1963	Olsen, Merlin 1982
+Battles, Cliff 1968	+Herber, Arnie 1966	Otto, Jim 1980
Baugh, Sammy 1963	+Hewitt, Bill 1971	
Bednarik, Chuck 1967	+Hinkle, Clarke 1964	Page, Alan 1988
Bell, Bobby 1983	Hirsch, Elroy (Crazylegs). . 1968	Parker, Clarence (Ace) 1972
Berry, Raymond 1973	Hornung, Paul 1986	Parker, Jim 1973
Biletnikoff, Fred 1988	Houston, Ken. 1986	Perry, Joe 1969
Blanda, George 1981	+Hubbard, Cal 1963	Pihos, Pete 1970
Blount, Mel 1989	Huff, Sam 1982	
Bradshaw, Terry 1989	Hutson, Don 1963	Ringo, Jim 1981
Brown, Jim 1971		Robustelli 1971
Brown, Roosevelt 1975	Johnson, John Henry 1987	
Brown, Willie. 1984	Jones, Deacon 1980	Sayers, Gale 1977
Buchanan, Buck 1990	Jurgensen, Sonny 1983	Schmidt, Joe 1973
Butkus, Dick 1979		Shell, Art 1989
	+Kinard, Frank (Bruiser) . . . 1971	Simpson, O.J. 1985
Canadeo, Tony 1974		Starr, Bart 1977
+Christiansen, Jack 1970	Lambert, Jack 1990	Staubach, Roger 1985
+Clark, Dutch 1963	Lane, Dick (Night Train) . . 1974	Stautner, Ernie 1969
Connor, George 1975	Langer, Jim 1987	St.Clair, Bob 1990
Csonka, Larry 1987	Lanier, Willie 1986	+Strong, Ken 1967
	Lary, Yale 1979	+Stydahar, Joe 1967
Davis, Willie 1981	Lavelli, Dante 1975	
Dawson, Len 1987	+Layne, Bobby 1967	Tarkenton, Fran 1986
Ditka, Mike 1988	+Leemans, Tuffy 1978	Taylor, Charley 1984
Donovan, Art 1968	Lilly, Bob 1980	Taylor, Jim 1976
+Driscoll, Paddy 1965	Luckman, Sid 1965	Thorpe, Jim 1963
Dudley, Bill 1966	Lyman, Roy (Link) 1964	Tittle, Y.A 1971
		+Trafton, George 1964
+Edwards, Turk 1969	Marchetti, Gino 1972	Trippi, Charley 1968
	Matson, Ollie 1972	+Tunnell, Emlen 1967
Fears, Tom 1970	Maynard, Don 1987	Turner, Clyde (Bulldog) . . . 1966
+Ford, Len 1976	McAfee, George 1966	
Fortmann, Dan 1985	McCormack, Mike 1984	Unitas, Johnny 1979
	McElhenny, Hugh 1970	Upshaw, Gene 1987
Gatski, Frank 1985	+McNally, Johnny (Blood) . 1963	
+George, Bill 1974	+Michalske, Mike 1964	+Van Brocklin, Norm 1971
Gifford, Frank 1977	+Millner, Wayne 1968	Van Buren, Steve. 1965
Graham, Otto 1965	Mitchell, Bobby 1983	
Grange, Red 1963	Mix, Ron 1979	Walker, Doak 1986
Greene, Joe 1987	Moore, Lenny 1975	Warfield, Paul 1983
Gregg, Forrest 1977	Motley, Marion 1968	+Waterfield, Bob 1965
Griese, Bob 1990	Musso, George 1982	Weinmeister, Arnie 1984
Groza, Lou 1974		Willis, Bill. 1977
+Guyon, Joe 1966	+Nagurski, Bronko 1963	Wilson, Larry 1978
	Namath, Joe 1985	Wojciechowicz, Alex 1968
Ham, Jack 1988		Wood, Willie 1989

Player and Coach

+Chamberlin, Guy 1965	Flaherty, Ray 1976	+Owen, Steve 1966
	+Kiesling, Walt 1966	

Player, Coach and Owner

+Halas, George 1963

Coaches

+Conzelman, Jimmy 1964	Gillman, Sid 1983	Landry, Tom 1990
	+Lambeau, Curly 1963	+Lombardi, Vince 1971
Brown, Paul. 1967		+Neale, Earle (Greasy) 1969
Ewbank, Weeb 1978		

Contributors

+ Bell, Bert 1963
+ Bidwill, Charles, Sr 1967
+ Carr, Joe 1963

Hunt, Lamar 1972
+ Mara, Tim 1963
+ Marshall, George Preston . 1963

+ Ray, Hugh (Shorty) 1966
+ Reeves, Dan 1967
+ Rooney, Art 1964
Rozelle, Pete 1985

Canadian Football Hall of Fame

Established in 1963. Current Hall opened in 1972. **Address:** 58 Jackson Street West, Hamilton, Ontario, L8P
1L4. **Telephone:** 416-528-7566.

Eligibility: nominated players must be retired three years and coaches must be retired. Voting done by
14-member panel of Canadian pro and amateur football officials.

Class of 1990: Players—DL **Jim Corrigall**, Toronto (1970-81); DL **Dave Fennell**, Edmonton (1974-83); DB-OE
Marv Luster, Montreal (1961-64,73-74), Toronto (1964-72). Builders—coach **Eagle Keys**, Edmonton (1959-
63), Saskatchewan (1965-1970), B.C.Lions (1971-75); general manager **Ken Preston**, Saskatchewan (1958-77).
Members are listed with year of induction; (+) indicates deceased members.

Players

Atchison, Ron 1978

Bailey, Byron 1975
Barrow, John 1976
+ Batstone, Harry 1963
+ Beach, Ormond 1963
Box, Ab 1965
+ Breen, Joseph 1963
+ Bright, Johnny 1970
Brown, Tom 1984

Casey, Tom 1964
Coffey, Tommy Joe 1977
+ Conacher, Lionel 1963
Copeland, Royal 1988
Corrigall, Jim 1990
+ Cox, Ernest 1963
+ Craig, Ross 1964
+ Cronin, Carl 1967
+ Cutler, Wes 1968

Dixon, George 1974

+ Eliowitz, Abe 1969
+ Emerson, Eddie 1963
Etcheverry, Sam 1969
Evanshen, Terry 1984

Faloney, Bernie 1974
+ Fear, A.H. (Cap) 1967
Fennell, Dave 1990
+ Ferraro, John 1966
Fieldgate, Norm 1979
Fleming, Willie 1982

Gabriel, Tony 1985
+ Gall, Hugh 1963
Golab, Tony 1964
Gray, Herbert 1983
Griffing, Dean 1965

Hanson, Fritz 1963

Harris, Wayne 1976
Helton, John 1986
Henley, Garney 1979
+ Huffman, Dick 1987

+ Isbister, Bob Sr 1965

Jackson, Russ 1973
+ Jacobs, Jack 1963
+ James, Eddie 1963
James, Gerry 1981
+ Kabat, Greg 1966
Kapp, Joe 1984
Keeling, Jerry 1989
+ Krol, Joe 1963
Kwong, Normie 1969

Lancaster, Ron 1982
+ Lawson, Smirle 1963
+ Leadlay, Frank 1963
+ Lear, Les 1974
Lewis, Leo 1973
Lunsford, Earl 1983
Luster, Marv 1990
Luzzi, Don 1986

+ McCance, Ches 1976
+ McGill, Frank 1965
McQuarters, Ed 1988
Miles, Rollie 1980
+ Molson, Percy 1963
Morris, Frank 1983
+ Morris, Ted 1964
Mosca, Angelo 1987

Nelson, Roger 1986
Neumann, Peter 1979

O'Quinn, John Red 1981

Pajaczkowski, Tony 1988
Parker, Jackie 1971

Patterson, Hal 1971
Perry, Gordon 1970
+ Perry, Norm 1963
Ploen, Ken 1975

Quilty, S.P.(Silver) 1966
Rebholz, Russ 1963
Reed, George 1979
+ Reeve, Ted 1963
Rigney, Frank 1985
+ Rodden, Michael 1964
Rowe, Paul 1964
Ruby, Martin 1974
+ Russel, Jeff 1963

Scott, Vince 1982
Shatto, Dick 1975
+ Simpson, Ben 1963
Simpson, Bob 1976
+ Sprague, David 1963
Stevenson, Art 1969
Stewart, Ron 1977
Stirling, Hugh (Bummer) . . 1966

Thelen, Dave 1989
+ Timmis, Brian 1963
Tinsley, Bud 1982
+ Tommy, Andy 1989
+ Trawick, Herb 1975
+ Tubman, Joe 1968

Urness, Ted 1989

Vaughan, Kaye 1978

Wagner, Virgil 1980
+ Welch, Hawley (Huck) . . . 1964
Wilkinson, Tom 1987
Wylie, Harvey 1980

+ Zock, William 1985

Builders

+ Back, Leonard 1971
+ Bailey, Harold 1965
+ Ballard, Harold 1987
+ Brook, Tom 1975
+ Brown, D.Wes 1963
Chipman, Arthur 1969
Clair, Frank 1981
Crighton, Hec 1986
Currie, Andrew 1974
+ Davies, Dr. Andrew 1969
+ DeGruchy, John 1963
Dojack, Paul 1978
+ Duggan, Eric 1981
+ DuMoulin, Seppi 1963
+ Foulds, Willliam 1963
Gaudaur, J.G.(Jake) 1984

Grant, Bud 1983
+ Grey, Lord Earl 1963
+ Griffith, Harry 1963
Halter, Sydney 1966
Hannibal, Frank 1963
+ Hayman, Lew 1975
+ Hughes, W.P.(Billy) 1974
Keys, Eagle 1990
Kramer, R.A. (Bob) 1987
+ Lieberman, M.I.(Moe) 1973
+ McBrien, Harry 1978
+ McCaffrey, Jimmy 1967
+ McCann, Dave 1966
+ McPherson, Don 1983
+ Metras, Johnny 1980
+ Montgomery, Ken 1970

+ Newton, Jack 1964
Preston, Ken 1990
+ Ritchie, Alvin 1963
+ Ryan, Joseph 1968
Sazio, Ralph 1988
+ Shaughnessy, Frank (Shag) 1963
+ Shouldice, W.T.(Hap) 1977
+ Simpson, Jimmie 1986
+ Slocomb, Karl 1989
+ Spring, Harry C 1976
Stukus, Annis 1974
+ Taylor, N.J.(Piffles) 1963
Tindall, Frank 1985
+ Warner, Clair 1965
+ Warwick, Bert 1964
+ Wilson, Seymour 1984

Golf Halls of Fame

There are two principal golf halls of fame: the PGA/World Golf Hall of Fame in Pinehurst, NC, and the LPGA Hall of Fame in Daytona Beach, FL. A third museum—the old PGA Hall—was abandoned in 1983 when the PGA took over the running of the World Golf Hall of Fame. Plans call for all members of the old PGA Hall to eventually be inducted into the PGA/World Hall.

PGA/World Golf Hall of Fame

Established in 1974 and taken over by PGA of America in 1983. **Address:** PGA Boulevard, P.O.Box 1908, Pinehurst, NC 28374. **Telephone:** 1-800-334-0178.
Eligibility: nominees can still be active. Voting done by Golf Writers Association of America.
Class of 1990: Men—**Gene Littler, Paul Runyan** and **Horton Smith.** Contributors—**William Campbell.**
Members are listed with year of induction; (+) indicates deceased members.

Men

+Anderson, Willie	1975	+Hagen, Walter	1974	Palmer, Arnold	1974
+Armour, Tommy	1976	+Hilton, Harold	1978	Player, Gary	1974
+Ball, John, Jr.	1977	Hogan, Ben	1974	Runyan, Paul	1990
+Barnes, Jim	1989	+Jones, Bobby	1974	Sarazen, Gene	1974
Boros, Julius	1982	+Little, Lawson	1980	+Smith, Horton	1990
+Braid, James	1976	Littler, Gene	1990	Snead, Sam	1974
Casper, Billy	1978	+Locke, Bobby	1977	+Taylor, John H	1975
+Cotton, Thomas	1980	Middlecoff, Cary	1986	Thomson, Peter	1988
+Demaret, Jimmy	1983	+Morris, Tom, Sr	1976	+Travers, Jerry	1976
DeVicenzo, Roberto	1989	+Morris, Tom, Jr	1975	+Travis, Walter	1979
+Evans, Chick	1975	Nelson, Byron	1974	Trevino, Lee	1981
Floyd, Ray	1989	Nicklaus, Jack	1974	+Vardon, Harry	1974
+Guldahl, Ralph	1981	+Ouimet, Francis	1974	Watson, Tom	1988

Women

Berg, Patty	1974	Lopez, Nancy	1989	+Wethered, Joyce	1975
+Howe, Dorothy C.H	1978	Rawls, Betsy	1987	Whitworth, Kathy	1982
Carner, JoAnne	1985	Suggs, Louise	1979	Wright, Mickey	1976
		+Vare, Glenna Collett	1975	+Zaharias, Babe Didrikson	1974

Contributors

Campbell, William	1990	Dey, Joseph	1975	Jones, Robert Trent	1987
+Corcoran, Fred	1975	+Graffis, Herb	1977	+Roberts, Clifford	1978
+Crosby, Bing	1978	+Harlow, Robert	1988	+Ross, Donald	1977
		Hope, Bob	1983		

LPGA Hall of Fame

Established in 1967 by the LPGA to replace the old Women's Golf Hall of Fame (founded in 1950). Originally located in Augusta, GA (1967-77), the Hall has been moved to Pinehurst, NC (1977-83), Sugar Land, TX (1983-89) and Daytona Beach, FL (since 1990). There is currently no museum to visit, but a new building is scheduled to open in October of 1992. **Address:** LPGA Headquarters, 2570 Volusia Ave., Suite B, Daytona Beach, FL, 32114.
Telephone: 904-254-8800.
Eligibility: players must have played 10 years and won 30 official events, including two major championships; or 35 official events and one major; or 40 official events and no majors.
Last inductee: Nancy Lopez in 1987 (10 years, 35 wins, one major).
Top two candidates going into 1990: Amy Alcott (28 wins, 4 majors) and Pat Bradley (23 wins, 6 majors).
Members are listed with year of induction; (+) indicates deceased members.

Berg, Patty	1951	Jameson, Betty	1951	Suggs, Louise	1951
Carner, JoAnne	1982	Lopez, Nancy	1987	Whitworth, Kathy	1975
Haynie, Sandra	1977	Mann, Carol	1977	Wright, Mickey	1964
		Rawls, Betsy	1960	+Zaharias, Babe Didrikson	1951

PGA Hall of Fame

Established in 1940 by PGA of America, but abandoned after 1982 inductions.

Men

+Anderson, Willie	1940	+Dutra, Olin	1962	Littler, Gene	1982
+Armour, Tommy	1940	+Evans, Chick	1940	+McDermott, John	1940
+Barnes, Jim	1940	+Farrell, Johnny	1961	+Mangrum, Lloyd	1964
Boros, Julius	1974	Ford, Doug	1975	+McLeod, Fred	1960
+Brady, Mike	1960	+Ghezzi, Vic	1965	Middlecoff, Cary	1974
+Burke, Billy	1966	+Guldahl, Ralph	1963	Nelson, Byron	1953
Burke, Jack, Jr	1975	+Hagen, Walter	1940	+Ouimet, Francis	1940
Casper, Billy	1982	Harbert, Chick	1968	Palmer, Arnold	1980
Cooper, Harry	1959	Harper, Chandler	1969	+Picard, Henry	1961
+Cruickshank, Bobby	1967	+Harrison, Dutch	1962	Revolta, Johnny	1963
+Demaret, Jimmy	1960	Hogan, Ben	1953	Runyan, Paul	1959
DeVicenzo, Roberto	1979	+Hutchison, Jock, Sr	1959	Sarazen, Gene	1940
+Diegel, Leo	1955	+Jones, Bobby	1940	+Shute, Denny	1957
+Dudley, Ed	1964	+Little, Lawson	1961	+Smith, Alex	1940

+ Smith, Horton 1958
+ Smith, Macdonald 1954

Snead, Sam 1953
+ Travers, Jerry 1940

+ Travis, Walter 1940
+ Craig Wood 1956

Women

Berg, Patty 1978
+ Zaharias, Babe Didrikson .1976

Hockey Hall of Fame

Established in 1945 by the National Hockey League and opened in 1961. **Current Address:** Exhibition Place, Toronto, Ontario, M6K 3C3. **New Address:** moving to downtown Toronto in May of 1992. **Telephone:** 416-595-1345.

Eligibility: nominated players and referees must be retired three years. Voting done by 12-member panel made up of NHL personalities and media representatives.

Class of 1990: Players—left wing **Bill Barber**, Philadelphia (1972-85); and center **Gilbert Perreault**, Buffalo (1970-87). Veterans—defenseman **Fernie Flaman**, Boston (1944-50,54-61), Toronto (1950-54). Builder—general manager **Bud Poile**, Philadelphia (1967-70), Vancouver (1970-73).

Members are listed with year of induction; (+) indicates deceased members.

Players

Abel, Sid 1969
+ Adams, Jack 1959
Apps, Syl 1961
Armstrong, George 1975

Bailey, Ace 1975
+ Bain, Dan 1945
+ Baker, Hobey 1945
Barber, Bill 1990
+ Barry, Marty 1965
Bathgate, Andy 1978
Beliveau, Jean 1972
+ Bentley, Doug 1964
+ Bentley, Max 1966
Blake, Toe 1966
Boivin, Leo 1986
+ Boon, Dickie 1952
Bouchard, Butch 1966
+ Boucher, Frank 1958
+ Boucher, George 1960
+ Bowie, Dubbie 1945
+ Broadbent, Punch 1962
Bucyk, John 1981
+ Burch, Billy 1974

+ Cameron, Harry 1962
+ Clancy, King 1958
+ Clapper, Dit 1945
Clarke, Bobby 1987
+ Cleghorn, Sprague 1958
+ Colville, Neil 1967
+ Conacher, Charlie 1961
+ Cook, Bill 1952
Coulter, Art 1974
Cournoyer, Yvan 1982
Cowley, Bill 1968
+ Crawford, Rusty 1962

+ Darragh, Jack 1962
+ Davidson, Scotty 1950
+ Day, Hap 1961
Delvecchio, Alex 1977
+ Denneny, Cy 1959
+ Drillon, Gordie 1975
+ Drinkwater, Graham 1950
+ Dunderdale, Tommy 1974
+ Dutton, Red 1958
+ Dye, Babe 1978

Esposito, Phil 1984

+ Farrell, Arthur 1965
+ Foyston, Frank 1958
+ Frederickson, Frank.....1958

Gadsby, Bill 1970
+ Gardiner, Herb 1958
+ Gardner, Jimmy 1962
Geoffrion, Bernie 1971

+ Gerard, Eddie 1945
Gilbert, Rod 1982
+ Gilmour, Billy 1962
+ Goheen, Moose 1952
+ Goodfellow, Ebbie 1963
+ Grant, Mike...........1950
+ Green, W.T.(Shorty) ...1962
+ Griffis, Si 1950

+ Hall, Joe 1975
+ Harvey, Doug 1973
+ Hay, George 1958
+ Hextall, Bryan 1969
+ Hooper, Tom 1962
Horner, Red 1965
+ Horton, Tim 1977
Howe, Gordie 1972
+ Howe, Syd 1965
Howell, Harry 1979
Hull, Bobby 1983
+ Hyland, Harry 1962
+ Irvin, Dick 1958

+ Jackson, Busher 1971
+ Johnson, Ching 1958
+ Johnson, Ernie 1952
Johnson, Tom 1970
+ Joliat, Aurel..........1947

+ Keats, Duke 1958
Kelly, Red 1969
Kennedy, Ted 1966
Keon, Dave 1986

Lach, Elmer 1966
Lafleur, Guy 1988
+ Lalonde, Newsy 1950
Laperrier, Jacques 1987
+ Laviolette, Jack 1962
Lemaire, Jacques 1984
Lindsay, Ted 1966

+ MacKay, Mickey 1952
Mahovlich, Frank 1981
+ Malone, Joe 1950
+ Mantha, Sylvio 1960
+ Marshall, Jack 1965
+ Maxwell, Steamer 1962
+ McGee, Frank 1945
+ McGimsie, Billy 1962
+ McNamara, George 1958
Mikita, Stan 1983
Moore, Dickie 1974
+ Morenz, Howie 1945
Mosienko, Bill 1965

+ Nighbor, Frank 1945
+ Noble, Reg 1962
+ Oliver, Harry 1967

Olmstead, Bert 1985
Orr, Bobby 1979
Park, Brad 1988
+ Patrick, Lester 1945
+ Patrick, Lynn 1980
Perreault, Gilbert 1990
+ Phillips, Tommy 1945
Pilote, Pierre 1975
+ Pitre, Didier 1962
+ Pratt, Babe 1966
+ Primeau, Joe 1963
Pronovost, Marcel 1978
+ Pulford, Harvey 1945

Quackenbush, Bill 1976

+ Rankin, Frank 1961
Ratelle, Jean 1985
Reardon, Ken 1966
Richard, Henri 1979
Richard, Maurice 1961
+ Richardson, George 1950
+ Roberts, Gordie.......1971
+ Ross, Art 1945
+ Russell, Blair 1965
+ Russell, Ernie 1965
+ Ruttan, Jack 1962

Savard, Serge 1986
+ Scanlan, Fred 1965
Schmidt, Milt 1961
Schriner, Sweeney 1962
+ Seibert, Earl 1963
+ Seibert, Oliver 1961
+ Shore, Eddie 1945
+ Siebert, Babe 1964
+ Simpson, Joe 1962
Sittler, Darryl 1989
+ Smith, Alf 1962
+ Smith, Hooley 1972
+ Smith, Tommy 1973
Stanley, Allan 1981
+ Stanley, Barney 1962
+ Stewart, Jack 1964
+ Stewart, Nels 1962
+ Stuart, Bruce 1961
+ Stuart, Hod 1945

+ Taylor, Cyclone 1945
+ Trihey, Harry 1950

Ullman, Norm 1982

+ Walker, Jack 1960
+ Walsh, Marty 1962
+ Watson, Harry 1962
+ Weiland, Cooney 1971
+ Westwick, Harry 1962
+ Whitcroft, Fred 1962
+ Wilson, Gordon 1962

Hockey Hall of Fame (Cont.)

Goaltenders

+Benedict, Clint 1965	+Gardiner, Chuck 1945	+Moran, Paddy 1958
Bower, Johnny 1976	Giacomin, Ed 1987	Parent, Bernie 1984
Brimsek, Frank 1966	+Hainsworth, George 1961	+Plante, Jacques 1978
+Broda, Turk 1967	Hall, Glenn 1975	Rayner, Chuck 1973
Cheevers, Gerry 1985	+Hern, Riley 1962	+Sawchuk, Terry 1971
+Connell, Alex 1958	+Holmes, Harry 1972	+Thompson, Tiny 1959
Dryden, Ken 1983	+Hutton, J.B (Bouse) 1962	Tretiak, Vladislav 1989
+Durnan, Bill 1964	+Lehman, Hughie 1958	+Vezina, Georges 1945
Esposito, Tony 1988	+LeSueur, Percy 1961	Worsley, Gump 1980
	Lumley, Harry 1980	+Worters, Roy 1969
Flaman, Fernie 1990		

Veterans

	Lewis, Herbie 1989	+O'Connor, Buddy 1988

Referees & Linesmen

Ashley, John 1981	+Hayes, George 1988	+Rodden, Mike 1962
Chadwick, Bill 1964	+Hewitson, Bobby 1963	+Smeaton, J. Cooper 1961
+Elliott, Chaucer 1961	+Ion, Mickey 1961	Storey, Red 1967
	Pavelich, Matt 1987	Udvari, Frank 1973

Builders

+Adams, Charles 1960	+Hay, Charles 1984	+Patrick, Frank 1958
+Adams, Weston 1972	+Hendy, Jim 1968	+Pickard, Allan 1958
+Ahearn, Frank 1962	+Hewitt, Foster 1965	Pilous, Rudy 1985
+Ahearn, J.F 1977	+Hewitt, W.A 1945	Poile, Bud 1990
+Allan, Montagu 1945	+Hume, Fred 1962	Pollock, Sam 1978
+Ballard, Harold 1977	+Imlach, Punch 1984	+Raymond, Donat 1958
+Bauer, Fr. David 1989	Ivan, Tommy 1964	+Robertson, John Ross 1945
+Bickell, J.P 1978		+Robinson, Claude 1945
+Brown, George 1961	+Jennings, William 1975	+Ross, Philip 1976
+Brown, Walter 1962	Juckes, Gordon 1979	
Buckland, Frank 1975		+Selke, Frank 1960
Butterfield, Jack 1980	+Kilpatrick, John 1960	Sinden, Harry 1983
		+Smith, Frank 1962
+Calder, Frank 1945	+Leader, Al 1969	+Smythe, Conn 1958
+Campbell, Angus 1964	LeBel, Robert 1970	Snider, Ed 1988
+Campbell, Clarence 1966	+Lockhart, Thomas 1965	+Stanley, Lord 1945
+Cattarinich, Joseph 1977	+Loicq, Paul 1961	+Sutherland, James 1945
+Dandurand, Leo 1963	+Mariucci, John. 1985	Tarasov, Anatoli 1974
Dilio, Frank 1964	+McLaughlin, Frederic 1963	+Turner, Lloyd 1958
+Dudley, George 1958	+Milford, Jake 1984	+Tutt, Thayer 1978
+Dunn, James 1968	Molson, Hartland 1973	
		Voss, Carl 1974
Eagleson, Alan 1989	+Nelson, Francis 1945	
	+Norris, Bruce 1969	+Waghorne, Fred 1961
Francis, Emile 1982	+Norris, James D 1962	+Wirtz, Arthur 1971
	+Norris, James, Sr 1958	Wirtz, Bill 1976
+Gibson, Jack 1976	+Northey, William 1945	
+Gorman, Tommy 1963		Ziegler, John 1987
	+O'Brien, J.A 1962	
Hanley, Bill 1986		

Lester Patrick Trophy

An annual award presented by the NHL and the New York Rangers "for outstanding service to hockey in the United States." The trophy is named after the former Rangers' coach and general manager; (*) indicates award was presented posthumously.

Year
1966 J.J.(Jack) Adams.
1967 Gordie Howe; Charles Adams*; James Norris, Sr*.
1968 Thomas Lockhart; Walter A.Brown*; Gen.John Kilpatrick.
1969 Bobby Hull; Eddie Jeremiah.
1970 Eddie Shore; James C.V.Hendy*.
1971 William Jennings; John Sollenberger*.
1972 Clarence Campbell; John Kelly; Cooney Weiland; James D.Norris*.
1973 Walter L.Bush, Jr.
1974 Alex Delvecchio; Murray Murdoch; Weston W. Adams, Sr*; Charles L.Crovat*.
1975 Donald Clark; Bill Chadwick; Tommy Ivan.
1976 Stan Mikita; George Leader; Bruce A. Norris.
1977 John Bucyk; Murray Armstrong; John Mariucci.

Year
1978 Phil Esposito; Tom Fitzgerald; William Tutt; William W.Wirtz.
1979 Bobby Orr.
1980 Bobby Clarke; Edward Snider; Fred Shero; 1980 US Olympic Hockey Team.
1981 Charles M.Schulz.
1982 Emile Francis.
1983 Bill Torrey.
1984 John Ziegler; Arthur Howie Ross*.
1985 Jack Butterfield; Arthur M.Wirtz.
1986 John MacInnes; Jack Riley.
1987 Hobey Baker*; Frank Mathers.
1988 Keith Allen; Fred Cusick; Bob Johnson.
1989 Dan Kelly; Lou Nanne; Lynn Patrick; Bud Poile.
1990 Len Ceglarski

U.S. Hockey Hall of Fame

Established in 1968 by the Eveleth (Minn.) Civic Association Project H Committee and opened in 1973. **Address:** 801 Hat Trick Ave., Eveleth, MN 55734. **Telephone:** 218-744-5167.

Eligibility: nominated players and referees must be American-born and retired five years; coaches must be American-born and must have coached predominantly American teams. Voting done by 12-member panel made up of Hall of Fame members and U.S. hockey officials.

Class of 1990: TBA.

Members are listed with year of induction; (+) indicates deceased members.

Players

+Abel, Clarence (Taffy) 1973
+Baker, Hobey 1973
Bartholome, Earl 1977
Bessone, Peter 1978
Blake, Robert 1985
Brimsek, Frank 1973
+Chaisson, Ray 1974
Chase, John P 1973
Christian, Bill 1984
Christian, Roger 1989
Cleary, Robert 1981
Cleary, William 1976
+Conroy, Anthony 1975
Dahlstrom, Carl (Cully) ..1973
DesJardins, Victor 1974
Desmond, Richard 1988

Dill, Robert 1979
Everett, Doug 1974
+Garrison, John B 1974
Garrity, Jack 1986
+Goheen, Frank (Moose) ..1973
Harding, Austin (Austie) ..1975
Iglehart, Stewart 1975
Johnson, Virgil 1974
Karakas, Mike 1973
Kirrane, Jack 1987
Lane, Myles 1973
+Linder, Joseph 1975
+LoPresti, Sam 1973
+Mariucci, John 1973
Mayasich, John 1976
McCartan, Jack 1983

Moe, William 1974
Moseley, Fred 1975
+Murray, Hugh (Muzz) Sr ..1987
+Nelson, Hubert (Hub) 1978
Olson, Eddie 1977
+Owen, George Jr 1973
+Palmer, Winthrop 1973
Paradise, Bob 1989
Purpur, Clifford (Fido) ...1974
Riley, William 1977
+Romnes, Elwin (Doc) ...1973
Rondeau, Richard 1985
Williams, Thomas 1981
+Winters, Frank (Coddy) ..1973
Yackel, Ken 1986

Coaches

+Almquist, Oscar 1983
+Gordon, Malcolm 1973
Heyliger, Vic 1974

+Jeremiah, Eddie 1973
+Kelley, John (Snooks) 1974
Riley, Jack 1979

Ross, Larry 1988
+Thompson, Clifford 1973
+Stewart, William 1982
+Winsor, Alfred (Ralph) ..1973

Administrators

+Brown, George V 1973
+Brown, Walter A 1973
Bush, Walter 1980
Clark, Donald 1978

+Gibson, J.C. (Doc) 1973
+Jennings, William 1981
+Kahler, Nick 1980
+Lockhart, Thomas 1973
Marvin, Cal 1982

Ridder, Robert 1976
Trumble, Harold 1970
+Tutt, William Thayer ...1973
Wirtz, William (Bill) 1967
+Wright, Lyle 1973

Referee

Chadwick, Bill 1974

National Horse Racing Hall of Fame

Established in 1950 by the Saratoga Springs Racing Association and opened in 1955. **Address:** National Museum of Racing and Hall of Fame, Union Ave., Saratoga Springs, NY 12866. **Telephone:** 518-584-0400.

Eligibility: nominated horses must be retired five years; jockeys must be active at least 15 years; trainers must be active at least 25 years. Voting done by 100-member panel of horse racing media.

Class of 1990: Jockeys—**Jorge Velasquez.** Trainers—**Ron McAnally** and **Jonathon Sheppard.** Horses—**All Along, Bimelech, John Henry** and **Zaccio.**

Members are listed with year of induction; (+) indicates deceased members.

Jockeys

+Adams, Frank (Dooley)* ..1970
+Adams, John 1965
+Aitcheson, Joe Jr.* 1978
Arcaro, Eddie 1958
Atkinson, Ted. 1957
Baeza, Braulio 1976
+Bassett, Carroll* 1972
+Blum, Walter 1987
+Bostwick, George H.* ..1968
+Boulmetis, Sam 1973
+Brooks, Steve 1963
+Burns, Tommy 1983
+Butwell, Jimmy 1984
+Coltiletti, Frank 1970
Cordero, Angel Jr. 1988
+Crawford, Robert (Specs)* 1973
+Fator, Laverne 1955
+Ensor, Lavelle (Buddy) ..1962
+Garner, Andrew (Mack) ..1969
+Garrison, Snapper 1955
+Griffin, Henry 1956
Guerin, Eric 1972

Hartack, Bill. 1959
+Johnson, Albert 1971
+Knapp, Willie 1969
+Kummer, Clarence 1972
+Kurtsinger, Charles 1967
+Loftus, John 1959
Longden, Johnny 1958
+Maher, Danny 1955
+McAtee, Linus 1956
McCarron, Chris 1989
+McCreary, Conn 1974
+McKinney, Rigan 1968
+McLaughlin, James 1955
+Miller, Walter 1955
+Murphy, Isaac 1955
+Neves, Ralph 1960
+Notter, Joe 1963
+Odom, George 1955
+O'Connor, Winnie 1956
+O'Neill, Frank 1956
+Parke, Ivan 1978
+Patrick, Gil 1970

Pincay, Laffit Jr 1975
+Purdy, Sam 1970
+Reiff, John 1956
+Robertson, Alfred 1971
Rotz, John L 1983
+Sande, Earl 1955
Schilling, Carroll 1970
Shoemaker, Bill 1958
+Simms, Willie 1977
+Sloan, Todhunter 1955
+Smithwick, A. Patrick* ..1973
+Stout, James 1968
+Taral, Fred 1955
+Tuckman, Bayard Jr.* ..1973
Turcotte, Ron 1979
+Turner, Nash 1955
Ussery, Robert 1980
Velasquez, Jorge 1990
+Woolfe, George 1955
+Workman, Raymond ..1956
Ycaza, Manuel 1977

*Steeplechase jockey

National Horse Racing Hall of Fame (Cont.)

Trainers

Barrera, Laz 1979	+Hyland, John 1956	Nerud, John 1972
+Bedwell, H.Guy 1971	+Jacobs, Hirsch 1958	+Parke, Burley 1986
+Brown, Edward D 1984	Jerkens, H. Allen 1975	Penna, Angel Sr 1988
Burch, Elliot 1980	+Johnson, William R 1986	+Pincus, Jacob 1988
+Burch, Preston M 1963	+Jolley, LeRoy 1987	+Rogers, John 1955
+Burch, W.P 1955	+Jones, Ben A 1958	+Rowe, James Sr 1955
+Burlew, Fred 1973	Jones, H.A.(Jimmy) 1959	Sheppard, Jonathan . . . 1990
+Byers, J.D. (Dilly) 1967	+Joyner, Andrew 1955	+Smith, Robert A 1976
+Childs, Frank E 1968	Laurin, Lucien 1977	+Smithwick, Mike 1976
Cocks, W. Burling 1985	+Lewis, J. Howard 1969	Stephens, Woody 1976
+Duke, William 1956	Luro, Horatio 1980	+Thompson, H.J 1969
+Feustel, Louis 1964	+Madden, John 1983	+Trotsek, Harry 1984
+Fitzsimmons, J.(Sunny Jim) 1958	+Maloney, John 1989	Van Berg, Jack 1985
+Gaver, John M 1966	Martin, Frank (Pancho) . . 1981	+Van Berg, Marion 1970
+Healey, Thomas 1955	McAnally, Ron 1990	+Veitch, Sylvester 1977
+Hildreth, Samuel 1955	+McDaniel, Henry 1956	+Walden, Robert 1970
+Hirsch, Max 1959	+Miller, MacKenzie 1987	+Ward, Sherrill 1978
+Hirsch, W.J.(Buddy) 1982	+Molter, William, Jr 1960	Whiteley, Frank Jr 1978
+Hitchcock, Thomas Sr . . . 1973	+Mulholland, Winbert 1967	Whittingham, Charlie . . . 1974
+Hughes, Hollie 1973	+Neloy, Eddie 1983	Winfrey, Carey 1971

Horses

Year foaled in parentheses.

+Ack Ack (1966) 1986	+Dr. Fager (1964) 1971	+Neji (1950) 1966
Affectionately (1960) 1989	+Elkridge (1938) 1966	+Oedipus (1941) 1978
Affirmed (1975) 1980	+Emperor of Norfolk (1885) 1988	+Old Rosebud (1911) 1968
All-Along (1979) 1990	+Equipoise (1928) 1957	+Omaha (1932) 1965
+Alsab (1939) 1976	+Exterminator (1915) 1957	
Alydar (1975) 1989		+Pan Zareta (1910) 1972
+American Eclipse (1814) . . 1970	+Fairmount (1921) 1985	+Parole (1873) 1984
+Armed (1941) 1963	+Fair Play (1905) 1956	+Peter Pan (1904) 1956
+Artful (1902) 1956	+Firenze (1885) 1981	
+Assault (1943) 1964	+Forego (1971) 1979	+Real Delight (1949) 1987
		+Regret (1912) 1957
+Battleship (1927) 1969	+Gallant Bloom (1966) . . . 1977	+Reigh Count (1925) 1978
+Bed O'Roses (1947) 1976	+Gallant Fox (1927) 1957	+Roamer (1911) 1981
+Beldame (1901) 1956	+Gallant Man (1954) 1987	+Roseben (1901) 1956
+Ben Brush (1893) 1955	+Gallorette (1942) 1962	+Round Table (1954) 1972
+Bewitch (1945) 1977	+Gamely (1964) 1980	+Ruffian (1972) 1976
+Bimelech (1937) 1990	Genuine Risk (1977) 1986	+Ruthless (1864) 1975
+Black Gold (1919) 1989	+Good and Plenty (1900) . 1956	
+Blue Larkspur (1926) 1957	+Grey Lag (1918) 1957	+Salvator (1886) 1955
+Bold Ruler (1954) 1973		+Sarazen (1921) 1957
+Bon Nouvel (1960) 1976	+Hamburg (1895) 1986	+Seabiscuit (1933) 1958
+Boston (1833) 1955	+Hanover (1884) 1955	+Searching (1952) 1978
+Broomstick (1901) 1956	+Henry of Navarre (1891) . 1985	Seattle Slew (1974) 1981
+Buckpasser (1963) 1970	+Hindoo (1878) 1955	+Secretariat (1970) 1974
+Busher (1942) 1964		+Shuvee (1966) 1975
+Bushranger (1930) 1967	+Imp (1894) 1965	+Silver Spoon (1956) 1978
		+Sir Archy (1805) 1955
+Cafe Prince (1970) 1985	+Jay Trump (1957) 1971	+Sir Barton (1916) 1957
+Carry Back (1958) 1975	John Henry (1975) 1990	+Stymie (1941) 1975
+Challendon (1936) 1977	+Jolly Roger (1922) 1965	+Susan's Girl (1969) 1976
+Chris Evert (1988) 1971		+Swaps (1952) 1966
+Cicada (1959) 1967	+Kingston (1884) 1955	+Sword Dancer (1956) . . . 1977
+Citation (1945) 1959	+Kelso (1957) 1967	+Sysonby (1902) 1956
+Coaltown (1945) 1983	+Kentucky (1861) 1983	
+Colin (1905) 1956		+Tim Tam (1955) 1985
+Commando (1898) 1956	+L'Escargot (1963) 1977	+Tom Fool (1949) 1960
+Count Fleet (1940) 1961	+Lexington (1850) 1955	+Top Flight (1929) 1966
	+Longfellow (1867) 1971	+Tosmah (1961) 1984
+Dahlia (1971) 1981	+Luke Blackburn (1877) . . . 1956	+Twenty Grand (1928) . . . 1957
+Damascus (1964) 1974		+Twilight Tear (1941) 1963
+Dark Mirage (1965) 1974	+Majestic Prince (1966) . . . 1988?	
+Davona Dale (1976) 1985	+Man O'War (1917) 1957	+War Admiral (1934) 1958
+Desert Vixen (1970) 1979	+Miss Woodford (1880) . . . 1967	+Whirlaway (1938) 1959
+Devil Diver (1939) 1980	+Myrtlewood (1933) 1979	+Whisk Broom II (1907) . . 1979
+Discovery (1931) 1969		
+Domino (1891) 1955	+Nashua (1952) 1965	Zaccio (1976) 1990
	Native Dancer (1950) 1963	+Zev (1920) 1983
	+Native Diver (1959) 1978	
	Northern Dancer (1961) . . 1976	

Exemplars of Racing

+Hanes, John W 1982	+Jeffords, Walter M 1973	+Widener, George D 1971

U.S. Olympic Hall of Fame

Established in 1983 by the United States Olympic Committee. **Current Address:** U.S. Olympic Committee, 1750 East Boulder Street, Colorado Springs, CO 80909. A permanent museum site is in the planning stages. **Telephone:** 719-578-4529.

Eligibility: Since 1986 nominated athletes must be five years removed from Olympic competition. Voting done by National Sportscasters and Sportswriters Association.

Class of 1990: Athletes—swimmer **Tracy Caulkins**; boxer **George Foreman**; figure skater **Scott Hamilton**; rower **Jack Kelly, Sr.**; weight lifter **Tommy Kono**; and diver **Sammy Lee**. Contributors—**Asa Bushnell**.

Members are listed with year of induction; (+) indicates deceased members.

Bobsled
+ Eagan, Eddie (see Boxing) . 1983

Boxing
Clay, Cassius* 1983	Foreman, George 1990	Leonard, Sugar Ray 1985
+ Eagan, Eddie (see Bobsled) 1983	Frazier, Joe 1989	Patterson, Floyd 1987

*Clay changed name to Muhammad Ali in 1964.

Figure Skating
Albright, Tenley 1988	Fleming, Peggy 1983	Hamilton, Scott 1990
Button, Dick 1983		

Gymnastics
Retton, Mary Lou 1985

Rowing
+ Kelly, Jack, Sr. 1990

Speed Skating
Heiden, Eric 1983

Swimming & Diving
Babashoff, Shirley 1987	Lee, Sammy 1990	Naber, John 1984
Caulkins, Tracy 1990	Louganis, Greg 1985	Schollander, Don 1983
+ Daniels, Charles 1988	McCormick, Pat 1985	Spitz, Mark 1983
de Varona, Donna 1987	Meyer, Debbie 1986	+ Weissmuller, Johnny 1983
+ Kahanamoku, Duke 1984		

Track & Field
Beamon, Bob 1983	+ Kraenzlein, Alvin 1985	Richards, Bob 1983
Boston, Ralph 1985	Lewis, Carl 1985	Rudolph, Wilma 1983
Davis, Glenn 1986	Mathias, Bob 1983	+ Sheppard, Mel 1989
+ Didrikson, Babe 1983	Mills, Billy 1984	Shorter, Frank 1984
Dillard, Harrison 1983	Morrow, Bobby 1989	+ Thorpe, Jim 1983
Evans, Lee 1989	Moses, Edwin 1985	Toomey, Bill 1984
+ Ewry, Ray 1983	O'Brien, Parry 1984	Tyus, Wyomia 1985
Jenner, Bruce 1986	Oerter, Al 1983	Whitfield, Mal 1988
Johnson, Rafer 1983	+ Owens, Jesse 1983	+ Wykoff, Frank 1984

Weight Lifting
Kono, Tommy 1990

Wrestling
Gable, Dan 1985

Contributors
Arledge, Roone 1989	Iba, Hank 1985	Miller, Don 1984
+ Brundage, Avery 1983	Kane, Robert 1986	Walker, Leroy 1987
+ Bushnell, Asa 1990	McKay, Jim 1988	

+ Davis, John 1989

Teams

1956 Basketball—Dick Boushka, Carl Cain, Chuck Darling, Bill Evans, Gib Ford, Burdy Haldorson, Bill Hougland, Bob Jeangerard, K.C.Jones, Bill Russell, Ron Tomsic, +Jim Walsh and coach +Gerald Tucker.

1960 Basketball—Jay Arnette, Walt Bellamy, Bob Boozer, Terry Dischinger, Burdy Haldorson, Darrall Imhoff, Allen Kelley, +Lester Lane, Jerry Lucas, Oscar Robertson, Adrian Smith, Jerry West and coach Pete Newell.

1964 Basketball—Jim Barnes, Bill Bradley, Larry Brown, Joe Caldwell, Mel Counts, Richard Davies, Walt Hazzard, Luke Jackson, John McCaffrey, Jeff Mullins, Jerry Shipp, George Wilson and coach Henry Iba.

1960 Ice Hockey—Billy Christian, Roger Christian, Billy Cleary, Bob Cleary, Gene Grazia, Paul Johnson, Jack Kirrane, John Mayasich, Jack McCartan, Bob McKay, Dick Meredith, Weldon Olson, Ed Owen, Rod Paavola, Larry Palmer, Dick Rodenheiser, Tom Williams and coach Jack Riley.

1980 Ice Hockey—Bill Baker, Neal Broten, Dave Christian, Steve Christoff, Jim Craig, Mike Eruzione, John Harrington, Steve Janaszak, Mark Johnson, Ken Morrow, Rob McClanahan, Jack O'Callahan, Mark Pavelich, Mike Ramsey, Buzz Schneider, Dave Silk, Eric Strobel, Bob Suter, Phil Verchota, Mark Wells and coach Herb Brooks.

National Sportscasters & Sportswriters Hall of Fame

Established in 1959 by the National Sportscasters and Sportswriters Association. **Temporary Address:** 322 East Innes Street, Salisbury, NC 28144. A permanent museum is scheduled to open in April of 1991. **Telephone:** 704-633-4275.

Eligibility: nominees must be active for at least 25 years. Voting done by NSSA membership and other media representatives.

Class of 1990: Sportscasters—**Jack Buck**, KMOX and CBS. Sportswriters—**Dave Anderson**, N.Y.Times; and **Alan Gould**, Associated Press. Memorable Athletes & Coaches—**Knute Rockne**, Notre Dame football coach (1918-30).

Members are listed with year of induction; (+) indicates deceased members.

Sportscasters

Allen, Mel 1972	Gowdy, Curt 1981	+McNamee, Graham 1964
Barber, Walter (Red) 1973	Harwell, Ernie 1989	Nelson, Lindsey 1979
Brickhouse, Jack 1983	+Hodges, Russ 1975	+Prince, Bob 1986
Buck, Jack 1990	+Husing, Ted 1963	Schenkel, Chris 1981
Caray, Harry 1989	+McCarthy, Clem 1970	Scott, Ray 1982
+Dean, Jay Hanna (Dizzy) . .1976	McKay, Jim 1987	+Stern, Bill 1974
Dunphy, Don 1986		

Sportswriters

Anderson, Dave 1990	+Grimsley, Will 1987	+Rice, Grantland 1962
Bisher, Furman 1989	+Kieran, John 1971	+Runyon, Damon 1964
Burick, Si 1985	+Lardner, Ring 1967	Russell, Fred 1988
+Cannon, Jimmy 1986	+Murphy, Jack 1988	+Smith, Walter (Red) 1977
+Considine, Bob 1980	Murray, Jim 1978	+Spink, J.G.Taylor 1969
+Daley, Arthur 1976	+Parker, Dan 1975	+Ward, Arch 1973
Gould, Alan 1990	Povich, Shirley 1984	+Woodward, Stanley 1974

Memorable Athletes & Coaches

+Lou Gehrig 1980	+Jesse Owens 1978	+Knute Rockne 1990

Contributors

Ronald Reagan 1989	+John Wayne 1979

International Tennis Hall of Fame

Originally the National Tennis Hall of Fame. Established in 1953 by James Van Alen and sanctioned by the U.S. Tennis Association in 1954. Renamed the International Tennis Hall of Fame in 1976. **Address:** 194 Bellevue Ave., Newport, RI 02840. **Telephone:** 401-849-3990.

Eligibility: nominated players must be five years removed from being a "significant factor" in competitive tennis. Voting done by members of the international tennis media.

Class of 1990: Players—**Jan Kodes**, Czechoslovakia. Contributors—**Joseph F. Cullman 3rd.**

Members are listed with year of induction; (+) indicates deceased members.

Players

Addie, Pauline Betz 1965	+Dod, Lottie 1983	Jacobs, Helen Hull 1962
+Adee, George 1964	+Doeg, John 1962	+Johnston, Bill 1958
+Alexander, Fred 1961	+Doherty, Lawrence 1980	Jones, Ann Haydon 1985
+Allison, Wilmer 1963	+Doherty, Reginald 1980	+Jones, Perry 1970
+Alonso, Manuel 1977	Drobny, Jaroslav 1983	
Ashe, Arthur 1985	du Pont, Margaret Osborne1967	King, Billie Jean 1987
+Atkinson, Juliette 1974	+Dwight, James 1955	Kodes, Jan 1990
		Kramer, Jack 1968
+Barger-Wallach, Maud . . .1958	Emerson, Roy 1982	
+Behr, Karl 1969	+Etchebaster, Pierre 1978	Lacoste, Rene 1976
Borg, Bjorn 1987		+Lambert Chambers, Dorothea1981
Borotra, Jean 1976	Falkenburg, Bob 1974	+Larned, William 1956
Bromwich, John 1984	Fraser, Neale 1984	Larsen, Art 1969
+Brookes, Norman 1977	Fry, Shirley (Irvin) 1970	Laver, Rod 1981
Brough, Louise (Clapp) 1967		+Lenglen, Suzanne 1978
+Browne, Mary 1957	+Garland, Chuck 1969	Lott, George 1964
+Brugnon, Jacques 1976	Gibson, Althea 1971	
Budge, Don 1964	Godfree, Kathleen McKane 1978	Mako, Gene 1973
Bueno, Maria 1978	Gonzales, Pancho 1968	+Mallory, Molla Bjurstedt . . .1958
	+Grant, Bryan (Bitsy) 1972	Marble, Alice 1964
+Cahill, Mabel 1976	+Griffin, Clarence 1970	+McKinley, Chuck 1986
+Campbell, Oliver 1955		+McLoughlin, Maurice 1957
Cawley, Evonne Goolagong1988	+Hackett, Harold 1961	McNeill, Don 1965
+Chace, Malcolm 1961	+Hansell, Ellen 1965	Moody, Helen Wills (Roark)1959
+Clark, Clarence 1983	Hard, Darlene 1973	+Moore, Elisabeth 1971
+Clark, Joseph 1955	Hart, Doris 1969	Mulloy, Gardnar 1972
+Clothier, William 1956	+Heldman, Gladys 1979	+Murray, Lindley 1958
+Cochet, Henri 1976	Hoad, Lew 1980	+Myrick, Julian 1963
+Connolly, Maureen (Brinker)1968	+Hovey, Fred 1974	
Court, Margaret Smith 1979	+Hunt, Joe 1966	Newcombe, John 1986
Crawford, Jack 1979	+Hunter, Frank 1961	+Nielsen, Arthur 1971
		+Nuthall, Betty (Shoemaker) 1977

Olmedo, Alex 1987
+Osuna, Rafael 1979

Palfrey, Sarah (Danzig) 1963
Parker, Frank 1966
+Patterson, Gerald 1989
Patty, Budge 1977
Perry, Fred 1975
+Pettitt, Tom 1982
Peitrangeli, Nicola 1986

Quist, Adrian 1984

Ralston, Dennis 1987
+Renshaw, Ernest 1983
+Renshaw, William 1983
+Richards, Vincent 1961
Riggs, Bobby 1967
Roche, Tony 1986
+Roosevelt, Ellen 1975

Rosewall, Ken 1980
+Round, Dorothy (Little) 1986
+Ryan, Elizabeth 1972

Santana, Manuel 1984
Savitt, Dick 1976
Schroeder, Ted 1966
+Sears, Eleonora 1968
+Sears, Richard 1955
Sedgman, Frank 1979
Segura, Pancho 1984
Seixas, Vic 1971
+Shields, Frank 1964
+Slocum, Henry 1955
Smith, Stan 1987
Stolle, Fred 1985
+Sutton, May (Bundy) 1956

Talbert, Bill 1967

+Tilden, Bill 1959
+Townsend, Bertha (Toulmin) 1974
Trabert, Tony 1970

Van Ryn, John 1963
Vines, Ellsworth 1962
+von Cramm, Gottfried 1977

Wade, Virginia 1989
+Wagner, Marie 1969
+Ward, Holcombe 1956
+Washburn, Watson 1965
+Whitman, Malcolm 1955
+Wightman, Hazel Hotchkiss 1957
+Wilding, Anthony 1978
+Williams, Richard 2nd 1957
Wood, Sidney 1964
+Wrenn, Robert 1955
+Wright, Beals 1956

Contributors

+Baker, Lawrence, Sr 1975
Cullman, Joseph F., 3rd . . .1990
+Danzig, Allison 1968
+Davis, Dwight 1956
+Gray, David 1985
+Gustaf, V (King of Sweden) 1980

Hester, Slew 1981
+Hopman, Harry 1978
+Laney, Al 1979
Martin, Alastair 1973
Martin, William McC. 1982

+Outerbridge, Mary 1981
+Pell, Theodore 1966
+Tingay, Lance 1982
+Tinling, Ted 1986
Van Alen, James 1965

National Track & Field Hall of Fame

Established in 1974 by The Athletics Congress. Originally located in Charleston, WV, the Hall moved to Indianapolis in 1983 and reopened at the Hoosier Dome in 1986. **Address:** One Hoosier Dome, Indianapolis, IN 46225. **Telephone:** 317-261-0483.

Eligibility: nominated athletes must be retired three years and coaches must have coached at least 20 years, if retired, or 35 years, if still coaching. Voting done by 800-member panel made up of Hall of Fame and TAC officials, Hall of Fame members, current U.S. champions and members of the Track & Field Writers of America.

Class of 1990: Men—middle distance runner **Jim Beatty**, high jumper **Charley Dumas** and half-miler **Rick Wohlhuter**. Women—distance runner and coach **Doris Brown Heritage**.

Members are listed with year of induction; (+) indicates deceased members.

Men

Albritton, Dave 1980
Ashenfelter, Horace 1975

+Bausch, James 1979
Beamon, Bob 1977
Beatty, Jim 1990
Bell, Greg 1988
+Boeckmann, Dee 1976
Boston, Ralph 1974

+Calhoun, Lee 1974
Campbell, Milt 1989
Connolly, Harold 1984
Courtney, Tom 1978
+Cunningham, Glenn 1974
+Curtis, William 1979

Davenport, Willie 1982
Davis, Glenn 1974
Davis, Harold 1974
Dillard, Harrison 1974
Dumas, Charley 1990

Evans, Lee 1983
Ewell, Barney 1986
+Ewry, Ray 1974

+Flanagan, John 1975
Fosbury, Dick 1981

+Gordien, Fortune 1979

+Hahn, Archie 1983
+Hardin, Glenn 1978
Hayes, Bob 1976

Held, Bud 1987
Hines, Jim 1979
Houser, Bud 1979
+Hubbard, DeHart 1979

Jenner, Bruce 1980
Johnson, Rafer 1974
Jones, Hayes 1976

Kelley, John 1980
Kiviat, Abel 1985
+Kraenzlein, Alvin 1974

Laird, Ron 1986

Mathias, Bob 1974
Matson, Randy 1984
Meredith, Ted 1982
+Metcalfe, Ralph 1975
Mills, Billy 1976
Moore, Tom 1988
Morrow, Bobby 1975
+Myers, Lawrence 1974

O'Brien, Parry 1974
Oerter, Al 1974
Osborn, Harold 1974
+Owens, Jesse 1974

+Paddock, Charley 1976
Patton, Mel 1985
Peacock, Eulace 1987
+Prefontaine, Steve 1976

+Ray, Joie 1976

Rice, Greg 1977
Richards, Bob 1975
+Rose, Ralph 1976
Ryun, Jim 1980

+Scholz, Jackson 1977
Seagren, Bob 1986
+Sheppard, Mel 1976
+Sheridan, Martin 1988
Shorter, Frank 1989
Sime, Dave 1981
+Simpson, Robert 1974
Smith, Tommie 1978
+Stanfield, Andy 1977
Steers, Les 1974

Thomas, John 1985
+Thomson, Earl 1977
+Thorpe, Jim 1975
+Tolan, Eddie 1982
Toomey, Bill 1975
Towns, Forrest 1976

Warmerdam, Cornelius 1974
White, Willye 1981
Whitfield, Mal 1974
Wohlhuter, Rick 1990
Woodruff, John 1978
Wottle, Dave 1982
+Wykoff, Frank 1977

Young, George 1981

National Track & Field Hall of Fame (Cont.)

Women

Coachman, Alice 1975	+Jackson, Nell 1989	Rudolph, Wilma 1974
+Didrikson, Babe 1974	Manning, Madeline......1984	Stephens, Helen 1975
Faggs, Mae.............1976	McDaniel, Mildred 1983	Tyus, Wyomia 1980
Ferrell, Barbara 1988	McGuire, Edith 1979	+Walsh, Stella 1975
Hall, Evelyne 1988	Robinson, Betty.........1977	Watson, Martha 1987
Heritage, Doris Brown 1990		

Coaches

Baskin, Weems 1982	+Hamilton, Brutus 1974	+Moakley, Jack 1988
Beard, Percy 1981	+Haydon, Ted 1975	+Murphy, Michael 1974
Botts, Tom 1983	+Hayes, Billy 1976	
Bowerman, Bill 1981	Haylett, Ward 1979	+Snyder, Larry 1978
Bush, Jim 1987	Higgins, Ralph 1982	Temple, Ed 1989
	+Hillman, Harry 1976	+Templeton, Dink 1976
+Cromwell, Dean 1974	+Hurt, Edward 1975	
Doherty, Ken...........1976	+Hutsell, Wilbur 1977	Walker, LeRoy 1983
		Wilt, Fred 1981
Easton, Bill 1975	+Jones, Thomas 1977	+Winter, Bud 1985
+Elliott, Jumbo 1981	Jordan, Payton 1982	
	+Littlefield, Clyde.........1981	Yancy, Joseph 1984
+Giegengack, Bob 1978		

Contributors

+Abramson, Jesse 1981	+Ferris, Dan 1974	Nelson, Cordner 1988
+Bakjian, Andy 1986	+Griffith, John 1979	+Sullivan, James 1977
+Brundage, Avery 1974		

Babe Didrickson Zaharias(left) and **Jim Thorpe** are each members of four major Halls of Fame. The Associated Press voted them Female and Male Athletes of the Half Century in 1950.

Retired Uniform Numbers
Major League Baseball

The New York Yankees have retired the most uniform numbers (12) in the Major Leagues; followed by Pittsburgh and the Brooklyn-Los Angeles Dodgers (8), the Chicago White Sox (7), the New York-San Francisco Giants (6), and the St.Louis Cardinals (5).

Three players and a manager have had their number retired by two teams: **Hank Aaron**—#44 by Atlanta and Milwaukee; **Rod Carew**—#29 by Minnesota and California; **Frank Robinson**—#20 by Cincinnati and Baltimore; and **Casey Stengel**—#37 by the New York Yankees and Mets.

Numbers retired in 1990: Cleveland #18, worn by pitcher **Mel Harder** (1928-47); and Philadelphia #20, worn by 3rd baseman **Mike Schmidt** (1972-89).

American League

Baltimore
4 Earl Weaver
5 Brooks Robinson
20 Frank Robinson
22 Jim Palmer
33 Eddie Murray

Boston Red Sox
1 Bobby Doerr
4 Joe Cronin
8 Carl Yastrzemski
9 Ted Williams

California Angels
26 Gene Autry
29 Rod Carew

Chicago White Sox
2 Nellie Fox
3 Harold Baines
4 Luke Appling
9 Minnie Minoso
11 Luis Aparicio
16 Ted Lyons
19 Billy Pierce

Cleveland Indians
3 Earl Averill
5 Lou Boudreau
18 Mel Harder
19 Bob Feller

Detroit Tigers
2 Charlie Gehringer
5 Hank Greenberg
6 Al Kaline

Kansas City Royals
10 Dick Howser

Milwaukee Brewers
44 Hank Aaron

Minnesota Twins
3 Harmon Killebrew
29 Rod Carew

New York Yankees
1 Billy Martin
3 Babe Ruth
4 Lou Gehrig
5 Joe DiMaggio
7 Mickey Mantle
8 Yogi Berra
  & Bill Dickey

9 Roger Maris
10 Phil Rizzuto
15 Thurman Munson
16 Whitey Ford
32 Elston Howard
37 Casey Stengel

Oakland Athletics
None

Seattle Mariners
None

Texas Rangers
None

Toronto Blue Jays
None

National League

Atlanta Braves
21 Warren Spahn
35 Phil Niekro
41 Eddie Mathews
44 Hank Aaron

Chicago Cubs
14 Ernie Banks
26 Billy Williams

Cincinnati Reds
1 Fred Hutchinson
5 Johnny Bench

Houston Astros
32 Jim Umbricht
40 Don Wilson

Los Angeles Dodgers
1 Pee Wee Reese
4 Duke Snider
19 Jim Gilliam
24 Walter Alston
32 Sandy Koufax
39 Roy Campanella
42 Jackie Robinson
53 Don Drysdale

Montreal Expos
None

New York Mets
14 Gil Hodges
37 Casey Stengel
41 Tom Seaver

Philadelphia Phillies
1 Richie Ashburn
20 Mike Schmidt
32 Steve Carlton
36 Robin Roberts

Pittsburgh Pirates
1 Billy Meyer
4 Ralph Kiner
8 Willie Stargell
9 Bill Mazeroski
20 Pie Traynor
21 Roberto Clemente
33 Honus Wagner
40 Danny Murtaugh

St.Louis Cardinals
6 Stan Musial
14 Ken Boyer

17 Dizzy Dean
20 Lou Brock
45 Bob Gibson

San Diego Padres
6 Steve Garvey

San Francisco Giants
* Christy Mathewson
* John McGraw
3 Bill Terry
4 Mel Ott
11 Carl Hubbell
24 Willie Mays
27 Juan Marichal
44 Willie McCovey

*Mathewson played and McGraw managed before numbers were worn on major league uniforms.

National Basketball Association

Boston has retired the most uniform numbers (15) in the NBA; followed by the New York Knicks (7); Milwaukee and the Rochester-Cincinnati-Kansas City-Omaha-Sacramento Royals-Kings (6); and Portland (5).

Three players have had their numbers retired by two teams: **Julius Erving**—#32 by New Jersey and #6 by Philadelphia; **Oscar Robertson**—#14 by Sacramento and #1 by Milwaukee; and **Nate Thurmond**—#42 by Golden State and Cleveland.

Numbers retired in 1990: Los Angeles Lakers #33, worn by **Kareem Abdul-Jabbar** (1975-89); Milwaukee #4, worn by guard **Sidney Moncrief** (1978-89); New York Knicks #12, worn by guard **Dick Barnett** (1965-74) and #613, the games won by coach **Red Holzman** (1967-77, 78-82); and Sacramento #11, worn by Rochester Royals' **Bob Davies** (1945-55).

Eastern Division

Atlanta Hawks
9 Bob Pettit
23 Lou Hudson

Boston Celtics
1 Walter A.Brown
2 Red Auerbach
6 Bill Russell
10 Jo Jo White
14 Bob Cousy
15 Tom Heinsohn

16 Tom (Satch) Sanders
17 John Havlicek
18 Dave Cowens
19 Don Nelson
21 Bill Sharman
22 Ed Macauley
23 Frank Ramsey
24 Sam Jones
25 K.C.Jones
Loscy Jim Loscutoff

Chicago Bulls
4 Jerry Sloan

Cleveland Cavaliers
7 Bingo Smith
34 Austin Carr
42 Nate Thurmond

Detroit Pistons
21 Dave Bing

Indiana Pacers
30 George McGinnis
34 Mel Daniels
35 Roger Brown

Miami Heat
None

National Basketall Association (Cont.)

Milwaukee Bucks
1 Oscar Robertson
2 Junior Bridgeman
4 Sidney Moncrief
14 Jon McGlocklin
16 Bob Lanier
32 Brian Winters

New York Knicks
10 Walt Frazier
12 Dick Barnett
15 Earl Monroe
19 Willis Reed
22 Dave DeBusschere
24 Bill Bradley
613 Red Holzman

New Jersey Nets
4 Wendell Ladner
25 Bill Melchionni
32 Julius Erving

Orlando Magic
None

Philadelphia 76ers
6 Julius Erving
15 Hal Greer
24 Bobby Jones
32 Billy Cunningham
Microphone Dave Zinkoff

Washington Bullets
11 Elvin Hayes
25 Gus Johnson
41 Wes Unseld

Western Division

Charlotte Hornets
None

Dallas Mavericks
None

Denver Nuggets
40 Byron Beck
44 Dan Issel

Golden St.Warriors
14 Tom Meschery
16 Al Attles
24 Rick Barry
42 Nate Thurmond

Houston Rockets
23 Calvin Murphy
45 Rudy Tomjanovich

LA Clippers
None

LA Lakers
13 Wilt Chamberlain
22 Elgin Baylor
33 Kareem Abdul-Jabbar
44 Jerry West

Minn. Timberwolves
None

Phoenix Suns
5 Dick Van Arsdale
33 Alvan Adams
42 Connie Hawkins
44 Paul Westphal

Portland Trail Blazers
13 Dave Twardzik
15 Larry Steele
20 Maurice Lucas
36 Lloyd Neal
45 Geoff Petrie

Sacramento Kings
6 Fans ("Sixth Man")
11 Bob Davies
12 Maurice Stokes
14 Oscar Robertson
27 Jack Twyman
44 Sam Lacey

San Antonio Spurs
13 James Silas
44 George Gervin

Seattle SuperSonics
19 Lenny Wilkens
32 Fred Brown

Utah Jazz
1 Frank Layden
7 Pete Maravich

National Football League

The Chicago Bears have retired the most uniform numbers (10) in the NFL; followed by the Baltimore-Indianapolis Colts, the New York Giants and San Francisco (7); the Portsmouth Spartans-Detroit Lions (6); and Cleveland, the Dallas Texans-Kansas City Chiefs and Philadelphia (5).

No NFL player has ever had his number retired by more than one team in the league.

Numbers retired in 1989: New England #57, worn by linebacker **Steve Nelson** (1974-87).

American Conference

Buffalo Bills
None

Cincinnati Bengals
54 Bob Johnson

Cleveland Browns
14 Otto Graham
32 Jim Brown
45 Ernie Davis
46 Don Fleming
76 Lou Groza

Denver Broncos
18 Frank Tripucka
44 Floyd Little

Houston Oilers
34 Earl Campbell
43 Jim Norton
65 Elvin Bethea

Indianapolis Colts
19 Johnny Unitas
22 Buddy Young
24 Lenny Moore
70 Art Donovan
77 Jim Parker
82 Raymond Berry
89 Gino Marchetti

Kansas City Chiefs
16 Len Dawson
28 Abner Haynes
33 Stone Johnson
36 Mack Lee Hill
78 Bobby Bell

Los Angeles Raiders
None

Miami Dolphins
12 Bob Griese

N.England Patriots
20 Gino Cappelletti
57 Steve Nelson
79 Jim Hunt
89 Bob Dee

New York Jets
12 Joe Namath
13 Don Maynard

Pittsburgh Steelers
None

San Diego Chargers
14 Dan Fouts

Seattle Seahawks
12 Fans ("12th Man")

National Conference

Atlanta Falcons
31 William Andrews
57 Jeff Van Note
60 Tommy Nobis

Chicago Bears
3 Bronko Nagurski
5 George McAfee
28 Willie Galimore
34 Walter Payton
41 Brian Piccolo
42 Sid Luckman
56 Bill Hewitt
61 Bill George
66 Bulldog Turner
77 Red Grange
GSH George Halas

Dallas Cowboys
None

Detroit Lions
7 Dutch Clark
22 Bobby Layne
37 Doak Walker
56 Joe Schmidt
85 Chuck Hughes
88 Charlie Sanders

Green Bay Packers
3 Tony Canadeo
14 Don Hutson
15 Bart Starr
66 Ray Nitschke

Los Angeles Rams
7 Bob Waterfield
74 Merlin Olsen

Minnesota Vikings
10 Fran Tarkenton

New Orleans Saints
31 Jim Taylor
81 Doug Atkins

New York Giants
1 Ray Flaherty
7 Mel Hein
14 Y.A.Tittle
32 Al Blozis
40 Joe Morrison
42 Charlie Conerly
50 Ken Strong

Philadelphia Eagles
15 Steve Van Buren
40 Tom Brookshier
44 Pete Retzlaff
60 Chuck Bednarik
70 Al Wistert

Phoenix Cardinals
8 Larry Wilson
77 Stan Mauldin
88 J.V.Cain
99 Marshall Goldberg

San Francisco 49ers
12 John Brodie
34 Joe Perry
37 Jimmy Johnson
39 Hugh McElhenny
70 Charlie Krueger
73 Lou Nomellini
87 Dwight Clark

Tampa Bay Bucs
63 Lee Roy Selmon

Wash. Redskins
33 Sammy Baugh

National Hockey League

The Boston Bruins have retired the most uniform numbers (7) in the NHL; followed by the Montreal Canadiens (6); Chicago (4); and the Boston-New England-Hartford Whalers, Philadelphia and St.Louis (3).

Two players have had their numbers retired by two teams: **Gordie Howe**—#9 by Detroit and Hartford; and **Bobby Hull**—#9 by Chicago and Winnipeg.

Numbers retired in 1990: Calgary #9, worn by **Lanny McDonald** (1981-89).

Campbell Conference

Calgary Flames
9 Lanny McDonald

Chicago Blackhawks
1 Glenn Hall
9 Bobby Hull
21 Stan Mikita
35 Tony Esposito

Detroit Red Wings
6 Larry Aurie
9 Gordie Howe

Edmonton Oilers
3 Al Hamilton

Los Angeles Kings
30 Rogie Vachon

Minn. North Stars
19 Bill Masterton

St.Louis Blues
3 Bob Gassoff
8 Barclay Plager
11 Brian Sutter

Toronto Maple Leafs
5 Bill Barilko
6 Ace Bailey

Vancouver Canucks
11 Wayne Maki

Winnipeg Jets
9 Bobby Hull

Wales Conference

Boston Bruins
2 Eddie Shore
3 Lionel Hitchman
4 Bobby Orr
5 Dit Clapper
7 Phil Esposito
8 Johnny Bucyk
15 Milt Schmidt

Buffalo Sabres
2 Tim Horton

Hartford Whalers
2 Rick Ley
9 Gordie Howe
19 John McKenzie

Montreal Canadiens
2 Doug Harvey
4 Jean Beliveau
   & Aurele Joliat
7 Howie Morenz
9 Maurice Richard
10 Guy Lafleur
16 Henri Richard
   & Elmer Lach

New Jersey Devils
None

New York Islanders
5 Denis Potvin

New York Rangers
1 Eddie Giacomin
7 Rod Gilbert

Philadelphia Flyers
1 Bernie Parent
4 Barry Ashbee
16 Bobby Clarke

Pitts. Penguins
21 Michel Briere

Quebec Nordiques
3 J.C.Tremblay
8 Marc Tardif

Wash. Capitals
7 Yvon Labre

Awards

Associated Press Athletes of the Year, 1931-89

Selected annually by A.P. newspaper sports editors since 1931.

Male

Multiple winners: Don Budge, Sandy Koufax, Carl Lewis and Byron Nelson (2).

Year		Year		Year	
1931	**Pepper Martin**, baseball	1950	**Jim Konstanty**, baseball	1970	**George Blanda**, pro football
1932	**Gene Sarazen**, golf	1951	**Dick Kazmaier**, football	1971	**Lee Trevino**, golf
1933	**Carl Hubbell**, baseball	1952	**Bob Mathias**, track	1972	**Mark Spitz**, swimming
1934	**Dizzy Dean**, baseball	1953	**Ben Hogan**, golf	1973	**O.J.Simpson**, pro football
1935	**Joe Louis**, boxing	1954	**Willie Mays**, baseball	1974	**Muhammad Ali**, boxing
1936	**Jesse Owens**, track & field	1955	**Hopalong Cassady**, football	1975	**Fred Lynn**, baseball
1937	**Don Budge**, tennis	1956	**Mickey Mantle**, baseball	1976	**Bruce Jenner**, track
1938	**Don Budge**, tennis	1957	**Ted Williams**, baseball	1977	**Steve Cauthen**, horse racing
1939	**Nile Kinnick**, football	1958	**Herb Elliot**, track	1978	**Ron Guidry**, baseball
1940	**Tom Harmon**, football	1959	**Ingemar Johansson**, boxing	1979	**Willie Stargell**, baseball
1941	**Joe DiMaggio**, baseball	1960	**Rafer Johnson**, track	1980	**US Olympic Hockey Team**
1942	**Frank Sinkwich**, football	1961	**Roger Maris**, baseball	1981	**John McEnroe**, tennis
1943	**Gunder Haegg**, track	1962	**Maury Wills**, baseball	1982	**Wayne Gretzky**, hockey
1944	**Byron Nelson**, golf	1963	**Sandy Koufax**, baseball	1983	**Carl Lewis**, track
1945	**Byron Nelson**, golf	1964	**Don Schollander**, swimming	1984	**Carl Lewis**, track
1946	**Glenn Davis**, football	1965	**Sandy Koufax**, baseball	1985	**Dwight Gooden**, baseball
1947	**Johnny Lujack**, football	1966	**Frank Robinson**, baseball	1986	**Larry Bird**, pro basketball
1948	**Lou Boudreau**, baseball	1967	**Carl Yastrzemski**, baseball	1987	**Ben Johnson**, track
1949	**Leon Hart**, football	1968	**Denny McLain**, baseball	1988	**Orel Hershiser**, baseball
		1969	**Tom Seaver**, baseball	1989	**Joe Montana**, football

Female

Multiple winners: Babe Didrikson Zaharias (6); Chris Evert (4); Patty Berg and Maureen Connolly (3); Tracy Austin, Althea Gibson, Billie Jean King, Nancy Lopez, Alice Marble, Martina Navratilova, Wilma Rudolph, Kathy Whitworth and Mickey Wright (2).

Year		Year		Year	
1931	**Helene Madison**, swimming	1938	**Patty Berg**, golf	1944	**Ann Curtis**, swimming
1932	**Babe Didrikson**, track	1939	**Alice Marble**, tennis	1945	**Babe Didrikson Zaharias**, golf
1933	**Helen Jacobs**, tennis	1940	**Alice Marble**, tennis	1946	**Babe Didrikson Zaharias**, golf
1934	**Virginia Van Wie**, golf	1941	**Betty Hicks Newell**, golf	1947	**Babe Didrikson Zaharias**, golf
1935	**Helen Wills Moody**, tennis	1942	**Gloria Callen**, swimming	1948	**Fanny Blankers-Koen**, track
1936	**Helen Stephens**, track	1943	**Patty Berg**, golf	1949	**Marlene Bauer**, golf
1937	**Katherine Rawls**, swimming				

Associated Press Athletes of the Year, 1931-89 (Cont.)
Female

Year		Year		Year	
1950	**Babe Didrikson Zaharias**, golf	1964	**Mickey Wright**, golf	1978	**Nancy Lopez**, golf
1951	**Maureen Connolly**, tennis	1965	**Kathy Whitworth**, golf	1979	**Tracy Austin**, tennis
1952	**Maureen Connolly**, tennis	1966	**Kathy Whitworth**, golf		
1953	**Maureen Connolly**, tennis	1967	**Billie Jean King**, tennis	1980	**Chris Evert Lloyd**, tennis
1954	**Babe Didrikson Zaharias**, golf	1968	**Peggy Fleming**, skating	1981	**Tracy Austin**, tennis
1955	**Patty Berg**, golf	1969	**Debbie Meyer**, swimming	1982	**Mary Decker Tabb**, track
1956	**Pat McCormick**, diving			1983	**Martina Navratilova**, tennis
1957	**Althea Gibson**, tennis	1970	**Chi Cheng**, track	1984	**Mary Lou Retton**, gymnastics
1958	**Althea Gibson**, tennis	1971	**Evonne Goolagong**, tennis	1985	**Nancy Lopez**, golf
1959	**Maria Bueno**, tennis	1972	**Olga Korbut**, gymnastics	1986	**Martina Navratilova**, tennis
		1973	**Billie Jean King**, tennis	1987	**Jackie Joyner-Kersee**, track
1960	**Wilma Rudolph**, track	1974	**Chris Evert**, tennis	1988	**Florence Griffith Joyner**, track
1961	**Wilma Rudolph**, track	1975	**Chris Evert**, tennis	1989	**Steffi Graf**, tennis
1962	**Dawn Fraser**, swimming	1976	**Nadia Comaneci**, gymnastics		
1963	**Mickey Wright**, golf	1977	**Chris Evert**, tennis		

James E. Sullivan Award, 1930-89

Presented annually by The Amateur Athletic Union since 1930. The James E. Sullivan Memorial Award is named after the former AAU president and given to the athlete who "by his or her performance, example and influence as an amateur, has done the most during the year to advance the cause of sportsmanship."
An athlete cannot win the award twice.

Year		Year		Year	
1930	**Bobby Jones**, golf	1950	**Fred Wilt**, track	1970	**John Kinsella**, swimming
1931	**Barney Berlinger**, track	1951	**Bob Richards**, track	1971	**Mark Spitz**, swimming
1932	**Jim Bausch**, track	1952	**Horace Ashenfelter**, track	1972	**Frank Shorter**, track
1933	**Glenn Cunningham**, track	1953	**Sammy Lee**, diving	1973	**Bill Walton**, basketball
1934	**Bill Bonthron**, track	1954	**Mal Whitfield**, track	1974	**Rich Wohlhuter**, track
1935	**Lawson Little**, golf	1955	**Harrison Dillard**, track	1975	**Tim Shaw**, swimming
1936	**Glenn Morris**, track	1956	**Pat McCormick**, diving	1976	**Bruce Jenner**, track
1937	**Don Budge**, tennis	1957	**Bobby Morrow**, track	1977	**John Naber**, swimming
1938	**Don Lash**, track	1958	**Glenn Davis**, track	1978	**Tracy Caulkins**, swimming
1939	**Joe Burk**, rowing	1959	**Parry O'Brien**, track	1979	**Kurt Thomas**, gymnastics
1940	**Greg Rice**, track	1960	**Rafer Johnson**, track	1980	**Eric Heiden**, speed skating
1941	**Leslie MacMitchell**, track	1961	**Wilma Rudolph**, track	1981	**Carl Lewis**, track
1942	**Cornelius Warmerdam**, track	1962	**Jim Beatty**, track	1982	**Mary Decker**, track
1943	**Gilbert Dodds**, track	1963	**John Pennel**, track	1983	**Edwin Moses**, track
1944	**Ann Curtis**, swimming	1964	**Don Schollander**, swimming	1984	**Greg Louganis**, diving
1945	**Doc Blanchard**, football	1965	**Bill Bradley**, basketball	1985	**Joan B. Samuelson**, track
1946	**Arnold Tucker**, football	1966	**Jim Ryun**, track	1986	**Jackie Joyner-Kersee**, track
1947	**John B. Kelly, Jr.**, rowing	1967	**Randy Matson**, track	1987	**Jim Abbott**, baseball
1948	**Bob Mathias**, track	1968	**Debbie Meyer**, swimming	1988	**Florence Griffith Joyner**, track
1949	**Dick Button**, skating	1969	**Bill Toomey**, track	1989	**Janet Evans**, swimming

Sports Illustrated Sportsman of the Year, 1954-89

Selected annually by **Sports Illustrated** magazine since 1954.

Year		Year		Year	
1954	**Roger Bannister**, track	1970	**Bobby Orr**, hockey	1983	**Mary Decker**, track
1955	**Johnny Podres**, baseball	1971	**Lee Trevino**, golf	1984	**Mary Lou Retton**, gymnastics
1956	**Bobby Morrow**, track	1972	**Billie Jean King**, tennis		& **Edwin Moses**, track
1957	**Stan Musial**, baseball		& **John Wooden**, basketball	1985	**K. Abdul-Jabbar**, basketball
1958	**Rafer Johnson**, track	1973	**Jackie Stewart**, auto racing	1986	**Joe Paterno**, football
1959	**Ingemar Johansson**, boxing	1974	**Muhammad Ali**, boxing	1987	**"8 Athletes Who Care"**
		1975	**Pete Rose**, baseball		**Bob Bourne**, hockey
1960	**Arnold Palmer**, golf	1976	**Chris Evert**, tennis		**Kip Keino**, track
1961	**Jerry Lucas**, basketball	1977	**Steve Cauthen**, horse racing		**Judi Brown King**, track
1962	**Terry Baker**, football	1978	**Jack Nicklaus**, golf		**Dale Murphy**, baseball
1963	**Pete Rozelle**, pro football	1979	**Terry Bradshaw**, football		**Chip Rives**, football
1964	**Ken Venturi**, golf		& **Willie Stargell**, baseball		**Patty Sheehan**, golf
1965	**Sandy Koufax**, baseball				**Rory Sparrow**, basketball
1966	**Jim Ryun**, track	1980	**US Olympic hockey team**		**Reggie Williams**, football
1967	**Carl Yastrzemski**, baseball	1981	**Sugar Ray Leonard**, boxing	1988	**Orel Hershiser**, baseball
1968	**Bill Russell**, basketball	1982	**Wayne Gretzky**, hockey	1989	**Greg LeMond**, cycling
1969	**Tom Seaver**, baseball				

Media

Peabody Awards

Presented annually since 1940 for outstanding achievement in radio and radio broadcasting. Only 10 Peabodys have been given for sports programming.

Named after Georgia banker and philanthropist George Foster Peabody, the awards are administered by the Henry W.Grady College of Journalism and Mass Communication at the University of Georgia.

Television (9)

Year

1960 **CBS** for coverage of 1960 Winter and Summer Olympic Games (for Outstanding Contribution to International Understanding).

1966 ABC's **"Wide World of Sports"** (for Outstanding Achievement in Promotion of International Understanding).

1968 **ABC Sports** coverage of both the 1968 Winter and Summer Olympic Games.

1972 **ABC Sports** coverage of the 1972 Summer Olympics in Munich.

1973 **Joe Garagiola** of NBC Sports (for "The Baseball World of Joe Garagiola").

1976 **ABC Sports** coverage of both the 1976 Winter and Summer Olympic Games.

1984 **Roone Arledge**, president of ABC News & Sports (for significant contributions to television news and sports programming.

1986 **WFAA-TV**, Dallas for its investigation of the Southern Methodist University football program.

1988 **Jim McKay** of ABC Sports (for pioneering efforts and career accomplishments in the world of TV sports).

Radio (1)

Year

1974 **WSB** radio in Atlanta for "Henry Aaron: A Man with a Mission."

National Emmy Awards

Eligibility period covered calendar year from 1949-50 and since 1988.

Multiple major award winners: ABC "Wide World of Sports" (17); ABC Olympic Games coverage (9); CBS NFL coverage (7); ABC Monday Night NFL Football, NFL Films football coverage (4); ABC "The American Sportsman" (3); ABC Kentucky Derby coverage, ABC Indianapolis 500 coverage, CBS NCAA basketball coverage, and NBC World Series coverage (2).

1949
Coverage—"Wrestling"(KTLA, Los Angeles)

1950
Program—"Rams Football" (KNBH-TV, Los Angeles)

1954
Program—"Gillette Cavalcade of Sports" (NBC)

1965-66
Programs—"Wide World of Sports" (ABC), "Shell's Wonderful World of Golf" (NBC) and "CBS Golf Classic" (CBS)

1966-67
Program—"Wide World of Sports" (ABC)

1967-68
Program—"Wide World of Sports" (ABC)

1968-69
Program—"1968 Summer Olympics" (ABC)

1969-70
Programs—"NFL Football" (CBS) and "Wide World of Sports" (ABC)

1970-71
Program—"Wide World of Sports" (ABC)

1971-72
Program—"Wide World of Sports" (ABC)

1972-73
News Special—"Coverage of Munich Olympic Tragedy" (ABC)
Sports Programs—"1972 Summer Olympics" (ABC) and "Wide World of Sports" (ABC)

1973-74
Program—"Wide World of Sports" (ABC)

1974-75
Non-Edited—"Jimmy Connors vs. Rod Laver Tennis Challenge" (CBS)
Edited—"Wide World of Sports" (ABC)

1975-76
Live Special—"1975 World Series" (NBC)
Live Special—"NFL Monday Night Football" (ABC)
Edited Specials—"1976 Winter Olympics" (ABC) and "Triumph and Tragedy: The Olympic Experience" (ABC)
Edited Series—"Wide World of Sports" (ABC)

1976-77
Live Special—"1976 Summer Olympics" (ABC)
Live Series—"The NFL Today/NFL Football" (CBS)
Edited Special—"1976 Summer Olympics Preview" (ABC)
Edited Series—"The Olympiad" (PBS)

1977-78
Live Special—"Muhammad Ali vs. Leon Spinks Heavyweight Championship Fight (CBS)
Live Series—"The NFL Today/NFL Football" (CBS)
Edited Special—"The Impossible Dream: Ballooning Across the Atlantic" (CBS)
Edited Series—"The Way It Was" (PBS)

1978-79
Live Special—"Super Bowl XIII—Pittsburgh vs Dallas" (NBC)
Live Series—"NFL Monday Night Football" (ABC)
Edited Special—"Spirit of '78: The Flight of Double Eagle II" (ABC)
Edited Series—"The American Sportsman" (ABC)

1979-80
Live Special—"1980 Winter Olympics" (ABC)
Live Series—"NCAA College Football" (ABC)
Edited Special—"Gossamer Albatross: Flight of Imagination" (CBS)
Edited Series—"NFL Game of the Week" (NFL Films)

National Emmy Awards (Cont.)

1980-81
Live Special—"1981 Kentucky Derby" (ABC)
Live Series—"PGA Golf Tour" (CBS)
Edited Special—"Wide World of Sports 20th Anniversary Show" (ABC)
Edited Series—"The American Sportsman" (ABC)

1981-82
Live Special—"1982 NCAA Basketball Final: North Carolina vs Georgetown" (CBS)
Live Series—"NFL Football" (CBS)
Edited Special—"1982 Indianapolis 500" (ABC)
Edited Series—"Wide World of Sports" (ABC)

1982-83
Live Special—"1982 World Series" (NBC)
Live Series—"NFL Football" (CBS)
Edited Special—"Wimbledon '83" (NBC)
Edited Series—"Wide World of Sports" (ABC)

1983-84
No awards given

1984-85
Live Special—"1984 Summer Olympics" (ABC)
Live Series—No award given
Edited Special—"Road to the Super Bowl '85" (NFL Films)
Edited Series—"The American Sportsman" (ABC)

1985-86
No awards given

1986-87
Live Special—"1987 Daytona 500" (CBS)
Live Series—"NFL Football" (CBS)
Edited Special—"Wide World of Sports 25th Anniversary Special" (ABC)
Edited Series—"Wide World of Sports" (ABC)

1987-88
Live Special—"1987 Kentucky Derby" (ABC)
Live Series—"NFL Monday Night Football" (ABC)
Edited Special—"Paris Roubaix Bike Race" (CBS)
Edited Series—"Wide World of Sports" (ABC)

1988
Live Special— "1988 Summer Olympics" (NBC)
Live Series—"1988 NCAA Basketball" (CBS)
Edited Special—"Road to the Super Bowl '88" (NFL Films)
Edited Series—"Wide World of Sports" (ABC)
Studio Show—"NFL GameDay" (ESPN)

1989
Live Special—"1989 Indianapolis 500" (ABC)
Live Series—"NFL Monday Night Football" (ABC)
Edited Special—"Trans-Antarctica! The International Expedition" (ABC)
Edited Series—"This is the NFL" (NFL Films)
Studio Show—"NFL Today" (CBS)

Outstanding Host/Analyst

First presented for 1967-68 season, and given annually since 1972-73. Split into two awards for the 1980-81 season. Eligibility period has covered calendar year since 1988.
  Multiple winners: Jim McKay (10); John Madden (7); Bob Costas, Dick Enberg, and Al Michaels (2).

Season	Host/Commentator	Season	Host	Season	Analyst
1967-68	Jim McKay, ABC	1980-81	Dick Enberg, NBC	1980-81	Dick Button, ABC
1968-69	No Award	1981-82	Jim McKay, ABC	1981-82	John Madden, CBS
		1982-83	Dick Enberg, NBC	1982-83	John Madden, CBS
1969-70	No Award	1983-84	No Award	1983-84	No Award
1970-71	Jim McKay, ABC & Don Meredith, ABC	1984-85	George Michael, NBC	1984-85	John Madden, CBS
		1985-86	No Award	1985-86	No Award
1971-72	No Award	1986-87	Al Michaels, ABC	1986-87	John Madden, CBS
1972-73	Jim McKay, ABC	1987-88	Bob Costas, NBC	1987-88	John Madden, CBS
1973-74	Jim McKay, ABC	1988	Bob Costas, NBC	1988	John Madden, CBS
1974-75	Jim McKay, ABC	1989	Al Michaels, ABC	1989	John Madden, CBS
1975-76	Jim McKay, ABC				
1976-77	Frank Gifford, ABC				
1977-78	Jack Whitaker, CBS				
1978-79	Jim McKay, ABC				
1979-80	Jim McKay, ABC				

Life Achievement Award
1989   Jim McKay, ABC

Note: Jim McKay has won 12 Emmys in all; the ten mentioned above, plus one for news commentary in 1972-73 and another for sports writing in 1987-88.

The Pulitzer Prize

The Pulitzer Prizes for journalism, letters and music have been presented annually since 1917 in the name of Joseph Pulitzer (1847-1911), the publisher of the New York World. Prizes are awarded by the president of Columbia University on the recommendation of a board of review.
  Since 1917, eight Pulitzers have been awarded for newspaper sportswriting or reporting on sports related general news. **1990 winner:** columnist **Jim Murray** of the LA Times.

Commentary
1976 **Red Smith,** NY Times, for his 1975 columns.
1981 **Dave Anderson,** NY Times, for his 1980 columns.
1990 **Jim Murray,** LA Times, for his 1989 columns.

General Reporting
1956 **Arthur Daley,** NY Times, for his 1955 "Sports of the Times" columns.

Investigative Reporting
1986 **Jeffrey Marx & Michael York,** Lexington (Ky.) Herald-Leader, for their 1985 investigation of the basketball program at the University of Kentucky and other major colleges.

News Coverage
1935 **Bill Taylor,** NY Herald Tribune, for reporting on the 1934 America's Cup yacht races.

Special Citation
1952 **Max Kase,** NY Journal-American, for his reporting on the 1951 college basketball point-shaving scandal.

Specialized Reporting
1985 **Randall Savage & Jackie Crosby,** Macon (Ga.) Telegraph and News, for their 1984 investigation of athletics and academics at the University of Georgia and Georgia Tech.

Murray gets his Pulitzer

by Scott Ostler

They gave Jim Murray a Pulitzer Prize in 1990, which should open the doors for a lot of other people overdue for awards.

Now they can give Beethoven a Grammy and Shakespeare a Tony. And how about that camping merit badge for Lewis and Clark?

Making James Patrick Murray wait until he was 70 years old to receive a Pulitzer was like withholding Custer's Purple Heart pending a review of the X-rays.

Of course, Murray didn't start writing a sports column until 1961, so it's possible the Pulitzer committee had been waiting to see if he was just a flash in the pan. After three decades they decided, hey, sometimes you gotta be impulsive, take a risk.

Lord knows Murray did. People laughed when he sat down at the typewriter in 1961, and that was the idea.

He was the new headliner for the *L.A. Times*, a newspaper which back then wore a monocle and didn't gossip or chew gum. Murray jumped off the page the way Michael Jordan jumps off the hardwood.

And he did this weird thing with his imagination—he used it. In those ancient days, you filed stories from a press box by handing your typed column to a Western Union operator. With Murray, the operator would read the lead, do a couple of Michael Jackson spins, hold the paper as if it was radioactive and beseech the author, "Mr. Murray, are you *sure* this is what you want to say?"

Murray painting word pictures of the sports world was like Dr. Seuss illustrating for the Audubon Society. It was—how you say?—a new approach to the craft.

Readers didn't know whether to laugh or cry, so they laughed till they cried. His columns dance like Astaire and hit like Tunney, soar like Dr. J and sing like Caruso. And he changed the sportswriting biz the way Ford changed the auto industry.

To Murray, the hallowed links of Royal St. George looked "like a Russian haircut." John Wooden was "so square, he was divisible by four." When Tom Harmon died in March, Murray wrote, "If he'd been carrying a football, God never would have touched him."

Jim has lousy eyesight, but he can spot an injustice a mile away. Long before Shoal

National Baseball Library, Cooperstown, N.Y.

Jim Murray (left) and Baltimore pitcher **Moe Drabowsky** after Game 1 of the 1966 World Series. Both are graduates of Trinity College in Hartford, Conn.

Creek became famous for the color of its membership, Murray lashed out at Augusta National for its exclusionary policies. He does not care for plantation-mentality sports owners. He simmers at Indy because drivers who are friends of his tend to get barbecued there, so he called The 500 "the run for the lilies," and wrote, "Gentlemen, start your coffins."

Subtle stuff.

Like DiMaggio and Mays, Murray makes it look easy. He swears he wrestles with his work just like the rest of us so-called sports columnists do, but how can we believe that? Judging from the product, column writing for Jim is as painful as a picnic, as arduous as singing in the shower, as wrenching as watching the sun set in the Pacific.

Murray's writing is as graceful as a swan dive or a chip-in from the sand. But to him it's still just typing, even when they give you a Pulitzer for it. As he said one day while standing in the clubhouse of a team that didn't particularly impress him, but whose players were passing around their championship trophy, "Well, I guess *somebody* had to win it."

I mean, the guy is still writing at age 70 because he wants to do it until he gets it right, until he perfects that art. I won't tell him if you don't.

Scott Ostler was a column-writing colleague of Jim Murray's at the Los Angeles Times from 1984-89. This piece is reprinted from The National.

Sportscasters & Sportswriters of the Year

Presented annually since 1959 by the National Sportscasters and Sportswriters Association, based in Salisbury, N.C. Voting is done by NSSA members and selected national media.

Sportswriter of the Year

Multiple winners: Jim Murray (14); Frank Deford (6); Red Smith (5); Will Grimsley (4).

Year		Year		Year	
1959	**Red Smith**, NY Herald-Trib	1970	**Jim Murray**, LA Times	1980	**Will Grimsley**, AP
1960	**Red Smith**, NY Herald-Trib	1971	**Jim Murray**, LA Times	1981	**Will Grimsley**, AP
1961	**Red Smith**, NY Herald-Trib	1972	**Jim Murray**, LA Times	1982	**Frank Deford**, Sports Ill.
1962	**Red Smith**, NY Herald-Trib	1973	**Jim Murray**, LA Times	1983	**Will Grimsley**, AP
1963	**Arthur Daley**, NY Times	1974	**Jim Murray**, LA Times	1984	**Frank Deford**, Sports Ill.
1964	**Jim Murray**, LA Times	1975	**Jim Murray**, LA Times	1985	**Frank Deford**, Sports Ill.
1965	**Red Smith**, NY Herald-Trib	1976	**Jim Murray**, LA Times	1986	**Frank Deford**, Sports Ill.
1966	**Jim Murray**, LA Times	1977	**Jim Murray**, LA Times	1987	**Frank Deford**, Sports Ill.
1967	**Jim Murray**, LA Times	1978	**Will Grimsley**, AP	1988	**Frank Deford**, Sports Ill.
1968	**Jim Murray**, LA Times	1979	**Jim Murray**, LA Times	1989	**Peter Gammons**, Sports Ill.
1969	**Jim Murray**, LA Times				

Sportscaster of the Year

Multiple winners: Keith Jackson (5); Lindsey Nelson and Chris Schenkel (4); Bob Costas, Dick Enberg, Al Michaels and Vin Scully (3); Curt Gowdy and Ray Scott (2).

Year		Year		Year	
1959	**Lindsey Nelson**, NBC	1970	**Chris Schenkel**, ABC	1980	**Dick Enberg**, NBC
1960	**Lindsey Nelson**, NBC	1971	**Ray Scott**, CBS		& **Al Michaels**, ABC
1961	**Lindsey Nelson**, NBC	1972	**Keith Jackson**, ABC	1981	**Dick Enberg**, NBC
1962	**Lindsey Nelson**, NBC	1973	**Keith Jackson**, ABC	1982	**Vin Scully**, LA Dodgers/NBC
1963	**Chris Schenkel**, CBS	1974	**Keith Jackson**, ABC	1983	**Al Michaels**, ABC
1964	**Chris Schenkel**, ABC	1975	**Keith Jackson**, ABC	1984	**John Madden**, CBS
1965	**Vin Scully**, LA Dodgers	1976	**Keith Jackson**, ABC	1985	**Bob Costas**, NBC
1966	**Curt Gowdy**, NBC	1977	**Pat Summerall**, CBS	1986	**Al Michaels**, ABC
1967	**Chris Schenkel**, ABC	1978	**Vin Scully**, LA Dodgers/CBS	1987	**Bob Costas**, NBC
1968	**Ray Scott**, CBS	1979	**Dick Enberg**, NBC	1988	**Bob Costas**, NBC
1969	**Curt Gowdy**, NBC			1989	**Chris Berman**, ESPN

The Sporting News Man of the Year, 1968-89

Selected annually by **The Sporting News** since 1968.

Year		Year		Year	
1968	**Denny McLain**, baseball	1975	**Archie Griffin**, football	1982	**Whitey Herzog**, baseball
1969	**Tom Seaver**, baseball	1976	**Larry O'Brien**, basketball	1983	**Bowie Kuhn**, baseball
1970	**John Wooden**, basketball	1977	**Steve Cauthen**, horse racing	1984	**Peter Ueberroth**, LA Olympics
1971	**Lee Trevino**, golf	1978	**Ron Guidry**, baseball	1985	**Pete Rose**, baseball
1972	**Charles O. Finley**, baseball	1979	**Willie Stargell**, baseball	1986	**Larry Bird**, pro basketball
1973	**O.J. Simpson**, pro football	1980	**George Brett**, baseball	1987	No award
1974	**Lou Brock**, baseball	1981	**Wayne Gretzky**, hockey	1988	**Jackie Joyner-Kersee**, track
				1989	**Joe Montana**, football

Honda Broderick Cup

To the outstanding collegiate woman athlete of the year in NCAA competition. Winner is chosen from nominees in each of the NCAA's 10 competitive sports. Final voting is done by member athletic directors. Award is named after founder and sportswear manufacturer Thomas Broderick.

Multiple winner: Tracy Caulkins (2).

Year		Year	
1976-77	**Lucy Harris**, Delta St . . . . basketball	1983-84	**Tracy Caulkins**, Florida . . . . swimming
1977-78	**Ann Meyers**, UCLA . . . . basketball		& **Cheryl Miller**, USC . . . . basketball
1978-79	**Nancy Lieberman**, Old Dom . . basketball	1984-85	**Jackie Joyner**, UCLA . . . . track & field
1979-80	**Julie Shea**, N.C. State . . . . . . track & field	1985-86	**Kamie Ethridge**, Texas . . . . basketball
1980-81	**Jill Sterkel**, Texas . . . . swimming	1986-87	**Mary T. Meagher**, California . . . swimming
1981-82	**Tracy Caulkins**, Florida . . . . swimming	1987-88	**Teresa Weatherspoon**, La.Tech basketball
1982-83	**Deitre Collins**, Hawaii . . . . volleyball	1988-89	**Vicki Huber**, Villanova . . . . track

Dr. James Naismith was a Canadian physical education instructor at the YMCA Training School in Springfield, Mass., when he invented basketball in 1891. The sport celebrates its 100th anniversary this year.

20TH CENTURY PERSONALITIES

Personalities

Five hundred and sixty-nine noteworthy names in sports dating back to 1900.

Hank Aaron (b.1934): Baseball OF, led NL in HRs and RBI 4 times each and batting twice, MVP in 1957, played in 24 All-Star games, all-time leader in HRs (755) and RBI (2,297), 3rd in hits (3,771).

Kareem Abdul-Jabbar (b.Lew Alcindor,1947): Basketball C, led UCLA to 3 NCAA titles (1967-69), tourney MVP 3 times, Player of Year twice; led Milwaukee (1) and LA Lakers (5) to 6 NBA titles, playoff MVP twice (1971,85), reg.season MVP 6 times (1971-72, 74,76-77, 80), retired after 20 seasons as all-time leader in over 20 categories.

Tenley Albright (b.1935): Figure skater, 2-time world champion (1953,55), won Olympic silver (1952) and gold (1956) medals.

Grover Cleveland Alexander (1887-1950): Baseball RHP, won 20 or more games 9 times, 373 career wins and 90 shutouts.

Vasily Alexeyev (b.1942): Soviet weightlifter, 8-time world champion, 2-time Olympic super-heavyweight champ (1972,76), set 80 world records between 1970-77.

Muhammad Ali (b.Cassius Clay,1942): Boxer, 1960 Olympic light-heavyweight champion; 3-time world heavyweight champ (1964-67,74-78,78-79), pro record 56-5 with 37 KOs, 19 successful title defenses.

Forrest (Phog) Allen (1885-74): Basketball, college coach 46 years, directed Kansas to NCAA title (1952), 746 career wins.

Bobby Allison (b.1937): Auto racer, 3-time winner of Daytona 500 (1978,82,88), NASCAR national champ in 1983.

Walter Alston (1911-84): Baseball, managed Brooklyn-LA Dodgers 23 years, won 7 pennants and 4 W.Series (1955,59,63,65).

Sparky Anderson (b.1934): Baseball, only manager to win World Series in each league—Cincinnati in NL (1975-76) and Detroit in AL (1984).

Mario Andretti (b.1940): Auto racer, only driver to win Daytona 500 (1967), Indy 500 (1969) and Formula One world championship (1978); 4-time USAC/CART national champ (1965-66,69,84).

Earl Anthony (b.1938): Bowler, 6-time PBA Bowler of Year, 41 career titles; first to earn $100,000 in 1 season (1975), first to earn $1 million in career.

Said Aouita (b.1960): Moroccan runner, world record holder in 5 events—1500m, 2000m, 3000m, 2-mile, 5000m—entering 1990.

Luis Aparicio (b.1934): Baseball SS, all-time leader in most games, assists, chances and double plays by shortstop; led AL in stolen bases 9 times (1956-64), 506 career steals.

Al Arbour (b.1932): Hockey, coached NY Islanders to 4 straight Stanley Cup titles (1980-83).

Eddie Arcaro (b.1916): Jockey, 2-time Triple Crown winner (Whirlaway in 1941, Citation in '48); won Kentucky Derby 5 times, Preakness and Belmont 6 times each.

Roone Arledge (b.1931): Sports TV innovator of live events, anthology shows, Olympic coverage and "Monday Night Football;" ran ABC Sports from 1968-86; has run ABC news since 1977.

Henry Armstrong (1912-88): Boxer, held feather-, light- and welterweight titles simultaneously in 1938; pro record 145-20-9 with 98 KOs.

Arthur Ashe (b.1943): Tennis, first black man to win US Championship (1968) and Wimbledon (1975), 1st US player to earn $100,000 in 1 year (1970), won Davis Cup as player (1968-70) and captain (1981-82).

Red Auerbach (b.1917): Basketball, winningest coach in NBA history (1,037 wins including playoffs), led Boston to 9 NBA titles, including 8 in a row (1959-66); still Celtics' GM.

Hobey Baker (1892-1918): Football and hockey star at Princeton (1911-14), member of college football and pro hockey halls of fame, college hockey Player of the Year award named after him.

Seve Ballesteros (b.1957): Spanish golfer, has won British Open 3 times (1979,84,88) and Masters twice (1980,83).

Ernie Banks (b.1931): Baseball SS-1B, led NL in home runs and RBI twice each, 2-time MVP (1958-59) with Chicago, 512 career HRs.

Roger Bannister (b.1929): British runner, first to run mile in less than 4 minutes (3:59.4 on May 6, 1954).

Walter (Red) Barber (b.1908): Radio-TV, renowned baseball play-by-play broadcaster for Cincinnati, Brooklyn and the N.Y. Yankees from 1934-67.

Rick Barry (b.1944): Basketball F, only player to lead both NBA and ABA in scoring, 5-time All-NBA 1st team; playoff MVP with Golden St. in 1975.

Sammy Baugh (b.1914): Football QB, led Washington to NFL titles in 1937 (his rookie year) and '42, led league in passing 6 times, punting 4 times and interceptions once.

Elgin Baylor (b.1934): Basketball F, MVP of NCAA tournament in 1958; led Minn.-LA Lakers to 8 NBA Finals, 10-time All-NBA 1st team (1959-65,67-69).

Bob Beamon (b.1946): Track & Field, won 1968 Olympic gold medal in long jump with world record (29 ft,2½ in.) that still stands.

Franz Beckenbauer (b.1945): Soccer, captain of West German World Cup champions in 1974 then coached West Germany to World Cup title in 1990, invented sweeper position, played in US for NY Cosmos (1977-80,83).

Boris Becker (b.1967): West German tennis player, 3-time Wimbledon champ (1985-86,89), youngest male (17) to win Wimbledon, led country to 1st Davis Cup win in 1988.

Jean Beliveau (b.1931): Hockey C, led Montreal to 10 Stanley Cups in 17 playoffs, playoff MVP (1965), 2-time reg.season MVP (1956,64).

Bert Bell (1895-1959): Football, team owner and 2nd NFL commissioner (1946-59), proposed college draft in 1935 and instituted TV blackout rule.

Johnny Bench (b.1947): Baseball C, led NL in HRs twice and RBIs 3 times, 2-time reg.season MVP (1970,72) with Cincinnati, W.Series MVP in 1976; 389 career HRs.

Patty Berg (b.1918): Golfer, 57 career pro wins including 15 Majors, 3-time AP Female Athlete of Year (1938,43,55).

Yogi Berra (b.1925): Baseball C, played on 10 W.Series winners with NY Yankees, 3-time AL MVP (1951,54-55), managed both Yankees (1964) and NY Mets (1973) to pennants.

Jay Berwanger (b.1915): Football HB, U.of Chicago star, won 1st Heisman Trophy in 1935.

Abebe Bikila (1932-1973): Ethiopian runner, 1st to win consecutive Olympic marathons (1960,64).

Matt Biondi (b.1965): Swimmer, won 5 gold medals (2 individual), 1 silver and 1 bronze in 1988 Olympics.

Larry Bird (b.1956): Basketball F, college Player of Year (1979); 9-time All-NBA 1st team, 3-time reg.season MVP (1984-86), led Boston to 3 NBA titles, playoff MVP (1984,86).

The Black Sox—8 Chicago White Sox players who were banned from baseball for life in 1921 for allegedly throwing the 1919 W.Series: RHP **Eddie Cicotte** (1884-1969), OF **Happy Felsch** (1891-1964), 1B **Chick Gandil** (1887-1970), OF **Shoeless Joe Jackson** (1887-1951), INF **Fred McMullan** (1891-1952), SS **Swede Risberg** (1894-1975), 3B-SS **Buck Weaver** (1890-1956), and LHP **Lefty Williams** (1893-1959).

Earl (Red) Blaik (1897-89): Football, coached Army to consecutive national titles in 1944-45, 166 career wins and 3 Heisman Trophy winners (Blanchard, Davis, Dawkins).

Bonnie Blair (b.1964): Speedskater, won 500m gold medal at 1988 Winter Olympics, World Sprint champion in 1989.

Toe Blake (b.1912): Hockey LW, led Montreal to 2 Stanley Cups as a player and 8 more as coach, regular season MVP in 1939.

Felix (Doc) Blanchard (b.1924): Football FB, 3-time All-America, led Army to national titles in 1944-45, Glenn Davis' running mate, won Heisman Trophy and Sullivan Award in 1945.

George Blanda (b.1927): Football QB-PK, NFL's all-time leading scorer (2,002 points), led Houston to 2 AFL titles (1960-61), played 26 pro seasons, retired at 48.

Fanny Blankers-Koen (b.1918): Dutch sprinter, 30 year-old mother of two who won 4 gold medals (100m, 200m,800m hurdles and 4x100m relay) at 1948 Olympics.

Wade Boggs (b.1958): Baseball 3B, entered 1990 season with 5 AL batting titles (1983,85-88) at Boston and .352 career average.

Brian Boitano (b.1963): Figure skater, 2-time world champion (1986,88), won gold medal at 1988 Olympics.

Bjorn Borg (b.1956): Swedish tennis player, 2-time Player of Year (1979-80), won 6 French Opens and 5 straight Wimbledons (1976-80), led Sweden to 1st Davis Cup win in 1975.

Mike Bossy (b.1957): Hockey RW, led NY Islanders to 4 Stanley Cups, playoff MVP in 1982, scored 50 goals or more 9 straight years, 573 career goals.

Ralph Boston (b.1939): Track & Field, medaled in 3 consecutive Olympic long jumps—gold (1960), silver (1964), bronze (1968).

Jack Brabham (b.1926): Australian auto racer, 3-time Formula One champion (1959-60,66), 14 career wins.

Bill Bradley (b.1943): Basketball F, 3-time All-America at Princeton, Player of Year and NCAA tourney MVP in 1965, led NY Knicks to 2 NBA titles (1970,73), US Senator (D,NJ) since 1979.

Terry Bradshaw (b.1948): Football QB, led Pittsburgh to 4 Super Bowl titles (1975-76,79-80), 2-time Super Bowl MVP (1979-80).

George Brett (b.1953): Baseball 3B-1B, has led AL in batting twice (1976,80), MVP in 1980, led KC to W.Series title in 1985.

Lou Brock (b.1939): Baseball OF, all-time stolen base leader (938), led NL in steals 8 times, led St.Louis to 2 W.Series titles (1964,67), had 3,023 career hits.

Jim Brown (b.1936): Football FB, led NFL in rushing 8 times, 8-time All-Pro (1957-61,63-65), 3-time MVP (1958,63,65) with Cleveland, ran for 12,312 yards and scored 756 points in just 9 seasons.

Paul Brown (b.1908): Football innovator, coached Ohio St. to national title in 1942; in pros, directed Cleve.Browns to 4 straight AAFC titles (1946-49) and 3 NFL titles (1950,54-55), formed Cinn.Bengals in 1968 (reached playoffs in '70).

Walter A. Brown (1905-64): member of both basketball and hockey halls of fame, succeeded father George as GM of Boston Garden in 1937, later became president of Garden and co-owner of both Bruins and Celtics.

Valery Brumel (b.1942): Soviet high jumper, dominated event from 1961-64, broke world record 5 times, won silver medal in 1960 Olympics and gold in 1964, highest jump 7-5¾.

Avery Brundage (1887-1975): Amateur sports' czar for over 40 years as president of AAU (1928-35), US Olympic Committee (1929-53) and Int'l Olympic Committee (1952-72).

Paul (Bear) Bryant (1913-1983): Football, coached at 4 colleges over 38 years, directed Alabama to 5 national titles (1961,64-65,78-79), 323 career wins, 15 bowl wins including 8 Sugar Bowls.

Sergei Bubka (b.1963): Soviet pole vaulter, has set 18 world records (in & outdoor), 2-time world champion (1983,87), won gold medal at 1988 Olympics; highest vault 19-10½.

Don Budge (b.1915): Tennis, in 1938 became 1st player to win the Grand Slam—the French, Wimbledon, US and Australian titles in 1 year; led US to 2 Davis Cups (1937-38); turned pro in late '38.

Maria Bueno (b.1939): Brazilian tennis player, won 4 US Championships (1959,63-64,66) and 3 Wimbledons (1959-60,64).

Dick Butkus (b.1942): Football LB, 2-time All-America at Illinois (1963-64); All-Pro 7 of 9 NFL seasons with Chicago.

Dick Button (b.1929): Figure skater, 5-time world champion (1948-52), 2-time Olympic champ (1948,52).

Walter Byers (b.1923): College athletics, 1st executive director of NCAA, served from 1951-88.

Frank Calder (1877-1943): Hockey, 1st NHL president (1917-43), guided league through its formative years, NHL's rookie of the year award named after him.

Lee Calhoun (1933-89): Track & Field: won consecutive Olympic gold medals in the 110m Hurdles (1956,60).

Walter Camp (1859-1925): Football coach and innovator, established scrimmage line, center snap, downs, 11 players per side; named 1st All-America team (1889).

Roy Campanella (b.1921): Baseball C, 3-time NL MVP (1951,53,55), led Brooklyn to 5 pennants and 1st W.Series title (1955).

Earl Campbell (b.1955): Football RB, won Heisman Trophy in 1977, led NFL in rushing 3 times, 3-time All-Pro, 2-time MVP (1978-80) at Houston.

Milt Campbell (b.1933): Track & field, won silver medal in 1952 Olympic decathlon and gold medal in '56.

Tony Canzoneri (1908-59): Boxer, 2-time world lightweight champion (1930-33,35-36); pro record 141-24-10 with 44 KOs.

Rod Carew (b.1945): Baseball 2B-1B, led AL in batting 7 times (1969,72-75,77-78) with Minnesota, MVP in 1977, had 3,053 career hits.

Steve Carlton (b.1944): Baseball LHP, won 20 or more games 6 times, 4-time Cy Young winner (1972,77, 80,82) with Phila., 329 career wins.

JoAnn Carner (b.1939): Golfer, 5-time US Amateur champion, 2-time US Open champ, 3-time LPGA Player of Year (1974,81-82).

Don Carter (b.1926): Bowler, 6-time Bowler of Year (1953-54,57-58,60-61), voted Greatest of All-Time in 1970.

Billy Casper (b.1931): Golfer, 2-time PGA Player of Year (1966,70), has won US Open (1959,66), Masters (1970), US Sr.Open (1983).

Tracy Caulkins (b.1963): Swimmer, won 3 gold medals (2 individual) at 1984 Olympics, set 5 world records and won 48 US national titles from 1978-84.

Evonne Goolagong Cawley (b.1951): Australian tennis player, won Australian Open 4 times, Wimbledon twice (1971-79), French once.

Florence Chadwick (b.1918): Dominant distance swimmer of 1950s, set English Channel records from France to England (1950) and England to France (1951 and '55).

Wilt Chamberlain (b.1936): Basketball C, led NBA in scoring 7 times and rebounding 11 times, 7-time All-NBA first team, 4-time MVP (1960,66-68) with Phila., scored 100 pts in one game (1962), led Phila. (1967) and LA (1972) to NBA titles, playoff MVP in 1972.

Waldemar Cierpinski (b.1950): East German runner, won consecutive Olympic marathons (1976,80).

Jim Clark (1936-68): Scottish auto racer, 2-time Formula One world champion (1963,65), won Indy 500 in 1965, killed in car crash.

Bobby Clarke (b.1949): Hockey C, led Philadelphia to consecutive Stanley Cups in 1974-75, 3-time reg. season MVP (1973,75-76).

Ron Clarke (b.1937): Australian runner, from 1963-70 set 17 world records in races from 2 miles to 20,000 meters, never won Olympic gold medal.

Roger Clemens (b.1962): Baseball RHP, fanned record 20 batters in 9-inning game (1986), 2 Cy Young Awards (1986-87) with Boston, AL MVP in 1986.

Roberto Clemente (1934-72): Baseball OF, hit .300 or better 13 times with Pittsburgh, led NL in batting 4 times, W.Series MVP in 1971, regular season MVP in 1966, had 3,000 career hits.

Ty Cobb (1886-1961): Baseball OF, all-time highest career batting average (.367), hit .400 or better 3 times, led AL in batting 12 times and stolen bases 6 times with Detroit, MVP in 1911, had 4,191 career hits and 892 steals.

Mickey Cochrane (1903-62): Baseball C, led Phila.A's (1929-30) and Detroit (1935) to 3 W.Series titles, 2-time AL MVP (1928,34).

Sebastian Coe (b.1956): British runner, won consecutive gold medals in 1,500m and silver medals in 800m at 1980 and '84 Olympics, held world records in 1,500m, mile and 800m in 1979.

Eddie Collins (1887-1951): Baseball 2B, led Phila.A's (1910-11) and Chi.White Sox (1917) to 3 W.Series titles, AL MVP in 1914, had 3,311 career hits and 743 stolen bases.

Nadia Comaneci (b.1961): Romanian gymnast, 1st to record perfect 10 in Olympics, won 3 individual gold medals at 1976 Olympics and 2 more in '80.

Lionel Conacher (1902-54): Canada's greatest all-around athlete, NHL hockey (2 Stanley Cups), CFL football (1 Grey Cup), minor league baseball, soccer, lacrosse, track, amateur boxing champion; also member of Parliament (1949-54).

Billy Conn (b.1917): Boxer, world light heavyweight champion (1939-41); pro record 63-11-1 with 14 KOs.

Dennis Connor (b.1942): Sailing, 2-time America's Cup-winning skipper (1980,87), but 1st American to lose Cup (1983).

Maureen Connolly (1934-69): Tennis, in 1953 1st woman to win Grand Slam (at age 19), riding accident ended her career in '54, won both Wimbledon and US titles 3 times (1951-53); 3-time AP Female Athlete of Year (1951-53).

Jimmy Connors (1952): Tennis, No.1 player in world 5 times (1974-78), has won 5 US Opens, 2 Wimbledons and 1 Australian.

Angel Cordero, Jr. (b.1942): Jockey, winner of more than 6,000 races, has won Kentucky Derby 3 times, Preakness twice and Belmont once, 2-time Eclipse winner (1982-83).

Howard Cosell (b.1920): Radio-TV, ABC commentator on "Monday Night Football" and "Wide World of Sports," who revolutionized TV sports journalism with "Tell it like it is" style, also hosted ill-fated ABC variety show in 1975.

James (Doc) Counsilman (b. 1920): coached Indiana men's swim team to 6 NCAA championships (1968-73), coached the 1964 and '76 US Men's Olympic teams that won a combined 21 of 24 gold medals (the Hoosiers' Mark Spitz won 7 in 1976), in 1979 became oldest person (59) to swim English Channel, retired in 1990 with dual meet record of 287-36-1.

Margaret Smith Court (b.1942): Australian tennis player, won Grand Slam in both singles (1970) and mixed doubles (1963 with Ken Fletcher); 26 G.Slam singles titles—11 Australian, 7 US, 5 French and 3 Wimbledon.

Bob Cousy (b.1928): Basketball G, led NBA in assists 8 times, 10-time All-NBA 1st team (1952-61), MVP in 1957, led Boston to 6 NBA titles (1957,59-63).

Joe Cronin (1906-84): Baseball SS, hit over .300 and drove in over 100 runs 8 times each, MVP in 1930, player-manager in Washington and Boston (1933-47); AL president (1959-73).

Glenn Cunningham (1910-88): Track & Field, dominant US miler of 1930s, ran sub-4:10 mile 12 times, lost Olympic 1,500m to Jack Lovelock in 1936.

Chuck Daly (b.1930): Basketball, has coached Detroit Pistons to consecutive NBA titles (1989-90), entered 1990-91 season with 440 wins in 8 years.

Stanley Dancer (b.1927): Harness racing, winner of 4 Hambletonians, trainer-driver of 2 Trotting Triple Crown winners (1968,72), one Pacing Triple Crown winner (1970).

Gary Davidson (b.1934): Entrepreneur, fueled boom in new sports leagues from 1967-75, 1st president of ABA, WHA and WFL.

Al Davis (b.1929): Football, GM-coach of Oakland 1963-66, helped force AFL-NFL merger as AFL commissioner (April-July,1966), returned to Oakland as managing general partner and directed club to 3 Super Bowl wins (1977,81,84); moved Raiders to LA in 1982.

Glenn Davis (b.1924): Football HB, 3-time All-America, led Army to national titles in 1944-45, Doc Blanchard's running mate, won Heisman Trophy in 1946.

John Davis (1921-84): Weightlifting, 6-time world champion, 2-time Olympic super-heavyweight champ (1948,52), undefeated 1938-53.

Pierre de Coubertin (1862-1940): of France, father of the Modern Olympic Games, IOC president from 1896-1925.

Dizzy Dean (1911-74): Baseball RHP, led NL in strikeouts and complete games 4 times, last NL pitcher to win 30 games (30-7 in 1934), MVP in 1934 with St. Louis, 150 career wins.

Frank Deford (b.1938): 6-time Sportswriter of the Year during 27 years at Sports Illustrated, left SI in 1989 to launch The National as editor in chief.

Anita DeFrantz (b.1952): one of two American delegates to International Olympic Committee, member of bronze medal-winning US women's eight-oared shell at Montreal in 1976.

Clarence DeMar (1888-58): Track & Field, only 7-time winner of Boston Marathon (1911,22-24,27-28, 30), Olympic bronze in 1924.

Jack Dempsey (1895-1983): Boxer, world heavyweight champion from 1919-26, lost title and rematch to Gene Tunney, pro record 62-6-10 with 49 KOs.

Klaus Dibiasi (b.1947): Italian diver, won 3 consecutive Olympic gold medals in Platform Diving (1968,72,76).

Eric Dickerson (b.1960): Football RB, has led NFL in rushing 4 times (1983-84,86,88), All-Pro 5 times, traded from LA Rams to Indianapolis (Oct.31,1987).

Harrison Dillard (b.1923): Track & Field, only man to win Olympic gold medals in both sprints (100m in 1948) and hurdles (110m in 1952).

Joe DiMaggio (b.1914): Baseball OF, hit safely in 56 straight games (1941), led AL in batting, HRs and RBI twice each, 3-time MVP (1939,41,47), led NY Yankees to 10 W.Series titles in 13 seasons.

Marcel Dionne (b.1951): Hockey C, scored 50 or more goals 6 times, led NHL in scoring in 1980, 2nd in all-time goals (731), 3rd in assists (1,348) and 3rd in points (1,771).

James (Buster) Douglas (b. 1960): Boxing, 50-1 shot who knocked out undefeated Mike Tyson in 10th round on Feb.10, 1990 to win heavyweight title in Tokyo, pro record after that fight 30-4-1 with 20 KOs.

Ken Dryden (b.1947): Hockey G, led Montreal to 6 Stanley Cup titles, playoff MVP as rookie in 1971, won or shared 5 Vezina Trophies.

Charley Dumas (b.1937): US high jumper, first man to clear 7 feet (7-0 ½) on June 29, 1956; won gold medal at 1956 Olympics.

Margaret Osborne du Pont (b.1918): Tennis, won 5 French, 7 Wimbledon and an unprecedented 24 US national titles in singles, doubles and mixed doubles from 1941-62.

Roberto Duran (b.1951): Panamanian boxer, world lightweight champion (1972-79), world welterweight champ (1980), entered 1990 with pro record of 86-8-0 and 60 KOs.

Leo Durocher (b.1905): Baseball, managed in NL 24 years, won 2,010 games, 3 pennants with Brooklyn (1941) and NY Giants (1951,54), won W.Series in 1954.

Eddie Eagan (1898-1967): Only US athlete to win gold medals in Summer and Winter Olympics (Boxing in 1920, Bobsled in 1932).

Alan Eagleson (b.1933): Hockey, executive dir. of NHL players union 1967-90, arranged Team Canada vs Soviet series (1972) and Canada Cup (1976,81, 84,87).

Dale Earnhardt (b.1952): Auto racer, 3-time NASCAR national champion (1980,86,87), yet to win Daytona 500.

Stefan Edberg (b.1966): Swedish tennis player, 2-time winner of both Wimbledon (1988,90) and Australian Open (1985,87).

Gertrude Ederle (b.1906): Swimmer, 1st woman to swim English Channel, breaking men's record by 2 hours in 1926, won 3 medals in 1924 Olympics.

Bill Elliott (b.1955): Auto racer, 2-time winner of Daytona 500 (1985,87), NASCAR national champ in 1988, won 11 races in '85.

Herb Elliott (b.1938): Australian runner, undefeated from 1958-60, ran 17 sub-4:00 miles, 3 world records, won gold medal in 1,500m of 1960 Olympics, retired at 22.

Roy Emerson (b.1936): Australian tennis player, won 12 Majors in singles—6 Australian, 2 French, 2 Wimbledon and 2 US from 1961-67.

Kornelia Ender (b.1958): East German swimmer, 1st woman to win 4 gold medals at one Olympics (1976), all in world record time.

Julius Erving (b.1950): Basketball F, in ABA (1972-76)—3-time MVP, 2-time playoff MVP, led NY Nets to 2 titles (1974-76); in NBA (1977-87)—5-time All-NBA 1st team, MVP in 1981, led Phila.76ers to title in 1983.

Phil Esposito (b.1942): Hockey C, 1st NHL player to score 100 points in a season (126 in 1969), 6-time All-NHL 1st team with Boston, 2-time MVP (1969,74), 5-time scoring champ, star of 1972 Canada-Soviet series.

Janet Evans (b.1971): Swimmer, won 3 individual gold medals (400m & 800m freestyle, 400m IM) at 1988 Olympics, 1989 Sullivan Award winner, entered 1990 with 3 world records.

Lee Evans (b.1947): Track & Field, dominant quarter-miler in world from 1966-72, world record in 400m at 1968 Olympics stood 20 years.

Chris Evert (b.1954): Tennis, No.1 player in world 5 times (1975-77,80-81), won at least 1 Grand Slam singles title every year from 1974-86, 18 Majors in all—7 French, 6 US, 3 Wimbledon and 2 Australian.

Patrick Ewing (b.1962): Basketball C, 3-time All-America, led Georgetown to 3 NCAA Finals, tourney MVP in 1984; NBA Rookie of Year with New York in 1986.

Ray Ewry (1873-1937): Track & Field, won 8 gold medals over 3 consecutive Olympics (1900,04,08); all events he won (Standing HJ,LJ and TJ) were discontinued in 1912.

Nick Faldo (b.1957): British golfer, 2-time winner of both Masters (1989-90) and British Open (1987,90).

Juan Manuel Fangio (b.1911): Argentine auto racer, 5-time Formula One world champion (1951,54-57), 24 career wins, retired in 1958.

Bob Feller (b.1918): Baseball RHP, led AL in strikeouts 7 times and wins 6 times with Cleveland, threw 3 no-hitters and 12 one-hitters, 266 career wins.

Tom Ferguson (b.1950): Rodeo, 6-time All-Around champion (1974-79), 1st cowboy to win $100,000 in one season (1978), 1st to win $1 million in career (1986).

Herve Filion (b.1940): Harness racing, 10-time Driver of the Year, all-time leader in races won with over 12,200.

Rollie Fingers (b.1946): Baseball RHP, all-time save leader with 341, won AL MVP and Cy Young awards in 1981 with Milwaukee, W.Series MVP in 1974 with Oakland.

Charles O.Finley (b.1918): Baseball owner, moved KC A's to Oakland in 1968, won 3 straight World Series from 1972-74; also owned teams in NHL and ABA.

Bobby Fischer (b.1943): Chess, only American to hold world championship (1972-75), resigned title in 1975.

Emerson Fittipaldi (b.1946): Brazilian auto racer, 2-time Formula One world champion (1972,74), won Indy 500 and overall CART title in 1989.

James (Sunny Jim) Fitzsimmons (1873-1966): Horse racing, trained horses that won over 2,275 races, including 2 Triple Crown winners—Gallant Fox in 1930 and Omaha in '35.

Larry Fleisher (1930-89): Basketball, led NBA players union from 1961-89; in that time, increased average yearly salary from $9,400 in 1967 to $600,000 without a strike.

Peggy Fleming (b.1948): Figure skating, 3-time world champion (1966-68), won Olympic gold medal in 1968.

Curt Flood (b.1938): Baseball OF, played 15 years (1956-71), lost challenge to MLB's reserve clause in Supreme Court in 1972 (see Peter Seitz).

Whitey Ford (b.1928): Baseball LHP, all-time leader in W.Series wins (10), led AL in wins 3 times, won both Cy Young and W.Series MVP in 1961 with NY Yankees.

George Foreman (b.1948): Boxer, 1968 Olympic heavyweight champion; world heavyweight champ (1973-74); returned to ring after 10-year hiatus in 1987, entered 1990 with pro record of 65-2-0 and 61 KOs.

Dick Fosbury (b.1947): Track & Field, revolutionized high jump with back-first "Fosbury Flop," won gold medal at 1968 Olympics.

Bob Foster (b.1938): Boxer, world light-heavyweight champion (1968-74); pro record 56-8-1 with 46 KOs.

The Four Horsemen—Senior backfield that led Notre Dame to national championship in 1924: HB **Jim Crowley** (1902-86), FB **Elmer Layden** (1903-73), HB **Don Miller** (1902-79) and QB **Harry Stuhldreher** (1901-65).

The Four Musketeers—French quartet that dominated men's world tennis in 1920s and '30s, winning 8 straight French singles titles (1925-32), 6 Wimbledons in a row (1924-29) and 6 consecutive Davis Cups (1927-32): **Jean Borotra** (b.1898), **Jacques Brugnon** (1895-1978), **Henry Cochet** (1901-1987), **Rene Lacoste** (b.1904).

Jimmie Foxx (1907-67): Baseball 1B, led AL in HRs 4 times and batting twice, won Triple Crown in 1933, 3-time MVP (1932-33,38) with Phila. and Boston, hit 30 HRs or more 12 years in a row, 534 career HRs.

A.J. Foyt (b.1935): Auto racer, 4-time Indy 500 winner (1961,64,67,77), 7-time USAC/CART national champ, only driver to win Indy 500, Daytona 500 (1972) and 24 Hours of LeMans (1967 with Dan Gurney).

Bill France, Sr. (b.1909): stock car pioneer and promoter, founded NASCAR in 1948, guided race circuit through formative years, built both Daytona (Fla.) International Speedway and Talladega (Ala.) Superspeedway.

Dawn Fraser (b.1937): Australian swimmer, won gold medals in 100m freestyle at 3 consecutive Olympics (1956,60,64).

Joe Frazier (b.1944): Boxer, 1964 Olympic heavyweight champion; world heavyweight champ (1970-73), fought Muhammad Ali 3 times, pro record 32-4-1 with 27 KOs.

Walt Frazier (b.1945): Basketball G, 4-time All-NBA 1st team, 7-time All-Defense 1st team, led New York to 2 NBA titles (1970,73).

Frankie Frisch (1898-1973): Baseball 2B, played on 8 NL pennant winners in 19 years with NY and St.Louis, hit .300 or better 11 years in a row (1921-31), MVP in 1931, player-manager from 1933-37.

Dan Gable (b.1948): Wrestling, 2-time NCAA champ at Iowa St., tourney MVP in 1969 (137 lbs.); won gold medal (149 lbs) at 1972 Olympics; coached Iowa to 9 straight NCAA titles (1978-86).

Eddie Gaedel (1925-61): Baseball PH, St.Louis Browns' midget whose career lasted one at bat (he walked) on Aug.19,1951.

Clarence (Bighouse) Gaines (b.1924): Basketball, entered 1990-91 season ranked 2nd on all-time college wins list with 806, trails Adolph Rupp by 69, has coached at Div.II Winston-Salem since 1947.

Lou Gehrig (1903-41): Baseball 1B, played in 2,130 consecutive games from 1923-39, led AL in RBI 5 times and HRs 3 times, drove in 100 runs or more 13 years in a row, 2-time MVP (1927,36), led NY Yankees to 7 W.Series titles.

Charlie Gehringer (b.1903): Baseball 2B, hit .300 or better 13 times, AL batting champion and MVP with Detroit in 1937.

A. Bartlett Giamatti (1938-89): Scholar and 7th commissioner of baseball, banned Pete Rose for life for betting on Major League games and associating with known gamblers and drug dealers; also served as president of Yale (1978-86) and National League (1986-89).

Althea Gibson (b. 1927): Tennis, won both Wimbledon and US championships in 1957 and '58, 1st black to play in either tourney and 1st to win each title.

Bob Gibson (b. 1935): Baseball RHP, won 20 or more games 5 times, won 2 NL Cy Young Awards (1968,70), MVP in 1968, led St. Louis to 2 W.Series titles, Series MVP twice (1964,67), 251 career wins.

Josh Gibson (1911-47): Baseball C, the "Babe Ruth of the Negro Leagues," Satchel Paige's battery mate with Pittsburgh Crawfords.

Frank Gifford (b. 1930): Football HB, 4-time All-Pro (1955-57,59), MVP in 1956, led NY Giants to 3 NL title games.

Sid Gillman (b.1911): Football innovator, coached LA Rams (1955-59) in NFL, then led LA-SD Chargers of AFL to 5 Western titles and 1 championship in the league's 1st six years.

George Gipp (1895-1920): Football FB, died of throat infection (Dec.14) 2 weeks before he made All-America (Notre Dame's 1st); rushed for 2,341 yards, scored 156 points and averaged 38 yards a punt in 4 years (1917-20).

Pancho Gonzalez (b.1928): Tennis, won consecutive US Championships in 1947-48 before turning pro at 21, dominated pro tour from 1950-61; in 1969 at age 41, played longest Wimbledon match ever (5:12) beating Charlie Pasarell 22-24,1-6,16-14,6-3,11-9.

Shane Gould (b.1956): Australian swimmer, set world records in 5 different freestyle events between July,1971 and Jan,1972; won 3 gold medals, a silver and bronze in 1972 Olympics then retired at age 16.

Steffi Graf (b.1969): West German tennis player, won Grand Slam in 1989 at age 19, No.1 player in world three times (1987-89).

Gillis Grafstrom (1894-1938): Swedish figure skater, 3-time world champ, won 3 straight gold medals then a silver in 4 Olympics (1920,24,28,32).

Otto Graham (b.1921): Football QB and basketball All-America at Northwestern; in pro ball, led Cleve. Browns to 7 league titles in 10 years, winning 4 AAFC championships (1946-50) and 3 NFL (1950,54-55), 5-time All-Pro, 2-time NFL MVP (1953,55).

Red Grange (b.1903): Football HB, 3-time All-America at Illinois who brought 1st huge crowds to pro football when he signed with Chicago in 1925; formed 1st AFL with manager C.C.Pyle in 1926, but league folded and he returned to NFL.

Hank Greenberg (1911-86): Baseball 1B, led AL in HRs and RBI 4 times each, 2-time MVP (1935,40) with Detroit, 331 career HRs.

Joe Greene (b.1946): Football DT, 5-time All-Pro (1972-74,77,79), led Pittsburgh to 4 Super Bowl titles.

Wayne Gretzky (b.1961): Hockey C, 9-time regular season MVP (1979-87,89), 8-time scoring champ, has scored 200 points or more in a season 4 times, led Edmonton to 4 Stanley Cups (1984-85,87-88), 2-time playoff MVP (1985,88), traded to LA Kings (Aug.9, 1988), all-time NHL leader in points (1,979) and assists (1,302).

Bob Griese (b.1945): Football QB, 2-time All-Pro (1971,77), led Miami to undefeated season (17-0) in 1972 and consecutive Super Bowl titles (1973-74).

Archie Griffin (b.1954): Football RB, only college player to win two Heisman Trophies (1974-75), rushed for 5,177 yards in career at Ohio St.

Emile Griffith (b.1938): Boxer, world welterweight champion (1961,62-63,63-65), world middleweight champ (1966-67,67-68), pro record 85-24-2 with 23 KOs.

Florence Griffith Joyner (b.1959): Track & Field, set world records in 100 and 200 meters in 1988, won 3 gold medals at '88 Olympics (100m,200m,4x100 relay).

Lefty Grove (1900-75): Baseball LHP, won 20 or more games 8 times, led AL in ERA 9 times and strikeouts 7 times, 31-4 record and MVP in 1931 with Phila., 300 career wins.

Lou Groza (b.1924): Football T-PK, 6-time All-Pro, played in 13 championship games for Cleveland from 1946-67, kicked winning field goal in 1950 NFL title game, 1,608 career points (1,349 in NFL).

Tony Gwynn (b.1960): Baseball OF, entered 1990 season with 4 NL batting titles (1984,87-89) at San Diego and .332 career average.

Harvey Haddix (b.1925): Baseball LHP, pitched 12 perfect innings for Pittsburgh but lost to Milwaukee in the 13th, 1-0 (May 26,1959).

Walter Hagen (1892-1969): Pro golf pioneer, won 2 US Opens (1914,19), 4 British Opens (1922,24,28-29), 5 PGA Championships (1921,24-27) and 5 Western Opens; US Ryder Cup captain 6 times.

Marvin Hagler (b.1954): Boxer, world middleweight champion 1980-87; pro record 62-3-2 with 52 KOs.

George Halas (1895-1983): Football pioneer, MVP in 1919 Rose Bowl; player-coach-owner of Chicago Bears from 1920-83, signed Red Grange in 1925, coached Bears for 40 seasons and won 7 NFL titles (1932-33,40-41,43,46,63), all-time leader in career wins (325).

Dorothy Hamill (b.1956): Figure skater, won Olympic gold medal and world championship in 1976.

Scott Hamilton (b.1958): Figure skater, 4-time world champion (1981-84), won gold medal at 1984 Olympics.

Franco Harris (b.1950): Football RB, ran for over 1,000 yards a season 8 times, rushed for 12,120 yards in 13 years, led Pittsburgh to 4 Super Bowl titles.

Bill Hartack (b.1932): Jockey, won Kentucky Derby 5 times (1957,60,62,64,69), Preakness 3 times (1956,64,69), but the Belmont only once (1960).

Doug Harvey (1924-90): Hockey D, 10-time All-NHL 1st team, won Norris Trophy 7 times (1955-58,60-62), led Montreal to 6 Stanley Cups.

Billy Haughton (1923-86): Harness racing, 4-time winner of Hambletonian, trainer-driver of one Pacing Triple Crown winner (1968), winner of 4,910 races in career.

John Havlicek (b.1940): Basketball, played in 3 NCAA finals at Ohio St.(1960-62); led Boston to 8 NBA titles (1963-66,68-69,74,76), playoff MVP in 1974; 4-time All-NBA 1st team.

Bob Hayes (b.1942): Track & Field/Football, won gold medal in 100m at 1964 Olympics, All-Pro SE for Dallas in 1966, convicted of drug trafficking in 1979 and served 18 months of a 5-year sentence.

Woody Hayes (1913-87): Football, coached Ohio St. to 3 national titles (1954,57,68) and 4 Rose Bowl victories, 238 career wins.

Eric Heiden (b.1958): Speed skater, 3-time overall world champion (1977-79), won all 5 men's gold medals at 1980 Olympics setting new records in each.

Mel Hein (b.1909): Football C, NFL All-Pro 8 straight years (1933-40), MVP in 1938 with NY Giants, didn't miss a game in 15 seasons.

John W.Heisman (1869-1936): Football, coached at 9 colleges from 1892-1927, won 185 games, Dir.of Athletics at Downtown Athletic Club in NYC (1928-36), DAC named Heisman Trophy after him.

Carol Heiss (b.1940): Figure skater, 5-time world champion (1956-60), won Olympic silver medal in 1956, gold in '60, married 1956 men's gold medalist Hayes Jenkins.

Robert Helmick (b.1937): president of US Olympic Committee since 1984, one of two American delegates to IOC.

Rickey Henderson (b.1958): Baseball OF, set single season base stealing record of 130 in 1982, has led AL in steals 9 times, entered 1990 with 871—just 67 behind all-time leader Lou Brock.

Sonja Henie (1912-69): Norwegian figure skater, 10-time world champion (1927-36), won 3 consecutive Olympic gold medals (1928,32,36).

Graham Hill (1929-75): British auto racer, 2-time Formula One world champion (1962,68), won Indy 500 in 1966, killed in plane crash.

Phil Hill (b.1927): Auto racer, first US driver to win Formula One championship (1961), 3 career wins (1958-64).

Edmund Hillary (b.1919): New Zealand explorer, one of first 2 men (with Sherpa guide Tenzing Norgay) to reach the top of Mt. Everest and return (May 29,1953).

Max Hirsch (1880-1969): Horse racing, trained 1,933 winners from 1908-68, won Triple Crown with Assault in 1946.

Tommy Hitchcock (1900-44): Polo, world class player at 20, achieved 10-goal rating 18 times from 1922-40.

Ben Hogan (b.1912): Golfer, 4-time PGA Player of Year; won 4 US Opens, 2 Masters, 2 PGA and 1 British Open between 1946-53; won 3 of 4 Majors (Masters, US Open, British Open) in 1953; 62 career wins.

Eleanor Holm (b.1913): Swimmer, won gold medal in 100m backstroke at 1932 Olympics, thrown off '36 US team for drinking champagne in public and shooting craps on boat to Germany.

Nat Holman (b.1896): Basketball pioneer, played pro with Original Celtics (1920-28); coached CCNY to both NCAA and NIT titles in 1950 (a year later, several of his players were caught up in a point-shaving scandal); 423 career wins.

Larry Holmes (b.1949): Boxer, heavyweight champion (WBC or IBF) from 1978-85, defended title 21 times, pro record 48-3 with 34 KOs.

Willie Hoppe (1887-1959): Billiards, dominant player from 1904-52; won over 50 world championship matches at 18.1 balkline, 18.2 balkline and 3-cushion billiards.

Rogers Hornsby (1896-1963): Baseball 2B, hit .400 three times, including .424 in 1924, led NL in batting 7 times, 2-time MVP (1925,29) with St. Louis, career average of .358 over 23 years is all-time highest.

Paul Hornung (b.1935): Football HB-PK, only Heisman Trophy winner to play for losing team (2-8 Notre Dame in 1956); 3-time NFL scoring leader (1959-61) at Green Bay, 176 points in 1960 all-time record, MVP in 1961.

Gordie Howe (b.1928): Hockey RW, played 32 seasons in NHL and WHA from 1946-80, led NHL in scoring 6 times, All-NHL 1st team 12 times, MVP 6 times in NHL (1952-53,57-58,60,63) with Detroit and once in WHA (1974) with Houston, all-time NHL leader in goals (801) and 2nd in points (1,850).

Cal Hubbard (1900-77): Member of college football, pro football and baseball halls of fame; 9 years in NFL, 4-time All-Pro at end and tackle; AL umpire for 15 years (1936-51).

Carl Hubbell (1903-88): Baseball LHP, led NL in wins and ERA 3 times each, 2-time MVP (1933,36) with NY Giants; fanned Ruth, Gehrig, Foxx, Simmons and Cronin in succession in 1934 All-Star Game, 253 career wins.

Miller Huggins (1880-1929): Baseball, managed NY Yankees to 6 pennants and 3 W.Series titles from 1921-27.

Bobby Hull (b.1939): Hockey LW, led NHL in scoring 3 times, 2-time MVP (1965-66) with Chicago, All-NHL first team 10 times; jumped to WHA in 1972, 2-time MVP there (1973,75) with Winnipeg, scored 913 goals in both leagues.

Jim (Catfish) Hunter (b.1946): Baseball RHP, won 20 games or more 5 times (1971-75), played on 5 W.Series winners with Oakland, NY Yankees; threw perfect game in 1968, won Cy Young Award in '74.

Don Hutson (b.1913): Football E-PK, led NFL in receptions 8 times and interceptions once, 9-time All-Pro (1936, 38-45) for Green Bay.

Hank Iba (b.1904): Basketball, coached Oklahoma A&M to 2 straight NCAA titles (1945-46), 767 career wins in 41 years; coached US Olympic team to 2 gold medals (1964,68) but lost to Soviets in controversial '72 final.

Punch Imlach (1918-1987): Hockey, directed Toronto to 4 Stanley Cups (1962-64,67) in 11 seasons as GM-coach.

Bo Jackson (b.1962): Baseball OF and Football RB, won Heisman Trophy in 1985 and MVP of baseball All-Star Game in 1989; starter for both baseball's KC Royals and NFL's LA Raiders in 1988 and '89.

Joe Jackson (1887-1951): Baseball OF, hit .300 or better 11 times, career average of .356 (see Black Sox).

Reggie Jackson (b.1946): Baseball OF, led AL in HRs 4 times, MVP in 1973, played on 5 W.Series winners with Oakland, NY Yankees; 1977 Series MVP with 5 HRs, 563 career HRs, all-time strikeout leader (2,597).

Helen Jacobs (b.1908): Tennis, 4-time winner of US Championship (1932-35), Wimbledon winner in 1936; lost 4 Wimbledon finals to arch-rival Helen Wills Moody.

Jim Jacobs (1930-88): Handball/Boxing, won 12 US Handball titles (6 singles and 6 doubles) from 1955-68; also managed 4 world champion boxers, including Mike Tyson (from 1985-88).

James J. Jeffries (1875-1953): Boxer, world heavyweight champion (1899-1905); retired undefeated but came back to fight Jack Johnson in 1910 and lost (KO,15th).

David Jenkins (b.1936): Figure skater, brother of Hayes, 3-time world champion (1957-59), won gold medal at 1960 Olympics.

Hayes Jenkins (b.1933): Figure skater, 4-time world champion (1953-56), won gold medal at 1956 Olympics, married 1960 women's gold medalist Carol Heiss.

Bruce Jenner (b.1949): Track & Field, won gold medal in 1976 Olympic decathlon.

Ben Johnson (b.1961): Canadian sprinter, set 100m world record (9.83) at 1987 World Championships; won 100m at 1988 Olympics, but flunked drug test and forfeited gold medal; 1987 world record revoked in '89 for admitted steroid use.

Earvin (Magic) Johnson (b.1959): Basketball G, led Mich.St. to NCAA title in 1979, tourney MVP; All-NBA 1st team 8 times, has led NBA in assists 4 times, 3-time MVP (1987,89-90), has led LA Lakers to 5 NBA titles, 3-time playoff MVP (1980,82,87).

Jack Johnson (1878-1946): Boxer, 1st black world heavyweight champion (1908-15), pro record 78-8-12 with 45 KOs.

Rafer Johnson (b.1935): Track & Field, won silver medal in 1956 Olympic decathlon and gold medal in 1960.

Walter Johnson (1887-1946): Baseball RHP, won 20 games or more 10 straight years; led AL in ERA 5 times, wins 6 times and strikeouts 12 times, twice MVP (1913, 24) with Washington; all-time leader in shutouts (113) and 2nd in wins (416).

Ben A. Jones (1882-1961): Horse racing, Calumet Farm trainer (1939-47), saddled 6 Kentucky Derby champions and 2 Triple Crown winners—Whirlaway in 1941 and Citation in '48.

Bobby Jones (1902-71): Won US and British Opens plus US and British Amateurs in 1930 to become golf's only Grand Slam winner ever; from 1922-30, won 4 US Opens, 5 US Amateurs, 3 British Opens, and played in 6 Walker Cups; founded Masters tournament in 1934.

Deacon Jones (b. 1938): Football DE, 5-time All-Pro (1965-69) with LA Rams.

Michael Jordan (b. 1933): Basketball G, College Player of Year in 1984; has led NBA in scoring 4 times (1987-90) with Chicago, 4-time All NBA 1st team, MVP in 1988.

Jackie Joyner-Kersee (b. 1962): Track & Field, entered 1989 as world record holder in heptathlon (7,291 pts); won gold medals in heptathlon and long jump at 1988 Olympics.

Alberto Juantorena (b. 1951): Cuban runner, won both 400m and 800m gold medals at 1976 Olympics.

Sonny Jurgensen (b.1934): Football QB, played 18 seasons with Phila. and Wash., led NFL in passing twice (1967,69), All-Pro in 1961, 255 career TD passes.

Duke Kahanamoku (1890-1968): Swimmer, won 3 gold medals and 2 silver over 3 Olympics (1912,20,24); also surfing pioneer.

Al Kaline (b.1934): Baseball, youngest player (20) to win batting title (led AL with .340 in 1955), had 3,007 hits, 399 HRs in 22 years with Detroit.

Anatoly Karpov (b.1951): Chess, Soviet world champion, 1975-85.

Gary Kasparov (b.1963): Chess, Soviet world champion since 1985; defeated Karpov for title.

Kip Keino (b.1940): Kenyan runner, won one gold medal in 1,500m at 1968 Olympics and another in steeplechase at 1972 Games.

Harmon Killebrew (b.1936): Baseball 3B-1B, led AL in HRs 6 times and RBI 4 times, MVP in 1969 with Minnesota, 573 career HRs.

Jean Claude Killy (b.1943): French alpine skier, 2-time World Cup champion (1967-68), won 3 gold medals 1968 Olympics.

Ralph Kiner (b.1922): Baseball OF, led NL in home runs 7 straight years (1946-52) with Pittsburgh, 369 career HRs.

Billie Jean King (b.1943): Tennis, Wimbledon singles champ 6 times, US champ 4 times, first woman athlete to earn $100,000 in one year (1971).

Bob Knight (b.1940): Basketball, has coached Indiana to 3 NCAA titles (1976,81,87); coached 1984 US Olympic team to gold.

Olga Korbut (b.1955): Soviet gymnast, 3 gold medals 1972 Olympics, first to perform back somersault on balance beam.

Sandy Koufax (b.1935): Baseball LHP, led NL in strikeouts 4 times and ERA 5 straight years, won 3 Cy Young Awards (1963,65,66) with LA Dodgers, MVP in 1963, 2-time W.Series MVP (1963,65); pitched 1 perfect game and 3 other no-hitters.

Alvin Kraenzlein (1876-1928): Track & Field, won 4 individual gold medals in 1900 Olympics (60m,long jump, and 110m & 200m hurdles).

Jack Kramer (b.1921): Tennis, Wimbledon singles champ 1947, US champ 1946-47; promoter and Open pioneer.

Ingrid Kristiansen (b.1956): Norwegian runner, 2-time Boston Marathon winner (1986,89), world record holder in 5,000m, 10,000m and marathon.

Bob Kurland (b.1924): Basketball C, 3-time All-America (1944-46), led Okla.A&M to 2 NCAA titles (1945-46) and US to 2 Olympic gold medals (1948,52), did not turn pro.

Marion Ladewig (b.1914): named Woman Bowler of the Year 9 times, (1950-54,57-59,63).

Guy Lafleur (b.1951): Hockey RW, has led NHL in scoring 3 times (1975-78), 2-time MVP (1977-78), played for 5 Stanley Cup winners in Montreal, playoff MVP in 1977; returned to NHL as player in 1988 after election to Hall of Fame.

Napoleon Lajoie (1875-1959): Baseball 2B, led AL in batting 4 times (1901-04), hit .422 in 1901, had 3,251 career hits.

Jack Lambert (b.1952): Football LB, 6-time All-Pro (1975-76,79-82), led Pittsburgh to 4 Super Bowl titles.

Kenesaw Mountain Landis (1866-1944): Baseball's first commissioner (1920-44), banned Black Sox for life.

Tom Landry (b.1924): Football, coached Dallas for 29 years (1960-88), won 2 Super Bowls (1972,78), 271 career wins.

Steve Largent (b.1954): Football WR, retired in 1989 after 14 years with Seattle as all-time NFL leader in passes caught (819) and TD passes caught (100).

Don Larson (b.1929): Baseball RHP, pitched only perfect game in W.Series history—NY Yankees 2, Brooklyn 0 (Oct.8,1956), Series MVP that year.

Larissa Latynina (b.1934): Soviet gymnast, won total of 18 medals, (9 gold) in 3 Olympics (1956,60,64).

Nikki Lauda (b.1949): Austrian auto racer, 3-time world Formula 1 champion (1975,77,84), 25 career wins from 1971-85.

Rod Laver (b.1938): Australian tennis player, only player to win Grand Slam twice (1962,69), Wimbledon champion 4 times, 1st to earn $1 million in prize money.

Andrea Mead Lawrence (b.1932): Alpine skier, won 2 gold medals at 1952 Olympics.

Bobby Layne (1926-86): Football QB, college star at Texas, led Detroit to 2 straight NFL titles (1952-53).

Frank Leahy (1908-73): Football, coached Notre Dame to four national titles (1943,46-47,49), career record of 107-13-9.

Sammy Lee (b.1920): US diver, 1st to repeat as Olympic diving champ (1948,52).

Greg LeMond (b.1962): Cyclist, 3-time Tour de France winner (1986,89-90), only American to win the event.

Mario Lemieux (b.1965): Hockey C, has led NHL in scoring twice (1988-89), 2-time All-NHL 1st team, MVP in 1988 with Pittsburgh.

Ivan Lendl (b.1960): Tennis, No.1 player in the world 4 times (1985-87,89), has won both French and US Opens 3 times.

Suzanne Lenglen (1899-1938): French tennis player, dominated women's tennis from 1919-26, won both Wimbledon and French singles titles 6 times.

Sugar Ray Leonard (b.1956): Boxer, light welterweight Olympic champ (1976), won world welterweight title 1979, four more titles since; entered 1990 with pro record of 36-1-1 and 25 KOs.

Carl Lewis (b.1961): Track & Field, won 4 gold medals in 1984 Olympics (100m,200m,400m relay and long jump), 2 more (100m, long jump) in 1988.

Sonny Liston (1932-70): Boxer, heavyweight champ (1962-64), lost title to Muhammad Ali (then Cassius Clay) in 1964; pro record 50-4 with 39 KOs.

Vince Lombardi (1913-70): Football, coached Green Bay to 5 NFL titles, won first 2 Super Bowls (1967-68).

Johnny Longden (b.1907): Jockey, first to win 6,000 races, rode Count Fleet to Triple Crown in 1943.

Nancy Lopez (b.1957): Golfer, 4-time LPGA Player of the Year (1978-79,85,88), reached Hall of Fame by age 30.

Greg Louganis (b.1960): US diver, won platform and springboard gold medals at both 1984 and '88 Olympics.

Joe Louis (1914-81): Boxer, world heavyweight champion (1937-49); reign of 11 years, 8 months longest in division history; pro record 63-3 with 49 KOs.

Sid Luckman (b.1916): Football QB, 6-time All-Pro, led Chicago Bears to 4 NFL titles (1940-41,43,46), MVP in 1943.

Hank Luisetti (b. 1916): Basketball F, 3-time All-America at Stanford (1935-38), revolutionized game with one-handed shot.

Johnny Lujack (b.1925): Football QB, led Notre Dame to three national titles (1943,46-47), won Heisman Trophy in 1947.

Larry MacPhail (1890-1975): Baseball executive, introduced major leagues to night games at Cincinnati on May 24,1935.

Connie Mack (1862-1956): Baseball owner, managed Phila.A's until he was 87 (1901-50), won 9 AL pennants and 5 W.Series (1910-11,13,29-30).

John Madden (b.1936): Football, won 112 games and a Super Bowl as coach of the Oakland Raiders, and has won 7 Emmy Awards as television analyst with CBS.

Larry Mahan (b.1943): Rodeo, 6-time All-Around Cowboy (1966-70,73).

Phil Mahre (b.1957): Alpine skier, 3-time World Cup overall champ (1981-83), finished 1-2 with twin brother Steve in 1984 Olympic slalom.

Moses Malone (b.1955): Basketball C, has led NBA in rebounding 6 times, 4-time All-NBA 1st team, 3-time NBA MVP (1979,82-83), playoff MVP with Phila. in 1983.

Mickey Mantle (b.1931): Baseball OF, led AL in home runs 4 times, won Triple Crown in 1956, 3-time MVP (1956-57,62), 536 career HRs, played on 7 W.Series winners with NY Yankees.

Pete Maravich (1948-88): Basketball, NCAA scoring leader 3 times (1968-70), averaged 44.2 points a game over career, Player of Year in 1970; NBA scoring champ in 1977.

Alice Marble (b.1913): Tennis, 4-time US champion (1936,38-40), won Wimbledon in 1939; swept US singles, doubles and mixed doubles from 1938-40.

Gino Marchetti (b.1927): Football DE, 8-time NFL All-Pro (1957-64) with Baltimore Colts.

Rocky Marciano (1923-69): Boxer, heavyweight champion (1952-56), retired undefeated, pro record of 49-0 with 43 KOs.

Juan Marichal (b.1937): Baseball RHP, won 21 or more games 6 times with S.F. Giants, 243 career wins.

Dan Marino (b.1961): Football QB, set NFL single-season records for TD passes (48) and passing yards (5,084) with Miami in 1984.

Roger Maris (1934-85): Baseball OF, broke Babe Ruth's single season HR record with 61 in 1961, 2-time AL MVP (1960-61) with NY Yankees.

Eddie Mathews (b.1931): Baseball 3B, led NL in HRs twice (1953,59), hit 30 or more home runs 9 straight years, 512 career HRs.

Christy Mathewson (1880-1925): Baseball RHP, won 22 or more games 12 straight years (1903-14), 373 career wins, pitched 3 shutouts in 1905 W.Series.

Bob Mathias (b.1930): Track & Field, first 2-time Olympic decathlon champion (1948,52).

Willie Mays (b.1931): Baseball OF, led NL in HRs and stolen bases 4 times each, 2-time MVP (1954,65) with NY-SF Giants, played in 24 All-Star games, 660 HRs and 3,283 hits in career.

Joe McCarthy (1887-1978): Baseball, managed NY Yankees to 8 pennants and 7 W.Series titles (1931-46).

Mark McCormick (b.1930): founder and CEO of International Management Group, the sports management conglomerate.

Pat McCormick (b.1930): US diver, won women's platform and springboard gold medals in both 1952 and '56 Olympics.

Willie McCovey (b.1938): led NL in HRs 3 times and RBI twice, MVP in 1969 with SF, 521 career HRs.

Terry McDermott (b.1940): Speed skater, first place in Men's 500m was only gold medal won by an American at 1964 Winter Olympics.

John McEnroe (b.1959): Tennis, No.1 player in the world from 1981-84, 4-time US Open singles champ (1979-81,84), 3-time Wimbledon champ (1981,83-84), played on 4 Davis Cup winners (1978-79,81-82).

John McGraw (1873-1934): Baseball, managed NY Giants to 10 NL pennants and 3 W.Series titles in 30 years, 4,879 career wins.

Jim McKay (b.1921): Radio-TV, host and commentator of ABC's Olympic coverage and "Wide World of Sports" show since 1961, 11-time Emmy winner, also given Peabody Award in 1988 and Life Achievement Emmy in 1990.

John McKay (b.1923): Football, coached Southern Cal to 3 national titles (1962,67,72), won Rose Bowl 5 times.

Tamara McKinney (b.1962): Alpine skier, only American woman to win World Cup overall title (1983).

Denny McLain (b.1944): Baseball RHP, last pitcher to win 30 games, (1968), 2-time Cy Young winner (1968-69) with Detroit; convicted of racketeering, extortion and drug possession in 1985, served 29 months of 25-year jail term, sentence overturned when court ruled he had not received a fair trial.

Debbie Meyer (b.1952): Swimmer, 1st swimmer to win 3 individual gold medals at one Olympics (1968).

George Mikan (b.1924): Basketball C, 3-time All-America (1944-46), led DePaul to NIT title (1945); led Minneapolis Lakers to 5 NBA titles in 6 years (1949-54). Commissioner of ABA (1967-69).

Stan Mikita (b.1940): Hockey C, led NHL in scoring 4 times, won both MVP and Lady Byng awards in 1967 and '68 with Chicago.

Cheryl Miller (b.1964): Basketball, 3-time college Player of Year (1984-86), led USC to NCAA title and US to Olympic gold medal in 1984.

Del Miller (b.1913): Harness racing—driver, trainer, owner, breeder, seller and track owner. Has driven over 2,400 winners since 1939.

Marvin Miller (b.1917): Baseball, executive dir. of Players' Assn. from 1966-82, increased average salary from $19,000 to over $240,000, led 13-day strike in 1972 and 50-day walkout in '81.

Billy Mills (b.1938): Track & Field, upset winner of 10,000m gold medal at 1964 Olympics.

Joe Montana (b.1956): Football QB, led Notre Dame to national title in 1977; has since led San Francisco to 4 Super Bowls (1982,85,89-90), NFL MVP in 1989, only 3-time Super Bowl MVP, QB rating of 94.0 all-time highest.

Helen Wills Moody (b.1905): Tennis, won 8 Wimbledon singles titles, 7 US and 4 French from 1923-38.

Archie Moore (b.1913): Boxer, world light-heavyweight champion (1952-60), pro record 199-26-8 with 145 KOs.

Howie Morenz (1902-37): Hockey C, 3-time NHL MVP (1928,31-32), led Montreal Canadiens to 3 Stanley Cups, voted Outstanding Player of the Half-Century in 1950.

Joe Morgan (b.1943): Baseball 2B, led NL in walks 4 times, regular season MVP both years he led Cincinnati to W.Series titles (1975-76).

Bobby Morrow (b.1935): Track & Field, won 3 gold medals at 1956 Olympics (100m,200m and 4x400m relay).

Willie Mosconi (b.1913): Pocket Billiards, 14-time world champion from 1941-57.

Edwin Moses (b.1955): Track & Field, won 400m hurdles at 1976 and '84 Olympics, bronze medal in '88, also winner of 122 consecutive races from 1977-87.

Stirling Moss (b.1929): Auto racer, won 194 of 466 career races and 16 Formula One events, but was never world champion.

Marion Motley (b.1920): Football FB, all-time leading AAFC rusher, rushed for over 4,700 yards and 31 TDs for Cleve.Browns (1946-53).

Shirley Muldowney (b.1940): Drag racer, 3-time Top Fuel champion (1977,80,82), first woman to win title.

Dale Murphy (b.1956): Baseball OF, led NL in HRs and RBI twice each, 2-time MVP (1982-83) with Atlanta.

Jim Murray (b.1919): sports columnist for *LA Times* since 1961, 14-time Sportswriter of the Year, won Pulitzer Prize for commentary in 1990.

Stan Musial (b.1920): Baseball OF-1B, led NL in batting 7 times, 3-time MVP (1943,46,48) with St. Louis, played in 24 All-Star games, had 3,630 career hits and .331 average.

John Naber (b.1956): Swimmer, won 4 gold medals and a silver in 1976 Olympics.

Bronko Nagurski (1908-90): Football FB-T, All-America at Minnesota (1929), All-Pro with Chicago Bears (1932-34), charter member of both college and pro halls of fame.

James Naismith (1861-1939): Canadian physical education instructor who invented basketball in 1891 at the YMCA Training School (now Springfield College) in Springfield, Mass.

Joe Namath (b.1943): Football QB, signed for unheard of $400,000 as rookie with AFL's NY Jets in 1965, 2-time All-AFL (1968-69) and All-NFL (1972), led Jets to Super Bowl title as MVP in '69.

Ilie Nastase (b.1946): Rumanian tennis player, No.1 in the world twice (1972-73), won US (1972) and French (1973) Opens.

Martina Navratilova (b.1956): Tennis, all-time money winner, No.1 player in the world 7 times (1978-79,82-86), won her record 9th Wimbledon singles title in 1990; has also won 4 US, 3 Australian and 2 French.

Byron Nelson (b.1912): Golfer, won Masters and PGA twice, US Open once; also won 11 consecutive tournaments (19 overall) in 1945.

Lindsey Nelson (b.1919): Radio-TV, all-purpose play-by-play broadcaster for CBS, NBC and others, 4-time Sportscaster of the Year (1959-62), voice of Cotton Bowl for 25 years and N.Y. Mets from 1962-78.

Ernie Nevers (1903-76): Football FB, earned 11 letters in four sports at Stanford; played pro football, baseball and basketball, scored 40 points for Chicago Cardinals in one NFL game (1929).

John Newcombe (b.1943): Australian tennis player, No.1 player in world 3 times (1967,70-71), won Wimbledon 3 times, US twice.

Jack Nicklaus (b.1940): Golfer, winner of 20 major tournaments, including 6 Masters, 5 PGAs, 4 US Opens and 3 British Opens; PGA Player of the Year 5 times (1967,72-73,75-76).

Chuck Noll (b.1931): Football, coached Pittsburgh to 4 Super Bowl titles (1975-76,79-80), entered 1990 regular season with 193 wins (including playoffs).

Leo Nomellini (b.1924): Football DT, played in 174 consecutive regular season games over 14 seasons with San Francisco (1950-63).

James D. Norris (1906-66): boxing promoter and NHL owner, president of International Boxing Club from 1949 until US Supreme Court ordered its break-up (for anti-trust violations) in 1958; only NHL owner to win Stanley Cups in two cities—Detroit (1936-37,43) and Chicago (1961).

Paavo Nurmi (1897-1973): Finnish runner, won 9 gold medals (6 individual) in 1920,'24 and'28 Olympics; from 1921-31 broke 23 world outdoor records in events ranging from 1,500 to 20,000 meters.

Parry O'Brien (b.1932): Track & field, in 4 consecutive Olympics, won two gold medals, a silver and placed 4th in the shot put (1952-64).

Al Oerter (b.1936): Track & Field, won 4 consecutive Olympic gold medals in discus (1956-68).

Sadaharu Oh (b.1940): Baseball 1B, led Japan League in HRs 15 times, 9-time MVP for Tokyo Giants, hit 868 HRs in 22 years.

Barney Oldfield (1878-1946): Auto racing pioneer, drove cars built by Henry Ford, first man to drive car a mile per minute (1903).

Walter O'Malley (1903-79): Baseball owner, moved Brooklyn Dodgers to Los Angeles after 1957 season.

Bobby Orr (b.1948) Hockey D, 8-time Norris Trophy winner as best defenseman, led NHL in scoring twice and assists 5 times, All-NHL 1st team 8 times, regular season MVP 3 times (1970-72), playoff MVP twice (1970,72) with Boston.

Mel Ott (1909-58): Baseball OF, joined NY Giants at age 16, led NL in HRs 6 times, had 511 HRs and 1,860 RBI in 22 years.

Kristin Otto (b.1966): East German swimmer, 1st woman to win 6 gold medals (4 individual) at one Olympics (1988).

Francis Ouimet (1893-1967): Golfer, won 1913 US Open as 20-year-old amateur playing on Brookline, Mass. course where he used to caddie; won US Amateur twice, 8-time Walker Cup player.

Jesse Owens (1913-80): Track & Field, won 4 gold medals (100m,200m,4x400 relay and long jump) at 1936 Olympics.

Satchel Paige (1906-82): Baseball RHP, pitched 55 career no-hitters in Negro Leagues, entered Major Leagues in 1948 at age 42.

Arnold Palmer (b.1929): Golfer, winner of 4 Masters, 2 British Opens and 1 US Open, PGA Player of the Year twice (1960,62), first player to earn over $1 million in career (1968).

Jim Palmer (b.1945): Baseball RHP, 3-time Cy Young Award winner (1973,75-76), won 20 or more games 8 times with Baltimore.

Bernie Parent (b.1945): Hockey G, led Philadelphia Flyers to 2 Stanley Cups as playoff MVP (1974,75), 2-time Vezina Trophy winner.

Joe Paterno (b.1926): Football, has coached Penn State to 2 national titles (1982,85) in 24 years; entered 1990 regular season with 220 career wins.

Lester Patrick (1883-1960): Pro hockey pioneer as player, coach and manager for 43 years, managed NY Rangers to their only Stanley Cups (1928,33,40).

Floyd Patterson (b.1935): Boxer, Olympic middleweight champ in 1952, world heavyweight champion (1956-59,60-62), 1st to regain heavyweight crown; pro record 55-8-1 with 40 KOs.

Walter Payton (b.1954): Football RB, NFL's all-time leading rusher with 16,726 yards, scored 109 TDs, All-Pro 7 times with Chicago, MVP in 1977.

Pele' (b.1940) Brazilian soccer F, given name—Edson Arantes do Nascimento; led Brazil to 3 World Cup titles (1958,62,70), came to US in 1975 to play for NY Cosmos in NASL, scored 1,281 goals in 22 years.

Willie Pep (b.1922): Boxer, 2-time world featherweight champion (1942-48,49-50); pro record 230-11-1 with 65 KOs.

Fred Perry (b.1909): British tennis player, 3-time Wimbledon champ (1934-36), last native to win All-England men's title.

Gaylord Perry (b.1938): Baseball RHP, won Cy Young Awards in each league, 314 wins and 3,534 strikeouts in 22 years.

Bob Pettit (b.1932): Basketball F, All-NBA 1st team 10 times (1955-64), 2-time MVP (1956,59) with St. Louis Hawks, first player to score 20,000 points.

Richard Petty (b.1937): Auto racer, 7-time winner of Daytona 500, 7-time NASCAR national champ (1964, 67,71-72,74-75,79), first stock car driver to win $1 million in career.

Laffit Pincay, Jr. (b.1946): Jockey, 5-time Eclipse award winner (1971-73-74,79,85), trails only Shoemaker in career wins, winner of 3 Belmonts and 1 Kentucky Derby (aboard Swale in 1984).

Nelson Piquet (b.1952): Brazilian auto racer, 3-time Formula One world champion (1981,83,87), entered 1990 win 20 career wins.

Jacques Plante (1929-86): Hockey G, led Montreal to 6 Stanley Cups (1953,56-60), won 7 Vezina Trophies, MVP in 1962, first goalie to regularly wear a mask.

Gary Player (b.1936): South African golfer, 3-time winner of Masters and British Open, also won 2 PGAs, a US Open and 2 US Senior Opens.

Jim Plunkett (b.1947): Football QB, Heisman Trophy winner in 1970, led Oakland-LA Raiders to Super Bowl wins in 1981 and '84, MVP in '81.

Maurice Podoloff (1890-85): Basketball, engineered merger of Basketball Assn. of America and National Basketball League into NBA in 1949, NBA commissioner (1949-63), league MVP trophy named after him.

Sam Pollock (b.1925): Hockey GM, managed Montreal to 9 Stanley Cups in 14 years (1965-78).

Denis Potvin (b.1953): Hockey D, won Norris Trophy 3 times (1976,78-79), 5-time All-NHL 1st-team, led NY Islanders to 4 Stanley Cups.

Annemarie Moser Proell (b.1953): Austrian alpine skier, won World Cup overall title 6 times (1971-75,79), won Downhill in 1980 Olympics.

Alain Prost (b.1955): French auto racer, 3-time Formula One world champion (1985-86,89), entered 1990 with 39 career wins.

Willis Reed (b.1942): Basketball C, led NY Knicks to NBA titles in 1970 and '73, playoff MVP both years, regular season MVP 1970.

Mary Lou Retton (b.1968): Gymnast, won gold medal in women's All-Around at the 1984 Olympics, also won a silver and 2 bronzes.

Grantland Rice (1880-54): first celebrated American sportswriter, chronicled the Golden Age of Sport in 1920s, immortalized Notre Dame's ''Four Horsemen.''

Jerry Rice (b.1962): Football WR, 4-time All-Pro, regular season MVP in 1987 and Super Bowl MVP in 1989 with San Francisco.

Maurice Richard (b.1921): Hockey RW, 8-time NHL 1st team All-Star, MVP in 1947, 1st to score 50 goals in one season (1945), 544 career goals, played on 8 Stanley Cup winners in Montreal.

Bob Richards (b.1926): Track & Field, only 2-time Olympic gold medalist in pole vault (1952,56).

Tex Rickard (1870-1929): Promoter who handled boxing's first $1 million gate (Dempsey vs Carpentier in 1921), built Madison Square Garden in 1925.

Branch Rickey (1881-1965): In baseball 59 years as player, manager and GM, made Jackie Robinson 1st black player in Majors (1947).

Bobby Riggs (b.1918): Tennis, won Wimbledon once (1939) and US title twice (1939,41) before turning pro in 1941, beat Margaret Court Smith but lost to Billie Jean King in 1973 exhibition matches.

Pat Riley (b.1945): Basketball, coached LA Lakers to 4 of their 5 NBA titles in 1980s (1982,85,87-88), all-time leader in playoff wins with 102.

Oscar Robertson (b.1938): Basketball G, 3-time college Player of Year (1958-60), 9-time All-NBA first team, MVP in 1964 with Cinn. Royals, record-holder for career assists (9,887).

Brooks Robinson (b.1937): Baseball 3B, led AL in fielding 12 times from 1960-72 with Baltimore, MVP in 1964, W.Series MVP in 1970.

Eddie Robinson (b.1919): Football, coaching at Grambling for over 45 years, winningest coach in college history; entered 1990 regular season with 358 career wins.

Frank Robinson (b.1935): Baseball OF, won MVP in both leagues (1961,66), Triple Crown and W.Series MVP in 1966 with Baltimore, 1st black manager in Major Leagues with Cleveland in 1975.

Jackie Robinson (1919-72): Baseball 2B, 4-sport athlete at UCLA; 1st black player in Majors with Brooklyn in 1947, Rookie of the Year in 1947, NL MVP in 1949.

Sugar Ray Robinson (1920-89): Boxer, world welterweight champion (1946-51), 5-time middleweight champ, retired at age 45 after 25 years in the ring; pro record 174-19-6 with 109 KOs.

Knute Rockne (1888-1931): Football, coached Notre Dame to 3 consensus national titles (1924,29,30), career record of 105-12-5 in 13 years.

Bill Rodgers (b.1947): Track & Field, won Boston and New York City marathons 4 times each from 1975-80.

Irina Rodnina (b.1953): Soviet figure skater, won 10 world championships and 3 Olympic gold medals in pairs competiton from 1971-80.

Art Rooney (1901-1988): Sportsman and pro football pioneer, owned Pittsburgh Steelers for 55 years.

Mauri Rose (1906-81): Auto racer, 3-time winner of Indy 500 (1941,47-48).

Murray Rose (b.1939): Australian swimmer, won 3 gold medals at 1956 Olympics; added a gold, silver and bronze in 1960.

Pete Rose (b.1941): Baseball OF-Inf., all-time hits leader with 4,256, led NL in batting 3 times, regular season MVP in 1973, W.Series MVP in 1975, had 44-game hitting streak in '78; managed Cincinnati (1984-89), banned for life in '89 for betting on baseball and associating with known gamblers and drug dealers; convicted of tax evasion in 1990 and sentenced to 5 months in prison and 1 yr. probation.

Ken Rosewall (b.1934): Tennis, won French singles title at age 17 and Australian at 18, US champ twice, but never won Wimbledon.

Pete Rozelle (b.1926): Football, NFL Commissioner from 1960-89. Presided over growth of league from 12 to 28 teams, merger with AFL, creation of Super Bowl and advent of huge TV rights fees.

Wilma Rudolph (b.1940): Track & Field, won 3 gold medals (100m,200m and 4x400m relay) at 1960 Olympics.

Adolph Rupp (1901-77) Basketball, all-time college wins leader with 875, coached Kentucky to 4 NCAA titles (1948-49,51,58).

Bill Russell (b.1934): Basketball C, won titles in college, Olympics and pros, 5-time NBA MVP, led Boston to 11 titles, also became first big league black head coach in 1966.

Babe Ruth (1895-1948): Baseball LHP-OF, 2-time 20-game winner with Boston Red Sox, sold to NY Yankees in 1920, led AL in HRs 12 times and RBI 6 times, hit 60 HRs in 1927, ended career in 1935 with 714 HRs, 2,211 RBI and batting average of .342.

Johnny Rutherford (b.1938): Auto racer, 3-time winner of Indy 500 (1974,76,80), CART national champion in 1980.

Nolan Ryan (b.1947): Baseball RHP, pitched 6th no-hitter and won 300th game in 1990; entered season as all-time leader in strikeouts (5,076).

Juan Antonio Samaranch (b.1920): of Spain, President of International Olympic Committee since 1980.

Joan Benoit Samuelson (b.1957): Track & Field, has won Boston marathon twice (1979,83), winner of first women's Olympic marathon in 1984.

Earl Sande (1889-1968): Jockey, rode Gallant Fox to Triple Crown in 1930, won 5 Belmonts and 3 Kentucky Derbys.

Gene Sarazen (b.1901): Golfer, won Masters, British Open, 2 US Opens and 3 PGA titles between 1922-35; invented sand wedge in 1930.

Glen Sather (b.1943): Hockey, GM-coach of 4 Stanley Cup winners in Edmonton (1984-85,87-88) and GM-only for another in 1990.

Terry Sawchuk (1929-1970): Hockey G, recorded 103 shutouts in 21 NHL seasons, 4-time Vezina Trophy winner, played on 4 Stanley Cup winners at Detroit and Toronto.

Gale Sayers (b.1943): Football HB, 5-time All-Pro with Chicago, scored then-record 22 TDs in rookie year (1965).

Mike Schmidt (b.1949): Baseball 3B, led NL in HRs 8 times, 3-time MVP (1980,81,86) with Phila., 548 career HRs, 10 gold gloves.

Don Schollander (b.1946): Swimming, won 4 gold medals at 1964 Olympics, plus one gold and one silver in 1968.

Dick Schultz (b.1929): executive director of NCAA since 1988, head coach of baseball (1964-70) and basketball (1970-74) at Iowa, athletic director at Cornell (1976-81) and Virginia (1981-87).

Bob Seagren (b.1946): Track & Field, won gold medal in pole vault at 1968 Olympics, broke world outdoor record 5 times.

Tom Seaver (b.1944): Baseball RHP, won 3 Cy Young Awards (1969,73,75), had 311 wins and 3,640 strikeouts over 20 years.

Peter Seitz (b.1905): Baseball arbitrator, ruled in 1975 (Dec.23) that players who perform for one season without a signed contract can become free agents; decision ushered in big money era for players.

Frank Selke (1893-1985): Hockey, GM of 6 Stanley Cup champions in Montreal (1953,56-60).

Wilbur Shaw (1902-54): Auto racer, 3-time winner and 3-time runner-up of Indy 500 from 1933-1940.

Bill Shoemaker (b.1931): Jockey, all-time career wins leader with 8,833; won Belmont 5 times, Kentucky Derby 4 times and Preakness twice.

Eddie Shore (1902-85): Hockey D, only defenseman (including Orr) to win MVP trophy 4 times (1933,35-36,38), all with Boston.

Frank Shorter (b.1947): Track & Field, won gold medal in marathon at 1972 Olympics, 1st US marathoner to win in 64 years.

Jim Shoulders (b.1928): Rodeo, 5-time All-Around Cowboy (1949,56-59), won record 16 different rodeo titles.

Don Shula (b.1930): Football, coached 6 teams to Super Bowl, won twice with Miami (1973-74); entered 1990 regular season with 287 career wins (including playoffs) second only to George Halas.

Al Simmons (1902-56): Baseball OF, led AL in batting twice (1930-31) and knocked in 100 runs or more 11 straight years (1924-34).

O.J.Simpson (b.1947): Football RB, won Heisman Trophy in 1966 at Southern Cal; ran for 2,003 yards in NFL in 1973, All-Pro 5 times, MVP in 1973, rushed for 11,236 career yards.

George Sisler (1893-73): Baseball 1B, hit over .400 twice (1920,22), 257 hits in 1920 still a major league record.

Mary Decker Slaney (b.1958): US middle distance runner, entered 1990 holding 7 separate American track & field records from the 800 to 10,000 meters, won both 1,500 and 3,000 meters at 1983 World Championships in Helsinki, but no Olympic medals.

Billy Smith (b.1950): Hockey G, led NY Islanders to 4 consecutive Stanley Cups (1979-83); won Vezina Trophy in 1982 and was Stanley Cup MVP in 1983.

Dean Smith (b.1931): Basketball, has coached North Carolina to 20 NCAA tournaments in 29 years, won title in 1982, coached US Olympic team to gold medal in 1976, entered 1990-91 season with more wins (688) than any other active Div.I coach.

Ozzie Smith (b.1954): Baseball SS, entered 1989 with 9 straight gold gloves, 7-time starter for NL in All-Star Game.

Walter (Red) Smith (1905-82): Sportswriter for newspapers in Philadelphia and New York from 1936-82, won Pulitzer Prize for commentary in 1976.

Conn Smythe (1895-80): Hockey pioneer, built Maple Leaf Gardens in 1931, managed Toronto to 7 Stanley Cups before retiring in 1961.

Sam Snead (b.1912): Golfer, won both Masters and PGA 3 times, British Open once, runner-up in US Open 4 times but never won, PGA Player of Year in 1949, PGA career victory leader with 84.

Peter Snell (b.1939): New Zealander who won gold medal in 800m at 1960 Olympics, then won both the 800m and 1,500m at 1964 Games.

Javier Sotomayor (b.1967): Cuban high jumper, first man to clear 8 feet (8-0) on July 29, 1989.

Warren Spahn (b.1921): Baseball LHP, led NL in wins 8 times, won 20 or more games 13 times, Cy Young winner in 1957, most career wins (363) by a left-hander.

Tris Speaker (1888-1958): Baseball OF, all-time leader in outfield assists (449) and doubles (793), had .344 career batting average and 3,515 hits.

J.G. Taylor Spink (1888-1962): Publisher of The Sporting News from 1914-62, Baseball Writers' Assn. annual meritorious service award named after him.

Mark Spitz (b.1950): Swimmer, set 23 world and 35 US records, won record 7 gold medals (4 individual, 3 relay) at 1972 Olympics.

Amos Alonzo Stagg (1862-1965): Football innovator, coached at U.of Chicago for 41 seasons and College of the Pacific for 14 more, won 314 games, elected to both college football and basketball halls of fame.

Willie Stargell (b.1941): Baseball OF-1B, led NL in home runs twice (1971,73), 475 career HRs, regular season and W.Series MVP in 1979.

Bart Starr (b.1934): Football QB, led Green Bay to 5 NFL titles and 2 Super Bowl wins from 1961-67, reg.season MVP in 1966, 2-time Super Bowl MVP (1967,68).

Roger Staubach (b.1942): Football QB, Heisman Trophy winner as Navy junior in 1963; led NFL in passing 4 times, led Dallas to 2 Super Bowl titles (1972,78), Super Bowl MVP in 1972.

George Steinbrenner (b.1930): principal owner of NY Yankees from 1973-90, teams won 2 World Series (1977-78), changed managers 19 times in 17 years, ordered by baseball commissioner Fay Vincent on July 30, 1990 to surrender control of club for dealings with small-time gambler Howard Spira.

Casey Stengel (1890-1975): Baseball, player for 14 years and manager for 25, guided NY Yankees to 10 pennants and 7 W.Series titles from 1949-60.

Ingemar Stenmark (b.1956): Swedish alpine skier, 3-time World Cup overall champ (1976-78), 86 World Cup wins in 16 years, won 2 gold medals at 1980 Olympics.

David Stern (b.1942): Basketball, marketing expert and NBA commissioner since 1984, has presided over growth of league from 23 to 27 teams, received unprecedented 5-year, $27.5 million contract extension in 1990.

Teofilo Stevenson (b.1951): Cuban boxer, won 3 consecutive gold medals as Olympic heavyweight (1972,76,80); did not turn pro.

Jackie Stewart (b.1939): Auto racer, won 27 Formula One races and 3 world driving titles from 1965-73.

Curtis Strange (b.1955): Golfer, won consecutive US Open titles (1988-89), first PGA player to win $1 million in one year (1988).

Louise Suggs (b.1923): Golfer, won 11 Majors and 50 LPGA events overall from 1949-62.

John L.Sullivan (1858-1918): Boxer, world heavyweight champion (1882-92), last of bare-knuckle champions.

Barry Switzer (b.1937): Football, coached Oklahoma to 3 national titles (1974-75,85), 157 career wins in 16 years.

Paul Tagliabue (b.1940): Football, NFL attorney who was elected league's 4th commissioner in 1989.

Anatoli Tarasov (b.1918): Hockey, coached USSR to 9 straight world championships and 3 Olympic gold medals (1964,68,72).

Fran Tarkenton (b.1940): Football QB, 2-time All-Pro (1973,75), threw for 47,003 yards and 342 TDs (both NFL records) in 18 seasons.

Gustave Thoeni (b.1951): Italian alpine skier, 4-time World Cup overall champion (1971-73,75), won Giant Slalom at 1972 Olympics.

Daley Thompson (b.1958): British decathlete, won consecutive gold medals in decathlon at 1980 and '84 Olympics.

Jim Thorpe (1888-1953): 2-time All-America in football, won 2 gold medals at 1912 Olympics, played major league baseball (1913-19), and pro football (1920-26,28); chosen "Athlete of the Half Century" by AP in 1950.

Bill Tilden (1893-1953): Tennis, won 7 US and 3 Wimbledon titles in 1920s, led US to 7 straight Davis Cup victories (1920-26).

Tinker to Evers to Chance—Chicago Cubs double play combination from 1903-08; SS **Joe Tinker** (1880-1948), 2B **Johnny Evers** (1883-1947) and 1B **Frank Chance** (1877-1924); all 3 managed the Cubs and made the Hall of Fame.

Y.A.Tittle (b.1926): Football QB, played 17 years in AFC and NFL, All-Pro 4 times, MVP with San Francisco (1957) and NY Giants (1962), passed for 28,339 career yards.

Bill Toomey (b.1939): Track & Field, won decathlon gold medal at 1968 Olympics.

Bill Torrey (b.1934): Hockey GM, managed NY Islanders to 4 Stanley Cups (1980-83).

Pie Traynor (1899-1972): Baseball 3B, hit .300 or better 10 times, led Pittsburgh to W.Series title in 1925.

Vladislav Tretiak (b.1952): Hockey G, led USSR to Olympic gold medals in 1972 and '76; starred for Soviets against Team Canada in 1972, and again in 2 Canada Cups (1976,81).

Lee Trevino (b.1939): Golfer, 2-time winner of 3 Majors—US Open (1968,71), British Open (1971-72) and PGA (1974,84); joined Seniors Tour in 1990 and won US Senior Open among other titles.

Bryan Trottier (b.1956): Hockey C, led NY Islanders to 4 straight Stanley Cups (1980-83), reg.season MVP in 1979, playoff MVP in 1980.

Gene Tunney (b.1897-78): Boxer, world heavyweight champion (1926-28), defeated Jack Dempsey twice on points, pro record 65-2-1 with 43 KOs.

Ted Turner (b.1938): Sportsman, skippered *Courageous* to America's Cup win in 1977, owner of both Atlanta Braves and Hawks, cable TV pioneer, founder of Goodwill Games.

Mike Tyson (b.1965): Boxer, youngest (age 19) to win heavyweight title (WBC, 1986), undisputed champ from 1987 until upset loss to Buster Douglas on Feb. 10, 1990; pro record after that fight 37-1-0 with 33 KOs.

Wyomia Tyus (b.1945): Track & Field, 1st woman or man to win consecutive Olympic gold medals in 100m (1964-68).

Peter Ueberroth (b.1937): Organizer of financially successful 1984 Summer Olympics in LA, 1984 Time Man of the Year, baseball commissioner from 1984-89.

Johnny Unitas (b.1933): Football QB, led Baltimore Colts to 2 NFL titles (1958-59) and a Super Bowl win (1971), All-Pro 5 times, 3-time MVP (1959,64,67), passed for 40,239 career yards and 290 TDs.

Al Unser,Sr. (b.1939): Auto racer, brother of Bobby, 4-time winner of Indy 500 (1970-71,78,87), 3-time USAC/CART national champ.

Bobby Unser (b.1934): Auto racer, brother of Al, 3-time winner of Indy 500 (1968,75,81), 2-time USAC-CART national champ.

Norm Van Brocklin (1926-83): Football QB, led NFL in passing 3 times and punting twice, led LA Rams (1951) and Philadelphia (1960) to NFL titles, MVP in 1960.

Steve Van Buren (b.1920): Football HB, led Philadelphia to 2 NFL titles (1948-49), league's top rusher 4 times.

Johnny Vander Meer (b.1914): Baseball LHP, only major leaguer to pitch consecutive no-hitters (June 11 & 15, 1938).

Harold S.Vanderbilt (1884-70): Sportsman, successfully defended America's Cup 3 times (1930,34,37), also invented contract bridge in 1926.

Glenna Collett Vare (1904-89): Golfer, won record 6 US Amateurs from (1922-35).

Andy Varipapa (1891-1984): Bowler, trick-shot artist, won consecutive All-Star match game titles (1947-48) at age 53.

Bill Veeck (1914-86): Maverick baseball executive, owned major league teams in Cleveland, St.Louis and Chicago from 1946-80, introduced ballpark giveaways, exploding scoreboards, and midget Eddie Gaedel.

Fay Vincent (b.1938): Baseball, became 8th commissioner after death of A.Bartlett Giamatti in 1989, has presided over World Series earthquake, owners' lockout and banishment of N.Y. Yankees owner George Steinbrenner in less than one year.

Lasse Viren (b.1949): Finnish runner, won gold medals in 5,000m and 10,000m at both the 1972 and '76 Olympics.

Honus Wagner (1874-1955): Baseball SS, hit .300 for 17 consecutive seasons (1897-1913) with Pittsburgh, led NL in batting 8 times, had 3,430 career hits.

Grete Waitz (b.1953): Norwegian runner, 9-time winner of New York City Marathon from 1978-88.

Doak Walker (b.1927): Football HB, won Heisman Trophy as SMU junior in 1948; led Detroit to 2 NFL titles (1952-53), All-Pro 4 times in 6 years.

Bill Walsh (b.1931): Football, coached San Francisco to 3 Super Bowl titles (1982,85,89).

Bill Walton (b.1950): Basketball C, 3-time college Player of Year (1972-74), led UCLA to 2 national titles (1972-73); led Portland to NBA title as MVP in 1977, regular season MVP in 1978.

Darrell Waltrip (b.1947): Auto racer, 3-time NASCAR national champion (1981-82,85), won 1989 Daytona 500.

Paul Waner (1903-65): Baseball OF, led NL in batting 3 times, MVP in 1927 with Pittsburgh, had 3,152 hits and .333 career average, brother of Lloyd.

Arch Ward (1896-55): Promoter and sports editor of Chicago Tribune from 1930-55, founder of baseball All-Star Game (1933), Chicago College All-Star Football Game (1934) and the All-America Football Conference (1946-49).

Cornelius (Dutch) Warmerdam (b.1915): Track & Field, 1st pole vaulter to clear 15 feet (1940).

Glenn (Pop) Warner (1872-54): Football innovator, coached at 7 colleges over 49 years, 313 career wins, produced 47 All-Americas, including Thorpe and Nevers.

Tom Watson (b.1949): Golfer, 6-time PGA player of the Year (1977-80,82,84), has won 5 British Opens, 2 Masters and 1 US Open.

Dick Weber (b.1929): Bowler, 3-time PBA Bowler of the Year (1961,63,65), won 30 PBA titles in 4 decades.

Johnny Weismuller (1904-84): Swimmer, won 3 gold medals at 1924 Olympics and 2 more at 1928 Games, became Hollywood's most famous Tarzan.

Jerry West (b.1938): Basketball G, 2-time All-America at W.Va.; 10-time All-NBA first-team, led LA Lakers to NBA title once as player (1972) and 5 times as GM.

Byron (Whizzer) White (b.1918): Football, All-America HB at Colorado (1935-37), signed with Pittsburgh in 1938 for the then largest contract in pro history ($15,800), took Rhodes scholarship in 1939, returned to NFL in 1940 to lead league in rushing and retired in 1941, named to US Supreme Court in 1962.

Kathy Whitworth (b.1939): Golf, 7-time LPGA Player of the Year (1966-69,71-73), won 6 Majors, 88 tour wins most on LPGA or PGA tour.

Hazel Hotchkiss Wightman (1886-1974): Tennis, won 16 US national titles, 4-time US Women's champion (1909-11,19), donor of Wightman Cup contested by US and Britain since 1923.

Mats Wilander (b.1964): Swedish tennis player, 1988 Player of the Year, has won Australian and French Opens 3 times each and US Open in 1988.

Bud Wilkinson (b.1916): Football, coached Oklahoma to 3 national titles (1950,55,56), 145 career wins in 17 years.

Ted Williams (b.1919): Baseball OF, led AL in batting 6 times, won Triple Crown twice (1942,47), MVP twice (1946,49), last player to hit .400 (1941), hit .344 with 521 HRs in 19 years.

Katarina Witt (b.1965): East German figure skater, 4-time world champion (1984-85,87-88), won consecutive Olympic gold medals (1984,88).

John Wooden (b.1910): Basketball, college Player of Year at Purdue in 1932, coached UCLA to 10 national titles (1964-65,67-73,75); only member of Basketball Hall of Fame inducted as player and coach.

Mickey Wright (b.1935): Golfer, won 3 of 4 Majors (LPGA, US Open, Titleholders) in 1961, 4-time winner of both US Open and LPGA titles, 82 career wins including 13 Majors.

Early Wynn (b.1920): Baseball RHP, won 20 games 5 times, Cy Young winner in 1959, 300 career wins in 23 years.

Cale Yarborough (b.1939): Auto racer, 4-time winner of Daytona 500 (1968,77,83-84), NASCAR national champ 3 times (1976-78).

Carl Yastrzemski (b.1939): Baseball OF, led AL in batting 3 times, won Triple Crown and MVP in 1967, had 3,419 hits and 452 HRs in 23 years with Boston.

Cy Young (1867-1955): Baseball RHP, won 20 games or more 16 times, holds record for career wins (511) and innings pitched (7,377).

Robin Yount (b.1955): Baseball SS-OF, 2-time AL MVP (1982,89) for Milwaukee, entered 1990 season with 2,602 hits at age 34.

Babe Didrikson Zaharias (1914-56): won 2 gold medals and a silver at 1932 Olympics; took up golf in 1935, won 55 pro & amateur events, helped found LPGA in 1949, won 10 Majors including 3 US Opens (1948,50,54) chosen female "Athlete of the Half Century" by AP in 1950.

Tony Zale (b.1913): Boxer, world middleweight champion (1941-47,48), pro record 67-18-2 with 44 KOs.

Emile Zatopek (b.1922): Czech runner, won total of 4 Olympic gold medals, including unprecedented triple (5,000m, 10,000m and marathon), in 1952.

John Ziegler (b.1934): Hockey, NHL president since 1977, negotiated settlement with rival WHA in 1979 that led to inviting four WHA teams (Edmonton, Hartford, Quebec and Winnipeg) to join NHL.

Pirmin Zurbriggen (b.1963): Swiss alpine skier, 4-time World Cup overall champ (1984,87,88,90) and 3-time runner-up, 40 World Cup wins in 10 years, won gold and bronze medals at 1988 Olympics.

NBC Sports

NBA commissioner **David Stern** (right) poses with NBC executives **Dick Ebersol** (left) and **Arthur Watson** after NBC won the 1991-94 NBA contract for $600 million.

BUSINESS & MEDIA

CBS Sports' schedule of dreams buffeted by routs, low ratings; Rights fees and player salaries escalate, but advertising off.

BUSINESS & MEDIA

1989-90 YEAR IN REVIEW

by John McManus

CBS called 1990 the "Dream Season."

The Big Event strategists at Black Rock in New York had a schedule that couldn't lose. Start off strong with the Super Bowl, then roll through the calendar with the Daytona 500, the NCAA basketball tournament, the Masters, the NBA playoffs, baseball's All-Star Game, U.S.Open tennis, NFL football, and baseball's playoffs and World Series. No single network ever monopolized sports' big ticket items so completely in one year.

CBS entered the new year determined to pull itself out of third place in network television's prime time ratings race and its sports division was going to lead the way. It was an expensive dream— securing baseball, football, and NCAA basketball rights cost over $3 billion— but CBS was desperate to attract viewers.

The stellar lineup of televised sports on CBS mirrored the bright prospects of the entire $63-billion sports business landscape going into 1990.

Signs of growth were everywhere. The NBA had successfully added four new franchises in the past two years, with new teams in Orlando, Miami, Charlotte and Minnesota packing their new arenas night after night. In 1989-90, spectators paid $3.5 billion for tickets to attend sports events. A new attendance record was set in the NBA, 33.6 million fans attended college basketball games, and despite an owners' lockout during Spring Training, baseball attendance was up as well.

Expansion was in the wind. The NFL announced it would add two new teams in the 1990s and prepared to launch its international spring circuit, the World League of American Football, in 1991. In baseball, the National League will have two more teams on the field by 1993. The lucky cities will be announced on Sept.30, 1991, and the entry fee is likely to reach $95 million per franchise. In hockey, the NHL announced the most expansive

John McManus is a staff writer with *Advertising Age* magazine and reports frequently on sports business and media.

plans of all: seven new clubs in place before the end of the century (at $50 million a pop). The league avoided an embarrassing franchise move early in the year when Minnesota owners George and Gordon Gund—who were threatening to relocate to San Jose—were allowed to sell the North Stars and get a Bay Area expansion team.

Another indicator of sports' prosperity was an Aug. 20 survey in **Forbes** magazine that named the world's 30 wealthiest athletes, based on 1990 salary, bonuses, endorsements and appearance fees. The Top 10 included four boxers, three golfers, two auto racers and Michael Jordan. Altogether, the Top 30 made $230 million for the year.

The rest of us spent more than $24 billion on leisure and participatory sports in 1989, shelling out about $7 billion for brand name athletic shoes, $11.6 billion on sports apparel and $10 billion on sports equipment. Boom times, right? Well, not exactly.

Take a closer look at CBS where the good ship Dream Season started taking on water before it even left port. On Nov. 9, 1989, NBC captured the rights to carry the NBA from 1991-94 for $600 million. While the deal didn't quite make up for losing the Major League Baseball contract to CBS in 1988, it did give NBC one of sports' only profitable television properties. Then came the Super Bowl and the San Francisco 49ers' 55-10 trashing of the Denver Broncos. The score was the most lopsided ever and CBS's 39.0 Nielsen rating was the lowest for a Super Bowl in more than two decades.

Two months later, more bad news, this time at the NCAA Final Four in Denver. On the eve of the championship game, CBS fired its No. 1 sportscaster Brent Musburger (see box), then, the next night, Nevada-Las Vegas annihilated Duke for the title—by a record 30 points. Ratings for the entire NCAA tournament were 9.5, down from a 10 in 1989.

Otherwise, post-season NBA games on CBS dropped to a 6.3 rating from a 7.5, as the L.A. Lakers were eliminated early and Detroit wiped out Portland in five games to win the NBA Finals. The Daytona 500 earned a 7.3 rating, compared with a 8.3 in 1989. And baseball ratings were also down. With CBS trying to sell

Wide World Photos

The 49ers' **Joe Montana** struck gold in August with a 4-year, $15 million contract that was signed after the Forbes' Top 30 went to press.

The Forbes' Top 30

The 30 highest-paid athletes of 1990 (including salary, signing bonus, winnings, endorsements, etc.) according to the Aug. 20, 1990 issue of **Forbes** magazine. Figures listed below are in millions of dollars.

		Salary/Purse	Other	Total
1	Mike Tyson	$27.0	$1.6	$28.6
2	Buster Douglas	25.0	1.0	26.0
3	Sugar Ray Leonard	12.0	1.0	13.0
4	Ayrton Senna	9.0	1.0	10.0
5	Alain Prost	8.0	1.0	9.0
6	Jack Nicklaus	0.6	8.0	8.6
7	Greg Norman	1.5	7.0	8.5
8	Michael Jordan	2.1	6.0	8.1
9	Arnold Palmer	0.1	8.0	8.1
10	Evander Holyfield	8.0	0.1	8.1
11	Boris Becker	1.2	6.0	7.2
12	Nigel Mansell	6.0	1.0	7.0
13	Steffi Graf	1.1	5.0	6.1
14	Jose Canseco	5.5	0.5	6.0
15	Wayne Gretzky	3.0	3.0	6.0
16	Andre Agassi	1.0	4.5	5.5
17	Stefan Edberg	1.5	4.0	5.5
18	Ivan Lendl	1.3	4.0	5.3
19	Diego Maradona	2.0	3.0	5.0
20	Don Mattingly	4.5	0.3	4.8
21	Bo Jackson	2.0	2.5	4.5
22	Gabriela Sabatini	0.5	4.0	4.5
23	Magic Johnson	2.5	2.0	4.5
24	Robin Yount	4.2	0.3	4.5
25	Joe Montana	1.4	3.0	4.4
26	Patrick Ewing	3.6	0.6	4.2
27	Greg LeMond	1.7	2.5	4.2
28	Gerhard Berger	3.0	1.0	4.0
29	Curtis Strange	0.8	3.0	3.8
30	Will Clark	3.7	0.1	3.8

advertising time for the league playoffs and World Series in the midst of the softest ad marketplace in five years, television industry analysts estimated that the network might lose as much as $100 million in the first year of its MLB contract.

Was the Dream Season turning into a nightmare? No, said CBS executives.

"Whether we make money on sports or don't isn't the only issue," said George Schweitzer, Senior V.P., Communications at CBS. "Affiliates want these events. We can build relationships with advertisers we don't normally have. Nothing has diminished our enthusiasm for sports and its use as a promotional tool for the network."

Controversy, ill will, and financial misfortune stalked the sports business throughout 1990 and laid waste to some formidable legends in the process. Mike Tyson lost the heavyweight title to 50-1 shot Buster Douglas in February. George Steinbrenner was effectively thrown out of baseball by commissioner Fay Vincent on July 30 for paying a small-time hood $40,000 to dig up some dirt on former Yankee Dave Winfield. Donald Trump, who was pummeled by his wife over a divorce, the tabloid press over his girlfriend, and his bankers over his debt load, had to get out of the sports promotion game (no more Tour de Trump). And Tom Werner, half of the Carsey-Werner production team that created TV's two biggest hits—"Roseanne" and "The Cosby Show"—bought the San Diego Padres from hamburger heiress Joan Kroc for $75 million in June. With his club 20 games out in late July, did Werner hire Bill Cosby to manage the team? No, he got Roseanne Barr to croak her version of the national anthem and do her best impersonation of a baseball player. The incident won national censure.

The sportswear business was also tarnished when media commentators began speaking out against high-priced sneakers and their possible link to increasing incidents of drug use and violence in urban ghettos. Charges flew that Nike, Reebok and other manufacturers of expensive footwear as well as their popular endorsers—Jordan, Bo Jackson, Spike Lee and others—were at least partially responsible for fostering the violence. The flames began to die down as manu-

The rise and fall and return of Brent Musburger

It was Super Bowl Sunday night in New Orleans and Brent Musburger was master of all he surveyed.

The San Francisco 49ers had just crushed the Denver Broncos by 45 points to win their second straight NFL title and there was Brent presiding over the postgame trophy presentation. Wearing the CBS blazer and working the CBS microphone, Musburger was in command.

The Dream Season—Musburger's Dream Season—had begun. Next stop: play-by-play at the NCAA Final Four in Denver, then host of NBA Finals, to be followed by baseball play-by-play at the All-Star Game, league playoffs and World Series. And if that wasn't enough to keep him busy—there was always the "The NFL Today" to anchor every Sunday in the fall and the Winter Olympics beckoning in 1992 and '94.

Musburger, 50, was as much CBS Sports as the unblinking eye on the network microphones. If CBS was there—anywhere —so was he. As network spokesperson Susan Kerr told **Sports Illustrated**, "Nobody ever looked at CBS without thinking of Brent Musburger, including the people who work here."

Even ABC's peripatetic Jim McKay, still spanning the globe after 25 years as host of "Wide World of Sports," didn't seem to get around as much as Musburger.

As luck would have it, just as Musburger's career was peaking after 15 years at CBS, his five-year, $10 million contract was running out. Negotiations had been under way since November between CBS Sports president Neal Pilson and Musburger's agent-brother Todd. In late March, the Musburgers arrived in Denver for the NCAA Final Four determined to wrap things up and go home with a big raise. CBS had to give Brent the money, he was the franchise. What was Pilson going to do, let him go?

Yes.

Realizing that he had a strong crop of young on-air talent waiting in the wings and a chance to hire a discontented Al Michaels away from ABC, Pilson felt that Musburger was no longer indispensable. In the last two years, in fact, CBS had cut back somewhat on its anchor's prodigious workload, taking him off college football play-by-play and

Former CBS Sports anchor **Brent Musburger** (left) shares last January's Super Bowl spotlight with 49ers' owner **Eddie DeBartolo** (center) and head coach **George Seifert.**

relieving him as host of Masters golf and U.S. Open tennis. There were two other factors: Musburger's growing reputation as being difficult to work with and a scheduled round of budget cuts at CBS Sports that called for reducing Brent's wages, not increasing them. So, when Todd gave him the ultimatum in Denver, Pilson gave Brent the axe—on April 1, the day before CBS was to go on the air with the UNLV-Duke final.

Keeping his composure, Musburger called the game then signed off with his arm around sidekick Billy Packer saying, "Folks, I've had the best seat in the house. Thanks for sharing it. I'll see you down the road."

Four weeks later, after lashing back at Pilson and CBS in an interview with Sam Donaldson on the ABC show "PrimeTime Live," Musburger was hired by ABC Sports. His six-year, $11 million contract called for him to work on college football and basketball broadcasts, as well as the new World League of American Football (for which ABC paid $24 million for two years of broadcast rights), "Wide World of Sports," the Hambletonian harness race and the Little League World Series.

Suddenly the spotlight fell on Al Michaels. Michaels had a public feud going with ABC Sports chief Dennis Swanson, and seemed headed toward arbitration to get out of the last three years of his contract. With CBS minus a No. 1 baseball play-by-play man

and ABC hiring Musburger, Michaels appeared headed for CBS. But on June 6, he decided to stay at ABC and signed a new contract for an annual salary of $2.5 million that runs through 1995. CBS, despite all that young talent waiting in the wings, gave the baseball play-by-play job to 65 year-old Jack Buck.

Still more broadcast booth excitement focused on NBC's earnest courtship of the NBA's two most successful coaches—Pat Riley of the Lakers and Chuck Daly of the Pistons—for analyst roles in the network's new NBA telecasts starting in November 1990. NBC wanted Riley and Daly to team with play-by-play men Marv Albert and Bob Costas. Both turned NBC down, although Riley did sign on for $400,000 a year as host of the pre-game, half-time and postgame shows. NBC ended up with former Atlanta Hawks coach Mike Fratello and Portland Trail Blazers' analyst Steve Jones.

Meanwhile, CBS named Greg Gumbel to replace Musburger as host of "The NFL Today," *Boston Globe* football writer Will McDonough jumped from "NFL Today" to the competition at NBC, and disgraced North Carolina State basketball coach Jim Valvano was hired by ABC and ESPN for $900,000 over three years.

Valvano and Musburger will be teamed on ABC college hoop broadcasts.

403

facturers pumped up their community relations and education advertising campaigns, and the outraged journalists realized that ghetto violence traces to deeper roots than sneaker commercials.

In late July, almost exactly 25 years after the signing of the 1965 Voting Rights Act, events at Shoal Creek Country Club in Birmingham, Ala., sent a chill through the golf world. Shoal Creek founder Hall Thompson set off a furor when he made racist remarks in connection with the club's exclusionary membership practices. Black groups reacted with threats of picketing and boycotts, while advertisers —ever fearful of becoming embroiled in controversy—began dropping out of ABC and ESPN's coverage of the PGA Championship in August.

Suddenly, the nation began to realize that exclusionary membership practices at golf's most prestigious clubs were the rule, not the exception. Advertisers, who annually pump more than $200 million into media advertising and sponsorship of professional golf, let it be known that they would not tolerate association with events that opened them up to public outcry. So just like that, the golf industry changed. Or at least a few private clubs, including Shoal Creek, began to admit black members.

The bidding for sports television rights that ended in 1990 closed a fierce 24-month period that cost networks $10 billion.

By late 1989, CBS was the king of the hill. It had baseball for four years, renewal options in place to retain the NBA and the NCAA, and down the road the 1992 and '94 Winter Olympics already locked up. ABC and NBC, left in the wake of the CBS spending spree, were forced to get out their checkbooks and go after some of the few sports properties still up for bids.

NBC got back in the game in November by winning the 1991-93 NBA contract at a 241 percent annual increase. With solid four-year commitments from automobile advertisers and the Miller Brewing Co. in place, NBC's NBA deal might be the only profitable professional sports rights contract for the next four years. TNT, meanwhile, held on to its NBA cable rights for $275 million through 1993, a 175 percent increase. Nobody

was happier with the two deals than David Stern, the NBA commissioner. Stern, the architect of the league's remarkable financial comeback in the 1980s, was rewarded by NBA owners with a 5-year contract extension in February worth $3.5 million a year.

Two weeks after NBC relieved CBS of the NBA, ABC made a run at the NCAA basketball tournament, but lost out when a determined CBS agreed to put up $1 billion over seven years for exclusive rights (i.e., no cable) to the event. The annual increase this time was 158 percent.

The deal, however, included new restrictions by NCAA executive director Dick Schultz on beer commercials. Instead of 90 seconds of beer ads per hour, CBS will be limited to one minute—and most of that time will be taken up with reminding viewers to know-when-to-say-when. In the past, beer advertising has accounted for as much as 25% of CBS's revenues during the coverage of the tournament. Anheuser-Busch and Miller Brewing executives see the NCAA restrictions as the beginning of the end of beer advertising on televised college sports— and possibly all of sports. The loss of beer commercials would take more than $250 million annually out of the sports television advertising marketplace.

As the fierce broadcast rights wars wore on into 1990, ABC finally enjoyed a moment of triumph in January, when it captured the 1991-95 CFA college football package from CBS for $175 million. ABC, which already had Big Ten and Pac-10 games, now had regular season college football all to itself, plus the Rose Bowl and Sugar Bowl games.

Not so fast, said NBC, which announced on Feb.5 that it had entered into a separate $38-million deal with Notre Dame University to televise Irish home football games from 1991-95.

Notre Dame's decision to cut its own TV deal coupled with an ongoing Federal Trade Commission investigation into whether the CFA had acted in violation of U.S. antitrust laws in its previous dealings with the networks made the CFA's 63 members nervous. As a consequence, college conferences began reshuffling their school lineups trying to build attractive television packages in the event of a CFA breakup (see "College Sports").

Notre Dame stunned big-time college football by signing a 5-year, $38 million home game contract with NBC.

Finally, on March 10, the NFL completed the biggest sports rights deal of all time: four years of NFL football on five networks for $3.6 billion. Commissioner Paul Tagliabue was able to increase the league's take 89 percent by lengthening the season to 16 games over 17 weeks, increasing the playoff field to 12 teams, including ABC in the playoffs, and giving TNT the first half-season of Sunday night games. Annual income for each of the NFL's 28 teams jumped from $17 million to $32 million per year.

When the smoke cleared, the network bills were as follows: CBS—$1.06 billion for the NFC; ABC—$950 million for Monday Night games; NBC—$752 million for the AFC; ESPN—$450 million for 8 Sunday night games and the Pro Bowl; and TNT—$450 million for 9 Sunday night games. The Super Bowls went to ABC (1991), CBS (1992) and NBC (1993) with the 1994 game to be bid on later.

NBC president Robert Wright was shocked at the price tag, telling *USA Today* that it was "extremely likely" that NBC would pass on the next round of negotiations. "I kind of wish I hadn't bid on this round."

Just as network sports executives were trying to justify their extravagance to the bottom-line oriented managements at CBS, ABC-Cap Cities and General Electric, advertisers let it be known that they intended to spend less on TV sports, not more.

Debt-ridden R.J. Reynolds has backed away from sponsoring golf, and longtime auto racing sponsors like Valvoline have cut back their event marketing as well. Recession and a newly restrictive advertising environment—which may well signal the imminent end of $105 million in cigarette sponsorship and signage in auto racing and at stadiums—are not the only forces cooling down the $1.7 billion sports sponsorship arena.

"The networks are fighting for dominance in programming," said Arthur Kesteloot, manager of advertising and media relations for Chrysler Corp., one of sports' top five advertisers. "They're not only fighting among themselves but with the various sanctioning bodies: professional baseball, the NFL, NBA and so on. The gist of the problem is rights fees. Sooner or later, we're going to see the marketing community start to pull back. Chrysler already is."

With the approach of 1991, the networks are sitting on several years' worth of high marquee sports broadcast licenses and the very real possibility of calamitous losses.

"The losses will be so great that (in a few years) you might not even recognize network sports as they are now," said a senior marketing executive with one of the networks. "Somebody's going to take a fall."

Some networks are already taking multi-million dollar hits. CBS, as previously noted, figures to lose a ton of money on baseball. ESPN, which bought exclusive cable rights to baseball through 1993 for $400 million, has said it will lose $40 million covering the sport in 1990. But at least it had three no-hitters to show for its four-nights-a-week, 170-game saturation coverage. Ted Turner lost $40 million on the Goodwill Games and had nothing to show for it.

Much worse losses may lie just ahead, however, as the new network contracts begin to kick in.

If this has been a Dream Season for anyone it's the players, the best of whom pocketed a lot of that new TV money.

After several years of gradual wage increases, salaries shot through the roof in late 1989. Between Thanksgiving and Christmas, seven baseball players signed contracts that averaged from $2.8 to $3.25 million a year. In all, five clubs—Minnesota, Oakland, California, San Diego, Kansas City and Milwaukee—committed $83 million in deals ranging from three to five years for the likes of Kirby Puckett, Rickey Henderson, Mark Langston, Joe Carter, Mark Davis and Robin Yount. Some of the investments were wise, some were not. By mid-August, Henderson was leading the A.L. in batting and Carter was first in the N.L. in runs batted in, but Langston was 5-15 with a 4.79 ERA and Davis was 1-5 with five saves.

Salaries continued to climb in all sports in 1990. Baseball's No.1 salary was topped by Oakland's Dave Stewart ($3.5 million), San Francisco's Will Clark ($3.75 million), Don Mattingly of the N.Y.Yankees ($3.86 million) and finally the A's Jose Canseco ($4.7 million). In the NFL, 49ers' quarterback Joe Montana struck gold and pocketed $4 million for 1990. The salary cap blew off the NBA in July and the L.A. Lakers promptly signed free agent Sam Perkins for $3.2 million a year, which is more than Magic Johnson makes. In August, Miami offered Cleveland's John (Hot Rod) Williams a $5 million a year contract making him the league's top paid player.

Even the NHL—which doesn't have a major network TV contract in the U.S.—showed signs of salary escalation. Wayne Gretzky of Los Angeles and Mario Lemieux of Pittsburgh earned raises to $3 and $2 million apiece, but 26-year-old Brett Hull of St.Louis replaced Detroit's Steve Yzerman as No.3 on the list. Hull also experienced the year's biggest boost in pay, cashing in on a 72-goal season to rise from $125,000 to $1.5 million a year. In a more significant deal that shook the NHL to its financial foundations, the Blues also signed free agent defenseman Scott Stevens of Washington for a million a year—twice what three-time Norris Trophy winner Ray Bourque of Boston makes.

In 1972, Brett Hull's father Bobby jumped from Chicago of the NHL to Winnipeg of the new World Hockey Association for the then unheard of figure of $1 million. In hockey, a million dollars a year is still a lot of money. But for how much longer? □

On June 27, 1972, **Bobby Hull** announced that he was leaving the NHL to become player-coach of the Winnipeg Jets in the new World Hockey Association. Eighteen years later, his son **Brett** (seen here right) signed a four-year, $7 million deal with the St.Louis Blues.

Western Canada Pictorial Index

Top 20 Prime Time TV Series, 1989-90

Six episodes or more. For period covering Sept.18, 1989 through April 15, 1990, according to Nielsen Media Research.

		Net	Rating	Share			Net	Rating	Share
1	Roseanne	ABC	23.4	35	11	Monday Night Football	ABC	18.1	32
2	The Cosby Show	NBC	23.1	38	12	Unsolved Mysteries	NBC	18.0	29
3	Cheers	NBC	22.9	36	13	Who's the Boss?	ABC	17.9	28
4	A Different World	NBC	21.1	34	14	L.A.Law	NBC	17.7	30
5	Funniest Home Videos	ABC	21.0	32	15	Murder, She Wrote	CBS	17.7	27
6	The Golden Girls	NBC	20.1	35	16	Grand	NBC	17.6	28
7	60 Minutes	CBS	19.7	33	17	Heat of the Night	NBC	17.3	26
8	The Wonder Years	ABC	19.2	29	18	Dear John	NBC	17.2	27
9	Empty Nest	NBC	19.1	33	19	Coach	ABC	17.0	26
10	Chicken Soup	ABC	18.2	29	20	Matlock	NBC	16.7	26

Top 35 TV Sports Events, 1989-90

For the period covering Oct.1, 1989 through Aug.1, 1990, according to Nielsen Media Research. Events are listed with date, network, ratings points and audience share (according to Nielsen Media Research).

		Date	Net	Rtg/Sh			Date	Net	Rtg/Sh
1	Super Bowl XXIV (SF vs Den.)	1/28	CBS	39.0/63	19	NL Playoffs, Game 1 (SF at Chi.)	10/4	NBC	15.4/26
2	NFC Championship (Rams at SF)	1/14	CBS	26.4/46	20	NL Playoffs, Game 3 (Chi.at SF)	10/7	NBC	15.3/29
3	AFC Championship (Clev.at Den.)	1/14	NBC	26.2/55	21	College Football (N.Dame at Miami)	11/25	CBS	14.9/27
4	AFC Semifinal (Pit.at Den.)	1/7	NBC	24.5/47	22	World Series, Game 4 (Oak.at SF)	10/28	ABC	14.7/28
5	NFC Semifinal (Rams at Giants)	1/7	CBS	22.3/52	23	NCAA Final Four (UNLV vs Ga.Tech)	3/31	CBS	14.1/25
6	AFC Wildcard (Pit.at Hou.)	12/31	NBC	21.4/43	24	NBA Finals, Game 4 (Det.at Port.)	6/12	CBS	13.4/25
7	NCAA Championship (UNLV vs Duke)	4/2	CBS	20.0/31	25	NBA Finals, Game 5 (Det.at Port.)	6/14	CBS	13.2/25
8	NFC Wildcard (Rams at Phi.)	12/31	CBS	19.7/46	26	AL Playoffs, Game 1 (Tor.at Oak.)	10/3	NBC	12.8/22
9	Orange Bowl (N.Dame vs Colo.)	1/1	NBC	18.5/29	27	NCAA Tournament (UNLV vs Loyola)	3/25	CBS	12.5/30
10	Baseball All-Star Game (at Chicago)	7/10	CBS	18.5/33*	28	AL Playoffs, Game 3 (Oak.at Tor.)	10/6	NBC	12.4/23
11	NFC Semifinal (Min.at SF)	1/6	CBS	17.7/36	29	NCAA Final Four (Duke vs Ark.)	3/31	CBS	12.3/27
12	World Series, Game 3 (Oak.at SF)	10/27	ABC	17.5/32	30	NBA Finals, Game 2 (Port.at Det.)	6/7	CBS	12.2/24
13	World Series, Game 2 (SF at Oak.)	10/15	ABC	17.4/28	31	NBA Finals, Game 1 (Port.at Det.)	6/5	CBS	11.8/22
14	NL Playoffs, Game 2 (SF at Chi.)	10/5	CBS	16.7/30	32	NCAA Tournament (Ga.Tech vs Min.)	3/25	CBS	10.9/31
15	NL Playoffs, Game 4 (Chi.at SF)	10/8	NBC	16.7/28	33	NBA Finals, Game 3 (Det.at Port.)	6/10	CBS	10.8/29
16	AFC Semifinal (Buf.at Clev.)	1/6	NBC	16.4/42	34	NL Playoffs, Game 5 (Chi.at SF)	10/9	NBC	10.7/28
17	World Series, Game 1 (SF at Oak.)	10/14	ABC	16.2/30	35	NBA East Final, Game 7 (Chi.at Det.)	6/3	CBS	10.5/32
18	Rose Bowl (USC vs Mich.)	1/1	ABC	15.6/24		Masters Golf (Final round)	4/8	CBS	10.5/25

*With the rain delay factored in, the overall rating for the Baseball All-Star Game was a 16.2.

Top 20 Highest Rated TV Shows Ever

Nine of the 20 highest rated individual shows ever seen on US television are Super Bowls. Shows are listed with ratings points and number of households watching, according to Nielsen Media Research.

	Program	Episode/Game	Network	Date	Rating	Households
1	M*A*S*H (series)	Final episode	CBS	2/28/83	60.2	50,150,000
2	Dallas (series)	"Who Shot J.R.?"	CBS	11/21/80	53.3	41,470,000
3	Roots (mini-series)	Part 8	ABC	1/30/77	51.1	36,380,000
4	Super Bowl XVI	San Fran. 26, Cincinnati 21	CBS	1/24/82	51.0	40,020,000
5	Super Bowl XVII	Washington 27, Miami 17	NBC	1/30/83	48.6	40,480,000
6	Super Bowl XX	Chicago 46, New England 10	NBC	1/26/86	48.3	41,490,000
7	Gone With the Wind (movie)	Part 1	NBC	11/7/76	47.7	33,960,000
8	Gone with the Wind (movie)	Part 2	NBC	11/8/76	47.4	33,750,000
9	Super Bowl XII	Dallas 27, Denver 10	CBS	1/15/78	47.2	34,410,000
10	Super Bowl XIII	Pittsburgh 35, Dallas 31	NBC	1/21/79	47.1	35,090,000

Top 20 Highest Rated TV Shows Ever (Cont.)

Program	Episode/Game	Network	Date	Rating	Households
11 Bob Hope Special	Christmas Show	NBC	1/15/70	46.6	27,260,000
12 **Super Bowl XVIII**	LA Raiders 38, Washington 9	CBS	1/22/84	46.4	38,800,000
Super Bowl XIX	San Francisco 38, Miami 16	ABC	1/20/85	46.4	39,390,000
14 **Super Bowl XIV**	Pittsburgh 31, LA Rams 19	CBS	1/20/80	46.3	35,330,000
15 ABC Theater (special)	"The Day After"	ABC	11/20/83	46.1	38,550,000
16 Roots (mini-series)	Part 6	ABC	1/28/77	45.9	32,680,000
The Fugitive (series)	Final episode	ABC	8/29/67	45.9	25,700,000
18 **Super Bowl XXI**	NY Giants 39, Denver 20	CBS	1/25/87	45.8	40,030,000
19 Roots (mini-series)	Part 5	ABC	1/27/77	45.7	32,540,000
20 Bob Hope Special	Christmas Show	NBC	1/14/71	45.0	27,050,000

Who Has What

The network-by-network roster of TV rights as of Sept.1, 1990.

ABC

Auto Racing—Indianapolis 500
Bowling—PBA Tour
NCAA Basketball—regular season
Cycling—Tour de France
NFL Football—Monday Night Football, Wild Card Playoffs, 1991 Super Bowl, WLAF Spring Football
College Football—Big 10/Pac-10 regular season, CFA (minus Notre Dame home games), Rose Bowl, Sugar Bowl
Men's Golf—US Open, British Open, PGA Skins, Seniors Skins, LPGA Skins
Horse Racing—Kentucky Derby, Preakness, Belmont Stakes
Pan Am Games—1991 Games (Havana)

CBS

Auto Racing—Daytona 500
Major League Baseball—regular season, All-Star Game, league playoffs, World Series
NCAA Basketball—regular season, NCAA Tournament
NFL Football—NFC regular season, NFC Playoffs, 1992 Super Bowl,
College Football—Cotton Bowl
Golf—Masters, PGA
Olympics—1992 and 1994 Winter Games
Tennis—US Open

SportsChannel America

NHL Hockey—regular season, Stanley Cup playoffs
Olympics—cable coverage of 1992 Summer Games

USA Network

NFL Football—WLAF Spring Football
Golf—Masters (early rounds)
Tennis—US Open (early rounds)

HBO

Boxing—Mike Tyson heavyweight fights
Tennis—Wimbledon (early rounds)

NBC

NBA Basketball—regular season, All-Star Game, playoffs, NBA Finals
NCAA Basketball—regular season
Figure Skating—World Championships
NFL Football—AFC regular season, AFC playoffs, 1993 Super Bowl
College Football—Notre Dame home games, Orange Bowl, Fiesta Bowl
Golf—Players Championship
Horse Racing—Breeders' Cup
Olympics—1992 Summer Games
Tennis—French Open, Wimbledon
World Track & Field Championships—1991 (Tokyo)

ESPN

Auto Racing—CART, NASCAR, Formula One
Major League Baseball—regular season
College Basketball—regular season
Bowling—PBA and LPBT tours
NFL Football—Sunday Night Football, Pro Bowl
College Football—regular season CFA, Big 10 and Pac-10
Golf—US Open, British Open (early rounds)
Horse Racing—The Hambletonian
Tennis—Australian Open, French Open (early rounds), ATP Masters, Va.Slims Championships, Davis Cup

Turner

Major League Baseball—Atlanta Braves (TBS)
NBA Basketball—regular season, playoffs (TNT); Atlanta Hawks (TBS)
NFL Football—Sunday Night Football (TNT)
College Football—SEC regular season (TBS)
Golf—PGA early rounds (TNT)
Goodwill Games—1994 (TBS)
Olympics—cable coverage of 1992 and '94 Winter Games (TNT)

Olympic Rights Fees, 1960-94

The reported cost of securing exclusive U.S. television rights for the Olympic Games has skyrocketed over the last 30 years. In 1960, CBS paid $50,000 for the Winter Olympics. In 1989, CBS agreed to pay $300 million for the 1994 Winter Games—an increase of 6000 percent. In the same time, the cost of the Summer Games has gone from just under $400,000 to just over $400 million.

Year	Games	Location	Rights Fee	Net	Year	Games	Location	Rights Fee	Net
1960	Winter—	Squaw Valley	$50,000	CBS	1980	Winter—	Lake Placid	$15.5 million	ABC
	Summer—	Rome	$394,000	CBS		Summer—	Moscow	$85 million	NBC
1964	Winter—	Innsbruck	$597,000	ABC	1984	Winter—	Sarajevo	$91.5 million	ABC
	Summer—	Tokyo	$1.5 million	NBC		Summer—	Los Angeles	$225 million	ABC
1968	Winter—	Grenoble	$2.5 million	ABC	1988	Winter—	Calgary	$309 million	ABC
	Summer—	Mexico City	$4.5 million	ABC		Summer—	Seoul	$300 million	NBC
1972	Winter—	Sapporo	$6.4 million	NBC	1992	Winter—	Albertville	$243 million	CBS
	Summer—	Munich	$7.5 million	ABC		Summer—	Barcelona	$401 million	NBC
1976	Winter—	Innsbruck	$10 million	ABC	1994	Winter—	Lillehammer	$300 million	CBS
	Summer—	Montreal	$25 million	ABC		Summer—	Atlanta	To be determined	

Directory
Listing of organizations, teams and media addresses and officials as of Sept. 1, 1990

Auto Racing

CART (Championship Auto Racing Teams)
390 Enterprise Court, Bloomfield Hills, MI 48302
313-334-8500
President .... John Capels
Director of Public Relations .... Mel Poole

Formula One
(Federation Internationale de Sport Automobile)
8 Rue de la Concorde, Paris 8E, France
331-426-599-51
President .... Jean Marie Balestre
Director of Public Relations .... Martin Whiticker

NASCAR
(National Assn. of Stock Car Auto Racing)
P.O. Box 2875, Daytona Beach, FL 32115
904-253-0611
President .... Bill France, Jr.
Director of Public Relations .... Bill Seaborn, Jr.

Major League Baseball

Office of the Commissioner
350 Park Ave., New York, NY 10022
212-371-7800
Commissioner .... Fay Vincent
Deputy Commissioner .... Steve Greenberg
Director of Public Relations .... Rich Levin

MLB Players Association
805 Third Ave., New York, NY 10022
212-826-0808
Exec. Director .... Donald Fehr
Special Assistant .... Mark Belanger

AL

American League Office
350 Park Ave., New York, NY 10022
212-339-7600
President .... Bobby Brown
Director of Public Relations .... Phyllis Merhige

Baltimore Orioles
Memorial Stadium, Baltimore, MD 21218
301-243-9800
Owners .... Eli Jacobs and Sargent Shriver
General Manager .... Roland Hemond
Director of Public Relations .... Rick Vaughn

Boston Red Sox
Fenway Park, 4 Yawkey Way, Boston, MA 02215
617-267-9440
Owners .... Jean Yawkey, Haywood Sullivan
and John Harrington
General Manager .... Lou Gorman
Director of Public Relations .... Dick Bresciani

California Angels
P.O. Box 2000, Anaheim, CA 92803
714-937-6700 or 213-625-1123
Owner .... Gene Autry
General Manager .... Mike Port
Director of Public Relations .... Tim Mead

Chicago White Sox
Comiskey Park, 333 W. 35th St., Chicago, IL 60616
312-924-1000
Owners ...... Jerry Reinsdorf and Eddie Einhorn
General Manager .... Larry Himes
Director of Public Relations .... Chuck Adams

Cleveland Indians
Cleveland Stadium, Cleveland, OH 44114
216-861-1200
Owners .... Richard and David Jacobs
General Manager .... Hank Peters
Director of Public Relations .... Bob DiBiasio

Detroit Tigers
Tiger Stadium, Detroit, MI 48216
313-962-4000
Owner .... Tom Monaghan
President .... Bo Schembechler
General Manager .... Bill Lajoie
Director of Public Relations .... Dan Ewald

Kansas City Royals
P.O. Box 419969, Kansas City, MO 64141
816-921-2200
Owner .... Ewing Kauffman
General Manager .... John Schuerholz
Director of Public Relations .... Dean Vogelaar

Milwaukee Brewers
County Stadium, 201 S. 46th St., Milwaukee, WI 53214
414-933-4114
Owner .... Bud Selig
General Manager .... Harry Dalton
Director of Public Relations .... Tom Skibosh

Minnesota Twins
Hubert H. Humphrey Metrodome
501 Chicago Ave. So., Minneapolis, MN 55415
612-375-1366
Owner .... Carl Pohlad
General Manager .... Andy MacPhail
Director of Public Relations .... Tom Mee

New York Yankees
Yankee Stadium, Bronx, NY 10451
212-293-4300
Managing General Partner ...... Robert Nederlander
General Manager .... Gene Michael
Director of Public Relations .... Arthur Richman

Oakland Athletics
Oakland Alameda County Coliseum
Oakland, CA 94621
415-638-4900
Owner .... Walter Haas, Jr.
General Manager .... Sandy Alderson
Director of Public Relations .... Jay Alves

Seattle Mariners
P.O. Box 4100, Seattle, WA 98104
206-628-3555
Owner .... Jeff Smulyan
General Manager .... Woody Woodward
Director of Public Relations .... Dave Aust

Texas Rangers
P.O. Box 1111, Arlington, TX 76010
Owners .... Geo. W. Bush and Edward Rose
General Manager .... Tom Grieve
Director of Public Relations .... John Blake

Toronto Blue Jays
300 Esplanade West, Suite 3200
Toronto, Ontario M5V 3B3 CAN
416-341-1000
Owner .... N.E. Hardy
General Manager .... Pat Gillick
Director of Public Relations .... Howie Starkman

NL

National League Office
350 Park Ave., New York, NY 10022
212-339-7700
President   Bill White
Director of Public Relations   Katy Feeney

Atlanta Braves
P.O. Box 4064, Atlanta, GA 30302
404-522-7630
Owner   Ted Turner
General Manager   Bobby Cox
Director of Public Relations   Jim Schultz

Chicago Cubs
1060 West Addison St., Chicago, IL 60613
312-404-2787
Owner   The Tribune Company
President   Don Grenesko
General Manager   Jim Frey
Director of Public Relations   Ned Colletti

Cincinnati Reds
100 Riverfront Stadium, Cincinnati, OH 45202
513-421-4510
Owner   Marge Schott
General Manager   Bob Quinn
Director of Public Relations   Jim Ferguson

Houston Astros
P.O. Box 288, Houston, TX 77001
713-799-9500
Owner   John McMullen
General Manager   Bill Wood
Director of Public Relations   Rob Matwick

Los Angeles Dodgers
1000 Elysian Park Ave., Los Angeles, CA 90012
213-224-1500
Owner   Peter O'Malley
General Manager   Fred Claire
Director of Public Relations   Mike Williams

Montreal Expos
P.O. Box 500, Station M, Montreal, Quebec H1V 3P2
514-253-3434
Owner   Charles Broufman
General Manager   Dave Dombrowski
Director of Public Relations   Richard Griffin

New York Mets
Shea Stadium, Flushing, NY 11368
718-507-6387
Owners   Nelson Doubleday and Fred Wilpon
General Manager   Frank Cashen
Director of Public Relations   Jay Horwitz

Philadelphia Phillies
P.O. Box 7575, Philadelphia, PA 19101
215-463-6000
Managing General Partner   Bill Giles
General Manager   Lee Thomas
Director of Public Relations   Larry Shenk

Pittsburgh Pirates
P.O. Box 7000, Pittsburgh, PA 15212
412-323-5000
Owners   Douglas Danforth and Carl Barger
General Manager   Larry Doughty
Director of Public Relations   Rick Cerrone

St. Louis Cardinals
250 Stadium Plaza, St. Louis, MO 63102
314-421-4040
Owner   Anheuser Busch Company
President   Fred Kuhlmann
General Manager   Dal Maxvill
Director of Public Relations   Jeff Wehling

San Diego Padres
P.O. Box 2000, San Diego, CA 92120
619-283-7294
Owner   Tom Werner
General Manager   Jack McKeon
Director of Public Relations   Mike Swanson

San Francisco Giants
Candlestick Park, San Francisco, CA 94124
415-468-3700
Owner   Bob Lurie
General Manager   Al Rosen
Director of Public Relations   Duffy Jennings

National Basketball Association

League Office
645 Fifth Ave.,
New York, NY 10022
212-826-7000
Commissioner   David Stern
Deputy Commissioner   Russell Granik
Director of Public Relations   Brian McIntyre

NBA Players Association
1775 Broadway, Suite 2401, New York, NY 10019
212-333-7510
Executive Director   Charles Grantham

Atlanta Hawks
One CNN Center, South Tower, Suite 405,
Atlanta, GA 30303
404-827-3800
Owner   Ted Turner
General Manager   Pete Babcock
Director of Public Relations   Arthur Triche

Boston Celtics
150 Causeway St., Boston, MA 02114
617-523-6050
Owners   Don Gaston, Paul Dupee
and Alan Cohen
President   Red Auerbach
General Manager   Dave Gavitt
Director of Public Relations   Jeff Twiss

Charlotte Hornets
Two First Union Center, Suite 2600
Charlotte, NC 28282
704-376-6430
Owner   George Shinn
General Manager   Allan Bristow
Director of Public Relations   Harold Kaufman

Chicago Bulls
One Magnificent Mile, 960 N. Michigan Ave.
Suite 1600, Chicago, IL 60611
312-943-5800
Owner   Jerry Reinsdorf
General Manager   Jerry Krause
Director of Public Relations   Tim Hallam

Cleveland Cavaliers
P.O. Box 5000, Richfield, OH 44286
216-659-9100
Owner   Gordon Gund
General Manager   Wayne Embry
Director of Public Relations   Bob Price

Dallas Mavericks
Reunion Arena, 777 Sports St., Dallas, TX 75207
214-988-0117
Owner   Donald Carter
General Manager   Norm Sonju
Director of Public Relations   Kevin Sullivan

Denver Nuggets
P.O. Box 4658, Denver, CO 80204
303-893-6700
Owners   Bertram Lee, Peter Bynoe
                              and Robert Wussler
General Manager   Bernie Bickerstaff
Director of Public Relations   Jay Clark

Detroit Pistons
The Palace of Auburn Hills
3777 Lapeer Road, Auburn Hills, MI 48057
313-377-0100
Owner   Bill Davidson
General Manager   Jack McCloskey
Director of Public Relations   Matt Dobek

Golden State Warriors
Oakland Coliseum Arena, Oakland, CA 94621
415-638-6300
Owner   James Fitzgerald
General Manager-Head Coach   Don Nelson
Director of Public Relations   Julie Gumlia-Marvel

Houston Rockets
P.O. Box 272349, Houston, TX 77277
713-627-0600
Owner   Charlie Thomas
General Manager   Steve Patterson
Director of Public Relations   Jay Goldberg

Indiana Pacers
300 East Market St., Indianapolis, IN 46204
317-263-2100
Owner   Herbert Simon
General Manager   Donnie Walsh
Director of Public Relations   Dale Ratermann

Los Angeles Clippers
L.A. Memorial Sports Arena
3939 S. Figueroa St., Los Angeles, CA 90037
213-748-8000
Owner   Donald Sterling
General Manager   Elgin Baylor
Director of Public Relations   Paul Feinberg

Los Angeles Lakers
P.O. Box 10, Inglewood, CA 90306
213-419-3100
Owner   Jerry Buss
General Manager   Jerry West
Director of Public Relations   John Black

Miami Heat
The Miami Arena, Miami, FL 33136
305-577-4328
Owner   Ted Arison
General Manager   Lewis Schaffel
Director of Public Relations   Mark Pray

Milwaukee Bucks
Bradley Center
1001 N. Fourth St., Milwaukee, WI 53203
414-227-0500
President   Herb Kohl
General Manager   John Steinmiller
Director of Public Relations   Bill King II

Minnesota Timberwolves
500 City Place, 730 Hennepin Ave.
Minneapolis, MN 55403
612-337-3865
Owners   Marv Wolfenson and Harvey Ratner
General Manager   Bob Stein
Director of Public Relations   Bill Robertson

New Jersey Nets
Meadowlands Arena, East Rutherford, NJ 07073
201-935-8888
Owners   Alan Aufzien, Bernard Mann
                              and David Gerstein
General Manager   Willis Reed
Director of Public Relations   John Mertz

New York Knickerbockers
Madison Square Garden
Four Pennsylvania Plaza, New York, NY 10001
212-563-8057
Owner   Paramount Communications
President   Richard Evans
General Manager   Al Bianchi
Director of Public Relations   John Cirillo

Orlando Magic
Orlando Arena, 1 Magic Place, Orlando, FL 32801
407-649-3200
Owner   William du Pont III
General Manager   Pat Williams
Director of Public Relations   Alex Martins

Philadelphia 76ers
Veterans Stadium
P.O. Box 25040, Philadelphia, PA 19147
215-339-7600
Owner   Harold Katz
General Manager   Gene Shue
Director of Public Relations   Zack Hill

Phoenix Suns
P.O. Box 1369, Phoenix, AZ 85001
602-266-5753
Owner-General Manager   Jerry Colangelo
Director of Public Relations   Barry Ringel

Portland Trail Blazers
Suite 950 Lloyd Building
700 Multnomah St., Portland, OR 97232
503-234-9291
Owner   Paul Allen
General Manager   Geoff Petrie
Director of Public Relations   John Lashway

Sacramento Kings
One Sports Parkway, Sacramento, CA 95834
916-928-0000
Owner   Gregg Lukenbill
General Manager   Jerry Reynolds
Director of Public Relations   Julie Fie

San Antonio Spurs
600 East Market St., Suite 102, San Antonio, TX 78205
512-224-4611
Owner   Red McCombs
General Manager   Bob Bass
Director of Public Relations   Wayne Witt

Seattle Supersonics
Box C 900911, Seattle WA 98109
206-281-5800
Owner   Barry Ackerley
General Manager   Bob Whitsitt
Director of Public Relations   Jim Rupp

Utah Jazz
5 Triad Center, 5th Floor, Salt Lake City, UT 84180
801-575-7800
Owner   Larry Miller
President   Frank Layden
General Manager   Tim Howells
Director of Public Relations   Kim Turner

Washington Bullets
One Harry S Truman Dr., Landover, MD 20785
301-773-2255
Owner	Abe Pollin
General Manager	John Nash
Director of Public Relations	Rick Moreland

Bowling

BPAA (Bowling Proprietors' Assn. of America)
P.O. Box 5802, Arlington, TX 76011
817-649-5105
President	Walter Hill
Director of Public Relations	Stuart Robinson

LPBT (Ladies Professional Bowlers Tour)
7171 Cherryvale Blvd., Rockford, IL 61112
815-332-5756
President	John Falzone
Director of Public Relations	TBA

PBA (Professional Bowlers Association)
1720 Merriman Road, P.O. Box 5118
Akron, OH 44313
216-836-5568
Commissioner	Joseph Antenora
Director of Public Relations	Kevin Shippy

Boxing

IBF (International Boxing Federation)
134 Evergreen Place, 9th Floor,
East Orange, NJ 07018
201-414-0300
President	Bob Lee
Director of Public Relations	Cy Roseman

WBA (World Boxing Association)
President	Gilberto Mendoza
General Counsel & U.S. Spokesman	Jimmy Binns

300 Walnut Street
Philadelphia, PA 19106
215-922-4000

WBC (World Boxing Council)
President	Jose Sulaiman
Treasurer & U.S. Contact	Haig Kelegian

850 W. Washington Blvd.
Los Angeles, CA 90015
213-742-0255

Canadian Football League

CFL Building
110 Eglinton Ave., 5th Floor
Toronto, Ontario M4R 1A3
416-322-9650
Chairman	Roy McMurtry
Commissioner	Donald Crump
Directors of Public Relations	Diane Cote and Norm Miller

B.C. Lions
B.C. Place Stadium, 765 Pacific Blvd. South
Vancouver, B.C. V6B 4Y9
604-681-5466
Owner	Murray Pezim
General Manager	Joe Kapp
Director of Public Relations	Roger Kelly

Calgary Stampeders
McMahon Stadium, 1817 Crowchild Tr. NW
Calgary, Alberta T2M 4R6
403-289-0205
Owner	Community owned
General Manager	Norman Kwong
Director of Public Relations	Kevin Gallant

Edmonton Eskimos
9023 — 111 Ave., Edmonton, Alberta T5B 0C3
403-429-2821
Owner	Community owned
General Manager	Hugh Campbell
Director of Public Relations	Allan Watt

Hamilton Tiger-Cats
P.O.Box 172, Hamilton, Ontario L8N 3A2
416-547-2418
Owner	David Braley
General Manager	Joe Zuger
Director of Public Relations	Chris Dowhun

Ottawa Rough Riders
Coliseum Building, Lansdowne Park
Ottawa, Ontario K1S 3W7
613-563-4551
Owner	Community owned
General Manager	Jo-Anne Polak
Director of Public Relations	Sal De Meo

Saskatchewan Roughriders
2940 — 10th Ave., P.O.Box 1277
Regina, Saskatchewan S4P 3B8
306-569-2323
Owner	Community owned
General Manager	Alan Ford
Director of Public Relations	Jim Dorash

Toronto Argos
Exhibition Place, Toronto, Ontario M6K 3C3
416-595-9600
Owner	Harry Ornest
General Manager	Mike McCarthy
Director of Public Relations	Shelly Hood

Winnipeg Blue Bombers
1465 Maroons Road, Winnipeg, Manitoba R3G 0L6
204-786-2583
Owner	Community owned
General Manager	Cal Murphy
Director of Public Relations	Kevin O'Donovan

National Football League

League Office
410 Park Ave., New York, NY 10022
212-758-1500
Commissioner	Paul Tagliabue
League Counsel	Jay Moyer
Director of Public Relations	Jim Heffernan

NFL Players Association
2021 L. Street NW, Washington, DC 20036
202-463-2200
Executive Director	Gene Upshaw
Assistant Director	Doug Allen
Director of Public Relations	Frank Woschitz

AFC

American Football Conference
President	Lamar Hunt
Director of Information	Pete Abitante

Buffalo Bills
One Bills Drive, Orchard Park, NY 14127
716-648-1800
Owner   Ralph Wilson,Jr.
General Manager   Bill Polian
Director of Public Relations   Denny Lynch

Cincinnati Bengals
200 Riverfront Stadium, Cincinnati, OH 45202
513-621-3550
Owner   John Sawyer
General Manager   Paul Brown
Director of Public Relations   Al Heim

Cleveland Browns
Tower B, Cleveland Stadium, Cleveland, OH 44114
216-696-5555
Owner   Art Modell
General Manager   Ernie Accorsi
Director of Public Relations   Kevin Byrne

Denver Broncos
13655 E. Dove Valley Parkway,
Englewood, CO 80112
303-649-9000
Owner   Pat Bowlen
General Manager   John Beake
Director of Public Relations   Jim Saccomano

Houston Oilers
6910 Fannin St., Houston, TX 77030
713-797-9111
Owner   Bud Adams
General Manager   Mike Holovak
Director of Public Relations   Chip Namias

Indianapolis Colts
P.O. Box 24100, Indianapolis, IN 46253
317-297-2658
Owner   Robert Irsay
General Manager   James Irsay
Director of Public Relations   Craig Kelley

Kansas City Chiefs
One Arrowhead Drive, Kansas City, MO 64129
816-924-9300
Owner   Lamar Hunt
General Manager   Carl Peterson
Director of Public Relations   Bob Moore

Los Angeles Raiders
332 Center St., El Segundo, CA 90245
213-322-3451
Managing General Partner   Al Davis
Director of Public Relations   Al LoCasale

Miami Dolphins
Joe Robbie Stadium
2269 NW 199th Street, Miami, FL 33056
305-620-5000
Owner   Tim Robbie
General Manager   Eddie Jones
Director of Public Relations   Harvey Greene

New England Patriots
Foxboro Stadium, Route 1, Foxboro, MA 02035
508-543-7911
Owner   Victor Kiam
General Manager   Pat Sullivan
Director of Public Relations   Dave Wintergrass

New York Jets
598 Madison Ave., New York, NY 10022
212-421-6600
Owner   Leon Hess
General Manager   Dick Steinberg
Director of Public Relations   Frank Ramos

Pittsburgh Steelers
Three Rivers Stadium
300 Stadium Circle, Pittsburgh, PA 15212
412-323-1200
Owner-General Manager   Dan Rooney
Director of Public Relations   Dan Edwards

San Diego Chargers
San Diego Jack Murphy Stadium
P.O. Box 20666, San Diego, CA 92120
619-280-2111
Owner   Alex Spanos
General Manager   Bobby Beathard
Director of Public Relations   Bill Johnston

Seattle Seahawks
11220 NE 53rd Street, Kirkland, WA 98033
206-827-9777
Owner   Ken Behring
General Manager   Tom Flores
Director of Public Relations   Gary Wright

NFC

National Football Conference
President   Wellington Mara
Director of Information   Reggie Roberts

Atlanta Falcons
Suwanee Road at I-85, Suwanee, GA 30174
404-945-1111
Owner   Rankin Smith, Sr.
General Manager   Rankin Smith, Jr.
Director of Public Relations   Charley Taylor

Chicago Bears
Halas Hall, 250 N. Washington, Lake Forest, IL 60045
312-295-6600
Owner   Edward McCaskey
President-General Manager   Mike McCaskey
Director of Public Relations   Bryan Harlan

Dallas Cowboys
Cowboys Center
One Cowboys Parkway, Irving, TX 75063
214-556-9900
Owner-General Manager   Jerry Jones
Director of Public Relations   Rich Dalrymple

Detroit Lions
Pontiac Silverdome
1200 Featherstone Road, Box 4200, Pontiac, MI 48057
313-335-4131
Owner   William Clay Ford
General Manager   Chuck Schmidt
Director of Public Relations   Bill Keenist

Green Bay Packers
1265 Lombardi Ave., Green Bay, WI 54307
414-496-5700
Owner   Community owned
Chairman   Robert Parins
General Manager   Tom Braatz
Director of Public Relations   Lee Remmel

Los Angeles Rams
2327 West Lincoln Ave., Anaheim, CA 92801
714-535-7267
Owner   Georgia Frontiere
General Manager   Jack Faulkner
Director of Public Relations   John Oswald

Minnesota Vikings
9520 Viking Drive, Eden Prairie, MN 55344
612-828-6500
Chairman   John Skoglund
General Manager   Mike Lynn
Director of Public Relations   Merrill Swanson

New Orleans Saints
6928 Saints Ave., Metairie, LA 70003
504-522-1500
Owner   Tom Benson
General Manager   Jim Finks
Director of Public Relations   Greg Suit

New York Giants
Giants Stadium, East Rutherford, NJ 07073
201-935-8111
Owners   Wellington Mara and Tim Mara
General Manager   George Young
Director of Public Relations   Ed Croke

Philadelphia Eagles
Veterans Stadium, Broad St. & Pattison Ave.
Philadelphia, PA 19148
215-463-2500
Owner   Norman Braman
General Manager   Harry Gamble
Director of Public Relations   Ron Howard

Phoenix Cardinals
P.O. Box 888, Phoenix, AZ 85001
602-967-1010
Owner   Bill Bidwill
General Manager   Larry Wilson
Director of Public Relations   Paul Jensen

San Francisco 49ers
4949 Centennial Blvd., Santa Clara, CA 95054
408-562-4949
Owner   Edward DeBartolo, Jr.
General Manager   John McVay
Director of Public Relations   Jerry Walker

Tampa Bay Buccaneers
One Buccaneer Place, Tampa, FL 33607
813-870-2700
Owner   Hugh Culverhouse
General Manager-Head Coach   Ray Perkins
Director of Public Relations   Rick Odioso

Washington Redskins
Redskin Park, P.O. Box 17247, Dulles Int'l Airport,
Washington, DC 20041
703-471-9100
Owner   Jack Kent Cooke
General Manager   Charlie Casserly
Director of Public Relations   Charlie Dayton

World League of American Football

405 Lexington Ave., 36th Floor
New York, NY 10174
212-973-6011
President   Tex Schramm
Director of Public Relations   Bob Rose

Golf

LPGA Tour
(Ladies Professional Golf Association)
2570 Volusia Ave., Daytona Beach, FL 32114
904-254-8800
Commissioner   William Blue
Director of Communications   Holly Geoghegan

PGA Tour
(Professional Golfer's Association)
Sawgrass, Ponte Vedra, FL 32082
904-285-3700
Commissioner   Deane Beman
Director of Information   Tom Place

USGA
(United States Golf Association)
Liberty Corner Road, Far Hills, NJ 07931
201-234-2300
President   Grant Spaeth
Executive Director   David Fay
Director of Communications   Bob Sommers

National Hockey League
President   John Ziegler
Executive Vice President   Brian O'Neill
General Counsel   Gilbert Stein
Dir. of Public Relations (Montreal)   Gary Meagher
Dir. of Public Relations (New York)   Gerry Helper
Montreal Office: 1155 Metcalfe St., Suite 960
                        Montreal, Quebec H3B 2W2
                        514-871-9220
New York Office: 650 Fifth Ave., 33rd Floor,
                        New York, NY 10019
                        212-398-1100

NHL Players' Association
37 Maitland St., Toronto, Ontario M4Y 1C8
416-924-7800
Executive Director   Alan Eagleson
Deputy Executive Director   Bob Goodenow
Director of Public Relations   Dolores Antonacci

Boston Bruins
Boston Garden, 150 Causeway St., Boston, MA 02114
617-227-3206
Owner   Jeremy Jacobs
General Manager   Harry Sinden
Director of Public Relations   Heidi Holland

Buffalo Sabres
Memorial Auditorium, 140 Main St.,
Buffalo, NY 14202
716-856-7300
Owner   Seymour Knox, III
General Manager   Gerry Meehan
Director of Public Relations   Budd Bailey

Calgary Flames
Olympic Saddledome, P.O. Box 1540 Station M,
Calgary, Alberta T2P 3B9
403-261-0475
Owners   Harley Hotchkiss, Norman Kwong
          Sonia Scarfield, Byron and Daryl Seamen
General Manager   Cliff Fletcher
Director of Public Relations   Rick Skaggs

Chicago Blackhawks
Chicago Stadium, 1800 W. Madison St.,
Chicago, IL 60612
312-733-5300
Owner   William Wirtz
General Manager-Head Coach   Mike Keenan
Director of Public Relations   Jim DeMaria

Detroit Red Wings
Joe Louis Sports Arena
600 Civic Center Drive, Detroit, MI 48226
313-567-7333
Owner   Mike Ilitch
General Manager-Head Coach   Bryan Murray
Director of Public Relations   Bill Jamieson

Edmonton Oilers
Northlands Coliseum
Edmonton, Alberta T5B 4M9
403-474-8561
Owner   Peter Pocklington
General Manager   Glen Sather
Director of Public Relations   Bill Tuele

Hartford Whalers
Hartford Civic Center Coliseum
One Civic Center Plaza, Hartford, CT 06103
203-728-3366
Managing General Partner   Richard Gordon
General Manager   Ed Johnston
Director of Public Relations   Phil Langan

Los Angeles Kings
The Forum, 3900 West Manchester Blvd.
Box 17013, Inglewood, CA 90306
213-419-3160
Owner   Bruce NcNall
General Manager   Rogie Vachon
Director of Public Relations   Sue Carpenter

Minnesota North Stars
Metropolitan Sports Center
7901 Cedar Ave. South, Bloomington, MN 55425
612-853-9333
Owners   Norman Green and Morris Belzberg
General Manager   Bobby Clarke
Director of Public Relations   Joan Preston

Montreal Canadiens
Montreal Forum, 2313 St. Catherine Street West,
Montreal, Quebec H3H 1N2
514-932-2582
Owner   Molson Companies Limited
President   Ronald Corey
General Manager   Serge Savard
Director of Public Relations   Michele Lapointe

New Jersey Devils
Byrne Meadowlands Arena
P.O. Box 504, East Rutherford, NJ 07073
201-935-6050
Owner   John McMullen
General Manager   Lou Lamoriello
Director of Public Relations   Dave Freed

New York Islanders
Nassau Veterans' Memorial Coliseum
Uniondale, NY 11553
516-794-4100
Owner   John Pickett, Jr.
General Manager   Bill Torrey
Director of Public Relations   Greg Bouris

New York Rangers
Madison Square Garden
4 Pennsylvania Plaza, New York, NY 10001
212-563-8000
Owner   Paramount Communications
President   Richard Evans
General Manager   Neil Smith
Director of Public Relations   Barry Watkins

Philadelphia Flyers
The Spectrum, Pattison Place, Philadelphia, PA 19148
215-465-4500
Owner   Ed Snider
General Manager   Russ Farwell
Director of Public Relations   Rodger Gottlieb

Pittsburgh Penguins
Civic Arena, Pittsburgh, PA 15219
412-642-1800
Owner   Edward DeBartolo, Sr.
General Manager   Craig Patrick
Director of Press Relations   Cindy Himes

Quebec Nordiques
Colisée de Quebec, 2205 Ave. du Colisée
Quebec City, Quebec G1L 4W7
418-529-8441
Owner   Marcel Aubut
General Manager   Pierre Page
Director of Public Relations   Jean Martineau

St. Louis Blues
St. Louis Arena
5700 Oakland Ave., St. Louis, MO 63110
314-781-5300
Owner   Michael Shanahan
General Manager   Ron Caron
Director of Public Relations   Susie Mathieu

Toronto Maple Leafs
Maple Leaf Gardens
60 Carlton St., Toronto, Ontario M5B 1L1
416-977-1641
Managing Director   Donald Giffen
General Manager   Floyd Smith
Director of Public Relations   Bob Stellick

Vancouver Canucks
Pacific Coliseum, 100 North Renfrew St.,
Vancouver, British Columbia V5K 3N7
604-254-5141
Owner   Frank Griffiths
General Manager   Pat Quinn
Director of Public Relations   Darcy Rota

Washington Capitals
Capital Centre, Landover, MD 20785
301-350-3400
Chairman   Abe Pollin
Owner-General Manager   Dave Poile
Director of Public Relations   Lou Corletto

Winnipeg Jets
Winnipeg Arena, 15-1430 Maroons Road,
Winnipeg, Manitoba R3G 0L5
204-783-5387
Owner   Barry Shenkarow
General Manager   Mike Smith
Director of Public Relations   Mike O'Hearn

Horse Racing

TRA
(Thoroughbred Racing Assn. of N.America)
3000 Marcus Ave., Suite 2W4
Lake Success, NY 11042
516-328-2660
President   Robert Levey
Director of Public Relations   Richard Schulhoff

USTA
(United States Trotting Association)
750 Michigan Ave., Columbus, OH 43215
614-224-2291
Exec. Vice President   Francis X. Ready
Director of Public Relations   John Pawlak

Media

DAILY NEWSPAPERS

The National
15 West 52nd St., New York, NY 10019
212-826-5400
Owner   Emilio Escaraga
Publisher   Peter Price
Editor   Frank Deford

USA Today
P.O. Box 500, Washington, DC 20044
703-276-3400
Owner   Gannett Company
Publisher   Cathleen Black
Managing Editor/Sports   Gene Policinski

WEEKLY MAGAZINES

Sports Illustrated
Time&Life Bldg., Rockefeller Ctr.,
New York, NY 10020
212-586-1212
Publisher   Donald Barr
Managing Editor   Mark Mulvoy

The Sporting News
1212 N.Lindbergh Blvd., St. Louis, MO 63132
314-997-7111
Chairman   Francis Pandolfi
Editor   John Rawlings

TELEVISION

ABC Sports
47 West 66th St., 13th Floor, New York, NY 10023
212-887-4867
President   Dennis Swanson
Senior V.P., Production   Dennis Lewin
Executive Producer   Geoffrey Mason
Director of Public Relations   Mark Mandel

CBS Sports
51 West 52nd St., 30th Floor, New York, NY 10019
212-975-5230
President   Neal Pilson
Executive Producer   Ted Shaker
V.P., Programming   Jay Rosenstein
Director of Information   Sandy Genelius

ESPN
ESPN Plaza, Bristol, CT 06010
203-585-2000
President   Roger Werner
Exec. V.P., Programming   Steve Bornstein
Director of Production   Steve Anderson
Managing Editor   John Walsh
Director of Communications   Chris LaPlaca

HBO Sports
1100 Ave. of the Americas, New York, NY 10036
212-512-1000
President   Seth Abraham
V.P., Executive Producer   Ross Greenburg
V.P., Programming   Bob Greenway

NBC Sports
30 Rockefeller Plaza, New York, NY 10112
212-664-4444
President   Dick Ebersol
Executive Vice President   Ken Schanzer
Executive Producer   Terry O'Neil
Director of Public Relations   Ed Markey

SportsChannel America
150 Crossways Park West, Woodbury, NY 11797
516-364-2222
President   Jeff Ruhe
V.P., Programming   Mike Lardner
Director of Information   Dan Martinsen

Turner Sports
One CNN Center, Suite 1300, Atlanta, GA 30303
404-827-1735
President   Terry McGuirk
Sr. V.P., Executive Producer   Don McGuire
Sr. V.P., Programming   Kevin O'Malley
Director of Public Relations   John Prenty

Olympics

**Albertville Olympic Organizing Committee
(1992 Winter Games)**
11 rue Pargoux, 73200 Albertville, France
Tel: (33.7)9379242
President   Michel Barnier

**Barcelona Olympic Organizing Committee
(1992 Summer Games)**
Edificio Hellos, C/Mejia Lequerica, S/N 08028,
Barcelona, Spain
Tel: (34.3)4321992
Chairman and President   M. Pasqual Maragall

**Atlanta Olympic Organizing Committee
(1996 Summer Games)**
1201 W. Peachtree St., Suite 3450
Atlanta, GA 30309
404-874-1996
President   Billy Payne
Executive Director   Doug Gatlin
Director of Public Relations   Bob Brennan

**COA
(Canadian Olympic Association)**
1600 James Naismith Dr., Ottawa, Ontario K1B 5N4
613-748-5647
President   Roger Jackson
IOC Members (2)   James Worrall & Richard Pound
Director of Communications   Frank Ratcliffe

**IOC
(International Olympic Committee)**
Chateau de Vidy, CH-1007 Lausanne, Switzerland
Tel.: (41.21)253271
President   Juan Antonio Samaranch
Director General   François Carrard
Director of Information   Michele Verdier

**USOC
(United States Olympic Committee)**
1750 East Boulder St., Colorado Springs, CO 80909
719-578-4529
President   Robert Helmick
IOC Members (2)   Robert Helmick & Anita DeFrantz
Director of Information   Mike Moran

**U.S. Olympic Festival
(1991 Organizing Committee)**
700 South Flower St., 20th Floor,
Los Angeles, CA 90017
213-489-1991
President & Exec. Dir.   Elizabeth Primrose Smith
Director of Public Relations   Jim Goyjer

Soccer

**FIFA
(Federation Internationale de Football Assn.)**
P.O. Box 85, CH-8030 Zurich, Switzerland
Tel: (01.5)55400
President   Joao Havelange (Brazil)
General Secretary   Joseph Blatter (Switz.)
Director of Public Relations   Guido Tognoni

**USSF
(United States Soccer Federation)**
1750 East Boulder St., Colorado Springs, CO 80909
719-578-4678
President   Alan Rothenberg
Director of Public Relations   John Polis

Major Soccer League
(Formerly the MISL)
7101 College Blvd., Suite 320
Overland Park, KS 66210
913-339-6475
Commissioner   Earl Foreman
Director of Public Relations   John Griffin

MSL Players Association
2021 L Street NW, 6th Floor, Washington 20036
202-463-2246
Executive Director   John Kerr
Special Assistant   Will Bray

MSL

Baltimore Blast
Baltimore Arena
1801 S. Clinton St., Baltimore, MD 21224
301-327-2100
Owner   Ed Hale
General Manager   John Borozzi
Director of Public Relations   Drew Forrester

Cleveland Crunch
One Crunch Place, 34200 Solon Road
Solon, OH 44139
216-349-2090
Owners   George Hoffman and Stuart Lichter
General Manager   Al Miller
Director of Public Relations   Jean Emser

Dallas Sidekicks
6116 N. Central Expressway, Suite 250
Dallas, TX 75206
214-361-5425
Owner   Phil Cobb
General Manager   Mike McCarthy
Director of Public Relations   Brian Briscoe

Kansas City Comets
Kemper Arena, 1800 Genessee St.
Kansas City, MO 64102
816-421-7770
Chairman   Chris Clouser
General Manager-Coach   Dave Clements
Director of Public Relations   Joe Horak

St. Louis Storm
St. Louis Arena, 5700 Oakland Ave.
St. Louis, MO 63110
314-781-6475
Owner   Milan Mandaric
General Manager   Dan Counce
Director of Public Relations   Jerry Lovelace

San Diego Sockers
San Diego Sports Arena
3500 Sports Arena Blvd., San Diego, CA 92110
Owner   Ron Fowler
General Manager   Ron Cady
Director of Public Relations   Tim Latta

Tacoma Stars
3630 South Cedar, Suite C, Tacoma, WA 98409
206-572-7827
Chairman   Richard Waltman
General Manager   Kent Russell
Director of Public Relations   Mike Vandenkolk

Wichita Wings
114 South Broadway, Wichita, KS 67202
316-262-3545
Managing Director   Bill Oliver
General Manager   Roy Turner
Director of Public Relations   Craig Smith

Tennis

ATP
(Association of Tennis Professionals)
200 Tournament Players Road
Ponte Vedra Beach, FL 32082
904-285-8000
Executive Director   Mark Miles
Director of Communications   Jay Beck

ITF
(International Tennis Federation)
Pallisert Road, Barons Court
London, England W14 9EN
011-4471-381-8060
President   Phillippe Chatrier
Director of Public Relations   Ians Barnes

USTA
(United States Tennis Association)
1212 Ave. of the Americas, 12th Floor, New York,
NY 10036
212-302-3322
Executive Director   Marshall Happer
Director of Public Relations   Edwin Fabricius

WTA
(Women's Tennis Association)
2665 S.Bayshore Dr., Suite 1002, Miami, FL 33133
305-856-4030
Executive Director   Gerard Smith
Director of Public Relations   Ana Leaird

College Sports

NAIA
(National Assn. of Intercollegiate Athletics)
1221 Baltimore Ave., Kansas City, MO 64105
816-842-5050
Executive Director   Jefferson Farris
Director of Communications   Mary Beth Brutton

NCAA
(National Collegiate Athletic Assn.)
6201 College Blvd., Overland Park, KS 66211
913-339-1906
Executive Director   Dick Schultz
Director of Enforcement   David Berst
Director of Communications   Jim Marchiony

Major NCAA Conferences

Atlantic Coast Conference
P.O. Drawer ACC
Greensboro, NC 27419
919-854-8787
Commissioner   Gene Corrigan
Director of Information   Tom Mickle

Big Eight Conference
104 West Ninth Street, Suite 408
Kansas City, MO 64105
816-471-5088
Commissioner   Carl James
Director of Information   Jeff Bollig

Big Ten Conference
1111 Plaza Drive, Suite 600
Schaumburg, IL 60173
708-605-8933
Commissioner   Jim Delany
Director of Information   Mark Rudner

Big West Conference
1700 East Dyer Road, Suite 140
Santa Ana, CA 92705
714-261-2525
Commissioner   Jim Haney
Director of Information   Jody McRoberts

Mid-American Conference
Four Seagate, Suite 102, Toledo, OH 43604
419-249-7177
Commissioner   Karl Benson
Director of Information   Allan Chamberlin

Pac 10 Conference
800 South Broadway, Suite 400
Walnut Creek, CA 94596
415-932-4411
Commissioner   Tom Hansen
Director of Information   Jim Muldoon

Southeastern Conference
3000 Galleria Tower, Suite 990
Birmingham, AL 35244
Commissioner   Roy Kramer
Director of Information   Mark Whitworth

Southwest Conference
P.O. Box 569420, Dallas, TX 75356
214-634-7353
Commissioner   Fred Jacoby
Director of Information   Bo Carter

Western Athletic Conference
14 West Dry Creek Circle
Littleton, CO 80120
303-795-1962
Commissioner   Joe Kearney
Director of Information   Jeff Hurd

Track & Field

AAU
(Amateur Athletic Union)
3400 W.86th St., Indianapolis, IN 46268
317-872-2900
President   Gussie Crawford
Executive Director   Stan Hooley
Director of Communications   David Morton

IAAF
(International Amateur Athletics Federation)
3 Hans Crescent, Knightsbridge
London, England SWIX 0LN
011-4471-581-8771
President   Primo Nebiolo
General Secretary   John Holt
Director of Information   John Wigley

TAC
(The Athletics Congress)
One Hoosier Dome, Suite 140
Indianapolis, IN 46225
317-261-0500
Executive Director   Ollan Cassell
Director of Information   Pete Cava

Commissioners & Presidents

Chief executives of established major sports organizations since 1876. Five names were added in 1989.

Major League Baseball

Commissioner	Tenure
Kenesaw Mountain Landis*	1920-44
Albert B.(Happy) Chandler	1945-51
Ford Frick	1951-65
William Eckert	1965-68
Bowie Kuhn	1969-84
Peter Ueberroth	1984-89
A.Bartlett Giamatti*	1989
Fay Vincent	1989-

*Died in office.

National League

President	Tenure
Morgan G.Bulkeley	1876
William A.Hulbart*	1877-82
A.G.Mills	1883-84
Nicholas Young	1885-1902
Henry Pulliam*	1903-09
Thomas J.Lynch	1910-13
John K.Tener	1914-18
John A.Heydler	1918-34
Ford Frick	1935-51
Warren Giles	1951-69
Charles (Chub) Feeney	1970-86
A.Bartlett Giamatti	1987-89
Bill White	1989-

*Died in office.

American League

President	Tenure
Bancroft (Ban) Johnson	1901-27
Ernest S.Barnard*	1927-31
William Harridge	1931-59
Joe Cronin	1959-73
Lee MacPhail	1974-83
Bobby Brown	1984-

*Died in office.

NBA

Commissioner	Tenure
Maurice Podoloff	1949-63
J.Walter Kennedy	1963-75
Larry O'Brien	1975-84
David Stern	1984-

NFL

President	Tenure
Jim Thorpe	1920
Joe Carr	1921-39
Carl Storck	1939-41
Commissioner	
Elmer Layden	1941-46
Bert Bell*	1946-59
Austin Gunsel†	1959-60
Pete Rozelle	1960-89
Paul Tagliabue	1989-

*Died in office. †Acting Commissioner.

NHL

President	Tenure
Frank Calder*	1917-43
Mervyn (Red) Dutton	1943-46
Clarence Campbell	1946-77
John Ziegler	1977-

*Died in office.

NCAA

Executive Director	Tenure
Walter Byers	1951-88
Richard (Dick) Schultz	1988-

IOC

President	Tenure
Demetrius Vikelas, Greece.	1894-96
Baron Pierre de Coubertin, France	1896-1925
Count Henri de Baillet-Latour, Belgium	1925-42
Vacant	1942-46
J.Sigfried Edstrom, Sweden	1946-52
Avery Brundage, USA	1952-72
Lord Michael Killanin, Ireland	1972-80
Juan Antonio Samaranch, Spain	1980-

Frank O'Brien/The Boston Globe

A new **Comiskey Park** will open in Chicago in 1991, replacing the old Comiskey after 80 years. Last summer, the new stadium could be seen rising in the background from the left field corner of the old yard.

ARENAS & BALLPARKS

A new generation of baseball fields looks to Wrigley for inspiration, While the influence of the Astrodome can be found at SkyDome and The Palace.

ARENAS & BALLPARKS

Architects Look Ahead to the Past

by Paul Goldberger

It seemed right, somehow, that baseball's All-Star Game for 1990 was played in Wrigley Field in Chicago: that magical, 77-year-old pile of steel that sums up all that is gentle and good about the game of baseball.

Playing the All-Star Game at Wrigley seemed almost like sending a signal, a message, to all of those owners and public officials and architects who have filled the landscape over the last generation with vast, hulking stadiums, those monstrous domes and arenas that sit like concrete whales in seas of automobiles, those places that manage to make New Orleans feel just like Houston and Pontiac feel just like Seattle or Minneapolis.

Wrigley isn't like those stadiums. It is small and intimate, not just in Chicago but of Chicago, and the people who watch the games from nearby rooftops are as

Paul Goldberger, who has been the architecture critic for the *New York Times* since 1973, won the Pulitzer Prize for criticism in 1984. He has also written several books on architecture and lectured widely.

much a part of its scene as the vendors and the kids in the bleachers. In a television interview the night before the All-Star game, first baseman Will Clark of the San Francisco Giants said of Wrigley that ''Being here, in this atmosphere, in this ballpark, it just adds to everything.'' Could he have said the same thing about an All-Star game in Anaheim?

Part of Wrigley's hold on baseball fans is that no games were played at night there until 1988—53 years after the first big league game went under the lights at Cincinnati's Crosley Field in 1935. Cub management held out until the economic reality of prime time televison forced them to wire the ballpark for night games. Without lights, Wrigley would not have been an acceptable site for either the All-Star Game or the 1989 National League playoffs.

When the lights went in, there was much talk about it being the end of Wrigley, but as things turned out, the main effect of the change was simply to focus more attention on the old ballyard's charms. That it's now okay to love the

Wide World Photos

After playing only day games for 74 years, **Wrigley Field** turned on the lights in 1988 and has hosted the National League playoffs and the All-Star Game in the last two years.

"friendly confines," to consider it, along with Fenway Park in Boston, the real life field of dreams, is probably the major development in stadium design of the last couple of years. For now, 25 years after the completion of the Astrodome—the first indoor, artificial-turf stadium that revolutionized sports architecture—the trend is moving sharply away from megastructures and firmly back toward the simpler, smaller fields of another era.

The most promising evidence of this is now rising in Baltimore, on a downtown site known as Camden Yards, where a new, 46,000-seat home for the Baltimore Orioles is scheduled for completion in 1992. Based largely on Wrigley Field, the new Baltimore ballpark will have neither a dome overhead or artificial turf underfoot. Instead of being an island in an ocean of parking, it will be closely integrated with the surrounding city, even to the point of being literally tied into an old warehouse next door, which will provide a backdrop for right field. From the outside, the Baltimore stadium will look like

a building, not like a chunk of Boulder Dam.

The Camden Yards stadium is not the only new ballpark to do away with the cookie cutter, but it looks to be the best. Buffalo's new Pilot Field, though smaller than a major-league stadium, also bases its design on the fields of an earlier era, here evoked with grace and common sense. The oldest stadium in major-league baseball, Comiskey Park in Chicago, which closed at the end of the 1990 season, is being replaced by a new field that, if not quite the determined return to the past that the Baltimore and Buffalo projects represent, is no Astrodome, either. If the new Comiskey Park is not an utter repudiation of the concrete hulks of recent years, it's at least a mild rebuke.

Why the change? There are a number of reasons, though it ought to be said at this point that the new-old style of ballparks hasn't been taken up everywhere; one of the major events of 1989 was the completion of Toronto's SkyDome, an extraordinary work of engineering that

Houston Sports Association

Judge Roy Hofheinz and the Houston Astrodome the year it opened in 1965. Hofheinz was the driving force behind the construction of baseball's first indoor stadium and is credited with inventing the luxury skybox.

pushed the stadium-as-megastructure idea to new heights. And the year before, the Detroit Pistons moved into the sprawling and lushly appointed Palace of Auburn Hills, a suburban arena complex with a name that sounds like a tract housing development, but which has been so successful that cities elsewhere are trying to imitate its design.

But if the Palace of Auburn Hills—about which more in a moment—has become the new model for basketball and hockey arenas, the Astrodome, which once looked like it was going to do the same thing for baseball, has now come to look sadly dated. At its quarter-century mark it's still an engineering marvel, this daring dome reaching 642 feet across and arching more than 18 stories over second base, and it perfectly caught the spirit of Houston, a city where bigger was always better, where technology reigned, and where no one wanted to be outdoors anyway. Houston in 1965 was a place more interested in celebrating the new than in turning back to the past—what good, after all, had the past done for

Houston anyway? This was a city that saw itself as freewheeling and inventive, and the Astrodome was as new and different as a baseball stadium could be. Add to that Astrodome builder Roy Hofheinz's idea of creating private boxes in the form of luxury suites around the upper tier of the stadium and it's easy to see how the Astrodome, in 1965, seemed truly revolutionary.

Judge Hofheinz's invention of skyboxes, which was so successful that it has been imitated in virtually every other stadium and arena around the country, even the old ones, may be the Astrodome's most potent legacy. So attractive is the lure of skyboxes that even the most determinedly old-style designs, like the Camden Yards stadium, include them. For in those luxury boxes, leased by the year to corporations for sums often well into six figures, is summed up the true role sports has come to play in the American culture. Once, it was a private box at the Metropolitan Opera; now, it's one at the Palace of Auburn Hills. (Indeed, at the Palace the boxholders even have their own separate

A model of the new 46,000-seat Baltimore ballpark at Camden Yards. Patterned after early 20th century stadiums, this downtown park will feature an asymmetrical field and an old warehouse over the right field wall.

entrance, their own private corridors and their own private dining facilities, so that they need never fear rubbing shoulders with the masses—just the way the classes were segregated at the opera houses of yore.)

But it's not hard to see why the Astrodome hasn't worked as a model for baseball. However much the indoors provides relief from Houston's soggy, humid climate, it's at odds with the spirit of baseball, a game of the outdoors, a game more naturally played on a field that in any kind of huge, enclosed stadium. It's no accident that the earlier stadiums were called fields or parks—they were fields or parks, with relatively simple surrounding structures intended to hold the spectators, who were all close enough to the field to have the intimate relationship to the action that is part of watching baseball. At Wrigley Field it's the field, the glowing, green grass, that grabs your attention and is the true heart of the place. At the Astrodome, it's the dome, the structure, that holds sway, and the experience is totally different. It is spectacular show-

manship—but baseball, for all the millions it brings in, has traditionally had its roots in something quieter, something more leisurely, than the kind of flamboyance represented by the Astrodome.

So it's no surprise that baseball has retreated into the past in its search for an ideal stadium form—or that throughout the country, veneration for older stadiums seems to be at an all-time high. A movement to save Detroit's Tiger Stadium (opened two years after Comiskey) is gathering steam, although the Tigers have thus far turned a deaf ear to proposals to restore it, preferring, management says, to build a new park elsewhere. Nonetheless, a new Tiger Stadium, if it is built, will be restricted to baseball, and this is a positive sign, since part of the problem of the last generation of mega-stadiums was the mistaken belief that a single immense structure could serve the needs of all sports. (It can, but only by compromising all of them, since the configurations and sightlines that are best for football work badly for baseball, and vice versa.)

An organization of fans called the

Toronto's **SkyDome** opened in 1989 with a retractable roof and a built-in hotel. As a mega-structure, it stands out from the crowd.

Society for American Baseball Research has built significant bridges to the architectural community, largely through the efforts of a Chicago architect named Philip Bess, a passionate student of baseball field design, and has become an outspoken national advocate of old-style ballparks. (Bess himself submitted a design for a traditionally-styled park called Armour Field to replace the doomed Comiskey Park, and while it was not accepted, the pressure to hold onto the best of the past surely had some impact in instilling what good elements there are in the new Comiskey.)

If baseball's return to tradition emerges largely from a sense that the ballparks of the last generation were too big, too impersonal, and too interchangeable, the change has come also from within the architectural world itself. As architecture has moved away from the glass box and the concrete bunker and toward urban buildings that strive to make less of a modernist statement and more of an accommodation with the mood and fabric of cities, sports facilities have stood as a kind of last frontier. Skyscrapers have been evolving away from glass boxes since Philip Johnson and John Burgee designed a Chippendale top for the AT&T Building in New York in 1978; shopping centers have been seeking softer, gentler images since the advent of such projects of the late '70s as Fanueil Hall Marketplace in Boston and Harborplace in Baltimore. And preserving the best of the old and seeking to integrate it into the new, once something of a radical notion, has become commonplace in American cities and towns. Perhaps the real question should be not why more traditionally-styled baseball parks have come into fashion, but why it took so long for the common wisdom of architecture to connect with sports.

If there's any simple answer, it has to be in the isolation architects have had from the sports hierarchy. Sports is for big business, politicians and athletes, groups to whom architecture has been less than relevant. No first-class architect with a national or international reputation has ever been hired to design a stadium or an arena—even today, those jobs invariably go to a couple of large, commercial architectural firms that have specialized in sports facilities, churning them out as fast, and usually with about as much imagination, as shopping centers or tract houses. (So complete is the lock these firms hold on the business that one of them, Hellmuth, Obata & Kassabaum, is even designing the Camden Yards in Baltimore—although with the guidance of Orioles' owner Eli S. Jacobs, an investor with a longstanding interest in architecture, and professional urban designer Janet Marie Smith, who was hired specifically to guide the architects to a different kind of design form from what they were accustomed to providing.)

If the Baltimore Stadium looks to be the ideal of the new old-style baseball park, surely the SkyDome in Toronto, home of the Blue Jays since 1989, is the culmination of the line that began with the Astrodome. What distinguishes the $360-million SkyDome from the Astrodome, however, beyond the fact that its dome is fully retractable (it consists of three moving panels that take roughly 20 minutes to slide open) is the way in which it connects to the city of Toronto. This is a megastructure, to be sure, and no one in any of its 50,000 seats loses a sense that he is in a massive piece of engineering first and a baseball stadium second, but there is at least not the feeling of total isolation from the surrounding cityscape, as there is in the Astrodome and in the dozens of suburban stadiums that took the Astrodome as a model. It is possible to walk from downtown to the SkyDome; restaurants, meeting rooms and other facilities are integrated into the structure, and there is even a hotel built into the complex with 70 of its rooms opening directly onto the stadium.

The hotel has caused a few minor scandals, such as the time unclad guests watching the game from their window became as big an attraction as the happenings on the field. But in a sense it's just the old style coming full circle—from the rooftops and tenements overlooking Ebbets Field, Yankee Stadium and Wrigley Field to the sleek new hotel rooms of the SkyDome. Those old stadiums had an urban context, and slid gracefully into it; the SkyDome, being too big to slide gracefully into anything, had to create an urban context for itself. Yet it does manage to do what few of the mega-stadiums manage, which is to stand apart from the crowd. When you are in the SkyDome, at least you know that you are in Toronto. The SkyDome, incidentally, is one of the few major facilities not done by an architect with a specialty in stadiums. Its designer was Roderick Robbie, who worked in conjunction with the engineer Michael Allen and the NORR Partnership, a large Toronto-based engineering and architecture firm.

The Palace of Auburn Hills, too, was designed by an architect without extensive sports-facility experience: Gino Rossetti, a Detroit and Los Angeles-based architect with a commercial practice that up to that point had been devoted largely to office buildings. Rossetti is an architect whose priority is serving the needs of business, however, and his success with the Palace tells much about what sports facilities have become. They are businesses, now more than ever, and their design is in and of itself a marketing tool. The Palace is clean, convenient, and luxurious so far as arenas go; even for the common folk who sit in regular seats and not in luxury boxes, it is a comfortable environment, with the same kind of appeal as an upscale suburban shopping mall. Indeed, it has more than a little bit in common with shopping malls—here, too, there is a sense that selling is as important as watching, and that attracting an upper middle-class suburban customer is the main goal of the architecture.

Not to sell the Palace short. Like the Astrodome 25 years ago, it pushes forward a design driven by a singleminded determination to reshape the marketplace. The Palace contains clubs, numerous restaurants, a four-sided video scoreboard, its own television studio, banquet and meeting facilities and a ''quiet room'' in which adults can seek refuge from the arena's state of the art sound system during rock concerts. The Palace has been so successful that it has earned Rossetti commissions to design similar arenas in Chicago, San Diego and Ottawa. (His major competition, the firm of Ellerbe Becket, is designing new indoor arenas for Phoenix, Oakland, Seattle, Boston and Santa Ana, Calif.)

The arena boom has been fueled largely by the continued growth of Judge Hofheinz's idea, the luxury suite, which Gino Rossetti brought quite literally to a new level in the Palace. The architect placed them lower in the structure, closer to the playing floor rather than up in the rafters where the earlier generations of luxury boxes had been stuffed, giving luxury suiteholders the best locations in the house—and, not incidentally, squeezing the regular ticketholders into less desirable locations. The 180 suites in the Palace yield roughly $12-million a year in rents, enough to cover debt service on the entire privately-owned complex. It's a triumph of economics, but it does raise some not very happy questions about just who this facility is for, and about how people relate to one another in it.

For at the Palace, the public place that all sports facilities are has become an essentially private place, the province of people who pay vast sums of money to avoid mixing with anyone else—to avoid having any sense that they are in a public place, in other words. One builder who has hoped to build a copy of the Palace in southern California was quoted in a news article as praising ''that living room feeling, that warm feeling you get'' in the Palace, and that's just what's disturbing about the place. It is a living room, a series of living rooms in which people gather to watch an event as if it were on television. When they watch the video scoreboard or the monitors inside their suites, they actually are watching television, further proof that the tube is more real than reality for many people.

Contrast this, for all the joys of its balance sheet, with the sheen of the grass at Wrigley Field, with the funky glory of the ''Green Monster'' in Fenway Park's outfield, with the palpable presence of history at Tiger Stadium, even with the rush of the crowds at Shea Stadium in New York. In these places, and others like them, there is a sense of shared experience, a sense of being in a public place, that transcends private identity. You and I, no matter where we sit, are the same, and are there for the same reason, to partake in the same pleasures.

So it was in all the stadiums and arenas of the past, and so it looks to be again in the realm of baseball, if the direction set by Baltimore continues strong. It's true, of course, that most old arenas, even the doomed Boston Garden, were not as beloved as the old baseball parks; they were dank and dirty, and can offer only history to prove their superiority over their replacements. But there has to be a way to get some of the magic into the design of new arenas—or have we really reached a time when duplicating the experience of a living room represents the ideal? □

The Palace of Auburn Hills offers a home court advantage not only to the NBA champion Detroit Pistons, but to luxury suite holders as well. The two-year-old arena has 180 suites spread over three levels with 52 suites only 16 rows up from courtside.

The Palace of Auburn Hills

Home, Sweet Home

The home fields, home courts and home ice of the NL, AL, NBA, NFL, CFL, NHL, Division I-A college football and Division I college basketball. Also, selected Auto Racing and Horse Racing tracks and Tennis center courts. Attendance figures are also provided for NL, AL, NBA, NFL and NHL teams.

Major League Baseball

National League

					Outfield Fences					
		Built	Capacity	LF	LCF	CF	RCF	RF	Field
Atlanta Braves	Atlanta-Fulton County Stadium	1966	**52,007**	330	385	402	385	330	Grass
Chicago Cubs	Wrigley Field	1914	**39,012**	355	368	400	368	353	Grass
Cincinnati Reds	Riverfront Stadium	1970	**52,392**	330	375	404	375	330	Turf
Houston Astros	The Astrodome	1965	**54,816**	330	378	400	378	330	Turf
Los Angeles Dodgers	Dodger Stadium	1962	**56,000**	330	385	400	385	330	Grass
Montreal Expos	Olympic Stadium	1977	**60,011**	325	375	404	375	325	Turf
New York Mets	Shea Stadium	1964	**55,601**	338	371	410	371	338	Grass
Philadelphia Phillies	Veterans Stadium	1971	**62,382**	330	371	408	371	330	Turf
Pittsburgh Pirates	Three Rivers Stadium	1970	**58,729**	335	375	400	375	335	Turf
St. Louis Cardinals	Busch Stadium	1966	**54,224**	330	383	414	383	330	Turf
San Diego Padres	San Diego/ Jack Murphy Stadium	1969	**59,022**	327	370	405	370	327	Grass
San Francisco Giants	Candlestick Park	1960	**60,000**	335	365	400	365	335	Grass

American League

					Outfield Fences					
		Built	Capacity	LF	LCF	CF	RCF	RF	Field
Baltimore Orioles	Memorial Stadium	1954	**54,017**	309	378	405	378	309	Grass
Boston Red Sox	Fenway Park	1912	**34,182**	315	379	390	380	302	Grass
California Angels	Anaheim Stadium	1966	**64,593**	333	386	404	386	333	Grass
Chicago White Sox	(New) Comiskey Park	1991	**43,000**	347	382	409	382	347	Grass
Cleveland Indians	Cleveland Stadium	1932	**74,483**	320	382	400	390	320	Grass
Detroit Tigers	Tiger Stadium	1912	**52,416**	340	365	440	375	325	Grass
Kansas City Royals	Royals Stadium	1973	**40,625**	330	385	410	385	330	Turf
Milwaukee Brewers	County Stadium	1953	**53,192**	315	392	402	392	315	Grass
Minnesota Twins	Hubert H. Humphrey Metrodome	1982	**55,884**	343	385	408	367	327	Turf
New York Yankees	Yankee Stadium	1923	**57,545**	318	399	408	385	314	Grass
Oakland Athletics	Oakland Coliseum	1968	**48,219**	330	375	400	375	330	Grass
Seattle Mariners	The Kingdome	1977	**58,150**	324	362	410	352	314	Turf
Texas Rangers	Arlington Stadium	1972	**43,508**	330	380	400	380	330	Grass
Toronto Blue Jays	SkyDome	1989	**50,516**	328	375	400	375	328	Turf

Note: As of Sept. 1, 1990, the White Sox estimate that the playing field dimensions for the new Comiskey Park will be the same as the old Comiskey.

Rank by Capacity

National League		American League	
Veterans	62,382	Cleveland	74,483
Olympic	60,011	Anaheim	64,593
Candlestick	60,000	Kingdome	58,150
Jack Murphy	59,022	Yankee	57,545
Three Rivers	58,729	Metrodome	55,884
Dodger	56,000	Memorial	54,017
Shea	55,601	County	53,192
Astrodome	54,816	Tiger	52,416
Busch	54,224	SkyDome	50,516
Riverfront	52,392	Oakland	48,219
Atlanta	52,007	Arlington	43,508
Wrigley	39,012	New Comiskey	43,000
		Royals	40,625
		Fenway	34,182

Rank by Age

National League		American League	
Wrigley	1914	Tiger	1912
Candlestick	1960	Fenway	1912
Dodger	1962	Yankee	1923
Shea	1964	Cleveland	1932
Astrodome	1965	Memorial	1949
Atlanta	1965	County	1953
Busch	1966	Arlington	1965
Jack Murphy	1967	Anaheim	1966
Riverfront	1970	Oakland	1966
Three Rivers	1970	Royals	1973
Veterans	1971	Kingdome	1977
Olympic	1976	Metrodome	1982
		Skydome	1989
		New Comiskey	1991

1990 MLB Attendance

See Baseball chapter.

Major League Baseball (Cont.)

Home Fields

Listed below are the principal home fields used through the years by current National and American League teams. The N.L. became a major league in 1876, the A.L. in 1901.

The capacity figures in the right hand column indicate the largest seating capacity of the ballpark while the club played there. Capacity figures before 1915 (and the introduction of concrete grandstands) are sketchy at best and have been left blank.

National League

Atlanta Braves
1876-94	South End Grounds I (Boston) . . .	—
1894-1914	South End Grounds II	—
1915-52	Braves Field	40,000
1953-65	County Stadium (Milwaukee)	43,394
1966-	Atlanta-Fulton County Stadium . .	52,007
	(1966 capacity—50,000)	

Chicago Cubs
1876-77	State Street Grounds	—
1878-84	Lakefront Park	—
1885-91	West Side Park	—
1891-93	Brotherhood Park	—
1893-1915	West Side Grounds	—
1916-	Wrigley Field	39,012
	(1916 capacity—16,000)	

Cincinnati Reds
1876-79	Avenue Grounds	—
1880	Bank Street Grounds	—
1890-1901	Redland Field I	—
1902-11	Palace of the Fans	—
1912-70	Crosley Field	29,603
1970-	Riverfront Stadium	52,392
	(1970 capacity—52,000)	

Houston Astros
1962-64	Colt Stadium	32,601
1965	The Astrodome	54,816
	(1965 capacity—45,011)	

Los Angeles Dodgers
1890	Washington Park I (Brooklyn) . . .	—
1891-97	Eastern Park	—
1898-1912	Washington Park II	—
1913-56	Ebbets Field	31,497
1957	Ebbets Field	31,497
	& Roosevelt Stadium	
	(Jersey City)	24,167
1958-61	Memorial Coliseum	
	(Los Angeles)	93,600
1962-	Dodger Stadium	56,000

Montreal Expos
1969-76	Jarry Park	28,000
1977-	Olympic Stadium	60,011
	(1977 capacity—58,500)	

New York Mets
1962-63	Polo Grounds	55,987
1964-	Shea Stadium	55,601
	(1964 capacity—55,101)	

Philadelphia Phillies
1883-86	Recreation Park	—
1887-94	Huntingdon Ave.Grounds	—
1895-1938	Baker Bowl	18,800
1938-70	Shibe Park	33,608
1971-	Veterans Stadium	62,382
	(1971 capacity—56,371)	

Pittsburgh Pirates
1887-90	Recreation Park	—
1891-1909	Exposition Park	—
1909-70	Forbes Field	35,000
1970-	Three Rivers Stadium	58,729
	(1970 capacity—50,235)	

St.Louis Cardinals
1876-77	Sportsman's Park I	—
1885-86	Vandeventer Lot	—
1892-1920	Robison Field	18,000
1920-66	Sportsman's Park II	30,500
1966-	Busch Stadium	54,224
	(1966 capacity—50,126)	

San Diego Padres
1969-	San Diego/Jack Murphy Stadium	59,022
	(1969 capacity—47,634)	

San Francisco Giants
1876	Union Grounds (Brooklyn)	—
1883-88	Polo Grounds I (New York)	—
1889-90	Manhattan Field	—
1891-1957	Polo Grounds II	55,987
1958-59	Seals Stadium (San Francisco) . . .	22,900
1960-	Candlestick Park	60,000
	(1960 capacity—42,553)	

Ballpark Name Changes: ATLANTA—**Atlanta Fulton County Stadium** originally Atlanta Stadium (1966-1974); CHICAGO— **Wrigley Field** originally Weeghman Park (1914-17), then Cubs Park (1918-25); CINCINNATI—**Redland Field** originally League Park (1890-93) and **Crosley Field** originally Redland Field II (1912-33); HOUSTON— **Astrodome** originally Harris County Domed Stadium before it opened in 1965; PHILADELPHIA—**Shibe Park** renamed Connie Mack Stadium in 1953; ST.LOUIS—**Robison Field** originally Vandeventer Lot, then League Park, then Cardinal Park all before becoming Robison Field in 1901, **Sportsman's Park** renamed Busch Stadium in 1953, and **Busch Stadium** originally Busch Memorial Stadium (1966-82); SAN DIEGO—**San Diego/Jack Murphy Stadium** originally San Diego Stadium (1967-81).

American League

Baltimore Orioles
1901	Lloyd Street Grounds (Milwaukee)	—
1902-53	Sportsman's Park II (St.Louis) . . .	30,500
1954-	Memorial Stadium (Baltimore) . . .	54,017
	(1954 capacity—47,866)	

Boston Red Sox
1901-11	Huntington Ave.Grounds	—
1912-	Fenway Park	34,182
	(1934 capacity—27,000)	

California Angels
1961	Wrigley Field (Los Angeles)	20,457
1962-65	Dodger Stadium	56,000
1966-	Anaheim Stadium	64,593
	(1966 capacity—43,250)	

Chicago White Sox
1901-10	Southside Park	—
1910-90	Comiskey Park I	43,931
1991-	Comiskey Park II	43,000

Cleveland Indians
1901-09	League Park I	—
1910-46	League Park II	21,414
1932-	Cleveland Stadium	74,483
	(1932 capacity—77,797)	

Detroit Tigers
1901-11	Bennett Park	—
1912-	Tiger Stadium	52,416
	(1912 capacity—23,000)	

Kansas City Royals
1969-72	Municipal Stadium	35,020
1973-	Royals Stadium	40,625
	(1973 capacity—40,762)	

Milwaukee Brewers
1969	Sick's Stadium (Seattle)	25,420
1970-	County Stadium (Milwaukee)	53,192
	(1970 capacity—46,625)	

Minnesota Twins
1901-02	American League Park (Wash.,DC)	—
1903-60	Griffith Stadium	27,410
1960-81	Metropolitan Stadium (Bloomington,MN)	45,919
1982-	HHH Metrodome (Minneapolis)	55,883
	(1982 capacity—54,000)	

New York Yankees
1901-02	Oriole Park (Baltimore)	—
1903-12	Hilltop Park (New York)	—
1913-22	Polo Grounds II	38,000
1923-73	Yankee Stadium I	67,224
1974-75	Shea Stadium	55,101
1976-	Yankee Stadium II	57,545
	(1976 capacity—57,145)	

Oakland Athletics
1901-08	Columbia Park (Philadelphia)	—
1909-54	Shibe Park	33,608
1955-67	Municipal Stadium (Kansas City)	35,020
1968-	Oakland Alameda County Coliseum	48,219
	(Original 1968 capacity—48,621)	

Seattle Mariners
1977-	The Kingdome	58,150
	(Original 1977 capacity—59,438)	

Texas Rangers
1961	Griffith Stadium (Wash.,DC)	27,410
1962-71	RFK Stadium	45,016
1972-	Arlington (TX) Stadium	43,508
	(Original 1972 capacity—35,698)	

Toronto Blue Jays
1977-89	Exhibition Stadium	43,737
1989-	SkyDome	50,516
	(Original 1989 capacity—49,500)	

Ballpark Name Changes: CHICAGO—**Comiskey Park I** originally White Sox Park (1910-12), then Comiskey Park in 1913, then White Sox Park again in 1962, then Comiskey Park again in 1976; CLEVELAND—**League Park** renamed Dunn Field in 1920, then League Park again in 1928; **Cleveland Stadium** originally Municipal Stadium (1932-74); DETROIT—**Tiger Stadium** originally Navin Field (1912-37), then Briggs Stadium (1938-60); LOS ANGELES—**Dodger Stadium** referred to as Chavez Ravine by AL while Angels played there (1962-65); PHILADELPHIA—**Shibe Park** renamed Connie Mack Stadium in 1953; ST.LOUIS—**Sportsman's Park** renamed Busch Stadium in 1953; WASHINGTON—**Griffith Stadium** originally National Park (1892-20), **RFK Stadium** originally D.C. Stadium (1961-68).

National Basketball Association

Eastern Conference

		Location	Built	Capacity
Atlanta Hawks	The Omni	Atlanta, GA	1972	16,003
Boston Celtics	Boston Garden	Boston, MA	1928	14,890
Chicago Bulls	Chicago Stadium	Chicago, IL	1929	17,339
Cleveland Cavaliers	The Coliseum	Richfield, OH	1974	20,273
Detroit Pistons	The Palace of Auburn Hills	Auburn Hills, MI	1988	21,454
Indiana Pacers	Market Square Arena	Indianapolis, IN	1974	16,912
Miami Heat	Miami Arena	Miami, FL	1988	15,008
Milwaukee Bucks	Bradley Center	Milwaukee, WI	1988	18,633
New Jersey Nets	Meadowlands Arena	East Rutherford, NJ	1981	20,089
New York Knicks	Madison Square Garden	New York, NY	1968	19,081
Orlando Magic	Orlando Arena	Orlando, FL	1989	15,500
Philadelphia 76ers	The Spectrum	Philadelphia, PA	1967	18,168
Washington Bullets	Capital Centre	Landover, MD	1973	18,756

Western Conference

		Location	Built	Capacity
Charlotte Hornets	Charlotte Coliseum	Charlotte, NC	1988	23,388
Dallas Mavericks	Reunion Arena	Dallas, TX	1980	17,007
Denver Nuggets	McNichols Arena	Denver, CO	1975	17,022
Golden St. Warriors	Oakland Coliseum Arena	Oakland, CA	1966	15,025
Houston Rockets	The Summit	Houston, TX	1975	16,611
Los Angeles Clippers	Memorial Sports Arena	Los Angeles, CA	1959	15,371
Los Angeles Lakers	Great Western Forum	Inglewood, CA	1967	17,505
Minnesota Timberwolves	Target Center	Minneapolis, MN	1990	18,500
Phoenix Suns	Veterans' Coliseum	Phoenix, AZ	1965	14,487
Portland Trail Blazers	Memorial Coliseum	Portland, OR	1960	12,880
Sacramento Kings	ARCO Arena	Sacramento, CA	1988	17,014
San Antonio Spurs	HemisFair Arena	San Antonio, TX	1968	15,861
Seattle SuperSonics	The Coliseum	Seattle, WA	1962	14,250
Utah Jazz	The Salt Palace	Salt Lake City, UT	1969	12,616

National Basketball Association (Cont.)

Rank by Capacity

Eastern Conference	Western Conference
The Palace 21,454	Charlotte Colis . .23,388
Clev.Coliseum . . .20,273	Target Ctr 18,500
Meadowlands . . .20,089	LA Forum 17,505
Mad.Sq.Garden . .19,081	McNichols Arena 17,022
Capital Centre. . .18,756	ARCO Arena . . .17,014
Bradley Center . .18,633	Reunion Arena . .17,007
The Spectrum . . .18,168	The Summit 16,611
Chicago Stadium . 17,339	HemisFair Arena . 15,861
Market Sq.Arena 16,912	LA Sports Arena . 15,371
The Omni 16,003	Oakland Arena . .15,025
Orlando Arena . .15,500	Phoe.Coliseum . .14,487
Miami Arena 15,008	Seat.Coliseum . . .14,250
Boston Garden . .14,890	Port.Coliseum . . .12,880
	Salt Palace 12,616

Rank by Age

Eastern Conference	Western Conference
Boston Garden . . .1928	LA Sports Arena . .1959
Chicago Stadium . .1929	Portland Coliseum .1960
The Spectrum 1967	Seattle Coliseum . .1962
Mad.Sq.Garden . .1968	Phoenix Coliseum .1965
The Omni 1972	Oakland Coliseum .1966
Capital Centre . . .1973	LA Forum 1967
Cleve.Coliseum . .1974	HemisFair Arena .1968
Market Sq.Arena . .1974	Salt Palace. 1969
NJ Meadowlands . .1981	McNichols Arena .1975
Miami Arena 1988	The Summit 1975
Bradley Center . . .1988	Reunion Arena . . .1980
The Palace 1988	Charlotte Colis. . . .1988
Orlando Arena . . .1989	ARCO Arena. 1988
	Target Center 1990

1989-90 NBA Attendance

Overall attendance in the NBA was 17,368,659 in 1107 games for an average per game crowd of 15,690. Teams in each conference are ranked by attendance over 41 home games.

Eastern Conference

		Attendance	Gm	Average
1	Detroit.	879,614	41	21,454
2	New York	730,432	41	17,815
3	Chicago	754,564	41	18,404
4	Cleveland	695,710	41	16,969
5	Milwaukee.	659,602	41	16,088
6	Miami	615,328	41	15,008
7	Orlando	617,468	41	15,060
8	Boston	611,537	41	14,916
9	Philadelphia	574,710	41	14,017
10	Atlanta	573,731	41	13,993
11	Indiana	528,275	41	12,885
12	New Jersey.	497,838	41	12,142
13	Washington	474,166	41	11,565
	TOTAL	8,212,975	533	15,409

Western Conference

		Attendance	Gm	Average
1	Minnesota	1,072,572	41	26,160
2	Charlotte	979,941	41	23,901
3	LA Lakers	712,498	41	17,378
4	Sacramento	697,574	41	17,014
5	Dallas	691,570	41	16,868
6	Houston.	649,697	41	15,846
7	Golden St	616,025	41	15,025
8	San Antonio	603,607	41	14,722
9	Phoenix	578,661	41	14,114
10	Portland	528,244	41	12,884
11	Denver	519,404	41	12,668
12	Utah	517,256	41	12,616
13	Seattle	502,014	41	12,244
14	LA Clippers	486,621	41	11,869
	TOTAL	9,155,684	574	15,951

Home Courts

Listed below are the principal home courts used through the years by current NBA teams. The largest capacity of each arena is noted in the right hand column. ABA arenas (1972-76) are included for Denver, Indiana, New Jersey and San Antonio.

Eastern Conference

Atlanta Hawks

1949-51	Wheaton Field House (Moline,IL) . . .6,000
1951-55	Milwaukee Arena 11,000
1955-68	Kiel Auditorium (St.Louis) 10,000
1968-72	Alexander Mem. Coliseum (Atlanta) .7,166
1972-	The Omni (Atlanta) 16,003
	(1972 capacity—16,818)

Boston Celtics

| 1946- | Boston Garden . . . . .14,890 |
| | (1946 capacity—13,909) |

Note: Since 1975-76, the Celtics have played several regular season games at the Hartford Civic Center.

Chicago Bulls

1966-67	Chicago Amphitheater. 11,002
1967-	Chicago Stadium 17,339
	(1967 capacity—17,374)

Cleveland Cavaliers

1970-74	Cleveland Arena 11,000
1974-	The Coliseum (Richfield,OH) 20,273
	(1974 capacity—19,500)

Detroit Pistons

1948-52	North Side H.S.Gym (Ft.Wayne,IN) .3,800
1952-57	Memorial Coliseum (Ft.Wayne). 9,306
1957-61	Olympia Stadium (Detroit). 14,000
1961-78	Cobo Arena. 11,147
1978-88	Silverdome (Pontiac,MI). 22,366
1988-	The Palace (Auburn Hills, MI) 21,454

Indiana Pacers

1967-74	State Fairgrounds (Indianapolis) 9,479
1974-	Market Square Arena 16,912
	(1974 capacity—17,287)

Miami Heat

| 1988- | Miami Arena . . . . .15,008 |
| | (1988 capacity—15,362) |

Milwaukee Bucks

| 1968-88 | Milwaukee Arena (The Mecca) . . . .11,052 |
| 1988- | Bradley Center. . . . . .18,633 |

New Jersey Nets

1967-68	Teaneck,NJ Armory	3,500
1968-69	Long Island Arena (Commack,NY)	6,500
1969-71	Island Garden (W.Hempstead,NY)	5,200
1971-77	Nassau Coliseum (Uniondale,NY)	15,500
1977-81	Rutgers Ath.Center (Piscataway,NJ)	9,050
1981-	Meadowlands Arena (E.Ruth.,NJ)	20,089

New York Knicks

1946-68	Madison Sq. Garden III (50th St)	18,496
1968-	Madison Sq. Garden IV (33rd St.)	19,081
	(1968 capacity—19,694)	

Orlando Magic

1989-	Orlando Arena	15,500

Philadelphia 76ers

1949-51	State Fair Coliseum (Syracuse,NY)	7,500
1951-63	Onondaga County (NY) War Memorial	8,000
1963-67	Convention Hall (Philadelphia)	12,000
	& Philadelphia Arena	7,777
1967-	The Spectrum	18,168
	(1967 capacity—15,205)	

Washington Bullets

1961-62	Chicago Amphitheater	11,000
1962-63	Chicago Coliseum	7,100
1963-73	Baltimore Civic Center	12,289
1973-	Capital Centre (Landover,MD)	18,756
	(1973 capacity—17,500)	

Western Conference

Charlotte Hornets

1988-	Charlotte Coliseum	23,388
	(1988 capacity—23,500)	

Dallas Mavericks

1980-	Reunion Arena	17,007
	(1980 capacity—17,828)	

Denver Nuggets

1967-75	Auditorium Arena	6,841
1975-	McNichols Sports Arena	17,022
	(1975 capacity—16,700)	

Golden State Warriors

1946-52	Philadelphia Arena	7,777
1952-62	Convention Hall (Philadelphia)	9,200
	& Philadelphia Arena	7,777
1962-64	Cow Palace (San Francisco)	13,862
1964-66	Civic Auditorium	7,500
	& (USF Memorial Gym)	6,000
1966-67	Cow Palace, Civic Auditorium	
	& Oakland Coliseum Arena	15,000
1967-71	Cow Palace	14,500
1971-	Oakland Coliseum Arena	15,025
	(1971 capacity—12,905)	

Houston Rockets

1967-71	San Diego Sports Arena	14,000
1971-72	Hofheinz Pavilion (Houston)	10,218
	& six other sites	
1972-73	Hofheinz Pavilion	10,218
	& HemisFair Arena (San Antonio)	10,446
1973-75	Hofheinz Pavilion	10,218
1975-	The Summit	16,611
	(1975 capacity—15,600)	

Note: During the 1971-72 season, the Rockets played 21 games at Hofheinz, 8 at Astrohall and 6 at the Astrodome in Houston, as well as 3 games in San Antonio, 2 in Waco and 1 in El Paso. In 1972-73, they played 28 games at Hofheinz and 13 at the HemisFair in San Antonio.

Los Angeles Clippers

1970-78	Memorial Auditorium (Buffalo)	17,300
1978-84	San Diego Sports Arena	12,167
1985-	Los Angeles Sports Arena	15,371

Los Angeles Lakers

1948-60	Minneapolis Auditorium	10,000
1960-67	Los Angeles Sports Arena	14,781
1967-	The Forum (Inglewood,CA)	17,505
	(1967 capacity—17,086)	

Minnesota Timberwolves

1989-90	Hubert H.Humphrey Metrodome	23,000
1990	Target Center	18,500

Phoenix Suns

1968-	Ariz.Veterans' Memorial Coliseum	14,487
	(1968 capacity—12,200)	

Portland Trail Blazers

1970-	Memorial Coliseum	12,880
	(1970 capacity—12,366)	

Sacramento Kings

1948-55	Edgarton Park Arena (Rochester,NY)	5,000
1955-58	Rochester War Memorial	10,000
1958-72	Cincinnati Gardens	11,438
1972-74	Municipal Auditorium (Kansas City)	9,929
	& Omaha,Neb. Auditorium	9,136
1974-78	Kemper Arena (Kansas City)	16,785
	& Omaha Civic Auditorium	9,136
1978-85	Kemper Arena	16,785
1985-88	ARCO Arena I	10,333
1988-	ARCO Arena II	17,014
	(1988 capacity—16,517)	

San Antonio Spurs

1967-70	Memorial Auditorium (Dallas)	8,088
	& Moody Coliseum (Dallas)	8,500
1970-71	Three courts—Moody Coliseum	8,500
	Tarrant Conven.Center(Ft.Worth)	13,500
	& Municipal Coliseum (Lubbock)	10,400
1971-73	Two courts—Moody Coliseum	9,500
	& Memorial Auditorium	8,088
1973-	HemisFair Arena (San Antonio)	15,861
	(1973 capacity—10,446)	

Seattle Supersonics

1967-78	Seattle Center Coliseum	14,098
1978-85	Kingdome	40,192
1985-	The Coliseum	14,250
	(1985 capacity—14,000)	

Utah Jazz

1974-75	Municipal Auditorium	7,853
	& Louisiana Superdome	47,284
1975-79	Superdome	47,284
1979-83	Salt Palace (Salt Lake City)	12,519
1983-84	Salt Palace	12,519
	& Thomas-Mack Center (Las Vegas)	18,500
1985-	Salt Palace	12,616
	(1979 capacity—12,519)	

National Football League

American Football Conference

		Location	Built	Capacity	Field
Buffalo Bills	Rich Stadium	Orchard Park, NY	1973	80,290	Turf
Cincinnati Bengals	Riverfront Stadium	Cincinnati, OH	1970	60,311	Turf
Cleveland Browns	Cleveland Stadium	Cleveland, OH	1932	80,098	Grass
Denver Broncos	Mile High Stadium	Denver, CO	1948	76,274	Grass
Houston Oilers	The Astrodome	Houston, TX	1965	60,502	Turf
Indianapolis Colts	The Hoosier Dome	Indianapolis, IN	1984	60,129	Turf
Kansas City Chiefs	Arrowhead Stadium	Kansas City, MO	1972	78,067	Turf
Los Angeles Raiders	Memorial Coliseum	Los Angeles, CA	1923	92,516	Grass
Miami Dolphins	Joe Robbie Stadium	Miami, FL	1987	73,000	Grass
New England Patriots	Foxboro Stadium	Foxboro, MA	1971	60,794	Turf
New York Jets	Giants Stadium	E.Rutherford, NJ	1976	77,152	Turf
Pittsburgh Steelers	Three Rivers Stadium	Pittsburgh, PA	1970	59,030	Turf
San Diego Chargers	San Diego/Jack Murphy Stadium	San Diego, CA	1967	60,750	Grass
Seattle Seahawks	The Kingdome	Seattle, WA	1976	64,984	Turf

National Football Conference

		Location	Built	Capacity	Field
Atlanta Falcons	Atlanta-Fulton County Stadium	Atlanta, GA	1965	59,643	Grass
Chicago Bears	Soldier Field	Chicago, IL	1924	66,946	Grass
Dallas Cowboys	Texas Stadium	Irving, TX	1971	65,024	Turf
Detroit Lions	Pontiac Silverdome	Pontiac, MI	1975	80,494	Turf
Green Bay Packers	Lambeau Field	Green Bay, WI	1957	59,543	Grass
	& County Stadium	Milwaukee, WI	1953	56,051	Grass
Los Angeles Rams	Anaheim Stadium	Anaheim, CA	1966	69,008	Grass
Minnesota Vikings	Hubert H.Humphrey Metrodome	Minneapolis, MN	1982	63,300	Turf
New Orleans Saints	Louisiana Superdome	New Orleans, LA	1975	69,065	Turf
New York Giants	Giants Stadium	E.Rutherford, NJ	1976	77,152	Turf
Philadelphia Eagles	Veterans Stadium	Philadelphia, PA	1971	67,011	Turf
Phoenix Cardinals	Sun Devil Stadium	Tempe, AZ	1958	74,865	Grass
San Francisco 49ers	Candlestick Park	San Francisco, CA	1960	66,252	Grass
Tampa Bay Buccaneers	Tampa Stadium	Tampa, FL	1967	74,315	Grass
Washington Redskins	Robert F.Kennedy Stadium	Washington, DC	1961	55,672	Grass

Rank by Capacity

AFC		NFC	
LA Coliseum	92,516	Silverdome	80,494
Rich	80,290	Giants	77,152
Cleveland	80,098	Sun Devil	74,865
Arrowhead	78,067	Tampa	74,315
Giants	77,152	Superdome	69,065
Mile High	76,274	Anaheim	69,008
Joe Robbie	73,000	Veterans	67,011
Kingdome	64,984	Soldier Field	66,946
Foxboro	60,794	Candlestick	66,252
Jack Murphy	60,750	Texas	65,024
Astrodome	60,502	Metrodome	63,300
Riverfront	60,311	Atlanta	59,643
Hoosier Dome	60,129	Lambeau Field	59,543
Three Rivers	59,030	Milw.County	56,051
		RFK	55,672

Rank by Age

AFC		NFC	
LA Coliseum	1923	Soldier Field	1924
Cleveland	1931	Milw.County	1953
Mile High	1948	Lambeau Field	1957
Astrodome	1965	Sun Devil	1958
Jack Murphy	1967	Candlestick	1960
Riverfront	1970	RFK	1961
Three Rivers	1970	Atlanta	1965
Foxboro	1971	Anaheim	1966
Arrowhead	1972	Tampa	1967
Rich	1973	Texas	1971
Giants	1976	Veterans	1971
Kingdome	1976	Silverdome	1975
Hoosier Dome	1984	Superdome	1975
Joe Robbie	1987	Giants	1976
		Metrodome	1982

1989 NFL Attendance

Overall attendance in the NFL was 12,850,545 in 224 games for an average per game crowd of 57,369. Teams in each conference are ranked by attendance over eight home games.

American Conference

		Attendance	Gm	Average
1	Buffalo	619,714	8	77,464
2	Cleveland	613,415	8	76,677
3	Denver	588,144	8	73,518
4	Kansas City	486,055	8	60,757
5	Seattle	481,233	8	60,154
6	Indianapolis	467,446	8	58,431
7	Miami	453,872	8	56,734
8	Houston	450,517	8	56,315
9	Cincinnati	440,906	8	55,113
10	NY Jets	429,465	8	53,683
11	LA Raiders	396,962	8	49,620
12	Pittsburgh	383,494	8	47,937
13	San Diego	376,434	8	47,054
14	New England	375,779	8	46,972
	TOTAL	6,563,436	112	58,602

National Conference

		Attendance	Gm	Average
1	NY Giants	596,319	8	74,540
2	San Francisco	510,600*	8	63,825
3	Philadelphia	501,479	8	62,685
4	Chicago	488,976	8	61,122
5	New Orleans	480,341	8	60,043
6	LA Rams	471,747	8	58,968
7	Minnesota	463,496	8	57,937
8	Green Bay	445,335*	8	55,667
9	Tampa Bay	439,685	8	54,961
10	Washington	420,106	8	52,513
11	Dallas	411,040	8	51,380
12	Detroit	392,396	8	49,050
13	Phoenix	345,198	8	43,150
14	Atlanta	320,391	8	40,049
	TOTAL	6,287,109	112	56,135

*Both San Francisco and Green Bay played home games in two stadiums in 1989: the 49ers played seven games at Candlestick Park (440,600 actual attendance) and one at Stanford Stadium (70,000) the week of the earthquake; the Packers, as usual, played five games at Lambeau Field (281,365) and three at Milwaukee County Stadium (163,970).

Home Fields

Listed below are the principal home fields used through the years by current NFL teams. The largest capacity of each stadium is noted in the right hand column. All-America Football Conference stadiums (1946-49) are included for Cleveland and San Francisco; and American Football League stadiums (1960-69) are included for Buffalo, Cincinnati, Denver, Houston, Kansas City, LA (Oakland) Raiders, Miami, New England (Boston), NY Jets and San Diego.

American Conference

Buffalo Bills

1960-72	War Memorial Stadium	45,748
1973-	Rich Stadium (Orchard Park,NY)	80,290
	(1973 capacity—80,020)	

Cincinnati Bengals

1968-69	Nippert Stadium (U.of Cincinnati)	26,500
1970-	Riverfront Stadium	60,311
	(1970 capacity—56,200)	

Cleveland Browns

1946-	Cleveland Stadium	80,098
	(1946 capacity—85,703)	

Denver Broncos

1960-	Mile High Stadium	76,274
	(1960 capacity—34,000)	

Houston Oilers

1960-64	Jeppesen Stadium	23,500
1965-67	Rice Stadium (Rice Univ.)	70,000
1968-	Astrodome	60,502
	(1968 capacity—52,000)	

Indianapolis Colts

1953-83	Memorial Stadium (Baltimore)	60,020
1984-	Hoosier Dome (Indianapolis)	60,129
	(1984 capacity—60,127)	

Kansas City Chiefs

1960-62	Cotton Bowl (Dallas)	72,000
1963-71	Municipal Stadium (Kansas City)	47,000
1972-	Arrowhead Stadium	78,067
	(1972 capacity—78,097)	

Los Angeles Raiders

1960	Kesar Stadium (San Francisco)	59,636
1961	Candlestick Park	42,500
1962-65	Frank Youell Field (Oakland)	20,000
1966-81	Oakland-Alameda County Coliseum	54,587
1982-	Memorial Coliseum (Los Angeles)	92,516

Miami Dolphins

1966-86	Orange Bowl	75,206
1987-	Joe Robbie Stadium	73,000
	(1987 capacity—75,500)	

New England Patriots

1960-62	Nickerson Field (Boston Univ.)	17,369
1963-68	Fenway Park	33,379
1969	Alumni Stadium (Boston College)	26,000
1970	Harvard Stadium	37,300
1971-	Foxboro Stadium	60,794
	(1971 capacity—61,114)	

New York Jets

1960-63	Polo Grounds	55,987
1964-83	Shea Stadium	60,372
1984-	Giants Stadium (E.Rutherford,NJ)	77,152
	(1984 capacity—76,891)	

Pittsburgh Steelers

1933-57	Forbes Field	35,000
1958-63	Forbes Field	35,000
	& Pitt Stadium	54,500
1964-69	Pitt Stadium	54,500
1970-	Three Rivers Stadium	59,030
	(1970 capacity—49,000)	

San Diego Chargers

1960	Memorial Coliseum (Los Angeles)	92,604
1961-66	Balboa Stadium (San Diego)	34,000
1967-	San Diego/Jack Murphy Stadium	60,750
	(1967 capacity—54,000)	

Seattle Seahawks

1976-	Kingdome	64,984
	(1976 capacity—65,000)	

Ballpark Name Changes: CLEVELAND—**Cleveland Stadium** originally Municipal Stadium (1932-74); DENVER —**Mile High Stadium** originally Bears Stadium (1948-66); NEW ENGLAND—**Foxboro Stadium** originally Schaefer Stadium (1971-82), then Sullivan Stadium (1983-89); SAN DIEGO—**San Diego/Jack Murphy Stadium** originally San Diego Stadium (1967-81).

National Football League (Cont.)

National Conference

Atlanta Falcons
1966-	Atlanta-Fulton County Stadium	 59,643
	(1966 capacity—58,850)	

Chicago Bears
1920	Staley Field (Decatur,IL)	.... —
1921-70	Wrigley Field (Chicago)	 37,741
1971-	Soldier Field	 66,946
	(1971 capacity—55,049)	

Dallas Cowboys
1960-70	Cotton Bowl	 72,132
1971-	Texas Stadium (Irving,TX)	 65,024
	(1971 capacity—65,101)	

Detroit Lions
1930-33	Spartan Stadium (Portsmouth,OH)	.. 8,200
1934-37	Univ.of Detroit Stadium	 25,000
1938-74	Tiger Stadium	 54,468
1975-	Pontiac Silverdome	 80,494
	(1975 capacity—80,638)	

Green Bay Packers
1921-22	Hagemeister Brewery Park	.... —
1923-24	Bellevue Park	.... —
1925-56	City Stadium I	 24,800
1957-	Lambeau Field	 59,543
	(1957 capacity—32,150)	

Note: The Packers have played some games in Milwaukee each season since 1933: at Borchert Field, State Fair Park and Marquette Stadium (1933-52), and County Stadium (56,051) since 1953.

Los Angeles Rams
1937-42	Municipal Stadium (Cleveland)	 85,703
1945	Suspended operations for one year	
1944-45	Municipal Stadium	 85,703
1946-79	Memorial Coliseum (Los Angeles)	.. 92,604
1980-	Anaheim Stadium	 69,008

Minnesota Vikings
1961-81	Metropolitan Stadium (Bloomington)	48,446
1982-	HHH Metrodome (Minneapolis)	... 63,300
	(1982 capacity—62,220)	

New Orleans Saints
1967-74	Tulane Stadium	 80,997
1975-	Louisiana Superdome	 69,065
	(1975 capacity—74,472)	

New York Giants
1925-55	Polo Grounds II	 55,200
1956-73	Yankee Stadium I	 63,800
1973-74	Yale Bowl (New Haven,CT)	 70,896
1975	Shea Stadium	 60,372
1976-	Giants Stadium (E.Rutherford,NJ)	.. 77,152
	(1976 capacity—76,800)	

Philadelphia Eagles
1933-35	Baker Bowl	 18,800
1936-39	Municipal Stadium	 73,702
1940	Shibe Park	 33,608
1941	Municipal Stadium	 73,702
1942	Shibe Park	 33,608
1943	Forbes Field (Pittsburgh)	 34,528
1944-57	Shibe Park	 33,608
1958-70	Franklin Field (Univ.of Penn.)	 60,546
1971-	Veterans Stadium	 67,011
	(1971 capacity—65,000)	

Phoenix Cardinals
1920-21	Normal Field (Chicago)	 7,500
1922-25	Comiskey Park	 28,000
1926-28	Normal Field	 7,500
1929-59	Comiskey Park	 52,000
1960-65	Busch Stadium (St.Louis)	 34,000
1966-87	Busch Memorial Stadium	 54,392
1988-	Sun Devil Stadium (Tempe,AZ)	... 73,500

San Francisco 49ers
1946-70	Kezar Stadium	 59,636
1971-	Candlestick Park	 66,252
	(1971 capacity—45,000)	

Tampa Bay Buccaneers
1976-	Tampa Stadium	 74,315
	(1976 capacity—71,951)	

Washington Redskins
1932	Braves Field (Boston)	 40,000
1933-36	Fenway Park	 27,000
1937-60	Griffith Stadium (Wash.,DC)	 35,000
1961-	RFK Stadium	 55,672
	(1961 capacity—55,004)	

Ballpark Name Changes: ATLANTA—**Atlanta-Fulton County Stadium** originally Atlanta Stadium (1966-74); CHICAGO—**Wrigley Field** originally Cubs Park (1916-25), also, **Comiskey Park** originally White Sox Park (1910-12); DETROIT— **Tiger Stadium** originally Navin Field (1912-37), then Briggs Stadium (1938-60), also, **Pontiac Silverdome** originally Pontiac Metropolitan Stadium (1975); GREEN BAY—**Lambeau Field** originally City Stadium II (1957-64); PHILADELPHIA—**Shibe Park** renamed Connie Mack Stadium in 1953; ST. LOUIS—**Busch Memorial Stadium** renamed Busch Stadium in 1983; WASHINGTON—**RFK Stadium** originally D.C.Stadium (1961-68).

Canadian Football League

Eastern Division

		Location	Built	Capacity	Field
Hamilton Tiger-Cats	**Ivor Wynne Stadium**	Hamilton, ONT.	1932	**29,183**	Turf
Ottawa Rough Riders	**Lansdowne Stadium**	Ottawa, ONT.	1967	**30,927**	Turf
Toronto Argos	**SkyDome**	Toronto, ONT.	1989	**53,595**	Turf
Winnipeg Blue Bombers	**Winnipeg Stadium**	Winnipeg, MAN.	1953	**32,946**	Turf

Western Division

		Location	Built	Capacity	Field
British Columbia Lions	**B.C.Place**	Vancouver, BC	1983	**59,478**	Turf
Calgary Stampeders	**McMahon Stadium**	Calgary, ALB.	1960	**38,200**	Turf
Edmonton Eskimos	**Commonwealth Stadium**	Edmonton, ALB.	1978	**60,081**	Grass
Saskatchewan Roughriders	**Taylor Field**	Regina, SASK.	1948	**27,637**	Turf

National Hockey League

Wales Conference

		Location	Built	Capacity
Boston Bruins	Boston Garden	Boston, MA	1928	14,637
Buffalo Sabres	Memorial Auditorium	Buffalo, NY	1940	16,433
Hartford Whalers	Civic Center Coliseum	Hartford, CT	1975	15,635
Montreal Canadiens	Montreal Forum	Montreal, Que	1924	16,084
New Jersey Devils	Byrne Meadowlands Arena	E.Rutherford, NJ	1981	19,040
New York Islanders	Veterans' Mem. Coliseum	Uniondale, NY	1971	16,297
New York Rangers	Madison Square Garden	New York, NY	1968	17,520
Philadelphia Flyers	The Spectrum	Philadelphia, PA	1967	17,425
Pittsburgh Penguins	Civic Arena	Pittsburgh, PA	1961	16,236
Quebec Nordiques	Colisée de Québec	Quebec City, Que	1951	15,399
Washington Capitals	Capital Centre	Landover, MD	1973	18,130

Campell Conference

		Location	Built	Capacity
Calgary Flames	Olympic Saddledome	Calgary, Alb.	1983	20,130
Chicago Blackhawks	Chicago Stadium	Chicago, IL	1929	17,317
Detroit Red Wings	Joe Louis Sports Arena	Detroit, MI	1979	19,275
Edmonton Oilers	Northlands Coliseum	Edmonton, Alb.	1974	17,313
Los Angeles Kings	Great Western Forum	Inglewood, CA	1967	16,005
Minnesota North Stars	Met Center	Bloomington, MN	1967	15,499
St.Louis Blues	St.Louis Arena	St.Louis, MO	1929	17,188
Toronto Maple Leafs	Maple Leaf Gardens	Toronto, Ont.	1931	16,864
Vancouver Canucks	Pacific Coliseum	Vancouver, B.C.	1968	16,123
Winnipeg Jets	Winnipeg Arena	Winnipeg, Man.	1954	15,393

Rank by Capacity

Wales Conference		Campbell Conference	
Meadowlands	19,040	Saddledome	20,130
Capital Centre	18,130	Joe Louis	19,275
Mad.Sq.Garden	17,520	Chicago Stadium	17,317
Spectrum	17,425	Northlands	17,313
Buffalo Aud	16,433	St.Louis	17,188
Nassau Coliseum	16,297	M.Leaf Gardens	16,864
Pitt.Civ.Arena	16,236	Pacific Col	16,123
Montreal Forum	16,084	LA Forum	16,005
Hart.Civ.Center	15,635	Met Center	15,499
Le Colisée	15,399	Winnipeg Arena	15,393
Boston Garden	14,637		

Rank by Age

Wales Conference		Campbell Conference	
Montreal Forum	1924	Chicago Stadium	1929
Boston Garden	1928	St.Louis Arena	1929
Buffalo Aud	1940	M.Leaf Gardens	1931
Le Colisée	1951	Winnipeg Arena	1954
Pitt Civic Arena	1961	Met Center	1967
Spectrum	1967	LA Forum	1967
Mad.Sq.Garden	1968	Pacific Coliseum	1968
Nassau Coliseum	1971	Northlands Col	1974
Capital Center	1973	Joe Louis Arena	1979
Hart.Civic Center	1975	Saddledome	1983
Meadowlands	1981		

Note: The Montreal Forum was rebuilt in 1968, the Hartford Civic Center in 1980.

1989-90 NHL Attendance

Overall attendance in the NHL was 13,251,254 in 840 games for an average per game crowd of 15,775. Teams in each conference are ranked by attendance over 40 home games.

Wales Conference

		Attendance	Gm	Average
1	Philadelphia	696,407	40	17,410
2	Washington	690,023	40	17,251
3	Montreal	684,696	40	17,117
4	NY Rangers	649,539	40	16,238
5	Pittsburgh	640,700	40	16,918
6	Buffalo	634,692	40	15,867
7	Quebec	602,060	40	15,052
8	New Jersey	580,187	40	14,505
9	Boston	572,571	40	14,314
10	Hartford	548,199	40	13,705
11	NY Islanders	508,388	40	12,710
	TOTAL	6,807,462	440	15,472

Campbell Conference

		Attendance	Gm	Average
1	Calgary	794,444	40	19,861
2	Detroit	781,229	40	19,531
3	Chicago	701,853	40	17,546
4	Edmonton	680,333	40	17,008
5	Toronto	647,867	40	16,197
6	Los Angeles	628,274	40	15,707
7	Vancouver	616,715	40	15,418
8	St.Louis	614,685	40	15,367
9	Winnipeg	524,235	40	13,106
10	Minnesota	454,157	40	11,354
	TOTAL	6,443,792	400	16,109

National Hockey League (Cont.)

Home Ice

Listed below are the principal home buildings used through the years by current NHL teams. The largest capacity of each arena is noted in the right hand column. World Hockey Association arenas (1972-76) are included for Edmonton, Hartford, Quebec and Winnipeg.

Wales Conference

Boston Bruins
1924-28	Boston Arena	6,200
1928-	Boston Garden	14,637
	(1928 capacity—14,500)	

Buffalo Sabres
| 1970- | Memorial Auditorium | 16,433 |
| | (1970 capacity—10,429) | |

Hartford Whalers
1972-73	Boston Garden	14,442
1973-74	Boston Garden (regular season)	14,442
	W.Springfield,MA Big E (playoffs)	5,513
1974-75	West Springfield Big E	5,513
	& Hartford (CT) Civic Center	10,507
1975-77	Hartford Civic Center	10,507
1977-78	Hartford Civic Center	10,507
	& Springfield (MA) Civic Center	7,725
1978-79	Springfield Civic Center	7,725
1979-80	Springfield Civic Center	7,725
	& Hartford Civic Center II	14,250
1980-	Hartford Civic Center II	15,635
	(1980 capacity—14,460)	

Note: The Hartford Civic Center roof caved in Jan,1978, forcing the Whalers to move their home games to Springfield,MA, for two years.

Montreal Canadiens
1910-20	Jubilee Arena	3,200
1913-18	Montreal Arena (Westmount)	6,000
1918-26	Mount Royal Arena	6,750
1926-68	Montreal Forum I	15,500
1968-	Montreal Forum II	16,084

Note: The Forum (original capacity: 9,200) was built in 1924 for Montreal's other NHL team, the Maroons, who were its only tenant from 1924-26. The Maroons, who folded after the 1937-38 season, shared the Forum with the Canadiens from 1924-38.

New Jersey Devils
1974-76	Kemper Arena (Kansas City)	16,300
1976-82	McNichols Arena (Denver)	15,900
1982-	Meadowlands Arena (E.Rutherford,NJ)	19,040
	(1982 capacity—19,023)	

New York Islanders
| 1972- | Nassau Veterans' Mem.Coliseum | 16,297 |
| | (1972 capacity—14,500) | |

New York Rangers
1925-68	Madison Square Garden III	15,925
1968-	Madison Square Garden IV	17,520
	(1968 capacity—17,250)	

Philadelphia Flyers
| 1967- | The Spectrum | 17,425 |
| | (1967 capacity—14,558) | |

Note: A section of Spectrum roof blew off in March,1968, forcing the Flyers to play their last seven regular season home games at Madison Sq.Garden (1 game), Maple Leaf Gardens (1) and Le Colisée in Quebec (1). The roof was fixed by the playoffs.

Pittsburgh Penguins
| 1967- | Civic Arena | 16,236 |
| | (1967 capacity—12,508) | |

Quebec Nordiques
| 1972- | Le Colisée de Québec | 15,399 |
| | (1972 capacity—10,004) | |

Washington Capitals
| 1974- | Capital Centre (Landover,MD) | 18,130 |

Campbell Conference

Calgary Flames
1972-80	The Omni (Atlanta)	15,278
1980-83	Calgary Corral	7,424
1983-	Olympic Saddledome	20,130
	(1983 capacity—16,674)	

Chicago Stadium
1926-29	Chicago Coliseum	5,000
1929-	Chicago Stadium	17,317
	(1929 capacity—16,500)	

Detroit Red Wings
1926-27	Border Cities Arena (Windsor,Ont.)	3,200
1927-79	Olympia Stadium (Detroit)	16,700
1979-	Joe Louis Arena	19,275

Edmonton Oilers
1972-74	Edmonton Gardens	7,200
1974-	Northlands Coliseum	17,313
	(1974 capacity—15,513)	

Los Angeles Kings
| 1967- | Great Western Forum | 16,005 |
| | (1967 capacity—15,651) | |

Note: The Kings played 17 games at Long Beach Sports Arena and LA Sports Arena at the start of the 1967-68 season.

Minnesota North Stars
| 1967- | Met Center | 15,499 |
| | (1967 capacity—14,400) | |

St.Louis Blues
| 1967- | St.Louis Arena | 17,188 |
| | (1967 capacity—14,200) | |

Toronto Maple Leafs
1917-31	Mutual Street Arena	8,000
1931-	Maple Leaf Gardens	16,864
	(1931 capacity—13,542)	

Vancouver Canucks
| 1970- | Pacific Coliseum | 16,123 |
| | (1970 capacity—15,760) | |

Winnipeg Jets
| 1972- | Winnipeg Arena | 15,393 |
| | (1972 capacity—10,177) | |

Building Name Changes: LOS ANGELES—**Great Western Forum** originally The Forum (1967-88); MINNESOTA—**Met Center** originally Metropolitan Sports Center (1967-82); ST.LOUIS—**St.Louis Arena** renamed The Checkerdome in 1977, then St.Louis Arena again in 1982.

Major College Football Stadiums

Stadiums played in by NCAA Division I-A football teams. Teams with home games in more than one stadium are noted.

Atlantic Coast Conference

	Stadium	Built	Seats	Field
Clemson	Memorial	1942	79,853	Grass
Duke	Wallace Wade	1929	33,941	Grass
Ga.Tech	Grant Field	1914	46,000	Turf
Maryland	Byrd	1950	45,000	Grass
N.Carolina	Kenan	1927	52,000	Grass
N.C.State	Carter-Finley	1966	53,500	Grass
Virginia	Scott	1931	42,000	Turf
Wake Forest	Groves	1968	31,500	Grass

Big Eight Conference

	Stadium	Built	Seats	Field
Colorado	Folsom Field	1924	51,463	Turf
Iowa St	Trice Field	1975	50,000	Turf
Kansas	Memorial	1927	50,250	Turf
Kansas St	KSU	1968	42,000	Turf
Missouri	Faurot Field	1926	62,000	Turf
Nebraska	Memorial	1923	73,650	Turf
Oklahoma	Owen Field	1923	75,004	Turf
Oklahoma St	Lewis Field	1920	50,440	Turf

Big Ten Conference

	Stadium	Built	Seats	Field
Illinois	Memorial	1923	69,200	Turf
Indiana	Memorial	1960	52,354	Turf
Iowa	Kinnick	1929	67,700	Grass
Michigan	Michigan	1927	101,701	Turf
Michigan St	Spartan	1957	76,000	Turf
Minnesota	Metrodome	1982	63,300	Turf
Northwestern	Dyche	1926	49,256	Turf
Ohio St	Ohio	1922	86,071	Grass
Purdue	Ross-Ade	1924	67,861	Grass
Wisconsin	Camp Randall	1917	77,745	Turf

Big West Conference

	Stadium	Built	Seats	Field
Fresno St	Bulldog	1980	30,000	Grass
CS-Fullerton	Santa Ana	1963	12,000	Grass
L.Beach St	Veterans	1966	12,500	Grass
N.Mexico St	Memorial	1978	30,343	Grass
Pacific	Stagg Memorial	1950	30,153	Grass
San Jose St	Spartan	1932	31,365	Grass
UNLV	Silver Bowl	1971	32,000	Turf
Utah St	Romney	1968	30,257	Grass

Mid-American Conference

	Stadium	Built	Seats	Field
Ball St	Ball State	1967	16,319	Grass
Bowl.Green	Perry Field	1966	30,599	Grass
Central Mich	Kelly/Shorts	1972	20,086	Turf
Eastern Mich	Rynearson	1969	19,800	Grass
Kent St	Dix	1969	30,520	Grass
Miami,OH	Yager	1983	25,183	Grass
Ohio Univ	Peden	1929	20,000	Grass
Toledo	Glass Bowl	1937	26,218	Turf
Western Mich	Waldo	1939	30,000	Turf

Pac-10 Conference

	Stadium	Built	Seats	Field
Arizona	Arizona	1928	57,000	Grass
Arizona St	Sun Devil	1958	74,865	Grass
California	Memorial	1923	75,630	Turf
Oregon	Autzen	1967	41,698	Turf
Oregon St	Parker	1953	39,597	Turf
Stanford	Stanford	1921	86,011	Grass
UCLA	Rose Bowl	1922	104,091	Grass
USC	LA Coliseum	1923	92,516	Grass
Washington	Husky	1920	72,500	Turf
Wash.St	Martin	1972	40,000	Turf

Southeastern Conference

	Stadium	Built	Seats	Field
Alabama	Bryant-Denny	1929	70,123	Turf
	Legion Field	1927	75,952	Turf
Auburn	Jordan-Hare	1939	85,214	Grass
Florida	Florida Field	1929	72,000	Grass
Georgia	Sanford	1929	82,122	Grass
Kentucky	Commonwealth	1973	57,800	Grass
LSU	Tiger	1924	80,140	Grass
Mississippi	Vaught-H'way	1941	42,000	Grass
	Memorial	1953	62,529	Grass
Miss.St	Scott Field	1935	41,200	Grass
	Memorial	1953	62,529	Grass
Tennessee	Neyland	1921	91,110	Turf
Vanderbilt	Vanderbilt	1981	41,000	Turf

Note: At **Alabama**, Bryant-Denny Stadium is in Tuscaloosa and Legion Field in Birmingham; at **Mississippi**, Vaught-Hemingway Stadium is in Oxford and Memorial Stadium in Jackson; at **Mississippi St.**, Scott Field is in Starkville and Memorial Stadium in Jackson.

Southwest Conference

	Stadium	Built	Seats	Field
Arkansas	Razorback	1938	52,860	Turf
	War Memorial	1948	53,250	Turf
Baylor	Baylor	1950	48,500	Turf
Houston	Astrodome	1965	60,502	Turf
Rice	Rice	1950	70,000	Turf
SMU	Ownby	1926	23,783	Grass
Texas	Memorial	1924	77,809	Turf
Texas A&M	Kyle Field	1925	72,387	Turf
TCU	Carter	1929	46,000	Turf
Texas Tech	Amon C. Jones	1947	47,000	Turf

Note: At **Arkansas**, Razorback Stadium is in Fayetteville and War Memorial Stadium in Little Rock; at **Texas**, Memorial Stadium is in Austin and the Cotton Bowl in Dallas.

Western Athletic Conference

	Stadium	Built	Seats	Field
Air Force	Falcon	1962	52,153	Grass
BYU	BYU	1964	65,000	Grass
Colorado St	Hughes	1968	30,000	Grass
Hawaii	Aloha	1975	50,000	Turf
New Mexico	University	1960	30,646	Grass
S.Diego St	Jack Murphy	1967	60,750	Grass
Utah	Rice	1927	35,000	Turf
UTEP	Sun Bowl	1963	52,000	Turf
Wyoming	War Memorial	1950	33,500	Grass

Major College Football Stadiums (Cont.)

I-A Independents

	Stadium	Built	Seats	Field
Akron	Rubber Bowl	1940	35,482	Turf
Army	Michie	1924	39,867	Turf
Boston Col	Alumni	1957	32,000	Turf
Cincinnati	Riverfront	1970	60,311	Turf
E.Carolina	Ficklen	1963	35,000	Grass
Florida St	Doak Campbell	1950	60,519	Grass
La.Tech	Aillet	1968	30,600	Grass
Louisville	Cardinal	1956	35,500	Turf
Memphis St	Liberty Bowl	1965	63,244	Grass
Miami,FL	Orange Bowl	1935	75,500	Grass
Navy	Navy-Marine Corps Memorial	1959	30,000	Grass
No.Illinois	Huskie	1965	30,998	Turf
N.Dame	Notre Dame	1930	59,075	Grass
Penn St	Beaver	1960	83,370	Grass
Pittsburgh	Pitt	1925	56,500	Turf
Rutgers	Rutgers	1938	23,000	Grass
	Giants	1976	77,152	Turf
S.Carolina	Williams-Brice	1934	72,400	Grass
SW La.	Cajun Field	1970	31,000	Grass
So.Miss	Roberts	1976	33,000	Grass
Syracuse	Carrier Dome	1980	50,000	Turf
Temple	Veterans	1971	67,011	Turf
Tulane	Superdome	1975	69,065	Turf
Tulsa	Skelly	1930	40,385	Turf
Va.Tech	Lane	1965	51,000	Grass
West Va	Mountaineer Fld	1980	63,500	Turf

Bowl Games

	Stadium	Built	Seats	Field
All-American	Legion Field	1927	75,952	Turf
Aloha	Aloha	1975	50,000	Turf
California	Bulldog	1980	30,000	Grass
Copper	Arizona	1928	57,000	Grass
Cotton	Cotton Bowl	1932	72,032	Turf
Fiesta	Sun Devil	1958	74,865	Grass
Fla.Citrus	Fla.Citrus Bowl-Orlando	1936	60,000	Grass
Freedom	Anaheim	1966	69,008	Grass
Gator	Gator Bowl	1949	82,000	Grass
Hall of Fame	Tampa	1967	74,314	Grass
Holiday	Jack Murphy	1967	60,750	Grass
John Hancock	Sun Bowl	1963	52,000	Turf
Independence	Independence	1936	50,560	Grass
Liberty	Liberty Bowl	1965	63,244	Grass
Orange	Orange Bowl	1935	75,500	Grass
Peach	Atlanta	1965	59,643	Grass
Rose	Rose Bowl	1922	104,091	Grass
Sugar	Superdome	1975	69,065	Turf
Sunshine	Joe Robbie	1986	73,000	Grass

Bowl Game Sites: All-American—Birmingham,AL; **Aloha**—Honolulu; **California**—Fresno; **Copper**—Tucson,AZ; **Cotton**—Dallas; **Fiesta**—Tempe,AZ; **Florida Citrus**—Orlando; **Freedom**—Anaheim,CA; **Gator**—Jacksonville,FL; **Hall of Fame**—Tampa,FL; **Holiday**—San Diego; **John Hancock**—El Paso,TX; **Independence**—Shreveport,LA; **Liberty**—Memphis,TN; **Orange**—Miami; **Peach**—Atlanta; **Rose**—Pasadena,CA; **Sugar**—New Orleans; **Sunshine**—Miami.

The 30 Largest Stadiums

The thirty largest home fields in Division I college football. Note that (*) indicates part-time home field.

		Seats	Home Team	Conference	Built	Field
1	Rose Bowl	104,091	UCLA	Pac-10	1922	Grass
2	Michigan Stadium	101,701	Michigan	Big Ten	1927	Turf
3	LA Coliseum	92,516	USC	Pac-10	1923	Grass
4	Neyland Stadium	91,110	Tennessee	SEC	1921	Turf
5	Ohio Stadium	86,071	Ohio St.	Big Ten	1922	Grass
6	Stanford Stadium	86,011	Stanford	Pac-10	1921	Grass
7	Jordan-Hare Stadium	85,214	Auburn	SEC	1939	Grass
8	Beaver Stadium	83,370	Penn St.	Independent	1960	Grass
9	Sanford Stadium	82,122	Georgia	SEC	1929	Grass
10	Tiger Stadium	80,140	LSU	SEC	1924	Grass
11	Memorial Stadium	79,853	Clemson	ACC	1942	Grass
12	Memorial Stadium	77,809	Texas	SWC	1924	Turf
13	Camp Randall Stadium	77,745	Wisconsin	Big Ten	1917	Turf
14	Giants Stadium	77,152	Rutgers*	Independent	1976	Turf
15	Spartan Stadium	76,000	Michigan St.	Big Ten	1957	Turf
16	Legion Field	75,952	Alabama*	SEC	1927	Turf
17	Memorial Stadium	75,630	California	Pac-10	1923	Turf
18	Orange Bowl	75,500	Miami, FL	Independent	1935	Grass
19	Owen Field	75,004	Oklahoma	Big Eight	1923	Turf
20	Sun Devil Stadium	74,865	Arizona St.	Pac-10	1958	Grass
21	Memorial Stadium	73,650	Nebraska	Big Eight	1923	Turf
22	Husky Stadium	72,500	Washington	Pac-10	1920	Turf
23	Williams-Brice Stadium	72,400	South Carolina	Independent	1934	Grass
24	Kyle Field	72,387	Texas A&M	SWC	1925	Turf
25	Florida Field	72,000	Florida	SEC	1929	Turf
26	Yale Bowl	70,896	Yale	Ivy	1914	Grass
27	Bryant-Denny Stadium	70,123	Alabama	SEC	1929	Turf
28	Kinnick Stadium	70,052	Iowa	Big 10	1929	Grass
29	Rice Stadium	70,000	Rice	SWC	1950	Turf
30	Memorial Stadium	69,200	Illinois	Big 10	1923	Turf

Major College Basketball Arenas

NCAA Division I basketball arenas with a seating capacity of at least 12,000.

Arena	Seats	Home Team	Arena	Seats	Home Team
Carrier Dome	32,683	Syracuse	Cole Fieldhouse	14,500	Maryland
Thompson-Boling Center	24,535	Tennessee	Joel Coliseum	14,500	W.Forest
Charlotte Coliseum	23,388	Davidson* & NC-Char.	Devaney Sports Center	14,478	Nebraska
Rupp Arena	23,000	Kentucky	University Center	14,287	Ariz.St.
Marriott Center	22,700	BYU	Maravich Center	14,236	LSU
Dean Smith Center	21,444	N.Carolina	Mackey Arena	14,123	Purdue
Meadowlands Arena	20,089	Seton Hall	Hilton Coliseum	14,020	Iowa St.
Madison Square Garden	19,081	St.John's*	WVU Coliseum	14,000	West Va.
Freedom Hall	18,865	Louisville	San Diego Sports Arena	13,741	S.D.St.
Capital Centre	18,756	Georgetown	Crisler Arena	13,609	Michigan
Bradley Center	18,633	Marquette	Bramlage Coliseum	13,500	Kansas St.
Thomas & Mack Center	18,500	UNLV	Myrl Shoemaker Center	13,500	Cinn.
The Spectrum	18,168	Villanova*	McKale Center	13,477	Arizona
Rosemont Horizon	17,500	DePaul & Loyola,IL	U.of Dayton Arena	13,455	Dayton
			Providence Civic Center	13,410	Providence & Rhode.Is.*
Assembly Hall	17,357	Indiana	St.John Arena	13,276	Ohio St.
The Pit	17,126	New Mexico	Pan American Center	13,222	N.Mex.St.
Pittsburgh Civic Arena	16,798	Pittsburgh*	Hearnes Center	13,143	Missouri
Williams Arena	16,434	Minnesota	Convocation Center	13,080	Ohio U.
Hartford Civic Center	16,294	UConn*	Pauley Pavilion	12,543	UCLA
Erwin Sp.Events Center	16,231	Texas	Leon County Civic Center	12,500	Fla.St.
Assembly Hall	16,153	Illinois	Eaves Mem.Coliseum	12,500	Auburn
Kibbie-Asui Dome	16,000	Idaho	Carolina Coliseum	12,401	S.Carolina
Allen Field.House	15,800	Kansas	Reynolds Coliseum	12,400	N.C.State
Memorial Gymnasium	15,646	Vanderbilt	Diddle Arena	12,370	Western Ky.
The Aud	15,564	Canisius*	Special Events Center	12,222	UTEP
Carver-Hawkeye	15,550	Iowa	Friel Court	12,058	Wash.St.
LA Sports Arena	15,371	USC	BSU Pavilion	12,000	Boise St.
Breslin Stud.Evts Center	15,100	Mich.St.	Cajundome	12,000	SW La.
Coleman Coliseum	15,043	Alabama	Dee Events Center	12,000	Weber St.
Arena-Auditorium	15,028	Wyoming	Long Beach Arena	12,000	L.Beach St.
Miami Arena	15,008	Miami	Memorial Center	12,000	E.Tenn.St.
Huntsman Center	15,000	Utah	O'Connell Center	12,000	Florida

*Teams that split schedule between large arenas and smaller home gyms.

Future NCAA Final Four Sites

Year	Arena	Seats	Location	Year	Arena	Seats	Location
1991	Hoosier Dome	38,000	Indianapolis	1995	Kingdome	40,000	Seattle
1992	HHH Metrodome	23,000	Minneapolis	1996	Meadowlands	20,089	E.Rutherford
1993	Superdome	65,000	New Orleans	1997	Hoosier Dome	38,000	Indianapolis
1994	Charlotte Coliseum	23,388	Charlotte				

Division I Basketball Arenas

Arenas played in by NCAA Men's Division I basketball teams. Teams with home games in more than one arena are noted.

American South

	Home Floor	Seats
Ark.St	Convocation Center	10,563
Lamar	Montagne Center	10,080
La.Tech	Thomas Assembly Center	8,000
N.Orleans	Lakefront Arena	10,000
SW La	Cajundome	12,000
Tex-Pan Am	Pan American Fieldhouse	5,500

Assn.of Mid-Continent Universities

	Home Floor	Seats
Akron	Rhodes Arena	7,000
Cleve.St	Woodling Gym & Public Hall	3,000 7,400
E.Illinois	Lantz Gym	6,500
Ill-Chicago	UIC Pavillion	10,000
No.Illinois	Evans Field House	6,076
No.Iowa	Uni-Dome	10,000
Valparaiso	Athletics Rec.Center	4,500
W.Illinois	Western Hall	5,139
Wisc-G.Bay	Brown County Arena	5,600

Atlantic Coast

	Home Floor	Seats
Clemson	Littlejohn Coliseum	11,020
Duke	Cameron Indoor Stadium	9,314
Ga.Tech	Alexander Mem.Coliseum	10,200
Maryland	Cole Field House	14,500
N.Carolina	Dean Smith Center	21,444
N.C.State	Reynolds Coliseum	12,400
Virginia	University Hall	8,800
Wake Forest	Lawrence Joel Coliseum	14,500

Atlantic 10

	Home Floor	Seats
Duquesne	A.J.Palumbo Center	6,200
Geo.Wash	Charles E.Smith Center	5,000
UMass	Curry Hicks Cage & Springfield Civic Center	4,024 8,200
Penn St	Rec Hall	7,200
Rhode Is	Keaney Gymnasium & Providence Civic Center	5,000 12,150
Rutgers	Louis Brown Ath.Center	8,000
St.Bona	Reilly Center	6,000
St.Joe's	Alumni Mem.Fieldhouse	3,200
Temple	McGonigle Hall	3,900
West Va	WVU Coliseum	14,000

Division I Basketball Arenas (Cont.)

Big East

Home Floor		Seats
Boston Col	Silvio O.Conte Forum	8,604
UConn	Gampel Pavilion	8,028
	& Hartford Civic Center	16,016
Georgetown	Capital Centre	18,756
Pittsburgh	Fitzgerald Field House	6,798
	& Pittsburgh Civic Arena	16,798
Providence	Providence Civic Center	13,410
St.John's	Alumni Hall	6,008
	& Madison Square Garden	19,081
Seton Hall	Walsh Gymnasium	3,200
	& Meadowlands Arena	20,089
Syracuse	Carrier Dome	32,683
Villanova	duPont Pavilion	6,500
	& The Spectrum	18,168

Big Eight

Home Floor		Seats
Colorado	Events Center	11,199
Iowa St	Hilton Coliseum	14,020
Kansas	Allen Field House	15,800
Kansas St	Bramlage Coliseum	13,500
Missouri	Hearnes Center	13,143
Nebraska	Devaney Sports Center	14,478
Oklahoma	Lloyd Noble Center	10,871
Okla.St	Gallagher-Iba Arena	6,381

Big Sky

Home Floor		Seats
Boise St	BSU Pavilion	12,000
E.Wash	Reese Court	5,000
Idaho	Kibbie-Asui Dome	16,000
Idaho St	Holt Arena	7,938
Montana	Dahlberg Arena	9,059
Montana St	Brick Breeden Field House	7,848
Nevada-Reno	Lawler Event Center	11,200
No.Arizona	Walkup Skydome	7,500
Weber St	Dee Events Center	12,000

Big South

Home Floor		Seats
Augusta	Augusta Gym	3,500
	& Richmond Civic Center	7,500
Baptist	Baptist Fieldhouse	2,500
Campbell	Carter Gym	1,500
	& Cumberland County Arena	5,500
C.Carolina	Kimbel Gym	1,800
NC-Ashvl	Justice Center	2,500
	& Ashville Civic Center	6,800
Radford	Dedmon Center	5,000
Winthrop	Winthrop Coliseum	6,100

Big Ten

Home Floor		Seats
Illinois	Assembly Hall	16,153
Indiana	Assembly Hall	17,357
Iowa	Carver-Hawkeye Arena	15,550
Michigan	Crisler Arena	13,609
Michigan St	Breslin Student Evts.Ctr.	15,100
Minnesota	Williams Arena	16,434
N'western	Welsh-Ryan Arena	8,117
Ohio St	St.John Arena	13,276
Purdue	Mackey Arena	14,123
Wisconsin	Wisconsin Field House	11,886

Big West

Home Floor		Seats
Fresno St	Selland Arena	10,159
Fullerton	Titan Gym	4,000
Irvine	Donald Bren Events Ctr.	5,000
L.Beach St	University Gym	2,200
	& Long Beach Arena	12,000
N.Mexico St	Pan American Center	13,222
Pacific	Alex G.Spanos Center	6,000
San Jose St	Recreation & Events Ctr.	4,800
S.Barbara	Campus Events Center	6,000
UNLV	Thomas & Mack Center	18,500
Utah St	The Spectrum	10,270

Colonial Athletic Assn

Home Floor		Seats
American	Bender Arena	5,000
E.Carolina	Minges Collisium	6,500
Geo.Mason	Patriot Center	10,000
J.Madison	JMU Convocation Center	7,612
Navy	Halsey Field House	5,000
NC-Wilm	Trask Coliseum	6,100
Richmond	Robbins Center	9,171
Wm.& Mary	Wm.& Mary Hall	10,000

East Coast

Home Floor		Seats
C.Conn.St	Kaiser Hall	4,500
Delaware	Delaware Field House	3,000
Drexel	Phys.Ed.Athletic Center	2,500
Hofstra	Phys.Fitness Center	3,500
MD-Balt.Co	UMBC Fieldhouse	4,024
Rider	Alumni Gymnasium	2,200
Towson St	Towson Center	5,200

Ivy League

Home Floor		Seats
Brown	Pizzitola Sports Center	2,800
Columbia	Levien Gymnasium	3,408
Cornell	Alberding Field House	5,000
Dartmouth	Leede Arena	2,100
Harvard	Briggs Athletic Center	3,000
Penn	The Palestra	8,700
Princeton	Jadwin Gymnasium	7,500
Yale	Payne Whitney Gymnasium	3,100

Metro

Home Floor		Seats
Cincinnati	Myrl Shoemaker Center	13,500
Florida St	Leon County Civic Ctr.	12,500
Louisville	Freedom Hall	18,865
Memphis St	Mid-South Coliseum	11,200
S.Carolina	Carolina Coliseum	12,401
So.Miss	Green Coliseum	8,532
Tulane	Fogelman Arena	6,000
Va.Tech	Cassell Coliseum	10,000

Metro Atlantic

Home Floor		Seats
Canisius	The Aud	15,564
	& Koessler Athletic Ctr.	1,800
Fairfield	Alumni Hall	3,022
Iona	Mulcahy Campus Center	3,200
La Salle	Phila.Civic Center	10,000
Loyola,MD	Reitz Arena	3,000
Manhattan	Draddy Gymnasium	3,000
Niagara	Niagara Falls Conv.Ctr.	6,000
	& Gallagher Center	3,400
St.Peter's	Yanitell Center	3,200
Siena	Alumni Recreation Ctr.	4,000

Mid-American

Home Floor		Seats
Ball St	University Gym	7,000
Bowl.Green	Anderson Arena	5,000
Cent.Mich	Rose Arena	6,000
East.Mich	Bowen Field House	5,800
Kent St	Memorial Gym	6,034
Miami,OH	Millett Hall	9,200
Ohio Univ	Convocation Center	13,080
Toledo	John F.Savage Hall	9,000
West.Mich	Read Fieldhouse	8,250

Mid-Eastern

Home Floor		Seats
Beth-Cook	Moore Gym	1,700
Coppin St	Pullen Gym	3,000
Delaware St	Memorial Hall	4,000
Fla.A&M	Gaither Gym	6,000
Howard	Burr Gym	3,900
MD-E.Shore	Tawes Gym	3,500
Morgan St	T.L.Hill Field House	7,500
N.Car.A&T	Corbett Sports Center	7,500
S.Car.St	Smith-Hammond-Middleton	3,200

Midwestern Collegiate

Home Floor		Seats
Butler	Hinkle Fieldhouse	10,700
Dayton	Univ.of Dayton Arena	13,455
Detroit	Cobo Arena	11,241
Evansville	Roberts Stadium	12,300
Loyola,IL	Rosemont Horizon	17,500
Marquette	Bradley Center	18,633
St.Louis	Kiel Auditorium	9,300
Xavier,OH	Cincinnati Gardens	10,400

Missouri Valley

Home Floor		Seats
Bradley	Carver Arena	10,401
Creighton	Omaha Civic Auditorium	9,800
Drake	Veterans Mem.Auditorium	9,564
Illinois St	Redbird Arena	10,500
Indiana St	Hulman Center	10,200
So.Illinois	SIU Arena	10,014
SW Mo.St	Hammons Student Ctr.	8,858
Tulsa	Maxwell Convention Ctr.	9,200
Wichita St	Levitt Arena	5,075

North Atlantic

Home Floor		Seats
Boston U	Walter Brown Arena	4,200
Hartford	Sports Center	4,675
Maine	Bangor Auditorium	6,500
New Hamp	Lund Holm Gym	3,500
N'eastern	Matthews Arena	6,500
Vermont	Patrick Gym	3,200

Northeast

Home Floor		Seats
FDU-Teaneck	Rothman Center	5,000
LIU-Bklyn	Schwartz Athletic Center	2,000
Marist	McCann Center	3,944
Monmouth	Alumni Memorial Gym	2,800
Mt.St.Mary's	Knot Arena	3,500
Robt.Morris	Charles Sewall Center	3,056
St.Fran.,NY	Phys.Ed Center	3,000
St.Fran.,PA	Maurice Stokes Bldg.	4,000
Wagner	Sutter Gym	1,650

Ohio Valley

Home Floor		Seats
Austin Peay	Dunn Center	9,000
Eastern Ky	Alumni Coliseum	6,500
Mid.Tenn.St	Murphy Athletic Center	11,520
Morehead St	Academic-Athletic Ctr.	6,500
Murray St	Racer Arena	5,550
Tenn.St	Gentry Center	10,000
Tenn.Tech	Eblen Center	10,150

Pacific-10

Home Floor		Seats
Arizona	McKale Center	13,477
Arizona St	Univ.Activity Center	14,287
California	Harmon Arena	6,578
Oregon	McArthur Court	10,063
Oregon St	GIll Coliseum	10,400
Stanford	Maples Pavilion	7,500
UCLA	Pauley Pavilion	12,543
USC	LA Sports Arena	15,371
Washington	Hec Edmundson Pavilion	8,000
Wash.St	Friel Court	12,058

Patriot League

Home Floor		Seats
Army	Cristl Arena	5,043
Bucknell	Davis Gym	2,000
Colgate	Cotterell Court	3,000
Fordham	Rose Hill Gymnasium	3,200
Holy Cross	Hart Center	4,000
Lafayette	Kirby Fieldhouse	3,500
Lehigh	Stabler Center	5,800

Southeastern

Home Floor		Seats
Alabama	Coleman Coliseum	15,043
Auburn	Eaves Mem.Coliseum	12,500
Florida	O'Connell Center	12,000
Georgia	Georgia Coliseum	10,400
Kentucky	Rupp Arena	23,000
LSU	Maravich Assembly Ctr.	14,236
Mississippi	Tad Smith Coliseum	8,135
Miss.St	Humphrey Coliseum	10,000
Tennessee	Thompson-Boling Arena	24,535
Vanderbilt	Memorial Gymnasium	15,646

Southern

Home Floor		Seats
Appalach.St	Varsity Gymnasium	8,000
Citadel	McAlister Field House	6,200
E.Tenn.St	Memorial Center	12,000
Furman	Greenville Auditorium	6,000
Marshall	Henderson Center	10,250
Tenn-Chatt	UTC Arena	11,218
VMI	Cameron Hall	5,029
W.Carolina	Ramsey Center	7,826

Southland

Home Floor		Seats
McNeese St	Burton Coliseum	8,000
North Texas	Super Pit	10,000
NE Louisiana	Ewing Coliseum	8,000
N'west.LA	Prather Coliseum	3,900
S.Hous.St	Johnson Coliseum	6,110
SW Texas St	Strahan Coliseum	7,500
S.F.Austin	SFA Coliseum	8,064
TX-Arlingtn	Texas Hall	4,200

Division I Basketball Arenas (Cont.)

Southwest

Home Floor		Seats
Arkansas	Barnhill Arena (F'ville)	9,000
	Barton Coliseum (L.Rock)	7,473
	Pine Bluff Conven.Ctr.	7,812
Baylor	Ferrell Center	10,084
Houston	Hofheinz Pavilion	10,060
Rice	Autry Court	5,400
SMU........	Moody Coliseum	9,007
Texas	Erwin Center	16,231
Texas A&M ..	G.Rollie White Coliseum	7,500
TCU	Daniel-Meyer Coliseum	7,166
Texas Tech ...	Lubbock Coliseum	8,174

Southwestern Athletic

Home Floor		Seats
Alabama St ..	L.J.Dunn Arena	3,200
Alcorn St	Scalpin' Grounds Arena	7,000
Grambling ...	Memorial Gym	4,500
Jackson St ...	Williams Activity Ctr.	8,000
Miss.Valley..	Henderson Ath.Complex	6,500
Prairie View ..	Little Dome	6,000
Southern U ..	F.G.Clark Activity Ctr	7,500
TX Southern ..	Health & Phys.Ed.Arena	7,500

Sun Belt

Home Floor		Seats
UAB........	Ala-Birm. Arena	8,500
Jack'ville	Jacksonville Coliseum	10,000
NC-Char	Charlotte Coliseum	23,388
Old Dom	Norfolk Scope	10,253
S.Alabama ..	Mobile Civic Center	10,000
S.Florida	Sun Dome	10,347
Va.Comm....	Richmond Coliseum	10,716
Western Ky ..	E.A.Diddle Arena	12,370

Trans America Athletic

Home Floor		Seats
Ark-L.Rock ...	Barton Coliseum	8,303
Centenary ...	Gold Dome	4,002
Ga.Southern .	Hanner Fieldhouse	5,500
Georgia St ...	GSU Sports Arena	5,500
Mercer	Macon Coliseum	9,000
Samford	Seibert Gym	4,000
Stetson	Edmunds Center	5,000
Texas-SA	Convocation Center	5,100

West Coast Athletic

Home Floor		Seats
Gonzaga	Martin Center	4,000
Loyola-Mmt ..	Gersten Pavilion	4,156
Pepperdine ..	Firestone Fieldhouse	3,104
Portland	Earle A.Chiles Center	5,000
St.Mary's	McKeon Pavilion	3,500
San Diego ...	USD Sports Center	2,500
San Fran	Memorial Gymnasium	5,300
Santa Clara .	Toso Pavilion	5,000

Western Athletic

Home Floor		Seats
Air Force	Cadet Field House	6,000
BYU	Marriott Center	22,700
Colo.St	Moby Arena	10,000
Hawaii	Neal Blaisdell Center	7,575
New Mexico .	The Pit	17,126
S.Diego St ...	San Diego Sports Arena	13,741
UTEP	Special Events Center	12,222
Utah........	Jon Huntsman Center	15,000
Wyoming	Arena-Auditorium	15,028

Independents

Home Floor		Seats
Brooklyn.....	Roosevelt Gym	1,500
Central Fla ...	Education Building	2,456
Chicago St ...	Phys.Ed.& Athletics Bldg	2,500
Davidson	Belk Arena	6,000
DePaul	Rosemont Horizon	17,500
Fla.Int'l	Sunblazer Arena	3,580
Liberty	Liberty Gym	4,000
MD-Balt.Co .	UMBC Fieldhouse	4,024
Miami,FL	Miami Arena	15,008
Missouri-KC .	Municipal Auditorium	10,000
No.Illinois ...	Chick Evans Field House	6,076
Notre Dame .	Joyce Convocation Ctr	11,418
Nicholls St ...	Stopher Gym	3,800
So.Utah	Centrum	5,300
US Int'l	San Diego Civic Center	4,100
Wright St	Phys.Ed.Building	2,750
Yngstown St ..	Beeghly Center	8,000

Miscellaneous

Auto Racing's two most famous 500-mile races, the Tennis Grand Slam, and Horse Racing's Triple Crown are all staged annually at the same sites.

Auto Racing

Official grandstand seating and estimated infield capacity for NASCAR's Daytona 500 and CART's Indianapolis 500.

Event	Speedway	Seats	
Daytona 500	Daytona	94,500	grstand
		55,000	infield
Indy 500	Indianapolis	265,000	grstand
		135,000	infield

Tennis

Official center court seating for the finals of the four Grand Slam events of men's and women's tennis.

Event	Main Stadium	Seats
Australian Open .	National Tennis Center	15,000
French Open ...	Stade Roland Garros	16,500
Wimbledon.....	Centre Court	13,107
U.S.Open	Stadium Court	20,000

Horse Racing

Official grandstand seating and estimated infield capacity for the three racetracks in thoroughbred racing's Triple Crown.

Event	Racetrack	Seats	
Kentucky Derby .	Churchill Downs	51,000	grstand
		100,000	infield
Preakness......	Pimlico	40,000	grstand
		50,000	infield
Belmont Stakes .	Belmont Park	32,491	grstand
		50,000	infield

Record crowds: Kentucky Derby—163,628 (1974); Preakness—90,145 (1989); Belmont Stakes—82,694 (1971).

Striker **Juergen Klinsmann** exults as he holds up the World Cup trophy following West Germany's 1-0 triumph over Argentina in the tournament final at Rome's Olympic Stadium, July 8. The West Germans have now won the Cup three times.

SOCCER

West Germany wins third World Cup as defense dominates Italia '90; Goals, creativity in short supply; Americans return, but exit early.

SOCCER

1989-90 YEAR IN REVIEW

by Paul Gardner

The harsh, metallic glare of the floodlights in Rome's Olympic Stadium was suddenly softened and turned into a rich, warm glow. All around the field, hundreds of flares sent a friendly red light into the night air as 73,000 fans watched West Germany begin their victory lap.

It was 10:07 P.M. on Sunday, July 8, and the beautifully staged final moments of the 1990 World Cup were under way, a colorful credit to the Italian organizers who had managed throughout the month-long tournament to combine efficiency with artistry.

But the beauty of the spectacle could not banish the ugliness of what had gone before. The ugliness of the one thing that the Italians could not control: the quality of the soccer. Just 15 minutes earlier, before the mellow red of the flares bathed

the stadium, the World Cup final between West Germany and Argentina had come to a close. And what a shabby game it had been.

Departing in a hurry from the stadium, as though fleeing the scene of some horrible crime, the famous Dutch coach Rinus Michels found time to turn round and comment: "This game you can forget. A disaster!"

Disaster indeed. The 90-minute game had seen nothing but grim defense from Argentina, which got off only *two* shots in the entire match! Meanwhile the Germans, virtually unchallenged until they neared the Argentine goal, had attacked ineffectually and eventually won on a highly dubious penalty kick awarded by referee Edgardo Codesal of Mexico.

The 1990 World Cup gave us the first ever 1-0 final (the average goal total for the 13 previous World Cup finals was 4.69 per game) and the first final in which one of the teams failed to score. Argentina was not only the first shutout victim but also the first team to have a player sent off (in fact, they had *two* players dismissed).

Paul Gardner has been a columnist for *Soccer America* since 1982. He has covered international soccer as a writer and broadcaster in Europe and the United States since 1964 and has written three books on the sport.

444

West German midfielder **Lothar Matthaeus** is sent flying by an Argentine defender as **Diego Maradona** looks on with obvious concern. Matthaeus and Maradona were the captains of the two Cup finalists.

As referee Codesal blew the final whistle, he was surrounded by protesting Argentine players, who hadn't thought much of his eccentric officiating. Captain Diego Maradona, his stricken face barely holding back the tears, went up for his second-place medal and refused to shake hands with Joao Havelange, the president of FIFA, the governing body of international soccer.

Later, Maradona was to accuse Havelange and FIFA of a vendetta against him, because he had criticized them for not giving more of the World Cup profits directly to the players. "I did not shake hands with Havelange and I will not do so in the future," he said. "There is a mafia within FIFA that did not want Argentina to win."

Even the West German coach, Franz Beckenbauer, tempered his rosier view of the match: "Well, you can't talk of an ex-*cellent* final game. It's not up to us to choose our opponents on the field. A 1-0

score is fine, but it should have been 3-0 or more. I can't think of a single dangerous opportunity by Argentina. It's too bad they didn't participate in the game."

Beckenbauer, who had announced before the World Cup began that he would retire after the tournament, joined Brazil's Mario Zalago as the only championship players to win again as coaches. The Kaiser, however, is the only man to ever captain one champion and coach another. West Germany has now won three World Cups, the others coming in 1954 and 1974. Brazil (1958, '62 and '70) and Italy (1934, '38 and '82) are the only other countries to win three times.

Back to Argentina. The Argentines had played in a dull, negative way throughout the tournament, yet managed to reach the final. They were simply the worst—and perversely, the most successful—example of soccer's problem: a marked reluctance on the part of coaches to play enterprising, attacking soccer. They believe—and the statistics back them up—that the name of the game is defense. Caution rules, risk-taking is out.

It went just as the West German star Pierre Littbarski had predicted: "It will be boring, there won't be too many good games. The majority of teams will concentrate on stopping their opponents from scoring."

Even the swashbuckling Brazilians, who had always embodied the very spirit of adventurous soccer, turned defensive. Under coach Sebastiao Lazaroni, they took the field with a European type formation that included a sweeper. Said midfielder Dunga: "Samba soccer and virtuosity with the ball, these are already old, out-of-date themes. We are the Brazil of sweat and sacrifice that is determined, above all, not to give up goals."

It didn't work. The Brazilians won their three first-round games unconvincingly, even struggling to beat little Costa Rica, 1-0. Then they went out to Argentina—by a 1-0 score, of course.

Brazil's new style of play was not popular with some of the country's all-time great players. Pele said he didn't like it, and Roberto Rivelino accused Lazaroni of wanting "to make history as the man who changed Brazilian soccer." Carlos Alberto remarked, "No one in Brazil was surprised at the elimination, they had no faith in this team. Now we must get back to Brazilian soccer, we must forget about the players who play in Europe, where the mentality has changed."

Fan humor said it all on a banner that appeared at the stadium in Turin after Brazil's loss to Argentina: "If Lazaroni Is a Coach, I'm the Pope."

What dominated the 1990 World Cup was fear. Fear of giving up a goal, fear of losing, even fear of sex ("Abstain during the World Cup," Italian coach Azaglio Vicini had told his players).

The West Germans, so spirited in the first round (nine goals scored in their first two games), became more tentative as they progressed toward the final. The presumably abstinent Italians, driven forward by the partisan home crowds, attacked with brio but without much luck. Their semifinal loss, on penalty kicks, to Argentina (who else?) ruined what had looked like a preordained Italy vs West

Germany final. The Italians had to be satisfied with third place and the tournament's Most Valuable Player award—given to Sicilian-born striker Toto Schillaci, the tournament's leading scorer with six goals.

Disappointments? Where do you start? The Dutch, the Swedes, the Russians, the Scots, the Uruguayans—flops, all of them. Holland and Uruguay failed to make it to the quarterfinals and the others didn't even survive the first round.

Ireland reached the quarterfinals, but the pedestrian Irish did it without actually winning a game—they had tied all three of their first round matches and then "beat" Romania on penalty kicks in the opening game of the second round. Italy beat them, 1-0 (naturally) in the quarterfinals.

The use of penalty kicks as a tie-breaker in the tournament came in for a good deal of criticism, but not from Irish coach Jackie Charlton, who at one point reckoned that, "We can probably win the World Cup without winning a game."

On the positive side, England did much better than expected, providing Italia '90 with two of its most dramatic games—a 3-2 overtime win against Cameroon in the quarterfinals and a tough semifinal loss on penalty kicks to West Germany. The English also unveiled one of the few discoveries of the tournament in midfielder Paul Gascoigne. Two veterans, goaltender Peter Shilton and striker Gary Lineker reached milestones in Italy. Shilton's seven games gave him 125 caps for international play, moving him past all-time leader Pat Jennings of Northern Ireland. Lineker, meanwhile, scored four goals for a World Cup career total of 10, tying him for fifth on the all-time list with West Germany's Helmut Rahn.

But it was Cameroon, and to a lesser extent Egypt, that truly livened the games up. Both teams emerged from the Africa zone preliminary competition without the fear and the blight of tactical discipline that seemed to paralyze so many European and South American sides. Cameroon, apart from a viciously physical opening game upset of defending champion Argentina, delighted everyone with its free-flowing skillful soccer and was unlucky to lose to England in a drama-packed quarterfinal.

Jon Van Woerden

Italian striker **Toto Schillaci** led the World Cup in scoring with six goals and was named the tournament MVP.

But Cameroon left its mark on FIFA, which announced that in future World Cup games African teams will get three, rather than two, of the 24 final berths. The Europeans, on the other hand, will get one less. In what has become an almost traditional announcement, FIFA president Havelange pronounced the 1990 World Cup the "best ever, both technically and organizationally." The organization, certainly, was first class, but the soccer, "technically" or otherwise, was alarmingly poor.

FIFA itself had shown some awareness of the situation by calling for the referees to clamp down on rough play, but the new hard-line approach led to confusion among players and coaches, and an unusually high number of player suspensions. Argentina went into the final without three of its regular starters, suspended for offenses in previous games. The referees—who, in soccer, have always been amateurs—also came in for sharp criticism.

Ridicule was heaped on Swedish referee Erik Fredriksson who, standing only a few feet away and staring straight at Maradona, did not see him use his hands to keep a Russian shot out of the Argentine goal in a first round game. Recalling Maradona's famous "Hand of God" goal against England in 1986, Brazilian coach Lazaroni remarked, "What a versatile player Maradona is. He scores goals with his left hand and saves them with his right!"

FIFA was not amused, and began to talk about creating a core of professional referees.

It seems certain that FIFA will have to continue its clampdown, for the evidence that soccer's defensive trend is accelerating can no longer be denied. The previous World Cup, the 1986 tournament in Mexico, had set a goal-scoring low of 2.5 per game. Italia '90, the World Cup of Fear, managed to do even worse, with a depressing 2.2 goals per game.

As the troubled 1990 World Cup tournament came to an end, with the smoke from the flares and fireworks drifting away and the red glow gently fading in the Olympic Stadium, the scoreboard lit up the message "Ciao Italia — Hello USA '94." In four years, the United States will host the World Cup and be the center of the soccer world for the first time ever.

The scrutiny had already started with the U.S. national team, present in the finals for the first time in 40 years. Coach Bob Gansler's team had qualified by finishing an unimpressive second to Costa Rica in the North and Central American region. In Italy, the Americans performed disastrously, losing all three of their Group A first round games by a combined 8-2 score. Paul Caligiuri and Bruce Murray had the only U.S. goals as the Americans lost to Czechoslovakia (5-1), Italy (1-0) and Austria (2-1).

The skeptics scoffed, confirmed in their opinion that America knew nothing of the sport, and went on to question its ability to stage a 1994 World Cup—an event that dwarfs even the Olympic Games in worldwide interest. Among the noisiest critics was former New York Cosmos star Giorgio Chinaglia, who openly called on the U.S. to renounce the tournament.

Immediately after Italia '90, Paul Breitner, the former West German star who is now a controversial journalist, wrote that he had been told by "one of the American organizing committee" that they would withdraw because of lack of television interest in the States, and that the '94 World Cup would go instead to West Germany.

"Completely untrue," said Scott LeTellier, the chairman of World Cup USA 1994. "There is a great deal of interest. We have 27 cities that have applied to stage games. And CBS, ABC and the cable networks TNT and ESPN are all very interested in the television rights."

LeTellier did not mention that NBC Sports president Dick Ebersol had given an emphatic "No!" when asked if his network had any interest in the World Cup, an event NBC carried in 1986. Low U.S. ratings certainly figured in NBC's decision, but so did previous dealings with the U.S.Soccer Federation. NBC and USSF president Werner Fricker worked out a World Cup contract in 1989, but it was nixed by FIFA after ABC and TNT complained that they had not been given a chance to bid. FIFA announced that it would hold an auction of the 1994 television rights later in 1990.

That was only one of Fricker's disagreements with FIFA—a running confrontation that climaxed with his sensational defeat when he stood for re-election as USSF president in August (see box).

Meanwhile, the USA's only professional soccer league, the indoor MISL, was won by the San Diego Sockers for the sixth time in eight years. Outdoors, Santa Clara and Virginia played to a 1-1 draw in double overtime to share the 1989 NCAA Division I title. Virginia (and national team) goaltender Tony Meola was the college Player of the Year.

In South America, FIFA had to deal with Roberto Rojas. Even by soccer's exaggerated standards, the "Rojas affair" went way over the top. It happened on Sept.3, 1989, at huge Maracana Stadium in Rio de Janeiro, where Brazil was playing Chile in a World Cup qualifying game. Brazil needed only to tie to qualify for Italy, while Chile had to win. With Brazil leading 1-0 and 20 minutes left in the game, a flare flew out of the crowd and dropped near Chilean goalkeeper Roberto Rojas. Rojas went down as if shot and was quickly surrounded by team-

Rothenberg takes control of U.S. soccer

In an astonishing upset, Werner Fricker, the president of the United States Soccer Federation, was swept out of office Aug. 5., at the USSF's Annual General Meeting in Orlando, Fla. He was comprehensively beaten by Los Angeles attorney Alan Rothenberg, who collected nearly two thirds of the votes.

While Fricker was able to claim credit for landing the 1994 World Cup and presiding over a national team program that saw the U.S. finally break a 40-year spell of futility and qualify for the 1990 World Cup in Italy, he had also turned many people off with his brusque and arrogant manner. Members of the USSF complained that he ignored the Federation's own regulations, and simply railroaded his pet projects through.

More significantly, Fricker had made the fatal mistake of antagonizing FIFA, international soccer's governing body. In the 25 months following FIFA's 1988 decision to award the 1994 World Cup to the U.S., Fricker repeatedly ignored FIFA's wishes (and FIFA is accustomed to having its wishes interpreted as demands) on marketing matters.

FIFA let it be widely known that they were extremely unhappy with the situation, and did not exactly leap forward to deny rumors in Italy that the World Cup tournament might be taken away from the U.S. As the USSF election neared, behind the scenes moves intensified. They culminated in the last-minute candidacy of Rothenberg, a man who was known to FIFA for his work as soccer commissioner during the 1984 Olympic Games in Los Angeles.

The key to Rothenberg's victory was outmaneuvering Fricker for the crucial votes of the Major Indoor Soccer League—which, as the only pro league in American soccer, commands one third of the total votes cast. Rothenberg never spelled out his platform, but backed by the MISL and most of the federation's anti-Fricker faction, he won easily.

A transition team was formed, which promptly made an extraordinary appoint-

New USSF president **Alan Rothenberg** (right) shakes hands with **Werner Fricker** after defeating Fricker by a 2-to-1 margin at the Federation's annual meeting in Orlando, Fla. Aug. 5.

ment: MISL commissioner Earl Foreman —notoriously scornful of outdoor soccer —was named to head a committee on the development of pro soccer.

The national team situation remained totally unsatisfactory. Coach Bob Gansler was still in charge—presumably temporarily—but his team was much depleted as players went off in search of European experience. Midfielder Tab Ramos joined Spanish second division team Figueras as a loan player, and goalkeeper Tony Meola signed a similar deal with Watford of the English second division. Defender John Doyle and midfielder Hugo Perez joined Orgryto IS of the Swedish first division, defender Steve Trittschuh went to Sparta Prague in Czechoslovakia, and forward Bruce Murray and midfielder John Harkes went to English clubs for tryouts.

While the exodus went on, Rothenberg & Co. attempted to talk former West German coach Franz Backenbauer into becoming the U.S. coach or technical director, or whatever. The USSF optimistically announced that "fruitful" talks had been held with Beckenbauer, and that "an agreement" has been reached.

Clearly, the USSF had jumped the gun, for Beckenbauer announced in August that he had signed a two-year, $2.9 million contract to be technical advisor to the French club Olympique de Marseille.

No problem, said the USSF, Beckenbauer, who had starred for the New York Cosmos in the old NASL, will come to the States in 1992. Again the USSF seemed to be ignoring reality. The owner of Marseille—business tycoon Bernard Tapie, who had stunned the sports world in July by purchasing the Adidas equipment company—was reported to be offering Beckenbauer a $3 million bonus if he led the team to victory in the European Cup. Said Beckenbauer: "If two years is not long enough to make Marseille the champions of Europe, then I may stay longer in France."

And so American soccer in general, and the USSF in particular, enters 1991 as they have entered so many other years: uncertain of their leadership, confused in their aims, wracked by internal dissension, but nevertheless full of hope that the game's long delayed millenium was imminent.

449

The United States qualified for the World Cup for the first time in 40 years, but was eliminated in the first round after three straight losses to Czechoslovakia, Italy and Austria.

mates who carried him off the field, with blood apparently pouring from a head wound. The Chileans refused to come back on the field—"Not safe", they claimed—and the game was abandoned.

After investigating the incident, FIFA awarded the game to Brazil and accused Rojas and other Chileans of faking the injury in "the biggest attempt at swindle in the history of the FIFA." The Chileans' idea, it seemed, had been to get the game replayed at a neutral site. Rojas protested his innocence but was banned from soccer for life. Six months later, he finally admitted that he had deliberately cut himself and implicated several teammates. They denied everything and invited Rojas to see a psychiatrist.

Back in Europe, Italy won all three European club championships in May. Sampdoria beat Anderlecht, 2-0 in overtime, to win the Cup Winners' Cup. Juventus clinched the UEFA Cup with a 3-1 win and a scoreless draw against fellow Italian club Fiorentina in the two-leg final. And AC Milan captured its second straight European Cup, beating Benfica, 1-0. Led by two-time European Player of the Year Marco Van Basten of Holland, Milan also won the 1989 Toyota Cup, played Dec.17 in Tokyo, beating South American champion Nacional Medellin of Colombia, 1-0.

English clubs were, rather surprising-ly, readmitted to European tournaments in 1990. They had been banned since 1985 when violence by Liverpool fans in Belgium had led to the deaths of 39 Italian fans. European soccer's governing body, UEFA, had stated that its decision would depend upon the behavior of English fans during the World Cup in Italy.

English fans were involved in numerous clashes with Italian police, yet UEFA decided that their behavior was no worse than that of Dutch or West German fans, and that it would therefore be unfair to continue the ban on English clubs.

In Olympic soccer, the International Olympic Committee agreed, without any great enthusiasm, to FIFA's demand that participation be limited to players under the age of 24. The IOC had wanted an open tournament, but FIFA insisted that the World Cup must remain the only true world championship.

Finally, there were the Albanians, all 37 of them—the national team, the under-21 team, the coaches and the doctors. On May 28, they were arrested at London's Heathrow Airport after some $8000 worth of merchandise went missing from the Duty Free shop. All were quickly released without being charged. A British police spokesman commented dryly: "It seems they did not quite understand the meaning of Duty Free." □

THE 1991 INFORMATION PLEASE SPORTS ALMANAC

SOCCER STATISTICS

THE SEASON IN REVIEW
1989-1990
INTERNATIONAL • USA

SEC A

PAGE 451

1989-90 International Champions

National Team Competition

WORLDWIDE

1990 World Cup Final: West Germany 1, Argentina 0 (July 8)
(see pages 452-53)

Club Team Competition

WORLDWIDE

1989 Toyota Cup Final: AC Milan 1, Nacional Medellin 0 (Dec 17)

EUROPE

1990 European Cup

Contested by league champions of countries belonging to the Union of European Football Associations (UEFA). Semifinals use two-game/total goals format. The final is one game.

Semifinals

AC Milan 2 . . . . Bayern Munich 2
(AC Milan wins 1-0, 1-2 on away goals)
Benfica 2 . . . . Marseille 2
(Benfica wins 1-2, 1-0 on away goals)

Final
(May 23 at Vienna)
AC Milan 1 . . . . Benfica 0

1990 European Cup Winners Cup

Contested by cup winners of countries belonging to the Union of European Football Associations (UEFA). Semifinals use two-game/total goals format. The final is one game.

Semifinals

Anderlecht 2 . . . . Dinamo Bucharest 0
(Anderlecht wins 1-0, 1-0)
Sampdoria 4 . . . . Monaco 2
(Sampdoria wins 2-2, 2-0)

Final
(May 9 at Gothenburg, Sweden)
Sampdoria 2 . . . . OT . . . . Anderlecht 0

1990 UEFA Cup

Contested by teams other than league champions and cup winners and selected by UEFA based on each country's previous performance in the tournament. Semifinals and final use two-game/total goals format.

Semifinals

Juventus 3 . . . . Cologne 2
(Juventus wins 3-2, 0-0)
Werder Bremen 1 . . . . Fiorentina 1
(Fiorentina wins 1-1, 0-0 on away goals)

Final
(May 2 at Turin; May 16 at Avellino)
Juventus 3 . . . . Fiorentina 1
(Juventus wins 3-1, 0-0)

National Champions

Country	League Champion	Cup Winner
Austria	FCS Tirol	Austria Vienna
Belgium	Club Bruges	FC Liege
Czech	Sparta Prague	Dukla Prague
England	Liverpool	Manchester United
France	Marseille	Montpellier
Holland	Ajax	PSV Eindhoven
Hungary	Dozsa Ujpest	MCS Pecs
Italy	Napoli	Juventus
Portugal	FC Porto	Estrela Amadora
Romania	Dinamo Bucharest	Dinamo Bucharest
Scotland	Rangers	Aberdeen
Spain	Real Madrid	Barcelona
USSR	Spartak Moscow	Dinamo Kiev
W.Germany	Bayern Munich	Kaiserslautern
Yugoslavia	Red Star	Red Star

SOUTH AMERICA

International Champions

1990 Cup	Date
Copa Libertadores Oct.3/10	
Olimpia (Paraguay) vs Barcelona (Ecuador)	

National Champions

Country	League
Argentina	River Plate
Brazil	Vasco da Gama
Chile	Colo Colo
Colombia	To be decided
Uruguay	Progresso

1990 World Cup

Contested over every four years; 24 teams qualified for tournament after two years of preliminary matches. Teams divided into six groups in first round and play three games each; (1) indicates top-seeded team in group; (*) indicates 16 teams advancing to single elimination bracket (below).

First Round

GROUP A	W	L	T	Pts	GF	GA
*Italy (1)	3	0	0	6	4	0
*Czechoslovakia	2	1	0	4	6	3
Austria	1	2	0	2	2	3
USA	0	3	0	0	2	8

Results
June 9—Italy 1, Austria 0 (at Rome); **June 10**—Czech. 5, USA 0 (Florence); **June 14**—Italy 1, USA 0 (Rome); **June 15**—Czech.1, Austria 0 (Florence); **June 19**—Italy 2, Czech.0 (Rome); Austria 2, USA 1 (Florence).

GROUP B	W	L	T	Pts	GF	GA
*Cameroon	2	1	0	4	3	5
*Romania	1	1	1	3	4	3
*Argentina (1)	1	1	1	3	3	2
Soviet Union	1	2	0	2	4	4

Results
June 8—Cameroon 1, Argentina 0 (at Milan); **June 9**—Romania 2, USSR 0 (Bari); **June 13**—Argentina 2, USSR 0 (Naples); **June 14**—Cameroon 2, Romania 1 (Bari); **June 18**—Argentina 1, Romania 1 (Naples); USSR 4, Cameroon 0 (Bari).

GROUP C	W	L	T	Pts	GF	GA
*Brazil (1)	3	0	0	6	4	1
*Costa Rica	2	1	0	4	3	2
Scotland	1	2	0	2	2	3
Sweden	0	3	0	0	3	6

Results
June 10—Brazil 2, Sweden 1 (at Turin); **June 11**—Costa Rica 1, Scotland 0 (Genoa); **June 16**—Brazil 1, Costa Rica 0 (Turin); Scotland 2, Sweden 1 (Genoa); **June 20**—Brazil 1, Scotland 0 (Turin); Costa Rica 2, Sweden 1 (Genoa).

GROUP D	W	L	T	Pts	GF	GA
*West Germany (1)	2	0	1	5	10	3
*Yugoslavia	2	1	0	4	6	5
*Colombia	1	1	1	3	3	2
U.A.Emirates	0	3	0	0	2	11

Results
June 9—Colombia 2, UAE 0 (at Bologna); **June 10**—W.Germany 4, Yugoslavia 1 (Milan); **June 14**—Yugoslavia 1, Colombia 0 (Bologna); **June 15**—W.Germany 5, UAE 1 (Milan); **June 19**—W.Germany 1, Colombia 1 (Milan); Yugoslavia 4, UAE 1 (Bologna).

GROUP E	W	L	T	Pts	GF	GA
*Spain	2	0	1	5	5	2
*Belgium (1)	2	1	0	4	6	3
*Uruguay	1	1	1	3	2	3
South Korea	0	3	0	0	1	6

Results
June 12—Belgium 2, S.Korea 0 (at Verona); **June 13**—Spain 0, Uruguay 0 (Udine); **June 17**—Belgium 3, Uruguay 1 (Verona); Spain 3, S.Korea 1 (Udine); **June 21**—Spain 2, Belgium 1 (Verona); Uruguay 1, S.Korea 0 (Udine).

GROUP F	W	L	T	Pts	GF	GA
*England (1)	1	0	2	4	2	1
*Ireland	0	0	3	3	2	2
*Holland	0	0	3	3	2	2
Egypt	0	1	2	2	1	2

Note: Ireland and Holland drew lots to decide 2nd place.

Results
June 11—England 1, Ireland 1 (at Cagliari); **June 12**—Holland 1, Egypt 1 (Palermo); **June 16**—England 0, Holland 0 (Cagliari); **June 17**—Ireland 0, Egypt 0 (Palermo); **June 21**—England 1, Egypt 0 (Cagliari); Ireland 1, Holland 1 (Palermo).

1990 WORLD CUP

FIRST ROUND	QUARTER-FINALS	SEMI-FINALS	FINALS	SEMI-FINALS	QUARTER-FINALS	FIRST ROUND

Cameroon 2 / Colombia 1 → Cameroon 2
England 1 / Belgium 0 → England 4
Cameroon 2 / England 4 → England 4
Czechoslovakia 4 / Costa Rica 1 → Czechoslovakia 0
W. Germany 2 / Holland 1 → W. Germany 1
Czechoslovakia 0 / W. Germany 5* → W. Germany 5*
England 4 / W. Germany 5*
West Germany 1 / Argentina 0
ITALIA '90

Brazil 0 / Argentina 1 → Argentina 3*
Spain 1 / Yugoslavia 2 → Yugoslavia 2
Argentina 3* / Yugoslavia 2 → Argentina 5*
Ireland 5* / Romania 4 → Ireland 0
Italy 2 / Uruguay 0 → Italy 1
Ireland 0 / Italy 1 → Italy 4
Argentina 5* / Italy 4

3rd Place
Italy 2
England 1

* Penalty kick shootout

Semifinals

Argentina 5, Italy 4 (Penalty kicks)

	1	2	OT—T	(PK)
July 3 Argentina	0	1	0 —1	(4)
Italy	1	0	0 —1	(3)

Scoring: Toto Schillaci, ITA (18th minute); Claudio Caniggia, ARG (68th).

Penalty kicks: Franco Baresi, ITA (goal); Jose Serrizuela, ARG (goal); Roberto Baggio, ITA (goal); Jorge Burruchaga, ARG (goal); Luigi DeAgostini, ITA (goal); Julio Olarticoechea, ARG (goal); Roberto Donadoni, ITA (save by Goycochea); Diego Maradona, ARG (goal); Aldo Serena, ITA (save by Goycochea).

Goaltenders: Sergio Goycochea, ARG; Walter Zenga, ITA.

Yellow cards: Italy (1)—Giuseppe Giannini (22nd minute); Argentina (5)—Ricardo Giusti (30th), Oscar Ruggeri (70th), Olarticoechea (76th), Claudio Caniggia (82nd), Sergio Batista (120th). **Referee:** Michel Vautrot (France).

Attendance: 59,978 (San Paulo Stadium at Naples).

West Germany 5, England 4 (Penalty kicks)

	1	2	OT—T	(PK)
July 4 West Germany	0	1	0 —1	(4)
England	0	1	0 —1	(3)

Scoring: Andreas Brehme, W.GER (60th minute); Gary Lineker, ENG (80th).

Penalty kicks: Lineker, ENG (goal); Brehme, W.GER (goal); Peter Beardsley, ENG (goal); Lothar Matthaeus, W.GER (goal); David Platt, ENG (goal); Karl-Heinz Riedle, W.GER (goal); Stuart Pearce, ENG (save by Illgner); Olaf Thon, W.GER (goal); Chris Waddle, ENG (high).

Goaltenders: Bodo Illgner, W.GER; Peter Shilton, ENG.

Yellow cards: England (2)—Paul Parker (65th), Paul Gascoigne (98th); W.Germany (1)—Brehme (110th). **Red cards:** Argentina (1)—Giusti (105th). **Referee:** Jose Wright (Brazil).

Attendance: 62,628 (Delle Alpi Stadium at Turin).

Third Place

Italy 2, England 1

	1	2—T
July 7 Italy (6-1)	0	2—2
England (3-2-2)	0	1—1

Scoring: Baggio, ITA (70th minute); Platt, ENG (80th); Schillaci, ITA (84th, penalty kick).

Italy: Walter Zenga, Franco Baresi, Giuseppe Bergomi, Ciro Ferrara, Paolo Maldini, Pietro Vierchowod, Luigi DeAgostini (Nicola Berti, 66th), Carlo Ancelotti, Giuseppe Giannini (Riccardo Ferri, 90th), Roberto Baggio, Toto Schillaci.

England: Peter Shilton, Mark Wright (Chris Waddle, 72nd), Paul Parker, Gary Stevens, Des Walker, Tony Dorigo, Trevor Steven, David Platt, Steve McMahon (Neil Webb, 72nd), Peter Beardsley, Gary Lineker.

Referee: Joel Quiniou (France).

Attendance: 51,426 (San Nicola Stadium at Bari).

Final World Cup Standings

Goals columns do not include goals scored in penalty kick shootouts.

	GP	W	L	T	Pts	—Goals— For	Opp
1 W.Germany	7	6	0	1	13	15	5
2 Argentina	7	4	2	1	9	5	4
3 Italy	7	6	1	0	12	10	2
4 England	7	3	2	2	8	8	6
Czechoslovakia	5	3	2	0	6	10	5
Yugoslavia	5	3	2	0	6	8	6
Cameroon	5	3	2	0	6	7	9
Ireland	5	1	1	3	5	2	3
Brazil	4	3	1	0	6	4	2
Spain	4	2	1	1	5	6	4
Belgium	4	2	2	0	4	6	4
Costa Rica	4	2	2	0	4	4	6
Romania	4	1	2	1	3	4	3
Colombia	4	1	2	1	3	4	4
Holland	4	0	1	3	3	3	4
Uruguay	4	1	2	1	3	2	5
Soviet Union	3	1	2	0	2	4	4
Austria	3	1	2	0	2	2	3
Scotland	3	1	2	0	2	2	3
Egypt	3	0	2	1	1	1	2
Sweden	3	0	3	0	0	3	6
South Korea	3	0	3	0	0	1	6
USA	3	0	3	0	0	2	8
U.A.Emirates	3	0	3	0	0	2	11

Final

West Germany 1, Argentina 0

	1	2—T
July 8 West Germany (6-0-1)	0	1—1
Argentina (4-2-1)	0	0—0

Scoring: Brehme, W.Ger.(85th minute, penalty kick).

West Germany: Bodo Illgner, Thomas Berthold (Stefan Reuter, 75th), Juergen Kohler, Klaus Augenthaler, Guido Buchwald, Andreas Brehme, Thomas Haessler, Lothar Matthaeus, Pierre Littbarski, Juergen Klinsmann, Rudi Voeller.

Argentina: Sergio Goycoechea, Oscar Ruggeri (Pedro Monzon, 46th), Juan Simon, Jose Serrizuela, Nestor Lorenzo, Jose Basualdo, Pedro Troglio, Jorge Burruchaga (Gabriel Calderon, 53rd), Roberto Sensini, Gustavo Dezotti, Diego Maradona. Suspended (starters unable to play in Final)— Sergio Batista, Claudio Caniggia, Ricardo Giusti, Julio Olarticoechea.

Yellow cards: Argentina (3)—Dezotti (5th minute), Troglio (84th), Maradona (86th); W.Germany (1)—Voeller (52nd). **Red Cards:** Argentina (2)—Monzon (64th), Dezotti (87th). **Referee:** Edgardo Codesal (Mexico).

Attendance: 73,603 (Olympic Stadium at Rome)

Most Valuable Player

Toto Schillaci, Italy

Leading Scorers

Top 10 goal scoring leaders in World Cup. Italy's Schillaci won Golden Shoe Award for scoring most goals. Goals scored in penalty kick shootouts do not count.

	G	A	Pts
Toto Schillaci, Italy	6	1	7
Lothar Matthaeus, W.Germany	4	3	7
Tomas Skuhravy, Czech	5	0	5
Michel, Spain	4	1	5
Roger Milla, Cameroon	4	1	5
Andreas Brehme, W.Germany	3	2	5
Juergen Klinsmann, W.Germany	3	2	5
Gary Lineker, England	4	0	4
Rudi Voeller, W.Germany	3	1	4

Six players tied with 3 points each.

U.S. Soccer

National Team

With an average age of 24 years and two months, the United States national team was the youngest at the 1990 World Cup, by a full year. The 22-man roster had five players, including starting goaltender and 1989 College Player of the Year Tony Meola, who were 20-years-old or younger.

Goalkeepers	Age	College
Kasey Keller	20	Portland
Tony Meola	20	Virginia
David Vanole	27	UCLA

Defenders	Age	College
Desmond Armstrong	25	Maryland
Marcelo Balboa	22	San Diego St.
Jimmy Banks	25	Wisc-Milwaukee
John Doyle	23	San Francisco
Paul Krumpe	26	UCLA
Steve Trittsch	24	SIU-Edwardsville
Mike Windischmann	24	Adelphi

Midfielders	Age	College
Brian Bliss	25	Southern Conn.
Paul Caligiuri	26	UCLA
Neil Covone	20	Wake Forest
John Harkes	22	Virginia
Chris Henderson	19	UCLA
Tab Ramos	23	N.C.State
John Stollmeyer	27	Indiana

Forwards	Age	College
Eric Eichmann	24	Clemson
Bruce Murray	24	Clemson
Chris Sullivan	25	Tampa
Peter Vermès	23	Rutgers
Eric Wynalda	20	San Diego St.

Captain: Mike Windischmann
Head Coach: Bob Gansler

1989-90 MISL
Final Standings

Division champions (*) and playoff qualifiers (†) are noted.

Eastern Division

	W	L	Pct	GB	GF	GA
*Baltimore	32	20	.615	—	231	188
†Kansas City	30	22	.577	2	208	205
†Wichita	26	26	.500	6	210	229
Cleveland	20	32	.385	12	201	237

Western Division

	W	L	Pct	GB	GF	GA
*Dallas	31	21	.596	—	217	190
†San Diego	25	27	.481	6	217	204
†St.Louis	24	28	.462	7	202	205
Tacoma	20	32	.385	11	191	217

Playoffs

Division Semifinals (Best-of-5): EAST—KC def. Wichita (3-1); WEST—SD def. St.Louis (3-1). **Finals** (Best-of-7): EAST—Baltimore def. KC (4-2); WEST—SD def. Dallas (4-2).

MISL Championship (Best-of-7): SD def. Baltimore (4-2).

1990 APSL
(American Professional Soccer League)

APSL East: Maryland
APSL West: San Francisco Bay
Playoff Champion: Maryland

World Cup Warm-Up Matches

The US national team played 15 international matches leading up to the World Cup, compiling a 7-7-1 record. The 4-team Marlboro Cup (Feb. 2-4) was played at the Orange Bowl in Miami and won by Uruguay, a 2-0 winner over Costa Rica in the final.

Date	Result	Site	Crowd
Feb. 2	C.Rica 2, USA 0	Marlboro Cup	25,392
Feb. 4	USA 1, Colombia 1	Marlboro Cup	15,231
	(Colombia won shootout, 9-8)		
Feb. 13	USA 1, Bermuda 0	Hamilton,Ber.	1,800
Feb. 24	USSR 3, USA 1	Stanford,CA	61,000
Mar.10	USA 2, Finland 1	Tampa	22,647
Mar.20	Hungary 2, USA 0	Budapest	9,000
Mar.28	E.Germany 3, USA 2	East Berlin	4,000
Apr. 8	USA 4, Iceland 1	St.Louis	3,287
Apr. 22	Colombia 1, USA 0	Miami	8,214
May 5	USA 1, Malta 0	Rutgers,NJ	8,604
May 9	USA 3, Poland 1	Hershey,PA	12,063
May 12	USA 1, Ajax 1	Washington,DC	18,243
May 20	USA 1, Partizan* 0	New Haven,CT	30,644
May 30	USA 4, Liech.1	Eschen-Mauren	2,400
Jun. 2	Switz. 2, USA 1	St.Gallen	4,500

*Yugoslavian club team Partizan Belgrade.

USA Scoring

Overall Goals—Murray and Wynalda (5); Vermes (4); Harkes and Sullivan (2); Balboa, Caligiuri, Henderson and Trittschuh (1).

World Cup Matches

Date	Result	Site	Crowd
Jun. 10	Czech 5, USA 1	Florence	33,266
Jun. 14	Italy 1, USA 0	Rome	73,423
Jun. 19	Austria 2, USA 1	Florence	34,857

USA Scoring

Vs Czechoslovakia—Caligiuri (61st minute); **vs Austria**—Murray (82nd minute).

1989 College
NCAA Division I Tournament

First Round: Columbia 4, FDU-Teaneck 1; Vermont 2, Connecticut 2; Yale 1, Hartwick 0; Phila.Textile 2, Princeton 1; Wake Forest 2, Old Dominion 1; South Carolina 2, Duke 1; Geo.Washington 3, George Mason 1; Howard 2, Penn St.1 (2 OT-penalty kicks); SMU 1, Evansville 0; Fresno St.2, St.Louis 1; Portland 1, Washington 0 (2 OT); UCLA 2, San Diego St.1 (2 OT-penalty kicks).

Second Round: Rutgers 3, Columbia 1; Vermont 1, Yale 0 (2 OT); Virginia 4, Phila.Textile 1; South Carolina 5, Wake Forest 1; Indiana 4, Geo.Washington 0; Howard 2, SMU 1 (2 OT); Santa Clara 2, Fresno St.1; UCLA 1, Portland 0 (2 OT-penalty kicks).

Quarterfinals: Rutgers 2, Vermont 1 (2 OT); Virginia 1, South Carolina 0 (2 OT); Indiana 1, Howard 0; Santa Clara 2, UCLA 0.

FINAL FOUR
At New Brunswick, NJ, Dec. 2-3.

Semifinals: Virginia 3, Rutgers 0; Santa Clara 4, Indiana 2.

Championship: 1-1 TIE (2 OT), Virginia vs Santa Clara. Cavaliers and Broncos are co-champions.

SOCCER
STATISTICS

THE 1991 INFORMATION PLEASE SPORTS ALMANAC

THROUGH THE YEARS 1930-1990 WORLD CUP • US CHAMPS

SEC B

PAGE 455

The World Cup

The Federation Internationale de Football Association (FIFA) began the World Cup championship tournament in 1930 with a 13-team field in Uruguay. Sixty years later, the 1990 World Cup in Italy marked the eighth time the competition has been held in Europe. Countries in South and Central America have hosted the Cup six times and the United States has been selected by FIFA as the tournament site for the first time in 1994.

Brazil retired the first World Cup (called the Jules Rimet Trophy for FIFA's first president) in 1970 after winning it for the third time. Since 1974, the award has been known as simply the World Cup.

The 1942 and '46 World Cup tournaments were cancelled because of World War II. European finalists are in capital LETTERS; (*) indicates score after extra time.

Multiple winners: Brazil, Italy and West Germany (3); Argentina and Uruguay (2).

Year Champion	Manager	Score	Runner-up	Host Country	Third Place
1930 Uruguay	Alberto Supicci	4-2	Argentina	Uruguay	No game
1934 ITALY	Vittorio Pozzo	2-1*	CZECHOSLOVAKIA	Italy	Germany 3, Austria 2
1938 ITALY	Vittorio Pozzo	4-2	HUNGARY	France	Brazil 4, Sweden 2
1942 Not held					
1946 Not held					
1950 Uruguay	Juan Lopez	2-1	Brazil	Brazil	No game
1954 W.GERMANY	Sepp Herberger	3-2	HUNGARY	Switzerland	Austria 3, Uruguay 1
1958 Brazil	Vicente Feola	5-2	SWEDEN	Sweden	France 6, W.Germany 3
1962 Brazil	Aymore Moreira	3-1	CZECHOSLOVAKIA	Chile	Chile 1, Yugoslavia 0
1966 ENGLAND	Alf Ramsey	4-2*	W.GERMANY	England	Portugal 2, USSR 1
1970 Brazil	Mario Zagalo	4-1	ITALY	Mexico	W.Ger. 1, Uruguay 0
1974 W.GERMANY	Helmut Schoen	2-1	HOLLAND	W.Germany	Poland 1, Brazil 0
1978 Argentina	Cesar Menotti	3-1*	HOLLAND	Argentina	Brazil 2, Italy 1
1982 ITALY	Enzo Bearzot	3-1	W.GERMANY	Spain	Poland 3, France 1
1986 Argentina	Carlos Bilardo	3-2	W.GERMANY	Mexico	France 4, Belgium 2*
1990 W.GERMANY	Franz Beckenbauer	1-0	Argentina	Italy	Italy 2, England 1

The United States in the World Cup

While the United States has fielded a national team every year of the World Cup, only four of those teams have been able to make it past the preliminary competition and qualify for the final World Cup tournament. The U.S. played in three of the first four World Cups (1930,'34 and '50) then not again until 1990.

The U.S. has won only three World Cup tournament matches—two opening round games in 1930 (which enabled the Americans to reach the semifinals) and a stunning first round, 1-0, upset of England in 1950. Center forward Joe Gaetjens scored the goal and goalkeeper Frank Borghi had the shutout against the English.

1930
1st Round Matches
United States 3 . . . . Belgium 0
United States 3 . . . . Paraguay 0
Semifinals
Argentina 6 . . . . United States 1

US Scoring—Bert Patenaude (3), Bart McGhee (2), James Brown, Ed Florie.

1934
1st Round Match
Italy 7 . . . . United States 1

US Scoring—Buff Donelli (who later became a noted college and NFL football coach).

1950
1st Round Matches
Spain 3 . . . . United States 1
United States 1 . . . . England 0
Chile 5 . . . . United States 2

US Scoring—John Souza (2), Joe Gaetjens, Gino Pariani.

1990
1st Round Matches
Czechoslovakia 5 . . . . United States 1
Italy 1 . . . . United States 0
Austria 2 . . . . United States 1

US Scoring—Paul Caligiuri, Bruce Murray.

World Cup All-Time Leaders

Career Goals

World Cup scoring leaders through 1990. Years listed are years played in World Cup. Players active in 1990 in **bold type**.

	No
Gerd Mueller, West Germany (1970,74)	14
Just Fontaine, France (1958)	13
Pele, Brazil (1958,70)	12
Sandor Kocsis, Hungary (1954)	11
Gary Lineker, England (1986,90)	10
Helmut Rahn, West Germany (1954,58)	10

Most Valuable Player

Officially, the Golden Ball Award, the Most Valuable Player of the World Cup tournament has been selected since 1982 by a panel of international soccer journalists.

Year
1982 Paolo Rossi, Italy
1986 Diego Maradona, Argentina
1990 Toto Schillaci, Italy

Single Tournament Goals

World Cup tournament scoring leaders through 1990.

Year		No
1930	Guillermo Stabile, Argentina	8
1934	Angelo Schiavio, Italy	4
	Oldrich Nejedly, Czechoslovakia	4
	& Edmund Conen, Germany	4
1938	Leonidas, Brazil	8
1942	Not held	
1946	Not held	
1950	Ademir, Brazil	7
1954	Sandor Kocsis, Hungary	11
1958	Just Fontaine, France	13
1962	Drazen Jerkovic, Yugoslavia	5
1966	Eusebio, Portugal	9
1970	Gerd Mueller, West Germany	10
1974	Grzegorz Lato, Poland	7
1978	Mario Kempes, Argentina	6
1982	Paolo Rossi, Italy	6
1986	Gary Lineker, England	6
1990	Toto Schillaci, Italy	6

World Cup Appearances

The World Cup tournament field has grown from 13 (1930) to 16 (1934-78) to 24 (since 1982). Brazil is the only team to have played in every World Cup tournament, but eight other countries have qualified teams at least nine times.

The following FIFA Table ranks all national teams by total points earned in World Cup play through 1990. Note that West Germany's appearances include two by Germany in 1934 and 1938.

	App	Gm	W	L	T	Pts			App	Gm	W	L	T	Pts
1 Brazil	14	66	44	11	11	99		16 Holland	5	20	8	6	6	22
2 West Germany	12	68	39	14	15	93		17 Belgium	8	25	7	14	4	18
3 Italy	12	54	31	11	12	74		Mexico	9	29	6	17	6	18
4 Argentina	10	48	24	15	9	57		19 Chile	6	21	7	11	3	17
5 England	9	41	18	11	12	48		20 Scotland	7	20	4	10	6	14
6 Uruguay	9	37	15	14	8	38		21 Portugal	2	9	6	3	0	12
7 Soviet Union	7	31	15	10	6	36		Switzerland	6	18	5	11	2	12
8 France	9	34	15	14	5	35		24 Peru	4	15	4	8	3	11
Yugoslavia	8	33	14	12	7	35		Northern Ireland	3	13	3	5	5	11
10 Hungary	9	32	15	14	3	33		25 Paraguay	4	11	3	4	4	10
Spain	8	32	13	12	7	33		26 Cameroon	2	8	3	2	3	9
12 Poland	5	25	13	7	5	31		Romania	5	12	3	6	3	9
13 Sweden	8	31	11	14	6	28		28 Denmark	1	4	3	1	0	6
14 Czechoslovakia	8	30	11	14	5	27		**United States**	4	10	3	7	0	6
15 Austria	6	26	12	12	2	26		East Germany	1	6	2	2	2	6

World Cup Finals

West Germany has appeared in the most World Cup championship games (6), winning three. Brazil (3-1), Italy (3-1) and Argentina (2-2) have each appeared in four finals. A four-team round robin decided the 1950 World Cup—fortunately, the deciding game turned out to be the last one of the tournament between Uruguay and Brazil.

1930

Uruguay 4, Argentina 2
(at Montevideo, Uruguay)

	1	2—T
July 30 Uruguay (4-0)	1	3—4
Argentina (4-1)	2	0—2

Goals: Uruguay—Pablo Dorado (12th minute), Pedro Cea (54th), Santos Iriarte (68th), Castro (89th); Argentina—Carlos Peucelle (20th), Guillermo Stabile (37th).

Uruguay—Ballestrero, Nasazzi, Mascheroni, Andrade, Fernandez, Gestido, Dorado, Scarone, Castro, Cea, Iriarte.

Argentina—Botasso, Della Torre, Paternoster, J.Evaristo, Monti, Suarez, Peucelle, Varallo, Stabile, M.Ferreyra, M.Evaristo.

Attendance: 90,000. **Referee:** Langenus (Belgium).

1934

Italy 2, Czechoslovakia 1 (OT)
(at Rome)

	1	2	OT—T
June 10 Italy (4-0-1)	0	1	1—2
Czechoslovakia (3-1)	0	1	0—1

Goals: Italy—Raimondo Orsi (80th minute), Angelo Schiavio (95th); Czechoslovakia—Puc (70th).

Italy—Combi, Monzeglio, Allemandi, Ferraris IV, Monti, Bertolini, Guaita, Meazza, Schiavio, Ferrari, Orsi.

Czechoslovakia—Planicka, Zenisek, Ctyroky, Kostalek, Cambal, Krcil, Junek, Svoboda, Sobotka, Nejedly, Puc.

Attendance: 55,000. **Referee:** Eklind (Sweden).

1938

Italy 4, Hungary 2
(at Paris)

	1	2—T
June 19 Italy (4-0)	3	1—4
Hungary (3-1)	1	1—2

Goals: Italy—Gino Colaussi (5th minute), Silvio Piola (16th), Colassi (35th), Piola (82nd); Hungary—Titkos (7th), Georges Sarosi (70th).

Italy—Olivieri, Foni, Rava, Serantoni, Andreolo, Locatelli, Biavati, Meazza, Piola, Ferrari, Colaussi.

Hungary—Szabo, Polgar, Biro, Szalay, Szucs, Lazar, Sas, Vincze, G.Sarosi, Szengeller, Titkos.

Attendance: 65,000. **Referee:** Capdeville (France)

1950

Uruguay 2, Brazil 1
(at Rio de Janeiro)

	1	2—T
July 16 Uruguay (3-0-1)	0	2—2
Brazil (4-1-1)	0	1—1

Goals: Uruguay—Juan Schiaffino (66th minute), Chico Ghiggia (79th); Brazil—Friaca (47th).

Uruguay—Maspoli, M.Gonzales, Tejera, Gambetta, Varela, Andrade, Ghiggia, Perez, Miguez, Schiaffino, Moran.

Brazil—Barbosa, Augusto, Juvenal, Bauer, Danilo, Bigode, Friaca, Zizinho, Ademir, Jair, Chico.

Attendance: 199,854. **Referee:** Reader (England)

1954

West Germany 3, Hungary 2
(at Berne, Switzerland)

	1	2—T
July 4 West Germany (5-1)	2	1—3
Hungary (4-1)	2	0—2

Goals: West Germany—Max Morlock (10th minute), Helmut Rahn (18th), Rahn (84th); Hungary—Ferenc Puskas (4th), Zoltan Czibor (9th).

West Germany—Turek, Posipal, Liebrich, Kohlmeyer, Eckel, Mai, Rahn, Morlock, O.Walter, F.Walter, Schaeffer.

Hungary—Grosics, Buzansky, Lorant, Lantos, Bozsik, Zakarias, Csibor, Kocsis, Higegkuti, Puskas, J.Toth.

Attendance: 60,000. **Referee:** Ling (England).

1958

Brazil 5, Sweden 2
(at Stockholm)

	1	2—T
June 29 Brazil (5-0-1)	2	3—5
Sweden (4-1-1)	1	1—2

Goals: Brazil—Vava (9th minute), Vava (32nd), Pele (55th), Mario Zagalo (68th), Pele (90th); Sweden—Nils Liedholm (3rd), Agne Simonsson (80th).

Brazil—Gilmar, D.Santos, N.Santos, Zito, Bellini, Orlando, Garrincha, Didi, Vava, Pele, Zagalo.

Sweden—Svensson, Bergmark, Axbom, Boerjesson, Gustavsson, Parling, Hamrin, Gren, Simonsson, Liedholm, Skoglund.

Attendance: 49,737. **Referee:** Guigue (France).

1962

Brazil 3, Czechoslovakia 1
(at Santiago, Chile)

	1	2—T
June 17 Brazil (5-0-1)	1	2—3
Czechoslovakia (3-2-1)	1	0—1

Goals: Brazil—Amarildo (17th minute), Zito (68th), Vava (77th); Czechoslovakia—Josef Masopust (15th).

Brazil—Gilmar, D.Santos, N.Santos, Zito, Mauro, Zozimo, Garrincha, Didi, Vava, Amarildo, Zagalo.

Czechoslovakia—Schroiff, Tichy, Novak, Pluskal, Popluhar, Masopust, Pospichal, Scherer, Kvasniak, Kadraba, Jelinek.

Attendance: 68,679. **Referee:** Latishev (USSR).

1966

England 4, West Germany 2 (OT)
(at London)

	1	2 OT—T
July 30 England (5-0-1)	1	1 2—4
West Germany (4-1-1)	1	1 0—2

Goals: England—Geoff Hurst (18th minute), Martin Peters (78th), Hurst (101st), Hurst (120th); West Germany—Helmut Haller (12th), Wolfgang Weber (90th).

England—Banks, Cohen, Wilson, Stiles, J.Charlton, Moore, Ball, Hurst, B.Charlton, Hunt, Peters.

West Germany—Tilkowski, Hottges, Schnellinger, Beckenbauer, Schulz, Weber, Haller, Seeler, Held, Overath, Emmerich.

Attendance: 93,802. **Referee:** Dienst (Switzerland).

1970

Brazil 4, Italy 1
(at Mexico City)

	1	2—T
June 30 Brazil (6-0)	1	3—4
Italy (3-1-2)	1	0—1

Goals: Brazil—Pele (18th minute), Gerson (65th), Jairzinho (70th), Carlos Alberto (86th); Italy—Roberto Boninsegna (37th).

Brazil—Felix, C.Alberto, Everaldo, Clodoaldo, Brito, Piazza, Jairzinho, Gerson, Tostao, Pele, Rivelino.

Italy—Albertosi, Burgnich, Facchetti, Bertini (Juliano, 73rd), Rosato, Cera, Domenghini, Mazzola, Boninsegna (Rivera, 84th), De Sisti, Riva.

Attendance: 107,412. **Referee:** Gloeckner (E.Germany).

1974

West Germany 2, Holland 1
(at Munich)

	1	2—T
July 7 West Germany (6-1)	2	0—2
Holland (5-1-1)	1	0—1

Goals: West Germany—Paul Breitner (25th minute, penalty kick), Gerd Mueller (43rd); Holland—Johan Neeskens (1st, penalty kick).

West Germany—Maier, Beckenbauer, Vogts, Breitner, Schwarzenbeck, Overath, Bonhof, Hoeness, Grabowski, Mueller, Holzenbein.

Holland—Jongbloed, Suurbier, Rijsbergen (De Jong, 58th), Krol, Haan, Jansen, Van Hanegem, Neeskens, Rep, Cruyff, Rensenbrink (R.Van de Kerkhof, 46th).

Attendance: 77,833. **Referee:** Taylor (England).

World Cup Finals (Cont.)

1978
Argentina 3, Holland 1 (OT)
(at Buenos Aires)

		1	2	OT	—T
June 25	Argentina (5-1-1)	1	0	2	—3
	Holland (3-2-2)	0	1	1	—1

Goals: Argentina—Mario Kempes (37th minute), Kempes (104th), Daniel Bertoni (114th); Holland—Dirk Nanninga (81st).
Argentina—Fillol, Olguin, L.Galvan, Passarella, Tarantini, Ardiles (Larrosa, 65th), Gallego, Kempes, Luque, Bertoni, Ortiz (Houseman, 77th).
Holland—Jongbloed, Jansen (Suurbier, 72nd), Brandts, Krol, Poortvliet, Haan, Neeskens, W.Van de Kerkhof, R.Van de Kerkhof, Rep (Nanninga, 58th), Rensenbrink.
Attendance: 77,000. **Referee:** Gonella (Italy).

1982
Italy 3, West Germany 1
(at Madrid)

		1	2—T
July 8	Italy (4-0-3)	0	3—3
	West Germany (4-2-1)	0	1—1

Goals: Italy—Paolo Rossi (57th minute), Marco Tardelli (68th), Alessandro Altobelli (81st); West Germany—Paul Breitner (83rd).
Italy—Zoff, Scirea, Gentile, Cabrini, Collovati, Bergomi, Tardelli, Oriali, Conti, Rossi, Graziani (Altobelli, 8th, and Causio, 89th).
West Germany—Schumacher, Stielike, Kaltz, Briegel, K.H.Foerster, B.Foerster, Breitner, Dremmler (Hrubesch, 61st), Littbarski, Fischer, Rummenigge (Mueller, 69th).
Attendance: 90,080. **Referee:** Coelho (Brazil).

1986
Argentina 3, West Germany 2
(at Mexico City)

		1	2—T
June 29	Argentina (6-0-1)	1	2—3
	West Germany (4-2-1)	0	2—2

Goals: Argentina—Jose Brown (22nd minute), Jorge Valdano (55th), Jorge Burruchaga (83rd); West Germany—Karl-Heinz Rummenigge (73rd), Rudi Voeller (81st).
Argentina—Pumpido, Cuciuffo, Olarticoechea, Ruggeri, Brown, Batista, Burruchaga (Trobbiani, 89th), Giusti, Enrique, Maradona, Valdano.
West Germany—Schumacher, Jakobs, K.H.Foerster, Berthold, Briegel, Eder, Brehme, Matthaeus, Rummenigge, Magath (Hoeness, 61st), Allofs (Voeller, 46th).
Attendance: 114,580. **Referee:** Arppi Filho (Brazil)

1990
West Germany 1, Argentina 0
(at Rome)

		1	2—T
July 8	West Germany (6-0-1)	0	1—1
	Argentina (4-2-1)	0	0—0

Goals: West Germany—Andreas Brehme (85th minute, penalty kick).
West Germany—Illgner, Berthold (Reuter, 75th), Kohler, Augenthaler, Buchwald, Brehme, Haessler, Matthaeus, Littbarski, Klinsmann, Voeller.
Argentina—Goycoechea, Ruggeri (Monzon, 46th), Simon, Serrizuela, Lorenzo, Basualdo, Troglio, Burruchaga (Calderon, 53rd), Sensini, Dezotti, Maradona.
Attendance: 73,603. **Referee:** Codesal (Mexico)

Other Worldwide Competition

The Olympic Games

Held every four years since 1896, except during World War I (1916) and World War II (1940-44). Soccer was not a medal sport in 1896 at Athens or in 1932 at Los Angeles. By agreement between FIFA and the IOC, Olympic soccer competition is currently limited to players under the age of 24.
Multiple winners: England and Hungary (3); USSR and Uruguay (2).

Year		Year		Year		Year	
1896	Not held	1920	Belgium	1944	Not held	1968	Hungary
1900	England	1924	Uruguay	1948	Sweden	1972	Poland
1904	Canada	1928	Uruguay	1952	Hungary	1976	East Germany
1906	Denmark	1932	Not held	1956	Soviet Union	1980	Czechoslovakia
1908	England	1936	Italy	1960	Yugoslavia	1984	France
1912	England	1940	Not held	1964	Hungary	1988	Soviet Union
1916	Not held						

The Under-20 World Cup

Held every two years since 1977. Officially called The World Youth Championship for the FIFA/Coca-Cola Cup.
Multiple winner: Brazil (2).

Year		Year	
1977	Soviet Union	1985	Brazil
1979	Argentina	1987	Yugoslavia
1981	West Germany	1989	Portugal
1983	Brazil		

The Under-17 World Cup

Held every two years since 1985. Officially called The FIFA U-17 World Tournament for the JVC Cup.

Year		Year	
1985	Nigeria	1989	Saudi Arabia
		1987	Soviet Union

Five-a-Side Championship

Inaugurated in 1989. FIFA's only indoor tournament.

Year	
1989	Brazil

Continental Competition

European Championship

Held every four years since 1960. Officially called the European Football Championship.
Multiple winner: West Germany (2).

Year		Year		Year		Year	
1960	Soviet Union	1968	Italy	1976	Czechoslovakia	1984	France
1964	Spain	1972	West Germany	1980	West Germany	1988	Holland

South American Championship

Held irregularly since 1916. Officially called the Copa America.
Multiple winners: Uruguay (13), Argentina (12), Brazil (4), Peru (2).

Year		Year		Year		Year	
1916	Uruguay	1926	Uruguay	1946	Argentina	1959	Uruguay
1917	Uruguay	1927	Argentina	1947	Argentina	1963	Bolivia
1919	Brazil	1929	Argentina	1949	Brazil	1967	Uruguay
1920	Uruguay	1935	Uruguay	1953	Paraguay	1975	Peru
1921	Argentina	1937	Argentina	1955	Argentina	1979	Paraguay
1922	Brazil	1939	Peru	1956	Uruguay	1983	Uruguay
1923	Uruguay	1941	Argentina	1957	Argentina	1987	Uruguay
1924	Uruguay	1942	Uruguay	1958	Argentina	1989	Brazil
1925	Argentina	1945	Argentina				

Club Competition

Toyota Cup

Contested annually in December between the winners of the previous year's European Cup and Libertadores Cup (see below).

Originally the **Intercontinental Cup** (1960-79). Best-of-three game format until 1968, then two-game/total-goal format was used. Toyota became sponsor in 1980, changed the format to one-game championship and moved it to Tokyo.

Multiple winners: Nacional and Penarol (3); AC Milan, Independiente, Inter-Milan and Santos (2).

Year		Year		Year	
1960	Real Madrid (Spain)	1970	Feyenoord (Holland)	1980	Nacional (Uruguay)
1961	Penarol (Uruguay)	1971	Nacional (Uruguay)	1981	Flamengo (Brazil)
1962	Santos (Brazil)	1972	Ajax (Holland)	1982	Penarol (Uruguay)
1963	Santos (Brazil)	1973	Independiente (Argentina)	1983	Gremio (Brazil)
1964	Inter-Milan (Italy)	1974	Atletico Madrid (Spain)	1984	Independiente (Argentina)
1965	Inter-Milan (Italy)	1975	Not held	1985	Juventus (Italy)
1966	Penarol (Uruguay)	1976	Bayern Munich (W.Germany)	1986	River Plate (Argentina)
1967	Racing Club (Argentina)	1977	Boca Juniors (Argentina)	1987	FC Porto (Portugal)
1968	Estudiantes (Argentina)	1978	Not held	1988	Nacional (Uruguay)
1969	AC Milan (Italy)	1979	Olimpia (Paraguay)	1989	AC Milan (Italy)

European Cup

Contested annually since the 1955-56 season by the league champions of the member countries of the Union of European Football Associations (UEFA).

On four occasions, the European Cup winner has refused to participate in the Intercontinental Cup (now Toyota Cup) against South America's Copa Libertadores winner. In each case, the European Cup runner-up went instead—Panathinaikos (Greece) in 1971, Juventus (Italy) in 1973, Atletico Madrid (Spain) in 1974, and Malmo (Sweden) in 1979.

Multiple winners: Real Madrid (6); AC Milan and Liverpool (4); Ajax Amsterdam and Bayern Munich (3); Benfica, Inter Milan and Nottingham Forest (2).

Year		Year		Year	
1956	Real Madrid (Spain)	1968	Manchester United (Eng.)	1980	Nottingham Forest (Eng.)
1957	Real Madrid (Spain)	1969	AC Milan (Italy)	1981	Liverpool (England)
1958	Real Madrid (Spain)			1982	Aston Villa (England)
1959	Real Madrid (Spain)	1970	Feyenoord (Holland)	1983	SV Hamburg (W.Germany)
		1971	Ajax Amsterdam (Holland)	1984	Liverpool (England)
1960	Real Madrid (Spain)	1972	Ajax Amsterdam (Holland)	1985	Juventus (Italy)
1961	Benfica (Portugal)	1973	Ajax Amsterdam (Holland)	1986	Steaua Bucharest (Rom.)
1962	Benfica (Portugal)	1974	Bayern Munich (W.Ger.)	1987	FC Porto (Portugal)
1963	AC Milan (Italy)	1975	Bayern Munich (W.Ger.)	1988	PSV Eindhoven (Holland)
1964	Inter Milan (Italy)	1976	Bayern Munich (W.Ger.)	1989	AC Milan (Italy)
1965	Inter Milan (Italy)	1977	Liverpool (England)		
1966	Real Madrid (Spain)	1978	Liverpool (England)	1990	AC Milan (Italy)
1967	Glasgow Celtic (Scotland)	1979	Nottingham Forest (Eng.)		

Club Competitions (Cont.)

Copa Libertadores

Contested annually since the 1955-56 season by the league champions of South America's football union.
Multiple winners: Independiente (7); Penarol (5); Estudiantes and Nacional-Uruguay (3); Boca Juniors and Santos (2).

Year		Year		Year	
1960	Penarol (Uruguay)	1970	Estudiantes (Argentina)	1980	Nacional (Uruguay)
1961	Penarol (Uruguay)	1971	Nacional (Uruguay)	1981	Flamengo (Brazil)
1962	Santos (Brazil)	1972	Independiente (Argentina)	1982	Penarol (Uruguay)
1963	Santos (Brazil)	1973	Independiente (Argentina)	1983	Gremio (Brazil)
1964	Independiente (Argentina)	1974	Independiente (Argentina)	1984	Independiente (Argentina)
1965	Independiente (Argentina)	1975	Independiente (Argentina)	1985	Argentinos Jrs.(Argentina)
1966	Penarol (Uruguay)	1976	Cruzeiro (Brazil)	1986	River Plate (Argentina)
1967	Racing Club (Argentina)	1977	Boca Juniors (Argentina)	1987	Penarol (Uruguay)
1968	Estudiantes (Argentina)	1978	Boca Juniors (Argentina)	1988	Nacional (Uruguay)
1969	Estudiantes (Argentina)	1979	Olimpia (Paraguay)	1989	Nacional Medellin (Colom.)
				1990	

European Cup Winners' Cup

Contested annually since the 1960-61 season by the cup winners of the member countries of the Union of European Football Associations (UEFA).
Multiple winners: Barcelona (3); AC Milan, Anderlecht and Dynamo Kiev (2).

Year		Year		Year	
1961	Fiorentina (Italy)	1970	Manchester City (England)	1980	Valencia (Spain)
1962	Atletico Madrid (Spain)	1971	Chelsea (England)	1981	Dynamo Tbilisi (USSR)
1963	Tottenham Hotspur (England)	1972	Glasgow Rangers (Scotland)	1982	Barcelona (Spain)
1964	Sporting Lisbon (Portugal)	1973	AC Milan (Italy)	1983	Aberdeen (Scotland)
1965	West Ham United (England)	1974	FC Magdeburg (E.Germany)	1984	Juventus (Italy)
1966	Borussia Dortmund (W.Ger.)	1975	Dynamo Kiev (USSR)	1985	Everton (England)
1967	Bayern Munich (W.Germany)	1976	Anderlecht (Belgium)	1986	Dynamo Kiev (USSR)
1968	AC Milan (Italy)	1977	SV Hamburg (W.Germany)	1987	Ajax Amsterdam (Holland)
1969	Slovan Bratislava (Czech.)	1978	Anderlecht (Belgium)	1988	Mechelen (Belgium)
		1979	Barcelona (Spain)	1989	Barcelona (Spain)
				1990	Sampdoria (Italy)

UEFA Cup

Contested annually since the 1957-58 season by teams other than league champions and cup winners of the Union of European Football Associations (UEFA). Teams selected by UEFA based on each country's previous performance in the tournament. Teams from England were banned from UEFA Cup play from 1985-90 for the criminal behavior of their supporters.
Multiple winners: Barcelona (3); Borussia Moenchengladbach, IFL Gothenburg, Juventus, Leeds United, Liverpool, Real Madrid, Tottenham Hotspur and Valencia (2).

Year		Year		Year	
1958	Barcelona (Spain)	1970	Arsenal (England)	1980	Eintracht Frankfurt (W.Ger.)
1959	Not held	1971	Leeds United (England)	1981	Ipswich Town (England)
		1972	Tottenham Horspur (England)	1982	IFK Gothenburg (Sweden)
1960	Barcelona (Spain)	1973	Liverpool (England)	1983	Anderlecht (Belgium)
1961	AS Roma (Italy)	1974	Feyenoord (Holland)	1984	Tottenham Hotspur (England)
1962	Valencia (Spain)	1975	Borussia Moenchen-	1985	Real Madrid (Spain)
1963	Valencia (Spain)		gladbach (W.Germany)	1986	Real Madrid (Spain)
1964	Real Zaragoza (Spain)	1976	Liverpool (England)	1987	IFK Gothenburg (Sweden)
1965	Ferencvaros (Hungary)	1977	Juventus (Italy)	1988	Bayer Leverksen (W.Ger.)
1966	Barcelona (Spain)	1978	PSV Eindhoven (Holland)	1989	Napoli (Italy)
1967	Dynamo Zagreb (Yugoslavia)	1979	Borussia Moenchen-		
1968	Leeds United (England)		gladbach (W.Germany)	1990	Juventus (Italy)
1969	Newcastle United (England)				

Awards

European Player of the Year

Officially, the "Ballon d'Or" and presented by *France Football* magazine since 1956. Candidates are limited to European players in European leagues and winners are selected by a panel of 27 European soccer journalists.
Multiple winners: Johan Cruyff and Michel Platini (3); Franz Beckenbauer, Alfredo di Stefano, Kevin Keegan, Karl-Heinz Rummenigge and Marco Van Basten (2).

Year		Nat'l Team	Year		Nat'l Team
1956	Stanley Matthews, Blackpool	England	1961	Enrique Sivori, Juventus	Arg./Italy
1957	Alfredo di Stefano, Real Madrid	Arg./Spain	1962	Josef Masopust, Dukla Praque	Czech.
1958	Raymond Kopa, Real Madrid	France	1963	Lev Yachin, Dynamo Moscow	Soviet Union
1959	Alfredo di Stefano, Real Madrid	Arg./Spain	1964	Denis Law, Manchester United	Scotland
1960	Luis Suarez, Barcelona	Spain	1965	Eusebio, Benfica	Portugal

Year		Nat'l Team	Year		Nat'l Team
1966	Bobby Charlton, Manchester United	England	1978	Kevin Keegan, SV Hamburg	England
1967	Florian Albert, Ferencvaros	Hungary	1979	Kevin Keegan, SV Hamburg	England
1968	George Best, Manchester United	N.Ireland			
1969	Gianni Rivera, AC Milan	Italy	1980	K.H.Rummenigge, Bayern Munich	W.Ger.
			1981	K.H.Rummenigge, Bayern Munich	W.Ger.
1970	Gerd Mueller, Bayern Munich	W.Ger.	1982	Paolo Rossi, Juventus	Italy
1971	Johan Cruyff, Ajax	Holland	1983	Michel Platini, Juventus	France
1972	Franz Beckenbauer, Bayern Munich	W.Ger.	1984	Michel Platini, Juventus	France
1973	Johan Cruyff, Barcelona	Holland	1985	Michel Platini, Juventus	France
1974	Johan Cruyff, Barcelona	Holland	1986	Igor Belanov, Dynamo Kiev	Soviet Union
1975	Oleg Blokhin, Dynamo Kiev	Soviet Union	1987	Ruud Gullit, AC Milan	Holland
1976	Franz Beckenbauer, Bayern Munich	W.Ger.	1988	Marco Van Basten, AC Milan	Holland
1977	Allan Simonsen, B.M'chengladbach	Denmark	1989	Marco Van Basten, AC Milan	Holland

South American Player of the Year

Presented by *El Pais* of Uruguay since 1971. Candidates are limited to South American players in South American leagues and winners are selected by a panel of 67 Latin American sports editors.

Multiple winners: Elias Figueroa and Zico (3); Diego Maradona (2).

Year		Nat'l Team	Year		Nat'l Team
1971	Tostao, Cruzeiro	Brazil	1980	Diego Maradona, Boca Juniors	Argentina
1972	Teofilo Cubillas, Alianza Lima	Peru	1981	Zico, Flamengo	Brazil
1973	Pele, Santos	Brazil	1982	Zico, Flamengo	Brazil
1974	Elias Figueroa, Internacional	Chile	1983	Socrates, Corinthians	Brazil
1975	Elias Figueroa, Internacional	Chile	1984	Enzo Francescoli, River Plate	Uruguay
1976	Elias Figueroa, Internacional	Chile	1985	Julio Cesar Romero, Fluminense	Paraguay
1977	Zico, Flamengo	Brazil	1986	Antonio Alzamendi, River Plate	Uruguay
1978	Mario Kempes, Valencia	Argentina	1987	Carlos Valderrama, Deportivo Cali	Colombia
1979	Diego Maradona, Argentinos Juniors	Argentina	1988	Ruben Paz, Racing Buenos Aires	Uruguay
			1989	Bebeto, Vasco da Gama	Brazil

Soccer in the United States

OUTDOOR

The NPSL and USA Leagues of 1967

The National Professional Soccer League was not sanctioned by FIFA, the international soccer governing body, and recruited individual players to fill its 10 rosters. The USA, which changed its original name from the North American Soccer League to avoid confusion with the NPSL, was sanctioned and imported entire teams from Europe to represent its 12 franchises.

League champions: Oakland Clippers (NPSL); L.A. Wolves (USA). The Wolves were actually the Wolverhampton Wanderers of the English League.

North American Soccer League, 1968-84

The NPSL and USA merged to form the NASL in 1968 and the new league lasted until 1985. The NASL championship was known as the Soccer Bowl from 1975-84. One game decided the NASL title every year but five. There were no playoffs in 1969; a two-game/aggregate goals format was used in 1968 and '70; and a best-of-three games format was used in 1971 and '84.

Multiple winners: NY Cosmos (5); Chicago (2).

Year	Champion	Score(s)	Runner-up	Year	Champion	Score	Runner-up
1968	Atlanta Chiefs	0-0,3-0	San Diego	1977	New York Cosmos	2-1	Seattle
1969	Kansas City Spurs	No game	Atlanta	1978	New York Cosmos	3-1	Tampa Bay
				1979	Vanc. Whitecaps	2-1	Tampa Bay
1970	Rochester Lancers	3-0,1-3	Washington				
1971	Dallas Tornado	2-1 (LWW)	Atlanta	1980	New York Cosmos	3-0	Ft.Lauderdale
1972	New York Cosmos	2-1	St.Louis	1981	Chicago Sting	1-0*	NY Cosmos
1973	Philadelphia Atoms	2-0	Dallas	1982	New York Cosmos	1-0	Seattle
1974	Los Angeles Aztecs	4-3*	Miami	1983	Tulsa Roughnecks	2-0	Toronto
1975	Tampa Bay Rowdies	2-0	Portland	1984	Chicago Sting	2-0	Toronto
1976	Toronto Metros	3-0	Minnesota		*Shootout		

Most Valuable Player

Regular season Most Valuable Player as designated by the NASL.

Year		Year		Year	
1968	John Kowalik, Chicago	1973	Warren Archibald, Mia.	1979	Johan Cruyff, LA
1969	Cirilio Fernandez, KC	1974	Peter Silvester, Bal.		
		1975	Steven David, Miami	1980	Roger Davis, Seattle
1970	Carlos Metidieri, Roch.	1976	Pele, New York	1981	Giorgio Chinaglia, NY
1971	Carlos Metidieri, Roch.	1977	Franz Beckenbauer, NY	1982	Peter Ward, Seattle
1972	Randy Horton, NY	1978	Mike Flanagan, N.Eng.	1983	Roberto Cabanas, NY
				1984	Steve Zungul, San Jose

U.S. Soccer (Cont.)

INDOOR

Major Soccer League

Originally the Major Indoor Soccer League from 1979-90. The MISL championship was decided by one game in 1980 and 1981; a best-of-three-games series in 1979, best-of-five games in 1982 and 1983; and best-of-seven games since 1984.

Multiple winners: San Diego (6); New York (4).

Year	Winner	Series	Loser	Playoff MVP	Season MVP
1979	NY Arrows	2-0	Philadelphia	Shep Messing, NY	Steve Zungul, NY
1980	NY Arrows	7-4	Houston	Steve Zungul, NY	Steve Zungul, NY
1981	NY Arrows	6-5	St.Louis	Steve Zungul, NY	Steve Zungul, NY
1982	NY Arrows	3-2	St.Louis	Steve Zungul, NY	Steve Zungul, NY & Stan Terlecki, Pit.
1983	San Diego	3-2	Baltimore	Juli Veee, SD	Alan Mayer, SD
1984	Baltimore	4-1	St.Louis	Scott Manning, Bal.	Stan Stamenkovic, Bal.
1985	San Diego	4-1	Baltimore	Steve Zungul, SD	Steve Zungul, SD
1986	San Diego	4-3	Minnesota	Brian Quinn, SD	Steve Zungul, SD/Tac.
1987	Dallas	4-3	Tacoma	Tatu, Dallas	Tatu, Dallas
1988	San Diego	4-0	Cleveland	Hugo Perez, SD	Erik Rasmussen, Wich.
1989	San Diego	4-3	Baltimore	Victor Nogueira, SD	Preki, Tac.
1990	San Diego	4-2	Baltimore	Brian Quinn, SD	Tatu, Dallas

College

NCAA Division I Champions

NCAA Division I champions since the first title was contested in 1959. The championship game has ended in a tie three times—in 1967, 1968 and 1989.

Multiple winners: St.Louis (10); San Francisco (5); Indiana (3); Clemson, Howard and Michigan St.(2).

Year	Champion	Score	Runner-up	Year	Champion	Score	Runner-up
1959	St.Louis	5-2	Bridgeport	1974	Howard	2-1*	St.Louis
1960	St.Louis	3-2	Maryland	1975	San Francisco	4-0	SIU-Edwardsville
1961	West Chester,PA	2-0	St.Louis	1976	San Francisco	1-0	Indiana
1962	St.Louis	4-3	Maryland	1977	Hartwick	2-1	San Francisco
1963	St.Louis	3-0	Navy	1978	San Francisco†	2-0	Indiana
1964	Navy	1-0	Michigan St.	1979	SIU-Edwardsville	3-2	Clemson
1965	St.Louis	1-0	Michigan St.	1980	San Francisco	4-3*	Indiana
1966	San Francisco	5-2	LIU	1981	Connecticut	2-1*	Alabama A&M
1967	Michigan St. & St.Louis	0-0	—tie—	1982	Indiana	2-1*	Duke
				1983	Indiana	1-0*	Columbia
1968	Michigan St. & Maryland	2-2*	—tie—	1984	Clemson	2-1	Indiana
				1985	UCLA	1-0*	American
1969	St.Louis	4-0	San Francisco	1986	Duke	1-0	Akron
				1987	Clemson	2-0	San Diego St.
1970	St.Louis	1-0	UCLA	1988	Indiana	1-0	Howard
1971	Howard†	3-2	St.Louis	1989	Santa Clara & Virginia	1-1	—tie—
1972	St.Louis	4-2	UCLA				
1973	St.Louis	2-1*	UCLA				

*Overtime games: 1968—two OT (game called a draw); 1973—one OT; 1974—four OT; 1980—one OT; 1981—one OT; 1982—eight OT; 1983—two OT; 1985—eight OT; 1989—two OT (game called a draw).
†Vacated titles: 1971—Howard; 1978—San Francisco.

Awards

Hermann Award

Named after Robert Hermann of St.Louis, one of the founders of the North American Soccer League. First presented to the U.S. College Player of the Year in 1967. Voting done by Division I college coaches and selected sportswriters.

Muliple winners: Mike Seerey and Al Trost (2).

Year		Year	
1967	Dov Markus, LIU	1978	Angelo DiBernardo, Indiana
1968	Manuel Hernandez, San Jose St.	1979	Jim Stamatis, Penn St.
1969	Al Trost, St.Louis	1980	Joe Morrone, Jr., Connecticut
1970	Al Trost, St.Louis	1981	Armando Betancourt, Ind.
1971	Mike Seerey, St.Louis	1982	Joe Ulrich, Duke
1972	Mike Seerey, St.Louis	1983	Mike Jeffries, Duke
1973	Dan Counce, St.Louis	1984	Amr Aly, Columbia
1974	Farrukh Quraishi, Oneonta	1985	Tom Kain, Duke
1975	Steve Ralbovsky, Brown	1986	John Kerr, Duke
1976	Glenn Myernick, Hartwick	1987	Bruce Murray, Clemson
1977	Billy Gazonas, Hartwick	1988	Ken Snow, Indiana
		1989	Tony Meola, Virginia

On Nov. 9, 1989, East Germany lifted restrictions on emigration and travel to the West and within hours thousands of Germans celebrated by climbing the Berlin Wall at Brandenburg Gate.

INTERNATIONAL SPORTS

*Wall falls on GDR medal machine
as change overtakes Eastern Bloc;
Zurbriggen retires, LeMond repeats;
Javelin record beaten four times.*

INTERNATIONAL SPORTS

1989-90 YEAR IN REVIEW

by Phil Hersh

For nearly two decades, the East German national anthem has been virtually the Olympic theme song so often was it played in honor of gold medalists at the Games. How strange it was, then, to listen to that anthem this summer and realize one might never again hear its familiar notes.

"I feel sad when I hear the anthem being played," said swimmer Manuela Stellmach of East Berlin, for whose victory it sounded in Seattle at the Goodwill Games. "It is an era coming to an end in which I didn't see just bad. I grew up in the GDR (East Germany). That is my homeland. If one's homeland is taken away, it has to be a reflective-type experience."

Reflections on what has happened to the world of Olympic sports in the year since the Berlin Wall fell in November, 1989, are blurred by both emotion and

confusion. Dramatic change is obviously underway, but its breakneck pace has confounded all attempts to analyze what the Olympics will look like in 1992. One thing is certain: the East German sports juggernaut, one of the most remarkable systems of all time, became a mere historical curiosity once the two Germanys reunified on Oct. 3, 1990.

But even before then, the East German medal machine had been all but dismantled. Its several hundred-million-dollar budget was down to pennies, its sports schools closed, most of its coaches out of work, its elite athletes desperately seeking western sponsors to continue careers previously underwritten by the state. Many of East Germany's individual sports federations had joined with their West German counterparts before actual reunification. The West, long the poor relation in terms of sports success, was making shrewd use of its economic might. In the new federations, West German bureaucracy, training methods and coaching staffs are in the ascendancy. However, the combined systems may

Phil Hersh has been the *Chicago Tribune's* full-time Olympics reporter since 1986. He covered his first Olympic Games at Lake Placid in 1980 for the *Chicago Sun-Times.*

prove something of a disappointment to those who naively add medal counts to conclude the unified Germany will be an Olympic colossus.

Although the effects may not be felt fully until 1994 or 1996, when few of the already developed East German elite will still be competing, the impact will be evident in 1992. It is unlikely, for instance, that the single German team at Albertville or Barcelona in 1992 will come close to matching the success of East Germany alone in Calgary or Seoul in 1988, when it was second to the Soviet Union in both gold and total medals. One simply cannot underestimate the demise of the East German system, whose ruthless efficiency, from determination to doping, turned the country of 16 million into a sporting rival of the two superpowers, the United States (pop.: 240 million) and Soviet Union (pop.: 280 million).

In its 42-year history, the East German sports organization achieved its goal of giving the new country a strong international identity. However, recent revelations of what went on within East Germany's repressive society have confirmed many western suspicions about the nature of the country's investment in sports. There were underground pressurized rooms for simulated altitude training; painstakingly kept logs of all training procedures; rewards of houses, cars and western currency for achievement ($17,000 for an Olympic gold in 1988); pregnancies terminated at the whim of coaches; and insider revelations of widespread use of performance-enhancing drugs, which may have differed from similar doping habits in the West only in terms of sophistication and organization.

In a nation where housing and living amenities have long been far below the standards of West Germany, the emphasis on sports obviously caused subrosa resentment for many years. When the Wall fell, so did the facade of national pride in sports achievement. The reaction that suddenly came to the surface was explosive. For example, the rink in Karl-Marx-Stadt where two-time Olympic gold medalist Katarina Witt trained was closed for lack of funds and being sold to a West German supermarket chain. Jutta Mueller, who coached Witt and 1980 gold

When the Berlin Wall came down, the status of **Jutta Mueller** (right), the coach of two-time Olympic figure skating champion **Katarina Witt,** went from socialist hero to reviled social parasite.

Wide World Photos

medalist Anett Poetzsch, came home one day to her four-room apartment and found these words spray-painted on her door: "You should give up this apartment. You need just one room. A jail cell."

Athletes and coaches whom East Germany elevated to the status of socialist heroes were suddenly seen by many as reviled social parasites. The athletes themselves, beneficiaries of a system that gave them privileges beyond the reach of most East Germans, suddenly accused the government of having exploited them, since almost all their financial gains had gone to the state.

Still, no one expected that East Germany would be making its last appearance in a major international competition as early as the European Track & Field Championships in Split, Yugoslavia, the last week of August. (It was an impressive farewell performance with the East Germans winning the most gold and total medals.) Even before then, East Germany had withdrawn from the qualifying rounds for the 1992 European Soccer Championship and agreed to compete in November, 1990, for spots on a unified team in the World Swimming Championships at Perth, Australia in January 1991. There will be one German track team at the 1991 indoor and outdoor World Championships. And, for the first time since 1964, there will be one German team at the Olympics in 1992.

East Germany, of course, was not the only Soviet Bloc country whose well-ordered sports programs were disturbed by the political transformation of Eastern Europe in the past year. In Bulgaria, Romania, and Hungary (which were 5th, tied for 8th, and 10th, respectively, in the overall medal count at Seoul) the notion of sports success as an affirmation of communist principles soon seemed like expensive nonsense.

Change was everywhere. Romanian athletes like miler Doina Melinte were soon chasing every dollar they could on the international track circuit rather than focusing their attention on major medals. Bulgaria's Olympic Committee president spent time in jail for a variety of abuses, real and perceived. And Czechoslovakia's new government issued a formal apology to its greatest Olympic hero,

runner Emil Zatopek, who had been made a non-person by the communist government for his role in the 1968 Prague Spring revolt.

Only in the Soviet Union and Cuba was the status relatively quo. The Soviets were trying to keep up their past levels of sporting achievement, although economic pressure and reform politics were likely to make that impossible.

Castro's athletes continued to toe the same hard line as always, vowing to defend socialism to the death and damning professionalism as, in the words of boxing champion Felix Savon, "trying to abolish humanity and society." Yet, even Castro allowed as how he might consider selling some of his prized baseball players to the *Yanquis* for desperately needed dollars.

The end result of the communist counter revolution will be to shift the balance of sporting power back to the West after nearly a quarter-century of Soviet Bloc pre-eminence. The 21st century could very well begin as the 20th did, with the Olympic Games dominated by the United States.

"From the Ruins of War," the East German national anthem, was a stirring combination of plaintive and martial theme. Now it has become the sound of silence.

Winter Sports

Bobsled: Swiss teams driven by Gustav Weder won the World Championships in both the two- and four-man sleds at St. Moritz, Switzerland. The top U.S. sled was 12th in the two-man and 13th in the four-man. The talk of the sport in the U.S. was an effort by track and/or football stars Willie Gault, Herschel Walker and Edwin Moses to put together a sled for the 1992 Olympics.

Figure Skating: Compulsory figures did not go quietly into their long goodbye. In fact, they decided the women's title in the Word Championships, the last senior event in which compulsories will be held.

By finishing 10th in the compulsories, Midori Ito of Japan could not retain her world title at Halifax, Nova Scotia, even though she was first in both segments of the freeskating. Jill Trenary of Minnetonka, Minn., won the world title by finishing first in the compulsories, fifth in the short program and second in the long

US bobsled driver **Brian Shimer** (seated) with team hopefuls (left to right) **Edwin Moses, Herschel Walker** and **Willie Gault.**

program. Holly Cook of Bountiful, Utah, was third and teammate Kristi Yamaguchi of Fremont, Calif., fourth—the first time one country has had three women in the top four at the worlds.

The other three world titles were won by the defending champions—Kurt Browning of Canada; Ekaterina Gordeeva and Sergei Grinkov of the Soviet Union (pairs); and Marina Klimova and Sergei Ponomorenko (ice dance). It was the 24th pairs title in the last 27 world meets for the Soviets.

At the U.S. championships in Salt Lake City, Trenary won her third national title, while Todd Eldredge, 18, of South Chatham, Mass., became a surprise men's champion when defender Christopher Bowman of Van Nuys, Calif., withdrew after the short program with a bad back.

After the World Championships, two-time U.S. pairs champions Yamaguchi and Rudi Galindo of San Jose, Calif., announced they were splitting up so Yamaguchi could concentrate on singles.

Also: famed coach Carlo Fassi, 60, announced he was leaving Colorado Springs after two decades to coach at a new rink in his native Milan, Italy. Fassi coached four Olympic champions—Peggy Fleming and Dorothy Hamill of the U.S. and John Curry and Robin Cousins of Great Britain. He also coaches

Trenary, who decided in August to remain a competitive amateur through the 1992 Olympics.

Ice Hockey: Despite losing some of its most famous veterans to the National Hockey League and stumbling through the preliminaries, the Soviet Union won the World Championship for the 22nd time since 1954. The Soviets lost their first preliminary-round game in 12 years but were unbeaten in medal-round play at Bern, Switzerland. It was the eighth world title for Viktor Tikhonov in a stormy 13-year reign as Soviet coach (see page 298). Tikhonov's teams have also won two Olympic titles during that period. Sweden finished second and Czechoslovakia was third. The United States took fifth place with a 6-4 record, its best finish since 1985.

Luge: East Germany's Gabi Köhlisch made her final race a memorable one, winning the women's world singles title on the Olympic track at Calgary. Cammy Myler of Lake Placid, N.Y., and Bonny Warner of Mt. Baldy, Calif., were 6th and 7th, the best-ever finishes for two U.S. women in the event. East Germany won the inaugural team event. Georg Hackl of West Germany won his second straight men's singles, and perennial runners-up Hansjoerg Raffl and Norbert Huber of Italy won the doubles.

Alpine Skiing: A World Cup season driven batty—and everywhere else—by the freakish European weather ended with a final triumph for Swiss great Pirmin Zurbriggen.

The weather, mainly lack of snow, forced 15 of 32 men's races and 11 of 32 women's events to be moved. The Hahnenkamm downhill in Kitzbuhel, Austria, skiing's most famous race, celebrated its 50th anniversary by being split into a mollycoddle two-run sprint.

And the omens weren't any better for 1990-91, after the August openers in New Zealand, where two of four scheduled races were canceled.

"This (1989-90) is the most terrible year in my 25 years following the World Cup," said Heinz Krecek, an International Ski Federation coordinator. "It was the toughest season I've experienced, but it was worth it," Zurbriggen said.

Zurbriggen, 27, retired after winning his fourth overall title, matching the

Swiss skier **Pirmin Zurbriggen** retired from alpine racing in 1990 after winning his fourth World Cup overall championship in seven years. His four overall titles match the record of Italy's Gustavo Thoeni.

record of Italy's Gustavo Thoeni. He also won the Super-G and combined titles. Zurbriggen's task was made easier when defending overall champion Marc Girardelli of Luxembourg went out for the season with a December injury and Alberto Tomba of Italy missed two months after fracturing a collarbone. Tomba came back to win the final two slaloms of the year in Scandinavia.

The women's tour also lost stars to injury. Tamara McKinney of Squaw Valley, Calif., one of the least fortunate athletes ever in the sport, broke a leg in training in October. Carole Merle of France tore up a knee in the Cup opener in Las Lenas, Argentina, in August. McKinney didn't come back, but Merle did in a big way, winning four straight races (two giants, two Super-Gs) to retain the Super-G crown and place fifth overall.

The 1989-90 season marked the end of the Swiss women's dynasty after seven seasons. Austria won the Nation's Cup for women, and Petra Kronberger of Austria, who turned 21 in February, took the overall title. Long-time Swiss stars Michela Figini and Maria Walliser, who had each won two overall crowns, retired at the end of the season.

The women provided the only good news for U.S. skiing. At 23, Diann Roffe of Williston, Vt., regained some of what made her the phenom giant slalom winner at the 1985 World Championships. She got two seconds and a third in Cup giant slaloms, finishing fourth for the season in the event and 10th in the overall standings. Meanwhile, Kristi Terzian, 22, of Salt Lake City, scored points (by finishing in the top 15) in 17 races, breaking McKinney's team record of scoring in 16.

Speedskating: A subpar result in the second of four races cost Bonnie Blair of Champaign, Ill., her world sprint title in Tromso, Norway. Blair was second to Angela Hauck of East Germany. Ki Tae Bae won the men's sprint title, becoming the first South Korean world champion and then retiring, while Dan Jansen of West Allis, Wis., was the top U.S. finisher (4th). Jacqueline Borner of East Germany and Johann Olav Koss of Norway took the all-around world titles.

Atlanta's Olympic Dream Comes True

William Porter (Billy) Payne, Esq., was sitting in church one day in early 1987 when the vision came to him.

Payne, an Atlanta real estate lawyer, had just finished a successful fund-raising drive for the church and was looking for another altruistic project to immerse himself in.

Then it came to him: why not bring the Olympic Games to Atlanta?

That dream seemed so improbable when Payne first suggested it to Andrew Young, then Atlanta's mayor, that hizzoner's first reaction was pretty much to pass off Billy as a good ol' boy with a goofy idea.

Payne wouldn't give up. He would soon convince Young to be a leading spokesman for a $7 million campaign that, astonishingly, turned one man's vision into a civic cause that succeeded.

On Sept. 18, 1990 in Tokyo, the International Olympic Committee chose Atlanta over five other candidates to be the host of the 1996 Summer Olympics, which will mark the centennial of the modern Games.

IOC president **Juan Antonio Samaranch** announcing selection of Atlanta as host of 1996 Summer Games.

The U.S. has staged the Summer Olympics on three previous occasions: 1904 in St.Louis, and 1932 and 1984 in Los Angeles.

It was a vote of pragmatism over sentiment. Among the beaten candidates was Athens, host of the 1896 games, which finished second in balloting that required the maximum five rounds.

Toronto finished third, followed by Melbourne, Australia; Manchester, England; and Belgrade, Yugoslavia.

Some of the losers, notably Athens, reacted bitterly to what they saw as a sellout of the Games to U.S. commercial interests, especially television, which will pay more for rights to Games with limitless programming potential.

"I express my deep regret that the international community did not respect history and the spirit of the Olympic Games and, yet again, committed an injustice against Greece," said Andreas Papandreou, former Greek prime minister.

The IOC's vote was a definite admission that the Olympics have become as materialistic and professionalized as the world around them. There was a clear feeling that Athens, given its pollution, struggling economy, and poor communications, was not a viable choice.

Atlanta had to overcome the problems of being a first-time bidder, of following so closely after the 1984 Games in Los Angeles, and of having an image as a crime-ridden city.

They did it with a powerful coalition of white and black leaders, led by Payne and Young, whose contacts as former U.S. ambassador to the U.N. were invaluable. Atlanta's ability to stage the Games was never in question, given its hotels, transportation and infrastructure. What sold the IOC was Atlanta's apparently unanimous civic desire to have the Games, scheduled for July 20-August 4, 1996.

Between now and then, Atlanta must build an Olympic Stadium, swimming pool, cycling velodrome and other facilities at a cost of $420 million. It projects a $150 million surplus on a $1 billion budget. When they come true, dreams aren't cheap.

Wide World Photos

Wide World Photos

Defending Tour de France champion **Greg LeMond** (left) raises the hand of runner-up **Claudio Chiappucci** of Italy after clinching his third Tour victory by 2 minutes, 16 seconds on July 22.

Summer Sports

Baseball: Cuba won its fourth straight World Championship in Edmonton, beating Nicaragua 11-5 in the final. Since the 1959 Castro revolution, Cuba has won all but two of the 16 World Championships in which it has played. In 1990, it rolled unbeaten through 10 games, outscoring the opposition 139-18, including a 23-1 rout of the United States. The U.S. team, a hastily assembled squad of young collegians, wound up seventh, its worst finish in a decade.

Basketball: Losses in the Goodwill Games and the World Championships—the first international championship events in which NBA players were eligible to compete—were just more evidence that the United States will need to use some of its pro players if it hopes to regain gold-medal status in international basketball.

In the Goodwill Games, the U.S. lost a preliminary-round game to a Soviet team missing four of its Lithuanian stars, including Sarunas Marchiulionis of the Golden State Warriors. The Lithuanians also refused to play in the World Championships in a protest to support their

homeland's independence movement.

Yugoslavia beat the U.S. in the Goodwill final and the World Championship semifinals, going on to beat the Soviets, 90-75, in the World title game in Argentina. The U.S., which had neither pros nor NBA draftees on its roster, was also beaten by Puerto Rico in the second-round round-robin at the Worlds.

Yugoslavia dressed two NBA regulars, Drazen Petrovic of Portland and Vlade Divac of the Lakers, plus Tony Kukoc, Chicago's first draft choice in 1990. It played so well in Argentina that an Italian sports daily headlined: "Yugoslavia, you are from the NBA!"

The U.S. women won their second straight world title, beating Yugoslavia, 88-78, in the final game in Kuala Lumpur, Malaysia.

Canoe/Kayak: The Eastern Europeans once again dominated the World Championships in Poznan, Poland, with the Soviet Union (9 gold-17 overall), East Germany (5-12) and Hungary (2-11) winning 16 of the 22 gold medals and 40 of the 66 total medals. The United States, blanked in the 1989 World Championships, came up with three silvers in kayak, two by Mike Herbert of Rogers, Ark., who was second in the K-1 500 meters and the K-2 500 with Terry Kent of Rochester, N.Y. Greg Barton of Bellingham, Wash., winner of two Olympic golds in 1988, ended his one-year retirement and won silver in the K-1 10,000.

Cycling: "LEMOND, ROI-SOLEIL" said L'Equipe, the French sports daily, in its headline the day after the 77th Tour de France ended July 22. "The Sun King" in question was not an 18th-century French royal but a contemporary American in Paris who wore the Tour's regal raiment—the yellow leader's jersey—for the second straight year.

Greg LeMond's victory in the 1990 Tour was a tribute to consistency. He won none of the race's 21 stages and did not lead until after the 20th. But, unlike 1989, no last-day dramatics were necessary for him to best Claudio Chiappucci of Italy by an aggregate 2 minutes, 16 seconds after 2112 miles of cycling. LeMond was able to turn the final stage to Paris into a triumphal procession. The only similarity with the 1989 Tour was that LeMond also began this one in questionable physical condition. He was sidelined nearly all April by a lingering virus, struggled badly to finish 78th in the Tour de Trump won by Mexico's Raul Alcala, then was 105th in the Tour of Italy won by Italy's Gianni Bugno. "I couldn't get out of my own way for four weeks," he said.

Critics said LeMond had gotten complacent over the winter after signing a fat three-year contract with the French "Z" team and being named 1989 Sportsman of the Year by *Sports Illustrated*. The one thing he certainly did get was rich: *Forbes* magazine ranked LeMond 26th among the world's 30th richest athletes, with an annual income estimated at $4.2 million.

LeMond began to silence the naysayers in late June, with a 10th-place finish in the Tour of Switzerland. His victory in July gave him three Tours de France. Only three other cyclists—Jacques Anquetil, Eddy Merckx and former LeMond teammate Bernard Hinault—have won more, all of them five-time champions.

"If all goes well, I could win five," said LeMond, 29, of Wayzata, Minn. Six weeks after the Tour, in the World Cycling Championships professional road race in Japan, defending champion LeMond never could make a serious challenge and wound up fourth, eight seconds behind surprise winner Rudy Dhaenens of Belgium. Dhaenens' previous record included nothing more impressive than a stage win in the Tour de France.

At the World Championships, the U.S. team had its best showing in history, with one gold medal, one silver and three bronze. Connie Paraskevin Young, 29, of Indianapolis, reclaimed the world match sprint title she had won three straight times from 1982-84, beating teammate Renee Duprel, 24, of Seattle, in the final. Ruthie Matthes, 24, of Ketchum, Idaho, whose career was previously so undistinguished her picture is missing from the U.S. press guide, was second to Catherine Marsal of France in the women's road race.

Gymnastics: Svetlana Boguinskaia, 17, of the Soviet Union became the first woman since Vera Caslavska of Czechoslovakia in 1967 to win the Grand Slam at the European Championships—gold medals in the team event, individual all-around and all four apparatus finals.

Kim Zmeskal, 14, of Houston, Bela Karolyi's newest prodigy, won both the McDonald's American Cup and the U.S. national all-around.

At the World Championships in October, 1989, Boguinskaia won the all-around, Igor Korobchinski took the men's title, and the Soviets won both team crowns. Brandy Johnson of Altamonte Springs, Fla., was seventh in the all-around (highest finish ever for a U.S. woman) and a silver medalist in the vault (the first medal for a U.S. gymnast since 1983). Johnson's 1990 season was ruined by injury.

Fencing: Italy was the big winner in the World Championships, with three gold medals and a bronze in five team events and three silvers and a bronze in the five individual events. None of the 1989 individual winners repeated.

Michael Marx of Portland, Ore., won a record seventh U.S. men's foil title, 11 years after he won his first.

Olympics: On Sept. 18, at the IOC meeting in Tokyo, Atlanta was selected over Athens and four other cities to host the 1996 Summer Games (see page 469).

The executive committee of the U.S. Olympic Committee induced USOC vice president George Steinbrenner to step aside indefinitely until the fallout from his baseball problems had settled. Steinbrenner's term runs through February, 1993.

Swimming: With the World Championships not taking place until January, 1991 (they are in Australia), 1990 was a slow year for swimming. Nevertheless, three long course world records were matched or bettered.

Tom Jager of Tijeras, N.M., broke his 50-meter mark (22.12) twice in one afternoon at the U.S. Sprint Championships in March, clocking 21.98 in the semifinals and 21.81 in the finals. In July, Mike Barrowman of Potomac, Md., lowered his 200-meter breaststroke mark by 1.36 seconds to 2:11.53 in the Goodwill Games. Adrian Moorhouse of Great Britain matched his own 100 breaststroke world mark, 1:01.49, in his national championships. It was the second time Moorhouse has equalled the mark he set in August, 1989.

Earlier in the year, Barrowman had lowered the oldest U.S. men's record on the books, clocking 1:53.77 in the 200-yard breaststroke to top Steve Lundquist's 1981 mark of 1:55.01.

Track & Field: In the 1990 outdoor track and field season, the times were out of joint from start to finish. The season began, unusually, in January when the

Randy Barnes reclaimed the world shotput record for the U.S. on May 20, with a heave of 75 feet, 10¼ inches.

Commonwealth Games took place in Australia. The year's final big meet, the European Championships in Yugoslavia (Aug.27-Sept.2), marked the last time an East German team will compete in an international championship.

During the months in between, times and distances were once again off previous levels, as the effects of random, out-of-competition drug testing seem to be having the desired effect. Through mid-September, world records had been set in only three championship events (not including walks)—and one of those, the javelin, was embroiled in a controversy that may not be resolved for a year.

Shotputter Randy Barnes began the record-setting in late May in Los Angeles, collecting a $50,000 bonus for a toss of 75 feet, 10¼ inches. That broke the 75-8 of East Germany's Ulf Timmermann and brought the shot record back to the U.S. for the first time since 1976. Prior to that, it had been held by U.S. putters for 42 years.

The French took away a record in the 4x100-meter relay that had been in the U.S. since 1968. Running in the European

Track & Field World Records Set in 1990

Eleven outdoor and nine indoor world records fell in 1990. Three events saw world marks lowered twice and the javelin distance lengthened four times.

Outdoor

MEN

Event	Holder.	Record	Old Mark	Former Holder
20,000 meters	Dionisio Castro, Portugal	57:18.4	57:24.2	Jos Hermens, Holland (1976)
Shot Put	Randy Barnes, United States	75-10¼	75- 8	Ulf Timmermann, E.Ger.(1988)
Javelin	Patrik Boden, Sweden	292- 4	287- 7	Jan Zelezny, Czech. (1987)
	Steve Backley, Britain	293-11		
	Jan Zelezny, Czech.	294- 2		
	Steve Backley, Britain	298- 6		
4x100-meter relay	France (Max Morniere, Daniel Sangouma, Jean-Charles Trouabel, Bruno Marie-Rose)	37.79	37.83	USA (Sam Graddy, Ron Brown, Calvin Smith, Carl Lewis), 1984

WOMEN

Event	Holder	Record	Old Mark	Former Holder
5-km walk	Kerry Saxby, Australia	20:17.19	20:32.75	Kerry Saxby, Australia (1989)
	Beate Anders, E.Germany	20:07.52		
10-km walk	Kerry Saxbe, Australia	42:25.2	42:39.2	Ileana Salvador, Italy (1989)
	Nadezhda Ryashkina,USSR	41:46.21		

Indoor

MEN

Event	Holder	Record	Old Mark	Former Holder
400 meters	Danny Everett, USA	45.04	45.05	Thomas Schonlebe, E.Ger.(1988)
1500 meters	Peter Elliott, England	3:34.21	3:35.6	Marcus O'Sullivan, Ireland (1989)
Pole vault	Sergei Bubka, USSR	19-10¼	19-9¼	Sergei Bubka, USSR (1989)

WOMEN

Event	Holder	Record	Old Mark	Former Holder
1500 meters	Doina Melinte, Romania	4:00.27	4:00.8	Mary Decker Slaney, USA (1980)
Mile	Doina Melinte, Romania	4:17.13	4:18.86	Doina Melinte, Romania (1988)
5000 meters	Lynn Jennings, USA	15:22.64	15:34.5	Margaret Groos, USA (1981)
60-meter hurdles	Lyudmila Narozhilenko,USSR	7.71	7.73	Cornelia Oschkenat, E.Ger. (1989)
	Lyudmila Narozhilenko,USSR	7.69		
3000-meter walk	Beate Anders, E.Germany	11:59.36	12:05.49	Olga Krishtop, USSR (1987)

For complete World Records list, see pages 480-81 and 483-484.

Championships, the quartet of Max Morniere, Daniel Sangouma, Jean-Charles Trouabel and Bruno-Marie Rose clocked 37.79, bettering the 37.83 by a Carl Lewis-anchored U.S. team at the 1984 Olympics. No French athletes had held a world record in a track event since 1975.

The javelin record was rewritten four times, but only the first two may stand without a new set of asterisks (all javelin records since 1986 already carry an asterisk, because the athletes began throwing a new, less aerodynamic javelin.)

The first record-breaker was Sweden's Patrick Boden, a University of Texas junior, who pitched the spear 292 feet, 4 inches on March 24, breaking the 287-7 set by Jan Zelezny of Czechoslovakia in 1987. The mark was then improved three times in 19 days in July—to 293-11 by Steve Backley of Great Britain, 294-2 by Zelezny, then 298-6 by Backley. But the last two were set with a rough-surface javelin that did not meet the implied specifications of smoothness for the implement, forcing the international track federation to consider the validity of the records at its 1991 congress and confusing javelin fans further.

At the European Championships, East Germany, which has competed as a separate nation since 1958, made its last stand a memorable one, leading the counts in both gold (12) and total medals (34). The East German women won nine golds, led by 100-200 champion Katrin Krabbe, 20, who also ran on the winning 4x100 relay. East German men won three golds, but the men's competition was dominated by Great Britain (8 gold) and Italy (4). The British took all the individual running events (including the two hurdles) at 800 meters or less, plus the 4x400 relay and the javelin. Led by Salvatore Antibo's 5000-10,000 double, Italy won all races over 1500 meters.

In a showdown of old and new, East German Jurgen Schult beat emigre East German Wolfgang Schmidt of West Germany in the discus. Sergei Bubka of the Soviet Union, bothered by a back, failed to win an international championship for the first time in his career when he finished sixth in the pole vault behind winning teammate Rodion Gataullin.

Merlene Ottey of Jamaica quickly let the world know what kind of year she would have by winning the 100 and 200 at the Commonwealth Games. Ottey, 31, went on to record season-leading times in the 100 (10.78) and 200 (21.66). Her 100 time has been bettered only by Florence Griffith-Joyner and Evelyn Ashford, the 200 time only by Griffith-Joyner.

After becoming the Goodwill Games only double winner, Ana Quirot of Cuba had her 39-race win streak in the 800 meters ended by a third-place finish to East Germans Sigrun Wodars and Christine Wachtel in Zurich on Aug. 15.

The revelations of 1990 were Michael Johnson, 23, of Baylor University, whose season-leading 19.85 in the 200 made him the fifth fastest ever at the distance; and high jumper Dragutin Topic, 19, of Yugoslavia, who set a world junior record (7-9¼) in early August then won a gold at the European Championships three weeks later with a leap of 7-8½.

In November, 1989, Pat Porter of Alamosa, Colo., won a record-breaking eighth straight national cross-country title, while Lynn Jennings went on to become the first U.S. woman to win the world cross-country title since Julie Brown in 1975. She also set an indoor world record in the 5000 meters.

Suzy Favor of Wisconsin finished perhaps the greatest collegiate career in women's track history by winning four NCAA titles—two outdoors and two indoors. In four years, Favor was unbeaten in nine NCAA finals, the only woman to win four straight NCAA titles in one event (the 1500 meters), the first to win the 800 and 1500 in the same NCAA meet, and the winner of a record 21 individual Big 10 titles.

Romania's Doina Melinte was the first Eastern Bloc athlete to personally cash a big check (the state sports federations kept most earnings in the past) when she broke indoor world records for both the

Will there be a Goodwill III?

The Goodwill Games are an international sporting event whose time has probably come and gone.

The political situation that led Ted Turner to cajole Soviet sports officials into creating the first Goodwill Games in Moscow in 1986 has changed dramatically since the fall of the Berlin Wall. It made the renewal in Seattle last summer seem nothing more than an exaggerated anachronism.

After consecutive superpower summer Olympic boycotts in 1980 and 1984, the Goodwill Games were a chance for Soviet and American athletes to renew their ideologically-charged rivalry. The notion of promoting both peace and his TV network made Turner more than willing to swallow a $26 million loss four years ago. The $44 million loss Turner Broadcasting Systems suffered in Seattle is not going to be as palatable to the TBS Board of Directors, which was to decide early this fall whether to underwrite Goodwill III, planned for 1994 in Moscow and Leningrad. Beyond Seattle, the event attracted little interest in the U.S. The TV ratings averaged barely half of the 5.0 promised advertisers by TBS. In major sports like track and basketball, Turner fell far short of the Games' motto, "Uniting the World's Best." And the competition dragged on at least a week too long.

There were only two world records set in Seattle, as compared with six in 1986. One came on the first day of competition, when Mike Barrowman of Potomac, Md., and the University of Michigan lowered his own mark in the 200-meter breaststroke by a whopping 1.36 seconds to 2 minutes, 11.53 seconds.

The other was in the women's 10-kilometer race walk, where Nadezha Ryashkina of the Soviet Union clocked 41:46.21, knocking 28 seconds off the mark held by Australia's Kerry Saxby, who was second.

The track and field competition was otherwise barely memorable. Only 41 percent of the world's top five 1990 performers made it to Seattle, and the list of

One of the few highlights at the Goodwill Games in Seattle came in the 100-meter final where **Leroy Burrell** (left) lunged at the tape to upset world record holder **Carl Lewis** (center) in 10.05 seconds. Mark Witherspoon was third.

late scratches was almost an International Who's Who.

"These are second-class athletes," said Zoya Ivanova of the Soviet Union after winning the women's marathon.

Yet the five-day meet drew an average of 23,000 fans to Husky Stadium. Excluding the 1984 Olympics, they were the largest multi-day track crowds in the U.S. since World War II. Those crowds saw Leroy Burrell beat Carl Lewis in the 100 meters; Lewis win his 64th straight long jump contest; and Ana Quirot of Cuba become the meet's only double winner (400 and 800 meters), then swear she would "defend socialism to death."

In swimming, the big stories other than Barrowman's record involved defeats. Matt Biondi was beaten again by Anthony Nesty of Surinam in the 100 butterfly, echoing the result of the Seoul Olympics. Janet Evans, now 18, lost to another Californian, Summer Sanders, 17, in the 400-meter individual medley—the first loss for Evans in that event since 1986. Sanders went on to win three individual events, as did Evans. Biondi won four golds (two on relays) and one silver.

East Germany's swimming wundermadchen, meanwhile, looked quite mortal, winning just one individual gold in 17 events and losing a relay in a major international meet for the first time since 1978.

The U.S. men's and women's basketball teams continued to go in opposite directions. The women romped to the gold over the Soviet Union, 82-70, extending their seven-year win streak to 41 in a row. The men lost to the Soviet Union in the preliminaries, 92-85, and Yugoslavia in the final, 85-79.

The young U.S. baseball team had fun (17-0) at the expense of a Soviet team making its international competition debut, but the Americans were later routed by Cuba 16-2 in the semifinals (the game stopped after 6½ innings by the 10-run "mercy" rule). Cuba won the title.

The U.S. hockey team came within 21 seconds of beating the Soviets before giving up a tying goal and losing in a shootout. The 3-3 tie in regulation was a marked improvement over the 10-1 loss to the Soviets during the preliminaries.

In diving, venerable Gao Min of China (she was 19 in Seattle) won both women's springboard events while her 11-year-old teammate, Fu Mingxia, took the platform.

Youth was also served in boxing and gymnastics: the youngest fighter in the tournament, 17-year-old Oscar dela Hoya of Los Angeles, was 125-pound gold medalist; Svetlana Boguinskaia, called the "Goddess" and looking old at 17, was toppled in the all-around by teammate Natalia Kalinina, 16, the latest munchkin prodigy.

Winning several controversial decisions, U.S. wrestlers beat the Soviets for the first time in a major international dual meet in 30 years. The Soviets protested, but not too loud or long. It wouldn't have been fitting for the Goodwill Games.

1500 meters (4:00.27) and the mile (4:17.13) at the Feb. 9 Vitalis Invitational at East Rutherford, N.J. Melinte set both marks in the same race and received a $100,000 bonus ($50,000 for each record). Melinte set the previous mile record (4:18.86) on the same track in 1988, while the old 1500 mark (4:00.8) was set by Mary Decker Slaney in 1980.

Other indoor world record-setters: Sergey Bubka of the Soviet Union, improving his 13-month-old pole vault mark by an inch to 19 feet, 10¼ inches; Peter Elliott of Great Britain in the 1500 (3:34.21), breaking Marcus O'Sullivan's two-year-old 3:35.4; and Lyudmila Narozhilenko of the Soviet Union, setting two 60-meter hurdles marks (7.71, then 7.69) in the same meet, bettering the 7.73 by Cornelia Oschkenat of East Germany in 1989.

Marathons: Olympic champion Gelindo Bordin of Italy proved patient enough to win the 94th Boston Marathon in 2 hours, 8 minutes, 19 seconds when Juma Ikangaa of Tanzania crossed the fine line between bravery and bravado. Ikangaa set a staggering pace for the first half and kept up a world-record pace for 19 miles but finished a badly beaten second in 2:09:52.

It was the third straight runner-up finish in Boston for Ikangaa, while Bordin became the first men's Olympic champion to win the race (nine others had failed before him). Bordin's time, second fastest ever at Boston behind Rob deCastella's 2:07:51 in 1986, was an Italian record. In the women's race, the other 1988 Olympic marathon champion—Rosa Mota of Portugal—won her third Boston in three tries in 2:25:24.

Ikangaa won the 1989 New York City Marathon in 2:08:01, a course record. Ingrid Kristiansen of Norway was the women's winner (2:25:30) then took 1990 off for the birth of her second child, a girl.

Bordin (2:14:02) and Mota (2:31.26) went on to win at the European Championships on a slow, hot course in Split, Yugoslavia. It was the second straight European title for Bordin and third straight for the amazing Mota, 31.

The long-distance running committee of The Athletics Congress/USA caused a controversy by adopting stricter course

Lynn Jennings won the world cross-country title in November, then went indoors to set a world record in the 5000.

standards for U.S. marathon records. The new standards would not allow records set on point-to-point courses like Boston's.

Drugs: Five of the world's best known track athletes ran afoul of testing in 1990. That group included two-time world champion and 1984 Olympic silver medal high hurdler Greg Foster of the U.S.; 1988 Olympic bronze medal long jumper Larry Myricks of the U.S.; 1983 world champion and 1988 Olympic bronze medal high jumper Tamara Bykova of the Soviet Union; 1987 world silver medal heptathlete Larisa Nikitina of the Soviet Union; and two-time Pan American discus champion Luis Delis of Cuba.

Nikitina and Delis were the more serious offenders, each getting a two-year suspension—the Soviet for amphetamine use at the Goodwill Games, the Cuban for steroids at two European meets. The other three received three-month bans for use of ephedrine-based stimulants.

The U.S. track federation, TAC/USA,

Three-time world champion **John Smith** of the U.S (top) on his way to victory over Bulgaria's Rossen Vasilev in the 136-pound finals at the World Freestyle Wrestling Championships in Tokyo.

suspended California coach Chuck DeBus for life after some of his former athletes testified he had given them banned substances.

TAC's administration of a short-notice, out-of-competition drug testing program came under such fire that its architects, including Olympic champion Edwin Moses, all resigned in May. There were charges that positives had been quashed by TAC executive director Ollan Cassell and that not enough had been done to close a loophole allowing athletes who live more than 75 miles from testers to be excused. The criticism led to a restructuring of TAC's operations designed to end Cassell's virtual dictatorship over the sport in the U.S.

Ben Johnson was cleared by the Canadian government to resume competition when his two-year international track suspension ended Sept. 24, 1990. Johnson had been banned since testing positive after he finished first in the 1988 Olympic 100 meters. He is expected to race again in the 1991 indoor season.

Volleyball: Italy won the inaugural title and $236,500 in the World League, beating the Dutch in the final. Team USA was last (1-11) in its pool of the eight-team league, which averaged 4856 spectators for its 51 matches.

At the quadrennial women's World Championships in Beijing, China, the Soviet Union beat the home team in the final, keeping China from a third straight crown. It was the Soviets' first title since 1970. The surprising United States women finished third, only the third time in nine appearances the U.S. has won a medal (third in 1982, second in 1967).

Weightlifting: The sport, in crisis since its doping problems at the 1988 Olympics, presented a 1989 World Championships in Athens in which drug controls kept results under 1987 levels in all but two of the three lowest weight classes. Soviet lifters won five of the 10 classes, Bulgaria four and Turkish Olympic hero Naim (Pocket Hercules) Suleymanoglu the other. Bulgaria won the team title, with the U.S. 15th of 31.

Wrestling: John Smith of Del City, Okla., became the first American wrestler to win four straight world-level titles when he took the 136-pound crown at September's World Freestyle Championships in Tokyo. Smith, 25, has now won three world championships (1987, '89, and '90) and an Olympic gold medal (1988). The Soviet Union won the meet with four gold medals and 80 overall points. The United States was second with 73 points and Bulgaria third with 72.□

Swimming
World & American Records
Through Oct.1, 1990

MEN

Freestyle

Distance	Record	Time	Record Holder	Date	Location
50 meters	World	21.18	**Tom Jager**, USA	Mar.24, 1990	Nashville
	American ...	same			
100 meters	World	48.42	**Matt Biondi**, USA	Aug.10, 1988	Austin, Texas
	American ...	same			
200 meters	World	1:46.69	**Giorgio Lamberti**, Italy	Aug.15, 1989	Bonn,W.Ger.
	American ...	1:47.72	**Matt Biondi**	Aug. 8, 1988	Austin, Texas
400 meters	World	3:46.95	**Uwe Dassler**, E.Germany	Sept.23, 1988	Seoul
	American ...	3:48.06	**Matt Cetlinski**	Aug.11, 1988	Austin, Texas
800 meters	World	7:50.64	**Vladimir Salnikov**, USSR	July 4, 1986	Moscow
	American ...	7:52.45	**Sean Killion**	July 27, 1987	Clovis, Calif.
1500 meters	World 14:54.76		**Vladimir Salnikov**, USSR	Feb. 22, 1983	Moscow
	American ...15:01.51		**George DiCarlo**	June 30, 1984	Indianapolis

Backstroke

Distance	Record	Time	Record Holder	Date	Location
100 meters	World	54.51	**David Berkoff**, USA	Sept.24, 1988	Seoul
	American ...	same			
200 meters	World	1:58.14	**Igor Poliansky**, USSR	Mar. 3, 1985	Erfurt, E.Ger.
	American ...	1:58.86	**Rick Carey**	June 27, 1984	Indianapolis

Breaststroke

Distance	Record	Time	Record Holder	Date	Location
100 meters	World	1:01.49	**Adrian Moorhouse**, Britain	Jan. 25, 1990	Aukland, N.Z.
	American ...	1:01.65	**Steve Lundquist**	July 29, 1984	Los Angeles
200 meters	World	2:11.53	**Mike Barrowman**, USA	Jul. 20, 1990	Seattle
	American ...	same			

Butterfly

Distance	Record	Time	Record Holder	Date	Location
100 meters	World	52.84	**Pablo Morales**, USA	June 23, 1986	Orlando, Fla.
	American ...	same			
200 meters	World	1:56.24	**Michael Gross**, W.Germany	June 27, 1986	Bonn,W.Ger.
	American ...	1:57.05	**Melvin Stewart**	Jul. 21, 1990	Seattle

Individual Medley

Distance	Record	Time	Record Holder	Date	Location
200 meters	World	2:00.11	**Dave Wharton**, USA	Aug.20, 1989	Tokyo
	American ...	same			
400 meters	World	4:14.75	**Tamas Darnyi**, Hungary	Sept.21, 1988	Seoul
	American ...	4:15.57	**Eric Namesnik**	Jul. 30, 1990	Austin, TX

Relays

Event	Record	Time	Record Holder	Date	Location
400-m free	World	3:16.53	**USA** (Chris Jacobs, Troy Dalbey, Tom Jager, Matt Biondi)	Sept.23, 1988	Seoul
	American ...	same			
800-m free	World	7:12.51	**USA** (Troy Dalbey, Matt Cetlinski, Doug Gjartsen, Matt Biondi)	Sept.21, 1988	Seoul
	American ...	same			
400-m medley	World	3:36.93	**USA** (David Berkoff, Rich Schroeder, Matt Biondi, Chris Jacobs)	Sept.25, 1988	Seoul
	American ...	same			

WOMEN

Freestyle

Distance	Record	Time	Record Holder	Date	Location
50 meters	World	24.98	**Yang Wenyi**, China	Mar. 24, 1990	Nashville
	American	25.50	**Leigh Ann Fetter**	Aug. 13, 1988	Austin, Texas
100 meters	World	54.73*	**Kristin Otto**, E. Germany	Aug. 19, 1986	Madrid, Spain
	American	55.30*	**Dara Torres**	Mar. 25, 1988	Orlando, Fla.
200 meters	World	1:57.55	**Heike Friedrich**, E. Germany	June 18, 1986	Berlin
	American	1:58.23	**Cynthia Woodhead**	Sept. 3, 1979	Tokyo
400 meters	World	4:03.85	**Janet Evans**, USA	Sept. 22, 1988	Seoul
	American	same			
800 meters	World	8:16.22	**Janet Evans**, USA	Aug. 20, 1989	Tokyo
	American	same			
1500 meters	World	15:52.10	**Janet Evans**, USA	Mar. 26, 1988	Orlando, Fla.
	American	same			

*Set on first leg of relay race.

Backstroke

Distance	Record	Time	Record Holder	Date	Location
100 meters	World	1:00.59*	**Ina Kleber**, E. Germany	Aug. 24, 1984	Moscow
	American	1:01.20	**Betsy Mitchell**	June 24, 1986	Orlando, Fla
200 meters	World	2:08.60	**Betsy Mitchell**, USA	June 27, 1986	Orlando, Fla
	American	same			

*Set on first leg of relay race.

Breaststroke

Distance	Record	Time	Record Holder	Date	Location
100 meters	World	1:07.91	**Silke Hoerner**, E. Germany	Aug. 21, 1987	Strasbourg, FRA
	American	1:08.91	**Tracey McFarlane**	Aug. 11, 1988	Austin, Texas
200 meters	World	2:26.71	**Silke Hoerner**, E. Germany	Sept. 21, 1988	Seoul
	American	2:29.58	**Amy Shaw**	Aug. 16, 1987	Brisbane, Aus.

Butterfly

Distance	Record	Time	Record Holder	Date	Location
100 meters	World	57.93	**Mary T. Meagher**, USA	Aug. 16, 1981	Brown Deer, WI
	American	same			
200 meters	World	2:05.96	**Mary T. Meagher**, USA	Aug. 13, 1981	Brown Deer, WI
	American	same			

Individual Medley

Distance	Record	Time	Record Holder	Date	Location
200 meters	World	2:11.73	**Uta Geweniger**, E. Germany	July 4, 1981	Berlin
	American	2:12.64	**Tracy Caulkins**	Aug. 3, 1984	Los Angeles
400 meters	World	4:36.10	**Petra Schneider**, E. Germany	Aug. 1, 1982	Guayaquil, EQU
	American	4:37.76	**Janet Evans**	Sept. 19, 1988	Seoul

Relays

Event	Record	Time	Record Holder	Date	Location
400-m free	World	3:40.57	**E.Ger.** (Kristin Otto, Manuella Stellmach, Sabine Schulze, Heike Friedrich)	Aug. 19, 1986	Madrid, Spain
	American	3:43.43	**USA** (Jenna Johnson, Carrie Steinseifer, Dara Torres, Nancy Hogshead)	July 31, 1984	Los Angeles
800-m free	World	7:55.47	**E.Ger.** (Manuella Stellmach, Astrid Strauss, Anke Mohring, Heike Friedrich)	Aug. 18, 1987	Strasbourg, FRA
	American	8:02.12	**USA** (Betsy Mitchell, Mary T. Meagher, Kim Brown, Mary Wayte)	Aug. 17, 1986	Madrid, Spain
400-m medley	World	4:03.69	**E.Ger.** (Ina Kleber, Sylvia Gerasch, Ines Geissler, Birgit Meineke)	Aug. 24, 1984	Moscow
	American	4:07.75	**USA** (Betsy Mitchell, Tracey McFarlane, Janet Jorgensen, Nicole Haislett)	Jul. 23, 1990	Seattle

Track & Field

World Outdoor Records
As of Oct.1, 1990.

World outdoor records officially recognized by the International Amateur Athletics Federation (IAAF).

MEN
Running

Event	World Mark	Record Holder	Date	Location
100 meters	9.92	**Carl Lewis,** USA	Sept.24, 1988	Seoul
200 meters	19.72	**Pietro Mennea,** Italy	Sept.17, 1979	Mexico City
400 meters	43.29	**Butch Reynolds,** USA	Aug.16, 1988	Zurich, Switzerland
800 meters	1:41.73	**Sebastian Coe,** Britain	June 10, 1981	Florence, Italy
1000 meters	2:12.18	**Sebastian Coe,** Britain	July 11, 1981	Oslo, Norway
1500 meters	3:29.46	**Said Aouita,** Morocco	Aug.23, 1985	West Berlin
One Mile	3:46.32	**Steve Cram,** Britain	July 27, 1985	Oslo, Norway
2000 meters	4:50.81	**Said Aouita,** Morocco	July 16, 1987	Paris
3000 meters	7:29.45	**Said Aouita,** Morocco	Aug.20, 1989	Cologne, W.Ger.
5000 meters	12:58.39	**Said Aouita,** Morocco	July 22, 1987	Rome
10,000 meters	27:08.23	**Arturo Barrios,** Mexico	Aug.18, 1989	West Berlin
20,000 meters	57:18.4	**Dionisio Castro,** Portugal	Mar.31, 1990	La Fleche, France
25,000 meters	1:13:55.8	**Toshihiko Seko,** Japan	Mar.22, 1981	Christchurch,N.Zea.
30,000 meters	1:29:18.8	**Toshihiko Seko,** Japan	Mar.22, 1981	Christchurch,N.Zea.
Marathon	2:06:50	**Belayneh Densimo,** Ethiopia	Apr. 17, 1988	Rotterdam, Holland

Note: The **One Mile** run is 1,609.344 meters and the **Marathon** is 42,194.988 meters (26 miles, 385 yards).

Hurdles

Event	World Mark	Record Holder	Date	Location
110-meter High	12.92	**Roger Kingdom,** USA	Aug.16, 1989	Zurich, Switzerland
400-meter Low	47.02	**Edwin Moses,** USA	Aug.31, 1983	Koblenz, W.Ger.

Note: The hurdles at 110 meters are 3 feet 6 inches high and the hurdles at 400 meters are 3 feet. There are 10 hurdles in each race.

Steeplechase

Event	World Mark	Record Holder	Date	Location
3000m Steeplechase	8:05.35	**Peter Koech,** Kenya	July 3, 1989	Stockholm

Note: The steeplechase course consists of 28 hurdles (3 feet high) and seven water jumps (12 feet long).

Walking

Event	World Mark	Record Holder	Date	Location
20 kilometers	1:18:40.0	**Ernesto Canto,** Mexico	May 5, 1984	Bergen, Norway
30 kilometers	2:07:59.8	**Jose Marin,** Spain	Aug. 4, 1979	Barcelona
50 kilometers	3:41:38.4	**Raul Gonzalez,** Mexico	May 25, 1979	Bergen, Norway

Relays

Event	World Mark	Record Holder	Date	Location
4x100-meter	37.79	**France** (Max Morniere, Daniel Sangouma, Jean-Charles Trouabel, Bruno Marie-Rose)	Sep. 1, 1990	Los Angeles
4x200-meter Relay	1:19.38	**USA** (Danny Everett, Leroy Burrell, Floyd Heard, Carl Lewis)	Aug.23, 1989	Koblenz, W.Ger.
4x400-meter Relay	2:56.16	**USA** (Vince Matthews, Ron Freeman, Larry James, Lee Evans)	Oct. 20, 1968	Mexico City
		USA (Danny Everett, Steve Lewis, Kevin Robinzine, Butch Reynolds)	Oct. 1, 1988	Seoul
4x800-meter Relay	7:03.89	**Britain** (Peter Elliott, Garry Cook, Steve Cram, Sebastian Coe)	Aug.30, 1982	London
4x1500-meter Relay	14:38.8	**West Germany**	Aug.14, 1977	Cologne, W.Ger.
4xMile	15:49.08	**Ireland**	Aug.17, 1985	Dublin

Decathlon

Event	World Mark	Record Holder	Date	Location
Decathlon	8,847 Pts	**Daley Thompson,** Britain	Aug.8-9, 1984	Los Angeles

Note: the Decathlon consists of 10 events—**100m** (10.44) **LJ** (26-3½) **SP** (51-7), **HJ** (6-8), **400m** (46.97), **100m H** (14.33), **Discus** (152-9), **PV** (16-4¾), **Javelin** (214-0), **1500m** (4:35.00).

Field Events

Event	World Mark	Record Holder	Date	Location
High Jump	8-0	**Javier Sotomayor,** Cuba	July 29, 1989	San Juan, P.R.
Pole Vault	19-10½	**Sergei Bubka,** USSR	July 10, 1988	Nice, France
Long Jump	29-2½	**Bob Beamon,** USA	Oct. 18, 1968	Mexico City
Triple Jump	58-11½	**Willie Banks,** USA	June 16, 1985	Indianapolis
Shot Put	75-10¼	**Randy Barnes,** USA	May 20, 1990	Los Angeles
Discus	243-0	**Jurgen Schult,** E.Germany	June 6, 1986	Neubrandenburg, EG
Javelin	298-0	**Steve Backley,** Britain	July 20, 1990	London
Hammer	284-7	**Yuri Sedykh,** USSR	Aug.30, 1986	Stuttgart, W.Ger.

Note: The international weights for men—**Shot** (16 lb), **Discus** (4 lb/6.55 oz), **Hammer** (16 lb), new **Javelin** (minimum 1 lb/12¼ oz).

WOMEN

Running

Event	World Mark	Record Holder	Date	Location
100 meters	10.49	**Florence Griffith Joyner,** USA	July 16, 1988	Indianapolis
200 meters	21.34	**Florence Griffith Joyner,** USA	Sept.29, 1988	Seoul
400 meters	47.60	**Marita Koch,** E.Germany	Oct. 6, 1985	Canberra, Australia
800 meters	1:53.28	**Jarmila Kratochvilova,** Czech.	July 26, 1983	Munich
1000 meters	2:30.6	**Tatyana Providokhina,** USSR	Aug.20, 1978	Podolsk, USSR
1500 meters	3:52.47	**Tatyana Providokhina,** USSR	Aug.13, 1980	Zurich
One Mile	4:15.61	**Paula Ivan,** Romania	July 10, 1989	Nice, France
2000 meters	5:28.69	**Maricica Puica,** Romania	July 11, 1986	London
3000 meters	8:22.62	**Tatyana Providokhina,** USSR	Aug.26, 1984	Leningrad, USSR
5000 meters	14:37.33	**Ingrid Kristiansen,** Norway	Aug. 5, 1986	Stockholm
10,000 meters	30:13.74	**Ingrid Kristiansen,** Norway	July 5, 1986	Oslo, Norway
Marathon	2:21:06	**Ingrid Kristiansen,** Norway	Apr. 21, 1985	London

Note: The **One Mile** run is 1,609.344 meters; and the **Marathon** is 42,194.988 meters (26 miles, 385 yards).

Hurdles

Event	World Mark	Record Holder	Date	Location
100-meter High	12.21	**Yordanka Donkova,** Bulgaria	Aug.21, 1988	Stara Zagora, Bulg.
400-meter Low	52.94	**Marina Stepanova,** USSR	Sept.17, 1986	Tashkent, USSR

Note: The hurdles at 100 meters are 2 feet 9 inches high and the hurdles at 400 meters are 2 feet 6 inches. There are 10 hurdles in each race.

Walking

Event	World Mark	Record Holder	Date	Location
5 kilometers	20:07.52	**Beate Anders,** E.Germany	June 23, 1990	Rostock, E.Ger.
10 kilometers	41:46.21	**Nadezhda Ryashkina,** USSR	July 24, 1990	Seattle

Relays

Event	World Mark	Record Holder	Date	Location
4x100-meter Relay	41.37	**East Germany**	Oct. 6, 1985	Canberra, Aus.
4x200-meter Relay	1:28.15	**East Germany**	Aug. 9, 1980	Jena, E.Germany
4x400-meter Relay	3:15.18	**USSR**	Oct. 1, 1988	Seoul
4x800-meter Relay	7:50.17	**USSR**	Aug. 5, 1984	Moscow

Heptathlon

Event	World Mark	Record Holder	Date	Location
Heptathlon	7,291 Pts	**Jackie Joyner-Kersee,** USA	Sept.23, 1988	Seoul

Note: Joyner-Kersee's record-setting times, distances and heights in the 7 heptathlon events, chronologically over 2 days—100m H (12.69), HF (6-1¼), SP (51-10), 200m (22.56), LJ (23-10)¼), Javelin (149-10), 800m (2:08.51).

Field Events

Event	World Mark	Record Holder	Date	Location
High Jump	6-10¼	**Stefka Kostadinova,** Bulgaria	Aug.30, 1987	Rome
Long Jump	24- 8¼	**Galina Chistyakova,** USSR	June 11, 1988	Leningrad, USSR
Triple Jump	47- 7¾	**Galina Chistyakova,** USSR	July 3, 1989	Stockholm
Shot Put	74- 3	**Natalya Lisovskaya,** USSR	June 7, 1987	Moscow
Discus	252- 0	**Gabriele Reinsch,** E.Germany	July 9, 1988	Neubrandenburg, EG
Javelin	262- 5	**Petra Felke,** E.Germany	Sept. 9, 1988	West Berlin

Note: The international weights for women—**Shot** (8 lb/13 oz), **Discus** (2 lb/3.27 oz), **Javelin** (minimum 1 lb/5.16 oz).

Track & Field (Cont.)

American Outdoor Records
As of Oct. 1, 1990.

American outdoor records officially recognized by The Athletics Congress (TAC) through Oct. 1, 1990. Note that (*) indicates a world record.

MEN

Running

Event	US Mark	Record Holder
100 m	9.92*	Carl Lewis (1988)
200 m	19.75	Carl Lewis (1983) & Joe DeLoach (1988)
400 m	43.29*	Butch Reynolds (1988)
800 m	1:42.60	Johnny Gray (1985)
1000 m	2:13.9	Rick Wohlhuter (1974)
1500 m	3:29.77	Sydney Maree (1985)
One Mile	3:47.69	Steve Scott (1982)
2000 m	4:52.44	Jim Spivey (1987)
3000 m	7:35.84	Doug Padilla (1983)
5000 m	13:01.15	Sydney Maree (1985)
10,000 m	27:20.56	Mark Nenow (1986)
20,000 m	58:25.0	Bill Rodgers (1977)
25,000 m	1:14:11.8	Bill Rodgers (1979)
30,000 m	1:31:49	Bill Rodgers (1979)
Marathon	2:08:52	Alberto Salazar (1982)

Hurdles

Event	US Mark	Record Holder
110-m High	12.92*	Roger Kingdom (1989)
400-m Low	47.02*	Edwin Moses (1983)

Steeplechase

Event	US Mark	Record Holder
3000 m	8:09.17	Henry Marsh (1985)

Walking

Event	US Mark	Record Holder
20 km	1:24:50	Tim Lewis (1988)
30 km	2:23:14	Goetz Klopfer (1970)
50 km	3:56:55	Marco Evoniuk (1988)

Relays

Event	US Mark	Record Holder
4x100 m	37.83*	Olympic team (1984)
4x200 m	1:19.38*	Santa Monica Track Club (1989)
4x400 m	2:56.16*	Olympic Team (1968) & Olympic Team (1988)
4x800 m	7:06.5	Santa Monica Track Club (1988)
4x1500 m	14:46.3	National Team (1979)

Decathlon

Event	US Mark	Record Holder
Decathlon	8,634 Pts	Bruce Jenner

Field Events

Event	US Mark	Record Holder
High Jump	7-10	Hollis Conway (1989)
Pole Vault	19-6½	Joe Dial (1987)
Long Jump	29-2½*	Bob Beamon (1968)
Triple Jump	58-11½*	Willie Banks (1985)
Shot Put	75-10¼	Randy Barnes (1990)
Discus	237-4	Ben Plucknett (1981)
Javelin	280-1	Tom Petranoff (1986)
Hammer	268-8	Jud Logan (1988)

Note: Tom Petranoff was suspended by TAC in early 1989 (for competing in a banned country), so even though he bettered his U.S. javelin record twice in 1990 (283-2 and 283-8), neither throw will be recognized.

WOMEN

Running

Event	US Mark	Record Holder
100 m	10.49*	F.Griffith Joyner (1988)
200 m	21.34*	F.Griffith Joyner (1988)
400 m	48.83	Valerie Brisco (1984)
800 m	1:56.90	Mary Slaney (1985)
1000 m	2:34.65	Mary Slaney (1988)
1500 m	3:57.12	Mary Slaney (1983)
One Mile	4:16.71	Mary Slaney (1985)
2000 m	5:32.7	Mary Slaney (1984)
3000 m	8:25.83	Mary Slaney (1985)
5000 m	14:59.99	PattiSue Pulmer (1989)
10,000 m	31:35.3	Mary Slaney (1982)
Marathon	2:21:21	Joan Samuelson (1985)

Hurdles

Event	US Mark	Record Holder
100-m High	12.61	Gail Devers (1988) & Jackie Joyner-Kersee (1988)
400-m Low	53.37	Sandra Farmer-Patrick (1989)

Walking

Event	US Mark	Record Holder
5 km	22:38.0	Teresa Vaill (1989)
10 km	46:10.26	Debbi Lawrence (1990)

Relays

Event	US Mark	Record Holder
4x100 m	41.55	National team (1987)
4x200 m	1:32.57	Louisiana St. (1989)
4x400 m	3:15.51	Olympic Team (1988)
4x800 m	8:17.09	Athletics West (1983)

Heptathlon

Event	US Mark	Record Holder
Heptathlon	7,291 Pts*	J.Joyner-Kersee (1988)

Field Events

Event	US Mark	Record Holder
High Jump	6-8 (twice)	Louise Ritter (1988)
Long Jump	24- 5½	J.Joyner-Kersee (1987)
Triple Jump	46- 0¼	Sheila Hudson (1990)
Shot Put	66- 2½	Ramona Pagel (1988)
Discus	216-10	Carol Cady (1986)
Javelin	227- 5	Kate Schmidt (1977)

World Indoor Records
As of Oct.1, 1990.

World indoor records officially recognized by the International Amateur Athletics Federation (IAAF).

MEN
Running

Event	World Mark	Record Holder	Date	Location
50 meters	5.61	Manfred Kokot, E.Germany	Feb. 4, 1973	East Berlin
	5.61	James Sanford, USA	Feb.20, 1981	San Diego
60 meters	6.50	Lee McRae, USA	Mar. 7, 1987	Indianapolis
200 meters	20.36	Bruno Marie-Rose, France	Feb.22, 1987	Lievin, France
400 meters	45.04	Danny Everett, USA	Feb. 4, 1990	Stuttgart, W.Ger
800 meters	1:44.84	Paul Ereng, Kenya	Mar. 4, 1989	Budapest, Hungary
1000 meters	2:16.4	Rob Druppers, Holland	Feb.20, 1988	The Hague, Holland
1500 meters	3:34.21	Peter Elliott, Britain	Feb.27, 1990	Seville, Spain
One Mile	3:49.78	Eammon Coghlan, Ireland	Feb.27, 1983	E.Rutherford, NJ
3000 meters	7:39.2	Emiel Puttemans, Belgium	Feb.18, 1973	West Berlin
5000 meters	13:20.4	Suleiman Nyambui, Tanzania	Feb. 6, 1981	New York City

Note: The One Mile run is 1,609.344 meters.

Hurdles

Event	World Mark	Record Holder	Date	Location
50 meters	6.25	Mark McKoy, CAN	Jan.27, 1985	Rosemont, IL
60 meters	7.36	Greg Foster, USA	Jan.31, 1987	Ottawa, Ontario
			Jan.16, 1987	Los Angeles

Note: The hurdles for both distances are 3 feet 6 inches high. There are four hurdles in the 50 and five in the 60.

Walking

Event	World Mark	Record Holder	Date	Location
5000 meters	18:27.10	Mikhail Shchennikov, USSR	Mar. 5, 1989	Budapest, Hungary

Relays

Event	World Mark	Record Holder	Date	Location
4x200-meters	1:22.32	Italy (Francesco Pavoni, Stefano Tilli, Giovanni Bongiorni, Carlo Simionato)	Feb.11, 1984	Torino, Italy
4x400-meters	3:05.21	USA (Clarence Daniel, Chip Jenkins, Ken Lowery, Mark Rowe)	Mar.10, 1989	Glasgow, Scotland

Field Events

Event	World Mark	Record Holder	Date	Location
High Jump	7-11½	Javier Sotomayor, Cuba	Mar. 4, 1989	Budapest, Hungary
Pole Vault	19-10¼	Sergei Bubka, USSR	Mar.17, 1990	Donyetsk, USSR
Long Jump	28-10¼	Carl Lewis, USA	Jan.27, 1984	New York City
Triple Jump	58- 3¼	Mike Conley, USA	Feb.27, 1987	New York City
Shot Put	74- 4¼	Randy Barnes, USA	Jan.20, 1989	Los Angeles

Note: The international weights for men—Shot (16 lbs).

WOMEN
Running

Event	World Mark	Record Holder	Date	Location
50 meters	6.06	Angella Issajenko, Canada	Feb. 2, 1980	Grenoble, France
60 meters	7.00	Nelli Cooman, Holland	Feb.23, 1986	Madrid, Spain
200 meters	22.27	Heike Drechsler, E.Germany	Mar. 7, 1987	Indianapolis
400 meters	49.59	Jarmila Kratochvilova, Czech.	Mar. 7, 1982	Milan, Italy
800 meters	1:56.40	Christine Wachtel, E.Germany	Feb.14, 1988	Vienna, Austria
1000 meters	2:34.8	Brigitte Kraus, W.Germany	Feb.19, 1978	Dortmund, W.Ger.
1500 meters	4:00.27	Doina Melinte, Romania	Feb. 9, 1990	E.Rutherford, NJ
One Mile	4:17.13	Doina Melinte, Romania	Feb. 9, 1990	E.Rutherford, NJ
3000 meters	8:33.82	Elly van Hulst, Holland	Feb. 8, 1986	Cosford, England
5000 meters	15:22.64	Lynn Jennings, USA	Jan. 7, 1990	Hanover, NH

Note: The One Mile run is 1,609.344 meters.

Hurdles

Event	World Mark	Record Holder	Date	Location
50-meter	6.58	Cornelia Oschkenat, E.Germany	Feb.20, 1988	East Berlin
60-meter	7.69	Lyudmila Narozhilenko, USSR	Feb. 4, 1990	Chelyabinsk, USSR

Note: The hurdles for both distances are 2 feet 9 inches high. There are four hurdles in the 50 and five in the 60.

Track & Field (Cont.)

World Indoor Records
WOMEN
Walking

Event	World Mark	Record Holder	Date	Location
3000 meters	11:59.36	Beate Anders, E.Germany	Mar. 4, 1990	Glasgow, Scotland

Relays

Event	World Mark	Record Holder	Date	Location
4x200-meters	1:32.55	W.Germany	Feb.20, 1988	Dortmund, W.Ger.
4x400-meters	3:34.38	W.Germany	Jan.30, 1981	Dortmund, W.Ger.

Field Events

Event	World Mark	Record Holder	Date	Location
High Jump	6- 9	Stefka Kostadinova, Bulgaria	Feb.20, 1988	Athens, Greece
Long Jump	24- 2¼	Heike Drechsler, E.Germany	Feb.14, 1988	Vienna, Austria
Shot Put	73-10	Helena Fibingerova, Czech.	Feb.19, 1977	Jablonec, Czech.

Note: The international weights for women—Shot (8 lb/13 oz).

American Indoor Records
As of Oct.1, 1990.

American indoor records officially recognized by The Athletics Congress (TAC) through Oct.1, 1990. Note that (*) indicates a world record.

MEN

Running

Event	US Mark	Record Holder
50 meters	5.61*	James Sanford (1981)
60 meters	6.50	Lee McRae (1987)
200 meters	20.59	Michael Johnson (1989)
400 meters	45.04	Danny Everett (1990)
800 meters	1:45.64	Johnny Gray (1990)
1000 meters	2:18.19	Ocky Clark (1989)
1500 meters	3:36.0	Steve Scott (1981)
One Mile	3:51.8	Steve Scott (1981)
3000 meters	7:39.94	Steve Scott (1989)
5000 meters	13:20.55	Doug Padilla (1982)

Note: The One Mile run is 1,609.344 meters.

Hurdles

Event	US Mark	Record Holder
50 meters	6.35*	Greg Foster (1985)
	6.35*	Greg Foster (1987)
60 meters	7.36*	Greg Foster (1987)

Note: The hurdles for both distances are 3 feet 6 inches high. There are four hurdles in the 50 and five in the 60.

Walking

Event	US Mark	Record Holder
5000 meters	19:18.40	Tim Lewis (1987)

Relays

Event	US Mark	Record Holder
4x200-meters	1:25.18	U.of Arkansas (1985)
4x400-meters	3:05.21*	National Team (1989)
4x800-meters	7:20.58	U.of Arkansas (1990)

Field Events

Event	World Mark	Record Holder
High Jump	7- 9¾	Hollis Conway (1989)
Pole Vault	19- 5½	Billy Olson (1986)
Long Jump	28-10 ¼*	Carl Lewis (1984)
Triple Jump	58- 3¼*	Mike Conley (1987)
Shot Put	74- 4¼*	Randy Barnes (1989)
Weight Throw	78- 0¼	Lance Deal (1990)

Note: The international weights for men—Shot (16 lbs); Weight Throw (35 lbs).

WOMEN

Running

Event	US Mark	Record Holder
50 meters	6.13	Jeanette Bolden (1981)
60 meters	7.07	Gwen Torrence (1989)
200 meters	22.87	Dawn Sowell (1989)
400 meters	51.77	Diane Dixon (1989)
800 meters	1:58.9	Mary Slaney (1980)
1000 meters	2:37.6	Mary Slaney (1989)
1500 meters	4:00.8	Mary Slaney (1980)
One Mile	4:20.5	Mary Slaney (1982)
3000 meters	8:40.45	Lynn Jennings (1990)
5000 meters	15:22.64	Lynn Jennings (1990)

Note: The One Mile run is 1,609.344 meters.

Hurdles

Event	World Mark	Record Holder
50 meters	6.84	Kim McKenzie (1989)
60 meters	7.81	J.Joyner-Kersee (1989)

Note: The hurdles for all three distances are 2 feet 9 inches high. There are four hurdles in the 50 and five in the 60.

Walking

Event	World Mark	Record Holder
3000 meters	12:45.38	Maryanne Torrellas (1988)

Relays

Event	World Mark	Record Holder
4x200-meters	1:36.8	Morgan St. (1981)
4x400-meters	3:35.92	U.of Florida (1990)
4x800-meters	8:25.5*	Villanova (1987)

Field Events

Event	World Mark	Record Holder
High Jump	6- 6¾	Coleen Sommer (1982)
Long Jump	23- 0½	J.Joyner-Kersee (1988)
Triple Jump	45- 3	Yvette Bates (1987)
Shot Put	65- 0¾	Romona Pagel (1987)

Note: The international weights for women—Shot (8 lb/13 oz).

World Track & Field Championships

While the Summer Olympic Games have usually served as the world outdoor championships for track and field throughout the century, a separate World Championship Meet for track and field was started in 1983 by the International Amateur Athletic Federation (IAAF). Quadrennial meets have been held in Helsinki in 1983 and Rome in 1987, with the 1991 championships schedule for Tokyo in 1991.

MEN

Helsinki, 1983

Running

Event	Champion	Time
100m	Carl Lewis, USA	10.07
200m	Calvin Smith, USA	20.14
400m	Bert Cameron, Jamaica	45.05
800m	Willi Wulbeck, W.Germany	1:43.65
1500m	Steve Cram, Britaln	3:41.59
5000m	Eamonn Coghlan, Ireland	13:28.53
10,000m	Alberto Cova, Italy	28:01.04
Marathon	Rob de Castella, Australia	2:10:03

Hurdles

Event	Champion	Time
110m	Greg Foster, USA	13.42
400m	Edwin Moses, USA	47.50

Steeplechase

Event	Champion	Time
3000m	Patriz Ilg, W.Germany	8:15.06

Walking

Event	Champion	Time
20 km	Ernesto Canto, Mexico	1:20:49
50 km	Ronald Weigel, E.Germany	3:43:08

Relays

Event	Champion	Time
4x100m	United States	37.86
4x400m	United States	3:00.79

Field Events

Event	Champion	Distance
High Jump	Gennadiy Avdeyenko, USSR	7-7¼
Pole Vault	Sergei Bubka, USSR	18-8¼
Long Jump	Carl Lewis, USA	28-0¾
Triple Jump	Zdzislaw Hoffmann, Poland	57-2
Shot Put	Edward Sarul, Poland	70-2¼
Discus	Imrich Bugar, Czech.	222-2
Hammer	Sergey Litvinov, USSR	271-3
Javelin	Detlef Michel, E.Germany	293-7

Decathlon

Champion	Points
Daley Thompson, Britain	8714

Rome, 1987

Running

Event	Chmpion	Time
100m	Ben Johnson, Canada	9.83
200m	Calvin Smith, USA	20.16
400m	Thomas Schonlebe, E.Ger.	44.33
800m	Billy Konchellah, Kenya	1:43.06
1500m	Abdi Bile, Somalia	3:36.80
5000m	Said Aouita, Morocco	13:26.44
10,000m	Paul Kipkoech, Kenya	27:38.63
Marathon	Douglas Wakiihuri, Kenya	2:11:48

Hurdles

Event	Champion	Time
110m	Greg Foster, USA	13.21
400m	Edwin Moses, USA	47.46

Steeplechase

Event	Champion	Time
3,000m	Francesco Panetta, Italy	8:08.57

Walking

Event	Champion	Time
20 km	Maurizio Damilano, Italy	1:20:45
50 km	Hartwig Gauder, E.Ger.	3:40:53

Relays

Event	Champion	Time
4x100m	United States	37.90
4x400m	United States	2:57.29

Field Events

Event	Champion	Distance
High Jump	Patrik Sjoberg, Sweden	7- 9¾
Pole Vault	Sergei Bubka, USSR	19- 2¼
Long Jump	Carl Lewis, USA	28- 5¼
Triple Jump	Khristo Markov, Bulgaria	58- 9½
Shot Put	Werner Gunthor, Switz.	72-11¼
Discus	Juergen Schult, E.Germany	225- 6
Hammer	Sergei Litvinov, USSR	272- 6
Javelin	Seppo Raty, Finland	274- 1

Decathlon

Champion	Points
Torsten Voss, E.Germany	8680

WOMEN

Helsinki, 1983

Running

Event	Champion	Time
100m	Marlies Gohr, E.Germany	10.97
200m	Marita Koch, E.Germany	22.13
400m	Jarmila Kratochvilova, Czech.	47.99
800m	Jarmila Kratochvilova, Czech.	1:54.68
1500m	Mary Decker, USA	4:00.90
3000m	Mary Decker, USA	8:34.62
10,000m	Not held	
Marathon	Grete Waitz, Norway	2:28:09

Hurdles

Event	Champion	Time
100m	Bettina Jahn, E.Germany	12.35
400m	Yekaterina Fesenko, USSR	54.14

Rome, 1987

Running

Event	Champion	Time
100m	Silke Gladisch, E.Germany	10.90
200m	Silke Gladisch, E.Germany	21.74
400m	Olga Bryzgina, USSR	49.38
800m	Sigrun Wodars, E.Germany	1:55.26
1500m	Tatyana Samolenko, USSR	3:58.56
3000m	Tatyana Samolenko, USSR	8:38.73
10,000m	Ingrid Kristiansen, Norway	31:05.85
Marathon	Rosa Mota, Portugal	2:25.17

Hurdles

Event	Champion	Time
100m	Ginka Zagorcheva, Bulgaria	12.34
400m	Sabine Busch, E.Germany	53.62

World Track & Field Championships (Cont.)
WOMEN

Helsinki, 1983
Walking

Event	Champion
10 km	Not held

Relays

Event	Champion	Time
4x100m	East Germany	41.76
4x400m	East Germany	3:19.73

Field Events

Event	Champion	Distance
High Jump	Tamara Bykova, USSR	6- 7
Long Jump	Heike Daute, E.Germany	23-10¼
Shot Put	Helena Fibingerova, Czech.	69- 0¾
Discus	Martina Opitz, E.Germany	226- 2
Javelin	Tiina Lillak, Finland	232- 4

Heptathlon

Champion	Points
Ramona Neubert, E.Germany	6770

Rome, 1987
Walking

Event	Champion	Time
10 km	Irina Strakhova, USSR	44:12

Relays

Event	Champion	Time
4x100m	United States	41.58
4x400m	East Germany	3:18.63

Field Events

Event	Champion	Distance
High Jump	Stefka Kostadinova, Bul.	6-10¼
Long Jump	Jackie Joyner-Kersee, USA	24- 1¾
Shot Put	Natalya Lisovskaya, USSR	69- 8¼
Discus	Martina O.Hellman, E.Ger.	235- 0
Javelin	Fatima Whitbread, Britain	251- 5

Heptathlon

Champion	Points
Jackie Joyner-Kersee, USA	7128

Boston Marathon

America's oldest regularly contested foot race, the Boston Marathon is held on Patriots' Day every April. It has been run at four different distances: 24 miles, 1232 yards (1897-1923); 26 miles, 209 yards (1924-26); 26 miles, 385 yards (1927-52); 25 miles, 958 yards (1953-56); and 26 miles, 385 yards (since 1957).

Multiple winners: Clarence DeMar (7); Gerard Cote and Bill Rodgers (4); Tarzan Brown, Jim Caffery, John A. Kelley, John Miles, Eino Oksanen, Leslie Pawson, Geoff Smith and Aurele Vandendriessche (2).

MEN

Year	Time	Year	Time
1897 John McDermott, New York	2:55:10	1932 Paul deBruyn, Germany	2:33:36
1898 Ronald McDonald, Massachusetts	2:42:00	1933 Leslie Pawson, Rhode Island	2:31:01
1899 Lawrence Brignolia, Massachusetts	2:54:38	1934 Dave Komonen, Canada	2:32:53
		1935 John A. Kelley, Massachusetts	2:32:07
1900 Jim Caffrey, Canada	2:39:44	1936 Ellison Brown, Rhode Island	2:33:40
1901 Jim Caffrey, Canada	2:29:23	1937 Walter Young, Canada	2:33:20
1902 Sam Mellor, New York	2:43:12	1938 Leslie Pawson, Rhode Island	2:35:34
1903 J.C. Lorden, Massachusetts	2:41:29	1939 Ellison (Tarzan) Brown, Rhode Is	2:28:51
1904 Mike Spring, New York	2:38:04		
1905 Fred Lorz, New York	2:38:25	1940 Gerard Cote, Canada	2:28:28
1906 Tim Ford, Massachusetts	2:45:45	1941 Leslie Pawson, Rhode Island	2:30:38
1907 Tom Longboat, Canada	2:24:24	1942 Joe Smith, Massachusetts	2:26:51
1908 Tom Morrissey, New York	2:25:43	1943 Gerard Cote, Canada	2:28:25
1909 Henri Renaud, New Hampshire	2:53:36	1944 Gerard Cote, Canada	2:31:50
		1945 John A.Kelley, Massachusetts	2:30:40
1910 Fred Cameron, Nova Scotia	2:28:52	1946 Stylianos Kyriakides, Greece	2:29:27
1911 Clarence DeMar, Massachusetts	2:21:39	1947 Yun Bok Suh, Korea	2:25:39
1912 Mike Ryan, Illinois	2:21:18	1948 Gerard Cote, Canada	2:31:02
1913 Fritz Carlson, Minnesota	2:25:14	1949 Karle Leandersson, Sweden	2:31:50
1914 James Duffy, Canada	2:25:01		
1915 Edouard Fabre, Canada	2:31:41	1950 Kee Yonh Ham, Korea	2:32:39
1916 Arthur Roth, Massachusetts	2:27:16	1951 Shigeki Tanaka, Japan	2:27:45
1917 Bill Kennedy, New York	2:28:37	1952 Doroteo Flores, Guatemala	2:31:53
1918 World War relay race		1953 Keizo Yamada, Japan	2:18:51
1919 Carl Linder, Massachusetts	2:29:13	1954 Veiko Karvonen, Finland	2:20:39
		1955 Hideo Hamamura, Japan	2:18:22
1920 Peter Trivoulidas, New York	2:29:31	1956 Antti Viskari, Finland	2:14:14
1921 Frank Zuna, New Jersey	2:18:57	1957 John J.Kelley, Connecticut	2:20:05
1922 Clarence DeMar, Massachusetts	2:18:10	1958 Franjo Mihalic, Yugoslavia	2:25:54
1923 Clarence DeMar, Massachusetts	2:23:37	1959 Eino Oksanen, Finland	2:22:42
1924 Clarence DeMar, Massachusetts	2:29:40		
1925 Charles Mellor, Illinois	2:33:00	1960 Paavo Kotila, Finland	2:20:54
1926 John Miles, Nova Scotia	2:25:40	1961 Eino Oksanen, Finland	2:23:39
1927 Clarence DeMar, Massachusetts	2:40:22	1962 Eino Oksanen, Finland	2:23:48
1928 Clarence DeMar, Massachusetts	2:37:07	1963 Aurele Vandendriessche, Belgium	2:18:58
1929 John Miles, Nova Scotia	2:33:08	1964 Aurele Vandendriessche, Belgium	2:19:59
		1965 Morio Shigematsu, Japan	2:16:33
1930 Clarence DeMar, Massachusetts	2:34:48	1966 Kenji Kimihara, Japan	2:17:11
1931 James Henigan, Massachusetts	2:46:45		

Year	Time	Year	Time
1967 David McKenzie, New Zealand	2:15:45	1980 Bill Rodgers, Massachusetts	2:12:11
1968 Amby Burfoot, Connecticut	2:22:17	1981 Toshihiko Seko, Japan	2:09:26
1969 Yoshiaki Unetani, Japan	2:13:49	1982 Alberto Salazar, Massachusetts	2:08:52
		1983 Greg Meyer, New Jersey	2:09:00
1970 Ron Hill, England	2:10:30	1984 Geoff Smith, England	2:10:34
1971 Alvaro Mejia, Colombia	2:18:45	1985 Geoff Smith, England	2:14:05
1972 Olavi Suomalainen, Finland	2:15:39	1986 Rob de Castella, Australia	2:07:51*
1973 Jon Anderson, Oregon	2:16:03	1987 Toshihiko Seko, Japan	2:11:50
1974 Neil Cusack, Ireland	2:13:39	1988 Ibrahim Hussein, Kenya	2:08:43
1975 Bill Rodgers, Massacusetts	2:09:55	1989 Abebe Mekonnen, Ethiopia	2:09:06
1976 Jack Fultz, Pennsylvania	2:20:19		
1977 Jerome Drayton, Canada	2:14:46	1990 Gelindo Bordin, Italy	2:08:19
1978 Bill Rodgers, Massachusetts	2:10:13		
1979 Bill Rodgers, Massachusetts	2:09:27		

*Record for distance.

WOMEN

Year	Time	Year	Time
1972 Nina Kuscsik, New York	3:08:58	1982 Charlotte Teske, West Germany	2:29:33
1973 Jacqueline Hansen, California	3:05:59	1983 Joan Benoit, Maine	2:22:43*
1974 Miki Gorman, California	2:47:11	1984 Lorraine Moller, New Zealand	2:29:28
1975 Liane Winter, West Germany	2:42:24	1985 Lisa Larsen Weidenbach, Mass	2:34:06
1976 Kim Merritt, Wisconsin	2:47:10	1986 Ingrid Kristiansen, Norway	2:24:55
1977 Miki Gorman, California	2:48:33	1987 Rosa Mota, Portugal	2:25:21
1978 Gayle Barron, Georgia	2:44:52	1988 Rosa Mota, Portugal	2:24:30
1979 Joan Benoit, Maine	2:35:15	1989 Ingrid Kristiansen, Norway	2:24:33
1980 Jacqueline Gareau, Canada	2:34:28	1990 Rosa Mota, Portugal	2:25:23
1981 Allison Roe, New Zealand	2:26:46		

*Record for distance.

New York City Marathon

Started in 1970, the New York City Marathon is run in the fall, through all of the city's five boroughs and finishes in Central Park.

Multiple winners: MEN—Bill Rodgers (4); Alberto Salazar (3); Tom Fleming and Orlando Pizzolato (2). WOMEN: Greta Waitz (9); Miki Gorman and Nina Kuscsik (2).

MEN / WOMEN

Year	Time	Year	Time
1970 Gary Muhrcke, USA	2:31:38	1970 No Finisher	
1971 Norman Higgins, USA	2:22:54	1971 Beth Bonner, USA	2:55:22
1972 Sheldon Karlin, USA	2:27:52	1972 Nina Kuscsik, USA	3:08:41
1973 Tom Fleming, USA	2:21:54	1973 Nina Kuscsik, USA	2:57:07
1974 Norbert Sander, USA	2:26:30	1974 Katherine Switzer, USA	3:07:29
1975 Tom Fleming, USA	2:19:27	1975 Kim Merritt, USA	2:46:14
1976 Bill Rodgers, USA	2:10:09	1976 Miki Gorman, USA	2:39:11
1977 Bill Rodgers, USA	2:11:28	1977 Miki Gorman, USA	2:43:10
1978 Bill Rodgers, USA	2:12:12	1978 Greta Waitz, Norway	2:32:30
1979 Bill Rodgers, USA	2:11:42	1979 Greta Waitz, Norway	2:27:33
1980 Alberto Salazar, USA	2:09:41	1980 Greta Waitz, Norway	2:25:41
1981 Alberto Salazar, USA	2:08:13	1981 Allison Roe, New Zealand	2:25:29
1982 Alberto Salazar, USA	2:09:29	1982 Greta Waitz, Norway	2:27:14
1983 Rod Dixon, New Zealand	2:08:59	1983 Greta Waitz, Norway	2:27:00
1984 Orlando Pizzolato, Italy	2:14:53	1984 Greta Waitz, Norway	2:29:30
1985 Orlando Pizzolato, Italy	2:11:34	1985 Greta Waitz, Norway	2:28:34
1986 Gianni Poli, Italy	2:11:06	1986 Greta Waitz, Norway	2:28:06
1987 Ibrahim Hussein, Kenya	2:11:01	1987 Priscilla Welch, Britain	2:30:17
1988 Steve Jones, Wales	2:08:20	1988 Greta Waitz, Norway	2:28:07
1989 Juma Ikangaa, Tanzania	2:08:01	1989 Ingrid Kristiansen, Norway	2:25:30

Cycling

1990 Tour de France

78th Tour de France (June 30-July 22); 27 stages covering 2121 miles; 198 rides. **Winning time**—90 hours, 443 mintues, 20 seconds. **Total purse**—$1,600,000; winner's share—$360,000.

	Behind		Behind
1 Greg LeMond, USA	—	7 Gianni Bugno, Italy	9:39
2 Claudio Chiappucci, Italy	2:16	8 Raul Alcala, Mexico	11:14
3 Eric Breukink, Holland	2:29	9 Claude Criquielion, Belgium	12:04
4 Pedro Delgado, Spain	5:01	10 Miguel Indurain, Spain	12:47
5 Marino Lejarrota, Spain	5:50	11 Andy Hampsten, USA	12:54
6 Eduardo Chozao, Spain	9:14		

Tour de France, 1903-90

The world's premier cycling event, the Tour de France is staged throughout the country (sometimes passing through neighboring countries) over four weeks. The 1946 Tour, however, the first after World War II, was only a five-day race.

Multiple winners: Jacques Anquetil, Bernard Hinault and Eddy Merckx (5); Louison Bobet, Gred LeMond and Philippe Thys (3); Gino Bertali, Ottavio Bottecchia, Gausto Coppi, Laurent Fignon, Nicholas Frantz, Firmin Lambot, Andred Leducq, Sylvere Maes, Antonin Magne, Lucien Petit-Breton (2).

Year		Year		Year	
1903	Maurice Garin, France	1933	Georges Speicher, France	1963	Jacques Anquetil, France
1904	Henri Cornet, France	1934	Antonin Magne, France	1964	Jacques Anquetil, France
1905	Louis Trousselier, France	1935	Romain Maes, Belgium	1965	Felice Gimondi, Italy
1906	Rene Pottier, France	1936	Sylvere Maes, Belgium	1966	Lucien Aimar, France
1907	Lucien Petit-Breton, France	1937	Roger Lapebie, France	1967	Roger Pingeon, France
1908	Lucien Petit-Breton, France	1938	Gino Bartali, Italy	1968	Jan Janssen, Holland
1909	Francois Faber, Luxembourg	1939	Sylvere Maes, Belgium	1969	Eddy Merckx, Belgium
1910	Octave Lapize, France	1940	Not held	1970	Eddy Merckx, Belgium
1911	Gustave Garrigou, France	1941	Not held	1971	Eddy Merckx, Belgium
1912	Odile Defraye, Belgium	1942	Not held	1972	Eddy Merckx, Belgium
1913	Philippe Thys, Belgium	1943	Not held	1973	Luis Ocana, Spain
1914	Philippe Thys, Belgium	1944	Not held	1974	Eddy Merckx, Belgium
1915	Not held	1945	Not held	1975	Bernard Thevenet, France
1916	Not held	1946	Jean Lazarides, France*	1976	Lucien van Impe, Belgium
1917	Not held	1947	Jean Robic, France	1977	Bernard Thevenet, France
1918	Not held	1948	Gino Bartali, Italy	1978	Bernard Hinault, France
1919	Firmin Lambot, Belgium	1949	Fausto Coppi, Italy	1979	Bernard Hinault, France
1920	Philippe Thys, Belgium	1950	Ferdinand Kubler, Switz.	1980	Joop Zoetemilk, Holland
1921	Leon Scieur, Belgium	1951	Hugo Koblet, Switzerland	1981	Bernard Hinault, France
1922	Firmin Lambot, Belgium	1952	Fausto Coppi, Italy	1982	Bernard Hinault, France
1923	Henri Pelissier, France	1953	Louison Bobet, France	1983	Laurent Fignon, France
1924	Ottavio Bottecchia, Italy	1954	Louison Bobet, France	1984	Laurent Fignon, France
1925	Ottavio Bottecchia, Italy	1955	Louison Bobet, France	1985	Bernard Hinault, France
1926	Lucien Buysse, Belgium	1956	Roger Walkowiak, France	1986	Greg LeMond, USA
1927	Nicholas Frantz, Lux'bourg	1957	Jacques Anquetil, France	1987	Stephen Roche, Ireland
1928	Nicholas Frantz, Lux'bourg	1958	Charly Gaul, Luxembourg	1988	Pedro Delgado, Spain
1929	Maurice Dewaele, Belgium	1959	Federico Bahamontes, Spain	1989	Greg LeMond, USA
1930	Andre Leducq, France	1960	Gastone Nencini, Italy	1990	Greg LeMond, USA
1931	Antonin Magne, France	1961	Jacques Anquetil, France		
1932	Andre Leducq, France	1962	Jacques Anquetil, France		

*The Tour de France was only a 5-day race in 1946.

Alpine Skiing
World Cup Champions, 1967-90

World Cup Overall Champions (downhill and slalom events combined) since the tour was organized in 1967.

Multiple winners: MEN—Gustavo Thoeni and Pirmin Zurbriggen (4); Marc Girardelli, Phil Mahre and Ingemar Stenmark (3); Jean Claude Killy, Karl Schranz (2). WOMEN—Annemarie Moser-Proell (6); Nancy Greene, Erica Hess, Michela Figini, Maria Walliser and Hanni Wenzel (2).

MEN

Year		Year		Year	
1967	Jean-Claude Killy, France	1975	Gustavo Thoeni, Italy	1983	Phil Mahre, USA
1968	Jean Claude Killy, France	1976	Ingemar Stenmark, Sweden	1984	Pirmin Zurbriggen, Switz.
1969	Karl Schranz, Austria	1977	Ingemar Stenmark, Sweden	1985	Marc Girardelli, Lux'bourg
		1978	Ingemar Stenmark, Sweden	1986	Marc Girardelli, Lux'bourg
1970	Karl Schranz, Austria	1979	Peter Luescher, Switz.	1987	Pirmin Zurbriggen, Switz.
1971	Gustavo Thoeni, Italy			1988	Pirmin Zurbriggen, Switz.
1972	Gustavo Thoeni, Italy	1980	Andreas Wenzel, Lichten.	1989	Marc Girardelli, Lux'bourg
1973	Gustavo Thoeni, Italy	1981	Phil Mahre, USA		
1974	Piero Gros, Italy	1982	Phil Mahre, USA	1990	Pirmin Zurbriggen, Switz.

WOMEN

Year	Winner	Year	Winner	Year	Winner
1967	Nancy Greene, Canada	1975	Annemarie Moser-Proell, Aust.	1983	Tamara McKinney, USA
1968	Nancy Greene, Canada	1976	Rosi Mittermaier, W.Germany	1984	Erika Hess, Switzerland
1969	Gertrud Gabi, Austria	1977	Lise-Marie Morerod, Switz.	1985	Michela Figini, Switz.
		1978	Hanni Wenzel, Lichtenstein	1986	Maria Walliser, Switz.
1970	Michele Jacot, France	1979	Annemarie Moser-Proell, Aust.	1987	Maria Walliser, Switz.
1971	Annemarie Proell, Austria			1988	Michela Figini, Switz.
1972	Annemarie Proell, Austria	1980	Hanni Wenzel, Lichtenstein	1989	Vreni Schneider, Switz.
1973	Annemarie Proell, Austria	1981	Marie-Theres Nadig, Switz.		
1974	Annemarie Proell, Austria	1982	Erika Hess, Switzerland	1990	Petra Kronberger, Austria

Figure Skating

MEN

World Champions

Skaters who won world and Olympic championships in the same year are listed in **bold** type.
Multiple winners: Ulrich Salchow (10); Karl Schafer (7); Dick Button (5); Wily Bockl, Scott Hamilton and Hayes Jenkins (4); Emmerich Danzor, Gillis Grafstrom, Gustav Hugel, David Jenkins, Fritz Kachler and Ondrej Nepela (3); Brian Boitano, Kurt Browning, Gilbert Fuchs, Jan Hoffmann, Felix Kaspar, Vladimir Kovalev and Tim Wood (2).

Year	Year	Year
1896 Gilbert Fuchs, Germany	1930 Karl Schafer, Austria	1963 Donald McPherson, Canada
1897 Gustav Hugel, Austria	1931 Karl Schafer, Austria	1964 **Manfred Schneldorfer**,W.Ger
1898 Henning Grenander, Sweden	1932 **Karl Schafer**, Austria	1965 Alain Calmat, France
1899 Gustav Hugel, Austria	1933 Karl Schafer, Austria	1966 Emmerich Danzer, Austria
1900 Gustav Hugel, Austria	1934 Karl Schafer, Austria	1967 Emmerich Danzer, Austria
1901 Ulrich Salchow, Sweden	1935 Karl Schafer, Austria	1968 Emmerich Danzer, Austria
1902 Ulrich Salchow, Sweden	1936 **Karl Schafer**, Austria	1969 Tim Wood, USA
1903 Ulrich Salchow, Sweden	1937 Felix Kaspar, Austria	
1904 Ulrich Salchow, Sweden	1938 Felix Kaspar, Austria	1970 Tim Wood, USA
1905 Ulrich Salchow, Sweden	1939 Graham Sharp, Britain	1971 Ondrej Nepela, Czech.
1906 Gilbert Fuchs, Germany		1972 **Ondrej Nepela**, Czech.
1907 Ulrich Salchow, Sweden	1940-46 Not held	1973 Ondrej Nepela, Czech.
1908 **Ulrich Salchow**, Sweden	1947 Hans Gerschwiler, Switz.	1974 Jan Hoffmann, E.Germany
1909 Ulrich Salchow, Sweden	1948 **Dick Button**, USA	1975 Sergie Volkov, USSR
1910 Ulrich Salchow, Sweden	1949 Dick Button, USA	1976 **John Curry**, Britain
1911 Ulrich Salchow, Sweden	1950 Dick Button, USA	1977 Vladimir Kovalev, USSR
1912 Fritz Kachler, Austria	1951 Dick Button, USA	1978 Charles Tickner, USA
1913 Fritz Kachler, Austria	1952 **Dick Button**, USA	1979 Vladimir Kovalev, USSR
1914 Gosta Sandhal, Sweden	1953 Hayes Jenkins, USA	
1915-21 Not held	1954 Hayes Jenkins, USA	1980 Jan Hoffmann, E.Germany
1922 Gillis Grafstrom, Sweden	1955 Hayes Jenkins, USA	1981 Scott Hamilton, USA
1923 Fritz Kachler, Austria	1956 **Hayes Jenkins**, USA	1982 Scott Hamilton, USA
1924 **Gillis Grafstrom**, Sweden	1957 David Jenkins, USA	1983 Scott Hamilton, USA
1925 Willy Bockl, Austria	1958 David Jenkins, USA	1984 **Scott Hamilton**, USA
1926 Willy Bockl, Austria	1959 David Jenkins, USA	1985 Alexander Fadeev, USSR
1927 Willy Bockl, Austria		1986 Brian Boitano, USA
1928 Willy Bockl, Austria	1960 Alan Giletti, France	1987 Brian Orser, Canada
1929 Gillis Grafstrom, Sweden	1961 Not Held	1988 **Brian Boitano**, USA
	1962 Donald Jackson, Canada	1989 Kurt Browning, Canada
		1990 Kurt Browning, Canada

U.S. Champions

Skaters who won U.S., world and Olympic championships in same year are in **bold type**.
Multiple winners: Dick Button and Roger Turner (7); Sherwin Badger, Robin Lee (5); Brian Boitano, Scott Hamilton, David Jenkins, Hayes Jenkins and Charles Tickner (4); Gordon McKellen, Nathaniel Niles and Tim Wood (3); Scott Allen, Eugene Turner and Gary Visconti (2).

Year	Year	Year
1914 Norman Scott	1940 Eugene Turner	1965 Gary Visconti
1915 Not held	1941 Eugene Turner	1966 Scott Allen
1916 Not held	1942 Robert Specht	1967 Gary Visconti
1917 Not held	1943 Arthur Vaughn	1968 Tim Wood
1918 Nathaniel Niles	1944 Not held	1969 Tim Wood
1919 Not held	1945 Not held	
	1946 Dick Button	1970 Tim Wood
1920 Sherwin Badger	1947 Dick Button	1971 John (Misha) Petkevich
1921 Sherwin Badger	1948 Dick Button	1972 Ken Shelley
1922 Sherwin Badger	1949 Dick Button	1973 Gordon McKellen
1923 Sherwin Badger		1974 Gordon McKellen
1924 Sherwin Badger	1950 Dick Button	1975 Gordon McKellen
1925 Nathaniel Niles	1951 Dick Button	1976 Terry Kubicka
1926 Chris Christenson	1952 Dick Button	1977 Charles Tickner
1927 Nathaniel Niles	1953 Hayes Jenkins	1978 Charles Tickner
1928 Roger Turner	1954 Hayes Jenkins	1979 Charles Tickner
1929 Roger Turner	1955 Hayes Jenkins	
	1956 Hayes Jenkins	1980 Charles Tickner
1930 Roger Turner	1957 David Jenkins	1981 Scott Hamilton
1931 Roger Turner	1958 David Jenkins	1982 Scott Hamilton
1932 Roger Turner	1959 David Jenkins	1983 Scott Hamilton
1933 Roger Turner		1984 Scott Hamilton
1934 Roger Turner	1960 David Jenkins	1985 Brian Boitano
1935 Robin Lee	1961 Bradley Lord	1986 Brian Boitano
1936 Robin Lee	1962 Monty Hoyt	1987 Brian Boitano
1937 Robin Lee	1963 Thomas Litz	1988 Brian Boitano
1938 Robin Lee	1964 Scott Allen	1989 Christopher Bowman
1939 Robin Lee		
		1990 Todd Eldredge

Figure Skating (Cont.)

WOMEN
World Champions

Skaters who won World and Olympic championships in the same year are listed in **bold** type.
Multiple winners: Sonja Henie (10); Carol Heiss and Herma Planck Szabo (5); Lily Kronberger and Katarina Witt (4); Sjoukje Dijkstra, Peggy Fleming, Meray Horvath (3); Tenley Albright, Linda Fratianne, Anett Poetzsch, Beatrix Schuba, Barbara Ann Scott, Gabriele Seyfert, Megan Taylor and Alena Vrzanova (2).

Year	Year	Year
1906 Madge Syers, Britain	1934 Sonja Henie, Norway	1962 Sjoukje Dijkstra, Holland
1907 Madge Syers, Britian	1935 Sonja Henie, Norway	1963 Sjoukje Dijkstra, Holland
1908 Lily Kronberger, Hungary	1936 **Sonja Henie**, Norway	1964 **Sjoukje Dijkstra**, Holland
1909 Lily Kronberger, Hungary	1937 Cecilia Colledge, Britain	1965 Petra Burka, Canada
	1938 Megan Taylor, Britain	1966 Peggy Fleming, USA
1910 Lily Kronberger, Hungary	1939 Megan Taylor, Britain	1967 Peggy Fleming, USA
1911 Lily Kronberger, Hungary		1968 **Peggy Fleming**, USA
1912 Meray Horvath, Hungary	1940 Not held	1969 Gabriele Seyfert, E.Germany
1913 Meray Horvath, Hungary	1941 Not held	
1914 Meray Horvath, Hungary	1942 Not held	1970 Gabriele Seyfert, E.Germany
1915 Not held	1943 Not held	1971 Beatrix Schuba, Austria
1916 Not held	1944 Not held	1972 **Beatrix Schuba**, Austria
1917 Not held	1945 Not held	1973 Karen Magnussen, Canada
1918 Not held	1946 Not held	1974 Christine Errath, E.Germany
1919 Not held	1947 Barbara Ann Scott, Canada	1975 Dianne DeLeeuw, Holland
	1948 **Barbara Ann Scott**, Canada	1976 **Dorothy Hamill**, USA
1920 Not held	1949 Alena Vrzanova, Czech.	1977 Linda Fratianne, USA
1921 Not held		1978 Anett Poetzsch, E.Germany
1922 Herma Planck-Szabo, Austria	1950 Alena Vrzanova, Czech.	1979 Linda Fratianne, USA
1923 Herma Planck-Szabo, Austria	1951 Jeannette Altwegg, Britain	
1924 **Herma Planck-Szabo**, Austria	1952 Jacqueline Du Bief, France	1980 **Anett Poetzsch**, E.Germany
1925 Herma Planck-Szabo, Austria	1953 Tenley Albright, USA	1981 Denise Biellmann, Switz.
1926 Herma Planck-Szabo, Austria	1954 Gundi Busch, W.Germany	1982 Elaine Zayak, USA
1927 Sonja Henie, Norway	1955 Tenley Albright, USA	1983 Rosalyn Sumners, USA
1928 **Sonja Henie**, Norway	1956 Carol Heiss, USA	1984 **Katarina Witt**, E.Germany
1929 Sonja Henie, Norway	1957 Carol Heiss, USA	1985 Katarina Witt, E.Germany
	1958 Carol Heiss, USA	1986 Debi Thomas, USA
1930 Sonja Henie, Norway	1959 Carol Heiss, USA	1987 Katarina Witt, E.Germany
1931 Sonja Henie, Norway		1988 **Katarina Witt**, E.Germany
1932 **Sonja Henie**, Norway	1960 **Carol Heiss**, USA	1989 Midori Ito, Japan
1933 Sonja Henie, Norway	1961 Not Held	
		1990 Jill Trenary, USA

U.S. Champions

Year	Year	Year
1914 Theresa Weld	1940 Joan Tozzer	1965 Peggy Fleming
1915 Not held	1941 Jane Vaughn	1966 Peggy Fleming
1916 Not held	1942 Jane Sullivan	1967 Peggy Fleming
1917 Not held	1943 Gretchen Merrill	1968 **Peggy Fleming**
1918 Rosemary Beresford	1944 Gretchen Merrill	1969 Janet Lynn
1919 Not held	1945 Gretchen Merrill	
	1946 Gretchen Merrill	1970 Janet Lynn
1920 Theresa Weld	1947 Gretchen Merrill	1971 Janet Lynn
1921 Theresa W.Blanchard	1948 Gretchen Merrill	1972 Janet Lynn
1922 Theresa W.Blanchard	1949 Yvonne Sherman	1973 Janet Lynn
1923 Theresa W.Blanchard		1974 Dorothy Hamill
1924 Theresa W.Blanchard	1950 Yvonne Sherman	1975 Dorothy Hamill
1925 Beatrix Loughran	1951 Sonya Klopfer	1976 **Dorothy Hamill**
1926 Beatrix Loughran	1952 Tenley Albright	1977 Linda Fratianne
1927 Beatrix Loughran	1953 Tenley Albright	1978 Linda Fratianne
1928 Maribel Vinson	1954 Tenley Albright	1979 Linda Fratianne
1929 Maribel Vinson	1955 Tenley Albright	
	1956 Tenley Albright	1980 Linda Fratianne
1930 Maribel Vinson	1957 Carol Heiss	1981 Elaine Zayak
1931 Maribel Vinson	1958 Carol Heiss	1982 Rosalyn Sumners
1932 Maribel Vinson	1959 Carol Heiss	1983 Rosalyn Sumners
1933 Maribel Vinson		1984 Rosalyn Sumners
1934 Suzanne Davis	1960 **Carol Heiss**	1985 Tiffany Chin
1935 Maribel Vinson	1961 Laurence Owen	1986 Debi Thomas
1936 Maribel Vinson	1962 Barbara Pursley	1987 Jill Trenary
1937 Maribel Vinson	1963 Lorraine Hanlon	1988 Debi Thomas
1938 Joan Tozzer	1964 Peggy Fleming	1989 Jill Trenary
1939 Joan Tozzer		1990 Jill Trenary

Billy Payne, the president of the Atlanta Olympic Organizing Committee, celebrates with fellow Atlantans in Tokyo, Sept. 18, after the IOC's announcement that their city will host the 1996 Summer Games.

OLYMPICS

Modern Olympic Games

First held in Athens in 1896, the modern Olympic Games were an attempt by French educator Pierre de Coubertin and others to revive the Greek tradition of a regularly scheduled athletic festival and to promote international good will among the youth of the world.

The International Olympic Committee (IOC) expanded the Olympics in 1924 by adding the Winter Games for cold weather sports. Both the Summer and Winter Games have been held at four-year intervals except during the century's two world wars.

Summer Olympics

Year	No.	Location	Dates	Nations	Most Medals	USA Medals
1896	I	Athens, Greece	Apr 6-15	13	Greece (10-19-18—47)	11-7-1—19 (2nd)
1900	II	Paris, France	May 20-Oct 28	22	France (29-41-32—102)	21-16-16—53 (2nd)
1904	III	St.Louis, Missouri	July 1-Nov 23	12	USA (80-86-72—238)	same
1906	—	Athens, Greece	Apr 22-May 2	20	France (15-9-16—40)	12-6-5—23 (4th)
1908	IV	London, Great Britain	Apr 27-Oct 31	23	Britain (56-50-39—145)	23-12-13—48 (2nd)
1912	V	Stockholm, Sweden	May 5-Jul 22	28	Sweden (24-24-17—65)	25-18-19—62 (2nd)
1916	VI	Not held†				
1920	VII	Antwerp, Belgium	Apr 20-Sept 12	29	USA (41-27-27—95)	same
1924	VIII	Paris, France	May 4-July 27	44	USA (45-27-27—99)	same
1928	IX	Amsterdam, Holland	May 17-Aug 12	46	USA (22-18-16—56)	same
1932	X	Los Angeles, California	July 30-Aug 14	37	USA (41-32-31—104)	same
1936	XI	Berlin, Germany	Aug 1-16	49	Ger. (33-26-30—89)	24-20-12—56 (2nd)
1940	XII	Not held†				
1944	XIII	Not held†				
1948	XIV	London, Great Britain	July 29-Aug 14	59	USA (38-27-19—84)	same
1952	XV	Helsinki, Finland	July 19-Aug 3	69	USA (40-19-17—76)	same
1956	XVI	Melbourne, Australia‡	Nov 22-Dec 8	67	USSR (37-29-32—98)	32-25-17—74 (2nd)
1960	XVII	Rome, Italy	Aug 25-Sept 11	83	USSR (43-29-31—103)	34-21-16—71 (2nd)
1964	XVIII	Tokyo, Japan	Oct 10-24	93	USA (36-26-28—90)	same
1968	XIX	Mexico City, Mexico	Oct 12-17	112	USA (45-28-34—107)	same
1972	XX	Munich, West Germany	Aug 26-Sept 10	122	USSR (50-27-22—99)	33-31-30—94 (2nd)
1976	XXI	Montreal, Canada	July 17-Aug 1	92	USSR (49-41-35—125)	34-35-25—94 (3rd)
1980	XXII	Moscow, USSR	July 19-Aug 3	81	USSR* (80-69-46—195)	Did not compete
1984	XXIII	Los Angeles, California	July 28-Aug 12	144	USA* (83-61-30—174)	same
1988	XXIV	Seoul, South Korea	Sept 17-Oct 2	159	USSR (55-31-46—132)	36-31-27—94 (3rd)
1992	XXV	Barcelona, Spain	July 25-Aug 9			
1996	XXVI	Atlanta, Georgia	July 20-Aug 4			

†The 1916 Games were scheduled for Berlin; the 1940 Games for Tokyo; and the 1944 Games for London. All were cancelled due to world wars.
‡In 1956, the equestrian events were held in Stockholm, June 10-17.
*The USA was among 64 nations that boycotted the 1980 Summer Games in Moscow; while the USSR, East Germany and most eastern bloc countries stayed away from the 1984 Summer Games in Los Angeles.

Winter Olympics

Year	No.	Location	Dates	Nations	Most Medals	USA Medals
1924	I	Chamonix, France	Jan 25-Feb 4	16	Norway (4-7-6—17)	1-2-1—4 (4th)
1928	II	St.Moritz, Switzerland	Feb 11-19	25	Norway (6-4-5—15)	2-2-2—6 (2nd)
1932	III	Lake Placid, New York	Feb 4-15	17	USA (6-4-2—12)	same
1936	IV	Garmisch-Partenkirchen, Germany	Feb 6-16	28	Norway (7-5-3—15)	1-0-3—4 (T-5th)
1940	—	Not held†				
1944	—	Not held†				
1948	V	St.Moritz, Switzerland	Jan 30-Feb 8	28	Norway (4-3-3—10) Sweden (4-3-3—10) Switz. (3-4-3—10)	3-4-2—9 (4th)
1952	VI	Oslo, Norway	Feb 14-25	30	Norway (7-3-6—16)	4-6-1—11 (2nd)
1956	VII	Cortina d'Ampezzo, Italy	Jan 26-Feb 5	32	USSR (7-3-6—16)	2-3-2—7 (T-4th)
1960	VIII	Squaw Valley, California	Feb 18-28	30	USSR (7-5-9—21)	3-4-3—10 (2nd)
1964	IX	Innsbruck, Austria	Jan 29-Feb 9	36	USSR (11-8-6—25)	1-2-3—6 (7th)
1968	X	Grenoble, France	Feb 6-18	37	Norway (6-6-2—14)	1-5-1—7 (T-7th)
1972	XI	Sapporo, Japan	Feb 3-13	35	USSR (8-5-3—16)	3-2-3—8 (6th)
1976	XII	Innsbruck, Austria‡	Feb 4-15	37	USSR (13-6-8—27)	3-3-4—10 (T-3rd)
1980	XIII	Lake Placid, New York	Feb 14-23	37	USSR (10-6-6—22)	6-4-2—12 (3rd)
1984	XIV	Sarajevo, Yugoslavia	Feb 7-19	49	USSR (6-10-9—25)	4-4-0—8 (T-5th)
1988	XV	Calgary, Canada	Feb 13-28	57	USSR (11-9-9—29)	2-1-3—6 (T-8th)
1992	XVI	Albertville, France	Feb 8-23			
1994	XVII*	Lillehammer, Norway	Feb 12-27			

†The 1940 Winter Games were scheduled first for Sapporo (Japan was stripped of the Games in 1937 when the Sino-Japanese war broke out), then St.Moritz (the Swiss felt ski instructors should not be considered professionals, the IOC disagreed), then finally Garmisch-Partenkirchen. The 1944 Games were scheduled for Cortina d'Ampezzo. Both were cancelled due to World War II.
‡The IOC originally granted the 1976 Winter games to Denver, but in 1972 Colorado voters rejected a $5 million bond issue to finance the undertaking. Denver immediately withdrew as host and the IOC designated Innsbruck, the site of the 1964 Games.
*Starting in 1994, the Winter Games will no longer be held in the same year as the Summer Games, but rather two years before.

SUMMER OLYMPICS
S T A T I S T I C S

THROUGH THE YEARS
1896-1988
GOLD MEDAL WINNERS

THE 1991 INFORMATION PLEASE SPORTS ALMANAC

SEC A

PAGE 493

Summer Games, 1896-1988

Gold medal winners in the following events: basketball, boxing, diving, field hockey, gymnastics, soccer, swimming, tennis, track & field, volleyball, water polo, freestyle wrestling and yachting.

Basketball

MEN

Year	Champion, 2nd, 3rd	Year	Champion, 2nd, 3rd
1936	**United States**, Canada, Mexico	1968	**United States**, Yugoslavia, Soviet Union
1948	**United States**, France, Brazil	1972	**Soviet Union**, United States, Cuba
1952	**United States**, Soviet Union, Uruguay	1976	**United States**, Yugoslavia, Soviet Union
1956	**United States**, Soviet Union, Uruguay	1980	**Yugoslavia**, Italy, Soviet Union
1960	**United States**, Soviet Union, Brazil	1984	**United States**, Spain, Yugoslavia
1964	**United States**, Soviet Union, Brazil	1988	**Soviet Union**, Yugoslavia, United States

WOMEN

Year	Champion, 2nd, 3rd	Year	Champion, 2nd, 3rd
1976	**Soviet Union**, United States, Bulgaria	1984	**United States**, South Korea, China
1980	**Soviet Union**, Bulgaria, Yugoslavia	1988	**United States**, Yugoslavia, Soviet Union

Boxing

Light Flyweight (106 lbs)

Year	Champion	Final Match	Year	Champion	Final Match
1968	Francisco Rodriguez, VEN	Decision, 3-2	1980	Shamil Sabyrov, USSR	Decision, 3-2
1972	György Gedó, HUN	Decision, 5-0	1984	Paul Gonzales, USA	Default
1976	Jorge Hernandez, CUB	Decision, 4-1	1988	Ivailo Hristov, BUL	Decision, 5-0

Flyweight (112 lbs)

Year	Champion	Final Match	Year	Champion	Final Match
1904	George Finnegan, USA	Stopped, 1st	1960	Gyula Török, HUN	Decision, 3-2
1920	Frank DiGennara, USA	Decision	1964	Fernando Atzori, ITA	Decision, 4-1
1924	Fidel LaBarba, USA	Decision	1968	Ricardo Delgado, MEX	Decision, 5-0
1928	Antal Kocsis, HUN	Decision	1972	Georgi Kostadinov, BUL	Decision, 5-0
1932	István Énekes, HUN	Decision	1976	Leo Randolph, USA	Decision, 3-2
1936	Willi Kaiser, GER	Decision	1980	Peter Lessov, BUL	Stopped, 2nd
1948	Pascual Perez, ARG	Decision	1984	Steven McCrory, USA	Decision, 4-1
1952	Nathan Brooks, USA	Decision, 3-0	1988	Kim Swang-Sun, KOR	Decision, 4-1
1956	Terence Spinks, GBR	Decision			

Bantamweight (119 lbs)

Year	Champion	Final Match	Year	Champion	Final Match
1904	Oliver Kirk, USA	Stopped, 3rd	1956	Wolfgange Behrendt, E.Ger	Decision
1908	A. Henry Thomas, GBR	Decision	1960	Oleg Grigoryev, USSR	Decision
1920	Clarence Walker, SAF	Decision	1964	Takao Sakurai, JPN	Stopped, 2nd
1924	William Smith, SAF	Decision	1968	Valery Sokolov, USSR	Stopped, 2nd
1928	Vittorio Tamagnini, ITA	Decision	1972	Orlando Martinez, CUB	Decision, 5-0
1932	Horace Gwynne, CAN	Decision	1976	Yong-Jo Gu, PRK	Decision, 5-0
1936	Ulderico Sergo, ITA	Decision	1980	Juan Hernandez, CUB	Decision, 5-0
1948	Tibor Csik, HUN	Decision	1984	Maurizio Stecca, ITA	Decision, 4-1
1952	Pentti Hämäläinen, FIN	Decision, 2-1	1988	Kennedy McKinney, USA	Decision, 5-0

Featherweight (125 lbs)

Year	Champion	Final Match	Year	Champion	Final Match
1904	Oliver Kirk, USA	Decision	1956	Vladimir Safronov, USSR	Decision
1908	Richard Gunn, GBR	Decision	1960	Francesco Musso, ITA	Decision, 4-1
1920	Paul Fritsch, FRA	Decision	1964	Stanislav Stepashkin, USSR	Decision, 3-2
1924	John Fields, USA	Decision	1968	Antonio Roldan, MEX	Won on Disq.
1928	Lambertus van Klaveren, HOL	Decision	1972	Boris Kousnetsov, USSR	Decision, 3-2
1932	Carmelo Robledo, ARG	Decision	1976	Angel Herrera, CUB	KO, 2nd
1936	Oscar Casanovas, ARG	Decision	1980	Rudi Fink, E.Ger	Decision, 4-1
1948	Ernesto Formenti, ITA	Decision	1984	Meldrick Taylor, USA	Decision, 5-0
1952	Jan Zachara, CZE	Decision, 2-1	1988	Giovanni Parisi, ITA	Stopped, 1st

Boxing (Cont.)

Lightweight (132 lbs)

Year	Champion	Final Match	Year	Champion	Final Match
1904	Harry Spanger, USA	Decision	1956	Richard McTaggart, GBR	Decision
1908	Frederick Grace, GBR	Decision	1960	Kazimierz Pazdzior, POL	Decision, 4-1
1920	Samuel Mosberg, USA	Decision	1964	Józef Grudzień, POL	Decision
1924	Hans Nielsen, DEN	Decision	1968	Ronnie Harris, USA	Decision, 5-0
1928	Carlo Orlandi, ITA	Decision	1972	Jan Szczepański, POL	Decision, 5-0
1932	Lawrence Stevens, SAF	Decision	1976	Howard Davis, USA	Decision, 5-0
1936	Imre Harangi, HUN	Decision	1980	Angel Herrera, CUB	Stopped, 3rd
1948	Gerald Dreyer, SAF	Decision	1984	Pernell Whitaker, USA	Foe quit, 2nd
1952	Aureliano Bolognesi, ITA	Decision, 2-1	1988	Andreas Zuelow, E.Ger	Decision, 5-0

Light Welterweight (139 lbs)

Year	Champion	Final Match	Year	Champion	Final Match
1952	Charles Adkins, USA	Decision, 2-1	1972	Ray Seales, USA	Decision, 3-2
1956	Vladimir Yengibaryan, USSR	Decision	1976	Ray Leonard, USA	Decision, 5-0
1960	Bohumil Nemeček CZE	Decision, 5-0	1980	Patrizio Oliva, ITA	Decision, 4-1
1964	Jerzy Kulej, POL	Decision, 5-0	1984	Jerry Page, USA	Decision, 5-0
1968	Jerzy Kulej, POL	Decision, 3-2	1988	Viatcheslav Janovski, USSR	Decision, 5-0

Welterweight (147 lbs)

Year	Champion	Final Match	Year	Champion	Final Match
1904	Albert Young, USA	Decision	1960	Nino Benvenuti, ITA	Decision, 4-1
1920	Albert Schneider, CAN	Decision	1964	Marian Kasprzki, POL	Decision, 4-1
1924	Jean Delarge, BEL	Decision	1968	Manfred Wolke, E.Ger	Decision, 4-1
1928	Edward Morgan, NZE	Decision	1972	Emilio Correa, CUB	Decision, 5-0
1932	Edward Flynn, USA	Decision	1976	Jochen Bachfeld, E.Ger	Decision, 3-2
1936	Sten Suvio, FIN	Decision	1980	Andrés Aldama, CUB	Decision, 4-1
1948	Julius Torma, CZE	Decision	1984	Mark Breland, USA	Decision, 5-0
1952	Zygmunt Chychla, POL	Decision, 3-0	1988	Robert Wangila, KEN	Stopped, 2nd
1956	Nicolae Linca, ROM	Decision, 3-2			

Light Middleweight (156 lbs)

Year	Champion	Final Match	Year	Champion	Final Match
1952	László Papp, HUN	Decision, 3-0	1972	Dieter Kottysch, W.Ger	Decision, 3-2
1956	László Papp, HUN	Decision	1976	Jerzy Rybicki, POL	Decision, 5-0
1960	Skeeter McClure, USA	Decision, 4-1	1980	Armando Martinez, CUB	Decision, 4-1
1964	Boris Lagutin, USSR	Decision, 4-1	1984	Frank Tate, USA	Decision, 5-0
1968	Boris Lagutin, USSR	Decision, 5-0	1988	Park Si-Hun, KOR	Decision, 3-2

Middleweight (165 lbs)

Year	Champion	Final Match	Year	Champion	Final Match
1904	Charles Mayer, USA	Stopped, 3rd	1956	Gennady Schatkov, USSR	KO, 1st
1908	John Douglas, GBR	Decision	1960	Edward Crook, USA	Decision, 3-2
1920	Harry Mallin, GBR	Decision	1964	Valery Popenchenko, USSR	Stopped, 1st
1924	Harry Mallin, GBR	Decision	1968	Christopher Finnegan, GBR	Decision, 3-2
1928	Piero Toscani, ITA	Decision	1972	Vyacheslav Lemechev, USSR	KO, 1st
1932	Carmen Barth, USA	Decision	1976	Michael Spinks, USA	Stopped, 3rd
1936	Jean Despeaux, FRA	Decision	1980	José Gomez, CUB	Decision, 4-1
1948	László Papp, HUN	Decision	1984	Joon-Sup Shin, KOR	Decision, 3-2
1952	Floyd Patterson, USA	KO, 1st	1988	Henry Maske, E.Ger	Decision, 5-0

Light Heavyweight (178 lbs)

Year	Champion	Final Match	Year	Champion	Final Match
1920	Eddie Eagan, USA	Decision	1960	Cassius Clay, USA	Decision, 5-0
1924	Harry Mitchell, GBR	Decision	1964	Cosimo Pinto, ITA	Decision, 3-2
1928	Victor Avendaño, ARG	Decision	1968	Dan Poznyak, USSR	Default
1932	David Carstens, SAF	Decision	1972	Mate Parlov, YUG	Stopped, 2nd
1936	Roger Michelot, FRA	Decision	1976	Leon Spinks, USA	Stopped, 3rd
1948	George Hunter, SAF	Decision	1980	Slobodan Kacar, YUG	Decision, 4-1
1952	Norvel Lee, USA	Decision, 3-0	1984	Anton Josipović, YUG	Default
1956	James Boyd, USA	Decision	1988	Andrew Maynard, USA	Decision, 5-0

Heavyweight (200 lbs)

Year	Champion	Final Match	Year	Champion	Final Match
1984	Henry Tillman, USA	Decision, 5-0	1988	Ray Mercer, USA	Stopped, 1st

Super Heavyweight (Unlimited)

Year	Champion	Final Match	Year	Champion	Final Match
1904	Samuel Berger, USA	Decision	1956	Pete Rademacher, USA	Stopped, 1st
1908	Albert Oldham, GBR	KO, 1st	1960	Franco De Piccoli, ITA	KO, 1st
1920	Ronald Rawson, GBR	Decision	1964	Joe Frazier, USA	Decision, 3-2
1924	Otto von Porat, NOR	Decision	1968	George Foreman, USA	Stopped, 2nd
1928	Arturo Rodriguez Jurado, ARG	Stopped, 1st	1972	Teófilo Stevenson, CUB	Default
1932	Santiago Lovell, ARG	Decision	1976	Teófilo Stevenson, CUB	KO, 3rd
1936	Herbert Runge, GER	Decision	1980	Teófilo Stevenson, CUB	Decision, 4-1
1948	Rafael Iglesias, ARG	KO, 2nd	1984	Tyrell Biggs, USA	Decision, 4-1
1952	Ed Sanders, USA	Won on Disq.	1988	Lennox Lewis, CAN	Stopped, 2nd

Diving

MEN

Springboard

Year	Champion	Points	Year	Champion	Points
1908	Albert Zürner, W.Ger	85.5	1956	Bob Clotworthy, USA	159.56
1912	Paul Günther, W.Ger	79.23	1960	Gary Tobian, USA	170.00
1920	Louis Kuehn, USA	675.4	1964	Ken Sitzberger, USA	159.90
1924	Albert White, USA	696.4	1968	Bernie Wrightson, USA	170.15
1928	Pete DesJardins, USA	185.04	1972	Vladimir Vasin, USSR	594.09
1932	Michael Galitzen, USA	161.38	1976	Phil Boggs, USA	619.05
1936	Richard Degener, USA	163.57	1980	Aleksandr Portnov, USSR	905.025
1948	Bruce Harlan, USA	163.64	1984	Greg Louganis, USA	754.41
1952	David Browning, USA	205.29	1988	Greg Louganis, USA	730.80

Platform

Year	Champion	Points	Year	Champion	Points
1904	George Sheldon, USA	12.66	1952	Sammy Lee, USA	156.28
1906	Gottlob Walz, W.Ger	156.0	1956	Joaquin Capilla Perez, MEX	152.44
1908	Hjalmar Johansson, SWE	83.75	1960	Bob Webster, USA	165.56
1912	Erik Adlerz, SWE	73.94	1964	Bob Webster, USA	148.58
1920	Clarence Pinkston, USA	100.67	1968	Klaus Dibiasi, ITA	164.18
1924	Albert White, USA	97.46	1972	Klaus Dibiasi, ITA	504.12
1928	Pete DesJardins, USA	98.74	1976	Klaus Dibiasi, ITA	600.51
1932	Harold Smith, USA	124.80	1980	Falk Hoffmann, E.Ger	835.650
1936	Marshall Wayne, USA	113.58	1984	Greg Louganis, USA	710.91
1948	Sammy Lee, USA	130.05	1988	Greg Louganis, USA	638.61

WOMEN

Springboard

Year	Champion	Points	Year	Champion	Points
1920	Aileen Riggin, USA	539.9	1960	Ingrid Krämer, E.Ger	155.81
1924	Elizabeth Becker, USA	474.5	1964	Ingrid Engel-Krämer, E.Ger	145.00
1928	Helen Meany, USA	78.62	1968	Sue Gossick, USA	150.77
1932	Georgia Coleman, USA	87.52	1972	Micki King, USA	450.03
1936	Marjorie Gestring, USA	89.27	1976	Jennifer Chandler, USA	506.19
1948	Vicki Draves, USA	108.74	1980	Irina Kalinina, USSR	725.910
1952	Pat McCormick, USA	147.30	1984	Sylvie Bernier, CAN	530.70
1956	Pat McCormick, USA	142.36	1988	Gao Min, CHN	580.23

Platform

Year	Champion	Points	Year	Champion	Points
1912	Greta Johansson, SWE	39.9	1960	Ingrid Krämer, E.Ger	91.28
1920	Stefani Fryland-Clausen, DEN	34.6	1964	Lesley Bush, USA	99.80
1924	Caroline Smith, USA	33.2	1968	Melina Duchkova, CZE	109.59
1928	Elizabeth Becker Pinkston, USA	31.6	1972	Ulrika Knape, SWE	390.00
1932	Dorothy Poynton, USA	40.26	1976	Elena Vaytsekhovskaya, USSR	406.59
1936	Dorothy Poynton Hill, USA	33.93	1980	Martina Jäschke, E.Ger	596.250
1948	Vicki Draves, USA	68.87	1984	Zhou Jihong, CHN	435.51
1952	Pat McCormick, USA	79.37	1988	Xu Yanmei, CHN	445.20
1956	Pat McCormick, USA	84.85			

Field Hockey

MEN

Year	Champion, 2nd, 3rd
1908	**Great Britain**, Ireland, Scotland
1920	**Great Britain**, Denmark, Belgium
1928	**India**, Holland, Germany
1932	**India**, Japan, United States
1936	**India**, Germany, Holland
1948	**India**, Great Britain, Holland
1952	**India**, Holland, Great Britain
1956	**India**, Pakistan, Germany

Year	Champion, 2nd, 3rd
1960	**Pakistan**, India, Spain
1964	**India**, Pakistan, Australia
1968	**Pakistan**, Australia, India
1972	**West Germany**, Pakistan, India
1976	**New Zealand**, Australia, Pakistan
1980	**India**, Spain, Soviet Union
1984	**Pakistan**, West Germany, Great Britain
1988	**Great Britain**, West Germany, Holland

WOMEN

Year	Champion, 2nd, 3rd
1980	**Zimbabwe**, Czechoslovakia, Soviet Union
1984	**Holland**, West Germany, United States

Year	Champion, 2nd, 3rd
1988	**Australia**, South Korea, Holland

Gymnastics

MEN

All-Around

Year	Champion	Points
1900	Gustave Sandras, FRA	302
1904	Julius Lenhart, AUT	69.80
1906	Pierre Paysse, FRA	116
1908	Alberto Braglia, ITA	317.0
1912	Alberto Braglia, ITA	135.0
1920	Giorgio Zampori, ITA	88.35
1924	Leon Stukelj, YUG	110.340
1928	Georges Miez, SWI	247.500
1932	Romeo Neri, ITA	140.625
1936	Alfred Schwarzmann, GER	113.100

Year	Champion	Points
1948	Veikko Huhtanen, FIN	229.7
1952	Viktor Chukarin, USSR	115.7
1956	Viktor Chukarin, USSR	114.25
1960	Boris Shakhlin, USSR	115.95
1964	Yukio Endo, JPN	115.95
1968	Sawao Kato, JPN	115.9
1972	Sawao Kato, JPN	114.650
1976	Nikolai Andrianov, USSR	116.65
1980	Aleksandr Dityatin, USSR	118.65
1984	Koji Gushiken, JPN	118.7
1988	Vladimir Artemov, USSR	119.125

Horizontal Bar

Year	Champion	Points
1896	Hermann Weingartner, GER	—
1904	Anton Heida, USA & Edward Hennig, USA	40
1924	Leon Stukelj, YUG	19.73
1928	Georges Miez, SWI	19.17
1932	Dallas Bixler, USA	18.33
1936	Aleksanteri Saarvala, FIN	19.367
1948	Josef Stalder, SWI	19.85
1952	Jack Günthard, SWI	19.55
1956	Takashi Ono, JPN	19.60

Year	Champion	Points
1960	Takashi Ono, JPN	19.60
1964	Boris Shakhlin, USSR	19.625
1968	Akinori Nakayama, JPN	19.55
1972	Mitsuo Tsukahara, JPN	19.725
1976	Mitsuo Tsukahara, JPN	19.675
1980	Stoyan Deltchev, BUL	19.825
1984	Shinji Morisue, JPN	20.00
1988	Vladimir Artemov, USSR & Valeri Lioukine, USSR	19.900

Parallel Bars

Year	Champion	Points
1896	Alfred Flatow, GER	—
1904	George Eyser, USA	44
1924	August Güttinger, SWI	21.63
1928	Ladislav Vácha, CZE	18.83
1932	Romeo Neri, ITA	18.97
1936	Konrad Frey, GER	19.067
1948	Michael Reusch, SWI	19.75
1952	Hans Eugster, SWI	19.65
1956	Viktor Chukarin, USSR	19.20

Year	Champion	Points
1960	Boris Shakhlin, USSR	19.40
1964	Yukio Endo, JPN	19.675
1968	Akinori Nakayama, JPN	19.475
1972	Sawao Kato, JPN	19.475
1976	Sawao Kato, JPN	19.675
1980	Aleksandr Tkachyov, USSR	19.775
1984	Bart Conner, USA	19.95
1988	Vladimir Artemov, USSR	19.925

Vault

Year	Champion	Points
1896	Karl Schumann, GER	—
1904	George Eyser, USA & Anton Heida, USA	36
1924	Frank Kriz, USA	9.98
1928	Eugen Mack, SWI	9.58
1932	Savino Guglielmetti, ITA	18.03
1936	Alfred Schwarzmann, GER	19.20
1948	Paavo Aaltonen, FIN	19.55
1952	Viktor Chukarin, USSR	19.20

Year	Champion	Points
1956	Helmut Bantz, W.Ger	18.85
1960	Takashi Ono, JPN	19.35
1964	Haruhiro Yamashita, JPN	19.60
1968	Makhail Voronin, USSR	19.00
1972	Klaus Köste, E.Ger	18.85
1976	Nikolai Andrianov, USSR	19.45
1980	Nikolai Andrianov, USSR	19.825
1984	Lou Yun, CHN	19.95
1988	Lou Yun, CHN	19.875

Pommel Horse

Year	Champion	Points	Year	Champion	Points
1896	Jules Zutter, SWI	—	1960	Eugen Ekman, FIN	19.375
1904	Anton Heida, USA	42	1964	Miroslav Cerar, YUG	19.525
1924	Josef Wilhelm, SWI	21.23	1968	Miroslav Cerar, YUG	19.325
1928	Hermann Hanggi, SWI	19.75	1972	Viktor Klimenko, SOV	19.125
1932	István Pelle, HUN	19.07	1976	Zoltán Magyar, HUN	19.70
1936	Konrad Frey, GER	19.333	1980	Zoltán Magyar, HUN	19.925
1948	Paavo Aaltonen, FIN	19.35	1984	Li Ning, CHN	19.95
1952	Viktor Chukarin, USSR	19.50	1988	Lyubomir Gueraskov, BUL	
1956	Boris Shakhlin, USSR	19.25		Dmitri Bilozertchev, USSR	
				& Zsolt Borkai, HUN	19.958

Rings

Year	Champion	Points	Year	Champion	Points
1896	Ioannis Mitropoulos, GRE	—	1960	Albert Azaryan, USSR	19.725
1904	Hermann Glass, USA	45	1964	Takuji Haytta, JPN	19.475
1924	Francesco Martino, ITA	21.553	1968	Akinori Nakayama, JPN	19.45
1928	Leon Stukelj, YUG	19.25	1972	Akinori Nakayama, JPN	19.35
1932	George Gulack, USA	18.97	1976	Nikolai Andrianov, USSR	19.65
1936	Alois Hudec, CZE	19.433	1980	Aleksandr Dityatin, USSR	19.875
1948	Karl Frei, SWI	19.80	1984	Koji Gushiken, JPN	19.85
1952	Grant Shaginyan, USSR	19.75	1988	Holger Behrendt, E.Ger	
1956	Albert Azaryan, USSR	19.35		& Dmitri Bilozertchev, USSR	19.925

Floor Exercise

Year	Champion	Points	Year	Champion	Points
1932	István Pelle, HUN	9.60	1968	Sawao Kato, JPN	19.475
1936	Georges Miez, SWI	18.666	1972	Nikolai Andrianov, USSR	19.175
1948	Ferenc Pataki, HUN	19.35	1976	Nikolai Andrianov, USSR	19.45
1952	William Thoresson, SWE	19.25	1980	Rolant Brückner, E.Ger	19.75
1956	Valentin Muratov, USSR	19.20	1984	Li Ning, CHN	19.925
1960	Nobuyuki Aihara, JPN	19.45	1988	Sergei Kharikov, USSR	19.925
1964	Franco Menichelli, ITA	19.45			

Team Combined Exercises

Year	Champion	Points	Year	Champion	Points
1904	United States	374.43	1952	Soviet Union	574.40
1906	Norway	19.00	1956	Soviet Union	568.25
1908	Sweden	438	1960	Japan	575.20
1912	Italy	265.75	1964	Japan	577.95
1920	Italy	359.855	1968	Japan	575.90
1924	Italy	839.058	1972	Japan	571.25
1928	Switzerland	1718.625	1976	Japan	576.85
1932	Italy	541.850	1980	Soviet Union	598.60
1936	West Germany	657.430	1984	United States	591.40
1948	Finland	1358.30	1988	Soviet Union	593.35

WOMEN

All-Around

Year	Champion	Points	Year	Champion	Points
1952	Maria Gorokhovskaya, USSR	76.78	1972	Lyudmila Tourischeva, USSR	77.025
1956	Larissa Latynina, USSR	74.933	1976	Nadia Comaneci, ROM	79.275
1960	Larissa Latynina, USSR	77.031	1980	Yelena Davydova, USSR	79.15
1964	Vera Cáslavská, CZE	77.564	1984	Mary Lou Retton, USA	79.175
1968	Vera Cáslavská, CZE	78.25	1988	Elena Shushunova, USSR	79.662

Vault

Year	Champion	Points	Year	Champion	Points
1952	Yekaterina Kalinchuk, USSR	19.20	1972	Karin Janz, E.Ger	19.525
1956	Larissa Latynina, USSR	18.833	1976	Nelli Kim, USSR	19.80
1960	Margarita Nikolayeva, USSR	19.316	1980	Natalya Shaposhnikova, USSR	19.725
1964	Vera Cáslavská, CZE	19.483	1984	Ecaterina Szabó, ROM	19.875
1968	Vera Cáslavská, CZE	19.775	1988	Svetlana Boguinskaya, USSR	19.905

Uneven Bars

Year	Champion	Points	Year	Champion	Points
1952	Margit Korondi, HUN	19.40	1972	Karin Janz, E.Ger	19.675
1956	Agnes Keleti, HUN	18.966	1976	Nadia Comaneci, ROM	20.00
1960	Polina Astakhova, USSR	19.616	1980	Maxi Gnauck, E.Ger	19.875
1964	Polina Astakhova, USSR	19.332	1984	Ma Yanhong, CHN	19.95
1968	Vera Cáslavská, CZE	19.65	1988	Daniela Silivas, ROM	20.00

Gymnastics (Cont.)
WOMEN

Balance Beam

Year	Champion	Points	Year	Champion	Points
1952	Nina Bocharova, USSR	19.22	1972	Olga Korbut, USSR	19.40
1956	Agnes Keleti, HUN	18.80	1976	Nadia Comaneci, ROM	19.95
1960	Eva Bosáková, CZE	19.283	1980	Nadia Comaneci, ROM	19.80
1964	Vera Cáslavská, CZE	19.449	1984	Simona Pauca, ROM	19.80
1968	Natalya Kuchinskaya, USSR	19.65	1988	Daniela Silivas, ROM	19.924

Floor Exercise

Year	Champion	Points	Year	Champion	Points
1952	Agnes Keleti, HUN	19.36	1972	Olga Korbut, USSR	19.575
1956	Agnes Keleti, HUN	18.733	1976	Nelli Kim, USSR	19.85
1960	Larissa Latynina, USSR	19.583	1980	Nadia Comaneci, ROM	19.875
1964	Larissa Latynina, USSR	19.599	1984	Ecaterina Szabó, ROM	19.975
1968	Vera Cáslavská, CZE	19.675	1988	Daniela Silivas, ROM	19.937

Team Combined Exercises

Year	Champion	Points	Year	Champion	Points
1928	Holland	316.75	1968	Soviet Union	382.85
1936	West Germany	506.50	1972	Soviet Union	380.50
1948	Czechoslovakia	445.45	1976	Soviet Union	466.00
1952	Soviet Union	527.03	1980	Soviet Union	394.90
1956	Soviet Union	444.800	1984	Romania	392.02
1960	Soviet Union	382.320	1988	Soviet Union	395.475
1964	Soviet Union	280.890			

Rhythmic All-Around

Year	Champion	Points	Year	Champion	Points
1984	Lori Fung, CAN	57.950	1988	Marina Lobatch, USSR	60.00

Soccer

Year	Champion, 2nd, 3rd	Year	Champion, 2nd, 3rd
1900	**Great Britain**, France, Belgium	1952	**Hungary**, Yugoslavia, Sweden
1904	**Canada**, USA I, USA II	1956	**Soviet Union**, Yugoslavia, Bulgaria
1906	**Denmark**, Smyrna (Int'l entry), Greece	1960	**Yugoslavia**, Denmark, Hungary
1908	**Great Britain**, Denmark, Holland	1964	**Hungary**, Czechoslovakia, E. Germany
1912	**Great Britain**, Denmark, Holland	1968	**Hungary**, Bulgaria, Japan
1920	**Belgium**, Spain, Holland	1972	**Poland**, Hungary, E. Germany
1924	**Uruguay**, Switzerland, Sweden	1976	**East Germany**, Poland, Soviet Union
1928	**Uruguay**, Argentina, Italy	1980	**Czechoslovakia**, E. Germany, Soviet Union
1936	**Italy**, Austria, Norway	1984	**France**, Brazil, Yugoslavia
1948	**Sweden**, Yugoslavia, Denmark	1988	**Soviet Union**, Brazil, W. Germany

Swimming
MEN

50-Meter Freestyle

Year	Champion	Time	Year	Champion	Time
1904	Zoltán Halmay, HUN	28.0	1988	Matt Biondi, USA	22.14 (WR)

100-Meter Freestyle

Year	Champion	Time	Year	Champion	Time
1896	Alfréd Hajós, HUN	1:22.2 (OR)	1952	Clarke Scholes, USA	57.4
1904	Zoltán Halmay, HUN	1:02.8	1956	Jon Henricks, AUS	55.4 (OR)
1906	Charles Daniels, USA	1:13.4	1960	John Devitt, AUS	55.2 (OR)
1908	Charles Daniels, USA	1:05.6 (WR)	1964	Don Schollander, USA	53.4 (OR)
1912	Duke Kahanamoku, USA	1:03.4	1968	Michael Wenden, AUS	52.2 (OR)
1920	Duke Kahanamoku, USA	1:00.4 (WR)	1972	Mark Spitz, USA	51.22 (WR)
1924	Johnny Weissmuller, USA	59.0 (OR)	1976	Jim Montgomery, USA	49.99 (WR)
1928	Johnny Weissmuller, USA	58.6 (OR)	1980	Jorg Woithe, E.Ger	50:40
1932	Yasuji Miyazaki, JPN	58.2	1984	Rowdy Gaines, USA	49.80 (OR)
1936	Ferenc Csik, HUN	57.6	1988	Matt Biondi, USA	48.63 (OR)
1948	Wally Ris, USA	57.3 (OR)			

200-Meter Freestyle

Year	Champion	Time	Year	Champion	Time
1900	Frederick Lane, AUS	2:25.2 (OR)	1976	Bruce Furniss, USA	1:50.29 (WR)
1904	Charles Daniels, USA	2:44.2	1980	Sergei Kopliakov, USSR	1:49.81 (OR)
1968	Michael Wenden, AUS	1:55.2	1984	Michael Gross, W.Ger	1:47.44 (WR)
1972	Mark Spitz, USA	1:52.78 (WR)	1988	Duncan Armstrong, AUS	1:47.25 (WR)

400-Meter Freestyle

Year	Champion	Time	Year	Champion	Time
1896	Paul Neumann, AUT	8:12.6	1952	Jean Boiteux, FRA	4:30.7 (OR)
1904	Charles Daniels, USA	6:16.2	1956	Murray Rose, AUS	4:27.3 (OR)
1906	Otto Scheff, AUT	6:23.8	1960	Murray Rose, AUS	4:18.3 (OR)
1908	Henry Taylor, GBR	5:36.8	1964	Don Schollander, USA	4:12.2 (WR)
1912	George Hodgson, CAN	5:24.4	1968	Mike Burton, USA	4:09.0 (OR)
1920	Norman Ross, USA	5:26.8	1972	Bradford Cooper, USA*	4:00.27
1924	Johnny Weissmuller, USA	5:04.2 (OR)	1976	Brian Goodell, USA	3:51.93 (WR)
1928	Alberto Zorilla, ARG	5:01.6 (OR)	1980	Vladimir Salnikov, USSR	3:51.31 (OR)
1932	Buster Crabbe, USA	4:48.4 (OR)	1984	George DiCarlo, USA	3:51.23 (OR)
1936	Jack Medica, USA	4:44.5 (OR)	1988	Ewe Dassler, E.Ger	3:46.95 (WR)
1948	Bill Smith, USA	4:41.0 (OR)			

*Cooper finished second to Rick DeMont of the U.S. who was disqualified when he flunked the post-race drug test (his asthma medication was on the IOC's banned list).

1500-Meter Freestyle

Year	Champion	Time	Year	Champion	Time
1896	Alfred Hajos, HUN	18:22.2 (OR)	1948	James McLane, USA	19:18.5
1900	John Arthur Jarvis, GBR	13:40.2	1952	Ford Konno, USA	18:30.3 (OR)
1904	Emil Rausch, W.Ger	27:18.2	1956	Murray Rose, AUS	17:58.9
1906	Henry Taylor, GBR	28:00.0	1960	John Konrads, AUS	17:19.6 (OR)
1908	Henry Taylor, GBR	22:48.4 (WR)	1964	Robert Windle, AUS	17:01.7 (OR)
1912	George Hodgson, CAN	22:00.0 (WR)	1968	Mike Burton, USA	16:38.9 (OR)
1920	Norman Ross, USA	22:23.2	1972	Mike Burton, USA	15:52.58 (WR)
1924	Boy Charlton, AUS	20:06.6 (WR)	1976	Brian Goodell, USA	15:02.40 (WR)
1928	Arne Borge, SWE	19:51.8 (OR)	1980	Vladimir Salnikov, USSR	14:58.27 (WR)
1932	Kusuo Kitamura, JPN	19:12.4 (OR)	1984	Mike O'Brien, USA	15:05.20
1936	Noboru Terada, JPN	19:13.7	1988	Vladimir Salnikov, USSR	15:00.40

100-Meter Backstroke

Year	Champion	Time	Year	Champion	Time
1904	Walter Brack, W.Ger	1:16.8	1952	Yoshinobu Oyakawa, USA	1:05.4 (OR)
1908	Arno Bieberstein, W.Ger	1:24.6 (WR)	1956	David Theile, AUS	1:02.2 (OR)
1912	Harry Hebner, USA	1:21.2	1960	David Theile, AUS	1:01.9 (OR)
1920	Warren Kealoha, USA	1:15.2	1968	Roland Matthes, E.Ger	58.7 (OR)
1924	Warren Kealoha, USA	1:13.2 (OR)	1972	Roland Matthes, E.Ger	56.58 (OR)
1928	George Kojac, USA	1:08.2 (WR)	1976	John Naber, USA	55.49 (WR)
1932	Masaji Kiyokawa, JPN	1:08.6	1980	Bengt Baron, SWE	56.33
1936	Adolf Kiefer, USA	1:05.9 (OR)	1984	Rick Carey, USA	55.79
1948	Allen Stack, USA	1:06.4	1988	Daichi Suzuki, JPN	55.05

200-Meter Backstroke

Year	Champion	Time	Year	Champion	Time
1900	Ernst Hoppenberg, W.Ger	2:47.0	1976	John Naber, USA	1:59.19 (WR)
1964	Jed Graef, USA	2:10.3 (WR)	1980	Sándor Wladár, HUN	2:01.93
1968	Roland Matthes, E.Ger	2:09.6 (OR)	1984	Rick Carey, USA	2:00.23
1972	Roland Matthes, E.Ger	2:02.82 (EWR)	1988	Igor Polianski, USSR	1:59.37

100-Meter Breaststroke

Year	Champion	Time	Year	Champion	Time
1968	Don McKenzie, USA	1:07.7 (OR)	1980	Duncan Goodhew, GBR	1:03.44
1972	Nobutaka Taguchi, JPN	1:04.94 (WR)	1984	Steve Lundquist, USA	1:01.65 (WR)
1976	John Hencken, USA	1:03.11 (WR)	1988	Adrian Moorhouse, GBR	1:02.04

200-Meter Breaststroke

Year	Champion	Time	Year	Champion	Time
1908	Frederick Holman, GBR	3:09.2 (WR)	1956	Masaru Furukawa, JPN	2:34.7 (OR)
1912	Walter Bathe, W.Ger	3:01.8 (OR)	1960	Bill Mulliken, USA	2:37.4
1920	Hakan Malmroth, SWE	3:04.4	1964	Ian O'Brien, AUS	2:27.8 (WR)
1924	Robert Skelton, USA	2:56.6	1968	Felipe Munoz, MEX	2:28.7
1928	Yoshiyuki Tsuruta, JPN	2:48.8 (OR)	1972	John Hencken, USA	2:21.55 (WR)
1932	Yoshiyuki Tsuruta, JPN	2:45.4	1976	David Wilkie, GBR	2:15.11 (WR)
1936	Tetsuo Hamuro, JPN	2:41.5 (OR)	1980	Robertas Zhulpa, USSR	2:15.85
1948	Joseph Verdeur, USA	2:39.3 (OR)	1984	Victor Davis, CAN	2:13.34 (WR)
1952	John Davies, AUS	2:34.4 (OR)	1988	Jozsef Szabo, HUN	2:13.52

Swimming (Cont.)

MEN

100-Meter Butterfly

Year	Champion	Time	Year	Champion	Time
1968	Doug Russell, USA	55.9 (OR)	1980	Par Arvidsson, SWE	54.92
1972	Mark Spitz, USA	54.27 (WR)	1984	Michael Gross, W.Ger	53.08 (WR)
1976	Matt Vogel, USA	54.35	1988	Anthony Nesty, SUR	53.0 (OR)

200-Meter Butterfly

Year	Champion	Time	Year	Champion	Time
1956	Bill Yorzyk, USA	2:19.3 (OR)	1976	Mike Bruner, USA	1:59.23 (WR)
1960	Mike Troy, USA	2:12.8 (WR)	1980	Sergei Fesenko, USSR	1:59.76
1964	Kevin Berry, AUS	2:06.6 (WR)	1984	Jon Sieben, AUS	1:57.04 (WR)
1968	Carl Robie, USA	2:08.7	1988	Michael Gross, W.Ger	1:56.94 (OR)
1972	Mark Spitz, USA	2:00.70 (WR)			

200-Meter Individual Medley

Year	Champion	Time	Year	Champion	Time
1968	Charles Hickcox, USA	2:12.0 (OR)	1984	Alex Baumann, CAN	2:01.42 (WR)
1972	Gunnar Larsson, SWE	2:07.17 (WR)	1988	Tamas Darnyi, HUN	2:00.17 (WR)

400-Meter Individual Medley

Year	Champion	Time	Year	Champion	Time
1964	Richard Roth, USA	4:45.4 (WR)	1980	Aleksandr Sidorenko, USSR	4:22.89 (OR)
1968	Charles Hickcox, USA	4:48.4	1984	Alex Baumann, CAN	4:17.41 (WR)
1972	Gunnar Larsson, SWE	4:31.98 (WR)	1988	Tamas Darnyi, HUN	4:14.75 (WR)
1976	Rod Strachan, USA	4:23.68 (WR)			

4x100-Meter Freestyle Relay

Year	Champion	Time	Year	Champion	Time
1964	United States	3:32.2 (WR)	1984	United States	3:19.03 (WR)
1968	United States	3:31.7 (WR)	1988	United States	3:16.53 (WR)
1972	United States	3:26.42 (WR)			

4x200-Meter Freestyle Relay

Year	Champion	Time	Year	Champion	Time
1906	Hungary	16:52.4	1956	Australia	8:23.6 (WR)
1908	Great Britain	10:55.6 (WR)	1960	United States	8:10.2 (WR)
1912	Australia/New Zealand	10:11.6 (WR)	1964	United States	7:52.1 (WR)
1920	United States	10:04.4 (WR)	1968	United States	7:52.33
1924	United States	9:53.4 (WR)	1972	United States	7:35.78 (WR)
1928	United States	9:36.2 (WR)	1976	United States	7:23.22 (WR)
1932	Japan	8:58.4 (WR)	1980	Soviet Union	7:23.50
1936	Japan	8:51.5 (WR)	1984	United States	7:15.69 (WR)
1948	United States	8:46.0 (WR)	1988	United States	7:12.51 (WR)
1952	United States	8:31.1 (OR)			

4x100-Meter Medley Relay

Year	Champion	Time	Year	Champion	Time
1960	United States	4:05.4 (WR)	1976	United States	3:42.22 (WR)
1964	United States	3:58.4 (WR)	1980	Australia	3:45.70
1968	United States	3:54.9 (WR)	1984	United States	3:39.30 (WR)
1972	United States	3:48.16 (WR)	1988	United States	3:36.93 (WR)

WOMEN

50-Meter Freestyle

Year	Champion	Time
1988	Kristin Otto, E.Ger	25.49 (OR)

100-Meter Freestyle

Year	Champion	Time	Year	Champion	Time
1912	Fanny Durack, AUS	1:22.2	1960	Dawn Fraser, AUS	1:01.2 (OR)
1920	Ethelda Bleibtrey, USA	1:13.6 (WR)	1964	Dawn Fraser, AUS	59.5 (OR)
1924	Ethel Lackie, USA	1:12.4	1968	Jan Henne, USA	1:00.0
1928	Albina Osipowich, USA	1:11.0 (OR)	1972	Sandra Neilson, USA	58.59 (OR)
1932	Helene Madison, USA	1:06.8 (OR)	1976	Kornelia Ender, E.Ger	55.65 (WR)
1936	Rie Mastenbroek, HOL	1:05.9 (OR)	1980	Barbara Krause, E.Ger	54.79 (WR)
1948	Greta Andersen, DEN	1:06.3	1984	Nancy Hogshead, USA	55.92
1952	Katalin Szöke, HUN	1:06.8		& Carrie Steinseifer, USA	55.92
1956	Dawn Fraser, AUS	1:02.0 (WR)	1988	Kristin Otto, E.Ger	54.93

200-Meter Freestyle

Year	Champion	Time	Year	Champion	Time
1968	Debbie Meyer, USA	2:10.5 (OR)	1980	Barbara Krause, E.Ger	1:58.33 (OR)
1972	Shane Gould, AUS	2:03.56 (WR)	1984	Mary Wayte, USA	1:59.23
1976	Kornelia Ender, E.Ger	1:59.26 (WR)	1988	Heike Friedrich, E.Ger	1:57.65 (OR)

400-Meter Freestyle

Year	Champion	Time	Year	Champion	Time
1920	Ethelda Bleibtrey, USA	4:34.0 (WR)	1960	Chris Von Saltza, USA	4:50.6 (OR)
1924	Martha Norelius, USA	6:02.2 (OR)	1964	Ginny Duenkel, USA	4:43.3 (OR)
1928	Martha Norelius, USA	5:42.8 (OR)	1968	Debbie Meyer, USA	4:31.8 (OR)
1932	Helene Madison, USA	5:28.5 (WR)	1972	Shane Gould, AUS	4:19.44 (WR)
1936	Rie Mastenbroek, HOL	5:26.4 (OR)	1976	Petra Thumer, E.Ger	4:09.89 (WR)
1948	Ann Curtis, USA	5:17.8 (OR)	1980	Ines Diers, E.Ger	4:08.76 (OR)
1952	Valeria Gyenge, HUN	5:12.1 (OR)	1984	Tiffany Cohen, USA	4:07.10 (OR)
1956	Lorraine Crapp, AUS	4:54.6 (OR)	1988	Janet Evans, USA	4:03.85 (WR)

800-Meter Freestyle

Year	Champion	Time	Year	Champion	Time
1968	Debbie Meyer, USA	9:24.0 (OR)	1980	Michelle Ford, AUS	8:28.90 (OR)
1972	Keena Rothhammer, USA	8:53.68 (WR)	1984	Tiffany Cohen, USA	8:24.95 (OR)
1976	Petra Thümer, E.Ger	8:37.14 (WR)	1988	Janet Evans, USA	8:20.20 (OR)

100-Meter Backstroke

Year	Champion	Time	Year	Champion	Time
1924	Sybil Bauer, USA	1:23.2 (OR)	1964	Cathy Ferguson, USA	1:07.7 (WR)
1928	Maria Braun, HOL	1:22.0	1968	Kaye Hall, USA	1:06.2 (WR)
1932	Eleanor Holm, USA	1:19.4	1972	Melissa Belote, USA	1:05.78 (OR)
1936	Nida Senff, HOL	1:18.9	1976	Ulrike Richter, E.Ger	1:01.83 (OR)
1948	Karen-Margrete Harup, DEN	1:14.4 (OR)	1980	Rica Reinisch, E.Ger	1:00.86 (WR)
1952	Joan Harrison, SAF	1:14.3	1984	Theresa Andrews, USA	1:02.55
1956	Judith Grinham, GBR	1:12.9 (OR)	1988	Kristin Otto, E.Ger	1:00.89
1960	Lynn Burke, USA	1:09.3 (OR)			

200-Meter Backstroke

Year	Champion	Time	Year	Champion	Time
1968	Lillian Watson, USA	2:24.8 (OR)	1980	Rica Reinisch, E.Ger	2:11.77 (WR)
1972	Melissa Belote, USA	2:19.19 (WR)	1984	Jolanda de Rover, HOL	2:12.38
1976	Ulrike Richter, E.Ger	2:13.43 (OR)	1988	Krisztina Egerszegi, HUN	2:09.29 (OR)

100-Meter Breaststroke

Year	Champion	Time	Year	Champion	Time
1968	Djurdjica Bjedov, YUG	1:15.8 (OR)	1980	Ute Geweniger, E.Ger	1:10.22
1972	Cathy Carr, USA	1:13.58 (WR)	1984	Petra van Staveren, HOL	1:09.88 (OR)
1976	Hannelore Anke, E.Ger	1:11.16	1988	Tania Dangalakova, BUL	1:07.95 (OR)

200-Meter Breaststroke

Year	Champion	Time	Year	Champion	Time
1924	Lucy Morton, GBR	3:33.2 (OR)	1964	Galina Prozumenshikova, USSR	2:46.4 (OR)
1928	Hilde Schrader, W.Ger	3:12.6	1968	Sharon Wichman, USA	2:44.4 (OR)
1932	Clare Dennis, AUS	3:06.3 (OR)	1972	Beverley Whitfield, AUS	2:41.71 (OR)
1936	Hideko Maehata, JPN	3:03.6	1976	Marina Koshevaia, USSR	2:33.35 (WR)
1948	Petronella van Vliet, HOL	2:57.2	1980	Lina Kaciusyte, USSR	2:29.54 (OR)
1952	Eva Szekely, HUN	2:51.7 (OR)	1984	Anne Ottenbrite, CAN	2:30.38
1956	Ursula Happe, W.Ger	2:53.1 (OR)	1988	Silke Hoerner, E.Ger	2:26.71 (WR)
1960	Anita Lonsbrough, GBR	2:49.5 (WR)			

100-Meter Butterfly

Year	Champion	Time	Year	Champion	Time
1956	Shelly Mann, USA	1:11.0 (OR)	1976	Kornelia Ender, E.Ger	1:00.13 (=WR)
1960	Carolyn Schuler, USA	1:09.5 (OR)	1980	Caren Metschuck, E.Ger	1:00.42
1964	Sharon Stouder, USA	1:04.7 (WR)	1984	Mary T. Meagher, USA	59.26
1968	Lyn McClements, AUS	1:05.5	1988	Kristin Otto, E.Ger	59.00 (OR)
1972	Mayumi Aoki, JPN	1:03.34 (WR)			

Swimming (Cont.)

WOMEN

200-Meter Butterfly

Year	Champion	Time	Year	Champion	Time
1968	Ada Kok, HOL	2:24.7 (OR)	1980	Ines Geissler, E.Ger	2:10.44 (OR)
1972	Karen Moe, USA	2:15.57 (WR)	1984	Mary T. Meagher, USA	2:06.90 (OR)
1976	Andrea Pollack, E.Ger	2:11.41 (OR)	1988	Kathleen Nord, E.Ger	2:09.51

200-Meter Individual Medley

Year	Champion	Time	Year	Champion	Time
1968	Claudia Kolb, USA	2:24.7 (OR)	1984	Tracy Caulkins, USA	2:12.64 (OR)
1972	Shane Gould, AUS	2:23.07 (WR)	1988	Daniela Hunger, E.Ger	2:12.59 (OR)

400-Meter Individual Medley

Year	Champion	Time	Year	Champion	Time
1968	Donna De Varona, USA	5:18.7 (OR)	1980	Petra Schneider, E.Ger	4:36.29 (WR)
1968	Claudia Kolb, USA	5:08.5 (OR)	1984	Tracy Caulkins, USA	4:39.24
1972	Gail Neall, AUS	5:02.97 (WR)	1988	Janet Evans, USA	4:37.76
1976	Ulrike Tauber, E.Ger	4:42.77 (WR)			

4x100-Meter Freestyle Relay

Year	Champion	Time	Year	Champion	Time
1912	Great Britain	5:52.8 (WR)	1960	United States	4:08.9 (WR)
1920	United States	5:11.6 (WR)	1964	United States	4:03.8 (WR)
1924	United States	4:58.8 (WR)	1968	United States	4:02.5 (OR)
1928	United States	4:47.6 (WR)	1972	United States	3:55.19 (WR)
1932	United States	4:38.0 (WR)	1976	United States	3:44.82 (WR)
1936	Holland	4:36.0 (WR)	1980	East Germany	3:42.71 (WR)
1948	United States	4:29.2 (OR)	1984	United States	3:43.43
1952	Hungary	4:24.4 (WR)	1988	East Germany	3:40.63 (OR)
1956	Australia	4:17.1 (WR)			

4x100-Meter Medley Relay

Year	Champion	Time	Year	Champion	Time
1960	United States	4:41.1 (WR)	1976	East Germany	4:07.95 (WR)
1964	United States	4:33.9 (WR)	1980	East Germany	4:06.67 (WR)
1968	United States	4:28.3 (WR)	1984	United States	4:08.34
1972	United States	4:20.75 (WR)	1988	East Germany	4:03.74 (OR)

Synchronized Swimming — Solo

Year	Champion	Points	Year	Champion	Points
1984	Tracie Ruiz, USA	198.467	1988	Carolyn Waldo, CAN	200.15

Synchronized Swimming — Duet

Year	Champion	Points	Year	Champion	Points
1984	Tracie Ruiz & Candy Costie, USA	195.584	1988	Carolyn Waldo & Michelle Cameron, CAN	197.717

Tennis

MEN

Singles

Year	Champion		Year	Champion	
1896	John Boland	Great Britain/Ireland	1908	(Indoor) Arthur Gore	Great Britain
1900	Hugh Doherty,	Great Britain	1912	Charles Winslow	South Africa
1904	Beals Wright	United States	1912	(Indoor) André Gobert	France
1906	Max Decugis	France	1920	Louis Raymond	South Africa
1908	Josiah Ritchie	Great Britain	1924	Vincent Richards	United States
			1988	Miloslav Mecir	Czechoslovakia

Doubles

Year	Champions	Year	Champions
1896	John Boland, IRL & Fritz Traun, GER	1912	Charles Winslow & Harold Kitson, SAF
1900	Hugh and Reggie Doherty, GBR	1912	(Indoor) André Gobert & Maurice Germot, FRA
1904	Edgar Leonard & Beals Wright, USA	1920	Noel Turnbull & Max Woosnam, GBR
1906	Max Decugis & Maurice Germot, FRA	1924	Vincent Richards & Frank Hunter, USA
1908	George Hillyard & Reggie Doherty, GRB	1988	Ken Flach & Robert Seguso, USA
1908	(Indoor) Arthur Gore & Herbert Barrett, GBR		

WOMEN

Singles

Year	Champion		Year	Champion	
1900	Charlotte Cooper	Great Britain	1912	Edith Hannam	Great Britain
1906	Esmee Simiriotu	Greece	1920	Suzanne Lenglen	France
1908	Dorothy Chambers	Great Britain	1924	Helen Wills	United States
1908	Gwendoline Eastlake-Smith	Great Britain	1988	Steffi Graf	West Germany
1912	Marguerite Broquedis	France			

Doubles

Year	Champions	Year	Champions
1920	Winifred McNair & Kitty McKane, GBR	1988	Pam Shriver & Zina Garrison, USA
1924	Hazel Wightman & Helen Wills, USA		

Track & Field

MEN

100 Meters

Year	Champion	Time	Year	Champion	Time
1886	Thomas Burke, USA	12.0	1948	Harrison Dillard, USA	10.3 (=OR)
1900	Frank Jarvis, USA	11.0	1952	Lindy Remigino, USA	10.4
1904	Archie Hahn, USA	11.0	1956	Bobby Morrow, USA	10.5
1906	Archie Hahn, USA	11.2	1960	Armin Hary, GER	10.2 (OR)
1908	Reggie Walker, SAF	10.8 (=OR)	1964	Bob Hayes, USA	10.0 (=WR)
1912	Ralph Craig, USA	10.8	1968	Jim Hines, USA	9.95 (WR)
1920	Charley Paddock, USA	10.8	1972	Valery Borzov, USSR	10.14
1924	Harold Abrahams, GBR	10.6 (=OR)	1976	Hasely Crawford, TRI	10.06
1928	Percy Williams, CAN	10.8	1980	Allan Wells, GBR	10.25
1932	Eddie Tolan, USA	10.3 (OR)	1984	Carl Lewis, USA	9.99
1936	Jesse Owens, USA	10.3	1988	Carl Lewis, USA	9.92 (WR)

200 Meters

Year	Champion	Time	Year	Champion	Time
1900	John Walter Tewksbury, USA	22.2	1952	Andrew Stanfield, USA	20.7
1904	Archie Hahn, USA	21.6 (OR)	1956	Bobby Morrow, USA	20.6 (OR)
1908	Bobby Kerr, CAN	22.6	1960	Livio Berruti, ITA	20.5 (=WR)
1912	Ralph Craig, USA	21.7	1964	Henry Carr, USA	20.3 (OR)
1920	Allen Woodring, USA	22.0	1968	Tommie Smith, USA	19.83 (WR)
1924	Jackson Scholz, USA	21.6	1972	Valery Borzov, USSR	20.00
1928	Percy Williams, CAN	21.8	1976	Donald Quarrie, JAM	20.23
1932	Eddie Tolan, USA	21.2 (OR)	1980	Pietro Mennea, ITA	20.19
1936	Jesse Owens, USA	20.7 (OR)	1984	Carl Lewis, USA	19.80 (OR)
1948	Mel Patton, USA	21.1	1988	Joe DeLoach, USA	19.75 (OR)

400 Meters

Year	Champion	Time	Year	Champion	Time
1896	Tom Burke, USA	54.2	1948	Arthur Wint, JAM	46.2
1890	Maxey Long, USA	49.4 (OR)	1952	George Rhoden, JAM	45.9
1904	Harry Hillman, USA	49.2 (OR)	1956	Charley Jenkins, USA	46.7
1906	Paul Pilgrim, USA	53.2	1960	Otis Davis, USA	44.9 (WR)
1908	Wyndham Halswelle, GBR	50.0	1964	Mike Larrabee, USA	45.1
1912	Charlie Reidpath, USA	48.2 (OR)	1968	Lee Evans, USA	43.86 (WR)
1920	Bevil Rudd, SAF	49.6	1972	Vince Matthews, USA	44.66
1924	Eric Liddell, GBR	47.6 (OR)	1976	Alberto Juantorena, CUB	44.26
1928	Raymond Barbuti, USA	47.8	1980	Viktor Markin, USSR	44.60
1932	Bill Carr, USA	46.2 (WR)	1984	Alonzo Babers, USA	44.27
1936	Archie Williams, USA	46.5	1988	Steve Lewis, USA	43.87

Track & Field (Cont.)
MEN
800 Meters

Year	Champion	Time	Year	Champion	Time
1896	Teddy Flack, AUS	2:11.0	1948	Mal Whitfield, USA	1:49.2 (OR)
1900	Alfred Tysoe, BFR	2:01.2	1952	Mal Whitfield, USA	1:49.2 (=OR)
1904	Hannes Lightbody, USA	1:56.0 (OR)	1956	Tom Courtney, USA	1:47.7 (OR)
1906	Paul Pilgrim, USA	2:01.5	1960	Peter Snell, NZE	1:46.3 (OR)
1908	Mel Sheppard, USA	1:52.8 (WR)	1964	Peter Snell, NZE	1:45.1 (OR)
1912	Ted Meredith, USA	1:51.9 (WR)	1968	Ralph Doubell, AUS	1:44.3 (=WR)
1920	Albert Hill, GBR	1:53.4	1972	Dave Wottle, USA	1:45.9
1924	Douglas Lowe, GRB	1:52.4	1976	Alberto Juantorena, CUB	1:43.50 (WR)
1928	Douglas Lowe, GBR	1:51.8 (OR)	1980	Steve Ovett, GBR	1:45.4
1932	Tommy Hampson, GBR	1:49.7 (WR)	1984	Joaquim Cruz, BRA	1:43.00 (OR)
1936	John Woodruff, USA	1:52.9	1988	Paul Ereng, KEN	1:43.45

1500 Meters

Year	Champion	Time	Year	Champion	Time
1896	Teddy Flack, AUS	4:33.2	1948	Henry Eriksson, SWE	3:49.8
1900	Charles Bennett, GBR	4:06.2 (WR)	1952	Josy Barthel, LUX	3:45.1 (OR)
1904	James Lightbody, USA	4:05.4 (WR)	1956	Ron Delany, IRL	3:41.2 (OR)
1906	James Lightbody, USA	4:12.0	1960	Herb Elliott, AUS	3:35.6 (WR)
1908	Mel Sheppard, USA	4:03.4 (OR)	1964	Peter Snell, NZE	3:38.1
1912	Arnold Jackson, GBR	3:56.8 (OR)	1968	Kip Keino, KEN	3:34.9 (OR)
1920	Albert Hill, GBR	4:01.8	1972	Pekkha Vasala, FIN	3:36.3
1924	Paavo Nurmi, FIN	3:53.6 (OR)	1976	John Walker, NZE	3:39.17
1928	Harry Larva, FIN	3:53.2 (OR)	1980	Sebastian Coe, GBR	3:38.4
1932	Luigi Beccali, ITA	3:51.2 (OR)	1984	Sebastian Coe, GBR	3:32.53 (OR)
1936	John Lovelock, NZE	3:47.8 (WR)	1988	Peter Rono, KEN	3:35.96

5000 Meters

Year	Champion	Time	Year	Champion	Time
1912	Hannes Kolehmainen, FIN	14:36.6 (WR)	1960	Murray Halberg, NZE	13:43.4
1920	Joseph Guillemot, FRA	14:55.6	1964	Bob Schul, USA	13:48.8
1924	Paavo Nurmi, FIN	14:31.2 (OR)	1968	Mohamed Gammoudi, TUN	14:05.0
1928	Ville Ritola, FIN	14:38.0	1972	Lasse Viren, FIN	13:26.4 (OR)
1932	Lauri Lehtinen, FIN	14:30.0 (OR)	1976	Lasse Viren, FIN	13:24.76
1936	Gunnar Höckert, FIN	14:22.2 (OR)	1980	Miruts Yifter, ETH	13:21.0
1948	Gaston Reiff, BEL	14:17.6 (OR)	1984	Said Aouita, MOR	13:05.59 (OR)
1952	Emil Zátopek, CZE	14:06.6 (OR)	1988	John Ngugi, KEN	13:11.70
1956	Vladimir Kuts, USSR	13:39.6 (OR)			

10,000 Meters

Year	Champion	Time	Year	Champion	Time
1912	Hannes Kolehmainen, FIN	31:20.8	1960	Pyotr Bolotnikov, USSR	28:32.2 (OR)
1920	Paavo Nurmi, FIN	31:45.8	1964	Billy Mills, USA	28:24.4 (OR)
1924	Ville Ritola, FIN	30:23.2 (WR)	1968	Naftali Temu, KEN	29:27.4
1928	Paavo Nurmi, FIN	30:18.8 (OR)	1972	Lasse Viren, FIN	27:38.4 (WR)
1932	Janusz Kusocinski, POL	30:11.4 (OR)	1976	Lasse Viren, FIN	27:40.38
1936	Ilmari Salminen, FIN	30:15.4	1980	Miruts Yifter, ETH	27:42.7
1948	Emil Zátopek, CZE	29:59.6 (OR)	1984	Alberto Cova, ITA	27:47.54
1952	Emil Zátopek, CZE	29:17.0 (OR)	1988	Brahim Boutaib, MOR	27:21.46
1956	Vladimir Kuts, USSR	28:45.6 (OR)			

Marathon

Year	Champion	Time	Year	Champion	Time
1896	Spiridon Louis, GRE	2:58:50	1948	Delfo Cabrera, ARG	2:34:51.6
1900	Michel Théato, FRA	2:59:45	1952	Emil Zátopek, CZE	2:23:03.2 (OR)
1904	Thomas Hicks, USA	3:28:63	1956	Alain Mimoun, FRA	2:25:00.0
1906	Billy Sherring, CAN	2:51:23.6	1960	Abebe Bikila, ETH	2:15:16.2 (WB)
1908	John Hayes, USA	2:55:18.4 (OR)	1964	Abebe Bikila, ETH	2:12:11.2 (WB)
1912	Kenneth McArthur, SAF	2:36:54.8	1968	Mamo Wolde, ETH	2:20:26.4
1920	Hannes Kolehmainen, FIN	2:32:35.8 (WB)	1972	Frank Shorter, USA	2:12:19.8
1924	Albin Stenroos, FIN	2:41:22.6	1976	Waldemar Cierpinski, E.Ger.	2:09:55.0 (OR)
1928	Boughêra El Ouafi, FRA	2:32:57.0	1980	Waldemar Cierpinski, E.Ger.	2:11:03.0
1932	Juan Carlos Zabala, ARG	2:31:36.0 (OR)	1984	Carlos Lopes, POR	2:09:21.0 (OR)
1936	Kee-Chung Sohn,* JPN	2:29:19.2 (OR)	1988	Gelindo Bordin, ITA	2:10:32

*Sohn was a Korean, but forced to compete for Japan, which occupied Korea at the time.
Note: Marathon distances—40,000 meters (1896,1904); 40,260 meters (1900); 41,860 meters (1906); 42,195 meters (1908 and since 1924); 40,200 meters (1912); 42,750 meters (1920). Current distance of 42,195 meters measures 26 miles, 385 yards.

110-Meter Hurdles

Year	Champion	Time	Year	Champion	Time
1896	Thomas Curtis, USA	17.6	1948	William Porter, USA	13.9 (OR)
1900	Alvin Kraenzlein, USA	15.4 (OR)	1952	Harrison Dillard, USA	13.7 (OR)
1904	Frederick Schule, USA	16.0	1956	Lee Calhoun, USA	13.5 (OR)
1906	Robert Leavitt, USA	16.2	1960	Lee Calhoun, USA	13.8
1908	Forrest Smithson, USA	15.0 (WR)	1964	Hayes Jones, USA	13.6
1912	Frederick Kelly, USA	15.1	1968	Willie Davenport, USA	13.3 (OR)
1920	Earl Thomson, CAN	14.8 (WR)	1972	Rod Milburn, USA	13.24 (=WR)
1924	Daniel Kinsey, USA	15.0	1976	Guy Drut, FRA	13.30
1928	Syd Atkinson, SAF	14.8	1980	Thomas Munkelt, E.Ger	13.39
1932	George Saling, USA	14.6	1984	Roger Kingdom, USA	13.20 (OR)
1936	Forrest (Spec) Towns, USA	14.2	1988	Roger Kingdom, USA	12.98 (OR)

400-Meter Hurdles

Year	Champion	Time	Year	Champion	Time
1900	John Walter Tewksbury, USA	57.6	1956	Glenn Davis, USA	50.1 (=OR)
1904	Harry Hillman, USA	53.0	1960	Glenn Davis, USA	49.3 (=OR)
1908	Charles Bacon, USA	55.0 (WR)	1964	Rex Cawley, USA	49.6
1920	Frank Loomis, USA	54.0 (WR)	1968	David Hemery, GBR	48.12 (WR)
1924	Morgan Taylor, USA	52.6	1972	John Akii-Bua, UGA	47.82 (WR)
1928	David Burghley, GBR	53.4 (OR)	1976	Edwin Moses, USA	47.64 (WR)
1932	Bob Tisdall, IRL	51.7	1980	Volker Beck, E.Ger	48.70
1936	Glenn Hardin, USA	52.4	1984	Edwin Moses, USA	47.75
1948	Roy Cochran, USA	51.1 (OR)	1988	Andre Phillips, USA	47.19 (OR)
1952	Charles Moore, USA	50.8 (OR)			

3000 Meter-Steeplechase

Year	Champion	Time	Year	Champion	Time
1900	George Orton, CAN/USA	7:34.4	1956	Chris Brasher, GBR	8:41.2 (OR)
1904	James Lightbody, USA	7:39.6	1960	Zdzislaw Krzyszkowiak, POL	8:34.2 (OR)
1908	Arthur Russell, GBR	10:47.8	1964	Gaston Roelants, BEL	8:30.8 (OR)
1920	Percy Hodge, GBR	10:00.4 (OR)	1968	Amos Biwott, KEN	8:51.0
1924	Ville Ritola, FIN	9:33.6 (OR)	1972	Kip Keino, KEN	8:23.6 (OR)
1928	Toivo Loukola, FIN	9:21.8 (WR)	1976	Anders Gärderud, SWE	8:08.2 (WR)
1932	Volmari Iso-Hollo, FIN*	10:33.4	1980	Bronislaw Malinowski, POL	8:09.7
1936	Volmari Iso-Hollo, FIN	9:03.8 (WR)	1984	Julius Korir, KEN	8:11.80
1948	Thore Sjöstrand, SWE	9:04.6	1988	Julius Kariuki, KEN	8:05.51 (OR)
1952	Horace Ashenfelter, USA	8:45.4 (WR)			

*Iso-Hollo ran one extra lap due to lap counter's mistake.

4x100-Meter Relay

Year	Champion	Time	Year	Champion	Time
1912	Great Britain	42.4 (OR)	1960	Germany	39.5 (=WR)
1920	United States	42.2 (WR)	1964	United States	39.0 (WR)
1924	United States	41.0 (=WR)	1968	United States	38.2 (WR)
1928	United States	41.0 (=WR)	1972	United States	38.19 (=WR)
1932	United States	40.0 (WR)	1976	United States	38.33
1936	United States	39.8 (WR)	1980	Soviet Union	38.26
1948	United States	40.6	1984	United States	37.83 (WR)
1952	United States	40.1	1988	Soviet Union	38.19
1956	United States	39.5 (WR)			

4x400-Meter Relay

Year	Champion	Time	Year	Champion	Time
1908	United States	3:29.4	1956	United States	3:04.8
1912	United States	3:16.6 (WR)	1960	United States	3:02.2 (WR)
1920	Great Britain	3:22.2	1964	United States	3:00.7 (WR)
1924	United States	3:16.0 (WR)	1968	United States	2:56.16 (WR)
1928	United States	3:14.2 (WR)	1972	Kenya	2:59.8
1932	United States	3:08.2 (WR)	1976	United States	2:58.65
1936	Great Britain	3:09.0	1980	Soviet Union	3:01.1
1948	United States	3:10.4 (WR)	1984	United States	2:57.91
1952	Jamaica	3:03.9 (WR)	1988	United States	2:56.16 (=WR)

20,000-Meter Walk

Year	Champion	Time	Year	Champion	Time
1956	Leonid Spirin, USSR	1:31:27.4	1976	Daniel Bautista Rocha, MEX	1:24:40.6 (OR)
1960	Vladimir Golubnichiy, USSR	1:34:07.2	1980	Maurizio Damilano, ITA	1:23:35.5 (OR)
1964	Kenneth Matthews, GBR	1:29:34.0 (OR)	1984	Ernesto Canto, MEX	1:23:13.0 (OR)
1968	Vladimir Golubnichiy, USSR	1:33:58.4	1988	Josef Pribilinec, CZE	1:19:57.0 (OR)
1972	Peter Frenkel, E.Ger	1:26:42.4 (OR)			

Track & Field (Cont.)

MEN

50,000-Meter Walk

Year	Champion	Time	Year	Champion	Time
1932	Thomas Green, GBR	4:50:10	1964	Abdon Pamich, ITA	4:11:12.4 (OR)
1936	Harold Whitlock, GBR	4:30:41.4 (OR)	1968	Christoph Höhne, E.Ger	4:20:13.6
1948	John Ljunggren, SWE	4:41.52	1972	Bernd Kannenberg, W.Ger	3:56:11.6 (OR)
1952	Giuseppe Dordoni, ITA	4:28:07.8 (OR)	1980	Hartwig Gauder, E.Ger	3:49:24.0 (OR)
1956	Norman Read, NZE	4:30:42.8	1984	Raúl González, MEX	3:47:26 (OR)
1960	Don Thompson, GBR	4:25:30.0 (OR)	1988	Vyacheslav Ivanenko, USSR	3:38:29.0 (OR)

High Jump

Year	Winner	Height	Year	Winner	Height
1896	Ellery Clark, USA	5-11¼	1948	John Winter, AUS	6-6
1900	Irving Baxter, USA	6-2¾ (OR)	1952	Walter Davis, USA	6-8½ (OR)
1904	Sam Jones, USA	5-11	1956	Charley Dumas, USA	6-11½ (OR)
1906	Cornelius Leahy, GBR/IRL	5-10	1960	Robert Shavlakadze, USSR	7-1 (OR)
1908	Harry Porter, USA	6-3 (OR)	1964	Valery Brumel, USSR	7-1¾ (OR)
1912	Alma Richards, USA	6-4 (OR)	1968	Dick Fosbury, USA	7-4¼ (OR)
1920	Richmond Landon, USA	6-4 (=OR)	1972	Yuri Tarmak, USSR	7-3¾
1924	Harold Osborn, USA	6-6 (OR)	1976	Jacek Wszola, POL	7-4½ (OR)
1928	Robert King, USA	6-4½	1980	Gerd Wessig, E.Ger	7-8¾ (WR)
1932	Duncan McNaughton, CAN	6-5½	1984	Dietmar Mögenburg, W.Ger	7-8½
1936	Cornelius Johnson, USA	6-8 (OR)	1988	Guennadi Avdeenko, USSR	7-9½ (OR)

Pole Vault

Year	Champion	Height	Year	Champion	Height
1896	William Hoyt, USA	10-10	1948	Guinn Smith, USA	14-1¼
1900	Irving Baxter, USA	10-10	1952	Bob Richards, USA	14-11 (OR)
1904	Charles Dvorak, USA	11-5¾	1956	Bob Richards, USA	14-11½ (OR)
1906	Fernand Gonder, FRA	11-5¾	1960	Don Bragg, USA	15-5 (OR)
1908	Edward Cooke, USA & Alfred Gilbert, USA	12-2 (OR)	1964	Fred Hansen, USA	16-8¾ (OR)
1912	Harry Babcock, USA	12-11½ (OR)	1968	Bob Seagren, USA	17-8½ (OR)
1920	Frank Foss, USA	13-5 (WR)	1972	Wolfgang Nordwig, E.Ger	18-½ (OR)
1924	Lee Barnes, USA	12-11½	1976	Tadeusz Slusarski, POL	18-½ (=OR)
1928	Sabin Carr, USA	13-9¼ (OR)	1980	Wladyslaw Kozakiewicz, POL	18-11½ (WR)
1932	Bill Miller, USA	14-1¾ (OR)	1984	Pierre Quinon, FRA	18-10¼
1936	Earle Meadows, USA	14-3¼ (OR)	1988	Sergei Bubka, USSR	19-9¼ (OR)

Long Jump

Year	Champion	Distance	Year	Champion	Distance
1896	Ellery Clark, USA	20-10	1948	Willie Steele, USA	25-8
1900	Alvin Kraenzlein, USA	23-6¾ (OR)	1952	Jerome Biffle, USA	24-10
1904	Meyer Prinstein, USA	24-1 (OR)	1956	Gregory Bell, USA	25-8¼
1906	Meyer Prinstein, USA	23-7½	1960	Ralph Boston, USA	26-7¾ (OR)
1908	Frank Irons, USA	24-6½ (OR)	1964	Lynn Davies, GBR	26-5¾
1912	Albert Gutterson, USA	24-11¼ (OR)	1968	Bob Beamon, USA	29-2½ (WR)
1920	William Petersson, SWE	23-5½	1972	Randy Williams, USA	27-½
1924	DeHart Hubbard, USA	24-5	1976	Arnie Robinson, USA	27-4¾
1928	Edward Hamm, USA	25-4½ (OR)	1980	Lutz Dombrowski, E.Ger	28-¼
1932	Ed Gordon, USA	25-¾	1984	Carl Lewis, USA	28-¼
1936	Jesse Owens, USA	26-5½ (OR)	1988	Carl Lewis, USA	28-7¼

Triple Jump

Year	Champion	Distance	Year	Champion	Distance
1896	James Connolly, USA	44-11¾	1948	Arne Ahman, SWE	50-6¼
1900	Meyer Prinstein, USA	47-5¾ (OR)	1952	Adhemar daSilva, BRA	53-2¾ (WR)
1904	Meyer Prinstein, USA	47-1	1956	Adhemar daSilva, BRA	53-7¾ (OR)
1906	Peter O'Connor, GBR/IRL	46-2¼	1960	Józef Schmidt, POL	55-2
1908	Timothy Ahearne, GBR/IRL	48-11¼ (OR)	1964	Józef Schmidt, POL	55-3½ (OR)
1912	Gustaf Lindblom, SWE	48-5¼	1968	Viktor Saneyev, USSR	57-¾ (WR)
1920	Vilho Tuulos, FIN	47-7	1972	Viktor Saneyev, USSR	56-11¼
1924	Nick Winter, AUS	50-11¼	1976	Viktor Saneyev, USSR	56-8¾
1928	Mikio Oda, JPN	49-11	1980	Jaak Uudmäe, USSR	56-11¼
1932	Chuhei Nambu, JPN	51-7 (WR)	1984	Al Joyner, USA	56-7½
1936	Naoto Tajima, JPN	52-6 (WR)	1988	Hristo Markov, BUL	57-9¼ (OR)

Shot Put

Year	Champion	Distance	Year	Champion	Distance
1896	Robert Garrett, USA	36-9¾	1948	Wilbur Thompson, USA	56-2 (OR)
1900	Richard Sheldon, USA	46-3¼ (OR)	1952	Parry O'Brien, USA	57-1½ (OR)
1904	Ralph Rose, USA	48-7 (WR)	1956	Parry O'Brien, USA	60-11¼ (OR)
1906	Martin Sheridan, USA	40-5¼	1960	Bill Nieder, USA	64-6¾ (OR)
1908	Ralph Rose, USA	46-7½	1964	Dallas Long, USA	66-8½ (OR)
1912	Patrick McDonald, USA	50-4 (OR)	1968	Randy Matson, USA	67-4¾
1920	Ville Pörhölä, FIN	48-7¼	1972	Wladyslaw Komar, POL	69-6 (OR)
1924	Bud Houser, USA	49-2¼	1976	Udo Beyer, E.Ger	69-¾
1928	John Kuck, USA	52-¾ (WR)	1980	Vladimir Kiselyo, USSR	70-½ (OR)
1932	Leo Sexton, USA	52-6 (OR)	1984	Alessandro Andrei, ITA	69-9
1936	Hans Woellke, GER	53-1¾ (OR)	1988	Ulf Timmermann, E.Ger	73-8¾ (OR)

Discus Throw

Year	Champion	Distance	Year	Champion	Distance
1896	Robert Garrett, USA	95-7½	1948	Adolfo Consolini, ITA	173-2 (OR)
1900	Rodulf Bauer, HUN	118-3 (OR)	1952	Sim Iness, USA	180-6 (OR)
1904	Martin Sheridan, USA	128-10½ (OR)	1956	Al Oerter, USA	184-11 (OR)
1906	Martin Sheridan, USA	136 ft	1960	Al Oerter, USA	194-2 (OR)
1908	Martin Sheridan, USA	134-2 (OR)	1964	Al Oerter, USA	200-1 (OR)
1912	Armas Taipale, FIN	148-3 (OR)	1968	Al Oerter, USA	212-6 (OR)
1920	Elmer Niklander, FIN	146-7	1972	Ludvik Daněk, CZE	211-3
1924	Bud Houser, USA	151-4 (OR)	1976	Mac Wilkins, USA	221-5
1928	Bud Houser, USA	155-3 (OR)	1980	Viktor Rashchupkin, USSR	218-8
1932	John Anderson, USA	162-4 (OR)	1984	Rolf Danneberg, W.Ger	218-6
1936	Ken Carpenter, USA	165-7 (OR)	1988	Jergen Schult, E.Ger	225-9¼ (OR)

Hammer Throw

Year	Champion	Distance	Year	Champion	Distance
1900	John Flanagan, USA	163-1	1952	József Csérmák, HUN	197-11 (WR)
1904	John Flanagan, USA	168-1 (OR)	1956	Harold Connolly, USA	207-3 (OR)
1908	John Flanagan, USA	170-4 (OR)	1960	Vasily Rudenkov, USSR	220-2 (OR)
1912	Matt McGrath, USA	179-7 (OR)	1964	Romuald Klim, USSR	228-10 (OR)
1920	Pat Ryan, USA	173-5	1968	Gyula Zsivótzky, HUN	240-8 (OR)
1924	Fred Tootell, USA	174-10	1972	Anatoly Bondarchuk, USSR	247-8 (OR)
1928	Pat O'Callaghan, IRL	168-7	1976	Yuri Sedykh, USSR	254-4 (OR)
1932	Pat O'Callaghan, IRL	176-11	1980	Yuri Sedykh, USSR	268-4 (WR)
1936	Karl Hein, W.Ger	185-4 (OR)	1984	Juha Tiainen, FIN	256-2
1948	Imre Németh, HUN	183-11	1988	Sergei Litinov, USSR	278-2½ (OR)

Javelin Throw

Year	Champion	Distance	Year	Champion	Distance
1908	Eric Lemming, SWE	179-10 (WR)	1956	Egil Danielson, NOR	281-2 (WR)
1912	Eric Lemming, SWE	198-11 (WR)	1960	Viktor Tsibulenko, USSR	277-8
1920	Jonni Myyrä, FIN	215-10 (OR)	1964	Pauli Nevala, FIN	271-2
1924	Jonni Myyrä, FIN	206-7	1968	Jänis Lüsis, USSR	295-7 (OR)
1928	Erik Lundkvist, SWE	218-6 (OR)	1972	Klaus Wolfermann, W.Ger	296-10 (OR)
1932	Matti Järvinen, FIN	238-6 (OR)	1976	Miklos Németh, HUN	310-4 (WR)
1936	Gerhard Stöck, W.Ger	235-8	1980	Dainis Kula, USSR	299-2
1948	Kai Tapio Rautavaara, FIN	228-10	1984	Arto Härkönen, FIN	284-8
1952	Cy Young, USA	242-1 (OR)	1988	Tapio Korjus, FIN	276-6

Decathlon

Year	Champion	Points	Year	Champion	Points
1904	Thomas Kiely, IRL	6036	1956	Milt Campbell, USA	7937 (OR)
1912	Jim Thrope, USA	8412 (WR)	1960	Rafer Johnson, USA	8392 (OR)
1920	Helge Lövland, NOR	6803	1964	Willi Holdorf, W.Ger	7887
1924	Harold Osborn, USA	7711 (WR)	1968	Bill Toomey, USA	8193 (OR)
1928	Paavo Yrjölä, FIN	8053 (WR)	1972	Nikolai Avilov, USSR	8454 (WR)
1932	Jim Bausch, USA	8462 (WR)	1976	Bruce Jenner, USA	8617 (WR)
1936	Glenn Morris, USA	7900 (WR)	1980	Daley Thompson, GBR	8495
1948	Bob Mathias, USA	7139	1984	Daley Thompson, GBR	8798 (=WR)
1952	Bob Mathias, USA	7887 (WR)	1988	Christian Schenk, E.Ger	8488

Track & Field (Cont.)
WOMEN
100 Meters

Year	Champion	Time	Year	Champion	Time
1928	Elizabeth Robinson, USA	12.2 (=WR)	1964	Wyomia Tyus, USA	11.4
1932	Stella Walsh, POL*	11.9 (=WR)	1968	Wyomia Tyus, USA	11.0 (WR)
1936	Helen Stephens, USA	11.5‡	1972	Renate Stecher, E.Ger	11.07
1948	Fanny Blankers-Koen, HOL	11.9	1976	Annegret Richter, W.Ger	11.08
1952	Marjorie Jackson, AUS	11.5 (=WR)	1980	Lyudmila Kondratyeva, USSR	11.06
1956	Betty Cuthbert, AUS	11.5	1984	Evelyn Ashford, USA	10.97 (OR)
1960	Wilma Rudolph, USA	11.0	1988	Florence Griffith Joyner, USA	10.54 (OR)

*An autopsy performed after Walsh's death in 1980 revealed that she was a man.
‡Wind-aided.

200 Meters

Year	Champion	Time	Year	Champion	Time
1948	Fanny Blankers-Koen, HOL	24.4	1968	Irena Szewinska, POL	22.5 (WR)
1952	Marjorie Jackson, AUS	23.7	1972	Renate Stecher, E.Ger	22.40 (=WR)
1956	Betty Cuthbert, AUS	23.4 (=OR)	1976	Bärbel Eckert, E.Ger	22.37 (OR)
1960	Wilma Rudolph, USA	24.0	1980	Bärbel Eckert Wöckel, E.Ger	22.03 (OR)
1964	Edith McGuire, USA	23.0 (OR)	1984	Valerie Brisco-Hooks, USA	21.81 (OR)
			1988	Florence Griffith Joyner, USA	21.34 (WR)

400 Meters

Year	Champion	Time	Year	Champion	Time
1964	Betty Cuthbert, AUS	52.0 (OR)	1980	Marita Koch, E.Ger	48.88 (OR)
1968	Colette Besson, FRA	52.0 (=OR)	1984	Valerie Brisco-Hooks, USA	48.43 (OR)
1972	Monika Zehrt, E.Ger	51.08 (OR)	1988	Olga Bryzgina, USSR	48.65
1976	Irena Szewinska, POL	49.29 (WR)			

800 Meters

Year	Champion	Time	Year	Champion	Time
1928	Lina Radke, W.Ger	2:16.8 (WR)	1976	Tatyana Kazankina, USSR	1:54.94 (WR)
1960	Lyudmila Shevtsova, USSR	2:04.3 (=WR)	1980	Nadezhda Olizarenko, USSR	1:53.42 (WR)
1964	Ann Packer, GBR	2:01.1 (OR)	1984	Doina Melinte, ROM	1:57.60
1968	Madeline Manning, USA	2:00.9 (OR)	1988	Sigrun Wodars, E.Ger	1:56.10
1972	Hildegard Falck, W.Ger	1:58.55 (OR)			

1500 Meters

Year	Champion	Time	Year	Champion	Time
1972	Lyudmila Bragina, USSR	4:01.4 (WR)	1984	Gabriella Doria, ITA	4:03.25
1976	Tatyana Kazankina, USSR	4:05.48	1988	Paula Ivan, ROM	3:53.96 (OR)
1980	Tatyana Kazankina, USSR	3:56.6 (OR)			

3000 Meters

Year	Champion	Time	Year	Champion	Time
1984	Maricica Puică, ROM	8:35.96 (OR)	1988	Tatyana Samolenko, USSR	8:26.53 (OR)

10,000 Meters

Year	Champion	Time
1988	Olga Boldarenko, USSR	31:44.69 (OR)

Marathon

Year	Champion	Time	Year	Champion	Time
1984	Joan Benoit, USA	2:24:52	1988	Rosa Mota, POR	2:25:39

100-Meter Hurdles

Year	Champion	Time	Year	Champion	Time
1932	Babe Didrikson, USA	11.7 (WR)	1968	Maureen Caird, AUS	10.3 (OR)
1936	Trebisonda Valla, ITA	11.7	1972	Annelie Ehrhardt, E.Ger	12.59 (WR)
1948	Fanny Blankers-Koen, HOL	11.2 (OR)	1976	Johanna Schaller, E.Ger	12.77
1952	Shirley Strickland, AUS	10.9 (WR)	1980	Vera Komisova, USSR	12.56 (OR)
1956	Shirley Strickland, AUS	10.7 (OR)	1984	Benita Fitzgerald-Brown, USA	12.84
1960	Irina Press, USSR	10.8	1988	Jordanka Donkova, BUL	12.38 (OR)
1964	Karin Balzer, E.Ger	10.5			

400-Meter Hurdles

Year	Champion	Time	Year	Champion	Time
1984	Nawal El Moutawakel, MOR	54.61 (OR)	1988	Debra Flintoff-King, AUS	53.17 (OR)

4x100-Meter Relay

Year	Champion	Time	Year	Champion	Time
1928	Canada	48.4 (WR)	1964	Poland	43.6
1932	United States	46.9 (WR)	1968	United States	42.8 (WR)
1936	United States	46.9	1972	West Germany	42.81 (=WR)
1948	Holland	47.5	1976	East Germany	42.55 (OR)
1952	United States	45.9 (WR)	1980	East Germany	41.60 (WR)
1956	Australia	44.5 (WR)	1984	United States	41.65
1960	United States	44.5	1988	United States	41.98

4x400 Meter Relay

Year	Champion	Time	Year	Champion	Time
1972	East Germany	3:23.0 (WR)	1984	United States	3:18.29 (OR)
1976	East Germany	3:19.23 (WR)	1988	Soviet Union	3:15.18 (WR)
1980	Soviet Union	3:20.2			

High Jump

Year	Champion	Height	Year	Champion	Height
1928	Ethel Catherwood, CAN	5-2½	1964	Iolanda Balas, ROM	6-2¾ (OR)
1932	Jean Shiley, USA	5-5¼ (WR)	1972	Ulrike Meyfarth, W.Ger	6-3½ (=WR)
1936	Ibolya Csák, HUN	5-3	1976	Rosemarie Ackermann, E.Ger	6-4 (OR)
1948	Alice Coachman, USA	5-6 (OR)	1980	Sara Simeoni, ITA	6-5½ (OR)
1952	Esther Brand, SAF	5-5¾	1984	Ulrike Meyfarth, W.Ger	6-7½ (OR)
1956	Mildred McDaniel, USA	5-9¼ (WR)	1988	Louise Ritter, USA	6-8 (OR)
1960	Iolanda Balas, ROM	6-¾ (OR)			

Long Jump

Year	Champion	Distance	Year	Champion	Distance
1948	Olga Gyarmati, HUN	18-8¼	1972	Heidemarie Rosendahl, W.Ger	22-3
1952	Yvette Williams, NZE	20-5¾ (OR)	1976	Angela Voigt, E.Ger	22-¾
1956	Elzbieta Krzesinska, POL	20-10 (=WR)	1980	Tatiana Kolpakova, USSR	23-2 (OR)
1960	Vyera Krepkina, USSR	20-10¾ (OR)	1984	Anisoara Cusmir-Stanciu, ROM	22-10
1964	Mary Rand, GBR	22-2¼ (WR)	1988	Jackie Joyner-Kersee, USA	24-3½ (OR)
1968	Viorica Viscopoleanu, ROM	22-4½ (WR)			

Shot Put

Year	Champion	Distance	Year	Champion	Distance
1948	Micheline Ostermeyer, FRA	45-1½	1972	Nadezhda Chizhova, USSR	69-(WR)
1952	Galina Zybina, USSR	50-1¾ (WR)	1976	Ivanka Hristova, BUL	69-5¼ (OR)
1956	Tamara Tyshkevich, USSR	54-5 (OR)	1980	Ilona Slupianek, E.Ger	73-6¼ (OR)
1960	Tamara Press, USSR	56-10 (OR)	1984	Claudia Losch, W.Ger	67-2¼
1964	Tamara Press, USSR	59-6¼ (OR)	1988	Natalya Lisovskaya, USSR	72-11½
1968	Margitta Gummel, E.Ger	64-4 (WR)			

Discus Throw

Year	Champion	Distance	Year	Champion	Distance
1928	Halina Konopacka, POL	129-11¾ (WR)	1964	Tamara Press, USSR	187-10 (OR)
1932	Lillian Copeland, USA	133-2 (OR)	1968	Lia Manoliu, ROM	191-2 (OR)
1936	Gisela Mauermayer, W.Ger	156-3 (OR)	1972	Faina Meinik, USSR	218-7 (OR)
1948	Micheline Ostermeyer, FRA	137-6	1976	Evelin Schlaak, E.Ger	226-4 (OR)
1952	Nina Romaschkova, USSR	168-8 (OR)	1980	Evelin Schlaak, E.Ger	229-6 (OR)
1956	Olga Fikotová, CZE	176-1 (OR)	1984	Ria Stalman, HOL	214-5
1960	Nina Ponomaryeva, USSR	180-9 (OR)	1988	Martina Hellmann, E.Ger	237-2¼ (OR)

Javelin Throw

Year	Champion	Distance	Year	Champion	Distance
1932	Babe Didrikson, USA	143-4 (OR)	1968	Angela Nemeth, HUN	198 ft
1936	Tilly Fleischer, W.Ger	148-3 (OR)	1972	Ruth Fuchs, E.Ger	209-7
1948	Herma Bauma, AUT	149-6	1976	Ruth Fuchs, E.Ger	216-4 (OR)
1952	Dana Zátopková, CZE	165-7	1980	Maria Colon Rueñes, CUB	224-5 (OR)
1956	Inese Jaunzeme, USSR	176-8	1984	Tessa Sanderson, GBR	228-2 (OR)
1960	Elvira Ozolina, USSR	183-8 (OR)	1988	Petra Felke, E.Ger	245 ft (OR)
1964	Mihaela Penes, ROM	198-7			

Heptathlon

Seven-event Heptathlon replaced five-event Pentathlon in 1984.

Year	Champion	Points	Year	Champion	Points
1964	Irina Press, USSR	5246 (WR)	1980	Nadezhda Tkachenko, USSR	5083 (WR)
1968	Ingrid Becker, W.Ger	5098	1984	Glynis Nunn, AUS	6390 (OR)
1972	Mary Peters, GBR	4801 (WR)	1988	Jackie Joyner-Kersee, USA	7215 (WR)
1976	Siegrun Siegl, E.Ger	4745			

Volleyball

MEN

Year	Champion, 2nd, 3rd
1964	**Soviet Union**, Czechoslovakia, Japan
1968	**Soviet Union**, Japan, Czechoslovakia
1972	**Japan**, E. Germany, Soviet Union
1976	**Poland**, Soviet Union, Cuba
1980	**Soviet Union**, Bulgaria, Romania
1984	**United States**, Brazil, Italy
1988	**United States**, Soviet Union, Argentina

WOMEN

Year	Champion, 2nd, 3rd
1964	**Japan**, Soviet Union, Poland
1968	**Soviet Union**, Japan, Poland
1972	**Soviet Union**, Japan, N. Korea
1976	**Japan**, Soviet Union, S. Korea
1980	**Soviet Union**, E. Germany, Bulgaria
1984	**China**, United States, Japan
1988	**Soviet Union**, Peru, China

Water Polo

Year	Champion, 2nd, 3rd
1900	**Great Britain**, Belgium, France
1904	**USA (NY)**, USA (Chi.), USA (Mo.)
1908	**Great Britain**, Belgium, Sweden
1912	**Great Britain**, Sweden, Belgium
1920	**Great Britain**, Belgium, Sweden
1924	**France**, Belgium, United States
1928	**Germany**, Hungary, France
1932	**Hungary**, Germany, United States
1936	**Hungary**, Germany, Belgium
1948	**Italy**, Hungary, Holland
1952	**Hungary**, Yugoslavia, Italy
1956	**Hungary**, Yugoslavia, Soviet Union
1960	**Italy**, Soviet Union, Hungary
1964	**Hungary**, Yugoslavia, Soviet Union
1968	**Yugoslavia**, Soviet Union, Hungary
1972	**Soviet Union**, Hungary, United States
1976	**Hungary**, Italy, Holland
1980	**Soviet Union**, Yugoslavia, Hungary
1984	**Yugoslavia**, United States, W. Germany
1988	**Yugoslavia**, United States, Soviet Union

Freestyle Wrestling

Light Flyweight (106 lbs)

Year	Champion	
1904	Robert Curry	United States
1972	Roman Dmitriev	Soviet Union
1976	Hasan Isaev	Bulgaria
1980	Claudio Pollio	Italy
1984	Bobby Weaver	United States
1988	Takashi Kobayashi	Japan

Flyweight (115 lbs)

Year	Champion	
1904	George Mehnert	United States
1948	Lennart Viitala	Finland
1952	Hasan Gemici	Turkey
1956	Mirian Tsalkalamanidze	Soviet Union
1960	Ahmet Bilek	Turkey
1964	Yoshikatsu Yoshida	Japan
1968	Shigeo Nakata	Japan
1972	Kiyoma Kato	Japan
1976	Yuji Takada	Japan
1980	Anatoly Beloglazov	Soviet Union
1984	Saban Trstena	Yugoslavia
1988	Mitsuru Sato	Japan

Bantamweight (126 lbs)

Year	Champion	
1904	Isidor Niflot	United States
1908	George Mehnert	United States
1924	Kustaa Pihlajamäki	Finland
1928	Kaarlo Mäkinen	Finland
1932	Robert Pearce	United States
1936	Ödön Zombori	Hungary
1948	Nasuh Akar	Turkey
1952	Shohachi Ishii	Japan
1956	Mustafa Dagistanli	Turkey
1960	Terry McCann	United States
1964	Yojiro Uetake	Japan
1968	Yojiro Uetake	Japan
1972	Hideaki Yanagida	Japan
1976	Vladimir Umin	Soviet Union
1980	Sergei Beloglazov	Soviet Union
1984	Hideaki Tomiyama	Japan
1988	Sergei Beloglazov	Soviet Union

Featherweight (137 lbs)

Year	Champion	
1904	Benjamin Bradshaw	United States
1908	George Dole	United States
1920	Charles Ackerly	United States
1924	Robin Reed	United States
1928	Allie Morrison	United States
1932	Hermanni Pihlajamäki	Finland
1936	Kustaa Pihlajamäki	Finland
1948	Gazanfer Bilge	Turkey
1952	Bayram Sit	Turkey
1956	Shozo Sasahara	Japan
1960	Mustafa Dagistanli	Turkey
1964	Osamu Watanabe	Japan
1968	Masaaki Kaneko	Japan
1972	Zagalav Abdulbekov	Soviet Union
1978	Jung-Mo Yang	Korea
1980	Magomedgasan Abushev	Soviet Union
1984	Randy Lewis	United States
1988	John Smith	United States

Lightweight (150 lbs)

Year	Champion		Year	Champion	
1904	Otto Roehm	United States	1956	Emamali Habibi	Iran
1908	George de Relwyskow	Great Britain	1960	Shelby Wilson	United States
1920	Kalle Anttila	Finland	1964	Enyu Dimov	Bulgaria
1924	Russell Vis	United States	1968	Abdollah Movahhed	Iran
1928	Osvald Käpp	Estonia	1972	Dan Gable	United States
1932	Charles Pacôme	France	1976	Pavel Pinigin	Soviet Union
1936	Károly Kárpáti	Hungary	1980	Saipulla Absaidov	Soviet Union
1948	Celal Atik	Turkey	1984	In-Tak You	Korea
1952	Olle Anderberg	Sweden	1988	Arsen Fadzaev	Soviet Union

Welterweight (163 lbs)

Year	Champion		Year	Champion	
1904	Charles Erickson	United States	1960	Doug Blubaugh	United States
1924	Hermann Gehri	Switzerland	1964	Ismail Ogan	Turkey
1928	Arvo Haavisto	Finland	1968	Mahmut Atalay	Turkey
1932	Jack Van Bebber	United States	1972	Wayne Wells	United States
1936	Frank Lewis	United States	1976	Jiichiro Date	Japan
1948	Yasar Dogu	Turkey	1980	Valentin Angelov	Bulgaria
1952	Bill Smith	United States	1984	Dave Schultz	United States
1956	Mitsuo Ikeda	Japan	1988	Kenny Monday	United States

Middleweight (181 lbs)

Year	Champion		Year	Champion	
1908	Stanley Bacon	Great Britain	1960	Hasan Güngör	Turkey
1920	Eino Leino	Finland	1964	Prodan Gardzhev	Bulgaria
1924	Fritz Hagmann	Switzerland	1968	Boris Gurevitch	Soviet Union
1928	Ernst Kyburz	Switzerland	1972	Levan Tediashvili	Soviet Union
1932	Ivar Johansson	Sweden	1976	John Peterson	United States
1936	Emile Poilvé	France	1980	Ismail Abilov	Bulgaria
1948	Glen Brand	United States	1984	Mark Schultz	United States
1952	David Tsimakuridze	Soviet Union	1988	Han Myang-Woo	South Korea
1956	Nikola Stanchev	Bulgaria			

Light Heavyweight (198 lbs)

Year	Champion		Year	Champion	
1920	Anders Larsson	Sweden	1960	Ismet Atli	Turkey
1924	John Spellman	United States	1964	Aleksandr Medved	Soviet Union
1928	Thure Sjöstedt	Sweden	1968	Ahmet Ayik	Turkey
1932	Peter Mehringer	United States	1972	Ben Peterson	United States
1936	Knut Fridell	Sweden	1976	Levan Tediashvili	Soviet Union
1948	Henry Wittenberg	United States	1980	Sanasar Oganesyan	Soviet Union
1952	Wiking Palm	Sweden	1984	Ed Banach	United States
1956	Gholam Reza Takhti	Iran	1988	Makharbek Khadartsev	Soviet Union

Heavyweight (220 lbs)

Year	Champion		Year	Champion	
1972	Ivan Yarygin	Soviet Union	1984	Lou Banach	United States
1976	Ivan Yarygin	Soviet Union	1988	Vasile Puscasu	Romania
1980	Ilya Mate	Soviet Union			

Freestyle Wrestling (Cont.)

Super Heavyweight (Unlimited)

Year	Champion		Year	Champion	
1904	Bernhuff Hansen	United States	1956	Hamit Kaplan	Turkey
1908	George Con O'Kelly	Great Britain/Ireland	1960	Wilfred Dietrich	West Germany
1920	Robert Roth	Switzerland	1964	Aleksandr Ivanitsky	Soviet Union
1924	Harry Steel	United States	1968	Aleksandr Medved	Soviet Union
1928	Johan Richthoff	Sweden	1972	Aleksandr Medved	Soviet Union
1932	Johan Richthoff	Sweden	1976	Soslan Andiev	Soviet Union
1936	Kristjan Palusalu	EST	1980	Soslan Andiev	Soviet Union
1948	Gyula Bóbis	Hungary	1984	Bruce Baumgartner	United States
1952	Arsen Mekokishvili	Soviet Union	1988	David Gobedjichvili	Soviet Union

Yachting

MEN

470 Class

Year		Points	Year		Points
1976	Frank Hubner, Harro Bode, W.Ger	42.4	1984	Luis Doreste, Roberto Molina, SPA	33.7
1980	M.R.Soares, Eduardo Penido, BRA	36.4	1988	Thierry Peponnet, Luc Pillot, FRA	34.70

WOMEN

470 Class

Year		Points
1988	Allison Jolly, Lynne Jewell, USA	26.70

OPEN

Windglider

Year		Points	Year		Points
1984	Stephan van denBerg, HOL	27.7	1988	Bruce Kendall, NZE	35.40

Finn

Year		Points	Year		Points
1920	(12-ft) Johannes and Franciscus Hin, HOL		1960	Paul Elvström, DEN	8171
	(18-ft) Francis Richards & T.Hedberg, GBR		1964	Wilhelm Kuhweide, W.Ger	7638
1924	Léon Huybrechts, BEL		1968	Valentin Mankin, USSR	11.7
1928	Sven Thorell, SWE		1972	Serge Maury, FRA	58.0
1932	Jacques Lebrun, FRA	87	1976	Jochen Schümann, E.Ger	35.4
1936	Daniel Kagchelland, HOL	163	1980	Esko Rechardt, FIN	36.7
1948	Paul Elvström, DEN	5543	1984	Russell Coutts, NZE	34.7
1952	Paul Elvström, DEN	8209	1988	Jose Luis Doreste, SPA	38.10
1956	Paul Elvström, DEN	7509			

Flying Dutchman

Year		Points	Year		Points
1960	Peder Lunde, Björn Bervall, NOR	6774	1976	Jörg and Eckart Diesch, W.Ger	34.7
1964	Helmer Pedersen, Earle Wells, NZE	6255	1980	Alesandro Abascal, M.Noguer, SPA	19.0
1968	Rod Pattison, I.Macd-Smith, GBR	3.0	1984	Jonathon McKee, W.C.Buchan, USA	19.7
1972	Rod Pattison, Chris Davies, GBR	22.7	1988	J.Bojsen-Möller, C.Grönberg, DEN	31.40

Star

Year		Points	Year		Points
1932	Gilbert Gray, Andrew Libano, USA	46	1964	Durward Knowles, Cecil Cooke, BAH	5664
1936	Peter Bischoff, Hans Weise, GER	80	1968	Lowell North, Peter Barrett, USA	14.4
1948	Hilary and Paul Smart, USA	5828	1972	David Forbes, John Anderson, AUS	28.1
1952	Agost.Straulio, Nicolo Rode, ITA	7635	1980	Valentin Mankin, A.Muzychenko, USSR	24.7
1956	Herb Williams, Lawrence Low, USA	5876	1984	Wm.Buchan, Steve Erickson, USA	29.7
1960	Timir Pinegin, Fyodor Shutkov	7619	1988	Michael McIntyre, P.B.Vaile, GBR	45.70

Tornado

Year		Points	Year		Points
1976	Reg White, John Osborn, GBR	18.0	1984	Rex Sellers, Chris Timms, NZE	14.7
1980	Alex Welter, Lars Björkström, BRA	21.4	1988	J.Y.Le Deroff, Nicolas Henard, FRA	16.00

Soling

Year		Points	Year		Points
1972	United States	8.7	1984	United States	33.7
1976	Denmark	46.7	1988	East Germany	11.70
1980	Denmark	23.0			

Note: Current events not included in this summary: archery, canoeing, cycling, equestrian, fencing, team handball, judo, modern pentathlon, rowing, shooting, table tennis, weightlifting, and Greco-Roman wrestling.

WINTER OLYMPICS
S T A T I S T I C S

THROUGH THE YEARS

1924-1988

GOLD MEDAL WINNERS

THE 1991
INFORMATION PLEASE
SPORTS ALMANAC

SEC **B**

PAGE **513**

Winter Olympics, 1924-88

Gold medal winners in all of the current events: alpine skiing, biathlon, bobsled, figure skating, ice hockey, luge, nordic skiing, and speed skating.

Alpine Skiing

MEN

Downhill

Year	Champion	Time	Year	Champion	Time
1948	Henri Oreiller, FRA	2:55.0	1972	Bernhard Russi, SWI	1:51.43
1952	Zeno Colo, ITA	2:30.8	1976	Franz Klammer AUT	1:45.73
1956	Toni Sailer, AUT	2:52.2	1980	Leonhard Stock, AUS	1:45.50
1960	Jean Vuarnet, FRA	2:06.0	1984	Bill Johnson, USA	1:45.59
1964	Egon Zimmermann, AUT	2:18.16	1988	Pirmin Zurbriggen, SWI	1:59.63
1968	Jean-Claude Killy, FRA	1:59.84			

Slalom

Year	Champion	Time	Year	Champion	Time
1948	Edi Reinalter, SWI	2:10.3	1972	Francisco Ochoa, SPA	1:49.27
1952	Othmar Schneider, AUT	2:00.0	1976	Piero Gros, ITA	2:03.29
1956	Toni Sailer, AUT	3:14.7	1980	Ingemar Stenmark, SWE	1:44.26
1960	Ernst Hinterseer, AUT	2:08.9	1984	Phil Mahre, USA	1:39.41
1964	Pepi Stiegler, AUT	2:11.13	1988	Alberto Tomba, ITA	1:39.47
1968	Jean-Claude Killy, FRA	1:39.73			

Giant Slalom

Year	Champion	Time	Year	Champion	Time
1952	Stein Eriksen, NOR	2:25.0	1972	Gustav Thöni, ITA	3:09.62
1956	Toni Sailer, AUS	3:00.1	1976	Heini Hemmi, SWI	3:26.97
1960	Roger Staub, SWI	1:48.3	1980	Ingemar Stenmark, SWE	2:40.74
1964	Francois Bonlieu, FRA	1:46.71	1984	Max Julen, SWI	2:41.18
1968	Jean-Claude Killy, FRA	3:29.28	1988	Alberto Tomba, ITA	2:06.37

Super Giant Slalom

Year	Champion	Time
1988	Frank Piccard, FRA	1:39.66

Alpine Combined

Year	Champion	Points	Year	Champion	Points
1936	Franz Pfnür, GER	99.25	1988	Hubert Strolz, AUT	36.55
1948	Henri Oreiller, FRA	3.27			

WOMEN

Downhill

Year	Champion	Time	Year	Champion	Time
1948	Hedy Schlunegger, SWI	2:28.3	1972	Marie-Theres Nadig, SWI	1:36.68
1952	Trude Jochum-Beiser, AUT	1:47.1	1976	Rosi Mittermaier, W.Ger	1:46.16
1956	Madeleine Berthod, SWI	1:40.7	1980	Annemarie Moser-Pröll, AUT	1:37.52
1960	Heidi Biebl, GER	1:37.6	1984	Michela Figini, SWI	1:13.36
1964	Christl Haas, AUT	1:55.39	1988	Marina Kiehl, W.Ger	1:25.86
1968	Olga Pall, AUT	1:40.87			

Alpine Skiing (Cont.)

WOMEN

Slalom

Year	Champion	Time	Year	Champion	Time
1948	Gretchen Fraser, USA	1:57.2	1972	Barbara Cochran, USA	1:31.24
1952	Andrea Mead Lawrence, USA	2:10.6	1976	Rosi Mittermaier, W.Ger	1:30.54
1956	Renée Colliard, SWI	1:52.3	1980	Hanni Wenzel, LIE	1:25.09
1960	Anne Heggtveit, CAN	1:49.6	1984	Paoletta Magoni, ITA	1:36.47
1964	Christine Goitschel, FRA	1:29.86	1988	Vreni Schneider, SWI	1:36.69
1968	Marielle Goitschel, FRA	1:25.86			

Giant Slalom

Year	Champion	Time	Year	Champion	Time
1952	Andrea Mead Lawrence, USA	2:06.8	1972	Marie-Theres Nadig, SWI	1:29.90
1956	Ossi Reichert, GER	1:56.5	1976	Kathy Kreiner, CAN	1:29.13
1960	Yvonne Rüegg, SWI	1:39.9	1980	Hanni Wenzel, LIE	2:41.66
1964	Marielle Goitschel, FRA	1:52.24	1984	Debbie Armstrong, USA	2:20.98
1968	Nancy Greene, CAN	1:51.97	1988	Vreni Schneider, SWI	2:06.49

Super Giant Slalom

Year	Champion	Time
1988	Sigrid Wolf, AUT	1:19.03

Alpine Combined

Year	Champion	Points	Year	Champion	Points
1936	Christl Cranz, GER	97.06	1988	Anita Wachter, AUT	29.25
1948	Trude Beiser, AUT	6.58			

Biathlon

10 Kilometers

Year	Champion	Time	Year	Champion	Time
1980	Frank Ullrich, E.Ger	32:10.69	1988	Frank-Peter Roetsch, E.Ger	25:08.1
1984	Erik Kvalfoss, NOR	30:53.8			

20 Kilometers

Year	Champion	Time	Year	Champion	Time
1960	Klas Lestander, SWE	1:33:21.6	1976	Nikolai Kruglov, USSR	1:14:12.26
1964	Vladimir Melanin, USSR	1:20:26.8	1980	Anatoly Alyabiev, USSR	1:08:16.31
1968	Magnar Solberg, NOR	1:13:45.9	1984	Peter Angerer, W.Ger	1:11:52.7
1972	Magnar Solberg, NOR	1:15:55.50	1988	Frank-Peter Roetsch, E.Ger	56:33.33

4x7.5-Kilometer Relay

Year	Champion	Time	Year	Champion	Time
1968	Soviet Union	2:13:02.4	1980	Soviet Union	1:34:03.27
1972	Soviet Union	1:51:44.92	1984	Soviet Union	1:38:51.7
1976	Soviet Union	1:57:55.64	1988	Soviet Union	1:22:30.0

Bobsled

Two-Man

Year	Champion (Driver)	Time	Year	Champion (Driver)	Time
1932	United States (Hubert Stevens)	8:14.74	1968	Italy (Eugenio Monti)	4:41.54
1936	United States (Ivan Brown)	5:29.29	1972	West Germany (Wolfgang Zimmerer)	4:57.07
1948	Switzerland (Felix Endrich)	5:29.2	1976	East Germany (Meinhard Nehmer)	3:44.42
1952	Germany (Andreas Ostler)	5:24.54	1980	Switzerland Erich Schärer	4:09.36
1956	Italy (Lamberto Dalla Costa)	5:30.14	1984	East Germany (Wolfgang Hoppe)	3:25.56
1964	Great Britain (Anthony Nash)	4:21.90	1988	Soviet Union (Janis Kipours)	3:54.19

Four-Man

Year	Champion (Driver)	Time	Year	Champion (Driver)	Time
1924	Switzerland (Eduard Scherrer)	5:45.54	1964	Canada (Vic Emery)	4:14.46
1928	United States (Billy Fiske)	3:20.5	1968	Italy (Eugenio Monti)	2:17.39
1932	United States (Billy Fiske)	7:53.68	1972	Switzerland (Jean Wicki)	4:43.07
1936	Switzerland (Pierre Musy)	5:19.85	1976	East Germany (Meinhard Nehmer)	3:40.43
1948	United States (Francis Tyler)	5:20.1	1980	East Germany (Meinhard Nehmer)	3:59.92
1952	West Germany (Andreas Ostler)	5:07.84	1984	East Germany (Wolfgang Hoppe)	3:20.22
1956	Switzerland (Franz Kapus)	5:10.44	1988	Switzerland (Ekkehard Fasser)	3:47.51

Figure Skating

MEN

Year	Champion		Year	Champion	
1908	Ulrich Salchow	Sweden	1960	David Jenkins	United States
1920	Gillis Grafström	Sweden	1964	Manfred Schnelldorfer	West Germany
1924	Gillis Grafström	Sweden	1968	Wolfgang Schwarz	Austria
1928	Gillis Grafström	Sweden	1972	Ondrej Nepela	Czechoslovakia
1932	Karl Schäfer	Austria	1976	John Curry	Great Britain
1936	Karl Schäfer	Austria	1980	Robin Cousins	Great Britain
1948	Dick Button	United States	1984	Scott Hamilton	United States
1952	Dick Button	United States	1988	Brian Boitano	United States
1956	Hayes Alan Jenkins	United States			

WOMEN

Year	Champion		Year	Champion	
1908	Madge Syers	Great Britain	1960	Carol Heiss	United States
1920	Magda Julin	Sweden	1964	Sjoukje Dijkstra	Holland
1924	Herma Planck-Szabó	Austria	1968	Peggy Fleming	United States
1928	Sonja Henie	Norway	1972	Beatrix Schuba	Austria
1932	Sonja Henie	Norway	1976	Dorothy Hamill	United States
1936	Sonja Henie	Norway	1980	Anett Pötzsch	E.Germany
1948	Barbara Ann Scott	Canada	1984	Katarina Witt	E.Germany
1952	Jeanette Altwegg	Great Britain	1988	Katarina Witt	E.Germany
1956	Tenley Albright	United States			

PAIRS

Year	Champion	Year	Champions
1908	Anna Hubler & Heinrich Burger, GER	1960	Barbara Wagner & Robert Paul, CAN
1920	Ludovika & Walter Jakobsson, FIN	1964	Lyudmila Belousova & Oleg Protopopov, USSR
1924	Helene Engelmann & Alfred Berger, AUT		
1928	Andrée Joly & Pierre Brunet, FRA	1968	Lyudmila Belousova & Oleg Protopopov, USSR
1932	Andrée & Pierre Brunet, FRA		
1936	Maxi Herber & Ernst Baier, GER	1972	Irina Rodnina & Aleksei Ulanov, USSR
1948	Micheline Lannoy & Pierre Baugniet, BEL	1976	Irina Rodnina & Aleksandr Zaitsev, USSR
1952	Ria & Paul Falk, W.Ger	1980	Irina Rodnina & Aleksandr Zaitsev, USSR
1956	Elisabeth Schwartz & Kurt Oppelt, AUT	1984	Elena Valova & Oleg Vasiliev, USSR
		1988	Ekaterina Gordeeva & Sergei Grinkov, USSR

ICE DANCE

Year	Champions	Year	Champion
1976	Lyudmila Pakhomova & Aleksandr Gorshkov, USSR	1984	Jayne Torvill & Christopher Dean, GBR
1980	Natalia Linichuk & Gennady Karponosov, USSR	1988	Natalia Bestemianova &Andrei Bukin, USSR

Ice Hockey

Year	Champion, 2nd, 3rd	Year	Champion, 2nd, 3rd
1920	**Canada,** United States Czechoslovakia	1960	**United States**, Canada, Soviet Union
1924	**Canada**, United States, Great Britain	1964	**Soviet Union**, Sweden, Czechoslovakia
1928	**Canada**, Sweden, Switzerland	1968	**Soviet Union**, Czechoslovakia, Canada
1932	**Canada**, United States, Germany	1972	**Soviet Union**, United States, Czechoslovakia
1936	**Great Britain**, Canada, United States	1976	**Soviet Union**, Czechoslovakia, W.Germany
1948	**Canada**, Czechoslovakia, Switzerland	1980	**United States**, Soviet Union, Sweden
1952	**Canada**, United States, Sweden	1984	**Soviet Union**, Czechoslovakia, Sweden
1956	**Soviet Union**, United States, Canada	1988	**Soviet Union**, Finland, Sweden

Luge

MEN

Singles

Year	Champion	Time	Year	Champion	Time
1964	Thomas Köhler, E.Ger	3:26.77	1980	Bernhard Glass, E.Ger	2:54.796
1968	Manfred Schmid, AUT	2:52.48	1984	Paul Hildgartner, ITA	3:04.258
1972	Wolfgang Scheidel, E.Ger	3:27.58	1988	Jens Mueller, E.Ger	3:05.548
1976	Dettlef Günther, E.Ger	3:27.688			

Doubles

Year	Champion	Time	Year	Champion	Time
1964	Austria	1:41.62	1976	East Germany	1:25.604
1968	East Germany	1:35.85	1980	East Germany	1:19.331
1972	East Germany & Italy	1:28.35	1984	West Germany	1:23.620
			1988	East Germany	1:31.940

Luge (Cont.)
WOMEN
Singles

Year Champion	Time	Year Champion	Time
1964 Ortrun Enderlein, E.Ger	3:24.67	1980 Vera Zozulia, USSR	2:36.537
1968 Erica Lechner, ITA	2:28.66	1984 Steffi Martin, E.Ger	2:46.570
1972 Anna-Maria Müller, E.Ger	2:59.18	1988 Steffi Martin Walter, E.Ger	3:03.973
1976 Margit Schumann, E.Ger	2:50.621		

Nordic Skiing
CROSS-COUNTRY, MEN
15 Kilometers
Event was held over 18 kilometers from 1924-52.

Year Champion	Time	Year Champion	Time
1924 Thorleif Haug, NOR	1:14:31.0	1964 Eero Mäntyranta, FIN	50:54.1
1928 Johan Gröttumsbraten, NOR	1:37:01.0	1968 Harald Grönningen, NOR	47:54.2
1932 Sven Utterström, SWE	1:23:07.0	1972 Sven-Ake Lundbäck, SWE	45:28.24
1936 Erik-August Larsson, SWE	1:14:38.0	1976 Nikolai Bazhukov, USSR	43:58.47
1948 Martin Lundström, SWE	1:13:50.0	1980 Thomas Wassberg, SWE	41:57.63
1952 Hallgeir Brenden, NOR	1:01:34.0	1984 Gunde Svan, SWE	41:25.6
1956 Hallgeir Brenden, NOR	49:39.0	1988 Mikhail Deviatiarov, USSR	41:18.9
1960 Hakon Brusveen, NOR	51:55.5		

30 Kilometers

Year Champion	Time	Year Champion	Time
1956 Veikko Hakulinen, FIN	1:44:06.0	1976 Sergei Saveliev, USSR	1:30:29.38
1960 Sixten Jernberg, SWE	1:51:03.9	1980 Nikolai Zimyatov, USSR	1:27:02.80
1964 Eero Mäntyranta, FIN	1:30:50.7	1984 Nikolai Zimyatov, USSR	1:28:56.3
1968 Franco Nones, ITA	1:35:39.2	1988 Alexi Prokourorov, USSR	1:24:26.3
1972 Vyacheslav Vedenine, USSR	1:36:31.15		

50 Kilometers

Year Champion	Time	Year Champion	Time
1924 Thorleif Haug, NOR	3:44:32.0	1964 Sixten Jernberg, SWE	2:43:52.6
1928 Per Erik Hedlund, SWE	4:52:03.0	1968 Ole Ellefsaeter, NOR	2:28:45.8
1932 Veli Saarinen, FIN	4:28:00.0	1972 Pal Tyldum, NOR	2:43:14.75
1936 Elis Wiklund, SWE	3:30:11.0	1976 Ivar Formo, NOR	2:37:30.05
1948 Nils Karlsson, SWE	3:47:48.0	1980 Nikolai Zimyatov, USSR	2:27:24.60
1952 Veikko Hakulinen, FIN	3:33:33.0	1984 Thomas Wassberg, SWE	2:15:55.8
1956 Sixten Jernberg, SWE	2:50:27.0	1988 Gunde Svan, SWE	2:04:30.9
1960 Kalevi Hämäläinen, FIN	2:59:06.3		

4x10-Kilometer Relay

Year Champion	Time	Year Champion	Time
1936 Finland	2:41:33.0	1968 Norway	2:08:33.5
1948 Sweden	2:32:08.0	1972 Soviet Union	2:04:47.94
1952 Finland	2:20:16.0	1976 Finland	2:07:59.72
1956 Soviet Union	2:15.30.0	1980 Soviet Union	1:57.03.46
1960 Finland	2:18.45.6	1984 Sweden	1:55:06.3
1964 Sweden	2:18:34.6	1988 Sweden	1:43:58.6

CROSS-COUNTRY, WOMEN
5 Kilometers

Year Champion	Time	Year Champion	Time
1964 Claudia Boyarskikh, USSR	17:50.5	1980 Raisa Smetanina, SOV	15:06.92
1968 Toini Gustafsson, SWE	16:45.2	1984 Marja-Liisa Hämäläinen, FIN	17:04.0
1972 Galina Kulakova, USSR	17:00.50	1988 Marjo Matikainen, FIN	15:04.0
1976 Helena Takalo, FIN	15:48.69		

10 Kilometers

Year Champion	Time	Year Champion	Time
1952 Lydia Wideman, FIN	41:40.0	1972 Galina Kulakova, USSR	34:17.82
1956 Lyubov Kosyreva, USSR	38:11.0	1976 Raisa Smetanina, USSR	30:13.41
1960 Maria Gusakova, USSR	39:46.6	1980 Barbara Petzold, E.Ger	30:31.54
1964 Claudia Boyarskikh, USSR	40:24.3	1984 Marja-Liisa Mämäläinen, FIN	31:44.2
1968 Toini Gustafsson, SWE	36:46.5	1988 Vida Ventsene, USSR	30:08.3

20 Kilometers

Year Champion	Time	Year Champion	Time
1984 Marja-Liisa Hämäläinen, FIN	1:01.45.0	1988 Tamara Tikhonova, USSR	55:53.6

4x5-Kilometer Relay

Year	Champion	Time	Year	Champion	Time
1956	Finland	1:09:01.0	1976	Soviet Union	1:07:49.75
1960	Sweden	1:04:21.4	1980	East Germany	1:02:11.10
1964	Soviet Union	59:20.2	1984	Norway	1:06:49.7
1968	Norway	57:30.0	1988	Soviet Union	59:51.1
1972	Soviet Union	48:46.15			

SKI JUMPING

Individual 70-Meter

Year	Champion	Points	Year	Champion	Points
1964	Veikko Kankkonen, FIN	229.9	1980	Anton Innauer, AUT	266.3
1968	Jiri Raska, CZE	216.5	1984	Jens Weissflog, E.Ger	215.2
1972	Yukio Kasaya, JPN	244.2	1988	Matti Nykänen, FIN	229.1
1976	Hans-Georg Aschenbach, E.Ger	252.0			

Individual 90-Meter

Year	Champion	Points	Year	Champion	Points
1924	Jacob Tullin Thams, NOR	18.960	1964	Toralf Engan, NOR	230.7
1928	Alf Andersen, NOR	19.208	1968	Vladimir Beloussov, USSR	231.3
1932	Birger Rudd, NOR	228.1	1972	Wojciech Fortuna, POL	219.9
1936	Birger Ruud, NOR	232.0	1976	Karl Schnabl, AUT	234.8
1948	Petter Hugsted, NOR	228.1	1980	Jouko Törmänen, FIN	271.0
1952	Arnfinn Bergmann, NOR	226.0	1984	Matti Nykänen, FIN	231.2
1956	Antti Hyvärinen, FIN	227.0	1988	Matti Nykänen, FIN	224.0
1960	Helmut Rechnagel, E.Ger	227.2			

Team 90-Meter

Year	Champion	Points
1988	Finland	634.4

NORDIC COMBINED (Ski Jump and Cross-Country)

Individual

Year	Champion	Points	Year	Champion	Points
1924	Thorleif Haug, NOR	18.906	1964	Tormod Knutsen, NOR	469.28
1928	Johan Gröttumsbraten, NOR	17.833	1968	Franz Keller, GER	449.04
1932	Johan Gröttumsbraten, NOR	446.00	1972	Ulrich Wehling, GDR	413.340
1936	Oddbjörn Hagen, NOR	430.3	1976	Ulrich Wehling, GDR	423.39
1948	Heikki Hasu, FIN	448.80	1980	Ulrich Wehling, GDR	432.200
1952	Simon Slattvik, NOR	451.621	1984	Tom Sandberg, NOR	422.595
1956	Sverre Stenersen, NOR	455.000	1988	Hippolyt Kempf, SWI	235.8
1960	Georg Thoma, GER	457.952			

Team

Year	Champion	Jump Pts	30-km Time
1988	West Germany	629.8	1:20:46

Speed Skating

MEN

500 Meters

Year	Champion	Time	Year	Champion	Time
1924	Charles Jewtraw, USA	44.0	1960	Yevgeny Grishin, USSR	40.2 (=WR)
1928	Bernt Evensen, NOR	43.4 (OR)	1964	Terry McDermott, USA	40.1 (OR)
	& Clas Thunberg, FIN	43.4 (OR)	1968	Erhard Keller, W.Ger	40.3
1932	John Shea, USA	43.4 (=OR)	1972	Erhard Keller, W.Ger	39.44 (OR)
1936	Ivar Ballangrud, NOR	43.4 (=OR)	1976	Yevgeny Kulikov, USSR	39.17 (OR)
1948	Finn Helgesen, NOR	43.1 (OR)	1980	Eric Heiden, USA	38.03 (OR)
1952	Kenneth Henry, USA	43.2	1984	Sergei Fokichev, USSR	38.19
1956	Yevgeny Grishin, USSR	40.2 (=WR)	1988	Jens-Uwe Mey, E.Ger	36.45 (WR)

1000 Meters

Year	Champion	Time	Year	Champion	Time
1976	Peter Mueller, USA	1:19.32	1984	Gaétan Boucher, CAN	1:15.80
1980	Eric Heiden, USA	1:15.18 (OR)	1988	Nikolai Guliaev, USSR	1:13.03 (OR)

Speed Skating (Cont.)

1500 Meters

Year	Champion	Time	Year	Champion	Time
1924	Clas Thunberg, FIN	2:20.8	1964	Ants Antson, USSR	2:10.3
1928	Clas Thunberg, FIN	2:21.1	1968	Kees Verkerk, HOL	2:03.4 (OR)
1932	Jack Shea, USA	2:57.5	1972	Ard Schenk, HOL	2:02.96 (OR)
1936	Charles Mathisen, NOR	2:19.2 (OR)	1976	Jan Egil Storholt, NOR	1:59.38 (OR)
1948	Sverre Farstad, NOR	2:17.6 (OR)	1980	Eric Heiden, USA	1:55.44 (OR)
1952	Hjalmar Andersen, NOR	2:20.4	1984	Gaétan Boucher, CAN	1:58.36
1956	Yevgeny Grishin, USSR	2:08.6 (WR)	1988	Andre Hoffman, E.Ger	1:52.06 (WR)
1960	Roald Aas, NOR	2:10.4			

5000 Meters

Year	Champion	Time	Year	Champion	Time
1924	Clas Thunberg, FIN	8:39.0	1964	Knut Johannesen, NOR	7:38.4 (OR)
1928	Ivar Ballangrud, NOR	8:50.5	1968	Fred Anton Maier, NOR	7:22.4 (WR)
1932	Irving Jaffee, USA	9:40.8	1972	Ard Schenk, HOL	7:23.61
1936	Ivar Ballangrud, NOR	8:19.6 (OR)	1976	Sten Stensen, NOR	7:24.48
1948	Reidar Liaklev, NOR	8:29.4	1980	Eric Heiden, USA	7:02.29 (OR)
1952	Hjalmar Andersen, NOR	8:10.6 (OR)	1984	Tomas Gustafson, SWE	7:12.28
1956	Boris Shilkov, USSR	7:48.7 (OR)	1988	Tomas Gustafson, SWE	6:44.63 (WR)
1960	Viktor Kosichkin, USSR	7:51.3			

10,000 Meters

Year	Champion	Time	Year	Champion	Time
1924	Julius Skutnabb, FIN	18:04.8	1964	Jonny Nilsson, SWE	15:50.1
1928	Irving Jaffee, USA	18:36.5	1968	Johnny Höglin, SWE	15:23.6 (OR)
1932	Irving Jaffee, USA	19:13.6	1972	Ard Schenk, HOL	15:01.35 (OR)
1936	Ivar Ballangrud, NOR	17:24.3 (OR)	1976	Piet Kleine, HOL	14:50.59 (OR)
1948	Ake Seyffarth, SWE	17:26.3	1980	Eric Heiden, USA	14:28.13 (WR)
1952	Hjallis Andersen, NOR	16:45.8 (OR)	1984	Igor Malkov, USSR	14:39.90
1956	Sigvard Ericsson, SWE	16:35.9 (OR)	1988	Tomas Gustafson, SWE	13:48.20 (WR)
1960	Knut Johannesen, NOR	15:46.6 (WR)			

WOMEN

500 Meters

Year	Champion	Points	Year	Champion	Time
1960	Helga Haase, E.Ger	45.9	1976	Sheila Young, USA	42.76 (OR)
1964	Lydia Skoblikova, USSR	45.0 (OR)	1980	Karin Enke, E.Ger	41.78 (OR)
1968	Lyudmila Titova, USSR	46.1	1984	Christa Rothenburger, E.Ger	41.02 (OR)
1972	Anne Henning, USA	43.33 (OR)	1988	Bonnie Blair, USA	39.10 (WR)

1000 Meters

Year	Champion	Time	Year	Champion	Time
1960	Klara Guseva, USSR	1:34.1	1976	Tatiana Averina, USSR	1:28.43 (OR)
1964	Lydia Skoblikova, USSR	1:33.2 (OR)	1980	Natalia Petruseva, USSR	1:24.10 (OR)
1968	Carolina Geijssen, HOL	1:32.6 (OR)	1984	Karin Enke, E.Ger	1:21.61 (OR)
1972	Monika Pflug, W.Ger	1:31.40 (OR)	1988	Christa Rothenburger, E.Ger	1:17.65 (WR)

1500 Meters

Year	Champion	Time	Year	Champion	Time
1960	Lydia Skoblikova, USSR	2:25.2 (WR)	1976	Galina Stepanskaya, USSR	2:16.58 (OR)
1964	Lydia Skoblikova, USSR	2:22.6 (OR)	1980	Annie Borckink, HOL	2:10.95 (OR)
1968	Kaija Mustonen, FIN	2:22.4 (OR)	1984	Karin Enke, E.Ger	2:03.42 (WR)
1972	Dianne Holum, USA	2:20.85 (OR)	1988	Yvonne Van Gennip, HOL	2:00.68 (OR)

3000 Meters

Year	Champion	Time	Year	Champion	Time
1960	Lydia Skoblikova, USSR	5:14.3	1976	Tatiana Averina, USSR	4:45.19 (OR)
1964	Lydia Skoblikova, USSR	5:14.9	1980	Bjorg Eva Jensen, NOR	4:32.13 (OR)
1968	Johanna Schut, HOL	4:56.2 (OR)	1984	Andrea Schöne, E.Ger	4:24.79 (OR)
1972	Christina Baas-Kaiser, HOL	4:52.14 (OR)	1988	Yvonne Van Gennip, HOL	4:11.94 (WR)

5000 Meters

Year	Champion	Time
1988	Yvonne Van Gennip, HOL	7:14.13 (WR)

Susan Butcher shares the victory stand in Nome, Alaska, with her lead dogs after winning the Iditarod Sled Dog Race in record time, March 14. The victory was Butcher's fourth in five years.

MISCELLANEOUS SPORTS

Directory

Baseball

Little League World Series

Twelve-year-old Sun Chao-Chi pitched a two-hitter and struck out 16 as Taipei, Taiwan routed Shippensburg, Pa., 9-0, on Aug.26 to win the Little League World Series at Williamsport, Pa. The victory marked the 14th time in 17 appearances that Taiwan has won the title. Since 1967, Asian ballclubs from Taiwan, Japan and South Korea have won 19 of 24 championships.

Year	Winner	Score	Loser	Year	Winner	Score	Loser
1947	Williamsport, PA	16-7	Lock Haven, PA	1970	Wayne, NJ	2-0	Campbell, CA
1948	Lock Haven, PA	6-5	St. Petersburg, FL	1971	Tainan, Taiwan	12-3	Gary, IN
1949	Hammonton, NJ	5-0	Pensacola, FL	1972	Taipei, Taiwan	6-0	Hammond, IN
				1973	Tainan City, Taiwan	12-0	Tucson, AZ
1950	Houston, TX	2-1	Bridgeport, CT	1974	Kao Hsiung, Taiwan	7-2	El Cajon, CA
1951	Stamford, CT	3-0	Austin, TX	1975	Lakewood, NJ	4-3*	Tampa, FL
1952	Norwalk, CT	4-3	Monongahela, PA	1976	Tokyo, Japan	10-3	Campbell, CA
1953	Birmingham, AL	1-0	Schenectady, NY	1977	Kao Hsiung, Taiwan	7-2	El Cajun, CA
1954	Schenectady, NY	7-5	Colton, CA	1978	Pin-Tung, Taiwan	11-1	Danville, CA
1955	Morrisville, PA	4-3	Merchantville, NJ	1979	Hsien, Taiwan	2-1	Campbell, CA
1956	Roswell, NM	3-1	Merchantville, NJ				
1957	Monterrey, Mex.	4-0	LaMesa, CA	1980	Hua Lian, Taiwan	4-3	Tampa, FL
1958	Monterrey, Mex.	10-1	Kankakee, IL	1981	Tai-Chung, Taiwan	4-2	Tampa, FL
1959	Hamtramck, MI	12-0	Auburn, CA	1982	Kirkland, WA	6-0	Hsien, Taiwan
				1983	Marietta, GA	3-1	Barahona, D.Rep.
1960	Levittown, PA	5-0	Ft. Worth, TX	1984	Seoul, S.Korea	6-2	Altamonte Sgs, FL
1961	El Cajon, CA	4-2	El Campo, TX	1985	Seoul, S.Korea	7-1	Mexicali, Mex.
1962	San Jose, CA	3-0	Kankakee, IL	1986	Tainan Park, Taiwan	12-0	Tucson, AZ
1963	Granada Hills, CA	2-1	Stratford, CT	1987	Hua Lian, Taiwan	21-1	Irvine, CA
1964	Staten Island, NY	4-0	Monterrey, Mex.	1988	Tai-Chung, Taiwan	10-0	Pearl City, HI
1965	Windsor Locks, CT	3-1	Stoney Creek, Can.	1989	Trumbull, CT	5-2	Kaohsiung, Taiwan
1966	Houston, TX	8-2	W.New York, NJ				
1967	West Tokyo, Japan	4-1	Chicago, IL	1990	Taipei, Taiwan	9-0	Shippensburg, PA
1968	Osaka, Japan	1-0	Richmond, VA				
1969	Taipei, Taiwan	5-0	Santa Clara,CA				

*Foreign teams were banned from the tournament in 1975. The ban was lifted the next year.

Chess

World Championship

The first World Chess Association (FIDE) World Championship contested in the United States will get underway Oct. 8, 1990, when champion Garry Kasparov of the Soviet Union meets former champion and countryman Anatoly Karpov in New York. The first half of the 24-game match will take place at the Macklowe Center in New York, while the second half is scheduled for Lyons, France.

Kasparov won the title on Nov.9, 1985, defeating Karpov, 5-3 (with 16 draws), in their second championship match. Their first match was declared void on Feb.15, 1985, after a record 48 games and 40 draws. Karpov led 5-3, but Kasparov had won the last two games when the match was called.

Kasparov has successfully defended his title twice, both times against Karpov—winning 12½-11½ (5 games to 4 with 15 draws) in 1986 and tying Karpov 12-12 (4 games to 4 with 16 draws) in 1987. The challenger must win the match outright to win the championship.

World Champions

Years		Years	
1866-94	Wilhelm Steinitz, Austria	1958-59	Mikhail Botvinnik, USSR
1894-		1960-61	Mikhail Tal, USSR
1921	Emanuel Lasker, Germany	1961-63	Mikhail Botvinnik, USSR
1921-27	Jose Capablanca, Cuba	1963-69	Tigran Petrosian, USSR
1927-35	Alexander Alekhine, France	1969-72	Boris Spassky, USSR
1935-37	Max Euwe, Holland	1972-75	Bobby Fischer, USA
1937-46	Alexander Alekhine, France	1975-85	Anatoly Karpov, USSR
1948-57	Mikhail Botvinnik, USSR	1985-	Garry Kasparov, USSR
1957-58	Vassily Smyslov, USSR		

Note: Fischer defaulted Championship in 1975.

U.S. Champions

Grandmaster Lev Alburt defeated grandmaster Larry Christiansen, 3-0, Aug. 16 in Jacksonville, Fla., to win the US championship for the second time. Alburt previously held the title from 1984-85.

For the first time in many years, the 16-player championship tournament was conducted on the knockout system. Note that US champions from 1857-91 are unofficial.

Years		Years		Years	
1857-71	Paul Morphy	1946-48	Samuel Reshevsky	1981-83	Walter Browne
1871-76	George Mackenzie	1948-51	Herman Steiner		& Yasser Seirawan
1876-80	James Mason	1951-54	Larry Evans	1983	Roman Dzindzichashvili,
1880-89	George Mackenzie	1954-57	Arthur Bisguier		Larry Christiansen
1889-90	Samuel Lipschutz	1957-61	Bobby Fischer		& Walter Browne
1890	Jackson Showalter	1961-62	Larry Evans	1984-85	Lev Alburt
1890-91	Max Judd	1962-68	Bobby Fischer	1986	Yasser Seirawan
1891-92	Jackson Showalter	1968-69	Larry Evans	1987	Joel Benjamin
1892-94	Samuel Lipshutz	1969-72	Samuel Reshevsky		& Nick DeFirmian
1894	Jackson Showalter	1972-73	Robert Byrne	1988	Michael Wilder
1894-95	Albert Hodges	1973-74	Lubomir Kavalek	1989	Roman Dzindzichashvili,
1895-97	Jackson Showalter		& John Grefe		Stuart Rachels
1897-		1974-77	Walter Browne		& Yasser Seirawan
1906	Harry Pillsbury	1978-80	Lubomir Kabalek	1990	Lev Alburt
1906-09	Vacant	1980-81	Larry Evans,		
1909-36	Frank Marshall		Larry Christiansen,		
1936-44	Samuel Reshevsky		& Walter Browne		
1944-46	Arnold Denker				

Dogs

Iditarod Sled Dog Race

Susan Butcher set a new record of 11 days, 1 hour, 53 minutes and 28 seconds on March 14, to win her fourth Iditarod Trail Dog Sled Race in five years. Butcher's 11-dog team finished ahead of defending champion Joe Runyan's sled to claim the $50,000 first prize.

The annual 1158-mile race stretches from Anchorage to Nome, Alaska. Begun in 1973, the course follows an old frozen river mail route and is named after a deserted mining town along the way. The Iditarod also commemorates a famous midwinter emergency mission to get medical supplies to Nome during a 1925 diptheria epidemic. Men and women mushers compete together.

Multiple winners: Susan Butcher and Rick Svenson (4); Rick Mackey (2).

Year	Winner	Elapsed Time	Year	Winner	Elapsed Time
1973	Dick Wilmarth	20 days, 00:49:41	1982	Rick Swenson	16 days, 04:40:10
1974	Carl Huntington	20 days, 15:02:07	1983	Rick Mackey	12 days, 14:10:44
1975	Emmitt Peters	14 days, 14:43:45	1984	Dean Osmar	12 days, 15:07:33
1976	Gerald Riley	18 days, 22:58:17	1984	Libby Riddles	18 days, 00:20:17
1977	Rick Swenson	16 days, 16:27:13	1986	Susan Butcher	11 days, 15:06:00
1978	Dick Mackey	14 days, 18:52:24	1987	Susan Butcher	11 days, 02:05:13
1979	Rick Swenson	15 days, 10:37:47	1988	Susan Butcher	11 days, 11:41:40
1980	Joe May	14 days, 07:11:51	1989	Joe Runyan	11 days, 05:24:34
1981	Rick Swenson	12 days, 08:45:02	1990	Susan Butcher	11 days, 01:53:23*

*Course record.

Westminster Kennel Club

A red, 3-year-old Pekingese, Champion Wendessa Crown Prince, was judged Best-in-Show at the 114th Westminster Kennel Club show, Feb.13, at Madison Square Garden in New York. The Peke, owned by Ed Jenner of Burlington, Wis., was the smallest of the 2903 dogs competing in the show and the first of his breed to win the top prize since 1982.

Best in Show

The Westminster show is the most prestigious canine event in America. Held every year since 1877, it is one of the oldest annual sporting events in the country.

Multiple winners: Ch.Warren Remedy (3); Ch.Chinoe's Adamant James, Ch.Comejo Wycollar Boy, Ch.Flornell Spicy Piece of Halleston; Ch.Matford Vic, Ch.My Own Brucie, Ch.Pendley Calling of Blarney, Ch.Rancho Dobe's Storm (2).

Year	Champion	Breed	Year	Champion	Breed
1907	Warren Remedy	Fox Terrier	1917	Comejo Wycollar Boy	Fox Terrier
1908	Warren Remedy	Fox Terrier	1918	Haymarket Faultless	Bull Terrier
1909	Warren Remedy	Fox Terrier	1919	Briergate Bright Beauty	Airedale
1910	Sabine Rarebit	Fox Terrier	1920	Comejo Wycollar Boy	Fox Terrier
1911	Tickle Em Jock	Scot.Terrier	1921	Midkiff Seductive	Cocker Spaniel
1912	Kenmore Sorceress	Airedale	1922	Boxwood Barkentine	Airedale
1913	Strathway Prince Albert	Bulldog	1923	No best-in-show award	
1914	Brentwood Hero	Old Eng.Sheepdog	1924	Barberryhill Bootlegger	Sealyham
1915	Matford Vic	Old Eng.Sheepdog	1925	Governor Moscow	Pointer
1916	Matford Vic	Old Eng.Sheepdog	1926	Signal Circuit	Fox Terrier

Dogs (Cont.)
Westminster K.C. Best in Show

Year	Champion	Breed
1927	Pinegrade Perfection	Sealyham
1928	Talavera Margaret	Fox Terrier
1929	Land Loyalty of Bellhaven	Collie
1930	Pendley Calling of Blarney	Fox Terrier
1931	Pendley Calling of Blarney	Fox Terrier
1932	Nancolleth Markable	Pointer
1933	Warland Protector of Shelterock	Airedale
1934	Flornell Spicy Bit of Halleston	Fox Terrier
1935	Nunsoe Duc de la Terrace of Blakeen	Standard Poodle
1936	St.Margaret Magnificent of Clairedale	Sealyham
1937	Flornell Spicy Bit of Halleston	Fox Terrier
1938	Daro of Maridor	English Setter
1939	Ferry v.Rauhfelsen of Giralda	Doberman
1940	My Own Brucie	Cocker Spaniel
1941	My Own Brucie	Cocker Spaniel
1942	Wolvey Pattern of Edgerstoune	W.Highland Terrier
1943	Pitter Patter of Piperscroft	Miniature Poodle
1944	Flornell Rarebit of Twin Ponds	Welsh Terrier
1945	Shieling's Signature	Scot.Terrier
1946	Hetherington Model Rhythm	Fox Terrier
1947	Warlord of Mazelaine	Boxer
1948	Rock Ridge Night Rocket	Bedling.Terrier
1949	Mazelaine's Zazarac Brandy	Boxer
1950	Walsing Winning Trick of Edgerstoune	Scot.Terrier
1951	Bang Away of Sirrah Crest	Boxer
1952	Rancho Dobe's Storm	Doberman
1953	Rancho Dobe's Storm	Doberman
1954	Carmor's Rise and Shine	Cocker Spaniel
1955	Kippax Fearnought	Bulldog
1956	Wilber White Swan	Toy Poodle
1957	Shirkhan of Grandeur	Afghan Hound

Year	Champion	Breed
1958	Puttencove Promise	Standard Poodle
1959	Fontclair Festoon	Miniature Poodle
1960	Chick T'Sun of Caversham	Pekingese
1961	Cappoquin Little Sister	Toy Poodle
1962	Elfinbrook Simon	W.Highland Terrier
1963	Wakefield's Black Knight	English Springer Spaniel
1964	Courtenay Fleetfoot of Pennyworth	Whippet
1965	Carmichaels Fanfare	Scottish Terrier
1966	Zeloy Mooremaides Magic	Fox Terrier
1967	Bardene Bingo	Scottish Terrier
1968	Stingray of Derryabah	Lakeland Terrier
1969	Glamoor Good News	Skye Terrier
1970	Arriba's Prima Donna	Boxer
1971	Chinoe's Adamant James	E.S.Spaniel
1972	Chinoe's Adamant James	E.S.Spaniel
1973	Acadia Command Performance	Stan.Poodle
1974	Gretchenhof Columbia River	German SH Pointer
1975	Sir Lancelot of Barvan	Old Eng.Sheepdog
1976	Jo Ni's Red Baron of Crofton	Lakeland Terrier
1977	Dersade Bobby's Girl	Sealyham
1978	Cede Higgens	Yorkshire Terrier
1979	Oak Tree's Irishtocrat	Irish Water Spaniel
1980	Sierra Cinnar	Siberian Husky
1981	Dhandy Favorite Woodchuck	Pug
1982	St.Aubrey Dragonora of Elsdon	Pekingese
1983	Kabik's The Challenger	Afghan Hound
1984	Seaward's Blackbeard	Newfoundland
1985	Braeburn's Close Encounter	Scot.Terrier
1986	Marjetta National Acclaim	Pointer
1987	Covy Tucker Hill's Manhattan	Ger.Sheperd
1988	Great Elms Prince Charming II	Pomeranian
1989	Royal Tudor's Wild As The Wind	Doberman
1990	Wendessa Crown Prince	Pekingese

Fishing
IGFA All-Tackle World Records
As of Sept. 1, 1990

All-tackle records are maintained for the heaviest fish of any species caught on any line up to 130-lb (60 kg) class and certified by the International Game Fish Association. **Address:** 3000 East Las Olas Blvd., Ft.Lauderdale, FL, 33316. **Telephone:** 305-467-0161.

FRESHWATER FISH

Species	Lbs-Oz	Where Caught	Date	Angler
Barramundi	59-12	Pt.Stuart, Australia	Apr. 7,1983	Andrew Davern
Bass, largemouth	22- 4	Montgomery Lake, GA	Jun. 2,1932	George W.Perry
Bass, peacock	26- 8	Matevini River, Colombia	Jan.26,1982	Rod Neubert
Bass, redeye	8- 3	Flint River, GA	Oct.23,1977	David A.Hubbard
Bass, rock	3- 0	York River, Ontario	Aug. 1,1974	Peter Gulgin
Bass, smallmouth	11-15	Dale Hollow Lake, KY	Jul. 9,1955	David L.Hayes
Bass, spotted	9- 4	Parris Lake, CA	Jan.24,1987	Steven West
	9- 4	Lake Perris, CA	Apr. 1,1987	Gilbert Rowe
Bass, striped (landlocked)	66- 0	O'Neill Forebay, Los Banos, CA	Jun.29,1988	Ted Furnish
Bass, Suwannee	3-14	Suwannee River, FL	Mar. 2,1985	Ronnie Everett
Bass, white	6-13	Lake Orange, VA	Jul.31,1989	Ronald L.Sprouse
Bass, whiterock	24- 3	Leesville Lake, VA	May 12,1989	David N.Lambert
Bass, yellow	2- 4	Lake Monroe, IN	Mar.27,1977	Donald L.Stalker
Bluegill	4-12	Ketona Lake, AL	Apr. 9,1950	T.S.Hudson
Bowfin	21- 8	Florence, SC	Jan.29,1980	Robert L.Harmon
Buffalo, bigmouth	70- 5	Bussey Brake, Bastrop, LA	Apr.21,1980	Delbert Sisk
Buffalo, black	55- 8	Cherokee Lake, TN	May 3,1984	Edward H.McLain
Buffalo, smallmouth	68- 8	Lake Hamilton, AR	May 16,1984	Jerry L.Dolezal
Bullhead, black	8- 0	Lake Waccabuc, NY	Aug. 1,1951	Kani Evans
Bullhead, brown	5- 8	Veal Pond, GA	May 22,1975	Jimmy Andrews
Bullhead, yellow	4- 4	Mormon Lake, AZ	May 11,1984	Emily Williams
Burbot	18- 4	Pickford, MI	Jan.31,1980	Tom Courtemanche

Fishing

Species	Lbs-Oz	Where Caught	Date	Angler
Carp	75-11	Lac de St.Cassien, France	May 21,1987	Leo van der Gugten
Catfish, blue	97- 0	Missouri River, SD	Sep.16,1959	Edward B.Elliott
Catfish, channel	58- 0	Santee-Cooper Res., SC	Jul. 7,1964	W.B. Whaley
Catfish, flathead	91- 4	Lake Lewisville, TX	Mar.28,1982	Mike Rogers
Catfish, white	17- 7	Success Lake, Tulare, CA	Nov.15,1981	Chuck Idell
Char, Arctic	32- 9	Tree River, Canada	Jul.30,1981	Jeffery Ward
Crappie, black	4- 8	Kerr Lake, VA	Mar. 1,1981	L.Carl Herring,Jr.
Crappie, white	5- 3	Enid Dam, MS	Jul.31,1957	Fred L.Bright
Dolly Varden	12- 0	Noatak River, AK	Jul.10,1987	Kenneth T.Alt
Dorado	51- 5	Corrientes, Argentina	Sep.27,1984	Armando Giudice
Drum, freshwater	54- 8	Nickajack Lake, TN	Apr.20,1972	Benny E.Hull
Gar, alligator	279- 0	Rio Grande, TX	Dec. 2,1951	Bill Valverde
Gar, Florida	21- 3	Boca Raton, FL	June 3,1981	Jeff Sabol
Gar, longnose	50- 5	Trinity River, TX	Jul.30,1954	Townsend Miller
Gar, shortnose	5- 0	Sally Jones Lake, OK	Apr.26,1985	Buddy Croslin
Gar, spotted	8-12	Tennessee River, AL	Aug.26,1987	Winston H.Baker
Grayling, Arctic	5-15	Katseyedie River, N.W.T.	Aug.16,1967	Jeanne P.Branson
Goldfish	3- 0	Southland Pk., Livingston, TX	May 8,1988	Kenneth R.Kinsey
Inconnu	53- 0	Pah River, AK	Aug.20,1986	Lawrence E.Hudnall
Kokanee	9- 6	Okanagan Lake, Brit.Columbia	Jun.18,1988	Norm Kuhn
Muskellunge	69-15	St. Lawrence River, NY	Sep.22,1957	Arthur Lawton
Muskellunge, tiger	51- 3	Lac Vieux-Desert, WI-MI	Jul.16,1919	John A.Knobla
Perch, Nile	152- 1	Tende Bay, Entebbe, Uganda	Jun. 4,1989	Kurt M.Fenster
Perch, white	4-12	Messalonskee Lake, ME	Jun. 4,1949	Mrs.Earl Small
Perch, yellow	4- 3	Bordentown, NJ	May, 1865	Dr.C.C.Abbot
Pickerel, chain	9- 6	Homerville, GA	Feb.17,1961	Baxley McQuaig, Jr.
Pike, northern	55- 1	Lake of Grefeerm, W.Germany	Oct.16,1986	Lothar Louis
Redhorse, greater	9- 3	Salmon River, Pulaski, NY	May 11,1985	Jason Wilson
Redhorse, river	5- 9	Mooresville, AL	Mar.27,1985	Don Hale
Redhorse, silver	11- 7	Plum Creek, WI	May 29,1985	Neal D.G.Long
Salmon, Atlantic	79- 2	Tana River, Norway	1928	Henrik Henriksen
Salmon, chinook	97- 4	Kenai River, AK	May 17,1985	Les Anderson
Salmon, chum	32- 0	Behm Canal, AK	Jun. 7,1985	Fredrick Thynes
Salmon, coho	33- 4	Salmon River, Pulaski, NY	Sep.27,1989	Jerry Lifton
Salmon, pink	12- 9	Morse & Kenai Rivers, AK	Aug.17,1974	Steven Alan Lee
Salmon, sockeye	15- 3	Kenai River, AK	Aug. 9,1987	Stan Roach
Sauger	8-12	Lake Sakakawea, ND	Oct. 6,1971	Mike Fischer
Shad, American	11- 4	Conn.River, S.Hadley, MA	May 19,1986	Bob Thibodo
Sturgeon, lake	92- 4	Kettle River, MN	Jun. 8,1986	James M.DeOtis
Sturgeon, white	468- 0	Benicia, CA	Jul. 9,1983	Joey Pallotta 3rd
Sunfish, green	2- 2	Stockton Lake, MO	Jun,18,1971	Paul M.Dilley
Sunfish, redbreast	1-12	Suwannee River, FL	May 29,1984	Alvin Buchanan
Sunfish, redear	4-13	Merritt's Pond, Mariana, FL	Mar.13,1986	Joey Floyd
Tigerfish	97- 0	Zaire River, Kinshasa, Zaire	Jul. 9,1988	Raymond Houtmans
Tilapia	6- 0	Lake Okeechobee, FL	Jun.24,1989	Joseph M.Tucker
Trout, Apache	2-10	White Mt.Apache Res., AZ	Jun.27,1989	Mike Shannon
Trout, brook	14- 8	Nipigon River, Ontario	July, 1916	Dr. W.J.Cook
Trout, brown	35-15	Nahuel Huapi, Argentina	Dec.16,1952	Eugenio Cavaglia
Trout, bull	32- 0	Lake Pond Orielle, ID	Oct.27,1949	N.L.Higgins
Trout, cutthroat	41- 0	Pyramid Lake, NV	Dec., 1925	John Skimmerhorn
Trout, golden	11- 0	Cooks Lake, WY	Aug. 5,1948	Charles S.Reed
Trout, lake	65- 0	Great Bear Lake, N.W.T.	Aug. 8,1970	Larry Daunis
Trout, rainbow	42- 2	Bell Island, AK	Jun.22,1970	David Robert White
Trout, tiger	20-13	Lake Michigan, WI	Aug.12,1978	Peter M.Friedland
Walleye	25- 0	Old Hickory Lake, TN	Apr. 1,1960	Mabry Harper
Warmouth	2- 7	Guess Lake, Holt, FL	Oct.19,1985	Tony D.Dempsey
Whitefish, lake	14- 6	Meaford, Ontario	May 21,1984	Dennis M.Laycock
Whitefish, mountain	5- 6	Rioh River, Saskatchewan	Jun.15,1988	John R.Bell
Whitefish, river	11- 2	Skrabean, Nymoua, Sweden	Dec. 9,1984	Jorgen Larsson
Whitefish, round	6- 0	Putahow River, Manitoba	Jun.14,1984	Allan J.Ristori
Zander	25- 2	Trosa, Sweden	Jun.12,1986	Harry Lee Tennison

SALTWATER FISH

Species	Lbs-Oz	Where Caught	Date	Angler
Albacore	88- 2	Gran Canaria, Canary Islands	Nov.19,1977	Siegfried Dickemann
Amberjack, greater	155-10	Challenger Bank, Bermuda	Jun.24,1981	Joseph Dawson
Amberjack, pacific	104- 0	Baja Calif., Mexico	Jul. 4,1984	Richard Cresswell
Barracuda, greater	83- 0	Lagos, Nigeria	Jan.13,1952	K.J.W.Hackett
Barracuda, Mexican	21- 0	Phantom Island, Costa Rica	Mar.27,1987	E.Greg Kent
Barracuda, slender	17- 4	Sitra Channel, Bahrain	Nov.21,1985	Roger Cranswick
Bass, barred sand	13- 3	Huntington Beach, CA	Aug.29,1988	Robert Halal
Bass, black sea	9- 8	Virginia Beach, VA	Jan. 9,1987	Joe Mizelle, Jr.

Fishing (Cont.)
FRESHWATER FISH

Species	Lbs-Oz	Where Caught	Date	Angler
Bass, European	20-11	Stes Maries de la Mer, France	May. 6,1986	Jean Baptiste Bayle
Bass, giant sea	563- 8	Anacapa Island, CA	Aug.20,1968	J.D.McAdam, Jr.
Bass, striped	78- 8	Atlantic City, NJ	Sep.21,1982	Albert R.McReynolds
Bluefish	31-12	Hatteras, NC	Jan.30,1972	James M.Hussey
Bonefish	19- 0	Zululand, South Africa	May 26,1962	Brian W.Batchelor
Bonito, Atlantic	18- 4	Faial Island, Azores	Jul. 8,1953	D.Gama Higgs
Bonito, Pacific	23- 8	Victoria, Mahe, Seychelles	Feb.19,1975	Anne Cochain
Cabezon	21- 0	Langora Island, Brit.Columbia	Sep.20,1989	Tadakazu Kumashiro
Cobia	135- 9	Shark Bay, W.Australia	Jul. 9,1985	Peter W.Goulding
Cod, Atlantic	98-12	Isle of Shoals, NH	Jun. 8,1969	Alphonse Bielevich
Cod, Pacific	30- 0	Andrew Bay, AK	Jul. 7,1984	Donald R.Vaughn
Conger	102- 8	Plymouth, Devon, England	Jul.18,1983	Raymond E.Street
Dolphin	87- 0	Papagallo Gulf, Costa Rica	Sep.25,1976	Manual Salazar
Drum, black	113- 1	Lewes, DE	Sep.15,1975	Gerald M.Townsend
Drum, red	94- 2	Avon, NC	Nov. 7,1984	David G.Deuel
Eel, African mottled	36- 1	Durban, S. Africa	Jun.10,1984	Ferdie van Nooten
Eel, American	4- 7	Lake Ronkonkoma, NY	Nov.15,1986	William C.Cummings
Flounder, southern	20- 9	Nassau Sound, FL	Dec.23,1983	Larenza Mungin
Flounder, summer	22- 7	Montauk, NY	Sep.15,1975	Charles Nappi
Flounder, winter	7- 0	Fire Island, NY	May 8,1986	Einar F.Grell
Grouper, warsaw	436-12	Gulf of Mexico, Destin, FL	Dec.22,1985	Steve Haeusler
Haddock	9-15	Perkins Cove, Ogunquit, ME	May 24,1988	Jim Donohue
Halibut, Atlantic	255- 4	Gloucester, MA	Jul.28,1989	Sonny Manley
Halibut, California	53- 4	Santa Rosa Island, CA	Jul. 7,1988	Russell J.Harmon
Halibut, Pacific	356- 8	Castineau Channel, Juneau, AK	Nov. 6,1986	Gregory C.Olsen
Jack, crevalle	54- 7	Port Michel, Gabon	Jan.15,1982	Thomas F.Gibson, Jr.
Jack, horse-eye	24- 8	Miami, FL	Dec.20,1982	Tito Schnau
Jack, almaco (Pacific)	132- 0	La Paz, Baja Calif., Mexico	Jul.21,1964	Howard H.Hahn
Jewfish	680- 0	Fernandina Beach, FL	May 20,1961	Lynn Joyner
Kawakawa	29- 0	Clarion Island, Mexico	Dec.17,1986	Ronald Nakamura
Lingcod	64- 0	Elfin Cove, AK	Aug. 2,1988	David L.Bauer
Mackerel, cero	17- 2	Islamorada, FL	Apr. 5,1986	G.Michael Mills
Mackerel, king	90- 0	Key West, FL	Feb.16,1976	Norton I.Thomton
Mackerel, Spanish	13- 0	Ocracoke Inlet, NC	Nov. 7,1987	Robert Cranton
Marlin, Atlantic blue	1282- 0	St.Thomas, Virgin Islands	Aug. 6,1977	Larry Martin
Marlin, Black	1560- 0	Cabo Blanco, Peru	Aug. 4,1953	A.C.Glassell, Jr.
Marlin, Pacific blue	1376- 0	Kaaiwi Point, Kona, HI	May 31,1982	Jay W.deBeaubien
Marlin, striped	494- 0	Tutakaka, New Zealand	Jan.16,1986	Bill Boniface
Marlin, white	181-14	Vitoria, Brazil	Dec. 8,1979	Evandro Luiz Coser
Permit	51- 8	Lake Worth, FL	Apr.28,1978	William M. Kenney
Pollack	26- 7	Salcombe, Devon, England	Dec.30,1984	Robert Perry
Pollock	46- 7	Brielle, NJ	May 26,1975	John Tomes Holton
Pompano, African	50- 8	Daytona Beach, FL	Apr.21,1990	Tom Sargent
Roosterfish	114- 0	La Paz, Baja Calif., Mexico	Jun. 1,1960	Abe Sackheim
Runner, blue	7- 0	Bimini, Bahamas	Jul.26,1989	Linda A.Schulz
Runner, rainbow	33-10	Clarion Island, Mexico	Mar.14,1976	Ralph A.Mikkelsen
Sailfish, Atlantic	128- 1	Luanda, Angola	Mar.27,1974	Harm Steyn
Sailfish, Pacific	221- 0	Santa Cruz Is., Ecuador	Feb.12,1947	C.W.Stewart
Seabass, white	83-12	San Felipe, Mexico	Mar.31,1953	L.C.Baumgardner
Seatrout, spotted	16- 0	Mason's Beach, VA	May 28,1977	William Katko
Shark, blue	437- 0	Catherine Bay, NSW, Australia	Oct. 2,1976	Peter Hyde
Shark, great white	2664- 0	Ceduna, S.Australia	Apr.21,1959	Alfred Dean
Shark, greenland	1708- 9	Trondheimsfjord, Norway	Oct.18,1987	Terje Nordtvedt
Shark, hammerhead	991- 0	Sarasota, FL	May 30,1982	Allen Ogle
Shark, mako	1115- 0	Black River, Mauritius	Nov.16,1988	Patrick Guillanton
Shark, porbeagle	465- 0	Padstow, Cornwall, England	Jul.23,1976	Jorge Potier
Shark, thresher	802- 0	Tutukaka, New Zealand	Feb. 8,1981	Dianne North
Shark, tiger	1780- 0	Cherry Grove, SC	Jun.14,1964	Walter Maxwell
Skipjack, black	20- 5	Alijos Rocks, Baja, Mexico	Oct.14,1983	Roger Torriero
Snapper, cubera	121- 8	Cameron, LA	Jul. 5,1982	Mike Hebert
Snapper, red	46- 8	Destin, FL	Oct. 1,1985	E.Lane Nichols, III
Snook	53-10	Parismina Ranch, Costa Rica	Oct.18,1978	Gilbert Ponzi
Spearfish	90-13	Madeira Island, Portugal	Jun. 2,1980	Joseph Larkin
Swordfish	1182- 0	Iquique, Chile	May 7,1953	L.Marron
Tanguigue	99- 0	Natal, S. Africa	Mar.14,1982	Michael Wilkinson
Tarpon	283- 0	Lake Maracaibo, Venezuela	Mar.19,1956	M.Salazar
Tautog	24- 0	Wachapreague, VA	Aug.25,1987	Gregory R.Bell
Toadfish, oyster	3-10	Ocracoke, NC	May 19,1990	Stuart C.Lee
Tuna, Atlantic bigeye	375- 8	Ocean City, MD	Aug.26,1977	Cecil Browne

Species	Lbs-Oz	Where Caught	Date	Angler
Tuna, blackfin	42- 0	Bermuda	Jun.2,1978	Alan J. Card
	42- 0	Challenger Bank, Bermuda	Jul.18,1989	Gilbert C.Pearman
Tuna, bluefin	1496- 0	Aulds Cove, Nova Scotia	Oct.26,1979	Ken Fraser
Tuna, longtail	79- 2	Montague Is., NSW, Australia	Apr.12,1982	Tim Simpson
Tuna, Pacific bigeye	435- 0	Cabo Blanco, Peru	Apr.17,1957	Dr.Russell Lee
Tuna, skipjack	41-14	Pearl Beach, Mauritius	Nov.12,1985	Edmund Heinzen
Tuna, southern bluefin	348- 5	Whakatane, New Zealand	Jan.16,1981	Rex Wood
Tuna, yellowfin	388-12	San Benedicto Island, Mexico	Apr. 1,1977	Curt Wiesenhutter
Tunny, little	35- 2	Cape De Garde, Algeria	Dec.14,1988	Jean Yves Chatard
Wahoo	149- 0	Cat Cay, Bahamas	Jun.15,1962	John Pirovano
Weakfish	19- 2	Jones Beach, Long Island, NY	Oct.11,1984	Dennis R.Rooney
	19- 2	Delaware Bay, DE	May 20,1989	William E.Thomas
Yellowtail, California	78- 0	Alijos Rocks, Baja, Mexico	Jun.27,1987	Richard W.Cresswell
Yellowtail, southern	114-10	Tauranga, New Zealand	Feb. 5,1984	Mike Godfrey

Lacrosse
NCAA Men's Division I

Led by three-time All-America midfielders and twin brothers Gary and Paul Gaits, Syracuse routed Loyola of Maryland, 21-9, on May 28 to become only the second team to win three straight NCAA Division I lacrosse titles. Gary Gaits scored a total of 15 goals for the Orangemen in the semifinals and the championship game while Paul had three goals and three assists in the final.

Johns Hopkins won three titles in a row from 1978-80. **Multiple winners:** Johns Hopkins (7); Syracuse (4); Cornell and North Carolina (3); Maryland (2).

Year	Champion	Score	Runner-up	Year	Champion	Score	Runner-up
1971	Cornell	12- 6	Maryland	1981	North Carolina	14-13	Johns Hopkins
1972	Virginia	13-12	Johns Hopkins	1982	North Carolina	7- 5	Johns Hopkins
1973	Maryland	10- 9**	Johns Hopkins	1983	Syracuse	17-16	Johns Hopkins
1974	Johns Hopkins	17-12	Maryland	1984	Johns Hopkins	13-10	Syracuse
1975	Maryland	20-13	Navy	1985	Johns Hopkins	11- 4	Syracuse
1976	Cornell	16-13*	Maryland	1986	North Carolina	10- 9*	Virginia
1977	Cornell	16- 8	Johns Hopkins	1987	Johns Hopkins	11-10	Cornell
1978	Johns Hopkins	13- 8	Cornell	1988	Syracuse	13- 8	Cornell
1979	Johns Hopkins	15- 9	Maryland	1989	Syracuse	13-12	Johns Hopkins
1980	Johns Hopkins	9- 8**	Virginia	1990	Syracuse	21- 9	Loyola,MD

*One overtime. **Two overtimes.

NCAA Men's Division III

There is no NCAA Men's Division II competition in lacrosse.

Year		Year		Year		Year		Year	
1980	Hobart	1982	Hobart	1984	Hobart	1986	Hobart	1988	Hobart
1981	Hobart	1983	Hobart	1985	Hobart	1987	Hobart	1989	Hobart
								1990	Hobart

Power Boat Racing
APBA Gold Cup

Tom D'Eath piloted Miss Budweiser to a second consecutive victory in the APBA Gold Cup finals, June 10 on the Detroit River. His average speed was 143.176 mph.

The American Power Boat Association Gold Cup for unlimited hydroplane racing is the oldest active motor sports trophy in North America. The first Gold Cup was competed for on the Hudson River in New York in June and September of 1904. Since then several cities have hosted the race, led by Detroit (25 times, including 1990) and Seattle (14). Note that (*) indicates driver was also owner of the winning boat.

Drivers with multiple wins: Bill Muncey (8); Chip Hanauer (7); Gar Wood (5); Dean Chenoweth (4); Caleb Bragg, Tom D'Eath, Lou Fageol, Ron Musson, George Reis and Jonathon Wainwright (3); Danny Foster, George Henley, Vic Kliesrath, E.J.Schroeder, Bill Schumacher, Zalmon G.Simmons Jr., Joe Taggart and George Townsend (2).

Year	Boat	Driver	Avg.MPH	Year	Boat	Driver	Avg.MPH
1904	Standard (June)	*Carl Riotte	23.160	1913	Ankle Deep	*Cas Mankowski	42.779
1904	Vingt-Et-Un II (Sept.)	*W.Sharpe Kilmer	24.900	1914	Baby Speed Demon II	Jim Blackton & Bob Edgren	48.458
1905	Chip I	*J.Wainwright	15.000	1915	Miss Detroit	Johnny Milot	
1906	Chip II	*J.Wainwright	25.000			& Jack Beebe	37.656
1907	Chip II	*J.Wainwright	23.903	1916	Miss Minneapolis	Bernard Smith	48.860
1908	Dixie II	*E.J.Schroeder	29.938	1917	Miss Detroit II	*Gar Wood	54.410
1909	Dixie II	*E.J.Schroeder	29.590	1918	Miss Detroit II	Gar Wood	51.619
				1919	Miss Detroit III	*Gar Wood	42.748
1910	Dixie III	*F.K.Burnham	32.473				
1911	MIT II	*J.H.Hayden	37.000	1920	Miss America I	*Gar Wood	62.022
1912	P.D.Q. II	*A.G.Miles	39.462	1921	Miss America I	*Gar Wood	52.825

Power Boat Racing (Cont.)
APBA Gold Cup

Year	Boat	Driver	Avg.MPH	Year	Boat	Driver	Avg.MPH
1922	Packard Chriscraft	*J.G.Vincent	40.253	1956	Miss Thirftaway	Bill Muncey	96.552
1923	Packard Chriscraft	Caleb Bragg	43.867	1957	Miss Thriftaway	Bill Muncey	101.787
1924	Baby Bootlegger	*Caleb Bragg	45.302	1958	Hawaii Kai III	Jack Regas	103.
1925	Baby Bootlegger	*Caleb Bragg	47.240	1959	Maverick	Bill Stead	104.481
1926	Greenwich Folly	*Geo.Townsend	47.984	1960	Not held		
1927	Greenwich Folly	*Geo.Townsend	47.662	1961	Miss Century 21	Bill Muncey	99.678
1928	No race			1962	Miss Century 21	Bill Muncey	100.710
1929	Imp	*Richard Hoyt	48.662	1963	Miss Bardahl	Ron Musson	105.124
1930	Hotsy Totsy	*Vic Kliesrath	52.673	1964	Miss Bardahl	Ron Musson	103.433
1931	Hotsy Totsy	*Vic Kliesrath	53.602	1965	Miss Bardahl	Ron Musson	103.132
1932	Delphine IV	Bill Horn	57.775	1966	Tahoe Miss	Mira Slovak	93.019
1933	El Lagarto	*George Reis	56.260	1967	Miss Bardahl	Bill Shumacher	101.484
1934	El Lagarto	*George Reis	55.000	1968	Miss Bardahl	Bill Shumacher	108.173
1935	El Lagarto	*George Reis	55.056	1969	Miss Budweiser	Bill Sterett	98.504
1936	Impshi	Kaye Don	45.735	1970	Miss Budweiser	DeanChenoweth	99.562
1937	Notre Dame	Clell Perry	63.675	1971	Miss Madison	Jim McCormick	98.043
1938	Alagi	*Theo Rossi	64.340	1972	Atlas Van Lines	Bill Muncey	104.277
1939	My Sin	*Z.G.Simmons,Jr	66.133	1973	Miss Budweiser	DeanChenoweth	99.043
1940	Hotsy Totsy III	*Sidney Allen	48.295	1974	Pay 'n Pak	George Henley	104.428
1941	My Sin	*Z.G.Simmons,Jr	52.509	1975	Pay 'n Pak	George Henley	108.921
1942	Not held			1976	Miss U.S.	Tom D'Eath	100.412
1943	Not held			1977	Atlas Van Lines	*Bill Muncey	111.822
1944	Not held			1978	Atlas Van Lines	*Bill Muncey	111.412
1945	Not held			1979	Atlas Van Lines	*Bill Muncey	100.765
1946	Tempo VI	*Guy Lombardo	68.132	1980	Miss Budweiser	DeanChenoweth	106.932
1947	Miss Peps V	Danny Foster	57.000	1981	Miss Budweiser	DeanChenoweth	116.932
1948	Miss Great Lakes	Danny Foster	46.845	1982	Atlas Van Lines	Chip Hanauer	120.050
1949	My Sweetie	Bill Cantrell	73.612	1983	Atlas Van Lines	Chip Hanauer	118.507
1950	Slo-Mo-Shun IV	Ted Jones	78.216	1984	Atlas Van Lines	Chip Hanauer	130.175
1951	Slo-Mo-Shun V	Lou Fageol	90.871	1985	Miller American	Chip Hanauer	120.643
1952	Slo-Mo-Shun V	Stan Dollar	79.923	1986	Miller American	Chip Hanauer	116.523
1953	Slo-Mo-Shun IV & Lou Fageol	Joe Taggart	99.108	1987	Miller American	Chip Hanauer	127.620
1954	Slo-Mo-Shun IV	Joe Taggart & Lou Fageol	92.613	1988	Miss Circus Circus	Chip Hanauer & Jim Prevost	123.756
1955	Gale V	Lee Schoenith	99.552	1989	Miss Budweiser	Tom D'Eath	131.209
				1990	Miss Budweiser	Tom D'Eath	143.176

Pro Rodeo
All-Around Champion Cowboys

Twenty-year-old Ty Murray became the youngest man ever to win the pro rodeo's World Champion All-Around Cowboy title in 1990. The Odessa, Tex., native combined his efforts in saddle bronc riding and bareback riding to lead all cowboys with $134,806 in earnings.

The Professional Rodeo Cowboys Association (PRCA) title of All-Around World Champion Cowboy goes to the rodeo athlete who wins the most prize money in a single year in two or more events. Only prize money earned in sanctioned PRCA rodeos is counted. From 1929-44, All-Around champions were named by the Rodeo Association of America (earnings for those years is not available).

Multiple winners: Tom Ferguson and Larry Mahan (6); Jim Shoulders (5); Lewis Feild and Dean Oliver (3); Everett Bowman, Lewis Brooks, Clay Carr, Bill Linderman, Phil Lyne, Gerald Roberts, Casey Tibbs and Harry Tompkins (2).

Year		Year		Year	
1929	Earl Thode	1935	Everett Bowman	1940	Fritz Truan
1930	Clay Carr	1936	John Bowman	1941	Homer Pettigrew
1931	John Schneider	1937	Everett Bowman	1942	Gerald Roberts
1932	Donald Nesbit	1938	Burel Mulkey	1943	Louis Brooks
1933	Clay Carr	1939	Paul Carney	1944	Louis Brooks
1934	Leonard Ward				

Year		Earnings	Year		Earnings	Year		Earnings
1945	No award		1955	Casey Tibbs	42,065	1965	Dean Oliver	33,163
1946	No award		1956	Jim Shoulders	43,381	1966	Larry Mahan	40,358
1947	Todd Whatley	$18,642	1957	Jim Shoulders	33,299	1967	Larry Mahan	51,996
1948	Gerald Roberts	21,766	1958	Jim Shoulders	32,212	1968	Larry Mahan	49,129
1949	Jim Shoulders	21,495	1959	Jim Shoulders	32,905	1969	Larry Mahan	57,726
1950	Bill Linderman	30,715	1960	Harry Tompkins	32,522	1970	Larry Mahan	41,493
1951	Casey Tibbs	29,104	1961	Benny Reynolds	31,309	1971	Phil Lyne	49,245
1952	Harry Tompkins	30,934	1962	Tom Nesmith	32,611	1972	Phil Lyne	60,852
1953	Bill Linderman	33,674	1963	Dean Oliver	31,329	1973	Larry Mahan	64,447
1954	Buck Rutherford	40,404	1964	Dean Oliver	31,150	1974	Tom Ferguson	66,929

Year		Earnings	Year		Earnings	Year		Earnings
1975	Tom Ferguson	50,300	1980	Paul Tierney	105,568	1985	Lewis Feild	130,347
1976	Tom Ferguson	87,908	1981	Jimmie Cooper	105,861	1986	Lewis Feild	166,042
1977	Tom Ferguson	65,981	1982	Chris Lybbert	123,709	1987	Lewis Feild	144,335
1978	Tom Ferguson	83,734	1983	Roy Cooper	153,391	1988	Dave Appleton	121,546
1979	Tom Ferguson	96,272	1984	Dee Picket	122,618	1989	Ty Murray	134,806

Rowing

Collegiate Varsity Eights

The Wisconsin men and Princeton women won the Collegiate Varsity Eights titles in 1990. Wisconsin won the Cincinnati Regatta on June 16, with a time of 5:52.5 over the 2000-meter course, beating Harvard by over four seconds. Princeton took the women's title June 3, in Madison, Wisc., with a time of 5:52.2 over a 1852-meter course. Radcliffe finished two seconds back.

MEN

National championship determined at Cincinnati Regatta over a 2000-meter course on Harsha Lake since 1982. Winner receives Herschede Cup.

Multiple winners: Harvard (5); Wisconsin (2).

Year	Champion	Time	Runner-up	Time
1982	Yale	5:50.8	Cornell	5:54.15
1983	Harvard	5:59.6	Washington	6:00.0
1984	Washington	5:51.1	Yale	5:55.6
1985	Harvard	5:44.4	Princeton	5:44.87
1986	Wisconsin	5:57.8	Brown	5:59.9
1987	Harvard	5:35.17	Brown	5:35.63
1988	Harvard	5:35.98	Northeastern	5:37.07
1989	Harvard	5:36.6	Washington	5:38.93
1990	Wisconsin	5:52.5	Harvard	5:56.84

WOMEN

National championship held over various distances at 10 different venues since 1979. Distances—1000 meters (1979-81); 1500 meters (1982-83); 1000 meters (1984); 1750 meters (1985); 2000 meters (1986-88); 1852 meters (since 1989).

Multiple winners: Washington (7).

Year	Champion	Time	Runner-up	Time
1979	Yale	3:06	California	3:08.6
1980	California	3:05.4	Oregon St.	3:05.8
1981	Washington	3:20.6	Yale	3:22.9
1982	Washington	4:56.4	Wisconsin	4:59.83
1983	Washington	4:57.5	Dartmouth	5:03.02
1984	Washington	3:29.48	Radcliffe	3:31.08
1985	Washington	5:28.4	Wisconsin	5:32.0
1986	Wisconsin	6:53.28	Radcliffe	6:53.34
1987	Washington	6:33.8	Yale	6:37.4
1988	Washington	6:41.0	Yale	6:42.37
1989	Cornell	5:34.9	Wisconsin	5:37.5
1990	Princeton	5:52.2	Radcliffe	5:54.2

The Harvard-Yale Regatta

Harvard won the 125th Harvard-Yale Regatta for varsity eights for the sixth year in a row, June 10, covering the 4-mile course in 19 minutes, 35 seconds. The Harvard-Yale Regatta is the country's oldest intercollegiate event and Harvard holds a 74-51 edge.

Intercollegiate Rowing Assn. Regatta

VARSITY EIGHTS

The Intercollegiate Rowing Association (IRA) was formed in 1895 by several northeastern schools, shortly after Harvard and Yale quit the Rowing Association (established in 1871) to stage an annual race of their own. Since then the IRA Regatta has been contested over courses of varying lengths in Poughkeepsie, N.Y., Marietta, Ohio, and Onondaga Lake in Syracuse, N.Y. The race has been over a 2000-meter course in Syracuse since 1968.

Distances: 4 miles (1895-97,1899-1916,1925-41); 3 miles (1898,1921-24,1947-49,1952-63,1965-67); 2 miles (1920,1950-51); 2000 meters (1964,since 1968).

Multiple winners: Cornell (24); Navy (12); California and Washington (10); Penn (8); Wisconsin (7); Syracuse (6); Brown and Columbia (4).

Year		Year		Year		Year	
1895	Columbia	1910	Cornell	1925	Navy	1940	Washington
1896	Cornell	1911	Cornell	1926	Washington	1941	Washington
1897	Cornell	1912	Cornell	1927	Columbia	1942	Not held
1898	Penn	1913	Syracuse	1928	California	1943	Not held
1899	Penn	1914	Columbia	1929	Columbia	1944	Not held
1900	Penn	1915	Cornell	1930	Cornell	1945	Not held
1901	Cornell	1916	Syracuse	1931	Navy	1946	Not held
1902	Cornell	1917	Not held	1932	California	1947	Navy
1903	Cornell	1918	Not held	1933	Not held	1948	Washington
1904	Syracuse	1919	Not held	1934	California	1949	California
1905	Cornell	1920	Syracuse	1935	California	1950	Washington
1906	Cornell	1921	Navy	1936	Washington	1951	Wisconsin
1907	Cornell	1922	Navy	1937	Washington	1952	Navy
1908	Syracuse	1923	Washington	1938	Navy	1953	Navy
1909	Cornell	1924	Washington	1939	California	1954	Navy*

Rowing (Cont.)
IRA Regatta

Year		Year		Year		Year	
1955	Cornell	1964	California	1973	Wisconsin	1982	Cornell
1956	Cornell	1965	Navy	1974	Wisconsin	1983	Brown
1957	Cornell	1966	Wisconsin	1975	Wisconsin	1984	Navy
1958	Cornell	1967	Penn	1976	California	1985	Princeton
1959	Wisconsin	1968	Penn	1977	Cornell	1986	Brown
		1969	Penn	1978	Syracuse	1987	Brown
1960	California			1979	Brown	1988	Northeastern
1961	California	1970	Washington			1989	Penn
1962	Cornell	1971	Cornell	1980	Navy		
1963	Cornell	1972	Penn	1981	Cornell	1990	Wisconsin

*In 1954, Navy was disqualified because of an ineligble coxwain; no trophies were given.

1990 University Boat Race
(on the Thames in London)

The Oxford heavyweight crew won the 136th renewal of the University Boat Race on March 31, 1990, easily outdistancing Cambridge for the fourth year in a row and 14th time in the last 15 meetings. Oxford covered the 4¼-mile course in 17 minutes and 15 seconds, the fastest time since 1985 but well off the record of 16:45 set by the Dark Blues in 1984. Despite this latest defeat, Cambridge still leads the series 69-66-1.

Sailing
The America's Cup

International yacht racing was launched in 1851 when England's Royal Yacht Squadron staged a 60-mile regatta around the Isle of Wight and offered a silver trophy to the winner. The 101-foot schooner **America**, sent over by the New York Yacht Club, won the race and the prize. Originally called the Hundred-Guinea Cup, the trophy was renamed The America's Cup after the winning boat's owners deeded it to the NYYC with instructions to defend it whenever challenged.

From 1870-1980, the NYYC successfully defended the Cup 25 straight times; first in large schooners and J-class boats that measured up to 140 feet in overall length, then in 12-meter boats.

A foreign yacht finally won the Cup in 1983 when **Australia II** beat defender **Liberty** in the seventh and deciding race off Newport, R.I. Four years later, the San Diego Yacht Club's **Stars & Stripes** won the Cup back, sweeping the four races of the final series off Fremantle, Australia.

Then in 1988, New Zealand's Mercury Bay Boating Club, unwilling to wait the usual three- to four-year period between Cup defenses, challenged the SDYC to a match contest, citing the Cup's 102-year-old Deed of Gift, which clearly stated that every challenge had to be honored. Mercury Bay announced it would race a 133-foot monohull. San Diego countered with a 60-foot catamaran. The resulting best-of-three series (Sept.7-8) was a mismatch as the SDYC's catamaran **Stars & Stripes** won two straight by margins of better than 18 and 21 minutes.

Mercury Bay syndicate leader Michael Fay protested the outcome and took the SDYC to court in New York State (where the Deed of Gift was first filed) claiming San Diego had violated the spirit of the deed by racing a catamaran instead of a monohull. N.Y.State Supreme Court judge Carmen Ciparick agreed and on March 28, 1989, ordered the SDYC to hand the Cup over to Mercury Bay. The SDYC refused, but did consent to the court's appointment of the New York Yacht Club as custodian of the Cup until an appeal was ruled on.

On Sept.19, 1989, the Appellate Division of the N.Y.Supreme Court overturned Ciparick's decision and awarded the Cup back to the SDYC. An appeal by Mercury Bay was denied by the N.Y.Court of Appeals on Apr.26, 1990, ending three years of legal wrangling.

The America's Cup will next be defended in May, 1992, off San Diego. To avoid the chaos of the last 12 months, a new class of boat—75-foot monohulls with 110-foot masts—has been agreed to by all potential competitors.

Note that (*) indicates skipper was also owner of the boat.

Schooners and J-Class Boats

Year	Winner	Skipper	Series	Loser	Skipper
1851	America	Richard Brown	—	—	—
1870	Magic	Andrew Comstock	1-0	Cambria, GBR	J.Tannock
1871	Columbia (2-1) & Sappho (2-0)	Nelson Comstock Sam Greenwood	4-0	Livonia, GBR	J.R.Woods
1876	Madeleine	Josephus Williams	2-0	Countess of Dufferin, CAN	J.E.Ellsworth
1881	Mischief	Nathanael Clock	2-0	Atalanta, CAN	Alexander Cuthbert*
1885	Puritan	Aubrey Crocker	2-0	Genesta, GBR	John Carter
1886	Mayflower	Martin Stone	2-0	Galatea, GBR	Dan Bradford
1887	Volunteer	Henry Haff	2-0	Thistle, GBR	John Barr
1893	Vigilant	William Hansen	3-0	Valkyrie II, GBR	Wm.Granfield
1895	Defender	Henry Haff	3-0	Valkyrie III, GBR	Wm.Granfield
1899	Columbia	Charles Barr	3-0	Shamrock I, GBR	Archie Hogarth
1901	Columbia	Charles Barr	3-0	Shamrock II, GBR	E.A.Sycamore
1903	Reliance	Charles Barr	3-0	Shamrock III, GBR	Bob Wringe
1920	Resolute	Charles F.Adams	3-2	Shamrock IV, GBR	William Burton
1930	Enterprise	Harold Vanderbilt*	4-0	Shamrock V, GBR	Ned Heard
1934	Rainbow	Harold Vanderbilt*	4-2	Endeavour, GBR	T.O.M.Sopwith
1937	Ranger	Harold Vanderbilt*	4-0	Endeavour II, GBR	T.O.M.Sopwith

12-Meter Boats

Year	Winner	Skipper	Series	Loser	Skipper
1958	Columbia	Briggs Cunningham	4-0	Sceptre, GBR	Graham Mann
1962	Weatherly	Bus Mosbacher	4-1	Gretel, AUS	Jock Sturrock
1964	Constellation	Bob Bavier & Eric Ridder	4-0	Sovereign, AUS	Peter Scott
1967	Intrepid	Bus Mosbacher	4-0	Dame Pattie, AUS	Jock Sturrock
1970	Intrepid	Bill Ficker	4-1	Gretel II, AUS	Jim Hardy
1974	Courageous	Ted Hood	4-0	Southern Cross, AUS	John Cuneo
1977	Courageous	Ted Turner	4-0	Australia	Noel Robins
1980	Freedom	Dennis Conner	4-1	Australia	Jim Hardy
1983	Australia II	John Bertrand	4-3	Liberty, USA	Dennis Conner
1987	Stars & Stripes	Dennis Conner	4-0	Kookaburra III, AUS	Iain Murray

60-ft Catamaran vs 133-ft Monohull

Year	Winner	Skipper	Series	Loser	Skipper
1988	Stars & Stripes	Dennis Conner	2-0	New Zealand, NZE	David Barnes

All-American Soap Box Derby

Mark Mihal of Valparaiso, Ind., won the Kit Division and Sami Jones of Salem, Ore., won the Masters Division of the 1990 Derby Aug.11 in Akron. Both drivers are 13 years old.

The All-American Soap Box Derby is a coasting race for small gravity-powered cars built by their drivers and assembled within strict guidelines on size, weight and cost. The Derby got its name in the 1930s when most cars were built from wooden soap boxes. Held every summer on the second Saturday of August at Derby Downs in Akron, Ohio, the Soap Box Derby is open to all boys and girls from 9 to 16 years old who qualify.

There are two competitive divisions: Kit Cars (ages 9-16), made up of racers assembled from Derby-approved car kits, and Masters (ages 12-16), made up of racers designed by drivers but constructed with Derby-approved hardware. The racing ramp at Derby Downs is 953.75 feet with an 11 percent grade.

Derby Champions

One champion was determined at the All-American Soap Box Derby each year from 1934-75, then Junior and Senior division champions from 1976-87, then Kit Car and Masters champions since 1989.

Year	Winner	Hometown	Age	Year	Winner	Hometown	Age
1934	Robert Turner	Muncie, IN	11	1970	Samuel Gupton	Durham, NC	13
1935	Maurice Bale, Jr.	Anderson, IN	13	1971	Larry Blair	Oroville, CA	13
1936	Herbert Muench, Jr.	St.Louis	14	1972	Robert Lange, Jr.	Boulder, CO	14
1937	Robert Ballard	White Plains, NY	12	1973	Bret Yarborough	Elk Grove, CA	11
1938	Robert Berger	Omaha, NE	14	1974	Curt Yarborough	Elk Grove, CA	11
1939	Clifton Hardesty	White Plains, NY	11	1975	Karren Stead	Lower Bucks, PA	11
1940	Thomas Fisher	Detroit	12	1976	JR: Phil Raber	Sugarcreek, OH	11
1941	Claude Smith	Akron, OH	14		SR: Joan Ferdinand	Canton, OH	14
1942	Not held			1977	JR: Mark Ferdinand	Canton, OH	10
1943	Not held				SR: Steve Washburn	Bristol, CT	15
1944	Not held			1978	JR: Darren Hart	Salem, OR	11
1945	Not held				SR: Greg Cardinal	Flint, MI	13
1946	Gilbert Klecan	San Diego	14	1979	JR: Russell Yurk	Flint, MI	10
1947	Kenneth Holmboe	Charleston, WV	14		SR: Craig Kitchen	Akron, OH	14
1948	Donald Strub	Akron, OH	13	1980	JR: Chris Fulton	Indianapolis	11
1949	Fred Derks	Akron, OH	15		SR: Dan Porul	Sherman Oaks, CA	12
1950	Harold Williamson	Charleston, WV	15	1981	JR: Howie Fraley	Portsmouth, OH	11
1951	Darwin Cooper	Williamsport, PA	15		SR: Tonia Schlegel	Hamilton, OH	13
1952	Joe Lunn	Columbus, GA	11	1982	JR: Carol A.Sullivan	Rochester, NH	10
1953	Fred Mohler	Muncie, IN	14		SR: Matt Wolfgang	Lehigh Val., PA	12
1954	Richard Kemp	Los Angeles	14	1983	JR: Tony Carlini	Del Mar, CA	10
1955	Richard Rohrer	Rochester, NY	14		SR: Mike Burdgick	Flint, MI	14
1956	Norman Westfall	Rochester, NY	14	1984	JR: Chris Hess	Hamilton, OH	11
1957	Terry Townsend	Anderson, IN	14		SR: Anita Jackson	St.Louis	15
1958	James Miley	Muncie, IN	15	1985	JR: Michael Gallo	Danbury, CT	12
1959	Barney Townsend	Anderson, IN	13		SR: Matt Sheffer	York, PA	14
1960	Fredric Lake	South Bend, IN	11	1986	JR: Marc Behan	Dover, NH	9
1961	Dick Dawson	Wichita, KS	13		SR: Tami Jo Sullivan	Lancaster, OH	13
1962	David Mann	Gary, IN	14	1987	JR: Matt Margules	Danbury, CT	11
1963	Harold Conrad	Duluth, MN	12		SR: Brian Drinkwater	Bristol, CT	14
1964	Gregory Schumacher	Tacoma, WA	14	1988	KIT: Jason Lamb	Des Moines, IA	10
1965	Robert Logan	Santa Ana, CA	12		MAS: David Duffield	Kansas City	13
1966	David Krussow	Tacoma, WA	12	1989	KIT: David Schiller	Dayton, OH	12
1967	Kenneth Cline	Lincoln, NE	13		MAS: Faith Chavarria	Ventura, CA	12
1968	Branch Lew	Muncie, IN	11	1990	KIT: Mark Mihal	Valparaiso, IN	12
1969	Steve Souter	Midland, TX	12		MAS: Sami Jones	Salem, OR	13

Softball

Men's and women's national champions since 1933 in Major Fast Pitch, Major Slow Pitch and Super Slow Pitch (men only). Sanctioned by the Amateur Softball Association of America.

MEN

Major Fast Pitch

Year	Year	Year
1933 J.L.Gill Boosters, Chicago	1954 Clearwater Bombers	1973 Clearwater Bombers
1934 Ke-Nash-A, Kenosha, WI	1955 Raybestos Cardinals,	1974 Gianella Bros, Santa Rosa, CA
1935 Crimson Coaches, Toledo, OH	Stratford, CT	1975 Rising Sun Hotel, Reading, PA
1936 Kodak Park, Rochester, NY	1956 Clearwater Bombers	1976 Raybestos Cardinals
1937 Briggs Body Team, Detroit	1957 Clearwater Bombers	1977 Billard Barbell, Reading, PA
1938 The Pohlers, Cincinnati	1958 Raybestos Cardinals	1978 Billard Barbell
1939 Carr's Boosters, Covington, KY	1959 Sealmasters, Aurora, IL	1979 McArdle Pontiac/Cadillac,
1940 Kodak Park, Rochester, NY	1960 Clearwater Bombers	Midland, MI
1941 Bendix Brakes, South Bend, IN	1961 Sealmasters	1980 Peterbilt Western, Seattle
1942 Deep Rock Oilers, Tulsa, OK	1962 Clearwater Bombers	1981 Archer Daniels Midland,
1943 Hammer Air Field, Fresno, CA	1963 Clearwater Bombers	Decatur, IL
1944 Hammer Air Field	1964 Burch Tool, Detroit	1982 Peterbilt Western
1945 Zollner Pistons, Ft.Wayne, IN	1965 Sealmasters	1983 Franklin Cardinals,
1946 Zollner Pistons	1966 Clearwater Bombers	Stratford, CT
1947 Zollner Pistons	1967 Sealmasters	1984 California Kings, Merced, CA
1948 Briggs Beautyware, Detroit	1968 Clearwater Bombers	1985 Pay'n Pak, Seattle
1949 Tip Top Tailors, Toronto	1969 Raybestos Cardinals	1986 Pay'n Pak
1950 Clearwater (FL) Bombers	1970 Raybestos Cardinals	1987 Pay'n Pak
1951 Dow Chemical, Midland, MI	1971 Welty Way, Cedar Rapids, IA	1988 TransAire, Elkhart, IN
1952 Briggs Beautyware	1972 Raybestos Cardinals	1989 Penn Corp, Sioux City, IA
1953 Briggs Beautyware		1990 Penn Corp

Super Slow Pitch

Year	Year	Year
1981 Howard's/Western Steer,	1984 Howard's/Western Steer	1988 Starpath, Monticello, KY
Denver, NC	1985 Steele's Sports, Grafton, OH	1989 Ritch's Salvage,
1982 Jerry's Catering, Miami	1986 Steele's Sports	Harrisburg, NC
1983 Howard's/Western Steer	1987 Steele's Sports	1990 Steele's Silver Bullets

Major Slow Pitch

Year	Year	Year
1953 Shields Construction,	1964 Skip Hogan A.C.	1978 Campbell Carpets, Concord, CA
Newport, KY	1965 Skip Hogan A.C.	1979 Nelco Mfg.Co., Okla.City
1954 Waldneck's Tavern, Cincinnati	1966 Michael's Lounge, Detroit	1980 Campbell Carpets
1955 Lang Pet Shop, Covington, KY	1967 Jim's Sport Shop, Pittsburgh	1981 Elite Coating, Gordon, CA
1956 Gatliff Auto Sales,	1968 County Sports, Levittown, NY	1982 Triangle Sports, Minneapolis
Newport, KY	1969 Copper Hearth, Milwaukee	1983 No.1 Electric & Heating,
1957 Gatliff Auto Sales	1970 Little Caesar's, Southgate, MI	Gastonia, NC
1958 East Side Sports, Detroit	1971 Pile Drivers, Va.Beach, VA	1984 Lilly Air Systems, Chicago
1959 Yorkshire Restaurant,	1972 Jiffy Club, Louisville, KY	1985 Blanton's Fayetteville, NC
Newport, KY	1973 Howard's Furniture,	1986 Non-Ferrous Metals, Cleveland
1960 Hamilton Tailoring,	Denver, NC	1987 Stapath, Monticello, KY
Cincinnati	1974 Howard's Furniture	1988 Bell Corp/FAF, Tampa, FL
1961 Hamilton Tailoring	1975 Pyramid Cafe, Lakewood, OH	1989 Ritch's Salvage, Harrisburg, NC
1962 Skip Hogan A.C., Pittsburgh	1976 Warren Motors, J'ville, FL	1990 New Construction, Shelbyville,IN
1963 Gatliff Auto Sales	1977 Nelson Painting, Okla.City	

WOMEN

Major Fast Pitch

Year	Year	Year
1933 Great Northerns, Chicago	1942 Jax Maids, New Orleans	1951 Orange Lionettes
1934 Hart Motors, Chicago	1943 Jax Maids	1952 Orange Lionettes
1935 Bloomer Girls, Cleveland	1944 Lind & Pomeroy, Portland, OR	1953 Betsy Ross Rockets, Fresno, CA
1936 Nat'l Screw & Mfg., Cleveland	1945 Jax Maids	1954 Leach Motor Rockets,
1937 Nat'l Screw & Mfg.	1946 Jax Maids	Fresno, CA
1938 J.J.Krieg's, Alameda, CA	1947 Jax Maids	1955 Orange Lionettes
1939 J.J.Krieg's	1948 Arizona Ramblers	1956 Orange Lionettes
1940 Arizona Ramblers, Phoenix	1949 Arizona Ramblers	1957 Hacienda Rockets, Fresno, CA
1941 Higgins Midgets, Tulsa, OK	1950 Orange (CA) Lionettes	1958 Raybestos Brakettes,
		Stratford, CT

Year		
1959 Raybestos Brakettes	1970 Orange Lionettes	1982 Raybestos Brakettes
1960 Raybestos Brakettes	1971 Raybestos Brakettes	1983 Raybestos Brakettes
1961 Gold Sox, Whittier, CA	1972 Raybestos Brakettes	1984 Los Angeles Diamonds
1962 Orange Lionettes	1973 Raybestos Brakettes	1985 Hi-Ho Brakettes, Stratford, CT
1963 Raybestos Brakettes	1974 Raybestos Brakettes	1986 So.California Invasion, LA
1964 Erv Lind Florists, Portland, OR	1975 Raybestos Brakettes	1987 Orange County Majestics, Anaheim, CA
1965 Orange Lionettes	1976 Raybestos Brakettes	
1966 Raybestos Brakettes	1977 Raybestos Brakettes	1988 Hi-Ho Brakettes (CT)
1967 Raybestos Brakettes	1978 Raybestos Brakettes	1989 Whittier (CA) Raiders
1968 Raybestos Brakettes	1979 Sun City (AZ) Saints	1990 Raybestos Brakettes
1969 Orange Lionettes	1980 Raybestos Brakettes	
	1981 Orlando (FL) Rebels	

Major Slow Pitch

Year		
1959 Pearl Laundry, Richmond, VA	1971 Gators, Ft.Lauderdale, FL	1981 Tifton (GA) Tomboys
1960 Carolina Rockets, High Pt.,NC	1972 Riverside Ford, Cincinnati	1982 Richmond (VA) Stompers
1961 Dairy Cottage, Covington, KY	1973 Sweeney Chevrolet, Cincinnati	1983 Spooks, Anoka, MN
1962 Dana Gardens, Cincinnati	1974 Marks Brothers Dots, Miami	1984 Spooks
1963 Dana Gardens	1975 Marks Brothers Dots	1985 Key Ford Mustangs, Pensacola, FL
1964 Dana Gardens	1976 Sorrento's Pizza, Cincinnati	
1965 Art's Acres, Omaha, NE	1977 Fox Valley Lassies, St.Charles, IL	1986 Sur-Way Tomboys, Tifton, GA
1966 Dana Gardens		1987 Key Ford Mustangs
1967 Ridge Maintenance, Cleveland	1978 Bob Hoffman's Dots, Miami	1988 Spooks
1968 Escue Pontiac, Cincinnati	1979 Bob Hoffman's Dots	1989 Canaan's Illusions, Houston
1969 Converse Dots, Hialeah, FL	1980 Howard's Rubi-Otts, Graham, NC	1990 Spooks
1970 Rutenschruder Floral, Cincinnati		

Women's NCAA Division I

Multiple winners: UCLA (5); Texas A&M (2).

Year	Year	Year	Year	Year
1982 UCLA	1984 UCLA	1986 CS-Fullerton	1988 UCLA	1990 UCLA
1983 Texas A&M	1985 UCLA	1987 Texas A&M	1989 UCLA	

Triathlon

Ironman Championship

Mark Allen won his second straight Ironman Triathlon World Championship, Oct. 6, 1990, at Kailua-Kona, Hawaii. Allen's time of 8 hours, 28 minutes and 17 seconds was 9:23 faster than runner-up Scott Tinley, a two-time former champion. Erin Baker won the women's division for the second time in four years with a 9:13:42.
   Multiple winners: Dave Scott (6); Paula Newby-Fraser (3); Mark Allen, Erin Baker, Sylviane Puntous and Scott Tinley (2).

MEN

Year	Date	Winner	Time	Runner-up	Margin	Start	Finish	Location
I	2/18/78	Gordon Haller	11:46	John Dunbar	34:00	15	12	Waikiki Beach
II	1/14/79	Tom Warren	11:15:56	John Dunbar	48:00	15	12	Waikiki Beach
III	1/10/80	Dave Scott	9:24:33	Chuck Neumann	1:08	108	95	Ala Moana Park
IV	2/14/81	John Howard	9:38:29	Tom Warren	26:00	326	299	Kailua-Kona
V	2/6/82	Scott Tinley	9:19:41	Dave Scott	17:16	580	541	Kailua-Kona
VI	10/9/82	Dave Scott	9:08:23	Scott Tinley	20:05	850	775	Kailua-Kona
VII	10/22/83	Dave Scott	9:05:57	Scott Tinley	0:33	964	835	Kailua-Kona
VIII	10/6/84	Dave Scott	8:54:20	Scott Tinley	24:25	1036	903	Kailua-Kona
IX	10/25/85	Scott Tinley	8:50:54	Chris Hinshaw	25:46	1018	965	Kailua-Kona
X	10/18/86	Dave Scott	8:28:37	Mark Allen	9:47	1039	951	Kailua-Kona
XI	10/10/87	Dave Scott	8:34:13	Mark Allen	11:06	1380	1284	Kailua-Kona
XII	10/22/88	Scott Molina	8:31:00	Mike Pigg	2:11	1277	1189	Kailua-Kona
XIII	10/15/89	Mark Allen	8:09:15	Dave Scott	0:58	1285	1231	Kailua-Kona
VIX	10/6/90	Mark Allen	8:28:17	Scott Tinley	9:23	1386	1255	Kailua-Kona

WOMEN

Year	Winner	Time	Runner-up	Year	Winner	Time	Runner-up
1978	No finishers			1984	Sylviane Puntous	10:25:13	Patricia Puntous
1979	Lyn Lemaire	12:55	None	1985	Joanne Ernst	10:25:22	Liz Bulman
1980	Robin Beck	11:21:24	Eve Anderson	1986	Paula Newby-Fraser	9:49:14	Sylviane Puntous
1981	Linda Sweeney	12:00:32	Sally Edwards				
1982	Kathleen McCartney	11:09:40	Julie Moss	1987	Erin Baker	9:35:25	Sylviane Puntous
1982	Julie Leach	10:54:08	Joann Dahlkoetter	1988	P.Newby-Fraser	9:01:01	Erin Baker
1983	Sylviane Puntous	10:43:36	Patricia Puntous	1989	P.Newby-Fraser	9:00:56	Sylviane Puntous
				1990	Erin Baker	9:13:42	P.Newby-Fraser

Wrestling

NCAA Division I Champions

Senior Chris Barnes (177 lbs) and freshman Pat Smith (158) won individual titles to lead Oklahoma St. to its second straight NCAA championship, March 24, at College Park, Md. Barnes, with a pin and two technical falls in his three matches, won his second 177-lb. title in a row and was voted the tournament's outstanding wrestler. OSU has now won 29 Division I championships.

Multiple winners: Oklahoma St.(29); Iowa (11); Iowa St.(8); Oklahoma (7). Note that champions in 1928 and from 1930-33 were unofficial.

Year	Champion	Pts	Runner-up	Pts	Year	Champion	Pts	Runner-up	Pts
1928	Oklahoma St.	—	—	—	1959	Oklahoma St.	73	Iowa St.	51
1929	Oklahoma St.	26	Michigan	18	1960	Oklahoma	59	Iowa St.	40
1930	Oklahoma St.	27	Illinois	14	1961	Oklahoma St.	82	Oklahoma	63
1931	Oklahoma St.	—	Michigan	—	1962	Oklahoma St.	82	Oklahoma	45
1932	Indiana	—	Oklahoma St.	—	1963	Oklahoma	48	Iowa St.	45
1933	Oklahoma St.	—			1964	Oklahoma St.	87	Oklahoma	58
	& Iowa St.	—			1965	Iowa St.	87	Oklahoma St.	86
1934	Oklahoma St.	29	Indiana	19	1966	Oklahoma St.	79	Iowa St.	70
1935	Oklahoma St.	36	Oklahoma	18	1967	Michigan St.	74	Michigan	63
1936	Oklahoma	14	Central,OK	10	1968	Oklahoma St.	81	Iowa St.	78
	& Okla.St.	10			1969	Iowa St.	104	Oklahoma	69
1937	Oklahoma St.	31	Oklahoma	13	1970	Iowa St.	99	Michigan St.	84
1938	Oklahoma St.	19	Illinois	15	1971	Oklahoma St.	94	Iowa St.	66
1939	Oklahoma St.	33	Lehigh	12	1972	Iowa St.	103	Michigan St.	72½
1940	Oklahoma St.	24	Indiana	14	1973	Iowa St.	85	Oregon St.	72½
1941	Oklahoma St.	37	Michigan St.	36	1974	Oklahoma	69½	Michigan	67
1942	Oklahoma St.	31	Michigan St.	26	1975	Iowa	102	Oklahoma	77
1943	Not held				1976	Iowa	123½	Iowa St.	85¾
1944	Not held				1977	Iowa St.	95½	Okla.St.	88¾
1945	Not held				1978	Iowa	94½	Iowa St.	94
1946	Oklahoma St.	25	No.Iowa	24	1979	Iowa	122½	Iowa St.	88
1947	Cornell Col.	32	No.Iowa	19	1980	Iowa	110¾	Oklahoma.St.	87
1948	Oklahoma St.	33	Michigan St.	28	1981	Iowa	129¾	Oklahoma	100¼
1949	Oklahoma St.	32	No.Iowa	27	1982	Iowa	131¾	Iowa St.	111
1950	No.Iowa	30	Purdue	16	1983	Iowa	155	Oklahoma St.	102
1951	Oklahoma	24	Oklahoma St.	23	1984	Iowa	123¾	Oklahoma St.	98
1952	Oklahoma	22	No.Iowa	21	1985	Iowa	145¼	Oklahoma	98½
1953	Penn St.	21	Oklahoma	15	1986	Iowa	158	Oklahoma	84¼
1954	Oklahoma St.	32	Pittsburgh	17	1987	Iowa St.	133	Iowa	108
1955	Oklahoma St.	40	Penn St.	31	1988	Arizona St.	93	Iowa	85½
1956	Oklahoma St.	65	Oklahoma	62	1989	Oklahoma St.	91¼	Arizona St.	70½
1957	Oklahoma	73	Pittsburgh	66	1990	Oklahoma St.	117¾	Arizona St.	104¾
1958	Oklahoma St.	77	Iowa St.	62					

Frances Genter, the 92-year-old owner of Unbridled, blows a kiss to the crowd at Churchill Downs after winning the Kentucky Derby for the first time.

HORSE RACING

Unbridled captures Kentucky Derby for Mrs. Genter; Injuries end Easy Goer-Sunday Silence rivalry; Shoe dismounts with 8833 wins.

HORSE RACING

1989-90 YEAR IN REVIEW

by Sharon Smith

The first commandment of horse racing being, "There's no such thing as a sure thing," no racing fan should have been surprised at what happened to the eagerly anticipated Easy Goer-Sunday Silence rivalry of 1990.

Their dramatic Breeders' Cup matchup provided the exclamation point to the 1980s, but Sunday Silence's win by a shrinking neck had ended just a paragraph, not a chapter. Although Sunday Silence won three of the four times the horses met as three-year-olds in 1989, his wins were hardly overwhelming. Followers of both horses were convinced that 1990 was the year when one would silence the other's claims to superiority.

Each started the year promisingly. Easy Goer was especially impressive, winning the May 16 Gold Stage Stakes at Belmont Park by seven and a half lengths. Sunday Silence had to work a little harder to win the June 3 Californian Stakes at

Sharon Smith is the Contributing Editor of *Horse Illustrated* magazine and has been an NBC-TV commentator at the Breeders' Cup since 1984.

Hollywood Park by three-quarters of a length.

Then each was stunned by a loss. Easy Goer was third to Criminal Type and Housebuster in Belmont's Metropolitan Handicap, and Sunday Silence ran second to Criminal Type in the Hollywood Gold Cup. But some of the glitter was restored with Easy Goer's third 1990 start—an easy win in one of the fastest Suburban Handicaps ever run.

"Bring them on!" said trainer Shug McGaughey after the Suburban. But two weeks before the first scheduled 1990 meeting of the rivals, Easy Goer developed a bone chip in an ankle and was retired from racing. Shortly after, Sunday Silence developed a ligament tear in his ankle and, in a space of two weeks, the rivalry and the careers of two of the great horses of the past decade were over. The emergence of Criminal Type as the only horse to beat them both provided solace for racing fans.

Although both were champions—Easy Goer at two and Sunday Silence at three—the two horses go off to stud (Sun-

Wide World Photos

Jockey **Chris McCarron** (right) straightens up in the saddle after **Sunday Silence** was able to hold off **Easy Goer** and win the 1989 Breeders' Cup Classic at Gulfstream Park.

day Silence to Japan) in an order that's clear to all but the most devout fans of Easy Goer. Sunday Silence was just a little better on the racetrack. Still, the fans and particularly the owners of Easy Goer can take comfort from one thought. After a previous equine rivalry ended in a similar fashion, Affirmed and Alydar went to stud in that order as racehorses. In retirement, the order has been reversed, and then some. Affirmed has been a good stallion, but Alydar has been nothing short of sensational. Among Alydar's brood of important offspring: Easy Goer and Criminal Type.

Criminal Type wasted no time after the retirement of his famous younger rivals to solidify his position as leading contender for Horse of the Year. Another cross country trip in August netted the late developing five-year-old the prestigious Whitney Handicap at Saratoga.

"I believe we've got the best horse in the country," said trainer D. Wayne Lukas after watching Criminal Type's effortless win. With the too-early absence of Sunday Silence and Easy Goer, few would disagree. But while a tinge of disappoint-

ment colored the year for older Thoroughbreds, a shadow of frustration, near disaster, and even tragedy darkened the three-year-old season. The bright moments shone all the more as a result.

The frustration began early. Rhythm, the two-year-old champion of 1989, made a disappointing three-year-old debut in February and was discovered to have a throat obstruction. He underwent surgery and missed the Triple Crown races. Rhythm did return to the track, capping his summer with a remarkably good Travers Stakes at Saratoga. His win gave him an outside chance of repeating as champion.

The runner-up for the 1989 two-year-old championship had no chance at all. Grand Canyon, who had run the fastest mile ever by a juvenile, suffered nagging injuries during the winter and also missed the Triple Crown. While training for a summer comeback, Grand Canyon developed laminitis, the incurable hoof disease that doomed the great Secretariat in 1989. He was humanely destroyed on July 14. Ironically, two months later, laminitis also claimed Fappiano, the 13-year-old sire of both Grand Canyon and Unbridled.

For several weeks, it appeared that the same fate might befall Mister Frisky, the rags-to-riches Puerto Rican import who earned the role of Triple Crown favorite in the absence of Rhythm and Grand Canyon. His unblemished early season campaign included an impressive win in the Santa Anita Derby, which emerged during the eighties as the prime predictor of success in the Kentucky Derby. But an eighth place at Churchill Downs left Mister Frisky's people shaking their heads.

"He ran a bad race. Why, I don't know," trainer Laz Barrera said. A so-so third in the Preakness provided no answers, but a fever and a sudden loss of weight a few weeks later did. Mister Frisky had developed a throat abscess that interfered with his breathing and eating. Doctors believed it started before the Kentucky Derby and, by the time it was discovered, was considered life-threatening. In spite of complications and fear for his survival, Mister Frisky recovered and was returned to California for further training. But the Triple Crown was gone forever.

If there was no storybook ending to Mister Frisky's Kentucky Derby quest, there certainly was one for another horse and—more dramatically—owner. Unbridled, the Florida Derby winner, came into the race as the fifth choice of 15 starters. He deserved that support and maybe a little more, being well conformed, well bred, professionally trained, and competently partnered by jockey Craig Perret.

But Unbridled had something else going for him—his 92-year-old owner, Frances Genter. For more than 50 years, Mrs. Genter had been one of the most admired and respected owners in racing, but she had never before started a horse in the Derby. Her failing eyesight required an impromptu race call from Unbridled's trainer Carl Nafzger, sitting next to her in the stands.

At the final turn: "He's third, Mrs. Genter!" Midway down the stretch: "He's taking the lead!" At the sixteenth pole: "He's going to win, Mrs. Genter! He's going to win!" And at the finish: "He won it, Mrs. Genter! You won the Kentucky Derby! Oh, Mrs. Genter, I love you!"

It was a scene witnessed by millions on ABC-TV, and a scene that prompted Pat Day, rider of the runner-up Summer Squall to say, "It brought tears to my eyes. It may just have been meant for her to win today."

Mrs. Genter did not make the trip to Baltimore to see Unbridled try to add the second jewel of the Triple Crown. She missed a good performance by her colt and a better one by Summer Squall. The Preakness saw the Derby order reversed, with Summer Squall sweeping past Unbridled midway down the stretch.

Hopes for a definitive showdown in the Belmont Stakes were dashed when Summer Squall's owners decided not to send the colt to New York, where rules prohibit the controversial anti-bleeding medication Lasix that he used at Churchill Downs and Pimlico (see box). "It would not be in the best interest of the horse," said managing partner Cot Campbell.

It was certainly in the best financial interest of Unbridled, who had merely to finish the Belmont Stakes to earn a million dollar bonus for the best composite finish in the Triple Crown. But Unbridled, too, usually runs on bleeder medication. He did not bleed in the Belmont, but he did run a dull race, finishing fourth for reasons not clear to anybody.

Go And Go, who arrived from Ireland just three days before the Belmont, found the mile and a half perfectly suited to his abilities and went home the winner. Flush with the victory, trainer Dermot Weld brought Go And Go back to New York in August, hoping a win in the Travers Stakes might make him the leading contender for a championship. But he finished well behind winner Rhythm, leaving the race for the Eclipse Award for three-year-old champion up in the air.

Two other three-year-old colts impressed fans during 1990. Housebuster, who enjoyed a finish in front of Easy Goer in the Metropolitan Handicap, emerged as the leading sprinter in the United States. Housebuster's people knew that he would have to stretch out to longer distances in the fall to have a serious chance for the three-year-old championship.

For the second year in a row, Canada had a Triple Crown winner. The handsome gray Izvestia earned honors as the

The year's closest race was May 21 at Arlington Park where **All Worked Up** (5), **Survival** (2) and **Marshua's Affair** dead-heated in the day's ninth race. It was the first triple dead heat in North America since 1981.

dominant horse in Canada with performances like his spectacular victory in the Queen's Plate, Canada's most prestigious race. That had Izvestia's trainer and owners talking about a trip south of the border in the fall to try their horse against the best in the U.S. and possibly earn an Eclipse Award.

Two of 1989's Eclipse champions did everything necessary to repeat as champions in 1990. The filly Go for Wand was even better at three than she had been at two. The highlight of her summer was a stakes-record performance in the Alabama at Saratoga, but her earlier performances there and at Belmont Park were nearly as good. The older mare Bayakoa took on everybody—mares and males alike—usually winning, rarely losing to the same horse twice, and never running a bad race.

Nineteen-ninety may be remembered as the year of the dead heat. Dead heats are rare, but dead heats in stakes races—particularly Grade One events—are even more uncommon. Among the too-close-to-call finishes was that of Beautiful Melody and Reluctant Guest in Hollywood Park's Beverly Hills Handicap. Trainer Richard Mandella didn't have to worry about sharing the 10 percent trainer's cut of first place; he trained both fillies.

On May 19, the Johnny Morris Handicap at Arlington International featured a dead heat between Dispersal and Pentelicus. But the very next day Arlington fans saw the rarest event of all— the first triple dead heat in American racing since 1981. Marshua's Affair, Survival, and All Worked Up could not be separated at the finish in the 9th race. It was the 18th triple dead heat in North America since the advent of the photo finish camera.

In harness racing, the pacer Beach Towel emerged as the summer star of 1990, with victories in such prestigious stakes as the Miller Memorial, the American-National, the Meadowlands Pace, and the Adios. Beach Towel cost $22,000 as a yearling and has rewarded his farsighted purchasers with over two million dollars in winnings.

The 1990 Hambletonian, trotting's most famous race, was won on Aug. 4 by a horse campaigned by owners who hadn't given up hope of winning the 1989 edition. In '89, Lindy Farm's Probe dead-heated for first place with Park Avenue Joe in the Hambletonian race-off, but was placed second in terms of prize money because of a composite finish rule. A year later, that decision was still being challenged in the courts. But Lindy Farm's colt Hamonious earned his owners a measure of revenge—and a whole lot of money—by winning the richest Hambletonian ever. The victory also gave driver John Campbell his third Hambletonian in four years.

In both harness and Thoroughbred racing, honors came in 1990 to people and horses who played dramatic and vital roles in their sports during the 1980s. Driver-trainer Clint Galbraith was joined by driver Buddy Gilmour in harness racing's Living Hall of Fame. Galbraith handled two-time Horse of the Year Niatross, who changed the face of harness racing in terms of prestige and pure speed.

Niatross himself was named Horse of the 80s in a poll conducted early in 1990, even though he had competed for only part of the first year of the decade. In October of 1980, Niatross took nearly three seconds off the world record for the mile, becoming the Roger Bannister of his sport. His name and record remain together in harness racing's memory, long after other horses have gone faster miles.

In Thoroughbred racing, honors went to another horse and trainer combination whose partnership epitomized the best of the 1980s. Among the 1990 inductees into the Thoroughbred Racing Hall of Fame were trainer Ron McAnally and the ageless John Henry, the one-time leading money winner who was named Horse of the year as a six-year-old in 1981 and again as a nine-year-old in '84. McAnally said during their joint induction ceremony, "It was a dream come true, having a horse of his caliber."

A much sadder event also brought back memories of the eighties. Gene Klein, whose stable had dominated racing for more than five years during the decade, died of a heart attack at 69 on

Vet study can't stanch Lasix debate

The use of artificial substances to improve the performance of race horses goes back almost as far as racing itself. The Greeks and Romans fermented a mixture of honey and water into a potent liquor called hydromel that they believed made race horses run faster when added secretly to pre-race feed. Secrecy was important; race fixing in Rome was punishable by crucifixion. Greek offenders had merely to erect a statue to Zeus at Mount Olympus.

Modern penalties for illegal drugging of race horses range from disqualification from purse money to suspension of license, depending on the state. What constitutes illegal drugging depends on the state, too. In the case of one controversial drug, that lack of uniformity has caused a long-term battle of nearly Olympian proportions.

The drug is furosemide, a diuretic developed to treat hypertensive humans. Under the trade name Lasix, the drug was one of several used during the 1960s and 1970s to treat bleeding from the lungs in horses. Bleeding is common, usually minor, and generally not painful. But it certainly affects performance.

The other drugs have mostly fallen by the wayside, but furosemide has established itself as the drug of choice for bleeders. By 1990, furosemide was a legal race day medication in 28 of the 34 racing states. Supporters believe so strongly that it helps prevent bleeding that many will keep their horse out of a non-Lasix state like New York—Belmont Stakes or no Belmont Stakes.

Preakness winner Summer Squall did not go to New York for the Belmont, even though he had a chance for a million dollar bonus if he finished in front of Kentucky Derby winner Unbridled in the final jewel of the Triple Crown. Summer Squall's owners were even prepared to keep their horse out of the 1990 Breeders' Cup in October, since the event was scheduled for Belmont Park.

Many Lasix supporters have long in-

Skip Dickstein

Kentucky Derby runner-up **Summer Squall**, Pat Day aboard, won the Preakness Stakes, but his owners refused to run him in the Belmont because New York is a non-Lasix state.

sisted that the drug should be permitted everywhere, since it affects only bleeding and does not improve performance in any other way.

Or does it? Why do the eyes of New Jersey bettors light up when they see a horse cross the Hudson River from New York? And why does the bettor's conventional wisdom insist, "Bet a horse first time on Lasix"?

Such questions prompted what was supposed to be the definitive study of the effects of furosemide on racing performance. Researchers at the University of Pennsylvania School of Veterinary Medicine received permission to give furosemide regardless of bleeding history to a group of Pennsylvania race horses, then monitored them over an eight-month period. The results, published in May, caused a furor.

Proven bleeders ran significantly faster on furosemide. No surprise there. But non-bleeders—particularly geldings— also ran measurably faster times the first time they received the drug. Moreover, post-race examination of the bleeders showed that most of them bled even though they were medicated. Many of the supposed non-bleeders also showed blood in the lungs in spite of having received furosemide.

The study seemed to prove what the drug's detractors had claimed: that it improves a horse's performance irrespective of bleeding, and that it doesn't do much to prevent bleeding anyway. The reaction was immediate. New York Racing and Wagering Board Chairman Richard Corbisiero said, "We are gratified that New York's position on the use of Lasix has been vindicated."

But Lasix supporters criticized the size and methodology of the study. The sample was too small and the analysis of speed was too subjective, they claimed. Many said they simply could not believe the results. "The conclusions are inappropriate," announced the American Association of Equine Practitioners. "Failure to completely eliminate a disease condition does not mean lack of usefulness." The veterinarians' organization stood by their support of moderate furosemide medication for proven bleeders four hours before race time.

So the study that hoped to quiet the argument merely led to more raised voices. Ironically, Hoechst Celanese, the manufacturer of Lasix, is a subsidiary of a multi-national corporation based in Europe, where race day medication is prohibited. Bleeders there are treated with good nutrition and rest.

March 12. Klein, who owned the NFL's San Diego Chargers from 1966-84, won eleven Eclipse Awards, including three as outstanding owner. He and trainer D. Wayne Lukas campaigned 1988 Kentucky Derby winner Winning Colors, 1986 Horse of the Year Lady's Secret, 1985 Preakness winner Tank's Prospect and dozens of other stakes winners. He had dispersed his racing and breeding operation in a $30 million dollar auction only four months before his death, hoping to be able to relax and spend more time with his family.

For legendary jockey Bill Shoemaker, the year marked the end of one career and the beginning of another. After six decades in the saddle (1949-90), the 58-year-old Shoemaker's last ride came on Feb. 3 in the fifth race at Santa Anita—a fourth place finish aboard Patchy Groundfog. When Shoe dismounted, one of the most remarkable racing careers ever was over. The final statistics: 8833 wins, $123 million in purses, four victories in the Kentucky Derby (the last in 1986 at age 53), two in the Preakness, and five in the Belmont. Within months of his retirement as a jockey, Shoemaker was a winning trainer.

In 1953, Shoemaker set the single season record for wins by a jockey, when he crossed the finish line first in 485 races. The record was broken a couple of times in the 1970s, but Chris McCarron's 1974 total of 546 wins in one year lasted until late in 1989. Kent Desormeaux, riding on the Maryland circuit, broke McCarron's record on November 30. The 19-year-old Cajun jockey finished the year with 597 wins. It was off to California and big-time racing for Desormeaux in 1990, so the wins were a little harder to come by. But his single season record won him Jockey of the Year honors and leaves him at the top of the list that includes some very big names.

Clouds of uncertainty darkened the year for some of racing's people and places. For the first time in recent memory, Hialeah Park did not conduct racing during 1990 and withdrew applications for racing dates for the 1990-91 season. Financial problems, competition with the two other South Florida tracks, and shrinking attendance had troubled Hialeah for years. There is hope that some kind of racing can resume at the beau-

Wide World Photos

All-time wins leader **Bill Shoemaker** retired as a jockey on Feb. 3, to train horses like three-year-old Star Child.

tiful old track, but it seems unlikely that Hialeah will ever be what it was when Citation and Nashua and Buckpasser raced among the flamingoes.

For many people in racing—owners, trainers, jockeys, and fans—the best part of any racing year comes during summer and fall when the two-year-olds begin their careers.

The first offspring of fine race horses add extra excitement. Racegoers in New York watched Meadow Star shine brightly. She is the daughter of Meadowlake, whose brilliant, brief racing career still has people wondering about what might have been. Racegoers in Europe felt the same way about Woodman, whose first sons included 1990 New York stakes winner Hansel.

Baby brothers also set racing people to dreaming. Two-year-olds like Summer Squall's half brother Honor Grades and Stephan's Odyssey's brother Walesa ran, won, and raised hopes that they just might be as good as their famous siblings. "Wait until next year" has a special meaning in horse racing, what with a Triple Crown coming up and a new generation of horses to compete. Anyone with a promising two-year-old in the barn is allowed an extra measure of dreaming.□

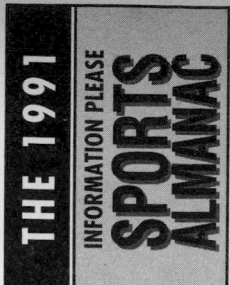

HORSE RACING
STATISTICS

THE SEASON IN REVIEW
1989-1990
THOROUGHBRED • HARNESS

THE 1991 INFORMATION PLEASE SPORTS ALMANAC

SEC A

PAGE 541

Thoroughbred Racing

1989-90 Major Stakes Races

Winners of major stakes races from Sept. 10, 1989, through Sept. 2, 1990; distances are listed by miles; (F) indicates furlongs.

Late 1989

Date	Race	Location	Miles	Winner	Jockey	Value to Winner
Sep.10	Molson Export Million	Woodbine	1¼	Prized	E.Delahoussaye	$600,000
Sep.16	Woodward Handicap	Belmont	1¼	Easy Goer	Pat Day	485,400
Sep.23	Man o'War Stakes	Belmont	1⅜	Yankee Affair	Jose Santos	282,240
Sep.24	Super Derby	La.Downs	1¼	Sunday Silence	Pat Valenzuela	600,000
Oct. 8	Arc de Triomphe	Longchamp	1½	Carroll House	Michael Kinane	828,000
Oct. 7	Jockey Club Gold Cup	Belmont	1½	Easy Goer	Pat Day	659,400
Oct. 8	Turf Classic	Belmont	1½	Yankee Affair	Jose Santos	392,550
Oct.13	Meadowlands Cup	Meadowlands	1¼	Mi Selecto	Jose Santos	300,000
Oct.14	Champagne Stakes	Belmont	1	Adjudicating	Jorge Vasquez	343,200
Oct.14	Oak Tree Invitational	Santa Anita	1½	Hawkster	Russell Baze	300,000
Oct.21	NYRA Mile Handicap	Aqueduct	1	Dispersal	Angel Cordero,Jr	348,600
Oct.22	Rothmans International	Woodbine	1½	Hodges Bay	Jean Cruguet	575,400
Oct.22	Budweiser International	Laurel	1¼	Caltech	R.R.Douglas	450,000
Oct.22	Fla.Stallion Stakes	Calder	1 1/16	Shot Gun Scott	Walter Guerra	270,000
Nov. 4	Breeders' Cup Classic	Gulfstream	1¼	Sunday Silence	Chris McCarron	1,350,000
Nov. 4	Breeders' Cup Turf	Gulfstream	1½	Prized	E.Delahoussaye	900,000
Nov. 4	Breeders' Cup Distaff	Gulfstream	1⅛	Bayakoa	Laffit Pincay,Jr	450,000
Nov. 4	Breeders' Cup Mile	Gulfstream	1	Steinlen	Jose Santos	450,000
Nov. 4	Breeders' Cup Fillies	Gulfstream	1 1/16	Go for Wand	Randy Romero	450,000
Nov. 4	Breeders' Cup Sprint	Gulfstream	6 F	Dancing Spree	Angel Cordero,Jr	450,000
Nov. 4	Breeders' Cup Juvenile	Gulfstream	1 1/16	Rhythm	Craig Perret	450,000
Dec. 3	Hollywood Starlet Stakes	Hollywood	1	Cheval Volant	Alex Solis	247,500
Dec.10	Hollywood Turf Cup	Hollywood	1½	Frankly Perfect	Chris McCarron	275,000
Dec.17	Hollywood Futurity	Hollywood	1	Grand Canyon	Angel Cordero,Jr	495,000

1990 (through Sept. 2)

Date	Race	Track/Park	Miles	Winner	Jockey	Value to Winner
Feb. 4	Charles H.Strub Stakes	Santa Anita	1¼	Fl.Continental	Corey Black	$275,000
Mar. 4	Santa Anita Handicap	Santa Anita	1¼	Ruhlmann	Gary Stevens	550,000
Mar.17	Florida Derby	Gulfstream	1⅛	Unbridled	Pat Day	300,000
Mar.31	Jim Beam Stakes	Turfway	1⅛	Summer Squall	Pat Day	300,000
Apr. 7	Santa Anita Derby	Santa Anita	1⅛	Mister Frisky	Gary Stevens	275,000
Apr.21	Wood Memorial	Aqueduct	1⅛	Thirty Six Red	Mike Smith	362,400
May 5	Kentucky Derby	Churchill Dns	1¼	Unbridled	Craig Perret	581,000
May 12	Pimlico Special Handicap	Pimlico	1 3/16	Criminal Type	Jose Santos	600,000
May 19	Preakness Stakes	Pimlico	1 3/16	Summer Squall	Pat Day	445,900
May 26	Acorn Stakes	Belmont	1	Stella Madrid	Angel Cordero,Jr	104,580
May 28	Metropolitan Handicap	Belmont	1	Criminal Type	Jose Santos	357,000
May 28	Hollywood Turf Handicap	Hollywood	1¼	Steinlen	Laffit Pincay,Jr	275,000
May 28	Jersey Derby	Garden State	1¼	Yonder	Jerry Bailey	300,000
Jun. 6	The Derby	Epsom Downs	1½	Quest For Fame	Pat Eddery	596,000
Jun. 9	Belmont Stakes	Belmont	1½	Go And Go	Michael Kinane	411,600
Jun.10	Mother Goose	Belmont	1⅛	Go for Wand	Randy Romero	136,560
Jun.24	Hollywood Gold Cup	Hollywood	1¼	Criminal Type	Jose Santos	550,000

Thoroughbreds (Cont.)

1989-90 Major Stakes Races

Date	Race	Location	Miles	Winner	Jockey	Value to Winner
Jul. 1	Irish Derby	Curragh	1½	Salsabil	Willie Carson	$501,235
Jul. 4	Suburban Handicap	Belmont	1¼	Easy Goer	Pat Day	239,400
Jul. 8	Queen's Plate	Woodbine	1¼	Izvestia	Don Seymour	235,200
Jul.28	Haskell Invitational	Monmouth	1⅛	Restless Con	Tim Doocy	300,000
Aug. 4	Whitney Handicap	Saratoga	1⅛	Criminal Type	Gary Stevens	140,640
Aug.11	Alabama Stakes	Saratoga	1¼	Go for Wand	Randy Romero	130,560
Aug.18	Travers Stakes	Saratoga	1¼	Rhythm	Craig Perret	707,100
Aug.19	Breeders' Stakes	Woodbine	1½	Izvestia	Don Seymour	1,183,600*
Sep. 1	Beverly D.Stakes	Arlington	1³⁄₁₆	Reluctant Guest	Robbie Davis	300,000
Sep. 2	Arlington Million	Arlington	1¼	Golden Pheasant	Gary Stevens	600,000

*Includes $1 million bonus for best overall showing in three races of Canadian Triple Crown.

Triple Crown Races

Thoroughbred racing's Triple Crown for 3-year-olds consists of the Kentucky Derby, Preakness Stakes and Belmont Stakes run over six weeks in May and June. Unbridled won the 1990 Triple Crown Challenge as the best overall performer entered in all three races by winning the Derby, placing second in the Preakness and finishing fourth in the Belmont. Summer Squall passed up the Belmont after finishing second in the Derby and winning the Preakness.

116th Kentucky Derby

Grade I for three-year-olds; 8th race at Churchill Downs in Louisville. **Date**—May 5, 1990; **Distance**—1¼ miles; **Stakes purse**—$756,000 ($581,000 to winner); **Track**—good; **Off**—5:34 P.M.

Winner—Unbridled; **Time**—2:02; **Won**—driving; **Bloodlines**—Bc, by Fappiano-Gana Facil, by Le Fabuleux; **Breeder**—Tartan Farms Corp.(Fla.).

	PP	Finish	To $1	Jockey	Trainer	Owner
Unbridled	8	1—3½	10.80	Craig Perret	Carl Nafzger	Frances A.Genter
Summer Squall	13	2—6	2.10	Pat Day	Neil Howard	Dogwood Stable
Pleasant Tap	9	3—3	40.70	Kent Desormeaux	Chris Speckert	Thomas Mellon Evans
Video Ranger	4	4—1¼	65.80	Ron Hansen	Ian Jory	Myung Kwon Cho
Silver Ending	10	5—1½	6.40	Chris McCarron	Ron McAnally	Debbie McAnally & Angelo Constanza
Killer Diller	2	6—1	60.90	James Bruin	Frank Alexander	Barry K.Schwartz
b-Land Rush	14	7—3	14.00	Angel Cordero,Jr	D.Wayne Lukas	W.T.Young&D.Wayne Lukas
Mister Frisky	5	8—3	1.90	Gary Stevens	Las Barrera	Jose & Marta Fernandez
Thirty Six Red	11	9—neck	5.80	Mike Smith	Nick Zito	B.Giles Brophy
b-Power Lunch	15	10—2½	14.00	Ron Romero	D.Wayne Lukas	Calumet Farm
b-Real Cash	6	11—¾	14.00	Alex Solis	D.Wayne Lukas	W.T.Young
f-Dr.Bobby A	1	12—2½	99.30	Nick Santagata	Steve DiMauro	Susan Rotondi & Kathryn Intrieri
a-Pendleton Ridge	3	13—15	33.80	Laffit Pincay,Jr	Bobby Frankel	Bruce McNall, Wayne Gretzky & Craig Stadler
a-Burnt Hills	12	14—6	33.80	Pat Valenzuela	Bobby Frankel	Edmund Gann
Fighting Fantasy	7	15	111.30	Shane Sellers	J.E.Churchman Jr.	Ray Cottrell

Times—0:22⅗; 0:46; 1:11; 1:37⅗; 2:02.
$2 Mutuel Prices—#7 Unbridled ($23.60, 7.80, 5.80); #11 Summer Squall ($3.80, 3.80), #8 Pleasant Tap ($12.00).
Scratched—Country Day; **Overweights**—none (all carried 126 lbs); **Attendance**—128,257; **TV Rating**—10.1/27 share (ABC).

115th Preakness Stakes

Grade I for three-year-olds; 10th race at Pimlico in Baltimore. **Date**—May 19, 1990; **Distance**—1³⁄₁₆ miles; **Stakes purse**—$686,000 ($445,900 to winner); **Track**—fast; **Off**—5:33 P.M.

Winner—Summer Squall; **Time**—1:53⅗; **Won**—driving; **Bloodlines**—Bc by Storm Bird-Weekend Surprise, by Secretariat; **Breeder**—WS Farish & WS Kilroy (Ky.).

	PP	Finish	To $1	Jockey	Trainer	Owner
Summer Squall	7	1—2¼	2.40	Pat Day	Neil Howard	Dogwood Stable
Unbridled	6	2—9	1.70	Craig Perret	Carl Nafzger	Frances A.Genter
Mister Frisky	9	3—½	2.50	Gary Stevens	Laz Barrera	Jose & Marta Fernandez
Music Prospector	1	4—2	61.10	Frank Olivares	Steve Miyadi	Silky Green Inc.
Fighting Notion	5	5—neck	35.50	Alberto Delgado	Nancy Heil	Arlene Kushner
Land Rush	2	6—nose	9.60	Angel Cordero,Jr	D.Wayne Lukas	D.Wayne Lukas & Overbrook Farm
Kentucky Jazz	4	7—1¾	11.10	Kent Desormeaux	D.Wayne Lukas	D.Wayne Lucas & Robert French
Baron de Vaux	3	8—½	37.00	Joe Rocco	Charles Peoples	Bayard Sharp
J.R.'s Horizon	8	9	74.40	Mark Johnston	Meredith Bailes	Marvin Champion

Times—0:23⅕; 0:47; 1:10⅘; 1:35⅗; 1:53⅗.
$2 Mutuel Prices—#7 Summer Squall ($6.80, 3.00, 2.60); #6 Unbridled ($3.00, 2.80), #9 Mister Frisky ($3.40).
Scratched—none; **Overweights**—none (all carried 126 lbs); **Attendance**—86,531; **TV Rating**—7.2/21 share (ABC).

122nd Belmont Stakes

Grade I for three-year-olds; 8th race at Belmont Park in Elmont, NY. **Date**—June 9, 1990; **Distance**—1½ miles; **Stakes purse**—$686,000 ($411,600 to winner); **Track**—fast; **Off**—5:31 pm.

Winner—Go And Go; **Time**—2:27⅕; **Won**—pulling away; **Bloodlines**—CHc by Be My Guest-Irish Edition, by Alleged; **Breeder**—Moyglare Std Farm Ltd (Ireland).

	PP	Finish	To $1	Jockey	Trainer	Owner
Go And Go	2	1—8	7.50	Michael Kinane	Dermot Weld	Moyglare Stud Farm
Thirty Six Red	1	2—2	3.70	Mike Smith	Nick Zito	B.Giles Brophy
Baron de Vaux	3	3—2	68.30	Joe Rocco	Charles Peoples	Bayard Sharp
Unbridled	5	4—head	1.10	Craig Perret	Carl Nafzger	Frances A.Genter
Yonder	8	5—7	6.30	Jerry Bailey	Angel Penna,Jr	Frank Stronach
Land Rush	9	6—12	12.00	Angel Cordero,Jr	D.Wayne Lukas	D.Wayne Lukas & Overbrook Farm
Video Ranger	6	7—6	10.30	Jose Santos	Ian Jory	M.K.Cho
Hawaiian Pass	7	8—neck	75.50	Art Madrid,Jr	Humberto Aguilera	C.N.& Anne Winner
Country Day	4	9	10.10	Chris Antley	John Parisella	James Scibelli

Times—0:23⅗; 0:48; 1:12⅕; 1:36⅖; 2:01⅘; 2:27⅕.

$2 Mutuel Prices—#2 Go And Go ($17.20, 6.20, 5.80); #1 Thirty Six Red ($4.40, 4.20), #3 Baron de Vaux ($12.60).

Scratched—none; **Overweights**—none (all carried 126 lbs); **Attendance**—50,123; **TV Rating**—5.3/16 share (ABC).

Points Change in Triple Crown Challenge

The point system used to determine the three-race, overall winner of the 11 million Triple Crown Challenge bonus has been changed for 1991. Instead of the 5-3 1 point system (in place since 1987) for win, place and show, the new system will use a 10-5-3-1 breakdown that strongly favors the horse or horses winning each race.

Under the new system, Unbridled would still have won the 1990 Challenge—but in 1987, Alysheba's two wins and a 4th would have beaten out Bet Twice's two seconds and a 1st, 21-20.

National Money Leaders

Official Top 10 standings for 1989 and unofficial Top 10 standings for 1990 (through Sept. 2), as compiled by *The Daily Racing Form*.

Final 1989

Horses	Age	Sts	1st	Purses
Sunday Silence	3	9	7	$4,578,454
Easy Goer	3	11	8	3,837,150
Prized	3	7	4	1,888,705
With Approval	3	10	6	1,772,150
Steinlen (GB)	6	11	7	1,521,378
Bayakoa (ARG)*	5	11	9	1,406,403
Yankee Affair	7	13	5	1,333,813
Blushing John	4	10	5	1,232,030
Open Mind*	3	11	8	1,120,308
Cryptoclearance	5	10	3	1,059,010

*Female

Jockeys	Mts	1st	Purses
Jose Santos	1459	285	$13,847,003
Pat Day	1349	383	13,313,946
Angel Cordero, Jr	1224	246	12,219,159
Chris McCarron*	1157	234	11,881,261
Eddie Delahoussaye	1371	248	11,511,616
Laffit Pincay, Jr	1594	298	11,361,610
Gary Stevens	1553	262	10,271,281
Kent Desormeaux	2312	598	9,114,623
Pat Valenzuela	984	147	8,209,535
Julie Krone	1673	368	8,031,445

*Includes foreign racing

Trainers	Sts	1st	Purses
D.Wayne Lucas	1398	305	$16,103,998
Charlie Whittingham	436	86	11,402,231
Shug McGaughey	178	55	8,306,888
Neil Drysdale	263	69	5,514,265
Ron McAnally	461	93	4,751,953
Roger Attfield	308	61	4,114,824
Scotty Schulhofer	410	59	3,560,624
William Mott	424	103	3,546,046
Robert Klesaris	729	187	2,746,417
Thomas Skiffington	427	82	2,746,269

1990 (through Sept. 2)

Horses	Age	Sts	1st	Purses
Criminal Type	5	10	7	$2,270,290
Unbridled	3	8	3	2,118,149
Izvestia	3	8	7	1,742,151
Ruhlmann	5	5	2	1,060,800
Summer Squall	3	5	3	1,042,356
Rhythm	3	8	3	888,172
Steinlen (GB)	7	8	3	830,104
Golden Pheasant	4	5	3	790,500
Thirty Six Red	3	10	3	716,535
Beau Genius	5	12	9	707,461

Jockeys	Mts	1st	Purses
Gary Stevens	1090	210	$9,879,704
Jose Santos	953	192	8,191,870
Craig Perret	555	132	8,126,438
Pat Day	1078	282	6,809,070
Angel Cordero, Jr	927	178	6,243,697
Pat Valenzuela	1061	177	6,123,704
Eddie Delahoussaye	962	128	5,749,542
Mike Smith	1175	160	5,565,357
Chris McCarron	583	113	5,282,749
Alex Solis	1079	141	5,151,749

Trainers	Sts	1st	Purses
D.Wayne Lucas	985	196	$11,171,000
Charlie Whittingham	287	42	4,420,925
Carl Nafzger	253	40	3,409,506
Ron McAnally	327	52	3,393,363
Roger Attfield	185	48	3,247,169
Richard Mandella	296	65	2,816,090
Shug McGaughey	102	35	2,756,620
Jerry Hollendorfer	632	165	2,111,549
Robert Frankel	213	37	2,037,549
Rusty Arnold	295	37	1,971,120

Harness Racing

1989-90 Major Stakes Races

Winners of major stakes races from Sept. 1, 1989, through Sept. 2, 1990; all paces and trots cover one mile: "BC" before a race indicates year-end Breeders' Crown series.

Late 1989

Date	Race	Raceway	Winner	Driver	Value to Winner
Sep. 1	BC Aged Mare Pace	Northfield Park	Armbro Feather	John Kopas	$143,843
Sep. 8	BC Aged Mare Trot	Hippodrome	Grades Signing	Olle Goop	144,925
Sep. 9	Messenger Stakes Pace	Freestate	Sandman Hanover	Bill O'Donnell	192,455
Sep. 15	BC Aged Horse/Geld.Pace .	Freehold	Matt's Scooter	Michel Lachance	139,119
Sep. 21	Little Brown Jug Pace	Delaware,OH	Goalie Jeff	Michel Lachance	151,310
Sep. 23	BC Aged Horse/Geld.Trot	Freestate	Delray Lobell	John Campbell	124,869
Oct. 6	Kentucky Futurity Trot	The Red Mile	Peace Corps	John Campbell	83,550
Oct. 27	BC 2-Yr-Old Filly Pace	Pompano Park	Town Pro	Doug Brown	219,106
Oct. 27	BC 2-Yr-Old Filly Trot	Pompano Park	Delphi's Lobell	Ron Waples	210,106
Oct. 27	BC 2-Yr-Old Colt Pace	Pompano Park	Til We Meet Again	Mickey McNichol	283,606
Oct. 27	BC 2-Yr-Old Colt Trot	Pompano Park	Royal Troubador	Carl Allen	178,205
Oct. 27	BC 3-Yr-Old Filly Pace	Pompano Park	Cherry Hello	John Campbell	142,850
Oct. 27	BC 3-Yr-Old Filly Trot	Pompano Park	Peace Corps	John Campbell	167,850
Oct. 27	BC 3-Yr-Old Colt Pace	Pompano Park	Goalie Jeff	Michel Lachance	188,850
Oct. 27	BC 3-Yr-Old Colt Trot	Pompano Park	Esquire Spur	Dick Stillings	161,138
Nov. 18	Governor's Cup	Garden St.	In the Pocket	John Campbell	340,550

1990 (through Sept. 2)

Date	Race	Raceway	Winner	Driver	Value to Winner
May 27	Elitlopp (Sweden)	Solvalla	Mack Lobell	Thomas Nilsson	170,000
Jun.23	North America Cup	Greenwood	Apache's Fame	William Fritz	500,000
Jul.13	Meadowlands Pace	Meadowlands	Bach Towel	Ray Remmen	575,750
Jul.14	Yonkers Trot	Yonkers	Royal Troubador	Carl Allen	100,291
Aug. 4	Hambletonian	Meadowlands	Harmonicus	John Campbell	637,000
Aug.17	Woodrow Wilson Pace	Meadowlands	Die Laughing	Richie Silverman	521,750
Aug.17	Sweetheart Pace...........	Meadowlands	Miss Easy	John Campbell	542,192
Aug.25	Cane Pace	Yonkers	Jake and Elwood	John Campbell	97,130

National Money Leaders

Official Top 10 standings for 1989 and unofficial Top 10 standings for 1990 (through Sept. 2), as compiled by the U.S. Trotting Association. Note that (f) indicates female; (m) indicates mare.

Final 1989

Horses	Age	Sts	1st	Purses
Goalie Jeff	3/P	31	17	$1,682,151
Matt's Scooter	4/P	30	23	1,140,994
Dexter Nukes	3/P	27	19	1,027,620
Peace Corps	3/T	19	16	1,002,701
In The Pocket	2/P	18	7	792,422
Sandman Hanover	3/P	31	18	767,153
Kentucky Spur	3/P	20	8	723,945
Park Avenue Joe	3/T	17	6	666,311
Bruce's Lady (f)	2/P	21	10	628,925
Armbro Feather (m)	5/P	32	21	587,405

1990 (through Sept. 2)

Horses	Age	Sts	1st	Purses
Beach Towel	3/P	15	13	$1,539,899
Jake and Elwood	3/P	18	10	1,031,251
Harmonious	3/T	11	9	1,024,150
Apache's Fame	3/P	18	13	979,471
Die Laughing	2/P	5	3	722,425
Embassy Lobell	3/T	11	5	698,420
Dorunrun Bluegrass	4/P	21	12	620,775
Mark Jonathan	3/P	22	10	596,068
Miss Easy (f)	2/P	12	11	580,109
In the Pocket	3/P	16	8	531,424

Drivers	Sts	1st	Purses
John Campbell	2071	425	$9,738,450
Michel Lachance	2183	369	7,477,749
Herve Filion	4076	814	5,258,920
Doug Brown............	1991	384	5,135,141
Bill O'Donnell	1707	244	4,881,195
Bill Fahy	1817	270	4,801,420
Cat Manzi	3729	687	4,479,193
Jack Moiseyev	3050	536	4,122,900
Steve Condren	1833	290	3,882,893
Ron Waples	1232	196	3,847,495

Drivers	Sts	1st	Purses
John Campbell	2064	471	$7,734,881
Michel Lachance	2087	289	5,342,892
Doug Brown	1291	252	4,020,787
Bill O'Donnell	1611	215	3,711,489
Cat Manzi	2643	425	3,570,223
Bill Fahy	1352	143	2,717,355
Herve Filion	2318	421	2,617,883
Ron Waples	936	141	2,396,617
Dave Magee	1014	203	2,344,390
Ray Remmen	426	65	2,146,190

1990 Steeplechase

Date	Race	Location	Miles	Fences	Winner	Jockey	Value to Winner
Apr. 7	Grand National (GB)	Liverpool	4½	30	Mr.Frisk	Marcus Armytage	$113,000

Thoroughbred Racing

Triple Crown Winners

Eleven horses have won the Kentucky Derby, Preakness Stakes and Belmont Stakes in the same year. Two trainers, James "Sunny Jim" Fitzsimmons and Ben A.Jones, won it twice, while Eddie Arcaro is the only jockey to have ridden two winners.

Year	Horse	Jockey	Trainer	Owner	Sire/Dam
1919	Sir Barton	Johnny Loftus	H.Guy Bedwell	J.K.L.Ross	Star Shoot/Lady Sterling
1930	Gallant Fox	Earle Sande	J.E. Fitzsimmons	Belair Stud	Sir Gallahad III/Marguerite
1935	Omaha	Willie Saunders	J.E. Fitzsimmons	Belair Stud	Gallant Fox/Flambino
1937	War Admiral	Chas.Kurtsinger	George Conway	Samuel Riddle	Man O'War/Brushup
1941	Whirlaway	Eddie Arcaro	Ben A.Jones	Calumet Farm	Blenheim II/Dustwhirl
1943	Count Fleet	Johnny Longden	Don Cameron	Mrs.J.D.Hertz	Reigh Count/Quickly
1946	Assault	Warren Mehrtens	Max Hirsch	King Ranch	Bold Venture/Igual
1948	Citation	Eddie Arcaro	Ben A.Jones	Calumet Farm	Bull Lea/Hydroplane II
1973	Secretariat	Ron Turcotte	Lucien Laurin	Meadow Stable	Bold Ruler/Somethingroyal
1977	Seattle Slew	Jean Cruguet	Billy Turner	Karen Taylor	Bold Reasoning/My Charmer
1978	Affirmed	Steve Cauthen	Laz Barrera	Harbor View Farm	Exclusive Native/Won't Tell You

Note: Gallant Fox (1930) is the only Triple Crown winner to sire another Triple Crown winner, Omaha (1935). Wm.Woodward Sr. owner of Belair Stud, was breeder-owner of both horses and both were trained by James (Sunny Jim) Fitzsimmons.

Triple Crown Near Misses

Thirty-eight horses have won two legs of the Triple Crown. Of those, a dozen won the Kentucky Derby (KD) and Preakness Stakes (PS) only to be beaten in the Belmont Stakes (BS). Two others, Burgoo King (1932) and Bold Venture (1936), each won the Derby and Preakness but were forced out of the Belmont with the same injury—a bowed tendon—that effectively ended their racing careers. In 1978, Alydar finished second to Affirmed in all three races, the only time that has happened.

Year	Horse	KD	PS	BS	Year	Horse	KD	PS	BS
1877	Cloverbrook	DNS	won	won	1956	Needles	won	2nd	won
1878	Duke of Magenta	DNS	won	won	1958	Tim Tam	won	won	2nd
1880	Grenada	DNS	won	won	1961	Carry Back	won	won	7th
1881	Saunterer	DNS	won	won	1963	Chateaugay	won	2nd	won
1895	Belmar	DNS	won	won	1964	Northern Dancer	won	won	3rd
1920	Man O'War	DNS	won	won	1966	Kauai King	won	won	4th
1922	Pillory	DNS	won	won	1967	Damascus	3rd	won	won
1923	Zev	won	12th	won	1968	Forward Pass	won*	won	2nd
1931	Twenty Grand	won	2nd	won	1969	Majestic Prince	won	won	2nd
1932	Burgoo King	won	won	DNS	1971	Canonero II	won	won	4th
1936	Bold Venture	won	won	DNS	1972	Riva Ridge	won	4th	won
1939	Johnstown	won	5th	won	1974	Little Current	5th	won	won
1940	Bimelech	2nd	won	won	1976	Bold Forbes	won	3rd	won
1942	Shut Out	won	5th	won	1979	Spectacular Bid	won	won	3rd
1944	Pensive	won	won	2nd	1981	Pleasant Colony	won	won	3rd
1949	Capot	2nd	won	won	1984	Swale	won	7th	won
1950	Middleground	won	2nd	won	1987	Alysheba	won	won	4th
1953	Native Dancer	2nd	won	won	1988	Risen Star	3rd	won	won
1955	Nashua	2nd	won	won	1989	Sunday Silence	won	won	2nd

*Won on disqualification.

The Triple Crown Challenge

Since 1987, a $5 million bonus has been guaranteed to any horse winning the Triple Crown and a $1 million bonus to the horse with the best overall showing in all three races. The top two point-getters each year have run in all three, except Summer Squall in 1990.

Year		KD	PS	BS	Pts	Year		KD	PS	BS	Pts
1987	1. Bet Twice	2nd	2nd	1st	— 11	1989	1. Sunday Silence	1st	1st	2nd	— 13
	2. Alysheba	1st	1st	4th	— 10		2. Easy Goer	2nd	2nd	1st	— 11
1988	1. Risen Star	3rd	1st	1st	— 11	1990	1. Unbridled	1st	2nd	4th	— 8
	2. Winning Colors	1st	3rd	6th	— 6		2. Summer Squall	2nd	1st	DNR	8

Kentucky Derby

For three-year-olds. Held the first Saturday in May at Churchill Downs in Louisville, Ky. Inaugurated in 1875. Originally run at 1½ miles (1875-95), shortened to present 1¼ miles in 1896.

Trainers with most wins: Ben A. Jones (6); H.J.Thompson (4); Sunny Jim Fitzsimmons and Max Hirsch (3).

Jockeys with most wins: Eddie Arcaro and Bill Hartack (5); Bill Shoemaker (4); Angel Cordero, Jr, Issac Murphy and Earl Sande (3).

Winning fillies: Regret (1915), Genuine Risk (1980) and Winning Colors (1988).

Year	Winner	Time	Jockey	Trainer	2nd place	3rd place
1875	**Aristides**	2:37¾	Oliver Lewis	Andy Anderson	Volcano	Verdigris
1876	**Vagrant**	2:38¼	Bobby Swim	James Williams	Creedmoor	Harry Hill
1877	**Baden-Baden**	2:38	Billy Walker	Ed Brown	Leonard	King William
1878	**Day Star**	2:37¼	Jimmy Carter	Lee Paul	Himyar	Leveler
1879	**Lord Murphy**	2:37	Charlie Shauer	George Rice	Falsetto	Strathmore
1880	**Fonso**	2:37½	George Lewis	Tice Hutsell	Kimball	Bancroft
1881	**Hindoo**	2:40	Jim McLaughin	James Rowe,Sr	Lelex	Alfambra
1882	**Apollo**	2:40¼	Babe Hurd	Green Morris	Runnymede	Bengal
1883	**Leonatus**	2:43	Billy Donohue	Raleigh Colston	Drake Carter	Lord Raglan
1884	**Buchanan**	2:40¼	Isaac Murphy	William Bird	Loftin	Audrain
1885	**Joe Cotton**	2:37¼	Babe Henderson	Alex Perry	Bersan	Ten Booker
1886	**Ben Ali**	2:36½	Paul Duffy	Jim Murphy	Blue Wing	Free Knight
1887	**Montrose**	2:39¼	Isaac Lewis	John McGinty	Jim Gore	Jacobin
1888	**MacBeth II**	2:38¼	Geo.Covington	John Campbell	Gallifet	White
1889	**Spokane**	2:34½	Thomas Kiley	John Rodegap	Proctor Knott	Once Again
1890	**Riley**	2:45	Isaac Murphy	Edward Corrigan	Bill Letcher	Robespierre
1891	**Kingman**	2:52¼	Isaac Murphy	Dud Allen	Balgowan	High Tariff
1892	**Azra**	2:41½	Lonnie Clayton	John Morris	Huron	Phil Dwyer
1893	**Lookout**	2:39¼	Eddie Kunze	Wm.McDaniel	Plutus	Boundless
1894	**Chant**	2:41	Frank Goodale	Eugene Leigh	Pearl Song	Sigurd
1895	**Halma**	2:37½	Soup Perkins	Byron McClelland	Basso	Laureate
1896	**Ben Brush**	2:07¼	Willie Simms	Hardy Campbell	Ben Eder	Semper Ego
1897	**Typhoon II**	2:12½	Buttons Garner	J.C.Cahn	Ornament	Dr. Catlett
1898	**Plaudit**	2:09	Willie Simms	John Madden	Lieber Karl	Isabey
1899	**Manuel**	2:12	Fred Taral	Robert Walden	Corsini	Mazo
1900	**Lieut. Gibson**	2:06¼	Jimmy Boland	Charles Hughes	Florizar	Thrive
1901	**His Eminence**	2:07¾	Jimmy Winkfield	F.B.VanMeter	Sannazarro	Driscoll
1902	**Alan-a-Dale**	2:08¾	Jimmy Winkfield	T.C.McDowell	Inventor	The Rival
1903	**Judge Himes**	2:09	Hal Booker	J.P.Mayberry	Early	Bourbon
1904	**Elwood**	2:08½	Shorty Prior	C.E.Durnell	Ed. Tierney	Brancas
1905	**Agile**	2:10¾	Jack Martin	Robert Tucker	Ram's Horn	Layson
1906	**Sir Huon**	2:08⅕	Roscoe Troxler	Pete Coyne	Lady Navarre	James Reddick
1907	**Pink Star**	2:12⅗	Andy Minder	W.H.Fizer	Zal	Ovelando
1908	**Stone Street**	2:15⅕	Arthur Pickens	J.W.Hall	Sir Cleges	Dunvegan
1909	**Wintergreen**	2:08⅕	Vincent Power	Charles Mack	Miami	Dr. Barkley
1910	**Donau**	2:06⅖	Fred Herbert	George Ham	Joe Morris	Fighting Bob
1911	**Meridian**	2:05	Geo.Archibald	Albert Ewing	Governor Gray	Colston
1912	**Worth**	2:09⅖	C.H.Shilling	Frank Taylor	Duval	Flamma
1913	**Donerail**	2:04⅘	Roscoe Goose	Thomas Hayes	Ten Point	Gowell
1914	**Old Rosebud**	2:03⅖	John McCabe	F.D.Weir	Hodge	Bronzewing
1915	**Regret**	2:05⅖	Joe Notter	James Rowe,Sr	Pebbles	Sharpshooter
1916	**George Smith**	2:04	Johnny Loftus	Hollie Hughes	Star Hawk	Franklin
1917	**Omar Khayyam**	2:04⅗	Charles Borel	C.T.Patterson	Ticket	Midway
1918	**Exterminator**	2:10⅘	William Knapp	Henry McDaniel	Escoba	Viva America
1919	**SIR BARTON**	2:09⅘	Johnny Loftus	H.Guy Bedwell	Billy Kelly	Under Fire
1920	**Paul Jones**	2:09	Ted Rice	Billy Garth	Upset	On Watch
1921	**Behave Yourself**	2:04⅕	Chas.Thompson	H.J.Thompson	Black Servant	Prudery
1922	**Morvich**	2:04⅗	Albert Johnson	Fred Burlew	Bet Mosie	John Finn
1923	**Zev**	2:05⅖	Earl Sande	D.J.Leary	Martingale	Vigil
1924	**Black Gold**	2:05⅕	John Mooney	Hedley Webb	Chilhowee	Beau Butler
1925	**Flying Ebony**	2:07⅗	Earl Sande	William Duke	Captain Hal	Son of John
1926	**Bubbling Over**	2:03⅗	Albert Johnson	H.J.Thompson	Bagenbaggage	Rock Man
1927	**Whiskery**	2:06	Linus McAtee	Fred Hopkins	Osmond	Jock
1928	**Reigh Count**	2:10⅖	Chick Lang	Bert Michell	Misstep	Toro
1929	**Clyde Van Dusen**	2:10⅘	Linus McAtee	Clyde Van Dusen	Naishapur	Panchio
1930	**GALLANT FOX**	2:07⅗	Earl Sande	Jim Fitzsimmons	Gallant Knight	Ned O.
1931	**Twenty Grand**	2:01⅘	Chas.Kurtsinger	James Rowe,Jr	Sweep All	Mate
1932	**Burgoo King**	2:05⅕	Eugene James	H.J.Thompson	Economic	Stepenfetchit
1933	**Brokers Tip**	2:06⅘	Don Meade	H.J.Thompson	Head Play	Charley O.
1934	**Cavalcade**	2:04	Mack Garner	Bob Smith	Discovery	Agrarian
1935	**OMAHA**	2:05	Willie Saunders	Jim Fitzsimmons	Roman Soldier	Whiskolo

Year	Winner	Time	Jockey	Trainer	2nd place	3rd place
1936	**Bold Venture**	2:03⅗	Ira Hanford	Max Hirsch	Brevity	Indian Brown
1937	**WAR ADMIRAL**	2:03⅕	Chas.Kurtsinger	George Conway	Pompoon	Reaping Reward
1938	**Lawrin**	2:04⅘	Eddie Arcaro	Ben Jones	Dauber	Can't Wait
1939	**Johnstown**	2:03⅖	James Stout	Jim Fitzsimmons	Challedon	Heather Broom
1940	**Gallahadion**	2:05	Carroll Bierman	Roy Waldron	Bimelech	Dit
1941	**WHIRLAWAY**	2:01⅖	Eddie Arcaro	Ben Jones	Staretor	Market Wise
1942	**Shut Out**	2:04⅖	Wayne Wright	John Gaver	Alsab	Valdina Orphan
1943	**COUNT FLEET**	2:04	Johnny Longden	Don Cameron	Blue Swords	Slide Rule
1944	**Pensive**	2:04⅕	Conn McCreary	Ben Jones	Broadcloth	Stir Up
1945	**Hoop Jr**	2:07	Eddie Arcaro	Ivan Parke	Pot o'Luck	Darby Dieppe
1946	**ASSAULT**	2:06⅗	Warren Mehrtens	Max Hirsch	Spy Song	Hampden
1947	**Jet Pilot**	2:06⅘	Eric Guerin	Tom Smith	Phalanx	Faultless
1948	**CITATION**	2:05⅖	Eddie Arcaro	Ben Jones	Coaltown	My Request
1949	**Ponder**	2:04⅕	Steve Brooks	Ben Jones	Capot	Palestinian
1950	**Middleground**	2:01⅗	William Boland	Max Hirsch	Hill Prince	Mr. Trouble
1951	**Count Turf**	2:02⅗	Conn McCreary	Sol Rutchick	Royal Mustang	Ruhe
1952	**Hill Gail**	2:01⅗	Eddie Arcaro	Ben Jones	Sub Fleet	Blue Man
1953	**Dark Star**	2:02	Hank Moreno	Eddie Hayward	Native Dancer	Invigorator
1954	**Determine**	2:03	Raymond York	Willie Molter	Hasty Road	Hasseyampa
1955	**Swaps**	2:01⅘	Bill Shoemaker	Mesh Tenney	Nashua	Summer Tan
1956	**Needles**	2:03⅖	David Erb	Hugh Fontaine	Fabius	Come On Red
1957	**Iron Liege**	2:02⅕	Bill Hartack	Jimmy Jones	Gallant Man	Round Table
1958	**Tim Tam**	2:05	I.Valenzuela	Jimmy Jones	Lincoln Road	Noureddin
1959	**Tomy Lee**	2:02⅕	Bill Shoemaker	Frank Childs	Sword Dancer	First Landing
1960	**Venetian Way**	2:02⅖	Bill Hartack	Victor Sovinski	Bally Ache	Victoria Park
1961	**Carry Back**	2:04	John Sellers	Jack Price	Crozier	Bass Clef
1962	**Decidedly**	2:00⅖	Bill Hartack	Horatio Luro	Roman Line	Ridan
1963	**Chateaugay**	2:01⅘	Braulio Baeza	James Conway	Never Bend	Candy Spots
1964	**Northern Dancer**	2:00	Bill Hartack	Horatio Luro	Hill Rise	The Scoundrel
1965	**Lucky Debonair**	2:01⅕	Bill Shoemaker	Frank Catrone	Dapper Dan	Tom Rolfe
1966	**Kauai King**	2:02	Don Brumfield	Henry Forrest	Advocator	Blue Skyer
1967	**Proud Clarion**	2:00⅗	Bobby Ussery	Loyd Gentry	Barbs Delight	Damascus
1968	**Forward Pass***	2:02⅕	I.Valenzuela	Henry Forrest	Francie's Hat	T.V. Commercial
1969	**Majestic Prince**	2:01⅘	Bill Hartack	Johnny Longden	Arts & Letters	Dike
1970	**Dust Commander**	2:03⅖	Mike Manganello	Don Combs	My Dad George	High Echelon
1971	**Canonero II**	2:03⅕	Gustavo Avila	Juan Arias	Jim French	Bold Reason
1972	**Riva Ridge**	2:01⅘	Ron Turcotte	Lucien Laurin	No Le Hace	Hold Your Peace
1973	**SECRETARIAT**	1:59⅖	Ron Turcotte	Lucien Laurin	Sham	Our Native
1974	**Cannonade**	2:04	Angel Cordero,Jr	Woody Stephens	Hudson County	Agitate
1975	**Foolish Pleasure**	2:02	Jacinto Vasquez	LeRoy Jolley	Avatar	Diabolo
1976	**Bold Forbes**	2:01⅗	Angel Cordero,Jr	Laz Barrera	Honest Pleasure	Elocutionist
1977	**SEATTLE SLEW**	2:02⅕	Jean Cruguet	Billy Turner	Run Dusty Run	Sanhedrin
1978	**AFFIRMED**	2:01⅕	Steve Cauthen	Laz Barrera	Alydar	Believe It
1979	**Spectacular Bid**	2:02⅖	Ron Franklin	Buddy Delp	General Assembly	Golden Act
1980	**Genuine Risk**	2:02	Jacinto Vasquez	LeRoy Jolley	Rumbo	Jaklin Klugman
1981	**Pleasant Colony**	2:02	Jorge Velasquez	John Campo	Woodchopper	Partez
1982	**Gato Del Sol**	2:02⅕	E.Delahoussaye	Eddie Gregson	Laser Light	Reinvested
1983	**Sunny's Halo**	2:02⅕	E.Delahoussaye	David Cross	Desert Wine	Caveat
1984	**Swale**	2:02⅖	Laffit Pincay,Jr	Woody Stephens	Coax Me Chad	At The Threshold
1985	**Spend A Buck**	2:00⅕	Angel Cordero,Jr	Cam Gambolati	Stephan's Odyssey	Chief's Crown
1986	**Ferdinand**	2:02⅘	Bill Shoemaker	Chas.Whittingham	Bold Arrangement	Broad Brush
1987	**Alysheba**	2:03⅖	Chris McCarron	Jack Van Berg	Bet Twice	Avies Copy
1988	**Winning Colors**	2:02⅕	Gary Stevens	D.Wayne Lukas	Forty Niner	Risen Star
1989	**Sunday Silence**	2:05	Pat Valenzuela	Chas.Whittingham	Easy Goer	Awe Inspiring
1990	**Unbridled**	2:02	Craig Perret	Carl Nafzger	Summer Squall	Pleasant Tap

*In 1968, Dancer's Image finished first but was disqualified after traces of prohibited medication were found in his system.

Preakness Stakes

For three-year-olds. Held two weeks after the Kentucky Derby at Pimlico Race Course in Baltimore, Md. Inaugurated 1873.

Originally run at 1½ miles (1873-88), then at 1¼ miles (1889), 1½ miles (1890), $1\frac{1}{16}$ miles (1894-1900), 1 mile & 70 yards (1901-07), $1\frac{1}{16}$ miles (1908), 1 mile (1909-10), 1⅛ miles (1911-24), and the present $1\frac{3}{16}$ miles since 1925.

Trainers with most wins: Robert W.Walden (7); T.J. Healey (5); Sunny Jim Fitzsimmons and Jimmy Jones (4); J. Whalen (3).

Jockeys with most wins: Eddie Arcaro (6); G. Barbee, Bill Hartack and Lloyd Hughes (3).

Winning fillies: Flocarline (1903), Whimsical (1906), Rhine Maiden (1915) and Nellie Morse (1924).

Year	Winner	Time	Jockey	Trainer	2nd place	3rd place
1873	**Survivor**	2:43	G.Barbee	A.D.Pryor	John Boulger	Artist
1874	**Culpepper**	2:56½	W.Donohue	H.Gaffney	King Amadeus	Scratch
1875	**Tom Ochiltree**	2:43½	L.Hughes	R.W.Walden	Viator	Bay Final

Preakness Stakes (Cont.)

Year	Winner	Time	Jockey	Trainer	2nd place	3rd place
1876	**Shirley**	2:44¾	G.Barbee	W.Brown	Rappahannock	Algerine
1877	**Cloverbrook**	2:45½	C.Holloway	J.Walden	Bombast	Lucifer
1878	**Duke of Magenta**	2:41¾	C.Holloway	R.W.Walden	Bayard	Albert
1879	**Harold**	2:40½	L.Hughes	R.W.Walden	Jericho	Rochester
1880	**Grenada**	2:40½	L.Hughes	R.W.Walden	Oden	Emily F.
1881	**Saunterer**	2:40½	T.Costello	R.W.Walden	Compensation	Baltic
1882	**Vanguard**	2:44½	T.Costello	R.W.Walden	Heck	Col. Watson
1883	**Jacobus**	2:42½	G.Barbee	R.Dwyer	Parnell	—
1884	**Knight of Ellerslie**	2:39½	S.Fisher	T.B.Doswell	Welcher	—
1885	**Tecumseh**	2:49	Jim McLaughlin	C.Littlefield	Wickham	John C.
1886	**The Bard**	2:45	S.Fisher	J.Huggins	Eurus	Elkwood
1887	**Dunboyne**	2:39½	W.Donohue	W.Jennings	Mahoney	Raymond
1888	**Refund**	2:49	F.Littlefield	R.W.Walden	Judge Murray	Glendale
1889	**Buddhist**	2:17½	W.Anderson	J.Rogers	Japhet	—
1890	**Montague**	2:36¾	W.Martin	E.Feakes	Philosophy	Barrister
1891	Not held					
1892	Not held					
1893	Not held					
1894	**Assignee**	1:49¼	F.Taral	W.Lakeland	Potentate	Ed Kearney
1895	**Belmar**	1:50½	F.Taral	E.Feakes	April Fool	Sue Kittie
1896	**Margrave**	1:51	H.Griffin	Byron McClelland	Hamilton II	Intermission
1897	**Paul Kauvar**	1:51¼	T.Thorpe	T.P.Hayes	Elkins	On Deck
1898	**Sly Fox**	1:49⅗	W.Simms	H.Campbell	The Huguenot	Nuto
1899	**Half Time**	1:47	R.Clawson	F.McCabe	Filigrane	Lackland
1900	**Hindus**	1:48⅖	H.Spencer	J.H.Morris	Sarmation	Ten Candles
1901	**The Parader**	1:47⅕	F.Landry	T.J.Healey	Sadie S.	Dr. Barlow
1902	**Old England**	1:45⅘	L.Jackson	G.B.Morris	Maj.Daingerfield	Namtor
1903	**Flocarline**	1:44⅘	W.Gannon	H.C.Riddle	Mackey Dwyer	Rightful
1904	**Bryn Mawr**	1:44⅕	E.Hildebrand	W.F.Presgrave	Wotan	Dolly Spanker
1905	**Cairngorm**	1:45⅘	W.Davis	A.J.Joyner	Kiamesha	Coy Maid
1906	**Whimsical**	1:45	Walter Miller	T.J.Gaynor	Content	Larabie
1907	**Don Enrique**	1:45⅖	G.Mountain	J.Whalen	Ethon	Zambesi
1908	**Royal Tourist**	1:46⅖	Eddie Dugan	A.J.Joyner	Live Wire	Robert Cooper
1909	**Effendi**	1:39⅘	Willie Doyle	F.C.Frisbie	Fashion Plate	Hilltop
1910	**Layminister**	1:40⅗	R.Estep	J.S.Healy	Dalhousie	Sager
1911	**Watervale**	1:51	Eddie Dugan	J.Whalen	Zeus	The Nigger
1912	**Colonel Holloway**	1:56⅗	C.Turner	D.Woodford	Bwana Tumbo	Tipsand
1913	**Buskin**	1:53⅖	James Butwell	J.Whalen	Kleburne	Barnegat
1914	**Holiday**	1:53⅘	A.Schuttinger	J.S.Healy	Brave Cunarder	Defendum
1915	**Rhine Maiden**	1:58	Douglas Hoffman	F.Devers	Half Rock	Runes
1916	**Damrosch**	1:54⅘	Linus McAtee	A.G.Weston	Greenwood	Achievement
1917	**Kalitan**	1:54⅖	E.Haynes	Bill Hurley	Al M. Dick	Kentucky Boy
1918	**War Cloud**	1:53⅗	Johnny Loftus	W.B.Jennings	Sunny Slope	Lanius
1918	**Jack Hare Jr**	1:53⅖	Charles Peak	F.D.Weir	The Porter	Kate Bright
1919	**SIR BARTON**	1:53	Johnny Loftus	H.Guy Bedwell	Eternal	Sweep On
1920	**Man o'War**	1:51⅗	Clarence Kummer	L.Feustel	Upset	Wildair
1921	**Broomspun**	1:54⅕	F.Coltiletti	James Rowe,Sr	Polly Ann	Jeg
1922	**Pillory**	1:51⅗	L.Morris	Thomas Healey	Hea	June Grass
1923	**Vigil**	1:53⅗	B.Marinelli	Thomas Healey	General Thatcher	Rialto
1924	**Nellie Morse**	1:57⅕	John Merimee	A.B.Gordon	Transmute	Mad Play
1925	**Coventry**	1:59	Clarence Kummer	William Duke	Backbone	Almadel
1926	**Display**	1:59⅘	John Maiben	Thomas Healey	Blondin	Mars
1927	**Bostonian**	2:01⅗	Whitey Abel	Fred Hopkins	Sir Harry	Whiskery
1928	**Victorian**	2:00⅕	Sonny Workman	James Rowe,Jr.	Toro	Solace
1929	**Dr. Freeland**	2:01⅗	Louis Schaefer	Thomas Healey	Minotaur	African
1930	**GALLANT FOX**	2:00⅗	Earl Sande	Jim Fitzsimmons	Crack Brigade	Snowflake
1931	**Mate**	1:59	George Ellis	J.W.Healey	Twenty Grand	Ladder
1932	**Burgoo King**	1:59⅘	John Maiben	Thomas Healey	Tick On	Boatswain
1933	**Head Play**	2:02	Chas.Kurtsinger	Thomas Hayes	Ladysman	Utopian
1934	**High Quest**	1:58⅕	Robert Jones	Bob Smith	Cavalcade	Discovery
1935	**OMAHA**	1:58⅖	Willie Saunders	Jim Fitzsimmons	Firethorn	Psychic Bid
1936	**Bold Venture**	1:59	George Woolf	Max Hirsch	Granville	Jean Bart
1937	**WAR ADMIRAL**	1:58⅖	Chas.Kurtsinger	George Conway	Pompoon	Flying Scot
1938	**Dauber**	1:59⅘	Maurice Peters	Dick Handlen	Cravat	Menow
1939	**Challedon**	1:59⅘	George Seabo	Louis Schaefer	Gilded Knight	Volitant
1940	**Bimelech**	1:58⅗	F.A.Smith	Bill Hurley	Mioland	Gallahadion
1941	**WHIRLAWAY**	1:58⅘	Eddie Arcaro	Ben A. Jones	King Cole	Our Boots
1942	**Alsab**	1:57	Basil James	Sarge Swenke	Requested	Sun Again

Year	Winner	Time	Jockey	Trainer	2nd place	3rd place
1943	**COUNT FLEET**	1:57⅖	Johnny Longden	Don Cameron	Blue Swords	Vincentive
1944	**Pensive**	1:59⅕	Conn McCreary	Ben A. Jones	Platter	Stir Up
1945	**Polynesian**	1:58⅘	W.D.Wright	Morris Dixon	Hoop Jr.	Darby Dieppe
1946	**ASSAULT**	2:01⅖	Warren Mehrtens	Max Hirsch	Lord Boswell	Hampden
1947	**Faultless**	1:59	Doug Dobson	Jimmy Jones	On Trust	Phalanx
1948	**CITATION**	2:02⅖	Eddie Arcaro	Jimmy Jones	Vulcan's Forge	Boyard
1949	**Capot**	1:56	Ted Atkinson	J.M.Gaver	Palestinian	Noble Impulse
1950	**Hill Prince**	1:59⅕	Eddie Arcaro	Casey Hayes	Middleground	Dooley
1951	**Bold**	1:56⅖	Eddie Arcaro	Preston Burch	Counter Point	Alerted
1952	**Blue Man**	1:57⅖	Conn McCreary	Woody Stephens	Jampol	One Count
1953	**Native Dancer**	1:57⅘	Eric Guerin	Bill Winfrey	Jamie K.	Royal Bay Gem
1954	**Hasty Road**	1:57⅖	Johnny Adams	Harry Trotsek	Carrilation	Hasseyampa
1955	**Nashua**	1:54⅗	Eddie Arcaro	Jim Fitzsimmons	Saratoga	Traffic Judge
1956	**Fabius**	1:58⅖	Bill Hartack	Jimmy Jones	Needles	No Regrets
1957	**Bold Ruler**	1:56⅕	Eddie Arcaro	Jim Fitzsimmons	Iron Liege	Inside Tract
1958	**Tim Tam**	1:57⅕	I.Valenzuela	Jimmy Jones	Lincoln Road	Gone Fishin'
1959	**Royal Orbit**	1:57	Wm.Harmatz	R. Cornell	Sword Dancer	Dunce
1960	**Bally Ache**	1:57⅗	Bobby Ussery	Jimmy Pitt	Victoria Park	Celtic Ash
1961	**Carry Back**	1:57⅗	Johnny Sellers	Jack Price	Globemaster	Crozier
1962	**Greek Money**	1:56⅕	John Rotz	V.W.Raines	Ridan	Roman Line
1963	**Candy Spots**	1:56⅕	Bill Shoemaker	Mesh Tenney	Chateaugay	Never Bend
1964	**Northern Dancer**	1:56⅘	Bill Hartack	Horatio Luro	The Scoundrel	Hill Rise
1965	**Tom Rolfe**	1:56⅕	Ron Turcotte	Frank Whiteley	Dapper Dan	Hail To All
1966	**Kauai King**	1:55⅖	Don Brumfield	H. Forrest	Stupendous	Amberoid
1967	**Damascus**	1:55⅕	Bill Shoemaker	Frank Whiteley	In Reality	Proud Clarion
1968	**Forward Pass**	1:56⅘	I.Valenzuela	Henry Forrest	Out Of the Way	Nodouble
1969	**Majestic Prince**	1:55⅗	Bill Hartack	Johnny Longden	Arts & Letters	Jay Ray
1970	**Personality**	1:56⅕	Eddie Belmonte	John Jacobs	My Dad George	Silent Screen
1971	**Canonero II**	1:54	Gustavo Avila	Juan Arias	Eastern Fleet	Jim French
1972	**Bee Bee Bee**	1:55⅗	Eldon Nelson	Red Carroll	No Le Hace	Key To The Mint
1973	**SECRETARIAT**	1:54⅖	Ron Turcotte	Lucien Laurin	Sham	Our Native
1974	**Little Current**	1:54⅗	Miguel Rivera	Lou Rondinello	Neapolitan Way	Cannonade
1975	**Master Derby**	1:56⅖	Darrel McHargue	Smiley Adams	Foolish Pleasure	Diabolo
1976	**Elocutionist**	1:55	John Lively	Paul Adwell	Play The Red	Bold Forbes
1977	**SEATTLE SLEW**	1:54⅖	Jean Cruguet	Billy Turner	Iron Constitution	Run Dusty Run
1978	**AFFIRMED**	1:54⅖	Steve Cauthen	Laz Barrera	Alydar	Believe It
1979	**Spectacular Bid**	1:54⅕	Ron Franklin	Buddy Delp	Golden Act	Screen King
1980	**Codex**	1:54⅕	Angel Cordero,Jr	D.Wayne Lukas	Genuine Risk	Colonel Moran
1981	**Pleasant Colony**	1:54⅗	Jorge Velasquez	John Campo	Bold Ego	Paristo
1982	**Aloma's Ruler**	1:55⅖	Jack Kaenel	John Lensini	Linkage	Cut Away
1983	**Deputed Testamony**	1:55⅖	Donald Miller	Bill Boniface	Desert Wine	High Honors
1984	**Gate Dancer**	1:53⅗	Angel Cordero,Jr	Jack Van Berg	Play On	Fight Over
1985	**Tank's Prospect**	1:53⅖	Pat Day	D.Wayne Lukas	Chief's Crown	Eternal Prince
1986	**Snow Chief**	1:54⅘	Alex Solis	Melvin Stute	Ferdinand	Broad Brush
1987	**Alysheba**	1:55⅘	Chris McCarron	Jack Van Berg	Bet Twice	Cryptoclearance
1988	**Risen Star**	1:56⅕	E.Delahoussaye	Louie Roussel	Brian's Time	Winning Colors
1989	**Sunday Silence**	1:53⅘	Pat Valenzuela	Chas.Whittingham	Easy Goer	Rock Point
1990	**Summer Squall**	1:53⅗	Pat Day	Neil Howard	Unbridled	Mister Frisky

Belmont Stakes

For three-year-olds. Held three weeks after Preakness Stakes at Belmont Park in Elmont, N.Y. Inaugurated in 1867 at Jerome Park, moved to Morris Park in 1890 and Belmont Park in 1905.

Originally run at 1 mile and 5 furlongs (1867-89), then 1¼ miles (1890-1905), 1⅜ miles (1906-25), and the present 1½ miles since 1926.

Trainers with most wins: James Rowe, Sr.(8); Sam Hildreth (7); Sunny Jim Fitzsimmons (6); Woody Stephens (5); Max Hirsch and Robert W. Walden (4); Elliott Burch, Lucien Laurin, F. McCabe and D. McDaniel (3).

Jockeys with most wins: Eddie Arcaro and Jim McLaughlin (6); Earl Sande and Bill Shoemaker (5); Braulio Baeza, Laffit Pincay, Jr and James Stout (3).

Winning fillies: Ruthless (1867) and Tanya (1905).

Year	Winner	Time	Jockey	Trainer	2nd place	3rd place
1867	**Ruthless**	3:05	J.Gilpatrick	A.J.Minor	De Courcy	Rivoli
1868	**General Duke**	3:02	Bobby Swim	A.Thompson	Northumberland	Fannie Ludlow
1869	**Fenian**	3:04¼	C.Miller	J.Pincus	Glenelg	Invercauld
1870	**Kingfisher**	2:59½	W.Dick	R.Colston	Foster	Midday
1871	**Harry Bassett**	2:56	W.Miller	D.McDaniel	Stockwood	By-the-Sea
1872	**Joe Daniels**	2:58½	James Rowe	D.McDaniel	Meteor	Shylock
1873	**Springbok**	3:01¾	James Rowe	D.McDaniel	Count d'Orsay	Strachino
1874	**Saxon**	2:39½	G.Barbee	W.Pryor	Grinstead	Aaron Pennington

Belmont Stakes (Cont.)

Year	Winner	Time	Jockey	Trainer	2nd place	3rd place
1875	**Calvin**	2:42¼	Bobby Swim	A.Williams	Aristides	Milner
1876	**Algerine**	2:40½	Billy Donohue	T.B.Doswell	Fiddlestick	Barricade
1877	**Cloverbrook**	2:46	C.Holloway	J.Walden	Loiterer	Baden-Baden
1878	**Duke of Magenta**	2:42¾	L.Hughes	R.W.Walden	Bramble	Sparta
1879	**Spendthrift**	2:42¾	George Evans	T.Puryear	Monitor	Jericho
1880	**Grenada**	2:47	L.Hughes	R.W.Walden	Ferncliffe	Turenne
1881	**Saunterer**	2:47	T.Costello	R.W.Walden	Eole	Baltic
1882	**Forester**	2:43	Jim McLaughlin	L.Stuart	Babcock	Wyoming
1883	**George Kinney**	2:42½	Jim McLaughlin	James Rowe,Sr	Trombone	Renegade
1884	**Panique**	2:42	Jim McLaughlin	James Rowe,Sr	Knight of Ellerslie	Himalaya
1885	**Tyrant**	2:43	Paul Duffy	C.Claypool	St.Augustine	Tecumseh
1886	**Inspector B**	2:41	Jim McLaughlin	F.McCabe	The Bard	Linden
1887	**Hanover**	2:43½	Jim McLaughlin	F.McCabe	Oneko	—
1888	**Sir Dixon**	2:40¼	Jim McLaughlin	F.McCabe	Prince Royal	—
1889	**Eric**	2:47	W.Hayward	J.Huggins	Diable	Zephyrus
1890	**Burlington**	2:07¾	Pike Barnes	A.Cooper	Devotee	Padishah
1891	**Foxford**	2:08¾	Ed Garrison	M.Donovan	Montana	Laurestan
1892	**Patron**	2:17	W.Hayward	L.Stuart	Shellbark	—
1893	**Comanche**	1:53¼	Willie Simms	G.Hannon	Dr.Rice	Rainbow
1894	**Henry of Navarre**	1:56½	Willie Simms	B.McClelland	Prig	Assignee
1895	**Belmar**	2:11½	Fred Taral	E.Feakes	Counter Tenor	Nanki Pooh
1896	**Hastings**	2:24½	H.Griffin	J.J.Hyland	Handspring	Hamilton II
1897	**Scottish Chieftain**	2:23½	J.Scherrer	M.Byrnes	On Deck	Octagon
1898	**Bowling Brook**	2:32	F.Littlefield	R.W.Walden	Previous	Hamburg
1899	**Jean Bereaud**	2:23	R.Clawson	Sam Hildreth	Half Time	Glengar
1900	**Ildrim**	2:21½	Nash Turner	H.E.Leigh	Petrucio	Missionary
1901	**Commando**	2:21	H.Spencer	James Rowe,Sr	The Parader	All Green
1902	**Masterman**	2:22½	John Bullman	J.J.Hyland	Ranald	King Hanover
1903	**Africander**	2:23⅕	John Bullman	R.Miller	Whorler	Red Knight
1904	**Delhi**	2:06⅖	George Odom	James Rowe,Sr	Graziallo	Rapid Water
1905	**Tanya**	2:08	E.Hildebrand	J.W.Rogers	Blandy	Hot Shot
1906	**Burgomaster**	2:20	Lucien Lyne	J.W.Rogers	The Quail	Accountant
1907	**Peter Pan**	—	G.Mountain	James Rowe,Sr	Superman	Frank Gill
1908	**Colin**	—	Joe Notter	James Rowe,Sr	Fair Play	King James
1909	**Joe Madden**	2:21⅗	E.Dugan	Sam Hildreth	Wise Mason	Donald MacDonald
1910	**Sweep**	2:22	James Butwell	James Rowe,Sr	Duke of Ormonde	—
1911	Not held					
1912	Not held					
1913	**Prince Eugene**	2:18	Roscoe Troxler	James Rowe,Sr	Rock View	Flying Fairy
1914	**Luke McLuke**	2:20	Merritt Buxton	J.F.Schorr	Gainer	Charlestonian
1915	**The Finn**	2:18⅖	George Byrne	E.W.Heffner	Half Rock	Pebbles
1916	**Friar Rock**	2:22	E.Haynes	Sam Hildreth	Spur	Churchill
1917	**Hourless**	2:17⅘	James Butwell	Sam Hildreth	Skeptic	Wonderful
1918	**Johren**	2:20⅖	Frank Robinson	A.Simons	War Cloud	Cum Sah
1919	**SIR BARTON**	2:17⅖	John Loftus	H.Guy Bedwell	Sweep On	Natural Bridge
1920	**Man o'War**	2:14⅕	Clarence Kummer	L.Feustel	Donnacona	—
1921	**Grey Lag**	2:16⅘	Earl Sande	Sam Hildreth	Sporting Blood	Leonardo II
1922	**Pillory**	2:18⅘	C.H.Miller	T.J.Healey	Snob II	Hea
1923	**Zev**	2:19	Earl Sande	Sam Hildreth	Chickvale	Rialto
1924	**Mad Play**	2:18⅘	Earl Sande	Sam Hildreth	Mr.Mutt	Modest
1925	**American Flag**	2:16⅘	Albert Johnson	G.R.Tompkins	Dangerous	Swope
1926	**Crusader**	2:32⅕	Albert Johnson	George Conway	Espino	Haste
1927	**Chance Shot**	2:32⅖	Earl Sande	Pete Coyne	Bois de Rose	Flambino
1928	**Vito**	2:33⅕	Clarence Kummer	Max Hirsch	Genie	Diavolo
1929	**Blue Larkspur**	2:32⅘	Mack Garner	C.Hastings	African	Jack High
1930	**GALLANT FOX**	2:31⅗	Earl Sande	Jim Fitzsimmons	Whichone	Questionnaire
1931	**Twenty Grand**	2:29⅗	Chas.Kurtsinger	James Rowe,Jr	Sun Meadow	Jamestown
1932	**Faireno**	2:32⅘	Tom Malley	Jim Fitzsimmons	Osculator	Flag Pole
1933	**Hurryoff**	2:32⅗	Mack Garner	H.McDaniel	Nimbus	Union
1934	**Peace Chance**	2:29⅕	W.D.Wright	Pete Coyne	High Quest	Good Goods
1935	**OMAHA**	2:30⅗	Willie Saunders	Jim Fitzsimmons	Firethorn	Rosemont
1936	**Granville**	2:30	James Stout	Jim Fitzsimmons	Mr.Bones	Hollyrood
1937	**WAR ADMIRAL**	2:28⅗	Chas.Kurtsinger	George Conway	Sceneshifter	Vamoose
1938	**Pasteurized**	2:29⅖	James Stout	George Odom	Dauber	Cravat
1939	**Johnstown**	2:29⅗	James Stout	Jim Fitzsimmons	Belay	Gilded Knight
1940	**Bimelech**	2:29⅗	Fred Smith	Bill Hurley	Your Chance	Andy K.
1941	**WHIRLAWAY**	2:31	Eddie Arcaro	Ben Jones	Robert Morris	Yankee Chance
1942	**Shut Out**	2:29⅕	Eddie Arcaro	John Gaver	Alsab	Lochinvar

Year	Winner	Time	Jockey	Trainer	2nd place	3rd place
1943	**COUNT FLEET**	2:28$\frac{1}{5}$	Johnny Longden	Don Cameron	Fairy Manhurst	Deseronto
1944	**Bounding Home**	2:32$\frac{1}{5}$	G.L.Smith	Matt Brady	Pensive	Bull Dandy
1945	**Pavot**	2:30$\frac{1}{5}$	Eddie Arcaro	Oscar White	Wildlife	Jeep
1946	**ASSAULT**	2:30$\frac{4}{5}$	Warren Mehrtens	Max Hirsch	Natchez	Cable
1947	**Phalanx**	2:29$\frac{2}{5}$	R.Donoso	Syl Veitch	Tide Rips	Tailspin
1948	**CITATION**	2:28$\frac{1}{5}$	Eddie Arcaro	Jimmy Jones	Better Self	Escadru
1949	**Capot**	2:30$\frac{1}{5}$	Ted Atkinson	John Gaver	Ponder	Palestinian
1950	**Middleground**	2:28$\frac{3}{5}$	William Boland	Max Hirsch	Lights Up	Mr.Trouble
1951	**Counterpoint**	2:29	David Gorman	Syl Veitch	Battlefield	Battle Morn
1952	**One Count**	2:30$\frac{1}{5}$	Eddie Arcaro	Oscar White	Blue Man	Armageddon
1953	**Native Dancer**	2:28$\frac{3}{5}$	Eric Guerin	Bill Winfrey	Jamie K.	Royal Bay Gem
1954	**High Gun**	2:30$\frac{4}{5}$	Eric Guerin	Max Hirsch	Fisherman	Limelight
1955	**Nashua**	2:29	Eddie Arcara	Jim Fitzsimmons	Blazing Count	Portersville
1956	**Needles**	2:29$\frac{3}{5}$	David Erb	Hugh Fontaine	Career Boy	Fabius
1957	**Gallant Man**	2:26$\frac{3}{5}$	Bill Shoemaker	John Nerud	Inside Tract	Bold Ruler
1958	**Cavan**	2:30$\frac{1}{5}$	Pete Anderson	Tom Barry	Tim Tam	Flamingo
1959	**Sword Dancer**	2:28$\frac{2}{5}$	Bill Shoemaker	Elliott Burch	Bagdad	Royal Orbit
1960	**Celtic Ash**	2:29$\frac{3}{5}$	Bill Hartack	Tom Barry	Venetian Way	Disperse
1961	**Sherluck**	2:29$\frac{1}{5}$	Braulio Baeza	Harold Young	Globemaster	Guadalcanal
1962	**Jaipur**	2:28$\frac{4}{5}$	Bill Shoemaker	B.Mulholland	Admiral's Voyage	Crimson Satan
1963	**Chateaugay**	2:30$\frac{1}{5}$	Braulio Baeza	James Conway	Candy Spots	Choker
1964	**Quadrangle**	2:28$\frac{2}{5}$	Manuel Ycaza	Elliott Burch	Roman Brother	Northern Dancer
1965	**Hail to All**	2:28$\frac{2}{5}$	John Sellers	Eddie Yowell	Tom Rolfe	First Family
1966	**Amberoid**	2:29$\frac{3}{5}$	William Boland	Lucien Laurin	Buffle	Advocator
1967	**Damascus**	2:28$\frac{4}{5}$	Bill Shoemaker	F.Y.Whiteley	Cool Reception	Gentleman James
1968	**Stage Door Johnny**	2:27$\frac{1}{5}$	Gus Gustines	John Gaver	Forward Pass	Call Me Prince
1969	**Arts And Letters**	2:28$\frac{4}{5}$	Braulio Baeza	Elliott Burch	Majestic Prince	Dike
1970	**High Echelon**	2:34	John Rotz	John Jacobs	Needles N Pins	Naskra
1971	**Pass Catcher**	2:30$\frac{2}{5}$	Walter Blum	Eddie Yowell	Jim French	Bold Reason
1972	**Riva Ridge**	2:28	Ron Turcotte	Lucien Laurin	Ruritania	Cloudy Dawn
1973	**SECRETARIAT**	2:24	Ron Turcotte	Lucien Laurin	Twice A Prince	My Gallant
1974	**Little Current**	2:29$\frac{1}{5}$	Miguel Rivera	Lou Rondinello	Jolly Johu	Cannonade
1975	**Avatar**	2:28$\frac{1}{5}$	Bill Shoemaker	Tommy Doyle	Foolish Pleasure	Master Derby
1976	**Bold Forbes**	2:29	Angel Cordero	Laz Barrera	McKenzie Bridge	Great Contractor
1977	**SEATTLE SLEW**	2:29$\frac{3}{5}$	Jean Cruguet	Billy Turner	Run Dusty Run	Sanhedrin
1978	**AFFIRMED**	2:26$\frac{4}{5}$	Steve Cauthen	Laz Barrera	Alydar	Darby Creek Road
1979	**Coastal**	2:28$\frac{3}{5}$	Ruben Hernandez	David Whiteley	Golden Act	Spectacular Bid
1980	**Temperence Hill**	2:29$\frac{4}{5}$	Eddie Maple	Joseph Cantey	Genuine Risk	Rockhill Native
1981	**Summing**	2:29	George Martens	Luis Barerra	Highland Blade	Pleasant Colony
1982	**Conquistador Cielo**	2:28$\frac{1}{5}$	Laffit Pincay,Jr	Woody Stephens	Gato Del Sol	Illuminate
1983	**Caveat**	2:27$\frac{4}{5}$	Laffit Pincay,Jr	Woody Stephens	Slew o'Gold	Barberstown
1984	**Swale**	2:27$\frac{1}{5}$	Laffit Pincay,Jr	Woody Stephens	Pine Circle	Morning Bob
1985	**Creme Fraiche**	2:27	Eddie Maple	Woody Stephens	Stephan's Odyssey	Chief's Crown
1986	**Danzig Connection**	2:29$\frac{4}{5}$	Chris McCarron	Woody Stephens	Johns Treasure	Ferdinand
1987	**Bet Twice**	2:28$\frac{1}{5}$	Craig Perret	Jimmy Croll	Cryptoclearance	Gulch
1988	**Risen Star**	2:26$\frac{2}{5}$	E.Delahoussaye	Louie Roussel	Kingpost	Brian's Time
1989	**Easy Goer**	2:26	Pat Day	Shug McGaughey	Sunday Silence	Le Voyageur
1990	**Go And Go**	2:27$\frac{1}{5}$	Michael Kinane	Dermot Weld	Thirty Six Red	Baron de Vaux

Breeders' Cup

Inaugurated on Nov. 10, 1984, the Breeders' Cup consists of seven races at one track on one day late in the year to determine thoroughbred racing's principal champions.

Breeders' Cup Day has been held at Hollywood Park (Calif.) in 1984, Aqueduct Racetrack (N.Y.) in 1985, Santa Anita Park (Calif.) in 1986, Hollywood Park in 1987, Churchill Downs (Ky.) in 1988 and Gulfstream Park (Fla.) in 1989. The 1990 running will be held at Belmont Park (N.Y.) on Oct. 27.

The steeplechase was added to the Breeders' Cup championship roster in 1986, but has been held each year at Fair Hill Race Course (Md.)

Trainers with most wins: D. Wayne Lukas (9); Neil Drysdale and Shug McCaughey (3).

Jockeys with most wins: Laffit Pincay, Jr (5); Pat Day and Angel Cordero, Jr (4); Chris McCarron, Randy Romero and Jose Santos (3).

Juvenile

Distances: one mile (1984-85, 87); 1$\frac{1}{16}$ miles (1986 and since 1988).

Year	Winner	Time	Jockey	Trainer	2nd place	3rd place
1984	**Chief's Crown**	1:36$\frac{1}{5}$	Don MacBeth	Roger Laurin	Tank's Prospect	Spend A Buck
1985	**Tasso**	1:36$\frac{1}{5}$	Laffit Pincay	Neil Drysdale	Storm Cat	Scat Dancer
1986	**Capote**	1:43$\frac{4}{5}$	Laffit Pincay	D.Wayne Lukas	Qualify	Alysheba
1987	**Success Express**	1:35$\frac{1}{5}$	Jose Santos	D.Wayne Lukas	Regal Classic	Tejano
1988	**Is It True**	1:46$\frac{3}{5}$	Laffit Pincay	D.Wayne Lukas	Easy Goer	Tagel
1989	**Rhythm**	1:43$\frac{3}{5}$	Craig Perret	Shug McGaughey	Grand Canyon	Slavic

Breeders' Cup (Cont.)

Juvenile Fillies

Distances: one mile (1984-85, 87); 1$\frac{1}{16}$ miles (1986 and since 1988).

Year	Winner	Time	Jockey	Trainer	2nd place	3rd place
1984	**Outstandingly**	1:37$\frac{4}{5}$	Walter Guerra	Pancho Martin	Dusty Heart	Fine Spirit
1985	**Twilight Ridge**	1:35$\frac{4}{5}$	Jorge Velasquez	D.Wayne Lukas	Family Style	Steal A Kiss
1986	**Brave Raj**	1:43$\frac{1}{5}$	Pat Valenzuela	Melvin Stute	Tappiano	Saros Brig
1987	**Epitome**	1:36$\frac{2}{5}$	Pat Day	Phil Hauswald	Jeanne Jones	Dream Team
1988	**Open Mind**	1:46$\frac{3}{5}$	Angel Cordero,Jr	D.Wayne Lukas	Darby Shuffle	Lea Lucinda
1989	**Go for Wand**	1:44$\frac{1}{5}$	Randy Romero	William Badgett	Sweet Roberta	Stella Madrid

Note: in 1984, winner **Fran's Valentine** was disqualified for interference in the stretch and placed 10th.

Sprint

Distance: six furlongs (since 1984).

Year	Winner	Time	Jockey	Trainer	2nd place	3rd place
1984	**Eillo**	1:10$\frac{1}{5}$	Craig Perret	Budd Lepman	Commemorate	Fighting Fit
1985	**Precisionist**	1:08$\frac{2}{5}$	Chris McCarron	R.Fenstermaker	Smile	Mt.Livermore
1986	**Smile**	1:08$\frac{2}{5}$	Jacinto Vasquez	S.Schulhofer	Pine Tree Lane	Bedside Promise
1987	**Very Subtle**	1:08$\frac{4}{5}$	Pat Valenzuela	Melvin Stute	Groovy	Exclusive Enough
1988	**Gulch**	1:10$\frac{2}{5}$	Angel Cordero,Jr	D.Wayne Lukas	Play The King	Afleet
1989	**Dancing Spree**	1:09	Angel Cordero,Jr	Shug McCaughey	Safely Kept	Dispersal

Mile

Year	Winner	Time	Jockey	Trainer	2nd place	3rd place
1984	**Royal Heroine**	1:32$\frac{3}{5}$	Fernando Toro	John Gosden	Star Choice	Cozzene
1985	**Cozzene**	1:35	Walter Guerra	Jan Nerud	Al Mamoon	Shadeed
1986	**Last Tycoon**	1:35$\frac{1}{5}$	Yves St.-Martin	Robert Collet	Palace Music	Fred Astaire
1987	**Miesque**	1:32$\frac{4}{5}$	Freddie Head	Francois Boutin	Show Dancer	Sonic Lady
1988	**Miesque**	1:38$\frac{3}{5}$	Freddie Head	Francois Boutin	Steinlen	Simply Majestic
1989	**Steinlen**	1:37$\frac{1}{5}$	Jose Santos	D.Wayne Lukas	Sabona	Most Welcome

Note: in 1985, 2nd place finisher **Palace Music** was disqualified for interference and placed 9th.

Distaff

Distances: 1$\frac{1}{4}$ miles (1984-87); 1$\frac{1}{8}$ miles (since 1988).

Year	Winner	Time	Jockey	Trainer	2nd place	3rd place
1984	**Princess Rooney**	2:02$\frac{2}{5}$	E.Delahoussaye	Neil Drysdale	Life's Magic	Adored
1985	**Life's Magic**	2:02	Angel Cordero,Jr	D.Wayne Lukas	Lady's Secret	DontstopThemusic
1986	**Lady's Secret**	2:01$\frac{1}{5}$	Pat Day	D.Wayne Lukas	Fran's Valentine	Outstandingly
1987	**Sacahuista**	2:02$\frac{4}{5}$	Randy Romero	D.Wayne Lukas	Clabber Girl	Oueee Bebe
1988	**Personal Ensign**	1:52	Randy Romero	Shug McGaughey	Winning Colors	Goodbye Halo
1989	**Bayakoa**	1:47$\frac{3}{5}$	Laffit Pincay,Jr	Ron McAnally	Gorgeous	Open Mind

Turf

Distance: 1$\frac{1}{2}$ miles (since 1984).

Year	Winner	Time	Jockey	Trainer	2nd place	3rd place
1984	**Lashkari**	2:25$\frac{1}{5}$	Yves St-Martin	De Royer-Dupre	All Along	Raami
1985	**Pebbles**	2:27	Pat Eddery	Clive Brittain	Strawberry Rd.II	Mourjane
1986	**Manila**	2:25$\frac{3}{5}$	Jose Santos	Leroy Jolley	Theatrical	Estrapade
1987	**Theatrical**	2:24$\frac{2}{5}$	Pat Day	Bill Mott	Trempolino	Village Star II
1988	**Grt.Communicator**	2:35$\frac{1}{5}$	Ray Sibille	Thad Ackel	Sunshine Forever	Indian Skimmer
1989	**Prized**	2:28	E.Delahoussaye	Neil Drysdale	Sierra Roberta	Star Lift

Classic

Distance: 1$\frac{1}{4}$ miles (since 1984).

Year	Winner	Time	Jockey	Trainer	2nd place	3rd place
1984	**Wild Again**	2:03$\frac{2}{5}$	Pat Day	V.Timphony	Slew O'Gold	Gate Dancer
1985	**Proud Truth**	2:00$\frac{4}{5}$	Jorge Velasquez	John Veitch	Gate Dancer	Turkoman
1986	**Skywalker**	2:00$\frac{2}{5}$	Laffit Pincay	M.Whittingham	Turkoman	Precisionist
1987	**Ferdinand**	2:01$\frac{2}{5}$	Bill Shoemaker	C.Whittingham	Alysheba	Judge Angelucci
1988	**Alysheba**	2:04$\frac{4}{5}$	Chris McCarron	Jack Van Berg	Seeking the Gold	Waquoit
1989	**Sunday Silence**	2:00$\frac{1}{5}$	Chris McCarron	C.Whittingham	Easy Goer	Blushing John

Note: in 1984, 2nd place finisher **Gate Dancer** was disqualified for interference and placed 3rd.

Steeplechase

Distances: 2$\frac{3}{8}$ miles (1986); 2$\frac{5}{8}$ miles (since 1987).

Year	Winner	Time	Jockey	Trainer	2nd place	3rd place
1986	**Census**	4:27$\frac{3}{5}$	Jeff Teter	Janet Elliott	Kesslin	Pont du Loup
1987	**Gacko**	5:15$\frac{1}{5}$	Roger Duchene	Xavier Guigand	Inlander	Gateshead
1988	**Jimmy Lorenzo**	5:12$\frac{2}{5}$	Graham McCourt	J.E.Sheppard	Kalankoe	Polar Pleasure
1989	**Highland Bud**	4:58$\frac{4}{5}$	Rich. Dunwoody	J.E.Sheppard	Polar Pleasure	Victorian Hill

All-Time Leading Money Winners

The all-time winning horses and jockeys of North America, through 1989, according to *The American Racing Manual*. Records include all available information on races in foreign countries.

Top 15 Horses

Note that (†) indicates horse raced in 1989; (*) indicates foreign-bred; (f) indicates female.

	Sts	1st	2nd	3rd	Purses
Alysheba	26	11	8	2	$6,679,242
John Henry	83	39	15	9	6,597,947
†Sunday Silence	12	8	4	0	4,600,154
†Easy Goer	17	12	5	0	4,534,650
Spend A Buck	15	10	3	2	4,220,689
†Creme Fraiche	64	17	12	13	4,024,727
Ferdinand	29	8	9	6	3,777,978
Slew o'Gold	21	12	5	1	3,533,534
Precisionist	46	20	10	4	3,485,393
Snow Chief	24	13	3	5	3,383,210
†Cryptoclearance	44	12	10	7	3,376,327
Bet Twice	26	10	6	4	3,308,599
Gulch	32	13	8	4	3,095,521
Lady's Secret (f)	45	25	9	3	3,021,425
*All Along (f)	21	9	4	2	3,015,764

Top 15 Jockeys

Note that (*) indicates jockey active in 1989.

	Yrs	Mounts	Wins	Purses
*Bill Shoemaker	41	40,343	8831	$123,300,009
*Laffit Pincay,Jr	24	33,660	7327	148,112,855
*Angel Cordero,Jr	28	35,899	6549	145,166,215
*Jorge Velasquez	27	35,288	6117	108,100,671
Johnny Longden	40	32,413	6032	24,665,800
*Larry Snyder	30	32,512	6011	42,400,943
*Sandy Hawley	22	26,184	5635	67,800,061
*Carl Gambardella	34	34,333	5515	23,612,504
*David Gall	33	31,493	5501	15,197,765
*Chris McCarron	15	23,578	5103	118,933,175
*Earlie Fires	25	32,667	4809	49,068,888
Eddie Arcaro	31	24,092	4779	30,039,543
*Jacinto Vasquez	30	32,894	4678	70,324,168
*Pat Day	17	22,353	4642	88,863,765
*Don Brumfield	37	33,228	4573	43,567,861

Note: Bill Shoemaker retired on Feb.3, 1990, with 40,350 mounts; 8833 wins; and purse earnings of $123,375,524.

Annual Money Leaders
HORSES

Annual money-leading horses since 1910, according to *The American Racing Manual*. **Multiple winners:** Round Table, Buckpasser and Alysheba (2).

Year		Age	Sts	1st	Purses	Year		Age	Sts	1st	Purses
1910	Novelty	2	16	11	$72,630	1950	Noor	5	12	7	$346,940
1911	Worth	2	13	10	16,645	1951	Counterpoint	3	15	7	250,525
1912	Star Charter	4	17	6	14,655	1952	Crafty Admiral	4	16	9	277,225
1913	Old Rosebud	2	14	12	19,057	1953	Native Dancer	3	10	9	513,425
1914	Roamer	3	16	12	29,105	1954	Determine	3	15	10	328,700
1915	Borrow	7	9	4	20,195	1955	Nashua	3	12	10	752,550
1916	Campfire	2	9	6	49,735	1956	Needles	3	8	4	440,850
1917	Sun Briar	2	9	5	59,505	1957	Round Table	3	22	15	600,383
1918	External	2	8	6	56,173	1958	Round Table	4	20	14	662,780
1919	Sir Barton	3	13	8	88,250	1959	Sword Dancer	3	13	8	537,004
1920	Man o'War	3	11	11	166,140	1960	Bally Ache	3	15	10	445,045
1921	Morvich	2	11	11	115,234	1961	Carry Back	3	16	9	565,349
1922	Pillory	3	7	4	95,654	1962	Never Bend	2	10	7	402,969
1923	Zev	3	14	12	272,008	1963	Candy Spots	3	12	7	604,481
1924	Sarazen	3	12	8	95,640	1964	Gun Bow	4	16	8	580,100
1925	Pompey	2	10	7	121,630	1965	Buckpasser	2	11	9	568,096
1926	Crusader	3	15	9	166,033	1966	Buckpasser	3	14	13	669,078
1927	Anita Peabody	2	7	6	111,905	1967	Damascus	3	16	12	817,941
1928	High Strung	2	6	5	153,590	1968	Forward Pass	3	13	7	546,674
1929	Blue Larkspur	3	6	4	153,450	1969	Arts and Letters	3	14	8	555,604
1930	Gallant Fox	3	10	9	308,275	1970	Personality	3	18	8	444,049
1931	Gallant Flight	2	7	7	219,000	1971	Riva Ridge	2	9	7	503,263
1932	Gusto	3	16	4	145,940	1972	Droll Role	4	19	7	471,633
1933	Singing Wood	2	9	3	88,050	1973	Secretariat	3	12	9	860,404
1934	Cavalcade	3	7	6	111,235	1974	Chris Evert	3	8	5	551,063
1935	Omaha	3	9	6	142,255	1975	Foolish Pleasure	3	11	5	716,278
1936	Granville	3	11	7	110,295	1976	Forego	6	8	6	401,701
1937	Seabiscuit	4	15	11	168,580	1977	Seattle Slew	3	7	6	641,370
1938	Stagehand	3	15	8	189,710	1978	Affirmed	3	11	8	901,541
1939	Challedon	3	15	9	184,535	1979	Spectacular Bid	3	12	10	1,279,334
1940	Bimelech	3	7	4	110,005	1980	Temperence Hill	3	17	8	1,130,452
1941	Whirlaway	3	20	13	272,386	1981	John Henry	6	10	8	1,798,030
1942	Shut Out	3	12	8	238,872	1982	Perrault (GB)	5	8	4	1,197,400
1943	Count Fleet	3	6	6	174,055	1983	All Along (FRA)	4	7	4	2,138,963
1944	Pavot	2	8	8	179,040	1984	Slew o'Gold	4	6	5	2,627,944
1945	Busher	3	13	10	273,735	1985	Spend A Buck	3	7	5	3,552,704
1946	Assault	3	15	8	424,195	1986	Snow Chief	3	9	6	1,875,200
1947	Armed	6	17	11	376,325	1987	Alysheba	3	10	3	2,511,156
1948	Citation	3	20	19	709,470	1988	Alysheba	4	9	7	3,808,600
1949	Ponder	3	21	9	321,825	1989	Sunday Silence	3	9	7	4,578,454

Annual Money Leaders (Cont.)

JOCKEYS

Annual money-leading jockeys since 1910, according to *The American Racing Manual*. **Multiple winners:** Bill Shoemaker (10); Laffit Pincay, Jr (7); Eddie Arcaro (6); Braulio Baeza (5); Jose Santos (4); Angel Cordero, Jr, Chris McCarron and Earl Sande (3); Ted Atkinson, Laverne Fator, Mack Garner, Bill Hartack, Charles Kurtsinger, Johnny Longden, Sonny Workman and Wayne Wright (2).

Year		Mts	Wins	Purses	Year		Mts	Wins	Purses
1910	Carroll Shilling	506	172	$ 176,030	1950	Eddie Arcaro	888	195	$1,410,160
1911	Ted Koerner	813	162	88,308	1951	Bill Shoemaker	1161	257	1,329,890
1912	Jimmy Butwell	684	144	79,843	1952	Eddie Arcaro	807	188	1,859,591
1913	Merritt Buxton	887	146	82,552	1953	Bill Shoemaker	1683	485	1,784,187
1914	J.McCahey	824	155	121,845	1954	Bill Shoemaker	1251	380	1,876,760
1915	Mack Garner	775	151	96,628	1955	Eddie Arcaro	820	158	1,864,796
1916	John McTaggart	832	150	155,055	1956	Bill Hartack	1387	347	2,343,955
1917	Frank Robinson	731	147	148,057	1957	Bill Hartack	1238	341	3,060,501
1918	Lucien Lyke	756	178	201,864	1958	Bill Shoemaker	1133	300	2,961,693
1919	John Loftus	177	65	252,707	1959	Bill Shoemaker	1285	347	2,843,133
1920	Clarence Kummer	353	87	292,376	1960	Bill Shoemaker	1227	274	2,123,961
1921	Earl Sande	340	112	263,043	1961	Bill Shoemaker	1256	304	2,690,819
1922	Albert Johnson	297	43	345,054	1962	Bill Shoemaker	1126	311	2,916,844
1923	Earl Sande	430	122	569,394	1963	Bill Shoemaker	1203	271	2,526,925
1924	Ivan Parke	844	205	290,395	1964	Bill Shoemaker	1056	246	2,649,553
1925	Laverne Fator	315	81	305,775	1965	Braulio Baeza	1245	270	2,582,702
1926	Laverne Fator	511	143	361,435	1966	Braulio Baeza	1341	298	2,951,022
1927	Earl Sande	179	49	277,877	1967	Braulio Baeza	1064	256	3,088,888
1928	Linus McAtee	235	55	301,295	1968	Braulio Baeza	1089	201	2,835,108
1929	Mack Garner	274	57	314,975	1969	Jorge Velasquez	1442	258	2,542,315
1930	Sonny Workman	571	152	420,438	1970	Laffit Pincay, Jr	1328	269	2,626,526
1931	Chas.Kurtsinger	519	93	392,095	1971	Laffit Pincay, Jr	1627	380	3,784,377
1932	Sonny Workman	378	87	385,070	1972	Laffit Pincay, Jr	1388	289	3,225,827
1933	Robert Jones	471	63	226,285	1973	Laffit Pincay, Jr	1444	350	4,093,492
1934	Wayne Wright	919	174	287,185	1974	Laffit Pincay, Jr	1278	341	4,251,060
1935	Silvio Coucci	749	141	319,760	1975	Braulio Baeza	1190	196	3,674,398
1936	Wayne Wright	670	100	264,000	1976	Angel Cordero, Jr	1534	274	4,709,500
1937	Chas.Kurtsinger	765	120	384,202	1977	Steve Cauthen	2075	487	6,151,750
1938	Nick Wall	658	97	385,161	1978	Darrel McHargue	1762	375	6,188,353
1939	Basil James	904	191	353,333	1979	Laffit Pincay, Jr	1708	420	8,183,535
1940	Eddie Arcaro	783	132	343,661	1980	Chris McCarron	1964	405	7,666,100
1941	Don Meade	1164	210	398,627	1981	Chris McCarron	1494	326	8,397,604
1942	Eddie Arcaro	687	123	481,949	1982	Angel Cordero, Jr	1838	397	9,702,520
1943	Johnny Longden	871	173	573,276	1983	Angel Cordero, Jr	1792	362	10,116,807
1944	Ted Atkinson	1539	287	899,101	1984	Chris McCarron	1565	356	12,038,213
1945	Johnny Longden	778	180	981,977	1985	Laffit Pincay, Jr	1409	289	13,415,049
1946	Ted Atkinson	1377	233	1,036,825	1986	Jose Santos	1636	329	11,329,297
1947	Douglas Dodson	646	141	1,429,949	1987	Jose Santos	1639	305	12,407,355
1948	Eddie Arcaro	726	188	1,686,230	1988	Jose Santos	1867	370	14,877,298
1949	Steve Brooks	906	209	1,316,817	1989	Jose Santos	1459	285	13,847,003

Awards

Horse of the Year, 1936-70

In 1971, *The Daily Racing Form*, the Thoroughbred Racing Associations, and the National Turf Writers Assn. joined forces to create the Eclipse Awards. Before then, however, the *Racing Form* (1936-70) and the TRA (1950-70) issued separate selections for Horse of the Year. Their picks differed only four times from 1950-70 and are so noted. Horses listed in capital LETTERS are Triple Crown winners; (f) indicates female.

1936 Granville	1946 ASSAULT	1955 Nashua	1964 Kelso
1937 WAR ADMIRAL	1947 Armed	1956 Swaps	1965 Roman Brother (DRF)
1938 Seabiscuit	1948 CITATION	1957 Bold Ruler (DRF)	Moccasin (TRA)
1939 Challedon	1949 Capot	Dedicate (TRA)	1966 Buckpasser
		1958 Round Table	1967 Damascus
1940 Challedon	1950 Hill Prince	1959 Sword Dancer	1968 Dr.Fager
1941 WHIRLAWAY	1951 Counterpoint		1969 Arts and Letters
1942 Whirlaway	1952 One Count (DRF)	1960 Kelso	
1943 COUNT FLEET	Native Dancer (TRA)	1961 Kelso	1970 Fort Marcy (DRF)
1944 Twilight Tear (f)	1953 Tom Fool	1962 Kelso	Personality (TRA)
1945 Busher (f)	1954 Native Dancer	1963 Kelso	

Eclipse Awards, 1971-89

The Eclipse Awards, honoring the Horse of the Year and other champions of the sport, are sponsored by *The Daily Racing Form*, the Thoroughbred Racing Associations and the National Turf Writers Assn.

The awards are named after the 18th century racehorse and sire, Eclipse, who began racing at age five and was unbeaten in 18 starts (eight wins were walkovers). As a stallion, Eclipse sired winners of 344 races, including three Epsom Derby champions.

Horses listed in capital LETTERS won the Triple Crown that year. Age of horse in parentheses where necessary.

Horse of the Year

1971 Ack Ack (5)	1976 Forego (6)	1981 John Henry (6)	1985 Spend A Buck (3)
1972 Secretariat (2)	1977 SEATTLE SLEW (3)	1982 Conquistador	1986 Lady's Secret (4)
1973 SECRETARIAT (3)	1978 AFFIRMED (3)	Cielo (3)	1987 Ferdinand (4)
1974 Forego (4)	1979 Affirmed (4)	1983 All Along (4)	1988 Alysheba (4)
1975 Forego (5)	1980 Spectacular Bid (4)	1984 John Henry (9)	1989 Sunday Silence (3)

Older Colt, Horse or Gelding

1971 Ack Ack (5)	1976 Forego (6)	1981 John Henry (6)	1985 Vanlandingham (4)
1972 Autobiography (4)	1977 Forego (7)	1982 Lemhi Gold (4)	1986 Turkoman (4)
1973 Riva Ridge (4)	1978 Seattle Slew (4)	1983 Bates Motel (4)	1987 Ferdinand (4)
1974 Forego (4)	1979 Affirmed (4)	1984 Slew o' Gold (4)	1988 Alysheba (4)
1975 Forego (5)	1980 Spectacular Bid (4)		1989 Blushing John (4)

Older Filly or Mare

1971 Shuvee (5)	1976 Proud Delta (4)	1981 Relaxing (5)	1985 Life's Magic (4)
1972 Typecast (6)	1977 Cascapedia (4)	1982 Track Robbery (6)	1986 Lady's Secret (4)
1973 Susan's Girl (4)	1978 Late Bloomer (4)	1983 Ambassador of	1987 North Sider (5)
1974 Desert Vixen (4)	1979 Waya (5)	Luck (4)	1988 Personal Ensign (4)
1975 Susan's Girl (6)	1980 Glorious Song (4)	1984 Princess Rooney (4)	1989 Bayakoa (5)

3-Year-Old Colt

1971 Canonero II	1976 Bold Forbes	1981 Pleasant Colony	1985 Spend A Buck
1972 Key to the Mint	1977 SEATTLE SLEW	1982 Conquistador Cielo	1986 Snow Chief
1973 SECRETARIAT	1978 AFFIRMED	1983 Slew o' Gold	1987 Alysheba
1974 Little Current	1979 Spectacular Bid	1984 Swale	1988 Risen Star
1975 Wajima	1980 Temperence Hill		1989 Sunday Silence

3-Year-Old Filly

1971 Turkish Trousers	1976 Revidere	1981 Wayward Lass	1985 Mom's Command
1972 Susan's Girl	1977 Our Mims	1982 Christmas Past	1986 Tiffany Lass
1973 Desert Vixen	1978 Tempest Queen	1983 Heartlight No. One	1987 Sacahuista
1974 Chris Evert	1979 Davona Dale	1984 Life's Magic	1988 Winning Colors
1975 Ruffian	1980 Genuine Risk		1989 Open Mind

2-Year-Old Colt

1971 Riva Ridge	1976 Seattle Slew	1981 Deputy Minister	1985 Tasso
1972 Secretariat	1977 Affirmed	1982 Roving Boy	1986 Capote
1973 Protagonist	1978 Spectacular Bid	1983 Devil's Bag	1987 Forty Niner
1974 Foolish Pleasure	1979 Rockhill Native	1984 Chief's Crown	1988 Easy Goer
1975 Honest Pleasure	1980 Lord Avie		1989 Rhythm

2-Year-Old Filly

1971 Numbered Account	1976 Sensational	1980 Heavenly Cause	1985 Family Style
1972 La Prevoyante	1977 Lakeville Miss	1981 Before Dawn	1986 Brave Raj
1973 Talking Picture	1978 Candy Eclair	1982 Landaluce	1987 Epitome
1974 Ruffian	& It's in the Air	1983 Althea	1988 Open Mind
1975 Dearly Precious	1979 Smart Angle	1984 Outstandingly	1989 Go for Wand

Champion Turf Horse

1971 Run the Gantlet (3)	1973 Secretariat (3)	1975 Snow Knight (4)	1977 Johnny D (3)
1972 Cougar II (6)	1974 Dahlia (4)	1976 Youth (3)	1978 Mac Diarmida (3)

Champion Male Turf Horse

1979 Bowl Game (5)	1982 Perrault (5)	1985 Cozzene (4)	1988 Sunshine Forever (3)
1980 John Henry (5)	1983 John Henry (8)	1986 Manila (3)	1989 Steinlen (6)
1981 John Henry (6)	1984 John Henry (9)	1987 Theatrical (5)	

Champion Female Turf Horse

1979 Trillion (5)	1982 April Run (4)	1985 Pebbles (4)	1988 Miesque (4)
1980 Just A Game II (4)	1983 All Along (4)	1986 Estrapade (6)	1989 Brown Bess (7)
1981 De La Rose (3)	1984 Royal Heroine (4)	1987 Miesque (3)	

Eclipse Awards (Cont.)

Sprinter

1971 Ack Ack (5)	1976 My Juliet (4)	1980 Plugged Nickle (3)	1985 Precisionist (4)
1972 Chou Croute (4)	1977 What A Summer (4)	1981 Guilty Conscience (5)	1986 Smile (4)
1973 Shecky Greene (3)	1978 Dr.Patches (4)	1982 Gold Beauty (3)	1987 Groovy (4)
1974 Forego (4)	& J.O.Tobin (4)	1983 Chinook Pass (4)	1988 Gulch (4)
1975 Gallant Bob (3)	1979 Star de Naskra (4)	1984 Eillo (4)	1989 Safely Kept (3)

Steeplechase or Hurdle Horse

1971 Shadow Brook (7)	1976 Straight & True (6)	1981 Zaccio (5)	1986 Flatterer (7)
1972 Soothsayer (5)	1977 Cafe Prince (7)	1982 Zaccio (6)	1987 Inlander (6)
1973 Athenian Idol (5)	1978 Cafe Prince (8)	1983 Flatterer (4)	1988 Jimmy Lorenzo (6)
1974 Gran Kan (8)	1979 Martie's Anger (4)	1984 Flatterer (5)	1989 Highland Bud (4)
1975 Life's Illusion (4)	1980 Zaccio (4)	1985 Flatterer (6)	

Outstanding Jockey

1971 Laffit Pincay,Jr	1976 Sandy Hawley	1981 Bill Shoemaker	1986 Pat Day
1972 Braulio Baeza	1977 Steve Cauthen	1982 Angel Cordero,Jr	1987 Pat Day
1973 Laffit Pincay,Jr	1978 Darrel McHargue	1983 Angel Cordero,Jr	1988 Jose Santos
1974 Laffit Pincay,Jr	1979 Laffit Pincay,Jr	1984 Pat Day	1989 Kent Desormeaux
1975 Braulio Baeza	1980 Chris McCarron	1985 Laffit Pincay,Jr	

Outstanding Apprentice Jockey

1971 Gene St. Leon	1976 George Martens	1981 Richard Migliore	1986 Allen Stacy
1972 Thomas Wallis	1977 Steve Cauthen	1982 Alberto Delgado	1987 Kent Desormeaux
1973 Steve Valdez	1978 Ron Franklin	1983 Declan Murphy	1988 Steve Capanas
1974 Chris McCarron	1979 Cash Asmussen	1984 Wesley Ward	1989 Michael Luzzi
1975 Jimmy Edwards	1980 Grank Lovato,Jr	1985 Art Madrid,Jr	

Outstanding Trainer

1971 Charlie Whittingham	1976 Laz Barrera	1981 Ron McAnally	1986 D.Wayne Lukas
1972 Lucien Laurin	1977 Laz Barrera	1982 Charlie Whittingham	1987 D.Wayne Lukas
1973 H.Allen Jerkens	1978 Laz Barrera	1983 Woody Stephens	1988 Shug McGaughey
1974 Sherrill Ward	1979 Laz Barrera	1984 Jack Van Berg	1989 Charlie Whittingham
1975 Steve DiMauro	1980 Bud Delp	1985 D.Wayne Lukas	

Outstanding Owner

1971 Mr.& Mrs.E.E. Fogleson	1976 Dan Lasater	1981 Dotsam Stable	1986 Mr.& Mrs. Eugene Klein
1972 No award	1977 Maxwell Gluck	1982 Viola Sommer	1987 Mr.& Mrs. Eugene Klein
1973 No award	1978 Harbor View Farm	1983 John Franks	1988 Ogden Phipps
1974 Dan Lasater	1979 Harbor View Farm	1984 John Franks	1989 Ogden Phipps
1975 Dan Lasater	1980 Mr.& Mrs. Bertram Firestone	1985 Mr.& Mrs. Eugene Klein	

Outstanding Owner-Breeder

1971 Paul Mellon	1972 Meadow Stable/ Meadow Stud	1973 Meadow Stable/ Meadow Stud

Outstanding Breeder

1974 John W.Galbreath	1978 Harbor View Farm	1982 Fred W.Hooper	1986 Paul Mellon
1975 Fred W.Hooper	1979 Claiborne Farm	1983 Edward P.Taylor	1987 Nelson Bunker Hunt
1976 Nelson Bunker Hunt	1980 Mrs. Henry Paxson	1984 Claiborne Farm	1988 Ogden Phipps
1977 Edward P. Taylor	1981 Golden Chance Farm	1985 Nelson Bunker Hunt	1989 North Ridge Farm

Man of the Year

1972 John W.Galbreath	1973 Edward P. Taylor	1974 William L.McKnight	1975 John A. Morris

Outstanding Achievement

1971* Charles Engelhard	1972* Arthur B.Hancock, Jr
*Awarded posthumously	

Award of Merit

1976 Jack J.Dreyfus	1979 Jimmy Kilroe	1984 John Gaines	1987 J.B.Faulconer
1977 Steve Cauthen	1980 John D.Schapiro	1985 Keene Daingerfield	1988 John Forsythe
1978 Dinny Phipps	1981 Bill Shoemaker	1986 Herman Cohen	1989 Michael Sandler

Special Award

1971 Robert J.Kleberg	1980 John T.Landry Pierre E. Bellocq (Peb)	1985 Arlington Park 1987 Anheuser-Busch	1988 Edward J. DeBartolo, Sr.
1974 Charles Hatton	1984 C.V.Whitney		1989 Richard Duchossois
1976 Bill Shoemaker			

Harness Racing

Triple Crown Winners

Trotters

Six 3-year-olds have won the Yonkers Trot, Hambletonian and Kentucky Futurity in the same year since the Trotting Triple Crown was established in 1955. Stanley Dancer is the only driver/trainer to win it twice.

Year	Horse	Driver/Trainer	Owner
1955	Scott Frost	Joe O'Brien	S.A. Camp Farms
1963	Speedy Scot	Ralph Baldwin	Castleton Farms
1964	Ayres	John Simpson, Sr.	Charlotte Sheppard
1968	Nevele Pride	Stanley Dancer	Nevele Acres & Lou Resnick
1969	Lindy's Pride	Howard Beissinger	Lindy Farms
1972	Super Bowl	Stanley Dancer	Rachel Dancer & Rose Hild Breeding Farm

Pacers

Seven 3-year-olds have won the Cane Pace, Little Brown Jug and Messenger Stakes in the same year since the Pacing Triple Crown was established in 1956. No trainer or driver has won it more than once.

Year	Horse	Driver	Trainer	Owner
1959	Adios Butler	Clint Hodgins	Paige West	Paige West & Angelo Pellillo
1965	Bret Hanover	Frank Ervin	Frank Ervin	Richard Downing
1966	Romeo Hanover	Bill Myer & George Sholty*	Jerry Silverman	Lucky Star Stable & Morton Finder
1968	Rum Customer	Billy Haughton	Billy Haughton	Kennilworth Farms & L.C. Mancuso
1970	Most Happy Fella	Stanley Dancer	Stanley Dancer	Egyptian Acres Stable
1980	Niatross	Clint Galbraith	Clint Galbraith	Niagara Acres, Niatross Stables & Clint Galbraith
1983	Ralph Hanover	Ron Waples	Stan Firlotte	Waples Stable, Pointsetta Stable, Grant's Direct Stable & P.J. Baugh

*Myer drove Romeo Hanover in the Cane, Sholty in the other two races.

Triple Crown Near Misses

Trotters

Five horses have won the first two legs of the Triple Crown—the Yonkers Trot (YT) and the Hambletonian (Ham)—but not the third. The eventual winner of the Ky. Futurity (KF) is listed.

Year	Horse	YT	Ham	KF
1962	AC's Viking	won	won	Safe Mission
1976	Steve Lobell	won	won	Quick Pay
1977	Green Speed	won	won	Texas
1978	Speedy Somolli	won	won	Doublemint
1987	Mack Lobell	won	won	Napoletano

Note: Green Speed (1977) was not eligible for Ky. Futurity.

Pacers

Five horses have won the first two legs of the Triple Crown, but not the third. The Cane Pace (CP), Little Brown Jug (LBJ), and Messenger Stakes (MS) have not always been run in the same order so numbers after races won indicate sequence for that year.

Year	Horse	CP	LBJ	MS
1957	Torpid	won,1	won,2	DNF
1960	Countess Adios	won,2	NE	won,1
1971	Albatross	won,2	2nd*	won,1
1976	Keystone Ore	won,1	won,2	2nd*
1986	Barberry Spur	won,1	won,2	2nd*

*Winning horses: Nansemond (1971), Windshield Wiper (1976), Amity Chef (1986).

Note: Torpid (1957) was scratched before the final heat; and Countess Adios (1960) was not eligible for Messenger.

The Hambletonian

For three-year-old trotters. Inaugurated in 1926 and has been held in Syracuse, N.Y.; Lexington, Ky.; Goshen, N.Y.; Yonkers, N.Y.; Du Quoin, Ill.; and, since 1981 at The Meadowlands in East Rutherford, N.J.

Run at one mile since 1947. Winning horse must win two heats.

Drivers with most wins: Ben White, Stanley Dancer and Bill Haughton (4); Del Cameron, John Campbell and Henry Thomas (3).

Year	Winner	Driver	Fastest Heat	Year	Winner	Driver	Fastest Heat
1926	Guy McKinney	Nat Ray	2:04¾	1940	Spencer Scott	Fred Egan	2:02
1927	Iosola's Worthy	Marvin Childs	2:03¾	1941	Bill Gallon	Lee Smith	2:05
1928	Spencer	W.H.Lessee	2:02½	1942	The Ambassador	Ben White	2:04
1929	Walter Dear	Walter Cox	2:02¾	1943	Volo Song	Ben White	2:02½
1930	Hanover's Bertha	Tom Berry	2:03	1944	Yankee Maid	Henry Thomas	2:04
1931	Calumet Butler	R.D.McMahon	2:03¼	1945	Titan Hanover	H.Pownall,Sr.	2:04
1932	The Marchioness	Wm. Caton	2:01¼	1946	Chestertown	Thomas Berry	2:02½
1933	Mary Reynolds	Ben White	2:03¾	1947	Hoot Mon	Sep Palin	2:00
1934	Lord Jim	Doc Parshall	2:02¾	1948	Demon Hanover	Harrison Hoyt	2:02
1935	Greyhound	Sep Palin	2:02¼	1949	Miss Tilly	Fred Egan	2:01.2
1936	Rosalind	Ben White	2:01¾	1950	Lusty Song	Del Miller	2:02
1937	Shirley Hanover	H.Thomas	2:01½	1951	Mainliner	Guy Crippen	2:02.3
1938	McLin Hanover	Henry Tomas	2:02¼	1952	Sharp Note	Bion Shively	2:02.3
1939	Peter Astra	Doc Parshall	2:04¼	1953	Helicopter	Harry Harvey	2:01.3

The Hambletonian (Cont.)

Year	Winner	Driver	Fastest Heat	Year	Winner	Driver	Fastest Heat
1954	Newport Dream	Del Cameron	2:02.4	1973	Flirth	Ralph Baldwin	1:57.1
1955	Scott Frost	Joe O'Brien	2:00.3	1974	Christopher T.	Bill Haughton	1:58.3
1956	The Intruder	Ned Bower	2:01.2	1975	Bonefish	Stanley Dancer	1:59
1957	Hickory Smoke	J.Simpson Sr.	2:00.1	1976	Steve Lobell	Bill Haughton	1:56.2
1958	Emily's Pride	Flave Nipe	1:59.4	1977	Green Speed	Bill Haughton	1:55.3
1958	Emily's Pride	Flave Nipe	1:59.4	1978	Speedy Somolli	H.Beissinger	1:55
1959	Diller Hanover	Frank Ervin	2:01.1	1979	Legend Hanover	George Sholty	1:56.1
1960	Blaze Hanover	Joe O'Brien	1:59.3	1980	Burgomeister	Bill Haughton	1:56.3
1961	Harlan Dean	James Arthur	1:58.2	1981	Shiaway St. Pat	Ray Remmen	2:01.1
1962	A.C.'s Viking	Sanders Russell	1:59.3	1982	Speed Bowl	Tommy Haughton	1:56.4
1963	Speedy Scot	Ralph Baldwin	1:57.3	1983	Duenna	Stanley Dancer	1:57.2
1964	Ayres	J.Simpson Sr.	1:56.4	1984	Historic Freight	Ben Webster	1:56.2
1965	Egyptian Candor	Del Cameron	2:03.4	1985	Prakas	Bill O'Donnell	1:54.3
1966	Kerry Way	Frank Ervin	1:58.4	1986	Nuclear Kosmos	Ulf Thoresen	1:55.2
1967	Speedy Streak	Del Cameron	2:00	1987	Mack Lobell	John Campbell	1:53.3
1968	Nevele Pride	Stanley Dancer	1:59.2	1988	Armbro Goal	John Campbell	1:54.3
1969	Lindys Pride	H.Beissinger	1:57.3	1989	Park Avenue Joe	Ron Waples	1:54.3
1970	Timothy T.	J.Simpson, Jr.	1:58.2		& Probe	Bill Fahy	
1971	Speedy Crown	H.Beissinger	1:57.2	1990	Harmonious	John Campbell	1:54.2
1972	Super Bowl	Stanley Dancer	1:56.2				

Note: In 1989, Park Avenue Joe and Probe finished in a dead heat in the race-off. They were later declared co-winners, but Park Avenue Joe was awarded 1st place money because his three-race summary (2-1-1) was better than Probe's (1-9-1).

All-Time Leading Money Winners

All-time money-winning trotters and pacers, through 1989, according to *The Trotting & Pacing Guide.* Purses for horses include foreign races, but starts and wins include only races in North America. Purses, starts and wins for drivers include only races in North America.

Top 5 Horses

Note that (*) indicates horse raced in 1989.

	T/P	Sts	1st	Purses
Ourasi (FRA)	T	—	32	$3,681,345
Nihilator	P	38	35	3,225,653
*Mack Lobell	T	58	41	3,073,214
Matt's Scooter	P	61	37	2,944,591
On the Road Again	P	61	44	2,819,102

Top 5 Drivers

All drivers were active in 1989.

	Yrs	Starts	Wins	Purses
John Campbell	17	24,323	4,593	$79,862,806
Bill O'Donnell	19	23,644	4,195	66,799,441
Herve Filion	29	59,664	12,007	66,696,221
Carmine Abbatiello	34	37,557	6,944	47,691,101
Michel Lachance	21	29,486	5,562	46,564,866

Horse of the Year

Selected since 1947 by U.S. Trotting Association and the U.S. Harness Writers Association; age of winning horse is noted; (t) indicates trotter and (p) indicates pacer. USTA added Trotter and Pacer of the Year awards in 1970.
   Multiple winners: Bret Hanover and Nevele Pride (3); Adios Butler, Albatross, Cam Fella, Good Time, Mack Lobell, Niatross and Scott Frost (2).

Year	Year	Year	Year
1947 Victory Song (4t)	1958 Emily's Pride (3t)	1969 Nevele Pride (4t)	1980 Niatross (3p)
1948 Rodney (4t)	1959 Bye Bye Byrd (4p)	1970 Fresh Yankee (7t)	1981 Fan Hanover (3p)
1949 Good Time (3p)	1960 Adios Butler (4p)	1971 Albatross (3p)	1982 Cam Fella (3p)
	1961 Adios Butler (5p)	1972 Albatross (4p)	1983 Cam Fella (4p)
1950 Proximity (8t)	1962 Su Mac Lad (8t)	1973 Sir Dalrai (4p)	1984 Fancy Crown (3t)
1951 Pronto Don (6t)	1963 Speedy Scot (3t)	1974 Delmonica Hanover (5t)	1985 Nihilator (3p)
1952 Good Time (6t)	1964 Bret Hanover (2p)	1975 Savoir (7t)	1986 Forrest Skipper (4p)
1953 Hi Lo's Forbes (5p)	1965 Bret Hanover (3p)	1976 Keystone Ore (3p)	1987 Mack Lobell (3t)
1954 Stenographer (3t)	1966 Bret Hanover (4p)	1977 Green Speed (3t)	1988 Mack Lobell (4t)
1955 Scott Frost (3t)	1967 Nevele Pride (2t)	1978 Abercrombie (3p)	1989 Matt's Scooter (4p)
1956 Scott Frost (4t)	1968 Nevele Pride (3t)	1979 Niatross (2p)	
1957 Torpid (3p)			

Driver of the Year

Determined by Universal Driving Rating System (UDR) and presented by the Harness Tracks of America since 1968. Eligible drivers must have at least 1000 starts for the season.
   Multiple winners: Herve Filion (10); Michel Lachance (3); John Campbell, Bill O'Donnell and Ron Waples (2).

Year	Year	Year	Year
1968 Stanley Dancer	1974 Herve Filion	1979 Ron Waples	1986 Michel Lachance
1969 Herve Filion	1975 Joe O'Brien	1980 Ron Waples	1987 Michel Lachance
	1976 Herve Filion	1981 Herve Filion	1988 John Campbell
1970 Herve Filion	1977 Donald Dancer	1982 Bill O'Donnell	1989 Herve Filion
1971 Herve Filion	1978 Carmine Abbatiello	1983 John Campbell	
1972 Herve Filion	& Herve Filion	1984 Bill O'Donnell	
1973 Herve Filion		1985 Michel Lachance	

Amleto Monicelli shared the Bowler and Player of the Year awards with Mike Aulby in 1989, but as the PBA leader in both earnings and average through the summer tour, he's aiming at a sweep in 1990.

BOWLING

*Despite bowling's popularity, pros
still not attracting TV megabucks;
Pencak, Palombi, Ferraro and Warren
win majors, but Monacelli tops PBA.*

BOWLING

1989-90 YEAR IN REVIEW

by Dave Petruska

The elite field at the Professional Bowlers Association's 1990 Firestone Tournament of Champions was surprised and pleased when the President dropped in to watch the finals of the event on April 28.

No, not George Bush, although he is acquainted with PBA member Walter Ray Williams Jr., because of their shared passion for horseshoe pitching. Bush and Williams, one of the nation's top pitchers, did some tossing in the presidential pit at the White House one weekend in 1989.

The president who mattered to the assembled PBA members in Akron was Dennis Swanson, the president of ABC Sports, who came by to let the pros know that ABC was very happy with its long-time association with the pro PBA tour.

At a question-and-answer session at the annual press breakfast before the finals were to be broadcast, PBA member

Mark Baker, who would finish in fifth place in the finals, beat the media to the No. 1 question: With the incredible amounts of rights fees being paid for the Olympics, major league baseball, the NFL and the NBA, would the PBA be seeing a substantial increase in TV payments?

Swanson proved to the just as adept as Bush at handling a political question. After a 10-minute history of the ratings and rights fees battles, he got to the point: Some of the other sports are loss-leaders; the PBA is a money maker. Therefore, don't expect a dramatic rise for bowling's rights fees.

"Bowling produces a profit," Swanson said. "We're not doing this as a hobby."

And although that wasn't the answer Baker was hoping to hear, he had no quarrel with Swanson.

"At least he was honest," Baker said. "I can't fault him. He shouldn't have to pay a nickel more than he wants to pay. It's just frustrating that there isn't more money out there for us. Our ratings are always good. We're beating golf head-

Dave Petruska of the Tucson (Ariz.) *Citizen* has written about professional and amateur bowling for 13 years and won 16 national awards. He also covers NFL football, PGA golf and college sports.

to-head almost every week, but we don't seem to be making any substantial headway."

To Baker and other pro bowlers, there seems to be a lack of respect for what they get paid to do.

"In our sport, we have amateurs who can make more money in one tournament than most pros do in a full year of touring," he said. "I just wish we could market ourselves better, get better sponsors. We have a strong product. I just don't feel we're aggressive enough."

But what Baker and the young lions of the tour are looking for might be unrealistic. The golf tours can add thousands of dollars to the prize funds at each tournament because of the large galleries they attract. Bowling tourneys will always be handicapped by the space restrictions of bowling centers.

"The other problem is that although we have better ratings than golf most of the time, we don't have the right demographics to get more money," points out PBA commissioner Joe Antenora. "I would love for us to have more auto companies sponsoring tourneys, getting soft-drink companies involved, but it's a struggle."

John Falzone, president of the Ladies Pro Bowlers Tour, would love to have the PBA's "problem." Only four of the LPBT's 22 tournaments are in the $100,000 purse range and the organization hasn't been able to land a spot on network television yet. It has slightly more than $1 million in prize funds, about seven times less than the PBA.

"But I feel we are on the verge of becoming an overnight success," said Falzone, ignoring the fact that the LPBT has been around for 10 years.

"We have a multi-year contract with ESPN to do all 22 tournaments and, in my book, ESPN is network television," Falzone continued. "We're trying to hold at 22 tournaments and make every single one of them a solid stop before we try to add extra stops."

The PBA can't complain about a lack of exposure. The winter and spring tours were televised by ABC, the summer by ESPN and the fall by NBC. In addition, ABC televised one of the senior tour events with ESPN picking up the rest. Every PBA event is on TV somewhere.

Sports File

Dave Ferraro picked up $50,000 for winning the Firestone Tournament of Champions in April.

In addition, PBA members found themselves as part of a sports collectors' card series for the first time. The Kingpins Collection, a set of 100 cards featuring past greats and present touring pros, was put out by Collect-A-Card Corp. of Greenville, N.C.

There was some concern, however, about the future of the Firestone Tournament of Champions. Firestone has been bought by Bridgestone, a Japanese tire company, and some cost cutting has already gone into effect. But Firestone officials maintain that the tourney is safe, at least for 1991, and the purse will stay at $250,000.

Both the PBA and LPBT got some very bad news in September when Seagram's Coolers dropped its sponsorship of the Bowling Proprietors' Association of America's United States Opens. Thanks to Seagram's, the U.S. Opens offered the largest purses on each tour—$400,000 for men and $120,000 for women. Without a new sponsor, the men's prize money will drop to $200,000 and the women's to $70,000.

The action on the lanes was just as interesting as what was going on off them. The 1989 PBA season ended with a split vote in the top two bowling awards for the first time since 1964. In 1964, Billy Hardwick won the Bowling Writers' Bowler of the Year award while Bob Strampe was the PBA Player of the Year. In 1989, Mike Aulby of Indianapolis won the writer's award and Amleto Monacelli of Barquisimeto, Venezuela, was the choice of the PBA membership. Aulby said he should have won both awards, although he added that Monacelli was also deserving.

"I felt Amleto had a great year, but look at what I accomplished—I set a record for season earnings ($298,237), won four PBA titles, including the U.S. Open, and won the (ABC) Masters, too. I was third at Firestone and 10th in the PBA National. I feel I had a very strong year."

Monacelli, who was second on the money list behind Aulby at $213,815, said his year-long consistency impressed his fellow tour members. He won four titles, cashed in on 24 of the 28 events he entered, made the television finals 10 times, was second in average at 215.049 and finished first on the points list.

"This is the award voted on by my peers and I feel I deserved it," Monacelli said. "I had a very, very good year from start to finish. I bowled well all year, not in spurts, not just in the majors. I feel winning any tournament is important. They're all majors in my book. If I had to win any award, this is the one I'd want to win."

And while Aulby continued a familiar pattern of following a great year with a so-so year—he earned $70,155 in 1986 after earning $201,200 in 1985 and was at $51,000 at the end of the 1990 summer tour—Monacelli has himself in serious contention to win both awards for 1990.

At the end of the summer tour, Monacelli led the money list with $174,825, just ahead of Chris Warren of Dallas with $172,275. He won two titles and his 218.59 average was more than two pins better than his closest challenger, Tony Westlake of Edmond, Okla. After repeating as the Wichita Open champion on Aug. 9, Monacelli said he didn't want to share top honors this year.

American Bowling Congress

The biggest victory so far in **Chris Warren's** remarkable season came in May when he won the ABC Masters.

"Player of the Year means a lot to me, but this year I hope to win both awards," he said.

While Monacelli emerged as the leader of the pack at the end of the summer, the early portion of the 1990 tour was dominated by Warren and Jim Pencak.

Warren, 27, nicknamed "Squeak" for his squeaky voice and 5 foot 5, 115-pound frame, entered his fourth year as a full-time touring pro with a goal for 1990 of being among the top 16 bowlers on the PBA list. The top 16 qualify for the Japan Cup competition in Tokyo, an annual event that pits 16 Japanese bowlers against 16 PBA members. Each PBA competitor is permitted to bring a guest and Warren wanted to take his mother, Mary, along if he qualified. Mrs. Warren is a native of Japan and hadn't been back to her homeland since the 1940s. Warren is the ninth of 10 children and his mother had to work two jobs to support the family because his father died when Warren was 10.

"I gave up football after my sophomore year in high school because I was getting banged around too much and I turned to bowling," Warren said.

No confusing this Masters with Augusta

Mention the Masters to a professional golfer and in hushed, reverent tones, he'll speak of Augusta National—about tradition, Amen Corner, and the prestige you gain if you're lucky enough to win the title.

Mention the Masters to a professional bowler and you're likely to get a shrug of indifference.

Traditionalists consider the American Bowling Congress Masters tournament to be one of the sport's Grand Slam events, along with the Triple Crown stops on the Pro Bowlers Tour—the PBA National, the BPAA U.S. Open and the Firestone Tournament of Champions. But a grand slam is what most PBA bowlers take at the Masters, despite the fact that it offers one of the biggest jackpots a pro can win.

"To me, it's a tournament where luck is more important than skill," says PBA Hall of Famer Joe Berardi. "The way the format is set up, you can just bowl great and be knocked out of action early on. If I'm averaging 220 at the Firestone, most likely I'll be leading the event. I could average 220 at the Masters but hit someone who is hot and find myself looking at the flight schedule home."

And those are not sour grapes. Berardi won the Masters in 1982.

Brian Voss, the PBA's Player of the Year in 1988, bowls in the Masters every year but doesn't think it should be considered a major tournament.

"To me, there just aren't enough quality bowlers in the field to consider it a major," Voss said. "It's a unique tournament but I don't like the format."

The American Bowling Congress has adapted the tournament, which began in 1951, to try to appease PBA members. There are now 15 games of qualifying, compared to the original eight, and the qualifiers bowl three-game matches instead of two. The Masters is also no longer a true double-elimination tourney. The top five players out of match play advance to the step-ladder finals format used in every PBA event.

The PBA tour works differently. Bowlers roll 18 games of qualifying in most tourneys. The field is then cut to the top 24 for the PBA version of match play.

Each qualifier is guaranteed to bowl 24 games—all one-game matches—once he qualifies. It is not a lose-two-matches-and-you're-gone format.

"If we ran the tourney, and ran it like a PBA event, I'd consider the Masters a major," PBA veteran Steve Cook says. "Until then, no."

Mike Aulby, the 1989 champion, disagrees. "I think the Masters is one of the most misunderstood tournaments we compete in," says Aulby. "True, you need some breaks to have a chance to win, but you can say that about any PBA event. I like it because the tournament is different and it's challenging. We bowl on very demanding lane conditions and we bowl in an arena before big crowds.

> ## "To me, it's a tournament where luck is more important than skill."
>
> — Joe Berardi
> PBA Hall of Famer

The Masters is held annually as part of the American Bowling Congress' National Tournament. The site varies every year and the ABC likes to set up lanes in convention centers, allowing for more fans to watch.

"We don't keep an official count, but the largest fan estimate for the Masters was in 1983 at Niagara Falls when we had more than 20,000 fans during the week and about 2500 for the finals," says Dan Matel of the ABC public relations staff. "We had big crowds there again in 1987."

Many touring pros believe that luck plays too big a part in the Masters, but PBA Hall of Famer George Pappas thinks the luck factor is overrated.

"In any tournament, the cream is going to come to the top," Pappas says. "Look at some of the guys who have won it—Aulby, Earl Anthony, Berardi, Del Ballard—just to mention a few. When you win the Masters, you get a one-year exemption into the Firestone Tournament of Champions. Obviously the people in our organization must think it's important."

Network TV didn't appreciate his penchant for black clothes, but **Mike Pencak** won the PBA National and 11 straight matches on the tube.

"I started getting good at it and began bowling a lot. Somehow, every month, my mom would find the money and I'd have a new bowling ball to use because I had worn out another one. Taking her to Tokyo is just one step in the many paybacks I owe her."

Warren won his first PBA title in Pinole, Calif., at the start of the '90 tour, won the ABC Masters title and $43,600 in Reno, and then survived a gutter ball in the ninth frame to win the Seattle Open over Brian Voss, 224-213.

Pencak, 31, who had bowled on and off the tour since 1980, entered the 1990 season with one pro title to his name. He struggled the first two months of the year but got hot in March, winning three titles in five weeks—the PBA National Championship, the Budweiser Open and the Showboat Open in Atlantic City.

What was most impressive during Pencak's hot streak was how he won, and what he wore when he won. Pencak won four straight matches to capture the PBA National, three straight to win the Budweiser Open and four straight to win in Atlantic City—a total of 11 straight victories on television. Combined with the four straight matches he won to win his first title in the summer of 1989 at Green Bay, Wis., Pencak was a PBA record 15-0 in championship round competition.

And while Pencak mastered the lanes on TV, he also violated one of the tube's cardinal rules—thou shalt not wear black—and got away with it. According to Chuck Pezzano, the PBA's television coordinator for ESPN broadcasts, the tour's reluctance to let bowlers wear black has nothing to do with making a fashion statement.

"We don't want guys to wear black or white shirts on the air simply because those colors don't show up well on TV," Pezzano said. "They're not good TV colors. If a guy wants to wear black with some bright, pink stripes, for example, that's not too bad, but black by itself doesn't register well. We very, very rarely agree to let someone wear black on the show."

Pencak's reason for wanting to wear black was much simpler: "I sweat so badly that black is the only color where you can't see me sweating."

When Pencak won in Green Bay, he said he got tired of hearing the broadcasting crew talk about how badly he was sweating.

"When I qualified for the show at the PBA Nationals, I asked to wear black," Pencak said. "I was nice about it, but persistent, and ABC finally agreed. Well, it turns out the network got a really good audience response about the 'Man in Black' winning on the show. When I made the show again the next week, I didn't have any problem getting to wear black again."

Pencak led the tour money list after the winter stops with $127,675 but he faltered badly and won barely over $2000 during the summer, leaving him fifth on the money list at $129,850.

Ron Palombi Jr., who topped the $100,000 mark for the first time in his career, won the 1990 U.S. Open and Dave Ferraro, who also topped the $100,000 mark, won the Firestone Tournament of Champions.

Dana Miller-Mackie, one of three double winners on the LPBT tour through the summer, became only the fourth woman since 1971 to win the U.S. Open twice when she edged Tish Johnson 190-189 with a strike on her final ball.

On the senior tour, Earl Anthony showed he still had the touch by winning three of the five tournaments he entered in 1990. John Handegard won twice, with Dave Soutar and John Hriscina also picking up titles.

On the women's tour, Robin Romeo won the 1989 Bowler of the Year title handily, setting a new LPBT standard for money won with $107,970. Lisa Wagner had set the old mark of $105,500 in 1988. But Romeo struggled through the first eight months of the 1990 tour. The 1990 race for Woman Bowler of the Year was wide open with Leanne Barrette leading the money list and Dana Miller-Mackie, Kim Terrell and Lisa Wagner all posting two victories apiece. Miller-Mackie became only the fourth woman to win the U.S. Open twice since 1971, but she needed a strike on her last ball to defeat Tish Johnson, 190-189. The other two-time Open winners are Paula Sperber Carter, Pat Costello and Donna Adamek.

Another prestigious title, the WIBC Queens title, went to amateur Patty Ann. Ann, 35, a former pro bowler from Appleton, Wis., was seeded third in the stepladder finals and beat fellow amateurs Chele Rutherford, 175-140, and Pat Costello, 267-169, before knocking off pro Vesma Grinfelds in the finals, 207-173, to earn the $10,000 winner's check.

Speaking of amateurs, Mike Neumann, 23, of Buffalo, N.Y. entered the record books by winning four titles in a single American Bowling Congress Championship Tournament, a feat that has been accomplished only two other times in the 88 years of the tourney. Neumann won the all-events title, teamed with Bob Ujvari to win the doubles and earned the other two titles with his team, Brunswick Rhinos No. 1. The Rhinos tied for the Regular Division team title and won the all-events crown. □

BOWLING STATISTICS

THE SEASON IN REVIEW
1989-1990
PBA • SENIORS • LPBT

SEC A

PAGE 566

1989-90 Results

Winners of stepladder finals in all PBA, Seniors and LPBT tournaments from the Fall Tours of 1989 through the Summer Tours of 1990; (a) indicates amateur.

PBA

1989 Fall Tour

Date	Event	Winner	Earnings	Final	Runner-up
Sep.24	No.7 PBA Invitational	Kevin West (a)	$ 7,000	192-186	Dave Ferraro
Oct.14	Japan Cup	Randy Pedersen	15,000	212-209	Amleto Monacelli
Oct.28	Budweiser Challenge	Joe Berardi	27,000	210-209	Marshall Holman
Nov.11	Toyota Classic	Charlie Tapp	27,000	228-190	Marshall Holman
Nov.18	Brunswick World Open	Parker Bohn III	33,000	217-190	Philip Ringener
Nov.25	Milwaukee Classic	David Ozio	18,000	236-226	Brian Voss
Dec. 2	Bud Touring Players Champ	Amleto Monacelli	27,000	235-209	Brian Voss
Dec. 7	Cambridge Pro Mixed Doubles	Amleto Monacelli & Tish Johnson	40,000	+177 pins	Mark Baker & Nikki Gianulias

1990 Winter Tour

Date	Event	Winner	Earnings	Final	Runner-up
Jan.13	AC-Delco Classic	Ron Williams	$35,000	232-212	Mark Thayer
Jan.20	Showboat Invitational	Dave Husted	33,000	190-190*	Marshall Holman
Jan.27	ARC Pinole Open	Chris Warren	20,000	201-188	Steve Cook
Feb. 3	Quaker State Open	Randy Pederson	28,000	201-167	Don Genalo
Feb.10	Don Carter Classic	Parker Bohn III	39,000	214-191	Mike Edwards
Feb.17	Budweiser Classic	Brian Voss	31,000	245-214	Scott Devers
Feb.24	Florida Space Coast Open	Robert Lawrence	24,000	274-199	Bob Learn, Jr.
Mar. 3	Fair Lanes Open	Danny Wiseman	28,000	255-201	Don Moser
Mar.10	Columbus Classic	Amleto Monacelli	20,000	232-222	Chris Warren
Mar.17	**PBA National Championship**	Jim Pencak	54,000	223-214	Chris Warren
Mar.24	Budweiser Open	Jim Pencak	31,000	247-209	John Mazza
Mar.31	True Value Open	Robert Lawrence	38,000	234-233	Steve Cook
Apr. 7	**BPAA US Open**	Ron Palombi, Jr.	80,000	269-205	Amleto Monacelli
Apr.14	Showboat Open	Jim Pencak	28,000	231-215	Purvis Granger
Apr.21	Greater Hartford Open	Mike Aulby	24,000	224-193	Dave Husted
Apr.28	**Firestone Tourn.of Champions**	Dave Ferraro	50,000	226-203	Tony Westlake
May 5	**ABC Masters**	Chris Warren	43,600	225-203	David Ozio

*Rolloff: Jan.20—Husted def. Holman, 39-36, in two frames. **Note:** The American Bowling Congress Masters is not a PBA Tour event.

1990 Spring/Summer Tour

Date	Event	Winner	Earnings	Final	Runner-up
May 19	Seattle Open	Chris Warren	$18,000	224-213	Brian Voss
May 26	Oregon Open	Mark Baker	27,000	255-230	Steve Wunderlich
Jun. 2	Showboat Doubles Classic	Steve Wunderlich & David Ozio	30,000	225-192	Parker Bohn III & Hugh Miller
Jun.16	Kessler Open	Butch Soper	23,000	220-192	Marc McDowell
Jun.23	Fresno Open	Hugh Miller	18,000	191-184	Joe Salvemini
Jun.30	Kessler Classic	Danny Wiseman	24,000	221-210	Ron Palombi, Jr.
Jul. 7	Fair Lanes Phoenix Classic	Ron Palombi, Jr.	18,000	219-173	Todd Thompson
Jul.14	Miller Lite Challenge	Bryan Goebel	24,000	184-173	Joe Salvemini
Jul.21	El Paso Open	Scott Devers	20,000	238-185	Joe Salvemini
Jul.28	Quality Inns Classic	Parker Bohn III	38,000	247-236	Hugh Miller
Aug. 2	Columbia 300 Open	Bob Handley	21,000	210-200	Steve Hoskins
Aug. 9	Wichita Open	Amleto Monacelli	20,000	222-203	W.R.Williams, Jr.
Aug.16	La Mode Classic	Pete Weber	20,000	257-251	Ron Williams
Aug.23	Senior Touring Pro Doubles	Rowdy Morrow & Dave Soutar	28,000	234-216	Jimmy Certain & Doug Kent

Seniors
Late 1989

Date	Event	Winner	Earnings	Final	Runner-up
Oct.19	Treasure Coast Open .... Teata Semiz		$7,500	254-231	John Hricsina

1990 (through Aug. 30)

Date	Event	Winner	Earnings	Final	Runner-up
Jun. 9	Showboat Invitational .... Earl Anthony		$13,000	180-149	Teata Semiz
Jun.21	St.Charles Bobact Classic .... John Hricsina		8,000	269-246	Jimmy Certain
Jul. 5	Hammer Open .... Earl Anthony		9,500	258-189	Bill Gaume
Jul.19	Hammond Open .... John Handegard		5,000	258-188	Richard Beattie
Jul.26	Battle Creek Open .... John Handegard		5,000	216-202	John Hricsina
Aug.23	Senior/Touring Pro Doubles .... Dave Soutar & Rowdy Morrow		28,000	234-216	Jimmy Certain & Doug Kent
Aug.30	Ebonite Championship .... Earl Anthony		17,000	244-192	John Hricsina

LPBT
1989 Fall Tour

Date	Event	Winner	Earnings	Final	Runner-up
Sep.13	Columbia 300 Open .... Donna Ademek		$10,000	213-162	Robin Romeo
Sep.20	AMF Virginia Classic .... Lisa Wagner		15,000	219-182	Nikki Gianulias
Sep.27	Hammer Eastern Open .... Aleta Sill		7,000	217-206	Nikki Gianulias
Oct. 4	Brunswick Open .... Carol Gianotti		8,000	217-208	Donna Adamek
Oct.11	Hammer Midwest Open .... Robin Romeo		10,000	208-166	Carolyn Hodge
Oct.18	Metroplex Open .... Leila Wagner		5,000	202-200	Carol Gianotti
Oct.25	Lady Fair Lanes Open .... Nikki Gianulias		7,000	203-158	Lisa Wagner
Nov. 1	Tempe Open .... Carol Norman		5,000	207-207*	Donna Adamek
Nov.11	**Sam's Town Invitational** .... Tish Johnson		25,000	210-183	Dede Davidson
Dec. 7	Cambridge Pro Mixed Doubles ..... Tish Johnson & Amleto Monacelli		40,000	+177 pins	Nikki Gianulias & Mark Baker

*Rolloff: Nov.1—Norman def. Adamek, 60-59 in two frames.

1990 Winter Tour

Date	Event	Winner	Earnings	Final	Runner-up
Feb.14	Robby's Open .... Dana Miller-Mackie		$6,000	213-177	Nikki Gianulias
Feb.21	Garland Open .... Leanne Barrette		5,000	227-182	Kim Terrell
Feb.28	Yuma Open .... Lisa Wagner		6,000	279-214	Kim Terrell

1990 Spring/Summer Tour

Date	Event	Winner	Earnings	Final	Runner-up
Apr. 5	Hoffman/Schaumburg Open .... Cindy Coburn-Carroll		$ 6,000	208-191	Leanne Barrette
Apr.12	Lady Fair Lanes Open .... Michelle Mullen		9,000	173-170	Nikki Gianulias
Apr.19	Carolina Classic .... Lisa Wagner		6,000	235-181	Lorrie Nichols
Apr.26	Greater Atlanta Open .... Jeri Edwards		6,000	245-168	Robin Romeo
May 3	Ebonite Thunderbolt Classic ...... Kim Terrell		7,000	189-182	Leanne Barrette
May 10	Clearwater Classic .... Kim Terrell		6,000	244-165	Lisa Wagner
May 17	**WIBC Queens Tournament** ...... Patty Ann (a)		10,000	207-173	Vesma Grinfelds
May 24	Ebonite Open .... Sandra Jo Shiery		7,000	259-212	Dede Davidson
May 31	**BPAA US Open** .... Dana Miller-Mackie		24,000	190-189	Tish Johnson
Aug.18	Gold Rush Mixed Doubles .... Leanne Barrette & Billy Young Jr.		7,000	424-408	Cheryl Daniels & Bill Straub
Aug.22	National Doubles .... Anne Marie Duggan & Stacy Rider		14,000	234-193	Diane Davenport & Nanci Johnson

Note: The Women's International Bowling Congress Queens Tournament is not a LPBT Tour event.

Fall Tour Schedules

PBA

Events (5)—Budweiser Challenge (Oct.29-Nov.3); Toyota Classic (Nov.5-10); Brunswick World Open (Nov.10-17); Touring Players Championship (Nov.26-Dec.1); Cambridge Mixed Doubles (Dec.7-10).

SENIORS

Events (1)—Treasure Coast Open (Oct. 18-25).

LPBT

Events (10)—AMF Cobra Classic (Sep.16-20); Columbia 300 Delaware Open (Sep.23-27); Hammer Eastern Open (Sep.30-Oct.4); Hammond Open (Oct.7-11); Hammer Midwest Open (Oct.14-18); Lady Ebonite Classic (Oct.21-25); Hammer Western Open (Oct.28-Nov.1); Los Angeles Open (Nov.4-8); Sam's Town Invitational (Nov.10-17); Cambridge Mixed Doubles (Dec.7-10).

Tour Leaders

Official Top 10 standings for 1989 and unofficial Top 10 standings (including summer tours) for 1990. PBA, Seniors and LPBT figures for 1990 reflect performances through Sept.1. Note that (TP) indicates tournaments played.

Final 1989

PBA

Top 10 Money Winners

	TP	Titles	Earnings
1 Mike Aulby	29	4	$298,237
2 Amleto Monacelli	28	4	213,815
3 Del Ballard Jr	24	3	193,668
4 Pete Weber	23	2	151,508
5 Dave Ferraro	30	0	137,907
6 Brian Voss	24	3	135,970
7 Parker Bohn, III	33	1	135,752
8 Tony Westlake	33	1	118,715
9 Randy Pedersen	29	2	113,932
10 Jess Stayrook	32	1	109,445

Top 5 Averages

	Gm	Pinfall	Avg
1 Pete Weber	851	183,333	215.43
2 Amleto Monacelli	1035	222,576	215.05
3 Del Ballard Jr	832	178,130	214.10
4 Dave Ferraro	942	201,587	214.00
5 Marshall Holman	841	178,928	212.76

Seniors

Top 10 Money Winners

	TP	Titles	Earnings
1 Jimmy Certain	5	1	$ 31,800
2 Les Zikes	5	1	23,870
3 Dick Weber	5	1	21,320
4 John Handegard	5	0	20,450
5 Teata Semitz	5	1	19,465
6 John Hricsina	5	0	12,900
7 Bob Helmbold	4	0	9,250
8 Allan Chodor	4	1	8,610
9 Carmen Salvino	4	0	8,570
10 Glenn Allison	4	0	6,900

Top 5 Averages

	Gm	Pinfall	Avg
1 Jimmy Certain	179	38,243	213.64
2 Teata Semiz	160	33,940	212.12
3 John Handegard	194	41,089	211.80
4 John Hricsina	177	37,445	211.55
5 Les Zikes	157	33,083	210.73

LPBT

Top 10 Money Winners

	TP	Titles	Earnings
1 Robin Romeo	24	5	$113,750
2 Lisa Wagner	23	2	83,060
3 Tish Johnson	24	3	74,302
4 Nikki Gianulias	23	1	67,645
5 Cheryl Daniels	25	4	64,390
6 Donna Adamek	20	1	60,725
7 Aleta Sill	22	2	54,775
8 Leanne Barrette	25	2	52,085
9 Carol Gianotti	21	2	47,805
10 Michelle Mullen	22	0	47,307

Top 5 Averages

	Gm	Pinfall	Avg
1 Lisa Wagner	934	197,887	211.87
2 Robin Romeo	1000	210,470	210.47
3 Nikki Gianulias	881	184,129	209.00
4 Tish Johnson	725	151,242	208.61
5 Lorie Nichols	724	150,773	208.25

1990 (through Sept.1)

PBA

Top 10 Money Winners

	TP	Titles	Earnings
1 Amleto Monacelli	23	2	$174,825
2 Chris Warren	27	2	172,275
3 Ron Palombi Jr	26	2	137,920
4 Brian Voss	23	1	130,280
5 Jim Pencak	24	3	129,850
6 Parker Bohn III	26	2	120,215
7 Robert Lawrence	27	2	108,390
8 Dave Ferraro	24	1	105,400
9 Tony Westlake	27	0	100,973
10 Dave Husted	26	1	96,105

Top 5 Averages

	Gm	Pinfall	Avg
1 Amleto Monacelli	825	180,336	218.59
2 Tony Westlake	860	185,891	216.15
3 W.Ray Williams Jr	698	150,775	216.01
4 Hugh Miller	724	156,384	216.00
5 Dave Ferraro	803	173,428	215.98

Seniors

Top 10 Money Winners

	TP	Titles	Earnings
1 Earl Anthony	5	3	$ 40,500
2 John Hricsina	7	1	30,750
3 Dave Soutar	6	1	24,910
4 John Handegard	7	2	24,700
5 Jimmy Certain	7	0	22,520
6 Teata Semiz	7	0	20,150
7 Bus Oswalt	6	0	11,630
8 Les Zikes	7	0	11,375
9 Robert Gibbs	5	0	10,840
10 Bob Hart	7	0	9,535

Top 5 Averages

	Gm	Pinfall	Avg
1 John Hricsina	256	55,522	216.88
2 Jimmy Certain	223	48,296	216.57
3 Richard Beattie	110	23,802	216.38
4 John Handegard	261	56,356	215.92
5 Earl Anthony	148	31,916	215.65

LPBT

Top 10 Money Winners

	TP	Titles	Earnings
1 Leanne Barrette	12	1	$ 42,055
2 Dana Miller-Mackie	12	2	41,580
3 Kim Terrell	12	2	34,555
4 Lisa Wagner	12	2	31,580
5 Tish Johnson	12	0	27,270
6 Robin Romeo	12	0	21,245
7 Nikki Gianulias	12	0	18,587
8 Stacy Rider	12	1	18,395
9 Michelle Mullen	9	1	17,755
10 Dede Davidson	12	0	17,290

Top 5 Averages

	Gm	Pinfall	Avg
1 Leanne Barrette	474	99,853	210.66
2 Lisa Wagner	452	94,274	208.57
3 Kim Terrell	450	93,069	206.82
4 Nikki Gianulias	398	81,833	205.61
5 Robin Romeo	468	96,141	205.43

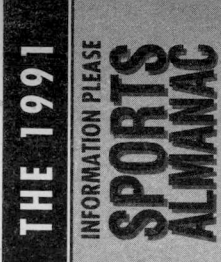
THE 1991 INFORMATION PLEASE SPORTS ALMANAC

BOWLING
STATISTICS

THROUGH THE YEARS
1941-1990
CHAMPIONS • AWARDS

SEC B

PAGE 569

Major Championships
MEN

BPAA U.S. Open

Started by the Bowling Proprietors' Association of America in 1941, eighteen years before the founding of the Professional Bowlers Association.

Originally the BPAA All-Star Tournament, it became the US Open in 1971. There were two BPAA All-Star tournaments in 1955, in January and December.

Multiple winners: Don Carter and Dick Weber (4); Marshall Holman, Junie McMahon, Connie Schwoegler and Andy Varipapa (2).

Year	Winner	Year	Winner	Year	Winner
1941	John Crimmons	1957	Not held	1974	Larry Laub
1942	Connie Schwoegler	1958	Don Carter	1975	Steve Neff
1943	Ned Day	1959	Billy Welu	1976	Paul Moser
1944	Buddy Bomar			1977	Johnny Petraglia
1945	Joe Wilman	1960	Harry Smith	1978	Nelson Burton, Jr
1946	Andy Varipapa	1961	Bill Tucker	1979	Joe Berardi
1947	Andy Varipapa	1962	Dick Weber		
1948	Connie Schwoegler	1963	Dick Weber	1980	Steve Martin
1949	Junie McMahon	1964	Bob Strampe	1981	Marshall Holman
		1965	Dick Weber	1982	Dave Husted
1950	Dick Hoover	1966	Dick Weber	1983	Gary Dickinson
1951	Junie McMahon	1967	Les Schissler	1984	Mark Roth
1952	Don Carter	1968	Jim Stefanich	1985	Marshall Holman
1953	Not held	1969	Billy Hardwick	1986	Steve Cook
1954	Don Carter			1987	Del Ballard, Jr
1955	Steve Nagy	1970	Bobby Cooper	1988	Pete Weber
1955	Bill Lillard	1971	Mike Lemongello	1989	Mike Aulby
1956	Don Carter	1972	Don Johnson		
		1973	Mike McGrath	1990	Ron Palombi, Jr

PBA National Championship

The Professional Bowlers Association was formed in 1958 and its first national championship tournament was held in Memphis in 1960. The tournament has been played in Toledo, Ohio, since 1981.

Multiple winners: Earl Anthony (6); Mike Aulby, Dave Davis, Mike McGrath and Wayne Zahn (2).

Year	Winner	Year	Winner	Year	Winner
1960	Don Carter	1970	Mike McGrath	1980	Johnny Petraglia
1961	Dave Soutar	1971	Mike Lemongello	1981	Earl Anthony
1962	Carmen Salvino	1972	Johnny Guenther	1982	Earl Anthony
1963	Billy Hardwick	1973	Earl Anthony	1983	Earl Anthony
1964	Bob Strampe	1974	Earl Anthony	1984	Bob Chamberlain
1965	Dave Davis	1975	Earl Anthony	1985	Mike Aulby
1966	Wayne Zahn	1976	Paul Colwell	1986	Tom Crites
1967	Dave Davis	1977	Tommy Hudson	1987	Randy Pedersen
1968	Wayne Zahn	1978	Warren Nelson	1988	Brian Voss
1969	Mike McGrath	1979	Mike Aulby	1989	Pete Weber
				1990	Jim Pencak

Firestone Tournament of Champions

The Tournament of Champions has been held in Akron, Ohio, since it began in 1965.

Multiple winners: Earl Anthony, Mike Durbin, Jim Godman, Marshall Holman and Mark Williams (2).

Year	Winner	Year	Winner	Year	Winner
1965	Billy Hardwick	1970	Don Johnson	1975	Dave Davis
1966	Wayne Zahn	1971	Johnny Petraglia	1976	Marshall Holman
1967	Jim Stefanich	1972	Mike Durbin	1977	Mike Berlin
1968	Dave Davis	1973	Jim Goodman	1978	Earl Anthony
1969	Jim Godman	1974	Earl Anthony	1979	George Pappas

Major Championships (Cont.)
Firestone Tournament of Champions

Year	Winner	Year	Winner	Year	Winner
1980	Wayne Webb	1984	Mike Durbin	1988	Mark Williams
1981	Steve Cook	1985	Mark Williams	1989	Del Ballard, Jr
1981	Steve Cook	1986	Marshall Holman	1990	Dave Ferraro
1982	Mike Durbin	1987	Pete Weber		
1983	Joe Berardi				

ABC Masters Tournament

Sponsored by the American Bowling Congress, the Masters is not a PBA event, but is open to qualified pros and amateurs.

Multiple winners: Earl Anthony, Billy Golembiewski, Dick Hoover, Billy Welu (2).

Year	Winner	Year	Winner	Year	Winner
1951	Lee Jouglard	1965	Billy Welu	1978	Frank Ellenburg
1952	Willard Taylor	1966	Bob Strampe	1979	Doug Myers
1953	Rudy Habetler	1967	Lou Scalia		
1954	Red Elkins	1968	Pete Tountas	1980	Neil Burton
1955	Buzz Fazio	1969	Jim Chestney	1981	Randy Lightfoot
1956	Dick Hoover			1982	Joe Berardi
1957	Dick Hoover	1970	Don Glover	1983	Mike Lastowski
1958	Tom Hennessey	1971	Jim Godman	1984	Earl Anthony
1959	Ray Bluth	1972	Bill Beach	1985	Steve Wunderlich
		1973	Dave Soutar	1986	Mark Fahy
1960	Billy Golembiewski	1974	Paul Colwell	1987	Rick Steelsmith
1961	Don Carter	1975	Eddie Ressler	1988	Del Ballard, Jr
1962	Billy Golembiewski	1976	Nelson Burton, Jr	1989	Mike Aulby
1963	Harry Smith	1977	Earl Anthony		
1964	Billy Welu			1990	Chris Warren

WOMEN

BPAA U.S. Open

Started by the Bowling Proprietors' Association of America in 1949, 11 years before the founding of the Professional Women's Bowling Association.

Originally the BPAA Women's All-Star Tournament, it became the US Open in 1971. There were two BPAA All-Star tournaments in 1955, in January and December. Note that (*) indicates amateur.

Multiple winners: Marion Ladewig (8); Donna Adamek, Paula Sperber Carter, Pat Costello, Dotty Fothergill, Dana Miller-Mackie and Sylvia Wene (2).

Year	Winner	Year	Winner	Year	Winner
1949	Marion Ladewig	1962	Shirley Garms	1977	Betty Morris
		1963	Marion Ladewig	1978	Donna Adamek
1950	Marion Ladewig	1964	LaVerne Carter	1979	Diana Silva
1951	Marion Ladewig	1965	Ann Slattery		
1952	Marion Ladewig	1966	Joy Abel	1980	Pat Costello
1953	Not held	1967	Gloria Bouvia	1981	Donna Adamek
1954	Marion Ladewig	1968	Dotty Fothergill	1982	Shinobu Saitoh
1955	Sylvia Wene	1969	Dotty Fothergill	1983	Dana Miller
1955	Anita Cantaline			1984	Karen Ellingsworth
1956	Marion Ladewig	1970	Mary Baker	1985	Pat Mercatanti
1957	Not held	1971	Paula Sperber*	1986	Wendy Macpherson
1958	Merle Matthews	1972	Lorrie Koch*	1987	Carol Norman
1959	Marion Ladewig	1973	Millie Martorella	1988	Lisa Wagner
		1974	Pat Costello	1989	Robin Romeo
1960	Sylvia Wene	1975	Paula Sperber Carter		
1961	Phyllis Notaro	1976	Patty Costello	1990	Dana Miller-Mackie

WPBA National Championship

The Women's Professional Bowling Association National Championship tournament was discontinued when the WPBA broke up in 1981. The WPBA changed its name from the Professional Women Bowlers Association (PWBA) in 1978.

Multiple winners: Patty costello (3); Dotty Fothergill (2).

Year	Winner	Year	Winner	Year	Winner
1960	Marion Ladewig	1968	Dotty Fothergill	1975	Pam Buckner
1961	Shirley Garms	1969	Dotty Fothergill	1976	Patty Costello
1962	Stevie Balogh			1977	Vesma Grinfelds
1963	Janet Harman	1970	Bobbe North	1978	Toni Gillard
1964	Betty Kuczynski	1971	Patty Costello	1979	Cindy Coburn
1965	Helen Duval	1972	Patty Costello		
1966	Judy Lee	1973	Betty Morris	1980	Donna Adamek
1967	Betty Mivelas	1974	Pat Costello	1981	Discontinued

WIBC Queens

Sponsored by the Women's International Bowling Congress, the Queens is a double elimination, match play tournament. It is not a LPBT event, but is open to qualified pros and amateurs. Note that (*) indicates amateur.

Multiple winners: Mille Martorella (3); Donna Adamek, Dotty Fothergill, Aleta Sill and Katsuko Sugimoto (2).

Year	Winner	Year	Winner	Year	Winner
1961	Janet Harman	1971	Millie Martorella	1981	Katsuko Sugimoto
1962	Dorothy Wilkinson	1972	Dotty Fothergill	1982	Katsuko Sugimoto
1963	Irene Monterosso	1973	Dotty Fothergill	1983	Aleta Sill
1964	D.D.Jacobsen	1974	Judy Soutar	1984	Kazue Inahashi
1965	Betty Kuczynski	1975	Cindy Powell	1985	Aleta Sill
1966	Judy Lee	1976	Pam Buckner	1986	Cora Fiebig
1967	Millie Martorella	1977	Dana Stewart	1987	Cathy Almeida
1968	Phyllis Massey	1978	Loa Boxberger	1988	Wendy Macpherson
1969	Ann Feigel	1979	Donna Adamek	1989	Carol Gianotti
1970	Millie Martorella	1980	Donna Adamek	1990	Patty Ann (a)

Sam's Town Invitational

Originally held in Milwaukee as the Pabst Tournament of Champions, but discontinued after one year (1981). The event was revived in 1984, moved to Las Vegas and renamed Sam's Town Tournament of Champions. Since then it has been known as the LPBT Tournament of Champions (1985), the Sam's Town National Pro/Am (1986-88) and the Sam's Town Invitational (since 1989).

Multiple winner: Aleta Sill (2).

Year	Winner	Year	Winner	Year	Winner
1981	Cindy Coburn	1986	Aleta Sill	1988	Donna Adamek
1984	Aleta Sill	1987	Debbie Bennett	1989	Tish Johnson
1985	Patty Costello				

All-Time Leaders

All-time leading money winners on the PBA and LPBT tours, through 1989. PBA figures date back to 1959, while LPBT figures date back to 1981.

Money Winners

PBA Top 10

		Titles	Earnings
1	Marshall Holman	21	$1,433,856
2	Mark Roth	33	1,378,756
3	Earl Anthony	41	1,302,226
4	Mike Aulby	18	1,081,740
5	Pete Weber	13	1,074,250
6	Wayne Webb	17	907,176
7	Dick Weber	26	812,584
8	Joe Berardi	10	780,879
9	George Pappas	10	779,684
10	Dave Husted	6	766,397

LPBT Top 10

		Titles	Earnings
1	Lisa Wagner	23	$380,739
2	Aleta Sill	16	355,744
3	Donna Adamek	17	352,089
4	Lorrie Nichols	13	334,509
5	Robin Romeo	12	313,065
6	Betty Morris	17	306,118
7	Nikki Gianulias	11	287,640
8	Cindy Coburn	12	252,187
9	Patty Costello	25	240,705
10	Pat Costello	11	236,056

Awards

MEN

BWAA Bowler of the Year

Winners selected by Bowling Writers Association of America.

Multiple winners: Earl Anthony and Don Carter (6); Mark Roth (4); Dick Weber (3); Mike Aulby, Buddy Bomar, Ned Day, Billy Hardwick, Don Johnson, Steve Nagy (2).

Year		Year		Year	
1942	Johnny Crimmins	1958	Don Carter	1974	Earl Anthony
1943	Ned Day	1959	Ed Lubanski	1975	Earl Anthony
1944	Ned Day			1976	Earl Anthony
1945	Buddy Bomar	1960	Don Carter	1977	Mark Roth
1946	Joe Wilman	1961	Dick Weber	1978	Mark Roth
1947	Buddy Bomar	1962	Don Carter	1979	Mark Roth
1948	Andy Varipapa	1963	Dick Weber		
1949	Connie Schwoegler	1964	Billy Hardwick	1980	Wayne Webb
		1965	Dick Weber	1981	Earl Anthony
1950	Junie McMahon	1966	Wayne Zahn	1982	Earl Anthony
1951	Lee Jouglard	1967	Dave Davis	1983	Earl Anthony
1952	Steve Nagy	1968	Jim Stefanich	1984	Mark Roth
1953	Don Carter	1969	Billy Hardwick	1985	Mike Aulby
1954	Don Carter			1986	Walter Ray Williams Jr.
1955	Steve Nagy	1970	Nelson Burton Jr.	1987	Marshall Holman
1956	Bill Lillard	1971	Don Johnson	1988	Brian Voss
1957	Don Carter	1972	Don Johnson	1989	Mike Aubly
		1973	Don McCune		

Awards (Cont.)

PBA Player of the Year

Winners selected by members of Professional Bowlers Association. The PBA Player of the Year has differed from the BWAA Bowler of the Year three times—1963-64 and 1989.

Multiple winners: Earl Anthony (6); Mark Roth (4); Billy Hardwick and Don Johnson (2).

Year		Year		Year	
1963	Billy Hardwick	1972	Don Johnson	1980	Wayne Webb
1964	Bob Strampe	1973	Don McCune	1981	Earl Anthony
1965	Dick Weber	1974	Earl Anthony	1982	Earl Anthony
1966	Wayne Zahn	1975	Earl Anthony	1983	Earl Anthony
1967	Dave Davis	1976	Earl Anthony	1984	Mark Roth
1968	Jim Stefanich	1977	Mark Roth	1985	Mike Aulby
1969	Billy Hardwick	1978	Mark Roth	1986	Walter Ray Williams, Jr
		1979	Mark Roth	1987	Marshall Holman
1970	Nelson Burton, Jr			1988	Brian Voss
1971	Don Johnson			1989	Amleto Monacelli

PBA Rookie of the Year

Winners selected by members of Professional Bowlers Association.

Year		Year		Year		Year	
1964	Jerry McCoy	1970	Denny Krick	1977	Steve Martin	1983	Toby Contreras
1965	Jim Godman	1971	Tye Critchlow	1978	Joseph Groskind	1984	John Gant
1966	Bobby Cooper	1972	Tommy Hudson	1979	Mike Aulby	1985	Tom Crites
1967	Mike Durbin	1973	Steve Neff	1980	Pete Weber	1986	Marc McDowell
1968	Bob McGregor	1974	Cliff McNealy	1981	Mark Fahy	1987	Ryan Shafer
1969	Larry Lichstein	1975	Guy Rowbury	1982	Mike Steinbach	1988	Rick Steelsmith
		1976	Mike Berlin			1989	Steve Hoskins

WOMEN

BWAA Bowler of the Year

Winners selected by Bowling Writers Association of America.

Multiple winners: Marion Ladewig (9); Donna Adamek (4); Betty Morris and Lisa Rathgeber Wagner (3); Patty Costello, Dotty Forthergill, Shirley Garms, Val Mikiel, Aleta Sill, Judy Soutar and Sylvia Wene (2).

Year		Year		Year	
1948	Val Mikiel	1962	Shirley Garms	1976	Patty Costello
1949	Val Mikiel	1963	Marion Ladewig	1977	Betty Morris
		1964	LaVerne Carter	1978	Donna Adamek
1950	Marion Ladewig	1965	Betty Kuczynski	1979	Donna Adamek
1951	Marion Ladewig	1966	Joy Abel		
1952	Marion Ladewig	1967	Millie Martorella	1980	Donna Adamek
1953	Marion Ladewig	1968	Dotty Fothergill	1981	Donna Adamek
1954	Marion Ladewig	1969	Dotty Fothergill	1982	Nikki Gianulias
1955	Sylvia Wene			1983	Lisa Rathgeber
1956	Anita Cantaline	1970	Mary Baker	1984	Aleta Sill
1957	Marion Ladewig	1971	Paula Sperber	1985	Aleta Sill
1958	Marion Ladewig	1972	Patty Costello	1986	Lisa Rathgeber Wagner
1959	Marion Ladewig	1973	Judy Soutar	1987	Betty Morris
		1974	Betty Morris	1988	Lisa Wagner
1960	Sylvia Wene	1975	Judy Soutar	1989	Robin Romeo
1961	Shirley Garms				

LPBT Player of the Year

Winners selected by members of Ladies Professional Bowlers Tour. The LPBT Player of the Year has differed from the BWAA Bowler of the Year twice—1985-86.

Multiple winner: Lisa Rathgeber Wagner (2).

Year		Year		Year	
1983	Lisa Rathgeber	1986	Jeanne Maiden	1988	Lisa Wagner
1984	Aleta Sill	1987	Betty Morris	1989	Robin Romeo
1985	Patty Costello				

WPBA and LPBT Rookies of the Year

Winners selected by members of Women's Professional Bowlers Association (1978-80) and the Ladies Professional Bowlers Tour (since 1981).

Year		Year		Year	
1978	Toni Gillard	1982	Carol Norman	1986	Wendy Macpherson
1979	Nikki Gianulias	1983	Anne Marie Pike	1987	Paula Drake
		1984	Paula Vidad	1988	Mary Martha Cerniglia
1980	Lisa Rathgeber	1985	Dede Davidson	1989	Kim Terrell
1981	Cindy Mason				

Martina Navratilova raises her ninth Wimbledon championship tray at centre court after beating Zina Garrison 6-4, 6-1 in the ladies singles final on July 7.

TENNIS

Grand Slam singles championships won by 8 different players; Navratilova wins 9th Wimbledon; Sampras a sensation at U.S. Open.

TENNIS

1989-90 YEAR IN REVIEW

by Jim Martz

It figured that during a year in which the planes stopped thundering over the U.S. Open and controversies erupted over Andre Agassi's neon clothes and Monica Seles' ear-splitting grunt, there would be eight different Grand Slam champions.

For the first time since the Open era of tennis began in 1968, no player—man or woman—won two or more singles titles in the Grand Slam tournaments. The last time there were eight different winners, in 1966, only amateurs were eligible to compete for the Australian, French, Wimbledon and United States championships.

In 1990, four players won their first Grand Slam titles—Andres Gomez and Seles at the French Open and Pete Sampras and Gabriela Sabatini at the U.S. Open. Ivan Lendl and Steffi Graf defended their Australian Open titles, while at Wimbledon, Martina Navratilova won a

Jim Martz is the Regional Sports Editor of the *Miami Herald* and has covered tennis for the paper since 1973.

record ninth championship and Stefan Edberg captured his second.

The year marked the heralded debut of Jennifer Capriati, a Floridian and former protege of Jimmy Evert, who signed endorsements worth more than a million dollars before she turned 14. New executive directors were hired by the Association of Tennis Professionals and the Women's Tennis Association—Mark Miles by the men and Gerard Smith by the women. The ATP also took over the control of the men's tour, supplanting the Men's Tennis Council and precipitating a power struggle with the International Tennis Federation.

The fact that eight different players won Grand Slam titles raised the question as to whether it was the start of a trend.

Yes and no, according to such observers as Chris Evert and Jack Kramer. It may have been a fluke among the women—mainly because Graf suffered an off year—but not the men.

"They say the men have more depth, so it's not surprising that no one dominated," said Evert, who was in the first year of her new role as retired player and television commentator. "It was a surprise among the women. Every year, from myself to Martina and Steffi, usually one of us would win two Grand Slams or more. Steffi didn't win two this year, but she made three finals. The competition's getting tougher for her, but watch out in 1991. This past year will spur her on."

Kramer, the Hall of Famer who won two U.S. titles and one Wimbledon in the mid-1940s, agreed. "The reason the women had four winners," he said, "is because Graf didn't play as well. She started out alright, then started having problems. But when she's on, her game is still the best in the game.

"The men's season figured to be wide open. Edberg was the only one who made two finals, so he sort of joined Becker and Lendl at the top."

There was no hint that 1990 would be so topsy-turvy when the 1989 season ended true to form. At the wrap-ups of the men's and women's circuits at New York City, Edberg defeated Becker to win the Nabisco Masters, 4-6, 7-6, 6-3, 6-1; while in the Virginia Slims Championships, Graf prevailed over Navratilova in the only best-of-five-sets women's title match, 6-4, 7-5, 2-6, 6-2.

Then in the Davis Cup finals at Stuttgart in mid-December, Becker lost only 12 games in six sets of singles to lead defending champion West Germany to a 3-2 victory over Edberg and Sweden.

Searing heat and John McEnroe's hot temper dominated headlines at the first Grand Slam of the 1990s—the Australian Open in January. As temperatures soared to 150 degrees Fahrenheit on the center court, the rubberized asphalt surface became sticky and intractable. Five players were forced to retire, including the second-seeded Sabatini, who twisted her ankle badly in the third round.

Lendl, who donned a white French Legionnaire's cap to keep cool, won the men's final when Edberg retired at 4-6, 7-6, 5-2. Edberg had pulled a stomach muscle in his semifinal victory over fellow Swede Mats Wilander. McEnroe wrapped a bandanna around his forehead to ward off the heat but lost his cool in a fourth-round match against Mikael Pernfors and was ejected from the tournament—a first in his stormy career. McEnroe led 6-1,

Stefan Edberg plants a kiss on his second Wimbledon men's singles trophy, won at Boris Becker's expense.

4-6, 7-5, 2-4, when the incident occurred.

The countdown to ejection went like this: a warning for intimidating a lineswoman; a point penalty when he slammed his racquet on the court; and default for cursing Ken Farrar, the International Tennis Federation chief of supervisors. McEnroe, who was also fined $6500, said he forgot the new ATP Tour rule, which reduces the process for default from four steps (warning, point penalty, game penalty, default) to three (warning, point, default).

"This is like a long story that culminates in me getting defaulted from a big tournament," said McEnroe. "I mean, I guess it was bound to happen."

On the women's side, Graf seemed out of synch throughout the tournament, making several uncharacteristic errors. Nevertheless, she won the championship for the third straight year, beating Mary Joe Fernandez, 6-3, 6-4. With four Grand Slam titles in 1988, three more in 1989 and one already tucked away in 1990, Graf left Melbourne on a definite roll.

In March, perhaps the most ballyhooed debut in tennis history occurred in Boca Raton, Fla., when Capriati, then 13,

Thirteen-year-old **Jennifer Capriati** (right) shakes hands with champion **Gabriela Sabatini** after a 6-4, 7-5 loss in the Virginia Slims of Florida final on Mar. 11. It was Capriati's first tournament as a pro.

played her first match as a professional in the Virginia Slims of Florida. Before an international press corps befitting Wimbledon and a near-capacity crowd of 6041, she bashed her way into the final, stunning 10th-ranked Helena Sukova, 6-1, 6-4, before losing to Sabatini, 6-4, 7-5.

"This wasn't a debut, it was a premiere," said Ted Tinling, the 79-year old tennis historian and chief of protocol for the Grand Slam tournaments. "Capriati has talent. She has rhythm and happiness. She also comes from a happy family and she lived up to her advanced billing. What a gift to American tennis."

Capriati went on to reach the semifinals of the French Open (losing to Seles) as well as the Round of 16 at Wimbledon and the U.S. Open (losing both times to Graf). She also teamed with Zina Garrison in singles to lead the U.S. to victory in the Federation Cup in Atlanta. By September, she had won more than $225,000 in prize money, vaulted to No. 11 on the WTA computer, and had signed three-year endorsement contracts worth more than $6 million.

Tinling, however, witnessed only the beginning of Capriati's career. In May, he died in London of a respiratory ailment and tennis had lost its most eloquent spokesman.

A week after Capriati's pro debut, Nick Bollettieri proteges Agassi and Seles won titles in the Lipton International Players Championships at Key Biscayne, Fla. Agassi thrashed a relatively lethargic Edberg, 6-1, 6-4, 0-6, 6-2, while Seles swept through a field that lacked Graf and Navratilova and crushed Judith Wiesner, 6-1, 6-2, in the final.

Seles soon ended her relationship with Bollettieri and his tennis academy in Bradenton, Fla. The Seles family wanted Bollettieri to spend more time with Monica. Bollettieri, who discovered Seles at the 1985 Orange Bowl tournament and invited her family to move from Yugoslavia to Bradenton, said, "It would be difficult for me to be with her totally," because of his travels with Agassi. The rift turned nasty for a while, Seles saying that her father, Karolj, was her real coach and declining to acknowledge Bollettieri when she won the

French. For his part, Bollettieri threatened to sue for $200,000, saying the Seles family owed him for housing, food and other expenses.

Through it all, the 16-year-old Seles, who had sprouted from 5-3 to 5-9½ the previous year, kept winning. She compiled a 33-match winning streak that didn't end until Garrison beat her in the quarterfinals at Wimbledon. When the streak ended, Seles had won five consecutive tournaments—the U.S. Hard Courts at San Antonio, the Eckerd Open in Tampa, the Italian Open (beating Navratilova), the German Open (ending Graf's 66-match winning streak) and the French Open (Graf again).

Meanwhile, the controversy over her grunting ("uunngh- iiieee!") on practically every shot grew louder. Players said it was distracting, but promotors loved it. An advertisement for a Seles exhibition in Germany said: "Come watch Monica Seles, 'The Grunt Person,' play."

Agassi's hot looks—the long hair and flashy outfits—got him into hot water at the French Open. Philippe Chatrier, the president of the French Tennis Federation, said his group was considering a dress code that would ban colorful garb such as Agassi's faded black shorts and "hot lava" tights. The 20-year-old Agassi responded by calling Chatrier a "bozo."

He also fought his way into his first Grand Slam final. But 30-year-old Gomez of Ecuador, also playing in his first Grand Slam final in 27 attempts, prevailed, 6-3, 2-6, 6-4, 6-4.

The real talk of the French Open, however, was about two former champions who were not there. Lendl and Navratilova shared one obsession in 1990—winning Wimbledon—and they used the two weeks of the French Open to train on grass.

Wimbledon is the only Grand Slam trophy that has eluded Lendl in his 13 years on the tour. He chased it gallantly, but came up short again, losing to Edberg in the semifinals, 6-1, 7-6, 6-3. Boris Becker joined Edberg in the final for the third year in a row, but only after holding off power-serving (105 aces) 18-year-old Goran Ivanisevic of Yugoslavia, 4-6, 7-6, 6-0, 7-6. Trailing two sets to love in the final, Becker almost became the first player since Henri Cochet in 1927 to

Monica Seles beat Steffi Graf twice in 1990, the second time to win the French Open.

come back and win, but Edberg hung on, 6-2, 6-2, 3-6, 3-6, 6-4.

At age 33, Navratilova came to Wimbledon aware that time was beginning to run out on her in her quest to move past Helen Wills Moody and become the tournament's first nine-time singles champion. Tied with Moody at eight wins, Navratilova caught a break when Garrison upset defending champion Graf, 6-3, 3-6, 6-4, in the semifinals. Navratilova beat Sabatini in the semis, 6-3, 6-4, then defeated Garrison, 6-4, 6-1, for title No.9.

"This tops it all," Navratilova said. "I've worked so long and so hard for this. This one means more than any of the others because I had to wait for it."

Agassi was a no-show at the All-England Club. Saying he wanted to take a break, and perhaps fearing staid Wimbledon wouldn't allow him to make a fashion statement, he skipped the tournament. The only year he has played Wimbledon, in 1987, Agassi lost in the first round.

In the weeks leading up to the U.S. Open, the United States women won the Federation Cup for the 14th time and Edberg became the No.1 men's player in the world.

On July 29 in Atlanta, a win by Capriati over Leila Meskhi in singles and a doubles victory by Garrison and Gigi

Fernandez over Natalia Zvereva and Larisa Savchenko enabled the defending champion Americans to defeat the Soviet Union, 2-1, in the Fed Cup.

On Aug. 13, following his victory in the ATP Championship in Cincinnati, Edberg became only the eighth player (and third Swede) to reach No. 1 in the 18-year history of the ATP Tour computer rankings. The other seven holders were Ilie Nastase (for 37 weeks), John Newcombe (7), Jimmy Connors (263), Bjorn Borg (104), John McEnroe (164), Ivan Lendl (267) and Mats Wilander (20). Lendl had been on top for 80 consecutive weeks when Edberg replaced him.

Edberg, however, seemed uncomfortable with his new status. In his second week as No. 1, he was stunned by 52nd-ranked Alexander Volkov of the Soviet Union, 6-3, 7-6, 6-2, in the first round of the U.S. Open. Edberg had also lost in the first round of the French Open (to Sergi Bruguera of Spain) giving him a roller-coaster year in Grand Slams—Australian final, Wimbledon title and quick exits in Paris and New York.

In essence, Edberg's erratic performance was the year in microcosm. So was the U.S. Open, where Gomez lost in the first round, Seles bowed out in the third and Navratilova in the fourth.

You sensed it would be an unusual U.S. Open when New York City Mayor (and tennis fan) David Dinkins helped U.S. Tennis Association officials persuade the Federal Aviation Administration to change the takeoff patterns at La Guardia Airport during the two weeks of the tournament. With rare exceptions, planes didn't roar overhead and disrupt play as they have every year since the championship moved to Flushing Meadows from Forest Hills in 1978.

The sounds of silence, however, gave way to some thunder created by Sampras, Sabatini and a resurgent McEnroe.

The 12th-seeded Sampras, a classic serve-and-volley player from California who began the year ranked 81st, jolted the men's bracket with victories over Lendl in the quarterfinals, McEnroe in the semifinals and Agassi in the final. Unable to stop the unheralded 19-year-old, McEnroe and Agassi kept shaking their heads in disbelief as Sampras blasted ace after ace past them.

Sun setting on McEnroe, Connors era

They were the dominant men's tennis players for much of the 1970s and 1980s, and they did it their way.

Talented, brash and controversial, Jimmy Connors, 38, and John McEnroe, 31, became the most notable players of their era. As the 1990s began, however, their careers were nearing a close. Connors, now an NBC-TV commentator at Wimbledon and the French Open, skipped all four Grand Slam tournaments this year. McEnroe, meanwhile, was thrown out of the Australian Open for cursing a ref, lost in the first round at Wimbledon and entered the U.S. Open unseeded for the first time in 12 years (he reached the semifinals).

From 1973 to 1985, either Connors or McEnroe (or both) was ranked among the top three players in the world on the ATP computer. Both spent four straight years at No.1—Connors from 1974-77 and McEnroe from 1981-84. Connors remained in the top 10 through 1988, while McEnroe was No.4 as recently as 1989.

Between them, they have won nine U.S. Opens, five Wimbledons and two NCAA singles titles. Connors is the all-time Grand Prix titleholder with 109, 26 more than runner-up Ivan Lendl and 34 more than McEnroe. McEnroe has won 74 doubles titles—54 of them with Peter Fleming—and led the U.S. to three Davis Cup championships.

With their careers now in eclipse, where do they rank among the greats of the game?

''I can't put them in my top five, but they're definitely in the top 10,'' says Jack Kramer, who speaks from the perspective of player, administrator and advisor in the game since the 1940s. ''The question is: How they would do against Don Budge, Bill Tilden, Ellsworth Vines, Pancho Gonzales and Rod Laver? That's my top five.

''Jimmy's groundstrokes were fantastic, but each of the five guys I've mentioned had a helluva serve, which Jimmy didn't have. His best game wasn't as good as

In their primes, **John McEnroe** (left) and **Jimmy Connors** each spent four years at No. 1 from 1974-84, yet they met only twice in a Grand Slam final. They split two showdowns at Wimbledon, Connors winning in 1982 and McEnroe in 1984.

seven or eight players I can think of, but you can't fault him on his heart. It carried him a long way.

"As for John, his serve and volley has been as good as anybody's, but my top five had more all-court ability and would have beaten him. The thing I admire about John, though, is his attitude toward the Davis Cup. It tests a player's nerves, knowing that people are counting on you. Connors made a mistake in not accepting that challenge."

Kramer, who turned pro in 1947 after winning Wimbledon and the U.S. Open, controlled pro tennis for 15 years and believes there should be asterisks beside the records of Connors and McEnroe for their on-court behavior.

"They played great, but they sure didn't act it," Kramer says. "Pancho had a lot of problems on the court. There's no getting around the fact that he could be a pretty cranky guy out there, but as far as creating disturbances, John and Jimmy were and are in a class by themselves."

Butch Buchholz, a former Davis Cup player and executive director of the ATP who is now chairman of the Lipton Players Championship, thinks Kramer is being a little too hard on both players.

"I used to love Ion Tiriac's comment that whenever you fine McEnroe $5000, you get $5 million worth of publicity," says Buchholz. "The fact is that John and Jimmy, whatever their behavior, have helped make tennis as popular as it is all over the world. Talk to any cab driver from Bombay to Budapest to Des Moines and they've all heard of McEnroe and Connors."

But how do they compare to the all-time greats?

"They certainly make the top 10," says Buchholz. "Top five, I don't know. McEnroe may be the most talented guy to ever play this game. There wasn't a shot he couldn't hit. And Connors lasted as long as he did, not because he was a great athlete, but because of his heart and his guts. Imagine what you'd get if you had someone with McEnroe's talent and Connors' heart."

Nineteen-year-old **Pete Sampras** routed Andre Agassi in three sets on Sept. 9, to become the youngest U.S. Open men's champion ever.

Sampras smacked his 100th ace of the tournament at championship point to finish off the overmatched Agassi, 6-4, 6-3, 6-2. With his booming serves averaging 120 miles per hour, the stoic Sampras, who grew up studying video tapes of Rod Laver, became the youngest man to win the U.S. Open and the first American to succeed since McEnroe in 1984.

Earlier in the tournament, McEnroe had recaptured some of his old magic before the hometown faithful. Ranked only 20th on the computer and unseeded for the first time since 1978, he knocked off 10th-seeded Andrei Chesnokov in the third round in straight sets. Then, revved up by the crowd, he came back from a two-sets-to-one deficit to beat 7th-seeded Emilio Sanchez, 7-6, 3-6, 4-6, 6-4, 6-3, and sailed into the semifinals with a 6-1, 6-4, 6-4 rout of David Wheaton.

"I had a great run," McEnroe said of his comeback after losing to Sampras in the semis. "I felt I had a great chance to take it all the way, but Pete played really well. I'm not there yet, but I'm not that far away."

Argentina's Sabatini, who had slipped from No.3 to No.5 in the rankings and had been criticized in the media for not fulfilling her potential, atoned for a so-so year by outlasting her longtime nemesis Graf, 6-2, 7-6 (7-4), in the women's final. Sabatini displayed a new fist-pumping feistiness and an aggressive net game that she credited to her new coach, Carlos Kirmayr of Brazil.

For Graf, the loss continued a frustrating year marked by injury and controversy—a broken thumb in a skiing mishap, a corrective operation on her sinuses, and her father Peter's highly publicized paternity suit. After Graf had won her first four tournaments of the year, the allegations surfaced that her father, who had been her first coach, had a relationship with a topless model. The stories clearly affected her play.

"I don't think (the losses) had anything to do with my tennis," she said. "I wasn't my usual self mentally. It was a difficult time for me."

In 1990 Davis Cup competition, West Germany's two-year reign as champion ended in Buenos Aires when Argentina ousted them from the quarterfinals, 3-2. The Germans obviously missed Becker, who didn't play, saying he wanted to concentrate on achieving the No. 1 ranking.

In the semifinals, the Argentines fell meekly (5-0) to Australia in Sydney, while in Vienna, 18-year-old Michael Chang of the United States came back from two sets down in the fifth and final match to defeat Austria's Horst Skoff, 3-6, 6-7, 6-4, 6-4, 6-3, sending the United States into its first Cup final since 1984. The loss erased a memorable performance by Thomas Muster, who beat both Chang and Andre Agassi in singles for Austria's two points.

The American and Australian teams will meet at the Sun Coast Dome in St. Petersburg, Fla., Nov. 30-Dec.2.

Finally, a feud between the ATP Tour and the ITF over control of the men's tour will result in two year-end tournaments. The $2 million ATP World Championship will be played Nov. 13-18, in Frankfurt, followed by the ITF's $6 million Grand Slam Cup, Dec. 11-16, in Munich.

The richer ITF tournament—the winner gets $2 million—is a clear attempt to split the players' allegiance to the ATP. □

THE 1991 INFORMATION PLEASE SPORTS ALMANAC

TENNIS
STATISTICS

THE SEASON IN REVIEW
1989-1990
MEN • WOMEN • WINNERS

SEC A

PAGE 581

1989-90 Tournament Results
Winners of selected men's and women's pro singles championships from Nov.1, 1989 through Sept.16, 1990.

Men's Tour
Late 1989

Finals	Tournament	Winner	Earnings	Loser	Score
Nov. 5	Paris Open	Boris Becker	$300,000	S.Edberg	64 63 63
Nov.12	Stockholm Open	Ivan Lendl	199,800	M.Gustafsson	75 60 63
Nov.12	Silk Cut Championships (London)	Michael Chang	80,000	G.Forget	62 61 61
Nov.12	Sao Paulo (Brazil) Grand Prix	Martin Jaite	20,000	J.Sanchez	76 63
Nov.19	South African Open (Johannesburg)	C.van Rensburg	59,500	P.Chamberlin	64 76 63
Nov.25	Citibank Open (Itapariça, Brazil)	Martin Jaite	55,000	J.Berger	64 64
Dec. 3	Nabisco Masters (New York)	Stefan Edberg	685,000	B.Becker	46 76 63 61

1990 (through Sept.16)

Finals	Tournament	Winner	Earnings	Loser	Score
Jan. 7	BP Nationals (Wellington)	Emilio Sanchez	$22,500	R.Reneberg	67 64 46 64 61
Jan. 7	Australian Hardcourts (Adelaide)	Thomas Muster	18,000	J.Arias	36 62 75
Jan. 14	New South Wales Open (Sydney)	Yannick Noah	21,600	C.Steeb	57 63 64
Jan. 14	New Zealand Open (Auckland)	Scott Davis	18,000	A.Chesnokov	46 63 63
Jan. 28	**Australian Open** (Melbourne)	Ivan Lendl	200,000	S.Edberg	46 76 52(wd)
Feb. 11	Stella Artois Indoor (Milan)	Ivan Lendl	78,000	T.Mayotte	63 62
Feb. 11	Chevrolet Classic (Brazil)	Martin Jaite	18,000	L.Mattar	36 64 63
Feb. 11	Volvo/San Francisco	Andre Agassi	32,400	T.Witsken	61 63
Feb. 18	SkyDome World Tennis (Toronto)	Ivan Lendl	167,500	T.Mayotte	63 60
Feb. 18	Belgian Indoor (Brussels)	Boris Becker	77,500	C.Steeb	75 62 62
Feb. 25	Eurocard Classics (Stuttgart)	Boris Becker	137,500	I.Lendl	62 62
Feb. 25	US Pro Indoor (Philadelphia)	Pete Sampras	135,000	A.Gomez	76 75 62
Mar. 4	ABN Wereld Toernooi (Rotterdam)	Brad Gilbert	65,000	J.Svensson	61 63
Mar. 4	Volvo Indoor (Memphis)	Michael Stich	32,000	W.Masur	67 64 76
Mar. 11	Newsweek Champions Cup (Indian Wells)	Stefan Edberg	125,000	A.Agassi	64 57 76 76
Mar. 11	Trophee Hassan II (Casablanca)	Thomas Muster	18,000	G.Perez-Roldan	61 67 62
Mar. 25	Lipton International (Key Biscayne)	Andre Agassi	179,000	S.Edberg	61 64 06 62
Apr. 8	Prudential-Bache Classic (Orlando)	Brad Gilbert	32,400	C.van Rensburg	62 61
Apr. 8	Estoril (Portugal) Open	Emilio Sanchez	32,400	F.Davin	63 61
Apr. 8	Banespa Open (Brazil)	Luiz Mattar	32,400	A.Sznajder	64 64
Apr. 15	Trofeo Conde de Godo (Barcelona)	Andres Gomez	62,500	G.Perez-Roldan	60 76 36 06 62
Apr. 15	Japan Open (Tokyo)	Stefan Edberg	137,500	A.Krickstein	64 75
Apr. 22	Philips Open (Nice)	Juan Aguilera	32,400	G.Forget	26 63 64
Apr. 22	KAL Cup Korea (Seoul)	Alex Antonitsch	20,160	P.Cash	76 63
Apr. 29	Volvo Monte Carlo Open	Andrei Chesnokov	125,000	T.Muster	75 63 63
Apr. 29	Salem Open (Hong Kong)	Pat Cash	26,640	A.Antonitsch	63 64
May 6	Madrid Grand Prix	Andres Gomez	40,400	M.Rosset	63 76
May 6	BMW Open (Munich)	Karel Novacek	32,400	T.Muster	64 76
May 6	Epson Singapore Super Tennis	Kelly Jones	32,400	R.Fromberg	64 26 76
May 13	German Open (Hamburg)	Juan Aguilera	125,000	B.Becker	61 60 76
May 13	US Clay Court Champs.(Kiawah Is.,SC)	David Wheaton	28,370	M.Kaplan	64 64
May 20	Italian Open (Rome)	Thomas Muster	160,000	A.Chesnokov	61 63 61
May 20	Yugoslav Open (Umag)	Goran Prpic	21,240	G.Ivanisevic	63 46 64
May 27	Internazionali di Tennis (Bologna)	Richard Fromberg	32,400	Marc Rosset	46 64 76
Jun. 10	**French Open** (Paris)	Andres Gomez	370,000	A.Agassi	63 26 64 64
Jun. 17	Stella Artois Grass Champs.(London)	Ivan Lendl	65,250	B.Becker	63 62
Jun. 17	Continental Grass Champs.(Holland)	Amos Mansdorf	32,400	A.Volkov	63 76
Jun. 24	Manchester Open	Pete Sampras	32,400	G.Bloom	76 76
Jul. 8	**Wimbledon** (London)	Stefan Edberg	366,068	B.Becker	62 62 36 36 64
Jul. 15	Swiss Open (Gstaad)	Martin Jaite	39,600	S.Bruguera	63 67 62 62

1989-90 Tournament Results (Cont.)

Men's Tour

Finals	Tournament	Winner	Earnings	Loser	Score
Jul. 22	Mercedes Cup (Stuttgart)	Goran Ivanisevic	$135,000	G.Perez-Roldan	67 61 64 76
Jul. 22	Sovran Bank Classic (Washington, DC)	Andre Agassi	70,000	Jim Grabb	61 64
Jul. 29	Canadian Open (Toronto)	Michael Chang	155,000	J.Berger	46 63 76
Aug. 5	Austrian Open (Kitzbukel)	Horacio dela Pena	48,000	K.Novacek	64 76 26 62
Aug. 5	Volvo/Los Angeles	Stefan Edberg	32,400	M.Chang	76 26 76
Aug. 12	ATP Championship (Cincinnati)	Stefan Edberg	170,200	B.Gilbert	61 61
Aug. 19	US Men's Hardcourts (Indianapolis)	Boris Becker	137,500	P.Lundgren	63 64
Aug. 19	Volvo International (New Haven)	Derrick Rostagno	137,500	T.Woodbridge	63 63
Aug. 26	Hamlet Challenge Cup (Long Island)	Stefan Edberg	32,800	G.Ivanisevic	76 63
Aug. 26	WCT Tourn.of Champions (Forest Hills)	Ivan Lendl		A.Krickstein	64 67 63
Sep. 9	**US Open** (Flushing)	Pete Sampras	350,000	A.Agassi	64 63 62
Sep. 16	Grand Prix Passing Shot (Bordeaux)	Guy Forget	38,800	G.Ivanisevic	64 63

Women's Tour

Late 1989

Finals	Tournament	Winner	Earnings	Loser	Score
Nov. 5	Va.Slims/New England (Worcester)	Mart.Navratilova	$60,000	Z.Garrison	62 63
Nov. 5	Va.Slims/Indianapolis	Katerina Maleeva	17,000	R.Reggi	64 64
Nov. 12	Va.Slims/Chicago	Zina Garrison	50,000	L.Savchenko	63 26 64
Nov. 12	Va.Slims/Nashville	Leila Meshki	17,000	H.Kelesi	62 63
Nov. 19	Va.Slims Championships (New York)	Steffi Graf	125,000	Navratilova	64 75 26 62

1990 (through Sept.16)

Finals	Tournament	Winner	Earnings	Loser	Score
Dec. 17	Rainha Classic (Guaruja, Brazil)	Federica Haumuller	$13,500	P.Tarabini	76 64
Jan. 7	Danone Women's (Brisbane)	Natalia Zvereva	27,000	R.McQuillan	64 60
Jan. 14	New South Wales Open (Sydney)	Natalia Zvereva	45,000	B.Paulus	46 61 63
Jan. 28	**Australian Open** (Melbourne)	Steffi Graf	176,700	M.J.Fernandez	63 64
Feb. 4	Toray Pan Pacific Open (Tokyo)	Steffi Graf	70,000	A.Sanchez	61 62
Feb. 4	Nutrimetics Open (Auckland, NZ)	Leila Meshki	13,500	S.Appelmans	61 60
Feb. 11	Breyers Classic (Wichita)	Dinky Van Rensburg	27,000	N.Tauziat	26 75 62
Feb. 11	Fernleaf Classic (Wellington, NZ)	Wiltrud Probst	13,500	L.Meshkki	16 64 60
Feb. 18	Va.Slims/Chicago	Mart.Navratilova	100,000	Man.Maleeva	63 62
Feb. 25	Va.Slims/Washington, DC	Mart.Navratilova	70,000	Z.Garrison	61 60
Feb. 25	Va.Slims/Oklahoma (Okla.City)	Amy Frazier	27,000	M.Bollegraf	64 62
Mar. 4	Va.Slims/Indian Wells, CA	Mart.Navratilova	70,000	H.Sukova	62 57 61
Mar. 11	Va.Slims/Florida (Boca Raton)	Gabriela Sabatini	70,000	J.Capriati	64 75
Mar. 25	Lipton International (Key Biscayne)	Monica Seles	112,500	J.Wiesner	61 62
Apr. 1	US Women's Hardcourts (San Antonio)	Monica Seles	45,000	Man.Maleeva	64 63
Apr. 1	Va.Slims/Houston	Katerina Maleeva	45,000	A.Sanchez	61 16 64
Apr. 8	Family Circle Cup (Hilton Head, SC)	Mart.Navratilova	100,000	J.Capriati	62 64
Apr. 15	Bausch & Lomb Champs.(Amelia Is.,FL)	Steffi Graf	70,000	A.Sanchez	61 60
Apr. 15	Japan Open (Tokyo)	Catarina Lindqvist	27,000	E.Smylie	63 62
Apr. 22	Eckerd Open (Tampa)	Monica Seles	45,000	K.Maleeva	61 60
Apr. 28	Singapore Open	Naoko Sawamatsu	27,000	S.Loosemoore	76 36 64
Apr. 29	Spain International (Barcelona)	Arantxa Sanchez	27,000	I.Cueto	64 62
May 6	Citizen Cup (Hamburg)	Steffi Graf	70,000	A.Sanchez	57 60 61
May 13	Italian Open (Rome)	Monica Seles	100,000	M.Navratilova	61 61
May 20	Lufthansa Cup (Berlin)	Monica Seles	100,000	S.Graf	64 63
May 27	Strasbourg (France) International	Mercedez Paz	27,000	A.Grossman	62 63
Jun. 10	**French Open** (Paris)	Monica Seles	293,000	S.Graf	76 64
Jun. 17	Dow Classic (Birmingham)	Zina Garrison	27,000	H.Sukova	64 61
Jun. 24	Pilkington Glass Champs.(Eastbourne)	Mart.Navratilova	70,000	G.Magers	60 62
Jul. 8	**Wimbledon** (London)	Mart.Navratilova	354,674	Z.Garrison	64 61
Jul. 22	Va.Slims/Newport, RI	Arantxa Sanchez	45,000	J.Durie	76 46 75
Aug. 5	Player's Canadian Open (Montreal)	Steffi Graf	100,000	K.Maleeva	61 67 63
Aug. 12	Great Amer.Bank Classic (San Diego)	Steffi Graf	45,000	Man.Maleeva	63 62
Aug. 12	Va.Slims/Albuquerque	Jana Novotna	27,000	L.Gildemeister	64 64
Aug. 19	Va.Slims/Los Angeles	Monica Seles	70,000	M.Navratilova	64 36 76
Sep. 9	**US Open** (Flushing)	Gabriela Sabatini	350,000	S.Graf	62 76
Sep. 16	Athens Open	Cecilia Dahlman	13,500	K.Piccolini	75 75

1990 Grand Slam Champions

Australian Open

Men's Singles . . . . Ivan Lendl
Men's Doubles . . . . Pieter Aldrich & Danie Visser
Women's Singles . . . . Steffi Graf
Women's Doubles . Jana Novotna & Helena Sukova
Mixed Doubles . . . . Jim Pugh & Natalia Zvereva

Wimbledon

Men's Singles . . . . Stefan Edberg
Men's Doubles . . . . Rick Leach & Jim Pugh
Women's Singles . . . . Martina Navratilova
Women's Doubles . Jana Novotna & Helena Sukova
Mixed Doubles . . . . Zina Garrison & Rick Leach

French Open

Men's Singles . . . . Andres Gomez
Men's Doubles . . . . . Sergio Casal & Emilio Sanchez
Women's Singles . . . . Monica Seles
Women's Doubles . Jana Novotna & Helena Sukova
Mixed Doubles . . . Arantxa Sanchez & Jorge Lozano

US Open

Men's Singles . . . . Pete Sampras
Men's Doubles . . . . Pieter Aldrich & Danie Visser
Women's Singles . . . . Gabriela Sabatini
Women's Doubles . . . . Gigi Fernandez
. . . . & Martina Navratilova
Mixed Doubles . . . . Elizabeth Smylie
. . . . & Todd Woodbridge

1989-90 Singles Leaders

Official Top 15 computer rankings and money leaders of men's and women's tours for 1989 and unofficial rankings and money leaders for 1990, as compiled by ATP (Association of Tennis Professionals) and WTA (Women's Tennis Association). Note that money list includes doubles earnings.

Final Computer Rankings & Money Won 1989

Listed are titles won (1st), match record (W-L), and earnings for the year.

MEN

	1st	W-L	Earnings
1 Ivan Lendl	10	79-7	$2,344,367
2 Boris Becker	5	64-8	2,216,823
3 Stefan Edberg	2	64-16	1,661,491
4 John McEnroe	3	47-11	946,023
5 Michael Chang	2	47-16	682,130
6 Brad Gilbert	5	60-17	900,848
7 Andre Agassi	1	41-19	478,901
8 Aaron Krickstein	3	50-20	582,651
9 Alberto Mancini	2	36-17	510,430
10 Jay Berger	1	40-19	332,168
11 Martin Jaite	4	51-15	419,209
12 Mats Wilander	0	33-19	295,158
13 Tim Mayotte	1	30-17	362,680
14 Jimmy Connors	2	31-13	250,827
15 Carl-Uwe Steeb	1	39-21	354,717

WOMEN

	1st	W-L	Earnings
1 Steffi Graf	14	83-2	$1,963,905
2 Martina Navratilova . . .	8	68-7	1,285,614
3 Gabriela Sabatini	4	58-12	780,801
4 Zina Garrison	3	59-15	590,653
5 Arantxa Sanchez	2	47-13	549,098
6 Monica Seles	1	33-8	239,361
7 Conchita Martinez	3	34-9	162,583
8 Helena Sukova	1	39-15	431,579
9 Manuela Maleeva	2	34-13	242,183
10 Chris Evert	0	27-9	231,683
11 Jana Novotna	1	50-16	430,896
12 Mary Joe Fernandez . . .	0	32-15	236,455
13 Helen Kelesi	0	36-17	151,569
14 Hana Mandlikova	0	33-19	220,415
15 Katerina Maleeva	3	31-11	143,055

Note: When Chris Evert retired after the U.S.Open she was ranked 4th in the world.

1990 Computer Rankings (through Sept.16)

Men's ATP Tour rankings based on total computer points from each player's 14 best tournaments. Women's WTA Tour rankings based on average computer points awarded for each tournament played. Listed are tournaments played (TP), titles won (1st), match record (W-L), total computer points (Pts), and average computer points (Avg).

MEN

	TP	1st	W-L	Pts
1 Stefan Edberg	18	6	48-10	3195
2 Boris Becker	16	3	50-12	2665
3 Ivan Lendl	15	4	42-7	2567
4 Andre Agassi	14	3	39-8	2292
5 Andres Gomez	24	3	37-17	1949
6 Pete Sampras	21	2	41-13	1718
7 Thomas Muster	23	3	44-13	1638
8 Emilio Sanchez	23	2	44-17	1552
9 Brad Gilbert	23	2	39-19	1512
10 Aaron Krickstein	23	0	30-17	1372
11 Goran Ivanisevic	22	2	38-16	1337
12 John McEnroe	15	0	25-12	1289
13 Michael Chang	18	1	26-13	1285
Andrei Chesnokov	21	1	37-16	1285
15 Guy Forget	22	0	34-18	1176

WOMEN

	TP	1st	W-L	Avg
1 Steffi Graf	13	6	54-4	287.0
2 Martina Navratilova . . .	15	6	48-5	218.3
3 Monica Seles	17	7	45-5	181.2
4 Gabriela Sabatini	15	2	36-10	135.5
5 Zina Garrison	18	1	41-15	120.8
6 Katerina Maleeva	14	1	35-10	116.8
7 Arantxa Sanchez	15	2	37-12	114.5
8 Mary Joe Fernandez . .	12	0	27-8	109.3
9 Manuela Maleeva	17	0	32-12	93.6
10 Jana Novotna	18	1	38-13	80.3
11 Jennifer Capriati	9	0	35-9	76.2
12 Helena Sukova	15	0	29-11	75.8
13 Natalia Zvereva	18	2	40-12	73.1
14 Conchita Martinez	11	0	24-8	68.4
15 Judith Wiesner	17	0	40-15	63.3

1989-90 Singles Leaders (Cont.)

1990 Money Won (through Sept.16)
Includes doubles earnings.

MEN

	Earnings		Earnings		Earnings
1 Stefan Edberg	$1,137,176	6 Pete Sampras	$732,697	10 Jim Courier	$383,845
2 Boris Becker	905,902	7 Goran Ivanisevic	593,285	11 Andrei Chesnokov	370,023
3 Ivan Lendl	797,802	8 Emilio Sanchez	529,839	12 Guy Forget	360,668
4 Andre Agassi	785,212	9 Thomas Muster	490,447	13 Michael Chang	351,512
5 Andres Gomez	784,055	10 Brad Gilbert	473,853	14 Jay Berger	343,184
				15 Jakob Hlasek	326,011

WOMEN

	Earnings		Earnings		Earnings
1 Mart.Navratilova	$1,027,030	6 Zina Garrison	$485,018	11 Mary Joe Fernandez	$281,616
2 Steffi Graf	999,070	7 Helena Sukova	401,684	12 Manuela Maleeva	249,874
3 Monica Seles	875,474	8 Arantxa Sanchez	398,299	13 Jennifer Capriati	225,815
4 Gabriela Sabatini	648,533	9 Natalia Zvereva	393,363	14 Nathalie Tauziat	221,756
5 Jana Novotna	513,482	10 Katerina Maleeva	282,163	15 Judith Wiesner	203,962

National Team Competition

1989 Davis Cup

West Germany successfully defended its Davis Cup title at home in Stuttgart, beating Sweden, 3-2. Boris Becker led the West Germans, winning two singles matches and one doubles.

FINAL

West Germany 3, Sweden 2
(at Stuttgart, Dec.15-17)

Day One—Mats Wilander (SWE) def. Carl-Uwe Steeb (WG), 5-7, 7-6, 6-7, 6-2, 6-3; Boris Becker (WG) def. Stefan Edberg (SWE), 6-2, 6-2, 6-4.

Day Two—Becker & Eric Jelen (WG) def. Anders Jarryd & Jan Gunnarsson (SWE), 7-6, 6-4, 3-6, 6-7, 6-4.

Day Three—Becker (WG) def. Wilander (SWE), 6-2, 6-0, 6-2; Edberg (SWE) def. Steeb (WG), 6-2, 6-4 (best-of-3).

1990 Davis Cup

The United States and Australia reached the final round and were scheduled to meet at the Sun Coast Dome in St.Petersburg, FL, Nov. 30-Dec. 2.

West Germany, playing without Boris Becker, was eliminated by Argentina in the quarterfinals of the 16-team tournament that began Feb. 2.

OPENING ROUND
(Feb. 2-5)

Winner	Loser
at West Germany 3	Holland 2
at Argentina 3†	Israel 0
at New Zealand 3	Yugoslavia 2
at Australia 3	France 2
at Czechoslovakia 5	Switzerland 0
at United States 3†	Mexico 0
Austria 3*	at Spain 2
at Italy 3*	Sweden 2

†Rain cancelled final two singles matches (Feb.4).
*Deciding singles match between Paolo Cane of Italy and Sweden's Mats Wilander was tied at 2 sets apiece when it was suspended due to darkness (Feb.4). It was concluded the next day with Cane beating Wilander, 7-5, in their final set at Cagliari, Italy.

QUARTERFINALS
(Mar.30-Apr.2)

Winner	Loser
Argentina 3*	at West Germany 2
at Australia 3	New Zealand 2
United States 4	at Czechoslovakia 1
at Austria 5	Italy 0

*Alberto Mancini of Argentina led West Germany's Carl-Uwe Steeb in the deciding singles match 7-5,6-3,3-3 when it was suspended due to darkness (Apr.1). Mancini won the final set 6-4 the next day. The defending Cup champion, West Germany, had to play the quarterfinal round without its best player, Boris Becker, who declined to play due to exhaustion.

SEMIFINALS

United States 3, Austria 2
(at Vienna, Sept. 21-24)

Day One—Thomas Muster (AUT) def. Michael Chang (US) 4-6,6-2,6-2,6-4; Andre Agassi (US) def. Horst Skoff (AUT) 7-6,6-0,6-1.

Day Two—Rick Leach & Jim Pugh (US) def. Muster & Alex Antonitsch (AUT) 7-6,3-6,6-0,7-5.

Day Three—Muster (AUT) def. Agassi (US) 6-2,6-2,7-6; Chang (US) def. Skoff (AUT) 3-6,6-7,6-4, 6-4,6-3. Match suspended by darkness after three sets, resumed the next day (Sept.24).

Australia 5, Argentina 0
(at Sydney, Sept. 21-23)

Day 1—Pat Cash (AUS) def. Alberto Mancini (ARG) 6-1,6-1,6-2; Wally Masur (AUS) def. Martin Jaite (ARG) 3-6,6-7,6-4,6-0,6-2.

Day 2—Mark Kratzmann & Darren Cahill (AUS) def. Javier Frana & Christian Miniussi (ARG) 3-6,7-6,7-6, 4-6,15-13. Australia clinches.

Day 3—Cash (AUS) def. Jaite (ARG) 7-5,6-2; Masur (AUS) def. Frana (ARG) 6-2,6-2.

FINAL

Australia at United States (Nov.30-Dec.2)

1990 Federation Cup

The United States women's team won the Federation Cup for the second straight year and the 14th time overall, beating the Soviet Union, 2-1, in Atlanta, July 23-29.

Unlike the Davis Cup, the Fed Cup is contested by 32 teams over seven consecutive days.

FINAL

United States 2, Soviet Union 1

Singles—Natalia Zvereva (USSR) def. Zina Garrison (US), 4-6,6-3,6-3; Jennifer Capriati (US) def. Leila Meskhi (USSR), 7-6,6-2.

Doubles—Garrison & Gigi Fernandez (US) def. Zvereva & Larisa Savchenko (USSR), 6-4,6-3.

THE 1991 INFORMATION PLEASE SPORTS ALMANAC

TENNIS STATISTICS

THROUGH THE YEARS
1900-1990
CHAMPIONS • LEADERS

SEC B

PAGE 585

Grand Slam Championships
MEN
Australian Open

Became an Open Championship in 1969. Two tournaments were held in 1977; the first in January, the second in December. Tournament moved back to January in 1987, so no championship was decided in 1986.
Surface: Synpave Rebound Ace (hardcourt surface composed of polyurethane and synthetic rubber).
First year: 1905. **Most wins:** Roy Emerson (6).
Multiple winners (since 1920): Roy Emerson (6); Jack Crawford, Ken Rosewall (4); Rod Laver, Adrian Quist and Mats Wilander (3); John Bromwich, Ashley Cooper, Stefan Edberg, Johan Kriek, Ivan Lendl, John Newcombe, Frank Sedgman and Guillermo Vilas (2).

Year	Winner	Loser	Score
1920	Pat Wood	R.Thomas	63 46 68 61 63
1921	Rhys Gemmell	A.Hedeman	75 61 64
1922	Pat Wood	G.Patterson	60 36 36 63 62
1923	Pat Wood	C.B.St.John	61 61 63
1924	James Anderson	R.Schlesinger	63 64 36 57 63
1925	James Anderson	G.Patterson	119 26 62 63
1926	John Hawkes	J.Willard	61 63 61
1927	Gerald Patterson	J.Hawkes	36 64 36 18 16 63
1928	Jean Borotra	R.O.Cummings	64 61 46 57 63
1929	John Gregory	R.Schlesinger	62 62 57 75
1930	Gar Moon	H.Hopman	63 61 63
1931	Jack Crawford	H.Hopman	64 62 26 61
1932	Jack Crawford	H.Hopman	46 63 36 63 61
1933	Jack Crawford	K.Gledhill	26 75 63 62
1934	Fred Perry	J.Crawford	63 75 61
1935	Jack Crawford	F.Perry	26 64 64 64
1936	Adrian Quist	J.Crawford	62 63 46 36 97
1937	V.B.McGrath	J.Bromwich	63 16 60 26 61
1938	Don Budge	J.Bromwich	64 62 61
1939	John Bromwich	A.Quist	64 61 63
1940	Adrian Quist	J.Crawford	63 61 62
1941-45	Not held		
1946	John Bromwich	D.Pails	57 63 75 36 62
1947	Dinny Pails	J.Bromwich	46 64 36 75 86
1948	Adrian Quist	J.Bromwich	64 36 63 26 63
1949	Frank Sedgman	K.McGregor	63 63 62
1950	Frank Sedgman	K.McGregor	63 64 46 61
1951	Richard Savitt	K.McGregor	63 26 63 61
1952	Ken McGregor	F.Sedgman	75 1210 26 62
1953	Ken Rosewall	M.Rose	60 63 64
1954	Mervyn Rose	R.Hartwig	62 06 64 62
1955	Ken Rosewall	L.Hoad	97 64 64
1956	Lew Hoad	K.Rosewall	64 36 64 75
1957	Ashley Cooper	N.Fraser	63 911 64 62
1958	Ashley Cooper	M.Anderson	75 63 64
1959	Alex Olmedo	N.Fraser	61 62 36 63
1960	Rod Laver	N.Fraser	57 36 62 86 86
1961	Roy Emerson	R.Laver	16 63 75 64
1962	Rod Laver	R.Emerson	86 06 64 64
1963	Roy Emerson	K.Fletcher	63 63 61
1964	Roy Emerson	F.Stolle	63 64 62
1965	Roy Emerson	F.Stolle	79 26 64 75 61
1966	Roy Emerson	A.Ashe	64 68 62 63
1967	Roy Emerson	A.Ashe	64 61 61
1968	Bill Bowrey	J.Gisbert	75 26 97 64
1969	Rod Laver	A.Gimeno	63 64 75
1970	Arthur Ashe	D.Crealy	64 97 62
1971	Ken Rosewall	A.Ashe	61 75 63
1972	Ken Rosewall	M.Anderson	76 63 75
1973	John Newcombe	O.Parun	63 67 75 61
1974	Jimmy Connors	P.Dent	76 64 46 63
1975	John Newcombe	J.Connors	75 36 64 75
1976	Mark Edmondson	J.Newcombe	67 63 76 61
1977	Roscoe Tanner	G.Vilas	63 63 63
	Vitas Gerulaitis	J.Lloyd	63 76 57 36 62
1978	Guillermo Vilas	J.Marks	64 64 36 63
1979	Guillermo Vilas	J.Sadri	76 63 62
1980	Brian Teacher	K.Warwick	75 76 63
1981	Johan Kriek	S.Denton	62 76 67 64
1982	Johan Kriek	S.Denton	63 63 62
1983	Mats Wilander	I.Lendl	61 64 64
1984	Mats Wilander	K.Curran	67 64 76 62
1985	Stefan Edberg	M.Wilander	64 63 63
1986	Not held		
1987	Stefan Edberg	P.Cash	63 64 36 57 63
1988	Mats Wilander	P.Cash	63 67 36 61 86
1989	Ivan Lendl	M.Mecir	62 62 62
1990	Ivan Lendl	S.Edberg	46 76 52 (ret)

French Open

Prior to 1925, entry was restricted to members of French clubs. From 1941-45, tournament was closed to all foreigners. Became an Open Championship in 1968, but closed to contract pros in 1972.
Surface: Red clay.
First year: 1891. **Most wins:** Max Decugis (8).
Multiple winners (since 1920): Bjorn Borg (6); Henri Cochet (4); Rene Lacoste, Ivan Lendl, Yvon Petra and Mats Wilander (3); Bernard Destremau, Jaroslav Drobny, Roy Emerson, Jan Kodes, Rod Laver, Frank Parker, Nicola Pietrangeli, Ken Rosewall, Manuel Santana, Tony Trabert and Gottfried von Cramm (2).

Year	Winner	Loser	Score	Year	Winner	Loser	Score
1925	Rene Lacoste	J.Borotra	75 61 64	1958	Mervyn Rose	L.Ayala	63 64 64
1926	Henri Cochet	R.Lacoste	62 64 63	1959	Nicola Pietrangeli	I.Vermaak	36 63 64 61
1927	Rene Lacoste	B.Tilden	64 46 57 63 119	1960	Nicola Pietrangeli	L.Ayala	36 63 64 46 63
1928	Henri Cochet	R.Lacoste	57 63 61 63	1961	Manuel Santana	N.Pietrangeli	4661366062
1929	Rene Lacoste	J.Borotra	63 26 60 26 86	1962	Rod Laver	R.Emerson	36 26 63 97 62
1930	Henri Cochet	B.Tilden	36 86 63 61	1963	Roy Emerson	P.Darmon	36 61 64 64
1931	Jean Borotra	C.Boussus	26 64 75 64	1964	Manuel Santana	N.Pietrangeli	63 61 46 75
1932	Henri Cochet	G.de Stefani	60 64 46 63	1965	Fred Stolle	T.Roche	36 60 62 63
1933	Jack Crawford	H.Cochet	86 61 63	1966	Tony Roche	I.Gulyas	61 64 75
1934	Gottfried vonCramm	J.Crawford	64 79 36 75 63	1967	Roy Emerson	T.Roche	61 64 26 62
1935	Fred Perry	G.vonCramm	63 36 61 63	1968	Ken Rosewall	R.Laver	63 61 26 62
1936	Gottfried vonCramm	F.Perry	60 26 62 26 60	1969	Rod Laver	K.Rosewall	64 63 64
1937	Henner Henkel	H.Austin	61 64 63	1970	Jan Kodes	Z.Franulovic	62 64 60
1938	Don Budge	R.Menzel	63 62 64	1971	Jan Kodes	I.Nastasi	86 62 26 75
1939	Don McNeill	B.Riggs	75 60 63	1972	Andres Gimeno	P.Proisy	46 63 61 61
1940	Not held			1973	Ilie Nastase	N.Pilic	63 63 60
1941	Bernard Destremau	n/a	n/a	1974	Bjorn Borg	M.Orantes	67 60 61 61
1942	Bernard Destremau	n/a	n/a	1975	Bjorn Borg	G.Vilas	62 63 64
1943	Yvon Petra	n/a	n/a	1976	Adriano Panatta	H.Solomon	61 64 46 76
1944	Yvon Petra	n/a	n/a	1977	Guillermo Vilas	B.Gottfried	60 63 60
1945	Yvon Petra	B.Destremau	75 64 62	1978	Bjorn Borg	G.Vilas	61 61 63
1946	Marcel Bernard	J.Drobny	36 26 61 64 63	1979	Bjorn Borg	V.Pecci	63 61 67 64
1947	Joseph Asboth	E.Sturgess	86 75 64	1980	Bjorn Borg	V.Gerulaitis	64 61 62
1948	Frank Parker	J.Drobny	64 75 57 86	1981	Bjorn Borg	I.Lendl	61 46 62 36 61
1949	Frank Parker	Budge Patty	63 16 61 64	1982	Mats Wilander	G.Vilas	16 76 60 64
1950	Budge Patty	J.Drobny	61 62 36 57 75	1983	Yannick Noah	M.Wilander	62 75 76
1951	Jaroslav Drobny	E.Sturgess	63 63 63	1984	Ivan Lendl	J.McEnroe	36 26 64 75 75
1952	Jaroslav Drobny	F.Sedgman	62 60 36 64	1985	Mats Wilander	I.Lendl	36 64 62 62
1953	Ken Rosewall	V.Seixas	63 64 16 62	1986	Ivan Lendl	M.Pernfors	63 62 64
1954	Tony Trabert	A.Larsen	64 75 61	1987	Ivan Lendl	M.Wilander	75 62 36 76
1955	Tony Trabert	S.Davidson	26 61 64 62	1988	Mats Wilander	H.Leconte	75 62 61
1956	Lew Hoad	S.Davidson	64 86 63	1989	Michael Chang	S.Edberg	61 36 46 64 62
1957	Sven Davison	H.Flam	63 64 64	1990	Andres Gomez	A.Agassi	63 26 64 64

Wimbledon

Officially called "The Lawn Tennis Championships" at the All-England Club, Wimbledon. Challenge round system (defending champion automatically qualifies for following year's final) used from 1877-1921. Became an Open Championship in 1968, but closed to contract pros in 1972.
Surface: Grass.
First year: 1877. **Most wins:** William Renshaw (7).
Multiple winners (since 1920): Bjorn Borg (5); Rod Laver (4); Bosris Becker, John McEnroe, John Newcombe, Fred Perry and Bill Tilden (3); Jean Borotra, Don Budge, Henri Cochet, Jimmy Connors, Stefan Edberg, Roy Emerson, Lew Hoad, Rene Lacoste and Gerald Patterson (2).

Year	Winner	Loser	Score	Year	Winner	Loser	Score
1920	Bill Tilden	G.Patterson	26 63 62 64	1936	Fred Perry	G.von Cramm	61 61 60
1921	Bill Tilden	B.Norton	46 26 61 60 75	1937	Don Budge	G.von Cramm	63 64 62
1922	Gerald Patterson	R.Lycett	63 64 62	1938	Don Budge	H.Austin	61 60 63
1923	Bill Johnston	F.Hunter	60 63 61	1939	Bobby Riggs	E.Cooke	26 86 36 63 62
1924	Jean Borotra	R.Lacoste	61 36 61 36 64	1940-45	Not held		
1925	Rene Lacoste	J.Borotra	63 63 46 86	1946	Yvon Petra	G.Brown	62 64 79 57 64
1926	Jean Borotra	H.Kinsey	86 61 63	1947	Jack Kramer	T.Brown	61 63 62
1927	Henri Cochet	J.Borotra	46 46 63 64 75	1948	Bob Falkenburg	J.Bromwich75 06 62 36 75
1928	Rene Lacoste	H.Cochet	61 46 64 62	1949	Ted Schroeder	J.Drobny	36 60 63 46 64
1929	Henri Cochet	J.Borotra	64 63 64	1950	Budge Patty	F.Sedgman	61 810 62 63
1930	Bill Tilden	W.Allison	63 97 64	1951	Dick Savitt	K.McGregor	64 64 64
1931	Sidney Wood	F.Shields	walkover	1952	Frank Sedgman	J.Drobny	46 63 62 63
1932	Ellsworth Vines	H.Austin	64 62 60	1953	Vic Seixas	K.Nielsen	97 63 64
1933	Jack Crawford	E.Vines	46 119 62 26 64	1954	Jaroslav Drobny	K.Rosewall	1311 46 62 97
1934	Fred Perry	J.Crawford	63 60 75	1955	Tony Trabert	K.Nielsen	63 75 61
1935	Fred Perry	G.von Cramm	62 64 64	1956	Lew Hoad	K.Rosewall	62 47 75 64

Year	Winner	Loser	Score
1957	Lew Hoad	A.Cooper	62 62 62
1958	Ashley Cooper	N.Fraser	36 62 64 1311
1959	Alex Olmedo	R.Laver	64 63 64
1960	Neale Fraser	R.Laver	64 36 97 75
1961	Rod Laver	C.McKinley	63 61 64
1962	Rod Laver	M.Mulligan	62 62 61
1963	Chuck McKinley	F.Stolle	97 61 64
1964	Roy Emerson	F.Stolle	64 1210 46 63
1965	Roy Emerson	F.Stolle	62 64 64
1966	Manuel Santana	D.Rolston	64 119 64
1967	John Newcombe	W.Bungert	63 61 61
1968	Rod Laver	T.Roche	63 64 62
1969	Rod Laver	J.Newcombe	64 57 64 64
1970	John Newcombe	K.Rosewall	57 63 62 36 61
1971	John Newcombe	S.Smith	63 57 26 64 64
1972	Stan Smith	I.Nastase	46 63 63 46 75
1973	Jan Kodes	A.Metreveli	61 98 63
1974	Jimmy Connors	K.Rosewall	61 61 64
1975	Arthur Ashe	J.Connors	61 61 57 64
1976	Bjorn Borg	I.Nastase	64 62 97
1977	Bjorn Borg	J.Connors	36 62 61 57 64
1978	Bjorn Borg	J.Connors	62 62 63
1979	Bjorn Borg	R.Tanner	67 61 36 63 64
1980	Bjorn Borg	J.McEnroe	16 75 63 67 86
1981	John McEnroe	B.Borg	46 76 76 64
1982	Jimmy Connors	J.McEnroe	36 63 67 76 64
1983	John McEnroe	C.Lewis	62 62 62
1984	John McEnroe	J.Connors	61 61 62
1985	Boris Becker	K.Curran	63 67 76 64
1986	Boris Becker	I.Lendl	64 63 75
1987	Pat Cash	I.Lendl	76 62 75
1988	Stefan Edberg	B.Becker	46 76 64 62
1989	Boris Becker	S.Edberg	60 76 64
1990	Stefan Edberg	B.Becker	62 62 36 36 64

U.S. Open

Challenge round system (defending champion automatically qualifies for following year's final) used from 1884-1911. Amateur and Open championships held in 1968 and '69. Became an exclusively Open championship in 1970.

Surface: Decoturf II (acrylic cement).

First year: 1881. **Most wins:** Richard Sears, William Larned and Bill Tilden (7).

Multiple winners (since 1920): Bill Tilden (7); Jimmy Connors (5); John McEnroe (4); Ivan Lendl and Fred Perry (3); Wilmer Allison, Arthur Ashe, Don Budge, Roy Emerson, Neale Fraser, Pancho Gonzales, Jack Kramer, Rene Lacoste, Rod Laver, John Newcombe, Frank Parker, Bobby Riggs, Ken Rosewall, Frank Sedgman, Stan Smith, Tony Trabert and Ellsworth Vines (2).

Year	Winner	Loser	Score
1920	Bill Tilden	B.Johnston	61 16 75 57 63
1921	Bill Tilden	W.Johnson	61 63 61
1922	Bill Tilden	B.Johnston	46 36 62 63 64
1923	Bill Tilden	B.Johnston	64 61 64
1924	Bill Tilden	B.Johnston	61 97 62
1925	Bill Tilden	B.Johnston	46 119 63 46 63
1926	Rene Lacoste	J.Borotra	64 60 64
1927	Rene Lacoste	B.Tilton	110 63 119
1928	Henri Cochet	F.Hunter	46 64 36 75 63
1929	Bill Tilden	F.Hunter	36 63 46 62 64
1930	John Doeg	F.Shields	108 16 64 1614
1931	Ellsworth Vines	G.Lott Jr.	79 63 97 75
1932	Ellsworth Vines	H.Cochet	64 64 64
1933	Fred Perry	J.Crawford	63 1113 46 60 61
1934	Fred Perry	W.Allison	64 63 16 86
1935	Wilmer Allison	S.Wood	62 62 63
1936	Fred Perry	D.Budge	26 62 86 16 108
1937	Don Budge	G.von Cramm	61 79 61 36 61
1938	Don Budge	G.Mako	63 68 62 61
1939	Bobby Riggs	S.van Horn	64 62 64
1940	Don McNeill	B.Riggs	46 68 63 63 75
1941	Bobby Riggs	F.Kovacs	57 61 63 63
1942	Fred Schroeder	F.Parker	86 75 36 46 62
1943	Joseph Hunt	J.Kramer	63 68 108 60
1944	Frank Parker	B.Talbert	64 36 63 63
1945	Frank Parker	B.Talbert	1412 61 62
1946	Jack Kramer	T.Brown, Jr.	97 63 60
1947	Jack Kramer	F.Parker	46 26 61 60 63
1948	Pancho Gonzales	E.Sturgess	62 63 1412
1949	Pancho Gonzales	F.Schroeder	1618 26 61 62 64
1950	Arthur Larsen	H.Flam	63 46 57 64 63
1951	Frank Sedgman	V.Seixas	64 61 61
1952	Frank Sedgman	G.Mulloy	61 62 63
1953	Tony Trabert	V.Seixas	61 62 63
1954	Vic Seixas	R.Hartwig	36 62 64 64
1955	Tony Trabert	K.Rosewall	97 63 63
1956	Ken Rosewall	L.Hoad	46 62 63 63
1957	Mal Anderson	A.Cooper	108 75 64
1958	Ashley Cooper	M.Anderson	62 36 46 108 86
1959	Neale Fraser	A.Olmedo	63 57 62 64
1960	Neale Fraser	R.Laver	64 64 97
1961	Roy Emerson	R.Laver	75 63 62
1962	Rod Laver	R.Emerson	62 64 57 64
1963	Rafael Osuna	F.Froehling	75 64 62
1964	Roy Emerson	F.Stolle	64 62 64
1965	Manuel Santana	C.Drysdale	62 79 75 61
1966	Fred Stolle	J.Newcombe	42 1210 63 64
1967	John Newcombe	C.Graebner	64 64 86
1968	Arthur Ashe	B.Lutz	46 63 810 60 64
1968	Arthur Ashe	T.Okker	1412 57 63 36 63
1969	Stan Smith	B.Lutz	97 63 61
1969	Rod Laver	T.Roche	79 61 63 62
1970	Ken Rosewall	T.Roche	26 64 76 63
1971	Stan Smith	J.Kodes	36 63 62 76
1972	Ilie Nastase	A.Ashe	36 63 67 64 63
1973	John Newcombe	J.Kodes	64 16 46 62 63
1974	Jimmy Connors	K.Rosewall	61 60 61
1975	Manuel Orantes	J.Connors	64 63 63
1976	Jimmy Connors	B.Borg	64 36 76 64
1977	Guillermo Vilas	J.Connors	26 63 76 60
1978	Jimmy Connors	B.Borg	64 62 62
1979	John McEnroe	V.Gerulaitis	75 63 63
1980	John McEnroe	B.Borg	76 61 67 57 64
1981	John McEnroe	B.Borg	46 62 64 63
1982	Jimmy Connors	I.Lendl	63 62 46 64
1983	Jimmy Connors	I.Lendl	63 67 75 60
1984	John McEnroe	I.Lendl	63 64 61
1985	Ivan Lendl	J.McEnroe	76 63 64
1986	Ivan Lendl	M.Mecir	64 62 60
1987	Ivan Lendl	M.Wilander	67 60 76 64
1988	Mats Wilander	I.Lendl	64 46 63 57 64
1989	Boris Becker	I.Lendl	76 16 63 76
1990	Pete Sampras	A.Agassi	64 63 62

Grand Slam Championships
WOMEN
Australian Open

Became an Open Championship in 1969. Two tournaments were held in 1977, the first in January, the second in December. Tournament moved back to January in 1987, so no championship was decided in 1986.
First year: 1922. Most wins: Margaret Smith Court (11).
Multiple winners: Margaret Smith Court (11); Nancye Wynne Bolton (6); Daphne Akhurst (5); Evonne Goolagong Cawley (4); Steffi Graf, Jean Hartigan and Martina Navratilova (3); Coral Buttsworth, Chris Evert Lloyd, Thelma Long, Hana Mandlikova and Mall Molesworth (2).

Year	Winner	Loser	Score	Year	Winner	Loser	Score
1922	Mall Molesworth	E.Boyd	63 108	1959	Mary Reitano	T.Schuman	62 63
1923	Mall Molesworth	E.Boyd	61 75	1960	Margaret Smith	J.Lehane	75 62
1924	Sylvia Lance	E.Boyd	63 36 64	1961	Margaret Smith	J.Lehane	61 64
1925	Daphne Akhurst	E.Boyd	16 86 64	1962	Margaret Smith	J.Lehane	60 62
1926	Daphne Akhurst	E.Boyd	61 63	1963	Margaret Smith	J.Lehane	62 62
1927	Esna Boyd	S.Harper	57 61 62	1964	Margaret Smith	L.Turner	63 62
1928	Daphne Akhurst	E.Boyd	75 62	1965	Margaret Smith	M.Bueno	57 64 52(ret)
1929	Daphne Akhurst	L.Bickerton	61 57 62	1966	Margaret Smith	N.Richey	walkover
1930	Daphne Akhurst	S.Harper	108 26 75	1967	Nancy Richey	L.Turner	61 64
1931	Coral Buttsworth	M.Crawford	16 63 64	1968	Billie Jean King	M.Smith	61 62
1932	Coral Buttsworth	K.LeMessurier	97 64	1969	Margaret S.Court	B.Jean King	64 61
1933	Joan Hartigan	C.Buttsworth	64 63	1970	Margaret S.Court	K.Melville	63 61
1934	Joan Hartigan	M.Molesworth	61 64	1971	Margaret S.Court	E.Goolagong	26 76 75
1935	Dorothy Round	N.Bolton	16 61 63	1972	Virginia Wade	E.Goolagong	64 64
1936	Joan Hartigan	N.Bolton	64 64	1973	Margaret S.Court	E.Goolagong	64 75
1937	Nancye Wynne	E.Westacott	63 57 64	1974	Evonne Goolagong	C.Evert	76 46 60
1938	Dorothy M.Bundy	D.Stevenson	63 62	1975	Evonne Goolagong	M.Navratilova	63 62
1939	Emily Westacott	N.Hopman	61 62	1976	E.Goolag.Cawley	R.Tomanova	62 62
1940	Nancye Wynne	T.Coyne	57 64 60	1977	K.Melville Reid	D.Balestrat	75 62
1941-45	Not held				E.Goolag.Cawley	H.Gourlay	63 60
1946	Nancye W.Bolton	J.Fitch	64 64	1978	Chris O'Neill	B.Nagelsen	63 76
1947	Nancye W.Bolton	N. Hopman	63 62	1979	Barbara Jordan	S.Walsh	63 63
1948	Nancye W.Bolton	M.Toomey	63 61	1980	Hana Mandlikova	W.Turnbull	60 75
1949	Doris Hart	N.Bolton	63 64	1981	M.Navratilova	C.Evert Lloyd	67 64 75
1950	Louise Brough	D.Hart	64 36 64	1982	Chris Evert Lloyd	M.Navratilova	63 26 63
1951	Nancye W.Bolton	T.Long	61 75	1983	M.Navratilova	K.Jordan	62 76
1952	Thelma Long	H.Angwin	62 63	1984	Chris Evert Lloyd	H.Sukova	67 61 63
1953	Maureen Connelly	J.Sampson	63 62	1985	M.Navratilova	C.Evert Lloyd	62 46 62
1954	Thelma Long	J.Staley	63 64	1986	Not held		
1955	Beryl Pemrose	T.Long	64 63	1987	Hana Mandlikova	M.Navratilova	75 76
1956	Mary Carter	T.Long	36 62 97	1988	Steffi Graf	C.Evert	61 76
1957	Shirley Fry	A.Gibson	63 64	1989	Steffi Graf	H.Sukova	64 64
1958	Angela Mortimer	L.Coghlan	63 64	1990	Steffi Graf	M.J.Fernandez	63 64

French Open

Prior to 1925, entry was restricted to members of French clubs. Became an Open Championship in 1968, but closed to contract pros in 1972.
First year: 1897. **Most wins:** Chris Evert Lloyd (7) and Suzanne Lenglen (6).
Multiple winners (since 1920): Christ Evert Lloyd (7); Margaret Smith Court (5); Helen Wills Moody (4); Hilde Sperling (3); Maureen Connolly, Steffi Graf, Margaret Osborne duPont, Doris Hart, Ann Haydon Jones, Suzanne Lenglen, Simone Mathieu, Margaret Scriven, Martina Navratilova and Lesley Turner (2).

Year	Winner	Loser	Score	Year	Winner	Loser	Score
1925	Suzanne Lenglen	K.McKane	61 62	1940-45	Not held		
1926	Suzanne Lenglen	M.Browne	61 60	1946	Margaret Osborne	P.Betz	16 86 75
1927	Kea Bouman	I.Peacock	62 64	1947	Patricia Todd	D.Hart	63 36 64
1928	Helen Wills	E.Bennett	61 62	1948	Nelly Landry	S.Fry	62 06 60
1929	Helen Wills	S.Mathieu	63 64	1949	M.Osborne duPont	N.Adamson	75 62
1930	Helen W. Moody	H.Jacobs	62 61	1950	Doris Hart	P.Todd	64 46 62
1931	Cilly Aussem	B.Nuthall	86 61	1951	Shirley Fry	D.Hart	63 36 63
1932	Helen W. Moody	S.Mathieu	75 61	1952	Doris Hart	S.Fry	64 64
1933	Margaret Scriven	S.Mathieu	62 46 64	1953	Maureen Connelly	D.Hart	62 64
1934	Margaret Scriven	H.Jacobs	75 46 61	1954	Maureen Connelly	G.Bucaille	64 61
1935	Hilde Sperling	S.Mathieu	62 61	1955	Angela Mortimer	D.Knode	26 75 108
1936	Hilde Sperling	S.Mathieu	63 64	1956	Althea Gibson	A.Mortimer	62 1210
1937	Hilde Sperling	S.Mathieu	62 64	1957	Shirley Bloomer	D.Knode	61 63
1938	Simone Mathieu	N.Landry	60 63	1958	Zsuzsi Kormoczy	S.Bloomer	64 16 62
1939	Simone Mathieu	J.Jedrzejowska	63 86	1959	Christine Truman	Z.Kormoczy	64 75

Year	Winner	Loser	Score
1960	Darlene Hard	Y.Ramirez	63 64
1961	Ann Hayden	Y.Ramirez	62 61
1962	Margaret Smith	L.Turner	63 36 75
1963	Lesley Turner	A.Jones	26 63 75
1964	Margaret Smith	M.Bueno	57 61 62
1965	Lesley Turner	M.Smith	63 64
1966	Ann Jones	N.Richey	63 61
1967	Francoise Durr	L.Turner	46 63 64
1968	Nancy Richey	A.Jones	57 64 61
1969	Margaret S.Court	A.Jones	61 46 63
1970	Margaret S.Court	H.Niessen	62 64
1971	E.Goolagong	H.Gourlay	63 75
1972	Billie Jean King	E.Goolagong	63 63
1973	Margaret S.Court	C.Evert	67 76 64
1974	Chris Evert	O.Morozova	61 62
1975	Chris Evert	M.Navratilova	26 62 61

Year	Winner	Loser	Score
1976	Sue Barker	R. Tomanova	62 06 62
1977	Mima Jausovec	F.Mihai	62 67 61
1978	Virginia Ruzici	M.Jausovec	62 62
1979	Chris Evert Lloyd	W.Turnbull	62 60
1980	Chris Evert Lloyd	V.Ruzici	60 63
1981	Hana Mandlikova	S.Hanika	62 64
1982	M.Navratilova	A.Jaeger	76 61
1983	Chris Evert Lloyd	M.Jausovec	61 62
1984	M.Navratilova	C.Evert Lloyd	63 61
1985	Chris Evert Lloyd	M.Navratilova	63 67 75
1986	Chris Evert Lloyd	M.Navratilova	26 63 63
1987	Steffi Graf	M.Navratilova	64 46 86
1988	Steffi Graf	N.Zvereva	60 60
1989	Arantxa Sanchez	S.Graf	76 36 75
1990	Monica Seles	S.Graf	76 64

Wimbledon

Officially called "The Lawn Tennis Championships" at the All-England Club, Wimbledon. Challenge round system (defending champion automatically qualifies for following year's final) used from 1886-1921. Became an Open Championship in 1968, but closed to contract pros in 1972.

First year: 1884. **Most wins:** Martina Navratilova (9).

Multiple winners (since 1920): Martina Navratilova (9); Helen Wills Moody (8); Billie Jean King (6); Suzanne Lenglen (6 since 1919); Louise Brough (4); Maria Bueno, Maureen Connolly, Margaret Smith Court and Chris Evert Lloyd (3); Evonne Goolagong Cawley, Althea Gibson, Steffi Graf and Dorothy Round (2).

Year	Winner	Loser	Score
1920	Suzanne Lenglen	D.Chambers	63 60
1921	Suzanne Lenglen	E.Ryan	62 60
1922	Suzanne Lenglen	M.Mallory	62 60
1923	Suzanne Lenglen	K.McKane	62 62
1924	Kathleen McKane	H.Wills	46 64 64
1925	Suzanne Lenglen	J.Fry	62 60
1926	Kathleen Godfree	L.de Alvarez	62 46 63
1927	Helen Wills	L.de Alvarez	62 64
1928	Helen Wills	L.de Alvarez	62 63
1929	Helen Wills	H.Jacobs	61 62
1930	Helen W.Moody	E.Ryan	62 62
1931	Cilly Aussem	H.Kranwinkel	75 75
1932	Helen W.Moody	H.Jacobs	63 61
1933	Helen W.Moody	D.Round	64 68 63
1934	Dorothy Round	H.Jacobs	62 57 63
1935	Helen W.Moody	H.Jacobs	63 36 75
1936	Helen Jacobs	H.K.Sperling	62 46 75
1937	Dorothy Round	J.Jedrzejowska	62 26 75
1938	Helen W.Moody	H.Jacobs	64 60
1939	Alice Marble	K.Stammers	62 60
1940-45	Not held		
1946	Pauline Betz	L.Brough	62 64
1947	Margaret Osborne	D.Hart	62 64
1948	Louise Brough	D.Hart	63 86
1949	Louise Brough	M.Osb.duPont	108 16 108
1950	Louise Brough	M.Osb.duPont	61 36 61
1951	Doris Hart	S.Fry	61 60
1952	Maureen Connolly	L.Brough	64 63
1953	Maureen Connolly	D.Hart	86 75
1954	Maureen Connolly	L.Brough	62 75
1955	Louise Brough	B.Fleitz	75 86
1956	Shirley Fry	A.Buxton	63 61
1957	Althea Gibson	D.Hard	63 62
1958	Althea Gibson	A.Mortimer	86 62

Year	Winner	Loser	Score
1959	Maria Bueno	D.Hard	64 63
1960	Maria Bueno	S.Reynolds	86 60
1961	Angela Mortimer	C.Truman	46 64 75
1962	Karen H.Susman	V.Sukova	64 64
1963	Margaret Smith	B.Jean Moffit	63 64
1964	Maria Bueno	M.Smith	64 79 63
1965	Margaret Smith	M.Bueno	64 75
1966	Billie Jean King	M.Bueno	63 36 61
1967	Billie Jean King	A.Haydon Jones	63 64
1968	Billie Jean King	J.Tegart	97 75
1969	Ann Jones	B.Jean King	36 63 62
1970	Margaret S.Court	B.Jean King	1412 119
1971	Evonne Goolagong	M.S.Court	64 61
1972	Billie Jean King	E.Goolagong	63 63
1973	Billie Jean King	C.Evert	60 75
1974	Chris Evert	O.Morozova	60 64
1975	Billie Jean King	E.Goolag.Cawley	60 61
1976	Chris Evert	E.Goolag.Cawley	63 46 86
1977	Virginia Wade	B.Stove	46 63 61
1978	M.Navratilova	Chris Evert	26 64 75
1979	M.Navratilova	Chris Evert Lloyd	64 64
1980	E.Goolag.Cawley	Chris Evert Lloyd	61 76
1981	Chris Evert Lloyd	H.Mandlikova	62 62
1982	M.Navratilova	Chris Evert Lloyd	61 36 62
1983	M.Navratilova	Andrea Jaeger	60 63
1984	M.Navratilova	Chris Evert Lloyd	76 62
1985	M.Navratilova	Chris Evert Lloyd	46 63 62
1986	M.Navratilova	H.Mandlikova	76 63
1987	M.Navratilova	Steffi Graf	75 63
1988	Steffi Graf	M.Navratilova	57 62 61
1989	Steffi Graf	M.Navratilova	62 67 61
1990	M.Navratilova	Z.Garrison	64 61

U.S. Open

Amateur and Open Championships held in 1968 and '69. Became an exclusively Open Championship in 1970.
First year: 1887. **Most wins:** Molla Bjurstedt Mallory (8, including the National Patriotic Tournament in 1917).
Multiple winners (since 1920): Helen Wills Moody (7); Chris Evert Lloyd (6); Margaret Smith Court (5); Pauline Betz, Mario Bueno, Helen Jacobs, Billie Jean King, Molla B.Mallory, Alice Marble and Martina Navratilova (4); Maureen Connolly and Margaret Osborne duPont (3); Tracy Austin, Sarah Palfrey Cooke, Darlene Hard, Doris Hart, Althea Gibson and Steffi Graf (2).

Year	Winner	Loser	Score	Year	Winner	Loser	Score
1920	Molla B.Mallory	M.Zinderstein	63 61	1957	Althea Gibson	L.Brough	63 62
1921	Molla B.Mallory	M.Browne	46 64 62	1958	Althea Gibson	D.Hard	36 61 62
1922	Molla B.Mallory	H.Wills	63 61	1959	Maria Bueno	C.Truman	61 64
1923	Helen Wills	M.B.Mallory	62 61	1960	Darlene Hard	M.Bueno	64 1012 64
1924	Helen Wills	M.B.Mallory	61 63	1961	Darlene Hard	A.Haydon	63 64
1925	Helen Wills	K.McKane	36 60 62	1962	Margaret Smith	D.Hard	97 64
1926	Molla B.Mallory	E.Ryan	46 64 97	1963	Maria Bueno	M.Smith	75 64
1927	Helen Wills	B.Nuthall	61 64	1964	Maria Bueno	C.Graebner	61 60
1928	Helen Wills	H.Jacobs	62 61	1965	Margaret Smith	B.Jean Moffit	86 75
1929	Helen Wills	P.Watson	64 62	1966	Maria Bueno	N.Richey	63 61
1930	Betty Nuthall	A.Harper	61 64	1967	Billie Jean King	A.Haydon Jones	119 64
1931	Helen W.Moody	E.Whitingstall	64 61	1968	Margaret S.Court	M.Bueno	62 62
1932	Helen Jacobs	C.Babcock	62 62	1968	Virginia Wade	B.Jean King	64 62
1933	Helen Jacobs	H.W.Moody 86 36	30(ret)	1969	Margaret S.Court	V.Wade	46 63 60
1934	Helen Jacobs	S.Palfrey	61 64	1969	Margaret S.Court	N.Richey	62 62
1935	Helen Jacobs	S.Palfrey Fabyan	62 64	1970	Margaret S.Court	R.Casals	62 26 61
1936	Alice Marble	H.Jacobs	46 63 62	1971	Billie Jean King	R.Casals	64 76
1937	Anita Lizane	J.Jedrzejowska	64 62	1972	Billie Jean King	K.Melville	63 75
1938	Alice Marble	N.Wynne	60 63	1973	Margaret S.Court	E.Goolagong	76 57 62
1939	Alice Marble	H.Jacobs	60 810 64	1974	Billie Jean King	E.Goolagong	36 63 75
1940	Alice Marble	H.Jacobs	62 63	1975	Chris Evert	E.Goola.Cawley	57 64 62
1941	Sarah P.Cooke	P.Betz	75 62	1976	Chris Evert	E.Goola.Cawley	63 60
1942	Pauline Betz	L.Brough	46 61 64	1977	Chris Evert	W.Turnbull	76 62
1943	Pauline Betz	L.Brough	63 57 63	1978	Chris Evert	P.Shriver	76 64
1944	Pauline Betz	M.Osborne	63 86	1979	Tracy Austin	C.Evert Lloyd	64 63
1945	Sarah P.Cooke	P.Betz	36 86 64	1980	Chris Evert Lloyd	H.Mandlikova	57 61 61
1946	Pauline Betz	P.Canning	119 63	1981	Tracy Austin	M.Navratilova	16 76 76
1947	Louise Brough	M.Osborne	86 46 61	1982	Chris Evert Lloyd	H.Mandlikova	63 61
1948	Margaret O.duPont	L.Brough	46 64 1513	1983	M.Navratilova	C.Evert Lloyd	61 63
1949	Margaret O.duPont	D.Hart	64 61	1984	M.Navratilova	C.Evert Lloyd	46 64 64
1950	Margaret O.duPont	D.Hart	64 63	1985	Hana Mandlikova	M.Navratilova	76 16 76
1951	Maureen Connolly	S.Fry	63 16 64	1986	M.Navratilova	H.Sukova	63 62
1952	Maureen Connolly	D.Hart	63 75	1987	M.Navratilova	S.Graf	76 61
1953	Maureen Connolly	D.Hart	62 64	1988	Steffi Graf	G.Sabatini	63 36 61
1954	Doris Hart	L.Brough	68 61 86	1989	Steffi Graf	M.Navratilova	36 75 61
1955	Doris Hart	P.Ward	64 62	1990	Gabriela Sabatini	S.Graf	62 76
1956	Shirley Fry	A.Gibson	63 64				

Grand Slam Summary

Men's and Women's singles winners of the four Grand Slam tournaments—Australian, French, Wimbledon and United States—since the French was opened to all comers in 1925. Note that there were two Australian Open championships in 1977 and none in 1986.

MEN

Only two men have won the Grand Slam—all four events in a single year: Don Budge in 1938 and Rod Laver in both 1962 and 1969.
Three wins in one year: Jack Crawford (1933); Fred Perry (1934); Tony Trabert (1955); Lew Hoad (1956); Ashley Cooper (1958); Roy Emerson (1964); Jimmy Connors (1974); Mats Wilander (1988).
Two wins in one year: Roy Emerson (4 times); Bjorn Borg (3 times); Rene Lacoste, Ivan Lendl, John Newcombe and Fred Perry (twice); Boris Becker, Don Budge, Henri Cochet, Jimmy Connors, Neale Fraser, Jack Kramer, John McEnroe, Alex Olmedo, Budge Patty, Bobby Riggs, Ken Rosewall, Dick Savitt, Frank Sedgman and Guillermo Vilas (once).

Year	Australia	French	Wmbldon	US	Year	Australia	French	Wmbldon	US
1925	Anderson	Lacoste	Lacoste	Tilden	1934	Perry	vonCramm	Perry	Perry
1926	Hawkes	Cochet	Borotra	Lacoste	1935	Crawford	Perry	Perry	Allison
1927	Patterson	Lacoste	Cochet	Lacoste	1936	Quist	vonCramm	Perry	Perry
1928	Borotra	Cochet	Lacoste	Cochet	1937	McGrath	Henkel	Budge	Budge
1929	Gregory	Lacoste	Cochet	Tilden	1938	**Budge**	**Budge**	**Budge**	**Budge**
1930	Moon	Cochet	Tilden	Doeg	1939	Bromwich	McNeill	Riggs	Riggs
1931	Crawford	Borotra	Wood	Vines	1940	Quist	—	—	McNeill
1932	Crawford	Cochet	Vines	Vines	1941	—	Destremau	—	Riggs
1933	Crawford	Crawford	Crawford	Perry					

Year	Australia	French	Wmbldon	US	Year	Australia	French	Wmbldon	US
1942	—	Destremau	—	Schroeder	1967	Emerson	Emerson	Newcombe	Newcombe
1943	—	Petra	—	Hunt	1968	Bowrey	Rosewall	Laver	Ashe
1944	—	Petra	—	Parker	1969	Laver	Laver	Laver	Laver
1945	—	Petra	—	Parker	1970	Ashe	Kodes	Newcombe	Rosewall
1946	Bromwich	Bernard	Petra	Kramer	1971	Rosewall	Kodes	Newcombe	Smith
1947	Pails	Asboth	Kramer	Kramer	1972	Rosewall	Gimeno	Smith	Nastase
1948	Quist	Parker	Falkenburg	Gonzales	1973	Newcombe	Nastase	Kodes	Newcombe
1949	Sedgman	Parker	Schroeder	Gonzales	1974	Connors	Borg	Connors	Connors
1950	Sedgman	Patty	Patty	Larse	1975	Newcombe	Borg	Ashe	Orantes
1951	Savitt	Drobny	Savitt	Sedgman	1976	Edmondson	Panatta	Borg	Connors
1952	McGregor	Drobny	Sedgman	Sedgman	1977	Tanner	Vilas	Borg	Vilas
1953	Rosewall	Rosewall	Seixas	Trabert		& Gerulaitis			
1954	Rose	Trabert	Drobny	Seixas	1978	Vilas	Borg	Borg	Connors
1955	Rosewall	Trabert	Trabert	Trabert	1979	Vilas	Borg	Borg	McEnroe
1956	Hoad	Hoad	Hoad	Rosewall	1980	Teacher	Borg	Borg	McEnroe
1957	Cooper	Davidson	Hoad	Anderson	1981	Kriek	Borg	McEnroe	McEnroe
1958	Cooper	Rose	Cooper	Cooper	1982	Kriek	Wilander	Connors	Connors
1959	Olmedo	Ptrangeli	Olmedo	Fraser	1983	Wilander	Noah	McEnroe	Connors
1960	Laver	Ptrangeli	Fraser	Fraser	1984	Wilander	Lendl	McEnroe	McEnroe
1961	Emerson	Santana	Laver	Emerson	1985	Edberg	Wilander	Becker	Lendl
1962	Laver	Laver	Laver	Laver	1986	—	Lendl	Becker	Lendl
1963	Emerson	Emerson	McKinley	Osuna	1987	Edberg	Lendl	Cash	Lendl
1964	Emerson	Santana	Emerson	Emerson	1988	Wilander	Wilander	Edberg	Wilander
1965	Emerson	Stolle	Emerson	Santana	1989	Lendl	Chang	Becker	Becker
1966	Emerson	Roche	Santana	Stolle	1990	Lendl	Gomez	Edberg	Sampras

WOMEN

Only three women have won the Grand Slam—all four events in a single year: Maureen Connolly in 1953, Margaret Smith Court in 1970 and Steffi Graf in 1988.

Three in one year: Helen Wills Moody (1928 and 1929); Margaret Smith Court (1962,1965,1969 and 1973); Billie Jean King (1972); Martina Navratilova (1983 and 1984); and Steffi Graf (1989).

Two in one year: Chris Evert Lloyd (5 times); Helen Wills Moody and Martina Navratilova (3 times); Maria Bueno, Maureen Connolly, Margaret Smith Court, Althea Gibson, Billie Jean King (twice); Cilli Aussem, Pauline Betz, Louise Brough, Evonne Goolagong Cawley, Shirley Fry, Darlene Hard, Margaret Osborne duPont, Suzanne Lenglen and Alice Marble.

Year	Australia	French	Wmbldon	US	Year	Australia	French	Wmbldon	US
1925	Akhurst	Lenglen	Lenglen	Wills	1959	Reitano	Truman	Bueno	Bueno
1926	Akhurst	Lenglen	Godfree	Mallory	1960	Smith	Hard	Bueno	Hard
1927	Boyd	Bouman	Wills	Wills	1961	Smith	Hayden	Mortimer	Hard
1928	Akhurst	Wills	Wills	Wills	1962	Smith	Smith	Susman	Smith
1929	Akhurst	Wills	Wills	Wills	1963	Smith	Turner	Smith	Bueno
1930	Akhurst	Moody	Moody	Nuthall	1964	Smith	Smith	Bueno	Bueno
1931	Buttswrth	Aussem	Aussem	Moody	1965	Smith	Turner	Smith	Smith
1932	Buttswrth	Moody	Moody	Jacobs	1966	Smith	Jones	King	Bueno
1933	Hartigan	Scriven	Moody	Jacobs	1967	Richey	Durr	King	King
1934	Hartigan	Scriven	Round	Jacobs	1968	King	Richey	King	Wade
1935	Round	Sperling	Moody	Jacobs	1969	Court	Court	Jones	Court
1936	Hartigan	Sperling	Jacobs	Marble	1970	Court	Court	Court	Court
1937	Bolton	Sperling	Round	Lizane	1971	Court	Goolagong	Goolagong	King
1938	Bundy	Mathieu	Moody	Marble	1972	Wade	King	King	King
1939	Westacott	Mathieu	Marble	Marble	1973	Court	Court	King	Court
1940	Bolton	—	—	Marble	1974	Goolagong	Evert	Evert	King
1941	—	—	—	Cooke	1975	Goolagong	Evert	King	Evert
1942	—	—	—	Betz	1976	Cawley	Barker	Evert	Evert
1943	—	—	—	Betz	1977	Reid	Jausovec	Wade	Evert
1944	—	—	—	Betz		& Cawley			
1945	—	—	—	Cooke	1978	O'Neil	Ruzici	Navtilova	Evert
1946	Bolton	Osborne	Betz	Betz	1979	Jordan	Lloyd	Navrtilova	Austin
1947	Bolton	Todd	Osborne	Brough	1980	Mandlkova	Lloyd	Cawley	Evert
1948	Bolton	Landry	Brough	duPont	1981	Navtilova	Mandlkova	Evert	Austin
1949	Hart	duPont	Brough	duPont	1982	Lloyd	Navtilova	Navtilova	Evert
1950	Brough	Hart	Brough	duPont	1983	Navtilova	Lloyd	Navtilova	Navtilova
1951	Brough	Fry	Hart	Connolly	1984	Lloyd	Navtilova	Navtilova	Navtilova
1952	Long	Hart	Connolly	Connolly	1985	Navtilova	Evert	Navtilova	Mandlkova
1953	Connolly	Connolly	Connolly	Connolly	1986	—	Evert	Navtilova	Navtilova
1954	Long	Connolly	Connolly	Hart	1987	Mandlkova	Graf	Navtilova	Navtilova
1955	Penrose	Mortimer	Brough	Hart	1988	Graf	Graf	Graf	Graf
1956	Carter	Gibson	Fry	Fry	1989	Graf	Sanchez	Graf	Graf
1957	Fry	Bloomer	Gibson	Gibson	1990	Graf	Seles	Navtilova	Sabatini
1958	Mortimer	Kormoczy	Gibson	Gibson					

Note: Because of space limitations, the last names of Martina Navratilova and Hana Mandlikova have been abbreviated to "Navtilova" and "Mandlkova."

All-Time Grand Slam Singles Wins

Men and Women with the most singles victories in the Australian, French, Wimbledon and U.S. championships, through 1990. Note that (*) indicates player did not play in that particular Grand Slam event; and players active in 1990 are in **bold type.**

Top 10 Men

	Aus	Fre	Wim	US	Total
Roy Emerson	6	2	2	2 —	12
Bjorn Borg	0	6	5	0 —	11
Rod Laver	3	2	4	2 —	11
Jimmy Connors	1	0	2	5 —	8
Ivan Lendl	2	3	0	3 —	8
Fred Perry	1	1	3	3 —	8
Ken Rosewall	4	2	0	2 —	8
Rene Lacoste	*	3	2	2 —	7
William Larned	*	*	*	7 —	7
John McEnroe	0	0	3	4 —	7
John Newcombe	2	0	3	2 —	7
William Renshaw	*	*	7	* —	7
Richard Sears	*	*	*	7 —	7
Mats Wilander	3	3	0	1 —	7

Top 10 Women

	Aus	Fre	Wim	US	Total
Margaret S.Court	11	5	3	5 —	24
Helen Wills Moody	*	4	8	7 —	19
Chris Evert Lloyd	2	7	3	6 —	18
Martina Navratilova	3	2	9	4 —	18
Billie Jean King	1	1	6	4 —	12
Maureen Connelly	1	2	3	3 —	9
Steffi Graf	3	2	2	2 —	9
Suzanne Lenglen	*	2	6	0 —	8
Molla Bjurstedt Malloy	*	*	0	8 —	8
Maria Bueno	0	0	3	4 —	7
Evonne Goolagong Cawley	4	1	2	0 —	7

Doubles Teams That Have Won Grand Slam

Only three doubles teams and two players with different partners have won the Grand Slam—all four events in a single year—in men's, women's and mixed doubles. No doubles team or single doubles player has done it more than once.

Men's Doubles

1951 Frank Sedgman, Australia
& Ken McGregor, Australia

Women's Doubles

1960 Maria Bueno, Brazil & two partners
1984 Martina Navratilova, USA & Pam Shriver, USA

Mixed Doubles

1963 Ken Fletcher, Australia
& Margaret Smith, Australia
1967 Owen Davidson, Australia & two partners

Notes: In Women's Doubles—Bueno won Australia with Christine Truman then took the French, Wimbledon and the US with Darlene Hard. In Mixed Doubles—Davidson won Australia with Lesley Turner then took the French, Wimbledon and the US with Billie Jean King.

Year-end Tournaments

MEN

The Masters

The year-end championship of the men's tour from 1970-89. Contested by the year's top eight players. Originally a round-robin, the Masters was revised in 1972 to include a round-robin to decide the four semifinalists then a single elimination format after that. Held at Madison Square Garden in New York from 1978-89, the event will be replaced by the ATP Tour World Championship, Nov. 13-18, in Frankfurt.

Year	Winner	Runner-Up
1970	Stan Smith (4-1)	Rod Laver (4-1)
1971	Ilie Nastase (6-0)	Stan Smith (4-2)

Year	Winner	Loser	Score
1972	Ilie Nastase	S.Smith	63 62 36 26 63
1973	Ilie Nastase	T.Okker	63 75 46 63
1974	Guillermo Vilas	I.Nastase	76 62 36 36 64
1975	Ilie Nastase	B.Borg	62 62 61
1976	Manuel Orantes	W.Fibak	57 62 06 76 61
1978*	Jimmy Connors	B.Borg	64 16 64
1979	John McEnroe	A.Ashe	67 63 75

Year	Winner	Loser	Score
1980	Bjorn Borg	V.Gerulaitis	62 62
1981	Bjorn Borg	I.Lendl	64 62 62
1982	Ivan Lendl	V.Gerulaitis	67 26 76 62 64
1983	Ivan Lendl	J.McEnroe	64 64 62
1984	John McEnroe	I.Lendl	63 64 64
1985	John McEnroe	I.Lendl	75 60 64
1986	Ivan Lendl	B.Becker	62 76 63
1986*	Ivan Lendl	B.Becker	64 64 64
1987	Ivan Lendl	M.Wilander	62 62 63
1988	Boris Becker	I.Lendl	57 76 36 62 76
1989	Stefan Edberg	B.Becker	46 76 63 61

*Tournament switched from December to January in 1977-78, then back to December in 1986.
Note: In 1970, Smith was declared the winner because he beat Laver in their round robin match (46 63 64).

WOMEN

Virginia Slims Championships

The year-end championship of the women's tour since 1977. Contested by the year's top 16 players. Since 1983, the tournament has featured the tour's only best-of-five set final.

Year	Winner	Loser	Score
1977	Chris Evert	B.J.King	62 62
1978	Chris Evert	M.Navratilova	63 63
1979	Martina Navratilova	T.Austin	62 61
1980	Tracy Austin	A.Jaeger	62 62
1981	Tracy Austin	M.Navratilova	26 64 62
1982	Martina Navratilova	C.Evert Lloyd	46 61 62
1983	Martina Navratilova	C.Evert Lloyd	63 75 64

Year	Winner	Loser	Score
1984	Martina Navratilova	H.Sukova	63 75 64
1985	Martina Navratilova	H.Mandlikova	62 60 36 61
1986	Martina Navratilova	S.Graf	76 63 62
1987	Steffi Graf	G.Sabatini	46 64 60 64
1988	Gabriela Sabatini	P.Shriver	75 62 62
1989	Steffi Graf	M.Navratilova	64 75 26 62

All-Time Leaders

Money Won

Men's and women's all-time money winners, from the arrival of open tennis in 1968 through 1989. Totals include doubles earnings.

MEN

		Earnings
1	Ivan Lendl	$15,626,336
2	John McEnroe	10,887,456
3	Jimmy Connors	8,094,670
4	Mats Wilander	7,123,221
5	Stefan Edberg	6,637,795
6	Boris Becker	6,572,705
7	Guillermo Vilas	4,897,967
8	Bjorn Borg	3,607,206
9	Tomas Smid	3,577,835
10	Andres Gomez	3,086,072
11	Anders Jarryd	3,049,671
12	Yannick Noah	3,006,218
13	Brian Gottfried	2,782,514
14	Vitas Gerulaitis	2,778,748
15	Wojtek Fibak	2,724,948

WOMEN

		Earnings
1	Martina Navratilova	$15,343,813
2	Chris Evert	8,896,195
3	Steffi Graf	5,251,345
4	Pam Shriver	4,272,521
5	Hana Mandlikova	3,291,186
6	Helena Sukova	2,910,382
7	Wendy Turnbull	2,748,624
8	Gabriela Sabatini	2,680,646
9	Zina Garrison	2,208,650
10	Billie Jean King	1,965,787
11	Claudia Kohde-Kilsch	1,937,864
12	Tracy Austin	1,925,415
13	Manuela Maleeva	1,600,390
14	Virginia Wade	1,542,278
15	Evonne Goolagong Cawley	1,399,431

Overall Wins

Tournaments

1	Jimmy Connors	109
2	Ivan Lendl	83
3	John McEnroe	75
4	Bjorn Borg	65
5	Guillermo Vilas	61
6	Ilie Nastase	57
7	Rod Laver	47
8	Stan Smith	39
9	Arthur Ashe	33
10	John Newcombe	32
	Manuel Orantes	32
	Ken Rosewall	32
	Mats Wilander	32
14	Tom Okker	29
15	Vitas Gerulaitis	27
16	Jose-Luis Clerc	25
	Brian Gottfried	25
18	Boris Becker	24
19	Eddie Dibbs	22
	Yannick Noah	22
	Harold Solomon	22

Matches

From 1968 through 1989. Note that Billie Jean King and Margaret Smith Court started their careers before Open tennis, so their records are incomplete.

		W	L	Pct
1	Chris Evert	1304	146	.899
2	Martina Navratilova	1211	166	.879
3	Virginia Wade	839	329	.718
4	Billie Jean King	695	155	.818
	Evonne Goolagong Cawley	695	158	.815
6	Wendy Turnbull	577	318	.644
7	Hana Mandlikova	559	186	.750
8	Pam Shriver	529	180	.746
9	Rosie Casals	528	306	.633
10	Virgina Ruzici	490	279	.637
11	Dianne Balestrat	468	269	.635
12	Margaret Smith Court	464	78	.906

Most tournaments won (since 1968); Chris Evert (157); Martina Navratilova (146); Evonne Goolagong Cawley (79); Billie Jean King (78); Virginia Wade (55).

National Team Competition

Davis Cup

Established in 1900 as an annual international tournament by American player Dwight Davis. Originally called the International Lawn Tennis Challenge Trophy. Challenge round system until 1972. Since 1981, the top 16 nations in the world have played a straight knockout tournament over the course of a year. The format is a best-of-five match of two singles, one doubles and two singles over three days. **Multiple winners:** USA (28); Australia (20); Australasia and France (6); British Isles (5); Britain and Sweden (4); West Germany (2).

Challenge Rounds

Year	Winner	Loser	Score	Site	Year	Winner	Loser	Score	Site
1900	USA	Brit. Isles	3-0	Boston	1913	USA	Brit. Isles	3-2	Wimbledon
1901	Not held				1914	Australasia	USA	3-2	New York
1902	USA	Brit. Isles	3-2	New York	1915-18	Not held			
1903	Brit. Isles	USA	4-1	Boston	1919	Australasia	Brit. Isles	4-1	Sydney
1904	Brit. Isles	Belgium	5-0	Wimbledon	1920	USA	Australasia	5-0	N. Zealand
1905	Brit. Isles	USA	5-0	Wimbledon	1921	USA	Japan	5-0	New York
1906	Brit. Isles	USA	5-0	Wimbledon	1922	USA	Australasia	4-1	New York
1907	Australasia	Brit. Isles	3-2	Wimbledon	1923	USA	Australasia	4-1	New York
1908	Australasia	USA	5-0	Melbourne	1924	USA	Australia	5-0	Philadelphia
1909	Australasia	USA	5-0	Sydney	1925	USA	France	5-0	Philadelphia
1910	Not held				1926	USA	France	4-1	Philadelphia
1911	Australasia	USA	5-0	N. Zealand	1927	France	USA	3-2	Philadelphia
1912	Brit. Isles	Australasia	3-2	Melbourne	1928	France	USA	4-1	Paris
					1929	France	USA	3-2	Paris

Davis Cup (Cont.)

Year	Winner	Loser	Score	Site	Year	Winner	Loser	Score	Site
1930	France	USA	4-1	Paris	1953	Australia	USA	3-2	Melbourne
1931	France	Britain	3-2	Paris	1954	USA	Australia	3-2	Sydney
1932	France	USA	3.2	Paris	1955	Australia	USA	5-0	New York
1933	Britain	France	3-2	Paris	1956	Australia	USA	5-0	Adelaide
1934	Britain	USA	4-1	Wimbledon	1957	Australia	USA	3-2	Melbourne
1935	Britain	USA	5-0	Wimbledon	1958	USA	Australia	3-2	Brisbane
1936	Britain	Australia	3-2	Wimbledon	1959	Australia	USA	3-2	New York
1937	USA	Britain	4-1	Wimbledon	1960	Australia	Italy	4-1	Sydney
1938	USA	Australia	302	Philadelphia	1961	Australia	Italy	5-0	Melbourne
1939	Australia	USA	3-2	Philadelphia	1962	Australia	Mexico	5-0	Brisbane
1940-1945	Not held				1963	USA	Australia	3-2	Adelaide
1946	USA	Australia	5-0	Melbourne	1964	Australia	USA	3-2	Cleveland
1947	USA	Australia	4-1	New York	1965	Australia	Spain	4-1	Sydney
1948	USA	Australia	5-0	New York	1966	Australia	India	4-1	Melbourne
1949	USA	Australia	4-1	New York	1967	Australia	Spain	4-1	Brisbane
1950	Australia	USA	4-1	New York	1968	USA	Australia	4-1	Adelaide
1951	Australia	USA	3-2	Sydney	1969	USA	Romania	5-0	Cleveland
1952	Australia	USA	4-1	Adelaide	1970	USA	W.Germany	5-0	Cleveland
					1971	USA	Romania	3-2	Charlotte

Final Rounds

Year	Winner	Loser	Score	Site	Year	Winner	Loser	Score	Site
1972	USA	Romania	3-2	Bucharest	1981	USA	Argentina	3-1	Cincinnati
1973	Australia	USA	5-0	Cleveland	1982	USA	France	4-1	Grenoble
1974	So.Africa	India	walkover	—	1983	Australia	Sweden	3-2	Melbourne
1975	Sweden	Czech.	3-2	Stockholm	1984	Sweden	USA	4-1	Gothenburg
1976	Italy	Chile	4-1	Santiago	1985	Sweden	W.Germany	3-2	Munich
1977	Australia	Italy	3-1	Sydney	1986	Australia	Sweden	3-2	Melbourne
1978	USA	Britain	4-1	Palm Springs	1987	Sweden	India	5-0	Gothenburg
1979	USA	Italy	5-0	San Francisco	1988	W.Germany	Sweden	4-1	Gothenburg
1980	Czech.	Italy	4-1	Prague	1989	W.Germany	Sweden	3-2	Stuttgart

The Federation Cup

Started in 1963 by the International Lawn Tennis Federation as the Davis Cup of women's tennis. The major difference is that all competing countries gather at one site to decide the Cup winner in one week.

Multiple winners: USA (14); Australia (7); Czechoslovakia (5).

Year	Winner	Loser	Score	Site	Year	Winner	Loser	Score	Site
1963	USA	Australia	2-1	London	1977	USA	Australia	2-1	Eastbourne
1964	Australia	USA	2-1	Philadelphia	1978	USA	Australia	2-1	Melbourne
1965	Australia	USA	2-1	Melbourne	1979	USA	Australia	3-0	Spain
1966	USA	Germany	3-0	Italy	1980	USA	Australia	3-0	W.Germany
1967	USA	Britain	2-0	W.Germany	1981	USA	Britain	3-0	Tokyo
1968	Australia	Holland	3-0	Paris	1982	USA	W.Germany	3-0	Santa Clara
1969	USA	Australia	2-1	Athens	1983	Czech.	W.Germany	2-1	Zurich
1970	Australia	Britain	3-0	W.Germany	1984	Czech.	Australia	2-1	Brazil
1971	Australia	Britain	3-0	Perth	1985	Czech.	USA	2-1	Japan
1972	So.Africa	Britain	2-1	Africa	1986	USA	Czech.	3-0	Prague
1973	Australia	So.Africa	3-0	W.Germany	1987	W.Germany	USA	2-1	Vancouver
1974	Australia	USA	2-1	Italy	1988	Czech.	USSR	2-1	Melbourne
1975	Czech.	Australia	3-0	France	1989	USA	Spain	3-0	Tokyo
1976	USA	Australia	2-1	Philadelphia	1990	USA	USSR	2-1	Atlanta

Hale Irwin, 45, became the oldest player to win the U.S. Open on June 18, when he beat Mike Donald in 19 extra holes at Medinah. Irwin has now won the Open three times.

GOLF

*Shoal Creek controversy forces PGA
to reevaluate tournament sites;
Faldo wins Masters, British Open;
Trevino and Nicklaus join Seniors.*

GOLF

1989-90 YEAR IN REVIEW

by Marino Parascenzo

Civil rights finally came in through golf's front door in 1990. Almost 25 years to the day after Congress passed the 1965 Voting Rights Act, a country club holding a major tournament on the PGA tour was forced to admit its first black member.

Shoal Creek Golf Club, outside Birmingham, Ala., host of the 74th PGA Championship (Aug.9-12), became the focus of national attention when club founder and president Hall Thompson said in a newspaper interview that the club would not admit blacks as members.

It should have surprised no one that most country clubs in America have exclusionary practices of one kind or another barring certain groups of people—blacks, Jews, other ethnics, even women—from membership. The focus at Shoal Creek was on the collision of two basic American rights: the right of free

association vs. the right not to be discriminated against on the basis of color, creed or anything else.

The pressure on Thompson, Shoal Creek, and the PGA of America was intense. Following the lead of IBM and Toyota, sponsors of ABC-TV's coverage of the PGA Championship withdrew a reported $2 million in advertising from the telecast. All kinds of groups, from the Southern Christian Leadership Conference to Ted Koppel and "Nightline," joined in the outcry. Civil rights activists threatened to picket the PGA if a black was not admitted. Thompson said Shoal Creek would not be forced into accepting a black. But it was, extending an honorary membership on July 31 to Birmingham businessman Louis J. Willie. That done, the PGA went on as scheduled.

But that wasn't the end of it. By August, all three major golf organizations—the U.S. Golf Association, the PGA Tour, and the PGA of America—issued policy statements saying, in effect, that future tournaments would not be held at clubs that discriminate. Even Augusta National,

Marino Parascenzo has been the *Pittsburgh Post-Gazette's* golf writer since 1975. He is also a contributing editor to *Golf Digest.*

John Pittman, the president of Shoal Creek Country Club, announcing membership policy changes on July 31 that included admitting a black member. The move enabled the club to host the PGA Championship without further controversy.

the home of the Masters, admitted its first black member.

Against this turbulent backdrop, a golf season was going on. The near-meltdown at Shoal Creek almost obscured some of the most exciting times golf has enjoyed in quite a while.

England's Nick Faldo established himself as the sport's premier player by becoming the first man since 1982 to win two majors—the Masters and the British Open—in one year (see box). Hale Irwin appeared from out of nowhere to force a playoff in the U.S. Open and then become the oldest player ever to win it. Wayne Grady of Australia emerged from countryman Greg Norman's shadow to capture the PGA Championship (he and Norman have now won the same number of majors—one). And an unsung, 13-year veteran named Wayne Levi reeled off four wins in 18 weeks to lead the tour in victories.

In European golf, it wasn't all Faldo. Jose Maria Olazabal, the other Span-

iard, was on the rise. Seve Ballesteros, married and with his first child on the way, spent the year spinning his wheels, but not Olazabal, a man whose name itself is a tough layout. Everybody likes to try to pronounce it in his native Basque (all together now: "OH-la-THA-bul") and they got a lot of practice at the World Series of Golf. Olazabal laid waste to punishing Firestone South in Akron, starting off with a 9-under-par 61 and finishing up with an 18-under 262. He won by 12 shots. How do you say "piece of cake" in Basque?

On the PGA's Senior tour, Jack Nicklaus and Lee Trevino both turned 50 and joined up. Nicklaus didn't like being a senior. Trevino loved it and quickly became "Senor Senior" by winning three tournaments before the middle of March and six before the first of July, including the U.S. Senior Open.

The LPGA tour was a mad scramble. By mid-September, Beth Daniel, in the second year of her revival, had won six events, including her first major—the LPGA Championship. Patty Sheehan won five times, and Betsy King won two majors—the U.S. Open and the Nabisco Dinah Shore.

Great golfers are ultimately measured by how they do in major tournaments. And in 1990, nobody measured up to Nick Faldo. In 1989, Faldo became only the second Englishman (after Sandy Lyle in '88) to win the Masters. A year later, on a gorgeous Palm Sunday afternoon in Georgia, he became only the second man to win back-to-back green blazers, equalling Jack Nicklaus' repeat of 1965-66.

Going into the final round, Faldo was three strokes behind leader Raymond Floyd. After opening with a double bogey-6, he was five down. Usually, when Floyd gets his teeth into a lead on the last day of a tournament you can forget about getting it away from him. Not this time. This time, he let go.

Floyd thought he was about to win his second Masters, and, at 47, surpass Nicklaus as the tournament's oldest champion. He led through the second round and the third, and was four up with six holes to play in the last round. "I think what happened was that nobody made a run at me early," Floyd said. "That dictated my play. I started playing for pars. Not consciously, but that's what I did."

Floyd went four shots in front with a birdie at No. 12, but as he headed home on automatic pilot, Faldo pulled to within one with birdies at 13, 15, and 16. Floyd then lost the lead on 17 when he left a simple approach about 50 feet from the hole and three-putted for bogey. Up ahead, Faldo parred the 18th and now Floyd needed a birdie to win or a par to tie. He got the par the hard way, after hitting into two bunkers, and the Masters had its second straight playoff.

Floyd and Faldo each parred the first extra hole, No. 10, and hit good drives on No. 11. But Floyd yanked his 7-iron approach dead left into the pond, while Faldo put an 8-iron 18 feet from the hole. It was over.

"I didn't think I could lose," Floyd said later. "You cannot imagine. I've never felt like this. Ever. I've never felt so devastated."

In June, Curtis Strange was in position

Men's golf has a dominant player again

Golf has a dominant player again.

Nick Faldo, a haughty, no-nonsense Englishman with a rebuilt swing, won both the Masters and the British Open in 1990. In doing so, he became golf's first certifiable main man since the fading of Tom Watson in the mid-1980s. He also answered to a description made by Jack Nicklaus.

At the British Open, Nicklaus, who ought to know, said that to be a dominant player you have to **feel** like a dominant player. You have to have an inner confidence that you're the best guy on the tour and then go out and prove it.

Are you that guy? Faldo was asked after completing his conquest of Augusta and St. Andrews in July—a double that gave him three majors in a year and a half.

"Well, yeah, I feel that way," said Faldo, after pondering the question for a millisecond. "I think what I've done over the past four years, winning four majors and being the first guy in a while (since Watson in 1982) to win two in the same year, says it. Now I feel I can win any tournament."

Faldo, 33, joined the European tour in 1976, won Rookie of the Year honors in 1977 and was the leading money winner in 1983. On the much tougher U.S. tour, however, he was much less successful. He used to be called Nick "Foldo," after his knack for blowing leads when the heat was turned up. Figuring that his problems were more mechanical than mental, in May of 1985 Faldo flew to Orlando, Fla., where countryman and teaching pro David Leadbetter helped him fashion a new swing.

"I wanted a swing that would hold up under pressure," Faldo said. He found it.

Two years later, Faldo won his first British Open. Since then his assault on Grand Slam tournaments reads as follows: 1988—a loss to Curtis Strange (75-71) in an 18-hole playoff for the U.S.Open, a third place at the British Open and a fourth in the PGA; 1989—

Nick Faldo celebrates the successful defense of his Masters title after beating **Raymond Floyd** on the second playoff hole.

victory at the Masters and a 9th at the PGA; and 1990—a second Masters title, a third at the U.S. Open (just missing a three-way playoff with Hale Irwin and Mike Donald), and another British Open trophy.

Some will argue that three of Faldo's four majors were American gifts. In the 1987 British Open, Paul Azinger had a one-shot lead with two holes to play and bogeyed both. In the 1989 Masters, Scott Hoch lost his one-shot lead when he missed a 3-foot par putt at No. 17. In the subsequent sudden death playoff, Hoch could have won the tournament with an 18-inch putt for par on the first extra hole, but he blew that one, too. Still, Faldo didn't give him a second chance, canning a 25-foot birdie putt on the next hole. Finally, in the 1990 Masters, Raymond Floyd led by four with six holes to play, got caught, and then with a clear shot to the green at the second playoff hole, smacked his approach to the left, into the water.

There was no question about the 1990 British Open, though. Faldo dusted Greg Norman in the third round, left Payne Stewart tagging along in the fourth, hit only one bunker all week, had no three-putt greens, and won by five shots with a record 18-under par at the Old Course at St. Andrews.

He got amazing efficiency out of his game. Heading into the '90 British Open, he had played in only seven of the 22 European tournaments and come away with two seconds, a 4th, 5th, 9th, 12th and 54th.

Faldo's outings on the 1990 U.S. tour were few, but profitable. He played in seven events, won the Masters, finished third in the U.S. Open, placed a disappointing 19th at the PGA, and won $345,262. His final American stop comes on Nov.24-25, at the Skins Game in La Quinta, Calif., where he joins Norman, Strange and Nicklaus in the annual $450,000, four-man shootout.

U.S. fans won't see that much more of Faldo in 1991. He was among the foreign golfers who quit the PGA tour this year when commissioner Deane Beman refused to relax the 15-tournament requirement. Count on the Grand Slam events, however. Faldo has yet to win the U.S. Open and the PGA and no one has ever won three straight Masters.

Can he dominate golf's major tournaments in the 1990s, as Nicklaus did from 1964-80? Consider the record he has to shoot at. Through 1990, Faldo trails Nicklaus in majors, 18-3.

to join Willie Anderson in the record book. As a young Scot, Anderson won three consecutive U.S. Opens from 1903-05, something no other golfer has ever done. Now Strange, Open champ in '88 and '89, could match him. And so, Medinah Country Club near Chicago awaited history. But it didn't come from Strange, who arrived having a so-so season and left with a tie for 21st place.

Destiny, as it turned out, chose to smile on Hale Irwin. The USGA often issues special invitations to the Open, and one went out this year to Irwin, a two-time winner in 1974 and '79, who had run out of automatic berths. Irwin returned the kindness by winning the tournament.

Going into the last nine holes of the final round, he trailed leader Mike Donald by six shots. Ordinarily a conservative player, he then ran off four straight birdies at 11, 12, 13 and 14. At 18, he added another by holing a cross-country putt that went 45 feet. When the ball dropped, he tore around the green in a victory lap, high-fiving the fans at the gallery rope.

"In my 22 years of pro golf," Irwin said, "I've never made a putt like that to win, or to give me a chance to win."

This one got him a tie with Donald and it was on to an 18-hole playoff the next day. The USGA is the only major organization that uses the 18-holer, and this one was to end up in sudden-death anyway—the first in Open history.

Irwin was two shots down and fast running out of holes when he pulled off probably the greatest shot of his career on No.16. From 207 yards out on the 436-yard, dogleg left, he hooked a 2-iron around the dogleg and put it six feet from the pin. Birdie. And Donald's lead was down to one.

At 18, Donald was still ahead by one, but hit his second hook of the week into the left rough. Bogey. Irwin made par and they were tied. Sudden death. Very sudden for Donald. Irwin dropped a 10-foot putt for a birdie on the first extra hole and at 45 he was the oldest Open champion ever. "I honest-to-God don't remember hitting that last putt," said Irwin. "All I remember is it going in the hole."

Said Donald, 35, who saw his first chance to win an Open evaporate in one bad swing, "No one will remember I finished second. Five years from now, no one will even remember I was here."

The 1990 British Open was held at the cradle of golf, the Old Course at St. Andrews. And it was there that Faldo removed all doubt that he was the best golfer around.

With an opening 67, he was one off the lead, behind Greg Norman and little-known American Mike Allen. On the second day, Faldo shot 65 and tied Norman for a four-stroke lead through 36 holes. On Saturday, while Norman ballooned to a 76, Faldo shot 67 and took a five-shot lead. A closing 71 gave him a five-stroke victory, his second British Open, and his second major of the year.

"I gotta tell you," Faldo said, "it's wonderful to win at St. Andrews. I really feel like I made history."

Three weeks later, Faldo's hot hand turned cold at Shoal Creek. His chances of tying Ben Hogan's record of three majors in one year faded with a 75 in the second round and an 80 in the third ("Faldo shot WHAT?" a Birmingham newspaper wanted to know).

Next question: Who is Wayne Grady?

Wayne Grady is a 33-year-old Australian who qualifies as one of golf's greatest bridesmaids by virtue of his 29 career second place finishes.

It looked like it was going to happen again in the final round of the PGA when he lost a two-shot lead to Fred Couples on the back nine. Couples, who started the day three strokes back, had birdied 11 and 12, and when Grady bogeyed 12, he took the lead.

After 10 years on the tour, Couples' first major was just over the horizon. But then, in a particularly brutal and sustained act of self-destruction, he reeled off four straight bogeys. In the first three, he blew putts of five feet or less.

"Boom, boom, boom," Couples said. "The bogeys happened so fast, it was kind of sickening." Grady closed with a par 72 for a six-under 282, and a three-stroke win. It was his first major, his second win in six years on the tour, and the fifth title of his career. Someone mentioned that the Shoal Creek discrimination flap would be all that anyone remembered about the 1990 PGA. Maybe so, said Grady, all he knew was that his

Lee Trevino (left) and **Jack Nicklaus** each turned 50 over the winter and became eligible for the Seniors tour. Trevino took the tour by storm, while Nicklaus played only a few tournaments.

name was going on the cup. "And no matter how much you scratch at it, you'll never get it off."

Another Wayne—Levi of upstate New York—had to pass up the PGA with a back injury and failed to make the cut at the Master's and U.S. Open. But nobody else on the men's tour won as many tournaments as he did. From June 10 to Sept. 16, Levi won four titles—the Atlanta Classic, the Western Open, the Greater Hartford Open and the Canadian Open—and found himself in third place on the PGA money list with $772,397. Not bad for a guy who hadn't won a thing since 1985.

Levi seemed as surprised as anyone at his sudden success after 13 years on the tour. "I didn't expect to win here," he said after taking the Canadian Open with a 10-under 278. "I was pretty rusty. I guess it just shows what can happen if you keep plugging away."

Meanwhile, there was the mid-life crisis of Jack Nicklaus. At 50, the Golden Bear would not go quietly into his golden years. Sure, he'd play a few senior tournaments, he said, but not many. Heck, he'd only be beating the same guys he used to beat 20 and 30 years ago.

The crack caused quite a fuss on the Seniors tour. "But nobody wrote the rest of what I said," Nicklaus protested. "I also said, 'And who were beating me.'"

Maybe turning 50 was the tough part. "Yeah, that's it," Nicklaus admitted.

Lee Trevino, on the other hand, couldn't wait to join the senior circuit. "Why should I play those flat-bellies when I can play all the round-bellies?" he said.

Trevino took the tour by storm, winning three times in his first five weeks and began sending Nicklaus flowers—thanks, pal, for not showing up. When Nicklaus did show, they had some interesting duels. At the Senior TPC in June, Nicklaus beat Trevino by six strokes. Three weeks later, they squared off in the final round of the U.S. Senior Open in Paramus, N.J. This time, Trevino shot a 67 and sat back while Nicklaus squandered his lead by turning an easy par-5 into a bogey on 17. Trevino won it in the clubhouse, becoming only the fifth player to win both the regular and Senior Opens (the other four are Arnold Palmer, Gary Player, Billy Casper and Orville Moody).

By mid-September, Trevino had six victories and led the Seniors money list with over $700,000. No wonder he was so happy—in his best year on the PGA tour (1980) he only earned $385,814.

The LPGA Tour was pretty much a

three-woman show by early fall—Daniel leading the pack with six wins, Sheehan with five, and King with three. Daniel and Sheehan had both earned over $640,000 to King's $470,000, but King had won two of the four women's majors—the U.S. Open and the Dinah Shore—both for the second time.

Sheehan was about to take her first major at the Open when she brought back memories of Arnold Palmer in 1966. Twenty-four years earlier, Palmer had led by seven strokes with nine holes to play, then blew sky-high and lost in a playoff to Billy Casper. In July, at the Atlanta Athletic Club, Sheehan led the Open by nine going into a 36-hole finale forced by rain delays. After going 11 up on King early in the day, Sheehan then proceeded to play the last 27 holes in eight over for a 75-76 finish. King, with rounds of 71-70, won by a stroke (284-to-285), becoming only the fifth woman to win back-to-back Opens.

"This sort of thing happens out here," King said. "Sometimes you win when you aren't playing that well. Other times, you play great and lose."

The outcome left Sheehan in tears. "I won't be able to forget this," she said. "It hurts. It hurts a lot."

Two weeks later, at Bethesda (Md.) Country Club, Daniel began the week of the LPGA Championship as the best player never to have won a major. She corrected that in a hurry, although a gruesome double bogey by Rosie Jones helped considerably. Still, it was Daniel's closing 66 against Jones's 72 that did it. Daniel won by a stroke.

"I didn't play as solidly as I needed to," Jones said, "and that's why I lost."

Said Daniel: "I've been second in all the majors. Winning a major was my No. 1 goal from the start of the year."

The year was a benchmark in other ways.

The square grooved clubs controversy went on. You may recall that the Karsten Manufacturing Co., makers of Ping irons, sued the USGA for $100 million a year ago for outlawing their clubs. Well, this year, Karsten and the USGA reached an interesting compromise: the USGA would pretend that the illegal Pings (their grooves were too close together) were now legal, provided Karsten started re-

Patty Sheehan reacts to another missed shot on her way to blowing a nine-stroke lead on the final day of the U.S. Women's Open.

tooling and producing clubs with legal grooves.

Karsten's suit against the PGA tour, which had banned all square grooves, no matter what the distance between them, was still alive as the '90 season wore down.

Elsewhere on the business side, RJR-Nabisco, the PGA tour's biggest single underwriter since 1986, withdrew some $5 million in annual sponsorships at the end of 1990, including the season-ending $2.5 million Nabisco Championship. Nabisco said it wanted a change in marketing strategy.

PGA Tour Commissioner Deane Beman didn't seem worried about losing all that prize money. Golf was still booming. Some 25 million Americans were now playing the game, and courses were sprouting everywhere. Presumably at golf clubs that don't discriminate. ☐

THE 1991 INFORMATION PLEASE SPORTS ALMANAC

G O L F
S T A T I S T I C S

THE SEASON IN REVIEW
1989-1990
PGA • SENIORS • LPGA

SEC A

PAGE 603

1989-90 Tournament Results

Winners of PGA, Seniors and LPGA tournaments from Oct.8, 1989 through Sept.16,1990.

PGA Tour
Late 1989

Last Rd	Tournament	Winner	Earnings	Runner-Up
Oct. 8	Nabisco Texas Open	Donnie Hammond (258)	$108,000	P.Azinger (265)
Oct.21	Disney World/Oldsmobile Classic ...	Tim Simpson (272)	144,000	D.Hammond (273)
Oct.29	Nabisco Championships	Tom Kite (276)*	450,000	P.Stewart (276)
Nov. 5	Asahi Glass Four Tours WCOG	United States (404)	390,000	Europe (416)
Nov.11	Isuzu Kapalua International	Peter Jacobsen (270)*	150,000	S.Pate (270)
Nov.19	RMCC Invitational..............	Curtis Strange/ Mark O'Meara (190)	250,000	Weiskopf/L.Wadkins & Langer/Mahaffey
Nov.28	Skins Game #7	Curtis Strange (11)	265,000	J.Nicklaus (4)
Dec. 3	JCPenney Classic	Bill Glasson/ Pat Bradley (267)*	100,000	D.Waldorf/ P.Sheehan (267)
Dec.10	Chrysler Team Championship	David Ogrin/ Ted Schulz (257)	100,000	B.McCallister/ C.Epps (259)

*Playoffs (3): **Nabisco**—Kite def. Stewart in 2 holes; **Kapalua**—Jacobsen def. Pate in 3 holes; **JCPenney**—Glasson/Bradley def. Waldorf/Sheehan in 4 holes.

1990 (through Sept.16)

Last Rd	Tournament	Winner	Earnings	Runner-Up
Jan. 7	MONY Tournament of Champions ..	Paul Azinger (272)	$135,000	I.Baker-Finch (273)
Jan.14	Northern Telecom Tucson Open	Robert Gamez (270)	162,000	M.Calcavecchia & J.Haas (274)
Jan.21	Bob Hope Chrysler Classic	Peter Jacobsen (339)	180,000	B.Tennyson & S.Simpson (340)
Jan.28	Phoenix Open..................	Tommy Armour III (267)	162,000	J.Thorpe (272)
Feb. 4	AT&T Pebble Beach Nat'l Pro-Am .	Mark O'Meara (281)	180,000	K.Perry (283)
Feb.11	Hawaiian Open	David Ishii (279)	180,000	P.Azinger (280)
Feb.18	Shearson Lehman Hutton Open	Dan Forsman (275)	162,000	T.Armour (277)
Feb.25	Nissan Los Angeles Open.........	Fred Couples (266)	180,000	G.Morgan (269)
Mar. 4	Doral Ryder Open	Greg Norman (273)*	252,000	3-way tie (273)
Mar.11	Honda Classic.................	John Huston (282)	180,000	M.Calcavecchia (284)
Mar.18	The Players Championship	Jodie Mudd (278)	270,000	M.Calcavecchia (279)
Mar.25	The Nestle Invitational	Robert Gamez (274)	162,000	G.Norman (275)
Apr. 1	Independent Insurance Agent Open.	Tony Sills (204)*	180,000	G.Morgan (204)
Apr. 8	**The Masters** (Augusta, GA)	Nick Faldo (278)*	225,000	R.Floyd (278)
Apr. 8	Deposit Guaranty Classic	Gene Sauers (268)	54,000	J.Ferenz (270)
Apr.15	MCI Heritage Classic	Payne Stewart (276)*	180,000	L.Mize & S.Jones (276)
Apr.22	K Mart Greater Greensboro Open .	Steve Elkington (282)	225,000	J.Sluman & M.Reid (284)
Apr.29	USF&G Classic	David Frost (276)	180,000	G.Norman (277)
May 6	GTE Byron Nelson Classic	Payne Stewart (202)	180,000	L.Wadkins (204)
May 13	Memorial Tournament	Greg Norman (216)†	180,000	P.Stewart (217)
May 20	SW Bell Colonial Invitational	Ben Crenshaw (272)	180,000	3-way tie (275)
May 27	BellSouth Atlanta Classic.........	Wayne Levi (275)	180,000	3-way tie (276)
Jun. 3	Kemper Open	Gil Morgan (274)	180,000	I.Baker-Finch (275)
Jun.10	Centel Western Open	Wayne Levi (275)	180,000	P.Stewart (279)
Jun.17	**United States Open** (Medinah,IL) .	Hale Irwin (280)*	220,000	M.Donald (280)
Jun.24	Buick Classic	Hale Irwin (269)	180,000	P.Azinger (271)
Jul. 1	Canon Greater Hartford Open	Wayne Levi (267)	180,000	4-way tie (269)
Jul. 8	Anheuser-Busch Classic	Lanny Wadkins (266)	180,000	P.Stewart (279)
Jul.15	Bank of Boston Classic	Morris Hatalsky (275)	162,000	S.Verplank (276)
Jul.22	**British Open** (St. Andrews)	Nick Faldo (270)	165,850	M.McNulty & P.Stewart (275)
Jul.29	Buick Open	Chip Beck (272)	180,000	3-way tie (273)

1989-90 Tournament Results (Cont.)

1990 (through Sept. 16)

Last Rd	Tournament	Winner	Earnings	Runner-Up
Aug. 5	Federal Express St.Jude Classic	Tom Kite (269)*	$180,000	J.Cook (269)
Aug.12	**PGA Championship** (Shoal Creek,AL)	Wayne Grady (282)	225,000	F.Couples (285)
Aug.19	The International	Davis Love III (+14)	180,000	3-way tie (+11)
Aug.26	NEC World Series of Golf	Jose M.Olazabal (262)	198,000	L.Wadkins (274)
Aug.26	Chattanooga Classic	Peter Persons (260)	108,000	R.Zokol (262)
Sep. 2	Greater Milwaukee Open	Jim Gallagher (271)*	162,000	E.Dougherty & B.Mayfair (271)
Sep. 9	Hardee's Classic	Joey Sindelar (268)*	180,000	W.Wood (268)
Sep.16	Canadian Open	Wayne Levi (278)	180,000	I.Baker-Finch & J.Woodward (279)

†Rain-shortened.
*Playoffs (8): **Doral**—Norman won on 1st hole; **Insurance**—Sills won on 1st hole; **Masters**—Faldo won on 2nd hole; **Heritage**—Stewart won on 2nd hole; **US Open**—Irwin won on 1st hole after he and Donald shot 74s in extra round; **St.Jude**—Kite won on 1st hole; **Milwaukee**—Gallagher won in 1st hole; **Hardee's**—Sindelar won on 1st hole.
  Second-place ties (3 players or more): 3-WAY—**Doral** (P.Azinger, M.Calcavecchia and T.Simpson lost playoff to Norman); **Colonial** (J.Mahaffey, C.Pavin, N.Price); **Atlanta** (K.Clearwater, L.Mize, N.Price); **Buick** (H.Irwin, M.Donald, F.Zoeller); **International** (S.Pate, P.Senior, E.Romero). 4-WAY—**GHO** (M.Calcavecchia, B.Fabel, R.Mediate, C.Perry).

Seniors Tour

Late 1989

Last Rd	Tournament	Winner	Earnings	Runner-Up
Oct. 8	RJR Championship	Gary Player (207)	$202,500	R.McBee (208)
Oct.15	Gatlin Bros.Southwest Classic	George Archer (209)	45,000	O.Moody & J.Powell (209)
Oct.22	TransAmerica Championship	Billy Casper (207)	60,000	A.Geiberger (210)
Nov.12	General Tire Las Vegas Classic	Charles Coody (205)	45,000	C.C.Rodriguez & B.Charles (205)
Nov.19	DuPont Cup (USA-Japan)	United States (1,493)	270,000	Japan (1,527)
Dec. 2	GTE West Classic	Walt Zembriski (197)	52,500	G.Archer & J.Dent (199)
Dec.10	GTE Kaanapali Classic	Don Bies (132)	45,000	D.Douglass (133)
Dec.17	Mazda Champions	Mike Hill/ Patti Rizzo (191)	500,000	Coody/Turner & Bies/Green (192)

1990 (through Sept.16)

Last Rd	Tournament	Winner	Earnings	Runner-up
Jan. 7	MONY Senior Tourn. of Champions	George Archer (283)	$ 37,500	B.Crampton & B.Nichols (300)
Jan.28	Senior Skins Game #3	Arnold Palmer (8)	240,000	J.Nicklaus (8)
Feb. 4	Royal Caribbean Classic	Lee Trevino (206)	60,000	B.Baird & J.Dent (207)
Feb.11	GTE Suncoast Classic	Mike Hill (207)	67,500	L.Trevino (209)
Feb.18	Aetna Challenge	Lee Trevino (200)	60,000	B.Crampton (201)
Feb.25	Chrysler Cup	United States (53½)		International (30½)
Mar. 4	Vintage Chrysler Invitational	Lee Trevino (205)	60,000	3-way tie (206)
Mar.18	Vantage at the Dominion	Jim Dent (205)	45,000	H.Henning (208)
Mar.25	Fuji Electric Grand Slam	Bob Charles (214)	72,000	H.Chi-san (216)
Apr. 1	The Tradition at Desert Mt	Jack Nicklaus (206)	120,000	G.Player (210)
Apr.15	**PGA Seniors Championship**	Gary Player (281)	75,000	C.C.Rodriguez (283)
Apr.22	Liberty Mutual Legends of Golf	Charles Coody/ Dale Douglass (249)	140,000	A.Geiberger/ H.Henning (256)
Apr.29	Murata Reunion Pro-Am	Frank Beard (207)	60,000	W.Zembriski (209)
May 6	Las Vegas Senior Classic	Chi Chi Rodriguez (204)	67,500	G.Archer & C.Coody (205)
May 13	Southwestern Bell Classic	Jimmy Powell (208)	67,500	4-way tie (211)
May 20	Doug Sanders Celebrity Classic	Lee Trevino (203)	45,000	G.Player (209)
May 27	Bell Atlantic Classic	Dale Douglass (206)*	75,000	G.Player (206)
Jun. 3	NYNEX/Golf Digest Commemorative	Lee Trevino (199)*	52,500	3-way tie (199)
Jun.10	Mazda Senior TPC	Jack Nicklaus (261)	150,000	L.Trevino (267)
Jun.17	MONY Syracuse Seniors Classic	Jim Dent (199)	60,000	G.Archer (200)
Jun.24	Digital Seniors Classic	Bob Charles (203)	52,500	L.Trevino (205)
Jul. 1	United States Senior Open	Lee Trevino (275)	90,000	J.Nicklaus (277)
Jul. 8	Northville Long Island Classic	George Archer (208)	67,500	F.Beard & C.Coody (209)
Jul.15	Kroger Senior Classic	Jim Dent (133)†	90,000	H.Henning (134)
Jul.22	Ameritech Senior Open	Chi Chi Rodriguez (203)	75,000	G.Archer & A.Kelley (210)
Jul.29	British Senior Open	Gary Player (280)	45,000	D.Beman & B.Waites (281)
Jul.29	Newport Cup	Al Kelley (134)	45,000	J.P.Cain & J.Dent (136)

Last Rd	Tournament	Winner	Earnings	Runner-Up
Aug. 5	PaineWebber Invitational	Bruce Crampton (205)	67,500	T.Shaw (206)
Aug.12	Sunwest Bank/Charley Pride Classic .	Chi Chi Rodriguez (205)	52,500	3-way tie (207)
Aug.19	Showdown Classic	Rives McBee (202)	52,500	L.Trevino
				& D.Bies (203)
Aug.26	GTE Northwest Classic	George Archer (205)	52,500	B.Crampton (207)
Sep. 2	GTE North Classic	Mike Hill (201)*	67,500	B.Crampton (201)
Sep. 9	Vantage Bank One Classic	Rives McBee (201)	45,000	M.Hill (205)
Sep.16	Greater Grand Rapids Open	Don Massengale (134)†	45,000	3-way tie (135)

†Rain-shortened.

*Playoffs (3): **Bell Atlantic**—Douglas won on 2nd hole; **Commemorative**—Trevino beat Fetchick on 5th hole (Rodriguez and Powell fell out after 1st hole); **GTE North**—M.Hill won on 1st hole.
    Second-place ties (3 players or more): 3-WAY—**Vintage** (D.Douglas, M.Hill, D.Massengale); **Commemorative** (M.Fetchick, J.Powell, C.C.Rodriguez); **Sunwest** (C.Coody, J.Dent, J.Ferree (207). 4-WAY—**SW Bell** (J.Dent, T.Dill, M.Hill, R.McBee).

LPGA Tour

Late 1989

Last Rd	Tournament	Winner	Earnings	Runner-Up
Oct.29	Nichirei International	Colleen Walker (71)	$ 80,000	H.Kobayashi (72)
Nov. 5	Mazda Japan Classic	Elaine Crosby (205)	75,000	D.Coe (208)
Dec. 3	JCPenney Classic	Pat Bradley/	100,000	P.Sheehan/
		Bill Glasson (267)*		D.Waldorf (267)
Dec.17	Mazda Champions	Patti Rizzo/	500,000	Turner/Coody
		Mike Hill (191)		& Green/Bies (192)

*Playoff: JCPenny—Bradley/Glasson won on 4th hole.

1990 (through Sept.16)

Last Rd	Tournament	Winner	Earnings	Runner-Up
Jan.21	Jamaica Classic	Patty Sheehan (212)	$75,000	3-way tie (215)
Feb. 4	Oldsmobile Classic	Pat Bradley (281)*	45,000	D.Eggeling (281)
Feb.18	Phar-Mor Inverrary Classic	Jane Crafter (209)	60,000	N.Lopez (210)
Feb.24	Orix Hawaiian Ladies Open	Beth Daniel (210)	52,500	P.Sheehan
				& A.Benz (213)
Mar. 4	Women's Kemper Open	Beth Daniel (283)	75,000	L.Davies
				& R.Jones (284)
Mar.11	Desert Inn International	Maggie Will (214)	60,000	3-way tie (215)
Mar.18	Circle K Tucson Open	Colleen Walker (276)	45,000	4-way tie (281)
Mar.25	Stan.Register Turquoise Classic	Pat Bradley (280)	75,000	A.Okamoto (281)
Apr. 1	**Nabisco Dinah Shore**...........	Betsy King (283)	90,000	K.Postelwait
				& S.Furlong (285)
Apr. 8	Red Robin Kyocera Inamori Classic . .	Kris Monaghan (276)	45,000	C.Gerring (278)
May 6	Sara Lee Classic	Ayako Okamoto (210)	63,750	5-way tie (211)
May 13	Crestar Classic	Dottie Mochrie (200)	52,500	C.Johnson (209)
May 20	Planters Pat Bradley International ...	Cindy Rarick (+25)	60,000	B.Daniel (+24)
May 27	JCPenney/LPGA Skins Game #1	Jan Stephenson (6 skins)	200,000	J.Carner (4)
May 27	Corning Classic	Pat Bradley (274)	52,500	P.Sheehan (277)
Jun. 3	Lady Keystone Open	Cathy Gerring (208)	45,000	P.Bradley
				& E.Crosby (209)
Jun.10	McDonald's Championship	Patty Sheehan (275)	97,500	4-way tie
Jun.16	Atlantic City Classic	Chris Johnson (275)	45,000	P.Wright (277)
Jun.24	Rochester International	Patty Sheehan (271)	60,000	A.Alcott (275)
Jul. 1	**du Maurier Classic**.............	Cathy Johnston (276)	90,000	P.Sheehan (278)
Jul. 8	Jamie Farr Toledo Classic	Tina Purtzer (205)	48,750	C.Johnson
				& J.Carner (209)
Jul.15	**United States Women's Open**	Betsy King (284)	85,000	P.Sheehan (285)
Jul.22	Phar-Mor Youngstown Classic	Beth Daniel (207)*	60,000	P.Sheehan (207)
Jul.29	**Mazda LPGA Championship**	Beth Daniel (280)	150,000	R.Jones (281)
Aug. 5	Boston Five Classic	Barb Mucha (277)*	52,500	L.Rittenhouse (277)
Aug.12	Stratton Mt. Classic	Cathy Gerring (281)*	67,500	C.Keggi (281)
Aug.19	Big Apple Classic	Betsy King (273)	60,000	B.Daniel (276)
Aug.26	Northgate Classic	Beth Daniel (203)	56,250	C.Johnson
				& P.Hammel (209)
Sep. 3	Rail Charity Classic	Beth Daniel (203)	45,000	S.Sanders (206)
Sep. 9	Cellular One-Ping Championship	Patty Sheehan (208)	52,500	D.Ammaccapane (209)
Sep.16	Safeco Classic	Patty Sheehan (208)	45,000	D.Richard (279)

*Playoffs (4): **Oldsmobile**—Bradley won on 1st hole; **Youngstown**—Daniels won on 1st hole; **Boston Five**—Mucha won on 2nd hole; **Stratton**—Gerring won on 1st hole.
    Second-place ties (3 players or more): 3-WAY—**Jamaica** (P.Bradley, L.Connelly, J.Geddes); **Desert Inn** (A.Okamota, P.Rizzo, V.Skinner). 4-WAY—**Tucson** (P.Bradley, H.Drew, B.King, K.Rogerson); **McDonald's** (K.Albers, C.Gerring, B.King, A.Okamoto). 5-WAY—**Sara Lee** (P.Bradley, J.Carner, D.Coe, B.King, C.Walker).

1989-90 Money Leaders

Official money leaders of PGA, Seniors and LPGA tours for 1989 and unofficial leaders for 1990, as compiled by PGA and LPGA. Listed are tournaments played (TP), titles won (1st), and earnings for the year.

PGA

Final 1989	TP	1st	Earnings	1990 (through Sept.16)	TP	1st	Earnings
1 Tom Kite	23	3	$1,395,278	1 Greg Norman	16	2	$907,977
2 Payne Stewart	24	2	1,201,301	2 Payne Stewart	22	2	826,063
3 Paul Azinger	25	1	951,649	3 Wayne Levi	20	4	772,397
4 Greg Norman	17	2	835,096	4 Hale Irwin	16	2	753,749
5 Mark Calcavecchia	25	2	807,741	5 Paul Azinger	22	1	746,681
6 Tim Simpson	30	2	761,597	6 Mark Calcavecchia	24	0	744,021
7 Curtis Strange	21	1	752,587	7 Fred Couples	21	1	682,499
8 Steve Jones	26	3	745,578	8 Gil Morgan	20	1	613,996
9 Chip Beck	23	0	694,087	9 Lanny Wadkins	21	1	604,433
10 Scott Hoch	27	1	670,680	10 Tom Kite	20	1	580,782
11 Fred Couples	24	0	653,944	11 Larry Mize	20	0	577,688
12 David Frost	26	1	620,430	12 Tim Simpson	23	0	501,189
13 Mark O'Meara	26	1	615,804	13 Peter Jacobsen	20	1	477,688
14 Mark McCumber	20	1	546,587	14 Ian Baker-Finch	21	0	438,463
15 Blaine McCallister	31	2	523,891	15 Wayne Grady	21	1	433,685
16 Wayne Levi	26	0	499,292	16 Chip Beck	23	1	432,816
17 Bob Tway	28	1	488,340	17 Steve Elkington	23	1	419,864
18 Mike Hulbert	34	1	477,621	18 Jim Gallagher Jr	29	1	413,382
19 Bill Glasson	23	1	474,511	19 Mark O'Meara	21	1	402,275
20 Donnie Hammond	25	1	458,741	20 Jodie Mudd	19	1	401,746

Other multiple winners: Robert Gamez and Nick Faldo (2).

SENIORS

Final 1989	TP	1st	Earnings	1990 (through Sept.16)	TP	1st	Earnings
1 Bob Charles	27	4	$725,887	1 Lee Trevino	21	6	$712,102
2 Orville Moody	31	2	647,985	2 George Archer	25	3	546,554
3 Al Geiberger	26	1	527,033	3 Jim Dent	24	3	530,877
4 Gary Player	18	2	514,116	4 Mike Hill	25	2	497,111
5 Dave Hill	26	2	488,541	5 Chi Chi Rodriguez	24	3	486,613
6 Harold Henning	35	0	453,163	6 Charles Coody	23	0	419,858
7 Bruce Crampton	29	2	443,582	7 Jack Nicklaus	4	2	340,000
8 Don Bies	25	3	421,769	8 Gary Player	16	1	336,071
9 Mike Hill	32	0	412,104	9 Bruce Crampton	17	1	319,644
10 Charles Coody	30	1	403,880	10 Rives McBee	29	2	311,141
11 Miller Barber	32	2	370,229	11 Harold Henning	26	0	301,988
12 Jim Dent	23	2	337,691	12 Dale Douglass	23	1	301,588
13 Larry Mowry	27	2	322,788	13 Dave Hill	21	0	281,421
14 Dale Douglass	32	0	313,275	14 Bob Charles	19	2	268,779
15 Walt Zembriski	33	1	291,861	15 Frank Beard	21	1	262,046

LPGA

Final 1989	TP	1st	Earnings	1990 (through Sept.16)	TP	1st	Earnings
1 Betsy King	25	6	$654,132	1 Beth Daniel	21	6	$661,578
2 Beth Daniel	25	4	504,851	2 Patty Sheehan	21	5	640,751
3 Nancy Lopez	21	3	487,153	3 Betsy King	24	3	470,760
4 Pat Bradley	26	1	423,714	4 Pat Bradley	24	3	439,076
5 Patty Sheehan	20	1	253,605	5 Rosie Jones	21	0	319,391
6 Ayako Okamoto	19	1	205,745	6 Ayako Okamoto	18	0	292,073
7 Colleen Walker	27	0	204,666	7 Cathy Gerring	25	2	280,931
8 Tammie Green	23	1	204,143	8 Cindy Rarick	25	1	217,221
9 Patti Rizzo	26	1	198,868	9 Danielle Ammaccapane	23	0	205,439
10 Sherri Turner	26	1	198,353	10 Dottie Mochrie	23	1	194,053
11 Cindy Rarick	30	1	196,611	11 Dawn Coe	22	0	192,728
12 Jane Geddes	25	0	186,485	12 Colleen Walker	23	0	191,881
13 Laura Davies	18	1	181,574	13 Deb Richard	23	0	172,110
14 Juli Inkster	21	2	180,848	14 Chris Johnson	13	1	168,362
15 Alice Ritzman	26	0	177,507	15 Jane Geddes	25	0	163,491

THE 1991 INFORMATION PLEASE SPORTS ALMANAC

GOLF STATISTICS

THROUGH THE YEARS 1860-1990
CHAMPIONS • LEADERS

SEC B

PAGE 607

Major Championships

MEN

The Masters

The Masters has been played every year since 1934 at the Augusta National Golf Club in Augusta, GA. Both the course (6905 yards, par 72) and the tournament were created by Bobby Jones.

Multiple winners: Jack Nicklaus (6); Arnold Palmer (4); Jimmy Demaret, Gary Player and Sam Snead (3); Seve Ballesteros, Nick Faldo, Ben Hogan, Byron Nelson, Horton Smith and Tom Watson (2).

Year	Winner	Year	Winner	Year	Winner	Year	Winner
1934	Horton Smith	1949	Sam Snead	1963	Jack Nicklaus	1977	Tom Watson
1935	Gene Sarazen*	1950	Jimmy Demaret	1964	Arnold Palmer	1978	Gary Player
1936	Horton Smith	1951	Ben Hogan	1965	Jack Nicklaus	1979	Fuzzy Zoeller*
1937	Byron Nelson	1952	Sam Snead	1966	Jack Nicklaus*		
1938	Henry Picard	1953	Ben Hogan	1967	Gary Brewer	1980	Seve Ballesteros
1939	Ralph Guldahl	1954	Sam Snead*	1968	Bob Goalby	1981	Tom Watson
		1955	Cary Middlecoff	1969	George Archer	1982	Craig Stadler*
1940	Jimmy Demaret	1956	Jack Burke, Jr.			1983	Seve Ballesteros
1941	Craig Wood	1957	Doug Ford	1970	Billy Casper*	1984	Ben Crenshaw
1942	Byron Nelson*	1958	Arnold Palmer	1971	Charles Coody	1985	Bernhard Langer
1943	Not held	1959	Art Wall, Jr.	1972	Jack Nicklaus	1986	Jack Nicklaus
1944	Not held			1973	Tommy Aaron	1987	Larry Mize*
1945	Not held	1960	Arnold Palmer	1974	Gary Player	1988	Sandy Lyle
1946	Herman Keiser	1961	Gary Player	1975	Jack Nicklaus	1989	Nick Faldo*
1947	Jimmy Demaret	1962	Arnold Palmer*	1976	Raymond Floyd		
1948	Claude Harmon					1990	Nick Faldo*

*PLAYOFFS

1935: Sarazen (144) def. Craig Wood (149) in 36 holes. **1942:** Nelson (69) def. Ben Hogan (70) in 18 holes. **1954:** Snead (70) def. Ben Hogan (71) in 18 holes. **1962:** Palmer (68) def. Gary Player (71) and Dow Finsterwald (77) in 18 holes. **1966:** Nicklaus (70) def. Tommy Jacobs (72) and Gay Brewer (78) in 18 holes. **1970:** Casper (69) def. Gene Littler (74) in 18 holes. **1979:** Zoeller (4-3) def. Ed Sneed (4-4) and Tom Watson (4-4) on 2nd hole of sudden death. **1982:** Stadler (4) def. Dan Pohl (5) on 1st hole of sudden death. **1987:** Mize (4-3) def. Greg Norman (4-4) and Seve Ballesteros (5) on 2nd hole of sudden death. **1989:** Faldo (5-3) def. Scott Hoch (5-4) on 2nd hole of sudden death. **1990:** Faldo (4-4) def. Raymond Floyd (4-x) on second hole of sudden death.

U.S. Open

Played at a different course each year, the US Open was launched by the new US Golf Association in 1895. The Open switched from a 3-day, 36-hole Saturday finish to 4 days of play in 1965.

Multiple winners: Willie Anderson, Ben Hogan, Bobby Jones and Jack Nicklaus (4); Hale Irwin (3); Julius Boros, Billy Casper, Ralph Guldahl, Walter Hagen, John McDermott, Cary Middlecoff, Andy North, Gene Sarazen, Alex Smith, Curtis Strange and Lee Trevino (2).

Year	Winner	Year	Winner	Year	Winner	Year	Winner
1895	Horace Rawlins	1910	Alex Smith*	1925	Willie Macfarlane*	1940	Lawson Little*
1896	James Foulis	1911	John McDermott*	1926	a-Bobby Jones	1941	Craig Wood
1897	Joe Lloyd	1912	John McDermott	1927	Tommy Armour*	1942	Not held
1898	Fred Herd	1913	a-Francis Ouimet*	1928	Johnny Farrell*	1943	Not held
1899	Willie Smith	1914	Walter Hagen	1929	a-Bobby Jones*	1944	Not held
		1915	a-Jerry Travers			1945	Not held
1900	Harry Vardon	1916	a-Chick Evans	1930	a-Bobby Jones	1946	Lloyd Mangrum*
1901	Willie Anderson*	1917	Not held	1931	Billy Burke*	1947	Lew Worsham*
1902	Laurie Auchterlonie	1918	Not held	1932	Gene Sarazen	1948	Ben Hogan
1903	Willie Anderson*	1919	Walter Hagen*	1933	a-John Goodman	1949	Cary Middlecoff
1904	Willie Anderson			1934	Olin Dutra		
1905	Willie Anderson	1920	Edward Ray	1935	Sam Parks, Jr.	1950	Ben Hogan*
1906	Alex Smith	1921	Jim Barnes	1936	Tony Manero	1951	Ben Hogan
1907	Alex Ross	1922	Gene Sarazen	1937	Ralph Guldahl	1952	Julius Boros
1908	Fred McLeod*	1923	a-Bobby Jones*	1938	Ralph Guldahl	1953	Ben Hogan
1909	George Sargent	1924	Cyril Walker	1939	Byron Nelson*	1954	Ed Furgol

U.S. Open (Cont.)

Year Winner	Year Winner	Year Winner	Year Winner
1955 Jack Fleck*	1964 Ken Venturi	1973 Johnny Miller	1982 Tom Watson
1956 Cary Middlecoff	1965 Gary Player*	1974 Hale Irwin	1983 Larry Nelson
1957 Dick Mayer*	1966 Billy Casper*	1975 Lou Graham*	1984 Fuzzy Zoeller*
1958 Tommy Bolt	1967 Jack Nicklaus	1976 Jerry Pate	1985 Andy North
1959 Billy Casper	1968 Lee Trevino	1977 Hubert Green	1986 Raymond Floyd
	1969 Orville Moody	1978 Andy North	1987 Scott Simpson
1960 Arnold Palmer		1979 Hale Irwin	1988 Curtis Strange*
1961 Gene Littler	1970 Tony Jacklin		1989 Curtis Strange
1962 Jack Nicklaus*	1971 Lee Trevino*	1980 Jack Nicklaus	
1963 Julius Boros*	1972 Jack Nicklaus	1981 David Graham	1990 Hale Irwin*

*PLAYOFFS

1901: Anderson (85) def. Alex Smith (86) in 18 holes. **1903:** Anderson (82) def. David Brown (84) in 18 holes. **1908:** McLeod (77) def. Willie Smith (83) in 18 holes. **1910:** A.Smith (71) def. John McDermott (75) & Macdonald Smith (77) in 18 holes. **1911:** McDermott (80) def. Mike Brady (82) & George Simpson (85) in 18 holes. **1913:** Ouimet (72) def. Harry Vardon (77) & Edward Ray (78) in 18 holes. **1919:** Hagen (77) def. Mike Brady (78) in 18 holes. **1923:** Jones (76) def. Bobby Cruickshank (78) in 18 holes. **1925:** Macfarlane (75-72) def. Bobby Jones (75-73) in 36 holes. **1927:** Armour (76) def. Harry Cooper (79) in 18 holes. **1928:** Farrell (143) def. Bobby Jones (144) in 36 holes. **1929:** Jones (141) def. Al Espinosa (164) in 36 holes. **1931:** Burke (149-148) def. George Von Elm (149-149) in 72 holes. **1939:** B.Nelson (68-70) def. Craig Wood (68-73) in 36 holes. **1940:** Little (70) def. Gene Sarazen (73) in 18 holes. **1946:** Mangrum (72-72) def. Byron Nelson (72-73) and Vic Ghezzi (72-73) in 36 holes. **1947:** Worsham (69) def. Sam Snead·(70) in 18 holes. **1950:** Hogan (69) def. Lloyd Mangrum (73) & George Fazio (75) in 18 holes. **1955:** Fleck (69) def. Ben Hogan (72) in 18 holes. **1957:** Mayer (72) def. Cary Middlecoff (79) in 18 holes. **1962:** Nicklaus (71) def. Arnold Palmer (74) in 18 holes. **1963:** Boros (70) def. Jacky Cupit (73) & Arnold Palmer (76) in 18 holes. **1965:** Player (71) def. Kel Nagle (74) in 18 holes. **1966:** Casper (69) def. Arnold Palmer (73) in 18 holes. **1971:** Trevino (68) def. Jack Nicklaus (71) in 18 holes. **1975:** L.Graham (71) def. John Mahaffey (73) in 18 holes. **1984:** Zoeller (67) def. Greg Norman (75) in 18 holes. **1988:** Strange (71) def. Nick Faldo (75) in 18 holes. **1990:** Irwin (74-3) def. Mike Donald (74-4) on 1st hole of sudden death after 18 holes.

British Open

The oldest of the Majors, the British Open began play in 1860 to determine ''the champion golfer of the world.'' Conducted by the Royal and Ancient Golf Club of St.Andrews, The Open is rotated among select golf courses in England.

Multiple winners: Harry Vardon (6); James Braid, J.H.Taylor, Peter Thomson and Tom Watson (5); Walter Hagen, Bobby Locke, Tom Morris Sr, Tom Morris Jr, and Willie Park (4); Jamie Anderson, Seve Ballesteros, Henry Cotton, Robert Ferguson, Bobby Jones, Jack Nicklaus and Gary Player; Nick Faldo, Harold Hilton, Bob Martin, Arnold Palmer, Willie Park Jr, Lee Trevino (2).

Year Winner	Year Winner	Year Winner	Year Winner
1860 Willie Park	1893 Wm.Auchterlinie	1926 a-Bobby Jones	1959 Gary Player
1861 Tom Morris, Sr.	1894 J.H.Taylor	1927 a-Bobby Jones	1960 Kel Nagle
1862 Tom Morris, Sr.	1895 J.H.Taylor	1928 Walter Hagen	1961 Arnold Palmer
1863 Willie Park	1896 Harry Vardon*	1929 Walter Hagen	1962 Arnold Palmer
1864 Tom Morris, Sr.	1897 a-Harold Hilton		1963 Bob Charles*
1865 Andrew Strath	1898 Harry Vardon	1930 a-Bobby Jones	1964 Tony Lema
1866 Willie Park	1899 Harry Vardon	1931 Tommy Armour	1965 Peter Thomson
1867 Tom Morris, Sr.		1932 Gene Sarazen	1966 Jack Nicklaus
1868 Tom Morris, Jr.	1900 J.H.Taylor	1933 Denny Shute*	1967 Roberto de Vicenzo
1869 Tom Morris, Jr.	1901 James Braid	1934 Henry Cotton	1968 Gary Player
	1902 Sandy Herd	1935 Alf Perry	1969 Tony Jacklin
1870 Tom Morris, Jr.	1903 Harry Vardon	1936 Alf Padgham	
1871 Not held	1904 Jack White	1937 Henry Cotton	1970 Jack Nicklaus*
1872 Tom Morris, Jr.	1905 James Braid	1938 Reg Whitcombe	1971 Lee Trevino
1873 Tom Kidd	1906 James Braid	1939 Dick Burton	1972 Lee Trevino
1874 Mungo Park	1907 Arnaud Massy		1973 Tom Weiskopf
1875 Willie Park	1908 James Braid	1940 Not held	1974 Gary Player
1876 Bob Martin*	1909 J.H.Taylor	1941 Not held	1975 Tom Watson*
1877 Jamie Anderson		1942 Not held	1976 Johnny Miller
1878 Jamie Anderson	1910 James Braid	1943 Not held	1977 Tom Watson
1879 Jamie Anderson	1911 Harry Vardon*	1944 Not held	1978 Jack Nicklaus
	1912 Ted Ray	1945 Not held	1979 Seve Balleteros
1880 Bob Ferguson	1913 J.H.Taylor	1946 Sam Snead	
1881 Bob Ferguson	1914 Harry Vardon	1947 Fred Daly	1980 Tom Watson
1882 Bob Ferguson	1915 Not held	1948 Henry Cotton	1981 Bill Rogers
1883 Willie Fernie*	1916 Not held	1949 Bobby Locke*	1982 Tom Watson
1884 Jack Simpson	1917 Not held		1983 Tom Watson
1885 Bob Martin	1918 Not held	1950 Bobby Locke	1984 Seve Ballesteros
1886 David Brown	1919 Not held	1951 Max Faulkner	1985 Sandy Lyle
1887 Willie Park, Jr.		1952 Bobby Locke	1986 Greg Norman
1888 Jack Burns	1920 George Duncan	1953 Ben Hogan	1987 Nick Faldo
1889 Willie Park, Jr.*	1921 Jock Hutchison*	1954 Peter Thomson	1988 Seve Ballesteros
	1922 Walter Hagen	1955 Peter Thomson	1989 Mark Calcavecchia
1890 a-John Ball	1923 Arthur Havers	1956 Peter Thomson	
1891 Hugh Kirkaldy	1924 Walter Hagen	1957 Bobby Locke	1990 Nick Faldo
1892 a-Harold Hilton	1925 Jim Barnes	1958 Peter Thomson*	

*PLAYOFFS

1876: Martin awarded title when David Strath refused playoff. **1883:** Fernie (158) def. Robert Ferguson (159) in 36 holes. **1889:** Park (158) def. Andrew Kirkaldy (163) in 36 holes. **1896:** Vardon (157) def. John H.Taylor (161) in 36 holes. **1911:** Vardon won when Arnaud Massy conceded at 35th hole. **1921:** Hutchison (150) def. Roger Wethered (159) in 36 holes. **1933:** Shute (149) def. Craig Wood (154) in 36 holes. **1949:** Locke (135) def. Harry Bradshaw (147) in 36 holes. **1958:** Thomson (139) def. Dave Thomas (143) in 36 holes. **1963:** Charles (140) def. Phil Rodgers (148) in 36 holes. **1970:** Nicklaus (72) def. Doug Sanders (73) in 18 holes. **1975:** Watson (71) def. Jack Newton (72) in 18 holes. **1989:** Calcavecchia (4-3-3-3—13) def. Wayne Grady (4-4-4-4—16) and Greg Norman (3-3-4-x) in 4 holes.

PGA Championship

The PGA Championship began in 1916 as a professional golfers match play tournament, but switched to stroke play in 1958. Conducted by the PGA of America, the tournament is played on a different course each year.

Multiple winners: Walter Hagen and Jack Nicklaus (5); Gene Sarazen and Sam Snead (3); Jim Barnes, Leo Diegel, Raymond Floyd, Ben Hogan, Byron Nelson, Larry Nelson, Gary Player, Paul Runyan, Denny Shute, Dave Stockton and Lee Trevino (2).

Year	Winner	Year	Winner	Year	Winner	Year	Winner
1916	Jim Barnes	1935	Johnny Revolta	1954	Chick Harbert	1973	Jack Nicklaus
1917	Not held	1936	Denny Shute	1955	Doug Ford	1974	Lee Trevino
1918	Not held	1937	Denny Shute	1956	Jack Burke, Jr.	1975	Jack Nicklaus
1919	Jim Barnes	1938	Paul Runyan	1957	Lionel Hebert	1976	Dave Stockton
		1939	Henry Picard	1958	Dow Finsterwald	1977	Lanny Wadkins*
1920	Jock Hutchison			1959	Bob Rosburg	1978	John Mahaffey*
1921	Walter Hagen	1940	Byron Nelson			1979	David Graham*
1922	Gene Sarazen	1941	Vic Ghezzi	1960	Jay Hebert		
1923	Gene Sarazen	1942	Sam Snead	1961	Jerry Barber*	1980	Jack Nicklaus
1924	Walter Hagen	1943	Not held	1962	Gary Player	1981	Larry Nelson
1925	Walter Hagen	1944	Bob Hamilton	1963	Jack Nicklaus	1982	Raymond Floyd
1926	Walter Hagen	1945	Byron Nelson	1964	Bobby Nichols	1983	Hal Sutton
1927	Walter Hagen	1946	Ben Hogan	1965	Dave Marr	1984	Lee Trevino
1928	Leo Diegel	1947	Jim Ferrier	1966	Al Geiberger	1985	Hubert Green
1929	Leo Diegel	1948	Ben Hogan	1967	Don January*	1986	Bob Tway
1930	Tommy Armour	1949	Sam Snead	1968	Julius Boros	1987	Larry Nelson*
1931	Tom Creavy			1969	Raymond Floyd	1988	Jeff Sluman
1932	Olin Dutra	1950	Chandler Harper			1989	Payne Stewart
1933	Gene Sarazen	1951	Sam Snead	1970	Dave Stockton		
1934	Paul Runyan	1952	Jim Turnesa	1971	Jack Nicklaus	1990	Wayne Grady
		1953	Walter Burkemo	1972	Gary Player		

*PLAYOFFS

1961: J.Barber (67) def. Don January (68) in 18 holes. **1967:** January (69) def. Don Massengale (71) in 18 holes. **1977:** L.Wadkins (4-4-4) def. Gene Littler (4-4-5) on 3rd hole of sudden death. **1978:** Mahaffey (4-3) def. Jerry Pate (4-4) and Tom Watson (4-5) on 2nd hole of sudden death. **1979:** D.Graham (4-4-2) def. Ben Crenshaw (4-4-4) on 3rd hole of sudden death. **1987:** Nelson (4) def. Lanny Wadkins (5) on 1st hole of sudden death.

Grand Slam Summary

MEN

The only golfer to ever win a recognized Grand Slam—four major championships in a single season—was Bobby Jones in 1930. That year, Jones won the US and British Opens as well as the US and British Amateurs.

The men's professional Grand Slam—the Masters, US Open, British Open and PGA Championship—did not gain acceptance until 30 years later when Arnold Palmer won the 1960 Masters and US Open. The media wrote that the popular Palmer was chasing the "new" Grand Slam and would have to win the British Open and the PGA to claim it. He did not, but then nobody has before or since.

Three wins in one year (11): Ben Hogan (1953).

Two wins in one year (16): Jack Nicklaus (5 times); Ben Hogan, Arnold Palmer and Tom Watson (twice); Nick Faldo, Gary Player, Sam Snead, Lee Trevino and Craig Wood (once).

Year	Masters	US Open	Brit.Open	PGA	Year	Masters	US Open	Brit.Open	PGA
1934	H.Smith	Dutra	Cotton	Runyan	1950	Demaret	Hogan	Locke	Harper
1935	Sarazen	Parks	Perry	Revolta	1951	Hogan	Hogan	Faulkner	Snead
1936	H.Smith	Manero	Padgham	Shute	1952	Snead	Boros	Locke	Turnesa
1937	B.Nelson	Guldahl	Cotton	Shute	1953	**Hogan**	**Hogan**	**Hogan**	Burkemo
1938	Picard	Guldahl	Whitcombe	Runyan	1954	Snead	Furgol	Thomson	Harbert
1939	Guldahl	B.Nelson	Burton	Picard	1955	Middlecoff	Fleck	Thomson	Ford
1940	Demaret	Little	—	B.Nelson	1956	Burke	Middlecoff	Thomson	Burke
1941	Wood	Wood	—	Ghezzi	1957	Ford	Mayer	Locke	L.Hebert
1942	B.Nelson	—	—	Snead	1958	Palmer	Bolt	Thomson	Finsterwald
1943	—	—	—	—	1959	Wall	Casper	Player	Rosburg
1944	—	—	—	Hamilton	1960	Palmer	Palmer	Nagle	J.Hebert
1945	—	—	—	B.Nelson	1961	Player	Littler	Palmer	J.Barber
1946	Keiser	Mangrum	Snead	Hogan	1962	Palmer	Nicklaus	Palmer	Player
1947	Demaret	Worsham	Daly	Ferrier	1963	Nicklaus	Boros	Charles	Nicklaus
1948	Harmon	Hogan	Cotton	Hogan	1964	Palmer	Venturi	Lema	Nichols
1949	Snead	Middlecoff	Locke	Snead	1965	Nicklaus	Player	Thomson	Marr

Grand Slam Summary (Cont.)

Year	Masters	US Open	Brit.Open	PGA	Year	Masters	US Open	Brit.Open	PGA
1966	Nicklaus	Casper	Nicklaus	Geiberger	1979	Zoeller	Irwin	Ballesteros	D.Graham
1967	Brewer	Nicklaus	DeVicenzo	January	1980	Ballesteros	Nicklaus	T.Watson	Nicklaus
1968	Goalby	Trevino	Player	Boros	1981	T.Watson	D.Graham	Rogers	L.Nelson
1969	Archer	Moody	Jacklin	Floyd	1982	Stadler	T.Watson	T.Watson	Floyd
1970	Casper	Jacklin	Nicklaus	Stockton	1983	Ballesteros	L.Nelson	T.Watson	Sutton
1971	Coody	Trevino	Trevino	Nicklaus	1984	Crenshaw	Zoeller	Ballesteros	Trevino
1972	Nicklaus	Nicklaus	Trevino	Player	1985	Langer	North	Lyle	H.Green
1973	Aaron	J.Miller	Weiskopf	Nicklaus	1986	Nicklaus	Floyd	Norman	Tway
1974	Player	Irwin	Player	Trevino	1987	Mize	S.Simpson	Faldo	L.Nelson
1975	Nicklaus	L.Graham	T.Watson	Nicklaus	1988	Lyle	Strange	Ballesteros	Sluman
1976	Floyd	J.Pate	Miller	Stockton	1989	Faldo	Strange	Calcav'chia	Stewart
1977	T.Watson	H.Green	T.Watson	L.Wadkins	1990	Faldo	Irwin	Faldo	Grady
1978	Player	North	Nicklaus	Mahaffey					

Major Championship Leaders

Through 1990; active players in **bold** type.

	US Open	British Open	PGA	Masters	US Am	British Am	Total
Jack Nicklaus	4	3	5	6	2	0	**20**
Bobby Jones	4	3	0	0	5	1	**13**
Walter Hagen	2	4	5	0	0	0	**11**
Ben Hogan	4	1	2	2	0	0	**9**
Gary Player	1	3	2	3	0	0	**9**
John Ball	0	1	0	0	0	8	**9**
Arnold Palmer	1	2	0	4	1	0	**8**
Tom Watson	1	5	0	2	0	0	**8**
Harold Hilton	0	2	0	0	1	4	**7**
Gene Sarazen	2	1	3	1	0	0	**7**
Sam Snead...........	0	1	3	3	0	0	**7**
Harry Vardon	1	6	0	0	0	0	**7**
Lee Trevino	2	2	2	0	0	0	**6**

Tournaments: US Open, British Open, PGA Championship, Masters, US Amateur, and British Amateur.

U.S. Amateur

Match play from 1895-64, stroke play from 1965-72, match play since 1972.

Multiple winners: Bobby Jones (5); Jerry Travers (4); Walter Travis (3); Deane Beman, Charles Coe, Gary Cowan, H.Chandler Egan, Chick Evans, Lawson Little, Jack Nicklaus, Francis Ouimet, Jay Sigel, William Turnesa, Bud Ward, Harvie Ward and H.J.Whigham (2).

Year	Winner	Year	Winner	Year	Winner	Year	Winner
1895	Charles Macdonald	1920	Chick Evans	1945	Not held	1970	Lanny Wadkins
1896	H.J.Whigham	1921	Jesse Guilford	1946	Ted Bishop	1971	Gary Cowan
1897	H.J.Whigham	1922	Jess Sweetser	1947	Skee Riegel	1972	Vinny Giles
1898	Findlay Douglas	1923	Max Marston	1948	William Turnesa	1973	Craig Stadler
1899	H.M.Harriman	1924	Bobby Jones	1949	Charles Coe	1974	Jerry Pate
1900	Walter Travis	1925	Bobby Jones	1950	Sam Urzetta	1975	Fred Ridley
1901	Walter Travis	1926	George Von Elm	1951	Billy Maxwell	1976	Bill Sander
1902	Louis James	1927	Bobby Jones	1952	Jack Westland	1977	John Fought
1903	Walter Travis	1928	Bobby Jones	1953	Gene Littler	1978	John Cook
1904	H.Chandler Egan	1929	Harrison Johnston	1954	Arnold Palmer	1979	Mark O'Meara
1905	H.Chandler Egan	1930	Bobby Jones	1955	Harvie Ward	1980	Hal Sutton
1906	Eben Byers	1931	Francis Ouimet	1956	Harvie Ward	1981	Nathanial Crosby
1907	Jerry Travers	1932	Ross Somerville	1957	Hillman Robbins	1982	Jay Sigel
1908	Jerry Travers	1933	George Dunlap	1958	Charles Coe	1983	Jay Sigel
1909	Robert Gardner	1934	Lawson Little	1959	Jack Nicklaus	1984	Scott Verplank
1910	W.C.Fownes, Jr.	1935	Lawson Little	1960	Deane Beman	1985	Sam Randolph
1911	Harold Hilton	1936	John Fischer	1961	Jack Nicklaus	1986	Buddy Alexander
1912	Jerry Travers	1937	John Goodman	1962	Labron Harris	1987	Billy Mayfair
1913	Jerry Travers	1938	William Turnesa	1963	Deane Beman	1988	Eric Meeks
1914	Francis Ouimet	1939	Bud Ward	1964	Bill Campbell	1989	Chris Patton
1915	Robert Gardner	1940	Richard Chapman	1965	Bob Murphy	1990	Phil Mickelson
1916	Chick Evans	1941	Bud Ward	1966	Gary Cowan		
1917	Not held	1942	Not held	1967	Bob Dickson		
1918	Not held	1943	Not held	1968	Bruce Fleisher		
1919	Davidson Herron	1944	Not held	1969	Steve Melnyk		

British Amateur

Match play since 1885.
Multiple winners: John Ball (8); Michael Bonallack (5); Harold Hilton (4); Joe Carr (3); Horace Hutchinson, Ernest Holderness, Trevor Homer, Johnny Laidley, Lawson Little, Peter McEvoy, Dick Siderowf, Frank Stranahan, Freddie Tait and Cyril Tolley (2).

Year	Winner	Year	Winner	Year	Winner	Year	Winner
1885	Allen MacFie	1912	John Ball	1939	Alexander Kyle	1966	Bobby Cole
1886	Horace Hutchinson	1913	Harold Hilton			1967	Bob Dickson
1887	Horace Hutchinson	1914	J.L.C. Jenkins	1940	Not held	1968	Michael Bonallack
1888	John Ball	1915	Not held	1941	Not held	1969	Michael Bonallack
1889	Johnny Laidley	1916	Not held	1942	Not held		
		1917	Not held	1943	Not held	1970	Michael Bonallack
1890	John Ball	1918	Not held	1944	Not held	1971	Steve Melnyk
1891	Johnny Laidlay	1919	Not held	1945	Not held	1972	Trevor Homer
1892	John Ball	1920	Cyril Tolley	1946	James Bruen	1973	Dick Siderowf
1893	Peter Anderson	1921	William Hunter	1947	William Turnesa	1974	Trevor Homer
1894	John Ball	1922	Ernest Holderness	1948	Frank Stranahan	1975	Vinny Giles
1895	Leslie Balfour	1923	Roger Wethered	1949	Samuel McCready	1976	Dick Siderowf
1896	Freddie Tait	1924	Ernest Holderness			1977	Peter McEvoy
1897	Jack Allen	1925	Robert Harris	1950	Frank Stranahan	1978	Peter McEvoy
1898	Freddie Tait	1926	Jesse Sweetser	1951	Richard Chapman	1979	Jay Sigel
1899	John Ball	1927	William Tweedell	1952	Harvie Ward		
		1928	Thomas Perkins	1953	Joe Carr	1980	Duncan Evans
1900	Harold Hilton	1929	Cyril Tolley	1954	Douglas Bachli	1981	Phillipe Ploujoux
1901	Harold Hilton			1955	Joe Conrad	1982	Martin Thompson
1902	Charles Hutchings	1930	Bobby Jones	1956	John Beharrell	1983	Philip Parkin
1903	Robert Maxwell	1931	Eric Smith	1957	Reid Jack	1984	Jose-Maria Olazabal
1904	Walter Travis	1932	John deForest	1958	Joe Carr	1985	Garth McGimpsey
1905	Arthur Barry	1933	Michael Scott	1959	Deane Beman	1986	David Curry
1906	James Robb	1934	Lawson Little			1987	Paul Mayo
1907	John Ball	1935	Lawson Little	1960	Joe Carr	1988	Christian Hardin
1908	E.A.Lassen	1936	Hector Thomson	1961	Michael Bonallack	1989	Stephen Dodd
1909	Robert Maxwell	1937	Robert Sweeny, Jr.	1962	Richard Davies		
		1938	Charles Yates	1963	Michael Lunt	1990	Rolf Muntz
1910	John Ball			1964	Gordon Clark		
1911	Harold Hilton			1965	Michael Bonallack		

Ryder Cup Matches

The Ryder Cup was presented by British businessman Samuel Ryder in 1927 for competition between professional golfers from Great Britain and the United States. Since 1979, the British have been joined by the rest of Europe in challenging the US. The US leads the series with a 21-6-1 record after 28 matches.

Year	Winner	Year	Winner	Year	Winner
1927	United States, 9½-2½	1951	United States, 9½-2½	1971	United States, 18½-13½
1929	Britain-Ireland, 7-5	1953	United States, 6½-5½	1973	United States, 19-13
		1955	United States, 8-4	1975	United States, 21-11
1931	United States, 9-3	1957	Britain-Ireland, 7½-4½	1977	United States, 12½-7½
1933	Britain-Ireland, 6½-5½	1959	United States, 8½-3½	1979	United States, 17-11
1935	United States, 9-3				
1937	United States, 8-4	1961	United States, 14½-9½	1981	United States, 18½-9½
1939	Not held	1963	United States, 23-9	1983	United States, 14½-13½
		1965	United States, 19½-12½	1985	Europe, 16½-11½
1941	Not held	1967	United States, 23½-8½	1987	Europe, 15-13
1943	Not held	1969	Draw, 16-16	1989	Draw, 14-14
1945	Not held				
1947	United States, 11-1			**Note:** Great Britain-Ireland became Europe in 1979.	
1949	United States, 7-5				

Walker Cup Matches

The Walker Cup was presented by American businessman George Herbert Walker in 1922 for competition between amateur golfers from Great Britain and the United States. The US leads the series with a 28-3-1 record after 32 matches.

Year	Winner	Year	Winner	Year	Winner
1922	United States, 8-4	1944	Not held	1967	United States, 15-9
1923	United States, 6-5	1946	Not held	1969	United States, 13-11
1924	United States, 9-3	1947	United States, 8-4		
1926	United States, 6½-5½	1949	United States, 10-2	1971	Britain-Ireland, 13-11
1928	United States, 11-1			1973	United States, 14-10
		1951	United States, 7½-4½	1975	United States, 15½-8½
1930	United States, 10-2	1953	United States, 9-3	1977	United States, 16-8
1932	United States, 9½-2½	1955	United States, 10-2	1979	United States, 15½-8½
1934	United States, 9½-2½	1957	United States, 8½-3½		
1936	United States, 10½-1½	1959	United States, 9-	1981	United States, 15-9
1938	Britain-Ireland, 7½-4½			1983	United States, 13½-10½
		1961	United States, 11-1	1985	United States, 13-11
1940	Not held	1963	United States, 14-10	1987	United States, 16½-7½
1942	Not held	1965	Draw, 12-12	1989	Britain-Ireland, 12½-11½

Major Championships
WOMEN

U.S. Women's Open

The US Women's Open began under the direction of the defunct Women's Professional Golfers Assn in 1946, passed to the LPGA in 1949 and to the USGA in 1953. The tournament used a match play format its first year then switched to stroke play.

Multiple winners: Betsy Rawls and Mickey Wright (4); Susie M.Berning, Hollis Stacy and Babe Zaharias (3); JoAnne Carner, Donna Caponi, Betsy King and Louise Suggs (2).

Year	Winner	Year	Winner	Year	Winner	Year	Winner
1946	Patty Berg	1958	Mickey Wright	1970	Donna Caponi	1981	Pat Bradley
1947	Betty Jameson	1959	Mickey Wright	1971	JoAnne Carner	1982	Janet Anderson
1948	Babe Zaharias	1960	Betsy Rawls	1972	Susie M.Berning	1983	Jan Stephenson
1949	Louise Suggs	1961	Mickey Wright	1973	Susie M.Berning	1984	Hollis Stacy
1950	Babe Zaharias	1962	Murle Lindstrom	1974	Sandra Haynie	1985	Kathy Baker
1951	Betsy Rawls	1963	Mary Mills	1975	Sandra Palmer	1986	Jane Geddes*
1952	Louise Suggs	1964	Mickey Wright*	1976	JoAnne Carner*	1987	Laura Davies*
1953	Betsy Rawls*	1965	Carol Mann	1977	Hollis Stacy	1988	Liselotte Neumann
1954	Babe Zaharias	1966	Sandra Spuzich	1978	Hollis Stacy	1989	Betsy King
1955	Fay Crocker	1967	a-Catherine Lacoste	1979	Jerilyn Britz	1990	Betsy King
1956	Kathy Cornelius*	1968	Susie M.Berning	1980	Amy Alcott		
1957	Betsy Rawls	1969	Donna Caponi				

*PLAYOFFS

1953: Rawls (71) def. Jackie Pung (77) in 18 holes. **1956:** Cornelius (75) def. Barbara McIntire (82) in 18 holes. **1964:** Wright (70) def. Ruth Jessen (72) in 18 holes. **1976:** Carner (76) def. Sandra Palmer (78) in 18 holes. **1986:** Geddes (71) def. Sally Little (73) in 18 holes. **1987:** Davies (71) def. Ayako Okamoto (73) and JoAnne Carner (74) in 18 holes.

LPGA Championship

Officially the Mazda LPGA Championship since 1987, the tournament began in 1955 and has had extended stays at the Stardust CC in Las Vegas (1961-66), Pleasant Valley CC in Sutton, MA (1967-68,70-74) and the Jack Nicklaus Sports Center at Kings Island, OH (1978-89).

Multiple winners: Mickey Wright (4); Nancy Lopez and Kathy Whitworth (3); Donna Caponi, Sandra Haynie, Mary Mills, Betsy Rawls and Patty Sheehan (2).

Year	Winner	Year	Winner	Year	Winner	Year	Winner
1955	Beverly Hanson	1964	Mary Mills	1973	Mary Mills	1982	Jan Stephenson
1956	Marlene Hagge*	1965	Sandra Haynie	1974	Sandra Haynie	1983	Patty Sheehan
1957	Louise Suggs	1966	Gloria Ehret	1975	Kathy Whitworth	1984	Patty Sheehan
1958	Mickey Wright	1967	Kathy Whitworth	1976	Betty Burfeindt	1985	Nancy Lopez
1959	Betsy Rawls	1968	Sandra Post*	1977	Chako Higuchi	1986	Pat Bradley
1960	Mickey Wright	1969	Betsy Rawls	1978	Nancy Lopez	1987	Jane Geddes
1961	Mickey Wright	1970	Shirley Englehorn*	1979	Donna Caponi	1988	Sherri Turner
1962	Judy Kimball	1971	Kathy Whitworth	1980	Sally Little	1989	Nancy Lopez
1963	Mickey Wright	1972	Kathy Ahern	1981	Donna Caponi	1990	Beth Daniel

*PLAYOFFS

1956: Hagge def. Patti Berg in sudden death. **1968:** Post (68) def. Kathy Whitworth (75) in 18-holes. **1970:** Englehorn def. Kathy Whitworth in sudden death.

du Maurier Classic

Formerly known as La Canadienne in 1973 and the Peter Jackson Classic from 1974-83, this Canadian stop on the LPGA Tour became the third designated major championship in 1979.

Multiple winner (as a major): Pat Bradley (3).

Year	Winner	Year	Winner	Year	Winner	Year	Winner
1973	Jocelyne Bourassa	1978	JoAnne Carner	1983	Hollis Stacy	1987	Jody Rosenthal
1974	Carole Jo Skala	1979	Amy Alcott	1984	Juli Inkster	1988	Sally Little
1975	JoAnne Carner	1980	Pat Bradley	1985	Pat Bradley	1989	Tammie Green
1976	Donna Caponi	1981	Jan Stephenson	1986	Pat Bradley*	1990	Cathy Johnston
1977	Judy Rankin	1982	Sandra Haynie				

*PLAYOFF

1986: Bradley def. Ayako Okamoto in sudden death.

Nabisco Dinah Shore

Formerly known as the Colgate Dinah Shore from 1972-81, the tournament become the LPGA's fourth designated major championship in 1983. Named after the entertainer, this tourney has been played at Mission Hills CC in Rancho Mirage, CA since it began.

Multiple winners (as a major): Amy Alcott, Juli Inkster and Betsy King (2).

Year	Winner	Year	Winner	Year	Winner	Year	Winner
1972	Jane Blalock	1978	Sandra Post	1983	Amy Alcott	1988	Amy Alcott
1973	Mickey Wright	1979	Sandra Post	1984	Juli Inkster*	1989	Juli Inkster
1974	Jo Ann Prentice			1985	Alice Miller	1990	Betsy King
1975	Sandra Palmer	1980	Donna Caponi	1986	Pat Bradley		
1976	Judy Rankin	1981	Nancy Lopez	1987	Betsy King*		
1977	Kathy Whitworth	1982	Sally Little				

*PLAYOFFS

1984: Inkster def. Pat Bradley in sudden death. **1987:** King def. Patty Sheehan in sudden death.

Titleholders Championship

The Titleholders was considered a major title on the women's tour until it was discontinued after the 1972 tournament. **Multiple winners:** Patty Berg (7); Louise Suggs (4); Babe Zaharias (3); Dorothy Kirby, Marilynn Smith, Kathy Whitworth and Mickey Wright (2).

Year	Winner	Year	Winner	Year	Winner	Year	Winner
1937	Patty Berg	1947	Babe Zaharias	1956	Louise Suggs	1965	Kathy Whitworth
1938	Patty Berg	1948	Patty Berg	1957	Patty Berg	1966	Kathy Whitworth
1939	Patty Berg	1949	Peggy Kirk	1958	Beverly Hanson	1967	Not held
1940	Betty Hicks	1950	Babe Zaharias	1959	Louise Suggs	1968	Not held
1941	Dorothy Kirby	1951	Pat O'Sullivan			1969	Not held
1942	Dorothy Kirby	1952	Babe Zaharias	1960	Fay Crocker		
1943	Not held	1953	Patty Berg	1961	Mickey Wright	1970	Not held
1944	Not held	1954	Louise Suggs	1962	Mickey Wright	1971	Not held
1945	Not held	1955	Patty Berg	1963	Marilynn Smith	1972	Sandra Palmer
1946	Louise Suggs			1964	Marilynn Smith	1973	Discontinued

Western Open

The Western Open was considered a major title on the women's tour until it was discontinued after the 1967 tournament. **Multiple winners:** Patty Berg (7); Louise Suggs and Babe Zaharias (4); Mickey Wright (3); Betty Jameson and Betsy Rawls (2).

Year	Winner	Year	Winner	Year	Winner	Year	Winner
1937	Betty Hicks	1945	Babe Zaharias	1953	Louise Suggs	1961	Mary Lena Faulk
1938	Bea Barrett	1946	Louise Suggs	1954	Betty Jameson	1962	Mickey Wright
1939	Helen Dettweiler	1947	Louise Suggs	1955	Patty Berg	1963	Mickey Wright
1940	Babe Zaharias	1948	Patty Berg	1956	Beverly Hanson	1964	Carol Mann
1941	Patty Berg	1949	Louise Suggs	1957	Patty Berg	1965	Susie Maxwell
1942	Betty Jameson	1950	Babe Zaharias	1958	Patty Berg	1966	Mickey Wright
1943	Patty Berg	1951	Patty Berg	1959	Betsy Rawls	1967	Kathy Whitworth
1944	Babe Zaharias	1952	Betsy Rawls	1960	Joyce Ziske	1968	Discontinued

Grand Slam Summary

WOMEN

The women's Grand Slam has consisted of four tournaments only 19 years. From 1955-66, the US Open, LPGA Championship, Western Open and Titleholders tournaments served du the major events. Since 1983, the US Open, LPGA, du Maurier Classic in Canada and Nabisco Dinah Shore have been the major events. No one has won a four-event Grand Slam on the women's tour.

Three wins in one year (3): Babe Zaharias (1950), Mickey Wright (1961) and Pat Bradley (1986).

Two wins in one year (13): Patty Berg and Mickey Wright (3 times); Louise Suggs (twice); Sandra Haynie, Juli Inkster, Betsy King, Betsy Rawls and Kathy Whitworth (once).

Year	LPGA	US Open	T'holders	Western	Year	LPGA	US Open	T'holders	Western
1937	—	—	Berg	Hicks	1948	—	Zaharias	Berg	Berg
1938	—	—	Berg	Barrett	1949	—	Suggs	Kirk	Suggs
1939	—	—	Berg	Dettweiler	1950	—	Zaharias	Zaharias	Zaharias
1940	—	—	Hicks	Zaharias	1951	—	Rawls	O'Sullivan	Berg
1941	—	—	Kirby	Berg	1952	—	Suggs	Zaharias	Rawls
1942	—	—	Kirby	Jameson	1953	—	Rawls	Berg	Suggs
1943	—	—	—	Berg	1954	—	Zaharias	Suggs	Jameson
1944	—	—	—	Zaharias	1955	Hanson	Crocker	Berg	Berg
1945	—	—	—	Zaharias	1956	Hagge	Cornelius	Suggs	Hanson
1946	—	Berg	Suggs	Suggs	1957	Suggs	Rawls	Berg	Berg
1947	—	Jameson	Zaharias	Suggs	1958	Wright	Wright	Hanson	Berg

Grand Slam Summary (Cont.)

WOMEN

Year	LPGA	US Open	T'holders	Western
1959	Rawls	Wright	Suggs	Rawls
1960	Wright	Rawls	Crocker	Ziske
1961	**Wright**	**Wright**	**Wright**	Faulk
1962	Kimball	Breer	Wright	Wright
1963	Wright	Mills	M.Smith	Wright
1964	Mills	Wright	M.Smith	Mann
1965	Haynie	Mann	Whitworth	Berning
1966	Ehret	Spuzich	Whitworth	Wright
1967	Whitworth	a-LaCoste	—	Whitworth
1968	Post	Berning	—	—
1969	Rawls	Caponi	—	—
1970	Englehorn	Caponi	—	—
1971	Whitworth	Carner	—	—
1972	Ahern	Berning	Palmer	—
1973	Mills	Berning	—	—
1974	Haynie	Haynie	—	—
1975	Whitworth	Palmer	—	—

Year	LPGA	US Open	T'holders	Western
1976	Burfeindt	Carner	—	—
1977	Higuchi	Stacy	—	—
1978	Lopez	Stacy	—	—

Year	LPGA	US Open	du Maurier	D.Shore
1979	Caponi	Britz	Alcott	—
1980	Little	Alcott	Bradley	—
1981	Caponi	Bradley	Stephenson	—
1982	Stephenson	Anderson	Haynie	—
1983	Sheehan	Stephenson	Stacy	Alcott
1984	Sheehan	Stacy	Inkster	Inkster
1985	Lopez	Baker	Bradley	Miller
1986	**Bradley**	Geddes	**Bradley**	**Bradley**
1987	Geddes	Davies	Rosenthal	King
1988	Turner	Neumann	Little	Alcott
1989	Lopez	King	Green	Inkster
1990	Daniel	King	Johnston	King

Major Championship Leaders

Through 1990; active players in **bold** type.

	US Open	LPGA	duM	Dinah	Title-holders	Western	US Am	Brit Am	Total
Patty Berg	1	0	0	0	7	7	1	0	**16**
Mickey Wright	4	4	0	0	2	3	0	0	**13**
Louise Suggs	2	1	0	0	4	4	1	1	**13**
Babe Zaharias	3	0	0	0	3	4	1	1	**12**
Betsy Rawls	4	2	0	0	0	2	0	0	**8**
JoAnne Carner	2	0	0	0	0	0	5	0	**7**
Kathy Whitworth	0	3	0	0	2	1	0	0	**6**
Pat Bradley	1	1	3	1	0	0	0	0	**6**
Julie Inkster	0	0	1	2	0	0	3	0	**6**
Glenna C.Vare	0	0	0	0	0	0	6	0	**6**

Tournaments: US Open, LPGA Championship, du Maurier Classic, Nabisco Dinah Shore, Titleholders (1937-72), Western Open (1937-67), US Amateur, and British Amateur.

U.S. Women's Amateur

Stroke play in 1895, match play since 1896. **Multiple winners:** Glenna Collett Vare (6); JoAnne Gunderson Carner (5); Margaret Curtis, Beatrix Hoyt, Dorothy Campbell Hurd, Juli Inkster, Alexa Stirling, Virginia Van Wie, Anne Quast Decker Welts (3); Kay Cockerill, Beth Daniel, Katherine Harley, Genevieve Hecker, Betty Jameson and Barbara McIntire (2).

Year	Winner	Year	Winner	Year	Winner
1895	Mrs.Chas.S. Brown	1920	Alexa Stirling	1945	Not held
1896	Beatrix Hoyt	1921	Marion Hollins	1946	Babe Didrikson Zaharias
1897	Beatrix Hoyt	1922	Glenna Collett	1947	Louise Suggs
1898	Beatrix Hoyt	1923	Edith Cummings	1948	Grace Lenczyk
1899	Ruth Underhill	1924	Dorothy Campbell Hurd	1949	Dorothy Porter
1900	Frances Griscom	1925	Glenna Collett	1950	Beverly Hanson
1901	Genevieve Hecker	1926	Helen Stetson	1951	Dorothy Kirby
1902	Genevieve Hecker	1927	Miriam Burns Horn	1952	Jacqueline Pung
1903	Bessie Anthony	1928	Glenna Collett	1953	Mary Lena Faulk
1904	Georgianna Bishop	1929	Glenna Collett	1954	Barbara Romack
1905	Pauline Mackay	1930	Glenna Collett	1955	Patricia Lesser
1906	Harriot Curtis	1931	Helen Hicks	1956	Marlene Stewart
1907	Margaret Curtis	1932	Virginia Van Wie	1957	JoAnne Gunderson
1908	Katherine Harley	1933	Virginia Van Wie	1958	Anne Quast
1909	Dorothy Campbell	1934	Virginia Van Wie	1959	Barbara McIntire
1910	Dorothy Campbell	1935	Glenna Collett Vare	1960	JoAnne Gunderson
1911	Margaret Curtis	1936	Pamela Barton	1961	Anne Quast Decker
1912	Margaret Curtis	1937	Estelle Lawson	1962	JoAnne Gunderson
1913	Gladys Ravenscroft	1938	Patty Berg	1963	Anne Quast Welts
1914	Katherine Harley	1939	Betty Jameson	1964	Barbara McIntire
1915	Florence Vanderbeck	1940	Betty Jameson	1965	Jean Ashley
1916	Alexa Stirling	1941	Elizabeth Hicks	1966	JoAnne Gunderson Carner
1917	Not held	1942	Not held	1967	Mary Lou Dill
1918	Not held	1943	Not held	1968	JoAnne Gunderson Carner
1919	Alexa Stirling	1944	Not held	1969	Catherine Lacoste

Year	Winner	Year	Winner	Year	Winner
1970	Martha Wilkinson	1978	Cathy Sherk	1985	Michiko Hattori
1971	Laura Baugh	1979	Carolyn Hill	1986	Kay Cockerill
1972	Mary Budke	1980	Juli Inkster	1987	Kay Cockerill
1973	Carol Semple	1981	Juli Inkster	1988	Pearl Sinn
1974	Cynthia Hill	1982	Juli Inkster	1989	Vicki Goetze
1975	Beth Daniel	1983	Joanne Pacillo	1990	Pat Hurst
1976	Donna Horton	1984	Deb Richard		
1977	Beth Daniel				

Curtis Cup Matches

Named after British golfing sisters Harriot and Margaret Curtis, the Curtis Cup was first contested in 1932 between teams of women amateurs from the US and the British Isles.

Competed for every other year since 1932 (except during World War II). The US leads the series with a 20-4-2 record after 26 matches.

Year	Winner	Year	Winner	Year	Winner
1932	United States, 5½-3½	1952	British Isles, 5-4	1972	United States, 10-8
1934	United States, 6½-2½	1954	United States, 6-3	1974	United States, 13-5
1936	Draw, 4½-4½	1956	British Isles, 5-4	1976	United States, 11½-6½
1938	United States, 5½-3½	1958	Draw 4½-4½	1978	United States, 12-6
1940	Not held	1960	United States, 6½-2½	1980	United States, 13-5
1942	Not held	1962	United States, 8-1	1982	United States, 14½-3½
1944	Not held	1964	United States, 10½-7½	1984	United States, 9½-8½
1946	Not held	1966	United States, 13-5	1986	British Isles, 13-5
1948	United States, 6½-2½	1968	United States, 10½-7½	1988	British Isles, 11-7
1950	United States, 7½-1½	1970	United States, 11½-6½	1990	United States, 14-4

Major Championships
SENIORS
PGA Seniors Championship

First played in 1937. Two championships played in 1979 and 1984. **Multiple winners:** Sam Snead (6); Gary Player and Eddie Williams (3); Julius Boros, Jock Hutchison, Don January, Arnold Palmer, Paul Runyan, Gene Sarazen and Al Watrous (2).

Year	Winner	Year	Winner	Year	Winner	Year	Winner
1937	Jock Hutchison	1951	Al Watrous*	1965	Sam Snead	1979	Jack Fleck*
1938	Fred McLeod*	1952	Ernest Newnham	1966	Fred Haas	1979	Don January
1939	Not held	1953	Harry Schwab	1967	Sam Snead	1980	Arnold Palmer*
1940	Otto Hackbarth*	1954	Gene Sarazen	1968	Chandler Harper	1981	Miller Barber
1941	Jack Burke	1955	Mortie Dutra	1969	Tommy Bolt	1982	Don January
1942	Eddie Williams	1956	Pete Burke	1970	Sam Snead	1983	Not Held
1943	Not held	1957	Al Watrous	1971	Julius Boros	1984	Arnold Palmer
1944	Not held	1958	Gene Sarazen	1972	Sam Snead	1984	Peter Thomson
1945	Eddie Williams	1959	Willie Goggin	1973	Sam Snead	1985	Not Held
1946	Eddie Williams*	1960	Dick Metz	1974	Robert de Vicenzo	1986	Gary Player
1947	Jock Hutchison	1961	Paul Runyan	1975	Charlie Sifford*	1987	Chi Chi Rodriguez
1948	Charles McKenna	1962	Paul Runyan	1976	Pete Cooper	1988	Gary Player
1949	Marshall Crichton	1963	Herman Barron	1977	Julius Boros	1989	Larry Mowry
1950	Al Watrous	1964	Sam Snead	1978	Joe Jiminez*	1990	Gary Player

*PLAYOFFS

1938: McLeod def. Otto Hackbarth in 18 holes. **1940:** Hackbarth def. Jock Hutchison in 36 holes. **1946:** Williams def. Jock Hutchison in 18 holes. **1951:** Watrous def. Jock Hutchison in 18 holes. **1975:** Sifford def. Fred Wampler on 1st extra hole. **1978:** Jiminez def. Joe Cheves and M.de la Torre on 1st extra hole. **1979:** Fleck def. Bill Johnston on 1st extra hole. **1980:** Palmer def. Paul Harney on 1st extra hole.

U.S. Senior Open

Established in 1980 for senior players 55 years-old and over, the minimum age was dropped to 50 (the PGA Seniors Tour entry age) in 1981. Arnold Palmer, Billy Casper, Orville Moody and Lee Trevino are the only golfers who have won both the US Open and US Senior Open. **Multiple winners:** Miller Barber (3); Gary Player (2).

Year	Winner	Year	Winner	Year	Winner	Year	Winner
1980	Roberto deVicenzo	1983	Bill Casper*	1986	Dale Douglass	1988	Gary Player*
1981	Arnold Palmer*	1984	Miller Barber	1987	Gary Player	1989	Orville Moody
1982	Miller Barber	1985	Miller Barber			1990	Lee Trevino

*PLAYOFFS

1981: Palmer (70) def. Bob Stone (74) and Billy Casper (77) in 18 holes. **1983:** Tied at 75 after 18-hole playoff, Casper def. Rod Funseth with a birdie on the 1st extra hole. **1988:** Player (68) def. Bob Charles (70) in 18 holes.

All-Time Leaders
PGA, Seniors and LPGA leaders through 1989.

Tournaments Won

PGA	No	SENIORS	No	LPGA	No
1 Sam Snead	81	1 Miller Barber	24	1 Kathy Whitworth	88
2 Jack Nicklaus	70	2 Don January	22	2 Mickey Wright	82
3 Ben Hogan	63	3 Bruce Crampton	15	3 Patty Berg	57*
4 Arnold Palmer	60	4 Gary Player	14	4 Betsy Rawls	55
5 Byron Nelson	52	5 Chi Chi Rodriguez	13	5 Louise Suggs	50
6 Billy Casper	51	Bob Charles	13	6 JoAnne Carner	42
7 Walter Hagen	40	7 Peter Thomson	11	Sandra Haynie	42
Cary Middlecoff	40	8 Arnold Palmer	10	Nancy Lopez	42
9 Gene Sarazen	38	9 Billy Casper	9	9 Carol Mann	38
10 Lloyd Mangrum	36	Orville Moody	9	10 Babe Zaharias	31
11 Horton Smith	32	11 Gene Littler	8	11 Jane Blaylock	29
Tom Watson	32	Lee Elder	8	12 Amy Alcott	28

*Includes 13 official pro wins prior to formation of LPGA in 1950.

Money Won

PGA	Earnings	SENIORS	Earnings	WOMEN	Earnings
1 Tom Kite	$5,600,691	1 Miller Barber	$2,214,603	1 Pat Bradley	$2,866,029
2 Tom Watson	5,160,243	2 Bob Charles	1,910,413	2 Nancy Lopez	2,725,209
3 Jack Nicklaus	5,102,420	3 Orville Moody	1,862,956	3 Betsy King	2,469,694
4 Curtis Strange	5,015,720	4 Bruce Crampton	1,682,961	4 Amy Alcott	2,392,647
5 Ben Crenshaw	4,115,074	5 Gary Player	1,604,659	5 JoAnne Carner	2,299,699
6 Lanny Wadkins	3,940,949	6 Don January	1,597,301	6 Patty Sheehan	2,097,846
7 Ray Floyd	3,616,587	7 Chi Chi Rodriguez	1,505,371	7 Beth Daniel	2,029,905
8 Payne Stewart	3,606,707	8 Gene Littler	1,473,677	8 Jan Stephenson	1,801,035
9 Lee Trevino	3,460,416	9 Harold Henning	1,348,536	9 Ayako Okamoto	1,739,582
10 Hale Irwin	3,227,831	10 Billy Casper	1,284,823	10 Kathy Whitworth	1,713,152
11 Bruce Lietzke	3,113,331	11 Dale Douglass	1,199,922	11 Hollis Stacy	1,406,579
12 Greg Norman	3,085,794	12 Lee Elder	1,164,104	12 Donna Caponi	1,387,235

Annual Money Leaders
PGA

Multiple leaders: Jack Nicklaus (8); Ben Hogan and Tom Watson (5); Arnold Palmer (4); Sam Snead and Curtis Strange (3); Julius Boros, Billy Casper, Tom Kite and Byron Nelson (2).

Year	Earnings	Year	Earnings	Year	Earnings
1934 Paul Runyan	$6,767	1953 Lew Worsham	$34,002	1972 Jack Nicklaus	$320,542
1935 Johnny Revolta	9,543	1954 Bob Toski	65,820	1973 Jack Nicklaus	308,362
1936 Horton Smith	7,682	1955 Julius Boros	63,122	1974 Johnny Miller	353,021
1937 Harry Cooper	14,139	1956 Ted Kroll	72,836	1975 Jack Nicklaus	298,149
1938 Sam Snead	19,534	1957 Dick Mayer	65,835	1976 Jack Nicklaus	266,438
1939 Henry Picard	10,303	1958 Arnold Palmer	42,608	1977 Tom Watson	310,653
1940 Ben Hogan	10,655	1959 Art Wall	53,168	1978 Tom Watson	362,429
1941 Ben Hogan	18,358	1960 Arnold Palmer	75,263	1979 Tom Watson	462,636
1942 Ben Hogan	13,143	1961 Gary Player	64,540	1980 Tom Watson	530,808
1943 No records kept		1962 Arnold Palmer	81,448	1981 Tom Kite	365,699
1944 Byron Nelson	37,968	1963 Arnold Palmer	128,230	1982 Craig Stadler	446,462
1945 Byron Nelson	63,336	1964 Jack Nicklaus	113,285	1983 Hal Sutton	426,668
1946 Ben Hogan	42,556	1965 Jack Nicklaus	140,752	1984 Tom Watson	476,260
1947 Jimmy Demaret	27,937	1966 Billy Casper	121,945	1985 Curtis Strange	542,321
1948 Ben Hogan	32,112	1967 Jack Nicklaus	188,998	1986 Greg Norman	653,296
1949 Sam Snead	31,594	1968 Billy Casper	205,169	1987 Curtis Strange	925,941
1950 Sam Snead	35,759	1969 Frank Beard	164,707	1988 Curtis Strange	1,147,644
1951 Lloyd Mangrum	26,089	1970 Lee Trevino	157,037	1989 Tom Kite	1,395,278
1952 Julius Boros	37,033	1971 Jack Nicklaus	244,490		

Note: In 1944-45, Nelson's winnings were in War Bonds.

SENIORS

Multiple leaders: Don January (3); Miller Barber and Bob Charles (2).

Year	Earnings	Year	Earnings	Year	Earnings
1980 Don January	$ 44,100	1984 Don January	$328,597	1988 Bob Charles	$533,929
1981 Miller Barber	83,136	1985 Peter Thomson	386,724	1989 Bob Charles	725,887
1982 Miller Barber	106,890	1986 Bruce Crampton	454,299		
1983 Don January	237,571	1987 Chi Chi Rodriguez	509,145		

LPGA

Multiple leaders: Kathy Whitworth (8); Mickey Wright (4); Patty Berg, JoAnne Carner and Nancy Lopez (3); Beth Daniel, Betsy King, Judy Rankin, Betsy Rawls, Louise Suggs and Babe Zaharis (2).

Year	Earnings	Year	Earnings	Year	Earnings
1950 Babe Zaharias	....$14,800	1964 Mickey Wright	....$29,800	1978 Nancy Lopez	....$189,814
1951 Babe Zaharias	15,087	1965 Kathy Whitworth	...28,658	1979 Nancy Lopez	197,489
1952 Betsy Rawls	14,505	1966 Kathy Whitworth	...33,517	1980 Beth Daniel	231,000
1953 Louise Suggs	19,816	1967 Kathy Whitworth	...32,937	1981 Beth Daniel	206,978
1954 Patty Berg	16,011	1968 Kathy Whitworth	...48,379	1982 JoAnne Carner	310,399
1955 Patty Berg	16,497	1969 Carol Mann	49,152	1983 JoAnne Carner	291,404
1956 Marlene Hagge	20,235	1970 Kathy Whitworth	...30,235	1984 Betsy King	266,771
1957 Patty Berg	16,272	1971 Kathy Whitworth	...41,181	1985 Nancy Lopez	416,472
1958 Beverly Hanson	12,639	1972 Kathy Whitworth	...65,063	1986 Pat Bradley	492,021
1959 Betsy Rawls	26,774	1973 Kathy Whitworth	...82,864	1987 Ayako Okamoto	...466,034
1960 Louise Suggs	16,892	1974 JoAnne Carner	87,094	1988 Sherri Turner	350,851
1961 Mickey Wright	22,236	1975 Sandra Palmer	76,374	1989 Betsy King	654,132
1962 Mickey Wright	21,641	1976 Judy Rankin	150,734		
1963 Mickey Wright	31,269	1977 Judy Rankin	122,890		

The Skins Game

The Skins Game is a made-for-TV, $450,000 shootout between four premier golfers playing 18 holes over two days (nine each day). Each hole is counted as a skin with the first six skins worth $15,000 apiece, the second six worth $25,000, and the last six worth $35,000. If a hole is tied, the money is added to the worth of the next hole. The PGA Skins Game was started in 1983, followed by the Senior Skins in 1988 and the LPGA Skins in 1990. Due to scheduling conflicts, the LPGA Skins will not be played in 1991, but is expected to return in 1992.

PGA Skins

Played in late November.

Total Winnings (7 years, through 1989): Fuzzy Zoeller ($625,000); Jack Nicklaus ($580,000); Lee Trevino ($435,000); Ray Floyd ($350,000); Curtis Strange ($265,000); Arnold Palmer ($245,000); Tom Watson ($230,000) and Gary Player ($170,000).

Year Winner	Earnings	Outskinned	
1983 Gary Player	$170,000	Palmer	$140,000
		Nicklaus	40,000
		Watson	10,000
1984 Jack Nicklaus	$240,000	Watson	$120,000
		Palmer	0
		Player	0
1985 Fuzzy Zoeller	$225,000	Watson	$100,000
		Palmer	80,000
		Nicklaus	15,000
1986 Fuzzy Zoeller	$370,000	Trevino	$55,000
		Palmer	25,000
		Nicklaus	0
1987 Lee Trevino	$310,000	Nicklaus	$70,000
		Zoeller	70,000
		Palmer	0
1988 Ray Floyd	$290,000	Nicklaus	$125,000
		Trevino	35,000
		Strange	0
1989 Curtis Strange	$265,000	Nicklaus	$90,000
		Floyd	60,000
		Trevino	35,000

Senior Skins

Played in early January.

Total Winnings (3 years, through 1990): Chi Chi Rodriguez ($420,000), Arnold Palmer ($330,000), Jack Nicklaus ($140,000), Gary Player ($130,000), Billy Casper ($80,000), Lee Trevino ($70,000) and Sam Snead (0).

Year Winner	Earnings	Outskinned	
1988 C.C.Rodriguez	$300,000	Player	$40,000
		Palmer	20,000
		Snead	0
1989 C.C.Rodriguez	$120,000	Player	$90,000
		Casper	80,000
		Palmer	70,000
1990 Arnold Palmer	$240,000	Nicklaus	$140,000
		Trevino	70,000
		Player	0

LPGA Skins

Played in late May; the second LPGA Skins Game has been postponed until 1992.

Total Winnings (1990): Jan Stephenson ($200,000); JoAnne Carner ($110,000); Nancy Lopez ($95,000) and Betsy King ($45,000).

Year Winner	Earnings	Outskinned	
1990 Jan Stephenson	$200,000	Carner	$110,000
		Lopez	95,000
		King	45,000

Awards

PGA Player of the Year

Awarded by the PGA of America; based on points scale that weighs performance in major tournaments, regular events, money earned and scoring average.

Multiple winners: Tom Watson (6); Jack Nicklaus (5); Ben Hogan (4); Julius Boros, Billy Casper and Arnold Palmer (2).

Year	Player	Year	Player	Year	Player	Year	Player
1948	Ben Hogan	1953	Ben Hogan	1959	Art Wall	1964	Ken Venturi
1949	Sam Snead	1954	Ed Furgol			1965	Dave Marr
		1955	Doug Ford	1960	Arnold Palmer	1966	Billy Casper
1950	Ben Hogan	1956	Jack Burke	1961	Jerry Barber	1967	Jack Nicklaus
1951	Ben Hogan	1957	Dick Mayer	1962	Arnold Palmer	1968	No award
1952	Julius Boros	1958	Dow Finsterwald	1963	Julius Boros	1969	Orville Moody

Awards (Cont.)

PGA Player of the Year

Year	Player	Year	Player	Year	Player	Year	Player
1970	Billy Casper	1976	Jack Nicklaus	1981	Bill Rogers	1987	Paul Azinger
1971	Lee Trevino	1977	Tom Watson	1982	Tom Watson	1988	Curtis Strange
1972	Jack Nicklaus	1978	Tom Watson	1983	Hal Sutton	1989	Tom Kite
1973	Jack Nicklaus	1979	Tom Watson	1984	Tom Watson		
1974	Johnny Miller	1980	Tom Watson	1985	Lanny Wadkins		
1975	Jack Nicklaus			1986	Bob Tway		

LPGA Player of the Year

Awarded by the LPGA; based on performance points accumulated during the year.
Multiple winners: Kathy Whitworth (7); Nancy Lopez (4); JoAnne Carner (3); Betsy King and Judy Rankin (2).

Year	Player	Year	Player	Year	Player	Year	Player
1966	Kathy Whitworth	1972	Kathy Whitworth	1978	Nancy Lopez	1984	Betsy King
1967	Kathy Whitworth	1973	Kathy Whitworth	1979	Nancy Lopez	1985	Nancy Lopez
1968	Kathy Whitworth	1974	JoAnne Carner	1980	Beth Daniel	1986	Pat Bradley
1969	Kathy Whitworth	1975	Sandra Palmer	1981	JoAnne Carner	1987	Ayako Okamoto
1970	Sandra Haynie	1976	Judy Rankin	1982	JoAnne Carner	1988	Nancy Lopez
1971	Kathy Whitworth	1977	Judy Rankin	1983	Patty Sheehan	1989	Betsy King

Colleges

NCAA Men's Division I Champions (since 1940)

Match play from 1897-1964, stroke plays since 1965.

Year	Team winner	Individual champion	Year	Team winner	Individual champion
1940	Princeton & LSU	Dixon Brooke, Virginia	1966	Houston	Bob Murphy, Florida
1941	Stanford	Earl Stewart, LSU	1967	Houston	Hale Irwin, Colorado
1942	LSU & Stanford	Frank Tatum Jr., Stanford	1968	Florida	Grier Jones, Oklahoma St.
1943	Yale	Wallace Ulrich, Carleton	1969	Houston	Bob Clark, Cal St.-LA
1944	Notre Dame	Louis Lick, Minnesota			
1945	Ohio State	John Lorms, Ohio St.	1970	Houston	John Mahaffey, Houston
1946	Stanford	George Hamer, Georgia	1971	Texas	Ben Crenshaw, Texas
1947	LSU	Dave Barclay, Michigan	1972	Texas	Ben Crenshaw, Texas
1948	San Jose St.	Bob Harris, San Jose St.			& Tom Kite, Texas
1949	North Texas	Harvie Ward, North Caro.	1973	Florida	Ben Crenshaw, Texas
1950	North Texas	Fred Wampler, Purdue	1974	Wake Forest	Curtis Strange, W.Forest
1951	North Texas	Tom Nieporte, Ohio St.	1975	Wake Forest	Jay Haas, Wake Forest
1952	North Texas	Jim Vichers, Oklahoma	1976	Oklahoma St.	Scott Simpson, USC
1953	Stanford	Earl Moeller, Oklahoma St.	1977	Houston	Scott Simpson, USC
1954	SMU	Hillman Robbins, Memphis St.	1978	Oklahoma St.	David Edwards, Okla.St.
1955	LSU	Joe Campbell, Purdue	1979	Ohio St.	Gary Hallberg, Wake Forest
1956	Houston	Rick Jones, Ohio St.	1980	Oklahoma St.	Jay Don Blake, Utah St.
1957	Houston	Rex Baxter Jr., Houston	1981	Brigham Young	Ron Commans, USC
1958	Houston	Phil Rodgers, Houston	1982	Houston	Billy Ray Brown, Houston
1959	Houston	Dick Crawford, Houston	1983	Oklahoma St.	Jim Carter, Arizona St.
			1984	Houston	John Inman, N.Carolina
1960	Houston	Dick Crawford, Houston	1985	Houston	Clark Burroughs, Ohio St.
1961	Purdue	Jack Nicklaus, Ohio St.	1986	Wake Forest	Scott Verplank, Okla.St.
1962	Houston	Kermit Zarley, Houston	1987	Oklahoma St.	Brian Watts, Oklahoma St.
1963	Oklahoma St.	R.H. Sikes, Arkansas	1988	UCLA	E.J.Pfister, Oklahoma St.
1964	Houston	Terry Small, San Jose St.	1989	Oklahoma	Phil Mickelson, Ariz.St.
1965	Houston	Marty Fleckman, Houston	1990	Arizona St.	Phil Mickelson, Ariz.St.

NCAA Women's Champions

Year	Team winner	Individual champion	Year	Team winner	Individual champion
1982	Tulsa	Kathy Baker, Tulsa	1987	San Jose St.	Caroline Keggi, N.Mexico
1983	TCU	Penny Hammel, Miami	1988	Tulsa	Melissa McNamara, Tulsa
1984	Miami,FL	Cindy Schreyer, Georgia	1989	San Jose St.	Pat Hurst, San Jose St.
1985	Florida	Danielle Ammaccapane, Ariz.St.	1990	Arizona St.	Susan Slaughter, Arizona
1986	Florida	Page Dunlap, Florida			

Surprise Daytona 500 winner **Derrike Cope** savors his first NASCAR victory on Feb.18. He won the race on the last lap after leader Dale Earnhardt shredded a tire.

AUTO RACING

Unheralded drivers Cope, Luyendyk win at Daytona and Indianapolis; Martin, Earnhardt in NASCAR battle; Senna, Al Unser, Jr., pace F-1, CART.

AUTO RACING

1989-90 YEAR IN REVIEW

by Mike Harris

The 1990 auto racing season could best be characterized as a year of surprises, highlighted by unexpected winners in America's two biggest races—the Daytona 500 and the Indianapolis 500.

Unheralded Derrike Cope, a 31-year-old NASCAR Winston Cup stock car apprentice, joined the big boys with a splashy victory at Daytona on Feb. 18, while 36-year-old Dutchman Arie Luyendyk shocked everyone on May 27 by running off the fastest Indianapolis victory ever. Neither driver had won any major race before coming up with the big one in his respective series.

Cope, who had not had as much as a top-five finish in 67 previous starts, needed a big break to win NASCAR's season-opener. Three-time Winston Cup series champion Dale Earnhardt dominated the first 499 miles of the race, leading 155

Mike Harris has been Motorsports Editor for the Associated Press since 1980. He has been covering the Indianapolis 500 since 1969 and covers more auto races during the year than any other writer in the country.

of the first 199 laps—only to run over a piece of debris that shredded his right rear tire two turns from the end on the 2.5-mile oval.

"It's like a dream," Cope said after dodging past Earnhardt's wiggling car and crossing the finish line ahead of veteran Terry Labonte. "But it wasn't totally luck, we had to be in position to take the win when we had the chance. And there we were in second place when Dale had his problems. Right place, right time and the right race."

The disconsolate Earnhardt, so close to his first Daytona 500 victory, said, "I was just sitting there and they couldn't touch me. They couldn't outrun me, but Derrike got some luck. You've got to get to the checkered flag to win this thing."

Cope solidified his status as a rising star in the NASCAR firmament in June when he won the Budweiser 500 at Dover, Del., for his second Winston Cup victory.

"There's always pressure on you to win that first one," said Cope. "But once you do that, the pressure really gets intense because people keep asking you, 'When are you going to win again?' There are no questions now. This team is going to win more races."

Luyendyk, considered a potential star for several years, broke through to his first CART victory under the biggest spotlight in motorsports. He didn't just win the Indy 500, he blew it away with a record-breaking average speed of 185.981 miles per hour. The previous record, set by Bobby Rahal in 1986, was a mere 170.722.

Like the Daytona 500, the Indy 500 was a race dominated by a veteran until tire problems spelled his ruin.

Defending champion Emerson Fittipaldi of Brazil set an Indy record by leading the first 92 laps and appeared to have things well in hand until he blistered two sets of tires and finished third. The same problem knocked the second-place Rahal out of the running late in the race.

Fittipaldi, the 1989 CART points champion, had established his 1990 credentials before the race by breaking Rick Mear's one- and four-lap qualifying records at Indy. His single fastest lap of 225.575 mph beat the 224.254 by Mears in 1988, and his eye-popping 10-mile qualifying average of 225.301 was considerably better than the 223.885 by Mears the previous year.

"It's unbelievable the way that we won," Luyendyk said, "Emerson looked really strong."

Luyendyk entered the race having never led a lap on the historic 2.5-mile oval in five previous starts. He stayed among the leaders all day, leading two laps in the early going and finally taking over the top spot for good with a strong pass on Rahal, 33 laps from the finish. Luyendyk won $1,090,940 at Indy, eclipsing the all-time single-race haul of $1,001,604 carried home by Fittipaldi in 1989. Before the race, Tom Monaghan, the principal sponsor of Luyendyk's Domino's Pizza Lola-Chevrolet, was determined to get out of the 16-race, $5 million-a-year Indy-car racing circuit where his team had enjoyed little success. Afterward, Monaghan, who also owns the Detroit Tigers, said he was reconsidering.

Not surprisingly, neither Luyendyk nor Cope was able to win consistently and did not challenge for either the CART or NASCAR championships.

Arie Luyendyk's first-ever triumph at the Indianapolis 500 was both the fastest and the richest in the 74-year history of the race.

Mark Martin, who came out of nowhere in 1989 to challenge longtime stars Rusty Wallace and Earnhardt for the Winston Cup title, was back for more in 1990. Running consistently at or near the front, Martin got into a season-long championship battle with Earnhardt, known to many in and around NASCAR as "The Intimidator."

Earnhardt lost the 1989 championship to Wallace by just 12 points—the closest margin since Richard Petty topped Darrell Waltrip by 11 in 1979. That whetted Earnhardt's appetite for his first title since 1987 and he came out smoking in 1990, winning eight races through mid-September.

But Martin wouldn't wilt. He took the points lead from Earnhardt at the halfway point in the season and held on determinedly to a small margin as the battle headed down the stretch of the 29-race season.

"You go out every race prepared to win," the 31-year-old Martin said. "If there's some reason you can't win, you try to finish as high as you can and get all the points you can get. We've been lucky enough to race consistently and let our preparation keep the pressure from affecting us."

That consistency was impressive, with Martin finishing on the lead lap in 20 of the first 24 races. During that period, he had 20 finishes in the Top 10 and 16 in the Top Five, including two victories.

Martin and his Roush Racing team also overcame a very disheartening situation in only the second race of the season.

The blossoming NASCAR star came back from a disappointing 21st place finish at the Daytona 500 to win the Pontiac 400 the following week at Richmond, Va. However, a technical inspection following the event detected an illegal carburetor spacer in Martin's Ford Thunderbird.

NASCAR let the victory stand but fined Martin's team $40,000 and 46 championship points—the latter a particular handicap in the battle for the $1 million title payoff.

"I don't think you're ever going to find a mechanic who says we got any real gain from that spacer," Martin said. "It was just a mistake, and one that really didn't make any difference in our performance. The whole thing was just a shame."

Martin was able to put the black day behind him and go on with his championship quest. He got a big boost when he won the Champion Spark Plug 400 at Michigan International Speedway in August.

"That win means a lot to our team," Martin said. "And this time there's no question about anything."

He added, "I've been saying since last January that this is the best team out there. Whether we win the championship this year or not, this is going to be the team of the 90s. We're in it for the long haul."

By the final stages of the Winston Cup season, Earnhardt not only had eight wins, but a surprising four poles as well. The 38- year-old driver's pole victory at Talladega Superspeedway in July was his first since March of 1988 at Atlanta International Speedway. Earnhardt won his second pole of the season the next weekend at Watkin's Glen, N.Y., took second the following week and added two more in succession.

Cruise movie not in sync with NASCAR

There was a lot of hope tied up in the 1990 movie Days of Thunder.

The people at Paramount Pictures put plenty of effort and money—an estimated $60 million—into this Tom Cruise vehicle about a hotshot racer trying to overcome his emotions and become a star stock car racer in NASCAR's Winston Cup series.

NASCAR, and particularly the folks at Daytona International Raceway and several other major tracks, cooperated as much as possible with the demanding Hollywood folks in hopes that the sport would benefit. After all, the movie would be seen by millions of people, many of them strangers to the bump, bang and bend world of the superspeedway ovals.

In the end, Days of Thunder, released with considerable fanfare in June, was not the explosive hit that Paramount, Cruise and NASCAR hoped it would be. Through September, it grossed about $80 million at the box office, or roughly $20 million more than it cost to make and market.

Still, it was entertaining (if a little far-fetched), according to most racing people who have seen it. And it did take NASCAR into places its stock cars have never been before.

"We know it isn't entirely realistic," said Chip Williams, NASCAR's media director. "There's quite a bit more bumping and crashing (in the movie) than really goes on, but it does show the scene and the excitement. I think people understand that and find it interesting."

Before the movie was even the germ of an idea in Cruise's mind, NASCAR was selling most of its seats and generating tremendous interest—and tremendous dollars—among corporate sponsors.

More seats are being added all the time and NASCAR officials say there's always room for more racing fans. But, while it may be somewhat glamorous, stock car racing is also a deadly serious business. People, including drivers, crewmen, track workers and spectators, can be seriously injured or killed if something goes wrong when these cars are roaring around the tracks.

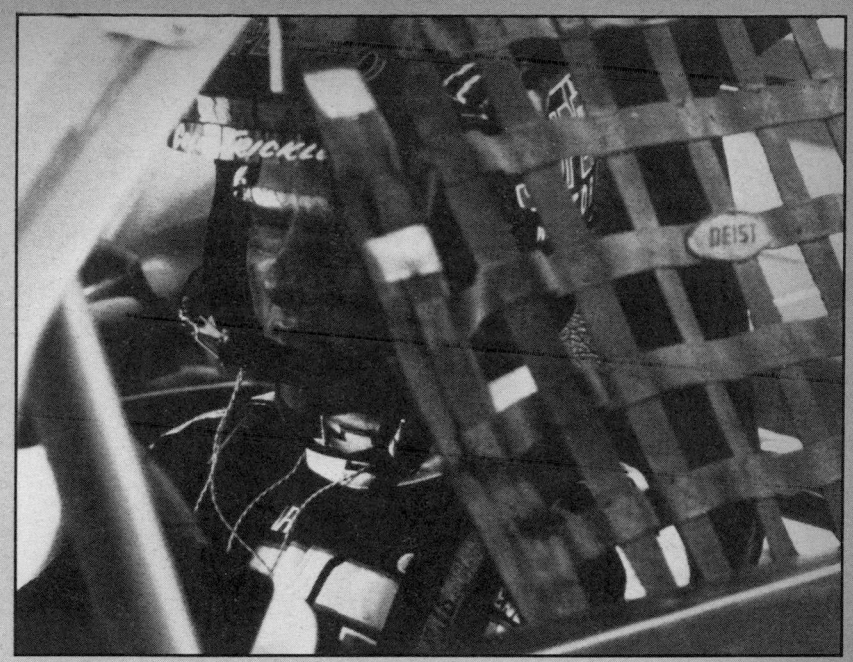

Stephen Vaughan/Paramount Pictures

Actor **Tom Cruise** may have played a daredevil stock car racer in Paramount Pictures' $60 million *Days of Thunder,* but in the real world, NASCAR is doing everything it can to make the sport less dangerous.

That's why NASCAR, while promoting the competitive aspects of its top series, is also fighting a serious battle to slow the cars down at its two fastest circuits—Daytona and Talladega Superspeedway.

Prior to the summer of 1987, laps of over 200 mph had become commonplace at those two tracks. Then, in a race at Talladega, veteran racer Bobby Allison lost control at about 210 mph, flew through the air, hit and tore down fencing protecting the spectators and very nearly went into the packed grandstand.

The sanctioning body was frightened by the specter of such a disaster, and its insurance company demanded changes. Before you could say "carburetor restrictor plate," NASCAR had taken steps to slow the cars down by cutting horsepower. The move, they said, was made in the interest of safety for everyone, including the spectators.

Nice irony. Here you have a sport built around speed and the prospect of danger and the governing body in that sport is trying its best to limit the speeds to eliminate some of the danger.

It's interesting that the wild crashes and daredevil moves that director Tony Scott tried to capture in *Days of Thunder* could be attracting more fans to the sport just when those things are being at least partially legislated out.

Darrell Waltrip, a three-time Winston Cup champion and the 1989 Daytona 500 winner, said, "I always thought that in racing the idea was to go as fast as you can to beat the other guy."

Dale Earnhardt, another three-time NASCAR champion and the winner of three of the four "restricted" races in 1990, has mixed feelings.

"I don't really agree with slowing the cars down because this is supposed to be racing," said Earnhardt. "But they (NASCAR) have got to think about the safety of those people in the stands and the image that racing needs to have. I can understand why they do it. I just don't like it. I'd rather just go out and race."

Dale Earnhardt won the IROC series title and eight NASCAR races through Sept.23, but he still trailed Mark Martin in Winston Cup points.

"I don't really know why we're winning poles this year when we haven't for so long," he said. "The team has always worked hard to get the car ready to win the pole and the race and that first part just wasn't working out for us for a while."

The shredded tired at Daytona, which set him back to fifth place, cost Earnhardt important championship points as well as a shot at Winston's $1 million bonus that goes to any driver who can win three of NASCAR's Big Four races.

He did earn a $100,000 bonus from the series sponsor for winning two of NASCAR's "Crown Jewels"—the Winston 500 at Talladega, Ala., and the Heinz Southern 500 at Darlington, S.C. NASCAR's other two jewels—the Daytona 500 and the Coca-Cola 600 at Charlotte, N.C.—were won by Cope and Wallace.

Earnhardt also outdueled English endurance racing star Martin Brundle for the 1990 International Race of Champions series title, winning two of the three events to take first-place money of $175,000. Brundle, who won the other race, was a first-time IROC performer.

The Indy-car series in 1990 belonged to a pair of second-generation drivers, who asserted their dominance and headed to the wire in a heated, see-saw battle for CART's championship.

Back in 1986, when Michael Andretti beat Al Unser, Jr. in the Long Beach Grand Prix for his first Indy-car victory, Andretti said, "The new generation has arrived."

Actually, it took four more years for both of the young racers to move to the forefront of the CART series. But both are firmly established now.

Unser, with six victories in the first 14 (of 16) races, took the upper hand in 1990, getting ahead by as many as 48 points before Andretti, with five victories, made a late-season run at him.

The big move by Unser was a spurt of four straight wins—the first time that's been done in CART's 12-year history. The streak, which ran from July 22 to Sept.2, included a record-smashing win in the Marlboro 500 at Michigan on August 5.

Andretti responded with two straight wins of his own following Unser's tear, keeping his title hopes alive with two races left.

"Al built his big lead over me by winning those four in a row," Michael said. "All we can do is try to win the last four and see if we can get those points back."

Unser, whose victory at Michigan was his first in a 500-mile event and only his second on an oval—the first coming in June at the Miller 200 in Milwaukee—said "I had a feeling at the beginning of the year that it was going to be Michael versus me for the championship. I'm glad to be in the position I'm in."

While neither Unser nor Andretti has yet won the points race for CART's PPG Cup, prior to 1990 each had finished second twice. In 1985, Unser lost by a point (151-150) to his father in the closest championship battle in CART history. Three years later, he came in 33 points behind champion Danny Sullivan. Andretti, the son of longtime racing great Mario Andretti, was runner-up to Bobby Rahal in both 1986 and '87—trailing by eight and 30 points, respectively.

Last year, Andretti placed third and Unser fifth as the points title went to Fittipaldi.

Wide World Photos

CART points leader **Al Unser, Jr.** won six races through September, including the fastest 500-mile race in history at the Marlboro 500.

Wide World Photos

With six victories in the first 13 Formula One races, **Ayrton Senna** was within reach of his second World Championship title in three years.

At Michigan, Unser fought off team-mate Rahal in a wheel-to-wheel duel at 220 mph and went on to win the race with an average speed of 189.727 mph—the fastest 500-mile race in history. The previous record was 186.288 set by stock car star Bill Elliott in the 1985 Winston 500.

"When you're racing somebody that close at those speeds," Unser said, "you have to trust them with your life. I trust Bobby with mine. . . but I'm glad it didn't go all the way to the end."

The 28-year-old Unser is well aware of the pitfalls that await race drivers. The same weekend he set the record on Michigan International Speedway's two-mile, high-banked oval, Al Unser, 51, a four-time Indianapolis winner, crashed in practice and broke his leg.

"I knew dad was in a lot of pain and that bothered me, but I also knew I had to go out and do the job I get paid to do," Unser said.

Another of the great names in racing wound up spending some time in the hospital late in the Indy-car season.

A.J. Foyt broke bones in both legs and put the continuation of his tremendous career in jeopardy when his brakes apparently failed during the Texaco 200 race at Road America in Elkhart Lake, Wis., on Sept.23. Foyt's Lola sped off the track, through a run-off area and across a field before slamming into an embankment and crushing the front of his car down on his legs and feet.

But even as track safety workers placed the 55-year-old legend in a helicopter for the ride to the hospital, the all-time Indy-car wins leader (he has 67) vowed, "I'll be back."

"Super Tex" made his record 33rd consecutive start at Indianapolis in May and finished a respectable sixth—his second straight Top 10 performance at Indy.

The Formula One season was another harrowing duel between Brazil's Ayrton Senna and Alain Prost of France—only this time they were on different teams and in very different cars.

The former teammates finally made up late in the 1990 season, publicly shaking hands after Senna's McLaren Honda beat Prost's Ferrari, Sept. 9, at Monza, Italy.

"We are both professionals, with much passion for our work," Senna said, defusing the feud that began two years earlier when they were McLaren teammates and constant adversaries.

Senna continued as the all-time master of pole victories, building his total to 49 late in the season. The former record, before Senna beat it in 1989, was 33 set by the late Jimmy Clark.

The brilliant Brazilian won six of the first 13 races in the 16-race series and was carrying a nearly insurmountable lead over Prost, winner of four races. Senna, aiming to unseat Prost as champion, was trying for his second world title.

"The championship is everything to me," Senna said. "It is the pinnacle and I want to climb it again."

Englishman Nigel Mansell, Prost's Ferrari teammate, shocked the Formula One world in August when he announced that he would retire at season's end. In September, however, after winning the Portuguese Grand Prix, the enigmatic Mansell hinted that he might change his mind and return in 1991, but not with Ferrari.

For the third straight year, the IMSA Camel GT Prototype sports car endurance series was dominated by Nissan and Australian driver Geoff Brabham.

Brabham, the son of former three-time Formula One champion Jack Brabham, was well on the way to his third consecutive title, chased only by teammate Chip Robinson, who appeared to be fighting a hopeless battle as the season waned.

The SCCA's Trans-Am season belonged to 24-year-old Tommy Kendall, a three-time IMSA GTU champ. Kendall wrapped up his first Trans-Am title early with six victories in the first 13 races.

In the World Sportscar Championship, Mercedes ran away with the manufacturer's championship for the second straight year, leaving the driver championship to be decided between its top driver Jean-Louis Schlesser of France and Mauro Baldi of Italy.

Finally, 1990 saw Jaguar prototypes win the two most prestigious 24-hour endurance races in the world. In February, Davy Jones, Jan Lammers and Andy Wallace combined to capture the Sun-Bank 24 at Daytona. And four months later, Brundle, Price Cobb and John Nielsen shared the wheel in winning the 24 Hours of Le Mans in France.

In fact, the Jaguars finished 1-2 in both races. Le Mans winners Jones, Lammers and Wallace came in second at Daytona, while Daytona winners Lammers and Wallace, driving with new number three man Franz Konrad, came in second at Le Mans. Meanwhile, Jaguar's win at Daytona made it the only manufacturer other than Porsche to win that twice-around-the-clock race more than once in its 23-year history. □

1990 Endurance Races
24 Hours of Daytona
(Feb. 3-4 at Daytona Beach FL)
Officially the SunBank 24 Hours of Daytona and first held in 1962 (as a 3-hour race). An IMSA Camel GT race for exotic prototype sports cars and contested over a 3.56-mile road course at Daytona International Speedway. Listed are drivers, hometowns or countries, car, prize money, and laps completed. Starting positions in parentheses.
1. (10) Jan Lammers of Holland, Andy Wallace of Britain and Davy Jones of McGraw, NY; JAGUAR XJR-10; $66,000; 761 laps (2709.160 miles) at 112.857 mph.
2. (9) John Nielsen of Denmark, Martin Brundle of Britain and Price Cobb of Evergreen, CO; JAGUAR XJR-10; $25,000; 757 laps.
3. (1) Bob Wollek of France, Sarel van der Merwe of South Africa and Dominic Dodson of Fairfax, CA; PORSCHE 962; $16,500; 755 laps.
4. (13) Rene Herzog of Switz., Harold Grohs and Hans Stuck of West Germany and Hurley Haywood of Jacksonville, FL; PORSCHE 962; $11,000; 704 laps.
5. (25) Robby Gordon of Los Angeles, Calvin Fish of Chicago and Lynn St.James of Ft.Lauderdale, FL; MERCURY COUGAR XR-7; $21,100; 689 laps.

24 Hours of Le Mans
(June 16-17 at Le Mans, France)
Officially the Le Mans Grand Prix d'Endurance and first held in 1923. Contested over the 8.5-mile circuit in Le Mans, France. Listed are drivers, countries, car, and laps completed.
1. John Nielsen of Denmark, Price Cobb of Evergreen,CO, and Martin Brundle of Britain; JAGUAR XJR-12; 358 laps; 3034 miles at 126.83 mph.
2. Jan Lammers of Holland, Andy Wallace of Britain, and Franz Konrad of W.Germany; JAGUAR XJR-12; 354 laps.
3. Tiff Needell, David Sears and Tony Reid of Britain; PORSCHE 962-C; 351 laps.
4. Hans Stuck of W.Germany, Derek Bell of Britain, and Frank Jelinski of W.Germany; PORSCHE 962-C; 349 laps.
5. Masahiro Hasemi, Kazuyoshi Hoshino and Toshio Suzuki of Japan; NISSAN GTP; 347 laps.
6. Geoff Lees of Britain, Masanori Sekiya and Hitoshi Ogawa of Japan; TOYOTA GTP; 346 laps.

Fastest lap: covered in 3 minutes, 40.03 seconds at 138.30 mph by Bob Earl of Larkspur,CA, Michael Roe of Ireland and Steve Millen of N. Zealand; NISSAN GTP.

THE 1991 INFORMATION PLEASE SPORTS ALMANAC

AUTO RACING
STATISTICS

THE SEASON IN REVIEW
1989-1990

NASCAR • CART • FORMULA 1

SEC A

PAGE 627

1989-90 NASCAR Results

Winners of NASCAR Winston Cup races from Oct.8, 1989 through Sept.23, 1990.

Late 1989

Date	Event	Winner (start pos.)	Avg.MPH	Earnings	Margin	Runner-up
Oct. 8	All Pro Auto Parts 500	Ken Schrader (2)	149.863*	$86,300	3.75s	H.Gant
Oct.15	Holly Farms 400	Geoff Bodine (11)	90.253	47,800	2.00s	M.Martin
Oct.22	AC Delco 500	Mark Martin (7)	114.079	52,800	3.02s	R.Wallace
Nov. 5	Autoworks 500	Bill Elliott (13)	105.683*	57,900	0.47s	T.Labonte
Nov.19	Atlanta Journal 500	Dale Earnhardt (3)	140.229	81,700	25.71s	G.Bodine

*New record.

Winning Cars: Chevrolet Lumina 3 (Schrader, Bodine, Earnhardt); Ford Thunderbird 2 (Martin, Elliott).

1990 (through Sept.23)

Date	Event	Winner (start pos.)	Avg.MPH	Earnings	Margin	Runner-up
Feb.18	**Daytona 500**	Derrike Cope (12)	165.761	$188,150	1½-L	T.Labonte
Feb.25	Pontiac 400	Mark Martin (6)	92.166	59,150	1.02s	D.Earnhardt
Mar. 4	Goodwrench 500	Kyle Petty (1)	122.842	302,050†	25.48s	G.Bodine
Mar.18	Motorcraft 500	Dale Earnhardt (1)	156.849*	85,000	0.32s	M.Shepherd
Apr. 1	TranSouth 500	Dale Earnhardt (15)	124.073	61,985	0.34s	M.Martin
Apr. 8	Valleydale Meats 500	Davey Allison (19)	87.257	50,100	6-in.	M.Martin
Apr.22	First Union 400	Brett Bodine (20)	83.900	50,682	0.85s	D.Waltrip
Apr.29	Hanes Sweatshirts 500	Geoff Bodine (1)	77.423	95,950†	4.21s	R.Wallace
May 6	**Winston 500**	Dale Earnhardt (5)	159.571	98,975	2-L	G.Sacks
May 27	**Coca-Cola 600**	Rusty Wallace (9)	137.650	151,000	1.76s	B.Elliott
Jun. 3	Budweiser 500	Derrike Cope (15)	123.993	55,050	1.30s	K.Schrader
Jun.10	Banquet Foods 300k	Rusty Wallace (11)	69.245	69,100	caution	M.Martin
Jun.17	Miller Genuine Draft 500	Harry Gant (16)	120.627	54,350	2.40s	R.Wallace
Jun.24	Miller Genuine Draft 400	Dale Earnhardt (5)	150.219	72,950	0.14s	E.Irvan
Jul. 7	Pepsi 400	Dale Earnhardt (3)	160.894	72,850	1.60s	A.Kulwicki
Jul.22	AC Spark Plug 500	Geoff Bodine (4)	124.103	58,500	1.29s	B.Elliott
Jul.29	Talladega DieHard 500	Dale Earnhardt (1)	174.429	152,975†	0.26s	B.Elliott
Aug.12	Budweiser at the Glen	Ricky Rudd (12)	92.440	55,000	6.54s	G.Bodine
Aug.19	Champion Spark Plug 400	Mark Martin (5)	138.821	71,200	1.75s	G.Sacks
Aug.25	Busch 500	Ernie Irvan (6)	91.728	49,600	1-L	R.Wallace
Sep. 2	**Heinz Southern 500**	Dale Earnhardt (1)	125.945*	240,750†	4.08s	E.Irvan
Sep. 9	Miller Genuine Draft 400	Dale Earnhardt (6)	95.567	59,225	0.43s	M.Martin
Sep.16	Peak Performance 500	Bill Elliott (7)	129.945*	98,300†	1.38s	M.Martin
Sep.23	Goody's 500	Geoff Bodine (14)	76.386	53,850	4.53s	D.Earnhardt

Remaining races (5): Holly Farms 400 (Sep.30); All-Pro Auto Parts 500 (Oct.7); AC Delco 500 (Oct.21); Autoworks 500k (Nov.4); and Atlanta Journal 500 (Nov.18).

*New record for event.

†Includes carryover Unocal 76 bonus for winning race from pole—Petty ($228,000); G.Bodine ($38,000); Earnhardt ($68,400 and $30,400); Elliott ($15,200). No bonus was given at Motorcraft 500 after qualifying was rained out (pole decided on owner points). Earnhardt also earned $100,000 Crown Jewel bonus for winning Southern 500.

Winning Cars: Ford Thunderbird 11 (G.Bodine 3, Martin 2, D.Allison and Elliott); Chevrolet Lumina (Earnhardt 8, Cope 2, Irvan and Rudd); Oldsmobile Cutlass (Gant); Buick Regal (B.Bodine); Pontiac Grand Prix (Wallace 2 and K.Petty).

Race Locations

February—Daytona 500 at Daytona Int'l Speedway; Pontiac 400 at Richmond,VA Int'l Raceway. **March**—GM 500 at North Carolina Motor Speedway in Rockingham; Motorcraft 500 at Atlanta Int'l Speedway. **April**—TranSouth 500 at Darlington,SC Int'l Raceway; Valleydale 500 at Bristol,TN Int'l Raceway; First Union 400 at North Wilkesboro,NC Speedway; Hanes 500 at Martinsville,VA Speedway. **May**—Winston 500 at Talladega,AL Superspeedway; Coca-Cola 600 at Charlotte Motor Speedway. **June**—Bud 500 at Dover,DE Downs Int'l Speedway; Banquet 300km at Sears Point Raceway in Somona, CA; Miller 500 at Pocono,PA Int'l Raceway; Miller 400 at Michigan Int'l Speedway in Brooklyn. **July**—Pepsi 400 at Daytona Int'l Speedway; AC 500 at Pocono Int'l Raceway in Long Pond,PA; DieHard 500 at Talladega,AL Superspeedway. **August**—Bud at the Glen in Watkins Glen,NY; Champion 400 at Michigan Int'l Speedway in Brooklyn; Busch 500 at Bristol,TN Int'l Raceway. **September**—Southern 500 at Darlington,SC Int'l Raceway; Miller 400 at Richmond,VA Int'l Raceway; Peak Perf.500 at Dover,DE Downs Int'l Speedway; Goody's 500 at Martinsville,VA Speedway; Holly Farms 400 at North Wilkesboro,NC Speedway. **October**—All Pro 500 at Charlotte Motor Speedway; AC Delco 500 at (Rockingham) North Carolina Motor Speedway. **November**—Autoworks 500km at Phoenix Int'l Raceway; Atlanta Journal 500 at Atlanta Int'l Raceway.

1990 Daytona 500

Date—Sunday, Feb.18, 1990, at Daytona, FL International Speedway. **Distance**—500 miles; **Course**—2.5 miles; **Field**—42 cars; **Average speed**—165.761 mph; **Margin of victory**—1½ car lengths; **Time of race**—3 hours, 59 seconds; **Caution flags**—3 for 15 laps; **Lead changes**—27 by 13 drivers; **Attendance**—150,000 (estimated).

Defending champion—Darrell Waltrip; **Pole sitter**—Ken Schrader won his 3rd consecutive Daytona 500 pole at 196.515 mph on Feb.10, but had to start in 41st position after crashing in the first of two 125-mile qualifying races on Feb.15; Geoff Bodine moved up to sit on pole.

Top 15 Finishers

Driver (start pos.)	Hometown	Car	Laps	Ended Race	Earnings
1 Derrike Cope (12)	Spanaway, WA	Chevrolet Lumina	200	Running	$188,150
2 Terry Labonte (20)	Corpus Christi, TX	Oldsmobile Cutlas	200	Running	117,800
3 Bill Elliott (4)	Dawsonville, GA	Ford Thunderbird	200	Running	114,100
4 Ricky Rudd (19)	Columbia, TN	Chevrolet Lumina	200	Running	77,050
5 Dale Earnhardt (2)	Kannapolis, NC	Chevrolet Lumina	200	Running*	109,325
6 Bobby Hillin (10)	Midland, TX	Buick Regal	200	Running	63,225
7 Rusty Wallace (38)	Hammonton, NJ	Pontiac Grand Prix	200	Running	59,682
8 Michael Waltrip (24)	Owensboro, KY	Pontiac Grand Prix	199	Running	46,200
9 Geoff Bodine (3)	Chemung, NY	Ford Thunderbird	199	Running	80,950
10 Morgan Shepherd (30)	Conover, NC	Ford Thunderbird	199	Running	44,125
11 Neil Bonnett (31)	Hueytown, AL	Ford Thunderbird	199	Running	38,400
12 Dick Trickle (32)	Wisc.Rapids, WI	Pontiac Grand Prix	199	Running	36,200
13 Ernie Irvan (18)	Modesto, CA	Ford Thunderbird	199	Running	31,455
14 Darrell Waltrip (9)	Franklin, TN	Chevrolet Lumina	199	Running	49,340
15 Jimmy Spencer (6)	Berwick, PA	Pontiac Grand Prix	199	Running	41,050

*Earnhardt was leading race with less than half a lap to go when his right rear tire blew after running over debris.

Winston Cup Point Standings

Official Top 10 NASCAR Winston Cup point leaders and Top 15 money leaders for 1989 and unofficial Top 10 point leaders and Top 15 money leaders for 1990 (through Sept.23). Points awarded for places 1 to 40 and lap leaders. Earnings include bonuses. Listed are starts (Sts), races won (1st), top five finishes (Top5) and points.

Final 1989

	Sts	1st	Top5	Points
1 Rusty Wallace	29	6	13	4176
2 Dale Earnhardt	29	5	14	4164
3 Mark Martin	29	1	14	4053
4 Darrell Waltrip	29	6	14	3971
5 Ken Schrader	29	1	10	3786
6 Bill Elliott	29	3	8	3774
7 Harry Gant	29	1	9	3610
8 Ricky Rudd	29	1	7	3608
9 Geoff Bodine	29	1	9	3600
10 Terry Labonte	29	2	9	3569

1990 (thru Sept.23)

	Sts	1st	Top5	Points
1 Mark Martin	24	2	15	3689
2 Dale Earnhardt	24	8	15	3673
3 Geoff Bodine	24	3	9	3360
4 Bill Elliott	24	1	9	3253
5 Rusty Wallace	24	2	9	3221
6 Kyle Petty	24	1	1	3004
7 Ricky Rudd	24	1	8	2993
8 Ernie Irvan	24	1	6	2934
9 Morgan Shepherd	24	0	4	2915
10 Ken Schrader	24	0	4	2894

Money Won

Final 1989

	Earnings		Earnings		Earnings
1 Rusty Wallace	$2,247,950	6 Bill Elliott	$854,570	11 Morgan Shepherd	$544,255
2 Dale Earnhardt	1,435,730	7 Terry Labonte	704,806	12 Ricky Rudd	534,824
3 Darrell Waltrip	1,313,079	8 Harry Gant	641,092	13 Alan Kulwicki	501,295
4 Ken Schrader	1,039,441	9 Davey Allison	640,956	14 Sterling Marlin	473,267
5 Mark Martin	1,019,250	10 Geoff Bodine	620,594	15 Dick Trickle	343,728

1990 (through Sept.23)

	Earnings		Earnings		Earnings
1 Dale Earnhardt	$1,569,930	6 Kyle Petty	$613,565	11 Harry Gant	$415,330
2 Mark Martin	767,695	7 Ken Schrader	609,110	12 Ernie Irvan	408,142
3 Rusty Wallace	746,444	8 Derrike Cope	480,530	13 Terry Labonte	371,689
4 Bill Elliott	713,965	9 Davey Allison	452,655	14 Darrell Waltrip	363,482
5 Geoff Bodine	696,785	10 Ricky Rudd	415,332	15 Morgan Shepherd	339,415

1989-90 CART Results

Winners of CART Indy car races from Oct.15,1989 through Sept.23,1990.

Late 1989

Date	Event	Winner (start pos.)	Avg.MPH	Earnings	Margin	Runner-up
Oct.15	Champion Spark Plug 300km	Rick Mears (1)	94.174	$66,160	1.85s	Ma.Andretti

Winning car: Penske PC-18 Chevrolet (Mears).

1990 (through Sept.23)

Date	Event	Winner (start pos.)	Avg.MPH	Earnings	Margin	Runner-up
Apr. 8	Autoworks 200	Rick Mears (1)	126.291	$88,708	7.26	B.Rahal
Apr.22	Toyota GP of Long Beach	Al Unser Jr.(1)	84.227	143,908	1.72	E.Fittipaldi
May 27	Indianapolis 500	Arie Luyendyk (3)	185.984*	1,090,940	10.7	B.Rahal
Jun. 3	Miller Genuine Draft 200	Al Unser,Jr (9)	133.670*	87,632	0.73	R.Mears
Jun.17	Valvoline Detroit GP	Michael Andretti (1)	84.902*	134,306	1:48.53	B.Rahal
Jun.24	Budweiser-G.I.Joe's 200	Michael Andretti (1)	110.673	77,333	3.92	Ma.Andretti
Jul. 8	Budweiser Cleveland GP	Danny Sullivan (5)	112.483	81.628	5.22	B.Rahal
Jul.15	Marlboro GP at Meadowlands	Michael Andretti (1)	97.290	80,781	38.18	R.Mears
Jul.22	Molson Indy Toronto	Al Unser,Jr (8)	75.997	138,908	38.1	Mi.Andretti
Aug. 5	Marlboro 500	Al Unser,Jr (5)	189.727**	172,684	25.46	B.Rahal
Aug.26	Texaco GP of Denver	Al Unser,Jr (2)	71.240	137,866	28.0	D.Sullivan
Sep. 2	Molson Indy Vancouver	Al Unser,Jr (6)	77.345	138,628	10.0	D.Sullivan
Sep.16	Red Roof Inns 200	Michael Andretti (1)	85.751	80,655	7.63	Ma.Andretti
Sep.23	Texaco-Havoline 200	Michael Andretti (5)	106.192	76,054	2.35	E.Fittipaldi

Remaining races (2): Bosch Spark Plug GP (Oct.7); Champion Spark Plug 300km (Oct.21).
*New track record.
**Fastest 500-mile race in history.
Winning cars: Lola-Chevrolet, 12 (Unser,Jr 6, Mi.Andretti 5, and Luyendyk); Penske-Chevrolet, 2 (Mears and Sullivan).

Race Locations

April—Autoworks 200 at Phoenix Int'l Raceway; Toyota GP in Long Beach,CA. **May**—Indianapolis 500 at Indianapolis Motor Speedway. **June**—Miller 200 at Wisconsin State Fair Park in West Allis; Detroit GP In Detroit; Bud-G.I.Joe's 200 at Portland,OR Int'l Raceway. **July**—Cleveland GP at Burke Lakefront Airport; Marlboro GP at Meadowlands Sports Complex in E.Rutherford, NJ; Molson Toronto at Exhibition Place.
August—Marlboro 500 at Michigan Int'l Speedway in Brooklyn; Texaco GP in Denver. **September**—Molson Vancouver in Vancouver; Red Roof Inns 200 at Mid-Ohio Sports Car Course in Lexington; Texaco 200 at Road America in Elkhart Lake,WI. **October**—Bosch GP at Pennsylvania Int'l Raceway in Nazareth; Champion 300km at Laguna Seca Raceway in Monterey,CA.

1990 Indianapolis 500

Date—Sunday, May 17, 1990, at Indianapolis Motor Speedway. **Distance**—500 miles; **Course**—2.5 miles oval; **Field**—33 cars; **Winner's average speed**—185.981 mph (record; old record, 170.722 mph by Bobby Rahal in 1986); **Margin of victory**—10.878 seconds; **Time of race**—2 hours, 41 minutes, 18.404 seconds; **Caution flags**—4 for 26 laps; **Lead changes**—7 by 3 drivers; **Attendance**—400,000 (estimated).
Defending champion—Emerson Fittipaldi; **Pole sitter**—Fittipaldi at 225.301 mph (record; old record, 223.885 by Rick Mears in 1989). **Most laps leading race**—Fittipaldi (128 of 200).

Top 15 Finishers

Driver (start pos.)	Hometown	Car	Laps	Ended Race	Earnings
1 Arie Luyendyk (3)	Holland	Lola-Chevrolet	200	Running	$1,090,940
2 Bobby Rahal (4)	Dublin,OH	Lola-Chevrolet	200	Running	488,566
3 Emerson Fittipaldi (1)	Brazil	Penske-Chevrolet	200	Running	592,874
4 Al Unser, Jr. (7)	Albuquerque	Lola-Chevrolet	199	Running	227,691
5 Rick Mears (2)	Bakersfield,CA	Penske-Chevrolet	198	Running	201,610
6 A.J. Foyt (8)	Houston	Lola-Chevrolet	194	Running	184,804
7 Scott Brayton (26)	Coldwater, MI	Lola-Chevrolet	194	Running	196,448
8 Eddie Cheever* (14)	Phoenix	Penske-Chevrolet	193	Running	172,786
9 Kevin Cogan (15)	Palos Verdes, CA	Penske-Buick	191	Running	150,572
10 Scott Goodyear* (21)	Toronto	Lola-Judd	191	Running	146,970
11 Dider Theys (20)	Belgium	Penske-Buick	190	Running	142,384
12 Tero Palmroth (16)	Finland	Lola-Cosworth	188	Running	138,756
13 Al Unser (30)	Albuquerque	March-Alfa Romeo	186	Running	141,387
14 Randy Lewis (12)	Hillsborogh,CA	Penske-Buick	186	Running	134,275
15 Jim Crawford (29)	Scotland	Lola-Buick	183	Running	130,022

*Rookies.

PPG Cup Point Standings

Official Top 10 CART PPG Cup point leaders and Top 15 money leaders for 1989 and unofficial Top 10 point leaders and Top 15 money leaders for 1990 (through Sept.23). Points awarded for places 1 to 12, fastest qualifier and overall lap leader. Listed are starts (Sts), races won (1st), races running at finish (RAF) and points.

Final 1989	Sts	1st	RAF	Points	1990 (thru Sept.23)	Sts	1st	RAF	Points
1 Emerson Fittipaldi	15	5	12	196	1 Al Unser, Jr	14	6	12	194
2 Rick Mears	15	3	14	186	2 Michael Andretti	14	5	9	157
3 Michael Andretti	15	2	10	150	3 Rick Mears	14	1	12	140
4 Teo Fabi	15	1	11	141	4 Bobby Rahal	14	0	12	128
5 Al Unser, Jr	15	1	11	136	5 Mario Andretti	14	0	10	124
6 Mario Andretti	15	0	10	110	6 Danny Sullivan	14	1	9	117
7 Danny Sullivan	13	2	10	107	7 Emerson Fittipaldi	14	0	11	115
8 Scott Pruett	15	0	12	101	8 Arie Luyendyk	14	1	11	86
9 Bobby Rahal	15	1	9	88	9 Eddie Cheever	14	0	9	69
10 Arie Luyendyk	15	0	11	75	10 John Andretti	14	0	7	46

1989-90 CART Leaders (Cont.)

Money Won

Final 1989

	Earnings		Earnings		Earnings
1 E.Fittipaldi	$2,166,078	6 Danny Sullivan	$790,234	11 Arie Luyendyk	$541,445
2 Al Unser,Jr	1,247,571	7 Mario Andretti	759,364	12 Scott Brayton	451,317
3 Darrell Waltrip	1,165,684	8 Scott Pruett	712,096	13 Derek Daly	410,279
4 Michael Andretti	931,793	9 Bobby Rahal	687,424	14 Kevin Cogan	401,325
5 Teo Fabi	802,463	10 Raul Boesel	662,821	15 Pancho Carter	382,976

1990 (through Sept.23)

	Earnings		Earnings		Earnings
1 Arie Luyendyk	$1,566,742	6 Rick Mears	$867,752	11 Scott Brayton	$533,250
2 Al Unser,Jr	1,318,441	7 Mario Andretti	773,779	12 Teo Fabi	515,843
3 Bobby Rahal	1,176,616	8 Danny Sullivan	757,003	13 Raul Boesel	498,691
4 E.Fittipaldi	1,131,442	9 Eddie Cheever	688,658	14 Dean Hall	424,627
5 Michael Andretti	912,255	10 A.J.Foyt	550,744	15 Didier Theys	418,010

1989-90 Formula One Results

Late 1989

Date	Grand Prix	Winner	Time	Avg.MPH	Runner-up	Behind
Oct. 1	Spain	Ayrton Senna	1:47:48.264	106.252	G.Berger	0:27.1
Oct.22	Japan	Alessandro Nannini	1:35:06.277	121.462	R.Patrese	0:11.9
Nov. 5	Australia	Thierry Boutsen	2:00:17.421	81.960	A.Naninni	0:28.7

Winning Constructors: Benetton-Ford (Nannini); McLaren-Honda (Senna); Williams-Renault (Boutsen).

1990 (through Sept.23)

Date	Grand Prix	Winner (start pos.)	Time	Avg.MPH	Runner-up	Behind
Mar.11	United States	Ayrton Senna (5)	1:52:32.829	90.586	J.Alesi	0:08.7
Mar.25	Brazil	Alain Prost (6)	1:37:21.258	117.56	G.Berger	0:13.6
May 13	San Marino	Riccardo Patrese (3)	1:30:55.478	125.783	G.Berger	0:05.1
May 27	Monaco	Ayrton Senna (1)	1:52:46.982	85.83	J.Acesi	0:01.1
Jun.10	Canada	Ayrton Senna (1)	1:42:56.400	111.946	N.Piquet	0:10.5
Jun.24	Mexico	Alain Prost (13)	1:32:35.783	123.540	N.Mansell	0:25.4
Jul. 8	France	Alain Prost (4)	1:33:29.606	121.67	I.Capelli	0:08.6
Jul.15	Britain	Alain Prost (5)	1:18:30.999	145.253	T.Boutsen	0:39.1
Jul.29	Germany	Ayrton Senna (1)	1:20:47.164	141.29	A.Nannini	0:06.5
Aug.12	Hungary	Thierry Boutsen (1)	1:49:30.597	104.00	A.Senna	0:00.3
Aug.26	Belgium	Ayrton Senna (1)	1:26:31.997	131.272	A.Prost	0:03.6
Sep. 9	Italy	Aryton Senna (1)	1:17:57.878	146.672	A.Prost	0:06.1
Sep.23	Portugal	Nigel Mansell (1)	1:22:11.014	120.110	A.Senna	0:02.8

Remaining races (3): Spain (Sept.30); Japan (Oct.21); Australia (Nov.4).
Winning Constructors: McLaren-Honda 6 (Senna 6); Ferrari 5 (Prost 4 and Mansell); Williams-Renault 2 (Boutsen and Patrese).

Race Locations

March—USA GP in downtown Phoenix; Brazilian GP at Jacarepagua. **May**—San Marino GP at Imola, Italy; Monaco GP in downtown Monaco. **June**—Canadian GP at Montreal; Mexican GP at Mexico City. **July**—French GP at Le Castellet; British GP at Silverstone; German GP at Hockenheim. **August**—Hungarian GP at Hungaroring; Belgian GP at Spa-Francorchamps. **September**—Italian GP at Monza; Portuguese GP at Estoril; Spanish GP at Jerez. **October**—Japanese GP at Suzuka. **November**—Australian GP at Adelaide.

World Championship Point Standings

Official Top 10 Formula One World Championship point leaders and unofficial Top 10 point leaders for 1990 (through Sept.23). Points awarded for places 1 to 6. Listed are starts (Sts), races won (1st), top six finishes (Top6); and points. Only 11 best race results were counted.
Note: Formula One does not keep Money Leader standings.

Final 1989

	Sts	1st	Top6	Pts
1 Alain Prost, FRA	16	4	13	76*
2 Ayrton Senna, BRA	16	6	7	60
3 Riccardo Patrese, ITA	16	0	9	40
4 Nigel Mansell, GBR	15	2	6	38
5 Thierry Boutsen, BEL	16	2	8	37
6 Alessandro Nannini, ITA	16	1	8	32
7 Gerhard Berger, AUT	15	1	3	21
8 Nelson Piquet, BRA	15	0	5	12
9 Jean Alesi, FRA	8	0	3	8
10 Derek Warwick, GBR	15	0	5	7

*Earned 81 points in 16 races, but only 11 best race results were counted.

1990 (thru Sept.23)

	Sts	1st	Top6	Pts
1 Ayrton Senna, BRA	13	6	11	78
2 Alain Prost, FRA	13	4	11	60
3 Gerhard Berger, AUT	13	0	11	40
4 Thierry Boutsen, BEL	13	1	7	27
5 Nelson Piquet, BRA	13	0	10	26
6 Nigel Mansell, GBR	13	1	5	25
7 Riccardo Patrese, ITA	13	1	5	17
Alessandro Nannini, ITA	13	0	5	17
9 Jean Alesi, FRA	13	0	3	13
10 Ivan Capelli, ITA	13	0	1	6

AUTO RACING
STATISTICS

THROUGH THE YEARS
1911-1990
CHAMPIONS • LEADERS

THE 1991 INFORMATION PLEASE SPORTS ALMANAC

SEC B

PAGE 631

NASCAR Circuit

The Crown Jewels

The four biggest races on the NASCAR circuit are the Daytona 500, the Winston 500, the Coca-Cola 600 and the Heinz Southern 500. The Winston Cup Media Guide lists them as the richest (Daytona), the fastest (Winston), the longest (Coca-Cola) and the oldest (Southern). Winston has offered a $1 million bonus since 1985 to any driver who can win three of the four races. The only drivers to win three of the races in a single year are LeeRoy Yarbrough (1969), David Pearson (1976) and Bill Elliott (1985).

Daytona 500

Held early in the NASCAR season; 200 laps around a 2.5-mile high-banked oval at Daytona International Speedway in Daytona Beach, FL. First race in 1959, although stock car racing at Daytona dates back to 1936.

Multiple winners: Richard Petty (7); Cale Yarborough (4); Bobby Allison (3); Bill Elliott (2). **Multiple poles:** Buddy Baker and Cale Yarborough (4); Bill Elliott, Fireball Roberts and Ken Schrader (3); Donnie Allison (2).

Year	Winner	Car	Owner	MPH	Fastest Qualifier	MPH
1959	Lee Petty	Oldsmobile	Petty Enterprises	135.521	Cotton Owens	143.198
1960	Junior Johnson	Chevrolet	Ray Fox	124.740	Fireball Roberts	151.556
1961	Marvin Panch	Pontiac	Smokey Yunick	149.601	Fireball Roberts	155.709
1962	Fireball Roberts	Pontiac	Smokey Yunick	152.529	Fireball Roberts	156.999
1963	Tiny Lund	Ford	Wood Brothers	151.566	Johnny Rutherford	165.183
1964	Richard Petty	Plymouth	Petty Enterprises	154.344	Paul Goldsmith	174.910
1965a	Fred Lorenzen	Ford	Holman-Moody	141.539	Darel Dieringer	171.151
1966b	Richard Petty	Plymouth	Petty Enterprises	160.627	Richard Petty	175.165
1967	Mario Andretti	Ford	Holman-Moody	149.926	Curtis Turner	180.831
1968	Cale Yarborough	Mercury	Wood Brothers	143.251	Cale Yarborough	189.222
1969	LeeRoy Yarbrough	Ford	Junior Johnson	157.950	David Pearson	190.029
1970	Pete Hamilton	Plymouth	Petty Enterprises	149.601	Cale Yarborough	194.015
1971	Richard Petty	Plymouth	Petty Enterprises	144.462	A.J.Foyt	182.744
1972	A.J.Foyt	Mercury	Wood Brothers	161.550	Bobby Issac	186.632
1973	Richard Petty	Dodge	Petty Enterprises	157.205	Buddy Baker	185.662
1974c	Richard Petty	Dodge	Petty Enterprises	140.894	David Pearson	185.017
1975	Benny Parsons	Chevrolet	L.G.DeWitt	153.649	Donnie Allison	185.827
1976	David Pearson	Mercury	Wood Brothers	152.181	A.J.Foyt	185.943
1977	Cale Yarborough	Chevrolet	Junior Johnson	153.218	Donnie Allison	188.048
1978	Bobby Allison	Ford	Bud Moore	159.730	Cale Yarborough	187.536
1979	Richard Petty	Oldsmobile	Petty Enterprises	143.977	Buddy Baker	196.049
1980	Buddy Baker	Oldsmobile	Ranier Racing	177.602*	A.J.Foyt	195.020
1981	Richard Petty	Buick	Petty Enterprises	169.651	Bobby Allison	194.624
1982	Bobby Allison	Buick	DiGard Racing	153.991	Benny Parsons	196.317
1983	Cale Yarborough	Pontiac	Ranier Racing	155.979	Ricky Rudd	198.864
1984	Cale Yarborough	Chevrolet	Ranier Racing	150.994	Cale Yarborough	201.848
1985	Bill Elliott	Ford	Melling Racing	172.265	Bill Elliott	205.114
1986	Geoff Bodine	Chevrolet	Hendrick Motorsports	148.124	Bill Elliott	205.039
1987	Bill Elliott	Ford	Melling Racing	176.263	Bill Elliott	210.364†
1988	Bobby Allison	Buick	Stavola Bros.Racing	137.531	Ken Schrader	193.823
1989	Darrell Waltrip	Chevrolet	Hendrick Motorsports	148.466	Ken Schrader	196.996
1990	Derrike Cope	Chevrolet	Whitcomb Racing	165.761	Ken Schrader	196.515

*Track and race record for Winning Time.
†Track and race record for Qualifying Time.
Notes: a—rain shortened 1965 to 332+ miles; b—rain shortened 1966 race to 495 miles; c—in 1974, race shortened 50 miles due to energy crisis.

Winston 500

Held at Talladega (Ala.) Superspeedway. **Multiple winners:** Bobby Allison, Buddy Baker and David Pearson (3); Davey Allison and Darrell Waltrip (2).

Year	Year	Year	Year
1970 Pete Hamilton	1976 Buddy Baker	1981 Bobby Allison	1987 Davey Allison
1971 Donnie Allison	1977 Darrell Waltrip	1982 Darrell Waltrip	1988 Phil Parsons
1972 David Pearson	1978 Cale Yarborough	1983 Richard Petty	1989 Davey Allison
1973 David Pearson	1979 Bobby Allison	1984 Cale Yarborough	1990 Dale Earnhardt
1974 David Pearson	1980 Buddy Baker	1985 Bill Elliott	
1975 Buddy Baker		1986 Bobby Allison	

Coca-Cola 500

Held at Charlotte (N.C.) Motor Speedway. **Multiple winners:** Darrell Waltrip (5); Buddy Baker, David Pearson (3); Bobby Allison, Neil Bonnett, Dale Earnhardt, Fred Lorenzen, Jim Paschal, Richard Petty (2).

Year	Year	Year	Year
1960 Joe Lee Johnson	1969 Lee Roy Yarbrough	1977 Richard Petty	1985 Darrell Waltrip
1961 David Pearson	1970 Donnie Allison	1978 Darrell Waltrip	1986 Dale Earnhardt
1962 Nelson Stacy	1971 Bobby Allison	1979 Darrell Waltrip	1987 Kyle Petty
1963 Fred Lorenzen	1972 Buddy Baker	1980 Benny Parsons	1988 Darrell Waltrip
1964 Jim Paschal	1973 Buddy Baker	1981 Bobby Allison	1989 Darrell Waltrip
1965 Fred Lorenzen	1974 David Pearson	1982 Neil Bonnett	
1966 Marvin Panch	1975 Richard Petty	1983 Neil Bonnett	1990 Rusty Wallace
1967 Jim Paschal	1976 David Pearson	1984 Bobby Allison	
1968 Buddy Baker			

Heinz Southern 500

Held at Darlington (S.C.) International Raceway. **Multiple winners:** Cale Yarborough (5); Bobby Allison (4); Buck Baker, Dale Earnhardt, David Pearson and Herb Thomas (3); Bill Elliott and Fireball Roberts (2).

Year	Year	Year	Year
1950 Johnny Mantz	1960 Buck Baker	1970 Buddy Baker	1980 Terry Labonte
1951 Herb Thomas	1961 Nelson Stacy	1971 Bobby Allison	1981 Neil Bonnett
1952 Fonty Flock	1962 Larry Frank	1972 Bobby Allison	1982 Cale Yarborough
1953 Buck Baker	1963 Fireball Roberts	1973 Cale Yarborough	1983 Bobby Allison
1954 Herb Thomas	1964 Buck Baker	1974 Cale Yarborough	1984 Harry Gant
1955 Herb Thomas	1965 Ned Jarrett	1975 Bobby Allison	1985 Bill Elliott
1956 Curtis Turner	1966 Darel Dieringer	1976 David Pearson	1986 Tim Richmond
1957 Speedy Thompson	1967 Richard Petty	1977 David Pearson	1987 Dale Earnhardt
1958 Fireball Roberts	1968 Cale Yarborough	1978 Cale Yarborough	1988 Bill Elliott
1959 Jim Reed	1969 LeeRoy Yarborough	1979 David Pearson	1989 Dale Earnhardt
			1990 Dale Earnhardt

All-Time Leaders

NASCAR's All-Time Top 20 drivers in victories, pole positions and earnings, based on records through 1989. Drivers active in 1990 in **bold type.**

Victories	Pole Positions	Earnings
1 **Richard Petty** 200	1 **Richard Petty** 127	1 **Darrell Waltrip** . . $9,996,542
2 David Pearson 105	2 David Pearson 113	2 **Dale Earnhardt** . . . 9,741,078
3 Bobby Allison 84	3 Cale Yarborough 70	3 **Bill Elliott** 9,160,139
4 Cale Yarborough 83	4 Bobby Allison 57	4 Bobby Allison 7,102,233
5 **Darrell Waltrip** 73	**Darrell Waltrip** 57	5 **Richard Petty** 6,971,494
6 Lee Petty 54	6 Bobby Issac 51	6 **Terry Labonte** 5,837,949
7 Ned Jarrett 50	7 Junior Johnson 47	7 **Rusty Wallace** 5,370,430
Junior Johnson 50	8 Buck Baker 44	8 Cale Yarborough . . . 5,003,616
9 Herb Thomas 48	9 Buddy Baker 40	9 **Ricky Rudd** 4,425,740
10 Buck Baker 46	10 Herb Thomas 38	10 **Harry Gant** 4,268,624
11 Tim Flock 40	11 **Bill Elliott** 37	11 Benny Parsons 3,926,539
12 **Dale Earnhardt** 39	Tim Flock 37	12 **Geoff Bodine** 3,867,649
13 Bobby Issac 37	Fireball Roberts 37	13 **Neil Bonnett** 3,784,546
14 Fireball Roberts 34	14 Ned Jarrett 36	14 Buddy Baker 3,486,776
15 **Bill Elliott** 32	Rex White 36	15 Dave Marcis 3,132,645
16 Rex White 28	15 **Bill Elliott** 35	16 **Ken Schrader** 2,509,255
17 Fred Lorenzen 26	16 Fred Lorenzen 33	17 **Kyle Petty** 2,500,409
18 Jim Paschal 25	17 Fonty Flock 30	18 David Pearson 2,483,201
19 Joe Weatherly 24	18 **Geoff Bodine** 25	19 Tim Richmond 2,288,568
20 Benny Parsons 21	Marvin Panch 25	20 **Morgan Shepherd** . 2,021,165
Jack Smith 21	20 Jack Smith 24	

Winston Cup Champions

Originally the Grand National Championship, 1949-70, and based on official NASCAR (National Association for Stock Car Auto Racing) records through the 1989 racing season.

Multiple winners: Richard Petty (7); Dale Earnhardt, David Pearson, Lee Petty, Darrell Waltrip and Cale Yarborough (3); Buck Baker, Tim Flock, Ned Jarrett, Herb Thomas and Joe Weatherly (2).

Year		Year		Year		Year	
1949	Red Byron	1960	Rex White	1970	Bobby Issac	1980	Dale Earnhardt
1950	Bill Rexford	1961	Ned Jarrett	1971	Richard Petty	1981	Darrell Waltrip
1951	Herb Thomas	1962	Joe Weatherly	1972	Richard Petty	1982	Darrell Waltrip
1952	Tim Flock	1963	Joe Weatherly	1973	Benny Parsons	1983	Bobby Allison
1953	Herb Thomas	1964	Richard Petty	1974	Richard Petty	1984	Terry Labonte
1954	Lee Petty	1965	Ned Jarrett	1975	Richard Petty	1985	Darrell Waltrip
1955	Tim Flock	1966	David Pearson	1976	Cale Yarborough	1986	Dale Earnhardt
1956	Buck Baker	1967	Richard Petty	1977	Cale Yarborough	1987	Dale Earnhardt
1957	Buck Baker	1968	David Pearson	1978	Cale Yarborough	1988	Bill Elliott
1958	Lee Petty	1969	David Pearson	1979	Richard Petty	1989	Rusty Wallace
1959	Lee Petty						

CART Circuit

Indianapolis 500

Held every Memorial Day weekend; 200 laps around a 2.5-mile oval at Indianapolis Motor Speedway. First race in 1911.

Multiple wins: A.J.Foyt and Al Unser (4); Rick Mears, Louis Meyer, Mauri Rose, Johnny Rutherford, Wilbur Shaw and Bobby Unser (3); Gordon Johncock, Tommy Milton, Bill Vukovich and Rodger Ward (2).

Multiple poles: Rick Mears (5); Mario Andretti, A.J.Foyt and Tom Sneva (4); Rex Mays (3); Billy Arnold, Ralph DePalma, Walt Faulkner, Parnelli Jones, Jack McGrath, Jimmy Murphy, Duke Nalon, Johnny Rutherford and Jimmy Snyder (2).

Year	Winner	Car	MPH	Fastest Qualifier	MPH
1911	Ray Harroun (28)	Marmon Wasp	74.602	Lewis Strang	—
1912	Joe Dawson (7)	National	78.719	David Bruce-Brown	88.45
1913	Jules Goux (7)	Peugeot	75.933	Jack Tower	88.33
1914	Rene Thomas (15)	Delage	82.474	Georges Boillot	99.86
1915	Ralph DePalma (2)	Mercedes	89.840	Howard Wilcox	98.90
1916a	Dario Resta (4)	Peugeot	84.001	John Aitken	96.69
1917-18	Not held				
1919	Howard Wilcox (2)	Peugeot	88.050	Rene Thomas	104.78
1920	Gaston Chevrolet (6)	Monroe	88.618	Ralph DePalma	99.15
1921	Tommy Milton (20)	Frontenac	89.621	Ralph DePalma	100.75
1922	Jimmy Murphy (1)	Murphy Special	94.484	Jimmy Murphy	100.50
1923	Tommy Milton (1)	H.C.S. Special	90.954	Tommy Milton	108.17
1924	L.L.Corum & Joe Boyer (21)	Duesenberg Special	98.234	Jimmy Murphy	108.037
1925	Peter DePaolo (2)	Duesenberg Special	101.127	Leon Duray	113.196
1926b	Frank Lockhart (20)	Miller Special	95.904	Earl Cooper	111.735
1927	George Souders (22)	Duesenberg	97.545	Frank Lockhart	120.100
1928	Louis Meyer (13)	Miller Special	99.482	Leon Duray	122.391
1929	Ray Keech (6)	Simplex Piston Ring Spl.	97.585	Cliff Woodbury	120.599
1930	Billy Arnold (1)	Miller-Hartz Special	100.448	Billy Arnold	113.268
1931	Louis Schneider (13)	Bowes Seal Fast Special	96.629	Billy Arnold	116.080
1932	Fred Frame (27)	Miller-Hartz Special	104.144	Lou Moore	117.363
1933	Louis Meyer (6)	Tydol Special	104.162	Bill Cummings	118.530
1934	William Cummings (10)	Boyle Products Special	104.863	Kelly Petillo	119.329
1935	Kelly Petillo (22)	Gilmore Speedway Special	106.240	Rex Mays	120.736
1936	Louis Meyer (28)	Ring-Free Special	109.069	Rex Mays	119.644
1937	Wilbur Shaw (2)	Shaw-Gilmore Special	113.580	Jimmy Snyder	125.287
1938	Floyd Roberts (1)	Burd Piston Ring Special	117.200	Ronney Householder	125.769
1939	Wilbur Shaw (3)	Boyle Special	115.035	Jimmy Snyder	130.138
1940	Wilbur Shaw (2)	Boyle Special	114.277	Rex Mays	127.850
1941	Floyd Davis & Mauri Rose (17)	Noc-Out Hose Clamp Special	115.117	Mauri Rose	128.691
1942-45	Not held				
1946	George Robson (15)	Thorne Engineering Special	114.820	Ralph Hepburn	133.944
1947	Mauri Rose (3)	Blue Crown Spark Plug Spl.	116.338	Bill Holland	128.755
1948	Mauri Rose (3)	Blue Crown Spark Plug Spl.	119.814	Duke Nalon	131.603
1949	Bill Holland (4)	Blue Crown Spark Plug Spl.	121.327	Duke Nalon	132.939
1950c	Johnnie Parsons (5)	Wynn's Friction Proofing	124.002	Walt Faulkner	134.343
1951	Lee Wallard (2)	Belanger Special	126.244	Walt Faulkner	136.872
1952	Troy Ruttman (7)	Agajanian Special	128.922	Chet Miller	139.034
1953	Bill Vukovich (1)	Fuel Injection Special	128.740	Bill Vukovich	138.392
1954	Bill Vukovich (19)	Fuel Injection Special	130.840	Jack McGrath	141.033

Indianapolis 500 (Cont.)

Year	Winner	Car	MPH	Fastest Qualifier	MPH
1955	Bob Sweikert (14)	John Zink Special	128.209	Jack McGrath	142.580
1956	Pat Flaherty (1)	John Zink Special	128.490	Pat Flaherty	145.596
1957	Sam Hanks (13)	Belond Exhaust Special	135.601	Paul Russo	144.817
1958	Jim Bryan (7)	Belond AP Parts Special	133.791	Dick Rathmann	145.974
1959	Rodger Ward (6)	Leader Card 500 Roadster	135.857	Johnny Thomson	145.908
1960	Jim Rathmann (2)	Ken-Paul Special	138.767	Jim Hurtubise	149.056
1961	A.J.Foyt (7)	Bowes Seal-Fast Special	139.131	Eddie Sachs	147.481
1962	Rodger Ward (2)	Leader Card 500 Roadster	140.293	Parnelli Jones	150.370
1963	Parnelli Jones (1)	Agajanian-Willard Special	143.137	Parnelli Jones	151.153
1964	A.J.Foyt (5)	Sheraton-Thompson Special	147.350	Jim Clark	158.828
1965	Jim Clark (2)	Lotus Ford	150.686	A.J.Foyt	161.233
1966	Graham Hill (15)	American Red Ball Special	144.317	Mario Andretti	165.899
1967d	A.J.Foyt (4)	Sheraton-Thompson Special	151.207	Mario Andretti	168.982
1968	Bobby Unser (3)	Rislone Special	152.882	Joe Leonard	171.559
1969	Mario Andretti (2)	STP Oil Treatment Special	156.867	A.J.Foyt	170.568
1970	Al Unser (1)	Johnny Lightning 500 Spl.	155.749	Al Unser	170.221
1971	Al Unser (5)	Johnny Lightning Special	157.735	Peter Revson	178.696
1972	Mark Donohue (3)	Sunoco McLaren	162.962	Bobby Unser	195.940
1973e	Gordon Johncock (11)	STP Double Oil Filters	159.036	Johnny Rutherford	198.413
1974	Johnny Rutherford (25)	McLaren	158.589	A.J.Foyt	191.632
1975f	Bobby Unser (3)	Jorgensen Eagle	149.213	A.J.Foyt	193.976
1976g	Johnny Rutherford (1)	Hy-Gain McLaren/Goodyear	148.725	Mario Andretti	189.404
1977	A.J.Foyt (4)	Gilmore Racing Team	161.331	Tom Sneva	198.884
1978	Al Unser (5)	FNCTC Chaparral Lola	161.363	Tom Sneva	202.156
1979	Rick Mears (1)	The Gould Charge	158.899	Rick Mears	193.736
1980	Johnny Rutherford (1)	Pennzoil Chaparral	142.862	Johnny Rutherford	192.256
1981h	Bobby Unser (1)	Norton Spirit Penske PC-9B	139.084	Tom Sneva	200.691
1982	Gordon Johncock (5)	STP Oil Treatment	162.029	Rick Mears	207.004
1983	Tom Sneva (4)	Texaco Star	162.117	Teo Fabi	207.395
1984	Rick Mears (3)	Pennzoil Z-7	163.612	Tom Sneva	210.029
1985	Danny Sullivan (8)	Miller American Special	152.982	Pancho Carter	212.583
1986	Bobby Rahal (4)	Budweiser/Truesports/March	170.722	Rick Mears	216.828
1987	Al Unser (20)	Cummins Holset Turbo	162.175	Mario Andretti	215.390
1988	Rick Mears (1)	Penske-Chevrolet V-8	149.809	Rick Mears	219.198
1989	Emerson Fittipaldi (3)	Penske-Chevrolet PC-18	167.581	Rick Mears	223.885
1990	Arie Luyendyk (3)	Domino's Pizza Chevrolet	185.981*	Emerson Fittipaldi	225.301†

*Track record for Winning Time.
†Track record for Qualifying Time.
Notes: a—1916 race scheduled for 300 miles; b—rain shortened 1926 race to 400 miles; c—rain shortened 1950 race to 345 miles; d—1967 race postponed due to rain after 18 laps (May 30), resumed next day (May 31); e—rain shortened 1973 race to 332+ miles; f—rain shortened 1975 race to 435 miles; g—rain shortened 1976 race to 255 miles; h—in 1981, runner-up Mario Andretti was awarded 1st place when winner Bobby Unser was penalized a lap after the race was completed for passing cars illegally under the caution flag. Unser and car-owner Roger Penske appealed the race stewards' decision to the U.S. Auto Club. Four months later, USAC overturned the ruling, saying that the penalty was too harsh and Unser should be fined $40,000 rather than stripped of his championship.

Indy 500 Rookie of the Year

Voted on by a panel of auto racing media. Award does not necessarily go to highest-finishing first year driver. Graham Hill won the race on this first try in 1966, but the rookie award went to Jackie Stewart.
Father and son winners: Mario and Michael Andretti (1965 and 1984); Bill and Billy Vukovich (1968 and 1988).

Year		Year		Year		Year	
1952	Art Cross	1962	Jimmy McElreath	1973	Graham McRae	1983	Teo Fabi
1953	Jimmy Daywalt	1963	Jim Clark	1974	Duane Carter, Jr	1984	Michael Andretti
1954	Larry Crockett	1964	Johnny White	1975	Bill Puterbaugh		& Robt. Guerrero
1955	Al Herman	1965	Mario Andretti	1976	Vern Schuppan	1985	Arie Luyendyk
1956	Bob Veith	1966	Jackie Stewart	1977	Jerry Sneva	1986	Randy Lanier
1957	Don Edmunds	1967	Denis Hulme	1978	Rick Mears	1987	Fabrizio Barbazza
1958	George Amick	1968	Bill Vukovich		& Larry Rice	1988	Billy Vukovich III
1959	Bobby Grim	1969	Mark Donohue	1979	Howdy Holmes	1989	Bernard Jourdain
1960	Jim Hurtubise	1970	Donnie Allison	1980	Tim Richmond		& Scott Pruett
1961	Parnelli Jones	1971	Denny Zimmerman	1981	Josele Garza	1990	Eddie Cheever
	& Bobby Marshman	1972	Mike Hiss	1982	Jim Hickman		

All-Time Leaders

CART's All-Time Top 20 drivers in victories, pole positions and earnings, based on records through 1989. Drivers active in 1990 in **bold type**.

Victories

1 **A.J.Foyt** 67
2 **Mario Andretti** 51
3 **Al Unser** 39
4 Bobby Unser 35
5 **Johnny Rutherford** 27
6 **Rick Mears** 26
   Rodger Ward 26
8 **Gordon Johncock** 25
9 Ralph DePalma 24
10 Tommy Milton 23
11 Tony Bettenhausen 22*
12 Earl Cooper 21
13 **Bobby Rahal** 19
   Jimmy Bryan 19
   Jimmy Murphy 19
16 Ralph Mulford 17
17 **Danny Sullivan** 13
   Tom Sneva 13
19 **Emerson Fittipaldi** 11
   Eddie Hearne 11
   Johnnie Parsons 11

*Bettenhausen won one race (in Milwaukee on Aug.29, 1948) as Myron Fohr's relief driver.

Pole Positions

1 **Mario Andretti** 64
2 **A.J.Foyt** 53
3 Bobby Unser 49
4 **Rick Mears** 31
5 **Al Unser** 27
6 **Johnny Rutherford** 23
7 **Gordon Johncock** 20
8 Rex Mays 19
9 Don Branson 15
   Danny Sullivan 15
10 Tom Sneva 14
   Tony Bettenhausen 14
13 **Bobby Rahal** 13
14 Parnelli Jones 12
15 Danny Ongais 11
   Rodger Ward 11
17 Dan Gurney 10
   Johnny Thomson 10
19 Bill Cummings 9
   Jud Larson 9

Earnings

1 **Mario Andretti** . .$6,937,915
2 **Al Unser** 6,853,821
3 **Rick Mears** 5,988,514
4 **Bobby Rahal** 5,954,349
5 **Danny Sullivan** . . .5,045,678
6 **Emerson Fittipaldi** 5,025,716
7 **Al Unser,Jr** 4,975,351
8 **Michael Andretti** . .4,528,671
9 **A.J.Foyt** 4,266,955
10 **Johnny Rutherford** 4,209,232
11 **Tom Sneva** 4,142,877
12 **Gordon Johncock** .3,009,721
13 **Kevin Cogan** 2,704,232
14 Bobby Unser 2,674,516
15 **Roberto Guerrero** .2,631,074
16 **Pancho Carter** . . .2,181,537
17 **Arie Luyendyk** . . .2,125,139
18 **Geoff Brabham** . . .2,124,944
19 **Raul Boesel** 2,029,945
20 Dick Simon 1,712,226

PPG Cup Champions

Officially the PPG Indy Car World Series Championship since 1979 and based on official AAA (American Automobile Assn., 1909-55), USAC (U.S.Auto Club, 1956-79), and CART (Championship Auto Racing Teams, 1979-present) records through the 1989 racing season.

Multiple titles: A.J.Foyt (7); Mario Andretti (4); Jimmy Bryan, Earl Cooper, Ted Horn, Rick Mears, Louis Meyer and Al Unser (3); Tony Bettenhausen, Ralph DePalma, Peter DePaolo, Joe Leonard, Rex Mays, Tommy Milton, Jimmy Murphy, Bobby Rahal, Wilbur Shaw, Tom Sneva, Bobby Unser and Rodger Ward (2).

AAA

Year Champion	Year Champion	Year Champion	Year Champion
1909 George Robertson	1921 Tommy Milton	1933 Louis Meyer	1945 No racing
1910 Ray Harroun	1922 Jimmy Murphy	1934 Bill Cummings	1946 Ted Horn
1911 Ralph Mulford	1923 Eddie Hearne	1935 Kelly Petillo	1947 Ted Horn
1912 Ralph DePalma	1924 Jimmy Murphy	1936 Mauri Rose	1948 Ted Horn
1913 Earl Cooper	1925 Peter DePaolo	1937 Wilbur Shaw	1949 Johnnie Parsons
1914 Ralph DePalma	1926 Harry Hartz	1938 Floyd Roberts	
1915 Earl Cooper	1927 Peter DePaolo	1939 Wilbur Shaw	1950 Henry Banks
1916 Dario Resta	1928 Louis Meyer		1951 Tony Bettenhausen
1917 Earl Cooper	1929 Louis Meyer	1940 Rex Mays	1952 Chuck Stevenson
1918 Ralph Mulford		1941 Rex Mays	1953 Sam Hanks
1919 Howard Wilcox	1930 Billy Arnold	1942 No racing	1954 Jimmy Bryan
	1931 Louis Schneider	1943 No racing	1955 Bob Sweikert
1920 Tommy Milton	1932 Bob Carey	1944 No racing	

USAC

Year Champion	Year Champion	Year Champion	Year Champion
1956 Jimmy Bryan	1962 Rodger Ward	1968 Bobby Unser	1974 Bobby Unser
1957 Jimmy Bryan	1963 A.J.Foyt	1969 Mario Andretti	1975 A.J.Foyt
1958 Tony Bettenhausen	1964 A.J.Foyt		1976 Gordon Johncock
1959 Rodger Ward	1965 Mario Andretti	1970 Al Unser	1977 Tom Sneva
	1966 Mario Andretti	1971 Joe Leonard	1978 Tom Sneva
1960 A.J.Foyt	1967 A.J.Foyt	1972 Joe Leonard	1979 A.J.Foyt
1961 A.J.Foyt		1973 Roger McCluskey	

CART

Year Champion	Year Champion	Year Champion	Year Champion
1979 Rick Mears	1981 Rick Mears	1984 Mario Andretti	1987 Bobby Rahal
1980 Johnny Rutherford	1982 Rick Mears	1985 Al Unser	1988 Danny Sullivan
	1983 Al Unser	1986 Bobby Rahal	1989 Emerson Fittipaldi

Formula One Circuit

All-Time Leaders

The All-Time Top 20 Grand Prix winning drivers, based on records through 1989. Listed are starts (Sts), poles won (Pole), wins (1st), second place finishes (2nd), and thirds (3rd). Drivers active in 1990 in **bold type**.

	Sts	Pole	1st	2nd	3rd		Sts	Pole	1st	2nd	3rd
1 **Alain Prost**	153	20	39	27	14	Emerson Fittipaldi	144	6	14	13	8
2 Jackie Stewart	99	17	27	11	5	Graham Hill	176	13	14	15	7
3 Jim Clark	72	33	25	1	6	13 Alberto Ascari	32	14	13	4	0
Niki Lauda	171	24	25	20	9	14 Alan Jones	116	6	12	8	5
5 Juan-Manuel Fangio	51	28	24	11	1	Mario Andretti	128	18	12	2	5
6 **Ayrton Senna**	94	42	20	15	8	Carlos Reutemann	146	6	12	13	20
Nelson Piquet	172	24	20	19	14	17 James Hunt	92	14	10	6	7
8 Stirling Moss	66	16	16	5	2	Jody Scheckter	112	3	10	14	9
9 **Nigel Mansell**	133	12	15	7	10	Ronnie Peterson	123	14	10	10	6
10 Jack Brabham	126	13	14	10	8	20 Denis Hulme	112	1	8	9	17
						Jackie Ickx	116	13	8	7	10

Note #1: the following drivers either died or were killed in their final year of competition—Clark in a Formula Two race in W.Germany in 1968; Hill in a plane crash in 1975; Ascari in a private practice run in 1955; and Peterson following an accident in the 1978 Italian Grand Prix.
Note #2: Fittipaldi and Andretti are still active, but driving on the CART circuit.

World Champions

Officially called the World Championship of Drivers and based on Formula One (Grand Prix) records through the 1989 racing season.
Multiple winners: Juan-Manuel Fangio (5); Jack Brabham, Niki Lauda, Nelson Piquet, Alain Prost and Jackie Stewart (3); Alberto Ascari, Jim Clark, Emerson Fittipaldi and Graham Hill (2).

Year Champion	Car	Year Champion	Car
1950 Guiseppe Farina, ITA	Alfa Romeo	1970 Jochen Rindt, AUT	Lotus Ford
1951 Juan-Manuel Fangio, ARG	Alfa Romeo	1971 Jackie Stewart, GBR	Tyrrell Ford
1952 Alberto Ascari, ITA	Ferrari	1972 Emerson Fittipaldi, BRA	Lotus Ford
1953 Alberto Ascari, ITA	Ferrari	1973 Jackie Stewart, GBR	Tyrrell Ford
1954 Juan-Manuel Fangio, ARG	Maserati & Mercedes	1974 Emerson Fittipaldi, BRA	McLaren Ford
1955 Juan-Manuel Fangio, ARG	Mercedes	1975 Niki Lauda, AUT	Ferrari
1956 Juan-Manuel Fangio, ARG	Ferrari	1976 James Hunt, GBR	McLaren Ford
1957 Juan-Manuel Fangio, ARG	Maserati	1977 Niki Lauda, AUT	Ferrari
1958 Mike Hawthorn, GBR	Ferrari	1978 Mario Andretti, USA	Lotus Ford
1959 Jack Brabham, AUS	Cooper Climax	1979 Jody Scheckter, SAF	Ferrari
1960 Jack Brabham, AUS	Cooper Climax	1980 Alan Jones, AUS	Williams Ford
1961 Phil Hill, USA	Ferrari	1981 Nelson Piquet, BRA	Brabham Ford
1962 Graham Hill, GBR	BRM	1982 Keke Rosberg, FIN	Williams Ford
1963 Jim Clark, GBR	Lotus Climax	1983 Nelson Piquet, BRA	Brabham BMW Turbo
1964 John Surtees, GBR	Ferrari	1984 Niki Lauda, AUT	McLaren TAG Porsche Turbo
1965 Jim Clark, GBR	Lotus Climax	1985 Alain Prost, FRA	McLaren TAG Porsche Turbo
1966 Jack Brabham, AUS	Brabham Climax	1986 Alain Prost, FRA	McLaren TAG Porsche Turbo
1967 Denis Hulme, NZE	Brabham Repco	1987 Nelson Piquet, BRA	Williams Honda Turbo
1968 Graham Hill, GBR	Lotus Ford	1988 Ayrton Senna, BRA	McLaren-Honda Turbo
1969 Jackie Stewart, GBR	Matra Ford	1989 Alain Prost, FRA	McLaren-Honda

Challenger **Buster Douglas** finishes off a five-punch flurry with a left that drops champion **Mike Tyson** to the canvas in the 10th round of their heavyweight championship fight in Tokyo on Feb. 10.

BOXING

*B*uster Douglas, a 42–1 underdog,
KOs Tyson for heavyweight crown;
Chavez stops Taylor in 12th round;
Whitaker unifies lightweight title.

BOXING

1989-90 YEAR IN REVIEW

by Bernard Fernandez

Boxing fans who had settled into comfortable expectations were jolted by the sweeping changes that hit the sport in 1990.

How sweeping? Well, the heavyweight champion who was going to reign forever fell to a 42-1 underdog in what was arguably the biggest upset in sports history; another unbeaten (and, some thought, unbeatable) titlist came within two seconds of what seemed to be a certain defeat; archrival promoters joined forces against a common enemy; and a fat, middle-aged relic from another era improbably rose to the fore while more contemporary legends began to fade from prominence.

And as if all that weren't enough, a number of long-time allegiances ended, a shrine was revisited and allegations of impropriety sullied boxing's image (again).

Bernard Fernandez joined the *Philadelphia Daily News* in 1984 and has been the paper's boxing writer since 1987. His father was a welterweight who fought on the undercard of several Archie Moore fights in the early 1940s.

Coming up with a pecking order of the year's most important events is no simple task, but by consensus some events were of more significance than others. It is quite possible that the three biggest stories of the first three months of 1990 will still be the three biggest stories at the end of the decade.

Unless something quite unforeseen happens with the old, fat guy, of course.

The top headline-grabber involved a fight halfway around the world. Undisputed heavyweight champion Mike Tyson, who at age 23 had been widely viewed as invincible, was taught a lesson Joe Louis and Muhammad Ali had learned before him: Any fighter, no matter how talented or fearsome, can be beaten if the circumstances are right.

We all should have known that, of course, but a succession of quick, brutal knockout victories by the man known as ''Iron Mike' had dulled any anticipation of a loss. Perhaps Tyson had begun to believe his own press clippings, which is one of the surest ways for an undefeated fighter to find out how the other half lives, or perhaps James "Buster" Douglas simply was better than advertised. Maybe it was a combination of both.

In any case, a worldwide television audience and 45,000 spectators in Tokyo's Korakuen Stadium were shocked when Douglas, who had dominated the action throughout, knocked out Tyson in the 10th round of their Feb. 11 fight with a five-punch combination punctuated by a jolting left cross.

As Tyson was counted out by referee Octavio Meyron, boxing historians were hailing Douglas' victory as the biggest upset ever, bigger even than Leon Spinks' decision over the legendary Ali in 1978 when Spinks had fought only eight professional bouts.

Given Douglas' background—he had lost to the undistinguished likes of David Bey and Mike "The Giant" White, and had flat-out quit in losing his only previous title bout to then-IBF heavyweight champion Tony Tucker in 1987—his dispatching of Tyson seemed all the more remarkable. Most Nevada sports books had refused even to accept bets on the fight, and the few that did had sent Tyson off as a 42-1 favorite.

But Douglas' moment of triumph was at least momentarily tarnished when promoter Don King persuaded officials of the WBA, WBC and Japanese Boxing Commission to delay recognition of Douglas as the new champion.

Douglas had been knocked down by a Tyson uppercut in the eighth round, and had risen at the count of nine—or at least the count of nine from Meyran. The referee, however, had been late to pick up the count from official timekeeper Kouichi Harano. Six hours after Tyson was counted out, WBC president Jose Sulaiman and WBA president Gilberto Mendoza announced at a press conference that they would not certify a winner until the executive committees of their respective organizations met later in the month.

The public smelled something rotten, and the immediate outcry got so loud that both Sulaiman and Mendoza did a quick about-face and said that Douglas was, indeed, the champion.

The damage, however, continued. Douglas, promoted by King, as was Tyson, charged that King had not acted in his best interests. Douglas and his

Wide World Photos

After Tyson's stunning defeat, promoter **Don King** (left) lobbied hard for the ex-champion and was sued by the new champion, whom he also promoted.

firebrand manager, John Johnson, filed a lawsuit in an attempt to cut their ties to King. The legal action against King had a ripple effect whose full ramifications have yet to be determined. The date of the new champion's first defense, against top-rated challenger Evander Holyfield, was delayed when the trial in New York cut into his training time.

Ultimately, the case was settled out of court, with King stepping aside from the Douglas-Holyfield fight in exchange for a multimillion-dollar fee. But more legal battles are still to be waged. Johnson and Douglas opted for a $24 million offer from The Mirage, Steve Wynn's new, $640 million gambling palace in Las Vegas, but in doing so opened up a large can of worms: Wynn does not believe in the concept of an outside promoter, which means he does not believe in doing business with men like King and Bob Arum.

Normally, King and Arum can't agree on whether the sun is shining. When confronted by the threat posed by Wynn, however, they forgot the animosity of the past and became fast friends, even co-promoting a heavyweight doubleheader in June at The Mirage's next-door neighbor, Caesar's Palace, involving Tyson and another former heavyweight champion, 42-year old George Foreman.

Tyson and Foreman are major players in a heavyweight scenario that also includes Douglas and Holyfield, who were to meet in late October (see Updates). Holyfield was an early 2-1 wagering favorite, perhaps because oddsmakers weren't sure if Douglas' triumph in Tokyo was a fluke.

Douglas' post-Tokyo actions were perplexing enough to raise doubts about his staying power. He didn't seem in any rush to return to action, and when he did begin training he appeared to be grossly overweight. The normally reticent Holyfield questioned Douglas' heart, saying, "If you see a man give up once, he'll do it again. When the pressure gets to him, I believe he will always give up. A quitter doesn't always quit, but you have to give him a reason to quit. There are some fighters who would rather die than give up. I don't think Buster Douglas is that kind of fighter."

Tyson, meanwhile, made some changes of his own. Assailed for being physically soft in the loss to Douglas, and with co-trainers Aaron Snowell and Jay Bright roundly criticized in that fight, Tyson returned in June with a new chief second, Richard Giachetti, and a rediscovered dedication. He destroyed Henry Tillman in less than one round, although skeptics would point out that Tillman hardly constituted much of a threat.

He was also talking like a man who still thinks he's the best fighter in the world.

"Buster Douglas did well that night in Tokyo, but how many times could he beat me if we fought three, four or five times?" Tyson asked after hammering Tillman. "That shows who's the best fighter. Can he beat me twice in a row? I doubt it. Nobody can beat me twice."

Foreman, meanwhile, continued to mow down a succession of outclassed opponents (see box). His two-round knockouts of Gerry Cooney in January and Adilson Rodrigues in June certified him as the people's choice to fight either Tyson or the Douglas-Holyfield winner in 1991.

The Preacher turns skeptics into believers

Logic has nothing to do with it. Logic almost never counts for much when you are dealing with someone with the rare gift of striking a chord with the public.

Someone like George Foreman, for instance.

It is wholly illogical that Foreman, the 42-year old former heavyweight champion of the world, should be in a position to again challenge for the most prestigious title in boxing. It is illogical for many reasons: He is too old, too fat, too slow, too far removed from his glory days. How far removed? Well, it has been 22 years since he won the Olympic super-heavyweight gold medal in Mexico City, 18 years since he pounded Joe Frazier in Jamaica to win the heavyweight title, 16 years since he lost it to Muhammad Ali in Zaire.

A lot of hamburgers and french fries have gone down the gullet of the Punching Preacher since he retired after a 1977 upset loss to Jimmy Young, a loss that prompted a "religious experience" in his dressing room and sent him to the pulpit.

Scoffers were legion when Foreman, a blubbery 263 pounds (down from 320), launched his improbable comeback after a 10-year absence from the ring with a fourth-round knockout of the justifiably unknown Steve Zouski on March 9, 1987. Only 5307 paying customers showed up in ARCO Arena in Sacramento that night, and they were so unimpressed by the sight of Big George's protruding belly that he left the ring to the sound of boos.

But Foreman does not discourage easily, as we were to find out. His first-round knockout of a one-time prospect named Terry Anderson Sept. 25 in London boosted his record to 68-2, with 64 KOs, and stretched his winning streak to 23 during the revival stage of his career.

And it really doesn't matter any more that for the most part his recent victims were blown-up light heavyweights and cruiserweights, has-beens or never-weres. From modest purses of $40,000 or so, George Foreman has become the Man of the People, a phenomenon who is looking at a payday of $10 million-plus when he arrives at his promised land, a title shot.

All his boxing congregation needed, it seemed, was the merest bit of tangible

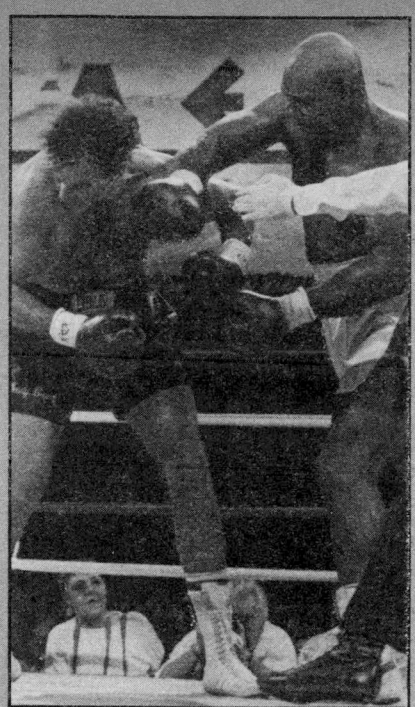

The illogical comeback of 41-year-old **George Foreman** gained credibility when he dispensed with Gerry Cooney in the second round of their Jan.15 bout.

evidence that Foreman could go back in time, like some gargantuan Marty McFly.

That proof was furnished last Jan. 15, when Foreman hammered Gerry Cooney en route to a second-round knockout win in Atlantic City. No matter that Cooney was 33, coming off a two-year retirement and burdened by failed expectations of his own; he tried to match cannon shots with a legendary bomber and found out, as so many others have, he was vastly outgunned.

"The Cooney fight legitimized George Foreman," said Bob Arum, who promotes Foreman. "Until then, I think there was a lot of hesitancy to accept his comeback. But after he took out Cooney, I think the attitude of the doubters went from, "There's no way he should be doing this" to 'Hmmm, maybe there really is something there.'"

Foreman added more converts with a second-round KO of Brazil's world-rated Adilson Rodrigues June 16 in Las Vegas,

an important fight in that it was packaged as part of an HBO doubleheader with Mike Tyson's first ring appearance after his shocking dethronement by James "Buster" Douglas in February. All of a sudden, the idea of Foreman and Tyson together (or Foreman and Douglas, or Foreman and Evander Holyfield) no longer seemed so ludicrous.

Foreman maintains that his goal is to regain the heavyweight title, and it doesn't matter from whom he takes it. But he regards a matchup with Tyson as especially intriguing.

"Mike Tyson and George Foreman is the most happening event on the boxing scene," Foreman said. "It's more important that Douglas-Holyfield or any title fight. If I could fight Tyson right now, I'd do it—with or without a title on the line."

What about Douglas and Holyfield?

"I'd be glad to whump on either one of them," Foreman said, "but they're colorless. Boxing would be a lot more interesting if I was the champ."

He just might be right. Good as he was, Foreman was no public relations prize in the '70s, a barely reformed street tough from Houston who learned how to glower from the late Sonny Liston.

"The guy I really wanted to imitate was Sonny Liston," Foreman said. "He'd sit back, stare everybody down and people would say, 'Man, that Sonny Liston. He's so bad.'

"I used to spar with Sonny, you know. He was the only guy I could never back up. I'd hit him with some monster shots and he'd just shake his head and say, 'No, son.' "

In one of the more remarkable transformations of public image boxing has ever seen, Foreman shed his Liston-like churlishness to become a quote machine, a lovable teddy bear who has become the standard bearer for Middle Aged America. The only vestige of his past that remains is that big punch, which might be even bigger than it was in his prime. Even Liston might not be able to shrug off one of the current Foreman's bombs.

"He is tremendously powerful," Arum said of Foreman. "He stuns guys when he hits 'em. Say what you will about him, but that hasn't changed.

"Is he slow? Sure, he's very slow. But at his peak he was slow. He's older and fatter than he was, too. But don't try telling the guys he's knocked out that he's too old or too fat."

Holyfield remained undefeated, but his tougher-than-expected eight-round TKO of 8-1 underdog Alex Stewart on Nov. 4, 1989, raised doubts as to whether he could stand up to the firepower of a Tyson, a Foreman or an at-his-peak Douglas.

Once the Big Four sort things out among themselves, the heavyweight who figures to be standing at the head of the line is Donovan "Razor" Ruddock, who had been scheduled to fight Tyson in November of 1989 in Edmonton. Tyson pulled out of that fight, claiming illness, and Ruddock was left to ponder the might-have-beens when the next challenger up, Douglas, pulled off the upset Ruddock is convinced he could have scored.

Ruddock and his promoter, Murah Muhammad, didn't simply shrug their shoulders at the missed opportunity. They filed a $75 million lawsuit against the oft-sued King, whom they depicted as the villain responsible for Tyson's cancellation.

When he wasn't having his attorneys file legal motions, Ruddock filled his time scoring a couple of knockouts in the ring, the most impressive and notable being a fourth round stop of former WBA champion Michael Dokes on Apr. 4. That fight, the first in Madison Square Garden's main arena in 3½ years, had a live gate of over $600,000 and demonstrated that casino sites did not have a lock on all major attractions.

"I think what this shows is that the big fights are back in New York," said Steve Griffith, director of public relations, marketing and operations for MSG Boxing. But the Garden did not host another major fight card for the rest of the year.

While the heavyweights held center stage for much of 1990, it was a classic match-up between two 140-pound champions that provided the year's best drama.

The long-anticipated meeting of WBC super lightweight champion Julio Cesar Chavez and IBF junior welterweight king Meldrick Taylor took place in Las Vegas on Mar. 17 and proved to be even more entertaining than expected.

Chavez, the Mexican great who entered the fight with a 68-0 record, was tested by Taylor as he had been tested by no other fighter. In fact, Taylor's blaz-

Julio Cesar Chavez rejoices after rallying to knock out Meldrick Taylor in the closing seconds of the title fight between WBC and IBF junior welterweight champions.

ing hand speed—he landed 457 of his 1176 punches, according to CompuBox statistics as compared to 258 of 701 for Chavez—enabled him to go into the 12th and final round with a wide edge on two of the three official scorecards.

But Taylor was advised, perhaps unwisely, that the outcome was still in doubt by co-manager Lou Duva. Taylor, his vision blurred from a blowout fracture of the orbit of his left eye, and queasy from having ingested two pints of his blood from a cut inside his mouth, tried to slug it out with Chavez to the finish—a strategy that backfired when Chavez decked him with a hard overhand right late in the round.

Taylor lurched to his feet at the count of six, but referee Richard Steele decided he was not able to continue and waved a halt to the fight with just two seconds remaining.

Steele's decision ignited a firestorm of

WBC and IBF lightweight champion **Pernell Whitaker** demonstrated new punching power on Aug.11, when he knocked out WBA champ Juan Nazario in the first round to unify the division's three major titles.

objections from the Taylor camp. Taylor said he was "fully conscious" and should have been given the benefit of the doubt. Duva and his son, promoter Dan Duva, argued that Steele had erred in not sending Chavez, who had wandered to the center of the ring, back to a neutral corner. Had Steele done so, the Duvas claimed, time would have expired and Taylor would have had his victory.

Opinion was divided on whether the well-respected Steele's actions were correct. Duane Ford, head of the Nevada State Athletic Commission, cited safety considerations as his reason for siding with Steele.

"We treat champions just like amateurs and six-round fighters," Ford said.

Taking the opposite viewpoint was HBO analyst Larry Merchant, who said, "These guys aren't normal people, they're real champions. Judges and cops on the beat don't treat everyone the same. A cop flags someone for going 85 miles per hour and finds the guy driving his pregnant wife to the hospital, he doesn't give him a ticket."

In any case, the Chavez-Taylor rematch will be even more eagerly awaited—provided, of course, neither man loses in the interim.

Two other fighters promoted by Dan Duva, Pernell "Sweet Pea" Whitaker and Hector "Macho" Camacho, might be in line for dates with Chavez. Whitaker, the IBF and WBC lightweight champion heading into the year, added the WBA crown to his collection in August with a stunning, one-punch knock-out of Juan Nazario. A stylist not previously known for his power, Whitaker said his workouts with strength instructor Bob Waering had given him another dimension.

"It might not show on the outside, but Bob muscled me up, bulked me up," said Whitaker, who used more conventional tactics in taking a unanimous decision over Vinny Pazienza in February.

Dan Duva said the mix-and-match possibilities involving Chavez, Taylor, Whitaker, Camacho and others were almost endless.

"In the '80s, there was an outstanding series of fights involving Sugar Ray

Leonard, Marvin Hagler, Roberto Duran and Tommy Hearns. All great fighters in or around the same weight class and all in their prime at the same time," Duva said. "I think you're going to see the same thing in the '90s with Meldrick, Pernell, Camacho, Chavez and possibly some of the welterweights like (IBF champion) Simon Brown."

Leonard, Duran and Hearns continued to hang around in 1990—maybe not the fighters they once were, but still commanding, for the most part, superstar purses.

Leonard and Duran opened The Mirage as a boxing venue on December 7, 1989, and their third meeting did a landslide business at the box office, even if it did not provide many fireworks inside the ropes. Duran, 38, spent much of the evening in fruitless pursuit of the 33-year-old Leonard, who was booed by action-starved fans who didn't appreciate his masterful boxing exhibition.

Leonard has not made a ring appearance since and even though he voluntarily relinquished his WBC super middleweight title early in 1990, he steadfastly denied that he was retired. At last report, Leonard's attorney, Mike Trainer, was negotiating for a fight with WBC junior middleweight champ Terry Norris in early 1991. Norris raised some eyebrows when he won his title by knocking out John "The Beast" Mugabi in one round in April.

Duran reportedly was angling for a shot at IBF super middleweight champ Lindell Holmes, although an ankle injury suffered in a car accident in September will likely idle him until 1991. Hearns, meanwhile, remained the WBO super middleweight titlist with a unanimous decision over Michael Olajide in April.

Hearns made his loudest noise out of the ring, however, when he and longtime manager-trainer Emanual Steward had an acrimonious split in September. Hearns announced he would manage himself, with Harold Rossfields Smith and Dennis Rappaport serving as his new advisers.

Hearns wasn't the only big-name fighter making changes. IBF middleweight champion Michael Nunn dropped manager Dan Goossen and trainer Joe Goossen and signed on with legendary trainer Angelo Dundee. Nunn, although still undefeated, needed some image-restoring after a yawn-inducing majority decision over WBC welterweight champion Marlon Starling in April.

Other notable fights saw WBA welterweight champ Mark Breland dethroned on a ninth-round knockout by Aaron Davis in July; Starling lose his title on a majority decision to Maurice Blocker in August; former IBF light heavyweight king Bobby Czyz resuscitate a flagging career with a seventh-round KO of previously unbeaten Andrew Maynard in June; and IBF junior lightweight champ Tony "The Tiger" Lopez take a unanimous decision over IBF featherweight champ Jorge Paez in September.

Boxing also made headlines in May when former middleweight champion Rocky Graziano died of heart failure and in June when the International Boxing Hall of Fame in Canastota, N.Y., welcomed 50 charter inductees—including such ring legends as Sugar Ray Robinson, Muhammad Ali, Joe Louis, Rocky Marciano, Jack Dempsey, Archie Moore and John L. Sullivan.

The stink raised by the delay in recognizing Douglas as heavyweight champion, and some questionable actions involving boxing by a state without a boxing commission, led to a renewed cry for the establishment of a federal boxing commission.

Wisconsin, which abolished its boxing commission in 1983, temporarily became a haven for fighters who could not obtain licenses in other states thanks to liberal interpretation of anti-discrimination laws. Vision-impaired Aaron Pryor, turned down for licenses in Nevada, California and New York, showed up in Madison in May for a fiasco of a fight with someone named Daryl Jones. And 45-year-old Jerry Quarry would have fought in Wisconsin a month later had he not suffered a cut above his eye in a confrontation with a co-promoter, of all people.

Finally, trivia buffs will want to note that the 1989 Nov. 27 WBA junior heavyweight fight between winner Robert Daniels and Dwight Muhammad Qawi in Nogent-Sur-Marne, France, became the first world title contest with three female judges—Carol Polis, Rose Grable and Patricia Jarman. □

BOXING STATISTICS

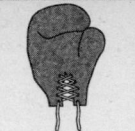

THE SEASON IN REVIEW
1989-1990
CHAMPIONS • BOUTS

SEC A

PAGE 645

Current Champions

WBA, WBC and IBF Titleholders (through Oct. 10, 1990)

The champions of professional boxing's 17 principal weight divisions, as recognized by the World Boxing Association (WBA), World Boxing Council (WBC) and International Boxing Federation (IBF). Heavyweight champion James (Buster) Douglas and lightweight champion Pernell (Sweet Pea) Whitaker are the only fighters currently holding all three titles.

	Weight Limit	WBA Champion	WBC Champion	IBF Champion
Heavyweight	—	Buster Douglas 30-4-1, 20 KO	Buster Douglas 30-4-1, 20 KO	Buster Douglas 30-4-1, 20 KO
Jr.Heavyweight	190 lbs	Robert Daniels 19-1-0, 17 KO	Massimiliano Duran 14-2-0, 6 KO	Jeff Lampkin 33-13-1, 28 KO
Light Heavyweight	175 lbs	Virgil Hill 28-0-0, 17 KO	Dennis Andries 38-8-2, 24 KO	Charles Williams 28-4-2, 20 KO
Super Middleweight	168 lbs	Christophe Tiozzo 26-0-0, 19 KO	Vacant	Lindell Holmes 42-5-1, 36 KO
Middleweight	160 lbs	Mike McCallum 38-1-0, 24 KO	Vacant	Michael Nunn 34-0-0, 23 KO
Jr.Middleweight	154 lbs	Julian Jackson 38-1-0, 36 KO	Terry Norris 25-3-0, 14 KO	Gianfranco Rosi 49-3-0, 16 KO
Welterweight	147 lbs	Aaron Davis 30-0-0, 18 KO	Maurice Blocker 32-1-0, 18 KO	Simon Brown 32-1-0, 24 KO
Jr.Welterweight	140 lbs	Loreto Garza 27-1-1, 23 KO	Julio Cesar Chavez 69-0-0, 56 KO	Julio Cesar Chavez 69-0-0, 56 KO
Lightweight	135 lbs	Pernell Whitaker 23-1-0, 13 KO	Pernell Whitaker 23-1-0, 13 KO	Pernell Whitaker 23-1-0, 13 KO
Jr.Lightweight	130 lbs	Brian Mitchell 42-1-2, 20 KO	Vacant	Tony Lopez 35-2-0, 22 KO
Featherweight	126 lbs	Antonio Esparragoza 30-1-4, 28 KO	Marcos Villasana 50-7-3, 44 KO	Jorge Paez 35-2-3, 25 KO
Jr.Featherweight	122 lbs	Luis Mendoza 27-2-2, 16 KO	Paul Banke 20-4-0, 11 KO	Welcome Ncita 27-0-0, 14 KO
Bantamweight	118 lbs	Luisito Espinoza 24-5-0, 12 KO	Raul Perez 47-1-1, 30 KO	Orlando Canizales 25-1-1, 21 KO
Jr.Bantamweight	115 lbs	Kaosai Galaxy 45-1-0, 40 KO	Sung-Kil Moon 12-1-0, 10 KO	Robert Quiroga 15-0-0, 11 KO
Flyweight	112 lbs	Leopard Tamakuma 27-4-0, 13 KO	Sot Chitalada 21-2-1, 13 KO	Dave McAuley 16-2-2, 7 KO
Jr.Flyweight	108 lbs	Myung-Woo Yuh 34-0-0, 13 KO	Humberto Gonzalez 28-0-0, 24 KO	Michael Carbajal 16-0-0, 10 KO
Strawweight	105 lbs	Bong-Jun Kim 20-5-3, 8 KO	Hideyuki Ohashi 14-3-0, 11 KO	Fahlan Lookmingkwan 16-0-0, 7 KO

Note: the following weight divisions are also known by these names—**Jr.Heavyweight** as Cruiserweight; **Jr.Middleweight** as Super Welterweight; **Jr.Welterweight** as Super Lightweight; **Jr.Lightweight** as Super Featherweight; **Jr.Featherweight** as Super Bantamweight; **Jr.Bantamweight** as Super Flyweight; **Jr.Flyweight** as Light Flyweight; and **Strawweight** as Mini-Flyweight.

Douglas-Tyson

Punch-Stat breakdown of punches thrown in the Feb.10, 1990, heavyweight championship fight between champion Mike Tyson and challenger James (Buster) Douglas in Tokyo. Statistics provided by CompuBox, Inc.

	Tyson	Douglas		Tyson	Douglas
Total punches thrown	214	441	Percentage connected	30%	53%
Punches connected	101	230	Power punches thrown	138	198
Percentage connected	47%	52%	Power punches connected	78	102
Jabs thrown	76	243	Percentage connected	57%	52%
Jabs connected	23	128	Knockdowns	1	1

Douglas-Tyson (Cont.)

The Judges' Cards

The round-by-round scoring of the three ringside judges in the Feb.10,1990, heavyweight championship fight between champion Mike Tyson and challenger James (Buster) Douglas in Tokyo. Note that Tyson knocked down Douglas in the 8th round and Douglas knocked out Tyson at 1:23 of the 10th. The referee was Octavio Meyran Sanchez.

Larry Rozadilla
(Douglas, 88-82)
Seven rounds to Douglas, one to Tyson and one even.

Round	Tyson		Douglas
1	9		10
2	9		10
3	9		10
4	9		10
5	9		10
6	9		10
7	10	(E)	10
8	10		8
9	8		10
Totals	**82**		**88**

Masakazu Uchida
(Even, 86-86)
Four rounds to Douglas, three to Tyson and two even.

Round	Tyson		Douglas
1	9		10
2	9		10
3	10		9
4	10	(E)	10
5	9		10
6	10		9
7	10	(E)	10
8	10		8
9	9		10
Totals	**86**		**86**

Ken Morita
(Tyson, 87-86)
Three rounds to Tyson, three to Douglas and three even.

Round	Tyson		Douglas
1	10	(E)	10
2	9		10
3	10		9
4	10	(E)	10
5	9		10
6	10	(E)	10
7	10		9
8	10		8
9	10		10
Totals	**87**		**86**

Major Bouts, 1989-90

Division by division, from Oct.16, 1989 through Oct. 10, 1990.

Heavyweights

Evander Holyfield knocked out Alex Stewart in 8th round (Atlantic City, Nov.4, 1989).

George Foreman gained a 2nd round TKO over Gerry Cooney (Atlantic City, Jan.15).

James (Buster) Douglas knocked out champion Mike Tyson at 1:23 of the 10th round to win WBA, WBC and IBF titles (Tokyo, Feb.10).

Razor Ruddock knocked out Michael Dokes in 4th round (New York, Apr.4).

James (Bonecrusher) Smith scored a 12-round unanimous decision over Mike Weaver (New York, Apr.4).

George Foreman knocked out Mike Jameson in 4th round (Lake Tahoe, Apr.17).

Evander Holyfield gained a 3rd round TKO over Seamus McDonagh (Atlantic City, June 1).

Mike Tyson knocked out Henry Tillman in 1st round (Las Vegas, June 16).

George Foreman knocked out Adilson Rodriguez in 2nd round (Las Vegas, June 16).

George Foreman knocked out Ken Lakusta in 3rd round (Edmonton, Alberta, July 31).

Razor Ruddock knocked out Kimmuel Odum in 3rd round (Atlantic City, Aug.19).

George Foreman knocked out Terry Anderson in 1st round (London, Sept.25).

Jr. Heavyweights
(Cruiserweights)

Glenn McCrory knocked out Siza Makhathini in 11th round to retain IBF title (Middlesboro, England, Oct.21, 1989).

Robert Daniels scored a 12-round split decision over Dwight Muhammad Qawi to win vacant WBA title (Paris, Nov.27, 1989).

Carlos de Leon fought Johnny Nelson to a 12-round draw to retain WBC title (Sheffield, England, Jan.27).

Jeff Lampkin gained a 3rd round TKO over champion Glenn McCrory to win IBF title (Gateshead, England, Mar.22).

Michael Moorer knocked out Mario Melo in 1st round to retain WBO title (Atlantic City, Apr.28).

Robert Daniels scored a 12-round unanimous decision over Craig Bodzianowski to retain WBA title (Seattle, July 19).

Massimiliano Duran won by disqualification in 11th round over champion Carlos de Leon to win WBC title (Capo D'Orlando, Italy, July 27).

Jeff Lampkin knocked out Siza Makhathini in 8th round to retain IBF title (St.Petersburg, FL, July 28).

Light Heavyweights

Virgil Hill knocked out James Kinchen in 1st round to retain WBA title (Bismarck, ND, Oct.24, 1989).

Jeff Harding gained a TKO over Tom Collins after 2 rounds—Collins quit in his corner—to retain WBC title (Brisbane, Oct.24, 1989).

(Prince) Charles Williams gained an 8th round TKO over Frankie Swindell to retain IBF title (Atlantic City, Jan.7).

Virgil Hill scored a 12-round unanimous decision over David Vedder to retain WBA title (Bismarck, ND, Feb.25).

Jeff Harding gained an 11th round TKO over Nestor Giovannini to retain WBC title (Atlantic City, Mar.18).

Virgil Hill scored a unanimous 12-round decision over Tyrone Frazier to retain WBA title (Bismarck, ND, July 7).

Dennis Andries knocked out champion Jeff Harding in 7th round to regain WBC title (Melbourne, Australia, July 28).

Dennis Andries gained a 5th round TKO over Daniel Merani to retain WBC title (London, Oct. 10).

Super Middleweights

Sugar Ray Leonard scored a unanimous 12-round decision over Roberto Duran to retain WBC title (Las Vegas, Dec.7, 1989).

In-Chul Baek gained an 8th round TKO over Yoshiaki Tajima to retain WBA title (Seoul, Jan.13).

Lindell Holmes scored a 12-round split decision over Frank Tate to win vacant IBF title (New Orleans, Jan.27).

Christophe Tiozzo gained a 6th round TKO over champion In-Chul Baek to win WBA title (Lyon, France, Mar.30).

Thomas Hearns scored a unanimous 12-round decision over Michael Olajide to retain WBO title (Atlantic City, Apr.28).

Lindell Holmes gained a 9th round TKO over Carl Sullivan to retain IBF title (Seattle, July 19).

Christophe Tiozzo gained an 8th round TKO over Paul Whitaker to retain WBA title (Arles, France, July 20).

Sugar Ray Leonard renouncement of WBC title acknowledged by WBC officials on Aug. 27. Leonard will continue to fight as a jr. middleweight.

Middleweights

John (The Beast) Mugabi, WBC junior middleweight champion, gained a 1st round TKO over Ricky Stackhouse in a non-title bout (Paris, Oct.30, 1989).

Roberto Duran stripped of title Jan.9 by WBC for failing to defend championship within 10 months of beating Iran Barkley on Feb.24, 1989.

Mike McCallum scored a unanimous 12-round decision over Steve Collins to retain WBA title (Boston, Feb.3).

Mike McCallum knocked out Michael Watson in 11th round to retain WBA title (London, Apr.14).

Michael Nunn scored a 12-round majority decision over WBC welterweight champion Marlon Starling to retain IBF title (Las Vegas, Apr.14).

Nigel Benn gained an 8th round TKO over champion Doug DeWitt to win WBO title (Atlantic City, Apr.29).

Nigel Benn knocked out Iran Barkley in 1st round to retain WBO title (Las Vegas, Aug.18).

Jr. Middleweights
(Super Welterweights)

Gianfranco Rosi scored a unanimous 12-round decision over Troy Waters to retain IBF title (St.Vincent, Italy, Oct.27, 1989).

John (The Beast) Mugabi, WBC champion, knocked out Carlos Antunes in 1st round of a non-title bout (London, Jan.10).

Terry Norris knocked out champion John Mugabi in 1st round to win WBC title (Tampa, Mar.31).

Gianfranco Rosi gained a 7th round TKO over Kevin Daigle to retain IBF title (Monte Carlo, Apr.14).

Terry Norris scored a unanimous 12-round decision over Rene Jacquot to retain WBC title (Annecy, France, July 13).

Gianfranco Rosi scored a unanimous 12-round decision over Darrin Van Horn to retain IBF title (Venice, Italy, July 14).

Welterweights

Simon Brown scored a unanimous 12-round decision over Luis Santana to retain IBF title (Springfield, MA, Nov.9, 1989).

Mark Breland gained a 4th round TKO over Fujio Ozaki to retain WBA title (Tokyo, Dec.10, 1989).

Mark Breland gained a 3rd round TKO over Lloyd Honeyghan to retain WBA title (London, Mar.3).

Simon Brown gained a 10th round TKO over Tyrone Trice to retain IBF title (Washington, DC, Apr.1).

Aaron Davis knocked out champion Mark Breland in 9th round to win WBA title (Reno, July 8).

Maurice Blocker scored a majority 12-round decision over champion Marlon Starling to win WBC title (Reno, Aug.19).

Jr. Welterweights
(Super Lightweights)

Julio Cesar Chavez gained an 11th round TKO over Sammy Fuentes to retain WBC title (Las Vegas, Nov.18, 1989).

Meldrick Taylor gained a 5th round TKO over Jaime (Rocky) Balboa to retain IBF title (Philadelphia, Nov.20, 1989).

Julio Cesar Chavez gained a 3rd round TKO over Alberto Cortes to retain WBC title (Mexico City, Dec.16, 1989).

Juan Martin Coggi knocked out Jesse Williams in 4th round to retain WBA title (France, Dec.30, 1989).

Meldrick Taylor knocked out Ramon Flores in 1st round to retain IBF title (Philadelphia, Jan.27).

Hector (Macho) Camacho scored a unanimous 12-round decision over Vinny Pazienza to retain WBO title (Atlantic City, Feb.3).

Julio Cesar Chavez gained a 12th round TKO over IBF champion Meldrick Taylor to unify WBC and IBF titles (Las Vegas, Mar.17).

Juan Martin Coggi scored a unanimous 12-round decision over Jose Luis Ramirez to retain WBA title (Ajaccio, Corsica, Mar.24).

Meldrick Taylor scored a unanimous 10-round decision over Primo Ramos (Lake Tahoe, Aug.11).

Hector (Macho) Camacho scored a unanimous 12-round decision over Tony Baltazar (Stateline, NV, Aug.11).

Loreto Garza scored a unanimous 12-round decision over champion Juan Martin Coggi to win WBA title (Nice, France, Aug.17).

Lightweights

Jorge Paez, IBF featherweight champion, gained a 6th round TKO over lightweight Allan Makitoki (Inglewood, CA, Oct.23, 1989).

Pernell Whitaker scored a unanimous 12-round decision over Freddie Pendleton to retain WBC and IBF titles (Atlantic City, Feb.3).

Juan Nazario gained an 8th round TKO over champion Edwin Rosario to win WBA title (New York, Apr.4).

Pernell Whitaker scored a unanimous 12-round decision over WBC jr.lightweight champion Azumah Nelson to retain WBC and IBF titles (Las Vegas, May 19).

Vinnie Pazienza scored a unanimous 12-round decision over Greg Haugen (Atlantic City, Aug.5).

Pernell Whitaker knocked out WBA champion Juan Nazario in 1st round to unite WBC, IBF and WBA titles (Stateline, NV, Aug.11).

Jr. Lightweights
(Super Featherweights)

John-John Molina gained a 10th round TKO over champion Tony (the Tiger) Lopez to win IBF title (Sacramento, CA, Oct.7, 1989).

Azumah Nelson gained a 12th round TKO over Jim McDonnell to retain WBC title (London, Nov.5, 1989). Nelson relinquished title in 1990 move up a weight class to fight Pernell Whitaker for the lightweight title on May 19.

Brian Mitchell scored a 10-round split decision over Felipe Orozco in a non-title bout (Callicoon, NY, Nov.11, 1989).

Jeff Fenech, WBC featherweight champion, scored a unanimous 12-round decision over Mario Martinez in elimination bout for vacant WBC title (Melbourne, Nov. 24, 1989). Relinquished featherweight title early in 1990.

John-John Molina gained a 6th round TKO over Lupe Suarez to retain IBF title (Atlantic City, Jan.28).

Brian Mitchell scored a unanimous 12-round decision over Jackie Beard to retain WBA title (Grosseto, Italy, Mar.14).

Tony (the Tiger) Lopez scored a 12-round split decision over champion John-John Molina to regain IBF title (Reno, May 20).

Tony (the Tiger) Lopez scored a unanimous 12-round decision over IBF featherweight champion Jorge Paez to retain IBF title (Sacramento, Sept.22).

Brian Mitchell scored a unanimous 12-round decision over Frank Mitchell to retain WBA title (Aosta, Italy, Sept.29).

Featherweights

Jorge Paez gained a 6th round TKO over Lupe Gutierrez to retain IBF title (Reno, Dec.9, 1989).

Jorge Paez scored a 12-round split decision over Troy Dorsey to retain IBF title (Las Vegas, Feb.4).

Jorge Paez scored a 12-round split decision over Louie Espinoza to retain IBF title (Las Vegas, Apr.7).

Antonio Esparragoza scored a unanimous 12-round decision over Park Chan-mok to retain WBA title (Seoul, May 12).

Marcos Villasana gained an 8th round TKO over Paul Hodkinson to win vacant WBC title (Manchester, England, June 2).

Jorge Paez fought Troy Dorsey to a 12-round draw to retain IBF title (Las Vegas, July 8).

Major Bouts (Cont.)

Jr. Featherweights
(Super Bantamweights)

Daniel Zaragoza scored a 12-round split decision over Chan-Yong Park to retain WBC title (Seoul, Dec.1, 1989).

Jesus Salud won by disqualification in 9th round over champion Juan Jose Estrada to win WBA title (Inglewood, CA, Dec.11, 1989). Salud later stripped of title.

Welcome Ncita scored a unanimous 12-round decision over champion Fabrice Benichou to win IBF title (Tel Aviv, Mar.10).

Paul Banke gained a 9th round TKO over champion Daniel Zaragoza to win WBC title (Inglewood, Apr.23).

Contenders **Luis Mendoza** and **Ruben Palacios** fought to a 12-round draw for vacant WBA title (Cartagena, Colombia, May 25).

Welcome Ncita gained an 8th round TKO over Ramon Cruz to retain IBF title (San Remo, Italy, June 2).

Jesus Salud knocked out Martin Ortegon in 11th round (Honolulu, June 16).

Paul Banke knocked out Lee Ki-Jun in 12th round to retain WBC title (Seoul, Aug.18).

Luis Mendoza knocked out Ruben Palacios in 3rd round to win vacant WBA title (Miami, Sept.11).

Welcome Ncita knocked out Gerardo Lopez in 8th round to retain IBF title (Aosto, Italy, Sept.29).

Bantamweights

Luisito Espinosa knocked out champion Kaokor Galaxy in 1st round to win WBA title (Bangkok, Oct.18, 1989).

Raul Perez scored a unanimous 12-round decision over Diego Avila to retain WBC title (Inglewood, Oct.24, 1989).

Luisito Espinosa knocked out Juan Mendoza in 3rd round to retain WBA title (Inglewood, Dec.1, 1989).

Raul Perez scored a unanimous 12-round decision over Gaby Canizales to retain WBC title (Inglewood, CA, Jan.22).

Orlando Canizales (Gaby's brother) scored a 12-round split decision over Billy Hardy to retain IBF title (Sunderland, England, Jan.24).

Raul Perez gained a 9th round TKO over Gerardo Martinez to retain WBC title (Inglewood, CA, May 7).

Luisito Espinosa gained a 9th round TKO over Hurley Snead to retain WBA title (Bangkok, May 30).

Orlando Canizales gained a 2nd round TKO over Paul Gonzalez to retain IBF title (El Paso, June 10).

Orlando Canizales knocks out Eddie Rangel in 5th round to retain IBF title (Saratoga Springs, NY, Aug.14).

Jr. Bantamweights
(Super Flyweights)

Juan Polo Perez scored a unanimous 12-round decision over champion Elly Pical to win IBF title (Roanoke, VA, Oct.14, 1989).

Kaosai Galaxy gained a 12th round TKO over Kenji Matsumura to retain WBA title (Tokyo, Oct.31, 1989).

Nana Yaw Konadu scored a unanimous 12-round decision over champion Gilberto Roman to win WBC title (Mexico City, Nov.7, 1989).

Sung-Kil Moon won by disqualification in 9th round over champion Nana Konadu to win WBC title (Accra, Ghana, Jan.20).

Kaosai Galaxy gained a 5th round TKO over Cobra Ari Blanca to retain WBA title (Bangkok, Mar.29).

Robert Quiroga scored a unanimous 12-round decision over champion Juan Polo Perez to win IBF title (Sunderland, England, Apr.21).

Sung-Kil Moon gained a 9th round TKO over Gilberto Roman to retain WBC title (Seoul, June 9).

Kaosai Galaxy gained an 8th round TKO over Shunichi Nakajima to retain WBA title (Bangkok, June 30).

Kaosai Galaxy knocked out Kim Yong-Kang in 6th round to retain WBA title (Bangkok, Sept.29).

Flyweights

Dave McAuley scored a 12-round split decision over Dodie Penalosa to retain IBF title (London, Nov.9, 1989).

Sot Chitalada scored a unanimous 12-round decision over Ric Siodoro to retain WBC title (Bangkok, Jan.27).

Yul-Woo Lee scored a 12-round split decision over champion Jesus Rojas to win WBA title (Seoul, Mar.10).

Dave McAuley scored a unanimous 12-round decision over Louis Curtis to retain IBF title (Belfast, Mar.17).

Sot Chitalada scored a unanimous 12-round decision over Carlos Salazar to retain WBC title (Bangkok, May 1).

Leopard Tamakuma gained a 10th round TKO over champion Yul-Woo Lee to win WBA title (Mita, Japan, July 29).

Dave McAuley scored a unanimous 12-round decision over Rodolfo Blanco to retain IBF title (Belfast, Ireland, Sept.24).

Jr. Flyweights
(Light Flyweights)

Humberto Gonzalez scored a unanimous 12-round decision over Jung-Koo Chang to retain WBC title (Taegu, S.Korea, Dec.9, 1989).

Myung-Woo Yuh gained a 7th round TKO over Hisashi Tokushima to retain WBA title (Inchon, S.Korea, Jan.14).

Muangshai Kittikasem knocked out Chung-Jae Lee in 3rd round to retain IBF title (Bangkok, Jan.19).

Myung-Woo Yuh scored a 12-round split decision over Leo Gamez to retain WBA title (Seoul, Apr.29).

Muangshai Kittikasem scored a unanimous 12-round decision over Abdi Pohan to retain IBF title (Bangkok, May 1).

Humberto Gonzalez knocked out Luis Monzote in 3rd round to retain WBC title (Inglewood, June 4).

Humberto Gonzalez gained a 5th round TKO over Jung-Keun Lim to retain WBC title (Inglewood, July 23).

Michael Carbajal gained a 7th round TKO over champion Muangshai Kittikasem to win IBF title (Phoenix, July 29).

Humberto Gonzalez knocked out Jorge Rivera in 9th round to retain WBC title (Cancun, Mexico, Aug.27).

Michael Carbajal knocked out Oscar Calzada in 3rd round in non-title bout (Las Vegas, Sept.20).

Strawweights
(Mini-Flyweights)

Bong-Jun Kim gained a 9th round TKO over John Arief to retain WBA title (Pohano, S.Korea, Oct.22, 1989).

Jum-Hwan Choi gained a 12th round TKO over champion Napa Kiatwanchai to win WBC title (Seoul, Nov.12, 1989).

Hideyuki Ohashi knocked out champion Jum-Hwan Choi in 9th round to win WBC title (Tokyo, Feb.7).

Bong-Jun Kim knocked out Petthai Chuvatana in 4th round to retain his WBA title (Seoul, Feb.10).

Fahlan Lookmingkwan gained a 7th round TKO over champion Eric Chavez to win IBF title (Bangkok, Feb.22).

Bong-Jun Kim gained a 5th round TKO over Silverio Barcenas to retain WBA title (Kunsan, S.Korea, May 13).

Hideyuki Ohashi scored a unanimous 12-round decision over Napa Katwanchai to retain WBC title (Tokyo, June 8).

Fahlan Lookmingkwan scored a unanimous 12-round decision over Joe Constantino to retain IBF title (Bangkok, June 14).

Fahlan Lookmingkwan scored a unanimous 12-round decision over Eric Chanez to retain IBF title (Bangkok, Aug.15).

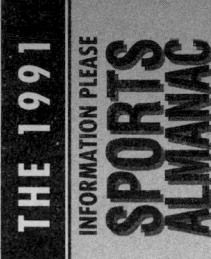

BOXING
STATISTICS

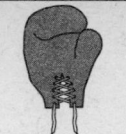

THROUGH THE YEARS
1884-1990
CHAMPIONS • BOUTS

THE 1991
INFORMATION PLEASE
SPORTS ALMANAC

SEC B

PAGE 649

World Heavyweight Championship Fights

Widely accepted world champions in **bold** type. Note following result abbreviations: KO (knockout), TKO (technical knockout), UD (unanimous decision), Maj (majority decision), Split (split decision), Ref (referee's decision), ND (no decision), Disq (won on disqualification).

Year Date	Winner	Age	Wgt	Loser	Wgt	Result	Location
1892 Sep. 7	James J.Corbett	26	178	**John L.Sullivan**	212	KO 21	New Orleans
1894 Jan. 25	**James J.Corbett**	27	184	Charley Mitchell	158	KO 3	Jacksonville, FL
1897 Mar. 17	Bob Fitzsimmons	24	167	**James J.Corbett**	183	KO 14	Carson City, NV
1899 Jun. 9	James J.Jeffries	24	206	**Bob Fitzsimmons**	167	KO 11	Coney Island, NY
1899 Nov. 3	**James J.Jeffries**	24	215	Tom Sharkey	183	Ref 25	Coney Island, NY
1900 Apr. 6	**James J.Jeffries**	24	NA	Jack Finnegan	NA	KO 1	Detroit
1900 May 11	**James J.Jeffries**	25	218	James J.Corbett	188	KO 23	Coney Island, NY
1901 Nov. 15	**James J.Jeffries**	26	211	Gus Ruhlin	194	TKO 6	San Francisco
1902 Jul. 25	**James J.Jeffries**	27	219	Bob Fitzsimmons	172	KO 8	San Francisco
1903 Aug. 14	**James J.Jeffries**	28	220	James J.Corbett	190	KO 10	San Francisco
1904 Aug. 25	**James J.Jeffries**	29	219	Jack Munroe	186	TKO 2	San Francisco
1905 Jul. 3	Marvin Hart	28	190	Jack Root	171	KO 12	Reno, NV
1906 Feb. 23	Tommy Burns	24	180	**Marvin Hart**	188	Ref 20	Los Angeles
1906 Oct. 2	**Tommy Burns**	25	NA	Jim Flynn	NA	KO 15	Los Angeles
1906 Nov. 28	**Tommy Burns**	25	172	Phila.Jack O'Brien	163½	Draw 20	Los Angeles
1907 May 8	**Tommy Burns**	25	180	Phila.Jack O'Brien	180	Ref 20	Los Angeles
1907 Jul. 4	**Tommy Burns**	26	181	Bill Squires	180	KO 1	Colma, Calif.
1907 Dec. 2	**Tommy Burns**	26	177	Gunner Moir	204	KO 10	London
1908 Feb. 10	**Tommy Burns**	26	NA	Jack Palmer	NA	KO 4	London
1908 Mar. 17	**Tommy Burns**	26	NA	Jem Roche	NA	KO 1	Dublin
1908 Apr. 18	**Tommy Burns**	26	NA	Jewey Smith	NA	KO 5	Paris
1908 Jun. 13	**Tommy Burns**	26	184	Bill Squires	183	KO 8	Paris
1908 Aug. 24	**Tommy Burns**	27	181	Bill Squires	184	KO 13	Sydney
1908 Sep. 2	**Tommy Burns**	27	183	Bill Lang	187	KO 6	Melbourne
1908 Dec. 26	Jack Johnson	30	192	**Tommy Burns**	168	TKO 14	Sydney
1909 Mar. 10	**Jack Johnson**	30	NA	Victor McLaglen	NA	ND 6	Vancouver
1909 May 19	**Jack Johnson**	31	205	Phila.Jack O'Brien	161	ND 6	Philadelphia
1909 Jun. 30	**Jack Johnson**	31	207	Tony Ross	214	ND 6	Pittsburgh
1909 Sep. 9	**Jack Johnson**	31	209	Al Kaufman	191	ND 10	San Francisco
1909 Oct. 16	**Jack Johnson**	31	205½	Stanley Ketchel	170¼	KO 12	Colma, Calif.
1910 Jul. 4	**Jack Johnson**	32	208	James J.Jeffries	227	KO 15	Reno, Nev.
1912 Jul. 4	**Jack Johnson**	34	195½	Jim Flynn	175	TKO 9	Las Vegas, NM
1913 Dec. 19	**Jack Johnson**	35	NA	Jim Johnson	NA	Draw 10	Paris
1914 Jun. 27	**Jack Johnson**	36	221	Frank Moran	203	Ref 20	Paris
1915 Apr. 5	Jess Willard	33	230	**Jack Johnson**	205½	KO 26	Havana
1916 Mar. 25	**Jess Willard**	34	225	Frank Moran	203	ND 10	NYC (Mad.Sq.Garden)
1919 Jul. 4	Jack Dempsey	24	187	**Jess Willard**	245	TKO 4	Toledo, Ohio
1920 Sep. 6	**Jack Dempsey**	25	185	Billy Miske	187	KO 3	Benton Harbor, Mich.
1920 Dec. 14	**Jack Dempsey**	25	188¼	Bill Brennan	197	KO 12	NYC (Mad.Sq.Garden)
1921 Jul. 2	**Jack Dempsey**	26	188	Georges Carpentier	172	KO 4	Jersey City, N.J.

World Heavyweight Championship Fights (Cont.)

Year Date	Winner	Age Wgt	Loser	Wgt	Result Location
1923 Jul. 4	**Jack Dempsey**	28 188	Tommy Givvons	175½	Ref 15 Shelby, Montana
1923 Sep. 14	**Jack Dempsey**	28 192½	Luis Firpo	216½	KO 2 NYC (Polo Grounds)
1926 Sep. 23	Gene Tunney	29 189½	**Jack Dempsey**	190	UD 10 Philadelphia
1927 Sep. 22	**Gene Tunney**	30 189½	Jack Dempsey	192½	UD 10 Chicago
1928 Jul. 26	**Gene Tunney**	31 192	Tom Heeney	203½	TKO 11 NYC (Yankee Stadium)
1930 Jun. 12	Max Schmeling	24 188	Jack Sharkey	197	Foul 4 NYC (Yankee Stadium)
1931 Jul. 3	**Max Schmeling**	25 189	Young Stribling	186½	TKO 15 Cleveland
1932 Jun. 21	Jack Sharkey	29 205	**Max Schmeling**	188	Split 15 Long Island City, N.Y.
1933 Jun. 29	Primo Carnera	26 260½	**Jack Sharkey**	201	KO 6 Long Island City, N.Y.
1933 Oct. 22	**Primo Carnera**	26 259½	Paulino Uzcudun	229¼	UD 15 Rome
1934 Mar. 1	**Primo Carnera**	27 270	Tommy Loughran	184	UD 15 Miami
1934 Jun. 14	Max Baer	25 209½	**Primo Carnera**	263¼	TKO 11 Long Island City, N.Y.
1935 Jun. 13	James J.Braddock	29 193¾	**Max Baer**	209½	UD 15 Long Island City, N.Y.
1937 Jun. 22	**Joe Louis**	23 197¼	James J.Braddock	197	KO 8 Chicago
1937 Aug. 30	**Joe Louis**	23 197	Tommy Farr	204¼	UD 15 NYC (Yankee Stadium)
1938 Feb. 23	**Joe Louis**	23 200	Nathan Mann	193½	KO 3 NYC (Mad.Sq.Garden)
1938 Apr. 1	**Joe Louis**	23 202½	Harry Thomas	196	KO 5 Chicago
1938 Jun. 22	**Joe Louis**	24 198¼	Max Schmeling	193	KO 1 NYC (Yankee Stadium)
1939 Jan. 25	**Joe Louis**	24 200¼	John Henry Lewis	180¾	KO 1 NYC (Mad.Sq.Garden)
1939 Apr. 17	**Joe Louis**	24 201¼	Jack Roper	204¾	KO 1 Los Angeles
1939 Jun. 28	**Joe Louis**	25 200¾	Tony Galento	233¾	TKO 4 NYC (Yankee Stadium)
1939 Sep. 20	**Joe Louis**	25 200	Bob Pastor	183	KO 11 Detroit
1940 Feb. 9	**Joe Louis**	25 203	Arturo Godoy	202	Split 15 NYC (Mad.Sq.Garden)
1940 Mar. 29	**Joe Louis**	25 201½	Johnny Paychek	187½	KO 2 NYC (Mad.Sq.Garden)
1940 Jun. 20	**Joe Louis**	26 199	Artoro Godoy	201¼	TKO 8 NYC (Yankee Stad.)
1940 Dec. 16	**Joe Louis**	26 202¼	Al McCoy	180¾	TKO 6 Boston
1941 Jan. 31	**Joe Louis**	26 202½	Red Burman	188	KO 5 NYC (Mad.Sq.Garden)
1941 Feb. 17	**Joe Louis**	26 203½	Gus Dorazio	193½	KO 2 Philadelphia
1941 Mar. 21	**Joe Louis**	26 202	Abe Simon	254½	TKO 13 Detroit
1941 Apr. 8	**Joe Louis**	26 203½	Tony Musto	199½	TKO 9 St. Louis
1941 May 23	**Joe Louis**	27 201½	Buddy Baer	237½	Disq 7 Washington, DC
1941 Jun. 18	**Joe Louis**	27 199½	Billy Conn	174	KO 13 NYC (Polo Grounds)
1941 Sep. 29	**Joe Louis**	27 202¼	Lou Nova	202½	TKO 6 NYC (Polo Grounds)
1942 Jan. 9	**Joe Louis**	27 206¾	Buddy Baer	250	KO 1 NYC (Mad.Sq.Garden)
1942 Mar. 27	**Joe Louis**	27 207½	Abe Simon	255½	KO 6 NYC (Mad.Sq.Garden)
1942 -45	World War II				
1946 Jun. 9	**Joe Louis**	32 207	Billy Conn	187	KO 8 NYC (Yankee Stadium)
1946 Sep. 18	**Joe Louis**	32 211	Tami Mauriello	198½	KO 1 NYC (Yankee Stadium)
1947 Dec. 5	**Joe Louis**	33 211½	Jersey Joe Walcott	194½	Split 15 NYC (Mad.Sq.Garden)
1948 Jun. 25	**Joe Louis**	34 213½	Jersey Joe Walcott	194¾	KO 11 NYC (Yankee Stadium)
1949 Jun. 22	Ezzard Charles	27 181¾	Jersey Joe Walcott	195½	UD 15 Chicago
1949 Aug. 10	**Ezzard Charles**	28 180	Gus Lesnevich	182	TKO 8 NYC (Yankee Stadium)
1949 Oct. 14	**Ezzard Charles**	28 182	Pat Valentino	188½	KO 8 San Francisco
1950 Aug. 15	**Ezzard Charles**	29 183¼	Freddie Beshore	184½	TKO 14 Buffalo
1950 Sep. 27	**Ezzard Charles**	29 184½	Joe Louis	218	UD 15 NYC (Yankee Stadium)
1950 Dec. 5	**Ezzard Charles**	29 185	Nick Barone	178½	KO 11 Cincinnati
1951 Jan. 12	**Ezzard Charles**	29 185	Lee Oma	193	TKO 10 NYC (Mad.Sq.Garden)
1951 Mar. 7	**Ezzard Charles**	29 186	Jersey Joe Walcott	193	UD 15 Detroit
1951 May 30	**Ezzard Charles**	29 182	Joey Maxim	181½	UD 15 Chicago
1951 Jul. 18	Jersey Joe Walcott	37 194	**Ezzard Charles**	182	KO 7 Pittsburgh
1952 Jun. 5	**Jersey Joe Walcott**	38 196	**Ezzard Charles**	191½	UD 15 Philadelphia
1952 Sep. 23	Rocky Marciano	29 184	**Jersey Joe Walcott**	196	KO 13 Philadelphia
1953 May 15	**Rocky Marciano**	29 184½	Jersey Joe Walcott	197¾	KO 1 Chicago
1953 Sep. 24	**Rocky Marciano**	30 185	Roland LaStarza	184¾	TKO 11 NYC (Polo Grounds)

Year	Date	Winner	Age	Wgt	Loser	Wgt	Result	Location
1954	Jun. 17	**Rocky Marciano**	30	187½	Ezzard Charles	185½	UD 15	NYC (Yankee Stadium)
1954	Sep. 17	**Rocky Marciano**	31	187	Ezzard Charles	192½	KO 8	NYC (Yankee Stadium)
1955	May 16	**Rocky Marciano**	31	189	Don Cockell	205	TKO 9	San Francisco
1955	Sep. 21	**Rocky Marciano**	32	188¼	Archie Moore	188	KO 9	NYC (Yankee Stadium)
1956	Nov. 30	Floyd Patterson	21	182¼	Archie Moore	187¾	KO 5	Chicago
1957	Jul. 29	**Floyd Patterson**	22	184	Tommy Jackson	192½	TKO 10	NYC (Polo Grounds)
1957	Aug. 22	**Floyd Patterson**	22	187¼	Pete Rademacher	202	KO 6	Seattle
1958	Aug. 18	**Floyd Patterson**	23	184½	Roy Harris	194	TKO 13	Los Angeles
1959	May 1	**Floyd Patterson**	24	182½	Brian London	206	KO 11	Indianapolis
1959	Jun. 26	Ingemar Johansson	26	196	**Floyd Patterson**	182	TKO 3	NYC (Yankee Stadium)
1960	Jun. 20	Floyd Patterson	25	190	**Ingemar Johansson**	194¾	KO 5	NYC (Polo Grounds)
1961	Mar. 13	**Floyd Patterson**	26	194¾	Ingemar Johansson	206½	KO 6	Miami Beach
1961	Dec. 4	**Floyd Patterson**	26	188½	Tom McNeeley	197	KO 4	Toronto
1962	Sep. 25	Sonny Liston	30	214	**Floyd Patterson**	189	KO 1	Chicago
1963	Jul. 22	**Sonny Liston**	31	215	Floyd Patterson	194½	KO 1	Las Vegas
1964	Feb. 25	Cassius Clay*	22	210½	**Sonny Liston**	218	TKO 7	Miami Beach
1965	Mar. 5	Ernie Terrell WBA	25	199	Eddie Machen	192	UD 15	Chicago
1965	May 25	**Muhammad Ali**	23	206	Sonny Liston	215¼	KO 1	Lewiston, Me.
1965	Nov. 1	Ernie Terrell WBA	26	206	George Chuvalo	209	UD 15	Toronto
1965	Nov. 22	**Muhammad Ali**	23	210	Floyd Patterson	196¾	TKO 12	Las Vegas
1966	Mar. 29	**Muhammad Ali**	24	214½	George Chuvalo	216	UD 15	Toronto
1966	May 21	**Muhammad Ali**	24	201½	Henry Cooper	188	TKO 6	London
1966	Jun. 28	Ernie Terrell WBA	27	209½	Doug Jones	187½	UD 15	Houston
1966	Aug. 6	**Muhammad Ali**	24	209½	Brian London	201½	KO 3	London
1966	Sep. 10	**Muhammad Ali**	24	203½	Karl Mildenberger	194¼	TKO 12	Frankfurt, W.Ger.
1966	Nov. 14	**Muhammad Ali**	24	212¾	Cleveland Williams	210½	TKO 3	Houston
1967	Feb. 6	**Muhammad Ali**	25	212¼	Ernie Terrell WBA	212½	UD 15	Houston
1967	Mar. 22	**Muhammad Ali**	25	211½	Zora Folley	202½	KO 7	NYC (Mad.Sq.Garden)
1968	Mar. 4	Joe Frazier	24	204½	Buster Mathis	243½	TKO 11	NYC (Mad.Sq.Garden)
1968	Apr. 27	Jimmy Ellis	28	197	Jerry Quarry	195	Maj 15	Oakland
1968	Jun. 24	Joe Frazier NY	24	203½	Manuel Ramos	208	TKO 2	NYC (Mad.Sq.Garden)
1968	Aug. 14	Jimmy Ellis WBA	28	198	Floyd Patterson	188	Ref 15	Stockholm
1968	Dec. 10	Joe Frazier NY	24	203	Oscar Bonavena	207	UD 15	Philadelphia
1969	Apr. 22	Joe Frazier NY	25	204½	Dave Zyglewicz	190½	KO 1	Houston
1969	Jun. 23	Joe Frazier NY	25	203½	Jerry Quarry	198½	TKO 8	NYC (Mad.Sq.Garden)
1970	Feb. 16	Joe Frazier NY	26	205	Jimmy Ellis WBA	201	TKO 5	NYC (Mad.Sq.Garden)
1970	Nov. 18	Joe Frazier	26	209	Bob Foster	188	KO 2	Detroit
1971	Mar. 8	Joe Frazier	27	205½	**Muhammad Ali**	215	UD 15	NYC (Mad.Sq.Garden)
1972	Jan. 15	**Joe Frazier**	28	215½	Terry Daniels	195	TKO 4	New Orleans
1972	May 26	**Joe Frazier**	28	217½	Ron Stander	218	TKO 5	Omaha, Neb.
1973	Jan. 22	George Foreman	25	217½	**Joe Frazier**	214	TKO 2	Kingston, Jamaica
1973	Sep. 1	**George Foreman**	25	219½	Jose (King) Roman	196½	KO 1	Tokyo
1974	Mar. 26	**George Foreman**	26	224¼	Ken Norton	212¼	TKO 2	Caracas, Venezuela
1974	Oct. 30	Muhammad Ali	32	216½	**George Foreman**	220	KO 8	Kinshasa, Zaire
1975	Mar. 24	**Muhammad Ali**	33	223½	Chuck Wepner	225	TKO 15	Cleveland
1975	May 16	**Muhammad Ali**	33	224½	Ron Lyle	219	TKO 11	Las Vegas
1975	Jul. 1	**Muhammad Ali**	33	224½	Joe Bugner	230	UD 15	Kuala Lumpur, Malaysia
1975	Oct. 1	**Muhammad Ali**	33	224½	Joe Frazier	215	TKO 15	Manila, Philippines
1976	Feb. 20	**Muhammad Ali**	34	226	Jean Pierre Coopman	206	KO 5	San Juan, P.R.
1976	Apr. 30	**Muhammad Ali**	34	230	Jimmy Young	209	UD 15	Landover, Md.
1976	May 24	**Muhammad Ali**	34	230	Richard Dunn	206½	TKO 5	Munich, W.Ger.
1976	Sep. 28	**Muhammad Ali**	34	221	Ken Norton	217½	UD 15	NYC (Yankee Stadium)
1977	May 16	**Muhammad Ali**	35	221¼	Alfredo Evangelista	209¼	UD 15	Landover, Md.
1977	Sep. 29	**Muhammad Ali**	35	225	Earnie Shavers	211¼	UD 15	NYC (Mad.Sq.Garden)
1978	Feb. 15	Leon Spinks	24	197¼	**Muhammad Ali**	224¼	Split 15	Las Vegas
1978	Jun. 9	Larry Holmes	28	209	Ken Norton WBC†	220	Split 15	Las Vegas
1978	Sep. 15	Muhammad Ali	36	221	**Leon Spinks**	201	UD 15	New Orleans
1978	Nov. 10	Larry Holmes WBC	29	214	Alfredo Evangelista	208¼	KO 7	Las Vegas

World Heavyweight Championship Fights (Cont.)

Year Date	Winner	Age	Wgt	Loser	Wgt	Result	Location
1979 Mar. 23	Larry Holmes WBC	29	214	Osvaldo Ocasio	207	TKO 7	Las Vegas
1979 Jun. 22	Larry Holmes WBC	29	215	Mike Weaver	202	TKO 12	NYC (Mad.Sq.Garden)
1979 Sep. 28	Larry Holmes WBC	29	210	Earnie Shavers	211	TKO 11	Las Vegas
1979 Oct. 20	John Tate	24	240	Gerrie Coetzee	222	UD 15	Pretoria, S.Africa
1980 Feb. 3	Larry Holmes WBC	30	213½	Lorenzo Zanon	215	TKO 6	Las Vegas
1980 Mar. 31	Mike Weaver	27	232	John Tate WBA	232	KO 15	Knoxville, Tenn.
1980 Mar. 31	Larry Holmes WBC	30	211	Leroy Jones	254½	TKO 8	Las Vegas
1980 Jul. 7	Larry Holmes WBC	30	214¼	Scott LeDoux	226	TKO 7	Minneapolis
1980 Oct. 2	Larry Holmes WBC	30	211¼	Muhammad Ali	217½	TKO 11	Las Vegas
1980 Oct. 25	Mike Weaver WBA	28	210	Gerrie Coetzee	226½	KO 13	Sun City, Boph'swana
1981 Apr. 11	**Larry Holmes**	31	215	Trevor Berbick	215½	UD 15	Las Vegas
1981 Jun. 12	**Larry Holmes**	31	212¼	Leon Spinks	200¼	TKO 3	Detroit
1981 Oct. 3	Mike Weaver WBA	29	215	Quick Tillis	209	UD 15	Rosemont, Ill.
1981 Nov. 6	**Larry Holmes**	32	213¼	Renaldo Snipes	215¾	TKO 11	Pittsburgh
1982 Jun. 11	**Larry Holmes**	32	212½	Gerry Cooney	225½	TKO 13	Las Vegas
1982 Nov. 26	**Larry Holmes**	33	217½	Randall (Tex) Cobb	234¼	UD 15	Houston
1982 Dec. 10	Michael Dokes	24	216	Mike Weaver WBA	209¾	TKO 1	Las Vegas
1983 Mar. 27	**Larry Holmes**	33	221	Lucien Rodriguez	209	UD 12	Scranton, Pa.
1983 May 20	Michael Dokes WBA	24	223	Mike Weaver	218½	Draw 15	Las Vegas
1983 May 20	**Larry Holmes**	33	213	Tim Witherspoon	219½	Split 12	Las Vegas
1983 Sep. 10	**Larry Holmes**	33	223	Scott Frank	211¼	TKO 5	Atlantic City
1983 Sep. 23	Gerrie Coetzee	28	215	Michael Dokes WBA	217	KO 10	Richfield, Ohio
1983 Nov. 25	**Larry Holmes**	34	219	Marvis Frazier	200	TKO 1	Las Vegas
1984 Mar. 9	Tim Witherspoon**	26	220¼	Greg Page	239½	Maj 12	Las Vegas
1984 Aug. 31	Pinklon Thomas	26	216	T. Witherspoon WBC	217	Maj 12	Las Vegas
1984 Nov. 9	**Larry Holmes** IBF	35	221½	Bonecrusher Smith	227	TKO 12	Las Vegas
1984 Dec. 1	Greg Page	26	236½	Gerrie Coetzee WBA	218	KO 8	Sun City, Boph'swana
1985 Mar. 15	**Larry Holmes**	35	223½	David Bey	233¼	TKO 10	Las Vegas
1985 Apr. 29	Tony Tubbs	26	229	Greg Page WBA	239½	UD 15	Buffalo
1985 May 20	**Larry Holmes**	35	222¼	Carl Williams	215	UD 15	Las Vegas
1985 Jun. 15	Pinklon Thomas	27	220¼	Mike Weaver	221¼	KO 8	Las Vegas
1985 Sep. 21	Michael Spinks	29	200	**Larry Holmes** IBF	221½	UD 15	Las Vegas
1986 Jan. 17	Tim Witherspoon	28	227	Tony Tubbs WBA	229	Maj 15	Atlanta
1986 Mar. 22	Trevor Berbick	33	218½	Pinklon Thomas WBC	222¾	UD 15	Las Vegas
1986 Apr. 19	**Michael Spinks**	29	205	Larry Holmes	223	Split 15	Las Vegas
1986 Jul. 19	Tim Witherspoon	28	234¾	Frank Bruno	228	TKO 11	Wembley, England
1986 Sep. 6	**Michael Spinks**	30	201	Steffen Tangstad	214¾	TKO 4	Las Vegas
1986 Nov. 22	Mike Tyson	20	221¼	Trevor Berbick WBC	218½	TKO 2	Las Vegas
1986 Dec. 12	Bonecrusher Smith	33	228½	T.Witherspoon WBA	233½	TKO 1	NYC (Mad.Sq.Garden)
1987 Mar. 7	Mike Tyson WBC	20	219	James Smith WBA	233	UD 12	Las Vegas
1987 May 30	Mike Tyson	20	218¾	Pinklon Thomas	217¾	TKO 6	Las Vegas
1987 May 30	Tony Tucker‡	28	222¼	Buster Douglas	227¼	TKO 10	Las Vegas
1987 Jun. 15	**Michael Spinks**	30	208¾	Gerry Cooney	238	TKO 5	Atlantic City
1987 Aug. 1	Mike Tyson	21	221	Tony Tucker IBF	221	UD 12	Las Vegas
1987 Oct. 16	Mike Tyson	21	216	Tyrell Biggs	228¾	TKO 7	Atlantic City
1988 Jan. 22	Mike Tyson	21	215¾	Larry Holmes	225¾	TKO 4	Atlantic City
1988 Mar. 20	Mike Tyson	21	216¼	Tony Tubbs	238¼	KO 2	Tokyo
1988 Jun. 27	Mike Tyson	21	218¼	**Michael Spinks**	212¼	KO 1	Atlantic City
1989 Feb. 25	**Mike Tyson**	22	218	Frank Bruno	228	TKO 5	Las Vegas
1989 Jul. 21	**Mike Tyson**	23	219¼	Carl Williams	218	TKO 1	Atlantic City
1990 Feb. 10	Buster Douglas	29	231½	**Mike Tyson**	220½	KO 10	Tokyo

Notes

*Muhammad Ali was known as Cassius Clay when he stopped Sonny Liston on Feb. 25, 1964.

†WBC recognized Ken Norton as world champion when Leon Spinks refused to meet Norton before Spinks' rematch with Muhammad Ali. Norton had scored a 15-round split decision over Jimmy Young on Nov. 5, 1977 in Las Vegas.

**WBC recognized winner of Mar. 9, 1984 fight between Tim Witherspoon and Greg Page as world champion after Larry Holmes relinquished title in dispute. IBF then recognized Holmes.

‡IBF recognized winner of May 30, 1987 fight between Tony Tucker and James (Buster) Douglas as world champion after Michael Spinks relinquished title in dispute.

All-Time Heavyweight Upsets

Buster Douglas' Feb. 10, 1990, knockout of unbeaten heavyweight champion Mike Tyson ranks as the biggest upset in boxing history. It tops 11 other well-known upsets in the annals of the heavyweight division. All were fights for the world championship except the Schmeling-Louis bout.

Note the following abbreviations: KO (knockout), UD (unanimous decision), TKO (technical knockout, fight stopped), SD (split decision).

Date	Winner	Loser	Result	KO Time	Location
9/7/1892	James J.Corbett	John L.Sullivan	KO 21	1:30	Olympic Club, New Orleans
4/5/1915	Jess Willard	Jack Johnson	KO 26	1:26	Mariano Race Track, Havana
9/23/26	Gene Tunney	Jack Dempsey	UD 10	—	Sesquicentennial Stadium, Phila.
6/13/35	James J.Braddock	Max Baer	UD 15	—	Mad.Sq.Garden Bowl, L.I.City
6/19/36	Max Schmeling	Joe Louis	KO 12	2:29	Yankee Stadium, New York
7/18/51	Jersey Joe Walcott	Ezzard Charles	KO 7	0:55	Forbes Field, Pittsburgh
6/26/59	Ingemar Johansson	Floyd Patterson	TKO 3	2:03	Yankee Stadium, New York
2/25/64	Cassius Clay†	Sonny Liston	TKO 7	*	Convention Hall, Miami Beach
10/30/74	Muhammad Ali	George Foreman	KO 8	2:58	20th of May Stadium, Zaire
2/15/78	Leon Spinks	Muhammad Ali	SD 15	—	Hilton Pavilion, Las Vegas
9/21/85	Michael Spinks	Larry Holmes	UD 15	—	Riviera Hotel, Las Vegas
2/10/90	Buster Douglas	Mike Tyson	KO 10	1:23	Korakuen Stadium, Tokyo

*Liston failed to answer bell for Round 7.
†Changed name to Muhammad Ali after winning title.

Major Titleholders

Note the following sanctioning body abbreviations: NBA (National Boxing Association), WBA (World Boxing Association), WBC (World Boxing Council), GBR (Great Britain), IBF (International Boxing Federation), plus other national and state commissions.

Fighters who retired as champion are indicated by (*) and champions who abandoned or relinquished their titles are indicated by (†).

Heavyweights

Widely accepted champions in capital LETTERS. Current champions in **bold** type.

Champion	Held Title	Champion	Held Title
JOHN L.SULLIVAN	1885-92	Jimmy Ellis (WBA)	1968-70
JAMES J.CORBETT	1892-97	JOE FRAZIER	1970-73
BOB FITZSIMMONS	1897-99	GEORGE FOREMAN	1973-74
JAMES J.JEFFRIES	1899-1905*	MUHAMMAD ALI	1974-78*
MARVIN HART	1905-06	LEON SPINKS	1978
TOMMY BURNS	1906-08	Ken Norton (WBC)	1978
JACK JOHNSON	1908-15	Larry Holmes (WBC)	1978-80
JESS WILLARD	1915-19	MUHAMMAD ALI	1978-79
JACK DEMPSEY	1919-26	John Tate (WBA)	1979-80
GENE TUNNEY	1926-28*	Mike Weaver (WBA)	1980-82
MAX SCHMELING	1930-32	LARRY HOLMES	1980-85
JACK SHARKEY	1932-33	Michael Dokes (WBA)	1982-83
PRIMO CARNERA	1933-34	Gerrie Coetzee (WBA)	1983-84
MAX BAER	1934-35	Tim Witherspoon (WBC)	1984
JAMES J.BRADDOCK	1935-37	Pinklon Thomas (WBC)	1984-86
JOE LOUIS	1937-49*	Greg Page (WBA)	1984-85
EZZARD CHARLES	1949-51	MICHAEL SPINKS	1985-87
JERSEY JOE WALCOTT	1951-52	Tim Witherspoon (WBA)	1986
ROCKY MARCIANO	1952-56*	Trevor Berbick (WBC)	1986
FLOYD PATTERSON	1956-59	Mike Tyson (WBC)	1986-87
INGEMAR JOHANSSON	1959-60	James (Bonecrusher) Smith (WBA)	1986-87
FLOYD PATTERSON	1960-62	Tony Tucker (IBF)	1987
SONNY LISTON	1962-64	Mike Tyson (WBC,WBA,IBF)	1987-88
CASSIUS CLAY (MUHAMMAD ALI)	1964-70	MIKE TYSON	1988-90
Ernie Terrell (WBA)	1965-67	**BUSTER DOUGLAS** (WBC, WBA, IBF)	1990-
Joe Frazier (NY)	1968-70		

Note: John L.Sullivan held the Bare Knuckle championship from 1882-85.

Light Heavyweights

Widely accepted champions in capital LETTERS. Current champions in **bold** type.

Champion	Held Title	Champion	Held Title
JACK ROOT	1903	MIKE McTIGUE	1923-25
GEORGE GARDNER	1903	PAUL BERLENBACH	1925-26
BOB FITZSIMMONS	1903-05	JACK DELANEY	1926-27†
PHILA.JACK O'BRIEN	1905-12*	Jimmy Slattery (NBA)	1927
JACK DILLON	1914-16	TOMMY LOUGHRAN	1927-29
BATTLING LEVINSKY	1916-20	JIMMY SLATTERY	1930
GEORGES CARPENTIER	1920-22	MAXIE ROSENBLOOM	1930-34
BATTLING SIKI	1922-23	George Nichols (NBA)	1932

Major Titleholders (Cont.)

Light Heavyweights

Champion	Held Title	Champion	Held Title
Bob Godwin (NBA)	1933	Mate Parlov (WBC)	1978
BOB OLIN	1934-35	Mike Rossman (WBA)	1978-79
JOHN HENRY LEWIS	1935-38	Marvin Johnson (WBC)	1978-79
MELIO BETTINA (NY)	1939	Matthew (Franklin) Saad Muhammad (WBC)	1979-81
Len Harvey (GBR)	1939-42	Marvin Johnson (WBA)	1979-80
BILLY CONN	1939-40†	Eddie (Gregory)	
ANTON CHRISTOFORIDIS (NBA)	1941	Mustapha Muhammad (WBA)	1980-81
GUS LESNEVICH	1941-48	Michael Spinks (WBA)	1981-83
Freddie Mills (GBR)	1942-46	Dwight (Braxton) Muhammad Qarvi (WBC)	1981-83
FREDDIE MILLS	1948-50	MICHAEL SPINKS	1983-85†
JOEY MAXIM	1950-52	J.B.Williamson (WBC)	1985-86
ARCHIE MOORE	1952-62	Slobodan Kacar (IBF)	1985-86
Harold Johnson (NBA)	1961	Marvin Johnson (WBA)	1986-87
HAROLD JOHNSON	1962-63	Dennis Andries (WBC)	1986-87
WILLIE PASTRANO	1963-65	Bobby Czyz (IBF)	1986-87
Eddie Cotton (Mich.)	1963-64	Leslie Stewart (WBA)	1987
JOSE TORRES	1965-66	**Virgil Hill (WBA)**	1987-
DICK TIGER	1966-68	**Prince Charles Williams (IBF)**	1987-
BOB FOSTER	1968-74*	Thomas Hearns (WBC)	1987
Vicente Rondon (WBA)	1971-72	Donny Lalonde (WBC)	1987-88
John Conteh (WBC)	1974-77	Sugar Ray Leonard (WBC)	1988
Victor Galindez (WBA)	1974-78	Dennis Andries (WBC)	1989
Miguel A.Cuello (WBC)	1977-78	Jeff Harding (WBC)	1989-90
		Dennis Andries (WBC)	1990-

Middleweights

Widely accepted champions in capital LETTERS. Current champions in **bold** type.

Champion	Held Title	Champion	Held Title
JACK (NONPAREIL) DEMPSEY	1884-91	ROCKY GRAZIANO	1947-48
BOB FITZSIMMONS	1891-97	TONY ZALE	1948
CHARLES (KID) McCOY	1897-98	MARCEL CERDAN	1948-49
TOMMY RYAN	1898-1907	JAKE LA MOTTA	1949-51
STANLEY KETCHEL	1908	SUGAR RAY ROBINSON	1951
BILLY PAPKE	1908	RANDY TURPIN	1951
STANLEY KETCHEL	1908-10	SUGAR RAY ROBINSON	1951-52*
FRANK KLAUS	1913	CARL (BOBO) OLSON	1953-55
GEORGE CHIP	1913-14	SUGAR RAY ROBINSON	1955-57
AL McCOY	1914-17	GENE FULLMER	1957
Jeff Smith (AUS)	1914	SUGAR RAY ROBINSON	1957
Mick King (AUS)	1914	CARMEN BASILIO	1957-58
Jeff Smith (AUS)	1914-15	SUGAR RAY ROBINSON	1958-60
Lee Darcy (AUS)	1915-17	Gene Fullmer (NBA)	1959-62
MIKE O'DOWD	1917-20	PAUL PENDER	1960-61
JOHNNY WILSON	1920-23	TERRY DOWNES	1961-62
Wm.Bryan Downey (Ohio)	1921-22	PAUL PENDER	1962-63
Dave Rosenberg (NY)	1922	Dick Tiger (WBA)	1962-63
Jock Malone (Ohio)	1922-23	DICK TIGER	1963
Mike O'Dowd (NY)	1922	JOEY GIARDELLO	1963-65
Lou Bogash (NY)	1923	DICK TIGER	1965-66
HARRY GREB	1923-26	EMILE GRIFFITH	1966-67
TIGER FLOWERS	1926	NINO BENVENUTI	1967
MICKEY WALKER	1926-31†	EMILE GRIFFITH	1967-68
GORILLA JONES	1931-32	NINO BENVENUTI	1968-70
MARCEL THIL	1932-37	CARLOS MONZON	1970-77*
Ben Jeby (NY)	1932-33	Rodrigo Valdez (WBC)	1974-76
Lou Brouillard (NBA,NY)	1933	RODRIGO VALDEZ	1977-78
Vince Dundee (NBA,NY)	1933-34	HUGO CORRO	1978-79
Teddy Yarosz (NBA,NY)	1934-35	VITO ANTUOFERMO	1979-80
Babe Risko (NBA,NY)	1935-36	ALAN MINTER	1980
Freddie Steele (NBA,NY)	1936-38	MARVELOUS MARVIN HAGLER	1980-87
FRED APOSTOLI	1937-39	SUGAR RAY LEONARD	1987
Al Hostak (NBA)	1938	Frank Tate (IBF)	1987-88
Solly Krieger (NBA)	1938-39	Sumbu Kalambay (WBA)	1987-89
Al Hostak (NBA)	1939-40	Thomas Hearns (WBC)	1987-88
CEFERINO GARCIA	1939-40	Iran Barkley (WBC)	1988-89
KEN OVERLIN	1940-41	**Michael Nunn** (IBF)	1988-
Tony Zale (NBA)	1940-41	Roberto Duran (WBC)	1989-90*
BILLY SOOSE	1941	**Mike McCallum** (WBA)	1989-
TONY ZALE	1941-47	*Duran stripped of WBC title for failing to defend within 10 months.

*Duran stripped of WBC title for failing to defend within 10 months.

Welterweights
Widely accepted champions in capital LETTERS. Current champions in **bold** type.

Champion	Held Title	Champion	Held Title
PADDY DUFFY	1888-90	SUGAR RAY ROBINSON	1946-51†
MYSTERIOUS BILLY SMITH	1892-94	JOHNNY BRATTON	1951
TOMMY RYAN	1894-98	KID GAVILAN	1951-54
MYSTERIOUS BILLY SMITH	1898-1900	JOHNNY SAXTON	1954-55
MATTY MATTHEWS	1900	TONY DeMARCO	1955
EDDIE CONNOLLY	1900	CARMEN BASILIO	1955-56
JAMES (RUBE) FERNS	1900	JOHNNY SAXTON	1956
MATTY MATHEWS	1900-01	CARMEN BASILIO	1956-57†
JAMES (RUBE) FERNS	1901	VIRGIL AKINS	1958
JOE WALCOTT	1901-04	DON JORDAN	1958-60
THE DIXIE KID	1904-05	BENNY (KID) PARET	1960-61
HONEY MELLODY	1906-07	EMILE GRIFFITH	1961
Mike (Twin) Sullivan	1907-08	BENNY (KID) PARET	1961-62
FRANK MANTELL	1907-08	EMILE GRIFFITH	1962-63
HARRY LEWIS	1908-13	LUIS RODRIGUEZ	1963
Jimmy Gardner	1908-09	EMILE GRIFFITH	1963-66†
Jimmy Clabby	1910-11	Charlie Shipes (Calif.)	1966-67
WALDEMAR HOLBERG	1914	CURTIS COKES	1966-69
TOM McCORMICK	1914	JOSE NAPOLES	1969-70
MATT WELLS	1914-15	BILLY BACKUS	1970-71
MIKE GLOVER	1915	JOSE NAPOLES	1971-75
JACK BRITTON	1915	Hedgemon Lewis (NY)	1972-73
TED (KID) LEWIS	1915-16	Angel Espada (WBA)	1975-76
JACK BRITTON	1916-17	JOHN H. STRACEY	1975-76
TED (KID) LEWIS	1917-19	CARLOS PALOMINO	1976-79
JACK BRITTON	1919-22	Pipino Cuevas (WBA)	1976-80
MICKEY WALKER	1922-26	WILFREDO BENITEZ	1979
PETE LATZO	1926-27	SUGAR RAY LEONARD	1979-80
JOE DUNDEE	1927-29	ROBERTO DURAN	1980
JACKIE FIELDS	1929-30	Thomas Hearns (WBA)	1980-81
YOUNG JACK THOMPSON	1930	SUGAR RAY LEONARD	1980-82
TOMMY FREEMAN	1930-31	Donald Curry (WBA)	1983-85
YOUNG JACK THOMPSON	1931	Milton McCrory (WBC)	1983-85
LOU BROUILLARD	1931-32	DONALD CURRY	1985-86
JACKIE FIELDS	1932-33	LLOYD HONEYGHAN	1986-87
YOUNG CORBETT III	1933	JORGE VACA (WBC)	1987-88
JIMMY McLARNIN	1933-34	LLOYD HONEYGHAN (WBC)	1988-89
BARNEY ROSS	1934	Mark Breland (WBA)	1987
JIMMY McLARNIN	1934-35	Marlon Starling (WBA)	1987-88
BARNEY ROSS	1935-38	Tomas Molinares (WBA)	1988-89
HENRY ARMSTRONG	1938-40	**Simon Brown** (IBF)	1988-
FRITZIE ZIVIC	1940-41	Mark Breland (WBA)	1989-90
Izzy Jannazzo (Md.)	1940-41	MARLON STARLING (WBC)	1989-90
Freddie (Red) Cochrane	1941-46	**Aaron Davis** (WBA)	1990-
MARTY SERVO	1946*	**Maurice Blocker** (WBC)	1990-

Lightweights
Widely accepted champions in capital LETTERS. Current champions in **bold** type.

Champion	Held Title	Champion	Held Title
JACK McAULIFFE	1886-94	HENRY ARMSTRONG	1938-39
GEORGE (KID) LAVIGNE	1896-99	LOU AMBERS	1939-40
FRANK ERNE	1899-02	Sammy Angott (NBA)	1940-41
JOE GANS	1902-04	LEW JENKINS	1940-41
JIMMY BRITT	1904-05	SAMMY ANGOTT	1941-42*
BATTLING NELSON	1905-06	Beau Jack (NY)	1942-43
JOE GANS	1906-08	Slugger White (Md.)	1943
BATTLING NELSON	1908-10	Bob Montgomery (NY)	1943
AD WOLGAST	1910-12	Sammy Angott (NBA)	1943-44
WILLIE RITCHIE	1912-14	Beau Jack (NY)	1943-44
FREDDIE WELSH	1915-17	Bob Montgomery (NY)	1944-47
BENNY LEONARD	1917-25*	Juan Zurita (NBA)	1944-45
JIMMY GOODRICH	1925	IKE WILLIAMS	1947-51
ROCKY KANSAS	1925-26	JAMES CARTER	1951-52
SAMMY MANDELL	1926-30	LAURO SALAS	1952
AL SINGER	1930	JAMES CARTER	1952-54
TONY CANZONERI	1930-33	PADDY DeMARCO	1954
BARNEY ROSS	1933-35†	JAMES CARTER	1954-55
TONY CANZONERI	1935-36	WALLACE (BUD) SMITH	1955-56
LOU AMBERS	1936-38	JOE BROWN	1956-62

Major Titleholders (Cont.)

Lightweights

Champion	Held Title	Champion	Held Title
CARLOS ORTIZ	1962-65	Andrew Ganigan (WAA)	1981-82
Kenny Lane (Mich.)	1963-64	Arturo Frias (WBA)	1981-82
ISMAEL LAGUNA	1965	Ray Mancini (WBA)	1982-84
CARLOS ORTIZ	1965-68	ALEXIS ARGUELLO	1982-83
CARLOS TEO CRUZ	1968-69	Edwin Rosario (WBC)	1983-84
MANDO RAMOS	1969-70	Choo Choo Brown (IBF)	1984
ISMAEL LAGUNA	1970	Livingstone Bramble (WBA)	1984-86
KEN BUCHANAN	1970-72	Harry Arroyo (IBF)	1984-85
Pedro Carrasco (WBC)	1971-72	Jose Luis Ramirez (WBC)	1984-85
Mando Ramos (WBC)	1972	Jimmy Paul (IBF)	1985-86
ROBERTO DURAN	1972-79†	Hector Camacho (WBC)	1985-86
Chango Carmona (WBC)	1972	Edwin Rosario (WBA)	1986-87
Rodolfo Gonzalez (WBC)	1972-74	Greg Haugen (IBF)	1986-87
Ishimatsu Suzuki (WBC)	1974-76	Julio Cesar Chavez (WBA)	1987-88
Esteban DeJesus (WBC)	1976-78	Jose Luis Ramirez (WBC)	1987-88
Jim Watt (WBC)	1979-81	JULIO CESAR CHAVEZ (WBC,WBA)	1988-89
Ernesto Espana (WBA)	1979-80	Vinny Pazienza (IBF)	1987-88
Hilmer Kenty (WBA)	1980-81	Greg Haugen (IBF)	1988-89
Sean O'Grady (WBA,WAA)	1981	Pernell Whitaker (IBF,WBC)	1989-90
Alexis Arguello (WBC)	1981-82	Edwin Rosario (WBA)	1989-90
Claude Noel (WBA)	1981	Juan Nazario (WBA)	1990
		PERNELL WHITAKER (IBF, WBC, WBA)	1990-

Featherweights

Widely accepted champions in capital LETTERS. Current champions in **bold** type.

Champion	Held Title	Champion	Held Title
TORPEDO BILLY MURPHY	1890	Sal Bartolo (NBA)	1944-46
YOUNG GRIFFO	1890-92	SANDY SADDLER	1948-49
GEORGE DIXON	1892-97	WILLIE PEP	1949-50
SOLLY SMITH	1897-98	SANDY SADDLER	1950-57*
Ben Jordan (GBR)	1898-99	HOGAN (KID) BASSEY	1957-59
Eddie Santry (GBR)	1899-1900	DAVEY MOORE	1959-63
DAVE SULLIVAN	1898	ULTIMINIO (SUGAR) RAMOS	1963-64
GEORGE DIXON	1898-1900	VICENTE SALDIVAR	1964-67*
TERRY McGOVERN	1900-01	Howard Winstone (GBR)	1968
YOUNG CORBETT II	1901-03	Raul Rojas (WBA)	1968
ABE ATTELL	1903-04	Jose Legra (WBC)	1968-69
BROOKLYN TOMMY SULLIVAN	1904-05	Shozo Saijyo (WBA)	1968-71
ABE ATTELL	1906-12	JOHNNY FAMECHON (WBC)	1969-70
JOHNNY KILBANE	1912-23	VICENTE SALDIVAR (WBC)	1970
Jim Driscoll (GBR)	1912-13	KUNIAKI SHIBATA (WBC)	1970-72
EUGENE CRIQUI	1923	Antonio Gomez (WBA)	1971-72
JOHNNY DUNDEE	1923-24†	CLEMENTE SANCHEZ (WBC)	1972
LOUIS (KID) KAPLAN	1925-26†	Ernesto Marcel (WBA)	1972-74
Dick Finnegan (Mass.)	1926-27	JOSE LEGRA (WBC)	1972-73
BENNY BASS	1927-28	EDER JOFRE (WBC)	1973-74
TONY CANZONERI	1928	Ruben Olivares (WBA)	1974
ANDRE ROUTIS	1928-29	Bobby Chacon (WBC)	1974-75
BATTLING BATTALINO	1929-32†	ALEXIS ARGUELLO (WBA)	1974-76†
Tommy Paul (NBA)	1932-33	Ruben Olivares (WBC)	1975
Kid Chocolate (NY)	1932-33	David (Poison) Kotey (WBC)	1975-76
Freddie Miller (NBA)	1933-36	DANNY (LITTLE RED) LOPEZ (WBC)	1976-80
Baby Arizmendi (MEX)	1935-36	Rafael Ortega (WBA)	1977
Mike Belloise (NY)	1936-37	Cecilio Lastra (WBA)	1977-78
Petey Sarron (NBA)	1936-37	Eusebio Pedroza (WBA)	1978-85
HENRY ARMSTRONG	1937-38†	SALVADOR SANCHEZ (WBC)	1980-82
Joey Archibald (NY)	1938-39	Juan LaPorte (WBC)	1982-84
Leo Rodak (NBA)	1938-39	Wilfredo Gomez (WBC)	1984
JOEY ARCHIBALD	1939-40	Min-Keun Oh (IBF)	1984-85
Petey Scalzo (NBA)	1940-41	Azumah Nelson (WBC)	1984-88
Jimmy Perrin (La.)	1940-41	Barry McGuigan (WBA)	1985-86
HARRY JEFFRA	1940-41	Ki-Young Chung (IBF)	1985-86
JOEY ARCHIBALD	1941	Steve Cruz (WBA)	1986-87
Richie Lemos (NBA)	1941-42	Antonio Rivera (IBF)	1986-88
CHALKY WRIGHT	1941-42	**Antonio Esparragoza** (WBA)	1987-
Jackie Wilson (NBA)	1941-43	Calvin Grove (IBF)	1988
WILLIE PEP	1942-48	**Jorge Paez** (IBF)	1988-
Jackie Callura (NBA)	1943	Jeff Fenech (WBC)	1988-90†
Phil Terranova (NBA)	1943-44	**Marcos Villasana** (WBC)	1990-

Bantamweights

Widely accepted champions in capital LETTERS. Current champions in **bold** type.

Champion	Held Title	Champion	Held Title
HUGHEY BOYLE	1887-88	HAROLD DADE	1947
CHAPPIE MORAN	1889-90	MANUEL ORTIZ	1947-50
TOMMY (SPIDER) KELLY	1890-92	VIC TOWEEL	1950-52
BILLY PLIMMER	1892-95	JIMMY CARRUTHERS	1952-54*
PEDLAR PALMER	1895-99	ROBERT COHEN	1954-56
TERRY McGOVERN	1899-1900	Raul Macias (NBA)	1955-57
DANNY DOUGHERTY	1900-01	MARIO D'AGATA	1956-57
HARRY FORBES	1901-03	ALPHONSE HALIMI	1957-59
FRANKIE NEIL	1903-04	JOE BECERRA	1959-60*
JOE BOWKER	1904-05	Johnny Caldwell (EBU)	1961-62
JIMMY WALSH	1905-06†	EDER JOFRE	1961-65
OWEN MORAN	1907-08	MASAHIKO FIGHTING HARADA	1965-68
MONTE ATTELL	1909-10	LIONEL ROSE	1968-69
FRANKIE CONLEY	1910-11	RUBEN OLIVARES	1969-70
JOHNNY COULON	1911-14	CHUCHO CASTILLO	1970-71
Digger Stanley (GBR)	1910-12	RUBEN OLIVARES	1971-72
Charles Ledoux (GBR)	1912-13	RAFAEL HERRERA	1972
Eddie Campi (GBR)	1913-14	ENRIQUE PINDER	1972-73
KID WILLIAMS	1914-17	ROMEO ANAYA	1973
Johnny Ertle	1915-18	Rafael Herrera (WBC)	1973-74
PETE HERMAN	1917-20	ARNOLD TAYLOR	1973-74
Memphis Pal Moore	1918-19	SOO-HWAN HONG	1974-75
JOE LYNCH	1920-21	Rodolfo Martinez (WBC)	1974-76
PETE HERMAN	1921	ALFONSO ZAMORA	1975-77
JOHNNY BUFF	1921-22	Carlos Zarate (WBC)	1976-79
JOE LYNCH	1922-24	JORGE LUJAN	1977-80
ABE GOLDSTEIN	1924	Lupe Pintor (WBC)	1979-83
CANNONBALL EDDIE MARTIN	1924-25	JULIAN SOLIS	1980
PHIL ROSENBERG	1925-27	JEFF CHANDLER	1980-84
Teddy Baldock (GBR)	1927	Albert Davila (WBC)	1983-85
BUD TAYLOR (NBA)	1927-28†	RICHARD SANDOVAL	1984-86
Willie Smith (GBR)	1927-28	Satoshi Shingaki (IBF)	1984-85
Bushy Graham (NY)	1928-29	Jeff Fenech (IBF)	1985
PANAMA AL BROWN	1929-35	Daniel Zaragoza (WBC)	1985
Sixto Escobar (NBA)	1934-35	Miguel (Happy) Lora (WBC)	1985-88
BALTAZAR SANGCHILLI	1935-36	GABY CANIZALES	1986
Lou Salica (NBA)	1935	BERNARDO PINANGO	1986-87
Sixto Escobar (NBA)	1935-36	Wilfredo Vasquez (WBA)	1987-88
TONY MARINO	1936	Kevin Seabrooks (IBF)	1987-88
SIXTO ESCOBAR	1936-37	Kaokor Galaxy (WBA)	1988
HARRY JEFFRA	1937-38	Moon Sung-Kil (WBA)	1988-89
SIXTO ESCOBAR	1938-39*	Kaokor Galaxy (WBA)	1989
Georgie Pace (NBA)	1939-40	**Raul Perez (WBC)**	1988-
LOU SALICA	1940-42	**Orlando Canizales (IBF)**	1988-
MANUEL ORTIZ	1942-47	**Luisito Espinosa (WBA)**	1989-

Flyweights

Widely accepted champions in capital LETTERS. Current champions in **bold** type.

Champion	Held Title	Champion	Held Title
SID SMITH	1913	Small Montana (NY,Calif.)	1935-37
BILL LADBURY	1913-14	PETER KANE	1938-43
PERCY JONES	1914	Little Dado (NBA,Calif.)	1938-40
JOE SYMONDS	1914-16	JACKIE PATERSON	1943-48
JIMMY WILDE	1916-23	RINTY MONAGHAN	1948-50*
PANCHO VILLA	1923-25	TERRY ALLEN	1950
FIDEL LaBARBA	1925-27*	SALVADOR (DADO) MARINO	1950-52
FRENCHY BELANGER (NBA,IBU)	1927-28	YOSHIO SHIRAI	1953-54
Izzy Schwartz (NY)	1927-29	PASCUAL PEREZ	1954-60
Johnny McCoy (Calif.)	1927-28	PONE KINGPETCH	1960-62
Newsboy Brown (Calif.)	1928	HIROYUKI EBIHARA	1963-64
FRANKIE GENARO (NBA,IBU)	1928-29	PONE KINGPETCH	1964-65
Johnny Hill (GBR)	1928-29	SALVATORE BURRINI	1965-66
SPIDER PLADNER (NBA,IBU)	1929	Horacio Accavallo (WBA)	1966-68
FRANKIE GENARO (NBA,IBU)	1929-31	WALTER McGOWAN	1966
Willie LaMorte (NY)	1929-30	CHARTCHAI CHIONOI	1966-69
Midget Wolgast (NY)	1930-35	EFREN TORRES	1969-70
YOUNG PEREZ (NBA,IBU)	1931-32	Hiroyuki Ebihara (WBA)	1969
JACKIE BROWN (NBA,IBU)	1932-35	Bernabe Villacampo (WBA)	1969-70
BENNY LYNCH	1935-38†	CHARTCHAI CHIONOI	1970

Major Titleholders (Cont.)

Flyweights

Champion	Held Title
Berkrerk Chartvanchai (WBA)	1970
Masao Ohba (WBA)	1970-73
ERBITO SALAVARRIA	1970-73
Betulio Gonzalez (WBC)	1972
Venice Borkorsor (WBC)	1972-73
VENICE BORKORSOR	1973
Chartchai Chionoi (WBA)	1973-74
Betulio Gonzalez (WBA)	1973-74
Shoji Oguma (WBC)	1974-75
Susumu Hanagata (WBA)	1974-75
Miguel Canto (WBC)	1975-79
Erbito Salavarria (WBA)	1975-76
Alfonso Lopez (WBA)	1976
Guty Espadas (WBA)	1976-78
Betulio Gonzalez (WBA)	1978-79
Chan-Hee Park (WBC)	1979-80
Luis Ibarra (WBA)	1979-80
Tae-Shik Kim (WBA)	1980
Shoji Oguma (WBC)	1980-81
Peter Mathebula (WBA)	1980-81
Santos Laciar (WBA)	1981
Antonio Avelar (WBC)	1981-82
Luis Ibarra (WBA)	1981
Juan Herrera (WBA)	1981-82
Prudencio Cardona (WBC)	1982
Santos Laciar (WBA)	1982-85
Freddie Castillo (WBC)	1982
Eleoncio Mercedes (WBC)	1982-83
Charlie Magri (WBC)	1983
Frank Cedeno (WBC)	1983-84
Soon-Chun Kwon (IBF)	1983-85
Koji Kobayashi (WBC)	1984
Gabriel Bernal (WBC)	1984
Sot Chitalada (WBC)	1984-88
Hilario Zapate (WBA)	1985-87
Chong-Kwan Chung (IBF)	1985-86
Bi-Won Chung (IBF)	1986
Hi-Sup Shin (IBF)	1986-87
Dodie Penalosa (IBF)	1987
Fidel Bassa (WBA)	1987-89
Choi Chang-Ho (IBF)	1987-88
Rolando Bohol (IBF)	1988
Yong-Kang Kim (WBC)	1988-89
Duke McKenzie (IBF)	1988-89
Dave McAuley (IBF)	1989-
Sot Chitalada (WBC)	1989-
Jesus Rojas (WBA)	1989-90
Yul-Woo Lee (WBA)	1990
Leopard Tamakuma (WBA)	1990-

Triple Champions

Fourteen fighters have won recognized world championships in three or more weight divisions. Sugar Ray Leonard has the most titles with five, while Roberto Duran and Thomas Hearns have four each. WBA, WBC and IBF titles are recognized, but WBO titles are not. Note that (*) indicates title claimant.

	Titles			Titles	
Terry McGovern	Bantamweight	1889-1900	**Alexis Arguello**	Featherweight (WBA)	1974-77
	Featherweight	1900-01		Jr.Lightweight (WBC)	1978-80
	Lightweight*	1900-01		Lightweight (WBC)	1981-82
Bob Fitzsimmons	Middleweight	1891-97	**Roberto Duran**	Lightweight	1972-79
	Light Heavyweight	1903-05		Welterweight (WBC)	1980
	Heavyweight	1987-99		Jr.Middleweight (WBA)	1983
				Middleweight (WBC)	1989-90
Stanley Ketchel	Welterweight*	1908, 08-10	**Sugar Ray Leonard**	Welterweight (WBC) .1979-80,80-82	
	Middleweight	1908-10		(undisputed from 1981-82)	
	Light Heavyweight*	1909-10		Jr.Middleweight (WBA)	1981
Tony Canzoneri	Featherweight	1928		Middleweight (WBC)	1987
	Lightweight	1930-33		Super Middleweight (WBC) .1988-90	
	Jr.Welterweight	1931-32,33		Light Heavyweight (WBC)	1988
Barney Ross	Lightweight	1933-35	**Thomas Hearns**	Welterweight (WBA)	1980-81
	Jr.Welterweight	1933-35		Jr.Middleweight (WBC)	1982-84
	Welterweight	1934-38		Middleweight (WBC)	1987-88
Henry Armstrong	Featherweight	1937-38		Light Heavyweight (WBC)	1987
	Welterweight	1938-40	**Julio Cesar Chavez**	Jr.Lightweight (WBC)	1984-87
	Lightweight	1938-39		Lightweight (WBA/WBC)	1987-89
Emile Griffith	Welterweight	1961,62-63,63-66		Jr.Welterweight (WBC/IBF)	1989-
	Jr.Middleweight	1962-63	**Jeff Fenech**	Bantamweight (IBF)	1985
	Middleweight	1966-67,67-68		Jr.Featherweight (WBC)	1986-88
Wilfredo Benitez	Jr.Welterweight	1976-79		Featherweight (WBC)	1988-90
	Welterweight	1979			
	Jr.Middleweight (WBC)	1981-82			

1934 Copyright Estate of Harold E. Edgerton

This famous 1934 stop-action photograph of a football player kicking a football was taken by MIT professor Harold E. (Doc) Edgerton, who died on Jan. 4. Edgerton invented the electronic flash, or strobe light, which revealed motion in segments never before seen by the human eye. It is hard to imagine modern sports photography without it.

DEATHS

November, 1989 to October, 1990

Wide World Photos

Harold Ballard

Wide World Photos

Mary Victor Bruce

Wide World Photos

Nat (Sweetwater) Clifton

Harold Ballard, 86; outspoken owner of the Toronto Maple Leafs and Maple Leaf Gardens since 1972; never won Stanley Cup; served a year in jail for fraud (for diverting money from Gardens' accounts to his own) in 1974; elected to Hockey Hall of Fame in 1977; also owned CFL Hamilton Tiger-Cats from 1978-88, winning the Grey Cup in 1986; of diabetes-related heart problems; in Toronto, Apr.11.

Charles (Red) Barrett, 75; holder of the major league record for fewest pitches thrown in a nine-inning game; as a member of the Boston Braves in 1944, he threw only 58 pitches to 27 Cincinnati batters and won, 2-0; led NL in wins with 23 in 1945, but was only 69-69 overall in 11 seasons; after a long illness, in Wilson, N.C., July 28.

Percy Beard, 82; silver medalist in 110-meter hurdles at 1932 Olympics in Los Angeles; set five world records in hurdles from 1931-34; track coach at Florida from 1936-64 and assistant AD from 1960-73; founded the Florida Relays; elected to Track & Field Hall of Fame in 1981; after a long illness, in Gainesville, Fla., Mar.27.

Johnny Beazley, 71; led St.Louis Cardinals to World Series title as a rookie pitcher in 1942; went 21-6 during the regular season, then beat the New York Yankees with two complete game wins in Series; injured in service, returned after war but won only nine games in four seasons; of cancer; in Nashville, Tenn., Apr.21.

Luigi Beccali, 83; Italian miler who came from behind to win the 1500-meter gold medal at the 1932 Olympics in Los Angeles; set 1500-meter world record (3:49.0) in 1933; placed third behind Jack Lovelace and Glenn Cunningham in 1500 at the 1936 Olympics in Berlin; of natural causes; in Rafaello, Italy, Aug.28.

Willis Peter Bilderback, 81; coached Naval Academy lacrosse teams to eight consecutive national championships from 1959-66; compiled a record of 132-26-2 in 14 years at Navy; cause of death undisclosed; in Annapolis, Md., June 12.

Dallas Bixler, 80; American gymnast who won gold medal in the horizontal bar competition at the 1932 Games in Los Angeles; of natural causes; in Buena Park, Calif., Aug.13.

Phil Boggs, 40; top American diver of the 1970s who won springboard gold medal at the 1976 Olympics in Montreal; three-time world champion and winner of nine U.S. titles; later became a commentator for CBS Sports and ESPN; of cancer; in Miami, July 4.

Richard Bond, 80; Philadelphia businessman and civic leader who chaired committees that oversaw the building of Veterans Stadium in 1971 and the organization of the Bicentennial celebration in 1976; of cancer and a cerebral hemorrhage; in Philadelphia, Nov.4, 1989.

Marshall (Sheriff) Bridges, 59; compiled a record of 23-15 with 25 saves in seven years with St.Louis, Cincinnati, the New York Yankees and Washington; 8-4 with 18 saves in 1962 as reliever with AL champion Yankees, then gave up the first grand slam ever hit by an NL player (Chuck Hiller of San Francisco) in the World Series; of cancer; in Jackson, Miss., Sept.3.

Arthur Brown, 78; retired trucking executive and original owner of ABA New Jersey Americans; moved team from Teaneck, N.J., to Commack, N.Y., in 1968 and changed name to Nets; sold club a year later; involved in harness racing for 45 years and won the Hambletonian with Historic Freight in 1984; of a heart attack; in Englewood, N.J., Dec.22, 1989.

Mary Victor Bruce, 94; pioneer racer of cars, boats and airplanes in the 1920s and '30s whose feats included: the 24-hour solo record by car which covered 2200 miles (1929), the 24-hour solo record by motorboat which covered 674 nautical miles (1929), the first solo flight from England to Japan (1930), and the fastest solo flight from India to French Indochina (1930); arrested in 1930 for flying tight circles around the Empire State Building in New York; at age 81 she came out of retirement to fly a loop-the-loop in a two-seater plane; of natural causes; in London, May 21.

Vern Buffey, 63; former hockey referee who co-founded, with Bruce Hood, the NHL referees' union and served as its first president; referee-in-chief and later supervisor of officials in the WHA from 1972-75; of a heart attack; in Toronto, Sept.11.

Robert (Bob) Carpenter, Jr., 74; owner and president of the Philadelphia Phillies for 29 years; made president at age 28 after his father bought the team in 1943; named Executive of the Year in 1949 for turning last place Phils into a contender; in 1950, the Phils won their first pennant in 35 years; succeeded by son Ruly in 1972; family sold club in 1981 after winning the franchise's one and only World Series in 1980; of cancer; in Montchanin, Del., July 8.

Stefano Casiraghi, 30; speedboat racer and husband of Princess Caroline of Monaco; killed, along with co-pilot Patrice Innocenti, defending his World Offshore Championship title when his 42-foot boat struck a wave and flipped at 90 mph; off Jean-Cap-Ferrat, near Monaco, Oct.3.

Spud Chandler, 82; college football and baseball star at Georgia from 1929-32; two-time 20-game winner with the New York Yankees; American League MVP in 1943 with a record of 20-4 and a 1.64 ERA; compiled a 109-43 record and pitched for six World Series champions in 11 seasons with New York; cause of death not disclosed; in St.Petersburg, Fla., Jan.9.

Wide World Photos

Tony Conigliaro

International Swimming Hall of Fame

Charlotte Boyle Clune

Wide World Photos

Bob Davies

Nat (Sweetwater) Clifton, 67; one of the first black players in the NBA; played college ball at Xavier in New Orleans then toured with the Harlem Globetrotters for two years before signing with the New York Knicks as a center-forward in 1950; led Knicks to the NBA Finals three times and made the All-Star team in 1957; ended career with Detroit in 1958; of a heart attack; in Chicago, Aug.31.

Joseph R. Cloutier, 81; president of Indianapolis Motor Speedway from 1977-79 and again from 1982-89; right hand man of speedway-owner Anton Hulman from 1926 until Hulman's death in 1977; presided over extensive track renovations and increase in prize money from $1.1 million in 1978 to $5.7 million in 1989; cause of death not disclosed; in Terre Haute, Ind., Dec.11, 1989.

Charlotte Boyle Clune, 91; pioneer women's swimming star who set four world records and eight American records between 1917-21; named all-American women's swimming champion in 1919; swam for USA in 1920 Olympics at Antwerp; helped develop six beat double trudgeon crawl, the freestyle stroke that became standard in racing; taught swimming until she was 83; elected to the International Swimming Hall of Fame in 1988; of cancer; in Scottsville, N.Y., Oct.3.

Herman Cohen, 95; president of Pimlico Race Course from 1952-86; of cancer; in Baltimore, May 17 (two days before the Preakness Stakes).

Leslie Combs II, 88; retired owner and breeder of thoroughbred horses; founder of Spendthrift Farm (1936-89) and pioneer in the syndication of race horses; of cancer; in Lexington, Ky., Apr.7.

Tony Conigliaro, 45; youngest player ever to win a major league home run title when he hit 32 for the Boston Red Sox in 1965; beaned by Jack Hamilton of California in 1967 and missed rest of that season and all of 1968 with blurred vision; returned in 1969 to hit 20 HRs, then had career-high 36 HRs and 116 RBI in 1970; vision problems returned after he was traded to California in '71; of kidney failure following debilitating 1982 heart attack; in Salem, Mass., Feb.24.

Casey Conner, 19, Charles Ford, 20 and **Michael Kimble, 18;** three Jackson St.(Miss.) football players; in an automobile accident, near Macon, Tenn., Apr.16. The three deaths marked the third straight year the Jackson St. team had players killed in car crashes.

Eddie Cotton, 64; light heavyweight contender in the 1960s who lost close 15-round decisions in title fights to Harold Johnson in 1961 and Jose Torres in 1966; compiled record of 58-23-2 in 21 years; later a Washington state boxing commissioner; of a blood disorder following a second liver transplant; in Seattle, June 24.

Ted Cox, 86; head football coach at Tulane from 1932-35 and at Oklahoma A&M (now Oklahoma St.) from 1936-39; compiled record of 35-33-2 in eight years; led Tulane to 20-14 victory over Temple in the inaugural Sugar Bowl of 1935; of natural causes, in Denver, Nov. 5, 1989.

Roger (Doc) Cramer, 85; outfielder who batted .296 over 20 AL seasons with Philadelphia, Boston, Washington and Detroit; one of several players to go 6-for-6 in a nine-inning game, but only AL player to do it twice; played in five All-Star Games; hit .379 to lead Detroit to a World Series title in 1945; of cancer; in Manahawkin, N.J., Sept. 9.

Frank Dascoli, 76; controversial NL umpire from 1948-61 who was known for his quick thumb; once threw 18 Philadelphia A's players out of an exhibition game; fired by NL president Warren Giles for published remarks questioning Giles' willingness to back up his umpires; of cancer; in Danielson, Conn., Aug.11.

Donald Davidson, 64; diminutive (4 feet tall) special assistant with the Houston Astros, whose baseball career spanned more than 40 years; began as a bat boy for the Boston Braves and Red Sox; held administrative jobs with Braves in Boston, Milwaukee and Atlanta from 1948-76; of cancer; in Houston, Mar.28.

Bob Davies, 70; All-America guard at Seton Hall who led Pirates to a three-year record of 55-5 through 1942; after the war, he led the Rochester Royals to NBL titles in 1946 and 1947 while also coaching Seton Hall to 24-3 record in 1946-47; Rochester joined the new NBA in 1948 and won the NBA championship in 1951; a five-time NBA All-Star before retiring in 1955; elected to Basketball Hall of Fame in 1969; uniform No.11 retired by Sacramento Kings (formerly Rochester Royals) in 1990; of cancer; in Hilton Head, S.C., Apr.22.

Victor Davis, 25; Canadian swimmer who won a gold medal in the 200-meter breaststroke and a silver in both the 100-meter breast and 400-meter medley relay at the 1984 Olympics in Los Angeles; twice set world record in 200-meter breaststroke; from injuries received when hit by a car; in Montreal, Nov.13, 1989.

Clarence (Hap) Day, 88; defenseman who was the only player to serve as captain, coach and general manager of the Toronto Maple Leafs; captain of first Maple Leafs team to win Stanley Cup in 1932, coached team to five more Cups between 1942-49; elected to the Hockey Hall of Fame in 1961; of natural causes; in St.Thomas, Ontario, Feb.17.

Georges de Mestral, 82; inventor of Velcro (1948), the fastener that revolutionized much of the clothing industry; of natural causes; in Commugny, Switzerland; Feb.10.

Wide World Photos

Victor Davis

Wide World Photos

Rocky Graziano

Wide World Photos

Fortune Gordien

George Dixon, 56; American running back for the Montreal Alouettes from 1959-65; named the CFL's Outstanding Player in 1962; set a pro football record with a 109-yard touchdown run from scrimmage (CFL fields are 110 yards long) in 1963; of cancer; in Montreal, Aug.6.

Augie Donatelli, 76; NL umpire for 24 years and founder of Major League Umpires Association in 1964; known for his combative style on the field; umpired five World Series and four All-Star Games; of natural causes; in St.Petersburg, Fla., May 24.

George Donnelly, 55; American soccer administrator who was on the U.S. Soccer Federation's board of directors and a member of the U.S. Soccer Hall of Fame; of a heart attack; in Nanuet, N.Y., Apr.7.

Harold (Doc) Edgerton, 86; professor emeritus of electrical measurements at MIT whose invention of the electrical flash in 1931 expanded the scope of photography; to popularize his invention he used a strobe light to take stop-action images of athletes, animals and machines; the famous photo of a football being kicked at the moment of impact is his (see p. 659); of a heart attack; in Cambridge, Mass., Jan.4.

Carl Ekern, 36; linebacker with the Los Angeles Rams from 1976-78 and 1980-88; named to NFC Pro Bowl squad following 1986 season; of injuries suffered in a single car accident; near Ridgecrest, Calif., Aug.1.

Charles (Chuck) Ewart, 74; star halfback at Yale with Heisman Trophy winners Larry Kelley and Clint Frank (1935-37); with FBI as national security agent (1942-46); backfield coach for the Philadelphia Eagles in 1946, then general manager in 1948 when Eagles won first NFL title; left in 1949 to coach NFL New York Bulldogs for one season; of cancer; in Elk Grove, Ill., Apr.30.

Lew Fonseca, 90; often-injured infielder who hit .369 for Cleveland in 1929 to win AL batting title; hit .316 over 14 years; managed the Chicago White Sox from 1932-34; best known for producing popular All-Star Game and World Series highlight films in the 1940s and '50s; after a long illness; in Ely, Iowa, Nov.26, 1989.

Malcolm Forbes, 70; chairman and editor-in-chief of Forbes magazine, whose extravagant pursuits included yachting, motorcycles (he owned 68) and ballooning; set six world records in hot-air balloons in 1973, then became the first person to pilot a hot-air balloon from coast to coast over the United States (Oregon to Maryland) in 1974; of a heart attack in his sleep; in Far Hills, N.J., Feb.24.

Hank Gathers, 23; All-America forward at Loyola Marymount who led NCAA Division I in scoring and rebounding as a junior in 1988-89; of heart failure after collapsing during West Coast Conference tournament game; in Los Angeles, Mar.4 (see pages 180-81).

Robert (Pappy) Gault, 68; first black coach of a U.S. Olympic boxing team when he got the job for the 1968 Games in Mexico City; led by lightweight Ron Harris and heavyweight George Foreman, the USA won two gold, one silver and four bronze medals; of a ruptured ulcer following a heart attack; in Westwood, Calif., May 18.

Glen Gorbous, 59; strong-armed, journeyman ballplayer who, as a minor leaguer with Omaha of the American Association, threw a baseball 445 feet, 10 inches on Aug. 1, 1957; the heave is still considered the longest ever by the Guinness Book of World Records; of a heart attack; in Calgary, Alberta, June 12.

Fortune Gordien, 67; held the world discus record for 10 years, from 1949-59; longest throw was 194 feet, 6 inches in 1953; three-time NCAA and six-time AAU champion; member of three U.S. Olympic teams, placing 3rd in 1948, 4th in 1952 and 2nd in 1956; of complications brought on by a blocked artery; in Fontana, Calif., Apr.10.

Rocky Graziano, 67; humorous reform school graduate who held middleweight championship from 1947-48; his three title fights with Tony Zale in 1946-47-48 are considered classic brawls; compiled 67-10-6 record from 1942-52; subject of 1956 Paul Newman film *Somebody Up There Likes Me*; later became an entertainer himself; of heart failure; in New York, May 22.

Ben Hill Griffin Jr., 79; leading figure in the Florida citrus industry and major benefactor of the University of Florida; Gators' football stadium named in his honor (Ben Hill Griffin Stadium at Florida Field); after a long illness; in Avon Park, Fla., Mar.1.

Homer Griffith, 77; tailback at Southern Cal from 1931-33 and MVP of 1933 Rose Bowl where unbeaten USC routed unbeaten Pitt, 35-0; of heart failure; in Tarzana, Calif., Jan.31.

Tom Harmon, 70; triple-threat tailback and two-time All-America at Michigan who led the nation in scoring in 1939 and '40; won 1940 Heisman Trophy after finishing second (to Iowa's Nile Kinnick) in 1939; first player chosen in the 1940 NFL Draft (by the Chicago Bears) but signed instead with rival AFL; won the Silver Star and Purple Heart as a fighter pilot in World War II; returned to play two years with the L.A. Rams after war, but retired in 1947; became radio and TV commentator; of a heart attack; in Los Angeles, Mar.15.

Wide World Photos

Doug Harvey

Wide World Photos

Tom Harmon

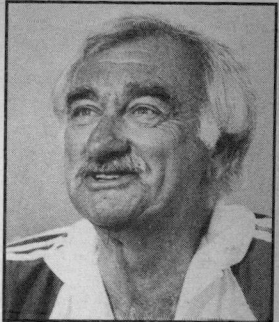

Wide World Photos

Gene Klein

Gypsy Joe Harris, 44; welterweight contender in the late 1960s; first boxer to make the cover of *Sports Illustrated* (June 19,1967) who was neither a heavyweight nor a world champion; 24-0 when he lost by decision to former champion Emile Griffith on Aug.6, 1968; it was his last fight—three months later, the Pennsylvania boxing commission discovered Harris had concealed the blindness of his right eye and revoked his license; of heart failure; in Philadelphia, Mar.6.

Marion Rice Hart, 98; sportswoman and author who sailed a ketch around the world in the late 1930s and logged more than 5,000 hours after taking up flying at age 54; flew seven solo flights across Atlantic after age 70; received aviation's prestigious Harmon International Trophy in 1976; of pneumonia; in Berkeley, Calif., July 2.

Doug Harvey, 65; an 11-time NHL All-Star who won the Norris Trophy as the league's top defenseman seven times; led the Montreal Canadiens to six Stanley Cups from 1953-60; retired in 1969 after 19 seasons (14 with Montreal); elected to the Hockey Hall of Fame in 1973; of cirrhosis of the liver; in Montreal, Dec.26, 1989.

Ralph Heikkinen, 72; consensus All-America guard at Michigan in 1938; played one year of pro football with the NFL Brooklyn Dodgers before going to law school; of heart failure; in Pontiac, Mich., Jan.11.

Carmen Hill, 94; won 22 games for the NL champion Pittsburgh Pirates in 1927; overall record of 49-33 in 10 years; of natural causes; in Indianapolis, Jan.1.

Bruce Hilkene, 64; tackle and captain of the unbeaten (10-0) Michigan football team that was declared the unofficial national champion in 1947; Notre Dame (9-0) was named No.1 in the final AP poll at the end of the regular season, but when Michigan routed No.8 Southern Cal, 49-0, in the Rose Bowl, AP was pressured into taking another vote and Michigan won by 226-119 (Notre Dame didn't play in a bowl); AP, however, ruled that the earlier poll would be the vote of record; of cancer; in La Quinta, Calif., Apr. 26.

Stan Isle, 66; member *The Sporting News* editorial staff since 1965 and a senior editor since 1984; of cancer; in St.Louis, Dec.28, 1989.

Larry Jackson, 59; pitcher who compiled a 196-183 record in 14 years with St.Louis, Chicago and Philadephia in the NL; he was 24-11 with the last place Cubs in 1964 and made the All-Star team three times; of cancer; in Boise, Idaho, Aug.28.

John Jardine, 53; head football coach at Wisconsin from 1970-77; guided the Badgers to a 37-47-3 record; of heart failure (he had received a heart transplant in June, 1989); in Madison, Wis., Mar.23.

Gene Johnson, 87; head basketball coach at Wichita St. from 1928-33 and assistant coach under Jim Needles of the gold medal-winning U.S. basketball team of the 1936 Olympics in Berlin; credited with inventing the zone press defense; cause of death not disclosed; in Overland Park, Kan., Dec.27, 1989.

Dick Jorgensen, 56; former Univ. of Wisconsin basketball captain (1955-56) and NFL referee since 1971; worked 12 postseason playoff games in career, including four conference title games and Super Bowl XXIV last Jan.28; did not work league games this season; president of Marine Bank in Champaign-Urbana, Ill., since 1978; of cancer; in Urbana, Ill., Oct. 10.

Charlie (King Kong) Keller, 73; outfielder who hit .286 with 189 home runs over a 13-year career with the New York Yankees and Detroit; hit at least 30 homers in a season three times; had .611 slugging average in four World Series with Yankees; never liked nickname given to him for his strength; retired in 1952 and became a successful breeder of standardbred horses (trotters and pacers); of cancer; in Frederick, Md., May 23.

Nick Kerbawy, 77; general manager of the Detroit Lions from 1950-58 when club won three NFL championships (1952-53,57); became GM of the NBA Detroit Pistons in 1958, was fired in 1961, then sued owner Fred Zollner for breach of contract and won nearly $1 million in 1967; of cancer; in Bloomfield Hills, Mich., June 7.

Gene Klein, 69; self-made millionaire and owner of the San Diego Chargers from 1966-84; bitterly opposed Al Davis when Raiders' owner moved team from Oakland to Los Angeles in 1982; gained real prominence as a horseman and winner of three Eclipse awards as Outstanding Owner; his filly, Winning Colors, won the 1988 Kentucky Derby; sold 114-horse stable in 1989 to travel; of a heart attack; in Rancho Sante Fe, Calif., Mar.12.

Barney Kremenko, 80; former sportswriter for the *N.Y. Journal-American* who gave Willie Mays the nickname "The Say Hey Kid" while covering the New York baseball Giants in the 1950s; also covered the Mets, Rangers, college basketball and track & field; cause of death not disclosed; in Mineola, N.Y., Jan.20.

Harry (Cookie) Lavagetto, 73; Brooklyn infielder who broke up New York Yankee pitcher Bill Bevins' no-hitter with two outs in the bottom of the 9th inning of Game 4 of the 1947 World Series; his pinch-hit double drove in two runs, won the game (3-2) and tied the Series; went on to manage Washington and Minnesota from 1957-61 and coached with the New York Mets under Casey Stengel from 1962-65; of a heart attack in his sleep; in Orinda, Calif., Aug.10.

Wide World Photos

Billy Martin

Wide World Photos

Bronko Nagurski

Wide World Photos

Harry (Cookie) Lavagetto

Donald Lourie, 91; former chairman of the Quaker Oats Company who was a consensus All-America quarterback at Princeton in 1920; of heart failure; in Longwood, Fla., Jan.15.

Lester Maitland, 91; aviation pioneer who co-piloted the first flight from the U.S. mainland to Hawaii with Albert Hegenberger in 1927; first pilot to fly at 200 mph and member of Army racing team that set the world speed record of 239.95 mph in a Curtiss racer in 1923; of natural causes; in Scottsdale, Ariz., Mar.27.

Earl Mann, 84; independent minor league baseball owner and promoter who was president of the old Atlanta Crackers of the Southern League from 1935-49; bought the team from the Coca-Cola Co. in 1949 and sold it in 1958; of pneumonia; in Palm Beach, Fla., Jan.5.

Billy Martin, 61; five-time manager of the New York Yankees who was frequently fired for drinking and brawling; also managed Minnesota, Detroit, Texas and Oakland over 16 years and won 2267 regular season games, five division titles, two pennants and one World Series (1977); also an infielder on Yankee teams that won four World Series in 1950s; of injuries suffered in a pickup truck crash in Binghamton, N.Y., Dec.25, 1989.

Bob Martin, 57; radio voice of the Denver Broncos from 1964 through the 1990 Super Bowl; released from hospital to call Super Bowl XXIV on Jan.28, then had to return; after a 2½-year battle with bone marrow cancer; in Denver, Feb.25.

Ettore Maserati, 96; founder and guiding force of the famous Italian racing and sports car company; produced first race car in 1926; won Indy 500 in 1939 and '40 with Wilbur Cross as driver; retired from car manufacturing business in 1972; cause of death not disclosed; in Bologna, Italy, Aug.4.

Rufus Mayes, 42; All-America tackle for the 1968 Ohio State team that won the national championship; played nine seasons with Cincinnati in the NFL; of bacterial meningitis; in Seattle, Jan.9.

Coyle Moore, 89; educator credited with bringing coeducation to Florida State College for Women (later, Florida State University) and introducing a football program in 1947; athletic center next to football stadium named in his honor; cause of death not disclosed; in Tallahassee, Fla., Feb.13.

Wally Moses, 80; American League outfielder who played for Philadelphia, Chicago and Boston from 1935-51; career .291 hitter with 2138 hits; led the AL in triples (12) in 1943 and doubles (35) in 1945; of a heart attack; in Vidalia, Ga., Oct.10.

Rob Moroso, 22; stock car driver and leading candidate for NASCAR's Winston Cup rookie of the year award; won Busch Grand National series championship in 1989; in a two-car accident that also killed the other driver; in Mooresville, N.C.; Sept.30.

Barney Nagler, 78; boxing and thoroughbred racing writer whose column ran for 40 years, first in *The Morning Telegraph* and then in *The Daily Racing Form;* also worked in television as a producer of sports events for NBC and ABC; of pneumonia; in Freehold, N.J., Oct.22.

Bronko Nagurski, 81; charter member of both the college and pro football halls of fame; fullback and defensive tackle at Minnesota where he was the only player ever to be named All-America at two positions in one year (1929); three-time All-Pro with the Chicago Bears; helped lead Bears to three NFL titles (1932-33, 43); cause of death not disclosed; in International Falls, Minn., Jan.7.

Isiah Nelson, 40; San Francisco police commander who supervised the safe evacuation of Candlestick Park and advised baseball commissioner Fay Vincent following the earthquake that postponed the 1989 World Series for 12 days; of injuries received in a motorcycle accident while on duty; in San Francisco, Apr.14.

Johnny Neun, 89; Detroit Tigers 1st baseman and one of only eight players in major league history to execute an unassisted triple play—on May 31, 1927 against Cleveland; managed the New York Yankees (14 games) and Cincinnati (2 years) in the 1940s; of cancer; in Baltimore, Mar.28.

Ralph Norwood, 23; former offensive tackle at LSU who had played 11 games as a rookie with the Atlanta Falcons; of injuries suffered in a car accident; in Suwanee, Ga., Nov.24, 1989.

Larry O'Brien, 73; veteran Democratic political wheeler-dealer who ran John F. Kennedy's presidential campaign in 1960 and served as Postmaster General under both Kennedy and Lyndon Johnson; two-time Democratic National Committee chairman, a post he held in 1972 when men broke into his office at Washington's Watergate complex (the subsequent scandal resulted in Richard Nixon's resigning as President); became NBA commissioner in 1975 and served until 1984; in his first year settled the so-called "Oscar Robertson suit" that led to free agency; ended NBA-ABA hostilities in 1976 as NBA agreed to absorb four ABA clubs; presided over introduction of three-point field goal in 1979; averted a players' strike late in the 1983 season by negotiating a new basic agreement that granted players a guaranteed percentage of the owners' gross income in exchange for a cap on salaries; of cancer; in New York, Sept.27.

Wide World Photos

Larry O'Brien

Wide World Photos

Joe Robbie

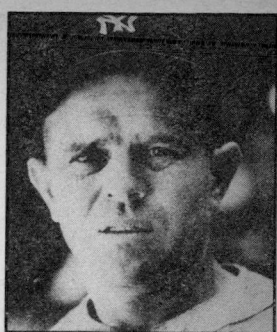

Wide World Photos

Joe Sewell

John Oliver, 75; federal judge who presided over the case that struck down baseball's reserve clause in 1976 and opened the free agent market for players; upheld arbitrator Peter Seitz's ruling in cases originated by pitchers Andy Messersmith and Dave McNally; of an aneurysm; in Kansas City, Mo., Apr.25.

Bennie Oosterbaan, 84; an All America in both football (3 times) and basketball (twice) at Michigan; also a Big Ten baseball star; coached both football (63-33-4) and basketball (58-56), led the Wolverines to their last national football title in 1948; after a long illness; in Ann Arbor, Mich., Oct. 25.

Bill Pace, 58; head football coach at Vanderbilt from 1967-72 and athletic director from 1971-72; compiled a record of 22-38-2 in six seasons; of a heart attack, in Nashville, Tenn., May 14.

Sherman Plunkett, 56; offensive tackle with the NFL champion Baltimore Colts in 1958-59; All-AFL with New York Jets in 1966; credited with giving Joe Namath the nickname "Broadway Joe;" of cancer; in Baltimore, Nov.18, 1989.

Frank Ramsey, 62; public address announcer for the Los Angeles Dodgers from 1958-82; announced at the L.A. Coliseum for the Rams, Raiders, NFL Pro Bowl, and USC football games; also announced at the L.A. Forum for the Lakers and Kings; of cardiac arrest brought on by diabetes; in Long Beach, Calif., Jan.25.

Walter Ris, 65; winner of two swimming gold medals at the 1948 Olympics in London—the 100-meter freestyle and 400-meter relay; of a heart attack; in Mission Viejo, Calif., Jan.1.

Joe Robbie, 73; successful trial lawyer who lost political campaigns for Governor in South Dakota and Congress in Minnesota before turning to pro football ownership; granted an AFL franchise in Miami in 1965; hired Don Shula as the Dolphins' second coach in 1970 and watched the team win back-to-back Super Bowls the seasons of 1972 and 1973; built privately-financed stadium for $115 million in 1987 and named it after himself; of respiratory failure; in Miami, Jan.7.

Robert Rodenkirchen, 74; world class sprinter who qualified at age 19 for the U.S. Olympic track team in 1936; forced to give up his spot, however, when it was learned he was an alien (his family had failed to obtain U.S. citizenship after moving from Cologne, Germany); he was then personally invited by Adolf Hitler to join the German Olympic team, but refused; following a heart attack; in Belleville, N.J., Aug.3.

Gilberto Roman, 29; two-time WBC super flyweight champion who held title from 1986-87 and 1988-89; of injuries received in a car accident; near Chilpancingo, Mexico, June 27.

Paul Rowe, 73; former fullback at Oregon in the 1930s who went on to star in the Canadian Football League; helped lead Calgary to the Grey Cup title in 1948; elected to the Canadian Football Hall of Fame in 1964; of cancer; in Calgary, Aug.27.

Sepp Ruschp, 81; Austrian-born alpine skier, who came to the U.S. in 1936 and helped develop the country's fledgling ski industry; former coach at both Vermont and Norwich; headed successful lobbying effort to bring 1960 Winter Olympics to Squaw Valley, Calif.; ran Mt.Mansfield Co. in Stowe, Vt., until 1978; of a self-inflicted gunshot wound after a long bout with Parkinson's disease; in Stowe, Vt., June 8.

Johnny Sanders, 68; general manager of the San Diego Chargers from 1976-87; his clubs won three AFC Western Division titles from 1979-81; in La Mesa, Calif.; Oct. 26.

Sweeney Schriner, 78; New York Americans' left wing who won Calder Cup as NHL rookie of the year in 1935 and consecutive scoring titles in 1936 and '37; later led Toronto to Stanley Cups in 1942 and '45; elected to Hockey Hall of Fame in 1962; after a long illness; in Montreal, July 5.

Doug Scovil, 62; quarterbacks coach for the Philadelphia Eagles; head coach at Pacific from 1966-69 and San Diego St. from 1981-85; compiled a college record of 45-51-3 in nine seasons; of a heart attack; in Philadelphia, Dec.9, 1989.

Earl Seibert, 79; All-Star defenseman with the New York Rangers and Chicago for 10 straight years from 1935-44; led Blackhawks to the Stanley Cup in 1938; elected to Hockey Hall of Fame in 1963; of cancer; in Agawam, Mass., May 20.

Joe Sewell, 91; AL shortstop for 14 seasons with Cleveland and the New York Yankees; member of World Series champions in 1920 and 1932; played in 1103 consecutive games from 1920-30 (then a record); lifetime .312 hitter who struck out only 114 times in 7132 at bats; college star and later baseball coach at Alabama; elected to Hall of Fame by veterans committee in 1977; cause of death not disclosed; Mobile, Ala., Mar.6.

Abram Shorin, 91; one of four brothers who founded the Topps Chewing Gum Company in Brooklyn, N.Y.; credited with the idea, in 1951, of packaging bubble gum with baseball cards featuring pictures of major league players and their statistics; of a heart attack; in Miami Beach, May 28.

Frank Sinkwich, 70; two-time consensus All-America halfback at Georgia and first player from SEC to win Heisman Trophy (in 1942); All-Pro with NFL Detroit Lions in 1944; after a long illness; in Athens, Ga., Oct. 22.

UPI/Bettmann

Ed Steitz

Wide World Photos

Horace Stoneham

Wide World Photos

Ted Tinling

Roger Stanton, 61; publisher of *Football News* and *Basketball Weekly*; after watching an NBC-TV special report on black athletes in 1989, he wrote a controversial letter to anchorman Tom Brokaw and the *Detroit Free Press* saying "black athletes traditionally lack discipline;" he later apologized for the letter; of cancer; in Detroit, June 23.

Max Starcevich, 78; consensus All-America guard for Washington football team in 1936; of heart failure in Bangor, Wash., Aug.9.

Ed Steitz, 68; secretary-editor of NCAA basketball rules committee since 1967; responsible for eliminating then reinstating the dunk, introducing the 45-second shot clock in 1986 and three-point field goal in 1987; basketball coach at Springfield College from 1956-66 and director of athletics from 1957-89; elected to Basketball Hall of Fame as contributor in 1983; of complications following a heart attack; in East Longmeadow, Mass., May 21.

Earl Stewart, 68; college golfer who won NCAA individual title in 1941 and led LSU to team title in 1942; won the 1953 Greensboro Open and 1961 Dallas Open as a pro, then coached at SMU from 1975-87; after a long illness, in Dallas, July 11.

Horace Stoneham, 86; New York baseball Giants owner who moved team to San Francisco in 1958; inherited the club at age 32 when his father died in 1936; served as principal owner and president for 41 years as Giants won one World Series (1954) and five pennants; sold team for $8 million in 1976 to a group of San Francisco investors led by Bob Lurie; of natural causes; in Scottsdale, Ariz., Jan.7.

Johnny Sylvester, 74; the most famous 11-year-old in America in 1926; kicked in the head by a horse in New Jersey and believed to be dying, he asked his father for a baseball autographed by Babe Ruth; reached in St.Louis during the World Series, Ruth promised Sylvester a home run on Oct.6 and actually hit three; cause of death not disclosed; in Mineola, N.Y., Jan.8.

Pat Tallman, 50; public address announcer for NBA San Antonio Spurs from 1973-85 and 88-90; of cancer; in San Antonio, June 7.

Billy (The Kid) Taylor, 71; center with Toronto, Detroit, Boston and the New York Rangers from 1939-48; one of only two NHL players (the other was Boston teammate Don Gallinger) ever banned for life (in 1949) for betting on league games (sometimes against Bruins); both players were reinstated in 1970; cause of death not disclosed; in Whitby, Ontario, June 12.

John (Cat) Thompson, 84; as a junior forward, led the Montana State basketball team to a national championship in 1929; Player of the Year in 1929 and a two-time consensus All-America in '29 and 1930; scored 1539 points in three seasons; elected to Basketball Hall of Fame in 1962; of a heart attack; in Idaho Falls, Idaho, Oct. 7.

Casey Tibbs, 60; flamboyant rodeo cowboy who won nine overall world championships from 1949-59; titles include two for All-Around Cowboy, six for saddle bronc riding and one for bareback riding; he swept all three titles in 1951; charter member of the ProRodeo Hall of Fame; of cancer; in Ramona, Calif., Jan.28.

Ted Tinling, 79; tennis historian and fashion designer, whose involvement in the game from ball boy to women's tour majordomo spanned from Suzanne Lenglen to Jennifer Capriati; the lace panties he designed for Gussie Moran made her a household name at Wimbledon in 1949; elected to Tennis Hall of Fame in 1986; of a respiratory ailment; in Cambridge, England, May 23.

Rich Vogler, 39; one of the busiest auto racers in the country; winner of 132 U.S.Auto Club national races, second only to A.J.Foyt's 138; five-time USAC midget car champion; drove in Indianapolis 500 five times from 1985-89; of head injuries following a crash in a sprint car race at Salem (Ind.) Speedway; July 21.

Brian Watkins, 22; former Utah state high school tennis champion and player at Idaho St.; stabbed to death coming to the aid of his parents who were being robbed at a subway stop in New York (they were all visiting New York to watch the U.S.Open), Sept.2.

George Wheeler, 75; gymnast who represented the U.S. at the 1936 Olympics in Berlin; was AAU all-around champion five straight years from 1937-41; of a cerebral hemorrhage; in New York, July 8.

Lew Worsham, 73; golfer who defeated Sam Snead by one stroke in an 18-hole playoff to win the 1947 US Open; also led PGA in earnings in 1953; after a long illness; in Poquoson, Va., Oct.19.

Lev Yashin, 60; the "Black Panther"; 4-time World Cup goalkeeper for Soviet Union (1958-70); led Russians to Olympic gold medal in 1956; gave up only 70 goals in 78 international matches; European Player of the Year in 1963 for Dynamo Moscow; received FIFA Gold Order of Merit in 1988; of cancer; in Moscow, Mar.21.

Barry Rabinowitz

BIBLIOGRAPHY

Many sources were used in the gathering of information for this almanac. Day-to-day material was almost always found in copies of *USA Today, The National, The Boston Globe,* and *The New York Times.*

Several weekly and bi-weekly periodicals were also used in the past year's pursuit of facts and figures, among them—*Baseball America, Boxing Illustrated, FIFA (Soccer) News, Inside Women's Tennis, International Tennis Weekly, The Hockey News, The NCAA News, Soccer America, Sports Illustrated, The Sporting News, Track & Field News.*

In addition, the following books provided a wealth of background material for one or more chapters of the almanac.

Baseball

The All-Star Game
(A Pictorial History, 1933 to Present)
By Donald Honig
The Sporting News Publishing Co. (1987)
St. Louis

The Baseball Encyclopedia
Fourth (1979), Seventh (1988)
and Eighth (1990) Editions
Joseph L. Reichler, Editor (4th & 7th)
Rick Wolff, Editorial Director (8th)
Macmillan Publishing Company
New York

Total Baseball
Edited by John Thorn and Pete Palmer
Warner Books (1989)
New York

Total Baseball 1990 Update
Edited by John Thorn and Pete Palmer
Warner Books (1990)
New York

The Sports Encyclopedia Baseball
Sixth Edition (1985)
Edited by David S. Neft and Richard M. Cohen
St. Martins's/Marek
New York

The Scrapbook History of Baseball
by Jordan A. Deutsch, Richard M. Cohen,
Roland T. Johnson, and David S. Neft
Bobbs-Merrill Company, Inc. (1975)
Indianapolis/New York

The Sporting News Official Baseball Guide
1990 Edition
Editor, Dave Sloan
The Sporting News Publishing Co.
St. Louis

The Sporting News Official Baseball Register
1990 Edition
Editor, Barry Siegel
The Sporting News Publishing Co.
St. Louis

The Complete Baseball Record Book
1990 Edition
Editor, Craig Carter
The Sporting News Publishing Co.
St. Louis

College Football

Football: A College History
by Tom Perrin
McFarland & Company, Inc. (1987)
Jefferson, N.C.

Football: Facts & Figures
by Dr. L.H. Baker
Farrar & Rinehart, Inc. (1945)
New York

Great College Football Coaches of the Twenties and Thirties
by Tim Cohane
Arlington House (1973)
New Rochelle, N.Y.

The Heisman, A Symbol of Excellence
by John T. Brady
Edited by John A. Walsh
Atheneum (1984)
New York

1989 NCAA Football
Compiled by Steve Boda, Jr. and
James M. Van Valkenburg
Edited by Michael V. Earle
NCAA Books
Mission, Kan.

Saturday Afternoon
by Richard Whittingham
Workman Publishing Co., Inc. (1985)
New York

Saturday's America
by Dan Jenkins
Sports Illustrated Books
Little, Brown & Company (1970)
Boston

Tournament of Roses, The First 100 Years
by Joe Hendrickson
Knapp Press (1989)
Los Angeles

Plus many college football guides, especially the 1989 guides compiled by Notre Dame, the Atlantic Coast Conference, Southeastern Conference and Southwest Conference.

Pro Football

The Official NFL Encyclopedia
by Beau Riffenburgh
New American Library (1986)
New York

The Official 1989 NFL Record and Fact Book
Edited by Pete Abitante and Chuck Garrity, Jr.
Produced by NFL Properties, Inc.
New York

The Scrapbook History of Pro Football
by Richard M. Cohen, Jordan A. Deutsch,
Roland T. Johnson and David S. Neft
Bobbs-Merrill Company, Inc. (1976)
Indianapolis/New York

The Sporting News Super Bowl Book
1989 Edition
Editor, Bob McCoy
The Sporting News Publishing Co.
St. Louis

CFL 89
(The Canadian Football League Facts Figures
& Records)
Editorial Director: John Iaboni
Toronto

College Basketball

All the Moves, A History of College Basketball
by Neil D. Issacs
J.B. Lippincott Company (1975)
New York

1989-90 Blue Ribbon College Basketball Yearbook
Edited by Chris Wallace
Christopher Publishing (1989)
Buckhannon, W.Va.

College Basketball, U.S.A. Since 1892
by John D.McCallum
Stein and Day (1978)
New York

Collegiate Basketball, facts and figures on the cage sport
by Edwin C. Caudle
The Paragon Press (1960)
Montgomery, Ala.

The Final Four
Compiled by Billy Reed
Host Communications, Inc. (1988)
Lexington, Ky.

Final Four Records, 1939-89
Compiled by Gary K. Johnson,
    Jim Van Valkenburg and Kerwin Hudson
Edited by Cheryl A. McElroy
NCAA Books
Overland Park, Kan.

The Modern Encyclopedia of Basketball
Second Revised Edition
Edited by Zander Hollander
Dolphins Books (1979)
Doubleday & Company, Inc
Garden City, N.Y.

1990 NCAA Basketball
Compiled by Gary K. Johnson, Richard M. Campbell,
    James F. Wright, and James M. Van Valkenburg
Edited by Michelle A. Pond
NCAA Books
Mission, Kan.

1990 NIT Tournament Guide
Madison Square Garden
New York

Plus many college basketball guides, especially the 1989-90 guides compiled by the Atlantic Coast Conference, Big East, Big Eight, Big Ten, Ivy League, Metro Conference, Missouri Valley Conference, Pac-10 Conference, Southeastern Conference, Southwest Conference and Western Athletic Conference.

Pro Basketball

The 1989-90 Philadelphia 76ers Statistical Yearbook
Edited by Harvey Pollack
Philadelphia 76ers
Philadelphia

From Peachbaskets to Slamdunks, A Story of Professional Basketball
by Robert D. Bole and Alfred C. Lawrence
Whitman Press (1987)
B & L Publishers
Canaan, N.H.

The Official NBA Basketball Encyclopedia
Edited by Zander Hollander and Alex Sachere
Villard Books (1989)
New York

The Sporting News Official NBA Guide
1989-90 Edition
Editors, Alex Sachare and Dave Sloan
The Sporting News Publishing Co.
St. Louis

The Sporting News Official NBA Register
1989-90 Edition
Editors, Alex Sachare and Dave Sloan
The Sporting News Publishing Co.
St. Louis

Hockey

Canada Cup '87—The Official History
No.1 Publications Ltd.
Toronto

Checking Back, A History of the National Hockey League
by Neil D. Issacs
W.W.Norton & Company, Inc. (1977)
New York

1989-90 Division I College Hockey Record Manual
Edited by Andrew K. Finnie
Andrew K. Finnie and Hockey East Association
Boston

The Hockey Encyclopedia
by Stan Fischler and Shirley Walton Fischler
Research Editor, Bob Duff
Macmillan Publishing Comnapy (1983)
New York

Hockey Hall of Fame, The Official History of the Game and Its Greatest Stars
By Dan Diamond and Joseph Romain
Doubleday (1988)
Dell Publishing Group, Inc.
New York

Hockey Twenty Years, The NHL Since 1967
By Dan Diamond and Lew Stubbs
Doubleday & Company, Inc. (1987)
Garden City, N.Y.

The National Hockey League
By Edward F Dolan Jr.
Bison Books Corp (1986)
W H Smith Publishers Inc.
New York

The NHL Official Guide & Record Book, 1989-90
Compiled by the NHL Communications Dept.
New York/Montreal

The Stanley Cup
by Joseph Romain and James Duplacey
Gallery Books (1989)
New York

The Trail of the Stanley Cup
Volumes I-III
By Charles L. Coleman
Progressive Publications (1969)
Sherbrooke, Quebec

College Sports

1990 NCAA Basketball
Compiled by Gary K. Johnson, Richard M.
    Campbell, Steve Boda, Jr., James F. Wright,
    and James M. Van Valkenburg
Edited by Michelle A. Pond
NCAA Books
Mission, Kan.

1989 NCAA Football
Compiled by Steve Boda, Jr. and James M.
Van Valkenburg
Edited by Michael V. Earle
NCAA Books
Mission, Kan.

1988-89 National Collegiate Championships
Edited by Theodore A. Breidenthal
NCAA Books
Mission, Kan.

NAIA Championship History and Records Book, 1988-89
National Assn. of Intercollegiate Athletics
NAIA Books
Kansas City, Mo.

Sports Personalities

Facts & Dates of American Sports
By Gorton Carruth & Eugene Ehrlich
Harper & Row, Publishers, Inc. (1988)
New York

101 Greatest Athletes of the Century
By Will Grimsley and the Associated Press Sports Staff
Bonanza Books (1987)
Crown Publishers, Inc.
New York

Superstars
By Frank Litsky
Vineyard Books, Inc. (1975)
Derbibooks Inc.
Secaucus, N.J.

Arenas & Ballparks

Ballparks of North America
by Michael Benson
McFarland & Company, Inc. (1989)
Jefferson, N.C.

The Ballparks
by Bill Shannon and George Kalinsky
Hawthorn Books, Inc. (1975)
New York

Green Cathedrals
by Philip Lowry
Society for American Baseball Research (1986)

The NFL's Encyclopedic History of Professional Football
Macmillan Publishing Co., Inc. (1977)
New York

Take Me Out to the Ballpark
by Lowell Reidenbaugh
The Sporting News Publishing Co. (1983)
St.Louis

24 Seconds to Shoot
(An Informal History of the NBA)
by Leonard Koppett
The Macmillan Company (1968)
New York

Plus many major league baseball, NBA, NFL, NHL
league and team guides, and major college football
and basketball guides.

Soccer

The American Encyclopedia of Soccer
Edited by Zander Hollander
Everest House Publishers (1980)
New York

The Guinness Book of Soccer Facts & Feats
By Jack Rollin
Guinness Superlatives Ltd (1978)
Middlesex, England

The History of the World Cup
By Brian Glanville
Faber and Faber Limited (1984)
London/Boston

History of Soccer's World Cup
By Michael Archer
Chartwell Books, Inc. (1978)
Secaucus, N.J.

MISL Official Guide, 1988-89
Major Indoor Soccer League
Overland Park, Kan.

International Sports

All That Glitters Is Not Gold
(An Irreverent Look at the Olympic Games)
By William O. Johnson, Jr.
G.P. Putnam's Sons (1972)
New York

An Illustrated History of the Olympics
Third Edition (1975)
By Dick Schaap
Alfred A. Knopf
New York

Athletics 1990, The International Track and Field Annual
Association of Track & Field Statisticians
Edited by Peter Matthews
Simon & Schuster
London/New York

The Complete Book of the Olympics
Revised Edition (1988)
By David Wallechinsky
Penguin Books
New York

Pursuit of Excellence, The Olympic Story
By The Associated Press and Grolier
Grolier Enterprises Inc. (1979)
Danbury, Conn.

United States Olympic Books
Seven Editions: 1936,48,52,56,60,61-65,68
U.S. Olympic Association
New York

Miscellaneous

The Encyclopedia of Sports
Fifth Revised Edition (1975)
By Frank G. Menke
Revisions by Suzanne Treat
A.S. Barnes and Co., Inc.
Cranbury, N.J.

The Great American Sports Book
By George Gipe
Doubleday & Company, Inc. (1978)
Garden City, N.Y.

Guinness Book of Sports Records, Winners & Champions
1982-83 Edition
By Norris McWhirter
Sterling Publishing Co., Inc.
New York

Official 1990 PRCA Media Guide
Editor, Steve Fleming
Professional Rodeo Cowboys Association
Colorado Springs, Colo.

"Ten Years of the Ironman"
Triathlete Magazine
October, 1988
Santa Monica, Cal.

Horse Racing

The American Racing Manual
1990 Edition
Compiled by the Daily Racing Form
Hightstown, N.J.

1990 Directory and Record Book
The Thoroughbred Racing Associations
Lake Success, N.Y.

The Trotting and Pacing Guide, 1989
Compiled and edited by John Pawlak
United States Trotting Association
Columbus, Ohio

Breeders' Cup 1989 Statistics
Breeders' Cup Limited
Lexington, Ky.

NYRA Media Guide 1990
The New York Racing Assn. Inc.
Jamaica, N.Y.

The 116th Kentucky Derby Media Guide, 1990
Churchill Downs Public Relations Dept.
Louisville, Ky.

The 115th Preakness Press Guide, 1990
Compiled and edited by Joe Kelly
Maryland Jockey Club
Baltimore, Md.

Bowling

Bowlers Journal 1988 Annual
January, 1989
Chicago, Ill.

LPBT 1990 Guide
Ladies Pro Bowlers Tour
Rockford, Ill.

PBA 1990 Press-Radio-TV Guide
Professional Bowlers Association
Akron, Ohio

Tennis

The Illustrated Encyclopedia of World Tennis
By John Haylett and Richard Evans
Exeter Books (1989)
New York

Official Encyclopedia of Tennis
Edited by the staff of the U.S. Lawn Tennis
    Association
Harper & Row (1972)
New York

Official 1990 ATP Player Guide
Edited by Michael Curet
Association of Tennis Professionals
Ponte Vedra Beach, Fla.

Official 1990 WITA Media Guide
Compiled by WITA Public Relations staff
Women's International Tennis Association
Miami, Fla.

Golf

1990 LPGA Player Guide
LPGA Tour
Daytona Beach, Fla.

Official 1990 PGA Tour Book
PGA Tour
Ponte Vedra, Fla.

Official 1990 Senior PGA Tour Book
PGA Tour
Ponte Vedra, Fla.

USGA Record Book
(1895-1959 and 1960-80)
U.S. Golf Association
Far Hills, N.J.

Guinness Golf Records, Facts and Champions
By Donald Steel
Guinness Superlatives Ltd (1987)
Middlesex, England

Auto Racing

CART 1990 Media Guide
Editor, Mel Poole
Championship Auto Racing Teams
Bloomfield Hills, Mich.

1990 Winston Cup Media Guide
Compiled and edited by Bob Kelly
NASCAR Winston Cup Series
Winston-Salem, N.C.

Indianapolis 500 Media Fact Book, 1990
Compiled Bob Laycock and Kurt Hunt
Indianapolis Motor Speedway
Indianapolis

Marlboro Grand Prix Guide, 1950-89
1990 Edition
Compiled by Jacques Deschenaux
Charles Stewart & Company Ltd
Brebtford, England

Boxing

1990 Computer Boxing Update
Compiled by Ralph Citro
Ralph Citro Inc.
Blackwood, N.J.

The Ring 1985 Record Book & Boxing Encyclopedia
Edited by Herbert G. Goldman
The Ring Publishing Corp.
New York

Other Reference Books

The New York Public Library Desk Reference
Editors, Felice Levy and Lisa Wolff
Webster's New World (1989)
Simon & Schuster
New York

TV Facts
Revised and Updated
by Cobbett Steinberg
Facts On File Publications (1985)
New York

The World Book Encyclopedia
1988 Edition
World Book, Inc.
Chicago

The World Book Yearbook
Annual Supplements, 1954-89
World Book, Inc.
Chicago

Olympics

Winter Games

Year	No.	Host City	Dates
1992	XVI	Albertville, France	Feb.8-23
1994	XVII	Lillehammer, Norway	Feb.12-27

Summer Games

Year	No.	Host City	Dates
1992	XXV	Barcelona, Spain	July 25-Aug.9
1996	XXVI	Atlanta, Georgia	July 20-Aug.4

All-Star Games

Baseball

Year	Site	Date
1991	SkyDome, Toronto	July 9
1992	Jack Murphy Stadium, San Diego	TBA
1993	Camden Yards, Baltimore	TBA
1994	Three Rivers Stadium, Pittsburgh	TBA

NBA Basketball

Year	Site	Date
1991	Charlotte (NC) Coliseum	Feb.10
1992	TBA	

NFL Pro Bowl

Year	Site	Date
1991	Aloha Stadium, Honolulu	Feb.3
1992	Aloha Stadium, Honolulu	Feb.2
1993	Aloha Stadium, Honolulu	Feb.7
1994	Aloha Stadium, Honolulu	Feb.6 or Feb.13

NHL Hockey

Year	Site	Date
1991	Chicago Stadium	Jan.19
1992	The Spectrum, Philadelphia	TBA
1993	Montreal Forum	TBA

Auto Racing

The Daytona 500 stock car race is usually held on the third Sunday in February, while the Indianapolis 500 is usually held on the Sunday of Memorial Day weekend in May. Except for 1991, the following dates are tentative.

Year	Daytona 500	Indianapolis
1991	Feb.17	May 26
1992	Feb.16	May 24
1993	Feb.21	May 30
1994	Feb.20	May 29

NCAA Basketball

Men's Final Four

Year	Site	Dates
1991	Hoosier Dome, Indianapolis	Mar.30-Apr.1
1992	HHH Metrodome, Minneapolis	April 4-6
1993	Superdome, New Orleans	April 3-5
1994	Charlotte (NC) Coliseum	April 2-4
1995	The Kingdome, Seattle	April 1-3
1996	Meadowlands (NJ) Arena	Mar.30-April.1
1997	Hoosier Dome, Indianapolis	March 29-31

Women's Final Four

Year	Site	Dates
1991	Lakefront Arena, New Orleans	March 30-31
1992	LA Sports Arena	April 4-5
1993	The Omni, Atlanta	April 3-4

NFL Football

Super Bowls

No.	Site	Date
XXV	Tampa Stadium, Tampa	Jan.27,1991
XXVI	HHH Metrodome, Minneapolis	Jan.26,1992
XXVII	Sun Devil Stadium, Tempe	Jan.31,1993
XXVIII	Georgia Dome, Atlanta	Jan.30 or Feb.6,1994

Golf

The Masters

Year	Site	Dates
1991	Augusta (GA) National GC	April 11-14
1992	Augusta (GA) National GC	April 9-12
1993	Augusta (GA) National GC	April 8-11
1994	Augusta (GA) National GC	April 7-10
1995	Augusta (GA) National GC	April 6-9

U.S. Open

Year	Site	Dates
1991	Hazeltine Nat'l GC, Chaska, MN	Jun.13-16
1992	Pebble Beach (CA) GC	June.18-21
1993	Baltunrol CC, Springfield, NJ	June.17-20
1994	Oakmont (PA) CC	June.16-19
1995	Shinnecock Hills (NY) GC	June.15-18

U.S. Women's Open

Year	Site	Dates
1991	Colonial CC, Ft.Worth,TX	Jul.11-14
1992	Oakmont (PA) CC	Jul.23-26
1993	TBA	
1994	Merion CC, Ardmore, PA	TBA

U.S. Senior Open

Year	Site	Dates
1991	Oakland Hills CC, Birmingham, MI	July.25-28
1992	Saucon Valley CC, Bethlehem,PA	Jul.9-12
1993	Cherry Hills, CC, Engelwood,CO	Jul.8-11
1994	Pinehurst (NC) CC, (No.2)	Jun.30-Jul.3

PGA Championship

Year	Site	Dates
1991	Crooked Stick GC, Carmel,IN	Aug.8-11
1992	Bellerive CC, St.Louis	Aug.13-16
1993	Aronimink CC, Newtown Sq.,PA	Aug.12-15
1994	Oak Tree CC, Edmond, OK	TBA

Horse Racing

The Triple Crown Races

The Kentucky Derby is always held at Churchill Downs in Louisville on the first Saturday in May, followed two weeks later by the Preakness Stakes at Pimlico Race Course in Baltimore and three weeks after that by the Belmont Stakes at Belmont Park in Elmont, NY.

Year	Ky Derby	Preakness	Belmont
1991	May 4	May 18	June 8
1992	May 2	May 16	June 6
1993	May 1	May 15	June 5
1994	May 7	May 21	June 11
1995	May 6	May 20	June 10

Sailing

America's Cup

All racing held off San Diego.

Year		Date
1992	Defender Selection Trials	January-May
	Challenger Selection Trials	January-May
	Final (Best-of-7)	starts May 9

Tennis

U.S. Open

Usually held from the last Monday in August through the second Sunday in September with Labor Day weekend being the midway point in the tournament.

Year	Site	Dates
1991	US Tennis Center, NYC	Aug.26-Sept.8
1992	US Tennis Center, NYC	Aug.31-Sept.13
1993	US Tennis Center, NYC	Aug.30-Sept.12
1994	US Tennis Center, NYC	Aug.29-Sept.11